AMERICAN
ENGLISH
STUDY
DICTIONARY

Pre-Intermediate
    Basic English Dictionary   1-901659-96-8
    Basic English Thesaurus   1-901659-98-4
Intermediate
    English Study Dictionary, paperback   1-901659-63-1
    English Study Dictionary, hardback   1-901659-64-X
    American English Study Dictionary, paperback   1-901659-69-0
    American English Study Dictionary, hardback   1-901659-70-4
Upper-Intermediate
    English Dictionary for Students, 2nd ed   1-903856-21-3
    English Thesaurus for Students   1-901659-31-3

Specialist English Dictionary Series:
Dictionary of Accounting   0-948549-27-0
Dictionary of Agrigulture, 2nd ed   0-948549-78-5
Dictionary of American Business, 2nd ed   1-901659-22-4
Dictionary of Astronomy, 2nd ed   0-948549-43-2
Dictionary of Automobile Engineering   0-948549-66-1
Dictionary of Banking & Finance, 2nd ed   1-901659-30-5
Dictionary of Business, 3rd ed   1-901659-50-X
Dictionary of Computing, 3rd ed   1-901659-04-6
Dictionary of Ecology & Environment, 4th ed   1-901659-61-5
Dictionary of Government & Politics, 2nd ed   0-948549-89-0
Dictionary of Hotels, Tourism, Catering Management   0-948549-40-8
Dictionary of Human Resources & Personnel, 2nd ed   0-948549-79-3
Dictionary of Information Technology, 2nd ed   0-948549-88-2
Dictionary of Law, 3rd ed   1-901659-43-7
Dictionary of Library & Information Management   0-948549-68-8
Dictionary of Marketing   0-948549-73-4
Dictionary of Medicine, 3rd ed   1-901659-45-3
Dictionary of Multimedia, 3rd ed   1-901659-51-8
Dictionary of PC & the Internet, 3rd ed   1-901659-52-6
Dictionary of Printing & Publishing, 2nd ed   0-948549-99-8
Dictionary of Science & Technology   0-948549-67-X

Workbooks to help test and improve vocabulary
Check your vocabulary for:
American Business   1-901659-32-1
Banking & Finance   0-948549-96-3
Business, 2nd ed   1-901659-27-5
Colloquial English   0-948549-97-1
Computing, 2nd ed   0-948549-72-6
English for FCE   1-901659-11-9
English for IELTS   1-901659-60-7
English for PET   1-903856-23-X
English for TOEFL   1-901659-68-2
Hotels, Tourism   0-948549-75-0
Human Resources   1-901659-79-8
Law, 2nd ed   1-901659-21-6
Marketing   1-901659-48-8
Medicine, 2nd ed   1-901659-47-X
Military English   1-901659-58-5

AMERICAN
ENGLISH
STUDY
DICTIONARY

General Editor
P.H. Collin

American Editors
B Kipfer
R Martinez
H Spradling

PETER COLLIN PUBLISHING

First published in Great Britain in 2002

Published by Peter Collin Publishing Ltd
32-34 Great Peter Street, London, SW1P 2DB

British Library Cataloguing-in-Publication Data

A catalogue record for this book is available from the British Library

ISBN 1-901659-69-0

Text processing and computer typesetting by PCP
Printed and bound in Italy by Legoprint

Preface

The aim of this dictionary is to provide a modern vocabulary of American English for the intermediate student.

The vocabulary of over 18,000 entries has been selected carefully according to various word frequency counts and syllabuses for national and international examinations.

Each word or term is clearly defined, and examples of each word and phrase are given in simple illustrative contexts (over 28,000 in all) , so as to show how the words can be used in practice.

Layout of the Dictionary

We have tried to lay the dictionary out as clearly as possible, in order to make it as easy as possible for the student to use.

Each entry begins with a main word, followed by the pronunciation in international phonetic symbols; this is followed by the part of speech. Entries where the same word occurs as two or more different parts of speech are split by numbers. Within each entry, major differences of meaning are highlighted by letter divisions.

The meanings of the words are written as simply as possible, using only a small defining vocabulary, supplemented as necessary by other words which appear in the dictionary. All words have examples of usage, and for the commonest words we give very many examples, all set in contexts which are easy to understand. Common idiomatic expressions and collocations are highlighted, explained, and examples are given for them also.

Throughout the book, usage notes (beginning with the word NOTE:) give irregular forms, constructions, words which can be confused, etc. These notes are also used to give information about the countries of the world which appear as entries.

Some words have fuller encyclopaedic comments in boxes, and these give more information than can be given within a simple definition.

Word frequency grading

Each main entry is preceded by a number. These refer to the frequency of the main word according to reliable international word counts. The most common 2,700 words are ①, the next 2,400 words are ②, the next 1,900 are ③ and the 1,800 remaining words are ④.

Phonetics

The following symbols have been used to show the pronunciation of the main words in the dictionary.

Stress has been indicated by a main stress mark ('), but these are only guides as the stress of the word may change according to its position in the sentence.

Vowels		*Consonants*	
æ	back	b	buck
ɑ	harm	d	dead
ɒ	stop	ð	other
aɪ	type	dʒ	jump
aʊ	how	f	fare
aɪə	hire	g	gold
aʊə	hour	h	head
ɔ	course	j	yellow
ɔɪ	loyalty	k	cab
e	head	l	leave
eə	fair	m	mix
eɪ	make	n	nil
ə	abroad	ŋ	bring
əʊ	float	p	post
əʊə	lower	r	rule
ɜ	word	s	save
i	keep	ʃ	shop
ɪ	fit	t	take
ɪə	near	tʃ	change
u	supreme	θ	theft
ʊ	book	v	value
ʌ	shut	w	work
		z	zone
		ʒ	measure

Aa

① **A, a**
[eɪ]
first letter of the alphabet, followed by B; *do you mean "been" with two Es or "bean" spelled EA?*; **from A to Z** = completely, all the way through

① **a, an**
[eɪ or æn] *article*
(a) one; *I want a glass of soda*; *she's bought a new automobile*; *an enormous hole*; *we had to wait an hour for the bus*; *a useful guidebook*
(b) for each or to each; *apples cost fifty cents a pound*; *the automobile was traveling at 30 miles an hour*; *he earns $150 a day* (NOTE: **an** is used in front of words beginning with **a, e, i, o, u** and with **h** if the **h** is not pronounced (**an apple**; **an hour**); **a** is used in front of all other letters and also in front of **u** where **u** is pronounced [ju] (**a useful guidebook**))

③ **abandon**
[ə'bændən] *verb*
(a) to leave; *he abandoned his wife and kids*; *the crew abandoned the sinking boat*
(b) to give up, to stop doing something; *the company has decided to abandon the project*; *we abandoned the idea of setting up a London office*

① **abandoned**
[ə'bændənd] *adjective*
no longer used or lived in; *two families of refugees moved into the abandoned house*

④ **abbot**
['æbət] *noun*
man in charge of a monastery

② **abbreviation**
[əbrivi'eɪʃn] *noun*
short form of a word; *"CD" is the abbreviation for "compact disc"*

④ **ABC**
[eɪbi'si] *noun*
the alphabet (from the first letters of the Roman alphabet)

④ **abdicate**
['æbdɪkeɪt] *verb*
to give up the throne

① **ability**
[ə'bɪlɪti] *noun*
(a) having the force to do something; *he has many abilities but singing isn't one of them* (NOTE: plural in this meaning is **abilities**)
(b) being clever; *he's a man of great or outstanding ability*; **I'll do it to the best of my ability** = I'll do it as well as I can

④ **ablaze**
[ə'bleɪz] *adverb*
(a) on fire; *the woodland was ablaze*
(b) shining brightly; *shops ablaze with lights*

① **able**
['eɪbl] *adjective*
to be able to do something = to have the capability or chance to do something; *she wasn't able to breathe*; *will you be able to come to the meeting?*; *they weren't able to find the house* (NOTE: **able** is only used with **to** and a verb)

② **aboard**
[ə'bɔrd] *adverb & preposition*
on a ship or vehicle; *the truck ran into a bus with twenty passengers aboard*; *the passengers went aboard the "Queen Elizabeth" at 10 P.M.*; *when the ship docked, customs officers came aboard to inspect the cargo*; **all aboard!** = everyone get on, please!

② **abolish**
[ə'bɒlɪʃ] *verb*
to get rid of (a law, a right); *Congress voted to abolish capital punishment*

③ **abolition**
[æbə'lɪʃn] *noun*
act of abolishing; *the abolition of the death penalty*

④ **abominable**
[ə'bɒmɪnəbl] *adjective*
horrible, disgusting; *abominable treatment*

④ **aboriginal**
[æbə'rɪdʒɪnəl] *noun*
original inhabitant

④ **abort**
[ə'bɔrt] *verb*
(a) to stop something taking place; *the space mission was aborted*
(b) *(of woman)* to have a miscarriage

④ **abortion**
[ə'bɔrʃn] *noun*
ending of a woman's pregnancy; *she did not want the baby, so asked to have an abortion*

④ **abortive**
[ə'bɔrtɪv] *adjective*
unsuccessful

① **about**
[ə'baʊt]
1 *preposition*
(a) referring to; *he told me all about his operation*; *what do you want to speak to the doctor about?*; *she's worried about her heart problems*
(b) to be about to do something = to be just going to do something; *we were about to go home when you arrived*
(c) in the process of doing something; *while you're about, can you mail this letter?*
(d) *(informal)* **how about** *or* **what about** = what do you think; *we can't find a new secretary for the club - what about Sarah?*; *how about a cup of coffee?* = would you like a cup of coffee?
2 *adverb*
(a) approximately; *the table is about 6 feet long*; *I've been waiting for about four hours*; *she's only about fifteen years old*
(b) in various places; *there were papers lying about on the floor*

① **above**
[ə'bʌv]
1 *preposition*
(a) higher than; *the plane was flying above the clouds*; *the temperature on the street was above 90 degrees*; *at prices above $9.00, nobody will buy it*
(b) older than; *if you are above 18, you have to pay the full fare*
(c) louder than; *I couldn't hear the telephone above the noise of the drills*
(d) earlier on (in a book); higher up (on a page); *see the section on computers on page 25 above*
2 *noun*
the above = people mentioned earlier; *all the above have passed the test*

④ **abrasion**
[ə'breɪʒn] *noun*
scraping off the skin; *cuts and abrasions*

④ **abrasive**
[ə'breɪzɪv] *noun*
substance which rubs away a surface

② **abroad**
[ə'brɔd] *adverb*
in another country; to another country; *he travels abroad a lot on business*; *they've gone abroad on vacation*; *vacations abroad are becoming more and more popular*; *she lives abroad and only comes back to the U.S. for her vacations*

④ **abrupt**
[ə'brʌpt] *adjective*
(a) sudden; *he made an abrupt change of plan*; *the bus made an abrupt turn to the right*
(b) not very polite; *his reply was abrupt and to the point*

② **absence**
['æbsəns] *noun*
(a) being away from a place; *she did not explain her absence from the meeting*; *the former president was sentenced in his absence*; **in the absence of** = without someone being there; *in the absence of the director, the assistant director took over*; **leave of absence** = permission to be away from work; *he asked for a leave of absence to visit his wife in the hospital*
(b) lack of something; *in the absence of any map of the town we had to ask our way*

① **absent**
['æbsənt] *adjective*
not there; *the chairman was absent from the meeting*; *ten of the staff are absent with flu*; *let's drink a toast to absent friends*

④ **absolute**
['æbsəlut] *adjective*
complete, total; *the general assumed absolute power*; *he's an absolute fool - he should have accepted the offer immediately*; **absolute majority** = majority over all the others; *the government has an absolute majority of fifteen*; **absolute zero** = the lowest possible temperature

③ **absolutely**
['æbsəlutli] *adverb*
completely, totally; *I am absolutely sure I left the keys in my coat pocket*

② **absorb**
[əb'zɔrb] *verb*
(a) to take in (a liquid, etc.); *the liquid should be absorbed by the paper*; *salt absorbs moisture from the air*
(b) to reduce a shock; *the car's springs are supposed to absorb any shock from the road surface*
(c) absorbed in = totally interested in; *he was absorbed in his newspaper and didn't notice that the toast had burned*

④ **absorption**
[əb'zɔrpʃən] *noun*
being absorbed; *the absorption of the drug into the bloodstream* (NOTE: the spellings: **absorb** but **absorption**)

③ **abstract**
['æbstrækt]
1 *adjective*
(a) which exists only in the mind; *she has lots of abstract theories about how to reorganize society*
(b) abstract art = art that does not reproduce something exactly; *an abstract painting by Picasso*
2 *noun*
(a) something that exists in your mind only; **in the abstract** = in a general way
(b) an abstract painting; *he started by painting abstracts and then turned to portraits*
(c) short form of a report or document; *he was asked to make an abstract of the report*

④ **absurd**
[əb'sɜrd] *adjective*
silly; *it's absurd to rely on winning the lottery*

④ **abundant**
[əˈbʌndənt] *adjective*
in large quantities; *abundant stocks of wood for the stove*

④ **abundantly**
[əˈbʌndəntlɪ] *adverb*
in large quantities

② **abuse**
1 *noun* [əˈbjus]
(a) bad use; *the senator's action is an abuse of power*; *demonstrators are protesting abuses of human rights in various parts of the world*
(b) **verbal abuse** = rude words; **a term of abuse** = a rude word
(c) very bad treatment; *she suffered physical abuse in prison*; *sexual abuse of children* (NOTE: no plural for meanings (b) and (c))
2 *verb* [əˈbjuz]
(a) to make the wrong use of; *he abused his position as finance director*; **he abused my confidence** = he took advantage of my trust in him
(b) to treat very badly, usually sexually; *as a child, she was abused by her uncle*
(c) to say rude things about someone; *the crowd sang songs abusing the president's wife*

④ **abyss**
[əˈbɪs] *noun*
deep hole; *she peered down into the abyss* (NOTE: plural is **abysses**)

④ **academic**
[ækəˈdemɪk]
1 *adjective*
(a) referring to study at a university; *members of the academic staff received a letter from the president*; **academic year** = school year or university year; *the new academic year starts next week*
(b) theoretical; *it is only of academic interest*
2 *noun*
a university teacher; *she teaches at a university and all her friends are academics*

③ **academy**
[əˈkædəmɪ] *noun*
(a) college where specialized subjects are taught; *a military academy*; *an academy of music*
(b) private society for the study of art or science; *the Russian Academy of Sciences*; *the award was from the American Academy of Arts and Sciences*

③ **accelerate**
[ækˈseləreɪt] *verb*
(a) to go faster; *he pressed down on the pedal and the car accelerated*; *don't accelerate when you get to traffic light*
(b) to make something go faster; *the drug accelerates the heart rate*

② **accent**
[ˈæksənt] *noun*
(a) particular way of saying words; *she has an Irish accent*; *he speaks with a Southern accent*
(b) sign over a printed letter; **an acute accent** = sign sloping forward over a vowel, such as é; *"résumé" has two acute accents*
(c) stress in speaking; *in the word "hotel", the accent is on "tel"*
(d) general stress; *the accent of the government's program is on youth unemployment*

④ **accentuate**
[əkˈsentjʊeɪt] *verb*
to emphasize; *he accentuated the importance of remaining calm*

① **accept**
[əkˈsept] *verb*
(a) to take a present; *we hope you will accept this little gift*
(b) to say "yes" or to agree to something; *she accepted the offer of a job in Australia*; *I invited her to come with us and she accepted*
(c) to agree to handle something; *only U.S. dollars are accepted on the cruise ship*; *"all major credit cards accepted"*; *do you accept traveler's checks?* (NOTE: do not confuse with **except**)

④ **acceptable**
[əkˈseptəbl] *adjective*
easily accepted; *a small gift of flowers would be very acceptable*; *the offer is not acceptable to the vendor*

④ **acceptance**
[əkˈseptəns] *noun*
(a) taking something that is offered; *he indicated his acceptance of the offer*
(b) agreement; *we received her letter of acceptance this morning*

① **accepted**
[əkˈseptɪd] *adjective*
which is taken as correct by most people; *this is not an antiseptic in the accepted sense of the word*

④ **access**
[ˈækses]
1 *noun*
(a) way of getting to a place; *the concert hall has access for wheelchairs*; *at present there is no access to the site*
(b) **to have (easy) access to** = to be able to get easily; *the company has access to substantial funds*
2 *verb*
to get information from a computer; *she tried to access the mailing list*

④ **accessible**
[əkˈsesɪbl] *adjective*
easily reached; *the island is only accessible by boat in fine weather*

④ **accessory**
[əkˈsesərɪ] *noun*
(a) useful piece of equipment, added to others; *photographic accessories*
(b) person who helps someone commit a crime (NOTE: plural is **accessories**)

① **accident**
['æksɪdənt] *noun*
(a) something that happens by chance; *he discovered the missing papers by accident*
(b) unpleasant thing that happens and causes damage; *the accident happened or took place at a dangerous intersection; she was involved in a car accident and had to go to the hospital; thirty people were killed in the train accident; he missed his flight, because his bus had an accident on the way to the airport*; **industrial accident** = accident that takes place at work

② **accidental**
[æksɪ'dentl] *adjective*
which happens by accident; *the police think his death was not accidental*

④ **accidentally**
[æksɪ'dentəli] *adverb*
by chance; *he discovered the missing papers accidentally*

④ **acclaim**
[ə'kleɪm]
1 *noun*
great praise; *his film was greeted with great acclaim*
2 *verb*
to greet with praise; *she was acclaimed as the best novelist of the decade*

④ **accommodation**
[əkɒmə'deɪʃən] *noun*
(a) **accommodations** = places to live; *all the available accommodations in town have been taken by journalists; visitors have difficulty in finding hotel accommodations during the summer*
(b) compromise, agreement; *he reached an accommodation with his creditors*

③ **accompany**
[ə'kʌmpni] *verb*
(a) to go with; *he accompanied his wife to the hospital; the pain was accompanied by a high temperature; Thanksgiving turkey is accompanied by cranberry sauce*
(b) to play a musical instrument, when someone else plays or sings; *she sang and was accompanied on the piano by her father* (NOTE: accompanied **by** someone or something)

② **accomplish**
[ə'kʌmplɪʃ] *verb*
to achieve something successfully; *what do you hope to accomplish at the meeting?; I don't think he has accomplished very much in his first year as head of the museum*

④ **accord**
[ə'kɔrd]
1 *noun*
(a) agreement; *they are still discussing the terms of the accord but we hope it will be signed today*
(b) **of your own accord** = without being ordered or forced by anyone; *of his own accord*

he decided to sell his business and retire to a Caribbean island
2 *verb*
(formal) to give as an honor; *he was accorded a civic reception*

④ **accordance**
[ə'kɔrdəns] *noun*
in accordance with = in agreement with *or* following; *in accordance with your instructions*

③ **according to**
[ə'kɔrdɪŋ tʊ] *adverb*
(a) as someone says or writes; *the washing machine was installed according to the manufacturer's instructions; according to the witness, the automobile was going too fast*
(b) in relation to; *the teachers have separated the children into classes according to their ages*

④ **accordingly**
[ə'kɔrdɪŋli] *adverb*
as a result of something just mentioned; *we have received your letter and have changed your flight booking accordingly; he's an experienced cook and should be paid accordingly*

① **account**
[ə'kaʊnt]
1 *noun*
(a) **bank account** = arrangement that you make with a bank to keep your money safely; *I put all my savings into my bank account; this type of bank account pays 10% interest*; **to open a bank account** = to start keeping money in a bank; **to close a bank account** = to stop keeping money in a bank; **checking account** = account that pays little or no interest but from which the customer can withdraw money when he wants by writing checks; **savings account** = account where you put money in regularly and which pays interest
(b) *(in a store)* arrangement that a customer has to buy goods and pay for them later; *put it on my account or charge it to my account*; *(of a customer)* **to open an account** = to ask a store to supply goods that you will pay for later; *(of a store)* **to open an account** *or* **to close an account** = to start or to stop supplying a customer on credit; **to settle an account** = to pay all the money owed on an account
(c) **on account** = as part of a total bill; **to pay money on account** = to pay to settle part of a bill
(d) **on account of** = because of, due to; *the trains are late on account of an accident; we don't use the automobile much on account of the price of gas*
(e) **I was worried on her account** = I was afraid something might happen to her; **on no account** = not under any circumstances
(f) **to take something into account** *or* **to take account of something** = to consider something; *we have to take the weather into account*

(g) story; *they were amused by his account of the journey*; by all accounts = as everyone says; *by all accounts, she is a very attractive woman*
(h) the accounts of a business *or* **a company's accounts** = detailed records of a company's financial affairs; **to keep the accounts** = to write each sum of money in the account book
2 *verb*
to account for = to explain; *he was asked to account for all his expenditures*

② **accountant**
[ə'kauntənt] *noun*
person who deals with accounts; *I send all my income tax queries to my accountant; she has an appointment with her accountant to go over her tax form*

③ **accounting**
[ə'kauntɪŋ] *noun*
(a) work of recording money paid, received, borrowed or owed; **accounting department** = department in a company which deals with money paid, received, borrowed or owed
(b) study of the work of being an accountant; *he is studying accounting* or *he is an accounting student*

④ **accredit**
[ə'kredɪt] *verb*
to make someone an official representative; *he is accredited to the United Nations*

④ **accumulate**
[ə'kjumjʊleɪt] *verb*
to grow larger, to pile up; *she allowed the interest in her account to accumulate*

④ **accumulation**
[əkjumjʊ'leɪʃn] *noun*
heap; *an accumulation of snow on the sidewalk*

④ **accuracy**
['ækjʊrəsɪ] *noun*
being correct in every detail; *accuracy is very important when drawing maps; the police doubt the accuracy of the witness' statements*

④ **accurate**
['ækjʊrət] *adjective*
correct in all details; *are the figures accurate?; we asked them to make an accurate copy of the plan of the house*

④ **accurately**
['ækjʊrətlɪ] *adverb*
correctly; *the TV weatherman accurately forecast the storm; it is very difficult to reproduce the sound of an owl accurately*

④ **accusation**
[ækjʊ'zeɪʃn] *noun*
statement that someone has done wrong; *the secretary made an accusation against her boss; he denied the accusations against him*

② **accuse**
[ə'kjuz] *verb*
to say that someone has done something wrong; *the police accused her of stealing the money; she was accused of stealing from the store*

where she worked (NOTE: you accuse someone **of** a crime or **of** doing something)

③ **accused**
[ə'kjuzd] *noun*
the accused = person or people charged with a crime; *all the accused pleaded not guilty; the police brought the accused into the court* (NOTE: can be singular or plural: **the six accused all appeared in court**)

③ **ace**
[eɪs] *noun*
(a) playing card with one spot; *he played the ace of spades*
(b) someone who is brilliant at doing something; *he's our ace salesman*
(c) *(in tennis)* service that the opposing player cannot touch; *Williams has served four aces so far*

② **achieve**
[ə'tʃiv] *verb*
to succeed in doing something; *what do you hope to achieve by writing to your congressman?; the theater company has achieved great success in Oregon; he achieved all his objectives*

② **achievement**
[ə'tʃivmənt] *noun*
thing which has been done successfully; *coming in sixth was a great achievement considering he had never raced before; she is excessively modest about her achievements*

① **acid**
['æsɪd]
1 *noun*
liquid chemical substance containing hydrogen, which burns; *the muggers threw acid in her face*
2 *adjective*
(a) sour; *the acid taste of lemons*
(b) acid rain = polluted rain which kills trees; *acid rain often falls a long distance away from the source of the pollution*

③ **acknowledge**
[ək'nɒlɪdʒ] *verb*
(a) to say that something has been received; *I am writing to acknowledge receipt of your letter dated June 15; he has still not acknowledged my letter of January 24*
(b) to admit that something is true; *in the end, they acknowledged defeat* or *they acknowledged that they were beaten; he acknowledged that what she said was true*

④ **acorn**
['eɪkɔrn] *noun*
fruit of an oak tree; *if you plant an acorn, don't expect an oak tree to grow overnight*

④ **acoustic**
[ə'kustɪk] *adjective*
referring to sound

④ **acoustics**
[ə'kustɪks] *noun*
quality of sound; *the acoustics in the concert hall*

④ **acquaintance**
[ə'kweɪntəns] *noun*
(a) knowing someone; **to make the acquaintance of someone** = to get to know someone for the first time; *I made her acquaintance when we were at college together*
(b) person you know; *she has many acquaintances in the newspaper industry but no real friends*

④ **acquiescence**
[ækwɪ'esəns] *noun*
(formal) agreement without protest; *all we need is the acquiescence of the local chief of police*

③ **acquire**
[ə'kwaɪər] *verb*
to obtain or to get; *she has acquired a large collection of shoes*; **acquired taste** = something that you come to like after a time; *sushi is something of an acquired taste*

④ **acquisition**
[ækwɪ'zɪ[n] *noun*
(a) act of acquiring; *his acquisition of half the shares in the company shocked the staff*
(b) thing that has been acquired; *the museum is very proud of its latest acquisition - a Picasso!*

② **acre**
['eɪkər] *noun*
measure of land, 4840 square yards or 0.4047 hectare (NOTE: the plural is used with figures, except before a noun: **he has bought a farm of 250 acres** *or* **he has bought a 250-acre farm**)

④ **acrid**
['ækrɪd] *adjective*
with a bitter smell; *acrid black smoke poured out the building*

④ **acrimony**
['ækrɪməni] *noun*
bitterness; *her acrimony showed in the letter she wrote*

④ **acrobat**
['ækrəbæt] *noun*
person who performs spectacular physical movements for the public; **circus acrobats** = people who perform exercises as part of a circus show

④ **acrobatic**
[ækrə'bætɪk] *adjective*
moving in an artistic way, like an acrobat; *acrobatic exercises*

④ **acrobatics**
[ækrə'bætɪks] *noun*
acrobatic exercises

① **across**
[ə'krɒs]
1 *preposition*
(a) from one side to the other; *he helped the old lady across the street; don't run across the road without looking to see if there is any traffic coming*

(b) on the other side; *he called to her from across the street; their house is across the street from ours* = it is just opposite our house
2 *adverb*
from one side to the other; *the river is only twenty feet across; the stream is very narrow - you can easily jump across*

① **act**
[ækt]
1 *noun*
(a) thing that is done; *he didn't forget the many acts of kindness she had shown him over the years; we caught him in the act* = we caught him as he was doing it
(b) part of a play, of a show; *Act II of the play takes place in the kitchen; the circus has acts with acrobats and wild animals*
(c) a law made by a legislative group; *an act of Congress; an act to ban the sale of weapons*
2 *verb*
(a) to take part in a movie, play, etc.; *she's acted on TV many times; he acted the part of Hamlet in the movie*
(b) to do something; *you will have to act quickly if you want to stop the fire; she acted in a very responsible way;* **to act on behalf of** = to represent; *the lawyer is acting on behalf of the old lady's family;* **to act as** = to do the work of; *the thick curtain acts as a screen to cut out noise from the street*
(c) to behave; *he's started acting very strangely*

① **acting**
['æktɪŋ]
1 *adjective*
taking the place of someone who is absent; *Mr. Smith is the acting chairman while Mr. Dempsey is in the hospital*
2 *noun*
profession of an actor; *he has decided on a career in acting*

① **action**
['æk[ən] *noun*
(a) doing something; *what action are you going to take to prevent accidents?*; **out of action** = not working; *the car has been out of action for a week; the goalkeeper broke his leg and will be out of action for some time*
(b) what happens in a play, movie, etc.; *the action of the play takes place in an LA apartment*
(c) instruction to start filming; *lights, camera, action!*
(d) case in a law court where someone sues someone else; *an action for libel or a libel action; to bring an action for damages against someone;* **to take legal action against someone** = to sue someone

④ **activate**
['æktɪveɪt] *verb*
(a) to make something start to work; *touching the door activated an alarm signal*
(b) to start a chemical reaction

② **active**
['æktɪv] *adjective*
(a) energetic or positive; *my grandmother is still very active at the age of 88; he didn't play an active part in the attack on the police station*
(b) *(volcano)* which is erupting; *scientists think the volcano is no longer active*
(c) on active duty = serving in the armed services in time of war; *he was killed during active service*
(d) form of a verb that shows that the subject is doing something (NOTE: if you say "the automobile hit him" the verb is active, but "he was hit by the automobile" is passive)

② **actively**
['æktɪvli] *adverb*
in an active way; *the store is actively recruiting new staff*

④ **activist**
['æktɪvɪst] *noun*
person who vigorously supports a political party; *the meeting was disrupted by an argument between the chairman and left-wing activists*

④ **activity**
[æk'tɪvɪti] *noun*
(a) being active; *there was a lot of activity on the stock market*
(b) occupation, thing you do to amuse yourself; *children are offered various summertime activities - sailing, windsurfing, water-skiing, etc.* (NOTE: plural in this meaning is **activities**)

① **actor** *or* **actress**
['æktər *or* 'æktrəs] *noun*
person who acts in the theater, in movies, on television; *a famous TV actor* (NOTE: the plural of **actress** is **actresses**)

② **actual**
['æktjʊəl] *adjective*
real; *it looks quite small but the actual height is 15 feet; her actual words were much stronger;* **in actual fact** = really; *in spite of what the newspapers said, in actual fact he did sell his condo*

④ **actuality**
[æktjʊ'ælɪti] *noun*
(formal) reality

③ **actually**
['æktjʊəli] *adverb*
really; *it looks pretty small, but actually it's over 40 feet high; he told his boss he was sick, but actually he wanted to go to the baseball game*

④ **acupuncture**
['ækjʊpʌŋktʃər] *noun*
(Chinese medicine) treatment where needles are inserted through the skin into nerve centres in order to relieve pain or to treat a disorder, etc.

③ **acute**
[ə'kjut] *adjective*
(a) (serious illness or pain) which starts suddenly and lasts for a short time; *he felt acute chest pains; the pain was very acute;* compare CHRONIC
(b) acute angle = angle that is less than 90º
(c) keen; *dogs have an acute sense of smell*
(d) acute accent = mark sloping forward over a vowel, indicating a change of sound; *"café" has an acute accent on the "e"*

③ **ad**
[æd] *noun*
(informal) = ADVERTISEMENT; *if you want to sell your automobile quickly, put an ad in the paper;* **classified ads** *or* **want ads** = newspaper advertisements that are listed under special headings, such as "help wanted" or "property for sale"; *look in the classified ads if you want a cheap stove*

④ **adage**
['ædɪdʒ] *noun*
old saying; *according to the old adage, time is the great healer*

④ **adagio**
[ə'dɑdʒɪəʊ] *noun*
slow piece of music

③ **adapt**
[ə'dæpt] *verb*
(a) to change something so that it fits; *the play has been adapted for television; she adapted the story for TV; the automobile has been adapted for a disabled driver*
(b) to change to become more suitable; *the country will have to adapt to the new political system*

③ **adaptable**
[ə'dæptəbl] *adjective*
able to change to deal with a new situation; *she's very adaptable, I'm sure that she won't mind teaching another subject*

④ **adaptation**
[ædæp'teɪʃn] *noun*
(a) change which fits new conditions; *the adaptation of the eye to different levels of brightness*
(b) film, play, etc., which has been adapted from another; *a new adaptation of 'Pickwick Papers' for television*

① **add**
[æd] *verb*
(a) to make a total of numbers; *if you add all these numbers together it should make fifty* (NOTE: **adding** is usually shown by the plus sign +: **10 + 4 = 14:** say "ten plus four equals fourteen")
(b) to join to something else; *interest is added to the account monthly; add two cupfuls of sugar; put a tea bag into the pot and add boiling water; by building the extension, they have added thirty rooms to the hotel; this paint is too thick - add some water to it*
(c) to say or to write something more; *I have nothing to add to what I put in my letter; she added that we still owed her some money for work she did last month*

④ **addict**
['ædɪkt] *noun*
person who cannot stop doing something, especially taking drugs; **drug addict** = person who takes drugs as a habit; *the clinic specializes in the treatment of drug addicts*

④ **addicted**
[ə'dɪktɪd] *adjective*
(person) who cannot stop doing something; *people addicted to alcohol can be treated at the clinic*

④ **addiction**
[ə'dɪkʃn] *noun*
not being able to stop doing something; *he hopes to cure her drug addiction*

① **addition**
[ə'dɪʃn] *noun*
(a) action of adding figures to make a total; *you don't need a calculator to do a simple addition*
(b) thing or person added; *the latest addition to the family*; *he showed us the additions to his collection of paintings*
(c) **in addition** = also; **in addition to** = as well as; *there are twelve letters to be mailed in addition to this package*

③ **additional**
[ə'dɪʃənəl] *adjective*
more; *additional tax will have to be paid*

③ **additionally**
[æ'dɪʃənəli] *adverb*
in addition; *the price includes the camera, the case and additionally six free rolls of film*

① **address**
[ə'dres]
1 *noun*
(a) details of the number of a house, the name of a street and the town where someone lives or works; *what is the doctor's address?*; *he wrote his address on a piece of paper*; **business address** = address of a business (as opposed to private address); *my business address and phone number are printed on the card*; **home address** *or* **private address** = address of a house or apartment where someone lives; *please send the plane tickets to my home address*; **address book** = special notebook, with columns printed in such a way that names, addresses and phone numbers can be entered; **address list** = list of addresses
(b) formal speech; *during the president's 'State of the Union' address he did not comment on the increase in violent crime* (NOTE: plural is **addresses**)
2 *verb*
(a) to write the details of name, street, town, etc., on a letter or package; *that letter is addressed to me - don't open it!*
(b) to speak to, to write to; *please address any comments or concerns to our main office*; *I was addressing the police officer, not you!*
(c) to make a formal speech; *the chairman addressed the meeting*

(d) to examine a problem; *this is an important issue which must be addressed at the next meeting*; *the committee failed to address the question of sexual harassment*

④ **adequate**
['ædɪkwət] *adjective*
enough; *his salary is barely adequate to support his family*; *we don't have adequate supplies for the whole journey*

③ **adhesive**
[əd'hizɪv]
1 *adjective*
which sticks; *she sealed the parcel with adhesive tape*; **self-adhesive** = which sticks to itself; *self-adhesive envelopes are easy to use*
2 *noun*
glue; *she bought a tube of adhesive*

② **adjective**
['ædʒektɪv] *noun*
word that describes a noun; *in the phrase "a big black cloud", "big" and "black" are both adjectives*

④ **adjoin**
[ə'dʒɔɪn] *verb*
to be next to; *a bedroom and an adjoining bathroom*

④ **adjourn**
[ə'dʒɜrn] *verb*
to postpone to a later date; *the meeting was adjourned until May 25*

① **adjust**
[ə'dʒʌst] *verb*
(a) to make a slight change to; *if the glasses are too tight, we can easily adjust the fitting*
(b) **to adjust to** = to change and adapt to; *it's difficult adjusting to living in a tropical climate*

④ **adjustment**
[ə'dʒʌstmənt] *noun*
slight change to make something work well; *a slight adjustment to the central heating pump*

④ **ad-lib**
['æd'lɪb] *(informal) verb*
to speak without a script (NOTE: **ad-libbing - ad-libbed**)

④ **administer**
[əd'mɪnɪstər] *verb*
(a) *(a country, an office, a company)* to manage, to organize; *the province was administered by Portugal for many years*
(b) *(formal)* to give; *to administer a drug to a patient*
(c) *(formal)* **to administer an oath** = to make someone swear an oath

③ **administration**
[ədmɪnɪ'streɪʃn] *noun*
(a) action of organizing; *hospital administration must be improved*; *who's in charge of administration here?*
(b) **the administration** = the government; *the Reagan Administration*

(c) the administration of justice = providing justice

③ **administrative**
[əd'mɪnɪstrətɪv] *adjective*
referring to administration; *his duties are almost entirely administrative*; *administrative expenses are rising all the time*; *there is more administrative staff than workers*

③ **admiration**
[ædmə'reɪʃn] *noun*
respect for; *I have great admiration for her*; *everyone looked on in admiration as she showed how to flip pancakes*

① **admire**
[əd'maɪər] *verb*
to look at someone or something with respect; *we admired his garden*; *everyone admires her paintings*; *he was admired for his skill as a violinist*; *a much-admired chief justice*

④ **admiringly**
[əd'maɪrɪŋli] *adverb*
in an admiring way; *we all watched admiringly as she danced*

① **admission**
[əd'mɪʃn] *noun*
(a) being allowed to go in; *there is a $5 admission charge*; *admission to the exhibition is free on Sundays*; *my friend was refused admission to the restaurant because he was not wearing a necktie*
(b) statement saying that something is true; *his admission of fraud*; *her admission that she had taken the watch*

② **admit**
[əd'mɪt] *verb*
(a) to allow someone to go in; *children are admitted free, but adults have to pay*; *this ticket admits three persons*
(b) to say that something is true; *he admitted stealing the car*; *she admitted she had taken the watch* (NOTE: **admitting - admitted**)

④ **admittance**
[əd'mɪtəns] *noun*
(formal) allowing someone to go into a place; *he gained admittance to the building by a door which had been left unlocked*

④ **admonition**
[ædmə'nɪʃn] *noun*
(formal) warning given to someone

④ **adolescence**
[ædə'lesns] *noun*
period between childhood and adulthood, between the ages of 12 and 18; *skin troubles in adolescence must be taken seriously*

④ **adolescent**
[ædə'lesənt]
1 *adjective*
referring to the period between being a child and being an adult; *she teaches a class of adolescent boys*

2 *noun*
young person between 12 and 18; *all adolescents rebel against the authority of their parents*

② **adopt**
[ə'dɒpt] *verb*
(a) to take legally as a son or daughter; *they have adopted a little boy*
(b) to take; *the opposition parties have adopted a different line of argument*; *he adopted an innocent air*
(c) to accept or begin to use (something); *the book has been adopted for use in all math classes*
(d) to vote to accept (something); *the motion was adopted*

④ **adoration**
[ædə'reɪʃn] *noun*
admiration, love; *his adoration for his young wife*

④ **adore**
[ə'dɔr] *verb*
to like very much; *she adores Italian food*

④ **adrift**
[ə'drɪft] *adverb*
drifting, not being steered by anyone; *the mutineers took over the ship and set the captain adrift in a small boat*

① **adult**
['ædʌlt]
1 *adjective*
(a) fully grown; *an adult tiger*
(b) referring to grown-up people; **adult education** = teaching people over the age of 20
2 *noun*
grown-up person; *children are admitted free, but adults have to pay*

④ **adulterate**
[ə'dʌltəreɪt] *verb*
(a) to add water to milk, wine
(b) to make something less pure by adding an inferior substance to it

④ **adulthood**
['ædʌlthʊd] *noun*
period when someone is adult; *young people reach adulthood at the age of 18*

② **advance**
[əd'væns]
1 *noun*
(a) movement forward; *the police have made some advances in their fight against crime*
(b) in advance = early; *if you want to get good seats for the play, you need to book three weeks in advance*; *you must phone well in advance to make an appointment*; *they asked us to pay $500 in advance*
(c) money paid as a loan or as a part of a payment to be made later; *she received an advance from the publisher for her book*; *can I have an advance of $100 against next month's salary?*

2 *verb*
(a) to go forward; *the police slowly advanced across the park*
(b) to pay as a loan; *he advanced me $200*
(c) to bring a date forward; *the date of the meeting has been advanced by a week*

② **advanced**
[əd'vænst] *adjective*
(a) which is studied after studying for several years; *he is taking advanced mathematics; she is studying for an advanced degree*
(b) which has moved forward; *in an advanced state of decay*

④ **advantage**
[əd'væntɪdʒ] *noun*
thing that will help you to be successful; *being able to drive an automobile is an advantage; knowledge of two foreign languages is an advantage in this job; she has several advantages over the other candidates for the job*; **to take advantage of** = to profit from; *they took advantage of the cheap fares being offered*; **to take advantage of someone** = to cheat someone; *he took advantage of the old lady*; **to advantage** = to make someone look perfect; *her dress shows off her figure to advantage*; **to use to great advantage** = to use in a way that helps you win

④ **advantageous**
[ædvən'teɪdʒəs] *adjective*
profitable, likely to help; *the contract would certainly be advantageous to us*

④ **advent**
['ædvent] *noun*
arrival; *the advent of spring; the advent of the industrial revolution changed the world*

① **adventure**
[əd'ventʃər] *noun*
new, exciting and dangerous experience; *I have to tell you about our adventures in Arizona*

③ **adverb**
['ædvɜrb] *noun*
word that modifies a verb, an adjective, another adverb or a whole sentence; *in the phrase "he walked slowly, because the snow was very thick", "slowly" and "very" are both adverbs*

④ **adversary**
['ædvərsəri] *noun*
opponent, the person you are fighting; *his first adversary in the ring was known as 'Man Mountain'* (NOTE: plural is **adversaries**)

④ **adverse**
['ædvɜrs] *adjective*
(conditions) which do not help, which go against you; *will the plan for the set of new traffic lights have any adverse effects on the village?*

① **advertise**
['ædvərtaɪz] *verb*
to make sure that people know that something is for sale, that something is going to happen, that a show is on; *there are posters all over the town advertising the movie; I sent away for a watch which I saw advertised in the paper; did you see that the new diner is advertising cheap meals on Sundays?; the company is advertising for secretaries*

② **advertisement**
[əd'vɜrtɪzmənt] *noun*
announcement which tries to make sure that people know that something is for sale, that something is going to happen, that a show is on; *he put an advertisement in the paper; she answered an advertisement in the paper*; **classified advertisements** = advertisements listed in a newspaper under special headings, such as "property for sale" or "help wanted"

④ **advertiser**
['ædvərtaɪzər] *noun*
person who advertises; *the advertiser will pay for postage on orders*

① **advertising**
['ædvərtaɪzɪŋ] *noun*
the action of making sure that people know that something is for sale, that something is going to happen, that a show is on; *they spent millions on the advertising campaign; the company has increased the amount of money it spends on advertising*; **advertising agency** = agency that organizes advertisements for other companies

① **advice**
[əd'vaɪs] *noun*
saying what should be done; *he went to the bank manager for advice on how to pay his debts; they would not listen to the doctor's advice; my grandfather gave me a very useful piece of advice; his mother's advice was to stay in bed; she took or followed the doctor's advice and stopped smoking* (NOTE: no plural: **some advice**; for one item say **a piece of advice**)

④ **advisable**
[əd'vaɪzəbl] *adjective*
which is recommended; *it is advisable to take warm clothing*

② **advise**
[əd'vaɪz] *verb*
to suggest what should be done; *he advised her to put all her money into a savings account*

② **advise against**
[əd'vaɪz ə'genst] *verb*
to suggest that something should not be done; *he advised against buying the house*

③ **adviser** *or* **advisor**
[əd'vaɪzər] *noun*
person who gives advice; *he is consulting his financial adviser*

④ **advocate**
1 *noun* ['ædvəkət]
person who pleads for a cause; *the advocates of capital punishment*
2 ['ædvəkeɪt] *verb*
to recommend; *she advocates the abolition of capital punishment*

③ **aerosol**
['eərəsɒl] *noun*
can which sends out a liquid such as an insect spray, medicine, etc., in the form of tiny drops; *it's much easier to use an aerosol to spray the kitchen*

④ **affable**
['æfəbl] *adjective*
pleasant and easy to talk to; *the boss always had an affable word for each member of staff*

③ **affair**
[ə'feər] *noun*
(a) thing that concerns someone; *that's his affair - it has nothing to do with me*; *it's an affair for the police*; *she's always sticking her nose into other people's affairs*; *his business affairs were very complicated*
(b) (**love**) **affair** = sexual relationship; *he's having an affair with his boss's wife*
(c) **state of affairs** = general situation; *the present state of affairs*
(d) **affairs of state** = government business

③ **affect**
[ə'fekt] *verb*
to have an influence on, to change; *the new regulations have affected our business*; *train services have been seriously affected by the strike*

③ **affection**
[ə'fekʃn] *noun*
liking or love; *she felt great affection for her youngest grandson*

④ **affidavit**
[æfi'deɪvɪt] *noun*
written statement which is signed and sworn before a lawyer and which can then be used as evidence in court

④ **affiliate**
[ə'filieɪt] *noun*
person or company linked to another one; *we have affiliates in several states*

④ **afflict**
[ə'flɪkt] *verb*
(a) to make someone very sad; *she was afflicted by the news of her father's death*
(b) to make someone suffer; *the country has been afflicted by natural disasters*

④ **affluence**
['æfluəns] *noun*
wealth

④ **affluent**
['æfluənt] *adjective*
very rich; **affluent society** = society where most people are rich

① **afford**
[ə'fɔrd] *verb*
to have enough money to pay for; *we can't afford to drive a large automobile these days*; *he couldn't afford the time to take a vacation* (NOTE: only used after **can, cannot, could, could not, able to**)

④ **affordable**
[ə'fɔrdəbl] *adjective*
which can be afforded; *the price of the meal was quite affordable*; *living in the center of Chicago is not affordable any more*

④ **afloat**
[ə'fləʊt] *adverb*
floating, not sinking; *she kept afloat by holding on to a piece of wood*

① **afraid**
[ə'freɪd] *adjective*
(a) **to be afraid of something** = to be frightened of something; *I am afraid of snakes*; *she is afraid of going out alone*; *he's too afraid to climb the ladder*
(b) **to be afraid (that)** = to be sorry to say; *I'm afraid that all the cookies have been sold*; *you can't see the boss - I'm afraid he's sick*; *do you have a pocket calculator? - no, I'm afraid not* (NOTE: **afraid** cannot be used in front of a noun: **the girl's afraid** but **a frightened girl**)

① **Africa**
['æfrɪkə] *proper noun*
large continent, to the south of the Mediterranean, between the Atlantic Ocean and the Indian Ocean; *they want to go to Africa on vacation*; *after ten days at sea, they saw the coast of North Africa in the distance*

② **African**
['æfrɪkən]
1 *adjective*
referring to Africa; *the African jungle*; **African elephant** = type of elephant with large ears (the other type is the Indian elephant)
2 *noun*
person from Africa; *the guitarist is an African*

② **African-American**
['æfrɪkənə'merɪkən] *noun*
American of African, especially black African, descent

① **after**
['æftər]
1 *preposition*
(a) following or next in order; *what's the letter after Q in the alphabet?*; *if today is Tuesday, the day after tomorrow is Thursday*; *they spoke one after the other*; **after you** = you go first
(b) later than; *we arrived after six o'clock*; *he should be in bed - it's after ten o'clock*; *we don't let the children go out alone after dark*
(c) **to be after someone** = (i) to be looking for someone; (ii) to be angry with someone; *the police are after him*; *if you leave mud all over the kitchen floor, your mother will be after you*; *what's she after?* = what does she want?
2 *conjunction*
later than a time; *after the snow fell, the freeways were closed*; *after the driver had got in, the bus started*; *phone me after you get home* (NOTE: **after** is used with many verbs: **look after, take after**, etc.)

① **after all**
['æftər'ɔl] *adverb*
(a) in spite of everything; *she changed her mind and decided to come with us after all*
(b) the fact is; *I think I'll go for a walk - after all, it's a nice day out and I've finished my work*

④ **aftermath**
['æftərmæθ] *noun*
time after a catastrophe; *they had to clear up in the aftermath of the storm*

① **afternoon**
[æftə'nun] *noun*
time between lunchtime and the evening; *he always has a little sleep in the afternoon; the store is closed on Wednesday afternoons; can we meet this afternoon?; there is an afternoon flight to Vancouver; I'm playing tennis tomorrow afternoon*

④ **afterthought**
['æftərθɔt] *noun*
thing which you only think of or do later; **as an afterthought** = showing that you have just thought of something new; *he signed the letter and as an afterthought added a row of kisses*

① **afterward** *or* **afterwards**
['æftəwəd *or* 'æftəwədz] *adverb*
later; *we'll have lunch first and go shopping afterward; she felt fine before dinner but was sick afterward*

① **again**
[ə'gen] *adverb*
(a) another time, once more; *he wrote again to say he was sick; we'd love to come to see you again; he had to take his driver's test again*
(b) back as you were before; *although I like going on vacation, I'm always glad to be home again; she brought the jeans back to the store again because they didn't fit*

◇ **once again**
['wʌns ə'gen]
another time; *once again, the train was late*

◇ **yet again**
['jet ə'gen]
once more after many times; *she's taking her driver's test yet again*

① **against**
[ə'genst] *preposition*
(a) touching; *he was leaning against the wall; she hit her head against the low doorway*
(b) not as someone suggests; **it's against the rules** *or* **against the law** = it's not as the rules say, not as the law says; *it's against the law to drive in the dark without lights; in soccer you mustn't hold the ball in your hands - it's against the rules; what do you have against the plan?* = why don't you agree with the plan?; *she was against the idea of going to the movie theater*
(c) opposite; *the San Antonio Spurs are playing against the Chicago Bulls tomorrow; it's hard cycling uphill against the wind*

(d) as part of; *can I have an advance against next month's salary?*

① **age**
[eidʒ] *noun*
(a) the number of years that you have lived; *what age will he be on his next birthday?; she is thirty years of age; he looks younger than his age;* **old age** = period when you are old; **under age** = younger than the legal age to do something; *the federal government is taking action against under-age drinking*
(b) **ages** = a very long time; *I've been waiting here for ages; it took us ages to get served*

① **aged**
adjective
(a) [eidʒd] with the age of; *a girl aged nine; she died last year, aged 83*
(b) ['eidʒid] very old; *an aged man* (NOTE: in this meaning, it comes before the noun)

② **agency**
['eidʒənsi] *noun*
office that represents another firm; *an advertising agency;* **real estate agency** = office that arranges for the sale of houses, apartments, etc.; **travel agency** = office that sells air tickets, organizes tours, etc. (NOTE: plural is **agencies**)

④ **agenda**
[ə'dʒendə] *noun*
list of points for discussion; *we will now discuss item five on the agenda; after two hours we were still discussing the first item on the agenda; what's on the agenda?* = what are we going to discuss?

② **agent**
['eidʒənt] *noun*
person who works for or represents someone else; *our head office is in New York City but we have an agent in Boston; it's easier to buy a house if you use a real estate agent;* **travel agent** = person who sells tickets, organizes tours, etc.; *I bought my plane tickets at the travel agent's*

④ **aggravate**
['ægrəveit] *verb*
(a) to make something worse; *playing football aggravated his knee injury*
(b) (*informal*) to annoy

④ **aggravating**
['ægrəveitiŋ] *adjective*
(*informal*) annoying; *it's really aggravating - every time I try to use the telephone the line is busy*

④ **aggravation**
[ægrə'veiʃn] *noun*
making worse; *his letter was a further aggravation to the quarrel*

③ **aggressive**
[ə'gresiv] *adjective*
ready to attack; *she's very aggressive toward her family; why are you getting so aggressive?*

④ **aggressor**
[ə'gresər] *noun*
person or country that attacks another; *they were the aggressors in the war*

④ **agile**
['ædʒəl] *adjective*
that can move easily; *he's very agile - he can climb up a rope easily*

④ **agitate**
['ædʒɪteɪt] *verb*
(a) to shake (a bottle)
(b) to worry (someone)

④ **agnostic**
[æg'nɒstɪk] *noun*
person who believes that no one can know if God exists

① **ago**
[ə'gəʊ] *adverb*
in the past; *he phoned a few minutes ago*; *she came to the U.S.A. two years ago*; *this all happened a long time ago* (NOTE: **ago** always follows a word meaning time)

④ **agonize**
['ægənaɪz] *verb*
to suffer; *to agonize over a decision* = to worry about a decision

① **agree**
[ə'gri] *verb*
(a) to say yes; *we asked her to come with us and she agreed*; *he nodded to show that he agreed*; *most of the group agreed with her suggestion*; *after some discussion he agreed to our plan* (NOTE: you agree **to** *or* **on** a plan)
(b) to agree with someone = to think the same way as someone; *I agree with you that most people drive too fast*
(c) not to agree with someone = to make someone ill; *I never eat shellfish - it doesn't agree with me*; *all this rich food doesn't agree with me*
(d) to agree to do something = to say that you will do something; *she agreed to baby-sit for us*; *the bank will never agree to lend the company $400,000*

① **agreement**
[ə'grimənt] *noun*
(a) thinking the same; *to reach an agreement or to come to an agreement on salaries*; *agreement between the two sides is still a long way off*; *they are in agreement with our plan* = they agree with our plan; *we discussed the plan with them and they are in agreement*
(b) contract; *we signed an agreement with the Canadian company*; *to draw up or to draft an agreement*

② **agricultural**
[ægrɪ'kʌltʃərəl] *adjective*
referring to agriculture; *agricultural machinery*

② **agriculture**
['ægrɪkʌltʃər] *noun*
growing crops or raising animals on farms; *not many people work in agriculture compared with fifty years ago*; *the country's agriculture is based on rice*

④ **agronomist**
[ə'grɒnəmɪst] *noun*
person who studies agronomy

④ **agronomy**
[ə'grɒnəmɪ] *noun*
scientific study of soil management and the cultivation of crops

② **ah**
[ɑ] *interjection showing surprise*
Ah! Jeff, how nice to see you!; *the audience let out "oohs" and "ahs" as they watched the performance*

① **ahead**
[ə'hed] *adverb*
in front; *our team was losing, but now we are ahead again*; *run on ahead and find some seats for us*; *you need to go straight ahead, and then make a left*; *full steam ahead!* = go forward as fast as possible; *to draw ahead* = to become the leader in a race, etc.

① **ahead of**
[ə'hed 'ɒv] *preposition*
in front of; *ahead of us was a steep hill*; *you have a mass of work ahead of you*; *they ran on ahead of the others*

④ **ahoy**
[ə'hɔɪ] *interjection*
used by sailors to call another ship

① **aid**
[eɪd] *noun*
(a) help; *aid to Third World countries*; *aid agency*; *aid worker*
(b) first aid = help for injured people; *we keep a first aid kit in the office*
(c) in aid of = to help; *we give money in aid of the Red Cross*; *they are collecting money in aid of refugees*
(d) device that helps; *he wears a hearing aid*; *food processors are useful aids in the kitchen*

④ **aide**
[eɪd] *noun*
assistant to an important person; *the president came with two of his aides*

④ **ailment**
['eɪlmənt] *noun*
illness, though not generally a very serious one; *measles is one of the common childhood ailments*

① **aim**
[eɪm]
1 *noun*
what you are trying to do; *his aim is to do well at school and then go to college*; *one of our aims is to increase the speed of service*
2 *verb*
(a) to plan to do something; *we aim to go on vacation in June*
(b) to point a weapon at something; *he was not aiming at the target*

④ **ain't**
['eɪnt] *verb*
(slang) = IS NOT

① **air**
[eər]
1 *noun*
(a) mixture of gases (mainly oxygen and nitrogen) which cannot be seen, but which is all around us and which every animal breathes; *his breath was like steam in the cold air*; *the mountain air feels cold*; *he threw the ball up into the air*
(b) method of traveling (or sending goods) using aircraft; **airfares** = different types of fares charged for travel on aircraft
(c) appearance or feeling; *there was an air of gloom over the meeting*
2 *verb*
to make (a room, clothes, etc.) fresher; *let's open the windows to air the bedroom*

◇ **by air**
['baɪ 'eər]
in an aircraft; *we are sending the goods by air, not by sea*; *send the letter by air if you want it to arrive before Christmas*

④ **airbase**
['eərbeɪs] *noun*
military airfield; *our planes bombed enemy airbases*

④ **air-conditioned**
['eər kən'dɪʃənd] *adjective*
having the temperature controlled by an air conditioner; *the office is air-conditioned*

① **air conditioner**
['eər kən'dɪʃənər] *noun*
device that cools the air in a room; *how can we turn the air conditioner off?*

① **air-conditioning**
['eər kən'dɪʃənɪŋ] *noun*
system of controlling the temperature in a room or office or train, etc.; *if you rent a car in Texas, make sure it has air-conditioning*; **to turn the air-conditioning on** = to start the making the air cooler; **to turn the air-conditioning off** = to stop the air being cooled; **to turn the air-conditioning down** = to make a room warmer; **to turn the air-conditioning up** = to make a room cooler

② **aircraft**
['eərkræft] *noun*
machine that flies in the air; *the passengers got into the aircraft*; *the airline has a fleet of ten aircraft*; *the president came down the aircraft steps* (NOTE: plural is **aircraft: one aircraft, six aircraft**)

④ **airfield**
['eərfild] *noun*
small, usually military, airport; *we landed at a military airfield*

② **air force**
['eər 'fɔrs] *noun*
the organization that runs a country's fighting planes; *he's joined the U.S. Air Force*

④ **airing**
['eərɪŋ] *noun*
action of putting something in fresh air

① **airline**
['eərlaɪn] *noun*
company that runs air services; *which airline are you flying with?*; *he's an airline pilot*; *the airline has been voted the most popular with business travelers*

① **airmail**
['eərmeɪl]
1 *noun*
way of sending letters or packages by air; *we sent the package by next-day airmail*; **airmail envelope** = very light envelope for sending airmail letters
2 *verb*
to send letters or packages by air; *we airmailed the documents to London*

① **airplane**
['eərpleɪn] *noun*
aircraft; *the president came down the airplane steps*

① **airport**
['eərpɔrt] *noun*
place where aircraft land and take off; *you can take the subway to the airport*; *we are due to arrive at O'Hare Airport at 6 P.M.*; *we leave from O'Hare Airport at 10:00 P.M.*; **airport shuttle** = bus that takes passengers to and from an airport; *there is an airport shuttle that takes passengers downtown*

④ **air raid**
['eər 'reɪd] *noun*
attack by military aircraft; *people hid underground during the air raid*

④ **airsick**
['eərsɪk] *adjective*
sick when traveling by air; *take one of these tablets if you feel airsick*

④ **airstrip**
['eərstrɪp] *noun*
small runway; *they landed on an airstrip in the jungle*

④ **airwaves**
['eərweɪvz] *noun*
way in which radio signals move through the air

④ **airy**
['eəri] *adjective*
full of fresh air; *light airy rooms*

③ **ajar**
[ə'dʒɑr] *adjective*
slightly open; *leave the door ajar to let in some air*

② **alarm**
[ə'lɑrm]
1 *noun*

(a) loud warning; *an alarm will sound if someone touches the wire*; **to raise the alarm** = to warn everyone of danger; **it was only a false alarm** = it was only a wrong warning
(b) **burglar alarm** = device that rings if a burglar enters a building; **fire alarm** = bell that sounds if there is a fire; **alarm bell** = bell that rings to warn people; **alarm clock** = clock that can be set to ring a bell at a certain time to wake you up; *I set my alarm for 5:30 because I had to catch the 7 o'clock plane*
(c) being afraid; *the expression on his face increased her alarm*; *there's no cause for alarm, the injection won't hurt at all*
2 *verb*
to warn or frighten; *I don't want to alarm you, but the police say a dangerous criminal has been seen in town*

④ **albeit**
[ɔl'biːt] *conjunction*
(formal) although; *an excellent concert, albeit rather long*

① **album**
['ælbəm] *noun*
(a) large book; *an album of photos or a photo album*; *he showed me his stamp album*
(b) collections of songs on a CD, cassette, etc.; *this is her latest album*

② **alcohol**
['ælkəhɒl] *noun*
liquid, such as beer, wine, etc., which can make you drunk; *the bar will not serve alcohol to anyone under the age of 21*

① **alcoholic**
[ælkə'hɒlɪk]
1 *adjective*
referring to alcohol; *they served alcoholic drinks as well as fruit juice*
2 *noun*
person who is addicted to alcohol; *she went to a clinic for alcoholics*

② **alert**
[ə'lɜrt]
1 *adjective*
(a) able to think clearly; *after a short sleep he was bright and alert*
(b) watching carefully; *the guard must remain alert at all times*
2 *noun*
warning signal; *he gave the alert*; **to be on the alert** = *to watch out for something*
3 *verb*
to alert someone to = to warn someone of something; *children are alerted to the dangers of smoking*

④ **algebra**
['ældʒɪbrə] *noun*
type of mathematics where letters are used to represent quantities

④ **alias**
['eɪliəs] *noun*

false name; *he traveled under the alias of Dupont* (NOTE: plural is **aliases**)

④ **alien**
['eɪliən]
1 *adjective*
foreign, different; *speaking foreign languages is alien to the American way of life*
2 *noun*
foreigner, a person who is not a citizen of the country; *aliens are not permitted to travel outside the capital*; *when you arrive at the airport, you must go through the door marked "aliens"*

④ **alight**
[ə'laɪt]
1 *verb*
(formal) to get off a bus, etc.; *alight here for the Post Office*
2 *adjective*
on fire; *after pouring gas on the heap of rubbish he set it alight*

① **alike**
[ə'laɪk] *adjective*
very similar; *the two sisters are very alike*

④ **alimony**
['ælɪmənɪ] *noun*
money paid regularly by someone to a divorced partner

① **alive**
[ə'laɪv] *adjective*
(a) not dead; *he was still alive when he was rescued, even though he had been in the sea for hours*; *when my grandfather was alive, there was no television* (NOTE: **alive** cannot be used in front of a noun: **the fish is alive** but **a live fish**)
(b) lively; *the fishing port is dead during the daytime, but really comes alive at night*

④ **alkali**
['ælkəlaɪ] *noun*
substance that neutralizes acids and forms salts; *an alkali plus an acid gives a salt* (NOTE: plural is **alkalies**)

④ **alkaline**
['ælkəlaɪn] *adjective*
containing more alkali than acid; *an alkaline solution*

① **all**
[ɔl]
1 *adjective & pronoun*
everything or everyone; *did you pick all (of) the tomatoes?*; *where are all the children?*; *they all like coffee or all of them like coffee*; **let's sing the song all together** = everyone at the same time
2 *adverb*
(a) completely; *the ground was all white after the snow fell*; *I forgot all about her birthday*
(b) **all by yourself** = all alone; *you can't do it all by yourself*; *I'm all by myself this evening - my girlfriend's gone out*; *he drove the truck all by himself*

◇ **not at all**
['nɒt ət 'ɔl]
certainly not; *do you mind waiting for a few minutes? - not at all!*; *she wasn't at all annoyed*

◇ **all along**
['ɔl ə'lɒŋ] *adverb*
(a) along the whole length of; *police were stationed all along the route of the parade*
(b) right from the beginning; *I knew all along that he was cheating me*; *we suspected all along that something was wrong*

◇ **all-American**
['ɔlə'merɪkən] *adjective*
typical of the United States; *an all-American football player*

◇ **all at once**
['ɔl ət 'wʌns] *phrase* suddenly; *all at once the telephone rang*

◇ **all the same**
['ɔl ðə 'seɪm] *phrase*
(a) in spite of this; *I'm not really keen on horror movies, but I'll go with you all the same*
(b) it's all the same = it makes no difference; *if it's all the same to you, I won't come to the party*

④ **allegation**
[ælɪ'geɪʃn] *noun*
suggestion that someone has possibly done something wrong; *she made several allegations about her boss*; *he denied the allegations made against him*

④ **allege**
[ə'ledʒ] *verb*
to suggest that someone may have done something wrong; *the police alleged that the accused was inside the building when the theft took place*

④ **alleged**
[ə'ledʒd] *adjective*
suggested; *the alleged victim refused to make a statement to the police*

④ **allegedly**
[ə'ledʒɪdlɪ] *adverb*
as has been suggested, but not proved; *the student allegedly offered her drugs*

③ **allergic**
[ə'lɜrdʒɪk] *adjective; to be allergic to* = to react badly to; *she is allergic to cats*; *he had an allergic reaction to peanuts*

③ **allergy**
['ælədʒɪ] *noun*
bad reaction to a substance; *she has an allergy to household dust*; *the baby has a tomato allergy*

④ **alley**
['ælɪ] *noun*
(a) narrow little street
(b) place for bowling

④ **alliance**
[ə'laɪəns] *noun*
formal link between two groups or countries; *the alliance between the United States and England*

④ **allied**
['ælaɪd] *adjective*
(a) linked in an alliance; *the allied powers*
(b) allied to = linked with; *his poor health allied to his age means that he will not be able to run the marathon*

④ **alligator**
['ælɪgeɪtər] *noun*
large reptile like a crocodile, found in the southern parts of the USA; *if you go to Florida you will see alligators*

④ **allocate**
['æləkeɪt] *verb*
to give out to various people; *we have allocated $2,500 to buying furniture for the office*; *our group was allocated rooms at the back of the hotel*

④ **allocation**
[ælə'keɪʃn] *noun*
giving as a share; *they set up a committee to decide the allocation of the money*

④ **all-out**
['ɔl'aʊt] *adjective*
total, involving a lot of work; *we must make an all-out effort*

③ **all over**
['ɔl 'əʊvər] *phrase*
(a) everywhere; *his coat was dirty all over*
(b) finished; *the show was all over by nine o'clock*

① **allow**
[ə'laʊ] *verb*
(a) to let someone do something; *she allowed me to borrow her book*; *smoking is not allowed in the restaurant*; *you are allowed to take two pieces of carry-on luggage onto the plane*
(b) to give; *we will allow you a discount*
(c) to agree or to accept legally; *to allow a claim for damages*

④ **allowable**
[ə'laʊəbl] *adjective*
which can be allowed

① **allowance**
[ə'laʊəns] *noun*
(a) money paid regularly; *she gets a weekly allowance from her father*
(b) something that is allowed; baggage allowance = weight of baggage that an air passenger is allowed to take free when he or she travels
(c) amount of money that you are allowed to earn without paying tax; *allowances against tax or tax allowances; personal allowances*
(d) to make allowances for = to take something into account; *you must make allowances for his age*

④ **allow for**
[ə'lau 'fɔr] *verb*
to allocate a certain amount of time or money; *to allow 10% extra for home delivery*

④ **alloy**
['ælɔɪ] *noun*
mixture of metals; *brass is an alloy of copper and zinc*

① **all right**
['ɔl 'raɪt]
1 *adjective*
well; *she was sick yesterday but is all right now*
2 *interjection; (meaning "yes") all right, here's your money; will you answer the telephone for me? - all right!* (NOTE: **OK** and **no problem** are often used in this meaning)

④ **all-star**
['ɔlstær] *adjective*
with many stars; *an all-star team*

④ **alluring**
[ə'ljʊrɪŋ] *adjective*
very attractive; *the alluring offer of a high salary*

④ **allusion**
[ə'luʒn] *noun*
referring indirectly to something; *I didn't understand his allusion*

④ **alluvial**
[ə'luviəl] *adjective*
deposited by rivers; *river deltas are created by alluvial deposits*

④ **alluvium**
[ə'luviəm] *noun*
silt deposited by rivers; *alluvium gives some of the most fertile soils*

④ **ally**
1 *noun* ['ælaɪ]
person or country which is on the same side; *he's a close ally of the leader of the opposition; when one of our allies is attacked, we have to come to their defense* (NOTE: plural is **allies**)
2 *verb* [ə'laɪ]
to ally yourself with *or* to someone = to join forces with someone; *the nationalists have allied themselves with the government party*

① **almost**
['ɒlməʊst] *adverb*
nearly; *London is almost as far from here as Paris; she's almost as tall as I am; she'll eat almost anything; hurry up, it's almost time for the train to leave*

① **alone**
[ə'ləʊn]
1 *adjective*
with no one else; *she lives alone with her cats; he was all alone in the store; we don't let the children go out alone after dark; I want to talk to you alone* = just the two of us together

2 *adverb*
(a) to leave someone alone = not to bother someone; *leave that cat alone and come and have your dinner*
(b) let alone = and certainly not; *he can't ride a bike let alone drive an automobile*

① **along**
[ə'lɒŋ]
1 *preposition*
(a) by the side of; *he planted fruit trees along both sides of the garden path; the river runs along one side of the railroad*
(b) from one end to the other; *she ran along the sidewalk; walk along the street until you come to the post office*
2 *adverb (with verbs)*
(a) to get along with someone = to agree with or to work well with someone; *she doesn't get along very well with her new boss; they don't get along very well together*
(b) to go with, to come with, etc.; *come along to the party; after the accident, she was taken along to the police station*

① **alongside**
[əlɒŋ'saɪd]
1 *preposition*
beside; *the ship was tied up alongside the dock*
2 *adverb*
beside; *we had stopped at a red light when a squad car pulled up alongside*

① **aloud**
[ə'laʊd] *adverb*
in a voice that can be heard; *she read the poem aloud*

① **alphabet**
['ælfəbet] *noun*
series of letters in order, A, B, C, etc.; *A is the first letter of the alphabet, and B is the second; G comes before L in the alphabet; if you're going to Greece on vacation, you ought to learn the Greek alphabet*

① **alphabetical**
[ælfə'betɪkl] *adjective*
referring to the alphabet; **in alphabetical order** = in order of the first letter of each word; *the words in the dictionary are in alphabetical order; the computer will sort out the addresses into alphabetical order*

② **already**
[ɔl'redɪ] *adverb*
(a) before now, before a certain time; *I've already done my shopping; it was already past ten o'clock when he arrived; I have seen that movie already* = I've seen that movie before
(b) sooner than expected; *have you finished your work already?*

② **also**
['ɔlsəʊ] *adverb*
too, as well as; *she sings well and can also play the violin; they came to visit us, and their kids also came*

④ **alter**
['ɒltər] *verb*
to change; *they wanted to alter the terms of the contract after they had signed it*; *he has altered the car so much I didn't recognize it*

③ **alteration**
[ɒltə'reɪʃn] *noun*
change; *she made some alterations to the design*

③ **alternate**
1 *adjective* [ɒl'tɜrnət]
every other one; *we see each other on alternate Sundays*
2 *verb* ['ɒltərneɪt]
to put something in place of something, then switch them around; *fill the pot with alternating layers of potato and onion*; *she alternated between excitement and gloom as she waited for her exam results*

④ **alternately**
[ɒl'tɜrnətli] *adverb*
by turns; one first and then the other

④ **alternative**
[ɒl'tɜrnətɪv]
1 *adjective*
(a) in place of something else; *if the plane is full, we will put you on an alternative flight*
(b) following a different way from usual; **alternative energy** = means of providing energy from the tide, the wind, the sun, etc., rather than by using coal, oil or nuclear power; **alternative medicine** = treating diseases by means which are not normally used by doctors (such as medicines made from herbs, etc.)
2 *noun*
something that takes the place of something else; *now that she has the measles, do we have any alternative to calling the vacation off?*; **there is no alternative** = there is nothing else we can do

② **although**
[ɒl'ðəʊ] *conjunction*
in spite of the fact that; *although it was freezing, she didn't put a jacket on*; *I've never been into that store although I've often walked past it*

④ **alto**
['æltəʊ] *noun*
low singing voice, lower than a soprano

④ **altogether**
[ɒltə'geðər] *adverb*
(a) taking everything together; *the food was $15 and the drinks $7, so that makes $22 altogether*; *the staff of the three stores come to 200 altogether*
(b) completely; *he's altogether a happier man since he got married*; *their situation is altogether different from ours*

④ **altruism**
['æltruɪzəm] *noun*
being unselfish

② **aluminum**
[ə'lumɪnəm] *noun*
extremely light silver metal; *we were given a set of aluminum saucepans for our wedding*; **aluminum foil** = very thin sheet of aluminum used for wrapping food before cooking; *wrap the fish in aluminum foil before putting it on the barbecue grill*; *cover the meat in a sheet of aluminum foil* (NOTE: Chemical element: chemical symbol: **Al**; atomic number: **13**)

④ **alumna**
[ə'lʌmnə] *noun*
a former woman student at a university or college or high school; *they are both alumnae of the same college* (NOTE: plural is **alumnae** [ə'lʌmni])

④ **alumnus**
[ə'lʌmnəs] *noun*
a former male student at a university or college or high school; *invitations to the concert were sent to all the alumni* (NOTE: plural is **alumni** [ə'lʌmnaɪ])

① **always**
['ɒlweɪz] *adverb*
(a) every time; *she is always late for work*; *why does it always rain when we want to go for a walk?*
(b) continually; *it's always hot in tropical countries*
(c) again and again; *she's always asking me to lend her money*

① **am**
[æm] *see* BE

① **A.M.**
['eɪ 'em] *adverb*
in the morning, before 12 o'clock; *I have to catch the 7 A.M. train to work every day*; *telephone calls made before 6 A.M. are charged at the cheap rate* (NOTE: **A.M.** is usually used to show the exact hour and the word **o'clock** is left out)

④ **amalgamation**
[əmælgə'meɪʃn] *noun*
act of combining together

③ **amateur**
['æmətər]
1 *noun*
(a) sportsman who is not paid to play; *the golf tournament is open to amateurs*
(b) someone who does something because he likes doing it; *for an amateur he's a very good painter*
2 *adjective*
(a) not paid; *he plays for the local amateur basketball team*
(b) doing something as a hobby rather than to earn money; *he's an amateur painter*; *our amateur theater club is putting on "Henry V"*

④ **amateurish**
['æmətərɪʃ] *adjective*
not well done, not done in a professional way; *his performance was quite amateurish*

① **amaze**
[ə'meɪz] *verb*
to surprise very much; *your attitude amazes me*; *they were amazed at the sounds and colors of the market*

① **amazement**
[ə'meɪzmənt] *noun*
great surprise; *to his amazement he won first prize*

① **amazing**
[ə'meɪzɪŋ] *adjective*
(a) very surprising; *it was amazing that she never suspected anything*
(b) extremely interesting and unusual; *it was an amazing experience, sailing down the Mississippi*

④ **ambassador**
[æm'bæsədər] *noun*
the representative of a country in another country; *His Excellency, the Japanese Ambassador*

④ **ambiguous**
[æm'bɪgjuəs] *adjective*
which has two meanings, which is not clear; *as it stands, the phrase is very ambiguous*

② **ambition**
[æm'bɪʃn] *noun*
desire to become great, rich or famous, or to do something special; *his great ambition is to ride on an elephant*

④ **ambitious**
[æm'bɪʃəs] *adjective*
with high aims; *she's a very ambitious young woman*

② **ambulance**
['æmbjuləns] *noun*
van that carries sick or injured people; *when she fell down the stairs, her husband called an ambulance*; *he pulled into the side of the road when he saw the ambulance coming*

② **ambush**
['æmbʊʃ]
1 *noun*
surprise attack by people who have been hiding; *the guerrillas lay in ambush beside the path* (NOTE: plural is **ambushes**)
2 *verb*
to wait hidden and attack someone by surprise; *the soldiers were ambushed as they went along the mountain path*

④ **amend**
[ə'mend] *verb*
to change for the better; *the president amended the text of the speech in several places*

③ **amendment**
[ə'mendmənt] *noun*
(a) change; *he has made several amendments to the text*
(b) proposed change to a law, to a proposal; *to propose an amendment to the constitution*; see also FIFTH

④ **amenity**
[ə'miniti] *noun*
ease of doing something; *the hotel has many amenities, that's why it is so popular* (NOTE: plural is **amenities**)

① **America**
[ə'merɪkə] *proper noun*
(a) one of two large continents between the Atlantic and Pacific Oceans; *in the year 1492 Columbus discovered America*; *they went to America by boat across the Atlantic*; see also CENTRAL AMERICA, NORTH AMERICA, SOUTH AMERICA
(b) the United States; *America is sometimes known as the Land of Opportunity*

① **American**
[ə'merɪkən]
1 *adjective*
referring to America or to the United States of America; *an American dollar*; *the American president*; *the bookstore has a huge selection of American literature*; *he's reading about American history*
2 *noun*
person from the United States of America; *I met a group of Americans on the train*; *the Americans won several gold medals at the Olympics*

④ **Americana**
[əmeri'kænə] *noun*
materials or objects that are characteristic of American culture; *this museum has an excellent collection of Americana*

② **Americanism**
[ə'merɪkənɪzm] *noun*
word or phrase which is used in American English and not in other forms of English; *Americanisms like "traffic circle" can be confusing to British people*

③ **Americanization**
[əmerɪkənaɪ'zeɪʃn] *noun*
the process of becoming Americanized

③ **Americanize**
[ə'merɪkənaɪz] *verb*
to make or become typical of America; *when immigrants settle here, the children often Americanize more quickly than their parents*

④ **amiable**
['eɪmiəbl] *adjective*
friendly and pleasant; *we had an amiable discussion about the project*

④ **amicable**
['æmɪkəbl] *adjective*
done in a friendly way; *following an amicable discussion the project was canceled*

④ **amid**
[ə'mɪd] *preposition*
(formal) in the middle of; *the family stood amid the ruins of their store*

④ **Amish**
['eimɪʃ or 'æmɪʃ]
1 *noun*
the Amish = members of a religious group who settled in America, especially in the 18th century; *the Amish live in their own communities*
2 *adjective*
relating to this religious group; *Amish crafts are beautiful*

③ **ammunition**
[æmjʊ'nɪʃn] *noun*
bullets, shells, etc.; *they fought all day until they started to run out of ammunition*; *the troublemakers used bottles as ammunition against the police* (NOTE: no plural)

② **among** *or* **amongst**
[ə'mʌŋ or ə'mʌŋst] *preposition*
(a) surrounded by, in the middle of; *to make a camp, we put up tents among the trees*; *among the people at the party was a woman who does the TV weather forecasts*; *he was standing amongst a crowd of tourists*
(b) between various people in a group; *the Christmas cookies were divided among the class of children*; *we had to share one towel amongst the three of us*

④ **amorphous**
[ə'mɔrfəs] *adjective*
with no particular shape; *an amorphous mass*

① **amount**
[ə'maʊnt] *noun*
quantity of something, such as money; *the amount in my bank account has reached $1500*; *this make of automobile uses by far the least amount of gas*; **a certain amount** = some; *the storm did a certain amount of damage*; *painting the house will take a certain amount of time*

① **amount to**
[ə'maʊnt tʊ] *verb*
(a) to make a total of; *the total bill amounts to over $150*
(b) **to amount to the same thing** = to mean the same, to be the same; *whether he took cash or free vacations, it all amounts to the same thing*

④ **amp** *or* **ampere**
[æmp or 'æmpeər] *noun*
measurement of electric current

③ **ample**
['æmpl] *adjective*
plenty, enough; *we have ample funds to pay for the development program*; *four hours should be ample time to get to Jefferson City*

④ **amplifier**
['æmplɪfaɪər] *noun*
device which makes sound louder; *the sound goes from the receiver through an amplifier to the loudspeakers*

④ **amplify**
['æmplɪfaɪ] *verb*
to make larger or louder; *the signal must be amplified*

④ **amputate**
['æmpjʊteɪt] *verb*
to cut off an arm, leg, finger or toe; *he developed gangrene and they had to amputate his leg*

④ **amputation**
[æmpjʊ'teɪʃn] *noun*
cutting off an arm, leg, finger or toe

② **amuse**
[ə'mjuz] *verb*
(a) to make someone laugh; *the story about the president's cat will amuse you*; *I was amused to hear that you and Jim are sharing an office*
(b) to make the time pass in a pleasant way; **to amuse yourself** = to play, to get pleasure from what you are doing; *the kids amused themselves quietly while their parents talked*

② **amusement**
[ə'mjuzmənt] *noun*
(a) pleasure; *when rain stopped the tennis match, the group sang for the crowd's amusement*; **amusement park** = open-air park with various types of entertainment, such as merry-go-rounds, shooting galleries, etc.
(b) **to someone's amusement** = making someone laugh; *much to her amusement, the band played "Happy Birthday to you!"*
(c) **amusements** = things that amuse people; *there are all sorts of amusements on the cruise ship*

② **amusing**
[ə'mjuzɪŋ] *adjective*
which makes you laugh; *it was amusing to hear about your journey*; *he stayed late, telling us amusing stories about his life in the army*

① **an**
[æn or ən]
see A

④ **analgesic**
[ænəl'dʒɪzɪk] *noun*
painkilling drug; *the doctor prescribed a strong analgesic to relieve the pain*

④ **analogy**
[ə'nælədʒi] *noun*
similarity between two things; **to draw an analogy between** = to show how two things are similar

④ **analysis**
[ə'næləsɪs] *noun*
close examination; *to make an analysis of the sales or a sales analysis*; *to carry out an analysis of the market* (NOTE: plural is **analyses** [ə'næləsiz])

④ **analyst**
['ænəlɪst] *noun*
(a) person who carries out analyses; *political analysts are examining the results of the election*; **systems analyst** = person who examines computer systems

(b) doctor who is trained in analyzing the psychology of patients; *I'm seeing an analyst about my problems*

③ **analyze**
['ænəlaɪz] *verb*
to examine closely and scientifically; *to analyze the market for computer games*; *when the food was analyzed it was found to contain bacteria*

④ **anarchist**
['ænərkɪst] *noun*
person who believes in anarchy, who tries to destroy a government by violent means, without planning to replace it in any way

④ **anarchy**
['ænərki] *noun*
absence of law and order, because the government has lost control or because there is no government; *when the president was assassinated, the country fell into anarchy*

① **ancestor**
['ænsestər] *noun*
member of your family a long time ago; *his ancestors built a castle here in the 13th century*

② **anchor**
['æŋkər]
1 *noun*
large metal hook which holds a ship in place; *the ship was at anchor in the harbor*; **to drop anchor** = to let the anchor fall to the bottom of the sea to hold a ship in the same place; *the ship dropped anchor in the harbor*
2 *verb*
(a) *(of ship)* to drop an anchor to stay in the same place; *the ship anchored in the mouth of the river*
(b) to hold firm; *the hot air balloon was anchored to the ground with cables*

④ **anchorman**
['æŋkərmæn] *noun*
(a) chief newscaster
(b) member of a relay team who is last to compete in a race (NOTE: **anchorperson** and **anchorwoman** are also used)

② **ancient**
['eɪnʃənt] *adjective*
very old; *she's studying ancient history*; *he was riding an ancient bicycle*; *see also* MONUMENT

① **and**
[ænd or nd] *conjunction used to join two words or phrases*
all my uncles and aunts live in Alabama; *use a knife and fork to eat your meat*; *the children were running and singing*; *come and sit down next to me* (NOTE: **and** is used to say numbers after 100: **seven hundred and two = 702**)

① **and so on**
[nd 'səʊ ɒn] *adverb*
with other things; *he talked about plants: flowers, vegetables, and so on*

④ **anemia**
[ə'nimiə] *noun*
condition where the level of red blood cells is less than normal; *the child who is always tired and pale may have anemia*

④ **anesthetic**
[ænəs'θetɪk] *noun*
substance given to a patient to remove feeling, so that he or she can have an operation without feeling pain; **general anesthetic** = substance given to make a patient lose consciousness so that a major operation can be carried out; *you will have to be given a general anesthetic for this operation*; **local anesthetic** = substance that removes the feeling in a certain part of the body only; *she had an operation to her leg under local anesthetic*; *this operation can be carried out under local rather than general anesthetic*

① **angel**
['eɪndʒl] *noun*
(a) being who lives in the sky; *she dreamt she was flying in the sky with the angels*
(b) *(informal)* sweet, kind person; *be an angel and get me my slippers*
(c) *(informal)* person who backs a new business or a theater production financially; *the play failed and the angels lost all their money*

① **anger**
['æŋgər]
1 *noun*
being annoyed; *I felt no anger, only great disappointment*
2 *verb*
to make someone annoyed; *her being late angered him*

② **angle**
['æŋgl] *noun*
(a) corner between two lines; *she planted the tree in the angle of the two walls*; **acute angle** = angle less than 90°; **right angle** = 90° angle
(b) point of view; *what's the government's angle on the story?*

④ **angora**
[æŋ'gɔrə] *noun*
animal with thick very soft wool; *a white angora rabbit*

① **angrily**
['æŋgrɪli] *adverb*
in an angry way; *he shouted angrily when the children climbed over his fence*

① **angry**
['æŋgri] *adjective*
upset and annoyed, and sometimes wanting to harm someone; *the storekeeper is angry with the schoolchildren because they broke his window*; *he gets angry if the mail is late*; *I am angry that the government is doing nothing to prevent crime*; *when the taxicab still hadn't arrived by 3 o'clock the boss got angrier and angrier* (NOTE: **angrier - angriest**)

① **animal**
['ænɪməl] *noun*
living and moving thing (but usually not people); *I like to have animals about the house: we have two dogs and three cats; the crowd behaved like animals*

④ **animated**
['ænɪmeɪtɪd] *adjective*
full of life and energy; *an animated discussion*; **animated cartoon** = a series of cartoon figures, each with slightly different poses, so that when the movie is projected the figures appear to move

① **ankle**
['æŋkəl] *noun*
part of the body, where your leg joins your foot; *I couldn't swim, the water only came up to my ankles; she twisted her ankle when she slipped on the stairs*; **ankle socks** = short socks

② **anniversary**
[ænɪ'vɜrsəri] *noun*
the same date as an important historical event; *the fiftieth anniversary of the end of the Second World War; July 4 1976 was the 200th anniversary of the United States' independence from Britain*; **wedding anniversary** = date that is the date of a wedding; *see also* GOLDEN, SILVER (NOTE: plural is **anniversaries**)

① **announce**
[ə'naʊns] *verb*
to say officially or in public; *he announced his resignation; she announced that she would be running for the Senate; she announced the results of the competition*

① **announcement**
[ə'naʊnsmənt] *noun*
statement made in public; *the director made an announcement to the staff; there were several announcements about flight changes*

④ **announcer**
[ə'naʊnsər] *noun*
person who reads the news or announces programs on radio or TV

③ **annoy**
[ə'nɔɪ] *verb*
to make someone irritated; *try not to annoy your father*

③ **annoyed**
[ə'nɔɪd] *adjective*
angry; *he was annoyed with his neighbors for making so much noise; I was annoyed to find someone had stolen my seat; you can tell he's annoyed by the way his ears get red; he gets very annoyed if you keep him waiting; the gas company wrote to say they were annoyed not to have gotten payment*

③ **annoying**
[ə'nɔɪɪŋ] *adjective*
that makes you angry; *it is highly annoying to have to try and get my automobile back from the police station; I find it very annoying that the mail doesn't come before 10 o'clock; how annoying! - I've got to go back to the supermarket because I forgot to buy some milk; the baby has an annoying cough that won't go away*

② **annual**
['ænjʊəl] *adjective*
happening once a year; *the town festival is an annual event; I get annual interest of 6% on my savings account*

④ **annul**
[ə'nʌl] *verb*
to cancel or stop something having a legal effect; *they have written to say that they want to annul the contract; his first marriage was annulled* (NOTE: annulling - annulled)

④ **anonymous**
[ə'nɒnɪməs] *adjective*
without giving a name; *the police have received several anonymous phone calls; the club has had a donation from a businessman who wants to remain anonymous*; **anonymous letter** = letter with no name or signature

① **another**
[ə'nʌðər] *adjective and pronoun*
(a) one more (like others); *would you like another drink?; I'd like another one of those cookies, please; there is only another week before we go on vacation*
(b) a different (one); *he's bought another automobile; can I have another plate, please, this one's dirty?; she tried on one dress after another, but couldn't find anything she liked*; *see also* EACH OTHER, ONE ANOTHER

① **answer**
['ænsər]
1 *noun*
reply, letter or conversation after someone has written or spoken to you, asking you a question; *I phoned his office but there was no answer; have you had an answer to your letter yet?*; **in answer to** = as a reply to; *I am writing in answer to your letter of October 6*
2 *verb*
(a) to reply, to speak or write words when someone has spoken to you or asked you a question; *he never answers my letters; when he asked us if we had enjoyed the meal we all answered "yes"*
(b) to answer the phone = to lift the telephone when it rings and listen to what the caller is saying; *when I called, it was his secretary who answered the phone*; **to answer the door** = to open the door when someone knocks or rings; *he leapt out of the bath and answered the door dripping wet with a towel around his waist*

④ **answering machine**
[ænsərɪŋ mə'ʃin] *noun*
machine that answers the telephone automatically when someone is not in the office or at home, and allows messages to be recorded; *I left a message for him on his answering machine*

① **ant**
[ænt] *noun*
small insect; *I found some ants in our kitchen*

② **antenna**
[æn'tenə] *noun*
(a) tube on the head of an insect, used to feel things; *a butterfly has two antennae which it uses to sense things* (NOTE: plural is **antennae** [æn'teni])
(b) device for receiving radio or TV signals; *a bigger TV antenna should give better reception* (NOTE: plural is **antennas**)

④ **antibiotic**
[æntibaɪ'ɒtɪk]
1 *adjective*
which kills bacteria; *she's taking a new antibiotic drug*
2 *noun*
substance that kills bacteria; *the doctor prescribed some antibiotics*; *he was given a course of antibiotics*

④ **anticipate**
[æn'tɪsɪpeɪt] *verb*
to expect something to happen; *we are anticipating bad weather*; *I don't anticipate taking a later flight*

④ **antiquated**
['æntɪkweɪtɪd] *adjective*
very old and out-of-date; *he was driving an antiquated Chevrolet*

③ **antique**
[æn'tik]
1 *adjective*
old and valuable; *an antique Chinese bowl*
2 *noun*
valuable old object; *their house is full of antiques*; **antique shop** = shop that sells antiques

④ **antiseptic**
[ænti'septɪk]
1 *adjective*
which prevents germs spreading or a wound becoming infected; *she put an antiseptic dressing on his knee*; *she gargled with an antiseptic mouthwash*
2 *noun*
substance that prevents germs growing or spreading; *the nurse painted his knee with antiseptic*

④ **anxiety**
[æŋ'zaɪəti] *noun*
(a) nervous worry about something; *her anxiety about her job prospects*
(b) being eager to do something; *in his anxiety to get away quickly, he forgot to lock the door*

② **anxious**
['æŋkʃəs] *adjective*
(a) nervous and very worried about something; *she's anxious about the baby*
(b) eager to do something; *the storekeeper is always anxious to please his customers*

② **anxiously**
['æŋkʃəsli] *adverb*
in a nervous worried way; *she peered anxiously through the window*; *they are waiting anxiously for the results of the tests*

① **any**
['eni]
1 *adjective and pronoun*
(a) it doesn't matter which; *take any book you like*; *I'm free any day next week except Tuesday*; *I don't like any of the paintings in the exhibition*
(b) a quantity; *do you have any money left?*; *is there any food for me?*; *would you like any more to eat?*; *will any of your friends be there?*
(c) not...any = none; *there isn't any food left - they've eaten it all*; *can you lend me some money? - sorry, I haven't got any*
2 *adverb; used to emphasize comparatives*
not...any = not even a little (more); *can't you sing any louder?*; *he can't pedal faster*; *she's been in the hospital for two weeks and isn't any better*

② **anybody**
['enibɒdi] *see* ANYONE

② **anyhow**
['enihaʊ] *adverb*
1 in a careless way; *he piled up the books anyhow*
2 = ANYWAY

③ **anymore**
[eni'mɔr] *adverb*
any longer; *do they make this model anymore?*; **not ... anymore** = no longer; *we don't go there anymore*

① **anyone** *or* **anybody**
['eniwʌn *or* 'enibɒdi] *pronoun*
(a) it doesn't matter who; *anyone can learn to ride a bike*; *anybody could tell you that*
(b) *(after questions, negatives)* any person; *can anybody lend me some money?*
(c) some person; *did anyone telephone while I was out?*; **we didn't meet with anybody we knew** = we met no one we knew; **hardly anybody came to the meeting** = very few people came to the meeting

③ **anyplace**
['enipleɪs] *adverb*
= ANYWHERE; *anyplace you want to go, she'll want to go too*

① **anything**
['eniθɪŋ] *pronoun*
(a) it doesn't matter what; *you can eat anything you want*; *our dog will bite anything that moves*
(b) *(in questions, negatives)* something; *are you doing anything interesting this weekend?*; *did you hear anything make a noise during the night?*; *has anything happened to their plans for a long vacation?*; *do you want anything more to drink?*; **he didn't eat anything** = he ate nothing

① **anything else**
['enɪθɪŋ 'els] *pronoun*
any other thing; *do you want anything else to drink?*; *is there anything else you would like to know about?*; *she must have a doll that closes its eyes - anything else won't do*

① **anyway**
['enɪweɪ] *adverb*
in any case; *I'm not supposed to drink during office hours, but I'll have a beer anyway*; *I think it's time to leave - anyway, the last bus is at 11:40 P.M.*

② **anywhere**
['enɪweər] *adverb*
(a) it doesn't matter where; *put the chair anywhere*
(b) *(in questions, negatives)* somewhere; *did you go anywhere over the weekend?*; *is there anywhere where I can sit down?*; *I can't see your wallet anywhere* (NOTE: Also used is **anyplace**)

② **apart**
[ə'part] *adverb*
(a) separated; *the two towns are about six miles apart*
(b) not living together; *they were married but now they're living apart*
(c) in separate pieces; **the watch came apart** = the watch came to pieces; *he took the watch apart*
(d) **to tell something** *or* **someone apart** = to identify two things or people that are similar; *the twins are very alike - how can you tell them apart?*

③ **apart from**
[ə'part from] *phrase*
except, other than; *do you have any special interests apart from your work?*; *I'm feeling fine, apart from a slight cold*

① **apartment**
[ə'partmənt] *noun*
separate set of rooms for living in; *she has an apartment in downtown New York*; **an apartment block** *or* **a block of apartments** = large building divided into many apartments; **apartment house** = large house that has been divided up into apartments; **a studio apartment** = apartment with one main room, plus kitchen and bathroom

① **ape**
[eɪp] *noun*
large monkey, such as a chimpanzee; *does man really come from the apes?*

② **apologize**
[ə'pɒlədʒaɪz] *verb*
to say you are sorry; *did you apologize to your mom for what you said?*; *he shouted at her and then apologized*; *she apologized for being late*

② **apology**
[ə'pɒlədʒi] *noun*
saying sorry; *he wrote a letter of apology*; *I enclose a check for $20 with apologies for the delay in answering your inquiry*; *my apologies for being so late*; *I expect we will receive an apology in due course* (NOTE: plural is **apologies**)

④ **apostrophe**
[ə'pɒstrəfi] *noun*
printing sign: (*'*); *when "it's" is written with an apostrophe means "it is"*

COMMENT: an apostrophe either shows that a letter has been left out ("weren't") or is used with "s" to show possession: before an "s" with singular words, after the "s" with plural words ("a boy's coat", "the girls' team")

④ **appall**
[ə'pæl] *verb*
to horrify, to shock; *the tourists were appalled by the dirt in the streets*

④ **apparatus**
[æpə'reɪtəs] *noun*
scientific or medical equipment; *he dropped an expensive piece of apparatus in the lab this morning*; *the firefighters had to wear breathing apparatus to enter the burning building* (NOTE: no plural: for one item say **a piece of apparatus**)

③ **apparent**
[ə'pærənt] *adjective*
obvious, which seems to be; *it was apparent to everyone that there had been an accident*; *there is an apparent mistake in the account*

③ **apparently**
[ə'pærəntli] *adverb*
as it seems; *apparently she took a taxicab home and then disappeared*; *he didn't come to work today - apparently he has a cold*

② **appeal**
[ə'pil]
1 *noun*
(a) asking for help; *the police have made an appeal for witnesses*; *the hospital is launching an appeal to raise $75,000*
(b) legal request to look at a decision again to see if it was correct; *his appeal to the Supreme Court was rejected*; *the verdict was overturned on appeal*
(c) attraction; *California has great appeal for tourists*; **sex appeal** = being attractive to the opposite sex
2 *verb*
(a) **to appeal to** = to ask for; *the charity appealed to us for money to continue their work*
(b) to make a legal request for a court to look again at a verdict; *will they appeal the verdict?*
(c) **to appeal to** = to attract; *these CDs appeal to the teenage market*; *the idea of working in Australia for six months appealed to her*

④ **appealing**
[ə'piliŋ] *adjective*
attractive; *the thought of a week in Florida is very appealing*

① **appear**
[ə'piər] *verb*
(a) to start to be seen; *a ship appeared through the fog*
(b) to seem; *there appears to be a mistake; he appears to have forgotten the time; she appeared kind of cross*
(c) to play a part in a movie or play; *his dream is to appear on Broadway*

② **appearance**
[ə'piərəns] *noun*
(a) look; *you could tell from his appearance that he had slept in a field*
(b) being present, being there; *this is her second appearance in a movie;* to put in an appearance = to arrive at, to come to a meeting, etc.

② **appearances**
[ə'piərənsiz] *noun*
looks; *appearances can be deceptive;* to keep up appearances = to try to show that you are still as rich or important as you were before

② **appetite**
['æpitait] *noun*
wanting to eat; *going for a long walk has given me an appetite; he's not feeling well and has lost his appetite;* good appetite = interest in eating food; *the baby has a good appetite;* poor appetite = lack of interest in eating food

② **applaud**
[ə'plɔd] *verb*
to bang your hands together to show that you like something; *the audience applauded the singers at the end of the concert*

① **applause**
[ə'plɔz] *noun*
banging your hands together; *at the end of the concert there was a storm of applause*

① **apple**
['æpl] *noun*
(a) common hard round sweet fruit, growing on a tree; *are the apples ripe?;* cooking apple = sour apple which is good for cooking, not for eating raw; eating apple = apple which is good to eat raw, rather than to be cooked
(b) apple (tree) = tree that apples grow on; *we have a field of apple trees next to our house*

④ **applesauce**
['æplsɒs] *noun*
dish of cooked mashed apples

② **appliance**
[ə'plaiəns] *noun*
machine, especially an electrical machine used in the home, such as a washing machine; *we bought new kitchen appliances*

④ **applicant**
['æplikənt] *noun*
person who applies for something; *applicants for visas will have to wait at least two weeks*

② **application**
[æpli'keiʃn] *noun*
(a) putting on (of medicine); *several applications of the cream will be necessary;* for external application only = to be used on the skin only
(b) applying for a job, etc.; *he wrote a letter of application; we received dozens of applications for the job of bartender;* application form = form to be filled out when applying; *she filled out an application form*

② **apply**
[ə'plai] *verb*
(a) to apply for a job = to ask for a job; *she applied for a job in the supermarket; he's applying for a job as a teacher;* to apply to take a course = to ask to be admitted to a course; *it's an encouraging sign that so many students have applied to take the course*
(b) to put on (paint); *wait until the first coat of paint is dry before you apply the second*
(c) to apply to = to affect or to relate to; *this rule only applies to non-U.S. residents*

② **appoint**
[ə'pɔint] *verb*
to give (a job) to someone; *he was appointed (as) manager or to the post of manager; we want to appoint someone to manage our sales department* (NOTE: you appoint a person to a job)

② **appointment**
[ə'pɔintmənt] *noun*
(a) being given a job; on her appointment as manager = when she was made manager; *she received a raise on her appointment as manager*
(b) agreed time for a meeting; *I want to make an appointment to see the doctor; she was late for her appointment; I have an appointment with Dr. Jones;* a dentist's appointment = arrangement to see a dentist; appointment book = book in which you write down the time and place of meetings

③ **appreciate**
[ə'priʃieit] *verb*
(a) to recognize the value of; *shoppers always appreciate good value; customers don't appreciate having to wait to be served*
(b) to increase in value; *the dollar has appreciated against the yen*

④ **appreciation**
[əpriʃi'eiʃn] *noun*
(a) showing that you recognize the value of something; *she is going to take a course on art appreciation*
(b) increase in value; *the appreciation of the dollar against the pound*

④ **appreciative**
['ə'priʃətɪv] *adjective*
full of gratitude; *she was very appreciative of our efforts to help*; *the audience burst into appreciative laughter*

④ **apprehend**
[æprɪ'hend] *verb*
(formal) to arrest a criminal; *he was apprehended as he was getting on the plane*

② **approach**
[ə'prəʊtʃ]
1 *noun*
(a) coming closer; *with the approach of winter we need to get the central heating serviced*
(b) way which leads to; *the approaches to the city were crowded with buses*; **approach road** = road leading to a main road
(c) way of dealing with a situation; *his approach to the question was different from hers*
(d) proposal; *he made approaches to her to leave her job and come to work for him* (NOTE: plural is **approaches**)
2 *verb*
(a) to come near; *the plane was approaching Atlanta airport when the lights went out*
(b) to deal with a problem; *he approached the question in an entirely new way*
(c) to make a proposal; *our company was approached with a takeover bid*; *he approached his bank with a request for a loan*

④ **approachable**
[ə'prəʊtʃəbl] *adjective*
easy to talk to; *the new boss is very approachable*

④ **appropriate**
1 *adjective* [ə'prəʊpriət] suitable; *those shoes are not really appropriate for gardening*; *we leave it to you to take appropriate action*
2 *verb* [ə'prəʊprieit]
(a) to seize property; *the authorities appropriated the land to build a new hospital*
(b) to put a sum of money aside for a special purpose; *they appropriated $150,000 to the reserve fund*

③ **approval**
[ə'pruvəl] *noun*
(a) agreeing with; *does the choice of color have your approval or meet with your approval?*; *the committee gave their approval to the plan*; **approval rating** = points system showing how many people approve of something, usually of a politician's work; *the president's approval rating has fallen to a new low*
(b) on approval = (merchandise) taken by a customer to use and see if he or she likes it; *the store let us have the machine for two weeks on approval*

④ **approve**
[ə'pruv] *verb*
(a) to approve of = to think something is good; *he doesn't approve of loud music*
(b) to agree to something officially; *the committee approved the plan*

③ **approximate**
1 *adjective* [ə'prɒksɪmət]
more or less correct; *the approximate cost will be $900*; *these figures are only approximate*
2 *verb* [ə'prɒksɪmeit]
to be nearly correct; *the cost of the sports stadium will approximate $12 million*

③ **approximately**
[ə'prɒksɪmətli] *adverb*
roughly; *it takes approximately 35 minutes to get to Baltimore by bus*

④ **approximation**
[əprɒksɪ'meiʃn] *noun*
approximate amount; *the figure is just a rough approximation*

② **apricot**
['eiprɪkɒt] *noun*
stone fruit with yellow flesh, like a small peach, but not as juicy; *you have a choice of marmalade or apricot jam for breakfast*

① **April**
['eiprəl] *noun*
the fourth month of the year, the month after March and before May; *her birthday is in April*; *we went on vacation last April*; *today is April 5*; **April 1** = *see* APRIL FOOLS' DAY (NOTE: **April 5:** say "April fifth")

① **April Fools' Day**
['eiprəl 'fulz dei] *noun*
April 1, the day when you play tricks on people

④ **apron**
['eiprən] *noun*
(a) cloth worn over your clothes when cooking or doing housework; *she came out of the kitchen in her apron*
(b) *(at an airport)* paved area where planes can be parked for unloading, waiting, cleaning, etc.

④ **apt**
[æpt] *adjective*
(a) which fits well; *she made some very apt comments*
(b) apt to = likely to; *our old auto was apt to break down on long journeys*

④ **aptitude**
['æptɪtjud] *noun*
skill or ability in doing something; *she shows great aptitude for Spanish*; **aptitude test** = test of someone's ability; *twenty young people will take the aptitude test this month*

④ **aquamarine**
[ækwəmə'rin] *adjective*
dark blue-green (color)

① **aquarium**
[ə'kweəriəm] *noun*
(a) tank for keeping tropical fish; *he keeps an aquarium with little blue fish in the kitchen*
(b) building with an exhibition of fish; *we went to the aquarium on Saturday afternoon*

④ **aquatic**
[æˈkwætɪk] *adjective*
(a) (animal or plant) which lives in water
(b) which takes place in water; *aquatic sports*

④ **arbitrary**
[ˈɑrbɪtrəri] *adjective*
done at random, without any reason; *an arbitrary decision*

④ **arbitration**
[ɑrbɪˈtreɪʃn] *noun*
settling of a dispute by an official judge, accepted by both sides; *to submit a dispute to arbitration*

③ **arch**
[ɑrtʃ] *noun*
(a) round structure forming a roof or doorway; *the church roof is formed of tall stone arches*
(b) triumphal arch = large building over a road, to celebrate a victory; *there are the ruins of a triumphal arch in the center of the square* (NOTE: plural is **arches**)

④ **archaic**
[ɑrˈkeɪɪk] *adjective*
old-fashioned; *her methods are quite archaic*

④ **archangel**
[ˈɑkeɪndʒl] *noun*
highest rank of angel; *the Archangel Gabriel*

④ **archer**
[ˈɑrtʃər] *noun*
person who shoots with a bow and arrows

③ **architect**
[ˈɑrkɪtekt] *noun*
person who designs buildings; *which architect designed the new city hall?*; *we've asked a local architect to draw up plans for a new house*

② **architecture**
[ˈɑrkɪtektʃər] *noun*
design of buildings; *she is studying architecture or she's an architecture student*; *he doesn't like modern architecture*

① **are**
[ɑr]
see BE

① **area**
[ˈeəriə] *noun*
(a) space; *the whole area around the city hall is going to be developed*; *we always sit in the "no smoking" area*
(b) measurement of the space taken up by something (calculated by multiplying how long it is by how wide it is); *the area of the room is 20 square feet*; *we are looking for a store with a sales area of about 1000 square feet*
(c) subject; *it's a problem area for the government*; *he's an expert in the area of crowd control*
(d) district, part of a town or country; *the industrial area is full of factories*; *the house is in a very good area for easy access to public transportation and good schools*

① **area code**
[ˈeəriəˈkəʊd] *noun*
3-digit number given before a telephone number to identify a particular area; *the area code for Cape Cod is 508*

② **arena**
[əˈrinə] *noun*
building with seats for spectators, where sports and fights are held; *the boxers entered the arena*

① **aren't**
[ɑrnt]
see BE

① **Argentina**
[ɑrdʒənˈtinə] *noun*
large country in South America; *our salesman is leaving for Argentina soon*; *we spent three weeks in Argentina, visiting relatives* (NOTE: capital: **Buenos Aires** people: **Argentinians**; language: **Spanish**; currency: **Argentinian peso**)

② **Argentinian**
[ɑrdʒənˈtɪnjən]
1 *adjective*
referring to Argentina; *we do a lot of business with an Argentinian importer*
2 *noun*
person from Argentina; *these Argentinians speak very good English*

② **argue**
[ˈɑrɡju] *verb*
to discuss without agreeing; *they argued over the prices*; *she argued with the waiter about the check*; *I could hear them arguing in the next room* (NOTE: you argue **with** someone **about** *or* **over** something)

② **argument**
[ˈɑrɡjumənt] *noun*
quarrel; *nobody would back her up in her argument with the boss*; *the argument took place in the restaurant*; **to get into an argument with someone** = to start to argue with someone; *he got into an argument with the customs officials*

④ **argumentative**
[ɑrɡjʊˈmentətɪv] *adjective*
who likes to argue; *he was very argumentative this morning*

④ **arid**
[ˈærɪd] *adjective*
extremely dry; where there is very little rain; *arid regions with less than 2 inches of rain per year*

② **arise**
[əˈraɪz] *verb*
(a) to start, to appear; *a problem has arisen in connection with the tickets*
(b) to arise from = to result from, to happen because of; *the misunderstanding arose from a mistake in her instructions* (NOTE: **arising - arose** [əˈrəʊz] **- arisen** [əˈrɪzn])

① **arithmetic**
[ə'rɪθmetɪk] *noun*
calculations with figures; *children must concentrate on reading, writing and arithmetic*

① **arm**
[ɑrm]
1 *noun*
(a) part of your body that goes from your shoulder to your hand; *he held the package under his arm; she tripped over the sidewalk and broke her arm; lift your arms up above your head;* **arm in arm** = with their arms linked; *they walked down the street arm in arm;* **to welcome someone with open arms** = to welcome someone eagerly; *the villagers welcomed the UN soldiers with open arms;* **to cost an arm and a leg** = to be very expensive; *see also* COST
(b) sleeve, the part of a coat, shirt, etc., that you put your arm into; *there was a hole under the arm of her favorite T-shirt*
(c) part of a chair which you can rest your arms on; *he put his coffee cup on the arm of his chair*
2 *verb*
to equip with weapons; *the farm workers have all been armed because of possible attacks; the soldiers were armed with guns*

④ **armament**
['ɑrməmənt] *noun*
heavy weapons; *the supply of armaments to the Middle Eastern countries*

① **armchair**
['ɑrmtʃeər] *noun*
chair with arms; *each room in the hotel is furnished with two armchairs and a TV; she settled down in a comfortable armchair to read*

① **armed**
[ɑrmd] *adjective*
(person) carrying weapons; *all our police officers are armed; an armed police officer guarded the house;* **the armed forces** = the army, navy and air force of a country; *(informal)* **armed to the teeth** = carrying lots of weapons; *the robbers were armed to the teeth*

② **armor**
['ɑrmər] *noun*
(a) metal clothes worn by medieval soldiers as protection; *knights wore suits of armor*
(b) thick metal covering to protect ships or tanks; *the gun is capable of piercing a tank's steel armor*

② **armored**
['ɑrməd] *adjective*
protected by armor; **armored car** = military vehicle which is protected by thick metal; **armored column** = series of armored cars or tanks in a line; *the armored column moved off down the road*

② **arms**
[ɑrmz] *noun*
(a) weapons, such as guns or bombs; *he's a well-known arms dealer; they were selling arms to African countries*
(b) **up in arms about** = very annoyed about; *they are up in arms about the new bus timetable*

① **army**
['ɑrmi] *noun*
all the soldiers of a country, trained for fighting on land; *he left school at 16 and joined the army; an army spokesman held a news conference* (NOTE: plural is **armies**)

① **around**
[ə'raʊnd]
1 *preposition*
(a) going all round something; *she had a gold chain around her neck; the flood water was all around the village; the squad car drove around the town*
(b) close to, nearby; *a few boys hung around the bus stop*
(c) in various places; *we have lots of computers scattered around the office; it's hard to find your way around Toronto without a map*
(d) more or less; *it will cost around $300; around sixty people came to the meeting*
2 *adverb*
(a) in various places; *papers were lying all around; the restaurants were all full, so we walked around for some time*
(b) all round; *a castle with water all around*
(c) close to, nearby; *the children stood around waiting for the bus; it's the only swimming pool for miles around*
(d) in existence; *she's one of the best eye surgeons around; the new coins have been around for some weeks now*

③ **arouse**
[ə'raʊz] *verb*
(a) to excite someone's emotions; *she only wanted to arouse our sympathy;* **he is easily aroused** = it is easy to make him angry
(b) to make someone interested, excited, etc.; *the proposal has aroused a lot of opposition among the locals; the painting has aroused the interest of several collectors*

④ **arpeggio**
[ɑr'pedʒɪəʊ] *noun*
chord where the notes are played one after the other and not all together (NOTE: plural is **arpeggios**)

① **arrange**
[ə'reɪndʒ] *verb*
(a) to put in order; *the chairs are arranged in rows; the books are arranged in alphabetical order; the ground floor is arranged as an open-plan area with a little kitchen at the side*
(b) to organize; *let's arrange to meet somewhere before we go to the movies; the tour has been arranged by the travel agent; she*

arranged for a taxicab to meet him at the airport; *I've arranged with my mom that she will feed the cat while we're away*

(c) to adapt a piece of music for different instruments; *the piece was written for the piano, but it has been arranged for full orchestra* (NOTE: you arrange **for** someone to do something; you arrange **for** something to be done; or you arrange **to** do something)

② **arrangement**
[ə'reɪndʒmənt] *noun*
(a) putting into an order; *the arrangement of the pictures in a book*
(b) organizing; *all the arrangements for the wedding were left to the bride's mother*
(c) general agreement; *we have an arrangement by which we meet for lunch every Tuesday*

② **arrest**
[ə'rest]
1 *noun*
holding someone for breaking the law; *the police made several arrests at the demonstration*; **under arrest** = held by the police; *after the demonstration, three people were under arrest*
2 *verb*
to hold someone for breaking the law; *the police arrested two men and took them to the police station*; *he ended up getting arrested as he tried to leave the country*; *he was arrested for stealing, but the judge let him off with a fine*

② **arrival**
[ə'raɪvl] *noun*
(a) action of reaching a place; *the arrival of flight AB 7174 from Chicago was announced*; *the time of arrival is 5 P.M.*; *she apologized for her late arrival*; **on arrival** = when you arrive; *on arrival at the hotel, members of the party will be allocated rooms*
(b) person who has arrived; *he's a new arrival on our staff*
(c) **arrivals** = part of an airport that deals with passengers who are arriving; *I'll wait for you in arrivals*; *compare* DEPARTURES
(d) birth of a baby; *the arrival of their son was announced in the newspapers*

① **arrive**
[ə'raɪv] *verb*
to reach a place; *the train from Paris arrives in London at 5 P.M.*; *when we arrived at the movie theater we found it was full*; *they arrived at the hotel in the middle of the night* (NOTE: that you arrive **in a town** or **in a country** but **at a place**)

④ **arrogant**
['ærəgənt] *adjective*
very proud in an unpleasant way; *because he was so arrogant, the people in his department refused to have anything to do with him*; *what an arrogant way to treat customers!*

① **arrow**
['ærəʊ] *noun*
(a) piece of wood with a sharp point, shot into the air with a bow; *the arrow missed the target by only a few inches*
(b) printed sign ( ) that points to something; *follow the arrows to the exhibition*

① **art**
[ɑrt] *noun*
painting, drawing, etc.; *she is taking art lessons*; *he went to an exhibition at the local art college*; *when you're in Washington, don't miss the Museum of Modern Art*; **art gallery** = museum of paintings, sculptures, etc.; *see also* ARTS

③ **artery**
['ɑrtəri] *noun*
tube carrying blood from the heart around the body; *a main artery runs down the side of the neck*; *compare* VEIN (NOTE: plural is **arteries**)

④ **artful**
['ɑrtfəl] *adjective*
clever, good at tricking people

③ **article**
['ɑrtɪkl] *noun*
(a) report in a newspaper; *there's an interesting article on fishing in the newspaper*; *did you read the article on skiing vacations in yesterday's paper?*
(b) section of a legal agreement; *see article 8 of the treaty*
(c) object, thing; *several articles of clothing were found near the road*
(d) one of the parts of speech; *"the" is the definite article; "a" is the indefinite article*

② **artificial**
[ɑrtɪ'fɪʃl] *adjective*
not real; *she was wearing artificial pearls*; **to give someone artificial respiration** = to revive someone who is almost dead by blowing air into their lungs (also called CPR)

① **artist**
['ɑrtɪst] *noun*
person who paints, draws, etc.; *he collects paintings by 19th-century artists*; **sidewalk artist** = artist who works for hire in public, on a sidewalk or in a mall

② **artistic**
[ɑr'tɪstɪk] *adjective*
with feeling for art; *her aunt is very artistic*; *he comes from an artistic family*

① **arts**
[ɑrts]
(a) all work connected with art; *funding for the arts has been cut this year*
(b) subject taught which is not a science; *she has an arts degree*

① **as**
[æz]
1 *conjunction*
(a) because; *as you can't drive, you'll have to go by bus*; *as it's cold, you should wear a warm coat*

(b) at the same time as; *as he was getting into the bath, the telephone rang; the little girl ran into the road as the fire engine was turning the corner*
(c) in this way; *leave everything as it is; you should take a vacation as the doctor told you*
2 *preposition*
(a) in a certain job; *he had a job as a bus driver*
(b) because you are; *as a doctor, he has to know the symptoms of all the common diseases*
(c) like; *she was dressed as a nurse; they treated him as a friend of the family*

◇ **as...as**
[æz]
(making comparative) like; *she is as tall as I am; as black as coal; I can't run as fast as you*

◇ **as for**
[ˈæz ˈfɔr] *preposition*
referring to; *as for him - he will have to take a cab; you play cards if you want to - as for me, I'm going to watch TV*

◇ **as from**
[ˈæz ˈfrɒm] *preposition* from a time; **as from next Friday** = starting from next Friday

◇ **as if** *or* **as though**
[əz ˈɪf or əz ˈðəʊ] in the same way as; *it looks as if it is going to be fine for the baseball game; she looked as if she was going to cry; he spoke very slowly, as though he was talking to a little child*

◇ **as well**
[ˈæz ˈwel] *phrase* in addition, also; *she came to have coffee and brought her sister as well; we visited the mansion and swam in the pool as well*

◇ **as well as**
[əz ˈwel æz] *phrase* in addition to, together with; *he has a house in the country as well as a condo in town; as well as being a math teacher, he is a part-time hairdresser*

④ **ascend**
[əˈsend] *verb*
(formal) to go up; *the balloon rapidly ascended*

④ **ascot**
[ˈæskət] *noun*
type of coloured scarf worn by men knotted round the neck inside the shirt; *ascots are not fashionable any more*

④ **ascribe**
[əˈskraɪb] *verb*
(formal) **to ascribe something to something** *or* **someone** = to say that something is caused by something *or* someone

④ **aseptic**
[eɪˈseptɪk] *adjective*
sterilized, with no infection

① **ash**
[æʃ] *noun*
gray dust left after a fire, the eruption of a volcano, etc.; *there was a pile of black ash left*

after we burned the garbage; a thick layer of ash from the volcano

② **ashamed**
[əˈʃeɪmd] *adjective*
embarrassed and sorry (for what you have done or not done); *I am ashamed to say that I have never been to this gallery before; she was ashamed of herself; it's nothing to be ashamed of*

② **ashtray**
[ˈæʃtreɪ] *noun*
little dish for cigarette ash; *there was no ashtray, so he asked the waiter for one*

② **Asia**
[ˈeɪʒə] *noun*
large continent running from the east of Europe to China and Japan; *the Trans-Siberian Railway crosses the deserts of central Asia*

② **Asian**
[ˈeɪʒən]
1 *adjective*
referring to Asia; *we went to a concert of Asian music*
2 *noun*
person coming from one of the countries of Asia; *more than half the children in the class are Asians*

② **aside**
[əˈsaɪd] *adverb*
(a) to one side; *he took me aside and whispered in my ear*; **to put aside** *or* **to set aside** = to save money; *he is putting $75 aside each week to pay for his automobile*
(b) *(usually U.S.)* **aside from** = apart from; *aside from a minor infection, his health has been remarkably good*

① **ask**
[æsk] *verb*
(a) to put a question to get information; *she asked a police officer how to get to the hospital; she went to the bus station to ask about cheap tickets; ask her how much her shoes cost*
(b) to put a question to get someone to do something; *ask your father to teach you how to drive; can I ask you not to make so much noise?*
(c) to invite; *we asked them over for dinner*; **to ask someone out** = to ask someone to go out to a restaurant, to a movie, etc., with you; *don't ask her out - she always orders the most expensive things on the menu*

① **ask for**
[ˈæsk ˈfɔr] *verb*
to say that you want something; *he asked Santa Claus for a new bike; she asked her boss for more money; someone came into the store and asked for the manager*; **he asked for his book back** = he said that he wanted to have the book that he had lent

① **asleep**
[ə'slip] *adjective*
sleeping; *he was asleep and didn't hear the fire alarm*; *they were asleep in the back seat*; *she fell asleep* = she began to sleep; *see also* FAST ASLEEP (NOTE: **asleep** cannot be used in front of a noun: **the cat is asleep** but **a sleeping cat**)

④ **aspect**
['æspekt] *noun*
(a) way of considering a situation, a problem; *I will examine several aspects of the problem*
(b) direction which a house faces; *the living room has a south-facing aspect*

④ **asphyxiation**
[əsfɪksɪ'eɪʃn] *noun*
death by being unable to breathe; *death was caused by asphyxiation from smoke inhalation*

② **aspirin**
['æsprɪn] *noun*
(a) common drug, used to stop the symptoms of flu, colds, headaches, etc.; *she always keeps a bottle of aspirin in her bag*
(b) one tablet of aspirin; *take a couple of aspirins and lie down*

② **ass**
[æs] *noun*
(informal) stupid person; *don't be such an ass!*; *he's an ass - he should have accepted right away* (NOTE: plural is **asses**)

③ **assassinate**
[ə'sæsɪneɪt] *verb*
to kill a famous person for political reasons; *do you remember the day when the president was assassinated?*

③ **assault**
[ə'sɔlt]
1 *noun*
attack; *troops are getting ready for the assault*; *he was accused of assault on a police officer*
2 *verb*
to attack; *he was arrested for assaulting a police officer*

② **assemble**
[ə'sembl] *verb*
(a) to come together; *the fans assembled at the gates of the football stadium*
(b) to put various pieces together; *the cars are assembled in Detroit*

③ **assembly**
[ə'semblɪ] *noun*
(a) meeting; *the General Assembly of the United Nations*; **school assembly** = meeting of all the children in a school (NOTE: plural in this meaning is **assemblies**)
(b) putting together; *the parts are shipped to Hong Kong for assembly*; **assembly line** = moving line in a factory, where the product moves slowly past workers who add pieces to it as it goes past; *he works on an assembly line* or *he is an assembly line worker*

④ **assert**
[ə'sɜrt] *verb*
to state firmly; *she continues to assert her innocence*; **to assert yourself** = to make your opinions felt

④ **assess**
[ə'ses] *verb*
(a) to calculate an amount to be paid; *damages were assessed at $1.5 m*
(b) to calculate the value of; *how do you assess the Denver Broncos' performance today?*; *teachers have to assess each student once per term*

④ **assessment**
[ə'sesmənt] *noun*
(a) calculation of an amount to be paid; *assessment of the damages will take about a week*
(b) calculation of value; *what's your assessment of the Denver Broncos' performance today?*; *student assessments showed that some were falling behind*

④ **asset**
['æsɪt] *noun*
(a) valuable quality; *knowing several languages is an asset*
(b) **assets** = valuable things which are owned; *they will have to sell some of their assets to repay the debt*

③ **assign**
[ə'saɪn] *verb*
(a) **to assign someone to** = to put someone in a position; *she was assigned to the ear, nose and throat section of the hospital*; *we are assigning you to work in the accounting department*
(b) **to assign something to someone** = to give something to someone; *he was assigned the job of cleaning the kitchen*; *she was assigned a bedroom on the first floor*

② **assignment**
[ə'saɪnmənt] *noun*
(a) appointment of someone to a job; *Detective Murray's assignment to the investigation did not please everyone*
(b) job of work; *he was given the assignment of reporting on the war*
(c) written work given to a student; *I have two assignments that must be in by the end of the week*

④ **assimilate**
[ə'sɪmɪleɪt] *verb*
(a) to learn and understand; *he quickly assimilated the instructions he had been given*
(b) to take in someone as part of a group; *the United States has assimilated people from many different nationalities*

② **assist**
[ə'sɪst] *verb*
(formal) to help; *he assists me with my income tax forms*; *I will be assisted in my work by Miss Smith* (NOTE: you assist someone **in** doing something or **with** something)

② **assistance**

[ə'sɪstəns] *noun*

help; *he was trying to change the tire, when a truck drove up and the driver offered his assistance*; *he asked if he could be of any assistance*; *she will need assistance with her baggage*; **financial assistance** = help in the form of money

② **assistant**

[ə'sɪstənt] *noun*

person who helps; *his assistant works in the office next door*; **store assistant** = person who serves the customers in a store; **assistant manager** = person who is second, after a manager

② **associate**

1 [ə'səʊsɪeɪt] *verb*

to associate with = to be linked with, to work with; *I don't want you to associate with that family - they've all been in trouble with the police*; *the government is closely associated with the project*

2 [ə'səʊsɪət] *noun*

person who works in the same business; *she is a business associate of mine*

② **associated**

[ə'səʊsɪeɪtɪd] *adjective*

linked with; *the sales division and all associated departments*

③ **association**

[əsəʊsɪ'eɪʃn] *noun*

(a) official group, group of companies in the same trade; *an association offering support to victims of street violence*

(b) connection between things; *for some people, a black cat has an association with luck*; *Des Moines has strong family associations for him*

(c) in **association with** = together with, sponsored by; *the guidebook is published in association with the local tourist board*; *this program is brought to you in association with American Airlines*

④ **assorted**

[ə'sɔrtɪd] *adjective*

various, mixed; *they come in assorted colors*

④ **assortment**

[ə'sɔrtmənt] *noun*

mixture of different shapes, colours, styles, etc.; *a wide assortment of women's clothes*

③ **assume**

[ə'sjum] *verb*

(a) to suppose; *let's assume that he is innocent*; *I assume you have enough money to pay for the meal?*

(b) to take on; *when she was twenty-one, she assumed complete control of the family business*; *he has assumed responsibility for fire safety*

④ **assumption**

[ə'sʌmpʃn] *noun*

(a) supposing something is true; *we must go on the assumption that she was murdered*

(b) *(formal)* **assumption of office** = starting your duties

④ **assurance**

[ə'ʃʊrəns] *noun*

(a) promise; *he gave her assurance that he would not do it again*

(b) guarantee; *there is no assurance that he will ever pay the damages*

(c) *(in Great Britain, Canada)* **life assurance** = insurance which pays if someone dies; *she took out a life assurance policy*

(d) calm, with a feeling of being sure; *his air of assurance hid the fact that he was very worried*

③ **assure**

[ə'ʃʊər] *verb*

(a) to state definitely; *I can assure you we will do everything to try to find your missing daughter*

(b) to make sure; *you are assured of a warm welcome in that hotel*

④ **assured**

[ə'ʃʊərd] *adjective*

very certain and confident; *she looks very assured up on the stage*

④ **asteroid**

['æstərɔɪd] *noun*

little planet

④ **asthma**

['æsmə] *noun*

breathing difficulty, often caused by an allergy; *she suffers from asthma*

④ **astigmatism**

[ə'stɪgmətɪzəm] *noun*

condition of the eyes where the image focuses correctly at one angle but not at another

② **astonish**

[ə'stɒnɪʃ] *verb*

to surprise someone a lot; *his success in math astonished the teacher - he never came to any of her classes*

② **astonished**

[ə'stɒnɪʃt] *adjective*

very surprised; *we were astonished to learn that he had died*; *she stood on a table and started to dance, watched by an astonished crowd*

② **astonishing**

[ə'stɒnɪʃɪŋ] *adjective*

very surprising; *they spent an astonishing amount of money buying Christmas presents*; *for an eight-year-old, the way she plays the piano is astonishing*

④ **astonishingly**

[ə'stɒnɪʃɪŋli] *adverb*

very surprisingly; *the teacher was astonishingly calm considering she was surrounded by screaming children*

② **astonishment**

[ə'stɒnɪʃmənt] *noun*

great surprise; *she could not hide her astonishment at the news*; *to my great astonishment they paid the bill in full*

④ **astounding**
['əstaʊndɪŋ] *adjective*
very surprising; *it was astounding that no one was killed in the accident*

④ **astronaut**
['æstrənɔt] *noun*
person who travels into space in a spacecraft; *one of the astronauts had to get out of the spacecraft to do some repair work*

④ **astronomer**
[ə'strɒnəmər] *noun*
person who studies the stars and planets; *a group of astronomers met to observe the new comet*

④ **astute**
[ə'stjut] *adjective*
clever at understanding things quickly; *a very astute businesswoman*; *the board was impressed by his astute answers to their questions*

① **at**
[æt] *preposition*
(a) *(showing time)* **we'll meet at eleven o'clock**; *you must put your lights on when you drive at night*; *we went to New Orleans at Easter*
(b) *(showing place)* **meet us at the ice-cream parlor**; *she's gotten a job at the supermarket*; *he's not at home, he's at work*
(c) *(showing speed)* *the train was traveling at 125 miles per hour*
(d) *(showing direction)* *they threw rotten eggs at the speaker* (NOTE: **at** is often used after verbs: **look at, point at**, etc.)

◇ **at least**
['æt 'list] *phrase*
(a) *(mentioning one good thing in a bad situation)* *it rained all day but at least we have brought our umbrellas*; *the children were very naughty but at least no windows were broken*
(b) *(to correct a statement)* *she lives in the Bahamas - at least, she used to*
(c) as a minimum; *try to tidy yourself up, at least comb your hair*
(d) not less than; *at least a third of the children are sick*; *she can't be sixty - she looks at least eighty*

◇ **at length**
['æt 'leŋθ] *phrase*
(a) for a long time and using many words; *he spoke at length about the results of the election*
(b) with a lot of details; *she explained at great length how the machine worked*

◇ **at once**
['æt 'wʌns] *adverb*
(a) immediately; *come here at once!*; *the ambulance came at once*
(b) at the same time; *don't all speak at once!*
(c) **all at once** = suddenly; *all at once the phone rang*

◇ **at sign**
['æt 'saɪn]
sign (@) used in email addresses; *my email address is peter@petercollin.com (say "peter at petercollin dot com")*

① **ate**
[eɪt] *see* eat

② **athlete**
['æθlit] *noun*
sportsman who competes in races, etc.; *the Olympic athletes marched around the stadium*

② **athletic**
[æθ'letɪk] *adjective*
(a) referring to sport; *the athletic events start at 2:30*
(b) fit, because you do a lot of sport; *her very athletic younger brother*

② **athletics**
[æθ'letɪks] *noun*
organized sports; *at school I hated athletics*; *we spent the afternoon watching athletics on TV*

④ **Atlantic (Ocean)**
[ət'læntɪk 'əʊʃən] *noun*
ocean between the Americas and Europe and Africa; *she sailed across the Atlantic on her own*

① **atlas**
['ætləs] *noun*
book of maps; *can you find Mexico in the atlas?* (NOTE: plural is **atlases**)

② **atmosphere**
['ætməsfɪər] *noun*
(a) air around the Earth; *the atmosphere surrounds the Earth to a height of several hundred kilometers*
(b) general feeling; *the atmosphere in the office was tense*; *I like the friendly atmosphere in our college*

② **atom**
['ætəm] *noun*
(a) basic bit of matter; *all substances are composed of atoms*; *splitting an atom releases energy*
(b) very small thing; *there's not an atom of evidence against him*

② **atomic**
[ə'tɒmɪk] *adjective*
referring to atoms; **atomic bomb** = bomb using nuclear energy; **atomic energy** = energy created during a nuclear reaction, as in a nuclear power station; **atomic number** = number of positive electric charges in an atom which give the element its place in the table of elements

② **attach**
[ə'tætʃ] *verb*
(a) to fasten; *the gate is attached to the post*; *I am attaching a copy of my previous letter*
(b) to consider that something has a particular quality; *she attaches great importance to food safety*

④ **attaché**
[ə'tæʃeɪ] *noun*
diplomat who deals with a special type of work; *a military attaché*

④ **attaché case**
[əˈtæʃeɪ ˈkeɪs] *noun*
small case for papers; *an elegant leather attaché case*

② **attached**
[əˈtætʃt] *adjective*
fond of; *he's very attached to his old car, and won't get a new one*

② **attachment**
[əˈtætʃmənt] *noun*
(a) thing that can be attached to something; *the camera has several attachments*; *I don't use half the attachments that come with the food processor*
(b) affection, liking for someone; *he formed an attachment to the girl next door*

② **attack**
[əˈtæk]
1 *noun*
(a) trying to hurt someone or something; *they made an attack on the town*; **under attack** = being attacked; *the town is under attack from guerrillas*
(b) criticism; *he launched an attack on the government*
(c) sudden illness; *she had a heart attack*
2 *verb*
to try to hurt someone or something; *three men attacked her and stole her watch*; *the old lady was attacked by muggers*; *they attacked the enemy camp*

④ **attainable**
[əˈteɪnəbl] *adjective*
which can be reached; *his objective seems quite easily attainable*

③ **attempt**
[əˈtempt]
1 *noun*
try; *he failed in his attempt to climb Mount Everest*; *all his attempts to get a job have failed*; *we closed down one store in an attempt to cut costs*; *she passed her driver's test on the second attempt*
2 *verb*
to try; *she attempted to commit suicide*

① **attend**
[əˈtend] *verb*
to be present at; *she attended the wedding*; *they organized a protest meeting but only one or two people attended*

② **attendance**
[əˈtendəns] *noun*
(a) *(formal)* being present at a ceremony; *your attendance at the opening ceremony is required*; **in attendance** = being present as helper; *the president unveiled the memorial, with most of the cabinet in attendance*
(b) the number of people present at a ceremony; *there was huge attendance on the first day of the show* (NOTE: no plural)

④ **attendant**
[əˈtendənt] *noun*

(a) person on duty; *ask the gas station attendant for the key to the restroom*; **flight attendant** = person who looks after passengers on a plane; *press the button to call the flight attendant*
(b) person on duty in a museum; *the attendant asked her to open her bag*
(c) person who helps someone during a ceremony; *one of the bride's attendants tripped over the flowers*

① **attention**
[əˈtenʃən] *noun*
(a) careful thinking; *don't distract the driver's attention*; **to the attention of** = words written on a letter to show that a certain person must see it and deal with it; *mark your letter "to the attention of the chief executive officer"*; **to pay attention to** = to note and think about something carefully; *pay attention to the instructions in the leaflet*; *don't pay any attention to what she says!*
(b) position of a soldier, standing straight, with heels together and looking straight ahead; *the guards stood at attention at the entrance of the palace*

③ **attentive**
[əˈtentɪv] *adjective*
(a) listening carefully; *the students were very attentive as the teacher explained the problem*
(b) being careful when dealing with someone; *the manager was very attentive to her needs*

④ **attentively**
[əˈtentɪvli] *adverb*
in an attentive way; *the children listened attentively while their teacher told them what to do*

② **attic**
[ˈætɪk] *noun*
room at the top of a house under a roof; *he slowly climbed up the stairs to the attic*

④ **attired**
[əˈtaɪərd] *adjective*
(formal) dressed; *they were attired more for the beach than for the office*

③ **attitude**
[ˈætɪtjud] *noun*
(a) way of standing, sitting, etc.; *his portrait shows him in a thoughtful attitude*
(b) way of thinking; *what is the government's attitude to the problem?*

③ **attorney**
[əˈtɜrni] *noun*
(a) lawyer; *after his arrest he tried to call his attorney*; see also DISTRICT ATTORNEY
(b) **power of attorney** = written document, which gives someone power to act on behalf of someone else; *she's going to her lawyer today to sign the power of attorney*

④ **Attorney-General**
[əˈtɜrni ˈdʒenrəl] *noun*
head of legal affairs in the federal government, in charge of the Department of Justice; *the new*

Attorney-General is well known in the legal world

② **attract**
[əˈtrækt] *verb*
to make someone come near; *the stores are lowering their prices to attract more customers*; *the exhibition attracted hundreds of visitors*; *we must see if we can attract more candidates for the job*; **to be attracted to someone** = to feel a sexual interest in someone; *I can't understand why she's attracted to him*

③ **attraction**
[əˈtrækʃn] *noun*
(a) the ability to attract; *the attraction of a large salary*; *what is the attraction of hockey?*
(b) something that attracts people; *the Statue of Liberty is a great tourist attraction*
(c) *(in physics)* act of attracting something; *the attraction of magnets*

② **attractive**
[əˈtræktɪv] *adjective*
(a) pleasant-looking; *they found Vermont very attractive*; *she's an attractive young girl*
(b) which attracts; *they offer some attractive bargains*; *the rival firm made him a very attractive offer*; **attractive salary** = good salary to make sure many people will apply for the job

② **auction**
[ˈɔkʃn]
1 *noun*
sale to the person who makes the highest bid in public; *the house was sold by auction*; *I bought the painting at an auction*; **to put something up for auction** = to offer something for sale at an auction
2 *verb*
to sell to the person who makes the highest bid in public; *they are auctioning all Grandma's possessions*; *the princess's dresses will be auctioned for charity*

④ **audacity**
[ɔˈdæsɪti] *noun*
great boldness; *he had the audacity to come in here and ask me for money, when he already owes me thousands*

② **audience**
[ˈɔdiəns] *noun*
(a) people at a theater, film, concert hall, watching TV or listening to the radio; *members of the audience cheered*; *there was a huge audience on the first night of the play*
(b) allowing you to speak to someone; *the ambassador had an audience with the president*

③ **audio**
[ˈɔdiəʊ] *prefix*
referring to sound; **audiotape** = special magnetic tape on which sounds can be recorded

④ **audit**
[ˈɔdɪt]
1 *noun*

official check of a company's accounts; *the auditors are carrying out the annual audit*
2 *verb*
(a) to check accounts officially; *the accounts have not yet been audited*
(b) to attend a college course without receiving credit; *he's auditing an art class*

④ **auditor**
[ˈɔdɪtər] *noun*
accountant who checks a company's accounts officially; *the IRS called in a tax auditor to go over the company's books*

① **August**
[ˈɔgəst] *noun*
eighth month of the year, the month after July and before September; *my birthday is in August*; *I left my job last August*; *today is August 15* (NOTE: **August 15**: say "August fifteenth")

① **aunt**
[ænt] *noun*
sister of mother or father; wife of an uncle; *say goodbye to Aunt Anne*; *she lives next door to my aunt*

④ **aura**
[ˈɔrə] *noun*
general feeling or quality

② **Australia**
[ɒsˈtreɪliə] *proper noun*
large country, covering a whole continent in the southwest of the Pacific Ocean; *they went to Australia by boat*; *she spent all her savings on a trip to Australia* (NOTE: capital: **Canberra**; people: **Australians**; language: **English**; currency: **Australian dollar**)

② **Australian**
[ɒsˈtreɪliən]
1 *adjective*
referring to Australia; *an Australian dollar*; *the Australian Prime Minister*; *I'm letting my house to an Australian family for the summer*; *his wife is Australian*
2 *noun*
person who lives in or comes from Australia; *I met an Australian on the train*

① **Austria**
[ˈɒstriə] *noun*
country in central Europe, south of Germany and east of Switzerland; *we often go skiing in Austria*; *they are moving to Austria as her father has a business in Vienna* (NOTE: capital: **Vienna**; people: **Austrians**; language: **German**; currency: **euro**)

② **Austrian**
[ˈɒstriən]
1 *adjective*
referring to Austria; *you can get Austrian wine in some supermarkets*; *an Austrian family has bought the house next door to us*
2 *noun*
person from Austria; *the group was made up mainly of Germans and Austrians*

① **author**
['ɔθər] *noun*
writer; *the books are written under the name "Mr. Big", and no one knows who the author is*; *she is the author of a popular series of children's books*

④ **authoritative**
[ɔ'θɒrɪtətɪv] *adjective*
(a) in a commanding way; *he spoke in an authoritative voice*
(b) which is an authority; *an authoritative book*

③ **authority**
[ɔ'θɒriti] *noun*
(a) power to do something; *he has no authority to act on our behalf*
(b) permission to do something; *he signed without having my authority to do so*
(c) source of information; *what is his authority for the story?*
(d) **the authorities** = the government; *the authorities have canceled his visa*
(e) expert; *he's an authority on Greek literature* (NOTE: plural is **authorities**)

④ **authorization**
[ɔθərai'zeɪʃn] *noun*
official permission; *she wrote the letter without our authorization*; *do you have authorization for this expenditure?*; *he has no authorization to act on our behalf*

④ **authorize**
['ɔθəraɪz] *verb*
to give permission for something to be done; *to authorize payment of $15,000*; *to authorize someone to act on the company's behalf*

① **auto**
['ɔtəʊ] *noun*
automobile; *he runs a small auto parts store*; **auto insurance** = insurance covering an automobile, the driver and passengers in case of accident

③ **autobiography**
[ɔtəbaɪ'ɒgrəfi] *noun*
story of the life of a person written by himself or herself; *he's writing his autobiography*; *I'm reading the autobiography of a ballet dancer*

④ **autocratic**
[ɔtə'krætɪk] *adjective*
ruling like a dictator; *his autocratic style annoyed the staff*

② **autograph**
['ɔtəgræf] *noun*
signature of a famous person; *he asked the football player for his autograph*

② **automatic**
[ɔtə'mætɪk]
1 *adjective*
which works by itself; *there is an automatic device that cuts off the electric current*; **automatic pilot** = device that flies a plane, allowing the pilot to rest
2 *noun*
(a) gun that goes on firing as long as the trigger is being pulled; *he was shot with an automatic*
(b) automobile that has automatic gear change; *I prefer driving automatics to manual models*

② **automatically**
[ɔtə'mætɪkli] *adverb*
working by itself; *the doors open automatically when someone comes near them*

① **automobile**
['ɔtəməbil] *noun*
car; *Ford is one of the main companies in the automobile industry*

④ **autonomous**
[ɔ'tɒnəməs] *adjective*
independent, which governs itself; *these former provinces have now become autonomous regions*

④ **autopsy**
['ɔtɒpsi] *noun*
examination of a corpse to find the cause of death; *the autopsy revealed nothing about the cause of death* (NOTE: plural is **autopsies**)

③ **available**
[ə'veɪləbl] *adjective*
(a) which can be obtained; *the tablets are available in most drugstores*
(b) **to make yourself available** = to arrange to be free to do something; *I can make myself available to meet with you next week*; *the manager is never available when customers want to complain*

③ **avalanche**
['ævəlænʃ] *noun*
fall of masses of snow down the side of a mountain; *two climbers were killed by an avalanche in the Rockies*

① **avenue**
['ævənju] *noun*
wide street in a town, often with trees along the side; *a suburban avenue lined with trees*; **Fifth Avenue** = famous shopping street in New York; *we went into the stores on Fifth Avenue* (NOTE: in names of streets, usually shortened to **"Ave"**: 15 Laurel Ave)

② **average**
['ævərɪdʒ]
1 *noun*
(a) number calculated by adding several figures and dividing by the number of figures added; *temperatures have been above average for this time of year*; *the average for the last three months or the last three months' average*
(b) **on average** = as a rule; *on average, $25 worth of goods are stolen every day*
2 *adjective*
(a) ordinary; *it was an average working day at the office*; *their daughter is of above average intelligence*
(b) calculated by dividing the total by the number of quantities; *his average speed was 30 miles per hour*

3 *verb*

to work out as an average; *price hikes have averaged 10% a year*

④ **aversion**

[əˈvɜːʃn] *noun*

aversion to *or* **towards** = dislike of; *she has a great aversion to men with mustaches*

④ **avert**

[əˈvɜːt] *verb*

to prevent something happening; *the negotiators are aiming to avert a strike*

④ **aviation**

[eɪvɪˈeɪʃn] *noun*

action of flying aircraft; *he's planning a career in aviation*; **aviation fuel** = special fuel used by aircraft

③ **avocado**

[ævəˈkɑːdəʊ] *noun*

dark green tropical fruit with yellow flesh and a very large stone, eaten as a salad or vegetable; *add slices of avocado to your salad* (NOTE: plural is **avocados**)

② **avoid**

[əˈvɔɪd] *verb*

(a) to keep away from; *travel early to avoid the traffic jams*; *aircraft fly high to avoid storms*; *you must avoid traveling on Friday evenings*

(b) to try not to do something; *he's always trying to avoid making a decision* (NOTE: you avoid something or avoid **doing** something)

④ **avoidable**

[əˈvɔɪdəbl] *adjective*

which could have been avoided; *the accident was completely avoidable*

④ **avoidance**

[əˈvɔɪdəns] *noun*

act of avoiding; *avoidance of danger amounts to cowardice*

② **await**

[əˈweɪt] *verb*

(formal) to wait for; *we are awaiting the decision of the court*; *your order is in the warehouse awaiting collection*

① **awake**

[əˈweɪk]

1 *verb*

(a) to stop somebody from sleeping; *he was awoken by the sound of the telephone*

(b) to wake up; *he awoke when he heard them knocking on the door*; *they awoke to find a rattlesnake in their tent* (NOTE: awaking - awoke [əˈwəʊk] - has awoken)

2 *adjective*

not asleep; *I can't get to sleep - it's 2 o'clock and I'm still awake*; **wide awake** = completely awake (NOTE: awake cannot be used in front of a noun)

① **award**

[əˈwɔːd]

1 *noun*

(a) prize; *the coffee maker has won a design award*; *the school has been nominated for an award*; *we all went to Augusta for the award-giving ceremony*

(b) decision that settles a dispute; *the latest court award has been announced*

2 *verb*

to give compensation, a prize, etc., to someone; *he was awarded first prize*; *she was awarded damages*

③ **aware**

[əˈweər] *adjective*

knowing; *is he aware that we have to decide quickly?*; *I am not aware of any problem*; **not that I am aware of** = not as far as I know; *has there ever been an accident here before? - not that I am aware of*

④ **awareness**

[əˈweənəs] *noun*

being aware; *the police are trying to increase public awareness of automobile crime*

① **away**

[əˈweɪ]

1 *adverb*

(a) at a distance; *they've gone away on vacation*; *the nearest store is five miles away*; *go away! - I don't want to see you*; *we all waved as the bus moved away*

(b) *(as emphasis, after verbs)* without stopping; *the birds were singing away in the garden*

(c) not here, somewhere else; *the chief executive officer is away on business*; *my secretary is away sick*

(d) *(in sports)* at your opponents' sports ground; *our team is playing away next Saturday* (NOTE: the opposite is **at home**)

2 *adjective*

away game = game played at your opponents' sports ground (NOTE: the opposite is **a home game**)

④ **awe**

[ɔː] *noun*

great fear; *he inspires considerable awe in the younger members of staff*; *she watched in awe as he dove off the rock*

① **awful**

[ˈɔːfəl] *adjective*

very bad, very unpleasant; *turn off the television - that program's awful!*; *she felt awful about missing the party*; *he has an awful cold*

① **awfully**

[ˈɔːfli] *adverb*

(informal) very; *she was awfully upset by the news*; *it was awfully cold in Moscow*

④ **awhile**

[əˈwaɪl] *adverb*

for a short time; *we will rest here awhile*

② **awkward**

[ˈɔːkwərd] *adjective*

(a) difficult to do; *I couldn't reach the handle - it's in a very awkward position*; *the lock is awkward and stiff*

(b) embarrassing; *it's awkward for us to invite him and his second wife, when his first wife is a friend of my sister*; *when he asked for the loan*

the bank started to ask some very awkward questions
(c) not convenient; *next Thursday is awkward for me - what about Friday?*

① **awoke, awoken**
[ə'wəuk or ə'wəukn]
see AWAKE

② **ax**
[æks] *noun*
tool with a heavy sharp metal head for chopping; *he chopped the tree down with an ax*

Bb

① **B, b**
[bi]
second letter of the alphabet, between A and C; *he initialed the document with a large "BB" for Ben Brown*

① **baby**
['beibi] *noun*
(a) very young child; *most babies start to walk when they are about a year old*; *I've known him since he was a baby*; **to have a baby** = to give birth to a baby; *she's going into the hospital to have her baby*; *see also* BATH WATER
(b) very young animal; *a baby rabbit* (NOTE: plural is **babies;** note also that if you do not know if a baby is a boy or a girl, you can always call it **it: the baby was sucking its thumb**)

① **baby-sit**
['beibisit] *verb*
to look after a child or children in a house, while their parents are out; *she baby-sits for me while I go to my evening classes*; *I'm baby-sitting my little brother tonight* (NOTE: **baby-sitting - baby-sat**)

① **baby-sitter**
['beibisitər] *noun*
person who baby-sits; *we have to find a baby-sitter for next Thursday evening*

④ **bachelor**
['bætʃələr] *noun*
(a) man who is not married; *he's still a bachelor and I'm beginning to wonder if he'll ever get married*
(b) person with a degree from a college given after completing the undergraduate program; **Bachelor of Arts (B.A.)** = first degree in an arts subject; **Bachelor of Science (B.Sc.)** = first degree in a science subject from a university

① **back**
[bæk]
1 *noun*
(a) part of your body that is not in front; *she went to sleep lying on her back*; *he carried his son on his back*; *don't lift that heavy box, you may hurt your back*; *she stood with her back to the wall*; **he did it behind my back** = he did it without telling me; **to put someone's back up** = to annoy someone
(b) the opposite part to the front; *he wrote his address on the back of his business card*; *she sat in the back of the bus and went to sleep*; *the dining room is at the back of the house*; **he put his pants on back to front** = he put them on the wrong way around
(c) *(in many sports)* person who defends the goal area
2 *adjective*
(a) on the opposite side to the front; *he knocked on the back door of the house*; *the back tire of my bicycle is flat*
(b) referring to the past; **back pay** = salary that has not been paid; *I am owed $750 in back pay*
3 *adverb*
(a) toward the back; *he stepped back from the edge of the platform*; *she leaned back in her armchair*; *can you please sit back, I can't see the screen*
(b) in the state where things were before; *put the telephone back on the table*; *she watched him drive away and then went back into the house*; *she gave me back the money she had borrowed*; *I'll phone you as soon as I get back to the office*
(c) in the past; *back in the 1950s, life was much less complicated than it is today* (NOTE: **back** is often used after verbs: **to give back, to go back, to pay back,** etc.)
4 *verb*
(a) to go backward; to make something go backward; *he backed (his car) out of the garage*; **to back away from** = to go backwards from something frightening; *the little girl backed away from the dog*
(b) to support with money; *she is backing her son's restaurant*
(c) to bet on something happening; *we're backing the Republican candidate to win the election*

④ **backache**
['bækeɪk] *noun*
pain in the back; *I've had a backache for several days*

④ **backer**
['bækər] *noun*
person who supports a person or a project with money; *one of our backers has withdrawn*

④ **backfire**
['bækfaɪər] *verb*
(a) *(of an automobile)* to make a loud bang, when unburnt gasoline explodes in the cylinder
(b) *(of a plan)* to go wrong, to turn out exactly the opposite to what was expected; *all their vacation plans backfired when their children got chickenpox*

③ **background**
['bækgraʊnd] *noun*
(a) part of a picture that seems farther away; *the photograph is of a house with mountains in the background*; *his white shirt stands out against the dark background*
(b) background music = music played quietly in a movie, restaurant, etc.; *the background music was too loud, so we asked for it to be turned down*
(c) past life or experience; *he comes from a working-class background*; *do you know anything about her background?*; *his background is in the restaurant business*
(d) past details; *he explained the background of the claim for damages*

④ **backing**
['bækɪŋ] *noun*
(a) financial support; *he has backing from an Australian bank*
(b) action of going backwards; *she finds backing into the ferry is difficult*

③ **backpack**
['bækpæk] *noun*
large bag carried on the back when walking; *I'll have to take something out of my backpack - it's much too heavy*

③ **backpacker**
['bækpækər] *noun*
person who goes walking, carrying a backpack; *we picked up two backpackers who were hitchhiking into the Rockies*

③ **backpacking**
['bækpækɪŋ] *noun*
going on a long distance walk, carrying a backpack; *we went backpacking around Europe*

① **back up**
['bæk 'ʌp] *verb*
(a) to help someone; *nobody would back her up when she complained about the service*; *will you back me up in the vote tomorrow?*
(b) to make a copy of a computer file; *don't forget to back up your work before you go home in the evening*

④ **backward**
['bækwəd] *adjective*
(a) not as advanced as is normal; *he is backward for his age*
(b) not having much industrial development; *poor and backward countries*

② **backward** *or* **backwards**
['bækwəd or 'bækwədz] *adverb*
from the front toward the back; *don't step backward*; *"tab" is "bat" spelled backward*; *she looked backward at the next person in the line*; **backward and forward** = in one direction, then in the opposite direction; *the police officer was walking backward and forward in front of the bank*; **he knows San Francisco backward and forward** = he knows San Francisco very well; *(informal)* **to bend over backward** *or* **to lean over backward to do something** = to do everything you can to be helpful; *we bent over backward to get her a mortgage, and then she decided not to buy the house*; *they leaned over backward to help the family*

① **bacon**
['beɪkən] *noun*
salted or smoked meat from a pig, usually cut in thin slices; **bacon and eggs** = fried bacon and fried eggs (served at breakfast) (NOTE: no plural: **some bacon; a pound of bacon**)

> COMMENT: bacon is cured in salt water for several days; some bacon is also smoked by hanging in smoke, which improves its taste

③ **bacteria**
[bæk'tɪərɪə] *noun*
tiny organisms, which can cause disease; *the cleaning fluid will kill harmful bacteria in the toilet*; *bacteria can move and reproduce very rapidly* (NOTE: the word is plural; the singular is **bacterium** [bæk'tɪərɪəm])

① **bad**
[bæd] *adjective*
(a) not good; *eating too much fat is bad for you*; *I think it would be a bad idea to go on vacation in November*
(b) of poor quality; *he's a bad driver*; *she's good at singing but bad at playing the piano*
(c) unpleasant; *he has a bad cold*; *she's in a bad mood*; *I've got some bad news for you*; *the weather was bad when we were on vacation in August*
(d) serious; *he had a bad accident on the freeway*
(e) *(food)* which is not fresh, which has started to rot; *the meat we bought yesterday has started to go bad* (NOTE: **bad - worse** [wɜrs] **- worst** [wɜrst])

◇ **not bad**
['nɒt 'bæd] quite good; *the food in this restaurant isn't bad*; *what did you think of the movie? - not bad!*

② **badge**
[bædʒ] *noun*

small sign pinned to someone's clothes (to show who he or she is, what company he or she belongs to, etc.); *all the staff at the exhibition must wear badges*

① **badly**
['bædli] *adverb*
(a) not well; *she did badly on her driver's test*
(b) seriously; *he was badly injured in the motorcycle accident*
(c) very much; *his hair badly needs cutting* (NOTE: **badly - worse** [wɜrs] **- worst** [wɜrst])

④ **badminton**
['bædmɪntən] *noun*
game for two or four people, similar to tennis, played with a different type of racket and a shuttlecock; *do you want a game of badminton?*

④ **baffle**
['bæfl] *verb*
to puzzle; *I'm baffled as to why the motorcycle won't start*; *the cause of the common cold has baffled scientists for years*

① **bag**
[bæg]
1 *noun*
(a) container made of paper, plastic, etc., in which you can carry things; *he put the apples in a paper bag*; *(informal)* **to let the cat out of the bag** = to tell a secret by accident; *her husband let the cat out of the bag and it was all over the newspapers the following morning*; *(informal)* **it's in the bag** = the deal has been agreed; **doggy bag** = bag in which you can put food that you didn't eat in a restaurant to take home; **shopping bag** = bag for carrying your shopping in; **shoulder bag** = bag that you carry on a strap over your shoulder; **sleeping bag** = comfortable warm bag for sleeping in, often used by people camping
(b) what is contained in a bag; *a bag of potatoes*; *a small bag of flour*
(c) = PURSE; *my keys are in my bag*
(d) suitcase, piece of baggage; *I always pack my bags at the last minute*
2 *verb*
(informal) to catch, kill or destroy; *we bagged a deer*; *he bagged three enemy planes* (NOTE: **bagging - bagged**)

③ **bagel**
['beɪgəl] *noun*
soft chewy ring-shaped bread; *we had bagels for breakfast*

① **baggage**
['bægɪdʒ] *noun*
cases and bags that you take with you when traveling; *she brought a huge amount of baggage with her*; **excess baggage** = cases that weigh more than you are allowed when traveling by air, and for which you must pay extra; **baggage allowance** = weight of baggage that an air passenger is allowed to take free when he or she travels; **baggage cart** = little cart with wheels that you use to carry your baggage at an

airport; *there's a row of baggage carts near where you claim your baggage*; **baggage room** = room at a train station, bus station, ferry terminal or airport where suitcases, bags and packages can be left (NOTE: **baggage** has no plural; to show one suitcase, etc., you can say **a piece of baggage**)

② **bail**
[beɪl]
1 *noun*
money paid to a court as guarantee that a prisoner who is released will return to the court to stand trial; *she was released on $5,000 bail*; **to jump bail** = not to appear in court after being released on bail; *the police are afraid he will jump bail*
2 *verb*
to scoop water out of a boat; *we're filling up with water - start bailing!*

④ **bail out**
['beɪl 'aut] *verb*
(a) to leave a difficult situation, etc.; *when his business stopped making a profit he decided to bail out*
(b) to pay money to a court to have a prisoner released; *he phoned his lawyer to see if someone could bail him out*
(c) to scoop water out of a boat; *I'll try to plug the hole, if you start to bail out*

① **bait**
[beɪt]
1 *noun*
something used to attract fish or animals so that you can catch them; *we should use some more bait to try to get rid of the mice*; **to take the bait** = to let yourself to get tricked into something or caught by a tempting offer
2 *verb*
to attach bait (to a hook); *he baited his line with a worm*; **to bait and switch** = to attract customers with a tempting offer, which is then replaced with something less attractive

① **bake**
[beɪk] *verb*
to cook in an oven; *Mom's baking a cake for my birthday*; *do you like baked potatoes?*; *bake the pizza for 35 minutes*

① **baked beans**
['beɪkt 'binz] *noun*
dried white beans cooked in tomato sauce; *we had Boston baked beans on our vacation in Massachusetts*; *when you go shopping, can you get me a can of baked beans?*

① **baker**
['beɪkər] *noun*
person who makes bread and cakes; *bakers start work very early in the morning*; **the baker's** = shop where you can buy bread and cakes; *can you go to the baker's and get me a loaf of brown bread?*

① **baking**
['beɪkɪŋ] *noun*

cooking in an oven, especially bread and cookies; *there was a wonderful smell of baking coming from the kitchen*; **baking dish** = dish that goes into the oven

② **balance**
['bæləns]
1 *noun*
(a) staying steady; *the cat needs a good sense of balance to walk along the top of a fence*; **to keep your balance** = not to fall over; **to lose your balance** = to fall down; *as he was crossing the river on the rope bridge he lost his balance and fell*
(b) money left in an account; *I have a balance of $35 in my bank account*; **balance of payments** = net amount of money received or paid by a country, resulting from its imports and exports; *the government is trying to reduce the balance of payments deficit*
(c) money left to be paid; *you can pay $150 down and the balance in three installments*; *the remaining balance to pay is now $5000*
(d) the result is hanging in the balance = you cannot tell which way the result will turn out
2 *verb*
(a) to stand without falling; *the cat balanced on the top of the fence*
(b) to make something stand without falling; *the waiter balanced a pile of dirty plates on his arm*
(c) to make accounts balance *or* **to balance the accounts** = to make income and expenditure equal in accounts

② **balanced**
['bælənst] *adjective*
(a) which does not contain too much of something; *children need a balanced diet*
(b) not in profit or loss; *we are aiming for a balanced budget this year*
(c) sensible, not extreme; *to express a balanced opinion*

② **balcony**
['bælkəni] *noun*
(a) small floor sticking out from the upper level of a building; *the apartment has a balcony overlooking the harbor*; *breakfast is served on the balcony*
(b) upstairs rows of seats in a theater or cinema; *we booked seats at the front of the balcony*
(NOTE: plural is **balconies**)

② **bald**
[bɔld] *adjective*
(a) who has no hair; *his grandfather is quite bald*; *he is beginning to go bald*; **bald eagle** = large eagle with a white head, the national symbol of the U.S.
(b) a bald tire = a tire that has been worn smooth; *this bald tire needs replacing*

④ **bale**
[beɪl] *noun*
large pack of wool, paper, cotton, etc.; *a bale of cotton*

① **ball**
[bɔl] *noun*
(a) round thing for throwing, kicking, playing games, etc.; *they played in the yard with an old tennis ball*; *he kicked the ball into the goal*; *he threw the ball and I caught it*; **to keep the ball rolling** = to keep everything moving, especially a conversation; *John kept the ball rolling by telling a long story about his trip to Egypt*; **I'll start the ball rolling** = I'll start things going; **he's on the ball** = he knows his job, he's clever in business; *I'll ask Marianne to do it - she's been here a long time and is really on the ball*; **they won't play ball** = they won't cooperate with us
(b) any round thing; *a ball of yarn*; *he crushed the paper up into a ball*
(c) formal dance; *Cinderella lost her shoe at the ball*; *(informal)* **to have a ball** = to enjoy yourself; *the kids don't want to go home - they're having a ball*

④ **ballad**
['bæləd] *noun*
simple romantic song; *a concert of country and western ballads*

② **ballet**
[bæ'leɪ] *noun*
(a) type of dance, given as a public entertainment, where dancers perform a story to music; *she's taking ballet lessons or she's going to ballet school*
(b) a performance of this type of dance; *Tchaikovsky's "Swan Lake" is a famous ballet*; *we went to the ballet last night*

① **balloon**
[bə'lun] *noun*
large ball that is blown up with air or gas; *he was blowing up balloons for the party*; **hot-air balloon** = very large balloon that rises into the air as the air inside it is heated, with people traveling in a basket attached underneath; *we went for a ride in a hot-air balloon*

③ **ballot**
['bælət]
1 *noun*
way of voting where voters mark papers with a mark; **ballot box** = box for putting voting papers into
2 *verb*
to vote by marking papers with a mark; *they balloted for the place on the committee*

③ **ballpark**
['bɔlpɑrk] *noun*
place for playing baseball; *the team's gone to the ballpark - they're playing baseball this afternoon*; **ballpark figure** = general figure which can be used as a basis for discussion

④ **ballplayer**
['bɔl'pleɪər] *noun*
person who plays baseball or football

④ **ball point pen**
['bɔl pɔint 'pen] *noun*
pen which writes using a small ball covered with
ink; *don't write in ball point, use a pencil*

④ **balm**
[bɑm] *noun*
soothing ointment; *apply some lip balm if your
lips are dry*

④ **baloney**
[bə'ləuni] *noun*
(slang) nonsense; *his speech was just a lot of
baloney*

④ **balsa**
['bɔlsə] *noun*
very light wood used for making models

② **bamboo**
[bæm'bu] *noun*
tropical plant, which grows very tall and of
which the stems are used as supports or in
making furniture; *we bought some bamboo
chairs for the living room*; **bamboo shoots** =
young shoots of bamboo, eaten especially in
Chinese cooking; *she fried some chicken and
bamboo shoots*

④ **ban**
[bæn]
1 *noun*
order that forbids something; *the government
has introduced a ban on smoking on domestic
flights*; *they imposed a ban on cycling in the
park*
2 *verb*
to forbid; *smoking has been banned on
domestic flights*; *she was banned from driving
for three years* (NOTE: **banning - banned**)

① **banana**
[bə'nænə] *noun*
(a) long yellow, slightly curved fruit which
grows in hot countries; *she was peeling a
banana*; *can I have a banana milkshake?*;
banana split = dessert made of a banana with
ice cream, whipped cream and chocolate sauce;
usually served in a long dish
(b) *(informal)* **to go bananas** = to go mad, to get
very annoyed; *when he saw what they had done
to his car, he went bananas*

① **band**
[bænd]
1 *noun*
(a) **rubber band** = thin circle of rubber for
holding things together; *the roll of papers was
held together with a rubber band*; *put a band
around the cards to stop them getting mixed*
(b) group of people; *bands of drunken football
fans wandered around the streets*
(c) group of people who play music together;
the band had two guitarists; *the dance band
played all night*
2 *verb*
to band together = to form a group; *they banded
together to form a pressure group*

② **bandage**
['bændidʒ]
1 *noun*
cloth for putting around a wound, an injured leg,
etc.; *the nurse put a bandage around his knee*;
his head was covered in bandages
2 *verb*
to put a cloth around a wound, an injured leg,
etc.; *she took him to the hospital and the nurse
bandaged his knee*

① **Band-Aid**
['bændeid] *noun*
(trademark) small strip of cloth which can be
stuck to the skin to cover a wound; *let me put a
Band-Aid on your finger*

② **bang**
[bæŋ]
1 *noun*
(a) sudden noise like that made by a gun; *the car
started with a series of loud bangs*; *there was a
bang and the tire went flat*
(b) **bangs** = hair cut in a fringe over your eyes
2 *verb*
to hit hard, so as to make a loud noise; *can't you
stop the door from banging?*; *he banged (on)
the table with his hand*
3 *interjection*
(showing the something makes a sudden noise) **a
firecracker suddenly went bang**
4 *adverb*
bang in the middle = directly, right in the
middle; *bang in the middle of the movie,
someone's cellular phone started to ring*

② **banister**
['bænistər] *noun*
rail on top of a series of poles along the side of
stairs; *the children love sliding down the
banister*

④ **banjo**
['bændʒəu] *noun*
stringed instrument with a round body and a
long neck; *the singer was accompanied by three
musicians playing banjos* (NOTE: plural is
banjos *or* **banjoes**)

① **bank**
[bæŋk]
1 *noun*
(a) business which holds money for its clients,
which lends money at interest and trades
generally in money; *I have to go to the bank to
get some money*; *how much money do you have
in the bank?*; *she took all her money out of the
bank to buy an automobile*
(b) land along the side of a river; *he sat on the
river bank all day, trying to catch fish*; *there is
a path along the bank of the canal*
(c) long heap of earth, sand, snow, etc.; *the road
was blocked by banks of snow blown by the
wind*
2 *verb*
(a) to put money away into a bank; *have you
banked the money yet?*

(b) to have an account with a bank; *I bank at Mutual Trust Bank*
(c) to pile up in a long mound; *the snow was banked up along both sides of the road*

① **bank account**
['bæŋk ə'kaʊnt] *noun*
arrangement that you make with a bank to keep your money safely, where you can deposit and withdraw money as you want; *I put all my savings into my bank account*; **to open a bank account** = to start keeping money in a bank; *he opened a bank account when he started his first job*; **to close a bank account** = to stop having an account with a bank

④ **bankbook**
['bæŋkbʊk] *noun*
book which records how much money you put in or take out of your savings or checking account; *next time, bring your bankbook so we can bring it up to date*

② **banker**
['bæŋkər] *noun*
person who has a senior post in a bank; *he works as a banker on Wall Street*

① **banking**
['bæŋkɪŋ] *noun*
(a) the profession of working in a bank; *he is planning a career in banking*
(b) the business of working in a bank; *some supermarkets now offer banking services*; **banking hours** = time when a bank is open for its customers; *you cannot get money out of the bank after banking hours unless you go to a cash machine*

③ **bankrupt**
['bæŋkrʌpt]
1 *adjective*
not able to pay your debts; *he was declared bankrupt, with debts totaling more than $1.5 m*
2 *verb*
to make someone bankrupt; *he was bankrupted in the Depression*

③ **bankruptcy**
['bæŋkrʌptsi] *noun*
being bankrupt; *when his business failed he faced bankruptcy*; *the number of bankruptcies increased during the recession* (NOTE: plural is **bankruptcies**)

② **banner**
['bænər] *noun*
(a) long flag; *they hung banners from the tops of buildings for the festival*
(b) large piece of cloth with a slogan on it; *the demonstrators carried banners with the words "Power to the People"*
(c) banner headline = newspaper headline printed in very large letters

④ **baptism**
['bæptɪzm] *noun*
religious ceremony where someone, usually a baby, is welcomed into the Christian church and given a Christian name after being sprinkled

with holy water; *all the family came together for the baptism*

④ **baptismal**
[bæp'tɪzməl] *adjective*
referring to a baptism

① **bar**
[bɑr]
1 *noun*
(a) long piece of something hard; *the yard was full of pieces of wood and metal bars*
(b) solid piece of material; *put a new bar of soap by the bath*; *she was eating a bar of chocolate*
(c) long piece of wood or metal that closes a door or window; **bars** = pieces of metal in front of a prison window; *the prisoners escaped by sawing through the bars*; **behind bars** = in prison; *he was put behind bars for several years*
(d) long metal or plastic key on a typewriter or computer keyboard; **space bar** = long bar at the bottom of the keyboard on a typewriter or computer which inserts a single space into text
(e) place where you can buy and drink alcohol; *let's meet in the bar before dinner*; *the salesmen met in the bar of the hotel*
(f) small store where you can buy food; **coffee bar** = small restaurant which sells coffee, cakes and sandwiches; **sandwich bar** = small store which mainly sells sandwiches; **snack bar** = small restaurant where you can eat simple meals; *she bought fries and a soda at the snack bar*
(g) thing which prevents something happening; *not having the right qualifications could be a bar to your promotion*; **color bar** = using the color of someone's skin as a reason to stop them from doing something
(h) the legal profession; **to be called to the bar** = to become a lawyer
(i) division within a piece of music; *let's play the first few bars again*
2 *preposition*
except; *all of the suppliers replied bar one*; *all bar two of the players on the team are American*
3 *verb*
(a) to block; *the road was barred by the police*; *the path is barred to cyclists*
(b) to bar someone from doing something = to prevent someone doing something; *she was barred from entering the exam* (NOTE: **barring - barred**)

② **barbecue**
['bɑrbɪkju]
1 *noun*
(a) food cooked on a metal grill; **barbecue sauce** = spicy tomato sauce eaten with barbecued food
(b) meal or party where food is cooked out-of-doors on a metal grill; *we had a barbecue for twenty guests*; *let's have a barbecue in our back yard*; *they've been invited to a barbecue*

(c) metal grill for cooking out-of-doors; *light the barbecue at least half an hour before you start cooking*

2 *verb*

to cook on a metal grill; *she was barbecuing burgers for lunch when it started to rain*; *here is a recipe for barbecued chicken*

④ **barber**

['bɑrbər] *noun*

person who cuts men's hair; **barber shop** = shop where men have their hair cut

② **bar code**

['bɑr 'kəʊd] *noun*

printed lines which can be read by a computer; *there doesn't seem to be a price on the packet - just a bar code*

② **bare**

['beər]

1 *adjective*

(a) naked, with no clothes on; *he walked on the beach in his bare feet*

(b) with no leaves on, no furniture inside, etc.; *in winter, the branches are all bare*; *they slept on the bare boards*; *they saw the bare bones of dead animals in the desert*

(c) bare minimum = the smallest amount needed; *the apartment is furnished with the bare minimum of furniture*

2 *verb*

to make part of the body bare by removing clothes; *men should bare their heads on entering the church* (NOTE: do not confuse with **bear**)

④ **bareback**

['beərbæk] *adjective & adverb*

without a saddle; *a bareback rider*; *she rode bareback along the beach*

④ **barefoot**

['beərfʊt] *adjective & adverb*

without shoes; *she walked barefoot in the grass*; *the children were barefoot*

④ **barelegged**

['beərlegd] *adjective & adverb*

not wearing clothes on your legs; *barelegged children were fishing for shrimps*

② **barely**

['beərli] *adverb*

scarcely, almost not enough; *she barely had enough money to pay for her ticket*; *he barely had time to get dressed before the police arrived*

② **bargain**

['bɑrgɪn]

1 *noun*

(a) an agreed deal; **to strike a bargain** = to agree terms; *we shook hands and the bargain was struck*; **he drives a hard bargain** = he is a tough negotiator

(b) in *or* **into the bargain** = as well as other things; *the plane was late and they lost my suitcase, in the bargain*

(c) something bought more cheaply than usual; *the automobile was a real bargain at $750*; **bargain basement** = cheap department in the basement of a store; *you'll find cheaper items in the bargain basement*; **bargain offer** *or* **bargain sale** = sale at a specially low price

2 *verb*

(a) to negotiate terms; *after bargaining with the man at the door, we managed to get into the club*

(b) to discuss a price; *if you bargain with the man in the antique shop, you'll probably get something knocked off the price*

(c) to bargain for something = to expect something to happen; *I hadn't bargained for him being away and leaving me to do all the work*; **I got more than I bargained for** = the deal had unpleasant results which I did not expect (NOTE: you bargain **with** someone **over** *or* **about** *or* **for** something)

② **barge**

[bɑrdʒ]

1 *noun*

cargo boat on a river or canal; *we watched the barges go past along the river*

2 *verb*

to barge in = to interrupt; *we were having a quiet chat when he came barging in*

① **bark**

[bɑrk]

1 *noun*

(a) hard outer layer of a tree; *the rough bark of a pine tree*; *the bark of birch trees comes off in strips*

(b) call of a dog; *the dog gave a bark to greet us as we came into the house*; **his bark is worse than his bite** = he is not as frightening as he seems; *don't be afraid of Aunt Bessie - her bark is much worse than her bite*

2 *verb*

to make a call like a dog; *the dog barks every time he hears the mailman*; **to bark up the wrong tree** = to be mistaken; *they don't know what the problem is - they're barking up the wrong tree*

① **barn**

[bɑrn] *noun*

large farm building for storing produce; *the barn is full of wheat*

④ **barometer**

[bə'rɒmɪtər] *noun*

instrument which measures changes in atmospheric pressure and can be used to forecast the weather

③ **barracks**

['bærəks] *noun*

building where soldiers live; *the soldiers marched into their barracks*; *the barracks were built in the 19th century* (NOTE: **barracks** is both singular and plural)

② **barrel**
['bærəl] *noun*
(a) round wooden container for liquid; *a barrel of beer*; *we sell wine by the barrel*; *he has me over a barrel* = I'm placed in very awkward situation
(b) amount contained in a barrel; *the price of oil has reached $30 a barrel*; *the oil well produces thousands of barrels of oil per day*
(c) firing tube of a gun; *you need to clean the barrel of a rifle very carefully*

③ **barrier**
['bæriər] *noun*
bar which blocks the way; thing which prevents the spread of a disease, the import of goods, etc.; *he lifted the barrier and we drove across the border*; **customs barriers** *or* **trade barriers** = special taxes to prevent imports; *to impose trade barriers on certain goods*

① **bartender**
['bɑrtendər] *noun*
person who mixes and serves drinks at a bar; *the bartender had never heard of the drink Mary ordered*

② **base**
[beɪs]
1 *noun*
(a) bottom part; *the table lamp has a flat base*
(b) place where you work from; *he lives in New York but uses London as his base when doing business in Europe*; **a military base** = a camp for soldiers; *he was posted to an air base in Germany*
(c) one of the marked spots in baseball where a player is safe; *players have to run from base to base*; **to touch base with someone** = to get in touch with someone again; *I'm calling because I wanted to touch base with you*
2 *verb*
to use as a base; *the company is based in Beijing*; *he based his article on work done at Harvard University*

① **baseball**
['beɪsbɔl] *noun*
(a) game for two teams of nine players, in which a player hits a ball with a bat and players from the other team try to catch it; he scores points by running around the field from base to base (there are four bases in all); *we went to the baseball game last Saturday*; **baseball cap** = soft cotton cap with a large peak; *she was wearing a baseball cap back to front*
(b) the hard ball used in playing baseball; *we lost yet another baseball in the river*

② **basement**
['beɪsmənt] *noun*
floor in a building below the ground level; *we keep the washing machine in the basement*; *she lives in a basement apartment*; see also BARGAIN

② **bash**
[bæʃ]

1 *noun*
(a) knock; *he got a bash in the head*
(b) *(informal)* big party; *are you going to Jane's bash tomorrow?* (NOTE: plural is **bashes**)
2 *verb*
to hit hard; *he bashed her over the head with a stick*; *she was bashing stakes into the ground with a hammer*

④ **bashful**
['bæʃfəl] *adjective*
shy and embarrassed; *he's bashful, and doesn't want to go up onto the stage to collect his prize*

② **basic**
['beɪsɪk] *adjective*
very simple, at the first level; *being able to swim is a basic requirement if you are going sailing*; *knowledge of basic Spanish will be enough for the job*; **basic vocabulary** = most common words in a language

④ **basically**
[beɪsɪkli] *adverb*
(used when stating the simplest fact) at the simplest level; *basically, he's fed up with his job*

② **basin**
['beɪsən] *noun*
(a) large bowl for holding liquids; *we filled the basin with water*
(b) land drained by a river and the streams that flow into it; *the Amazon basin covers a huge area*

④ **basis**
['beɪsɪs] *noun*
(a) general facts on which something is based; *what is the basis for these proposals?*; **on the basis of** = based on; *the calculations are done on the basis of an exchange rate of 1.6 dollars to the pound*
(b) general terms of an agreement; *she is working for us on a freelance basis*; *many of the helpers at the children's home work on a voluntary basis* (NOTE: plural is **bases** ['beɪsiz])

① **basket**
['bæskɪt] *noun*
container made of thin pieces of wood, wire, grass, etc., woven together; **shopping basket** = basket used for carrying purchases; *if you're going shopping, don't forget your shopping basket*; **wastepaper basket** = container into which paper or pieces of garbage can be put; *he threw the letter into the wastepaper basket*

① **basketball**
['bæskɪtbɔl] *noun*
(a) game played by two teams of five players, who try to throw a ball into a basket placed high on the back wall; *he plays on the college basketball team*
(b) the ball used when playing basketball

② **bass**
1 [beɪs] *adjective*
referring to a low-pitched voice or music; *he has a pleasant bass voice*; **bass guitar** = guitar that

plays a lower range of notes; *he plays bass guitar in a pop group*

2 [beɪs] *noun*

(a) singer with deep voice; *the famous Russian bass*

(b) (double) bass = very large musical instrument like a big cello; *she plays the double bass in the city orchestra* (NOTE: plural is **basses**; do not confuse with **base**)

(c) [bæs] edible fish found in both fresh and salt waters; *we cooked the bass that we had caught*

④ **bastard**
['bæstəd]

1 *adjective*

with parents who are not married; *the bastard son of the last king*

2 *noun*

(a) person whose parents are not married; *many children are born bastards nowadays*

(b) *(informal) (generally offensive)* nasty person, nasty thing; *the bastard walked out of the restaurant without paying*

① **bat**
[bæt]

1 *noun*

(a) piece of wood used for hitting a ball; *a baseball bat*; **at bat** = having one's turn batting; **right off the bat** = immediately; *he did it right off the bat*

(b) little animal, similar to a mouse, which can fly; *bats were flying all around the trees in the yard*; *bats hang upside down*

2 *verb*

(a) *(in baseball)* to be the player who is hitting the ball; *I watched him batting on TV this afternoon*; **to go to bat for** = to help or support someone; *I went to bat for my friend when I heard what they were saying*

(b) *he never batted an eye or an eyelid* = he showed no surprise at all (NOTE: **batting - batted**)

② **batch**
[bætʃ] *noun*

number of things made at one time; *he baked a batch of cookies*; *the department processed a batch of orders*; **batch number** = number printed on a batch of units made at one time; *when making a complaint, please quote the batch number on the packet* (NOTE: plural is **batches**)

① **bath**
[bæθ]

1 *noun*

(a) washing your whole body; *he took a bath when he came home from work*; *my father has a cold bath every morning*

(b) bathtub, a large container in which you can sit and wash your whole body; *there's a washbowl and a bath in the bathroom*; *the bath has not been cleaned properly* (NOTE: you say **one bath** [bæθ] but **two baths** [bæðz])

2 *verb*

to wash all over; *she's bathing the baby* (NOTE: do not confuse with **bathe**; note also **baths** [bæθs] - **bathing** ['bæθɪŋ] - **bathed** [bæθt])

② **bathe**
[beɪð] *verb*

(a) to wash a wound carefully; *the nurse bathed his wound before applying a dressing*

(b) to have a bath; *I just have enough time to bathe before my dinner guests arrive*

(c) *(formal)* to go swimming in a pool, lake, the sea, etc.; *we decided to bathe a while in the warm river waters*; **bathing suit** = swim suit, the clothing worn by women or children when swimming; *don't forget to bring your bathing suit* (NOTE the pronunciation (and compare to **bath**): **bathes** [beɪðz] - **bathing** ['beɪðɪŋ] - **bathed** [beɪðd])

① **bathroom**
['bæθrum] *noun*

(a) room in a house with a bath, a washbowl and usually a lavatory; *the house has two bathrooms*

(b) *(said instead of)* toilet; *where's the bathroom?*; *can I use your bathroom, please?*

① **bathtub**
['bæθtʌb] *noun*

bath, the large container in which you can sit and wash your body; *I'd rather have a shower than a bathtub in the bathroom*

② **batter**
['bætər]

1 *noun*

(a) liquid mixture of flour and milk; *the fish are coated in batter and fried*

(b) *(in baseball)* the player who has the bat and hits the ball

2 *verb*

to hit someone often; *he was accused of battering the baby to death*

② **battery**
['bætəri] *noun*

little device for storing electric energy; *my calculator needs a new battery*; *the battery has given out so I can't use my cellular phone*

① **battle**
['bætl]

1 *noun*

(a) important fight between armed forces; *many of the soldiers died in battle*; *the Battle of Gettysburg*; **pitched battle** = battle where the opposing sides stand and face each other; **running battle** = battle that moves around; *the police were engaged in running battles with the protesters*

(b) fight against something; *the government's constant battle against inflation*; *he lost his battle against cancer*

2 *verb*

to battle against = to fight against; *she had to battle against the other members of the board*; *his last years were spent battling against cancer*

② **battlefield**
['bætəlfiəld] *noun*
site where a battle took place; *we went to visit the battlefields of northern Alabama*

④ **battleground**
['bætəlgraʊnd] = BATTLEFIELD

④ **battleship**
['bætəlʃɪp] *noun*
largest type of warship with big guns; *after the World War II, most battleships were scrapped*

③ **bay**
[beɪ] *noun*
(a) large curve in a coast; *the Bay of Biscay*
(b) **bay window** = window that sticks out from a flat wall; *can we sit at that table in the bay window?*
(c) **loading bay** = place for loading trucks in a warehouse
(d) **to keep someone at bay** = to stop someone from attacking; *he tried to keep the bank manager at bay by promising to repay the loan in ten days' time; farmers use guns to protect their lambs and keep foxes at bay*
(e) shrub with leaves used in cooking; *add a bay leaf to the soup*

④ **bazaar**
[bə'zɑr] *noun*
(a) Indian or Middle Eastern market; *we visited the busy bazaar to try to buy spices*
(b) **charity bazaar** = sale of goods donated by people to be sold for charity; *we're organizing a bazaar for the hospital*

④ **bazooka**
[bə'zukə] *noun*
small anti-tank gun; *the guerrillas were armed with bazookas and hand grenades*

① **be**
[bi]
1 *verb*
(a) *(describing a person or thing)* *our house is older than yours; she is bigger than her brother; lemons are yellow; the soup is hot; are you tired after your long walk?; put on your coat - it is cold outside; I'm cold after standing and waiting for the bus*
(b) *(showing age or time)* *he's twenty years old; she will be two next month; it is nearly ten o'clock; it is time to get up; September is the beginning of fall*
(c) *(showing price)* *onions are 80 cents a pound; the cookies are 75 cents each; my automobile was worth $15,000 when it was new*
(d) *(showing a job)* *his father is a bus driver; she wants to be a teacher*
(e) *(showing size, weight, height, etc.)* *he's six feet tall; the room is 30 square feet; our house is ten miles from the nearest station*
(f) *(meaning to add up to)* *two and two are four*
(g) *(showing that something exists)* *where are we?; there's your hat!; there was a crowd of people waiting for the store to open; there were only two people left on the bus*
(h) *(meaning to go or visit)* *the police have been into every room; have you ever been to Italy?; we have been to see the movie three times*
2 *(making part of a verb)*
(a) *(making a present tense)* *don't make a noise when he's watching football on TV; I'm waiting for the bank to open; we are hoping to go on vacation in June*
(b) *(making a past tense)* *he was singing in the shower; we were walking toward the post office when we met her*
(c) *(making a future tense)* *we will be going to Malaysia next week*
(d) *(showing a passive)* *he was killed by a train; the children were sent home by the teacher*

① **beach**
[bitʃ]
1 *noun*
area of sand or little stones by the edge of the sea; *they spent the afternoon on the beach; many of the beaches are covered with oil from the tanker; we walked along the beach and looked for shells; beach towel* = large towel normally used on the beach; *she was wrapped in a bright blue and yellow beach towel; beach umbrella* = large colored umbrella to use on a beach (NOTE: plural is **beaches**)
2 *verb*
to bring onto a beach; *they beached the boat near the harbor; at high tide we will try to return the beached whale to the sea*

④ **bead**
[biːd] *noun*
(a) little decorative piece of wood, plastic, glass, etc., with a hole in it, used to make a necklace; *she was wearing a string of red beads*
(b) small drop of liquid; *beads of sweat formed on his brow*

① **beak**
[bik] *noun*
hard part of a bird's mouth; *the bird was carrying the worm in its beak*

① **beam**
[bim]
1
(a) long block of wood or metal that supports part of a building, especially a roof; *you can see the old beams in the ceiling*
(b) ray of light; *beams of sunlight came through the windows of the church; the beam from the car's headlights shone into the room*
2 *verb*
to give a wide smile; *the little girl beamed at him*

① **bean**
[bin] *noun*
(a) long thin green vegetable, of which you eat the outside or the seeds; *can you go to the grocery store and get me some beans?*
(b) *(informal)* **full of beans** = (i) full of energy; (ii) wrong, not knowing anything; *she's full of*

beans today; *don't listen to him - he's just full of beans*; *see also* BAKED BEANS, SPILL
(c) coffee beans = seeds of the coffee bush, which are roasted and ground to make coffee; **soy beans** = beans of the soy plant, which have a high protein and fat content and are low in carbohydrates; *soy sauce is made from soy beans*

④ **bean bag**
['biːn 'bæg] *noun*
little bag with beans inside, used for throwing; *she was playing with her bean bag*

④ **beanie**
['biːni] *noun*
sort of small cap, worn by freshmen or sports fans

④ **bean sprouts**
['biːn 'spraʊts] *noun*
small sprouts of various types of beans, used as food; *stir-fry some bean sprouts in the wok*

① **bear**
[beər]
1 *noun*
large wild animal covered with fur; *they say that bears like honey*; *there are bears near the camp in the mountains*; **polar bear** = big white bear which lives in the snow near the North Pole; *the explorers were attacked by polar bears*; **teddy bear** = toy bear; *she was carrying her favorite teddy bear* (NOTE: usually simply called a **teddy**)
2 *verb*
(a) to carry, to produce; *this apple tree has borne fruit every year for the last twenty years*; *my deposits bear 5% interest*
(b) not to bear = not to like; *I can't bear the smell of cooking fish*
(c) to turn slightly; *bear right when the road divides* (NOTE: **bearing - bore** [bɔːr] **- has borne** [bɔːrn])

② **beard**
['biərd] *noun*
hair growing on a man's chin; *Santa Claus has a long white beard*

④ **bearing**
['beəriŋ] *noun*
(a) (ball) bearings = set of little balls inside which a wheel turns; *the bearings inside the brake drums had to be replaced*
(b) calculation to show where you are; **to get your bearings** = to find out where you are; *give me a few moments to get my bearings*; **to lose your bearings** = to get lost; *I'm sorry I'm late, but I didn't have a map and lost my bearings*
(c) bearing on something = connection to something; *the letter had no bearing on the result of the trial*

① **beat**
[biːt]
1 *noun*
(a) regular sound; *the patient's heart has a beat that is not regular*
(b) *(in music)* regular sound of a piece of music; *they danced to the beat of the steel band*

(c) area patrolled by a police officer on foot; *here police officers on the beat have to go around in pairs*
2 *verb*
(a) to do better than someone else, than another team in a game; *they beat us at our own game*; *our football team beat Dallas 21-3*; *they beat us by 10 goals to 2*; *we beat the Canadians at hockey last year*
(b) to make a regular sound; *his heart was still beating when the ambulance arrived*; *her heart beat faster as she went into the interview*
(c) to hit hard; *he used to drink and then beat his wife*; *she hung the carpet on the line and beat it with a stick to remove the dust*
(d) *(informal)* **beat it!** = go away! (NOTE: **beating - beat - has beaten**)

② **beaten**
['biːtən] *adjective*
(a) defeated; *the beaten team went home*
(b) off the beaten track = in a place that is away from main roads and not normally visited by many people; *luckily, our town is off the beaten track*

② **beating**
['biːtiŋ] *noun*
act of hitting or defeating; *they gave our team a beating*

② **beat up**
['biːt 'ʌp] *verb*
to attack someone; *three muggers beat him up and stole his credit cards*

① **beautiful**
['bjuːtɪfəl] *adjective*
very nice, especially to look at; *the beautiful colors of the leaves in fall*; *Mr. Smith and his three beautiful daughters*; *what beautiful weather!*; *they have a beautiful house in the country*

④ **beautifully**
['bjuːtɪfəli] *adverb*
in a very pleasing way; *she sang the song beautifully*

① **beauty**
['bjuːti] *noun*
(a) quality of being beautiful; *her beauty was famous*; *the beauty of the trees against the background of the blue lake*
(b) beautiful thing; *at 18 she was a real beauty*; *his motorbike is a beauty - I must buy one like it*; *look at these apples, they're real beauties*

④ **beauty parlor** *or* **salon** *or* **shop**
['bjuːti 'pɑːrlər *or* 'sælɒn *or* 'ʃɒp] *noun*
place which offers styling and treatments for hair, nails, skin, etc., to help women look more beautiful

④ **beaver**
['biːvər] *noun*
animal with sharp teeth and a broad flat tail, which lives in water; *beavers cut down young*

trees to build their homes; **eager beaver** = person who is very enthusiastic

① **became**
[bɪˈkeɪm]
see BECOME

① **because**
[bɪˈkɒz] *conjunction* for this reason; *I was late because I missed the train*; *the dog's wet because he's been in the river*; *just because I'm lending you my automobile this time, it doesn't mean you can borrow it when you like*

① **because of**
[bɪˈkɒz ɒv] *preposition*
on account of, due to; *flights are delayed because of the fog*; *we don't often use the automobile because of the price of gas*

③ **beckon**
[ˈbekən] *verb*
to beckon to someone = to make a sign with your hand telling someone to come; *the nurse beckoned to her to come into the room*

② **become**
[bɪˈkʌm] *verb*
(a) to change to something different; *the sky became dark and the wind became stronger*; *they became good friends*; *as she got older she became rather deaf*; *it soon became obvious that he didn't understand a word of what I was saying*
(b) to start to work as; *he wants to become a doctor*
(c) to become of = to happen to; *I never saw her brother again, I wonder what became of him* (NOTE: **becoming - became** [bɪˈkeɪm] - **has become**)

① **bed**
[bed]
1 *noun*
(a) piece of furniture for sleeping on; *lie down on my bed if you're tired*; **double bed** = bed for two people; **single bed** = bed for one person; **to go to bed** = to get into your bed for the night; *she always goes to bed at 9 o'clock*; **to be in bed** = to be sitting or lying in bed; *she's in bed with a cold*; *he was sitting up in bed drinking a cup of coffee*; **to make a bed** = to make it tidy or change the sheets after someone has slept in it; *have you made your bed?*; *you can't go into your hotel room because the beds haven't been made*; **to get up on the wrong side of the bed** = to start the day badly
(b) piece of ground specially for plants; *a strawberry bed*; *a bed of roses*; *her life isn't a bed of roses* = she leads a life full of difficulties
(c) ground at the bottom of water; *the sandy bed of a river*
2 *verb*
to bed out plants = to put plants into a garden bed; *it's still too cold to start bedding out the summer flowers*

① **bedroom**
[ˈbedrum] *noun*
room where you sleep; *my bedroom is on the first floor*; *the hotel has twenty-five bedrooms*; *lock your bedroom door if you don't want to be disturbed*

② **bedside**
[ˈbedsaɪd] *noun*
the side of a bed; *his wife was sitting at his bedside*; *there's a small lamp on the bedside table*; **bedside manner** = way in which a doctor behaves toward a patient, especially with kindness and understanding; **he has a good bedside manner** = he comforts and reassures his patients

④ **bedspread**
[ˈbedspred] *noun*
decorated cloth cover put over a bed; *she bought a pink and white bedspread to match her bedroom curtains*

① **bedtime**
[ˈbedtaɪm] *noun*
time when you go to bed; *10 o'clock is my bedtime*; *she read the children a bedtime story*; **go to bed - it's past your bedtime** = it's later than the time when you normally go to bed

① **bee**
[bi] *noun*
insect that makes honey, and can sting you if it is annoyed; *the bee moved from flower to flower*

COMMENT: in a bee colony, the main female bee is the **queen;** the other females are the **workers,** and the males are the **drones**

③ **beech**
[bitʃ] *noun*
(a) beech (tree) = common large tree; *beeches are common in the south*
(b) wood from this tree; *the floor is made of beech* (NOTE: do not confuse with **beach**)

① **beef**
[bif]
1 *noun*
meat from a cow or bull; *a plate of roast beef and mashed potatoes* (NOTE: no plural)
2 *verb*
(informal) **to beef about** = to grumble about; *what's he beefing about, tell him to shut up!*; **to beef up** = to make bigger or stronger; *we will have to beef up our advertising budget*

① **beehive**
[ˈbihaɪv] *noun*
box for bees to make a nest in; *he took the honey carefully out of the beehive*

④ **beekeeper**
[ˈbikipər] *noun*
person who keeps bees for their honey; *the beekeeper opened one of the hives*

① **been**
[bin]
see BE

② **beer**
[biər] *noun*
(a) alcoholic drink made from grain and water; *can I have a glass of beer?*; *what beers do you have on tap?*
(b) a glass of beer; *three beers, please* (NOTE: the plural **beers** is used to mean **glasses of beer**)

④ **beeswax**
['bizwæks] *noun*
wax produced by bees, used as a polish

① **beet**
[bit] *noun*
vegetable with a dark red root, often cooked or pickled with vinegar; *their main crop was beets*; **beet red** = very red in the face; *he turned beet red when we showed his girlfriend his baby pictures*

① **beetle**
['bitl] *noun*
insect with hard covers on its wings; *waiter, there's a beetle in the salad!*; *ladybugs are a type of beetle*

① **before**
[bɪ'fɔr]
1 *adverb*
earlier; *why didn't you tell me before?*; *I didn't see him last week, I saw him the week before*
2 *preposition*
earlier than; *they should have arrived before now*; *you must be home before 9 o'clock*; *G comes before H in the alphabet*
3 *conjunction*
earlier than; *before you sit down, can you switch on the light?*; *the police got there before I did*; *think carefully before you start to answer the exam questions*; *wash your hands before you have your dinner*

② **beforehand**
[bɪ'fɔrhænd] *adverb*
in advance; *you must tell me beforehand if you want to borrow any more money*

② **beg**
[beg] *verb*
(a) to ask for money, food, clothes, etc.; *she sat begging on the steps of the station*; *children were begging for food*
(b) to ask someone in an emotional way to do something, to give something; *his mother begged him not to go*; *he begged for more time to find the money*
(c) to beg a favor of someone = to ask someone to do something for you
(d) I beg your pardon! = excuse me, forgive me; *I beg your pardon, I didn't hear what you said*; *I do beg your pardon - I didn't know you were busy*; *see also* DIFFER (NOTE: **begging - begged**)

① **began**
[bɪ'gæn]
see BEGIN

① **begin**
[bɪ'gɪn] *verb*
to start; *the children began to cry*; *she has begun to knit a red pullover for her father*; *the house is beginning to warm up*; *his surname begins with an S*; *the meeting is due to begin at ten o'clock sharp*; **to begin again** = to start a second time; *he forgot to save his file and had to begin keyboarding all over again* (NOTE: **beginning - began** [bɪ'gæn] **- has begun** [bɪ'gʌn])

② **beginner**
[bɪ'gɪnər] *noun*
person who is starting; *he can't paint well, he's only a beginner*

① **beginning**
[bɪ'gɪnɪŋ] *noun*
first part; *the beginning of the movie is kind of slow*; *hurry up if you want to see the beginning of the news*

① **begun**
[bɪ'gʌn]
see BEGIN

④ **begrudge**
[bɪ'grʌdʒ] *verb*
(a) to feel resentment because of something someone has or does; *I don't begrudge him his money*
(b) to give money unwillingly; *I begrudge every dollar I pay in tax*

④ **behalf**
[bɪ'hæf] *noun*
(a) on behalf of = acting for someone; *she is speaking on behalf of the association of retired public service employees*; *he was chosen to speak on behalf of the other workers in the factory*
(b) acting on my behalf = acting as my representative; *the lawyer acting on my behalf*
(c) don't worry on my behalf = don't worry about me

② **behave**
[bɪ'heɪv] *verb*
to act in a certain way with someone; *he behaved very pleasantly toward his staff*; *she was behaving in a funny way*; *(of children)* **to behave (yourself)** = to be good; *if you don't behave (yourselves) you won't get any ice cream*

② **behavior**
[bɪ'heɪvjər] *noun*
way of doing things; *the police asked him for an explanation of his strange behavior*; *visitors complained about the behavior of the kids*

① **behind**
[bɪ'haɪnd]
1 *preposition*
(a) at the back of; *they hid behind the door*; *I dropped my pen behind the sofa*; *he was*

second, only three meters behind the winner; **she's behind the rest of the class** = not as advanced as the others; *see also* TIME

(b) responsible for; *the police believe they know who is behind the bombing campaign*

(c) supporting; *all his colleagues were behind his decision*; *we're behind you!*

2 *adverb*

(a) at the back; *he was first, the rest of the runners were a long way behind*; **he left his umbrella behind** = he forgot to take his umbrella with him; **when the others went out, he stayed behind to watch TV** = he stayed at home when the others went out

(b) later than you should be; *I am behind with my correspondence*; *the company has fallen behind with its deliveries*

3 *noun*

(informal) part of the body that you sit on; *there was some water on the chair and my behind's all wet*; *I'll kick his behind if he doesn't get a move on*; *he's so lazy! - he needs a good kick in the behind*

② **being**
['biːŋ]
see HUMAN, TIME

③ **Belgian**
['beldʒən]

1 *adjective*

referring to Belgium; *we ordered pancakes and the kids had Belgian waffles*

2 *noun*

person from Belgium; *there were ten people at the meeting, and two of them were Belgians*

① **Belgium**
['beldʒəm] *noun*

country on the North Sea, between France and Holland; *if you're driving to Denmark, it is quicker to drive through Belgium into Germany* (NOTE: capital: **Brussels**; people: **Belgians**; languages: **Flemish, French**; currency: **Belgian franc, euro**)

① **belief**
[bɪˈliːf] *noun*

feeling sure that something is true; *his firm belief in the power of law*; *her strong belief in God*; **it is my belief** = I believe; *it's my belief that the problems with the engine are caused by the rain*; **beyond belief** = quite incredible; *that she did not know that there were drugs in the package is quite beyond belief*

① **believe**
[bɪˈliːv] *verb*

(a) to be sure that something is true, although you can't prove it; *people used to believe that the Earth was flat*; *don't believe anything he tells you*

(b) not to be absolutely sure; *I don't believe I have ever met your father*; *I believe I have been here before*

(c) to believe in = to be sure that something exists; *do you believe in flying saucers?*; *some people believe in miracles*

(d) can't *or* **couldn't believe your eyes** *or* **ears** = be very surprised to see *or* hear something; *I couldn't believe my ears when I heard my name read out as the winner*; *she couldn't believe her eyes when she saw the automobile he had bought her*

① **bell**
[bel] *noun*

metal object, like a cup, that makes a ringing noise when hit; electric device that makes a ringing noise if you push a button; *the alarm bell rings if you touch the door*; *the mail carrier rang the door bell*; *you ought to have a bell on your bicycle*; *they rang the church bells at the wedding*; **that rings a bell** = that reminds me of something; *does the name Forsyth ring a bell with you?*

① **belly**
['beli] *noun*

(informal) stomach and the front part of the body below the chest; *the little boy lifted his T-shirt and showed his round belly* (NOTE: plural is **bellies**)

④ **bellyache**
['belieɪk]

1 *noun*

pain in the abdomen or stomach; *she had a bellyache after eating green apples*

2 *verb*

(informal) **to bellyache about something** = to complain about something; *nothing seems to make her happy - she's always bellyaching about something*

① **belong**
[bɪˈlɒŋ] *verb*

(a) to belong to someone = to be the property of someone; *does the car really belong to you?*

(b) to belong to a group or club = to be a member of a group or club; *which tennis club do you belong to?*

(c) to belong with = to be part of, to be stored with; *these plates belong with the big dinner service*

① **belongings**
[bɪˈlɒŋɪŋz] *noun*

personal property; *her belongings were scattered all over the room*; *please be sure to take all personal belongings with you when you leave the aircraft*

② **beloved**
[bɪˈlʌvɪd] *adjective*

(person or place) which someone loves very much; *she doesn't want to leave her beloved childhood home*; *he was very upset at the death of his beloved grandpa*

① **below**
[bɪˈləʊ]

1 *adverb*

lower down; *I looked down from the hill at the town below; these toys are for children of two years and below*

2 *preposition*

lower down than; *the temperature was below freezing; in Singapore, the temperature never goes below 80°F; can you see below the surface of the water?; do not write anything below this line; this medication should not be given to children below the age of twelve*

② **belt**
['belt]

1 *noun*

(a) strap that goes around your waist (to hold up a skirt or pants); *she wore a bright red belt; this silver belt comes from Japan*

(b) seat belt *or* safety belt = belt that you wear in an automobile or a plane to stop you from being hurt if there is an accident; *please fasten your seat belts as we are preparing to land; the police caught him driving without a seat belt*

(c) area with a particular characteristic; *the Bible Belt refers to the southern states*

2 *verb*

to hit someone hard; *he belted the guy*

① **bench**
['bentʃ] *noun*

(a) long wooden seat; *we sat down on one of the park benches*

(b) (work) bench = table in a workshop at which someone works; *the shoe repairer was standing at his bench*

(c) the bench = magistrates sitting in court; *he was up before the bench for speeding* (NOTE: plural is **benches**)

① **bend**
['bend]

1 *noun*

curve (in a road, line, etc.); *don't drive too fast, there's a sudden bend in the road; the pipe under the sink has an awkward S-bend*

2 *verb*

(a) to make something curved; *you will have to bend the pipe to fit around the corner*

(b) to curve; *the road bends sharply after the bridge* (NOTE: **bending** - **bent** ['bent])

① **bend down** *or* **bend over**
['bend 'daʊn *or* 'əʊvər] *verb*

to bend your body so that your head is lower than your waist; *he dropped his pen and bent down to pick it up; she was bending over the sink*; *see also* BACKWARDS

① **beneath**
[bɪ'niːθ]

1 *adverb*

underneath; *from the bridge we watched the river flowing beneath*

2 *preposition*

(a) under; *there are dangerous rocks beneath the surface of the lake; the river flows very fast beneath the bridge*

(b) not suitable, not important enough; *he thinks it is beneath him to make the coffee himself*

④ **benefactor**
['benɪfæktər] *noun*

person who gives money to an organization such as a charity; *the college welcomes any financial help from overseas benefactors*

④ **beneficial**
[benɪ'fɪʃl] *adjective*

which helps, which is a benefit; *a regular walk every morning is beneficial to your general health*

③ **benefit**
['benɪfɪt]

1 *noun*

(a) advantage; *what are the benefits of joining the club?*

(b) payment made by the state; *he receives unemployment benefits*

2 *verb*

(a) to be useful to someone; *the book will benefit anyone who is planning to do some home repairs*

(b) to benefit from *or* by something = to get an advantage from; *American tourists will benefit from the strong dollar; he benefits from the senior free bus pass because he is over 65*

① **bent**
['bent]

1 *adjective*

(a) curved; *these nails are bent so we can't use them*; *see also* BEND

(b) to be bent on = to be very keen on doing something; *he is bent on buying the automobile even if he can't afford it*

2 *noun*

instinct; *she has a natural bent to be a nurse; he followed his bent and joined the navy*

① **berry**
['beri] *noun*

small fruit; *they spent the afternoon picking berries in the woods* (NOTE: plural is **berries**; do not confuse with **bury**)

④ **bequeath**
[bɪ'kwɪð] *verb*

to bequeath something to someone = to leave property to someone in your will; *he bequeathed his house to his son*

④ **bereaved**
[bɪ'riːvd] *noun*

the bereaved = family or friends of a person who has died; *the priest was trying to console the bereaved after the ceremony*

④ **beseech**
[bɪ'siːtʃ] *verb*

(formal) to beseech someone to do something = to ask someone earnestly to do something; *she beseeched them to think again*

① **beside**

[bɪ'saɪd] *preposition*

(a) at the side of someone or something; *come and sit down beside me*; *the office is just beside the train station*; *it's beside the point* = it has nothing to do with the main subject; *whether or not the coat matches your hat is beside the point - it's simply too big for you*

(b) to be beside yourself with = to be frantic; *the parents were beside themselves with worry when their daughter did not come home from school*; *she was beside herself with grief*

② **besides**

[bɪ'saɪdz]

1 *preposition*

as well as; *they have two other automobiles besides the big Ford*; *besides the football team, our town also has a hockey team*; *besides managing the store, he also teaches in the evening*

2 *adverb*

(a) as well; *he paints, plays chess and has lots of other interests besides*

(b) in any case; *I don't want to go for a picnic - besides, it's starting to rain*

① **best**

[best]

1 *adjective*

(a) very good, better than anything else; *she's my best friend*; *what is the best way of getting to Elm Street from here?*; *he put on his best suit to go to the interview*

(b) for the best part of = for most of; *she's been in bed for the best part of a week*

2 *noun*

(a) thing which is better than anything else; *the picture shows her at her best*; *to do your best* = to do as well as you can; *she did her best, but didn't win*

(b) to make the best of something = to take any advantage you can from something; *they say it will rain this afternoon, so we'd better make the best of the sunshine while it's here*; *to make the best of a bad job* = to do something in spite of terrible conditions; *it was raining when we stopped for a picnic, so we made the best of a bad job and had our sandwiches in the automobile*

(c) *(informal)* best clothes; *the children were all in their Sunday best*

3 *adverb*

in the best way; *which of you knows Tallahassee best?*; *the engine works best when it's warm*; *oranges grow best in hot countries*; *as best you can* = in the best way you can, even though this may not be perfect; *he repaired the dent in the car door as best he could* (NOTE: **best** is the superlative of both **good** and **well**)

② **best man**

['best 'mæn] *noun*

man who helps the bridegroom at a wedding; *the best man had put the wedding rings in his pocket*; *the best man gave a speech and told some funny stories about the bridegroom when he was a student*

④ **best-seller**

['best'selər] *noun*

thing that sells very well; *her book was a best-seller*

② **best wishes**

['best 'wɪʃɪz] *noun*

greeting sent to someone; *give my best wishes to your father*

① **bet**

[bet]

1 *noun*

money that is risked by trying to say which horse will come first in a race, which side will win a competition, etc.; *he placed a bet on his friend's horse but lost when the horse came in last*; *I've got a bet on Lewis to win the next contest*; safe bet = bet that you are not likely to lose; *it's a safe bet that if we decide to go camping it will rain*

2 *verb*

(a) to risk money by saying which horse you think will come first in a race, which team will win, etc.; *he bet me $10 the Bulls would lose the game*

(b) to be sure of something; *I bet you she's going to be late*; *(informal)* you bet! = of course; *do you want to go to a bar? - you bet!* (NOTE: betting - bet)

③ **betray**

[bɪ'treɪ] *verb*

(a) to harm someone by telling a secret about them; *he was betrayed to the enemy by his best friend*; *the scientist was accused of betraying secrets to the enemy*

(b) to show a feeling that you want to keep hidden; *the tears in her eyes betrayed her emotion*

① **better**

['betər]

1 *adjective*

(a) good when compared to something else; *the weather is better today than it was yesterday*; *his latest book is better than the first one he wrote*; *she's better at math than English*; *whole-wheat bread is better for you than white*; *we will shop around to see if we can get a better price*

(b) healthy again; *I had a cold last week but I'm better now*; *I hope your sister will be better soon*

2 *adverb*

well as compared to something else; *she sings better than her sister*; *my old knife cuts better than the new one*; *to think better of something* = to decide that something is not a good idea; *he was going to drive to Trenton, but thought better of it when he heard the traffic report on the news* (NOTE: **better** is the comparative of both **good** and **well**)

3 *noun*

to get the better of someone = to beat someone; *no one can get the better of him at cards*; **for the better** = which makes the situation better; *he's earning more money now, and his financial situation has changed for the better*; *he took a turn for the better* = his health began to improve

◇ **had better**

['hæd 'betər] *phrase*

it would be a good thing if; *you had better wear a coat - I think it's starting to snow*; *she'd better go to bed if she has flu*; *hadn't you better answer the phone?*

③ **betting**
['betɪŋ]
see BET

① **between** [bɪ'twin] *preposition*

(a) placed with things on both sides; *there's only a thin wall between his office and mine, so I hear everything he says*; *don't sit between him and his girlfriend*

(b) connecting two places; *the coach goes between Pierre and Bismarck*

(c) in the interval separating two times; *I'm have a meeting between 10 o'clock and 12*; *can you come to see me between now and next Monday?*

(d) in the space separating two amounts; *the package weighs between eight and nine pounds*; *cherries cost between $1.50 and $2.00 per pound*

(e) showing a difference; *she's color-blind - she can't tell the difference between red and green*

(f) sharing; *we only had $15 between the three of us*

(g) among; *she could choose between courses in German, Chinese or Russian*

(h) between you and me = speaking privately; *between you and me, I don't think he's very good at his job*

◇ **in between**
[ɪn bɪ'twin]

in the middle, with things on both sides; *the hotel looks over the river, with a park in between*; *he had two meetings in the morning but managed to fit in a game of tennis in between*

② **beverage**
['bevrɪdʒ] *noun*

drink; *you get a free beverage with your meal*

③ **beware**
[bɪ'weər] *verb*

watch out for; *beware of the dog!*; *beware of pickpockets!*

④ **bewilder**
[bɪ'wɪldər] *verb*

to make someone puzzled; *all these road signs just bewilder tourists*

① **beyond**
[bɪ'jɒnd]

1 *preposition*

(a) further away than; *the post office is beyond the bank*; **it is beyond my means** = it is too expensive for me to buy it; *I'd love to buy a sports car, but I think it would be beyond my means*

(b) later than; *the party went on till beyond midnight*

2 *adverb*

further away, on the other side; *she stared through the window at the fields beyond*

④ **bias**
['baɪəs] *noun*

fixed opinion in favor of something or against something; *the judges in the beauty competition were accused of bias*; *she had a bias against men with beards*

④ **biased**
['baɪəst] *adjective*

too much in favor of something or against something; *we felt the decision was biased*; *the court was biased in favor of the president's daughter*

④ **bib**
[bɪb] *noun*

(a) little piece of cloth which is tied round a baby's neck, under its chin; *don't forget to put his bib on when he's eating spinach*

(b) top part of an apron or dungarees, covering your chest

① **Bible**
['baɪbl] *noun*

(a) Christian and Jewish book of holy writing; *he reads from the Bible every evening*

(b) important and useful reference book; *she keeps an old French cookbook in the kitchen - it's her bible*

COMMENT: the Bible is formed of the Old Testament (the Jewish holy book) and New Testament, the writings concerned with the life and works of Christ and the early Christian church

① **bicycle**
['baɪsɪkl] *noun*

vehicle with two wheels which is ridden by one person who makes it go by pushing on the pedals; *he goes to school by bicycle every day*; *she's going to do the shopping on her bicycle*; *he's learning to ride a bicycle*; **bicycle pump** = small hand pump for blowing up bicycle tires; *we blew up the mattress with a bicycle pump*; *see also* BIKE (NOTE: also called a **bike**. The person who rides a bicycle is a **cyclist**)

② **bid**
[bɪd]

1 *noun*

(a) offer to buy at an auction; *his bid for the painting was too low*

(b) attempt to do something; **he made a bid for power** = he tried to seize power; **takeover bid** = attempt to take over a company by offering to buy most of its shares

2 *verb*

(a) to make an offer to buy something at an auction; *he bid $750 for the automobile* (NOTE: **bidding - bid**)

(b) *(formal)* to wish; *he bade me farewell* (NOTE: **bid** *or* **bade** [bæd] **- has bidden**)

ⓐ **bidder**
['bɪdər] *noun*
person who makes an offer to buy something, especially at an auction; *several bidders made offers for the house*; **the highest bidder** = the person who makes the best offer

ⓞ **big**
[bɪg] *adjective*
of a large size; *I don't want a small car - I want a big one*; *his father has the biggest restaurant in town*; *I'm not afraid of him - I'm bigger than he is*; *we had a big order from Germany*; **big toe** = the largest of your five toes (NOTE: **bigger - biggest**)

ⓞ **big deal**
['bɪg 'dil] *noun*
(a) important business transaction; *it's one of the biggest deals we have ever signed*

(b) *(informal)* **big deal!** = that's not a very good deal; *he offered me $30 for the automobile - big deal!*

ⓐ **big shot**
['bɪg 'ʃɒt] *noun*
(informal) important person; *she's marrying some big shot in the music business*

ⓞ **bike**
[baɪk] *noun*
(informal) = BICYCLE; *he goes to school by bike*; *she was knocked off her bike by an automobile*; *although he is over eighty he still rides a bike* or *goes for a bike ride every day*; **exercise bike** = bicycle fixed to the floor, which you can pedal on as exercise; *he does ten minutes on his exercise bike before breakfast*; **mountain bike** = strong bicycle with wider tires, used for country cycling; *she rode her mountain bike along the hill paths*

ⓞ **bill**
[bɪl] *noun*
(a) piece of paper showing the amount of money you have to pay (for repairs, etc.); *the total bill came to more than $300*; *don't forget to pay the gas bill*; **to foot the bill** = to pay the costs

(b) hard part of a bird's mouth; *the bird was picking up food with its bill*

(c) piece of paper money; *a 10-dollar bill*

(d) draft of a new law which will be discussed in a legislature; *Congress will consider two bills this week*

(e) advertising poster; **to fill the bill** = to be what is needed

ⓐ **billfold**
['bɪlfəʊld] *noun*
small flat leather case for credit cards and money, carried in your pocket; *his billfold was stolen from his back pocket*

ⓐ **billiards**
['bɪljədz] *noun*
game where two players with long cues hit their own white ball against a red ball or the opponent's ball, scoring points; *they played a game of billiards*; *the club has bought a new billiard table* (NOTE: the word **billiards** loses the "s" when it is in front of another noun)

> COMMENT: The game is played on a table covered with smooth green cloth and with raised edges (or "cushions") and six small net bags (or "pockets") at each corner and in the middle of the two long sides

ⓐ **billion**
['bɪljən] *noun*
(a) one thousand millions; *the government raises billions in taxes each years*

(b) a great many; *billions of Christmas cards are sent every year* (NOTE: with figures it is usually written **bn**: **$5bn** say "five billion dollars")

ⓐ **Bill of Rights**
['bɪl əv 'raɪts] *noun*
the first ten amendments to the constitution of the United States, which refer to the rights and privileges of individual citizens

ⓐ **billy goat**
['bɪli 'gəʊt] *noun*
(children's word) male goat

ⓐ **bimonthly**
[baɪ'mʌnθli]
1 *adjective*
(a) every two months; *a bimonthly meeting*

(b) twice a month; *a bimonthly meeting*

2 *noun*
magazine appearing every two months

ⓑ **bin**
[bɪn] *noun*
large storage container; *the farmer stored the grain in bins*

ⓒ **bind**
[baɪnd] *verb*
(a) to force someone to do something; *the contract binds him to make regular payments*

(b) to put a cover on a book; *the book is bound in blue leather*

(c) to tie; *they bound her to the tree with ropes*; *see also* BOUND (NOTE: **binding - bound** [baʊnd])

ⓒ **binding**
['baɪndɪŋ] *adjective*
which has legal power; *this contract is binding on both parties*

ⓐ **binge**
[bɪndʒ]
1 *noun*

(informal) time when you drink alcohol, eat or do something else to excess; *after last night's binge he had to stay in bed*; *she went on a chocolate binge that lasted the whole summer*
2 *verb*
to binge on something = to eat or drink far too much of something; *I felt sick after bingeing on chocolate*

④ **bingo**
['bɪŋɡəʊ]
1 *noun*
game of chance, where each player has a card with numbers on it, numbers are called out and when you have marked off a whole row of numbers, you win; *she goes to play bingo every Friday night*
2 *interjection showing surprise*; *you want me to clean my room? - Bingo!*

④ **biochemistry**
[baɪəʊ'kemɪstri] *noun*
science and study of the chemistry of living things (animals, plants, etc.); *he majored in biochemistry*

④ **biodegradable**
[baɪəʊdi'greɪdəbl] *adjective*
which can easily be decomposed by organisms such as bacteria, or by sunlight, sea water, etc.; *biodegradable packaging*

③ **biography**
[baɪ'ɒɡrəfi] *noun*
the story of someone's life; *have you read the new biography of Kennedy?*; *she's the author of a biography of Jackson* (NOTE: plural is **biographies**)

④ **biological**
[baɪə'lɒdʒɪkl] *adjective*
(a) referring to living things; *the biological balance along the Pacific Coast*
(b) using bacteria; *a treaty to ban biological warfare*
(c) biological parent = mother or father who was responsible for the birth of a child

③ **biologist**
[baɪ'ɒlədʒɪst] *noun*
scientist who specializes in biology; *Darwin was a famous biologist*

③ **biology**
[baɪ'ɒlədʒi] *noun*
study of living things; *she took biology and chemistry as exam subjects*; *biology students spend some of their time in the research lab*

④ **biomass**
['baɪəʊmæs] *noun*
the weight of all living organisms in a certain place

④ **biopsy**
['baɪɒpsi] *noun*
operation to remove a small piece of tissue for examination; *the biopsy showed that the growth was not cancerous*

② **birch**
[bɜrtʃ] *noun*
northern tree, with small leaves, thin branches and white bark; *the birch forests of Russia*; *the bark of birch trees comes off in strips* (NOTE: plural is **birches**)

① **bird**
[bɜrd] *noun*
animal with wings and feathers; *most birds can fly, but some can't*; *she keeps a little bird in a cage*; **bird house** = wooden box with a small hole in it, placed in a tree to attract birds to nest; **a little bird told me** = someone told me the secret, but I can't tell you who it was; **a bird in the hand is worth two in the bush** = be satisfied with what you have, rather than hope for something better which may never come; *see also* EARLY

① **birth**
[bɜrθ] *noun*
being born; *he was a big baby at birth*; **to give birth to** = to have a baby; *she gave birth to a boy last week*; **birth certificate** = official document that says when and where someone was born; **date of birth** = day, month and year when a person was born; *he put his date of birth as June 15, 1985*

② **birthday**
['bɜrθdeɪ] *noun*
date on which you were born; *April 23 is Shakespeare's birthday*; *my birthday is on June 25*; *what do you want for your birthday?*; *he'll be 10 years old next birthday* = on his next birthday he will be 10 years old; **birthday cake** = cake made specially for a birthday and decorated with icing, candles, etc.; **birthday card** = card sent to someone to wish him or her good luck on their birthday; *remind me to send her a birthday card, it's her birthday next Tuesday*; **birthday party** = party held for a birthday; **birthday present** = present given to someone for his or her birthday; *the watch was a birthday present from my father*

◇ **Happy Birthday**
['hæpi 'bɜrθdeɪ]
greeting said to someone on their birthday; **"Happy Birthday to you!"** = song sung at a birthday party; *we all sang "Happy Birthday to you" and then she blew out the candles on her cake*

④ **birthmark**
['bɜrθmɑrk] *noun*
mark on skin which a baby has from birth and which usually cannot be removed; *he has a birthmark on his stomach*

② **biscuit**
['bɪskɪt] *noun*
(a) small soft raised bread, made with baking soda; *we're having biscuits with gravy for dinner*
(b) *GB* (i) cracker, a small flat hard cake; (ii) cookie; *a pack of chocolate biscuits*

② **bishop**
['bɪʃəp] *noun*
(a) Christian church leader; *the bishop visited our church*
(b) piece in chess, which looks like a bishop's hat; *she took both his bishops in three moves*

① **bit**
[bɪt]
1 *noun*
(a) little piece; *he tied the bundle of sticks together with a bit of string; would you like another bit of cake?;* **to come to bits** = to fall apart; *the chair has come to bits;* **to take something to bits** = to put it in pieces to mend it; *he's taking my old clock to bits*
(b) a bit = a little; *the painting is a bit too dark; let him sleep a little bit longer; do you have a piece of wood a bit bigger than this one?; can you wait a bit, I'm not ready yet;* **a bit much** = not fair; *being told it was my fault when I wasn't even there is a bit much;* **not the slightest bit** = not at all; *she didn't sound the slightest bit worried*
(c) tool which fits into a drill, used for making holes; *have you seen the bit for the drill anywhere?*
(d) metal rod which is in a horse's mouth, and which the rider uses to control the horse
2 *verb*
see BITE

◇ **bit by bit**
['bɪt baɪ 'bɪt] *phrase*
not all at the same time, little by little; *he paid back the money he owed, bit by bit; he inched forward, bit by bit, toward the edge of the cliff*

① **bite**
[baɪt]
1 *noun*
(a) mouthful; *all I had for lunch was a bite of bread and cheese; she took a big bite out of the sandwich*
(b) place where someone has been bitten; **insect bite** = sting caused by an insect which goes through the skin and hurts; *some insect bites can be very painful; her arms were covered with mosquito bites*
2 *verb*
(a) to cut with your teeth; *the dog tried to bite the mail carrier; she bit a piece out of the pie*
(b) *(of an insect)* to sting; *she's been bitten by a mosquito* (NOTE: biting - bit [bɪt] - has bitten ['bɪtn])

① **bitten**
['bɪtn]
see BITE

② **bitter**
['bɪtər]
adjective
(a) not sweet; *this black coffee is too bitter*
(b) angry and annoyed; *she was very bitter about the way the company treated her;* **to the**
bitter end = to the very end; *they resisted the changes to the bitter end*
(c) very cold; *a bitter December night; bitter weather coming from the Arctic*

④ **bitterly**
['bɪtəli] *adverb*
(a) deeply; *he bitterly regrets what he said*
(b) bitterly cold = very cold; *it was bitterly cold in the tent*

④ **bizarre**
[bɪ'zɑr] *adjective*
very strange; *I find it bizarre that no one told her that the house had been sold; she's started to wear the most bizarre clothes*

① **black**
[blæk]
1 *adjective*
(a) very dark color, the opposite to white; *he was wearing a black suit; a black and white photograph;* **black coffee** = coffee without milk or cream in it; *do you want your coffee black or with cream?*
(b) black economy = goods and services that are paid for in cash, and not declared to the income tax authorities
(c) with a dark-colored skin; *our landlady is a very friendly black lady* (NOTE: **blacker - blackest**)
2 *noun*
(a) the color of black; **in the black** = in credit, in profit; *the company went into the black last year; my bank account is still in the black*
(b) person whose skin is dark colored

① **blackberry**
['blækbəri] *noun*
(a) small black fruit that grows on a bush; *for dessert we're having blackberry and apple pie*
(b) the bush this fruit grows on; *we had to struggle through blackberry bushes which had grown over the path*

① **blackbird**
['blækbɜrd] *noun*
bird with black feathers; *listen to the blackbird singing*

① **blackboard**
['blækbɔrd] *noun*
dark board on the wall of a classroom, etc., which you can write on with chalk; *he wrote the instructions for the exam on the blackboard; some dishes are not on the menu, but are written on a blackboard*

③ **blackcurrant**
[blæk'kʌrənt] *noun*
(a) garden fruit with little black berries which are usually eaten cooked; *a jar of blackcurrant jam; the blackcurrants need more sugar - they're very sour*
(b) the small bush this fruit grows on; *I planted six blackcurrants in the garden*

④ **blacken**

['blækən] *verb*

to make black; *the walls of the cave were blackened with smoke*

④ **blackjack**

['blækdʒæk] *noun*

card game where the aim is to hold cards worth 21 points

④ **blacklist**

['blæklɪst]

1 *noun*

list of people, companies or countries which are banned or disapproved of; *we added his name to the blacklist*

2 *verb*

to forbid trading in certain goods or with certain suppliers; *three firms were blacklisted by the government*

② **blackmail**

['blækmeɪl]

1 *verb*

to threaten to harm someone unless a demand is met, to threaten to reveal a secret unless money is paid; *her former cook tried to blackmail her; they tried to blackmail the government into releasing prisoners of war*

2 *noun*

act of blackmailing; *the government will not give in to blackmail*

④ **black market**

['blæk 'mɑːkɪt] *noun*

buying and selling goods in a way which is not allowed by law (as when goods are rationed); *we bought some gold coins on the black market*

② **blade**

[bleɪd] *noun*

(a) sharp cutting part; *the blades of a pair of scissors; be careful - that knife has a very sharp blade*

(b) shoulder blade = one of two large flat bones covering the top part of your back; *he fell when skiing and broke his shoulder blade*

(c) thin leaf of grass; *she sat in the shade of an apple tree, chewing a blade of grass*

(d) long piece of wood with a flat part at the end, used for rowing (it is the flat part of an oar or paddle)

② **blame**

[bleɪm]

1 *noun*

criticism for having done something (even if you did not do it); *I'm not going to take the blame for something I didn't do;* **to get the blame for** = to be accused of; *who got the blame for breaking the window? - me, of course!*

2 *verb*

to blame someone for something *or* **to blame something on someone** = to say that someone is responsible for something; *blame my sister for the awful food, not me; he blamed the accident on the bad weather;* **I don't blame you** = I think you're right to do that; *I don't blame you for*

being annoyed, when everyone else got a present and you didn't; **he has only himself to blame** = no one else is responsible for what happened; *he has only himself to blame if he missed the chance of a free ticket to Thailand;* **to be to blame for** = to be responsible for; *the manager is to blame for the bad service*

④ **blanch**

[blɑːntʃ] *verb*

(a) to cook for a short time in boiling water; *blanch the asparagus for two minutes; blanch the tomatoes first to remove the skin*

(b) to turn white with fright or worry; *she blanched at the news*

④ **bland**

[blænd] *adjective*

(a) without much flavor; *some people don't like rice because they find it too bland; the sauce needs more herbs - it's far too bland*

(b) dull and not very interesting, not giving any information; *he gave a bland reply to the questions from the reporters*

① **blank**

[blæŋk]

1 *adjective*

(a) (paper) with no writing on it; *she took a blank piece of paper and drew a map*

(b) he looked blank = he didn't seem to know anything about it; *when she mentioned the money he owed, he just looked blank*

2 *noun*

(a) empty space (on a piece of paper); *just fill in the blanks on the form*

(b) my mind is a blank = I can't remember anything about it; **to draw a blank** = not to be able to remember something; *when she wanted to call her father, she drew a blank on his number*

3 *verb*

to blank out = (i) to cover up something (which has been written); (ii) to forget; *he showed her the letter with the signature blanked out; she blanked out memories of childhood*

① **blanket**

['blæŋkɪt]

1 *noun*

(a) thick cover which you put over you to keep warm; *he woke up when the blankets fell off the bed; she wrapped the children up in blankets to keep them warm;* **wet blanket** = miserable person who spoils a party, etc.; *don't ask her to your birthday - she's such a wet blanket*

(b) thick layer; *a blanket of snow covered the fields; the freeway was covered in a blanket of fog*

2 *verb*

to cover with something; *the whole area was blanketed with snow*

① **blankly**

['blæŋkli] *adverb*

not showing any reaction; *when the teacher*

asked him about his homework he just stared at her blankly

④ **blasphemy**
['blæsfəmi] *noun*
being rude about God, religion or established principles; *he was accused of blasphemy*

① **blast**
[blæst]
1 *noun*
(a) explosion; *windows were broken by the blast*
(b) strong wind; *a cold blast from the north*
(c) sharp blow on a signal or whistle; *three blasts of the alarm means that passengers should go on deck*
(d) going full blast = going at full power; *they kept the heating going full blast even on warmer days*
2 *verb*
(a) to destroy with an explosive or bullets; *the burglars blasted their way into the safe; they blasted their way out of the police trap*
(b) to ruin; *the accident blasted his hopes of a career in sports*

② **blaze**
[bleiz]
1 *noun*
(a) large bright fire; *five fire engines were called to the blaze*
(b) to work like blazes = to work very hard; *they worked like blazes to get the house ready*
2 *verb*
(a) to burn fiercely; *the campfire was blazing and everyone sang songs*
(b) to blaze away = to shoot fiercely; *they blazed away at the enemy for several minutes*

④ **blazer**
['bleizər] *noun*
jacket which is worn with pants of a different material, often with a club badge stitched to the pocket; *she was wearing a blue blazer with brass buttons;* **college blazer** = blazer of a special color with the badge of the college on it; *a crowd of boys and girls in college blazers got onto the bus*

④ **bleach**
[blitʃ] *verb*
to remove colour; *he's bleached his hair; her hair was bleached by the sun*

④ **bleachers**
['blitʃərz] *noun*
open-air seats in a sports stadium; *the crowd in the bleachers soon started shouting and throwing cans*

④ **bleak**
[blik] *adjective*
(a) cold and miserable; *the path led across bleak mountains*
(b) showing no sign of hope or encouragement; *she gave him a bleak stare; with no qualifications, his job prospects are bleak* (NOTE: **bleaker - bleakest**)

① **bled**
[bled]
see BLEED

① **bleed**
[blid] *verb*
to lose blood; *his chin bled after he cut himself while shaving; he was bleeding heavily from his wound* (NOTE: **bleeding - bled** ['bled])

④ **blemish**
['blemiʃ]
1 *noun*
mark which makes something look less perfect; *the fruit must have no blemishes*
2 *verb*
to spoil something; *being arrested for theft blemished his reputation*

① **blend**
[blend]
1 *noun*
mixture; *Colombian blends of coffee*
2 *verb*
(a) to mix; *blend the eggs, milk and flour together*
(b) *(of color)* to go well together, not to contrast with each other; *the gray curtains blend with the pale wallpaper*

① **bless**
[bles] *verb*
(a) to make holy by prayers, etc.; *the church was blessed by the bishop*
(b) to bring happiness or good fortune; *their marriage was blessed with two fine sons*
(c) *(informal) (said when someone sneezes)* *bless you!* (NOTE: **blessing - blessed** [blest])

④ **blessing**
['blesiŋ] *noun*
(a) prayer which blesses; *the priest gave his blessing to the bride and groom*
(b) to give your blessing to something = to approve something officially; *the chairman gave his blessing to the new design*

① **blew**
[blu]
see BLOW

① **blind**
[blaind]
1 *adjective*
not able to see; *he's not only blind, he's also very deaf;* **to turn a blind eye to something** = not to bother about something, even if you know it exists; *we turn a blind eye to minor cases of theft in the office*
2 *noun*
(a) covering over a window that can be pulled up and down; *they must still be asleep - their blinds are closed; he closed the blinds to keep out the sun*
(b) the blind = people who cannot see; *the town hall has excellent facilities for the blind*
3 *verb*
to make someone unable to see; *she was blinded by the bright lights of the automobiles*

① **blindfold**
['blaɪndfəʊld]
1 *noun*
cloth put over someone's eyes to prevent him or her seeing; *the people who kidnapped her did not let her take off the blindfold*
2 *verb*
to put a piece of cloth over someone's eyes to prevent him or her seeing; *he was blindfolded and pushed into the back of a car; I could find my way around Washington blindfolded*

④ **blindly**
['blaɪndli] *adverb*
without being able to see; *he groped blindly around the room, feeling for a light switch*

① **blink**
[blɪŋk]
1 *noun*
(informal) **on the blink** = not working, out of action; *the telephone's on the blink*
2 *verb*
(a) to close your eyelids very quickly; *he blinked when the light was switched on; she watched the bull come toward her without blinking*
(b) *(of lights)* to go on and off; *the turn signal is blinking*

④ **blinker**
['blɪŋkər] *noun*
light which goes on and off to show when a car is planning to turn; *my right blinker doesn't work*

② **blister**
['blɪstər] *noun*
swelling on your skin where the skin has been rubbed; *I can't run - I've got a blister on my heel*

④ **blitz**
[blɪts] *noun*
(informal) sudden effort to do something; *we had an advertising blitz*

① **block**
[blɒk]
1 *noun*
(a) section of buildings surrounded by streets; *he lives two blocks away*
(b) large piece; *blocks of ice were floating in the river*
(c) group of things together; *they booked a block of seats in the middle of the plane*
2 *verb*
to prevent something passing along something; *the pipe is blocked with dead leaves; roads are blocked by snow throughout the state*

③ **blockage**
['blɒkɪdʒ] *noun*
something which blocks; *there was a blockage in the pipe*

① **blond, blonde**
[blɒnd]
1 *adjective*
fair, or with fair hair; *is her blond hair natural?; two little blond children; she has lovely long blonde hair*
2 *noun*
blonde = woman with fair hair; *he came to the party with a gorgeous blonde*

① **blood**
[blʌd] *noun*
red liquid in the body; *blood was pouring out of the wound on his head; she can't stand the sight of blood*

COMMENT: blood is mainly formed of red and white cells. It circulates around the body, going from the heart and lungs around the body and back again. As it moves around the body, blood takes oxygen to the tissues and removes waste matter which is cleaned through the kidneys. An adult has about 10-12 pints of blood in his or her body

④ **bloodhound**
['blʌdhaʊnd] *noun*
large dog which can follow a trail by scent

② **blood pressure**
['blʌd 'preʃər] *noun*
pressure at which the heart pumps blood; *he has to take pills for his high blood pressure*

④ **bloodshot**
['blʌdʃɒt] *adjective*
red (eyes)

④ **bloodstained**
['blʌdsteɪnd] *adjective*
covered with marks of blood; *they found a bloodstained shirt in his suitcase*

① **bloodstream**
['blʌdstrim] *noun*
flow of blood around the body; *the antibiotics are injected into the bloodstream; hormones are carried by the bloodstream to various parts of the body*

② **blood type**
['blʌd 'taɪp] *noun*
(a) classification of blood into a certain group
(b) people with the same type of blood

④ **bloody**
['blʌdi] *adjective*
(a) with much blood; *a bloody battle*
(b) *GB (slang)* awful, terrible; *stop that bloody noise!*
(c) *(slang)* **Bloody Mary** = alcoholic drink, a mixture of vodka and tomato juice (NOTE: **bloodier - bloodiest**)

① **bloom**
[blum]
1 *verb*
to have flowers; *the cherry trees are blooming in the park*
2 *noun*
flower; *the apple trees are in full bloom* = the apple trees are in flower

① **blossom**
['blɒsəm]
1 *noun*
mass of flowers on trees; *the hedges are covered with blossom*; *the trees are in full blossom*
2 *verb*
(a) to flower; *the roses were blossoming around the garden*
(b) to do well; *she's really blossomed since she got married*

① **blot**
[blɒt]
1 *noun*
drop of ink; *the boy with blots of ink on his shirt is my kid brother*
2 *verb*
to blot something out = to hide something completely; *the thick fog blotted out the details of the landscape* (NOTE: **blotting - blotted**)

④ **blouse**
[blaʊz] *noun*
loose shirt; *she wore a pink blouse and white jeans*

① **blow**
[bləʊ]
1 *noun*
knock or punch; *he received a blow to the head in the fight*
2 *verb*
to make air move; *the wind had been blowing hard all day*; *blow on your soup if it's too hot*; **to blow your nose** = to clear a blocked nose by blowing down it into a handkerchief; *she has a cold and keeps having to blow her nose* (NOTE: **blowing - blew** [blu] **- has blown** [bləʊn])

① **blow away**
['bləʊ ə'weɪ] *verb*
(a) to go away by blowing; *his hat blew away*
(b) to make something go away by blowing; *the wind will blow the fog away*

① **blow down**
['bləʊ 'daʊn] *verb*
(a) to make something fall down by blowing; *six trees were blown down in the storm*
(b) to fall down by blowing; *the school fence has blown down*

① **blow off**
['bləʊ 'ɒf] *verb*
to make something go away by blowing; *the wind blew his hat off*; *the wind has blown all the leaves off the trees*

① **blow out**
['bləʊ 'aʊt] *verb*
to make something go out by blowing; *she blew out the candles on her birthday cake*

① **blow up**
['bləʊ 'ʌp] *verb*
(a) to make something get bigger by blowing into it; *he blew up balloons for the party*; *your front tire needs blowing up*
(b) to destroy something in an explosion; *the soldiers blew up the bridge*

(c) to make a photograph bigger; *the article was illustrated with a blown-up picture of the little girl and her uncle*
(d) to make something seem more important than it really is; *the story has been blown up by the papers*

④ **blubber**
['blʌbər] *noun*
fat of a whale or seal; *whales were killed and their blubber melted down*

① **blue**
[blu]
1 *adjective*
(a) colored like the color of the sky; *he wore a pale blue shirt*; *they live in the house with the dark blue door*; *all their children have got blue eyes*
(b) sad or miserable; *when you're feeling blue just sing a song and you'll feel better* (NOTE: **bluer - bluest**)
2 *noun*
(a) the color of the sky; *do you have you a cloth of a darker blue than this?*; *she was dressed all in blue*
(b) out of the blue = suddenly; *out of the blue came an offer of a job in Washington*

② **blueberry**
['bluberi] *noun*
wild berry, which is dark blue or purple when ripe; *my mom made a pie with the blueberries we picked*

① **bluebird**
['blubɜrd] *noun*
small North American bird with blue feathers; *bluebirds are common in the Midwest*

④ **blue-collar**
['blu'kɒlər] *noun*
referring to manual labor, to work in a factory; *a blue-collar job*

② **blues**
[bluz] *plural noun*
(a) type of slow, sad music that developed from African-American songs in the southern states; *the blues are popular in Louisiana*
(b) sad mood; *she had the blues after her sister died*

④ **bluff**
[blʌf]
1 *noun*
(a) threat to do something which cannot be carried out; *don't believe what he says, it's all just bluff*
(b) steep rocky hill; *the soldiers climbed the bluff and found the enemy waiting for them on top*
2 *adjective*
straightforward, not very sensitive; *he's a bluff individual, but you can trust what he says*
3 *verb*
to do something by trickery; *he said he was a naval officer, but he was just bluffing*

③ **blunt**
[blʌnt]
1 *adjective*
(a) not sharp; *he tried to cut the meat with a blunt knife*; **blunt instrument** = something used as a weapon such as a piece of wood or hammer, which is not sharp; *the doctor says the wounds were caused by a blunt instrument*
(b) almost rude (way of speaking); *his blunt manner made people think he was being rude* (NOTE: **blunter - bluntest**)
2 *verb*
to make blunt; *using the knife to open cans has blunted it*

④ **bluntly**
[ˈblʌntli] *adverb*
quite rudely; *he told her bluntly that she had failed her exam*; *to put it bluntly, you're just no good at your job*

③ **blur**
[blɜr]
1 *verb*
to become less clear, to make less clear; *his vision became blurred*; *the paper printed a rather blurred photograph of the house* (NOTE: **blurring - blurred**)
2 *noun*
picture that is not very clear; *he was hit on the head, and everything became a blur*; *he tried to take a picture of the plane as it flew past but it was just a blur*

④ **blurred** *or* **blurry**
[blɜrd *or* ˈblɜri] *adjective*
not clear; *the paper printed a blurred photograph of the suspect*

② **blush**
[blʌʃ] *verb*
to go red in the face because you are ashamed, embarrassed or hot; *she blushed when he spoke to her*

① **board**
[bɔrd]
1 *noun*
(a) long flat piece of wood, etc.; *the floor of the bedroom was just bare boards*; **ironing board** = long narrow table for ironing; **board games** = games (like chess) that are played on a flat piece of wood
(b) blackboard; *the teacher wrote on the board*
(c) food; **room and board** = meals and accommodations; **full board** = rate for bedroom and all meals in a boardinghouse; **half board** = rate for breakfast and dinner at a boardinghouse, but not lunch
(d) group of directors; *she was asked to join the board*; *the board meets every month*
(e) to go on board = to go on to a ship, train, plane, etc.; *we went on board at 9:30 and the ship sailed at 12:00*
2 *verb*
to go on to a ship, train, plane, etc.; *six passengers boarded at Belgrade*; *customs officials boarded the ship in the harbor*; *the 4:50 P.M. plane to Salt Lake City is now ready for boarding*

② **boardinghouse**
[ˈbɔrdɪŋhaʊs] *noun*
private house that provides rooms and meals for paying customers

④ **boardwalk**
[ˈbɔrdwɔk] *noun*
walk along a beach, made of wooden planks; *we strolled down the boardwalk*

③ **boast**
[bəʊst]
1 *noun*
act of boasting; *their boast is that they never surrendered*
2 *verb*
(a) to boast of *or* **about something** = to say how good, etc., you are; *he was boasting of how he had climbed the three mountains in a day*
(b) to have something good; *the house boasts an indoor swimming pool*; *the town boasts an 18-hole golf course*

① **boat**
[bəʊt] *noun*
small ship; *they sailed their boat across the lake*; *they went to Spain by boat*; *when is the next boat to the island?*; **rowboat** = small boat that is rowed with long wooden oars; *we hired a rowboat and went down the river*; **sailboat** = boat that has sails; *two sailboats sank during the race*; **fishing boat** = boat used for catching fish at sea; *the fishing boats are back, let's go down to the harbor and buy some fish*; *(informal)* **we're all in the same boat** = we're all in the same situation; *it's a shame about the layoffs, but if the firm goes bust we'll all be in the same boat*

④ **bob**
[bɒb] *verb*
to move up and down; *pieces of wood were bobbing about on the water* (NOTE: **bobbing - bobbed**)

④ **bobcat**
[ˈbɒbkæt] *noun*
wild mountain cat

① **body**
[ˈbɒdi] *noun*
(a) the whole of a person or of an animal; *he had pain throughout his body*; *the dead man's body was found in the river*
(b) the main part of an animal or person, but not the head and arms and legs; *she was beaten on the arms and the upper part of her body*
(c) the main part of an automobile, plane, text, etc.; *the automobile has an all-steel body*; *the body of the text is printed in black* (NOTE: plural is **bodies** for meanings (a), (b) and (c))
(d) being strong or solid; *the conditioner will give your hair body*; *the wine has good body*

① **bodyguard**
['bɒdigɑːd] *noun*
person who guards someone; *the attacker was seized by the president's bodyguards*

② **boil**
[bɔɪl]
1 *noun*
(a) infected swelling; *he has a boil on the back of his neck*
(b) when water is boiling; **bring the water to a boil** = to heat the water until it boils
2 *verb*
(a) *(of water or other liquid)* to bubble and change into steam or gas because of being very hot; *put the egg in when you see that the water's boiling*; *don't let the milk boil*; **the kettle's boiling** = the water in the kettle is boiling
(b) to heat water (or another liquid) until it changes into steam; *can you boil some water so we can make some tea?*; *boil the water before you drink it*
(c) to cook (vegetables, eggs, etc.) in boiling water; *small potatoes do not take long to boil*; *would you like a boiled egg for breakfast?*; **soft-boiled egg** = egg cooked by boiling in water until it is hot, but with the yolk still more or less liquid; **hard-boiled egg** = egg that has been boiled until it is hard; *I need two hard-boiled eggs for the salad*

② **boiler**
['bɔɪlər] *noun*
apparatus for boiling water; heater for central heating; *naturally the boiler broke down just before Christmas*

② **boiling**
['bɔɪlɪŋ]
1 *noun*
action of heating a liquid to the point where it becomes steam or gas; *boiling water for five minutes will kill germs in it*
2 *adjective*
(a) which has started to boil (i.e., for water, at 212°F); *put the potatoes in a pan of boiling water*
(b) very hot; *it is boiling in this room*
3 *adverb*
boiling hot = very hot; *it's boiling hot in our office*; *a pan of boiling hot oil fell on her foot*

② **boiling point**
['bɔɪlɪŋ 'pɔɪnt] *noun*
temperature at which a liquid boils, i.e. when it turns into steam or gas; *212°F is the boiling point of water*

② **boil over**
['bɔɪl 'əʊvər] *verb*
(of liquid) to rise up when boiling and run over the side of the pan; *the pasta boiled over and made a mess*

② **bold**
[bəʊld]
1 *adjective*

(a) strong in color or design; *she likes bold colors*; *the wallpaper is a bold design of dark green leaves*
(b) brave; *she was bold enough to say "no" to her boss*; *may I be so bold as to ask if you are free for dinner this evening?* (NOTE: **bolder - boldest**)
2 *noun*
printing type with thick black letters; *the main words in this dictionary are printed in bold*; *compare* ITALIC

④ **boldly**
['bəʊldli] *adverb*
in a brave way; *she boldly went up to the boss and asked him for a raise*

① **Bolivia**
[bə'lɪviə] *noun*
country in the Andes in South America (NOTE: capital: **La Paz**; people: **Bolivians**; language: **Spanish**; currency: **boliviano**)

② **Bolivian**
[bə'lɪviən]
1 *adjective*
referring to Bolivia
2 *noun*
person from Bolivia

④ **boll**
[bɒl] *noun*
seed head of the cotton plant; **boll weevil** = insect which attacks cotton plants

① **bolt**
[bəʊlt]
1 *noun*
(a) long metal rod with a screw thread, fastened with a nut; *the table was secured to the floor with two bolts*
(b) long metal rod that is pushed into a hole to close a door firmly; *she looked through the window and after a long pause pulled back the bolts*
(c) flash of lightning; *he had taken shelter under a tree that was hit by a bolt of lightning*; **it came as a bolt from the blue** = it came as a complete surprise
(d) **to make a bolt for** = to rush toward; *at the end of the show everyone made a bolt for the door*; **to make a bolt for it** = to run away; *when the guards weren't looking two prisoners tried to make a bolt for it*
2 *verb*
(a) to fasten with a bolt; *he bolted the door when he went to bed*; *the tables are bolted to the floor*
(b) to run fast, to escape; *the horse bolted*
(c) to eat quickly; *don't bolt your food*
3 *adverb*
sitting bolt upright = sitting with your back very straight

① **bomb**
[bɒm]
1 *noun*

weapon that explodes, dropped from an aircraft or placed by hand; *the bomb was left in a suitcase in the middle of the station*; *they phoned to say that a bomb had been planted in the building*; *enemy aircraft dropped bombs on the army base*

2 *verb*

(a) to drop bombs on something; *enemy aircraft bombed the power station*

(b) *(informal)* to fail completely; *I really bombed the test this semester*

② **bomber**
['bɒmər] *noun*

(a) person who plants bombs; *the bombers managed to escape after planting the bomb*

(b) aircraft for dropping bombs; *the bombers were out during the night, attacking enemy targets*

④ **bonanza**
[bə'nænzə] *noun*

situation where you can make a lot of money; *he won the lottery - it was a real bonanza for the family*

③ **bond**
[bɒnd]

1 *noun*

(a) document showing a loan to the government; *government bonds are a very safe form of investment*; **savings bond** = document showing you have invested money in a government savings plan

(b) link between two people; *there is a close bond between her and her sister*

(c) contract; *his word is his bond*

(d) **goods in bond** = goods which are held by customs until duty has been paid

(e) money paid as a bail; *he had to pay a $15,000 bond*

2 *verb*

to stick together tightly; *cover the two surfaces with glue and hold them tightly until they bond*

② **bone**
[bəʊn]

1 *noun*

(a) one of the solid pieces in the body, which make up the skeleton; *he fell over and broke a bone in his leg*; *be careful when you're eating fish - they have lots of little bones*; *the two dogs were fighting over a bone*; **I've got a bone to pick with you** = I want to complain about something you have done

(b) **bone dry** = extremely dry; *don't put your shirt on until it is bone dry*

2 *verb*

to remove bones from meat; *a boned leg of lamb*

② **bonfire**
['bɒnfaɪər] *noun*

outdoor fire; *he put the dead leaves on the bonfire*; *they sat around the bonfire singing songs*

② **bonus**
['bəʊnəs] *noun*

(a) extra money; *salesmen earn a bonus if they sell more than their quota*

(b) advantage; *it was an added bonus that the plane arrived early, as we were able to catch an earlier bus home* (NOTE: plural is **bonuses**)

③ **bony**
['bəʊni] *adjective*

(a) thin, with bones which you can see easily; *he grabbed her arm with his bony hand*

(b) with many bones; *I don't like that kind of fish - it is usually too bony* (NOTE: **bonier - boniest**)

① **book**
[bʊk]

1 *noun*

(a) sheets of printed paper attached together, usually with a stiff cover; *I'm reading a book on the history of Peru*; *he wrote a book about butterflies*; **coffee table book** = heavy expensive book with many illustrations, which can be left on a table for people to look at; **phone book** *or* **telephone book** = book that lists names of people and businesses in alphabetical order with their addresses and telephone numbers; *he looked up the number of the company in the phone book*; **picture book** = book with mainly pictures and not much text; *the book store has a few picture books for the under twos*; **reference book** = book (such as a dictionary or directory) where you can look up information; **school book** = book used when learning a subject in school; *I've lost one of my school books*

(b) sheets of paper attached together; **account book** = book that records sales and purchases; **checkbook** = set of blank checks attached together in a cover; *don't leave your checkbook on the counter*; **a book of matches** = set of cardboard matches attached together in a paper cover; *he collects books of matches*

(c) **books** = business records; *her job is to keep the firm's books up to date*; *we have no one on our books with that name*; *we have ten houses for sale on our books*

2 *verb*

(a) to reserve a place, a seat, a table in a restaurant or a room in a hotel; *we have booked a table for tomorrow evening*; *I want to book two seats for Friday evening*; *I'm afraid the dentist is fully booked until the end of next week*; *I'm sorry, the concert is sold out - all the seats have been booked*

(b) to charge someone with an offense; *the police officer booked him for speeding*

④ **bookcase**
['bʊkkeɪs] *noun*

cupboard with shelves for keeping books; *he keeps his best books in the bookcase*

② **booking**
['bʊkɪŋ] *noun*

reservation of seats, places, etc.; *we had to cancel our booking and travel the next day*; **to make a booking** = to reserve a room, a seat, a table, etc.; *we tried to make a booking for the week beginning May 1, but the hotel was full*

④ **bookshelf**
['bukʃelf] *noun*
shelf for keeping books; *his study was lined with bookshelves* (NOTE: plural is **bookshelves**)

① **bookstore**
['bukstɔr] *noun*
store that sells books; *there's a good bookstore just across the street from our apartment*

① **boom**
[bum]
1 *noun*
(a) increase in wealth for everyone; *the economy is improving and everyone is forecasting a boom for next year*
(b) loud noise, like a deep bang; *there was such a loud boom that everyone jumped*
(c) long rod for holding a microphone over the heads of speakers
2 *verb*
(a) to become more prosperous, to increase; *sales to Europe are booming*
(b) to make a loud deep noise; *his voice boomed across the square*

② **boost**
[bust]
1 *noun*
help or increase; *the advertising campaign gave a boost to our sales*
2 *verb*
to help to increase; *the TV commercial should boost our sales*

① **boot**
[but]
1 *noun*
(a) strong shoe that covers your foot and goes above your ankle; *the police officers were wearing long black boots*; *put on your boots if you're going to dig the garden*; *bring walking boots with you as we will be climbing in the hills*; **soccer boots** = boots to wear when playing soccer; **ski boots** = boots to wear when skiing
(b) *GB* trunk of an automobile
2 *verb*
(a) to kick (someone or something); *he booted the cat across the room*
(b) to start a computer; *you'll have to boot up the computer first*

② **booth**
[buð] *noun*
(a) small place for one person to stand or sit; **polling booth** = small enclosed space in a polling station, where the voter goes to mark his ballot paper in private; **telephone booth** = public box with a telephone; *there's a telephone booth near the supermarket - we can phone from there*; **ticket booth** = place outdoors where a person sells tickets
(b) separate section of a commercial fair where a company shows its products or services; *the*

Spanish publisher wants us to meet him at his booth

④ **bootleg**
['butleg]
1 *adjective*
illegal; *a shipment of bootleg whisky*
2 *verb*
to make or transport something illegally; *they bootlegged music disks*

④ **bootlegger**
['butlegər] *noun*
person who makes or transports illegal spirits

② **border**
['bɔrdər]
1 *noun*
(a) frontier between countries; *they managed to cross the border into Guatemala*; *there was nothing to show that we had crossed the border*; *she was stopped at the border because her passport was invalid*; *the enemy shelled several border towns*; *he was killed by the border guards*
(b) edge; **flower border** = flower bed by the side of a path or lawn
2 *verb*
to be along the edge of something; *the path is bordered with rose bushes*

② **bore**
[bɔr]
1 *noun*
(a) thing which makes you bored; *he went on talking non-stop and in the end it became a bit of a bore*; **what a bore!** = what a nuisance
(b) dull person who is not very interesting; *I don't want to sit next to him, he's such a bore*
(c) measurement of the inside of a pipe or gun barrel; *a small-bore gun*
2 *verb*
(a) to make a round hole in something; *bore three holes two inches apart*
(b) to make someone fed up with what you are saying or doing; *I won't bore you with the details of my operation*
(c) *see also* BEAR

② **bored**
[bɔrd] *adjective*
fed up, not interested in what is happening; *you get very bored having to do the same work every day*; *I'm bored - let's go out to the club*; **bored with** = fed up with; *I'm bored with this program, can't we change to another channel* (NOTE: do not confuse with **board**)

② **boring**
['bɔrɪŋ] *adjective*
dull, not interesting; *I don't want to watch that boring TV show*

① **born**
[bɔrn] *verb*
to be born = to begin to live; *he was born in New Hampshire*; *she was born in 1962*; *he's American-born but was brought up in Canada*; *the baby was born last week*; *(informal)* **I**

wasn't born yesterday = I'm not as stupid as you think (NOTE: **born** is usually only used with **was** or **were**)

④ **borne**
['bɔrn]
see BEAR

④ **borough**
['bʌrər] *noun*
town or a district within a town that is a unit of government; *she lives in the borough of Manhattan*

② **borrow**
['bɒrəʊ] *verb*
(a) to take something for a short time, usually with the permission of the owner; *can I borrow your car to go shopping?; she borrowed three books from the school library; he wants to borrow one of my CDs*
(b) to take money for a time, usually paying interest; *he borrowed $15 from me and never paid it back; companies borrow from banks to finance their business; she borrowed $150,000 from the bank to buy a condo; compare* LEND

② **borrower**
['bɒrəʊwər] *noun*
person who borrows; *the interest rate for borrowers is 18.5%*

② **borrowing**
['bɒrəʊwɪŋ] *noun*
(a) action of taking money for a time; **borrowing power** = amount of money which a company or person can borrow; *he has enormous debts, so his borrowing power is very limited*
(b) **borrowings** = money that is borrowed; *the company has borrowings of over $300,000*

② **boss**
[bɒs]
1 *noun*
(*informal*) person in charge, owner (of a business); *if you want a day off, ask the boss; I left because I didn't get along with my boss* (NOTE: plural is **bosses**)
2 *verb*
to boss someone around = to tell someone what to do all the time; *she's always bossing her little brother around; stop bossing me around!*

① **both**
[bəʊθ] *adjective & pronoun*
(a) two people together, two things together; *hold on to the handle with both hands; both my shoes have holes in them; both her brothers are very tall; she has two brothers, both of them in Canada; she and her brother both go to the same school; I'm talking to both of you*
(b) (*for emphasis*) *she is both clever and modest*

② **bother**
['bɒðər]
1 *noun*
trouble or worry; *we found the store without any bother; it was such a bother getting packed that we nearly didn't go on vacation*

2 *verb*
(a) to annoy, to cause trouble; *stop bothering me, I'm trying to read*; **to be hot and bothered** = to be annoyed and nervous about something
(b) **to bother to do something** = to take the time or trouble to do something; *don't bother to come with me to the station - I can find my way easily*
(c) **can't be bothered to** = don't have the time to, don't have the energy to; *I can't be bothered to iron the sheets; he couldn't be bothered to answer my letters*

① **bottle**
['bɒtl]
1 *noun*
(a) tall plastic or glass container for liquids; *he bought two bottles of red wine; she drank the water straight out of the bottle; he bought his wife a bottle of perfume*
(b) **hot water bottle** = rubber bottle filled with hot water, for warming the bed
2 *verb*
to put in bottles; *the wine is bottled in California; only bottled water is safe to drink; she perfected a process for speeding up the bottling system*

① **bottom**
['bɒtəm]
1 *noun*
(a) lowest point; *is there any honey left in the bottom of the jar?; the ship sank to the bottom of the sea; make a left at the bottom of the hill*; **he's at the bottom of his class** = he gets the worst marks; **to get to the bottom of a problem** = to find the real cause of a problem
(b) far end; *go down to the bottom of the street and you will see the post office on your left; the greenhouse is at the bottom of the garden*
(c) part of the body on which you sit; *if you are naughty again, you will get a smack on the bottom; see also* BEHIND
(d) lower part of a piece of clothing; *he was wearing just his track suit bottoms*
(e) **from the bottom of my heart** = deeply and sincerely; *I want to thank you all from the bottom of my heart*
2 *adjective*
lowest; *the jam is on the bottom shelf; he was standing on the bottom rung of the ladder*

① **bought**
[bɔt]
see BUY

① **bounce**
[baʊns]
1 *noun*
(a) movement up and down; *he hit the ball on the second bounce*
(b) energy; *she's always full of bounce*
2 *verb*
(a) to spring up and down or off a surface; *the ball bounced down the stairs; he kicked the ball but it bounced off the post*

(b) *(informal)* **his check bounced** = there was not enough money in his account to pay the sum on the check

② **bound**
[baʊnd]
1 *noun*
great jump; **in leaps and bounds** = very rapidly; *the project is going forward in leaps and bounds*
2 *adjective*
(a) **bound for** = on the way to; *a ship bound for the Gulf*
(b) tied up; *the boy was left bound to a tree; the burglars left him bound hand and foot; a bundle of old letters bound in pink ribbon*
(c) obliged; *he felt bound to help her; he is bound by the contract he signed last year*
(d) very likely; *they are bound to be late*
(e) see also BIND
3 *verb*
to leap; to run fast; *she bounded into the room; he bounded out of his chair; the dog bounded into the bushes*

③ **boundary**
[ˈbaʊndri] *noun*
limit of property, knowledge, etc.; *the white fence marks the boundary between our land and his*; **the boundaries of knowledge** *or* **of science** = the furthest point in human knowledge; *scientists are trying to push back the boundaries of human knowledge* (NOTE: plural is **boundaries**)

④ **bout**
[baʊt] *noun*
(a) fight or contest, especially a boxing match; *Lewis won that bout*
(b) attack of illness; *she had a bout of flu*

① **bow**
1 [ˈbəʊ] *noun*
(a) ribbon knotted in a shape like a butterfly; *the present was tied up with red bows*; **bow tie** = tie which is tied in the shape of a butterfly; *he always wears a bow tie*
(b) piece of wood with strings, used for playing a string instrument; *he slowly drew the bow across the strings of his double bass*
2 [baʊ] *noun*
(a) bending the body forward as a mark of respect; *he made a deep bow to the queen*; **to take a bow** = to step forward on a stage and bow to the audience to thank them for their applause; *the actors took their bows one after the other*
(b) *(also;* **bows)** front part of a ship; *the captain posted a sailor in the bow(s) to look out for rocks*; **bow wave** = big wave that forms at the front of a boat
(c) the person rowing who sits nearest to the bow of a boat; *he rowed bow for Princeton*; *compare* STROKE
3 [baʊ] *verb*
to bend forward in salute; *he bowed to the queen*

③ **bowels** *or* **bowel**
[ˈbaʊəlz] *noun*
(a) the tube from the stomach in which food is digested as it passes through; **bowel movement** = action of passing solid waste matter from the bowel; *the patient had a bowel movement this morning*
(b) **in the bowels of the earth** = deep underground

① **bowl**
[bəʊl]
1 *noun*
(a) wide container for food, water, etc.; *put the egg whites in a bowl and beat them*; **salad bowl** = special bowl for salad; **soup bowl** = special bowl for soup
(b) the food or liquid contained in a bowl; *he was eating a bowl of rice; give the dog a bowl of water; a bowl of hot thick soup is just what you need in this cold weather*
(c) large heavy ball, used for playing the game of lawn bowls or the game of bowling; *she picked up the bowl and stepped up to take her turn*
(d) a special football game; *the Super Bowl is the U.S.A.'s professional football championship*
2 *verb*
(in a game of lawn bowls) to roll a bowl (to try to get close to the target)

④ **bow-legged**
[bəʊˈlegɪd] *adjective*
with legs which curve apart at the knee

② **bowling**
[ˈbəʊlɪŋ] *noun*
game where your roll a large ball to knock down a set of pieces of wood standing at the end of a wooden stage; *we're going bowling tomorrow night*

① **box**
[bɒks]
1 *noun*
(a) container made of wood, plastic, metal, etc., with a lid; *she put the cookies into a cardboard box*; **cash box** = metal box for keeping cash in
(b) a container and its contents; *he took a box of matches from his pocket; he gave her a box of chocolates for her birthday*
(c) **mailbox** = container for mailing letters; *she put her cards in the mailbox on the corner of the street*; **box number** = address with a number at a post office
(d) line that runs around a section of text or an illustration; *in this dictionary, the comments are in boxes*
(e) small separate section in a theater; *they took a box for the performance of the "Marriage of Figaro"* (NOTE: plural is **boxes**)
(f) tree with very small leaves, used to make hedges; *the beds of flowers are edged with box* (NOTE: no plural in this meaning)
2 *verb*

to fight by punching; *he learned to box at a gym near his office*

④ **boxcar**
['bɒkskɑr] *noun*
enclosed freight car on a train

① **boxer**
['bɒksər] *noun*
fighter who fights by punching; *the two boxers came together in the ring*; **boxer shorts** = men's underwear shaped like sports shorts

① **boxing**
['bɒksɪŋ] *noun*
sport in which two opponents fight each other in a ring by punching with thick gloves; **boxing gloves** = thick padded gloves, laced at the wrist, worn for boxing; **boxing ring** = square area, surrounded with a rope fence, in which boxing matches take place; *the two boxers climbed into the (boxing) ring*

> COMMENT: a fight lasts a certain number (usually 10 or 15 in professional boxing) of 3-minute rounds with a 1-minute rest between rounds, the object being to knock out or score more points than your opponent. Blows must land above the waist on the front and sides of the body and on the head. A referee in the ring supervises the fight. If one boxer is knocked down he is allowed ten seconds, counted out loud by the referee, to get up; if at the end of ten seconds he is still down, he is counted out and as a result he is declared to have lost by being knocked out

① **boy**
[bɔɪ] *noun*
(a) male child; *a boy from our school won the tennis match*; *when I was a boy, hardly anyone in the town had a television set*; *I knew him when he was a boy*; **paper boy** = boy who delivers newspapers to your house; *the paper boy comes every morning at seven o'clock*; **boys' school** = a school for boys only; *see also* OLD BOY
(b) a son; *her three boys are all in college*

③ **boycott**
['bɔɪkɒt]
1 *verb*
to refuse to deal with someone, usually for political reasons; *we are boycotting all food imports from that country*
2 *noun*
action of refusing to deal with someone, usually for political reasons; *the boycott of the company lasted three months*

② **boyfriend**
['bɔɪfrend] *noun*
man, usually young, that a girl is having a relationship with; *she has a new boyfriend*; *she brought her boyfriend to the party*; *compare* GIRLFRIEND

② **bra**
[brɑ] *noun*
(informal) = BRASSIERE a piece of clothing worn by women to hold the breasts; *don't wear a black bra under that white shirt*

② **brace**
[breɪs]
1 *noun*
(a) support which makes a bone straight; *he had his leg in a brace*; *she wears braces on her teeth*
(b) **a brace and bit** = a drill, the tool holding a bit
2 *verb*
to brace yourself for = to prepare yourself for something nasty to happen; *when the phone rang, she braced herself for the shock of hearing his voice again*; *the pilot told us to brace ourselves for a crash landing*

④ **bracelet**
['breɪslət] *noun*
chain or other ornament worn round your wrist or arm; *he gave her a bracelet for her birthday*

③ **bracing**
['breɪsɪŋ] *adjective*
cool and fresh; *the bracing climate of the east coast*

④ **brag**
[bræg] *verb*
to boast about something; *he's always bragging about his business deals* (NOTE: **bragging - bragged**)

④ **braid**
[breɪd]
1 *noun*
(a) decoration made of twisted ribbon or thread; *admirals have gold braid on their caps*
(b) twisted woven hair; *this is a picture of her when she was ten and still had her hair in braids*
2 *verb*
to trist (hair, ribbon, etc.); *she braided her hair before going swimming*

③ **Braille**
['breɪl] *noun*
system of writing using raised dots on paper to show the letters, which allows a blind person to read by passing his or her fingers over the page; *the book has been published in Braille*

① **brain**
[breɪn] *noun*
(a) nerve center in the head, which controls all the body; *the brain is the most important part of the body*
(b) intelligence; **use your brain** = think hard; *she has brains or she has a good brain* = she's intelligent

④ **brainy**
['breɪni] *adjective*
(informal) very intelligent; *she was always the brainiest of the family* (NOTE: **brainier - brainiest**)

④ **braise**
[breɪz] *verb*
to cook food in a pot with very little liquid; *why don't you braise the ham?*

① **brake**
[breɪk]
1 *noun*
device for stopping a vehicle or making it go slower; *put the brake on when you go down a hill*; *the brakes aren't working!*; **hand brake** = brake that is worked by hand; *he managed to stop the automobile safely using the hand brake*; *release the hand brake before you start*; **foot brake** = brake that is worked by foot, using a pedal; **brake lights** = red lights at the back of an automobile which light up when you put the brakes on; *do you know that one of your brake lights isn't working?*; **brake pedal** = pedal in an automobile that you press with your foot to make the brakes work; *see also* JAM
2 *verb*
to slow down by pressing the brakes; *the driver of the little white van braked hard* (NOTE: do not confuse with **break**)

① **branch**
[brɑːnʃ]
1 *noun*
(a) part of a tree, growing out of the trunk; *he hit his head against a low branch*
(b) local office of an organization; *he's the manager of our local branch*; *the store has branches in most towns in the south of the country* (NOTE: plural is **branches**)
2 *verb*
to branch off = to come off a main road; *drive along for about a mile and you will see a small road branching off on the left*; **to branch out** = to start to do something different, as well as what you normally do; *the business has branched out and now sells flowers*

② **brand**
[brænd]
1 *noun*
(a) product with a name; *a well-known brand of soap*
(b) mark burned with a hot iron on an animal's skin, to show who owns the animal
2 *verb*
(a) to name in public; *he was branded as a thief*; *the minister was branded a crook in the newspaper*
(b) to mark an animal's skin with a hot iron; *the cattle were branded before being sent to market*

④ **brandish**
['brændɪʃ] *verb*
to wave something about; *the cook ran out of the kitchen brandishing a knife*; *she burst into the room brandishing a letter*

① **brand-new**
[brænd'njuː] *adjective*
completely new; *these shoes are brand-new - I bought them for the wedding*

② **brass**
[brɑːs] *noun*
(a) mixture of copper and zinc; *the doctor has a brass nameplate on his door*
(b) musical instruments made of brass; *a brass band led the parade*; **the brass section** *or* **the brass** = section of an orchestra with brass instruments; *compare* STRINGS, WIND

④ **brassiere**
['bræziər] *noun*
(formal) see BRA

④ **brat**
[bræt] *noun*
badly-behaved child; *her children are just spoiled brats*

② **brave**
[breɪv]
1 *adjective*
full of courage; *it was very brave of him to dive into the river to try to rescue the little girl* (NOTE: **braver - bravest**)
2 *verb*
to be brave enough to do something dangerous; *the ambulance braved the snowstorm to answer the emergency call*

① **bravely**
['breɪvlɪ] *adverb*
in a brave way; *she bravely volunteered to go back into the burning house*

① **Brazil**
[brə'zɪl] *noun*
large country on the Atlantic coast of South America; *don't just go to Rio de Janeiro, you must visit the rest of Brazil* (NOTE: capital: **Brasilia**; people: **Brazilians**; language: **Portuguese**; currency: **rial**)

② **Brazilian**
[brə'zɪlɪən]
1 *adjective*
referring to Brazil
2 *noun*
person from Brazil

④ **breach**
[briːtʃ]
1 *noun*
breaking the law, or a promise; *this is a breach of the promise they made last year*; **breach of the peace** = noisy behavior; *they were arrested for a breach of the peace*; **breach of faith** = going back on a promise; **in breach of** = breaking; *in breach of their agreement, they started negotiating with our rivals behind our backs* (NOTE: plural is **breaches**)
2 *verb*
(a) to go against rules, etc.; *the pay settlement has breached the government's rules*; *he was arrested for breaching the peace*
(b) to make a hole; *the enemy guns breached the town's defenses*

① bread
[bred] *noun*
food made from flour and water baked in an oven; *can you get a loaf of bread from the supermarket?*; *she cut thin slices of bread for sandwiches*; **bread and butter** = slices of bread covered with butter; **white bread** = bread made from white flour; **whole-wheat bread** = bread made from whole wheat flour; **French bread** = bread in the form of a long thin stick (NOTE: do not confuse with **bred**; note also there is no plural: **some bread**; for one piece say **a loaf of bread, a slice of bread**, etc.)

④ breadcrumbs
['bredkrʌmz] *noun*
little pieces of dried bread; *the fish is covered in breadcrumbs and fried*

④ breadth
[bredθ] *noun*
(a) *(formal)* measurement of how broad something is; *the breadth of the plot of land is over 30 ft*
(b) how wide your knowledge is; *his answers show the breadth of his knowledge of the subject*

① break
[breɪk]
1 *noun*
(a) space; *you can see blue sky through a break in the clouds*
(b) short rest; *there will be a 15-minute break in the middle of the meeting*; *they worked for three hours without a break* = they worked without stopping; **to take a break** = to have a short rest; *we'll take a break now, and start again in fifteen minutes*; **coffee break** = short rest in the middle of work when you drink coffee; *we'll have a coffee break now*
(c) short vacation; **school break** = short vacation, as at Christmas
(d) move away from someone or something; *I thought they were in love, so the break came as a surprise*; *it's not always easy to make a break with the past*
(e) **(commercial) break** = short period between TV programs or parts of programs when advertisements are shown; *we will continue with the news after this break*
(f) crack in a broken bone, piece of china, etc.; *the break is clean so it should heal quite quickly*
(g) stop in something regular; *there's a break in the pattern that shouldn't be there*
(h) *he had a lucky break* = his bad luck changed
2 *verb*
(a) to make something come apart in pieces; *he dropped the plate on the floor and broke it*; *she broke her leg when she was skiing*
(b) to come apart in pieces; *the clock fell on the floor and broke*
(c) **to break a record** = to do better than a previous record; *he broke the record for the 2000 meters*
(d) **to break your journey** = to stop for a while before going on; *we'll break for lunch at Lafayette*
(e) **to break a silence** = to make a noise; *the silence was broken by a cellular phone*; **to break your silence** = to talk about something which has been kept secret for a long time; *at long last he broke his silence about the affair*
(f) **to break with the past** = to cut your links with people you used to know, places you used to visit; *they decided to break with the past and go to live in New Zealand*
(g) to fail to carry out the duties of a contract; *the company has broken its agreement*; **to break a promise** = not to do what you had promised to do; *he broke his promise and wrote to her again*; **to break a contract** = to cancel a contract
(h) to start; *we woke up as day was breaking*; *she suddenly broke out in spots after eating fish*
(i) **to break the news to someone** = to tell someone bad news; *we will have to break the news to her as gently as possible*; **breaking news** = item of news broadcast on TV or radio as it is happening (NOTE: do not confuse with **brake**; note also **breaking - broke** [brəʊk] **- has broken** ['brəʊkn])

③ break down
['breɪk 'daʊn] *verb*
(a) *(of machine)* to stop working; *the bus broke down on the bridge*
(b) to show all the items in a total list; *can you break down this invoice into travel costs and extras?*

② breakdown
['breɪkdaʊn] *noun*
(a) failure of a system to work properly; *there has been a breakdown in communications between them*
(b) collapse of the body or mind; **nervous breakdown** = severe depression; *he had a nervous breakdown after the layoff*
(c) *(of machine)* stopping working; *there was a breakdown on the freeway and we arrived late*; *a breakdown truck came to tow the automobile to the garage*
(d) showing details item by item; *give me a breakdown of the travel costs*

① breakfast
['brekfəst] *noun*
first meal of the day; *I had waffles and eggs for breakfast*; *she didn't have any breakfast because she was in a hurry*; *the hotel serves breakfast from 7:30 to 9:30 every day*

② break in
['breɪk 'ɪn] *verb*
to break in *or* **to break into a building** = to use force to get into a building; *burglars broke into the office during the night*

④ **break-in**
['breɪkɪn] noun
burglary; *they had a break-in when they were away on vacation*; *the police reported a series of break-ins during the weekend*

④ **breakneck**
['breɪknek] adjective
at breakneck speed = extremely fast

④ **breakthrough**
['breɪkθru] noun
sudden success; *we have had or have made a breakthrough in our search for a cure for cancer*

③ **break up**
['breɪk 'ʌp] verb
(a) to come to pieces; *the oil tanker was breaking up on the rocks*
(b) to stop being together; *we broke up last year*; *their marriage broke up after 25 years*
(c) to stop being in a group; *the meeting broke up at 3 P.M.*; *the group broke up when the lead singer left*
(d) come on, break it up! = stop fighting!

④ **breakup**
['breɪkʌp] noun
coming to pieces, stopping being together; *the board has recommended the breakup of the company into smaller independent divisions*; *the breakup of their marriage was a surprise to everyone*

① **breast**
[brest] noun
(a) one of two parts on a woman's chest which produce milk; **breast cancer** = tumor in the breast
(b) meat from the front part of a bird; *do you want a wing or a slice of breast?*; *we bought some chicken breasts to fry*

③ **breaststroke**
['breststroʊk] noun
swimming stroke where you face downwards, pushing your arms out in front and bringing them back to the sides while your feet are kicking; *she won the 200 m breaststroke*

① **breath**
[breθ] noun
(a) air which goes into and out of the body through the nose or mouth; *you should smell his breath - he must have eaten garlic last night*; **out of breath** or **gasping for breath** = having difficulty in breathing; *he ran all the way to the station, got there out of breath, and then saw the train leaving*; **to get your breath back** = to breathe normally again, after exercise; *first get your breath back, then tell me all about it*; **to hold your breath** = to keep air in your lungs to go under water, as a test or because you are afraid that something will happen; *she held her breath under water for a minute*; **we're all holding our breath to see if he wins** = we're all waiting anxiously to see if he wins; **to take a deep breath** = to breathe in as much air as you can; *take a deep breath for the X-ray*; **to take someone's breath away** = to make someone very surprised; *the view of the mountains took my breath away*; **under your breath** = quietly; *he cursed under his breath*
(b) a breath of wind = slight movement of air; *there wasn't a breath of wind all day*

① **breathe**
[brið] verb
to take air into the lungs or let it out; *take your hand off my mouth, I can't breathe*; *I want to listen to your chest, so breathe in and then out when I tell you to*; *do you know how fish breathe?*; *she breathed a sigh of relief*; **breathe deeply** = take in a lot of air; **he's breathing down my neck all the time** = he's always watching how I'm working

① **breathless**
['breθləs] adjective
out of breath; finding it difficult to breathe; *she was breathless after running upstairs*

③ **bred**
[bred]
see BREED
(NOTE: do not confuse with **bread**)

③ **breed**
[brid]
1 noun
race of animal or plant; *Alsatians and other large breeds of dog*
2 verb
(a) to produce young (animals); *rabbits breed very rapidly*
(b) I was born and bred in the country = I was born and grew up in the country; **well-bred** = polite, well-educated
(c) to raise new plants; *they are breeding new varieties of wheat* (NOTE: **breeding - bred** [bred])

② **breeder**
['bridər] noun
person who breeds animals or plants; *a racehorse breeder*

① **breeze**
[briz]
1 noun
slight wind; *a cool breeze is welcome on a hot day like this*; **a stiff breeze** = a strong wind; *there was a stiff breeze blowing from the south*
2 verb
to walk around looking very pleased with yourself; *he breezed into the meeting carrying a cup of coffee*

④ **breezy**
['brizi] adjective
windy; *it's a little too breezy on the beach*

③ **brew**
[bru]
1 verb
(a) to make beer; *they've been brewing beer in this town for over two hundred years*

(b) to make tea or coffee; *let's brew some tea before we sit down and talk*

(c) there's trouble brewing = there will soon be trouble; *the police moved in when they felt trouble brewing in the crowd*

2 *noun*

a brew = beer or another drink made by brewing; *he makes a good strong brew*

③ **bribe**
['braɪb]
1 *noun*
illegal payment to someone to get something done; *he offered me a bribe to say nothing to the police*
2 *verb*
to give an illegal payment to someone; *she had to bribe customs officials to get her box through customs*

① **brick**
[brɪk] *noun*
hard block of baked clay used for building; *you need more than eighty bricks to build the wall*

① **bride**
[braɪd] *noun*
woman who is getting married; *the bride wore white; the bride was given away by her father; it is usual for the bride to arrive a few minutes late*

② **bridegroom**
['braɪdgrum] *noun*
man who is getting married; *the bridegroom looked nervously over his shoulder; the parents of the bridegroom came all the way from Hawaii*

② **bridesmaid**
['braɪdzmeɪd] *noun*
girl who is one of the bride's attendants at a wedding; *three little bridesmaids followed the bride into the church*

① **bridge**
[brɪdʒ] *noun*
(a) construction built over a road, river, etc., so that you can walk or drive from one side to the other; *the most famous bridge in the United States is the Golden Gate Bridge*; **railway bridge** = bridge that carries a railroad
(b) part of a ship where the captain and crew can keep watch and steer; *the captain was on the bridge when the accident occurred*
(c) card game for four people; *they played bridge until midnight*

② **brief**
[brif]
1 *adjective*
short; *he wrote a brief note of thanks; the meeting was very brief; tell me what happened, but be brief as we don't have much time*
2 *noun*
instructions given to a professional person; *his brief was to modernize the accounting system*
3 *verb*

to give information or instructions to someone; *he briefed the staff on the latest stage in the negotiations*

② **briefcase**
['brifkeɪs] *noun*
thin case for carrying papers, documents, etc.; *he put all the files into his briefcase*

② **briefly**
['brifli] *adverb*
for a short time; *she spoke briefly about the work of the hospital*

④ **brigade**
[brɪ'geɪd] *noun*
(a) fire brigade = group of fire fighters; *she called the fire brigade when she saw smoke coming out of the windows*
(b) section of the army; *the general sent an infantry brigade to the region*

① **bright**
[braɪt] *adjective*
(a) shining strongly; *bright sunshine*
(b) with a very strong color; *they have painted their front door bright orange*
(c) intelligent; *he's a bright little boy; both their children are very bright; she's the brightest of the class*; **bright idea** = clever thought; *I've had a bright idea - let's all go to the beach!*
(d) clear and sunny; *there will be bright periods during the afternoon*
(e) cheerful; *she gave me a bright smile* (NOTE: **brighter - brightest**)

④ **brighten**
['braɪtən] *verb*
to make bright; *light-colored paint would brighten the room*

③ **brightly**
['braɪtli] *adverb*
(a) in a bright way; *a children's book with brightly painted pictures; the streets were brightly lit for Christmas*
(b) cheerfully; *she smiled brightly as she went into the hospital*

④ **brilliance**
['brɪljəns] *noun*
being very intelligent; *because of his brilliance at math, several colleges offered him places*

③ **brilliant**
['brɪljənt] *adjective*
(a) extremely clever; *he's the most brilliant student of his year; she had a brilliant idea*
(b) *(informal)* very good; *the graphics on this video are brilliant*
(c) shining brightly; *she stepped out into the brilliant sunshine*

④ **brilliantly**
['brɪljəntli] *adverb*
in a brilliant way; *the gold roofs of the temples shone brilliantly in the sun; he did brilliantly at college*

① **bring**
[brɪŋ] *verb*
to come with someone or something to this place; *she brought the books to school with her; he brought his girlfriend home for dinner; are you bringing any friends to the party?* (NOTE: bringing - brought [brɔt])

④ **brink**
[brɪŋk] *noun*
edge; **on the brink of** = very close to; *the company is on the brink of collapse; she was on the brink of a nervous breakdown*

③ **brisk**
[brɪsk] *adjective*
rapid; *we went for a brisk walk along the beach* (NOTE: brisker - briskest)

① **Britain**
[ˈbrɪtən] *noun*
(Great) Britain = country formed of England, Scotland and Wales (which with Northern Ireland makes up the United Kingdom); *we flew to Britain first as it is English-speaking; in 1814 Britain was at war with France or Britain and France were at war; in Britain, cars drive on the left-hand side of the road; see also* GREAT BRITAIN, UNITED KINGDOM (NOTE: the word England is often used instead of Britain, and this is a mistake, as England is only one part of Britain; note also the capital: London; people: British; language: English; currency: pound sterling (£))

① **British**
[ˈbrɪtɪʃ]
1 *adjective*
referring to Great Britain; *a British citizen; the British press reported a plane crash in Africa; the ship was flying a British flag;* **the British government** = the government of the United Kingdom; **the British Isles** = the islands that make up Great Britain and Ireland (NOTE: the word English is often used instead of British, and this is a mistake, as England is only one part of Great Britain; you say the British Prime Minister and not the English Prime Minister)
2 *noun*
the British = the people of Great Britain

② **broad**
[brɔd] *adjective*
(a) very wide; *a broad river*
(b) *(as an emphasis)* **in broad daylight** = when it is light during the day; *the gang attacked the bank in broad daylight* (NOTE: broader - broadest)

① **broadcast**
[ˈbrɔdkæst]
1 *noun*
radio or TV program; *the broadcast came live from Madison Square;* **outside broadcast** = program not done in the studio
2 *verb*
(a) to send out on radio or TV; *the program will be broadcast on Monday at 8 P.M.; the police broadcast an appeal for information*
(b) to tell everyone; *don't broadcast the fact* = keep it a secret (NOTE: broadcasting - broadcast)

② **broadcasting**
[ˈbrɔdkæstɪŋ] *noun*
sending out on radio or TV; *many companies now have broadcasting licenses*

④ **broaden**
[ˈbrɔdən] *verb*
(a) to make something wider; to become wider; *part of their plan is to broaden the road; the river broadens to form a small lake*
(b) **to broaden the mind** = to increase knowledge; *travel broadens the mind*

④ **broadly**
[ˈbrɔdli] *adverb*
widely; *he smiled broadly as he handed her the ring;* **broadly speaking** = speaking in a general way; *broadly speaking, you can calculate that 15 pounds equals ten dollars*

④ **broad-minded**
[ˈbrɔdˈmaɪndɪd] *adjective*
not shocked by other people's behavior or words; *you can tell him the story - he's very broad-minded*

④ **brochure**
[ˈbrəʊʃər] *noun*
small publicity leaflet; *I picked up a brochure about ferry services; the travel agent could not give a guarantee that the accommodation would be in the hotel shown in the brochure; can you get some brochures from the travel agent?*

③ **broil**
[brɔɪl] *verb*
to cook something close to the flame or direct heat; *we will broil the fish*

② **broke**
[brəʊk] *adjective*
(informal) with no money; *it's the end of the month and, as usual, I'm broke;* **to be flat broke** = to have no money at all; *see also* BREAK

① **broken**
[ˈbrəʊkən] *adjective*
(a) in pieces; *she tried to fix the broken vase;* a **broken home** = a family where the parents have separated; *the girl comes from a broken home*
(b) not working; *they came to repair the broken TV; we can't use the elevator because it's broken*
(c) not complete; *after so many broken nights, she's looking forward to the day when the baby will sleep all night without waking*
(d) **broken English** = English spoken with a foreign accent and mistakes; *he only spoke broken English when he arrived, but was soon speaking like a native*

(e) discouraged; *he was pardoned, but came out of prison a broken man*; see also BREAK

④ **brokenhearted**
[brəʊkən'hɑːtɪd] *adjective*
very sad; *she was brokenhearted when her cat died*

③ **broker**
['brəʊkər] *noun*
dealer in shares or insurance; *he works as an insurance broker*; **to play the honest broker** = to try to solve the problems of other people

④ **bronco**
['brɒŋkəʊ] *noun*
wild horse (NOTE: plural is **broncos**)

② **bronze**
[brɒnz] *noun*
(a) mixture of copper and tin; *they put up a bronze statue of the emperor on a horse*
(b) bronze (medal) = medal given to someone who finishes third in a race or competition; *the U.S.A. won a gold and three bronzes at the track meet*; see also GOLD, SILVER

④ **brood**
[bruːd] *noun*
family of chicks or small children; *some birds raise only one brood of chicks a year*; *my son and his brood came for lunch yesterday*

④ **brook**
[brʊk] *noun*
small stream; *they jumped over the brook and walked on up the hill*

④ **broom**
[bruːm] *noun*
long-handled brush used to sweep floors; *she swept the kitchen with a broom*

④ **broth**
[brɒθ] *noun*
light meat soup; *use freshly made chicken broth for this dish*

① **brother**
['brʌðər] *noun*
boy or man who has the same mother and father as someone else; *my brother John is three years older than me*; *she came with her three brothers*

② **brought**
[brɔːt]
see BRING

② **brow**
[braʊ] *noun*
(a) forehead; *she wrinkled or knit her brow as she tried to understand the guidebook*; **by the sweat of your brow** = with a lot of hard work; *he became a millionaire by the sweat of his brow*
(b) top of a hill; *having reached the brow of the hill they stopped to look at the view*

① **brown**
[braʊn]
1 *adjective*
with a color like the earth or wood; *she has brown hair and blue eyes*; *it's fall and the leaves are turning brown*; *he's very brown - he must have been sitting in the sun*; *I like brown bread better than white* (NOTE: **browner - brownest**)
2 *noun*
(a) the color brown; *I'd prefer a darker brown than this*
(b) hash browns = boiled potatoes, diced or mashed and fried till crisp and brown
3 *verb*
to cook until brown; *brown the onions in a little butter*

① **brownie**
['braʊni] *noun*
(a) small square of chocolate cake, often with nuts; *I ordered brownies and ice cream for dessert*
(b) Brownie = member of the Girl Scouts for girls from first through third grades in school; *she will become a Brownie this year*

④ **browse**
[braʊz] *verb*
(a) to wander around looking at things for sale; *she browsed along the racks of clothes*
(b) to look through a book, newspaper or magazine, without reading it properly; *I browsed through several magazines in the lounge*

② **bruise**
[bruːz]
1 *noun*
dark, painful area on the skin, following a blow; *she had bruises all over her arms*
2 *verb*
(a) to make a bruise; *she bruised her knee on the corner of the table*
(b) to bruise easily = to get bruises easily because your skin is delicate; *she bruises easily, even a little blow gives her a bruise*; *peaches are delicate fruit - they bruise easily*

④ **brunt**
[brʌnt] *noun*
to bear the brunt of = to suffer most effects of; *the west coast bore the brunt of the storm*

② **brush**
[brʌʃ]
1 *noun*
(a) tool made of a handle and hairs or wire, used for cleaning, painting, etc.; *you need a stiff brush to get the mud off your shoes*; *she used a very fine brush to paint the details*; *he was painting the front of the house with a large brush*
(b) act of cleaning with a brush; *she gave the coat a good brush*
(c) land covered with bushes or low trees; *they walked through the brush for several miles until they came to a lake*
(d) near miss, when something nearly happens to harm you; *they had a brush with death on the freeway*

(e) short argument or fight with someone; *he's had several brushes with the police recently* (NOTE: plural is **brushes**)
2 *verb*
(a) to clean with a brush; *he brushed his shoes before going to the office; always remember to brush your teeth before you go to bed*
(b) to go past something touching it gently; *she brushed against me as she came into the café*

③ **brutal**
['bruːtəl] *adjective*
cruel and violent; *the police said it had been a particularly brutal murder, and that they were looking for an ax*

① **bubble**
['bʌbl]
1 *noun*
ball of air or gas trapped in liquid; *bubbles of gas rose to the surface of the lake; he blew bubbles in his drink;* **bubble bath** = bath with special liquid soap which makes lots of bubbles; *she relaxed in a hot bubble bath*
2 *verb*
to make bubbles, to have bubbles inside; *the soup was bubbling in the pan;* **to bubble up** = to come to the surface as bubbles; *gas was bubbling up out of the hot mud*

② **buck**
[bʌk]
1 *noun*
(a) male animal, particularly a male deer; *a buck rabbit*
(b) *(informal)* dollar; *it'll cost you ten bucks; you couldn't lend me 100 bucks, could you?;* **to make a quick buck** = to get rich quickly; *all he wants is to make a quick buck*
(c) *(informal)* **to pass the buck** = to pass responsibility to someone else; *the manager is a very weak character, he's always passing the buck;* **the buck stops here** = I am the person who is responsible
2 *verb*
(a) **to buck the trend** = to go against the trend; *sales of books have bucked the trend and risen sharply*
(b) *(of horse)* to jump in the air; *the horses bucked at the sound of gunfire*

① **bucket**
['bʌkɪt] *noun*
(a) round container with a handle but no lid, used mainly for liquids; *throw the water on the fire and pass the empty bucket back to me; (informal)* **to kick the bucket** = to die; *don't worry - I don't intend to kick the bucket just yet!;* **the rain came down in buckets** = it was raining heavily
(b) the contents of a bucket; *he brought a bucket of water from the river; they threw buckets of water on the fire*

① **buckle**
['bʌkl]
1 *noun*

metal fastener for a strap; *she wore a black leather belt with a big gold buckle*
2 *verb*
(a) to attach with a buckle; *he buckled on his seat belt*
(b) to bend and collapse, to become bent; *the whole bridge buckled under the weight of the traffic; the front wheel of my bicycle has buckled*

① **bud**
[bʌd] *noun*
(a) place where a new shoot comes on a plant; *it was spring and the buds on the trees were beginning to open;* **in bud** = flower that has not yet opened; *the roses are in bud; (informal)* **to nip something in the bud** = to stop something before it develops any further; *we must try to nip the student protests in the bud*
(b) *(informal)* friend, buddy; *hey bud! come and have a beer!*

④ **Buddhist**
['buːdɪst]
1 *adjective*
referring to the teaching of Buddha; *a Buddhist temple*
2 *noun*
person who follows the teaching of Buddha; *life in Nepal suits him so much that he's become a Buddhist*

④ **buddy**
['bʌdɪ] *noun*
(informal) friend; *he's gone fishing with a couple of his old buddies* (NOTE: plural is **buddies**)

④ **budge**
[bʌdʒ] *verb*
(informal) to move; *this box is so heavy that I can't budge it; he sits in front of the TV after dinner and doesn't budge*

② **budget**
['bʌdʒɪt]
1 *noun*
proposed expenditures; *there isn't enough money in the household budget to pay for a new carpet;* **publicity budget** = money allowed for expected expenditures on publicity; *we've increased the publicity budget by 50%*
2 *adjective*
cheap; **budget prices** = low prices; **budget travel** = cheap travel
3 *verb*
to plan how you will spend money in the future; *they are having to budget carefully before going on vacation in Europe;* **to budget for** = to plan to spend money on something; *we're budgeting for a 10% increase in electricity prices*

① **buffalo**
['bʌfələu] *noun*
large wild animal with long hair, like a large bull, which used to be common in North America but is now much less common; *buffalo*

used to roam the plains of the Midwest (NOTE: the plural is **buffaloes** *or* **buffalo**)

① bug
[bʌg]
1 *noun*
(a) insect; *what are these bugs on the roses?*
(b) *(informal)* germ; *she got a stomach bug on vacation*
(c) hidden microphone; *the secret services left a bug in her bedroom*
(d) error in a computer program; *you need a special program to detect bugs in the system*
2 *verb*
(a) *(informal)* to plant a hidden microphone; *they met in Central Park because he was afraid his apartment had been bugged*
(b) *(informal)* to annoy, to bother; *what's bugging him?* (NOTE: **bugging - bugged**)

① buggy
['bʌgi] *noun*
(a) light folding baby carriage; *she pushed the buggy across the busy road*; **double buggy** = buggy for two children
(b) a little car for one or two people; *beach buggies have very large tires so that they can drive on sand* (NOTE: the plural is **buggies**)

① build
[bɪld]
1 *noun*
shape of the body; *a girl of slight build*; *he has the same build as his dad*
2 *verb*
to make something by putting things together; *the house was only built last year*; *they are planning to build a new freeway across the state*; *the children built sand castles on the beach* (NOTE: **building - built** [bɪlt])

① builder
['bɪldər] *noun*
person who builds houses, blocks of apartments, etc.; *he works for a local builder*; *the builders are starting work on the kitchen today*

① building
['bɪldɪŋ] *noun*
(a) something which has been built, such as a house, train station, factory, etc.; *the flood washed away several buildings*; *his office is on the top floor of the building*; *they will have to knock several buildings down to build the new freeway*
(b) *(used in names of large office blocks)* **the Shell Building**
(c) action of constructing something; *the building of the church must have taken many years*

④ built-in
['bɪltɪn] *adjective*
made as part of a room or machine; *the kitchen has built-in cupboards*

① bulb
[bʌlb] *noun*
(a) fat underground part of a plant, from which

leaves and flowers grow; *she planted bulbs all around the yard*
(b) glass ball that gives electric light; *you'll need a ladder to change the bulb*

③ bulge
[bʌldʒ] *verb*
to bulge with = to be fat with; *her pockets were bulging with pieces of paper*

④ bulk
[bʌlk] *noun*
large amount; **in bulk** = in large quantities; *it is cheaper to buy food in bulk for the school*; **bulk purchase** = buying in large quantities; *bulk purchase is much cheaper*; **the bulk of** = most of; *the bulk of our sales are in Europe*; *she finished the bulk of the work before lunch*

③ bulky
['bʌlki] *adjective*
awkward and large; *the post office does not take very bulky packages* (NOTE: **bulkier - bulkiest**)

① bull
[bʊl] *noun*
(a) male animal of the cow family; *be careful when you cross the field - there's a bull in it*; *(informal)* **to take the bull by the horns** = to tackle a difficult problem; *he decided to take the bull by the horns and tell his father that he was leaving the family firm*
(b) male of some other animals; *a bull elephant*

④ bulldozer
['bʊldəʊzər] *noun*
large powerful tractor with a curved plate in front for pushing or moving earth, rubble, etc.; *they hired bulldozers to clear the site*

① bullet
['bʊlɪt] *noun*
piece of metal fired from a gun; *he loaded his gun with bullets*; *two bullets had been fired*

③ bulletin
['bʊlɪtɪn] *noun*
information given to the public about a situation; *the hospital issued a daily news bulletin on the condition of the accident victims*

① bulletin board
['bʊlɪtɪn 'bɔrd] *noun*
(a) board on which notices can be pinned; *she pinned a notice on the bulletin board*
(b) *(on the Internet)* system of sending messages, advertising events, etc.; *she advertised the concert on a bulletin board*

④ bull's eye
['bʊlz 'aɪ] *noun*
(a) center of the target which you try to hit when shooting, etc.; *it is not easy to hit the target, the bull's eye is very small*
(b) hitting in the center of a target; *no one scored a bull's eye*

① bully
['bʊli]
1 *noun*

person who hurts or is not kind to weaker people; *he's just a big bully - always trying to frighten the little children* (NOTE: plural is **bullies**)

2 *verb*

to treat someone who is weaker badly; *she was bullied by the other children in school* (NOTE: **bullying - bullied**)

④ **bum**

[bʌm]

1 *noun*

(informal)

(a) person who sits around doing nothing; *can't you bums find something to do?*

(b) person who is very keen on something; *a ski bum*

2 *verb*

(informal) to ask someone to give you something; *he always trying to bum cigarettes from his friends*

① **bump**

[bʌmp]

1 *noun*

(a) slight knock; *the boat hit the landing stage with a bump*

(b) raised place; *the field was covered with bumps and the team managers complained to the referee*; **speed bump** = small raised part in a road; *they have built speed bumps in the road to slow down the traffic*

(c) raised place on your body, where something has hit it; *he has a bump on the back of his head*

2 *verb*

to hit; *he's crying because he bumped his head on the door*

④ **bumper**

['bʌmpər]

1 *adjective*

very large; *a bumper crop of apples*; *we're publishing a bumper edition of children's stories*; *last year was a bumper year for sales of cellular phones*

2 *noun*

protective bar on the front and rear of an automobile; *the rear bumper of the car was damaged when the bus hit it*; *the traffic was bumper-to-bumper*

④ **bumpy**

['bʌmpi] *adjective*

uneven (path or flight); *the road is so bumpy that you can't drive fast*; *the flight was not bumpy at all* (NOTE: **bumpier - bumpiest**)

① **bun**

[bʌn] *noun*

little round bread or cake; *hamburgers are made of ground beef cooked and served in a bun*

② **bunch**

[bʌntʃ] *noun*

(a) group of things taken together; *he carries a bunch of keys attached to his belt*; *he brought her a bunch of flowers*; *I work with a nice bunch of people*

(b) cluster of fruit on the same stem; *a bunch of grapes*; *a bunch of bananas* (NOTE: plural is **bunches**)

① **bundle**

['bʌndl]

1 *noun*

package of things wrapped up or tied up together; *a bundle of clothes was all she possessed*; *he produced a bundle of papers tied up with green string*; *she left her clothes in a bundle on the floor*

2 *verb*

(a) to put things somewhere roughly; *he bundled the papers into a drawer*; *she bundled the children off to school*; *the police bundled him into the back of their van*

(b) to sell a software program at the same time as you sell hardware, both sold together at a special price; *the word processing package is bundled with the computer*

③ **bungalow**

['bʌŋgələʊ] *noun*

small house with only one story; *my grandparents have bought a bungalow by the sea*

① **bunk**

[bʌŋk] *noun*

(a) bed attached to a wall, as in a ship, etc.; *he climbed up into his bunk and fell asleep*; *do you want the top bunk or the bottom one?*; **bunk beds** = two beds one on top of the other, with a ladder to climb to the top one; *we put the children in bunk beds because they take up less space*

(b) *(informal)* nonsense; *I've heard a lot of bunk*

④ **bunker**

['bʌŋkər] *noun*

(a) fortified room, often underground; *as the enemy approached, the president hid in a bunker*

(b) open pit filled with sand placed on a golf course to trap balls and make difficulties for the players; *that's the second time he's in a bunker on this round*

① **bunny**

['bʌni] *noun*

child's name for a rabbit; *what a sweet little bunny!*; *look at all the bunnies in the field*; **bunny slopes** = gentle snow-covered mountain slopes where people learn to ski (NOTE: plural is **bunnies**)

③ **burden**

['bɜrdn]

1 *noun*

(a) heavy load; *he relieved her of her burden*

(b) something hard to bear; *I think he finds running the office at the age of seventy-five something of a burden*; **to make someone's life a burden** = to make someone's life difficult

2 *verb*

to weigh down with a load; *the whole town was burdened with grief*; *the company is burdened with debt*

② **bureau**

['bjʊərəʊ] *noun*

(a) office; *he filed the report from the New York bureau*; **(tourist) information bureau** = office that gives information to tourists; *ask for a list of bed and breakfasts at the information bureau*

(b) chest of drawers; *my socks are in the bureau in the bedroom*

(c) department of the government; *the Federal Bureau of Investigation*

④ **bureaucracy**

[bjʊə'rɒkrəsi] *noun*

(a) official system that is run by civil servants; *red tape and bureaucracy slow down our export business*; *I'm fed up with all this bureaucracy, just to get an export license*

(b) group of officials working for central or local government, or for an international body; *the investigation of complaints is in the hands of the local bureaucracy*

④ **bureaucrat**

['bjʊərəkræt] *noun*

civil servant; *bureaucrats in Brussels are still trying to decide on what to do*

④ **burgeon**

['bɜrdʒn] *verb*

to grow fast; *the population of the town has burgeoned rapidly*

① **burger**

['bɜrgər] *noun*

chopped beef grilled and served in a toasted roll; *he had a burger and fries for lunch* (NOTE: also called **hamburger**)

① **burglar**

['bɜrglər] *noun*

person who tries to get into a building to steal; *burglars broke in during the night*; *she saw the burglar as he was climbing out of the window*; **burglar alarm** = device that rings a loud bell if someone enters a building

② **burglarize**

['bɜrgləraɪz] *verb*

to enter a building and steal things from it; *their apartment was burglarized while they were on vacation*; *someone tried to burglarize our house*

① **burglary**

['bɜrgləri] *noun*

robbery by a burglar; *he was charged with burglary*; *there are many more burglaries during the summer vacation when houses are empty*

④ **burlap**

['bɜrlæp] *noun*

thick canvas

① **burn**

[bɜrn]

1 *noun*

burnt area of the skin or a surface; *she had burns on her face and hands*; *there's a burn on the edge of the table where he left his cigarette*

2 *verb*

(a) to damage or destroy by fire; *all our clothes were burned in the hotel fire*; *she burned her finger on the hot frying pan*; *the house was burned to the ground last year*; *(informal)* **to burn the candle at both ends** = to work much too hard; *he gets up early to go to the office, and comes home late - he's burning the candle at both ends*; *see also* MONEY

(b) to be on fire; *the firemen were called to the burning school*

(c) to use as a fuel; *the stove burns gas*; **a wood-burning stove** = heater that burns wood (NOTE: **burning - burned**)

④ **burner**

['bɜrnər] *noun*

part of a stove for making fire; heater

① **burnt**

[bɜrnt] *adjective*

black with fire; *the kitchen smells of burnt toast*; *all that remained of the house were some burnt walls*

④ **burp**

[bɜrp]

1 *noun*

noise when bringing up air from the stomach; *pat the baby gently on the back until he makes a burp*

2 *verb*

(a) to make a burp; *fizzy drinks make you burp*

(b) **to burp a baby** = to make a baby burp by gently patting it on the back until it burps; *burp the baby after he's had his bottle*

④ **burro**

['bʌrəʊ] *noun*

little donkey

① **burst**

[bɜrst]

1 *noun*

(a) sudden loud sound; *there was a burst of gunfire and then silence*; *bursts of laughter came from the office*

(b) sudden effort or activity; *he put on a burst of speed*; *in one of her bursts of efficiency she sorted out the cluttered closet*

2 *verb*

(a) to explode suddenly; *a water main burst on Main Street*; *when she picked up the balloon it burst*

(b) **to burst in** = to go in with force; *three masked men burst into the room* (NOTE: **bursting - burst**)

② **bury**

['beri] *verb*

to put into the ground; *he was buried in the local cemetery*; *they buried the gold in the garden*; *(informal)* **to bury your head in the sand** = to pretend that a danger or problem doesn't exist (NOTE: do not confuse with **berry**)

① **bus**
[bʌs] *noun*
large motor vehicle that carries passengers; *he goes to work by bus*; *she takes the 8 o'clock bus to school every morning*; *we missed the last bus and had to walk home*; *the number 6 bus will take you there*; *there's hourly bus service to the casino*; *the bus driver fell asleep while driving*; **airport bus** = bus that takes passengers between a town and an airport; **school bus** = bus that takes schoolchildren to school; *the children were waiting for the school bus* (NOTE: plural is **buses**)

① **bush**
[buʃ] *noun*
(a) small tree; *an animal was moving in the bushes*; *a holly bush with red berries* (NOTE: plural is **bushes**)
(b) *(in Africa, India, etc.)* **the bush** = land covered with bushes or low trees; *they walked through the bush for several days before finding a village* (NOTE: no plural in this meaning)

① **business**
['bɪznəs] *noun*
(a) occupation or trade, the work of buying or selling things; *she works in the electricity business*; *they do a lot of business with European countries*; **business college** *or* **business school** = place where commercial studies are taught; *he's going to a business school in September*; **business letter** = letter about business matters; **business trip** = trip to do with your business; *he's on a business trip to Japan*; **on business** = on commercial work; *the sales director is in Europe on business*
(b) commercial company; *she runs a photography business*; *he runs a used-car business*; **business address** = details of number, street and town where a company is located; **business card** = card showing a businessman's name and the name and address of the company he works for; **business hours** = time (usually 9 A.M. to 5:00 P.M.) when a business is open (NOTE: plural in this meaning is **businesses**)
(c) affair, concern; **it's none of your business** = it's nothing to do with you

① **businessman, businesswoman**
['bɪznəsmæn or 'bɪznəswumən] *noun*
person who is engaged in business, who runs a business; *the early morning flights to Los Angeles are full of businessmen*; *even the cleverest businesspeople can make mistakes* (NOTE: plural is **businessmen, businesswomen, businesspeople**)

① **bus stop**
['bʌs 'stɒp] *noun*
place where a bus stops and passengers can get on or off; *there were ten people waiting at the bus stop*

③ **bust**
[bʌst]
1 *noun*
(a) sculpture of the head and shoulders of a person; *there's a bust of Shakespeare at the museum*
(b) woman's breasts; **bust size** *or* **bust measurement** = measurement around a woman's breasts
2 *adjective*
(informal) **to go bust** = to fail, to be bankrupt; *thousands of people lost their savings when the bank went bust*
3 *verb*
(informal) to break; *she busted my precious vase!*; *he hit the ball hard and it busted a window* (NOTE: **busting - busted**)

④ **bustle**
['bʌsl]
1 *noun*
rushing around; *I like to sit quietly at home after the bustle of the office*
2 *verb*
to rush around doing things; *she bustled about the kitchen getting dinner ready*

② **busy**
['bɪzi]
1 *adjective*
working on something, doing something; *he was busy mending the automobile*; *I was too busy to phone my aunt*; *the busiest time for stores is the week before Christmas*; **the line is busy** = the telephone line is being used (NOTE: **busier - busiest**)
2 *verb*
to busy yourself with something = to occupy yourself, to keep yourself busy with something; *my sister likes to busy herself with the garden now she's retired*

① **but**
[bʌt]
1 *conjunction*
(coming before a contrast) *he is very tall, but his wife is quite short*; *we would like to come to your party, but we're doing something else that evening*; *I'm sorry, but there are no seats left*
2 *preposition*
except; *everyone but me is allowed to go to the movie theater*; *they had eaten nothing but apples*

② **butcher**
['butʃər]
1 *noun*
person who prepares and sells meat; *ask the butcher for some steak*; *the butcher shop is closed because he's on vacation*
2 *verb*
to kill in a brutal way; *the soldiers set fire to the village and butchered the people living in it*

④ **butt**

['bʌt]

1 *noun*

(a) end of a cigarette which has been smoked; *he picked up old butts from the sidewalk*

(b) end of the handle of a rifle which presses against the shoulder of the person firing it; *the prisoners were beaten with rifle butts*

(c) person who is teased; *he is always the butt of their criticism*

(d) *(informal)* buttocks; *to give someone a kick in the butt*

2 *verb*

(a) to push with the head; *the goat lowered its head and butted him*

(b) to butt in = to interrupt; *he always butts in while I'm trying to tell a story*

① **butter**

['bʌtər]

1 *noun*

(a) yellow fat made from cream, used on bread or for cooking; *can I have some more butter, please?*; *don't spread the butter so thick*; *fry the mushrooms in butter*

(b) spread; *I like peanut butter*; *she spread apple butter on her toast* (NOTE: no plural: **some butter**; **a knob of butter**)

2 *verb*

(a) to spread butter on something; *she was busy buttering slices of bread for the sandwiches*

(b) *(informal)* **to butter someone up** = to flatter someone, to praise someone without really believing it to be true; *just butter up the boss a bit - tell him how good his golf game is*

③ **buttercup**

['bʌtəkʌp] *noun*

common yellow flower found in fields; *she picked buttercups in the field*

① **butterfly** ['bʌtərflaɪ] *noun*

(a) insect with large brightly colored wings which comes out in daylight; *butterflies come out in the sunshine*

(b) *(informal)* **to have butterflies in the stomach** = to be very nervous; *she had butterflies in the stomach before the interview* (NOTE: plural is **butterflies**)

④ **butterscotch**

['bʌtərskɒtʃ] *noun*

candy made from butter and sugar; *butterscotch ice cream*

① **button**

['bʌtən]

1 *noun*

(a) little round disk for fastening clothes; *the wind is cold - do up the buttons on your coat*; *a button's come off my shirt*

(b) little round disk that you push to ring a bell, etc.; *press the "up" button to call the elevator*; *push the red button to set off the alarm*; *push the button marked "black" if you want coffee without cream*

(c) button mushroom = small round white mushroom

2 *verb*

to fasten with buttons; *he buttoned up his coat because it was cold*

④ **buttonhole**

['bʌtənhəʊl]

1 *noun*

hole made in a piece of clothing to push a button through

2 *verb*

to force someone to stop and listen to you, as if you were holding him by a buttonhole; *he was buttonholed by a journalist from the local newspaper*

① **buy**

[baɪ]

1 *verb*

to get something by paying money; *I bought a newspaper on my way to the station*; *she's buying a condo*; *she bought herself a pair of ski boots*; *what did you buy your mother for her birthday?* (NOTE: **buying - bought** [bɔt])

2 *noun*

a good buy = something which you have bought which is worth the money spent; *that camera you bought was a very good buy*

③ **buyer**

['baɪər] *noun*

person who buys; *there were no buyers for his house*; *she works as the shoe buyer in a department store*; **head buyer** = most important buyer in a store; **a buyer's market** = market where products are sold cheaply because there are more sellers than buyers; *compare* SELLER'S MARKET

① **buzz**

[bʌz]

1 *noun*

(a) noise like the noise made by a bee; *I can hear a buzz but I can't see the bee*; *the buzz of an electric chainsaw in the yard next door*

(b) *(informal)* excitement; *she gets a buzz from skiing fast downhill*

(c) *(informal)* telephone call; *give me a buzz tomorrow*

(d) the feeling of being slightly drunk; *he got a buzz from the beer* (NOTE: plural is **buzzes**)

2 *verb*

to make a noise like a bee; *flies were buzzing around the jam*

② **buzzard**

['bʌzərd] *noun*

large bird of prey; *one of the great birds of prey, the buzzard, is no longer as common in America as it was*

① **by**

[baɪ]

1 *preposition*

(a) near; *the house is just by the bus stop*; *sit down here by me*

(b) before, not later than; *they should have arrived by now, I hope there hasn't been an accident*; *you must be home by eleven o'clock*; *we must finish this piece of work by Friday*
(c) *(showing means or way)* *send the package by airmail*; *get in touch with the office by phone*; *they came by bus*; *she caught a cold by standing in the rain*; *she paid by check, not by credit card*
(d) *(showing the person or thing that did something)* *a painting by van Gogh*; *"Hamlet" is a play by Shakespeare*; *a CD recorded by our local group*; *the dog was bitten by the mail carrier*; *she was knocked down by a truck*
(e) by yourself = alone; *don't sit at home all by yourself*; *she made the hat all by herself*; *can he find his way to the station by himself?*
(f) *(showing how much)* *we sell tomatoes by the pound*; *eggs are sold by the dozen*; *prices have been increased by 5%*; *they won by 4 goals to 2*
(g) *(showing dimensions)* *the table is 25 inches long by 10 wide*
2 *adverb*
past; *she drove by without seeing us*

◇ **by and large**
['baɪ n 'lɑrʒ]
in general; *by and large, the trains run on time*

◇ **by the way**
['baɪ ðə 'weɪ]
(used to mention something not very important) *by the way, did you see the TV show on cars yesterday?*; *by the way, I shall be home late tonight*

③ **bye** *or* **bye-bye**
[baɪ or 'baɪbaɪ] *interjection*
goodbye; *bye! see you next week!*

③ **bypass**
['baɪpæs]
1 *noun*
(a) road around a town; *take the bypass if you want to avoid traffic hold-ups downtown*
(b) heart bypass = operation to put pieces of vein around a part near the heart which is not functioning properly; *she had a heart bypass ten years ago and is still going strong*
2 *verb*
to go around a town, avoiding the center; *the main road bypasses the town center*

Cc

① **C, c**
[sɪ]
third letter of the alphabet, between B and D; *remember the rhyme: I before E except after C: so write "receive" and not "recieve"*

① **cab**
[kæb] *noun*
(a) taxicab, a car that takes people from one place to another for money; *he took a cab to the airport*; *can you phone for a cab, please?*; *the office is only a short cab ride from the train station*; *cab fares are very high in New York*
(b) separate section for a driver in a large vehicle, such as a truck; *the truck driver climbed into his cab and started the engine*

① **cabbage**
['kæbɪdʒ] *noun*
vegetable with large pale green or red leaves which you eat; *we had red cabbage with our lunch*; *the school always smells of boiled cabbage*; *he was planting cabbages in his garden* (NOTE: as food, **cabbage** does not have a plural: **some cabbage; a helping of cabbage**; as plants you can count **one cabbage, two cabbages,** etc.)

① **cabin**
['kæbɪn] *noun*
(a) small room on a ship; *we reserved a first-class cabin on the cruise*; *she felt sick and went to lie down in her cabin*
(b) small hut; *he has a cabin by a lake where he goes fishing*
(c) inside of an aircraft; *the aircraft is divided into three separate cabins*; *the first-class cabin is in the front of the plane*; **the cabin crew** *or* **cabin staff** = the flight attendants on a plane

③ **cabinet**
['kæbɪnət] *noun*
(a) piece of furniture with shelves; *a china cabinet*; **filing cabinet** = piece of office furniture with drawers for storing files
(b) committee formed of the most important members of a government; *the cabinet met at 10 o'clock this morning*; *there's a cabinet meeting every Thursday morning*

③ **cable**
['keɪbl] *noun*
(a) wire for carrying electricity; *he ran a cable out into the yard so that he could use his electric saw*
(b) thick rope or wire; *the ship was attached to*

the dock by cables; *the cable snapped and ten passengers died when the cable car fell to the floor of the valley*; **cable railway** = railway where the cars are pulled by a cable

(c) wire for sending messages underground or under the sea; *they've been digging up the sidewalks to lay cables*; **cable TV** = TV where the programs are sent by wires from distant stations to people who have paid a subscription to the service

③ **cable car**
['keɪbl 'kar] *noun*
(a) vehicle that goes up a mountain, hanging on a wire cable; *ten people were killed when the cable car fell to the floor of the valley*
(b) *(in San Francisco)* type of trolley that is pulled by a metal cable set in a channel in the road; *we took the cable car down to Fisherman's Wharf*

① **cactus**
['kæktəs] *noun*
plant with thorns which grows in the desert; *cacti don't need much water* (NOTE: plural is **cactuses** *or* **cacti** ['kæktaɪ])

① **café**
['kæfeɪ] *noun*
small restaurant selling snacks or light meals; *we had a snack in the outdoor café*

① **cage**
['keɪdʒ] *noun*
box made of wire or with metal bars for keeping birds or animals so they cannot get out; *the rabbit got out of its cage*; *don't put your hand into the cage*

① **cake**
['keɪk]
1 *noun*
(a) food made by mixing flour, eggs, sugar, etc., and baking it; *a piece of cherry cake*; *she had six candles on her birthday cake*; *have another slice of pound cake*; *would you like some chocolate cake?*; **wedding cake** = special cake usually made of layers covered with icing and eaten at a wedding reception; **cake mix** = main ingredients for a cake that are bought ready mixed in a pack; *(slang)* **it's a piece of cake** = it's very easy; *the exam was a piece of cake - I finished it in half-an-hour!*; **you can't have your cake and eat it too** = you can't benefit from two opposing things (NOTE: as food, cake sometimes has no plural: **some cake, a piece of cake**; when it means one single item of food it can have a plural: **she made twenty cakes; a plate of cakes; there are no cakes left in the store**)
(b) small round or square piece of something; *a cake of soap*
(c) food made by mixing ingredients together into small round pieces which are then fried; *a meal of fish cakes and hush puppies*
2 *verb*

to dry and form a hard crust; **to be caked with** = to be covered with something that has dried hard; *his boots were caked with mud*

③ **calcium**
['kælsiəm] *noun*
(a) chemical element that is a major component of bones and teeth; *their diet does not have enough calcium* (NOTE: chemical symbol: **Ca**; atomic number: **20**)
(b) white substance found in water, which makes a white deposit; *calcium deposits form inside pipes and kettles*

> COMMENT: calcium is an important element in a balanced diet. Milk, cheese, eggs and certain vegetables are its main sources

③ **calculate**
['kælkjuleɪt] *verb*
to find the answer to a problem using numbers; *the bank clerk calculated the rate of exchange for the dollar*; *I calculate that we have enough money left for a meal*; *he calculated that it would take us six hours to get to Atlanta*

④ **calculated**
['kælkjuleɪtɪd] *adjective*
planned; *his speech was calculated to make his opponents very angry*; **a calculated insult** = insult which was made on purpose; **a calculated risk** = risk which you think you can afford to take

④ **calculation**
[kælkju'leɪʃn] *noun*
act of calculating; *according to my calculations, we have enough fuel left for only twenty miles*; **rough calculation** = approximate answer to a problem using numbers; *I made some rough calculations on the back of an envelope*

③ **calculator**
['kælkjuleɪtər] *noun*
machine for doing sums; *he worked out the price on his calculator*; **pocket calculator** = small calculator that you can put in your pocket

④ **calendar**
['kæləndər] *noun*
paper showing the days and months of the year, which can be pinned on a wall; *he pinned the calendar to the wall next to his desk*; *turn to the next page of the calendar - today is November 1*; **calendar month** = month from the first day to the last; **calendar year** = twelve months from January 1 to December 31

④ **caliber**
['kælɪbər] *noun*
(a) interior diameter of a gun; *the two bullets come from same caliber guns*
(b) intellectual or other ability; *it's work which he thinks is beneath a person of his caliber*

① **call**
[kɔl]
1 *noun*

(a) telephone conversation; trying to get in touch with someone by telephone; *were there any calls for me while I was out?*; **collect call** = call where the person receiving the call agrees to pay for it; **local call** = call to a number in the same area; **long-distance call** = call to a number in a different area; **overseas call** *or* **international call** = call to another country; **person-to-person call** = call where you ask the operator to connect you with a named person; **to make a call** = to dial and speak to someone on the telephone; *she wanted to make a (phone) call to Australia*; **to take a call** = to answer the telephone

(b) telephone call or shout to wake someone; *he asked for an early morning call*; **I want a wake-up call at 7 o'clock** = I want someone to wake me at 7 o'clock

(c) visit; *the doctor made three calls on patients this morning*; **on call** = available for duty

2 *verb*

(a) to say something loudly to someone who is some distance away, to tell someone to come; *call the kids when dinner's ready*

(b) to give someone or something a name; *they're going to call the baby Sam*; *his name is John but everyone calls him Jack*; *our cat's called Felix*; *what do you call this computer program?*

(c) to telephone; *if he comes back, tell him I'll call him when I'm in the office*; *Mr. Smith is out - shall I ask him to call you back?*; *call the police - the store has been robbed!*; *can you call me a cab, please?*; **call me at 7 o'clock** = phone me to wake me up at 7

(d) to visit; *the doctor called at the house, but there was no one there*; *the whole family called to see if she was better*

③ **caller**
['kɔlər] *noun*
(a) person who comes to visit; *she can't see any callers today*
(b) person who telephones; *I picked up the phone and the caller asked for my father*

③ **call for**
['kɔl 'fər] *verb*
(a) to call for someone = to fetch someone before going somewhere; *he called for me to take me to the theater*
(b) to call for help = to shout to ask for help; *we could hear people calling for help from under the ruins*
(c) to need or to require; *rescuing people with a helicopter calls for particular flying skills*

② **call off**
['kɔl 'ɒf] *verb*
to decide not to do something which had been planned; *he called off the visit to the museum*; *the picnic has been called off because it is raining*; *when the chairman heard about the deal he called it off*

③ **call on**
['kɔl 'ɒn] *verb*

(a) to visit someone; *she called on her mother to see how she was*
(b) to ask someone to do something; *the police have called on everyone to watch out for the escaped prisoner*

③ **call up**
['kɔl 'ʌp] *verb*
to tell someone to join the army, navy or air force; *thousands of men were called up at the beginning of the war*

② **calm**
[kɑm]
1 *adjective*
quiet, not rough or excited; *the sea was perfectly calm and no one was sick*; *keep calm, everything will be all right* (NOTE: **calmer - calmest**)
2 *noun*
period of quiet; *the calm of the Sunday afternoon was broken by the sound of jazz from the house next door*
3 *verb*
to calm (down) = to make someone quieter; to become quieter and less annoyed; *she stroked his hand to try to calm him down*; *after shouting for some minutes he finally calmed down*

② **calmly**
['kɑmli] *adverb*
quietly, not in an excited way; *the doctor explained calmly what would happen during the operation*

③ **calorie**
['kæləri] *noun*
(a) unit of measurement of energy in food; *she's counting calories to try to lose weight*; *there are 250 calories in a bottle of beer*
(b) unit of measurement of heat or energy (the heat needed to raise the temperature of 1g of water by 1°C)

③ **camcorder**
['kæmkɔrdər] *noun*
small portable camera for taking video pictures with sound; *he took a film of the wedding on his camcorder*

① **came**
[keɪm]
see COME

① **camel**
['kæml] *noun*
desert animal with long legs and one or two humps; *when we were on vacation in Kuwait we went to camel races in the desert*

COMMENT: there are two breeds of camel: the Bactrian camel has two humps and lives in Asia; the Arabian camel has one hump, and is common in North Africa and the Arab countries

① **camera**
['kæmrə] *noun*
machine for taking photographs; *he took a picture of the garden with his new camera; they went on vacation and forgot to take their camera; did you remember to put a film in your camera?*

① **camp**
[kæmp]
1 *noun*
place where people live in tents in the open air; *we set up camp halfway up the mountain*
2 *verb*
to spend a vacation or a period of time in a tent; *we go camping in Yosemite every summer; they had camped by the side of the lake*

② **campaign**
[kæm'peɪn]
1 *noun*
(a) organized military attack; *Napoleon's Russian campaign of 1812*
(b) organized attempt to achieve something; *a publicity campaign or an advertising campaign; he's organizing a campaign against the new freeway; the government's anti-smoking campaign isn't working*
2 *verb*
to work in an organized way to achieve something; *the party is to campaign against nuclear reactors; they are campaigning for women's rights*

④ **campaigner**
['kæmpeɪnər] *noun*
person who campaigns; *the anti-freeway campaigners are protesting outside City Hall; she's a well-known campaigner for women's rights*

① **campfire**
['kæmpfaɪər] *noun*
small bonfire at a camp; *the campfire was blazing and everyone sang songs*

③ **camping site** *or* **campsite**
['kæmpɪŋ saɪt *or* 'kæmpsaɪt] *noun*
area specially arranged for camping and trailers, with special places for tents, washing and toilet facilities, etc.; *there are several well-equipped campsites near the lake*

③ **campus**
['kæmpəs] *noun*
land on which a university or college is built, and the buildings on it; *the campus covers an area of about 25 square miles*; **to live on campus** = to live in accommodations for students; *all students live on campus during their first year at college* (NOTE: plural is **campuses**)

① **can**
[kæn]
1 *noun*
(a) round metal container for food or drink; *he opened a can of lemonade; empty beer cans were all over the sidewalk; can you open a can of beans?*
(b) **watering can** = container similar to a bucket, with a long tube for pouring, used to give water to plants
2 *verb used with other verbs*
(a) *(to mean "be able")* *he can swim well but he can't ride a bike; she can't run as fast as I can; can you remember what the doctor told us to do?; I can't bear to watch this movie any longer*
(b) *(to mean "be allowed")* *children under 16 can't drive; he says we can go in; the police officer says we can't park here*
(c) *(in asking politely)* *can we come in, please?; can you shut the door, please?* (NOTE: negative: **cannot**, usually **can't**; past: **could, could not,** usually **couldn't; can** and **could** are only used with other verbs, and are not followed by the word **to**)
3 *verb*
to put food in cans; *the town has a factory where they can peas* (NOTE: **canning - canned**)

① **Canada**
['kænədə] *noun*
very large country in North America, to the north of the United States; *we are going to Canada for vacation this year* (NOTE: capital: **Ottawa**; people: **Canadians**; languages: **English, French**; currency: **the Canadian dollar**)

② **Canadian**
[kə'neɪdjən]
1 *adjective*
referring to Canada; *his mother is Canadian and so is he; she is a Canadian citizen; the ticket costs 250 Canadian dollars*
2 *noun*
person from Canada; *how many Canadians are living in Seattle?*

② **canal**
[kə'næl] *noun*
(a) artificial river made to allow boats to go from one place to another; *you can take a boat trip round the canals of Amsterdam*
(b) tube in the body

② **cancel**
['kænsl] *verb*
(a) to stop something which has been planned; *the singer was sick, so the show had to be canceled; there is no refund if you cancel less than three weeks before the date of departure; the trip was canceled because the weather was too bad*
(b) to mark a postage stamp with a rubber stamp to show that it has been used

② **cancer**
['kænsər] *noun*
disease in which cells grow in a wrong way; *she developed skin cancer; he died of lung cancer*

③ **candidate**
['kændɪdət] *noun*
(a) person who applies for a job; *there are six candidates for the position of assistant*

manager; we have asked three candidates to come for an interview
(b) person who is standing for election; *she accompanied the candidate around the constituency*
(c) person who is taking an examination; *all candidates should answer three questions; candidates are given three hours to complete the exam*

① **candle**
['kændl] *noun*
stick of wax with a thread in the center, which you light to make a flame; *he blew out all the candles on his birthday cake; we lit a candle in her memory*

① **candy**
['kændi] *noun*
(a) sweet food, made with sugar; *eating candy is bad for your teeth*
(b) one piece of this food; *she bought a box of candies* (NOTE: plural is **candies**)

① **cane**
[keɪn] *noun*
(a) walking stick cut from the stem of a plant; *she was leaning on a cane as she walked up the path*
(b) strong stem of a plant, especially used of tall thin plants; *a field of sugar cane*

① **cannon**
['kænən] *noun*
(a) large gun; *the sailors hauled a huge cannon across the ship's deck*
(b) water cannon = machine for spraying water against demonstrators, etc.; *the police turned the water cannon on the group of protesters* (NOTE: plural is usually **cannons**)

① **cannot**
['kænɒt]
see CAN

② **canoe**
[kə'nu]
1 *noun*
boat with two pointed ends, which is moved forward by one or more people using paddles; *she paddled her canoe across the lake*
2 *verb*
to travel in a canoe; *they canoed down the river*

② **can opener**
['kæn 'əʊpnər] *noun*
device for opening cans; *there's a can opener on the wall of the kitchen by the telephone*

① **can't**
[kænt]
see CAN

③ **canvas**
['kænvəs] *noun*
(a) thick cloth for making tents, sails, etc.; *he was wearing a pair of old canvas shoes* (NOTE: no plural in this meaning)
(b) a painting; *three canvases by Picasso* (NOTE: plural is **canvases**)

① **cap**
[kæp]
1 *noun*
(a) flat hat with a flat hard piece in front; *the bus driver was wearing an old black cap; an officer's cap with a gold badge*
(b) top which covers something; *screw the cap back on the medicine bottle; a red pen with a black cap*
2 *verb*
to put a cap on top of something; to fix a cover on something to stop it from leaking; *they tried to cap the broken pipe* (NOTE: **capping - capped**)

④ **capability**
[keɪpə'bɪlɪti] *noun*
being able to do something; **beyond your capabilities** = too difficult for you to do; *I'm afraid this job is way beyond my capabilities* (NOTE: plural is **capabilities**)

② **capable**
['keɪpəbl] *adjective*
competent, able to work well; *she's an extremely capable secretary;* **capable of** = able to do something; *the automobile is capable of very high speeds; she isn't capable of running the department on her own* (NOTE: you are capable **of** something or **of doing** something)

③ **capacity**
[kə'pæsɪti] *noun*
(a) amount that something can hold; *this barrel has a larger capacity than that one; the movie theater was filled to capacity;* **a capacity audience** = an audience that fills a cinema, theater, etc.; **seating capacity** = number of seats in a bus, cinema, etc.; **to work at full capacity** = to do as much work as possible
(b) engine capacity = output of an engine or electric motor
(c) being able to do something easily; *he has a capacity for making friends with anyone he meets*
(d) position; **acting in his capacity as manager** = acting as a manager; **speaking in an official capacity** = speaking officially (NOTE: no plural)

② **cape**
[keɪp] *noun*
(a) piece of high land sticking out into the sea; *we rounded the cape on June 21 at 8 A.M.;* **the Cape (of Good Hope)** = the point at the very south of the African continent; *they almost sank in a storm when they were rounding the Cape*
(b) long piece of clothing with no sleeves; *she wrapped her cape more tightly around her*

COMMENT: the cape at the southern tip of South America is Cape Horn

② **capital**
['kæpɪtəl]
1 *noun*
(a) main city of a country, usually where the government is based; *the capital is in the*

eastern part of the country; *Madrid is the capital of Spain*; *the Italian capital is full of tourists at Easter*; *the capital's traffic has ground to a halt*
(b) money that is invested; *company with $150,000 capital* or *with a capital of $150,000*; **capital gains** = profit made when selling stocks or other investments
(c) carved top part of a column; *we visited the cathedral and looked at the carvings on the capitals*
2 *adjective*
(a) capital letters = letters written as A, B, C, D, etc., and not a, b, c, d; *write your name in capital letters at the top of the form*
(b) capital punishment = killing someone as a punishment for a crime; *capital punishment will never be restored in this state*

④ **capitalism**
['kæpɪtəlɪzm] *noun*
economic system based on the ownership of resources by individuals or companies and not by the state; *capitalism gives us all greater freedom*

④ **capitalist**
['kæpɪtəlɪst]
1 *noun*
(a) person who supports the theory of capitalism; *capitalists are in favor of free enterprise*
(b) businessman or businesswoman who invests money in a business; *he's a young capitalist who is only twenty-one, but on the way to becoming a millionaire*
2 *adjective*
working according to the principles of capitalism; *a capitalist economy*; *the capitalist system*

④ **Capitol**
['kæpɪtəl] *noun*
(a) building in Washington, D.C., where the U.S. Congress meets; **Capitol Hill** = hill on which the Capitol building stands, together with other important government buildings; **on Capitol Hill** = in the U.S. Senate or House of Representatives; *the feeling on Capitol Hill is that the president will veto the proposal*
(b) state capitol = building in the main city of a state, housing the state legislature

③ **capping, capped**
['kæpɪŋ or kæpt]
see CAP

① **captain**
['kæptən] *noun*
(a) person in charge of a team; *the two captains shook hands at the beginning of the match*
(b) person in charge of a ship or of an aircraft; *go and see the captain if you want to use the radio phone*; *Captain Smith is flying the plane*
(c) rank in the army above a lieutenant and below a major; *a lieutenant has to report to his*

captain (NOTE: used as a title with names, and often shortened to **Capt.**)

④ **caption**
['kæpʃn] *noun*
words printed beneath a picture; *the caption read "blaze leaves dozens homeless"*

② **capture**
['kæptʃər]
1 *noun*
being captured; *we must do everything to avoid capture*
2 *verb*
(a) to take someone or something as a prisoner; *they captured the enemy capital very quickly*; *four soldiers were captured in the attack*
(b) to take a share of sales from another company; *they have captured 10% of the market*

① **car**
[kɑr] *noun*
(a) small private vehicle for carrying people; *she bought a new car*; *my car was stolen while I was shopping*; *he drove his car into the garage*; *he goes to his office every morning by car*; **car ferry** = boat that carries vehicles and passengers from one place to another
(b) vehicle forming part of a train; *is there a dining car on the train?*; **freight car** = car that carries freight; **observation car** = special car with a glass roof, so that passengers can see more of the scenery

③ **caravan**
['kærəvæn] *noun*
group of animals or vehicles traveling together, one behind the other; *a caravan of camels crossing the desert*; *we joined a caravan of trucks going to Romania*

④ **carbohydrate**
[kɑrbəʊ'haɪdreɪt] *noun*
chemical substance containing carbon, hydrogen and oxygen; *she eats too many carbohydrates*

> COMMENT: carbohydrates are found in particular in sugar, potatoes and bread; they provide the body with energy. Compare proteins

③ **carbon**
['kɑrbən] *noun*
(a) chemical element found in coal; *carbon is an essential part of all living matter* (NOTE: Chemical element: chemical symbol: **C**; atomic number: **6**)
(b) carbon (paper) = paper with a black coating on one side, used for making copies; *you forgot to put a carbon in the typewriter*
(c) carbon copy; *make a top copy and two carbons*

④ **carbon copy**
['kɑrbən 'kɒpɪ] *noun*
copy of a document; *give me the original, and file the carbon copy*

① **card**
[kɑrd] *noun*
(a) flat piece of stiff paper (often with a picture on one side) which you send to someone with a short message on it; *they sent us a card from Italy*; *how much does it cost to send a card to Hong Kong?*; *see also* POSTCARD
(b) piece of stiff paper, folded so that a message can be written inside; **birthday card** = card that you send someone to wish them a happy birthday; **Christmas card** = card that you send someone at Christmas
(c) one of a set of 52 pieces of stiff paper, with a picture or pattern on it, used to play games; *a pack of cards*; *they were playing cards in the bar*; *would you like a game of cards?*
(d) piece of stiff paper with your name and address printed on it; *he gave me his business card*
(e) piece of stiff plastic used for payment; *do you want to pay cash or with a card?*; **cash card** = plastic card used to obtain money from a cash machine; **charge card** = plastic card that you use for buying things (you pay off the total sum charged at the end of each month); **credit card** = plastic card that allows you to buy goods without paying for them immediately; *he paid for the hotel with his credit card*; **smart card** = card with a chip, used for storing records or data; **store card** = credit card issued by a department store which can only be used for purchases within that store; *see also* PHONECARD
(f) **index card** = card used to make a card index; *she tipped all the index cards out onto the table*

① **cardboard**
['kɑrdbɔrd] *noun*
thick card; *do you have a piece of cardboard that I can use to make this model?*; *we put the glasses into cardboard boxes* (NOTE: no plural: **some cardboard; a piece of cardboard**)

① **care**
[keər]
1 *noun*
(a) serious attention; *he handled the glass with great care*; **to take care** = to be very careful; *take care when you cross the road*; *he took great care with the box of glasses*; *take care not to be late*
(b) *(on a letter)* **in care of** = words to show that the person is living at the address, but only as a visitor; **Mr. Brown, in care of Mrs. Green** = to Mr. Brown at the address of Mrs. Green (NOTE: usually written **c/o** on the envelope)
(c) looking after someone; *the care of the elderly*; **child care** = looking after children; **to take care of someone** = to look after someone; *who will take care of mother while I'm away?*
2 *verb*
to be worried; *I don't care if my automobile is dirty*; *she cares a lot about the environment*; *he couldn't care less* = he doesn't worry at all about it

③ **career**
[kə'rɪər]
1 *noun*
life of professional work; *she is starting her career as a librarian*; *he gave up his career in the military and bought a farm*; *go and see the school careers adviser - she will give you advice on how to become a dentist*; **career woman** *or* **girl** = woman who is working and does not plan to stop working to look after the house or children
2 *verb*
to rush forward out of control; *the automobile careered off the road into a ditch*

② **care for**
['keər'fɔr] *verb*
(a) *(formal)* to like; *I never did care for Lydia very much*; *I don't care for this music very much*
(b) to look after; *nurses cared for the injured people after the accident*; *people who have to care for their elderly relatives should get a grant from the state*

① **careful**
['keərfəl] *adjective*
taking care; *be careful not to make any noise, the baby is asleep*; *be careful when you're packing those glasses, they're very valuable!*; *she is very careful about what she eats*; *the project needs very careful planning*

① **carefully**
['keərfəli] *adverb*
with great care; *carry the box of eggs carefully!*; *drive more carefully in the future!*; *it poured and spoiled her carefully arranged hair*

① **careless**
['keərləs] *adjective*
without taking care; *he is careless about his work*; *he made several careless mistakes when he took his driving test*

② **carelessly**
['keərləsli] *adverb*
without taking care; *he carelessly dropped his bag of shopping and broke the eggs*

② **caretaker**
['keərteɪkər] *noun*
person who looks after a garden; *the city is advertising for a caretaker in the Parks Department*

② **cargo**
['kɑrgəʊ] *noun*
goods carried (especially on a ship); *the ship was taking on cargo*; **cargo boat** *or* **cargo ship** *or* **cargo plane** = ship or plane that carries only cargo and not passengers (NOTE: plural is **cargoes**)

② **Caribbean (Sea)**
[kə'rɪbiən] *noun*
sea that is to the south of the U.S., and to the west of the East Indies

④ **caribou**
['kærɪbu] *noun*
deer of North America

③ **caring**
['keərɪŋ] *adjective*
loving and helping; *she's a very caring person*; *his caring attitude toward his students*

② **carnival**
['kɑrnɪvl] *noun*
festival, often with music, dancing and eating in the open air; *the carnival procession arrived in the main square*

① **carpet**
['kɑrpɪt]
1 *noun*
thick material for covering the floor, stairs, etc.; *he spilled his coffee on our new white carpet*
2 *verb*
(a) to cover with a carpet; *a thickly carpeted hotel room*
(b) to cover with something as if with a carpet; *the path through the woods is carpeted with wild flowers*

① **carriage**
['kærɪdʒ] *noun*
horse-drawn carriage = open vehicle pulled by a horse; *the queen rode in an open carriage*

① **carried, carries**
['kærɪd or 'kærɪz]
see CARRY

③ **carrier**
['kæriər] *noun*
(a) thing or person that carries; *a procession of water carriers with jars on their heads*
(b) person who carries the germ of a disease without showing any signs of it, and who can infect others with it; *the disease is transmitted by a carrier through infected food or drink*
(c) **aircraft carrier** = large ship which carries aircraft; *we sent an aircraft carrier to the Middle East*

① **carrot**
['kærət] *noun*
vegetable with a long orange root which can be eaten; *boiled carrots*; *carrot soup*

① **carry**
['kæri] *verb*
(a) to take something and move it to another place; *there was no elevator, so they had to carry the sofa up the stairs*; *the plane was carrying 120 passengers*; *that suitcase is too heavy for me to carry*
(b) to vote to approve; **the motion was carried** = the motion was accepted after a vote; *her proposal was not carried*
(c) to keep in stock; *a supermarket will carry about 5,000 different lines of goods*
(d) *(of sound)* to be heard at a distance; *the sound of the bells carried across the marsh*

② **carry on**
['kæri 'ɒn] *verb*
to go on doing something; *when the police officer came into the restaurant, they all carried on talking as if nothing had happened*; *they carried on with their work even though the office was on fire*

③ **carry-on**
['kæri'ɒn] *adjective*
carry-on luggage = suitcases which you take with you onto a plane, as opposed to those you check in; *you are allowed to take two pieces of carry-on luggage onto the plane*

① **cart**
[kɑrt]
1 *noun*
(a) vehicle pulled by a horse; *a cart piled high with furniture*; **to put the cart before the horse** = to deal with things the wrong way round
(b) **baggage cart** = little cart with wheels that you use to carry your baggage at an airport; *there's a row of baggage carts near where you claim your luggage*; **golf cart** = little motor buggy for driving around a golf course; **shopping cart** = metal basket on wheels, used by shoppers to put their purchases in as they go round a supermarket
2 *verb*
to carry a big or heavy thing; *why do we have to cart this folding bed around with us?*; *they carted all their equipment up three flights of stairs*; *the police came and carted him off to jail*

② **carton**
['kɑrtən] *noun*
container made of cardboard; *a carton of yogurt*; *a milk carton*

① **cartoon**
[kɑr'tun] *noun*
(a) funny, often political, drawing in a newspaper; *he draws a cartoon for the "Examiner"*; **cartoon strip** = cartoon story made of a series of small drawings inside little boxes side by side
(b) program made of moving drawings; *I like watching Simpsons cartoons*

① **carve**
[kɑrv] *verb*
(a) to cut a large piece of meat up at table; *who's going to carve?*; *Father sat at the end of the table, carving a chicken*
(b) to cut stone or wood to make a shape; *he carved a bird out of wood*

① **carving**
['kɑrvɪŋ] *noun*
(a) cutting up cooked meat; **carving knife** = large sharp knife, used for carving; *it would be easier to carve the chicken with a proper carving knife*
(b) art of cutting stone or wood into shapes; *stone carving is an option at art school*
(c) an object that has been made by carving; *he gave me a wood carving for my birthday; the*

stone carvings in the church date from the 19th century

① case
[keɪs] *noun*
(a) suitcase, a box with a handle, for carrying your clothes, etc., in when traveling; *she was still packing her case when the taxi came*; *my plane went to Chicago, but my case went to New York by mistake*; *customs made him open his case*
(b) special box for something; *put the gun back in its case*; *I've lost my red eyeglasses case*
(c) large wooden box for goods; *he bought a case of wine*; **a packing case** = large wooden box for carrying items that can be easily broken; *the moving men are bringing their packing cases tomorrow*
(d) situation, way in which something happens; *your case is very similar to mine*; *it was a case of first come, first served*
(e) **court case** = legal action or trial; **the case is being heard next week** = the case is coming to court next week

◇ **in any case**
[ɪn ˈeni ˈkeɪs]
anyway, whatever may happen; *she missed the bus but in any case it didn't matter because the movie started late*; *they scored a late penalty, but it didn't matter, we were losing 3-0 in any case*

◇ **in case**
[ɪn ˈkeɪs]
because something might happen; *take your gloves in case it's cold on the mountain*; *I always carry an umbrella in case it rains*; **in case of fire, break the glass** = if there is a fire, break the glass; **just in case** = because something might happen; *it's still sunny, but I'll take my umbrella just in case*

◇ **in that case**
[ɪn ˈðæt ˈkeɪs]
if that happens or if that is the situation; *there is a bus strike - in that case, you'll have to take a taxi*

① cash
[kæʃ]
1 *noun*
money in coins and notes, not in checks; *we don't keep much cash in the house*; *I'd prefer to use up my spare cash, rather than pay with a credit card*; **cash box** = metal box for keeping cash; **cash machine** = machine that gives out money when a special card is inserted and instructions given; **cash on delivery (COD)** = payment in cash when goods are delivered; **cash register** = machine at a cash desk where you pay, with a drawer for cash (NOTE: no plural)
2 *verb*
to cash a check = to change a check into cash; *he tried to cash a check for nine hundred dollars*

③ cash flow
[ˈkæʃ ˈfləʊ] *noun*
rate at which money comes into and is paid out of a business; **the company is suffering from cash flow problems** = cash income is not coming in fast enough to pay the cash expenditure going out

③ casket
[ˈkæskɪt] *noun*
(a) long wooden box in which a dead person is buried; *they watched in silence as the casket was lowered into the ground*
(b) small box or chest; *the thief stole a casket of jewels from beside her bed*

④ cassette
[kəˈset] *noun*
magnetic tape in a plastic case which can fit directly into a playing or recording machine; *do you want it on cassette or CD?*; *he bought a cassette of folk songs*; **cassette player** = machine that plays cassettes; **cassette recorder** = machine that records and plays back cassettes

③ cast
[kæst]
1 *noun*
(a) all the actors in a play or movie; *after the first night the cast went to celebrate in a restaurant*
(b) **plaster cast** = shape made by pouring liquid plaster into a mold
2 *verb*
(a) to make a metal or plaster object from a mold; *he cast the statue in copper*
(b) to choose actors for a play or movie; *he was cast as a soldier in "Henry V"*
(c) **to cast a vote** = to vote; *the process of counting all the votes cast in the election has just begun*
(d) *(formal)* to throw; **to cast doubts on** = to say that you are doubtful about something; *he cast doubts on the whole proposal*; **to cast light on something** = to make something easier to understand; *the papers cast some light on how the president reached his decision* (NOTE: casting - cast)

① castle
[ˈkæsl] *noun*
(a) large building with strong walls; *the king and queen are living in the castle*; *the soldiers shut the castle gate*; *see also* SAND CASTLE
(b) one of two pieces used in chess, shaped like a little castle tower; *she took my last castle*

③ casual
[ˈkæʒjuəl] *adjective*
not formal; *he just walked in without knocking in a very casual way*; *she tried to appear casual at the interview, even though she was very nervous*; **casual labor** = temporary workers; **casual shoes** = light shoes, which are not office shoes; **casual work** = work where workers are hired for a short period

④ **casualty**
['kæʒjʊəlti] *noun*
person injured or killed in a battle or in an accident; *casualties were taken to the hospital by ambulance and helicopter; there was only one casualty in the accident* (NOTE: plural is **casualties**)

① **cat**
[kæt] *noun*
animal with soft fur and a long tail, kept as a pet; *she asked her neighbors to feed her cat when she went on vacation; don't forget to get some cans of cat food* (NOTE: cats are often called **Puss** *or* **Pussy**; a baby cat is a **kitten**)

② **catalog** *or* **catalogue**
['kætəlɒg]
1 *noun*
list of things for sale or in a library or museum; *look up the title in the library catalog; an office equipment catalog*
2 *verb*
to make a list of things that exist somewhere; *she spent months cataloging or cataloguing his correspondence*

④ **catastrophe**
[kə'tæstrəfi] *noun*
disaster, very bad accident; *it's a natural catastrophe on the same scale as the earthquake last year; this is the latest catastrophe to hit the family*

① **catch**
[kætʃ]
1 *noun*
(a) thing which has been grabbed or taken; *the boat brought back a huge catch of fish*
(b) action of grabbing a ball in the air; *he made a marvelous catch; he dropped an easy catch*
(c) hidden disadvantage; *it seems such a good deal, there must be a catch in it somewhere;* **catch-22** = circle of events in which the outcome gives you two equally unwanted results
(d) little hook that holds a door shut (NOTE: plural is **catches**)
2 *verb*
(a) to grab hold of something moving in the air; *can you catch a ball with your left hand?; when he knocked a glass off the table he managed to catch it before it hit the floor*
(b) to grab hold of something; *she caught him by the sleeve as he turned away; as he slipped, he caught the rail to stop himself from falling;* **to catch someone's eye** = to look at someone who is looking at you; *she caught his eye and nodded toward the door*
(c) to get hold of an animal, especially to kill it; *he sat by the river all day but didn't catch anything; our cat is no good at catching mice: she's too lazy*
(d) to get on a bus, plane, train, etc., before it leaves; *you will have to run if you want to catch the last bus; he caught the 10 o'clock plane to Atlanta*

(e) to get an illness; *he caught a cold from standing watching the soccer game; the baby has caught the measles*
(f) to find someone doing something wrong; *she caught the boys stealing in her store; the police caught the burglar as he was climbing out of the window*
(g) to arrest someone; *after months of searching, the police finally caught the gang*
(h) to hear; *I didn't quite catch what she said* (NOTE: **catching - caught** [kɔt] **- has caught**)

② **catcher**
['kætʃər] *noun*
baseball player who catches the balls not hit by the batter; *the catcher threw the ball back to the pitcher*

③ **category**
['kætɪgərɪ] *noun*
classification of things or people; *we only sell the most expensive categories of watches; if there is no room in the hotel mentioned in the leaflet, we will put you into a similar category of hotel* (NOTE: plural is **categories**)

④ **cater**
['keɪtər] *verb*
(a) to supply food and drink at a party, etc.; *our firm caters receptions of up to 250 guests*
(b) to provide for; *the college caters mainly to older students; we cater to private individuals as well as for groups*

② **caterpillar**
['kætərpɪlər] *noun*
(a) insect worm with many legs, which turns into a moth or butterfly; *caterpillars have eaten most of the leaves on our trees*
(b) *(Trademark)* **Caterpillar tractor** = tractor with continuous chain treads

③ **cathedral**
[kə'θidrəl] *noun*
large church where a bishop sits; *we went on a tour of cathedrals in Europe; they went to St. Patrick's Cathedral in New York*

② **catholic**
['kæθlɪk]
1 *adjective*
(a) Catholic = referring to the Roman Catholic Church; *the Catholic communion service is called Mass; our local Catholic priest is leaving to go to Colombia; there's a Catholic church at the end of the block*
(b) wide, general (taste); *his interests have always been quite catholic*
2 *noun*
Catholic = member of the Roman Catholic Church; *she became a Catholic when she married; the war between Protestants and Catholics*

① **cattle**
['kætl] *noun*
animals of the cow family; *a herd of cattle; cattle farmers are complaining about the high*

cost of foodstuffs; *the cattle were brought inside for the winter* (NOTE: the word is plural)

① **caught**
[kɔt]
see CATCH

② **cauliflower**
['kɒlɪflaʊər] *noun*
vegetable with hard white flowers, which are eaten cooked; *would you like some more cauliflower?* (NOTE: no plural when referring to the food: **some cauliflower; we had cauliflower with the meat**)

① **cause**
[kɔz]
1 *noun*
(a) thing which makes something happen; *what is the chief cause of traffic accidents?*; *the police tried to find the cause of the fire*
(b) organization that people support; *she is fighting for the cause of working mothers*
2 *verb*
to make something happen; *the accident caused a traffic jam on the freeway*; *the loud bang caused her to drop the cup she was carrying*

② **caution**
['kɔʃn]
1 *noun*
(a) care; *the sidewalk is covered with ice - please proceed with great caution* (NOTE: no plural in this meaning)
(b) warning not to do something again; *the judge let him off with a caution*
2 *verb*
to warn; *he was cautioned by the police*; *the doctor cautioned him against working too hard*

② **cautious**
['kɔʃəs] *adjective*
careful, not rushing; *we were warned to be cautious when driving through the crowded streets*; *she's a very cautious driver*; *he has adopted a cautious approach to his investments*

② **cautiously**
['kɔʃəsli] *adverb*
in a cautious way; *she walked cautiously along the top of the wall*

① **cave**
[keɪv]
1 *noun*
large underground hole in rock or earth; *when the tide went out we could explore the cave*; **cave paintings** = paintings done by ancient peoples on the walls of caves
2 *verb*
to cave in = to collapse; *the beam cracked and the roof caved in*

② **CD**
['si 'di] *abbreviation for*
compact disc; *I don't like his new CD - do you?*; *some CDs are expensive so I borrow them from the music library*; *you can get it on CD or cassette*; **CD player** = machine that plays CDs

② **CD-ROM**
['si di 'rɒm] *noun*
= COMPACT DISK READ ONLY MEMORY
small plastic disk that can store data, sounds or pictures; **CD-ROM drive** = disk drive that allows a computer to read data stored on a CD-ROM; *most PCs have CD-ROM drives*

④ **cease**
[sis] *verb*
to stop; *at long last the drilling noise has ceased*; **to cease to exist** = to stop being in existence; *the diner on the corner ceased to exist some time ago*

② **ceasefire**
['sisfaɪər] *noun*
agreement to stop shooting (in a war); *they agreed a two-week ceasefire to allow negotiations to start*

① **ceiling**
['silɪŋ] *noun*
(a) inside roof over a room; *he's so tall, he can easily touch the ceiling*; *flies can walk on the ceiling*; *he painted the kitchen ceiling*; *watch out when you go into the bedroom - it has a very low ceiling*
(b) highest point, such as the highest interest rate, the highest amount of money that you can invest, etc.; *output has reached its ceiling*; *there is a ceiling of $30,000 on the amount you can hold in state bonds*

① **celebrate**
['selɪbreɪt] *verb*
(a) to have a party or do special things because something good has taken place, or because of something that happened in the past; *our team won, so we're all going out to celebrate*; *today we celebrate the 400th anniversary of the founding of our college*; *they celebrated their wedding anniversary quietly at home*
(b) to perform a religious ceremony; *the priest was celebrating Mass*

④ **celebrated**
['selɪbreɪtɪd] *adjective*
very famous; *a concert by a celebrated pianist*

① **celebration**
[selɪ'breɪʃn] *noun*
action of celebrating something; *we had my birthday celebration in a local bar*; *after our team won, the celebrations went on late into the night*

② **celery**
['seləri] *noun*
plant with a white or green stem, eaten as a vegetable or raw as a salad; *she bought a stalk of celery in the market*; **a stick of celery** = a piece of the stem of the celery plant (often served raw with cheese) (NOTE: no plural)

② **cell**
[sel] *noun*
(a) room in a prison; *he was arrested downtown and spent the night in a cell at the police station*

(b) basic unit of an organism; *you can see the cancer cells under a microscope* (NOTE: do not confuse with **sell**)

① **cellar**
['selər] *noun*
underground room beneath a house; *we keep our wine in the cellar*

③ **cello**
['tʃeləʊ] *noun*
large stringed musical instrument smaller than a double bass; *a quartet made up of two violins and two cellos* (NOTE: plural is **cellos**)

③ **cellular phone** *or* **cell phone**
['seljʊlər 'fəʊn] *noun*
small telephone which you can carry around; *the sound is bad because I'm calling on my cell phone*; *cellular phones won't work on the subway*; *the battery has given out so I can't use my cellular phone*; *cellular phones are commonly banned in restaurants*

③ **Celsius**
['selsiəs] *adjective & noun*
scale of temperature where the freezing point of water is 0° and the boiling point is 100°; *do you use Celsius or Fahrenheit in the weather forecasts?*; *what is 75° Fahrenheit in Celsius?* (NOTE: used in many countries, but not in the U.S.A., where the Fahrenheit system is preferred. Normally written as a **C** after the degree sign: **32°C** (say: "thirty-two degrees Celsius"). It was formerly called **centigrade**.)

> COMMENT: to convert Celsius temperatures to Fahrenheit, multiply by 1.8 and add 32. So 20°C is equal to 68°F. To convert Fahrenheit to Celsius, subtract 32 and divide by 1.8.

③ **cement**
[sɪ'ment]
1 *noun*
(a) powder made from lime and clay, which is mixed with water and dries hard; *he was mixing cement to make a path around the house*
(b) strong glue; *she stuck the handle back on the cup with cement*
2 *verb*
to attach strongly; *he cemented some bricks on the top of the wall*; *the two halves should be cemented together*

② **cemetery**
['semətri] *noun*
place where people are buried; *he is buried in the cemetery next to the church*; *there are two cemeteries in the city* (NOTE: plural is **cemeteries**)

④ **census**
['sensəs] *noun*
official count of a country's population; *the next census will be taken in ten years' time* (NOTE: plural is **censuses**)

① **cent**
[sent] *noun*
(a) small coin, one-hundredth part of a dollar; *the stores are only a 25-cent bus ride away*; *they sell oranges at 99 cents each* (NOTE: do not confuse with **sent, scent**; **cent** is usually written (¢) in prices: (**25¢**,) but not when a dollar price is mentioned: **$1.25**)
(b) *see also* PERCENT

① **center**
['sentər]
1 *noun*
(a) middle; *they planted a rose bush in the center of the lawn*; *chocolates with coffee cream centers*; **center of gravity** = the point in an object at which it will balance; *a bus has a very low center of gravity*
(b) large building containing several different sections; *an army training center*; **health center** *or* **medical center** = building with various doctors and specialists; **sports center** = place where several different sports can be played; **shopping center** = several stores in one big building
(c) important town; *Detroit is the center for the automobile industry*; *Hollywood is the center for aspiring young film stars*
(d) group or political party between the left and right; *the Center combined with the Right to defeat the proposal*; *the cabinet is formed of right-of-center supporters of the president*
2 *verb*
(a) to put something in the middle; *make sure you center the picture in the frame*
(b) to concentrate on; *the opposition's attack was centered on the government's reorganization of the social services*; *our report centers on some aspects of the sales team*

④ **centigrade**
['sentɪɡreɪd] *noun*
scale of temperature where the freezing point of water is 0° and the boiling point is 100°; *do you use centigrade or Fahrenheit in the weather forecasts?*; *what is 75° Fahrenheit in centigrade?*; *see note at* CELSIUS

③ **centimeter**
['sentɪmitər] *noun*
measure of length, one hundredth part of a meter; *I need a short piece of string - about 25 centimeters long* (NOTE: written **cm** with numbers: **25cm**: say: "twenty-five centimeters")

③ **central**
['sentrl] *adjective*
in the center; *the hall has one central pillar*; *his offices are very central*; **central government** = the main government of a country, as opposed to local government; **central heating** = heating of a whole house from one main heater and several radiators; *the house has gas central heating*

③ **Central America**
['sentrəl ə'merɪkə] *noun*
part of the American continent between North and South America, containing Mexico, Costa

Rica, etc.; *our cruise took us to several ports in Central America*

③ **Central Intelligence Agency (CIA)**
['sentrəl ɪn'telɪdʒəns 'eɪdʒənsi] *noun*
the government intelligence agency in the U.S.A., specializing in espionage

② **century**
['sentʃəri] *noun*
(a) one hundred years; **his legal career spanned over half a century**
(b) period of time that begins every 100 years, starting with the year of the birth of Jesus Christ; **the eighteenth century** = the period from 1700 to 1799; *an 18th-century church*; *the church dates from the 19th century* (NOTE: plural is **centuries;** note also that the number of a century is always one more than the date number: so the period from **1900 to 1999** is the **20th century,** and the period starting in the year **2000** is the **21st century**)

③ **CEO**
= CHIEF EXECUTIVE OFFICER

① **cereal**
['sɪriəl] *noun*
(breakfast) cereal = food made from corn, oats, etc., eaten with milk for breakfast; *would you like some cereal for breakfast?* (NOTE: do not confuse with **serial**)

③ **ceremony**
['serɪməni] *noun*
important official occasion when something special is done in public; *they held a ceremony to remember the victims of the train crash*; **to stand on ceremony** = to be formal and not relaxed; *don't stand on ceremony* (NOTE: plural is **ceremonies**)

② **certain**
['sɜrtən] *adjective*
(a) sure; *are you certain that you locked the door?*; *I'm not certain where she lives*; **to make certain that** = to do something to be sure that something with happen; *he put the money in his safe to make certain that no one could steal it*
(b) without any doubt; *our team is certain to win the prize*
(c) a certain quantity *or* a certain amount = some; *the fire did a certain amount of damage*; *rebuilding the house took a certain amount of time*; *you need to add a certain quantity of water to the paint*
(d) which you don't know or are not sure about; *the manager is a certain Mr. Arbuthnot*; *certain mushrooms can make you sick if you eat them*

② **certainly**
['sɜrtənli] *adverb*
(a) *(after a question or order)* of course; *can you give me a lift to the station? - certainly*; *tell him to write to me immediately - certainly, sir*; *give me a kiss - certainly not!*
(b) definitely; *she certainly impressed the judges*; *he certainly knows how to score goals*

③ **certificate**
[sər'tɪfɪkət] *noun*
official document that proves or shows something; *she has been awarded a certificate for swimming*; *he has a teaching certificate*; **birth certificate** = official paper showing the date on which someone was born, together with details of the parents; **death certificate** = paper signed by a doctor which shows that someone has died and what was the cause of death; **insurance certificate** = document from an insurance company showing that an insurance policy has been issued; **marriage certificate** = official paper to confirm that two people are married; **share certificate** = document proving that you own shares

① **chain**
[tʃeɪn]
1 *noun*
(a) series of metal rings joined together; *she wore a gold chain around her neck*; *he stopped when the chain came off his bike*; **chain reaction** = series of reactions that follow on from an event; **chain saw** = saw made of a chain with teeth in it, which turns very fast when driven by a motor
(b) series of stores, restaurants, bars, hotels, etc., belonging to the same company; *a chain of hotels or a hotel chain*; *a supermarket chain*; *she runs a chain of shoe stores*
(c) row (of large mountains); *the Rockies are a chain of mountains running down from Canada through the western states*
(d) series of people, each buying another's house; *there is a chain of six families, so the sale will take some time*
2 *verb*
to attach with a chain; *I chained my bike to the fence*

① **chair**
[tʃeər]
1 *noun*
(a) piece of furniture which you can sit on, with a back; *someone has been sitting in my chair, said the father bear*; *he pulled up a chair and started to write*; *these dining-room chairs are very hard*; **easy chair** = comfortable chair; *see also* ARMCHAIR
(b) the chairman, the person who presides over a meeting; *please address all your comments to the chair*
(c) position of professor at a university; *he has been appointed to the chair of history*
2 *verb*
to preside over a meeting; *Mr. Jones chaired the meeting*; *the meeting was chaired by Mrs. Smith*

② **chairman**
['tʃeəmən] *noun*
(a) person who is in charge of a meeting; *Mrs. Jones was the chairman at the meeting*
(b) person who presides over a board of directors; *the chairman of the bank* (NOTE:

plural is **chairmen**; also called **chairperson** *or* **chairwoman**)

① **chalk**
[tʃɔk]
1 *noun*
(a) type of soft white rock made of calcium; *these white cliffs are formed of chalk*
(b) stick of white or colored material for writing on a blackboard; *he wrote the dates on the board in colored chalk*
2 *verb*
to mark or write with chalk; *she chalked an outline on the canvas*

② **challenge**
['tʃæləndʒ]
1 *noun*
(a) test of skill, strength, etc.; *the action by the union is another challenge to the authority of the government*; **to pose a challenge to someone** = to be a difficult task; *getting the piano up the stairs will pose a challenge to the removal men*
(b) invitation to a fight or match; *our team accepted the challenge to play another game*; **to take up a challenge** = to agree to fight
2 *verb*
(a) to ask someone to prove that he is right; *when challenged, he admitted that he had seen her get into a car*; *the committee's conclusions have been challenged by other experts*
(b) **to challenge someone to a fight** = to ask someone to fight you

③ **chamber**
['tʃeɪmbər] *noun*
(a) *(formal)* official room; *we saw the king's meeting chamber*
(b) a law-making group or a room where they meet; *the Senate is the upper chamber of the legislature*
(c) **chambers** = office of a judge in a courthouse; *the lawyers met in the judge's chambers*
(d) **chamber music** = music for a few instruments that can be played in a small room; **chamber orchestra** = small orchestra that plays chamber music
(e) empty space inside the heart; *blood collects inside the chambers of the heart and is then pumped out*

③ **champagne**
[ʃæm'peɪn] *noun*
sparkling white wine from the northeast of France; *they opened a bottle of champagne to celebrate the baby's birth*

② **champion**
['tʃæmpiən]
1 *noun*
best in a particular competition; *a champion cow; she was champion two years in a row; he's the world champion in the 100 meters*
2 *verb*

to champion a cause = to support a cause strongly; *they are championing the cause of women's rights*

② **championship**
['tʃæmpjənʃɪp] *noun*
(a) contest to find who is the champion; *the schools' tennis championship was won by a boy from Hartford*
(b) support for a cause; *her constant championship of the homeless*

② **chance**
[tʃæns]
1 *noun*
(a) possibility; *does our team have any chance of winning? - yes, I think they have a good chance; is there any chance of our getting home tonight?; there is no chance of rain in August; what are their chances of survival in this weather?*
(b) opportunity; *I've been waiting for a chance to speak to the mayor; I wish I had the chance to visit South Africa*
(c) luck; *it was pure chance or it was purely by chance that we were traveling on the same flight* (NOTE: the meanings: **chance of +ing** = possibility of doing something; **chance to** = opportunity to do something)
2 *verb*
(a) to do something by chance; *he chanced to look around as she came up to him; the automobile in front of us chanced to make a right*
(b) **to chance it** = to try to do something that is risky; *the sky looks gray, but I think I'll chance it without an umbrella*
(c) **to chance upon** = to find something by accident; *as he was searching in the library he chanced upon an unknown play by Shakespeare*

◇ **by any chance**
phrase by luck, by accident; *do you by any chance happen to know where the nearest post office is?; have you by any chance seen my glasses?*

④ **chancellor**
['tʃænsələr] *noun*
(a) important official; *he became chancellor of the university in 1999*
(b) *(in Germany and Austria)* head of the government; *Helmut Kohl was Chancellor of Germany until 1998*

① **change**
[tʃeɪndʒ]
1 *noun*
(a) making something different or becoming different; *there was a last-minute change of plan; we've seen a lot of changes over the years; I think it's a change for the better* = I think it has made things better than they were
(b) something different; *we usually go on vacation in summer, but this year we're taking a winter vacation for a change; a cup of tea is a*

nice change after all those glasses of orange juice; *a change of scenery will do you good*; *he took a change of clothes with him* = he took a set of clean clothes with him; *see also* RING

(c) money in coins or notes; *I need some change for the parking meter*; *do you have change for a $10 bill?*; **small change** = coins, especially ones with a low value; *I have only two $10 bills - I have no small change at all*

(d) money that you get back when you have given more than the correct price; *the book is $15.95, so if you give me $20, you should get $4.05 change*; *the storekeeper gave me the wrong change*; **keep the change** = keep it as a tip (said to waiters, etc.) (NOTE: no plural for meanings (c) and (d))

2 *verb*

(a) to make something different; to become different; *living in the country has changed his attitude toward towns*; *Providence has changed a lot since we used to live there*; *he's changed so much since I last saw him that I hardly recognized him*; **I've changed my mind** = I've decided to do something different

(b) to put on different clothes; *I'm just going upstairs to change or to get changed*; *go into the bathroom if you want to change your dress*; **changing room** = room where you can change into or out of sports clothes; **to change a bed** = to put clean sheets, etc., on a bed; *the girl has come in to change the beds*

(c) to use or have something in place of something else; *you ought to change your automobile tires if they are worn*; *can we change our room for one with a view of the sea?*; *she's recently changed her job or changed jobs*; *you will have to change in Chicago and take another plane to the coast*

(d) to give smaller coins or notes for a larger one; **can you change a $10 bill?** = can you give me small change for it?

(e) to give one type of currency for another; *I had to change $2,000 into pounds sterling*; *we want to change some traveler's checks*

① **channel**

['tʃænl]

1 *noun*

(a) piece of water connecting two seas; **the (English) Channel** = the sea between England and France; *many people use the Channel Tunnel to get to France*; *the boat only takes 50 minutes to cross the Channel*

(b) way in which information or goods are passed from one place to another; *the matter was sorted out through the normal diplomatic channels*; **channels of communication** = ways of communicating

(c) frequency range for radio or TV; station using this range of frequencies; *can you switch to Channel 36 for the news?*; *the new chat show is scheduled to compete with the gardening program on the other channel*

2 *verb*

to send in a certain direction; *they are channeling their funds into research*; *the money from the sale of the farm has been channeled into the building project*

④ **chaos**

['keɪɒs] *noun*

confusion; *there was total chaos when the electricity failed*; **chaos theory** = theory that things happen at random, and one should plan for the unexpected to happen

④ **chaotic**

[keɪ'ɒtɪk] *adjective*

confused, without any order; *there were chaotic scenes after the train crash*

④ **chap**

[tʃæp] *verb*

(of the skin) to crack; *rub an ointment on your chapped lips* (NOTE: **chapping - chapped**)

② **chapel**

['tʃæpl] *noun*

(a) separate part of a large church; *there are three chapels on the west side of the cathedral dedicated to St. Teresa*

(b) small church; *the chapel is an ancient monument and is protected*; *they were buried in the prison chapel*

② **chapter**

['tʃæptər] *noun*

(a) division of a book; *the first chapter is kind of slow, but after that the story gets exciting*; *don't tell me how it ends - I'm only up to chapter three*; *see also* VERSE

(b) **a chapter of accidents** = a series of accidents

(c) group of priests who run a cathedral; **chapter house** = special room where a chapter meets

② **character**

['kærəktər] *noun*

(a) the part of a person that makes him or her different from all others; *his character is quite different from yours*; *she is a very strong character*

(b) person in a play or novel; *the leading character in the movie is an old blind man*

(c) letter or symbol used in writing or printing; *the book is printed in Chinese characters*

③ **characteristic**

[kærəktə'rɪstɪk]

1 *adjective*

special, typical; *you can recognize him by his characteristic way of walking*; *that is characteristic of this type of flower* (NOTE: something is characteristic **of** something)

2 *noun*

typical feature; *the two cars have very similar characteristics*

④ **characterize**

['kærəktəraɪz] *verb*

(a) to be a typical feature of something; *California is characterized by economic strength and cultural diversity*

(b) to describe something as; *he didn't like being characterized as weak and inefficient*; *how would you characterize her reaction to the movie?*

① **charge**
[tʃɑrdʒ]
1 *noun*
(a) money that you have to pay; *there is no charge for delivery*; *we require a small charge for rental*; **we will send the package free of charge** = without asking you to pay for postage; **admission charge** *or* **entry charge** = price to be paid before going into an exhibition, etc.; **service charge** = charge added to a check in a restaurant to pay for service; *a 10% service charge is added*; *does the check include a service charge?*
(b) claim by the police that someone has done something wrong; *he was kept in prison on a charge of trying to blow up the White House*
(c) in charge = being in control of; *he is in charge of the sales department*; *who's in charge here?*; **to take charge of something** = to start to be responsible for something; *he took charge of the class while the teacher was out of the room*
(d) electric current; *he was killed by an electric charge from the wires*
(e) running attack; *the captain led the charge against the enemy camp*
2 *verb*
(a) to ask someone to pay; *the restaurant charged me $10 for two glasses of water*; *how much did the garage charge for fixing the car?*; *can I charge the restaurant check to my room number?*; **to charge the packing to the customer** = to ask the customer to pay for the packing
(b) *(of the police)* to say that someone has done something wrong; *he was charged with stealing the jewels*
(c) to attack while running; *the police charged the group of protesters*; *if the elephant charges, run as fast as you can!*
(d) to run violently; *the children charged into the kitchen*
(e) to give someone responsibility; *she was charged with organizing the club's dinner dance* .
(f) to put electricity into a battery; *you can charge your phone battery by plugging it into the outlet overnight*; *my cellular phone doesn't work - the battery probably needs charging*

④ **charisma**
[kəˈrɪzmə] *noun*
personal appeal; *the president's lack of charisma is rather disappointing*

② **charity**
[ˈtʃærɪti] *noun*
(a) organization that collects money to help the poor or to support some cause; *charities do not pay tax*; **charity shop** = shop run by a charity, where you can take old clothes, china, etc., which are then sold and the money given to charity (NOTE: plural is **charities**)
(b) help, usually money, given to the poor; *he lost his job and his family has to rely on the charity of neighbors* (NOTE: no plural in this meaning)

① **charm**
[tʃɑrm]
1 *noun*
(a) being attractive; *she has great personal charm*; *the charm of the Pennsylvanian countryside*
(b) object that is supposed to be magic; *she wears a lucky charm around her neck*
2 *verb*
(a) to put under a spell; *the old man played a pipe and charmed a snake out of its basket*
(b) to attract someone, to make someone pleased; *he always manages to charm the girls at the office*; *I was charmed by their cabin in the woods*

④ **charming**
[ˈtʃɑrmɪŋ] *adjective*
attractive; *she looks charming in her pink dress*; *he was such a charming young man*; *the effect of the little lights in the trees was charming*

② **chart**
[tʃɑrt]
1 *noun*
(a) map of the sea, a river or a lake; *you will need an accurate chart of the entrance to the river*
(b) diagram showing statistics; *a chart showing the increase in cases of lung cancer*; **bar chart** = diagram where quantities are shown as thick columns of different heights; **pie chart** = diagram where information is shown as a circle cut up into sections of different sizes
(c) the charts = list of the most popular records; *his single is going up in the charts*
2 *verb*
(a) to make a map of the sea, a river or lake; *he charted the coast of southern California in the 18th century*
(b) to describe or make a diagram of something to show information; *the book charts the rise of the new political party*

④ **charter**
[ˈtʃɑrtər]
1 *noun*
(a) charter flight = flight in an aircraft that has been hired specially; *our charter flight to the island was two hours late*; **charter plane** = plane that has been chartered
(b) legal document giving rights or privileges to a town or a university; *the university received its charter in 1846*
2 *verb*
to hire an aircraft, bus or boat for a particular trip; *we chartered a boat for a day trip to the island*

chase

[tʃeɪs]

1 *noun*

running after someone to try to catch him; *he was caught after a three-hour chase along the freeway*; **to give chase** = to run after someone; *the police gave chase to the robbers*; *see also* WILD GOOSE CHASE

2 *verb*

to run after someone to try to catch him; *the police officer chased the burglars down the street*; *the mail carrier was chased by a dog*

chassis

['ʃæsi] *noun*

metal framework of a car; *the car's chassis was damaged in the accident* (NOTE: plural is **chassis** ['ʃæsiz])

chat

[tʃæt]

1 *noun*

casual friendly talk; *he likes to drop in for a cup of coffee and a chat*; *I'd like to have a chat with you about your work*

2 *verb*

to talk in a casual and friendly way; *they were chatting about their vacations when the bus arrived* (NOTE: **chatting - chatted**)

cheap

[tʃip]

1 *adjective*

which does not cost a lot of money; *if you want a cheap radio you ought to shop around*; *why do you go by bus? - because it's cheaper than by cab*; *buses are by far the cheapest way to travel*; **dirt cheap** = extremely cheap; *oranges are dirt cheap in the street markets* (NOTE: **cheaper - cheapest**)

2 *adverb*

at a low price; *I bought them cheap in the local market*

cheaply

['tʃipli] *adverb*

without paying much money; *you can live quite cheaply if you don't go out to eat in restaurants*

cheat

[tʃit]

1 *noun*

person who acts in an unfair way in order to win; *I won't play cards with him again, he's a cheat*

2 *verb*

(a) to act in an unfair way in order to be successful; *they don't let him play any more since they found he was cheating*; *they are sure he cheated on his exam, but can't find out how he did it*

(b) to cheat someone out of something = to get something by tricking someone; *he was furious, saying that he had been cheated out of the first prize*

check

[tʃek]

1 *noun*

(a) examination or test; *the police are carrying out checks on all cars*; *a routine check of the fire equipment*; **baggage check** = examination of passengers' baggage to see if it contains bombs or other dangerous devices

(b) *(in a restaurant)* piece of paper showing the amount of money you have to pay; *I'll ask for the check*

(c) note to a bank asking for money to be paid from one account to another; *I paid for the jacket by check*; *he made out the check to Mr. Smith*; *he's forgotten to sign the check*; **paycheck** *or* **salary check** = regular check by which an employee is paid; **traveler's check** = check which you buy at a bank before you travel and which you can then use in a foreign country; *most stores in the U.S.A. accept traveler's checks*; *the hotel will cash traveler's checks for you*; *the bank guarantees replacement of stolen traveler's checks*

(d) mark on paper to show that something is correct; *put a check in the box marked "R"*

(e) in check = under control; *we must keep our spending in check*

(f) check (pattern) = pattern made of small squares; *the restaurant has red check tablecloths*

2 *verb*

(a) to make sure; to examine; *I'd better check with the office if there are any messages for me*; *did you lock the door? - I'll go and check*; *you must have your automobile checked every 10,000 miles*

(b) to mark with a sign to show that something is correct, 3; *check the box marked "R"*

(c) to bring someone or something to a halt; *bad weather checked the expedition's progress*

checkbook

['tʃekbʊk] *noun*

set of blank checks attached together in a cover; *I need a new checkbook*

checkers

['tʃekərz] *noun*

(a) game played by two people with twelve pieces each and a black and red checked board; *checkers is a much simpler game than chess*

(b) checker = one of the pieces used in this game; *one of the checkers is missing*

check in

['tʃek ɪn] *verb*

(a) *(at a hotel)* to arrive at a hotel and sign for a room; *he checked in at 12:15*

(b) *(at an airport)* to give in your ticket to show you are ready to take the flight; *please check in two hours before your departure time*

(c) to check baggage in = to pass your baggage to be put on the plane for you; *my bag hasn't been checked in yet*

check-in

['tʃekɪn] *noun*

place where passengers give in their tickets and baggage for a flight; *the check-in is on the first floor*; **holders of valid tickets can go straight through the check-in**; **check-in counter** *or* **desk** = counter where passengers check in; **check-in time** = time at which passengers should check in

② **check out**
['tʃek 'aʊt] *verb*
(a) *(at a hotel)* to leave and pay for a room; *we will check out before breakfast*
(b) to take baggage out of safekeeping; *the ticket shows that he checked out his bag at 9:15*
(c) to see if something is all right; *I thought I heard a noise in a kitchen - I'll go and check it out*

② **checkout**
['tʃekaʊt] *noun*
(a) *(in a supermarket)* **checkout (counter)** = desk where you pay for the goods you have bought; *there were huge lines at the checkouts*; *take your purchases to the nearest checkout counter*
(b) *(in a hotel)* **checkout time is 12:00** = time by which you have to leave your room

① **checkup**
['tʃekʌp] *noun*
(a) test to see if someone is fit; general examination by a doctor or dentist; *he had a heart checkup last week*; *he made an appointment with the dentist for a checkup*
(b) general examination of a machine; *I'm taking the car to the garage for its six-month checkup*

② **cheek**
[tʃik] *noun*
fat part of the face on either side of the nose and below the eye; *a baby with red cheeks*; *see also* TONGUE

① **cheer**
['tʃiər]
1 *noun*
shout of praise or encouragement; *when he scored the touchdown there was a big cheer from the crowd*; **three cheers** = three shouts of praise for someone; *three cheers for the captain! hip! hip! hooray!*
2 *verb*
to shout encouragement; *the crowd cheered when the first cyclists appeared*

① **cheerful**
['tʃiərfəl] *adjective*
happy; *you're looking very cheerful today*; *"hi!" he said in a cheerful voice*

① **cheerfully**
['tʃiərfəli] *adverb*
in a happy way; *they marched cheerfully along, singing songs*

③ **cheers!**
['tʃiərz] *interjection said when drinking*
good health!; *they all lifted their glasses and said "cheers!"*

① **cheer up**
['tʃiər'ʌp] *verb*
to become happier; **cheer up!** = don't be miserable!; **to cheer someone up** = to make someone happier; *she made him a good meal to try to cheer him up*

① **cheese**
[tʃiz] *noun*
solid food made from milk; *she ordered a cheese sandwich and salad*; *can I have a pound of Cheddar cheese, please?*; **cream cheese** = soft white cheese; **blue cheese** = cheese with blue mold in it (NOTE: the plural **cheeses** is only used to mean different types of cheese or several large round whole blocks of cheese; usually there is no plural: **some cheese; a piece of cheese**)

② **cheeseburger**
['tʃizbɜrgər] *noun*
hamburger with melted cheese

② **chef**
[ʃef] *noun*
cook in a restaurant; *they've got a new chef at this restaurant and the food is much better*; **chef's special** = special dish, sometimes one which the chef is famous for, which is listed separately on the menu

② **chemical**
['kemɪkl]
1 *adjective*
referring to chemistry; *if you add acid it sets off a chemical reaction*
2 *noun*
substance that is formed by reactions between elements; *rows of glass bottles containing chemicals*; *chemicals are widely used in agriculture*

② **chemist**
['kemɪst] *noun*
scientist who studies chemical substances; *he works as a chemist in a nuclear laboratory*

② **chemistry**
['kemɪstri] *noun*
(a) science of chemical substances and their reactions; *she's studying chemistry at college*; *he passed his chemistry exam*
(b) **personal chemistry** = reaction of one person to another; *the personal chemistry of the two leaders was very good* (NOTE: no plural)

① **cherry**
['tʃeri] *noun*
(a) tree that produces small, round, sweet red fruit; *we have a beautiful cherry tree in the middle of the lawn*
(b) small, round, sweet red fruit, growing usually in pairs on a tree; *she ate a half a pound of cherries*; *a jar of cherry jam* (NOTE: plural is **cherries**)

② **chess**
[tʃes] *noun*
game for two people played on a board with sixteen pieces on each side; *would you like a*

game of chess?; *they played chess all evening* (NOTE: no plural)

> COMMENT: the game is played on a board with 64 black and white squares. Each player has sixteen pieces: eight pawns, two castles, two knights, two bishops, one queen and one king. The object is to capture and remove your opponent's pieces, and finally to put your opponent's king in a position where he cannot move without being captured

① **chest**
[tʃest] *noun*
(a) the top front part of the body, where the heart and lungs are; *if you have pains in your chest or if you have chest pains, you ought to see a doctor*; *the doctor listened to the patient's chest*; *she was rushed to the hospital with chest wounds*; *he has a 48-inch chest*; **to get something off your chest** = to speak frankly about a problem
(b) piece of furniture, like a large box; *he keeps his old clothes in a chest under the bed*; **chest of drawers** = piece of furniture with several drawers for clothes

② **chestnut**
['tʃesnʌt] *noun*
large tree, with large shiny red-brown seeds; *there is an avenue of chestnuts in the middle of the park*; *in winter, men stand at street corners selling roasted chestnuts*

① **chew**
[tʃu] *verb*
to make something soft with your teeth; *you must chew your meat well, or you will get sick to your stomach*; *the dog was lying in front of the fire chewing a bone*

① **chewing gum**
['tʃuɪŋ gʌm] *noun*
sweet substance which you chew but do not swallow; *would you like a piece of chewing gum?*; *I've got some chewing gum stuck to my shoe*

② **Chicano**
[tʃɪ'kɑnəʊ] *noun*
American who was born in Mexico or has Mexican ancestors

① **chick**
[tʃɪk] *noun*
baby bird, especially a baby hen; *all the chicks hatched on the same day*; *the chicks came running along in a line behind the mother hen*

① **chicken**
['tʃɪkɪn] *noun*
(a) young hen; *chickens were running everywhere in the yard*
(b) meat from a hen; *we're having roast chicken for lunch*; *would you like another slice of chicken?*; *we bought some chicken salad sandwiches* (NOTE: no plural for this meaning: **some chicken; a piece** *or* **a slice of chicken**)

② **chickenpox**
['tʃɪkɪnpɒks] *noun*
infectious disease of children, with fever and red spots that itch; *he got chickenpox and couldn't go to school*

① **chief**
[tʃif]
1 *adjective*
most important; *what are the country's chief exports?*; *what is the chief cause of air accidents?*
2 *noun*
(a) person in charge in a group of people or in a business; *he's been made the new chief of our department*; *the fire chief warned that the building was dangerous*; **chief executive officer (CEO)** = executive in charge of a company, responsible to the board of directors for its profits and operations
(b) the leader of a tribe; *all the chiefs came together at a meeting*

③ **chiefly**
['tʃifli] *adverb*
mainly; *our town is famous chiefly for its pork sausages*

① **child**
[tʃaɪld] *noun*
(a) young boy or girl; *there was no TV when my mother was a child*; *here's a photograph of the president as a child*; *a group of children were playing on the beach*; **child's play** = something which is very easy; *building a wall may look like child's play, but it's not as easy as you think*
(b) son or daughter; *whose child is that?*; *how many children do they have?*; *they have six children - two boys and four girls* (NOTE: plural is **children** ['tʃɪldrən])

② **childhood**
['tʃaɪldhʊd] *noun*
time when someone is a child; *he spent his childhood in the country*; *she had a happy childhood living on a farm in Canada*; *she's had all the usual childhood diseases - measles, etc.*; *he married his childhood sweetheart*

② **childish**
['tʃaɪldɪʃ] *adjective*
like a child; *it was a bit childish of her to start to cry when the boss told her off*

② **chili**
['tʃɪli] *noun*
(a) dry seed pod of the pepper plant, used to make very hot sauces; *the sauce contains chili*
(b) chili (con carne) = mixture of meat and beans in a sauce made with chilies; *we had chili for lunch* (NOTE: plural is **chilies**)

① **chill**
[tʃɪl]
1 *noun*
illness caused by cold; *you'll catch a chill if you don't wear a coat*
2 *verb*

to make something cool; *he asked for a glass of chilled orange juice*

② **chilly**
['tʃɪlɪ] *adjective*
quite cold; *even summer evenings can be chilly in the mountains* (NOTE: chillier - chilliest)

② **chime**
[tʃaɪm]
1 *noun*
ringing of bells; *the chimes of the church bell rang out*
2 *verb*
(of bells) to ring; *the church clock has just chimed four*

① **chimney**
['tʃɪmnɪ] *noun*
tall brick column for taking smoke away from a fire; *the house has two tall chimneys*; *if you look up the chimney in an old house you can see the sky*

① **chin**
[tʃɪn] *noun*
front part of the bottom jaw; *she suddenly stood up and hit him on the chin*; **to keep your chin up** = to stay confident; *even if everything seems to be going wrong, try to keep your chin up!*

① **china**
['tʃaɪnə] *noun*
fine white cups, plates, etc.; *she got out her best china tea service because she had visitors*; *a china cup and saucer*; *all our china was broken when we moved* (NOTE: no plural)

① **China**
['tʃaɪnə] *noun*
very large country in Asia; *we went to China on business last year*; *visitors to China always go to see the Great Wall* (NOTE: capital: **Beijing**; people: **the Chinese**; language: **Chinese**; currency: **renminbi** *or* **yuan**)

② **Chinese**
[tʃaɪˈniːz]
1 *adjective*
referring to China; *her husband is Chinese*; *we often go to a Chinese restaurant in the evening*
2 *noun*
(a) person from China; *the Chinese are very good at mathematics* (NOTE: plural is **Chinese**)
(b) language spoken in China; *she had been taking Chinese lessons for some weeks*; *the book has been translated into Chinese*

① **chip**
[tʃɪp]
1 *noun*
(a) thin slice of potato, fried till crisp and eaten cold as a snack; *he ordered a beer and a bag of chips*
(b) small piece of something hard, such as wood or stone; *chips of stone flew all over the studio as he was carving the statue*; **chocolate chip** = small piece of hard chocolate, used in ice cream, cookies or cakes; *a chocolate chip cookie*; *mint chocolate chip ice cream*

(c) **a computer chip** = a small piece of a substance which can store data, used in a computer; *computer chip manufacturers are doing very well*
(d) **a chip on your shoulder** = a feeling of being constantly annoyed because you feel you have lost an advantage; *he has a chip on his shoulder because his brother has a better job than he has*
(e) counter, piece of plastic or metal which stands in for money in gambling; *he put a pile of chips on the table*; *(informal)* **when the chips are down** = when the situation is serious and important decisions have to be made
(f) *GB* **chips** = French fries
2 *verb*
to break a small piece off something hard; *he banged the cup down on the plate and chipped it* (NOTE: chipping - chipped)

② **chisel**
['tʃɪzl] *noun*
metal tool which you hit with a hammer to cut small pieces of wood or stone; *he tapped the chisel very carefully with his hammer*

① **chocolate**
['tʃɒklət] *noun*
(a) sweet brown food made from the crushed seeds of a tropical tree; *can I buy a bar of chocolate?*; *her mother made a chocolate cake*; **dark chocolate** *or* **plain chocolate** = dark brown chocolate which is quite bitter; **milk chocolate** = light brown sweet chocolate
(b) a single sweet made from chocolate; *there are only three chocolates left in the box*; *who's eaten the last chocolate?*
(c) drink made from chocolate powder and milk; *I always have a cup of hot chocolate before I go to bed*
(d) dark brown color, like chocolate; *we have a chocolate-colored carpet in the sitting room* (NOTE: no plural, except for meaning (b))

② **choice**
[tʃɔɪs]
1 *noun*
(a) thing which is chosen; *Cape Cod was our first choice for our honeymoon*
(b) act of choosing something; *you must give the customer time to make his choice*
(c) range of items to choose from; *the store has a huge choice of furniture*; **I hadn't any choice** *or* **I had no choice** = there was nothing else I could do
2 *adjective*
specially selected food; *choice meat*; *choice peaches*

② **choir**
['kwaɪər] *noun*
group of people who sing together; *he sings in the church choir*

① **choke**
[tʃəʊk]
1 *noun*

(in an automobile engine) valve that increases the flow of air to the engine; ***this model has an automatic choke***

2 *verb*

(a) to block a pipe, etc.; ***the river was choked with weeds***

(b) to stop breathing properly because you have swallowed something which blocks your throat; ***don't talk with your mouth full or you'll choke***; ***he choked on a piece of bread*** *or* ***a piece of bread made him choke***

① **choose**
[tʃuz] *verb*

(a) to pick something which you like best; ***have you chosen what you want to eat?***; ***they chose him as team leader***; ***don't take too long choosing a book to read on vacation***; ***there were several good candidates to choose from***; ***you must give customers plenty of time to choose***

(b) to decide to do one thing when there are several things you could do; ***in the end, they chose to go to the movies*** (NOTE: **choosing - chose** [tʃəuz] **- has chosen** [ˈtʃəuzn])

① **chop**
[tʃɒp]

1 *noun*

piece of meat with a bone attached; ***we had lamb chops for dinner***

2 *verb*

to cut into small pieces; ***he spent the afternoon chopping wood for the fire*** (NOTE: **chopping - chopped**)

① **chop down**
[ˈtʃɒp ˈdaun] *verb*

to cut down a tree, etc.; ***they chopped down hundreds of trees to make way for the freeway***

① **chop off**
[ˈtʃɒp ˈɒf] *verb*

to cut off; ***he chopped off the dead branch***; ***the table was too high for the children, so we chopped 6 inches off the legs***

① **chopsticks**
[ˈtʃɒpstiks] *noun*

pair of small sticks used to eat Asian food or to stir food when cooking; ***he said he didn't know how to use chopsticks and asked for a knife and fork instead***

① **chop up**
[ˈtʃɒp ˈʌp] *verb*

to cut into pieces; ***chop the vegetables up into little pieces***

② **chorus**
[ˈkɔrəs] *noun*

part of a song which is repeated later in the song; ***I'll sing the verses and everyone can join in the chorus*** (NOTE: plural is **choruses**)

① **chose, chosen**
[tʃəuz *or* ˈtʃəuzən]
see CHOOSE

③ **chowder**
[ˈtʃaudər] *noun*

thick soup, usually made with milk and seafood; ***we ordered clam chowder***

① **Christ**
[kraist]

1 *noun*

Jesus Christ, the person on whose life and teachings the Christian religion is based

2 *interjection*

(informal) showing that you are annoyed; ***Christ! it's eight o'clock already and I haven't started cooking dinner***

② **Christian**
[ˈkristʃn]

1 *noun*

person who believes in the teaching of Christ and follows the Christian religion; ***the early Christians were victims of the Roman emperors***

2 *adjective*

referring to the teachings of Jesus Christ; ***there are several Christian churches in the town***

② **Christianity**
[kristiˈæniti] *noun*

religion based on the teaching of Jesus Christ and followed by Christians ever since; ***the course on religious studies covers both Christianity and Islam***

③ **Christian name**
[ˈkristʃn ˈneim] *noun*

a person's first name, the special name given to someone as a child; ***I know his surname's Smith, but what's his Christian name?***

② **Christmas**
[ˈkrisməs] *noun*

Christian festival on December 25th, the birthday of Jesus Christ; ***have you opened your Christmas presents yet?***; ***we're going to Grandpa's for Christmas Day***; ***what did you get for Christmas?*** = what presents were you given?; **Christmas card** = special card sent to friends at Christmas to wish them a happy time; **Christmas stockings** = large colored stockings, which children hang up by their beds or under the Christmas tree, and which are filled with presents by Santa Claus; **Christmas tree** = evergreen tree which is brought into the house at Christmas and decorated with ornaments and lights; **Merry Christmas!** *or* **Happy Christmas!** = way of greeting someone on Christmas Day

② **Christmas Eve**
[ˈkrisməs ˈiv] *noun*

(a) December 24th, the day before Christmas Day; ***the office is closed on Christmas Eve***

(b) the evening of December 24th; ***Christmas Eve party***

④ **chronic**
[ˈkrɒnik] *adjective*

(a) (illness, etc.) which is continual, which comes back often; ***chronic asthma sufferers need to use special drugs***; *compare* ACUTE

(b) always very bad; *we have a chronic shortage of skilled staff*

④ **chuck**
[tʃʌk]
1 *noun*
part of a drill that holds the bit; *he released the chuck and put in a bigger bit*
2 *verb*
(informal) to throw; *chuck me that newspaper, can you?*; *she chucked the book out of the window*

① **chuckle**
['tʃʌkl] *verb*
to give a quiet laugh; *he chuckled when she said she wanted a good steady job*

① **church**
[tʃɜrtʃ] *noun*
building where Christians go to pray; *we usually go to church on Sunday mornings*; *the oldest building in the town is the church*; *the times of the church services are given on the board outside* (NOTE: plural is **churches**)

② **CIA**
['si'aɪ'eɪ]
abbreviation for CENTRAL INTELLIGENCE AGENCY

② **cigarette**
[sɪgə'ret] *noun*
chopped dried tobacco rolled in very thin paper, which you can light and smoke; *a pack of cigarettes*; *he's trying to cut down on the number of cigarettes he smokes*; *the room was full of cigarette smoke*; **cigarette machine** = machine which sells packs of cigarettes when you put the right money in; *do you have any change for the cigarette machine?*

④ **cinema**
['sɪnəmə] *noun*
(a) art of making motion pictures; *he is a well-known cinema critic*
(b) movie theater, a building where you go to watch movies; *we went to the cinema on Friday night*; **what's on at the cinema this week?** = which movie is being shown?

① **circle**
['sɜrkl]
1 *noun*
(a) line forming a round shape; *he drew a circle on the blackboard*
(b) thing forming a round shape; *the children sat in a circle around the teacher*; *the soldiers formed a circle around the prisoner*
(c) group of people or society; *she went to live abroad and lost contact with her old circle of friends*; *he moves in the highest government circles*
(d) row of seats above the ground floor in a theater; *we got tickets for the upper circle*
2 *verb*
to go around in a ring; *big birds were circling in the air above the dead deer*

③ **circuit**
['sɜrkɪt] *noun*
(a) trip around something; *his first circuit of the track was very slow*
(b) path of electricity; *he designed a circuit for a burglar alarm*; **printed circuit board** = card with metal tracks printed on it, which forms a connection when other electronic elements are fitted onto it; **short circuit** = electrical fault where two wires touch or where the electric current passes through another channel; *the fallen electricity cable caused a short circuit that blacked out half the town*

② **circular**
['sɜrkjʊlər]
1 *adjective*
round in shape; *a circular table*
2 *noun*
publicity leaflet; *the restaurant sent a circular around offering a 10% discount*

③ **circulate**
['sɜrkjʊleɪt] *verb*
(a) to send to various people; *they circulated a new list of prices to all their customers*
(b) to move around; *blood circulates around the body*; *waiters circulated around the room carrying trays of drinks*
(c) to go around from person to person; *the rumor quickly circulated through the office*

② **circulation**
[sɜrkjʊ'leɪʃn] *noun*
(a) act of circulating; *the circulation of the new price list to all departments will take several days*; **bills that are in circulation** = bills that have been issued and are in use
(b) movement of blood around the body; *rub your hands together to get the circulation going*; *he has poor circulation*
(c) number of copies of a magazine, newspaper, etc., that are sold; *the new editor hopes to increase the circulation numbers*

③ **circumference**
[sər'kʌmfərəns] *noun*
distance round the outside edge of a circle; *you can calculate the circumference of a circle by multiplying the radius by 2π*

③ **circumstances**
['sɜrkəmstænsɪz] *noun*
(a) way in which something happened; *he described the circumstances leading up to the accident*; *she died in very suspicious circumstances*; **in the circumstances** *or* **under the circumstances** = as this is the case; *under the circumstances, it would probably be wiser to cancel the meeting*
(b) state of your finances; *she's been in difficult circumstances since the death of her husband* (NOTE: usually used in the plural)

① **circus**
['sɜrkəs] *noun*
traveling show, often given under a large tent, with animals and other entertainments; *we went*

to the circus last night; the circus is coming to town next weekend (NOTE: plural is **circuses**)

④ **cite**
[saɪt] *verb*
(a) to quote a reference, a person, etc., as proof; *she cited several passages from his latest book*
(b) to call someone to appear in court; *I was cited for speeding* (NOTE: do not confuse with **sight, site**)

② **citizen**
['sɪtɪzən] *noun*
(a) person who comes from a certain country or has the same right to live there as someone who was born there; *all U.S. citizens have a duty to vote*; *he was born in Germany, but is now a U.S. citizen*; **senior citizen** = person who is 65 or older
(b) person who lives in a certain city; *the citizens of Los Angeles complained about their taxes*

① **city**
['sɪti] *noun*
large town; *walking around the hot city streets can be very tiring*; *which is the largest city in Vermont?*; *traffic is a problem in big cities*; **city center** = the central part of a town; *he has an office in the city center*; **city hall** = main building in a city where the mayor has his office (NOTE: plural is **cities**)

④ **civic**
['sɪvɪk] *adjective*
referring to a city; *we must try to encourage a sense of civic pride*; **civic center** = building with social and sports facilities for a town

② **civil**
['sɪvɪl] *adjective*
(a) belonging to the general public and not to the armed forces; *he left the air force and became a civil airline pilot*; **civil engineer** = person who builds roads, bridges, etc.
(b) referring to ordinary people; *there have been civil disturbances again today*; **civil defense** = defense of a country by civilians; **civil law** = laws relating to people's rights and agreements between individuals (NOTE: the opposite, laws relating to crimes against the law of the land punished by the state, is **criminal law**); **civil rights** = rights of a citizen; *she campaigned for civil rights in the 1960s*; **civil rights movement** = campaign for equal rights for all citizens; **civil war** = situation inside a country where groups of armed people fight against each other or against the government; **the Civil War** = war between the northern and southern states of the U.S.A. from 1861 to 1865
(c) polite; *she wasn't very civil to the police officer*; **please keep a civil tongue in your head** = please be polite

② **civilian**
[sɪ'vɪljən]
1 *adjective*
not in the armed forces; *both the military and civilian personnel will be involved*; *the civilian population was advised to take shelter underground*
2 *noun*
private citizen who is not in the armed forces; *it is certain that civilians will be affected by the war*; *many civilians were killed in the air raids*

② **civilization**
[sɪvɪlaɪ'zeɪʃn] *noun*
society or way of organizing society; *the civilization of Ancient Greece*; *she is studying Chinese art and civilization*

② **civil servant**
['sɪvɪl 'sɜrvənt] *noun*
person who works in a government department; *as a cleaner in a government office, I am considered to be a civil servant*

② **civil service**
[sɪvɪl 'sɜrvɪs] *noun*
the organization and its staff who administer a country; *you have to pass an examination to get a job in the civil service or to get a civil service job*

② **claim**
[kleɪm]
1 *noun*
(a) asking for money; *his claim for a pay increase was turned down*; **wage claim** = asking for an increase in wages
(b) statement; *his claim that the automobile belonged to him was correct*
(c) demand for money against an insurance policy; *after the floods, insurance companies received hundreds of claims*; **to put in or to submit a claim** = to ask the insurance company officially to pay damages; *to put in a claim for repairs to the car*; *she submitted a claim for $375,000 damages against the driver of the other car*
2 *verb*
(a) to demand as a right; *steelworkers have claimed huge pay raises*; *if they charged you too much you must claim a refund*
(b) to state, but without any proof; *he claims he never received the letter*; *she claims that the automobile belongs to her*
(c) to say you own something that has been left behind or lost; *no one has claimed the umbrella found in my office, so I am going to keep it*

④ **claimant**
['kleɪmənt] *noun*
person who claims; *the insurance company is agreeing to pay the claimants*; *the court decided in favor of the claimant*

② **clam**
[klæm] *noun*
edible sea animal, living in a double shell; *clam chowder contains milk and clams*

② **clap**
[klæp] *verb*
to beat your hands together to show you are pleased; *at the end of her speech the audience stood up and clapped* (NOTE: **clapping - clapped**)

④ **clarify**
['klærɪfaɪ] *verb*
to make clear; *we will have to clarify the situation before taking any further decisions*

③ **clash**
[klæʃ]
1 *noun*
(a) loud noise of metal things hitting each other; *she heard a loud clash like two saucepans being banged together*
(b) battle, argument; *there were clashes outside the stadium between supporters of the two teams*; *we are getting reports of clashes between government forces and guerrillas* (NOTE: plural is **clashes**)
2 *verb*
(a) to bang together making a loud noise; *he clashed the two trash can lids together*
(b) to argue violently; *she clashed with her mother about wearing a ring in her nose*; *the opposition deputies clashed with the government*
(c) to fight; *rioting fans clashed with the police*
(d) *(of colors)* to shock when put side by side; *that bright pink necktie clashes with your green shirt*

① **class**
[klæs] *noun*
(a) group of people who go to school or college together; *there are 30 children in my son's class*
(b) group of people who were at the same school or college at the same time in the past; *she's organizing a dinner for the class of '76*
(c) lesson; **evening classes** = lessons given in the evening (usually to adults); *I am going to evening classes to learn Portuguese*; *we have two math classes a week*
(d) people of the same group in society; *people from different social classes mixed at the reception*; **working class** = people who mainly work with their hands; **middle class** = people who have taken exams for their jobs, such as doctors, teachers, etc., or people in business; also some farmers and skilled workers
(e) certain level of quality; *always buy the best class of product*; *these peaches are Class 1*; **first-class** = very good; *he is a first-class tennis player*; **second-class** = not as good as first class
(f) quality of seats or service on a plane, train, etc.; **first class** = best quality (and most expensive); *if you travel first class, you get free drinks*; **business class** = less expensive than first class; **economy class** *or* **tourist class** = cheapest; *they are staying in a first-class hotel*; *first-class passengers get free drinks with their meal*; *the tourist-class fare is much less than the first-class*; *I travel economy class because it is cheaper* (NOTE: plural is **classes**)

③ **classic**
['klæsɪk]
1 *noun*
(a) great book, play, piece of music, etc.; *"the Maltese Falcon" is a Hollywood classic*; *we have to study several classics of English literature for our course*
(b) **Classics** = study of the languages, literature, philosophy, etc., of Ancient Greece and Rome; *she studied Classics at Harvard*; *he is majoring in Classics*
2 *adjective*
(a) (style) which is elegant and traditional; *the classic little black dress is always in fashion*; *the style of the store is classic, simple and elegant*
(b) *(style of architecture)* which is based on that of Greek or Roman architecture; *this is built in classic Greek style*
(c) typical; *he couldn't decide if he wanted white or wheat bread - it was a classic example of his inability to make decisions*

③ **classical**
['klæsɪkl] *adjective*
(a) which is elegant and based on the style of Greek or Roman architecture, literature, etc.; *a classical eighteenth-century villa*
(b) referring to Ancient Greece and Rome; *classical Greek literature*
(c) referring to traditional, serious music; *a concert of classical music*

③ **classification**
[klæsɪfɪ'keɪʃn] *noun*
way of arranging things into categories; *the classification of social classes into various categories*; *the hotel has received three stars under the new classification system*

③ **classified**
['klæsɪfaɪd] *adjective*
(a) which has been put into a category; **classified ads** *or* **classified advertisements** = newspaper advertisements which are listed under special headings, such as "jobs wanted" or "household goods for sale"; *look in the classified ads if you want a cheap stove*; **classified directory** = directory of business addresses listed under various headings, such as "hairdressers", "bookstores", etc.; *look for his address under "builders" in the classified directory*
(b) secret; **classified documents** *or* **classified information** = documents or information marked "secret"; *he left a box of classified documents in the back of his car*; *this is classified information, and only a few people can see it*

③ **classify**
['klæsɪfaɪ] *verb*
to arrange things into groups; *the hotels are classified according to a star system*; *now that*

these plants have been classified, please write a label for each one

① **classroom**
['klæsrum] *noun*
room in a school where children are taught; *when the teacher came into the classroom all the children were shouting and throwing books*

③ **clause**
[klɔz] *noun*
(a) paragraph in a treaty or legal document; *according to clause six, payments will not be due until next year*
(b) part of a sentence; *the sentence has two clauses, separated by the conjunction "and"*; **main clause** = main part of a sentence; **subordinate clause** = clause that depends on the main clause

① **claw**
[klɔ] *noun*
nail on the foot of an animal or bird; *our cat scratches the furniture with its claws*

① **clay**
[kleɪ] *noun*
stiff soil used for making bricks or china; *he put a lump of clay onto his wheel and started to make a pot*

① **clean**
[klin]
1 *adjective*
(a) not dirty; *wipe your glasses with a clean handkerchief*; *the bedrooms must be clean before the guests arrive*; *tell the waitress these cups aren't clean*; *the girl forgot to put clean towels in the bathroom*; *(informal)* **to come clean** = to confess to a crime, etc.; *he came clean and owned up to stealing the watch*
(b) with no record of offenses; *candidates should have a clean record*
(c) fair, according to the rules; *we played a good clean of game of football* (NOTE: **cleaner - cleanest**)
2 *verb*
to make clean, by taking away dirt; *remember to clean your ears when bathing*; *she was cleaning the kitchen when the telephone rang*; *he cleans his automobile every Saturday morning*
3 *adverb*
(informal) completely; *I clean forgot to send the letter*
4 *noun*
(informal) action of cleaning; *the restaurant kitchen needs a good clean*

① **cleaner**
['klinər] *noun*
(a) machine that removes dirt; **vacuum cleaner** = machine that sucks up dirt from floors
(b) substance that removes dirt; *this new oven cleaner doesn't get rid of the worst stains*; *can you buy another bottle of window cleaner?*
(c) person who cleans (a house, office, etc.); *the cleaners didn't empty my waste basket*

③ **cleaner's**
['klinərz] *noun*
(a) shop where you take clothes to be cleaned; *when I got my suit back from the cleaner's there was a button missing*
(b) *(slang)* **to take someone to the cleaner's** = to take all someone's money; *I played cards last night and got taken to the cleaner's*

② **clean up**
['klin 'ʌp] *verb*
(a) to make everything clean and tidy after a party, etc.; *it took us three hours to clean up after her birthday party*
(b) to remove corruption; *the police are going to have a hard job cleaning up this town*
(c) *(informal)* to make a lot of money; *David cleaned up at the races*

③ **cleanup**
['klinʌp] *noun*
making clean; *after the flooding had stopped, the cleanup took weeks*

② **clear**
[klɪər]
1 *adjective*
(a) with nothing in the way; *you can cross the road - it's clear now*; *from the window, she had a clear view of the street*
(b) with no clouds, mist, etc.; *a clear blue sky*; *on a clear day, you can see the other side of the lake*
(c) easily understood; *she made it clear that she wanted us to go*; *the instructions on the computer screen are not very clear*; *will you give me a clear answer - yes or no?*
(d) which is not covered and which you can easily see through; *a clear glass window* (NOTE: **clearer - clearest**)
2 *verb*
(a) to remove something which is in the way; *snowploughs cleared the highway of snow or cleared the snow from the highway*; *we'll get a plumber to clear the blocked pipe in the bathroom*; **to clear the table** = to take away knives, forks, plates, etc., after a meal
(b) *(of a check)* to pass through the banking system, so that the money is transferred from one account to another; *the check took ten days to clear*
(c) to sell cheaply in order to get rid of stock; *"demonstration models to clear"*; *if we reduce the price we'll clear the stock in no time*
(d) *(of a court)* to find that someone is not guilty; *the court cleared him of all the charges*
(e) to go over the top of something without touching it; *she cleared 6 feet in the high jump*
3 *adverb*
(a) not close; *stand clear of the doors, please*; *I would advise you to stay clear of that dog*
(b) completely, all the way; *we walked clear across town*

① **clearing**
['klɪərɪŋ] *noun*
(a) act of removing things that are in the way;

the clearing of the wreckage from the crash will take several days

(b) area in a wood where the trees have been cut down; *they set up camp in a clearing in the middle of the forest*

① **clearly**
['klɪərli] *adverb*
(a) in a way which is easily understood or heard; *he didn't speak clearly, and I couldn't catch the address he gave*
(b) obviously; *he clearly didn't like being told he was too fat*

② **clear up**
['klɪər ʌp] *verb*
(a) to solve a problem; *in the end, we cleared up the mystery of the missing computer disk*
(b) to get better; *I hope the weather clears up because we're going on vacation tomorrow; he has been taking aspirins, but his cold still hasn't cleared up*

② **clench**
[klentʃ] *verb*
to close tightly; *he clenched his fists, ready for a fight*

② **clerk**
klɜrk] *noun*
person who works in an office; *a ticket clerk; a bank clerk*

② **clever**
['klevər] *adjective*
intelligent, able to learn quickly; *he's the cleverest person in the family; she's very clever with money; he is very clever at spotting bargains; he's clever with his hands* = he's good at making things with his hands (NOTE: **cleverer - cleverest**)

③ **cleverly**
['klevərli] *adverb*
in a clever way; *the dog had cleverly figured out how to open the door*

③ **click**
[klɪk]
1 *noun*
short sharp sound; *she heard a click and saw the door start to open*
2 *verb*
(a) to make a short sharp sound; *the cameras clicked as she came out of the church; he clicked his fingers to attract the waiter's attention*
(b) *(informal)* to become clear and easily understood; **suddenly everything clicked** = suddenly it all became clear
(c) to press the button on a mouse quickly to start a computer function; *the menu is displayed by clicking on the menu bar at the top of the screen; click twice on the mouse to start the program*

④ **client**
['klaɪənt] *noun*
person who you give a service to; *a personal trainer who visits his clients in their own*

homes; how often do your salesmen visit their major clients?

② **cliff**
[klɪf] *noun*
steep or vertical face of rocks, usually by the sea; *he went for a walk along the top of the cliffs; these white cliffs are formed of chalk; huge heads of presidents are cut into the cliff face*

① **climate**
['klaɪmət] *noun*
(a) general weather conditions in a certain place; *the climate in the south of the country is generally milder than in the north; the climate in the Midwest is hot in the summer and cold in the winter*
(b) general atmosphere; *the current economic climate makes an interest rate rise very likely; she wants to change jobs - she thinks she could do with a change of climate*

④ **climax**
['klaɪmæks] *noun*
most important and exciting point; *the celebrations reached their climax with a parade down Market Street; the movie was reaching its climax when the electricity failed* (NOTE: plural is **climaxes**)

① **climb**
[klaɪm]
1 *noun*
going up; *it's a steep climb to the top of the hill*
2 *verb*
(a) to go up (or down) using arms and legs; *the cat climbed up the apple tree; the burglars climbed over the wall; he escaped by climbing out of the window*
(b) to go up; *the road climbs up to 3,000 feet above sea level*
(c) to go up mountains as a sport; *when you have climbed Everest, there is no higher mountain left to climb; he goes climbing every weekend*

① **climb down**
['klaɪm 'daʊn] *verb*
to come down a mountain, a ladder, etc.; *he climbed down from the roof; the firemen helped the hotel guests climb down the ladder*

② **climber**
['klaɪmər] *noun*
person who climbs mountains; *the climbers roped themselves together and set off up the slope*

③ **clinch**
[klɪntʃ]
1 *noun*
(a) position where two people hold each other tightly; *he found his girlfriend in a clinch with another man*
(b) *(in boxing)* position where both boxers hold on to each other; *the referee tried to separate the two boxers who were in a clinch* (NOTE: plural is **clinches**)

2 *verb*
to settle (a deal); *he offered an extra 5% to clinch the deal*

③ **cling**
[klɪŋ] *verb*
to cling (on)to something = to hold tight; *she survived by clinging onto a piece of wood*; *he clung tightly to his mother's arm* (NOTE: clinging - clung [klʌŋ])

② **clinic**
['klɪnɪk] *noun*
specialized medical center or hospital; *a family planning clinic*; *she had treatment in a private clinic in Switzerland*

④ **clinical**
['klɪnɪkl] *adjective*
(a) medical; **clinical medicine** = treatment of patients in a hospital or a doctor's office (as opposed to an operating room); *I'm more interested in clinical medicine than in surgery*
(b) to look at things in a clinical way = to look at something in a detached way, without any prejudices

① **clip**
[klɪp]
1 *noun*
(a) paper clip = piece of bent wire for attaching papers, etc., together; *he attached the check to the letter with a paper clip*
(b) piece of jewelry which clips onto your clothes; *he wore a gold clip on his necktie*; *she has a diamond clip on her dress*
(c) (*informal*) short piece of film; *here is a clip of the president getting into the car*
(d) (*informal*) a quick, sharp blow; *a clip on the jaw*
2 *verb*
(a) to attach things together with a clip; *she clipped the invoice and the check together and put them in an envelope*; *these earrings are made to clip onto your ears*
(b) to cut with scissors; *the dog has its fur clipped once a month*; *he carefully clipped the article out of the newspaper*
(c) to hit slightly; *the wing of the plane clipped the top of the tree before it crashed* (NOTE: clipping - clipped)

① **clock**
[klɒk]
1 *noun*
large instrument which shows the time; *the station clock is always right*; *your clock is 5 minutes slow*; *the office clock is fast*; *the clock has stopped - it needs winding up*; **alarm clock** = clock which can be set to ring a bell at a certain time to wake you up; *see also* GRANDFATHER, O'CLOCK (NOTE: a small instrument for showing the time, which you wear, is a **watch**)
2 *verb*
to clock in = to arrive for work and register by putting a card into a timing machine; **to clock out** = to leave work and register by putting a card into a timing machine

③ **clockwise**
['klɒkwaɪz] *adjective & adverb*
in the same direction as the hands of a clock; *turn the lid clockwise to tighten it* (NOTE: the opposite is **counterclockwise**)

① **close**
1 [kləʊs] *adjective*
(a) very near, just next to something; *our office is close to a freeway exit*; *this is the closest I've ever been to a movie star!*
(b) where only a few votes separate the winner from the other candidates; *the election was very close*; *it was a close contest*
(c) hot, with no air; *it's very close in here, can someone open a window?*
2 [kləʊs] *adverb*
very near; *keep close by me if you don't want to get lost*; *go further away - you're getting too close*; *they stood so close (together) that she felt his breath on her cheek*; *the sound came closer and closer* (NOTE: closer - closest)
3 [kləʊz] *verb*
(a) to shut; *would you mind closing the window, there's a draft?*; *he closed his book and turned on the TV*
(b) to make something come to an end; *she closed her letter by saying she was coming to see us*; **to close a meeting** = to end a meeting
(c) to come to an end; *the meeting closed with a vote of thanks*
(d) to close an account = to take all the money out of a bank account and stop the account; *he closed his checking account*
4 [kləʊz] *noun*
end, final part; *the century was drawing to a close*

① **closed**
[kləʊzd] *adjective*
shut; *the store is closed on Sundays*; *the office will be closed for the Christmas vacation*; *there was a "closed" sign hanging in the window*

③ **close down**
['kləʊz 'daʊn] *verb*
to shut a business; *the store closed down last week*; *they're going to close down the factory because they haven't enough work*

④ **closely**
['kləʊsli] *adverb*
(a) with a lot of attention; *she studied the timetable very closely*
(b) very close together; *the photographers moved in closely around the car*; *the prisoners were closely guarded by armed soldiers*

③ **close on**
['kləʊz 'ɒn] *verb*
(a) to close on someone = to come closer to someone, to catch someone up; *the horse in second place was closing on the leader*
(b) to close on a deal = to complete a deal; *they closed on their new house last Friday*

② **closet**
['klɒzɪt]
1 *noun*
small room or space in a wall for storing things; *the sheets are in the linen closet*
2 *adjective*
secret; *he's been a closet artist for years*

④ **close-up**
['kləʊsʌp] *noun*
photograph taken very close to the subject; *flowers are ideal subjects for close-up photography*; *he has a framed close-up of his daughter on his desk*; *using a zoom lens can give you close-ups of lions from quite a long way away*

① **cloth**
[klɒθ] *noun*
(a) material; *do you have a cloth of a darker blue than this?*; *this cloth is of a very high quality*
(b) piece of material for cleaning; *he wiped up the spill with a damp cloth*
(c) piece of material that you put on a table to cover it; *the waiter spread a white cloth over the table*; *she spilled some red wine on the cloth*

① **clothes**
[kləʊðz] *noun*
(a) things (such as shirts, pants, dresses, etc.) which you wear to cover your body and keep you warm; *he walked down the street with no clothes on or without any clothes on*; *the doctor asked him to take his clothes off*; *the children haven't had any new clothes for years*
(b) **clothes horse** = frame for hanging wet clothes on to dry; **clothes rack** = rack for hanging clothes on in a store

① **clothesline**
['kləʊðzlaɪn] *noun*
rope for hanging wet clothes on to dry

② **clothespin**
['kləʊðzpɪn] *noun*
little wooden clip, used to attach wet clothes to a washing line

① **clothing**
['kləʊðɪŋ] *noun*
clothes; *take plenty of warm clothing on your trip to the mountains*; *an important clothing manufacturer* (NOTE: no plural: **some clothing**; **a piece of clothing**)

① **cloud**
[klaʊd] *noun*
(a) mass of white or gray mist floating in the air; *do you think it's going to rain? - yes, look at those gray clouds*; *the plane was flying above the clouds*
(b) (*informal*) **on cloud nine** = very happy; *they were on cloud nine when she won the lottery*; **under a cloud** = suspected of having done something wrong; *he was under a cloud for some time after the thefts were discovered*; *see also* LINING

(c) similar mass of smoke; *clouds of smoke poured out of the burning building*

① **cloudy**
['klaʊdi] *adjective*
(a) with clouds; *the weather was cloudy in the morning, but cleared up in the afternoon*; *when it's very cloudy it isn't easy to take good photographs*
(b) not clear, not transparent; *this beer is cloudy*; *the water in the tank turned cloudy and the fish died* (NOTE: **cloudier - cloudiest**)

② **club**
[klʌb]
1 *noun*
(a) group of people who have the same interest or form a team; *she's a member of a photography club*; *I'm joining a tennis club*
(b) place where a club meets; *the sports club is near the river*; *he goes to the golf club every Friday*
(c) **clubs** = one of the black suits in a pack of cards, shaped like a leaf with three parts; *he had the five of clubs in his hand* (NOTE: the other black suit is **spades**; **hearts** and **diamonds** are the red suits)
(d) large heavy stick; *she was knocked to the ground by a blow from a club*; **a golf club** = stick for playing golf (NOTE: **a golf club** can either mean the place where you play golf, or the stick used to hit the ball)
2 *verb*
to hit with a club; *she was clubbed to the ground* (NOTE: **clubbing - clubbed**)

① **clubhouse**
['klʌbhaʊs] *noun*
building in which members of club meet; *it started to rain, so the golfers went quickly back to the clubhouse*

④ **club sandwich**
['klʌb 'sændwɪtʃ] *noun*
sandwich made of three slices of bread, with chicken or other meat, lettuce, tomato and mayonnaise

③ **clue**
[klu] *noun*
information that helps you solve a mystery or puzzle; *the detective had missed a vital clue*; **I don't have a clue** = I don't know at all; *the police still don't have a clue who did it*

③ **clumsy**
['klʌmzi] *adjective*
who frequently breaks things or knocks things over; *don't let Ben set the table - he's so clumsy, he's bound to break something* (NOTE: **clumsier - clumsiest**)

③ **clung**
[klʌŋ] *verb*
see CLING

③ **cluster**
['klʌstər]
1 *noun*

group of objects close together; *he photographed a cluster of stars*

2 *verb*

to cluster (together) = to form a group; *they clustered around the bulletin board to read their exam results*

② **clutch**
[klʌtʃ]

1 *noun*

(a) holding tight; *she felt the clutch of his fingers on her sleeve*; **in the clutches of** = under the control of; *if the company were to get into their clutches it would be a disaster*

(b) mechanism for changing gear in an automobile; *the car has just had a new clutch fitted*; **clutch pedal** = pedal that operates the clutch and allows the driver to shift gears; **to let in the clutch** = to make the clutch engage the gears; *let the clutch in slowly, or you'll stall the car* (NOTE: plural is **clutches**)

2 *verb*

to grab hold of; *she clutched my arm as we stood on the edge of the cliff*

③ **cm**
['sentɪmitərz]

see CENTIMETER; *yesterday we had 3 cm of rain; 25 cm of snow had fallen during the night*

③ **co.**
[kəʊ or 'kʌmpəni]

abbreviation for COMPANY; *J. Smith & Co.*

③ **c/o**
['siː'əʊ]

(in addresses) = CARE OF; *Jane Smith, c/o Mr. & Mrs. Jonas, 1450 North St*

② **coach**
[kəʊtʃ]

1 *noun*

(a) large bus; *there's a coach from the airport to the city center*

(b) railroad passenger car; *the seats in this rail coach are dirty*

(c) category of seat on a plane that is cheaper than first class; *we went coach to Washington*

(d) person who trains tennis players, etc.; *the coach told them that they needed to spend more time practicing; he's a professional football coach* (NOTE: plural is **coaches**)

2 *verb*

(a) to train tennis players, football players, etc.; *she was coached by a runner who won a gold medal in the Mexico Olympics*

(b) to give private lessons to someone; *all the actors had to be coached separately*

② **coal**
[kəʊl]

noun

(a) black rock which is dug out of the ground and which you can burn to make heat; **coal-fired power station** = electric power station that burns coal (NOTE: no plural in this meaning: **some coal; a piece of coal** *or* **a lump of coal**)

(b) a lump of this substance; *put some more coals on the fire*

④ **coalition**
[kəʊə'lɪʃn] *noun*

combination of several political parties to form a government; *they formed a coalition government*

③ **coarse**
[kɔrs] *adjective*

(a) not fine, not small; *coarse grains of sand; a coarse net*

(b) rough, not polite; *he gave a coarse laugh; he could hear her coarse voice booming down the corridor*

(c) rude (joke); *he made a coarse gesture and walked out; don't make any coarse remarks in front of my mother* (NOTE: **coarser - coarsest;** do not confuse with **course**)

① **coast**
[kəʊst] *noun*

land by the sea; *after ten weeks at sea, Columbus saw the coast of America; the south coast is the warmest part of the country; let's drive down to the coast this weekend;* **from coast to coast** = from the sea on one side of a country to the sea on the other side; *he crossed the U.S.A. from coast to coast*

② **coastline**
['kəʊstlaɪn] *noun*

edge of land along a coast; *the coastline here is very rocky*

① **coat**
[kəʊt]

1 *noun*

(a) piece of clothing that you wear on top of other clothes when you go outside; *you'll need to put your winter coat on - it's just started to snow; she was wearing a black fur coat*

(b) **coat of paint** = layer of paint covering something; *that window frame needs a coat of paint;* **we gave the door two coats of paint** = we painted the door twice

2 *verb*

to cover with a layer of something; *we coated the metal disk with silver*

④ **cobbler**
['kɒblər] *noun*

large fruit pie; *my mom is making an apple cobbler for dessert*

① **cobweb**
['kɒbweb] *noun*

net made by a spider to catch insects; *the bedroom hadn't been cleaned and everything was covered with cobwebs*

① **Coca-Cola**
['kəʊkə 'kəʊlə] *noun*

trademark for a popular fizzy soft drink; *two Coca-Colas, please, and a vanilla milkshake* (NOTE: often just called **coke: two cokes, please**)

③ **cockroach**
['kɒkrəʊtʃ] *noun*

big black or brown insect, a common household pest; *in hot damp climates, cockroaches are often found in kitchens* (NOTE: also called a **roach**; plural is **cockroaches**)

① **cocktail**
['kɒkteɪl] *noun*
(a) mixed alcoholic drink; *a Bloody Mary is a cocktail of vodka with tomato juice*; **cocktail lounge** = bar in a hotel or club; **cocktail party** = party where drinks and snacks are served, but not a full meal; **cocktail snacks** = little snacks eaten with drinks
(b) mixture of various things; *she died after taking a cocktail of drugs*; **fruit cocktail** = mixture of little pieces of fruit

① **cocoa**
['kəʊkəʊ] *noun*
(a) brown chocolate powder, used for making a drink; *there's a tin of cocoa on the top shelf*
(b) drink made with cocoa powder and hot water or milk; *he always has a cup of cocoa before going to bed*

① **coconut**
['kəʊkənʌt] *noun*
(a) large nut from a type of palm tree
(b) white flesh from a coconut; *a coconut cake; I don't like cookies with coconut in them* (NOTE: no plural in this meaning)

② **code**
[kəʊd] *noun*
(a) set of laws, rules of behavior; *the hotel has a strict dress code, and people wearing jeans are not allowed in*; **code of practice** = general rules for a group of people, such as lawyers
(b) secret words or system agreed in advance for sending messages; *we're trying to break the enemy's code; he sent the message in code*; **code word** = secret word that allows you to do something
(c) system of numbers or letters that mean something; *the code for San Francisco's airport is SFO*; **area code** = numbers that indicate an area when telephoning; **bar code** = system of lines printed on a product that can be read by a computer to give a reference number or price; **international dialing code** = numbers that indicate a country when telephoning; *what's the international dialing code for Israel?*; *see also* ZIP CODE

② **code of conduct**
['kəʊd əv 'kɒndʌkt] *noun*
informal (sometimes written) rules by which a group of people work

④ **co-ed**
['kəʊ'ed] *noun*
female college student

① **coffee**
['kɒfi] *noun*
(a) bitter drink made from the seeds of a tropical plant; *would you like a cup of coffee?; I always take sugar with my coffee; the doctor told me to avoid tea and coffee*; **black coffee** = coffee without milk or cream in it; **instant coffee** = drink that you make by pouring hot water onto a

special coffee powder; **coffee machine** = automatic machine that gives a cup of coffee or other drink when you put in a coin and press a button; **coffee spoon** = very small spoon, used with small cups of coffee
(b) a cup of coffee; *I'd like a coffee with cream, please; three coffees and two teas, please*
(c) pale brown color; *we have a coffee-colored carpet in our sitting room* (NOTE: usually no plural; **coffees** means **cups of coffee**)

③ **coffee shop**
['kɒfi 'ʃɒp] *noun*
small restaurant (often in a hotel) serving tea, coffee and snacks; *it will be quicker to have lunch in the coffee shop than in the restaurant*

② **coffin**
['kɒfin] *noun*
casket, a long wooden box in which a dead person is buried; *they watched in silence as the coffin was lowered into the ground*

④ **coherent**
[kəʊ'hɪərənt] *adjective*
clear and logical (ideas, story, etc.); *she gave a very coherent description of what had happened*

③ **coil**
[kɔɪl]
1 *noun*
one ring in something twisted round and round; *they surrounded the machine part with coils of wire*
2 *verb*
to twist round something to form a ring; *the sailors coiled the ropes on the deck*

① **coin**
[kɔɪn]
1 *noun*
piece of metal money; *I found a coin on the street; he hid the gold coins under his bed; this machine only takes certain coins*
2 *verb*
to invent a new word or phrase; *they coined the phrase "surfing the net" to mean searching for information on the Internet; (informal)* **to coin a phrase** = to emphasize that you are saying something which everyone says; *"when it rains it pours" - to coin a phrase*

④ **coincide**
[kəʊɪn'saɪd] *verb*
to coincide with something = to happen by chance at the same time as something else; *this year, my exams don't coincide with my birthday; do our trips to Alaska coincide? - if they do, we can meet while we're both there*

③ **coincidence**
[kəʊ'ɪnsɪdəns] *noun*
two things happening at the same time by chance; *the two of us happening to be at the same party was pure coincidence; by coincidence, she was at the drugstore too; what a coincidence, I went to that school too!*

② **coke**

[kəʊk] *noun*

(a) fuel processed from coal, which produces a very strong heat; *the steel is produced in coke ovens* (NOTE: no plural in this meaning)

(b) *(informal)* Coca-Cola, trademark for a type of fizzy soft drink; a glass of this drink; *he drinks nothing but coke; three cokes and a beer, please* (NOTE: plural is **cokes**)

④ **cola**

[ˈkəʊlə] *noun*

fizzy sweet drink made from the seeds of a tropical tree; *the kids would like two colas please*

① **cold**

[kəʊld]

1 *adjective*

(a) with a low temperature; not hot or not heated; *they say that cold showers are good for you; the weather turned colder after Christmas; it's too cold to go for a walk; if you're hot, have a glass of cold water; start eating, or your soup will get cold; he had a plate of cold beef and salad; put your slippers on if your feet are cold; (informal)* **to give someone the cold shoulder** = not to give someone a friendly welcome; **to get cold feet** = to begin to feel afraid that a plan is too risky; *we wanted to buy an old house and start a bed and breakfast, but my husband got cold feet*

(b) not friendly; *he got a very cold reception from the rest of the staff; she gave him a cold nod* (NOTE: **colder - coldest**)

2 *noun*

(a) illness, when you sneeze and cough; *he caught a cold by standing in the rain at a football game; my sister's in bed with a cold; don't come near me - I've got a cold*

(b) cold temperature (outdoors); *he got sick from standing in the cold waiting for a bus; houseplants can't stand the cold;* **to be left out in the cold** = not to be part of a group anymore

③ **coldly**

[ˈkəʊldli] *adverb*

in an unfriendly way; *she greeted him coldly*

④ **cole slaw**

[ˈkəʊl ˈslɔ] *noun*

salad made from raw white cabbage and mayonnaise

③ **collapse**

[kəˈlæps]

1 *noun*

(a) sudden fall; *the collapse of the old wall buried two workmen*

(b) sudden fall in price; *the collapse of the dollar on the foreign exchange markets*

(c) sudden failure of a company; *investors lost thousands of dollars in the collapse of the bank*

2 *verb*

(a) to fall down suddenly; *the roof collapsed under the weight of the snow*

(b) to fail suddenly; *the company collapsed with $35,000 in debts*

① **collar**

[ˈkɒlər]

1 *noun*

(a) part of a shirt, coat, dress, etc., that goes around your neck; *I can't do up the top button on my shirt - the collar's too tight; she turned up her coat collar because the wind was cold; he has a winter coat with a fur collar;* **to get hot under the collar** = to get angry or worried about something

(b) leather ring round the neck of a dog or cat; *the cat has a collar with an ID tag*

2 *verb*

to catch hold of someone; *I managed to collar him as he was leaving the hotel*

④ **colleague**

[ˈkɒliɡ] *noun*

person who works in the same company, office, school, etc. as you; *his colleagues gave him a present when he got married; I know Jane Gray - she was a colleague of mine at my last job*

① **collect**

[kəˈlekt]

1 *verb*

(a) to fetch something or bring things together; *your coat is ready for you to collect from the cleaner's; the mail is collected from the mailbox twice a day; I must collect the children from school*

(b) to buy things or bring things together as a hobby; *he collects stamps and old coins*

(c) to gather money for charity; *they're collecting for the Salvation Army*

(d) to come together; *a crowd collected at the scene of the accident*

2 *adverb*

to call collect = to ask the person being phoned to pay for the call; *if you don't have any money you can always try calling collect*

① **collection**

[kəˈlekʃən] *noun*

(a) group of things brought together as a hobby; *he allowed me to see his stamp collection; the museum has a large collection of Italian paintings*

(b) money that has been gathered; *we're taking a collection for the Salvation Army*

(c) action of bringing things together; **debt collection** = collecting money that is owed

(d) fetching of goods; *your order is in the warehouse awaiting collection*

(e) taking of letters from a mailbox or post office for dispatch; *there are six collections a day from the mailbox on the corner of the block; the last collection is at 6 P.M.*

④ **collective**

[kəˈlektɪv]

1 *adjective*

done together; *they had a meeting and soon reached a collective decision*; **collective bargaining** = wage negotiations between management and unions

2 *noun*

business run by a group of workers; *the owner of the garage sold out and the staff took it over as a workers' collective*

① **college**
['kɒlɪdʒ] *noun*

(a) place of education that is entered after high school and grants degrees; *Peter plans to go to college after he has graduated from high school*

(b) one of the separate parts into which some universities are divided; *she graduated from the College of Business Administration*

③ **collide**
[kə'laɪd] *verb*

to collide with something = to bump into something; *he lost control of the automobile and collided with a bus*

② **collision**
[kə'lɪʒən] *noun*

action of bumping into something; *two people were injured in the collision*; *a collision between a truck and a bus closed the main road for some time*

① **Colombia**
[kə'lʌmbiə] *noun*

country in central South America (NOTE: capital: **Bogotá**; people: **Colombians**; language: **Spanish**; currency: **Colombian peso**)

② **Colombian**
[kə'lʌmbiən]

1 *adjective*

referring to Colombia

2 *noun*

person from Colombia

③ **colon**
['kəʊlən] *noun*

printing sign (:); *use a colon before starting a list*

③ **colonel**
['kɜːnl] *noun*

officer in the army, a rank above lieutenant-colonel; *he married the colonel's daughter*; *is Colonel Davis in?* (NOTE: used as a title before a surname: **Colonel Davis**; often shortened to **Col.: Col. Davis**)

③ **colonial**
[kə'ləʊniəl] *adjective*

referring to a colony; *Britain was once an important colonial power*; *the colonial status of Hong Kong ended in 1997*

② **colonize**
['kɒlənaɪz] *verb*

to take possession of an area or country and rule it as a colony; *the government was accused of trying to colonize the region around the South Pole*

② **colony**
['kɒləni] *noun*

(a) territory ruled by another country; people who live in this territory; *Roman colonies were established in North Africa and along the shores of the Black Sea*; *the former French colonies in Africa are now all independent countries*

(b) group of animals or human beings living together; *a colony of ants*; *an artists' colony* (NOTE: plural is **colonies**)

① **color**
['kʌlər]

1 *noun*

(a) shade that an object has in light (red, blue, yellow, etc.); *what color is your bathroom?*; *I don't like the color of his shirt*; *his socks are the same color as his shirt*

(b) not black or white; *the book has pages of color pictures*

(c) shade of a person's skin; *people must not be discriminated against on grounds of sex, religion or color*; **color bar** = using the color of someone's skin as an obstacle to something

(d) local color = amusing or unusual details that go with a certain place; *elephants working in the forests lend some local color to the scene*

(e) with flying colors = with great success; *she passed her test with flying colors*

2 *verb*

to add color to something; *the children were given felt pens and told to color the trees green and the earth brown*

① **color-blind**
['kʌlər'blaɪnd] *adjective*

not able to tell the difference between certain colors, such as red and green; *he can't become a pilot because he's color-blind*

① **colored**
['kʌlərd] *adjective*

(a) in color; *a colored postcard*; *a book with colored illustrations*

(b) *(offensive)* with a skin that is not white; *colored children make up over 90% of this class*

② **colorfast**
['kʌlərfæst] *adjective*

(yarn, cloth, etc.) with colors which do not run when washed; *this shirt is colorfast, so you can wash it in the washing machine*

① **colorful**
['kʌlərfəl] *adjective*

(a) with bright colors; *I'm trying to create a bed of flowers that will remain colorful all year round*; *she tied a colorful silk scarf around her hair*

(b) full of excitement and adventure; *she lived a colorful existence as a dancer in an Egyptian club*; *a colorful account of life in Vienna before World War I*

② **column**
['kɒləm] *noun*
(a) tall pillar; *there is a row of huge columns at the entrance to the museum*; *these are Roman columns*
(b) thing that is tall and thin; *a thin column of smoke rose from the bonfire*; **control column** = handle for steering an aircraft; **steering column** = the pillar that holds a steering wheel in a car, bus, etc.
(c) line of people, one after the other; *a column of prisoners came into the camp*; *columns of refugees crossed the border*
(d) *(in the army)* line of soldiers, tanks, etc., moving forward; *two columns of soldiers advanced toward the enemy positions*; *a column of tanks entered the town*
(e) thin block of printing going down a page; *his article ran to three columns on the first page of the paper*; *"continued on page 7, column 4"*
(f) series of numbers, one under the other; *to add up a column of figures*; *put the total at the bottom of the column*
(g) regular article in a newspaper; *she writes a gardening column for the local newspaper*; *regular readers of this column will know about my problems with drains*; **gossip column** = regular article about famous people and their private lives

③ **columnist**
['kɒləmɪst] *noun*
journalist who writes a regular column for a paper; *our regular columnist is on vacation, so the editor had to write the science feature this week*; **gossip columnist** = person who writes a gossip column

① **comb**
[kəum]
1 *noun*
instrument with long teeth used to make your hair smooth; *her hair is in such a mess that you can't get a comb through it*
2 *verb*
(a) to smooth your hair with a comb; *she was combing her hair in front of the mirror* verb
(b) to search; *police combed the woods for clues*

② **combat**
['kɒmbæt]
1 *noun*
fighting; *these young soldiers have no experience of combat*; *they exercise with periods of unarmed combat*
2 *verb*
to fight against; *they have set up a special police squad to combat drugs*

② **combination**
[kɒmbɪˈneɪʃn] *noun*
(a) several things taken together; *a combination of cold weather and problems with the car made our vacation in Maryland a disaster*
(b) series of numbers that open a lock; *the safe has a combination lock*; *I've forgotten the combination to my case*

② **combine**
1 *noun* ['kɒmbaɪn]
(a) large financial or commercial group; *a German industrial combine*
(b) large farm machine that cuts grain and cleans it; *a row of combines moved across the huge field*
2 *verb* [kəmˈbaɪn]
to combine with = to join together with; *the cold weather combined with high winds has made it a dreadful harvest*

① **come**
[kʌm] *verb*
(a) to move to or toward this place; *come and see us when you're in Los Angeles*; *the doctor came to see him yesterday*; *some of the children come to school on foot*; *don't make any noise - I can hear someone coming*; *come up to my room and we'll talk about the problem*
(b) to happen; *how did the door come to be open?*; *(informal)* **how come?** = why?; *how come the front door was left open?*
(c) to occur; *what comes after R in the alphabet?*; *P comes before Q*; *what comes after the news on TV?* (NOTE: **coming - came** [keɪm] **- has come**)

③ **come across**
['kʌm əˈkrɒs] *verb*
to find by chance; *we came across this little restaurant when we were out walking*

③ **come along**
['kʌm əˈlɒŋ] *verb*
(a) to go with someone; *if you walk, the children can come along with us in the car*
(b) to hurry; *come along, or you'll miss the bus*
(c) to progress; *how is your new book coming along?*

③ **come apart**
['kʌm əˈpɑrt] *verb*
to break into pieces; *the toy simply came apart in my hands*

③ **come back**
['kʌm ˈbæk] *verb*
to return; *they left the house in a hurry, and then had to come back to get their passports*; *they started to walk away, but the police officer shouted at them to come back*

② **comedy**
['kɒmədi] *noun*
play or movie that makes you laugh; *"A Midsummer Night's Dream" is one of Shakespeare's comedies* (NOTE: plural is comedies)

③ **come in**
['kʌm ˈɪn] *verb*
to enter; *please come in, and make yourself at home*; *why didn't you ask him to come in?*

③ come off

['kʌm 'ɒf] verb

(a) to stop being attached; *the button has come off my coat; I can't use the kettle, the handle has come off*

(b) to be removed; *the paint won't come off my coat*

(c) to do well or badly; *our team came off badly in the competition*

③ come on

['kʌm 'ɒn] verb

(a) to hurry; *come on, or we'll miss the start of the movie*

(b) to arrive; *a storm came on as we were fishing in the bay; night is coming on; she thinks she has a cold coming on*

④ comet

['kɒmɪt] noun

body which moves in space, which you can see at night because of its bright tail; *Halley's Comet returns every 76 years*

③ come to

['kʌm 'tu] verb

(a) to add up to; *the bill comes to $20*

(b) to become conscious again; *when he came to, he was in a hospital*

① comfort

['kʌmfət]

1 noun

(a) thing which helps to make you feel happier; *it was a comfort to know that the children were safe*

(b) state of being comfortable; *they live in great comfort; you expect a certain amount of comfort on a luxury liner; she complained about the lack of comfort in the second-class seats; see also* CREATURE

2 verb

to make someone happier, when they are in pain or miserable, etc.; *she tried to comfort the little girl; he felt comforted by the gentle words of the priest*

① comfortable

['kʌmftəbl] adjective

(a) soft and relaxing; *this chair isn't very comfortable - it has a wooden seat; there are more comfortable chairs in the lounge*

(b) to make yourself comfortable = to relax; *she made herself comfortable in the chair by the fire*

④ comfortably

['kʌmftəbli] adverb

(a) in a comfortable or relaxing way; *if you're sitting comfortably, I'll explain to you what the work involves; make sure you're comfortably dressed because it is kind of cold outside*

(b) comfortably off = having plenty of money; *her husband left her comfortably off when he died*

① comic

['kɒmɪk]

1 noun

(a) children's paper with cartoon stories; *he spends his pocket money on comics and sweets*

(b) man who tells jokes to make people laugh; *he's a well-known TV comic*

2 adjective

funny; **comic book** = children's book with cartoon stories; **comic strip** = cartoon story made of a series of small drawings inside little boxes side by side

① coming

['kʌmɪŋ]

1 adjective

which is approaching; *the newspaper tells you what will happen in the coming week in the Senate; they are preparing for their coming silver wedding anniversary*

2 noun

arrival; **comings and goings** = lots of movement; *the photographers watched the comings and goings at the palace*

① comma

['kɒmə] noun

punctuation mark (,) showing a break in the meaning of a sentence; *use a comma between each item listed in this sentence*

① command

[kə'mand]

1 noun

(a) order; *the general gave the command to attack*; **in command of** = in charge of; **second-in-command** = person serving under the main commander

(b) knowledge (of a language); *she has a good command of French*

2 verb

(a) to order; *he commanded the troops to open fire on the rebels*

(b) to be in charge of; *he commands a group of guerrillas*

① commander

[kə'mandər] noun

officer in charge of a group of soldiers or a ship; *the commander must make sure that all his soldiers know exactly what they must do*

④ commencement

[kə'mensmənt] noun

ceremony at a college or university when degrees are awarded to successful students

③ comment

['kɒment]

1 noun

(a) words showing what you feel about something; *his comments were widely reported in the newspapers; the man made a rude comment accompanied by some very offensive gestures;* **"no comment"** = I refuse to discuss it in public

(b) discussion of a question; *the scandal aroused considerable comment in the press*

(c) explanation; *it is a sad comment on modern values that we spend more money on arms than*

on helping the poor (NOTE: no plural in this meaning)
2 *verb*
to comment on something = to make a remark about something; *he commented on the lack of towels in the bathroom*

④ **commentary**
['kɒməntri] *noun*
(a) spoken report on an event; *the Olympic Games are being shown on the TV with live commentary*
(b) remarks about a book, a problem, etc.; *for intelligent commentary on current events you should read this magazine* (NOTE: plural is **commentaries**)

④ **commentator**
['kɒmənteɪtər] *noun*
person who reports events as they happen, on the radio or TV; *radio commentators are much better than those on TV*

④ **commerce**
['kɒmɜrs] *noun*
business, the buying and selling of goods and services; *a trade mission went to South America to boost U.S. commerce in the region*

② **commercial**
[kə'mɜrʃl]
1 *adjective*
(a) referring to business; *he is a specialist in commercial law*
(b) used for business purposes, not private or military; *he left the air force and became a commercial airline pilot*; *the company makes commercial vehicles such as taxis and buses*
(c) profitable; *our commercial future looks doubtful*; *not a commercial proposition* = not likely to make a profit
2 *noun*
advertisement on television; *our TV commercial attracted a lot of interest*

③ **commission**
[kə'mɪʃn]
1 *noun*
(a) group of people which investigates problems of national importance; *the president has appointed a commission to look into the problem of drugs in schools*
(b) order for something to be made or to be used; *he received a commission to paint the portrait of the president*
(c) percentage of sales value given to the salesman; *she gets 15% commission on everything she sells*; *he charges 10% commission*
(d) order making someone an officer; *he has a commission in the air force*
(e) *out of commission* = not working; *the elevator's out of commission so you'll have to use the stairs*
2 *verb*
(a) to authorize an artist or architect, etc., to do a piece of work; to authorize a piece of work to be

done; *the magazine commissioned him to write a series of articles on Germany*
(b) to make someone an officer; *he was commissioned into the National Guard*

① **commissioner**
[kə'mɪʃnər] *noun*
representative of authority; **police commissioner** = officer in charge of a police department

④ **commit**
[kə'mɪt] *verb*
(a) to carry out a crime; *the gang committed six robberies before they were caught*; *he said he was on vacation in Nevada when the murder was committed*
(b) *to commit suicide* = to kill yourself
(c) *to commit someone for trial* = to send someone to prison; *she has been committed to the state prison for women*
(d) *to commit funds to a project* = to agree to spend money on a project; *the party pledged to commit more funds to the health service*
(e) *to commit yourself* = to promise to do something; to give your opinion; *he refused to commit himself*; *I can't commit myself to anything until I have more details* (NOTE: **committing - committed**)

④ **commitment**
[kə'mɪtmənt] *noun*
(a) promise to pay money; *he has difficulty in meeting his commitments*
(b) agreement to do something; *she made a firm commitment to arrive early for work in future*; *we have the fax machine on one week's trial, with no commitment to buy*

② **committee**
[kə'mɪti] *noun*
official group of people who organize or discuss things for a larger group; *the town council has set up a committee to look into sports facilities*; *committee members will be asked to vote on the proposal*; *to be on a committee* = to be a member of a committee; *he's on the finance committee*

④ **commodity**
[kə'mɒdɪti] *noun*
thing sold in very large quantities, especially raw materials (such as silver and tin) and food (such as corn or coffee); **basic commodities** = food and raw materials; *the country's basic commodities are coffee and timber*; *because of the drought, even basic commodities have to be imported* (NOTE: plural is **commodities**)

③ **common**
['kɒmən]
1 *adjective*
(a) which happens often, which you find everywhere; *bluebirds are common in the Midwest*; *it's very common for people to get colds in winter*; *it is common knowledge* = everyone knows it; *it is common knowledge that he is having an affair with his secretary*

(b) belonging to two or more people; *the two countries have a common border*; *blue eyes are not common to all the members of our family*; **common ownership** = ownership of a property by a group of people; **in common** = shared by two or more people; *they have two things in common - they are both Irish and they are both left-handed* (NOTE: commoner - commonest)

2 *noun*

an open area of land that belongs to a community; *we went walking on the commons*

③ **commonly**
['kɒmənli] *adverb*
often; *bluebirds are commonly found in the Midwest*; *cellular phones are commonly banned in restaurants*

④ **commonplace**
['kɒmənpleɪs] *adjective*
ordinary, standard; *it is a commonplace occurrence*

④ **common sense**
['kɒmən 'sens] *noun*
ordinary good sense; *use some common sense - switch the machine off before you start working on it with a screwdriver*; *at least she had the common sense to call the police*

④ **commonwealth**
['kɒmənwelθ] *noun*
Commonwealth = (part of) the official name of some U.S. states, including Kentucky, Massachusetts, Pennsylvania and Virginia; *the Commonwealth of Virginia welcomes you*; **the (British) Commonwealth** = an association of independent countries linked to Britain; *the Queen is the head of the Commonwealth*

② **commotion**
[kə'məʊʃən] *noun*
confusion or trouble; *there was a sudden commotion on the playground and the head teacher went to see what was the matter*

② **communicate**
[kə'mjuːnɪkeɪt] *verb*
(a) to send or give information to someone; *although she is unable to speak, she can still communicate by using her hands*; *he finds it impossible to communicate with his staff*; *communicating with our office in Toronto has been quicker since we installed the fax*; *he communicated his wishes to his children*
(b) to connect with; **communicating rooms** = rooms with a connecting door between them; **communicating door** = door between two rooms; *the communicating door is kept locked at all times*

② **communication**
[kəmjuːnɪ'keɪʃn] *noun*
(a) passing of information; *e-mail is the most rapid means of communication*; *it is not a happy school - there is no communication between the principal and the other members of staff*; **to enter into communication with someone** = to start discussing something with

someone, usually in writing; *we have entered into communication with their attorneys*
(b) official message; *we had a communication from the factory inspector*
(c) **communications** = being able to contact people; *after the flood all communications with the outside world were cut off*

④ **communism**
['kɒmjʊnɪzm] *noun*
political and social system in which all property is owned by the state and shared by the society as a whole and not by individual people

④ **communist**
['kɒmjʊnɪst]
1 *adjective*
referring to communism; *the Communist Party is holding its annual meeting this weekend*
2 *noun*
person who believes in communism; member of the Communist Party; *he was a Communist all his life*

② **community**
[kə'mjuːnɪti] *noun*
group of people living in one area; *the local community is worried about the level of violence on the streets*; **rural community** = people living in a small area of the countryside; *we grew tired of the big city and moved to a quiet rural community*; **urban community** = a town's inhabitants; **community college** = local two-year college at which students can learn a technical subject or prepare to enter a college or university (NOTE: plural is **communities**)

④ **commute**
[kə'mjuːt] *verb*
(a) to travel to work from home each day; *he commutes from Oakland to his office in downtown San Francisco*
(b) to reduce a legal penalty; *the prison sentence was commuted to a fine*; *his death sentence was commuted to life imprisonment*
(c) to exchange one type of payment for another; *his pension has been commuted to a lump sum payment*

④ **commuter**
[kə'mjuːtər] *noun*
person who travels to work in town every day; *commuters face a 10% increase in bus fares*; **commuter train** = train which commuters take in the morning and evening; *the commuter trains are full every morning*

② **compact**
1 *adjective* [kəm'pækt]
small; close together; *the computer system is small and very compact*
2 *noun* ['kɒmpækt]
(a) small family car; *they sold the four-wheel drive and bought a compact*
(b) *(formal)* agreement; *the two companies signed a compact to share their research findings*

(c) small box with face powder in it; *she always carries a compact in her purse*

② **compact disk (CD)**
['kɒmpækt 'dɪsk] *noun*
metal recording disc, which can hold a large amount of data, pictures or music, and which is read by a laser in a special player; *the sound quality on CDs is better than on vinyl records*

② **companion**
[kəm'pænjən] *noun*
person or animal who lives with someone; *his constant companion was his old white dog*; **traveling companion** = person who travels with someone; *he and his traveling companions were arrested as they tried to cross the border*

② **company**
['kʌmpni] *noun*
(a) commercial firm; *it is company policy not to allow smoking anywhere in the offices*; *the company has taken on three secretaries*; *she runs an electrical company*; *he set up a computer company* (NOTE: usually written **Co.** in names: **Smith & Co.** Note also the plural **companies** in this meaning)
(b) being together with other people; *I enjoy the company of young people*; *she went to Boston in company with or in the company of three other girls from college*; **he is good company** = he's a very entertaining person to be with; **to keep someone company** = to be with someone to prevent them feeling lonely; *would you like to come with me to keep me company?*; **to part company** = to split up; *we all set off together, but we parted company when we got to Boston*
(c) guests; *I cannot talk right now, I have company to entertain*
(d) group of people who work together; **a ship's company** = the crew of a ship; **a theater company** = the actors and directors of a theater
(e) *(in the army)* a group of men commanded by a captain

④ **comparative**
[kəm'pærətɪv]
1 *adjective*
when considered next to something else; *judging by last year's performance it is a comparative improvement*
2 *noun*
form of an adjective or adverb showing an increase in level compared to something else; *"happier", "better" and "more often" are the comparatives of "happy", "good" and "often"*

> COMMENT: comparatives are usually formed by adding the suffix -er to the adjective: "quicker" from "quick", for example; in the case of long adjectives, they are formed by putting "more" in front of the adjective: "more comfortable", "more expensive", and so on.

④ **comparatively**
[kəm'pærətɪvli] *adverb*
to a certain extent, more than something else; *the country is comparatively rich in minerals*; *she is comparatively well-off*; *comparatively speaking, he's quite tall*

③ **compare**
[kəm'peər] *verb*
(a) to compare something with *or* **to something else** = to look at two things side by side to see how they are different; *if you compare the situation in the U.S. with that in Britain*
(b) to compare something with *or* **to something else** = to say that something is like something else; *he compared his mother's cake to a brick*

② **compared**
[kəm'peəd] *adjective*
compared to *or* **with** = when you compare it to; *compared with my limousine, your automobile is tiny*; *compared to last year, this summer was cold*

② **comparison**
[kəm'pærɪsən] *noun*
act of comparing; *this year, July was cold in comparison with last year*; **there is no comparison between them** = one is much better than the other

② **compass**
['kʌmpəs] *noun*
(a) device with a floating needle which points to the north; **the points of the compass** = the different directions, north, south, east and west
(b) a pair of compasses = device for drawing a circle; *set your compasses to 10 mm and draw a circle with a diameter of 20 mm*

④ **compassion**
[kəm'pæʃn] *noun*
feeling of sympathy for someone who is in an unfortunate situation; *the soldiers showed no compassion in separating families and driving them away from their homes*

④ **compatible**
[kəm'pætəbl] *adjective*
(a) compatible with something = able to fit or work with something; *make sure the two computer systems are compatible*
(b) compatible with someone = able to live or work happily with someone; *how their marriage has lasted so long no one knows - they were not at all compatible*

④ **compel**
[kəm'pel] *verb*
to force; *he compelled her to sign the paper* (NOTE: **compelling - compelled**)

④ **compensate**
['kɒmpenseɪt] *verb*
to compensate someone for something = to pay for damage, for a loss; *they agreed to compensate her for damage to her car*; *the*

airline refused to compensate him when his baggage was lost

④ **compensation**
[kɒmpenˈseɪʃn] *noun*
(a) payment for damage or loss; *the airline refused to pay any compensation for his lost baggage*; *you must submit a claim for compensation to the insurance company within two weeks*
(b) something that makes up for something bad; *working in downtown Chicago has its compensations*; *four weeks' vacation is no compensation for a year's work in that office*

④ **compete**
[kəmˈpiːt] *verb*
to compete with someone = to try to beat someone in sport, trade, etc.; *he is competing in both the 100 and 200 meters*; *we have to compete with cheap imports from the Far East*

④ **competent**
[ˈkɒmpɪtənt] *adjective*
(a) efficient; *she is a very competent manager*
(b) quite good, but not brilliant; *he's quite competent at math*; *she's a competent golfer*
(c) legally able to do something; **the court is not competent to deal with this case** = the court is not legally able to deal with the case

③ **competition**
[kɒmpəˈtɪʃn] *noun*
(a) sport or game where several teams or people enter and each tries to win; *France was the winner of the competition*; *he won first prize in the piano competition*; *the competition is open to everybody* (NOTE: plural in this meaning is **competitions**)
(b) trying to do better than someone in business; *our main competition comes from the big supermarkets*; *we have to keep our prices low because of competition from cheap imports*
(c) the competition = people or companies who are trying to do better than you; *we have lowered our prices to try to beat the competition*; *the competition is planning to reduce their prices*

④ **competitive**
[kəmˈpetɪtɪv] *adjective*
(a) liking to win competitions; *he's very competitive*; **competitive sports** = sports which are based on competition between people or teams
(b) competitive prices = prices which are lower or no higher than those of rival firms; *we must keep our prices competitive if we want to stay in business*

② **competitor**
[kəmˈpetɪtər] *noun*
(a) person who enters a competition; *all the competitors lined up for the start of the race*
(b) company that competes; *two German firms are our main competitors*

② **complain**
[kəmˈpleɪn] *verb*
to say that something is no good or does not work properly; *the shop is so cold the staff has started complaining*; *she complained about the service*; *they are complaining that our prices are too high*; *she complained that no one spoke English in the hotel* (NOTE: you complain **to** someone **about** something or **that** something is no good)

② **complaint**
[kəmˈpleɪnt] *noun*
(a) saying that something is wrong; *she sent her letter of complaint to the chief executive officer*; *you must file your complaint with the relevant department*; **complaints department** = department that deals with complaints from customers
(b) illness; *she was admitted to the hospital with a kidney complaint*

② **complete**
[kəmˈpliːt]
1 *adjective*
with all its parts; *he has a complete set of the new stamps*; *we have to study the complete works of Shakespeare*
2 *verb*
to finish; *the builders completed the whole job in two days*

② **completely**
[kəmˈpliːtli] *adverb*
totally; *the building was completely destroyed in the earthquake*; *I completely forgot about my dentist appointment*

③ **completion**
[kəmˈpliːʃn] *noun*
act of finishing; *the building of the bridge is nearing completion*

④ **complex**
[ˈkɒmpleks]
1 *adjective*
complicated; *the committee is discussing the complex problem of the site for the new hospital*; *the specifications for the machine are very complex*
2 *noun*
(a) series of buildings; *the town council has built a new sports complex*; *an industrial complex is planned on the site of the old steelworks*
(b) *(in the mind)* group of ideas which are based on an experience that you had in the past, and which influence the way you behave; *he has a complex about going bald*; *stop talking about her height - you'll give her a complex about it* (NOTE: plural is **complexes**)

② **complexion**
[kəmˈplekʃn] *noun*
color of the skin on your face; *she has a beautiful pale complexion*

③ **complicated**
['kɒmplɪkeɪtɪd] *adjective*
with many small details; difficult to understand; *it is a complicated subject; it's all getting too complicated - let's try and keep it simple; chess has quite complicated rules; the route to get to our house is complicated, so I'll draw you a map*

③ **complication**
[kɒmplɪ'keɪʃn] *noun*
(a) illness occurring because of or during another illness; *she appeared to be getting better, but complications set in*
(b) trouble, complicated problem; *it all seems quite simple to me - what's the complication?; all these forms that we have to fill out just create further complications*

③ **compliment**
1 *noun* ['kɒmplɪmənt]
(a) remark that praises someone or something; *she turned red when she read his compliments on her dancing*; **to be fishing for compliments** = to try to get someone to say nice things about you; **to pay someone a compliment** = to praise someone, to do something that shows you appreciate someone; *they paid her the compliment of asking her to speak to the meeting*
(b) **compliments** = good wishes; **send him my compliments** = give him my good wishes; **with the compliments of Apple Co.** = with good wishes from Apple Co.; *a box of chocolates with the compliments of the manager or with the manager's compliments; please accept these flowers with my compliments*
2 *verb* ['kɒmplɪment]
to praise; *the management compliments the staff on its excellent work this year; I would like to compliment the chef on an excellent meal*

④ **complimentary**
[kɒmplɪ'mentəri] *adjective*
(a) that praises; *he was very complimentary about her dress; the reviews of his book are very complimentary*
(b) **complimentary ticket** = free ticket, sent to a friend or business associate; *the club does not allow you to sell complimentary tickets*

④ **comply (with)**
[kəm'plaɪ] *verb*
(a) to observe a rule; *does it comply with all the relevant regulations?*
(b) to obey an order; *if you fail to comply with the court order you may be prosecuted*

④ **component**
[kəm'pəʊnənt]
1 *adjective*
which forms part of a larger machine, etc.; *they supply component parts for washing machines*
2 *noun*

small piece in a larger machine; *a components manufacturer; the assembly line stopped because they ran out of components*

② **compose**
[kəm'pəʊz] *verb*
(a) to write a piece of music; *it took Mozart only three days to compose this piece; who composed the music to "Doctor Zhivago"?*
(b) to write something, using your intelligence; *he sat down to compose a letter to his family*

② **composer**
[kəm'pəʊzər] *noun*
person who writes music; *Elgar, Copland and other British and American composers; that was a marvelous piece, but who was the composer?*

③ **composition**
[kɒmpə'zɪʃn] *noun*
(a) how something is made up; *scientists are trying to establish the composition of the rock sample from the Moon*
(b) something which has been composed, a poem, piece of music, etc.; *we will now play a well-known composition by Dowland*
(c) essay, piece of writing on a special subject; *we had three hours to write a composition on "pollution"*

② **compound**
1 *adjective* ['kɒmpaʊnd]
made up of several parts; **compound interest** = interest calculated on the original total plus any previous interest; *compare* SIMPLE INTEREST
2 *noun* ['kɒmpaʊnd]
(a) chemical made up of two or more elements; *water is a compound of hydrogen and oxygen*
(b) buildings and land enclosed by a fence; *guard dogs patrol the compound at night; soldiers were guarding the embassy compound*
3 *verb* [kəm'paʊnd]
to make something worse; *the plane's late arrival was compounded by fog at the airport; the problems of getting across New York will be compounded by today's bus strike*

④ **comprehensive**
[kɒmprɪ'hensɪv] *adjective*
which includes everything; *she was given a comprehensive medical examination before being allowed back to work; the police made a comprehensive search of all the files; the list is really comprehensive - I don't think we've left anything out*; **comprehensive insurance** = insurance policy that covers you against all risks which are likely to happen

② **compress**
1 *noun* ['kɒmpres]
pad of cloth, sometimes soaked in hot or cold liquid, placed on the skin to relieve pain or to force infected matter out of a wound; *she applied a cold compress to the bruise; the nurse applied a dry compress to his bleeding knee* (NOTE: plural is **compresses**)

2 *verb* [kəmˈpres]
(a) to squeeze into a small space; *the garden center sells soil compressed into plastic bags*; *I tried to compress the data onto one page, but couldn't do it*
(b) compressed air = air under pressure; *the cleaning machine uses a jet of compressed air*

④ **comprise**
[kəmˈpraɪz] *verb*
to be made up of; *the course comprises three years at an American university and one year's study abroad*; to be comprised of = to be made up of; *the exam is comprised of two written papers and an oral test*

④ **compromise**
[ˈkɒmprəmaɪz]
1 *noun*
agreement between two opposing sides, where each side gives way a little; *they reached a compromise after some discussion*; *there is no question of a compromise with the terrorists*
2 *verb*
(a) to come to an agreement by giving way a little; *he asked $20 for it, I offered $10, and we compromised on $15*; *the government has refused to compromise with the terrorists*
(b) to put someone in a difficult position; *now that he has been compromised, he has had to withdraw as a candidate*
(c) to do something that reveals a secret; *the security code has been compromised*

④ **compulsory**
[kəmˈpʌlsəri] *adjective*
which everyone is forced to do; *a compulsory injection against a tropical disease*; *it is compulsory to wear a crash helmet on a motorcycle*

① **computer**
[kəmˈpjutər] *noun*
electronic machine that calculates and keeps information automatically; *all the company's records are on computer*; personal computer **(PC)** *or* home computer = small computer that can be used in the home; *he wrote his book on his home computer*; computer error = mistake made by a computer; computer file = section of information on a computer, such as a list of addresses, a letter, etc.; computer game = game that you can play on a computer, using a special program; *the boys spent the weekend playing computer games*; computer program = instructions to a computer, telling it to do a particular piece of work

④ **computerize**
[kəmˈpjutəraɪz] *verb*
(a) to equip a business, school, etc., with computers; *the school is being computerized, but we still have only one computer per class*; *all our supermarket checkouts are fully computerized*
(b) to change from a manual system to one using computers; *our booking system has been*

completely computerized; *we get computerized paychecks*

③ **computing**
[kəmˈpjutɪŋ] *noun*
using a computer; *all children learn computing at school*; *computing is a very important skill*

③ **conceal**
[kənˈsil] *verb*
to hide something, to put something where it cannot be seen; *she concealed the loss from her manager*; *he tried to conceal the camera by putting it under his coat*

④ **concede**
[kənˈsid] *verb*
(a) to admit that you are wrong; *she conceded that this time she had been mistaken*
(b) to concede defeat = to admit that you have lost; *with half the votes counted, the presidential candidate conceded defeat*; *after sixteen moves, the chess champion had to concede defeat*

④ **conceivable**
[kənˈsivəbl] *adjective*
which can be imagined; *it is quite conceivable that he will be forced to resign*

④ **conceivably**
[kənˈsivəbli] *adverb*
in a conceivable way; *she couldn't conceivably have been in Florida last month*

④ **conceive**
[kənˈsiv] *verb (formal)*
(a) to imagine; *I can't conceive of any occasion where I would wear a dress like that*; *it is difficult to conceive how people can be so cruel*
(b) *(formal)* to become pregnant; *after two years of marriage she began to think she would never conceive*; *(of a child)* to be conceived = to start existence inside the mother; *our little girl was conceived during a power outage in New York*

③ **concentrate**
[ˈkɒnsəntreɪt]
1 *verb*
(a) to be very attentive; *the exam candidates were all concentrating hard when someone started to giggle*; to concentrate on something = to pay special attention to something; *don't talk - he's trying to concentrate on his homework*; *the salespeople are supposed to concentrate on getting orders*
(b) to put everything together in one place; *the enemy guns are concentrated on top of that hill*
2 *noun*
substance which is concentrated, after water has been removed; *lemon concentrate*

③ **concentrated**
[ˈkɒnsəntreɪtɪd] *adjective*
(a) (juice) from which water has been removed, so giving a very strong taste; *a bottle of concentrated orange juice*
(b) very determined to do something; *with a little concentrated effort we should be able to do it*

③ **concentration**
[kɒnsən'treɪʃn] *noun*
(a) thinking carefully about something; *a loud conversation in the next room disturbed my concentration*; *his concentration slipped and he lost the next two games*
(b) grouping of a lot of things in one area; *the concentration of computer companies in California's Silicon Valley*; *the concentration of wild animals around the water hole makes it easy for lions to find food*
(c) concentration camp = harsh camp, often for political prisoners

④ **concept**
['kɒnsept] *noun*
philosophical idea; *it is difficult for some countries to grasp the concept of democratic government*; *the concept of grammar is completely foreign to her*; *our children have absolutely no concept of what peace and quiet is*

③ **concern**
[kən'sɜrn]
1 *noun*
(a) worry; *she's a cause of great concern to her family*
(b) interest; *my main concern is to ensure that we all enjoy ourselves*; *the teachers showed no concern at all for the children's safety*; **it is no concern of yours** = it's nothing to do with you; *I don't care what they do with the money - it's not my concern*
(c) company, business; *a big German chemical concern*
2 *verb*
(a) to have as the subject; **the letter concerns you** = the letter is about you; **that does not concern him** = it has nothing to do with him; **as far as money is concerned** = referring to money; **to concern yourself with** = to deal with; *you don't need to concern yourself with cleaning the store*
(b) to worry; *it concerns me that he is always late for work*

③ **concerned**
[kən'sɜrnd] *adjective*
worried; *she looked concerned*; *I could tell something was wrong by the concerned look on her face*; *we are concerned about her behavior - do you think she is having problems at school?*

④ **concerning**
[kən'sɜrnɪŋ] *preposition* dealing with; *can you answer some questions concerning vacations?*; *I'd like to speak to Mr. Robinson concerning his application for insurance*; *anyone with information concerning this person should get in touch with the police*

② **concert**
['kɒnsərt] *noun*
program of music played in public; *I'm sorry, the concert is sold out*; *I couldn't go to the concert, so I gave my ticket to a friend*; **concert hall** = large building where concerts are given

④ **concession**
[kən'seʃn] *noun*
(a) allowing someone do something that you do not really want them to do; *we insist that the children are home by 8 P.M. on weekdays, but as a concession, we let them stay out until 11 P.M. on Saturdays*
(b) to make concessions to someone = to change your plans so as to please someone; *the president has said that no concessions will be made to the terrorists*

③ **conclude**
[kən'klud] *verb*
(a) to end; to come to an end; *he concluded by thanking all those who had helped arrange the exhibition*; *the concert concluded with a piece by Mozart*
(b) to come to an opinion; *the police concluded that the thief had got into the building through the kitchen window*
(c) to conclude an agreement with someone = to arrange an agreement or treaty with someone

③ **conclusion**
[kən'kluʒn] *noun*
(a) end; *at the conclusion of the trial all the defendants were found guilty*
(b) opinion which you reach after careful thought; *she came to or reached the conclusion that he had found another girlfriend*; *what conclusions can you draw from the evidence before you?*

② **concrete**
['kɒnkrit]
1 *noun*
mixture of cement and sand, used in building; *concrete was invented by the Romans*; *the sidewalk is made of blocks of concrete*
2 *adjective*
(a) made of cement and sand; *a concrete path*
(b) real, important; *he had no concrete proposals to offer*; *the police are sure he is guilty, but they have no concrete evidence against him*

③ **condemn**
[kən'dem] *verb*
(a) to say that you do not approve of something; *she condemned the court's decision*
(b) to sentence a criminal; *he was condemned to death*
(c) to declare a house to be not in good enough state to live in; *the whole block of apartments has been condemned and will be pulled down*

④ **condense**
[kən'dens] *verb*
(a) to reduce the size of something; *we sent the article back to the author asking her to condense it*
(b) *(of steam)* to form drops of water; *vapor will condense when it is cooled*

② **condition**
[kənˈdɪʃn] *noun*
(a) state that something is in; *the automobile is in very good condition considering it is over thirty years old*; *he was taken to the hospital when his condition got worse*
(b) state of the surroundings in which someone is living or working; *conditions in the refugee camps are very bad*; *the 7 o'clock news forecast poor weather conditions*
(c) illness; *he is being treated for a heart condition*
(d) term of a deal; something which has to be agreed before something else is done; *they didn't agree with some of the conditions of the contract*; *one of conditions of the deal is that the company pays all travel costs*; **on condition that** = only if; *I will come on condition that you pay my fare*

④ **conditioner**
[kənˈdɪʃənər] *noun*
liquid that puts hair into good condition; *the hairdresser asked me if I wanted some conditioner after the shampoo*; *I always use a combined shampoo and conditioner*; *see also* AIR CONDITIONER

④ **condominium**
[kɒndəˈmɪniəm] *noun*
(a) building in which each owner of an apartment shares in the ownership of the roof, elevators, etc.; *the developer plans to build two condominiums*
(b) apartment in such a building; *his cousin has just bought an expensive condominium in Malibu* (NOTE: often shortened to **condo**)

② **conduct**
1 *noun* [ˈkɒndʌkt] way of behaving; *his conduct in class is becoming a cause of concern*; *her conduct during the trial was remarkably calm*; *he was arrested for noisy conduct on Main Street*
2 *verb* [kənˈdʌkt]
(a) to guide; *the guests were conducted to their seats*; **conducted tour** = tour led by a guide
(b) to direct an orchestra; *the orchestra will be conducted by a Russian*
(c) to allow electricity, heat, etc., to pass through; *copper conducts electricity very well*
(d) to carry out; *they are conducting an experiment into the effect of TV advertising*
(e) to lead, to direct; *the chairman conducted the negotiations very efficiently*; **to conduct a meeting** = to be chairman of a meeting; *as he was going away on business, he asked his deputy to conduct the meeting*

① **conductor**
[kənˈdʌktər] *noun*
(a) metal, or other substance that conducts heat or electricity; *copper is a good conductor but plastic is not*; **conductor rail** = the electric rail for trains

(b) person who directs an orchestra; *as the orchestra reached the end of the piece, the conductor started to sing*; *the orchestra has appointed a new conductor*
(c) person in charge of a train, bus, streetcar, etc.

② **conference**
[ˈkɒnfərəns] *noun*
(a) discussion; *the managers had a quick conference to decide what action to take*; **to be in conference** = to be in a meeting; **conference call** = telephone link arranged that several people can speak at the same time from different places; **press conference** = meeting where newspaper, radio and TV reporters are invited to hear news of something or to talk to a famous person; *he gave a press conference outside the White House*; **sales conference** = meeting of sales managers, representatives, publicity staff, etc., to discuss future sales plans
(b) meeting of a group or society; *the annual conference of the Electricians Union*; *the conference agenda was drawn up by the secretary*; *many people attended the conference on the effects of global warming*

② **confess**
[kənˈfes] *verb*
(a) to admit that you have done something wrong; *he confessed to six burglaries*; *she confessed that she had forgotten to lock the door*
(b) to admit your sins to a priest; *she went to church to confess to the priest*

② **confession**
[kənˈfeʃn] *noun*
(a) admission of fault; *the prisoner said his confession had been forced from him by the police*
(b) **to make your confession** = to admit your sins to a priest

② **confidence**
[ˈkɒnfɪdəns] *noun*
(a) feeling sure; *the staff do not have much confidence in their manager*; *I have total confidence in the pilot*; *see also* VOTE
(b) being secret; **in confidence** = as a secret; *he showed me the report in confidence*
(c) **confidence game** = a trick to get money by making someone believe something

④ **confident**
[ˈkɒnfɪdənt] *adjective*
sure that you or something will be successful; *I am confident (that) the show will go off well*; *she's confident of doing well in the exam*

④ **confidential**
[kɒnfɪˈdenʃl] *adjective*
secret, private; *please mark the letter "Private and Confidential"*; **confidential secretary** = secretary who deals with her employer's private matters

④ **confidentially**
[kɒnfɪˈdenʃəli] *adverb*
in a confidential way; *he told me confidentially that I had won the prize*

③ **confine**
[kən'faɪn] *verb*
(a) to keep in one small place; *the tigers were confined in a small cage with no room to move around*; **confined to bed** = forced to stay in bed; *she wanted to get up, but the doctor has confined her to bed*
(b) to restrict; *make sure you confine your answer to the subject in the question*

④ **confirm**
[kən'fɜrm] *verb*
(a) to say that something is certain; *the dates of the concerts have been confirmed by the pop group's manager*; *the photograph confirmed that the result of the race was a dead heat*; *we have been told that she left the country last month - can you confirm that?*
(b) **to confirm someone in a job** = to say that someone is now permanently in the job; **to be confirmed in office** = to be kept in your job by a new management
(c) **to be confirmed** = to be admitted as a full member of a church; *he was confirmed when he was twelve*

④ **confirmation**
[kɒnfə'meɪʃn] *noun*
(a) making sure; *we are awaiting official confirmation of the figures*
(b) document that confirms something; *we have had confirmation from the bank that the payment has been made*
(c) ceremony where a person is admitted as a full member of a church; *when is your daughter's confirmation?*

③ **conflict**
1 *noun* ['kɒnflɪkt]
(a) fighting; *the army is engaged in armed conflict with rebel forces*; *the border conflict escalated into an full-scale war*
(b) angry situation between people; *the demand for equal treatment for all classes can lead to social conflict*; **to come into conflict with someone** = to start to fight someone; *the decision brought the union into conflict with the management*; **conflict of interest** = situation where a person may profit personally from decisions which he makes as an official
2 *verb* [kən'flɪkt]
to conflict with = to contradict; *the defendant's version of events conflicts with that of the witness*; **conflicting advice** = pieces of advice from different people which are the opposite of each other

④ **confront**
[kən'frʌnt] *verb*
(a) to try to tackle someone; *don't confront a burglar on your own - he may be armed*
(b) **to confront someone with the evidence** = to show the evidence to someone; *when the police confronted him with the photographs he confessed*

④ **confrontation**
[kɒnfrʌn'teɪʃn] *noun*
angry meeting between opposing sides; *to avoid confrontation, the fans of the two opposing teams will be kept as far apart as possible*; *there have been some violent confrontations between students and the police*

② **confuse**
[kən'fjuz] *verb*
(a) to muddle; *she was confused by all the journalists' questions*
(b) to mix up; *the twins are so alike I am always confusing them*; *I always confuse him with his brother - they are very alike*

② **confused**
[kən'fjuzd] *adjective*
not clear in your mind; *I'm a bit confused - did we say 8:00 or 8:30 P.M.?*; *my grandma used to get confused in her old age*

② **confusing**
[kən'fjuzɪŋ] *adjective*
which is difficult to make clear; *she found the instructions on the computer very confusing*

③ **confusion**
[kən'fjuʒn] *noun*
disorder; *there were scenes of confusion at the airport when the snowstorm stopped all flights*

② **congratulate**
[kən'grætjʊleɪt] *verb*
to give someone good wishes on a special occasion or for having done something; *he congratulated them on their silver wedding anniversary*; *I want to congratulate you on your promotion*

③ **congratulations**
[kəngrætjʊ'leɪʃnz] *noun*
good wishes to someone who has done well; *congratulations - you're our millionth customer!*; *congratulations on passing your exam!*; *the office sent him their congratulations on his wedding*

④ **congress**
['kɒŋgres] *noun*
meeting of a group; *the annual congress of a scientific society*

③ **Congress**
['kɒŋgres] *noun*
legislative body of the U.S.A., formed of the House of Representatives and the Senate; *the President has to persuade Congress to pass his budget*

④ **congressional**
[kən'greʃənəl] *adjective*
referring to the U.S. Congress; *a congressional hearing*

④ **congressman** *or* **congresswoman**
['kɒŋgresmən *or* 'kɒŋgrəwʊmən] *noun*
member of the United States House of Representatives (NOTE: plural is **congressmen**, **congresswomen**; note also that it can be used as

a title with a name: **Congressman Smith, Congresswoman Murphy**)

③ **conjunction**
[kən'dʒʌŋkʃn] *noun*
word which links different words together to make phrases or sentences; *"and" and "but" are conjunctions*

① **connect**
[kə'nekt] *verb*
(a) to join; *the computer should have been connected to the printer; has the telephone been connected yet?; connect the two red wires together*
(b) to link up with; **the flight from New York connects with a flight to Athens** = the plane from New York arrives in time for passengers to catch the plane to Athens; **this train connects with the 12:45** = this train allows passengers to catch the 12:45

② **connection**
[kə'nekʃn] *noun*
(a) link; *there is a definite connection between smoking and lung cancer; he said that there was no connection between how much he had had to drink and his falling over on the street;* **in connection with your visit** = referring to your visit
(b) train, plane, etc., which you catch after getting off another train or plane; *my plane was late and I missed my connection to Los Angeles*
(c) **connections** = people you know; *he has business connections in Argentina*

② **conquer**
['kɒŋkər] *verb*
to defeat with an army; *England was conquered by the Normans in 1066; the Romans conquered most of Europe*

③ **conscience**
['kɒnʃəns] *noun*
feeling that you have that you have done right or wrong; *I can say with a clear conscience that I have done nothing wrong; why can't you look me in the eye - do you have a guilty conscience?; he refused to serve in the army as a matter of conscience*

④ **conscientious**
[kɒnʃi'enʃəs] *adjective*
working carefully and well; *she's a very conscientious worker*

③ **conscious**
['kɒnʃəs] *adjective*
aware of things happening around you; *she was conscious during the whole operation;* **a conscious decision** = a decision that you have thought about; *refusing the offer was a conscious decision on his part; he made a conscious decision to try to avoid her in future*

④ **consciousness**
['kɒnʃəsnəs] *noun*
being conscious; **to lose consciousness** = to become unconscious; **to regain consciousness** = to become conscious again; *he never regained consciousness after the accident*

④ **consecutive**
[kən'sekjutɪv] *adjective*
one after the other; *the bank sent him reminders for two consecutive weeks*

② **consent**
[kən'sent]
1 *noun*
agreement; *doctors must obtain a patient's consent before operating;* **to withhold your consent** = not to agree; *her parents withheld their consent to the marriage;* **the age of consent** = age at which someone can legally agree to have sex
2 *verb*
to consent to something = to agree to something; *the judge consented to the prosecution's request*

③ **consequence**
['kɒnsɪkwəns] *noun*
(a) something which follows, a result; *we walked all day in the rain, with the consequence that all of us got colds*
(b) importance; **it is of no consequence** = it is not important

④ **consequently**
['kɒnsɪkwəntli] *adverb*
because of this; *we walked all day in the rain and consequently all caught colds*

② **conservation**
[kɒnsə'veɪʃn] *noun*
saving of energy, natural resources, old buildings, etc.; *the company is spending more money on energy conservation*

④ **conservative**
[kən'sɜrvətɪv] *adjective*
(a) not wanting to change; *he has very conservative views*
(b) probably too low; *a conservative estimate of sales; at least two hundred people came to the flower show, and that is a conservative estimate*

② **consider**
[kən'sɪdər] *verb*
(a) to think carefully about something; *please consider seriously the offer which we are making; we have to consider the position of the children after the divorce*
(b) to think; *do you consider him the right man for the job?; she is considered (to be) one of the best lawyers in town*
(c) **all things considered** = on the whole; *all things considered, the evening went off quite well*

④ **considerable**
[kən'sɪdrəbl] *adjective*
quite large; *he lost a considerable amount of money on the horse races*

④ **considerably**
[kən'sɪdrəbli] *adverb*
quite a lot; *it is considerably hotter than it was last week*

② **consideration**
[kənsɪdə'reɪʃn] *noun*
(a) careful thought; *we are giving serious consideration to the possibility of moving our main office to Houston*; **to take something into consideration** = to think about something when making a decision; *the age of the children has to be taken into consideration*; **under consideration** = being thought about; *the matter is under consideration*
(b) thing which has an effect on a decision; *the safety of the children is our most important consideration*
(c) *(formal)* small sum of money; **for a small consideration** = for a small fee or payment

② **considering**
[kən'sɪdrɪŋ] *conjunction & preposition*
when you think (of); *he plays the piano extremely well, considering he's only five*; *he ought to be more grateful, considering the amount of help you have given him*

③ **consist**
[kən'sɪst] *verb*
(a) **to consist of** = to be formed of; *the package tour consists of air travel, six nights in a luxury hotel, all meals and visits to places of interest*
(b) **to consist in** = to be, to mean; *for him, dieting consists in having two chocolates instead of three*

④ **consistent**
[kə'sɪstənt] *adjective*
(a) **consistent with something** = which does not contradict something; *the measures taken must be consistent with government policy*
(b) always at the same level; *some of his work is very good, but he's not consistent*

④ **consistently**
[kən'sɪstəntli] *adverb*
always, without changing; *she has been consistently supportive of our work*

④ **consolidate**
[kən'sɒlɪdeɪt] *verb*
(a) to make firm or sure; *having entered the market, the company spent a year consolidating its position; the team consolidated their lead with a second goal*
(b) to join together to make one single unit or one single shipment; *the two businesses consolidated to form one group; the shipment to India is being consolidated, and will leave the Port of Oakland early next week*

② **consonant**
[ˈkɒnsənənt] *noun*
letter representing a sound that is made using the teeth, tongue or lips; *"b" and "t" are consonants, while "e" and "i" are vowels*

COMMENT: the five vowels are "a", "e", "i", "o" and "u". All the other letters of the alphabet are consonants

④ **conspicuous**
[kən'spɪkjʊəs] *adjective*
very obvious; *he is very conspicuous because he is so tall*; **he was conspicuous by his absence** = it was very obvious that he was not there (NOTE: the opposite is **inconspicuous**)

④ **conspicuously**
[kən'spɪkjʊəsli] *adverb*
in a very obvious way; *she was conspicuously absent from the list of prize-winners*

③ **constant**
[ˈkɒnstənt]
1 *adjective*
(a) not changing or stopping; *the constant noise of music from the bar next door drives me mad*
(b) always there; *his dog was his constant companion*
(c) with a value that does not change; *the calculations are constant digits*
2 *noun*
number or thing that does not change; *the speed of light is a constant; death and taxes are the only constants in life*

③ **constantly**
[ˈkɒnstəntli] *adverb*
all the time; *he is constantly changing his mind; the telephone rang constantly*

④ **constituency**
[kən'stɪtjʊənsi] *noun*
(a) voters in an electoral district; *the senator was returned to office by his constituency*
(b) area or district represented by an elected official; *the constituency comprises four counties* (NOTE: plural is **constituencies**)

④ **constitute**
[ˈkɒnstɪtjut] *verb*
to be or form; *selling the photographs to a newspaper constitutes a serious breach of security; women now constitute the majority of the committee*

② **constitution**
[kɒnstɪˈtjuʃn] *noun*
(a) ability of a person to stay healthy; *she has a very strong constitution*
(b) laws and principles under which a country is ruled, which give the people rights and duties, and which give the government powers and duties; *most states have a written constitution; freedom of speech is guaranteed by the U.S. Constitution*
(c) written rules or regulations of a society, club, etc.; *under the society's constitution, the chairman is elected for two years*

③ **constitutional**
[kɒnstɪˈtjʃənl]
1 *adjective*

(a) according to a country's constitution; *such action by the secretary of defense is not constitutional*

(b) according to a society's constitution; *the election of the chairman for a third term of office is not constitutional*

2 *noun*

short walk that is good for your health; *after a big lunch I went for a constitutional; he always takes his early morning constitutional in the park*

④ **constraint**
[kən'streɪnt] *noun*

something which limits your ability to act; *the financial constraints placed on a country by the international banking system; the legal constraints of my position do not allow me to make any comment*

② **construct**
[kən'strʌkt] *verb*

to build; *we have tendered for the contract to construct the new airport; the wings are constructed of light steel*

② **construction**
[kən'strʌkʃn] *noun*

(a) the act of building; *the construction of the new stadium took three years;* **construction company** = company that specializes in building; **under construction** = being built; *the airport is under construction*

(b) thing that has been built; *the new stadium is a magnificent construction; planning regulations ban any construction more than 10 stories high in the older part of the town*

④ **constructive**
[kən'strʌktɪv] *adjective*

which aims to help or improve; *she made some constructive suggestions for improving the store layout*

③ **consult**
[kən'sʌlt] *verb*

(a) to ask someone for advice; *he consulted his accountant about his tax*

(b) to look at something to get information; *after consulting the map they decided to go north; he consulted his watch and said that they had enough time to catch the train*

④ **consultant**
[kən'sʌltənt] *noun*

specialist who gives advice; *his tax consultant advised him to sell the shares*

④ **consultation**
[kɒnsʌl'teɪʃn] *noun*

(a) act of consulting; *after consultations with the police, the government has decided to ban the protest march; a 30-minute consultation with my lawyer cost me more than I earn in a week!*

(b) act of visiting a doctor for advice; *she had a consultation with an eye surgeon*

④ **consume**
[kən'sjum] *verb*

(a) to eat or drink; *the guests consumed over 100 hamburgers*

(b) to use up; *the factory consumes a vast quantity of energy*

③ **consumer**
[kən'sjumər] *noun*

person or company that buys goods or services; *gas consumers are protesting the increase in prices; consumers are buying more from supermarkets and less from small stores;* **consumer goods** = goods bought by members of the public

④ **consumption**
[kən'sʌmpʃn] *noun*

(a) act of consuming; *the meat was condemned as not fit for human consumption; the consumption of alcohol on the premises is not allowed*

(b) quantity consumed; *unless you reduce your consumption of fat, you risk having a heart attack;* **gas consumption** = amount of gas used by an automobile to go a certain distance; *an automobile with low gas consumption*

② **contact**
['kɒntækt]

1 *noun*

(a) touch; *avoid any contact between the oil and the skin; anyone who has been in physical contact with the patient must consult their doctor immediately;* **contacts** *or* **contact lenses** = tiny lenses worn directly on your eyes instead of eyeglasses

(b) act of communicating with someone; *we don't have much contact with our old friends in Arkansas;* **to get in contact with someone** = to communicate with someone you have not spoken to or written to; *he put me in contact with a good lawyer* = he told me the name and address of a good lawyer; **I have lost contact with them** = I do not communicate with them any longer; **contact number** = phone number which you can call to speak to someone

(c) person whom you know; *he has a lot of contacts in the newspaper world; who is your contact in the cabinet?*

2 *verb*

to get into communication with someone; *he tried to contact his office by telephone; can you contact the ticket office immediately?*

③ **contagious**
[kən'teɪdʒəs] *adjective*

(a) *(disease)* which can be passed by touching an infected person or objects which an infected person has touched; *did you have any contagious diseases when you were a child?; your child is no longer contagious and can go back to school* (NOTE: compare **infectious**)

(b) which can be passed on to someone else; *he's a great music teacher and his enthusiasm for music is very contagious*

② contain
[kən'teɪn] *verb*
(a) to hold, to have inside; *the bottle contains acid*; *the envelope contained a check for $1500*; *a barrel contains 250 liters*; *I have lost a bag containing important documents*
(b) to restrict; *the army tried to contain the advance of the enemy forces*; *the party is attempting to contain the revolt among its members*

② container
[kən'teɪnər] *noun*
(a) box or bottle, etc., that holds something else; *we need a container for all this garbage*; *the gas is shipped in strong metal containers*
(b) special very large case for easy loading onto a ship, truck, etc.; *the crane was loading the containers onto the ship*; *we had our furniture shipped out to Singapore in a container*; **a container-load of spare parts** = a shipment of spare parts sent in a container; **container port** = port which only deals with containers; **container ship** = ship which only carries containers

④ contaminate
[kən'tæmɪneɪt] *verb*
to make something dirty by touching it or by adding something to it; *supplies of drinking water were contaminated by refuse from the factories*; *a party of tourists fell sick after eating contaminated food*

④ contemporary
[kən'temprəri]
1 *adjective*
(a) **contemporary with someone** *or* **something** = existing at the same time as someone or something; *most of the people I was contemporary with at college already have jobs*
(b) modern, present-day; *a museum of contemporary art*
2 *noun*
person who lives at the same time as someone; *he is one of my contemporaries from school*; *Shakespeare and his contemporaries lived and worked in London*

④ contempt
[kən'tempt] *noun*
feeling of not respecting someone; *you have shown contempt for the feelings of our family*; *the reviewer had nothing but contempt for the author of the novel*; **to hold someone in contempt** = not to respect someone; *they hold all foreigners in contempt and won't have anything to do with them*

③ content
1 *adjective* [kən'tent]
content to = happy to; *she was content to sit in the sun and wait*; **content with** = satisfied with; *if you are not content with the way the automobile runs, bring it back and we will look at it again*
2 *noun*

(a) [kən'tent] satisfaction; **to your heart's content** = as much as you want; *you can play billiards to your heart's content*; *living by the sea, they can go sailing to their heart's content*
(b) ['kɒntent] thing or amount which is contained; *dried fruit has a higher sugar content than fresh fruit*; **the mineral content of water** = the percentages of different minerals contained in a sample of water

② contents
['kɒntents] *noun*
things which are inside something, which are in a container; *he dropped the bottle and the contents spilled onto the carpet*; *the burglars took the entire contents of the safe*; *the customs officials inspected the contents of the packing case*; *she kept the contents of the letter secret*; **table of contents** = list of chapters in a book, usually printed at the beginning of the text

④ contest
1 *noun* ['kɒntest]
fight, competition; *only two people entered the contest for the party leadership*; **beauty contest** = competition to see which girl is most beautiful
2 *verb* [kən'test]
(a) to fight an election; *there are four candidates contesting the seat*
(b) to query a will, or argue that a will is invalid; *when she died and left all her money to a cats' home, her family contested the will*

④ context
['kɒntekst] *noun*
phrase in which a word occurs which helps to show what it means; *even if you don't know what a word means, you can sometimes guess its meaning from the context*; **taken out of context** = quoted without surrounding text; *my words have been taken out of context - if you read the whole speech you will see that I meant something quite different*

② continent
['kɒntɪnənt] *noun*
(a) one of the major land areas in the world (Africa, North America, South America, Asia, Australia, Europe, etc.)
(b) *(in Britain)* **the Continent** = the rest of Europe, as opposed to Britain itself, which is an island; **on the Continent** = in Europe; **to the Continent** = to Europe; *when you drive on the Continent remember to drive on the right*; *they go to the Continent on vacation each year, sometimes to France, sometimes to Switzerland*

④ continental
[kɒntɪ'nentl]
1 *adjective*
(a) referring to a continent; **continental climate** = climate of hot dry summers and very cold winters; *the Midwest has a continental climate, which is quite different from the climate in Florida*; **continental shelf** = area of shallow sea around the edges of a continent; *oil companies*

are very interested in exploring the waters of the continental shelf
(b) referring to Europe (excluding the British Isles); **continental breakfast** = light breakfast
2 *noun*
(informal) **Continental** = European person; *the Continentals seem to play a different type of soccer from us*

② **continual**
[kən'tɪnjuəl] *adjective*
which goes on all the time; *I am getting fed up with her continual complaints*; *the computer has given us continual problems ever since we bought it*

② **continually**
[kən'tɪnjuəli] *adverb*
very often, again and again, almost all the time; *the photocopier is continually breaking down*

② **continue**
[kən'tɪnju] *verb*
to go on doing something or go on happening; *he continued working, even though the house was on fire*; *the engine continued to send out clouds of black smoke*; *the meeting started at 10 A.M. and continued until 6 P.M.*; *the show continued with some children's dances*

② **continuous**
[kən'tɪnjuəs] *adjective*
with no break; *she has been in continuous pain for three days*; *a continuous white line means that you are not allowed to pass*; **continuous tense** = form of a verb showing that something is going on and has not stopped; *"is going" is a continuous form of the verb "to go"*; *continuous tenses in English are formed using the ending -ing*

② **continuously**
[kən'tɪnjuəsli] *adverb*
without stopping; *the children behind me ate popcorn continuously during the movie*; *the lead singer was on stage continuously for four hours*

④ **contraceptive**
[kɒntrə'septɪv]
1 *adjective*
which prevents pregnancy; *the contraceptive pill is available from doctors and clinics*
2 *noun*
drug or device which prevents pregnancy; *the drugstore sells various types of contraceptives*; *an oral contraceptive such as the Pill*

② **contract**
1 ['kɒntrækt] *noun*
legal agreement; *I don't agree with some of the conditions of the contract*; **under contract** = bound by the terms of a contract; *the company is under contract to a French supermarket*; **breach of contract** = breaking the terms of a contract; **the company is in breach of contract** = the company has failed to do what was agreed in the contract
2 [kən'trækt] *verb*

(a) to agree to do some work under a legally binding contract; *to contract to supply spare parts or to contract for the supply of spare parts*
(b) to sign an agreement with a contractor; *the corporation has contracted the garbage collection service to a private company*
(c) to become smaller; *metal contracts when it gets cold, and expands when it is hot*

③ **contractor**
[kən'træktər] *noun*
person who does work according to a signed agreement; *a building contractor*; *an electrical contractor*

④ **contradict**
[kɒntrə'dɪkt] *verb*
to say that what someone else says is not true; to be different from what has been said before; *why do you always contradict me?*; *the witness contradicted herself several times*; *what you have just said contradicts what you said yesterday*

③ **contradiction**
[kɒntrə'dɪkʃn] *noun*
stating or being the opposite; *there is a basic contradiction between the government's policies and what it actually does*; **a contradiction in terms** = phrase that is formed of two parts which contradict each other, and so have no meaning; *a politician who tells the truth is a contradiction in terms*

④ **contradictory**
[kɒntrə'dɪktəri] *adjective*
which states or is the opposite; *we were given various contradictory orders*

④ **contrary**
['kɒntrəri]
1 *adjective*
(a) opposite; *most people agreed with the speaker, but one or two expressed contrary views*; **contrary winds** = winds blowing in the opposite direction; *the ship could not leave harbor because of contrary winds*
(b) **contrary to** = in opposition to; *contrary to what you would expect, the desert gets quite cold at night*
(c) [kən'treəri] always doing the opposite of what you want; *she's such a contrary child*
2 *noun*
the contrary = the opposite; **on the contrary** = just the opposite; *I'm not mad at her - on the contrary, I think she has done the right thing*; **to the contrary** = stating the opposite; *we will go on with the plans for the exhibition unless we hear to the contrary*; *smoking used to be considered harmless, but now the evidence is to the contrary*

③ **contrast**
1 *noun* ['kɒntræst]
sharp difference between two things; *the contrast in weather between the north and the south of the country*; **in contrast to** = as opposed to; *he is quite short, in contrast to his*

sister who is very tall; the north of the country is green and wooded in contrast to the south which is dry and sandy; the two cities are in sharp contrast
2 verb [kən'træst]
to be quite obviously different from; *his rude letter contrasted with his friendly conversation on the telephone*

② **contribute**
[kən'trıbjut] verb
(a) to help toward; *the government's policies have contributed to a feeling of worry among teachers*
(b) to give money to; *we were asked to contribute to a charity; everyone was asked to contribute to the secretary's going away present*
(c) to contribute to a magazine = to write articles for a magazine

② **contribution**
[kɒntrı'bjuʃn] noun
(a) money, etc., given to help something; *she makes monthly contributions to the charity*
(b) article submitted to a newspaper; *the deadline for contributions is December 1*

① **control**
[kən'trəʊl]
1 noun
(a) keeping in order, being able to direct something; *the club is under the control of three shareholders; he lost control of his business and resigned; the teacher has no control over the class;* **control button** = on a TV, radio, etc., the button that switches it on, changes channel, increases volume, etc.; **control column** = handle for steering an aircraft; **control key** = key on a computer which works part of a program
(b) restricting something; **under control** = restricted; *we try to keep expenses under tight control;* **to bring something under control** = to reduce or restrict something; *the firemen quickly brought the fire under control;* **out of control** = not restricted; *the automobile ran down the hill out of control; our spending has got out of control; the fire started in the roof and quickly got out of control; soccer fans got out of control and started breaking windows in the center of town*
(c) control group = group against which the results of a test on another group can be compared
2 verb
(a) to keep in order, to direct or restrict; *the police couldn't control the crowds; there was nobody there to control the traffic; we must try to control the sales of foreign cars; the government controls the price of meat*
(b) to control a business = to have the power to direct the way a business is run; *the business is controlled by a company based in Austin*
(NOTE: **controlling - controlled**)

③ **controller**
[kən'trəʊlər] noun
person who controls; **air traffic controller** = person who directs planes from a control tower; *the strike by air traffic controllers disrupted air services*

④ **controversial**
[kɒntrə'vɜrʃl] adjective
which starts violent discussions; *he made a highly controversial speech; making drugs legal is a very controversial issue; she has controversial views on abortion*

④ **controversy**
['kɒntrəvɜrsi] noun
sharp discussion; *there is a lot of controversy about the funding of political parties*

④ **convenience**
[kən'viniəns] noun
(a) being convenient; *I like the convenience of working from home; we bought the house because of the convenience of the area for shopping;* **at your earliest convenience** = as soon as you can easily do it; *please return this form at your earliest convenience*
(b) public conveniences = public toilets; **all modern conveniences** = all modern facilities such as central heating, telephone, electricity, etc.; *the apartment is advertised for sale with all modern conveniences*
(c) convenience food = food which is prepared by the shop before it is sold, so that it needs only heating to be made ready to eat; *sales of convenience food are booming;* **convenience store** = small local store which stays open long hours and stocks a wide range of necessary goods

③ **convenient**
[kən'viniənt] adjective
which does not cause any practical problems; *6:30 in the morning is not a very convenient time for a meeting; a bank draft is a convenient way of sending money abroad*

③ **conveniently**
[kən'viniəntli] adverb
in a useful way; *the hotel is conveniently placed next to the railway station*

② **convention**
[kən'venʃn] noun
(a) the usual way of doing things; *it is a convention that the bride wears white to her wedding*
(b) contract or treaty; *an international convention on human rights*
(c) general meeting of an association or political party; *they are holding their annual convention in Chicago;* **convention center** = building with a series of meeting rooms, hotel bedrooms, restaurants, etc., built specially for holding large meetings

④ **conventional**
[kən'venʃənəl] adjective
ordinary, usual; *they're a very conventional*

family; *he arrived at the office wearing a very conventional gray suit*; **conventional weapons** = ordinary weapons such as guns, not nuclear or biological weapons

② **conversation**
[kɒnvə'seɪʃn] *noun*
talk; *we had a long conversation with the bank manager*; *why did he suddenly change the subject of the conversation?*; **to carry on a conversation with someone** = to talk to someone; *she tried to carry on a conversation with him while he was working*; *it's difficult to carry on a conversation with Uncle Harry because he's deaf*

④ **conversion**
[kən'vɜrʃn] *noun*
(a) changing of one thing into another; *the conversion of the old chapel into a modern house*; *I need a calculator to work out the conversion of $800 into pesos*
(b) turning of a person to another set of ideas or religion; *she underwent a sudden conversion to Islam*

③ **convert**
1 *noun* ['kɒnvɜrt]
person who has changed his ideas or religion; *he has become a convert to Islam*
2 *verb* [kən'vɜrt]
(a) to turn or to make someone turn from one set of ideas or religion to another; *when she got married she converted to Islam*; *she tried to convert her husband to a vegetarian*; *see also* PREACH
(b) to change; *we are converting the shed into a studio*; *these panels convert the heat of the sun into electricity*
(c) to change money of one country for money of another; *we converted our dollars into Swiss francs*

③ **convertible**
[kən'vɜrtəbl]
1 *noun*
automobile with a roof which folds back or can be removed; *you can rent a small convertible for $100 a day*
2 *adjective*; *(especially of a currency)* which can easily be changed into another currency; *the dollar, the yen and other convertible currencies can be bought easily at banks*

④ **convey**
[kən'veɪ] *verb*
(a) to transport, to carry; *the supplies were being conveyed in trucks*
(b) to give a message or to express something; *please convey my good wishes to the team*

② **convict**
1 *noun* ['kɒnvɪkt]
criminal who has been sent to prison; *the police are searching for two escaped convicts*
2 *verb* [kən'vɪkt]
to find someone guilty; *she was convicted of theft*

③ **conviction**
[kən'vɪkʃn] *noun*
(a) being found guilty; *his lawyers are appealing his conviction*
(b) being certain that something is true; *it was a common conviction in the Middle Ages that the Earth was flat*; *her religious convictions do not allow her to eat pork*
(c) being likely, able to convince someone; *she gave a string of excuses which completely lacked conviction*

② **convince**
[kən'vɪns] *verb*
to convince someone of something = to persuade someone that something is true; *the lawyer has to convince the jury that his client is innocent*; *at an interview, you have to convince the employer that you are the right person for the job*

② **convinced**
[kən'vɪnst] *adjective*
very certain; *I am convinced that she knows something about the robbery*; *I'm still not convinced she is telling the truth*

① **cook**
[kʊk]
1 *noun*
person who gets food ready; *she worked as a cook in a restaurant during the summer*; *he's a very good cook* = he makes very good food
2 *verb*
(a) to get food ready for eating, especially by heating it; *if you want to learn how to cook Chinese food, watch the TV program*; *don't bother your mother when she's cooking the dinner*; *how do you cook cabbage?*; *see also* BAKE, BOIL, FRY, etc.
(b) *(of food)* to be got ready by heating; *the chicken is cooking in the oven*; *how long do these vegetables take to cook?*

③ **cookbook**
['kʊkbʊk] *noun*
book containing recipes, showing you how to cook dishes; *I gave her a Thai cookbook for her birthday*; *if you're not sure how long to cook turkey, look it up in the cookbook*

④ **cooker**
['kʊkər] *noun*
device run on gas, electricity, etc., for cooking food; *I used a pressure cooker to cook the jam*

① **cookie**
['kʊki] *noun*
small flat hard sweet cake; *she bought a pack of cookies*; **chocolate chip cookie** = small flat hard sweet cake made with little pieces of hard chocolate inside

① **cooking**
['kʊkɪŋ] *noun*
(a) action of getting food ready to eat, especially by heating it; *he does the cooking, while his wife serves in the restaurant*; **cooking apple** =

sour apple which can be cooked but not eaten raw

(b) particular way of preparing food; *the restaurant specializes in French provincial cooking*

① **cookout**
['kʊkaʊt] *noun*
meal or party where food is cooked out-of-doors; *we had a cookout for twenty guests*; *let's have a cookout in our backyard*; *they've been invited to a cookout*

① **cool**
[kuːl]
1 *adjective*
(a) quite cold; *blow on your soup to make it cool*; *it was hot on deck but cool down below*; *wines should be stored in a cool place*; *it gets cool in the evenings in September*
(b) not enthusiastic; *I got a cool reception when I arrived half an hour late*; *the board was cool to his proposal*
(c) calm; *the nurses remained cool and professional when dealing with all the accident victims* (NOTE: **cooler - coolest**)
2 *verb*
to make cool; to become cool; *she cooked the jam for several hours and then put it to one side to cool*
3 *noun*
(a) colder area which is pleasant; *after the heat of the front lawn, it is nice to sit in the cool of the patio*
(b) *(informal)* state of being calm; **to lose your cool** = to become angry; *he lost his cool when they told him there were no tables free*; *as soon as the reporters started to ask her questions she lost her cool*

④ **co-op**
['kəʊɒp] *noun*
(informal) cooperative store; *we do all our shopping at the local co-op*

② **cooperate**
[kəʊ'ɒpəreɪt] *verb*
to cooperate with someone = to work with someone; *several governments are cooperating in the fight against international drug smuggling*

② **cooperation**
[kəʊɒpə'reɪʃn] *noun*
action of working together with someone else; *the school is run with the cooperation of the local church*; *he wrote the book in cooperation with one of his students*

② **cooperative**
[kəʊ'ɒprətɪv]
1 *adjective*
(a) working with the profits shared between the workers; *a cooperative farm*; *a cooperative store*
(b) helpful, willing to work with someone; *the bank manager was not at all cooperative when I asked for a loan*

2 *noun*
business that works on the basis that all profits are shared; *a workers' cooperative*

④ **coordinate**
1 *verb* [kəʊ'ɔːdɪneɪt]
to make people or things work together or fit in with each other; *his job is to coordinate with the work of the various relief agencies*; *the election campaign was coordinated by the party headquarters*
2 *noun* [kəʊ'ɔːdɪnət]
set of figures that fix a point on a map or graph; *what are the coordinates for that hill? I don't think it is marked on the map*; *draw the X - Y coordinates*

④ **coordination**
[kəʊɔːdɪ'neɪʃn] *noun*
(a) action of coordinating people or things; *better coordination between departments would have allowed everyone to know what was happening*
(b) being able to move parts of your body at the same time properly; *she has excellent coordination for a little girl who is only two years old*

① **cop**
[kɒp] *noun*
(informal) police officer; *he was stopped by a cop*; *when the cops came to arrest him he had disappeared*; *watch out! there's a cop coming*

④ **cope**
[kəʊp] *verb*
to cope with something = to manage to deal with something; *she can cope perfectly well on her own*; *we are trying to cope with a sudden mass of orders*

④ **copier**
['kɒpjər] *noun*
machine which makes photocopies; **copier paper** = special paper used in photocopiers

② **copper**
['kɒpər] *noun*
(a) reddish metal that turns green when exposed to air; *copper is a good conductor of electricity*; *the end of the copper wire should be attached to the terminal* (NOTE: Chemical element: chemical symbol: **Cu**; atomic number: **29**)
(b) reddish brown color

① **copy**
['kɒpi]
1 *noun*
(a) something made to look the same as something else; *this is an exact copy of the painting by Picasso*; **carbon copy** = copy made with carbon paper
(b) one book; one newspaper; *where's my copy of today's "Wall Street Journal"?*; *I lent my old copy of Shakespeare to my brother and he never gave it back*; *can I borrow your copy of the telephone directory?*
(c) text written to be used in a newspaper or advertisement; *he sent in his copy three days*

late; *we need more copy for this page* (NOTE: plural is **copies** in meanings (a) and (b))

2 *verb*

to make something which looks like something else; *to knit the pullover, just copy this pattern*; *I get very annoyed because he copies everything I do*; **copying machine** = a machine that photocopies

ⓐ **copyright**

['kɒpɪraɪt] *noun*

an author's right to publish a book, put on a play, etc., and not to have it copied without permission; *who holds the copyright for the play?*; *she is being sued for breach of copyright*; **book that is in copyright** = book that is protected by the copyright laws; **book that is out of copyright** = book by a writer who has been dead for more than seventy years

① **cord**

[kɔrd] *noun*

(a) strong thin rope; *the box was tied with cord*; *in an emergency, pull the cord to stop the train*

(b) thick electric wire; *I need an extension cord for the electric saw*

③ **core**

[kɔr]

1 *noun*

central part; **apple core** = hard part in the middle of an apple, containing the seeds; *he threw the apple core into the lake*; **rotten to the core** = completely rotten; *the local police force is rotten to the core*; **to take a core sample** = to cut a long cylindrical sample of soil or rock for testing

2 *verb*

to cut out the central part of an apple, etc.; *peel and core the apples before putting them in the oven*

① **cork**

[kɔrk]

1 *noun*

(a) piece of light wood from the bark of a tree, which closes wine bottles; *he pulled the cork out of the bottle*; *the little boat went up and down on the surface of the water like a cork*

(b) material made from the very light bark of a type of oak tree; *she placed little cork mats on the table to stop the wine glasses marking it*; **cork oak** = type of oak tree with thick light bark; *cork oaks are common in Spain and Portugal*

2 *verb*

to put a cork into a bottle; *when they had drunk half the bottle, she corked it up to use the following day*

① **corn**

[kɔrn] *noun*

(a) cereal plants such as wheat, etc.; *a field of corn*

(b) in particular maize, a widely grown very tall cereal crop; **sweet corn** = sweet variety of corn, which you can eat as a vegetable; **corn cob** = head of corn with seeds; **corn on the cob** = a

piece of corn, with seeds on it, boiled and served hot, with butter and salt

(c) hard painful lump of skin, usually on your foot, where something, such as a tight shoe, has rubbed it; *he has a corn on his little toe*

④ **corned beef**

['kɔrnd 'bif] *noun*

beef which has been preserved in salt water

① **corner**

['kɔrnər]

1 *noun*

(a) place where two walls, sides or streets meet; *the bank is on the corner of Main Street and Lincoln Street*; *put the plant in the corner of the room nearest the window*; *the number is in the top right-hand corner of the page*; *the motorcycle went around the corner at top speed*; **to paint yourself into a corner** = to get yourself into a situation that you cannot get out of; **to turn the corner** = (i) to go round a corner; (ii) to get better after being ill or in difficulties; *as she turned the corner she saw the bus coming*; *he has been in bed for weeks, but he seems to have turned the corner*

(b) *(in games, such as soccer)* free kick taken from the corner of the field near the opponent's goal

2 *verb*

(a) to turn a corner; *this new car corners very well*

(b) **to corner the market** = to own most or all of the supply of a certain thing and so control the price; *the group tried to corner the market in silver*

① **cornflakes**

['kɔrnfleɪks] *noun*

breakfast cereal of crisp pieces of roasted corn; *I'll just have a bowl of cornflakes and a cup of coffee for breakfast*

② **corporal**

['kɔrprəl]

1 *adjective*

referring to the body; **corporal punishment** = punishment by beating someone; *corporal punishment is illegal in public schools*

2 *noun*

rank in the army and marines below sergeant; *the major ordered the corporal to take down the flag* (NOTE: can be used with the surname: **Corporal Jones**)

③ **corporate**

['kɔrpərət] *adjective*

referring to a body such as a corporation; *corporate responsibility rests with the whole management*; *corporate profits are down this year*; **corporate plan** = plan for a whole corporation

③ **corporation**

[kɔrpə'reɪʃn] *noun*

large business organization; *working for a big corporation can pay better than working for a small family firm*; **corporation tax** = tax on profits made by companies

③ **corpse**
[kɔrps] *noun*
dead body; *after he had killed her he didn't know what to do with the corpse*

① **correct**
[kə'rekt]
1 *adjective*
right; without any mistakes; *can you tell me the correct time?*; *you have to give correct answers to all the questions if you want to win first prize*; *you are correct in thinking that the weather in Greece is hot*; *would it be correct to say that the store has not made a profit for years?*
2 *verb*
to take away mistakes in something; *the boss had to correct the letter which his secretary had typed*; *you must try to correct your driving mistakes, or you will never pass the test*; *the computer keeps switching itself off - can you correct this fault?*

② **correction**
[kə'rekʃn] *noun*
showing a mistake in something, making something correct; *he made a few small corrections to the letter*

② **correctly**
[kə'rektlɪ] *adverb*
in a correct way; *you must answer all the questions correctly if you want to win the prize*

③ **correspond**
[kɒrɪ'spɒnd] *verb*
(a) to correspond to = to fit with; *the findings correspond to my own research*
(b) to correspond with someone = to write letters to someone; *she corresponded for years with this man living in New York whom she had never met*

④ **correspondence**
[kɒrɪ'spɒndəns] *noun*
letters; *they had been carrying on a correspondence for years*; *she was told by her father to break off the correspondence*; **correspondence course** = lessons given by mail; **business correspondence** = letters concerned with a business; **to be in correspondence with someone** = to write letters to someone and receive letters back; *I have been in correspondence with the company about a refund but with no success*

② **correspondent**
[kɒrɪ'spɒndənt] *noun*
(a) journalist who writes articles for newspapers or reports for TV or radio on a particular subject; *he is the London correspondent for the "Washington Post"*; *the report has come from our news correspondent in the area*; *a report from our financial correspondent*
(b) person who writes letters; *a correspondent in Australia sent us an e-mail*

③ **corresponding**
[kɒrɪ'spɒndɪŋ] *adjective*
which corresponds; *the approach of winter brings a corresponding rise in the number of people wanting to go on vacation in warm countries*

③ **corridor**
['kɒrɪdɔr] *noun*
long, narrow passage; *the ladies' room is straight ahead at the end of the corridor*; *there is an underground corridor to the next building*

④ **corrupt**
[kə'rʌpt]
1 *adjective*
(a) who is not honest, who takes bribes; *the senator promised to fire any officials who were found to be corrupt*
(b) (data on a computer disk) which is faulty; *he sent us a disk with corrupt data*
2 *verb*
(a) to make dishonest; *he was corrupted by his rich friends from college*; *"power corrupts, absolute power corrupts absolutely"*
(b) to make data faulty; *the data on this disk has been corrupted*

④ **corruption**
[kə'rʌpʃn] *noun*
(a) paying money or giving a favor to someone (usually an official) so that he does what you want; *government corruption is difficult to control*; *corruption in the civil service will be rooted out*
(b) making data faulty; *you have to watch out for corruption of data*

② **cosmetic**
[kɒz'metɪk]
1 *adjective*
which improves someone's or something's appearance; *she uses a cosmetic cream to remove the lines round her eyes*; *the changes to the organization were purely cosmetic*; **cosmetic surgery** = surgery to improve the appearance of someone
2 *noun*
cosmetics = substances like skin cream, which improve your appearance; *my wife keeps all her cosmetics in a little bag*

② **cost**
[kɒst]
1 *noun*
(a) price that you have to pay for something; *what is the cost of a round-trip to Dayton?*; *computer costs are falling each year*
(b) **costs** = expenses involved in a court case; **to pay costs** = to pay the expenses of a court case; *he lost his case and was ordered to pay costs*; **the judge awarded costs to the defendant** = the judge said that the defendant would not have to pay the cost of the case
2 *verb*
to have a price; *potatoes cost 40 cents a pound*; *gas seems to cost more all the time*; **what does**

it cost? = how much is it?; **to cost an arm and a leg** = to be very expensive; *don't buy your kitchen there - it'll cost you an arm and a leg*; *the repairs to his car cost him an arm and a leg*; *tropical fruit costs an arm and a leg in winter*; *see also* FORTUNE, SMALL (NOTE: **costing - cost - has cost**)

③ **costly**
['kɒstli] *adjective*
very expensive; *our new automobile is not very costly to run*; **costly mistake** = mistake which results in a lot of money being spent; *telling them we would pay all their expenses was a costly mistake* (NOTE: **costlier - costliest**)

② **cost of living**
['kɒst əv 'lɪvɪŋ] *noun*
money that has to be paid for food, heating, rent, etc.; *higher interest rates increase the cost of living*; **cost-of-living increase** = increase in salary to allow it to keep up with the increased cost of living; **cost-of-living index** = way of measuring the cost of living which is shown as a percentage increase on the figure for the previous year

② **costume**
['kɒstjum] *noun*
(a) set of clothes worn by an actor or actress in a play or movie or on TV; *the costumes for "Henry V" are magnificent*
(b) **national costume** = special clothes worn by people of a certain country; *they all came to the wedding in national costume*

① **cottage**
['kɒtɪdʒ] *noun*
little house in the country; *we have a cottage in the mountains that we use in the summer*; **cottage cheese** = type of moist white cheese

① **cotton**
['kɒtən] *noun*
(a) thread from the soft seed heads of a tropical plant; *she put a new spool of cotton thread on the sewing machine*
(b) cloth made of cotton; *he was wearing a pair of cotton pants*; *I bought some cotton material to make a skirt*
(c) **absorbent cotton** = cotton fibers used to clean wounds, to clean the skin, to apply cream, etc.; *she dabbed the cut with absorbent cotton*; *the nurse put a pad of absorbent cotton over the graze*

② **couch**
[kaʊtʃ] *noun*
long comfortable seat with a soft back; *she lay down on a couch in the lounge*; *(informal)* **couch potato** = person who lies on a sofa all day, watching TV or videos (NOTE: plural is **couches**)

② **cough**
[kɒf]
1 *noun*
sending the air out of your lungs suddenly, for example when you are sick; *take some cough*

medicine if your cough is bad; *he ought to see the doctor if his cough is no better*; *he gave a little cough to attract the waitress's attention*; **cough drops** = candies with medicine inside against coughs; *she always carries a pack of cough drops in her bag*
2 *verb*
to send air out of your lungs suddenly because your throat hurts; *the smoke from the fire made everyone cough*; *people with the flu go around coughing and sneezing*

① **could**
[kʊd] *verb used with other verbs*
(a) *(meaning "was" or "would be able")* *the old lady fell down and couldn't get up*; *you could still catch the train if you ran*
(b) *(meaning "was allowed")* *the police officer said we could go into the house*
(c) *(in asking)* *could you pass me the salt, please?*; *could you shut the window?*
(d) *(meaning "might happen")* *the new shopping center could be finished by Christmas*
(e) *(making a suggestion)* *you could always try borrowing money from the bank* (NOTE: negative is **could not**, usually **couldn't**; note also that **could** is the past of **can**; **could** is only used in front of other verbs and is not followed by the word **to**)

② **council**
['kaʊnsəl] *noun*
(a) elected committee; **city council** = elected committee which runs a town; *the city council has decided to sell this building*; *see also* SECURITY COUNCIL
(b) official group chosen to advise on a problem (NOTE: do not confuse with **counsel**)

③ **councilor**
['kaʊnsələr] *noun*
elected member of a town council; *the local paper has exposed corruption among the councilors* (NOTE: do not confuse with **counselor**)

④ **counsel**
['kaʊnsl]
1 *noun*
lawyer(s) acting for one of the parties in a legal action; *defense counsel*; *prosecution counsel*
2 *verb*
to advise; *she counseled us against buying the house*

③ **counselor**
['kaʊnsələr] *noun*
adviser; *he was advised to see a counselor about his drinking problem*; **marriage counselor** = person who gives advice to couples whose marriage is in difficulties (NOTE: do not confuse with **councilor**)

① **count**
[kaʊnt]
1 *noun*

(a) action of counting or of adding; **to lose count** = to no longer have any idea of how many there are; *I tried to add up all the sales figures but lost count and had to start again*; *I've lost count of the number of times he's left his umbrella on the train*
(b) adding up the votes after an election; *the candidates paced up and down during the count*
(c) large amount of something, calculated in a scientific way; *today there is a high pollution count*
(d) accusation, charge read out against someone in court; *she was found guilty on two counts of theft*
2 *verb*
(a) to say numbers in order (1, 2, 3, 4, etc.); *she's only two and she can count up to ten*; *count to five and then start running*; **to count backward** = to say numbers in the opposite order (9, 8, 7, 6, etc.)
(b) to find out a total; *did you count how many books there are in the library?*; *he counted up the sales for the twelve months*
(c) to include when finding out a total; *there were sixty people on the boat if you count the children*; *did you count my trip to New York as part of my expenses?*; **not counting** = not including; *there are three of us, not counting the baby*; *we have three computers, not counting the old ones that don't work anymore*
(d) to be important; *your appearance counts for a lot in an interview*; *every little bit of energy saved counts*

② **counter**
['kauntər]
1 *noun*
(a) long flat surface in a store for displaying goods, or in a bank for placing money; *she put her purse down on the counter and took out her checkbook*; *the cheese counter is over there*; **bargain counter** = counter where things are sold cheaply; **checkout counter** = desk in a store where you pay for the goods you have bought; *take your purchases to the nearest checkout counter*; **ticket counter** = place where tickets are sold; **sold over the counter** = sold without a prescription; *some drugs are sold over the counter, but for most you need a prescription*
(b) long flat surface on which food is got ready; *he had his breakfast standing at the counter in the kitchen*
(c) small round disk used in games; *you've thrown a six - you can move your counter six places*; *she placed a pile of counters on the board*
2 *verb*
to reply in an opposing way; *he accused her of theft and she countered with an accusation of sexual harassment*

③ **counterclockwise**
[kauntər'klɒkwaɪz] *adverb & adjective*
in the opposite direction to the hands of a clock;

he was driving counterclockwise round the rotary when the accident took place (NOTE: the opposite is **clockwise**)

④ **counterpart**
['kauntərpart] *noun*
person who has a similar job or who is in a similar situation; *the secretary of state had talks with his Japanese counterpart*; **John is my counterpart at Smith's** = John has the same job at Smith's as I have here

③ **count on**
['kaunt 'ɒn] *verb*
to be sure that someone will do something; *can I count on you to help wash the dishes?*; *don't count on having good weather for the baseball game*

① **country**
['kʌntri] *noun*
(a) land that is separate and governs itself; *the countries of South America*; *some African countries voted against the plan* (NOTE: plural in this meaning is **countries**)
(b) land that is not the town; *he lives in the country*; *we went walking in the hill country*; *road travel is difficult in country areas* (NOTE: no plural in this meaning)
(c) **country music** *or* **country and western** = style of popular music from the Southern U.S.; *she's the queen of country and western*

② **countryside**
['kʌntrisaɪd] *noun*
land away from towns, with fields, woods, etc.; *the countryside in West Virginia is beautiful in the fall*; *the countryside is in danger of being covered in new houses* (NOTE: no plural)

③ **county**
['kaunti] *noun*
administrative division of a state or country; *I live in Cook County*; *the city and county of Los Angeles*; **county court** = court which hears minor civil cases (NOTE: plural is **counties**)

④ **coup**
[ku] *noun*
(a) the overthrow of a government by force; *the army took over after yesterday's coup*; *the officers who planned the failed coup were all executed*
(b) great success, successful move; *getting the Education Secretary to open the school exhibition was a coup for the organizers*

① **couple**
['kʌpl]
1 *noun*
(a) two things together; **a couple of** = (i) two; (ii) a few; *I have a couple of jobs for you to do*; *can you move the chairs a couple of feet to the left?*; *do you mind waiting a couple of minutes while I make a phone call?*; *the movie lasted a couple of hours*
(b) two people together; *they are a charming couple*; *several couples strolled past hand in hand*; **married couple** = husband and wife

2 *verb*

(a) to link; *high tides coupled with strong winds caused flooding along the coast*

(b) to join two machines together; *couple the trailer to the back of the truck*

② **coupon**
['kupɒn] *noun*
piece of paper that is used in place of money or in place of a ticket; *cut out the six coupons from the paper and send them to this address to receive your free travel bag; collect all ten coupons and cross the Atlantic for $150!; gift coupon* = coupon from a store which is given as a gift and which must be exchanged in that store

② **courage**
['kʌrɪdʒ] *noun*
being brave when in a dangerous situation; *she showed great courage in attacking the burglar* (NOTE: no plural)

① **course**
[kɔrs] *noun*
(a) over the course of = during; *he's gotten much richer over the course of the last few years*

(b) series of lessons; *I'm taking a math course; she's going on a painting course; she has finished her computing course; the hotel offers weekend courses in art*

(c) series of treatments, medicines, etc.; *he's taking a course of antibiotics*

(d) separate part of a meal; *a five-course meal; the first course is soup, and then you can have either fish or roast lamb*

(e) golf course = area of land specially designed for playing golf; *there is a golf course near the hotel*

◇ **in due course**
[ɪn 'dju 'kɔrs]
after a certain amount of time; *if you study for several years at college, in due course you will get a degree; put a coin in the slot and in due course the machine will produce a ticket*

◇ **of course**
[ɒf 'kɔrs]
(a) *(used to say "yes" or "no" more strongly)* *are you coming with us? - of course I am!; do you want to lose all your money? - of course not!*

(b) naturally; *he is rich so, of course, he lives in a big house*

② **court**
[kɔrt]
1 *noun*
(a) tribunal where a judge tries criminals, sometimes with a jury; *the court was packed for the opening of the murder trial; please tell the court what you saw when you opened the door; the defendant was in court for three hours; court case* = legal action or trial; *the court case is expected to last two weeks;* **to take someone to court** = to tell someone to appear in court to settle an argument

(b) area where a game of tennis, basketball, etc., is played; *the tennis courts are behind the hotel;* **to be on court** = to be playing tennis; *they were on court for over three hours*

(c) group of people living around a king or queen; *the people at court were very cold toward the young princess; it was dangerous to be a pretty young girl at the court of Henry VIII*

2 *verb*
(a) *(old)* to try to persuade a woman to marry you; *the man courted her for some months*

(b) to be often together before getting married; *do you remember when we were courting and you took me to see the sun setting over the ocean in San Diego?; they've been courting for three years, and there are still no signs of them getting married*

(c) to try to get someone to support you; *he has been courting the major stockholders to win their approval for the scheme*

(d) to court disaster = to risk disaster happening; *you are courting disaster if you try to drive a sports car without a license*

③ **courtesy**
['kɜrtəsi] *noun*
(a) being polite, having good manners; *the hotel staff showed us every courtesy; she might have had the courtesy to apologize; children should show some courtesy toward their grandparents*

(b) (by) courtesy of = as a gift from; with the kind permission of; *a box of chocolates by courtesy of the management; he arrived home two hours late, courtesy of the train service;* **courtesy bus** *or* **car** *or* **van** = bus, car or coach that is provided for people free of charge as a service; *a courtesy van will pick you up at the airport; the garage lent me a courtesy car to use while mine was being repaired*

① **courtroom**
['kɔrtrʊm] *noun*
room where a judge presides over a trial; *the jury left the courtroom to deliberate*

④ **courtyard**
['kɔrtjɑrd] *noun*
small square yard surrounded by buildings; *the hotel is built round a courtyard with fountains and palm trees*

① **cousin**
['kʌzɪn] *noun*
son or daughter of your uncle or aunt; *our cousins from Canada are coming to stay with us for Christmas; we didn't have a Christmas card from cousin Charles this year*

① **cover**
['kʌvər]
1 *noun*
(a) thing put over something to keep it clean, etc.; *keep a cover over your computer when you are not using it; put a cover over the meat to keep the flies off*

(b) front and back of a book, magazine, etc.; *she read the book from cover to cover*
(c) place where you can hide or shelter; *they ran for cover when it started to rain*; **under cover** = under a roof, not in the open air; *if it rains the meal will be served under cover*; **under cover of night** *or* **of darkness** = at night, when everything is hidden; *they crept out of the city under cover of darkness*; *the Marines attacked under cover of night*; **to take cover** = to shelter; *it started to rain and they took cover under a tree*; *when the robbers started shooting, the police officer took cover behind a wall*
(d) *(in a restaurant)* **cover charge** = charge per person in addition to the charge for food; *there is a $5 cover charge*
(e) envelope; **to send something under separate cover** = in a separate envelope; **to send a magazine under plain cover** = in a regular envelope with no company name printed on it; **cover letter** = COVERING LETTER
2 *verb*
(a) to put something over something to keep it clean, etc.; *you should cover the furniture with sheets before you start painting the ceiling*
(b) to hide something; *he covered the hole in the ground with leaves*; *she covered her face with her hands*
(c) to provide enough money to pay for something; *the damage was covered by the insurance*; *the prize covers all the costs of the vacation*
(d) to write a report on an event for a newspaper, radio program, etc.; *the journalists covering the story were briefed by the police*
(e) to travel a certain distance; *they made good progress, covering twenty miles a day*

④ **coverage**
['kʌvrɪdʒ] *noun*
press coverage *or* **media coverage** = amount of space or time given to an event in newspapers or on TV; *the company had good media coverage for the launch of its new car*; *coverage of the U.S. Open continues at 3 P.M.*
(NOTE: no plural)

② **covering**
['kʌvrɪŋ] *noun*
(a) thing which covers; *there was a light covering of snow*; *you need a really hard floor covering in a kitchen*
(b) **covering letter** = letter explaining what is enclosed with it, sometimes referred to as a cover letter; *further details of the job are given in the covering letter*

① **cow**
[kaʊ] *noun*
(a) large female farm animal, kept to give milk; *a field of cows*; *the farmer was milking a cow*
(NOTE: the meat from a cow is **beef**)
(b) female of other animals; *a cow elephant*; *a cow whale*

② **coward**
['kaʊərd] *noun*
person who is not brave; *when it comes to going to the dentist, I'm a coward*

① **cowboy**
['kaʊbɔɪ] *noun*
man who looks after cows in the west of the U.S.A.; **a cowboy movie** = movie about the west of the U.S.A. in the late 19th century; **cowboy hat** = large wide-brimmed hat

② **cozy**
['kaʊzi] *adjective*
comfortable and warm; *she wrapped herself up in a blanket and made herself cozy on the sofa*
(NOTE: **cozier - coziest**)

② **crab**
[kræb] *noun*
(a) sea animal which walks sideways and has eight legs and two large pincers; *they caught several little crabs in the rock pool*
(b) meat of this animal, used as food; *he ate some crab cakes*

② **crack**
[kræk]
1 *noun*
(a) sharp sound; *the crack of a branch behind her made her turn around*
(b) long thin break in something hard; *a crack appeared in the ceiling*; *her ring fell down a crack in the grating*; *the field is so dry it is full of cracks*; **at (the) crack of dawn** = as soon as it starts to be light; *if we want to miss the traffic we must set off at (the) crack of dawn*
(c) *(informal)* **to have a crack at something** = to try to do something; *I've never tried sailing before but I'm willing to have a crack at it*
(d) *(informal)* joke; *she made some crack about his bald spot*
2 *verb*
(a) to make a sharp sound; *a piece of wood cracked as he stepped on it*
(b) to make a long thin break in something; *the rock cracked the glass*
(c) **to crack jokes** = to tell jokes; *he spent all lunch cracking jokes*
(d) to find out how to read a secret code; *they spent months trying to crack the enemy codes*

① **cracker**
['krækər] *noun*
dry thin and crispy wafer made of flour and water; *after the main course they served cheese and crackers*

③ **craft**
[kræft] *noun*
(a) using skills to make something by hand; *he learned the craft of furniture-making as a boy*; *we went to a demonstration of traditional country crafts*
(b) *(formal)* ship; *his little craft slipped out of harbor*; *all sizes of craft took part in the rescue*
(NOTE: plural in this meaning is **craft**)

④ **crafty**
['kræfti] *adjective*
planning something in secret; *I could tell from the crafty look on her face that she was going to play a trick on me; I have a crafty plan for making a lot of money* (NOTE: **craftier - craftiest**)

④ **cramped**
[kræmt] *adjective*
too small; *on some planes, the seats in tourist class can be very cramped*

① **cranberry**
['krænbəri] *noun*
bitter wild red berry, used to make a sharp sweet sauce; *she drank a glass of cranberry juice; don't forget to make some cranberry sauce to eat with the turkey* (NOTE: plural is **cranberries**)

② **crane**
[kreın]
1 *noun*
tall metal construction for lifting heavy weights; *the container slipped as the crane was lifting it onto the ship; they had to hire a crane to get the piano into the upstairs room*
2 *verb*
to crane your neck = to stretch your neck; *he craned his neck to try to see the parade*

① **crash**
[kræʃ]
1 *noun*
(a) accident where cars, planes, etc., are damaged; *he was killed in a train crash; none of the passengers were hurt in the bus crash; his automobile was badly damaged in the crash*; **crash barrier** = strong fence by the side of a road to prevent cars from running off the road; **crash helmet** = hard hat worn by motorcyclists, etc.; *it is illegal to ride a motorcycle without a crash helmet*
(b) loud noise when something falls over; *the ladder fell down with a crash; he said he would go and wash the dishes, and then there was a crash in the kitchen*
(c) collapse of a company; *he lost all his savings in the bank crash*
(d) complete breakdown of a computer (NOTE: plural is **crashes**)
2 *verb*
(a) *(of vehicles)* to hit something and be damaged; *the bus crashed into a wall; the plane crashed four miles from the airport*
(b) to move, making a loud noise; *the wall came crashing down; the ladder crashed onto the floor*
(c) *(of a company)* to collapse; *he lost all his savings when the bank crashed*
(d) *(of a computer)* to stop working; *the hard disk has crashed but we think the data can be saved*
3 *adjective*
crash course = course of rapid, hard study; *he took a crash course in Spanish*; **crash diet** = severe rapid diet

② **crate**
[kreıt] *noun*
(a) large rough wooden box; *the china arrived safely, carefully packed in a wooden crate*
(b) container for bottles; *the school orders a crate of milk every day*

① **crawl**
[krɔːl]
1 *noun*
very slow speed; *the traffic on the freeway was reduced to a crawl* (NOTE: no plural)
2 *verb*
(a) to move around on your hands and knees; *the baby has just started to crawl*
(b) to go along slowly; *the traffic was crawling along*
(c) **to be crawling with** = to be covered with (insects, etc.); *the place was crawling with ants; the streets were crawling with police*

② **crazy**
['kreızı] *adjective*
mad; *it was a crazy idea to go mountain climbing in beach shoes*; **to drive someone crazy** = to have an effect on someone so that they become very annoyed; *the noise is driving me crazy; all this work is driving her crazy*; **crazy about** = very enthusiastic about; *he's crazy about her; she's crazy about dancing* (NOTE: **crazier - craziest**)

② **creak**
[kriːk]
1 *noun*
noise like a little squeak; *she heard a creak on the stairs and sat up in bed*
2 *verb*
to make a little noise; *the shed door creaked and banged all night in the high wind*

② **cream**
[kriːm]
1 *noun*
(a) top part of milk, full of fat; *I like strawberries and cream*; **whipped cream** = cream, beaten until it is stiff, flavored with sugar; **cream cake** = any cake or pastry filled with whipped cream; **cream cheese** = rich soft cheese
(b) soft stuff for cleaning, oiling, etc.; *she bought a tube of face cream; he uses lime shaving cream*
(c) the top few; *the cream of the medical students*
2 *adjective*
colored like cream, a very pale brown; *he was wearing a cream shirt; do you like our new cream carpet?*

② **crease**
[kriːs]
1 *noun*
(a) fold made by ironing; *trousers should have a crease in front*
(b) fold made accidentally; *she ironed his shirts to remove the creases*

2 *verb*

to make folds accidentally in something; *after two hours in the car, my skirt was badly creased*

③ **create**
['krɪ'eɪt] *verb*

to make, to invent; *do you believe that God created the world?; a government scheme which aims at creating new jobs for young people*

② **creation**
[krɪ'eɪʃn] *noun*

(a) thing which has been made; *for dessert they served some sort of chocolate and cream creation; the model appeared wearing a pink and blue creation*

(b) act of creating; *the aim is the creation of new jobs for young unemployed people*

③ **creative**
[krɪ'eɪtɪv] *adjective*

full of ideas; always making something; *he's a very creative child*

③ **creator**
[krɪ'eɪtər] *noun*

person who makes or invents something; *he's the creator of the radio that doesn't use electric power*

① **creature**
['krɪtʃər] *noun*

(a) *(formal)* animal; *lift any stone and you'll find all sorts of little creatures underneath; we try not to harm any living creature; some sea creatures live in holes in the sand*

(b) creature comforts = things which make life comfortable for you; *he likes his little creature comforts - his pipe and his glass of beer*

④ **credible**
['kredɪbl] *adjective*

which can be believed; *the jury did not find the witnesses' stories at all credible; the plot of the movie is not entirely credible*

③ **credit**
['kredɪt]

1 *noun*

(a) praise for something which is well deserved; *the professor took all the credit for the invention; to his credit, he owned up immediately; it does you credit* = you must be proud of it; *your daughter does you both credit; he's a credit to the school* = he's done well and this gives honor to the school where he studied

(b) time given to pay; *we give customers six months' credit with no interest to pay; credit check* = check on a customer's credit rating; **credit controller** = member of staff whose job is to try to get payment of invoices; **on credit** = without paying immediately; *we bought the dining room furniture on credit*

(c) side of an account showing money in hand or which is owed to you; *we paid in $150 to the credit of Mr. P. Smith;* **credit note** = note showing that money is owed; *she took the sweater back to the store and got a credit note;*

the company sent the wrong items and had to issue a credit note

(d) credits = list of people who helped to make a movie, TV program, etc.; *she sued the company when her name did not appear in the credits*

(e) unit of study completed; *this course gives two credits toward your degree*

2 *verb*

(a) **to credit someone with** = to say that someone has done something good; *he has been credited with making the company profitable again*

(b) to believe; *I find that hard to credit; would you credit it? - she's gotten married again!*

(c) to pay money into an account; *to credit an account with $150* or *to credit $150 to an account*

② **credit card**
['kredɪt 'kɑrd] *noun*

plastic card that allows you to borrow money and to buy goods without paying for them immediately; *how do you want to pay - cash, check or credit card?; I bought a fridge and put it on my credit card*

④ **creditor**
['kredɪtər] *noun*

person who is owed money; *he is trying to pay off his creditors*

② **creep**
[krip]

1 *verb*

(a) to move around quietly; *they crept softly down the stairs;* **to creep up on someone** = to come up close behind someone without making any noise; *the idea is to creep up on the gang as they are loading the stolen goods into the truck*

(b) to go along slowly; *the traffic was creeping along the freeway because of the fog* (NOTE: creeping - crept [krept])

2 *noun*

(a) *(informal)* unpleasant person who does things in secret

(b) **to give someone the creeps** = to make someone shiver with disgust; *I don't like that bank manager - he gives me the creeps*

② **crew**
[kru] *noun*

people who work together on a boat, aircraft, bus, etc.; *the helicopter rescued the crew of the sinking ship; the plane was carrying 125 passengers and a crew of 6;* **stage crew** = workers who move things around on a theater stage; *the stage crew worked all night to get the set ready for the following morning*

③ **crib**
[krɪb] *noun*

small bed for a baby; *the baby threw its rattle out of the crib*

④ **cricket**
['krɪkɪt] *noun*

(a) game played in England, Australia, New Zealand, the West Indies, and many other

countries, between two teams of eleven players using bats and a hard ball; *we haven't played much cricket this year - the weather has been too bad*; *we are going to a cricket match this afternoon*
(b) *(informal)* **it's not cricket** = it is not fair

① **cried, cries**
[kraɪd or kraɪz] *see* CRY

① **crime**
[kraɪm] *noun*
illegal act or acts; *we must try to reduce the levels of crime in the inner cities*; *the government is trying to deal with the problem of teenage crime* or *with the teenage crime problem*; *more crimes are committed at night than during the day*

② **criminal**
[ˈkrɪmɪnəl]
1 *adjective*
referring to illegal acts; *he has a criminal record*; *stealing is a criminal offense*; *the criminal justice system*; **criminal law** = laws that deal with crimes against the law of the land, which are punished by the state (NOTE: the opposite, actions relating to people's rights and freedoms, and to agreements between individuals, is **civil law**)
2 *noun*
person who commits a crime; *the police think two well-known criminals did it*

① **cripple**
[ˈkrɪpl]
1 *noun*
(offensive) person who is disabled and has difficulty in walking
2 *verb*
(a) to make someone disabled; *he was crippled in a mining accident*
(b) to prevent something from working; *the explosion crippled the tanker and she drifted toward the rocks*; *the bus and train strike has crippled the capital's transport system*

③ **crisis**
[ˈkraɪsɪs] *noun*
serious situation where decisions have to be made quickly; *an international crisis*; *a banking crisis*; **to take crisis measures** = to take measures rapidly to stop a crisis from developing; *the government had to take crisis measures to stop the collapse of the currency* (NOTE: plural is **crises** [ˈkraɪsiz])

① **crisp**
[krɪsp] *adjective*
(a) hard, which can be broken into pieces easily; *these crackers are not crisp anymore, they have gone soft*; *pick an apple off the tree, they're really very crisp*
(b) sharp and cold; *it was a beautiful crisp morning, with snow on the mountains*; *she could see her breath in the crisp mountain air* (NOTE: **crisper - crispest**)

④ **criterion**
[kraɪˈtɪəriən] *noun*
standard by which things are judged; *does the candidate satisfy all our criteria?*; *this is not a reliable criterion on which to base our decision* (NOTE: plural is **criteria**)

③ **critic**
[ˈkrɪtɪk] *noun*
(a) person who examines something and comments on it, especially a person who writes comments on new plays and movies for a newspaper; *she's the TV critic of "The New York Times"*; *the movie was praised by all the critics*
(b) person who says that something is bad or wrong; *the chairman tried to answer his critics at the meeting*

④ **critical**
[ˈkrɪtɪkəl] *adjective*
(a) dangerous and difficult; *with the enemy attacking on all sides, our position was becoming critical*
(b) extremely important; *he made a critical decision to break off the negotiations*; *critical relief supplies have been held up at customs*
(c) very serious; *the driver of the automobile was in a critical condition last night*; *the hospital said that her condition was critical*; *after the accident, she was on the critical list for some hours*
(d) which criticizes; *the report was highly critical of the authorities*

③ **criticism**
[ˈkrɪtɪsɪzm] *noun*
(a) comment; *if you have any constructive criticism to make, I will be glad to hear it*; **literary criticism** = criticism of works of literature
(b) comment which criticizes; *there was a lot of criticism of the government's plan*

③ **criticize**
[ˈkrɪtɪsaɪz] *verb*
to say that something or someone is bad or wrong; *she criticized the sales assistant for not being polite*; *the design of the new automobile has been criticized*

① **crook**
[krʊk] *noun*
dishonest person, a criminal; *I don't trust the government - they're a bunch of crooks*; *that used-car dealer is a bit of a crook*

② **crooked**
[ˈkrʊkɪd] *adjective*
(a) bent, not straight; *that picture is crooked*; *I don't think the wallpaper has been put on straight - it looks crooked to me*
(b) *(informal)* dishonest; *the police chief promised to remove any crooked officers in his force*

① **crop**
[krɒp]
1 *noun*

plants, such as vegetables or cereals, grown for food; *the bad weather has set the crops back by three weeks*; *we had a wonderful crop of potatoes* or *a wonderful potato crop this year*; *see also* GENETICALLY

2 *verb*

(a) to cut short; *the photograph had to be cropped to fit the space on the page*

(b) *(of plant)* to cause to have fruit; *we cropped two acres of pear trees this year* (NOTE: cropping - cropped)

④ **crop up**
['krɒp 'ʌp] *verb*
to happen suddenly; *get in touch if any problem should crop up*; *a little difficulty has cropped up - we've lost the key to the safe*

① **cross**
[krɒs]
1 *adjective*
(a) angry, annoyed; *the teacher will be cross with you for missing school*; *don't be cross - the children were only trying to help*
(b) opposed; *they were at cross purposes* = they were in total disagreement
2 *noun*
(a) shape made where one line goes straight across another; *write your name where I have put a cross*; *there is a cross on the top of the church tower*; **the Red Cross** = international organization that provides medical help; *Red Cross officials have been allowed into the war zone*
(b) breed of plant or animal which comes from two different varieties; *a cross between two types of cattle* (NOTE: plural is **crosses**)
3 *verb*
(a) to go across to the other side; *she just crossed the road without looking to see if there was any traffic coming*; *he crossed the lake in a small boat*; *the road crosses the railroad about 6 miles from here*; *the Concorde only took three hours to cross the Atlantic*
(b) to put one thing across another; *he crossed his arms and looked annoyed*; *she sat down and crossed her legs*; **crossed line** = fault on a telephone line, where you can hear a conversation from another line; *I can't hear you properly - we've got a crossed line*; *see also* FINGER
(c) to breed a new animal or plant, etc., from two varieties; *he crossed two strains of rice to produce a variety that is resistant to disease*

① **crossing**
['krɒsɪŋ] *noun*
(a) action of going across to the other side of an area of water; *how long is the crossing to the island?*; **they had a rough crossing** = the sea was rough when they traveled
(b) place where you go across safely; *cars have to take care at the railroad crossing*; **grade crossing** = place where a road crosses a railroad

without a bridge or tunnel; *the grade crossing gates opened when the train had passed*

① **cross off** *or* **cross out**
['krɒs 'ɒf or 'krɒs 'aut] *verb*
to draw a line through something which has been written to show that it should not be there; *he's sick, so you can cross him off the list for the party*; *I had difficulty reading her letter - she'd crossed out so many words*; *she crossed out $400 and put in $750*

② **crossroads**
['krɒsrəudz] *noun*
place where one road crosses another; *make a right at the crossroads*

① **crosswalk**
['krɒswɔk] *noun*
place where you can walk across a street; *it's safer to use the crosswalk when you're crossing a busy intersection*

② **crossword**
['krɒswɜrd] *noun*
puzzle where small squares have to be filled with letters to spell words; *I can't do today's crossword - it's too hard*; *he finished the crossword in 25 minutes*

② **crouch**
[krautʃ] *verb*
to bend down low; *she sat crouched down in the bottom of the boat*

① **crowd**
[kraud]
1 *noun*
mass of people; *she was cut off from her friends by a crowd of school children*; *after the election, the crowds were dancing on the streets*; *someone in the crowd threw an egg at the speaker on the platform*; *if you travel early, you will avoid the crowds of Christmas shoppers*
2 *verb*
to group together; *all the baseball fans crowded into the sports bar*; *the kids were crowding around their teacher*

② **crowded**
['kraudɪd] *adjective*
with a large number of people; *the town gets very crowded during the vacation season*; *the stands were crowded before the game started*

② **crown**
[kraun]
1 *noun*
(a) gold hat decorated with jewels, worn by an emperor, king, queen, etc.; *the bishop placed the crown on the head of the young king*; *the queen received the ambassadors wearing a heavy gold crown*
(b) *(in Britain)* king or queen representing the state; *in England, all swans belong to the crown*
(c) false top attached to a broken tooth; *I'm going to the dentist to have a crown fitted*
2 *verb*

(a) to make someone king, queen, emperor, etc., by placing a crown on his or her head; *the Queen of England was crowned in Westminster Abbey*

(b) to be a splendid end to something; *to crown it all, he won the lottery*

(c) to attach a false top to a broken tooth; *the dentist said that the tooth was so badly broken that he would have to crown it instead of trying to fill it*

④ **crucial**
['kruʃl] *adjective*
extremely important; *it is crucial that the story be kept out of the papers*

③ **crude**
[krud]
1 *adjective*
(a) not processed; *beaches were covered in crude oil from the tanker*
(b) rude, with no manners; *he made some crude gestures at the fans* (NOTE: cruder - crudest)
2 *noun*
raw oil, taken from the ground; *the price of Arabian crude has fallen*

① **cruel**
['kruəl] *adjective*
who causes pain, who makes a person or animal suffer; *don't be so cruel to your new puppy*; *it was cruel of him to mention her weight problem* (NOTE: crueler - cruelest)

② **cruelty**
['kruəlti] *noun*
act of being cruel; *the zookeeper was accused of cruelty to animals*; *cases of cruelty to children are increasing*; **mental cruelty** = being cruel to someone in a way that does not hurt them physically

② **cruise**
[kruz]
1 *noun*
long voyage in a ship calling at different places; *when he retired he went on a cruise around the Mediterranean*
2 *verb*
(a) to go in a boat from place to place; *they spent May cruising in the Mediterranean*; *the ship cruised from island to island*
(b) to travel at an even speed; *the automobile cruises very comfortably at 100 miles per hour*
(c) to win without much difficulty; *he cruised to victory in the race*

① **crumb**
[krʌm] *noun*
small piece of bread, cake, etc.; *they left crumbs all over the table*

① **crumble**
['krʌmbl]
1 *noun*
hot cooked dessert made of fruit covered with a mixture of flour, fat and sugar; *we are having apple crumble for pudding*

2 *verb*
to break up into small pieces; *he picked up a lump of dry earth and crumbled it between his fingers*

① **crunch**
[krʌntʃ]
1 *noun*
(a) sound of something dry being crushed; *the crunch of new snow under his boots*
(b) *(informal)* crisis point; *the crunch will come when the firm has no cash to pay the wages*; **if it comes to the crunch** = if crisis point is reached; *when it came to the crunch, the other side backed down*
2 *verb*
(a) to crush something dry; *the snow crunched under his boots*
(b) to chew something hard which makes a noise when you are eating; *she was crunching on a potato chip when the phone rang*

② **crush**
[krʌʃ]
1 *verb*
(a) to press flat; *she was crushed against the wall by the car*; *crush a piece of garlic and add it to the soup*
(b) to end completely; *government troops crushed the student rebellion*; *all her hopes of getting a better job were crushed by the report of the interviewer*
2 *noun*
(a) mass of people; *she was hurt in the crush of people trying to get to the exit*; *he lost his case in the crush on the train*
(b) *(informal)* **to have a crush on someone** = to have a feeling of love for someone you do not know very well; *she had a crush on her tennis coach*

① **crust**
[krʌst] *noun*
hard outside layer of bread, the earth, etc.; *you can cut the crusts off the sandwiches*; *the Earth's crust is over 30 km thick*

① **cry**
[kraɪ]
1 *noun*
(a) loud shout; *no one heard her cries for help*
(b) sharp sound made by a bird or animal; *the cry of the birds overhead*; *we could hear the cries of monkeys in the trees* (NOTE: plural is cries)
2 *verb*
(a) to have tears coming out of your eyes; *the baby cried when her mother took away her toys*; *cutting up onions makes me cry*; *many people were crying when they left the movie theater*; *(informal)* **to cry over spilled milk** = to be upset because of something which you couldn't prevent; *it's no use crying over spilled milk - what's happened has happened*
(b) *(formal)* to call out; *"hi there", she cried*

③ **crystal**
['krɪstl] *noun*
(a) solid chemical substance with a regular shape; *the salt formed crystals at the bottom of the jar*
(b) very clear bright glass; *a crystal wine glass*; **crystal clear** = very clear and simple to understand; *I want to make this crystal clear: anyone who gets into trouble with the police will be sent home immediately*

① **cub**
[kʌb] *noun*
young animal, especially a bear or fox; *the bear led her cubs down to the river*

① **Cuba**
['kjubə] *noun*
independent country, a large island in the Caribbean Sea; *we went to Cuba for vacation last year*; *Cuba is famous for its cigars* (NOTE: capital: **Havana**; people: **Cubans**; language: **Spanish**; currency: **Cuban peso**)

② **Cuban**
['kjubn]
1 *adjective*
referring to Cuba; *Cuban cigars are very famous*
2 *noun*
person from Cuba; *two Cubans came onto the plane*

② **cube**
[kjub]
1 *noun*
(a) shape where all six sides are square and join each other at right angles; *the design for the library is nothing more than a series of cubes*
(b) piece of something shaped like a cube; *he put two cubes of sugar in his tea*; *put the ice cubes in the glasses and then add orange juice*
(c) *(mathematics)* the result when a number is multiplied by itself twice; *27 is the cube of 3*; **cube root of a number** = number which when multiplied twice by itself will equal the number; *the cube root of 1728 is 12 (12 x 12 x 12 = 1728)*
2 *verb*
(a) to cut into little cubes; *wash, peel and then cube the potatoes*
(b) to multiply a number twice by itself; *if you cube 6 the result is 216 (6 x 6 x 6)*

③ **cubic**
['kjubɪk] *adjective*
measured in volume by multiplying length, depth and width; *the packing case holds six cubic feet* (NOTE: cubic is written in figures as ^{3}: **6 m^3 =** six cubic meters; **10 ft^3 =** ten cubic feet)

② **cuckoo**
['kʊku] *noun*
common bird which makes a repeated call; *the cuckoo lays its eggs in the nests of other birds*; **cuckoo clock** = wooden clock where a small bird comes out at each hour and makes a noise like a cuckoo

③ **cucumber**
['kjukʌmbər] *noun*
long dark green vegetable used in salads; *we had cucumber sandwiches for tea*; *(informal)* **as cool as a cucumber** = very calm and relaxed; *he walked out of the prison as cool as a cucumber*

② **cuddle**
['kʌdl]
1 *noun*
a hug; *she picked up her daughter and gave her a cuddle*
2 *verb*
to hug someone; *the little girl was cuddling her teddy bear*

③ **cue**
[kju] *noun*
(a) *(in a play)* words after which you have to speak or act; *he missed his cue and had to be prompted*; *the sound of the gun is your cue to rush onto the stage screaming*; **to take your cue from someone** = to do as someone does; *watch the chief executive officer during the negotiations and take your cue from him*
(b) long stick for playing pool or billiards; *before playing his shot, he put some chalk on the tip of his cue*; **cue ball** = the white ball which a billiards player hits with his cue (NOTE: do not confuse with **queue**)

④ **culprit**
['kʌlprɪt] *noun*
person who has done something wrong; *the police say that they have not yet caught the culprits*

④ **cult**
[kʌlt] *noun*
small religious group; *I'm worried about my daughter - she left home two years ago and has joined a cult*; **cult hero** = person who is admired by a group

② **cultivate**
['kʌltɪveɪt] *verb*
(a) to dig and water the land to grow plants; *fields are cultivated in early spring, ready for sowing corn*
(b) to grow plants; *this field is used to cultivate new strains of wheat*

② **cultivated**
['kʌltɪveɪtɪd] *adjective*
(a) who has been well educated in music, art, literature, etc.; *the new principal is a really cultivated person*
(b) *(land)* prepared on which crops are grown; *from the air, the cultivated fields were a pattern of brown and green*

④ **cultivation**
[kʌltɪ'veɪʃn] *noun*
(a) act of cultivating land or plants; *the cultivation of soft fruit is very dependent on the weather*; **land under cultivation** = land that is being cultivated; *he has sixty acres under cultivation*

(b) good education; *his lack of cultivation was apparent as soon as he began to speak*

④ **cultural**
['kʌltʃərəl] *adjective*
referring to culture; *a French cultural delegation visited the exhibition*; *his cultural interests are very wide-ranging - from Mexican art to 12th-century Greek paintings*

③ **culture**
['kʌltʃər] *noun*
(a) a country's civilization, including music, art, literature, etc.; *he is taking a course in Russian culture*; *is a TV in every home really the peak of Western culture?*; **culture shock** = shock that you feel when moving from one type of society to another which is very different; *going from California to live with hill tribes in India was something of a culture shock*
(b) cultivation of plants; *the culture of some greenhouse plants must be done in warm damp conditions*
(c) bacteria grown in a laboratory; *the first part of the experiment is to grow a culture in the lab*

④ **cunning**
['kʌnɪŋ] *adjective*
clever and full of tricks; *they had a cunning plan to get into the exhibition free*

① **cup**
[kʌp] *noun*
(a) small bowl with a handle, used for drinking tea, coffee, etc.; *she put out a cup and saucer for everyone*; **tea cup** = a cup for drinking tea; **coffee cup** = a cup for drinking coffee
(b) liquid in a cup; *he drank two cups of coffee*; *can I have a cup of tea?*; **to make a cup of tea** = to prepare tea, usually in a pot; *I'll make you all a cup of tea*; *(informal)* **it's not my cup of tea** = it's not something I like very much; *modern art isn't really my cup of tea*
(c) tall silver bowl given as a prize for winning a competition; *he has won three cups for golf*

① **cupboard**
['kʌbəd] *noun*
piece of furniture with shelves and doors; *put the jam in the kitchen cupboard*; *the best plates are in the dining room cupboard*; *she painted the cupboard doors white*

④ **curative**
['kjurətɪv] *adjective*
which can cure; *the plant has certain curative properties*

② **curb**
[kɜrb]
1 *noun*
(a) something which holds something back; *the company needs to put a curb on its spending*
(b) stone edge to a sidewalk; *he sat on the curb and watched the cars go past*; *try not to hit the curb when you park*
2 *verb*
to hold back; *she needs to curb her enthusiasm to spend money*

② **cure**
[kjuər]
1 *noun*
something which makes a disease better; *doctors are still trying to find a cure for colds*
2 *verb*
(a) to make a patient or a disease better; *I don't know what's in the medicine, but it cured my cough very fast*
(b) to preserve meat or fish, as by putting it in salt; *a piece of cured ham*; *this bacon has been cured in salt water*

③ **curfew**
['kɜrfju] *noun*
period when no one is allowed out into the street; *the government is proposing to impose a curfew for young people*

④ **curiosity**
[kjuərɪ'ɒsɪti] *noun*
wanting to know about something; *I just asked out of sheer curiosity* (NOTE: no plural)

② **curious**
['kjuəriəs] *adjective*
(a) strange; *she has a curious high-pitched voice*
(b) wanting to know; *I'm curious to know if anything happened at the party*

① **curl**
[kɜrl]
1 *noun*
(a) lock of hair which twists; *the little girl looked so sweet with her golden curls*
(b) twist in the hair; *my hair has a natural curl*
2 *verb*
(a) to make hair twist around; *she curled her hair around her finger*; *she went to the hairdresser's to have her hair curled*
(b) to twist; *my hair curls naturally*
(c) to curl up = to bend your body into a round shape; *she curled up on the sofa and went to sleep*

② **curly**
['kɜrli] *adjective*
curly hair = hair with natural waves in it; *she has naturally curly hair* (NOTE: **curlier - curliest**)

④ **currant**
['kʌrənt] *noun*
(a) small dried black grape; *currants are smaller and blacker than raisins or sultanas, but they are all sorts of dried grapes*
(a) small black or red soft fruit, such as a blackcurrant; *I have planted some currant bushes* (NOTE: do not confuse with **current**)

③ **currency**
['kʌrənsi] *noun*
(a) money used in a certain country; *I want to change my dollars into Italian currency*; **foreign currency** = the money of other countries; *the bank will change your foreign currency for you*; **hard currency** = money that is stable and is easily exchanged for foreign

currency; *people in some countries will do anything to get hold of hard currency*; *developing countries need to sell raw materials for hard currency*; **soft** **currency** = currency of a country with a weak economy, which is cheap to buy and difficult to exchange for other currencies

(b) *(formal)* state of being known or accepted; **to gain currency** = to become better known or more accepted; *the idea that the world was round began to gain currency in the later Middle Ages*

② **current**
['kʌrənt]
1 *noun*
(a) flow of water or air; *don't go swimming in the river - the current is very strong*; *a warm current of air is flowing across the country*; *big black birds were circling in rising currents of warm air*
(b) flow of electricity; *switch the current off at the fuse box*
2 *adjective*
(a) referring to the present time; *what is your current position?*; *who is the current Prime Minister of Japan?*; *do you have a current timetable - mine is out-of-date?*; **the current rate of exchange** = today's rate of exchange; *the current rate of exchange is 1.50 dollars to the pound*
(b) widely believed; *the idea that the world was flat was current in the Middle Ages*

④ **currently**
['kʌrəntlī] *adverb*
at the present time; *he is currently the manager of our Atlanta office*; *we are currently in the process of buying a house*

④ **curriculum**
[kə'rɪkjʊləm] *noun*
subjects studied in a school, etc.; *I am very glad that music and drama have been added to the curriculum*

④ **curry**
['kʌrī]
1 *noun*
(a) **curry powder** *or* **curry paste** = hot spicy powder or paste, used to make Indian dishes
(b) Indian food prepared with spices; *I would like a mild curry, please*; *we ordered chicken curry and rice* (NOTE: plural is **curries**)
2 *verb*
to curry favor with someone = to try to please someone; *he's just trying to curry favor with the boss by coming in at seven o'clock in the morning*

② **curse**
[kɜrs]
1 *noun*
(a) swear word; *he threw the letter down with a curse*

(b) magic word to make something unpleasant happen to someone; *the wicked sister put a curse on the whole family*
(c) something which causes you problems; *being on call 24 hours a day is the curse of being a doctor*; *pollution is the curse of industrial societies*
2 *verb*
(a) to swear; *he cursed under his breath and marched out of the room*
(b) to cast an evil spell on someone; *we must be cursed - everything we do seems to go wrong*

② **cursor**
['kɜrsər] *noun*
little arrow or a bright spot on a screen which shows where the next character will appear; *to print your text, point your cursor at "print" and click twice*

② **curtain**
['kɜrtən] *noun*
(a) long piece of cloth hanging in front of a window, etc.; *can you close the curtains, please?*; **to draw the curtains** = (i) to open the curtains; (ii) to close the curtains; *draw the curtains - it's getting cold*
(b) long piece of cloth hanging in front of the stage at a theater; **the curtain will go up at 8:30** = the play begins at 8:30; **safety curtain** = special curtain in front of the stage in a theater, which protects against fire; *the safety curtain is lowered and raised at the beginning of each performance*; **it will be curtains for him** = he will be devastated, ruined, etc.

② **curve**
[kɜrv]
1 *noun*
(a) round shape like part of a circle; *the road makes a sharp curve to the left*
(b) rounded shape on a graph; **learning curve** = gradual process of learning; **a steep learning curve** = having to learn new skills fast; **sales curve** = graph showing how sales increase or decrease
2 *verb*
to make a rounded shape; *the road curves around the side of the mountain*

② **cushion**
['kʊʃən]
1 *noun*
(a) bag filled with feathers, etc., for sitting or leaning on; *feel how soft this cushion is*; *put a cushion behind your back if you find your chair is too hard*
(b) money that allows you to get through a difficult period; *we have a little money in the bank which is a useful cushion when money is tight*
2 *verb*
to make soft something which could be hard or painful; *luckily when he fell off the ladder there was a hedge underneath to cushion his fall*; *she made no attempt to cushion the blow, but just*

told them straight out that they were all being laid off

③ **custody**
['kʌstədɪ] *noun*
(a) keeping; *the jewels were in the custody of the manager, and he had placed them in the hotel safe*; **to take someone into custody** = to arrest someone; *the three fans were taken into police custody*
(b) right of keeping and looking after a child; *when they were divorced, she was granted custody of the children* (NOTE: no plural)

② **custom**
['kʌstəm] *noun*
(a) habit, thing which is usually done; *it's a local custom in this part of the world*
(b) **custom-built** *or* **custom-made** = made to order for a customer; *he drives a custom-built sports car*

② **customer**
['kʌstəmər] *noun*
(a) person who buys something in a store; *the stores are lowering their prices to attract customers*; *she was locking up the store when a customer came in*; *his store is always full of customers*; **satisfied customer** = someone who is happy with what he has bought
(b) person who uses a service, such as a train passenger; *we apologize to customers waiting on Platform 5 for the late arrival of their train*

④ **customs**
['kʌstəmz] *noun*
(a) money paid to the government when a person takes certain goods from one country to another; *we had to pay $500 in customs*
(b) place at a port, airport or border where travelers' baggage may be searched for illegal or taxable goods; **to go through customs** = to pass through the area of a port or airport where customs officials examine goods; *when you come into the country, you have to go through customs*; **to take something through customs** = to carry something through the customs area without always declaring it; *she said that her boyfriend had asked her to take the case through customs for him*

① **cut**
[kʌt]
1 *verb*
(a) to make an opening using a knife, scissors, etc.; to remove something using a knife, scissors, etc.; *the meat is very tough - I can't cut it with my knife*; *he needs to get his hair cut*; *there were six children, so she cut the cake into six pieces*
(b) to hurt yourself by making a wound in the skin; *she cut her finger on the broken glass*; *he cut himself while shaving*
(c) to reduce the size of something; *we are trying to cut the number of staff*; *accidents have been cut by 10%*; *the article is too long, so I asked the author to cut 500 words*

(d) **to cut across** *or* **to cut through** = to take a shortcut to get somewhere; *it's quicker if you cut across* *or* *through the park*
(e) **to cut a corner** = to try to go around a corner quickly, by driving on the sidewalk; *he was trying to cut the corner and hit a fence*; **to cut corners** = to do things rapidly and cheaply; *she tried to cut corners and the result was that the whole job had to be done again*
(f) to look at someone and pretend not to recognize him or her; *when I held out my hand she cut me dead*
(g) to miss (a lecture); *she cut her history lecture and went shopping* (NOTE: **cutting - cut - has cut**)
2 *noun*
(a) place that bleeds when your skin has been broken; *she had a bad cut on her leg*; *put a Band-Aid on your cut*
(b) **shortcut** = shorter way; *he took a shortcut through the park*
(c) sudden lowering of a price, salary, etc.; *price cuts* *or* *cuts in prices*; **job cuts** = reductions in the number of jobs; *the union is forecasting huge job cuts*; **he took a cut in salary** *or* **a salary cut** = he accepted a lower salary
(d) piece of meat; *you can use a cheaper cut of meat if you cook it slowly*
(e) *(informal)* share (of profits, etc.); *each salesman gets a cut of what he can sell for cash*
(f) *(computing)* **cut and paste** = taking a section of text from one point and putting it in at another

③ **cut back**
['kʌt 'bæk] *verb*
to reduce spending; *we are having to cut back on staff costs*

③ **cut down**
['kʌt 'daʊn] *verb*
(a) to make a tree fall down with a saw, etc.; *he cut the tree down* *or* *he cut down the tree*
(b) **to cut down (on)** = to reduce; *we are trying to get him to cut down the number of cigarettes he smokes each day*; *she's trying to cut down on chocolates*

② **cute**
[kjut] *adjective*
(informal) nice; *what a cute little kitten!*; *Doreen may look cute now, but you should see her when she's in a temper*

④ **cutlery**
['kʌtləri] *noun*
knives, forks, spoons; *put the cutlery out on the tables, please*

③ **cut off**
['kʌt 'ɒf] *verb*
(a) to take away a small part of something using a knife, etc.; *she cut off a little piece of string*; *he cut off two slices of ham*
(b) to stop someone from being with someone or reaching a place; *she was cut off from her friends by a crowd of police officers*; *the farm*

was cut off by the snow; the tide came in and cut off a party of schoolchildren
(c) to stop a phone call before it is finished; *we were cut off in the middle of our conversation*
(d) to stop electricity or water from reaching someone; *he didn't pay the bill, so the company cut off his electricity; the lightning hit the cable and caused the electricity to be cut off*

③ **cut out**
['kʌt 'aʊt] *verb*
(a) to remove a small piece by cutting it from a large piece (of paper, etc.); *she cut an advertisement out of the newspaper; he used a pair of scissors to cut out the picture*
(b) to stop doing or eating something; *she's decided to cut out candy so as to lose weight*; **cut it out!** = stop doing that!
(c) *(of an engine)* to stop working; *one of the engines cut out as the plane came in to land*
(d) **to be cut out for** = to be ideally suited for; *I don't think he's cut out for a job in the post office*

③ **cut-rate**
['kʌt'reɪt] *adjective*
sold at a cheaper price than usual; *supermarkets attract customers with cut-rate goods*; **cut-rate store** = store selling goods at cheaper prices

② **cutting**
['kʌtɪŋ]
1 *noun*
little piece of a plant which will grow roots if it is pushed into the ground; *the cuttings I took from your plant are all growing well*
2 *adjective*
cutting remark = sharply critical remark

③ **cut up**
['kʌt 'ʌp] *verb*
to make into small pieces by cutting; *she cut the old towel up into little pieces; can you cut up the meat for the children?*

③ **cycle**
['saɪkl]
1 *noun*
(a) bicycle; *if your bike's got a flat tire, take it to the cycle shop*; **cycle path** = special path for cyclists; *there are thousands of cycle paths in Holland*
(b) period during which something develops and then returns to its starting point; *global warming is starting to affect the natural cycle of the seasons; the washing machine broke down in the middle of the spin cycle*; **business cycle** *or* **economic cycle** *or* **trade cycle** = period during which trade expands, then slows down, then expands again; **life cycle** = life of an animal or plant from birth to death, which is repeated by the next generation
2 *verb*
to go on a bicycle; *it's hard cycling against the wind; he thinks nothing of cycling ten miles to work every day*

④ **cyclist**
['saɪklɪst] *noun*
person who rides a bicycle; *the police told the crowds to stand back as the cyclists were passing*

② **cyclone**
['saɪkləʊn] *noun*
tropical storm in the Indian Ocean and Pacific, where the air moves very fast in a circle around a central area; *according to the shipping forecasts, a cyclone is approaching* (NOTE: in the Far East this is called a **typhoon;** in the Caribbean area a **hurricane**)

③ **cylinder**
['sɪlɪndər] *noun*
(a) object shaped like a round tube closed at both ends; **gas cylinder** = metal tube containing gas; *the divers carried oxygen cylinders on their backs*
(b) part of an engine; *the automobile has a six-cylinder engine; the engine seems to lack power - maybe it's not firing on all six cylinders*

Dd

③ **D, d**
['di]
fourth letter of the alphabet, between C and E; *you don't spell "riding" with two Ds*

③ **DA**
['di 'eɪ] = DISTRICT ATTORNEY

① **dad** *or* **daddy**
[dæd or 'dædi] *noun*
child's name for father; *Hi Daddy! look at my exam results!; my dad has bought me a new bike; compare* MOM, MOMMY, POP

① **daily**
['deɪli]
1 *adjective*
happening every day; *I read daily newspapers such as "The New York Times" and "The*

Washington Post"; *the stove has been in daily use for ten years*; *there's a daily flight to Washington*

2 *noun*

newspaper published every weekday; *the story was carried on the front page of most of the dailies* (NOTE: plural is **dailies**)

3 *adverb*

every day; **twice daily** = two times a day

② **dairy**
['deəri] *noun*

place where milk, cream and butter are processed or sold; *you can buy butter and cheese from the dairy*; **dairy farm** = farm that produces milk, cheese, etc.; **dairy products** = milk, butter, cream, etc. (NOTE: plural is **dairies**)

② **daisy**
['deɪzi] *noun*

small white and yellow flower; *the lawn was covered with daisies* (NOTE: plural is **daisies**)

① **dam**
[dæm]

1 *noun*

wall of earth or concrete that blocks a river to make a lake; *after the thunderstorm people were afraid the dam would burst*

2 *verb*

to block a river with a wall of earth or concrete; *when they built the power station, the river had to be dammed* (NOTE: **damming - dammed**)

② **damage**
['dæmɪdʒ]

1 *noun*

(a) harm (done to things not to people); *the storm did a lot of damage*; *it will take us months to repair the damage to the restaurant*; *the fire caused damage estimated at $150,000*; **fire damage** = damage caused by a fire; **flood damage** = damage caused by a flood; **storm damage** = damage caused by a storm; **to suffer damage** = to be harmed; *the automobile suffered serious damage in the accident* (NOTE: no plural in this meaning)

(b) **damages** = payment to someone who has been hurt or whose property has been damaged; *the accident victim claimed $350,000 in damages*; *after his operation went wrong, he sued the hospital for damages*; *the court awarded the girl damages against the driver of the car*

2 *verb*

to harm something; *a large number of stores were damaged in the fire*; *glasses need to be packed carefully as they are easily damaged*

① **damp**
[dæmp]

1 *adjective*

rather wet; *she'd just taken a shower and her hair was still damp*; *the basement room has cold damp walls* (NOTE: **damper - dampest**)

2 *noun*

moisture in the air, on a surface; *the damp makes my rheumatism worse* (NOTE: no plural)

① **dance**
[dæns]

1 *noun*

(a) way of moving in time to music; *she teaches dance or she's a dance teacher*; *we learned a new dance today*; *she's taking dance lessons*

(b) evening entertainment for a group of people where you can dance; *the club is holding a New Year's dance*; *they met at a youth club dance*; **dance floor** = specially polished floor for dancing on

2 *verb*

(a) to move in time to music; *there he is - he's dancing with that tall girl*; *she often goes to clubs but never dances*

(b) to move or jump around happily; *she danced into the room and announced she's gotten the job*; *the fans were dancing on the streets*

② **dancer**
['dænsər] *noun*

person who dances; *she trained as a dancer*; *the dancers hold hands and form a circle*

① **dancing**
['dænsɪŋ] *noun*

action of moving to music; *she goes to dancing classes*

① **danger**
['deɪndʒər] *noun*

possibility of damage, failure, getting hurt, etc.; *when it rains, there's a danger of flooding*; *the broken window is a danger to office security*; *there's a danger we won't get there in time*; *we were warned of the dangers of traveling alone in the desert*; **danger money** = payment for a dangerous job; *the workers said the job was very dangerous and asked for danger money*; **out of danger** *or* **off the danger list** = not likely to die; *she was very ill, but she's off the danger list now*

◇ **in danger**
['ɪn 'deɪndʒər] *phrase*

likely to be harmed; *get an ambulance - her life is in danger*; *I don't think the children are in any danger*; *the whole building was in danger of catching fire*

① **dangerous**
['deɪndʒərəs] *adjective*

which can cause injury or damage; *be careful - those old stairs are dangerous!*; *these electric wires are dangerous*; *children are warned that it is dangerous to go out alone at night*

② **dangerously**
['deɪndʒərəsli] *adverb*

in a dangerous way; *she was standing dangerously close to the edge of the cliff*; **to be dangerously ill** = to be very ill

② **Danish**
['deɪnɪʃ]

1 *adjective*

referring to Denmark; **Danish pastry** = sweet pastry cake with jam or fruit folded in it (NOTE: also called simply **a Danish: an apple Danish**)

2 *noun*

language spoken in Denmark

ⓘ **dare**

['deər]

1 *verb*

(a) to be brave enough to do something; *I bet you wouldn't dare put your hand into the cage and stroke that tiger*; **I dare say** = very probably; *I dare say you're right*

(b) *(negative)* *I dare not go out into the street or I don't dare go out into the street while that man is standing there*

(c) to challenge someone to do something by suggesting he is too afraid to do it; *I dared him to go the meeting without his necktie*

2 *noun*

act of challenging someone to do something; *he only climbed on the roof for a dare*

ⓘ **dark**

[dɑrk]

1 *adjective*

(a) with little or no light; *the sky turned dark and it started to rain*; *can you switch the light on - it's getting too dark to see*; *in Sweden in the summer it gets dark very late*

(b) not a light color; *her eyes are dark*; *she was wearing a dark blue coat*; **a dark horse** = someone who may succeed unexpectedly

(c) with black or brown hair; *he's quite dark, but his sister has red hair*

(d) **to keep something dark** = to keep something a secret; *they kept their plans dark from the rest of the family* (NOTE: **darker - darkest**)

2 *noun*

(a) absence of light; *little children are afraid of the dark*; *they say cats can see in the dark*; *in the dark, everything looks different*; **after dark** = during the nighttime; *you must turn on your headlights after dark*

(b) **in the dark** = not knowing anything about something; *I'm completely in the dark about the whole business*; *we want to keep everyone in the dark about our plans*

ⓘ **darkness**

['dɑrknəs] *noun*

not having any light; *the cat's eyes glowed in the darkness*; *the sun had set and the darkness was closing in*; **the building was in complete darkness** *or* **in total darkness** = there were no electric lights on in the building (NOTE: no plural)

ⓘ **darling**

['dɑrlɪŋ]

1 *adjective*

which you can love; *what a darling little baby!*

2 *noun*

(a) name used to talk to someone you love; *Darling! I'm back from the shops*

(b) person who is loved; *she's an absolute darling!*; *be a darling and fetch me the newspaper*

ⓘ **dart**

[dɑrt]

1 *noun*

(a) small heavy arrow with plastic feathers, used for playing the game of darts; *each player takes turn to throw his three darts*

(b) **darts** = game for two or more people, played by each player throwing three darts in turn at a round target; *they had a game of darts*; *I'm not very good at darts*; *he plays darts every evening in the neighborhood bar* (NOTE: not plural, and takes a singular verb)

2 *verb*

to rush; *the little boy darted across the street*; *we sat by the river and watched the fish darting about chasing flies*

ⓘ **dash**

[dæʃ]

1 *noun*

(a) little line written to join two figures or phrases; *the reference number is one four six dash seven (146-7)*

(b) sudden rush; *there was a mad dash to buy tickets*; *while the police officer wasn't looking she made a dash for the door*

(c) small amount; *a glass of tomato juice with a dash of Tabasco* (NOTE: plural is **dashes**)

2 *verb*

to rush; *I can't stop now - I must dash to catch the last mail collection*; *I dashed home to watch the football game on television*; *she dashed into a store so that he wouldn't see her*

③ **data**

['deɪtə] *noun*

information in the form of statistics; *the data is stored in our main computer*; *we spent months gathering data on hospital waiting times*; *the data shows that, on average, a murder is committed every two weeks*; **data bank** = store of information on a computer; **data protection** = making sure that information on a computer does not get into the wrong hands (NOTE: **data** is usually singular: **the data is easily available**)

③ **database**

['deɪtəbeɪs] *noun*

data stored in a computer, which can be used to provide information of various kinds; *we can extract the lists of possible customers from our database*; *I'll just add your details to our customer database*

③ **data processing**

['deɪtə 'prəʊsesɪŋ] *noun*

selecting and examining data in a computer to produce special information; *she's a data processing manager*

ⓘ **date**

[deɪt]

1 *noun*

(a) number of a day in a month or year (when something happens or happened); *put today's date on the check*; *what's the date next Wednesday?*; *the dates of the exhibition have been changed*; *the date of the next meeting has been fixed for Wednesday, June 10*; *do you remember the date of your girlfriend's birthday?*; **date of birth** = date on which someone was born; *please write your date and place of birth on the registration form*; **arrival date** *or* **date of arrival** = day on which you arrive; **departure date** *or* **date of departure** = day on which you leave

(b) time agreed for a meeting, usually a romantic meeting; *we made a date to meet at the Italian restaurant*; *he asked her out for a date*; **blind date** = meeting arranged between two people who have never met before

(c) small sweet brown fruit of the date palm; **date palm** = a tall tropical tree with very large leaves and sweet fruit

2 *verb*
(a) to write the date on something; *the check was dated June 15*; *you forgot to date the check*
(b) **to date from** = to exist since; *this house dates from* *or* *dates back to the eighteenth century*
(c) to give the date of an old piece of wood, a monument, an antique, etc.; *the bowl has been dated to 1500 BC*
(d) to meet someone of the opposite sex regularly; *he's dating my sister*

◇ **out of date**
['aut əv 'deɪt]
not containing recent information; *this guidebook is out of date*; *the information in it is two years out of date*

◇ **up to date**
['ʌp tə 'deɪt]
containing very recent information; *the new telephone directory is completely up to date*; *he is bringing the guidebook up to date*; **to keep someone up to date on** *or* **with something** = to tell someone all the latest information about something; *while I'm on vacation, you must keep me up to date on what's happening at the office*

① **daughter**
['dɔtər] *noun*
girl child of a mother or father; *they have two sons and one daughter*; *my daughter Mary goes to the local school*

② **dawn**
[dɔn]
1 *noun*
beginning of a day, when the sun rises; *we must set off for the Pyramids at dawn, so you'll have to get up very early*; **at the crack of dawn** = as soon as it starts to be light; *the plane leaves at 6:30 A.M. - which means I'll have to get up at the crack of dawn*
2 *verb*

(a) *(of day)* to begin; *the day of the tennis match dawned wet and windy*
(b) **it dawned on him that** = he began to realize that; *it gradually dawned on him that someone else was opening his mail*

① **day**
[deɪ] *noun*
(a) period of time lasting 24 hours; *there are 365 days in a year and 366 in a leap year*; *New Year's Day is January 1*; *they went on a ten-day tour of Southern Spain*; *I spoke to him on the phone the day before yesterday*; *we are planning to meet the day after tomorrow*; **what day is it today?** = is it Monday, Tuesday, etc.
(b) **every other day** = every two days (i.e., on Monday, Wednesday, Friday, etc.); *he calls his mother every other day*; **the other day** = quite recently; *the other day I went for a walk by the river*; **one day** *or* **some day** = at some time in the future; *one day we'll have enough money to go on vacation*; **day by day** = gradually; *day by day her condition improved*
(c) period from morning until night, when it is light; *he works all day in the office, and then helps his wife with the children in the evening*; *it took the workmen four days to build the wall*; **day tour** *or* **day trip** = tour that leaves in the morning and returns the same day in the evening
(d) work period from morning to night; *she took two days off* = she did not come to work for two days; *he works three days on, two days off* = he works for three days, then has two days' vacation; **to work an eight-hour day** = to spend eight hours at work each day; **to work a four-day week** = to work four days each week; **to make someone's day** = to make someone happy; *she smiled at me - that made my day*
(e) **days** = time in the past; *in the days of Henry VIII, kings were very powerful*; **those were the days** = they were good times we had in the past; *do you remember spending all night going to clubs in New York? - ah! those were the days!*

◇ **a day**
[ə 'deɪ]
every day; *an apple a day keeps the doctor away*; *you should drink a quart of water a day*

◇ **all day**
['ɔl 'deɪ]
the whole day; *it's been raining hard all day*

① **daylight**
['deɪlaɪt] *noun*
light from the sun during the day; *he pulled back the curtains to let in the daylight*; **in broad daylight** = openly, in the middle of the day; *three men robbed the bank in broad daylight* (NOTE: no plural)

③ **dazzle**
['dæzl] *verb*
to make someone blind for a moment; *she was dazzled by the lights of the cars coming toward her*

① **dead**

[ded]

1 *adjective*

(a) not alive anymore; *his parents are both dead*; *dead fish were floating in the water*; *he brushed the dead leaves into piles*; *six people were dead as a result of the accident*; **to drop dead** = to die suddenly; *he dropped dead in the middle of Main Street*

(b) complete; *there was dead silence in the exam room*; *the train came to a dead stop*

(c) not working; **the line went dead** = the telephone line suddenly stopped working; *I was talking on the phone when suddenly the line went dead*

(d) not lively, not exciting; *seaside towns can be quite dead in winter*

2 *adverb*

(a) completely; *he was dead tired after his long walk*

(b) exactly; *you're dead right*; *the train arrived dead on time*

3 *noun*

(a) **the dead** = dead people; *a list of the names of the dead of the two world wars*

(b) **the dead of night** = the middle of the night; *he woke up in the dead of night and thought he heard a noise downstairs*

② **deadline**

['dedlaɪn] *noun*

date by which something has to be done; *we've been given an October deadline to finish the job*; **to meet a deadline** = to finish something in time; *I don't think we can meet the deadline*; **to miss a deadline** = not to finish something in time; *they worked as fast as they could but missed the deadline by two days*

③ **deadly**

['dedli]

1 *adjective*

(a) which will kill; *the female spider is deadlier than the male*

(b) very serious or bitter; *a deadly rival* (NOTE: **deadlier - deadliest**)

2 *adverb*

extremely; *don't eat those mushrooms - they're deadly poisonous*; *he was deadly serious*

② **deaf**

[def]

1 *adjective*

(person) who cannot hear, who has difficulty in hearing; *the old lady is going deaf*; *he's deafer than he used to be*; **stone deaf** = completely deaf (NOTE: **deafer - deafest**)

2 *noun*

the deaf = people who cannot hear; *their son goes to a school for the deaf*

① **deal**

[diːl]

1 *noun*

(a) **a good deal** *or* **a great deal** = much; *he's feeling a good deal better after two days off work*; *she didn't say a great deal*; **a good deal of** *or* **a great deal of** = a lot of; *he made a good deal of money from his business*; *there's a great deal of work still to be done*

(b) business affair, agreement, contract; *we've signed a deal with a German firm*; *they did a deal to supply envelopes*; *the vice president set up a deal with a Russian bank*; **bad deal** *or* **rough deal** *or* **raw deal** = bad treatment; *she got a rough deal from the company*; **package deal** = agreement where several different items are agreed at the same time

2 *verb*

(a) **to deal in** = to buy and sell; *she deals in carpets and rugs imported from India*

(b) to hand out cards to players; *it's my turn to deal*; *he dealt me two kings* (NOTE: **dealing - dealt** [delt])

② **dealer**

['diːlər] *noun*

person who buys and sells; *he bought his automobile from a used-car dealer*; *she's an antiques dealer with a store in Seattle*; **drug dealer** = person who sells illegal drugs to other people

② **deal with**

['diːl 'wɪθ] *verb*

to concern yourself with, to handle; *the job involves dealing with the public*; *leave it to the filing clerk - he'll deal with it*; *we will deal with your order as soon as we can*; *this administration has to deal with the problem of teenage crime*

① **dear**

[dɪər]

1 *adjective*

(a) well liked, loved; *she's a very dear friend of mine*; *we had a letter from dear old Mrs. Smith*

(b) *(used at the beginning of a letter)* **Dear Sir** *or* **Dear Madam** = addressing a man or woman whom you do not know, or addressing a company; **Dear Sirs** = addressing a company; **Dear Mr. Smith** *or* **Dear Mrs. Smith** *or* **Dear Miss Smith** = addressing a man or woman whom you know; **Dear James** *or* **Dear Julia** = addressing a friend or a person you do business with

(c) costing a lot of money; *fresh fruit is always dearer in the winter*; *that restaurant is too dear for me* (NOTE: **dearer - dearest**)

2 *interjection*

(meaning how annoying) **oh dear!** *it's starting to rain*

3 *noun*

(way of referring to someone you like) *be a dear, and pass me my glasses*; *did you have a good day at the office, Dear?* (NOTE: do not confuse with **deer**)

① **death**

[deθ] *noun*

(a) act of dying; *she never got over her mother's death*; *traffic accidents caused over*

/152

1000 deaths last year; **death rate** = percentage of deaths per thousand of population; *the region has a death rate of 15 per thousand*; *an increase in the death rate due to accidents*; **death tax** = tax paid on the value of the things left by a dead person

(b) *(informal)* **to death** = completely; *she was bored to death sitting watching football on television*; *she's sick to death of always having to do the housework*

② **debate**
[dɪ'beɪt]
1 *noun*
formal discussion; *after his talk the scientist had a lively debate with the students*; *there has been some debate among experts about whether global warming is really taking place*
2 *verb*
to discuss; *we sat in the rain and debated what to do next*; *they debated the motion to cut taxes*

④ **debilitating**
[dɪ'bɪlɪteɪtɪŋ] *adjective*
which makes you weak; *he suffers from a debilitating illness*

④ **debit**
['debɪt]
1 *noun*
money that is paid out, or taken out of an account; *your bank statement gives a list of credits and debits at the end of each month*
2 *verb*
to deduct money from an account; *my account was debited for the entire amount*

④ **debris**
[də'bri] *noun*
pieces of a building that is being knocked down, aircraft that has crashed, etc.; *debris from the crash littered the ground*; *she was hit by flying debris* (NOTE: no plural)

③ **debt**
[det] *noun*
money owed to someone; *her debts are piling up*; **to be in debt** = to owe money; *he is in debt to the tune of $3,750*; **to get into debt** = to start to owe money; **to be out of debt** = not to owe money; *see also* RED; **debt collector** = person who collects money owed to other people, informally, a bill collector

④ **debut**
['deɪbju] *noun*
first appearance of an actor, etc.; *she made her debut on the stage in the role of Ophelia*

④ **decade**
['dekeɪd] *noun*
period of ten years; *during the last decade of the 20th century*

② **decay**
[dɪ'keɪ]
1 *noun*
rotting, falling into ruin; *the mayor has plans to deal with inner city decay*; *tooth decay is especially bad in children who eat sweets*; *you*

must treat the wood to prevent decay (NOTE: no plural)
2 *verb*
to rot, to fall into ruin; *sugar makes your teeth decay*; *the jungle path was blocked by decaying branches*

③ **deceive**
[dɪ'siv] *verb*
to trick someone, to make someone believe something which is not true; *he deceived everyone into thinking that he was a police officer*

① **December**
[dɪ'sembər] *noun*
twelfth and last month of the year, after November and before January; *she was born in December*; *his birthday is December 25 - Christmas Day!*; *they always go on a skiing vacation in December*; *today is December 6* (NOTE: **December 6:** say "December sixth")

④ **decent**
['disənt] *adjective*
(a) honest; *the boss is a hard-working decent man*
(b) quite good; *she earns a decent salary*
(c) *(informal)* properly dressed, wearing clothes; *you can't come in yet - I'm not decent*

④ **deceptive**
[dɪ'septɪv] *adjective*
not as it seems; *the distance is deceptive - it is much farther away than you think*; **appearances are deceptive** = things are not always what they appear to be on the surface

① **decide**
[dɪ'saɪd] *verb*
to make up your mind to do something; *have you decided which restaurant to go to?*; *they decided to stay at home and watch TV*; *she decided not to spend her money on a new car*

① **decide against**
[dɪ'saɪd ə'genst] *verb*
to make up your mind not to do something; *we've decided against going to Maine this year*

② **decimal**
['desɪml]
1 *adjective*
decimal system = system of counting based on the number 10
2 *noun*
fraction expressed as tenths, hundredths and thousandths; *three-quarters is 0.75 in decimals*; **to three decimal places** = with three figures shown after the decimal point; *67 divided by 13 gives 5.154 to three decimal places*; **decimal point** = dot used to show the division between whole numbers and parts of numbers; *to multiply by ten, simply move the decimal point one place to the right* (NOTE: three and a half is written: **3.5** (say "three point five"))

COMMENT: the decimal point is used in the U.S.A. and Britain. In most European countries a comma is used to show the decimal, so 4,75% in Germany is written 4.75% in the U.S.A.

② **decision**
[dɪˈsɪʃn] *noun*
act of making up your mind to do something; **to come to a decision** *or* **to reach a decision** *or* **to make a decision** = to decide to do something; *they talked for hours but didn't come to any decision; he thought about the job offer, but, in the end, made the decision to stay where he was*; **decision-making process** = the process involved in making up your mind to do something; *we involve all the staff in the decision-making process*

④ **decisive**
[dɪˈsaɪsɪv] *adjective*
(a) firm (tone of voice); *he was nervous but tried to sound decisive*
(b) which brings about a result; *the second and decisive round of voting takes place next Sunday; her action was decisive in obtaining the release of the hostages*

② **deck**
[dek] *noun*
(a) floor of a ship, bus, etc.; *I'll stay on deck because I'm feeling seasick; the sailors were washing down the deck; let's go up to the upper deck of the bus - you can see the sights better from there*; **main deck** = deck on a ship with the most important facilities, such as the restaurant, bars, etc.
(b) set of playing cards; *she shuffled the deck*
(c) wooden platform outside a house; *we had drinks outside on the deck*

③ **declaration**
[deklǝˈreɪʃn] *noun*
(a) official statement; *the senator's declaration was broadcast at 6 o'clock*
(b) list of goods declared to customs; *don't forget to fill out your declaration before the plane lands in London*

② **declare**
[dɪˈkleǝr] *verb*
(a) to state officially; *Mr. Bush declared his intention to run for president; she was declared dead on arrival at the hospital; it was declared that Mrs. Broom was elected chairman by 46 votes*; **to declare war on a country** = to state formally that a war has begun with a country
(b) *(at customs)* **to declare goods to customs** = to list the goods you are carrying on which you may need to pay customs duty; *the customs officials asked him if he had anything to declare; go through that line if you have nothing to declare*

③ **decline**
[dɪˈklaɪn]
1 *noun*
going downwards; *sales figures have gone into a sharp decline; the decline in the value of the franc; a welcome decline in the number of cases of pollution*
2 *verb*
(a) to refuse or to turn down (an invitation); *she declined their request; he declined to come to lunch*
(b) to become weaker; *he declined rapidly after he went into the hospital*
(c) to become less in numbers or amount; *our sales declined over the last year; the fish population has declined sharply*

② **decorate**
[ˈdekǝreɪt] *verb*
(a) to paint (a room or a building); to put new wallpaper in (a room); *she can't come to the phone - she's decorating the kitchen*; **interior decorating** = arranging and decorating the inside of a house (drapes, paint, wallpaper, carpets, etc.)
(b) to cover something with pretty or colorful things to make it look attractive, or to celebrate an occasion; *the streets were decorated with flags*
(c) to put colored icing on a cake; *the wedding cake was decorated with bells and flowers*
(d) to award someone a medal; *he was decorated for his brave rescue of the children*

④ **decoration**
[dekǝˈreɪʃn] *noun*
(a) action of decorating; *she is in charge of the decoration of the church for the wedding*
(b) action of painting a room, etc.; *the decoration of the town hall took over a year*
(c) things added to make something more attractive; *the only decoration allowed was a pattern of red and blue squares*
(d) **decorations** = flags or lights, etc., used to celebrate an occasion; *we put up the Christmas decorations at the beginning of the vacation*
(e) medal; *he went to the White House to receive his decoration from the president; old soldiers were wearing their decorations for the Veterans Day parade*

② **decorative**
[ˈdekǝrǝtɪv] *adjective*
pleasant to look at; serving as a decoration; *she stuck a decorative border around the edge*

② **decrease**
1 *noun* [ˈdikris]
falling, becoming less; *a decrease in traffic; sales show a 10% decrease for last year; there has been a decrease of 20% in applications to join the club*; **to be on the decrease** = to be falling; *traffic accidents are on the decrease*
2 *verb* [dɪˈkris]
to fall, to become less; *the number of traffic accidents is decreasing; applications to join have decreased by 20%*

④ **decree**
[dɪˈkriː]
1 *noun*
legal order that has not been voted; *the president has issued a decree that June 1 should be a national holiday*
2 *verb*
to state as a legal order; *the president has decreed that everyone must work on Saturdays*

③ **dedicate**
[ˈdedɪkeɪt] *verb*
(a) to spend all your life doing something; *she dedicated her life to the service of the poor*
(b) to name a church after a saint; *the chapel is dedicated to St. Christopher*
(c) to offer a book to someone as a mark of respect or love; *he dedicated his collection of poems to his wife*

③ **deduct**
[dɪˈdʌkt] *verb*
to remove something from a sum of money; *we made $90 at the sale, but if we deduct our expenses, we only made $35*; *the landlord deducted some money from our deposit to cover broken items*

③ **deduction**
[dɪˈdʌkʃn] *noun*
(a) sum of money that is taken away from a total sum; *there is an automatic deduction for insurance*; *net wages are wages after deduction of tax and social security payments*; **tax deductions** = money removed from your salary to pay tax
(b) conclusion that is reached; **by a process of deduction** = by looking at the evidence and reaching a conclusion

③ **deed**
[diːd] *noun*
legal document; **title deeds** *or* **the deed to a house** = legal documents showing who owns a house; *we have deposited the deed to the house in the bank*

① **deep**
[diːp]
1 *adjective*
(a) which goes a long way down; *the water is very deep in the middle of the river*; *this is the deepest lake in North America*; *in the shallow end of the pool, the water is only a few inches deep* (NOTE: the use with figures: **the pool is six feet deep; a lake 50 m deep**)
(b) dark (color); *a deep brown carpet*
(c) felt very strongly; *we want to express our deepest thanks for what you have done*; *she sat in a corner, deep in thought*
(d) low-pitched, bass (voice); *who's been sitting on my chair, said Father Bear in his deep voice* (NOTE: **deeper - deepest**)
2 *adverb*
a long way down; *the mine goes deep under the sea*

③ **deepen**
[ˈdiːpən] *verb*
(a) to make something become deeper; *they're going to deepen the channel so that bigger boats can use the harbor*
(b) to become deeper; *the water deepened as he walked out into the lake*

③ **deeply**
[ˈdiːpli] *adverb*
(a) very much; *we deeply regret having to lay so many people off*
(b) **to sleep deeply** = to sleep without waking; *after taking the drug she slept deeply for ten hours*

① **deer**
[dɪər] *noun*
wild animal of which the male has long horns, often hunted; *there is a herd of deer in the park* (NOTE: do not confuse with **dear**; the plural is **deer**)

④ **default**
[dɪˈfɒlt]
1 *noun*
(a) **he is in default** = he has failed to carry out the terms of the contract
(b) **by default** = because someone else fails to do something; *his opponent withdrew and he won by default*
(c) *(computers)* set way of working; **default drive** = the drive that is accessed first
2 *verb*
to fail to carry out the terms of a contract; **to default on payments** = not to make payments which are due; *he paid regularly for six months and then defaulted on his loan*

② **defeat**
[dɪˈfiːt]
1 *noun*
loss of a fight, a vote, a game; *the chief executive officer offered to resign after the defeat of the proposal at the stockholders' meeting*; *it was the team's first defeat for two years*
2 *verb*
to beat someone in a fight, game or vote; *the proposal was defeated by 10 votes to 3*; *the ruling party was heavily defeated in the presidential election*; *our team has not been defeated so far this season*

④ **defect**
1 *noun* [ˈdiːfekt]
fault; *there must be a defect in the computer program*
2 *verb* [dɪˈfekt]
to leave your country to live in an opposing one; *she defected while on a tour of Southeast Asia*

① **defend**
[dɪˈfend] *verb*
(a) to protect someone who is being attacked; *he jumped forward to defend his wife against the robbers*; *she couldn't defend herself against the muggers*

(b) *(in a law court)* to speak on behalf of an accused person; *he hired the best lawyers to defend him*; *the lawyer who is defending my uncle*; **to defend a lawsuit** = to appear in court to state your case when accused of something

③ **defendant**
[dɪˈfendənt] *noun*
(in a law court) person who is accused of doing something illegal; person who is sued in a civil case; *the defendant says he is innocent*

> COMMENT: in a civil case, the defendant faces a complaint from the plaintiff. In a criminal case, the defendant (also called the accused) is being prosecuted for a crime by the prosecution

① **defense**
[dɪˈfens] *noun*
(a) protection against attack, infection, etc.; *several people ran to her defense when she was attacked by muggers*; *these tablets offer a limited defense against the disease*
(b) protection provided by the armed forces; *some countries spend more on defense than on education*; **the Defense Department** = government department dealing with the army, navy and air force
(c) *(in games)* part of a team whose job is to protect the goal; *the U.S. defense came under attack from the Brazilian forwards*
(d) defenses = strong walls, etc., that are built to protect something; *the town is strengthening its defenses by building thicker walls*; **when your defenses are down** = when you are not prepared for an attack; *burglars often strike when you're relaxing and your defenses are down*
(e) *(in a law court)* **the defense** = lawyers acting for the accused person; **defense counsel** = lawyer who represents the defendant in a lawsuit (NOTE: the opposing side in a court is the **prosecution**)

④ **defensive**
[dɪˈfensɪv]
1 *adjective*
which protects; *they built a defensive wall around the camp*
2 *noun*
to be on the defensive about something = to feel you need to give reasons for having done something; *she's always on the defensive when newspapers mention her huge salary*

④ **deficiency**
[dɪˈfɪʃənsi] *noun*
lack of; *their diet has a deficiency in vitamins or has a vitamin deficiency*

④ **deficit**
[ˈdefɪsɪt] *noun*
amount by which expenditures are more than receipts in a company's or a country's accounts; *the company announced a $3 million deficit*; **to make good a deficit** = to put money into an account to balance it; **balance of payments**

deficit *or* **trade deficit** = situation when a country imports more than it exports; *the U.S.'s trade deficit has fallen by $9 billion*

③ **define**
[dɪˈfaɪn] *verb*
(a) to explain clearly, to give the meaning of something; *how would you define environmental?*; *the memo tried to define the way in which the two departments should work together*
(b) to indicate the limits of something; *the police operate within limits that have been clearly defined*

③ **definite**
[ˈdefɪnət] *adjective*
(a) very clear, very sure; *I need a definite answer*; *he was quite definite that he had seen the girl at the bus stop*
(b) definite article = "the" (as opposed to the indefinite article "a" or "an")

③ **definitely**
[ˈdefɪnətli] *adverb*
certainly, surely; *I'll definitely be there by 7 o'clock*

③ **definition**
[defɪˈnɪʃn] *noun*
(a) clear explanation (of a word); *an English-German dictionary doesn't give definitions, only translations*; *look up the definition of "democracy" in the dictionary*
(b) *(of a photograph)* being clear and with sharp lines; *the portrait shots are clear, but your landscape photos lack definition* (NOTE: no plural in this meaning)

④ **definitive**
[dɪˈfɪnɪtɪv] *adjective*
final and best, which cannot be made better; *this is the definitive production of "Macbeth"*

② **defrost**
[diˈfrɒst] *verb*
(a) to melt ice which has formed; *I must defrost the freezer*
(b) *(frozen food)* to stop being frozen; *a large turkey will take 24 hours to defrost*

④ **defy**
[dɪˈfaɪ] *verb*
(a) to refuse to obey the law; *he should never have tried to defy the university authorities*
(b) *(formal)* **to defy someone to do something** = to challenge someone to do something; *I defy you to jump higher than that*

② **degree**
[dɪˈgri] *noun*
(a) division of a scale; *the temperature of the water is above 20 degrees*; *an angle of 80°* (NOTE: with figures, **degree** is usually written °: **25°**)
(b) level; *to what degree do you think the driver was to blame for the accident?*; **to a certain degree** = partly; *it's his own fault to a certain degree*

(c) diploma from a university; *she has a degree in mathematics from Harvard*

② **delay**
[dɪˈleɪ]
1 *noun*
length of time that something is late; *there will be a delay of ten minutes before the meeting starts*; *we are sorry for the delay in replying to your letter*
2 *verb*
(a) to make late; *the train has been delayed by ice*; *he was delayed because his taxi had an accident*
(b) to put something off until later; *we will delay making a decision until we see the result of the election*; *the company has delayed payment of all invoices*

③ **delegate**
1 *noun* [ˈdelɪgət]
person who represents others at a meeting; *the vice president met delegates from the union*
2 *verb* [ˈdelɪgeɪt]
to pass authority or responsibility on to someone else; *she finds it difficult to delegate*; *he delegated the job of locking up the store to the assistant manager*

③ **delegation**
[delɪˈgeɪʃn] *noun*
(a) group of representatives; *the board met with a union delegation*
(b) passing authority or responsibility to someone else; *the secret of good management is delegation* (NOTE: no plural in this meaning)

③ **deliberate**
1 *adjective* [dɪˈlɪbərət]
(a) done on purpose; *it was a deliberate attempt to spoil her birthday party*; *the fans came with the deliberate intention of stirring up trouble*
(b) slow and thoughtful in speaking or doing something; *she has a very deliberate way of signing her name*
2 *verb* [dɪˈlɪbəreɪt]
(a) to debate, to discuss; *the city council deliberated all morning*; *the jury left the courtroom to deliberate*
(b) to think carefully about something; *I'll need some time to deliberate on the possible ways of solving the problem*

③ **deliberately**
[dɪˈlɪbərətli] *adverb*
(a) on purpose; *it was an accident - I didn't hit her deliberately*; *he deliberately left the cage door open*; *the police think that the fire was started deliberately*
(b) slowly and carefully; *she walked deliberately up the steps onto the platform*

③ **delicate**
[ˈdelɪkət] *adjective*
(a) easily damaged; *a delicate china bowl*
(b) liable to get illnesses; *little babies are very delicate*
(c) very soft and fine; *a delicate silk dress*

(d) possibly difficult; *he is in a delicate situation*

② **delicious**
[dɪˈlɪʃəs] *adjective*
which tastes very good; *can I have another piece of that delicious cake?*

② **delight**
[dɪˈlaɪt]
1 *noun*
pleasure; *their singing was a pure delight*; *the news was greeted with delight by the waiting crowd*; **to take great delight in something** = to take great pleasure in something
2 *verb*
to delight in something = to take great pleasure in something; *she delights in teasing her little brother*

① **delighted**
[dɪˈlaɪtɪd] *adjective*
very pleased; *she's delighted with her present*; *we are delighted that you were able to come*; *I'm delighted to meet you at last*

② **delightful**
[dɪˈlaɪtfəl] *adjective*
very pleasant; *we had a delightful picnic by the river*

① **deliver**
[dɪˈlɪvər] *verb*
(a) to bring something to someone; *has today's newspaper been delivered?*; *he delivered the letter himself so as to save buying a stamp*
(b) **to deliver a baby** = to help a mother when a baby is born; *the twins were delivered by the nurse*
(c) **to deliver a speech** = to make a speech; *this is the full text of the speech the president delivered at the meeting*

① **delivery**
[dɪˈlɪvri] *noun*
(a) bringing something to someone; *there is no charge for delivery within the Manhattan area*; *use the rear entrance for deliveries*; *the next delivery will be on Thursday*; **delivery van** = goods van for delivering goods to retail customers
(b) birth of a child; *the doctor supervised the delivery*

② **demand**
[dɪˈmænd]
1 *noun*
(a) asking for something; *they made a demand for payment*; *her latest demands are quite impossible to meet*
(b) need for goods or services at a certain price; **to meet a demand** *or* **to fill a demand** = to supply what is needed; *the factory had to increase production to meet the extra demand*; *we cannot keep up with the demand for our services*; **there is not much demand for this item** = not many people want to buy it; **this item is in great demand** = many people want to buy it; **law of supply and demand** = general rule

that the amount of a product which is available is linked to the amount which is wanted by customers

2 *verb*

to ask for something in a firm way; *she demanded a refund*; *I demand an explanation*

④ **demanding**
['dɪ'mædɪŋ] *adjective*
which takes up much time and energy; *he has a very demanding job*; *looking after little children is very demanding*

② **democracy**
[dɪ'mɒkrəsi] *noun*
(a) country governed by elected representatives of the people; *we live in a democracy* (NOTE: plural is **democracies**)
(b) system of government by elected representatives of the people; *the people want democracy, not a military government* (NOTE: no plural in this meaning)

③ **democrat**
['deməkræt] *noun*
(a) person who believes in democracy; *all true democrats will unite against the military rulers*
(b) Democrat = a member of the Democratic Party; *the Democrats lost the election to the Republicans*

④ **democratic**
[demə'krætɪk] *adjective*
referring to democracy; *they promised to restore democratic government*

③ **Democratic Party**
[demə'krætɪk 'pɑrti] *noun*
one of the two main political parties in the U.S.A., which is in favor of some social change and state aid for poor people; *the Democratic Party's candidate for the presidency*; *compare* REPUBLICAN PARTY

④ **demonstrate**
['demənstreɪt] *verb*
(a) to show; *this demonstrates how little he has changed*; *he demonstrated how the machine worked*
(b) to demonstrate against something = to protest something in public; *a group was demonstrating against the new freeway*

③ **demonstration**
[demən'streɪʃn] *noun*
(a) showing (how something works); *can you give me a demonstration of how it works?*; **demonstration model** = automobile, or other piece of equipment, which has been used by a store to show how it works, and is then sold at a lower price
(b) crowd of people who are protesting something; *we went shopping and got mixed up in a demonstration in front of City Hall*; *they staged demonstrations against the government in several cities*

③ **demonstrator**
['demənstreɪtər] *noun*
(a) person who shows how to do something or how pieces of equipment work; *the demonstrator showed how to work the electric saw*
(b) person who marches, or who forms part of a crowd protesting something; *a crowd of demonstrators blocked the road*; *the police used tear gas to clear demonstrators from in front of the White House*

④ **denial**
[dɪ'naɪəl] *noun*
statement that something is not true; *despite his repeated denials, people still suspect he is the man responsible for planting the bomb*; *the company issued a denial that it was planning to close down the factory*

① **Denmark**
['denmɑrk] *noun*
country in northern Europe, south of Sweden and Norway, and north of Germany; *Legoland is one of the tourist attractions of Denmark* (NOTE: capital: **Copenhagen**; people: **the Danes**; language: **Danish**; currency: **Danish krone**)

③ **dense**
[dens] *adjective*
(a) very thick; *dense fog closed the airport*
(b) crowded together; *they tried to find their way through dense forest*; *I find it difficult to read through 100 pages of dense text*
(c) *(informal)* stupid; *how can anybody be so dense?* (NOTE: **denser - densest**)

③ **dent**
[dent]
1 *noun*
slight hollow made by hitting something; *someone has made a dent in my car door*
2 *verb*
to make a slight hollow mark in something; *he backed into a tree and dented the bumper*

② **dental**
['dentəl] *adjective*
referring to teeth; *he's a dental student*; **dental practice** = a dentist's office

① **dentist**
['dentɪst] *noun*
person who looks after your teeth; *one of my teeth has started to hurt - I need to make an appointment to see the dentist*; *he hates going to the dentist*; *the dentist filled two of my teeth*

③ **deny**
[dɪ'naɪ] *verb*
(a) to state that something is not correct; *you were there, weren't you? - don't deny it!*; *she denied that she had ever seen him*; *he denied stealing the car*
(b) to deny someone something = to prevent someone having something; *he was denied access to the secret government papers*; **to deny oneself** = not to eat, not to do something, which you would like to do; *she denied herself a*

vacation in order to earn enough to pay off her mortgage

② **depart**
[dɪˈpɑrt] *verb*
(a) to go away, to leave; *the bus departs from the depot at 9:00*
(b) to depart from the normal procedure = to act in a different way from the normal practice

③ **department**
[dɪˈpɑrtmənt] *noun*
(a) specialized section of a large company; *he is in charge of the marketing department*; *write to the complaints department about the service*; **accounting department** = section in a company which deals with money paid or received, borrowed or owed; *if you have a question about the invoice, ask to speak to the accounting department*
(b) one of the sections of the government; *the Department of Agriculture*
(c) part of a large store; *if you want cheese you have to go to the dairy department*; *you will find beds in the furniture department*

② **department store**
[dɪˈpɑrtmənt ˈstɔr] *noun*
a large store with many departments; *Tiffany's is one of the largest department stores in New York*

② **departure**
[dɪˈpɑrtʃər] *noun*
(a) leaving; *the departure time is 3 o'clock*; *the plane's departure was delayed by two hours*
(b) departures = (i) list of trains, planes, etc., that are leaving; (ii) part of an airport terminal that deals with passengers who are leaving; **departure lounge** = waiting area at an airport for people who are about to leave
(c) departure from = working in a different way from usual; *this is a departure from our usual practice* = we are doing something in a different way from the usual one

② **depend**
[dɪˈpend] *verb*
(a) to happen because of something or someone; *the success of the book will depend on the publicity campaign*; *I can't be sure that we will come for lunch - it depends on what time we get home from the party the night before*; *(informal)* **that depends** *or* **it (all) depends** = it is not certain; *we may go to Massachusetts on vacation, or New Hampshire, that depends*
(b) to depend on someone *or* **something** = to rely on someone or something, to be sure of someone or something; *you can't depend on Jack - he's always too busy to help*; *you can depend on her to do her best*

③ **dependent**
[dɪˈpendənt]
1 *adjective*
(a) supported with money by someone; *she has five dependent relatives*

(b) relying on someone else; *the patients become very dependent on the hospital staff*
2 *noun*
person who is supported by someone else

② **depending**
[dɪˈpendɪŋ] *adjective*
depending on = which varies according to something; *it takes around one hour to drive to downtown Cincinnati, depending on the traffic*

④ **deplete**
[dɪˈplit] *verb*
to reduce available stocks or stores; *stocks of oil have been seriously depleted by the cold weather*

④ **deport**
[dɪˈpɔrt] *verb*
to expel someone from a country; *the refugees were deported*

② **deposit**
[dɪˈpɑzɪt]
1 *noun*
(a) money placed (in a bank); *her deposits to the bank had grown over the years*; **deposit slip** = piece of paper stamped by the bank to prove that you have paid money into your account
(b) money given in advance so that the thing which you want to buy will not be sold to someone else; *she had to put down a deposit on the watch*; *can you leave $75 as a deposit?*; *I paid a 30% deposit and don't have to pay anything more for six months*; *the money is on deposit for the purchase*
(c) layer of mineral in the ground; *coal deposits occur in several parts of the country*; *the North Sea oil deposits yield 100,000 barrels a month*
2 *verb*
to put money into a bank account; *he deposited $150 in his checking account*; *the check arrived at long last, and I deposited it immediately*; *I deposited the check as soon as it arrived*

③ **depressed**
[dɪˈprest] *adjective*
(a) sad, miserable; *she's been feeling depressed since the accident*
(b) depressed area = part of a country where people are poor and unemployed and living conditions are bad

③ **depressing**
dɪˈpresɪŋ] *adjective*
gloomy; *a depressing November day*; *that movie is deeply depressing - it just made me want to cry*

④ **depression**
[dɪˈpreʃn] *noun*
(a) mental state where you feel miserable and hopeless; *he was in a state of depression after the exams*; *she is subject to fits of depression*
(b) low pressure area bringing bad weather; *the depression coming from the Atlantic will bring rain to most parts of the country*; *winds move rapidly around the center of a depression*

(c) economic crisis; *an economic depression*; **the (Great) Depression** = the world economic crisis of 1929-1933; *all economies suffered during the Depression*
(d) place which is lower than the area around it; *a pool of water had formed a depression in the rocks*

③ **deprive**
[dɪ'praɪv] *verb*
to deprive someone of something = to take something away from someone, not to let someone have something; *as an artist, it was dreadful for him to be deprived of his paints in prison*

③ **dept.**
= DEPARTMENT

③ **depth**
[depθ] *noun*
(a) how deep something is; *the depth of the lake is 60 ft; the submarine dove to a depth of 200 m*
(b) deepest or most extreme point; *in the depth of the Russian winter, temperatures can reach -45°F; they have a house in the depths of rural Wyoming*; **the depths of despair** = complete lack of hope; *he lay in bed in the depths of despair and thought of committing suicide*

◇ **out of your depth**
phrase
(a) to be in deep water and not be able to touch the bottom; *she swam out of her depth and had to be rescued by the beach guards*
(b) to be unable to understand; *he's quite out of his depth in discussions about economic theory*

② **deputy**
['depjuti] *noun*
person who can take the place of another person; *he appointed her as his deputy; she's acting as deputy chairman while the chairman is in the hospital*

④ **derive**
[dɪ'raɪv] *verb*
(a) to derive from *or* **to be derived from** = to come from originally; *the name of the plant "fuchsia" is derived from the name of the German scientist, Fuchs*
(b) to get; *the local people derive a good deal of pleasure from watching the tourists riding on camels*

③ **descend**
[dɪ'send] *verb*
(a) to go down (a ladder, etc.); *the president seemed to trip as he descended the steps of the plane*
(b) to descend from someone = to have someone as an ancestor; *he is descended from Irish immigrants*
(c) to descend on = to visit in large numbers; *my wife's family descended on us for Christmas*

① **describe**
[dɪ'skraɪb] *verb*
to say or write what something or someone is like; *can you describe the automobile that hit the old lady?; she described how the bus suddenly left the road; he described the mugger as a tall man with a black beard; the police asked him to describe what happened*

② **description**
[dɪ'skrɪpʃn] *noun*
saying or writing what something or someone is like; *she gave the police a clear description of the car*; **job description** = official document from a company which says what a job involves

② **desert**
1 ['dezərt] *noun*
very dry area of the world; *from Los Angeles you can drive into the Mojave Desert; she plans to cross the Sahara Desert on a motorcycle; it hardly ever rains in the desert; we watched a TV program on desert animals* (NOTE: do not confuse with **dessert**)
2 *verb* [dɪ'zɜrt]
(a) to leave the armed forces without permission; *the general ordered that all soldiers who had deserted should be captured and shot*
(b) to leave someone all alone; *he deserted his wife when she was expecting their second child*

③ **deserted**
[dɪ'zɜrtɪd] *adjective*
with no one in, with no people; *the restaurant was completely deserted; the center of town is quite deserted on Sunday afternoons*

③ **deserve**
[dɪ'zɜrv] *verb*
to earn something because of what you have done; *he didn't deserve to win because he cheated; I've been on my feet all day - I think I deserve a rest; I'm sure she deserved to be punished*; see also TURN

① **design**
[dɪ'zaɪn]
1 *noun*
(a) plan or drawing of something, before it is made or built; *here are the designs for the book cover; the architect has produced the designs for the new city hall*
(b) to have designs on something = to plan to try to take something; *I think he has designs on my job*
2 *verb*
to draw plans for the shape or appearance of something before it is made or built; *he designed the new college library; she designs garden furniture*

③ **designer**
[dɪ'zaɪnər] *noun*
artist who plans the shape or appearance of goods, clothes, rooms, etc.; *we've chosen an interior designer to plan the inside of the house*; **designer clothes** = clothes designed by a

famous designer; *she was wearing designer jeans*; **designer label** = label attached to clothes made by a designer; *see also* INTERIOR DESIGNER

③ **desirable**
[dɪˈzaɪrəbl] *adjective*
which a lot of people want; *this has become a very desirable part of the town to live in*

② **desire**
[dɪˈzaɪər]
1 *noun*
something that you want very much; *it's difficult to satisfy the public's desire for information*; *she had a sudden desire to lie down and go to sleep*
2 *verb*
(a) *(formal)* to want; *he will get you anything you desire*
(b) to leave a lot to be desired = not to be of the right standard, not to be acceptable; *the bathrooms in the hotel leave a lot to be desired*

① **desk**
[desk] *noun*
(a) table for writing (often with drawers); *he put the papers away in his desk drawer*; *she was sitting at her desk when the telephone rang*; **desk pad** = pad of paper kept on a desk for writing notes
(b) section of a bank dealing with a particular type of business; *foreign exchange desk*
(c) section of a newspaper office; *city desk* = department that deals with local news

③ **despair**
[dɪˈspeər]
1 *noun*
lack of hope; *when he lost his job and his girlfriend left him, he was filled with despair*; **the depths of despair** = complete lack of hope (NOTE: no plural)
2 *verb*
to despair of something = to give up all hope of something; *after two months in the jungle, he despaired of ever being rescued*

④ **despatch**
[dɪsˈpætʃ]
see DISPATCH

② **desperate**
[ˈdesprət] *adjective*
(a) hopeless; *food ran out and the situation on the ship was becoming desperate*
(b) urgent; *there is a desperate need of medical supplies*
(c) wild with despair; *when he didn't phone she became desperate with worry*

③ **despise**
[dɪˈspaɪz] *verb*
to look down on someone, to think someone is not worth much; *I despise people who always agree with the boss*; *she despised his attempts to speak French when ordering food in a restaurant*

④ **despite**
[dɪˈspaɪt] *preposition*
in spite of; *despite the wet weather we still enjoyed our vacation*

① **dessert**
[dɪˈzɜrt] *noun*
sweet course at the end of a meal; *the meal will end with a dessert of strawberries and cream*; *what's for dessert?*; **dessert menu** = special separate menu for desserts in a restaurant; *may I see the dessert menu please?*; **dessert spoon** = spoon that is larger than a teaspoon, but smaller than a soup spoon, used for eating desserts (NOTE: do not confuse with **desert**)

③ **destination**
[destɪˈneɪʃn] *noun*
place to which a person or vehicle is going; *we reached our destination at eight o'clock*; *the destination is shown on the front of the bus*

④ **destiny**
[ˈdestɪni] *noun*
(a) what will happen to you in the future; *the war affected the destinies of many people*
(b) power that controls what happens to you in the future; *you never know what destiny has in store for you*

① **destroy**
[dɪˈstrɔɪ] *verb*
to ruin completely; *the bomb destroyed several buildings*; *a lot of private property was destroyed in the war*

③ **destruction**
[dɪˈstrʌkʃn] *noun*
action of ruining completely, of causing a lot of damage; *the volcano caused enormous destruction*; *the destruction of the town by enemy bombs*; *after the bomb attack there was a scene of total destruction* (NOTE: no plural)

③ **destructive**
[dɪˈstrʌktɪv] *adjective*
which destroys, which causes a lot of damage; *the destructive power of an earthquake*

③ **detached**
[dɪˈtætʃt] *adjective*
(a) not personally involved or interested; *he was just a detached observer*; *it's better to look at something in a detached way, without any prejudices*
(b) not connected to a main building; *they live in a pleasant house with a detached garage*

③ **detail**
[ˈditeɪl]
1 *noun*
(a) small item of information; *send in your résumé including full details of your past experience*; *can you give me further details of when the accident took place?*; *I can't make out the details in the photo because the light is bad*
(b) in detail = with plenty of details; *the catalog lists all the furniture in detail*; *please describe*

the circumstances of the accident in as much detail as possible

2 *verb*

(a) to list all the small items; *he detailed the work that had to be done*

(b) to detail someone to do something = to tell someone to do a job; *he was detailed to wash the kitchen floor*

④ **detailed**

['diteıld] *adjective*

in detail, giving a lot of details; *we need a detailed list of the items that have been stolen; the police issued detailed descriptions of the two men*

③ **detect**

[dı'tekt] *verb*

to discover; to notice; *a little device detects the presence of smoke; if breast cancer is detected early enough, it can be cured; do I detect a note of optimism in your report?*

① **detective**

[dı'tektıv] *noun*

police officer who investigates crimes; *detectives have interviewed four suspects;* **private detective** = detective who is not part of a police force, and works for a fee; *we hired a private detective to track them down*

④ **deter**

[dı'tзr] *verb*

to deter someone from doing something = to put someone off doing something; *the heavy rain didn't deter the tourists from visiting the castle; we have installed cameras to deter shoplifters* (NOTE: **deterring - deterred**)

④ **deteriorate**

[dı'tıərıəreıt] *verb*

to become bad; to get worse; *her health has deteriorated since the accident; deteriorating weather conditions make driving difficult*

③ **determination**

[dıtзrmı'neıʃn] *noun*

strong wish to do something, and not to let anyone stop you doing it; *his determination to win the prize; the government needs to show more determination in their fight against drugs* (NOTE: no plural)

④ **determine**

[dı'tзrmın] *verb*

(a) to fix (a date, etc.); *the meeting will be at a date still to be determined*

(b) *(formal)* **to determine to do something** = to make up your mind to do something; *I determined not to make the same mistake again*

② **determined**

[dı'tзrmınd] *adjective*

decided; *he had a very determined expression on his face as he entered the ring; she is determined to win the prize*

② **detour**

['ditur] *noun*

temporary road system that sends traffic another way; *all traffic has to take a detour and join the highway again 6 miles further on*

④ **deuce**

[djus] *noun*

score of 40 - 40 in tennis

④ **devastating**

['devəsteıtıŋ] *adjective*

(a) causing a lot of damage; *the country has still not recovered from the devastating effects of the storm*

(b) which shocks or upsets; *the news from Paris was devastating*

② **develop**

[dı'veləp] *verb*

(a) to grow and change; *eventually, that little plant will develop into a giant oak*

(b) to make larger; *she does exercises to develop her leg muscles*

(c) to start a disease, etc.; *she developed a cold from standing in the rain*

(d) to produce and fix a photograph from film; *we can develop your film in an hour*

(e) to plan and produce; *to develop a new product*

(f) to plan and build; *they are planning to develop the site as an industrial project; the company is developing a chain of service stations*

③ **developer**

[dı'veləpər] *noun*

(a) person or company that plans and builds roads, airports, houses, factories or office buildings; *the land has been acquired by developers for a housing project;* **property developer** = person who plans and builds property

(b) liquid for developing photographs; *she put the film into a bath of developer*

② **developing**

[dı'veləpıŋ] *adjective*

(a) growing; *his rapidly developing network of contacts in government; her developing knowledge of the English language*

(b) developing countries = countries with growing industries

③ **development**

[dı'veləpmənt] *noun*

(a) growth; *the development of the little plant takes place rapidly;* **economic development** = process by which a country's economy changes and its industries grow; **industrial development** = planning and building of new industries in special areas

(b) developments = things which happen; *the police are waiting for further developments in the case*

(c) planning the production of a new product; *the development of new drugs will take some time*

(d) planning and building on an area of land; *they are planning a large-scale development on the site of the former docks*; **housing development** = group of houses built at the same time

② **device**
[dɪ'vaɪs] *noun*
(a) small useful machine; *he invented a device for screwing tops on bottles*; *the engineers brought in a device for taking samples of soil*
(b) left to your own devices = left to do whatever you want, left to look after yourself; *their parents were away and the children were left to their own devices*

① **devil**
['devl] *noun*
(a) powerful evil spirit; *he believes in ghosts and devils and all that sort of thing*
(b) *(informal: showing surprise)* **what the devil?** = what on earth?; *what the devil has been going on here while we've been away?*
(c) *(informal)* person; *he won the lottery, the lucky devil!*; *poor devil! I must go and see him in the hospital*; **little devil** = naughty child; *that little devil has been pulling the cat's tail*

③ **devise**
[dɪ'vaɪz] *verb*
to think up, to invent; *we've devised a new timetable for the summer term*; *he devised a plan for making more money out of the farm*

④ **devote**
[dɪ'vəʊt] *verb*
to devote time to something = to spend precious time on something; *don't you think you've devoted enough time to your model trains?*; **to devote yourself to** = to spend all your time on; *she devoted herself to looking after refugee children*

③ **devoted**
[dɪ'vəʊtɪd] *adjective*
(a) devoted to someone = loving someone; *he is devoted to his children*; *he died suddenly, leaving his devoted wife and six children*
(b) devoted to something = spending all your time on something; *she's devoted to her charity work*

② **dew**
[dju] *noun*
water which forms at night on objects in the open air; *the grass was wet with dew* (NOTE: do not confuse with **due**)

③ **diabetes**
[daɪə'biːtiz] *noun*
illness where the body cannot control the rate at which sugar is absorbed; *some people with diabetes give themselves daily injections* (NOTE: no plural)

③ **diabetic**
[daɪə'betɪk]
1 *adjective*
referring to diabetes; *the hospital provides a special diet for diabetic patients*; *he's on a strict*

diabetic diet; **diabetic food** = special food with a low sugar content which can be eaten by people with diabetes
2 *noun*
person with diabetes; *she is a diabetic and has to be careful about what she eats*

④ **diagnose**
[daɪəg'nəʊz] *verb*
to identify a patient's illness by examining him or her and noting symptoms; *the doctor diagnosed cancer*

④ **diagnosis**
[daɪəg'nəʊsɪs] *noun*
action of identifying an illness; *tests confirmed the doctor's diagnosis; the doctor's diagnosis was cancer, but the patient asked for a second opinion* (NOTE: plural is **diagnoses**)

③ **diagonal**
[daɪ'ægənl] *adjective*
going from one corner to another opposite; *he drew a diagonal line on the floor, running from one corner of the room to the other*

③ **diagram**
['daɪəgræm] *noun*
sketch, plan or accurate drawing; *she drew a diagram to show how to get to her house; the book gives a diagram of the circulation of blood*

① **dial**
['daɪəl]
1 *noun*
round face of a clock, meter, telephone, etc.; *modern telephones don't have dials - just buttons*
2 *verb*
to call a telephone number; *to call the police you must dial 911*; *dial 0 to reach an operator*; **to dial direct** = to contact a phone number yourself without asking the operator to do it for you; *you can dial New York direct from London*

④ **dialogue** *or* **dialog**
['daɪəlɒg] *noun*
(a) conversation between two people; *the storekeeper and the customer had an interesting dialogue*
(b) spoken words in a movie or TV drama; *turn the volume up so that we can hear the dialogue more clearly*
(c) political talks or negotiations; *the government is trying to encourage greater dialogue in the Middle East*

③ **diameter**
[daɪ'æmɪtər] *noun*
distance across the center of a circle; *each rod is one inch in diameter*

② **diamond**
['daɪəmənd] *noun*
(a) very hard precious stone; *he gave her a diamond ring*; *diamonds sparkled on her crown*; **diamond wedding** = 60th anniversary of a wedding day

(b) one of the red suits in a pack of cards; *he held the ten of diamonds* (NOTE: the other red suit is **hearts; clubs** and **spades** are the black suits)

(c) *(in baseball)* (i) the area formed by the three bases and home plate; (ii) the whole playing field; *the pitcher stands in the center of the baseball diamond*

② **diaper**
['daɪəpər] *noun*
cloth that is wrapped around a baby's bottom; *she changed the baby's diaper*

③ **diary**
['daɪəri] *noun*
(a) description of what has happened in your life day by day; *he kept a diary for years*; *she kept a diary of the places she visited on vacation*

(b) small book in which you write notes or make appointments for each day of the week; *I've noted the appointment in my desk diary*; *I can't fix the date immediately because I haven't got my diary with me* (NOTE: plural is **diaries**)

① **dice**
[daɪs]
1 *noun*
small cube with one to six dots on each side, used for playing games; *shake the dice in the cup and then throw them onto the board*; *he lost hundreds of dollars playing dice* (NOTE: plural is **dice**)

2 *verb*
to cut food into small cubes; *a cup of diced potato*

③ **dictate**
[dɪk'teɪt] *verb*
(a) to say something to someone who writes down your words; *she dictated a letter to her secretary*; *he dictated his address to me over the phone*

(b) to tell someone what to do; *the army commander dictated the terms of the surrender*; *she's always trying to dictate to us how to run the business*

② **dictation**
[dɪk'teɪʃn] *noun*
act of speaking something which is to be written down; *I got an A in French dictation*; **to take dictation** = to write down what someone is saying; *the secretary was taking dictation from the chief executive officer*

③ **dictator**
[dɪk'teɪtər] *noun*
person who rules a country alone; *the country was ruled by a military dictator*

② **dictionary**
['dɪkʃənri] *noun*
book that lists words, giving their meanings or translations into other languages; *look up the word in the dictionary if you don't know what it means*; **college dictionary** = book with most words needed by a college student; **pocket**

dictionary = small dictionary that you can put in your pocket (NOTE: plural is **dictionaries**)

① **did, didn't**
[dɪd or dɪdnt]
see DO

① **die**
[daɪ] *verb*
to stop living; *his mother died in 1995*; *she died in an automobile crash*; *if you don't water the plants they'll die*; *see also* DYING (NOTE: do not confuse with **dye**; note also **dies - dying**)

① **die out**
['daɪ 'aʊt] *verb*
to disappear gradually; *the habit of having a cooked breakfast is dying out*; *this butterfly is likely to die out unless measures are taken to protect it*

① **diet**
['daɪət]
1 *noun*
(a) kind of food you eat; *he lives on a diet of bread and beer*; *during the war, people were much healthier than now because their diet was simpler*

(b) eating only certain types of food, either to become thinner or to cure an illness; *the doctor told her to follow a strict diet*; *because she is pregnant she has to follow a diet*; **salt-free diet** = diet that does not contain salt; **to be on a diet** = to eat only certain types of food, especially in order to become thin or to deal with an illness; *he's been on a diet for some weeks, but still hasn't lost much weight*; **to go on a diet** = to start to eat less; *she went on a diet before going on vacation*

2 *verb*
to eat less food or only one kind of food; *she dieted for two weeks before going on vacation*; *he is dieting to try to lose weight*

③ **differ**
['dɪfər] *verb*
(a) not to be the same as something else; *the two machines differ considerably - one has an electric motor, the other runs on oil*; **to differ from** = to be different from, not to be the same as; *this automobile differs from the earlier model*; *their business differs from ours in one important way*

(b) **I beg to differ** = I do not agree

① **difference**
['dɪfrəns] *noun*
(a) way in which two things are not the same; *can you tell the difference between an apple and a pear with your eyes shut?*; *what is the difference in price between these two cars?*; *it doesn't make any difference* = it's not important; *you can use any color you like - it doesn't make any difference*; **to split the difference** = to agree on a figure which is halfway between two figures suggested; *twenty's too many, ten's not enough, let's split the difference and say fifteen*; *you are offering*

$30 and he wants $60, so why don't you split the difference and settle on $45?
(b) differences = arguments between people; *they had a meeting to try to settle their differences*

① **different**
['dɪfrənt] *adjective*
not the same; *living in the city is very different from living in the country; I went to three different clothing stores but I couldn't find anything in my size; he looks different now that he has a beard;* **that's quite a different matter** = it's not at all the same thing

① **differently**
['dɪfrəntli] *adverb*
not in the same way; *the same subject is treated quite differently in the three paintings*

① **difficult**
['dɪfɪkʌlt] *adjective*
not easy; which is hard to do; *the German exam was very difficult - half the class got poor grades; finding a parking space is difficult on Saturday mornings; the company is finding it difficult to sell their cars in the European market; it's difficult for me to judge my own sister from an objective point of view;* **to make things** *or* **life difficult for someone** = to create problems for someone; *his main aim at the office seems to be to make life as difficult as possible for his assistants*

① **difficulty**
['dɪfɪkʌlti] *noun*
(a) to have difficulty with something *or* **in doing something** to find it hard to do something; *she has difficulty in paying the rent;* **with difficulty** = not easily; *she climbed out of the hole with difficulty*
(b) problem; *the difficulty is that nobody has a driver's license; he is in financial difficulties; she went swimming in the rough sea and got into difficulties;* **to create** *or* **make difficulties for someone** = to make problems for someone; *she doesn't realize that going on vacation now is going to create difficulties for everyone*
(NOTE: plural is **difficulties**)

① **dig**
[dɪg]
1 *verb*
to make a hole in the ground (with a spade); *she's been digging in the garden all morning; the prisoners dug a tunnel to try to escape; digging holes in the ground is hard work*
(NOTE: **digging - dug** [dʌg] **- has dug**)
2 *noun*
(a) making holes in the ground to find something old; *they are working on a dig to find the remains of a Roman town*
(b) cutting, sarcastic remark; *he made a dig about my clothes*

③ **digest**
verb [daɪ'dʒest]

(a) to break down food in the stomach and convert it into elements that can be absorbed by the body; *I find beans difficult to digest*
(b) to think about something and understand it fully; *give me time to digest the news*

③ **digestion**
[dɪ'dʒestʃən] *noun*
process by which food is broken down and the elements in it are absorbed into the body; *high-fiber cereal helps digestion*

③ **digital**
['dɪdʒɪtəl] *adjective*
(a) which involves figures; **digital clock** = clock where the time is shown by figures, such as 11:52:02, and not by hands on a dial
(b) digital TV = TV where the picture has been changed into a form which a computer can process

③ **dignified**
['dɪgnɪfaɪd] *adjective*
solemn, looking important; *a dignified old gentleman came out of the bank; she was walking at a dignified pace*

④ **dignitary**
['dɪgnɪtri] *noun*
important person; *various dignitaries attended the opening ceremony and made speeches*
(NOTE: plural is **dignitaries**)

① **dig up**
['dɪg 'ʌp] *verb*
(a) to find by digging; *we dug up an old coin in the garden*
(b) to break a solid surface by digging; *the workmen had to dig the road up to mend the gas pipe*
(c) to find information with difficulty; *he managed to dig up some old government statistics*

④ **dilemma**
[dɪ'lemə] *noun*
serious problem, where a choice has to be made between several alternatives none of which is really acceptable; *how can we ever solve this awful dilemma?;* **in a dilemma** = not sure what action to take

④ **dilute**
[daɪ'ljut] *verb*
(a) to add a liquid, usually water, to another liquid to make it weaker; *dilute the acid with water*
(b) to make something weaker and less effective; *the president's proposals were thought too radical and so had to be diluted before being announced to the press*

① **dim**
[dɪm]
1 *adjective*
(a) weak (light); *the lights grew dimmer;* **to take a dim view of something** = to disapprove of something; *the boss takes a very dim view of people who arrive late for work*

(b) rather stupid; *he must be the dimmest sales manager we've ever had* (NOTE: **dimmer - dimmest**)

2 *verb*

(a) to make a light less bright; *they dimmed the cabin lights before the plane took off*

(b) to become less bright; *the movie theater lights dimmed before the program started* (NOTE: **dimming - dimmed**)

① **dime**
[daɪm] *noun*
ten cent coin; *ten dimes equal one dollar*

④ **dimension**
[daɪˈmenʃn] *noun*
(a) **dimensions** = measurements of length, height, etc.; *what are the dimensions of the hall?*

(b) size of a problem; *the international dimension of the refugee issue; the task is taking on huge dimensions*

④ **diminish**
[dɪˈmɪnɪʃ] *verb*
(a) to make something smaller or weaker; *nothing will ever diminish his enthusiasm for fast cars*

(b) to become smaller or weaker; *my income has diminished over the last few years*

④ **din**
[dɪn] *noun*
loud noise; *the children are making such a din I didn't hear the phone ring*

② **dine**
[daɪn] *verb*
(formal) to have dinner; *we normally dine at 8:30;* **to dine out** = to have dinner away from home; *we're dining out tonight;* **dining car** = section of a train where you can eat a full meal

① **dining room**
[ˈdaɪnɪŋ ˈruːm] *noun*
room in a house or hotel where you usually eat; *we were sitting in the dining room having supper; he was doing his homework on the dining room table*

② **dinner**
[ˈdɪnər] *noun*
(a) main meal of the day, eaten in the evening or at midday; *we were having dinner when the telephone rang; would you like to come to dinner on Saturday?; he ate his dinner quickly because there was a TV program he wanted to watch; what are we having for dinner? or what's for dinner?; the restaurant is open for dinner or serves dinner from 7:30 to 11:30;* **dinner party** = private dinner to which guests are invited; **dinner plate** = wide flat plate for serving the main course on

(b) formal evening meal; *the club is organizing a dinner and dance on Saturday;* **dinner jacket** = a man's formal black jacket (worn with a bow tie) (NOTE: also called a **tuxedo**)

③ **dinnertime**
[ˈdɪnətaɪm] *noun*
time when you usually have dinner; *hurry up, it's almost dinnertime*

① **dinosaur**
[ˈdaɪnəsɔːr] *noun*
large animal that lived many millions of years ago, and whose bones are found in rock; *at the time when dinosaurs lived, California was a tropical forest*

② **dip**
[dɪp]
1 *noun*
(a) sudden drop of a road, of land; *watch out - there's a dip in the road that makes it difficult to see cars coming in the opposite direction*

(b) soft food into which crackers, etc., can be dipped as snacks; *a bowl of smoked salmon dip*

(c) short swim; *we went for a quick dip in the lake before breakfast; are you coming for a dip in the pool?*

(d) sudden small fall; *last year there was a dip in our sales*

2 *verb*
(a) **to dip something into** = to put something quickly into a liquid; *he dipped his hand into the stream*

(b) to fall suddenly; *stocks dipped sharply on the stock exchange; the bird flew overhead then dipped behind the trees* (NOTE: **dipping - dipped**)

③ **diploma**
[dɪˈpləʊmə] *noun*
document which shows that a person has reached a certain level of skill in a subject; *she has a diploma in personnel management; he is studying for a diploma in engineering; at the end of the course she was awarded a diploma*

④ **diplomacy**
[dɪˈpləʊməsi] *noun*
art of negotiating between different sides, especially between different countries; *civil servants skilled in diplomacy are dealing with the negotiations;* **shuttle diplomacy** = going backward and forward between countries to try to solve an international crisis (NOTE: no plural)

④ **diplomat**
[ˈdɪpləmæt] *noun*
person (such as an ambassador) who represents his or her country abroad and discusses matters with representatives from other countries; *the ambassador had invited diplomats from other countries to the reception*

③ **diplomatic**
[dɪpləˈmætɪk] *adjective*
(a) referring to diplomats; *we are looking for a diplomatic solution to the crisis, rather than sending in troops;* **diplomatic immunity** = being outside the control of the laws of the country you are living in because of being a diplomat; *he refused to pay his parking fines and claimed diplomatic immunity; the*

diplomatic service = the government department concerned with relations with other countries; *he has decided on a career in the diplomatic service*
(b) careful not to give offense; *it wouldn't be very diplomatic to arrive late for the wedding*

② **direct**
[daɪˈrekt]
1 *adjective*
(a) straight, without any bends or stops; *this phone number will give you a direct line to the senator*; **direct flight** = flight without any stops; *there are direct flights every day to Washington*
(b) not involving another person or organization; **direct debit** = system where a customer allows a company to charge costs to his bank account automatically and where the amount charged can be increased or decreased with the agreement of the customer; *I pay my electric bills by direct debit*; **direct mail** = selling something by sending publicity material to possible buyers by mail; **direct taxation** = tax, such as income tax, that is paid straight to the government
(c) not trying to hide the meaning or make a meaning weaker; *I want a direct answer to a direct question*
2 *verb*
(a) to manage or to organize; *he directs our New York operations*; *the police officer was directing the traffic*
(b) to aim toward a point; *can you direct me to the nearest post office?*; *he directed his remarks to the head of the complaints department*
(c) to tell someone to do something; *the spray has to be used as directed on the bottle*; *he did as he had been directed, and took the plane to Chicago*
3 *adverb*
(a) straight, without stopping; *you can phone New York direct from here*; *the plane flies direct to Anchorage*
(b) not involving other people; *they sell insurance direct to the public*

② **direction**
[dɪˈrekʃn] *noun*
(a) point toward which you are going; *you are going in the wrong direction if you want to get to the station*; *the post office is in the opposite direction*; **in all directions** = everywhere; *the wind was blowing bits of old newspapers in all directions*; *see also* SENSE OF DIRECTION
(b) **directions** = instructions how to do something; *we couldn't find the train station, so we asked a police officer for directions*; *I can't use the computer because there are no directions telling me how to put it together*; **directions for use** = instructions showing how to use something
(c) organizing or managing; *he took over the direction of the group*

③ **directly**
[daɪˈrektli] *adverb*
(a) straight, without anything or anyone between; *this door opens directly into the kitchen*; *she reports directly to the chief executive officer himself*
(b) soon; *I'll be with you directly*

② **director**
[daɪˈrektər] *noun*
(a) person who is appointed to help run a firm, or to be in charge of an organization, a project, an official institute, etc.; *she's just started her job as director of an international charity*
(b) person in charge of making a movie or a play; *who was the first female director to win this award?*

COMMENT: a director organizes the actual making of the movie or play, giving instructions to the actors, dealing with the lighting, sound, etc. The producer is in general charge, especially of the finances of the movie or play, but does not deal with the technical details

② **directory**
[daɪˈrektəri] *noun*
book giving lists of professional people, organizations or businesses with their addresses and telephone numbers; **classified directory** = book listing companies classified into groups; **street directory** = map of a town with all the streets listed in an index; **telephone directory** = book that lists names of people and businesses with their phone numbers and addresses; *look up his number in the telephone directory*; **directory lookup** = telephone service that finds phone numbers which you do not know or cannot find; *call directory lookup at 411*

① **dirt**
[dɜrt] *noun*
(a) mud; earth; *children were playing in the dirt*; *his clothes were covered with dirt from handling potatoes*
(b) *(informal)* **dirt cheap** = very cheap; *I got the shoes dirt cheap at the flea market*

① **dirty**
[ˈdɜrti] *adjective*
(a) not clean; *if you play in the mud, you'll get your clothes dirty*; *after the party, someone has to wash all the dirty plates*; *don't come into the kitchen with your dirty boots on*
(b) not honest, not done according to the rules; *he never uses violence himself, he just gets other people to do his dirty work for him*; *the other team fought dirty*
(c) referring to sex; *he keeps the dirty magazines on the top shelf*; *he makes his money selling dirty postcards to tourists* (NOTE: **dirtier - dirtiest**)

① **dirty trick**
['dɜrti 'trɪk] *noun*
(a) nasty action that upsets someone; *that was a dirty trick to play on an old lady*
(b) method of spoiling someone's plans or of ruining his reputation by spreading rumors; *they mounted a dirty tricks campaign against the rival company*

③ **disability**
[dɪsə'bɪlɪti] *noun*
physical handicap; *being deaf is a disability that affects many old people; people with severe disabilities can receive assistance from the government*; **learning disability** = mental handicap, being unable to learn as fast as others

③ **disabled**
[dɪs'eɪbld]
1 *adjective*
(a) physically handicapped; *a hospital for disabled soldiers; the automobile crash left him permanently disabled*
(b) not able to work properly; *a tug went to the help of the disabled cruise ship*
2 *noun*
the disabled = handicapped people; *the library has facilities for the disabled;* **access for the disabled** = entrances with sloping paths instead of steps, which are easier for people in wheelchairs to use (NOTE: more polite or formal terms for the **disabled** are **people with disabilities** or **people with special needs**)

③ **disadvantage**
[dɪsəd'væntɪdʒ] *noun*
factor that makes someone or something less likely to succeed; *her main disadvantage is her lack of experience; it was a disadvantage not to be able to get to the airport quickly; there are certain disadvantages to leaving at 5:30 in the morning;* **at a disadvantage** = handicapped by something, suffering from a disadvantage; *we are at a disadvantage compared with our competitors because we have no salesmen*

② **disagree**
[dɪsə'gri] *verb*
(a) not to agree, to say that you do not think the same way as someone; *we all disagreed with the chairman; they all disagreed about what to do next*
(b) **to disagree with someone** = to make someone feel sick; *raw onions disagree with me*

③ **disagreeable**
[dɪsə'griəbl] *adjective*
unpleasant; *he's a very disagreeable old man; we had a disagreeable meeting with the tax inspectors*

② **disagreement**
[dɪsə'grimənt] *noun*
argument; *they had a disagreement about who should sit in the front row; nothing could be decided because of the disagreement between the chairman and the secretary*

① **disappear**
[dɪsə'piər] *verb*
to vanish, not to be seen anymore; *he hit the ball hard and it disappeared into the bushes; there was a bottle of orange juice in the fridge this morning and now it's disappeared; the two boys disappeared on their way home from school*

② **disappointed**
[dɪsə'pɔɪntɪd] *adjective*
sad, because things did not turn out as expected; *she is disappointed with her exam results; he was disappointed because his ticket didn't win a prize; you should have seen the disappointed expression on his face*

② **disappointing**
[dɪsə'pɔɪntɪŋ] *adjective*
which makes you sad because it does not turn out as expected; *the results of the tests were disappointing; it's disappointing to see so few young people come to our meetings*

② **disappointment**
[dɪsə'pɔɪntmənt] *noun*
(a) sadness because what was expected did not take place; *she tried hard not to show her disappointment; to his great disappointment, he didn't win first prize* (NOTE: no plural in this meaning)
(b) something that disappoints someone; *it was a disappointment to his parents when he failed his exam; after many disappointments she finally won a race*

③ **disapproval**
[dɪsə'pruvəl] *noun*
act of disapproving; *my Mom could not hide her disapproval of my new boyfriend*

② **disapprove**
[dɪsə'pruv] *verb*
to disapprove of something = to show that you do not approve of something, that you do not think something is good; *the principal disapproves of members of staff wearing jeans to school*

② **disaster**
[dɪ'zæstər] *noun*
(a) catastrophe, very bad accident; *the disaster was caused by fog or due to fog; ten people died in the air disaster; insurance companies are paying out millions for flood disaster damage; we're insured against natural disasters such as storms and floods*
(b) something that is completely unsuccessful; *the advertising campaign was a disaster - our sales went down; if it rains on Saturday the county fair will be a complete disaster*
(c) financial collapse; **the company is heading for disaster** *or* **is on a disaster course** = the company is going to collapse

③ **disastrous**
[dɪ'zæstrəs] *adjective*
very bad; *there have been disastrous floods in the region before; the country had a disastrous harvest; it would be disastrous if the car didn't*

start just when we need to get to the church on time

③ **disc**
[dɪsk]
= DISK

② **discard**
[dɪs'kard] *verb*
to put something on one side because it is no longer useful, to throw something away; *discard any damaged or burned items*

④ **discernible**
[dɪ'sɜrnəbl] *adjective*
which can be seen; *a barely discernible movement*

② **discharge**
1 *verb* [dɪs'tʃardʒ]
(a) to get rid of waste; *the factory is discharging wastewater into the river*
(b) to send someone away; *the judge discharged the jury; he was discharged from the hospital* = he was sent home from the hospital
(c) to let a prisoner go free; *the prisoners were discharged by the judge; he was discharged after having served eleven months in jail*
(d) *(formal)* to dismiss, to lay off; *he was discharged for being late*
2 *noun* [dɪs'tʃardʒ]
(a) liquid which comes out of a pipe, etc.; *the discharge from the factory flows into the river*
(b) release (of a prisoner); *he was arrested again within a month of his discharge from prison*

③ **discipline**
['dɪsɪplɪn]
1 *noun*
(a) keeping people under control; *the tour leaders are trying to keep discipline among the teenagers; we need to enforce stricter discipline in the school* (NOTE: no plural in this meaning)
(b) branch of learning; *chemistry and other related disciplines*
2 *verb*
to control someone, to punish someone; *as a result of the investigation, one employee was dismissed and three were disciplined; she was disciplined for swearing at her supervisor*

④ **disclose**
[dɪs'kləʊz] *verb*
to reveal a secret; *the journalists refused to disclose their sources to the police; the bank has no right to disclose details of my account to the auditors*

③ **disco**
['dɪskəʊ] *noun*
(informal) place where people dance to recorded music; *they spent the evening in the disco next door; you can't have a conversation in the disco because the music is too loud* (NOTE: plural is **discos**)

② **discomfort**
[dɪs'kʌmfət] *noun*
lack of comfort; *we suffered acute physical discomfort on the flight back from our vacation because it was so crowded*

③ **discount**
1 *noun* ['dɪskaʊnt]
percentage by which a full price is reduced to a buyer by the seller; *the store gives a discount on bulk purchases; we give a discount on summer vacations booked before Christmas*; **to sell goods at a discount** *or* **at a discount price** = to sell goods below the normal price; **10% discount for cash** *or* **10% cash discount** = you pay 10% less if you pay in cash; **student discount** = reduction in price to students; **discount store** = store selling cheap goods
2 *verb* [dɪs'kaʊnt]
(a) to reduce a price; *we are discounting many items in our January sales*
(b) not to pay any attention to something; *don't discount all his advice - he is very experienced*

② **discourage**
[dɪs'kʌrɪdʒ] *verb*
not to encourage; *we try to discourage people from coming in without tickets; don't be discouraged if people in the audience start to go to sleep*

④ **discourse**
['dɪskɔrs] *noun*
(formal) talk, speech; *we listened politely to a lengthy discourse on the history of the southern states; grammar mistakes are common in spoken discourse*

② **discover**
[dɪ'skʌvər] *verb*
to find something new; *in the year 1492 Columbus discovered America; who discovered aspirin?; we discovered that the real estate agent had sold the house twice; the auditors discovered some errors in the accounts*

① **discovery**
[dɪ'skʌvəri] *noun*
(a) act of finding something new; *they congratulated him on his discovery of a new planet; her discovery that someone had been in her house while she was away*
(b) new thing which has been found; *the first discovery they made was that the lake contained salt water; look at his latest discovery - an old oak table which he found in a shed*

④ **discreet**
[dɪs'krit] *adjective*
careful, not intending to attract attention; *you can tell her, she is very discreet; I had a discreet word with him before the meeting*

③ **discreetly**
[dɪs'kritli] *adverb*
quietly, without anyone noticing; *he discreetly left the meeting*

④ **discretion**
[dɪˈskreʃn] *noun*
(a) power to decide or choose what to do; **I leave it to your discretion** = I leave it for you to decide what to do; *tips are left to the discretion of the customer*
(b) wisdom, or good sense; *he showed great discretion in his handling of the family crisis*
(c) ability to keep a secret, not to give information about someone; *the chairman's secretary is known for her discretion* (NOTE: no plural)

④ **discriminate**
[dɪˈskrɪmɪneɪt] *verb*
to distinguish; **to discriminate between** = to treat two things in different ways; *the board must not discriminate between men and women candidates; we discriminate between part-time and full-time staff*; **to discriminate against** = to be biased against; *she accused the management of discriminating against female members of staff*

④ **discrimination**
[dɪskrɪmɪˈneɪʃn] *noun*
(a) treating people in different ways because of class, religion, race, language, color or sex; *we try to avoid discrimination against older applicants*; **racial discrimination** = bad treatment of someone because of their race; **sexual discrimination** *or* **sex discrimination** *or* **discrimination on grounds of sex** = treating men and women in different ways
(b) judgment, good taste; *the store sells gifts that appeal to people of discrimination* (NOTE: no plural)

② **discuss**
[dɪˈskʌs] *verb*
to talk about a serious matter or problem; *the point of the meeting is to discuss how to save money; they spent hours discussing the details of the wedding*

② **discussion**
[dɪˈskʌʃn] *noun*
talking about a serious matter or problem; *most problems can be solved by discussion; the next program will feature a discussion between environmental experts; the discussion led to a violent argument; she had a heated discussion with the bus driver*

② **disease**
[dɪˈziz] *noun*
serious illness (of people, animals, plants, etc.); *hundreds of people caught the disease; it is a disease that can be treated with antibiotics*

① **disgrace**
[dɪsˈgreɪs]
1 *noun*
(a) having lost someone's respect because of errors, scandal, corruption, etc.; *the senator's disgrace followed the discovery of the papers in his office*; **the minister fell into disgrace** = he became out of favor

(b) thing which brings shame; *he's a disgrace to the teaching profession; it was a disgrace to see her lying on the sidewalk like that; you say it is acceptable behavior - I would call it a disgrace* (NOTE: no plural)
2 *verb*
to bring shame on; *he disgraced all his family by arriving drunk at the birthday party*; **to disgrace yourself** = to do something that brings shame on you; *he disgraced himself by throwing sandwiches at the speakers at the conference*

① **disgraceful**
[dɪsˈgreɪsfəl] *adjective*
which you should be ashamed of; *people living near the football stadium complained about the disgraceful behavior of the fans; it's disgraceful that you have to pay $2 for a cup of coffee in the museum café*

③ **disguise**
[dɪsˈgaɪz]
1 *noun*
clothes, false hair, etc., to make a person look like someone else; *I didn't recognize him as he was wearing a disguise*; **in disguise** = dressed to look like someone else; *the burglar turned out to be a police officer in disguise*
2 *verb*
to dress so as to look like someone else; *he entered the country disguised as a student; she had her hair cut short to disguise her appearance*

③ **disgust**
[dɪsˈgʌst]
1 *noun*
(a) strong dislike, feeling sick; *the sight of the flies on the meat in the market filled her with disgust*
(b) strong feeling of being annoyed; *to my disgust, the driver's test examiner passed my teenage brother and not me*; **in disgust** = because you are upset and annoyed; *she walked out of the interview in disgust*
2 *verb*
to give someone a strong feeling of dislike or disapproval; *I'm disgusted that no one went to see her in the hospital; the rudeness of the waiters disgusts me*

③ **disgusting**
[dɪsˈgʌstɪŋ] *adjective*
that fills you with disgust; *there's a disgusting smell in here; a disgusting display of violence on the part of the fans*

① **dish**
[dɪʃ] *noun*
(a) large plate for serving food; *she carefully arranged the slices of meat on a dish*
(b) **dishes** = plates and cups, etc.; **to wash the dishes** *or* **to do the dishes** = to wash plates, glasses, knives and forks, etc., after a meal; *he's offered to do the dishes; can you dry the dishes for me?*

(c) part of a meal; plate of prepared food; *we are trying a new Mexican dish*; **side dish** = small dish served on a side plate; *he had a green salad as a side dish*

(d) round device, shaped like a plate, used to get signals from satellites; *almost every house on the street has a satellite dish* (NOTE: plural is **dishes**)

③ **dishonest**
[dɪsˈɒnɪst] *adjective*

not honest; *it was quite dishonest of him to tell his wife that he'd given up smoking*; *he has a record of dishonest business deals*

② **dish out**
[ˈdɪʃ ˈaʊt] *verb*

(informal) to hand out in a free manner; *he dished out advice to anyone who asked for it*; *they were dishing out free tickets for the concert*

③ **dish up**
[ˈdɪʃ ˈʌp] *verb*

(informal) to serve food; *she dished up the food with a large spoon*; *he was dishing up the meal*

③ **dishwasher**
[ˈdɪʃwɒʃər] *noun*

machine for washing dishes, knives, forks, spoons, etc.; *I never put the saucepans in the dishwasher* (NOTE: a machine for washing clothes is a **washing machine**)

④ **dishwashing**
[ˈdɪʃwɒʃɪŋ] *noun*

action of washing dishes; **dishwashing liquid** = liquid soap used to wash dishes; *don't squirt so much dishwashing liquid into the bowl*

④ **disintegrate**
[dɪsˈɪntɪɡreɪt] *verb*

to fall to pieces; *the library book had been borrowed so much that its cover was disintegrating*; *most satellites disintegrate when they enter Earth's atmosphere*

③ **disk** *or* **disc**
[dɪsk] *noun*

(a) any round flat object, especially a piece of plastic used in computers to record information; *the setting sun was a huge orange disk on the horizon*; **floppy disk** = small disk that can be inserted and removed from a computer; *all the data is on two floppy disks*; **hard disk** = large fixed disk; **disk jockey (DJ)** = person who plays recorded music at a nightclub; *the DJ played another track from the album*

(b) flat round bone which links with others to make the spine; **slipped disk** = painful back, caused by a disk having moved out of line

③ **diskette**
[dɪˈsket] *noun*

small floppy disk; *the data came on a diskette*

② **dislike**
[dɪsˈlaɪk]
1 *noun*

(a) not liking something or someone; *she had never felt such a dislike for someone before*; **to take a dislike to** = to hate; *their dog took a sudden dislike to the mail carrier*

(b) thing which you do not like; *we try to take account of the likes and dislikes of individual customers*
2 *verb*

not to like; *I dislike it when the people behind me at the theater start whispering*; *he dislikes people who arrive for work late*; **I don't dislike Mozart** = I quite like Mozart

④ **dismay**
[dɪsˈmeɪ]
1 *noun*

anxiety, great disappointment; *to her dismay she couldn't find her passport*; *to the dismay of the supporters, the team played extremely badly*
2 *verb*

to strike someone with alarm; *his reaction to her letter dismayed her*; *she was dismayed to find that her passport had been stolen*

② **dismiss**
[dɪsˈmɪs] *verb*

(a) **to dismiss an employee** = to remove an employee from a job; *he was dismissed for being late*; *when they found him taking money from the cash register he was dismissed immediately*

(b) to send someone away; *at the end of the interview he dismissed her with a brief "good afternoon"*

(c) to refuse to consider an idea; *her plan was dismissed as being quite impossible*; *all his suggestions were dismissed by the CEO*

(d) to refuse a request; *they dismissed my application for a loan*

② **dismissal**
[dɪsˈmɪsəl] *noun*

removal from a job; *he had only been working there three months when he received notice of dismissal*; **unfair dismissal** = removing of a person from his or her job for reasons which do not appear to be reasonable; *he appealed to the tribunal on the grounds of unfair dismissal*

② **disorder**
[dɪsˈɔrdər] *noun*

(a) lack of order; *the whole office is in a state of disorder*

(b) riot, disturbance on the streets; *violent public disorders broke out on the streets*

(c) illness; *she suffers from a stomach disorder*; *a doctor who specializes in disorders of the kidneys or in kidney disorders*

④ **dispatch**
[dɪˈspætʃ]
1 *noun*

(a) sending; *dispatch of the merchandise will be delayed until Monday*

(b) message sent; *the reporters send regular dispatches from the war zone*; *we received a*

dispatch from our Calcutta office (NOTE: plural is **dispatches**)
2 *verb*
(a) to send; *they dispatched the message to all commanding officers*; *the goods were dispatched to you this morning*
(b) to finish doing something quickly; *she got to work on the files and dispatched most of them by lunchtime*

④ **dispenser**
[dɪˈspensər] *noun*
machine that automatically provides something, when money is put in or a button is pushed; *there is a liquid soap dispenser in the men's washroom*

④ **disperse**
[dɪˈspɜrs] *verb*
(a) to clear away; *the sun will soon disperse the mist*; *the police were called in to disperse the crowds of angry fans*
(b) to scatter in different directions; *the crowd dispersed rapidly once the parade was over*

② **display**
[dɪˈspleɪ]
1 *noun*
(a) show, exhibition; *they have a fine display of Chinese art*; *a display of local crafts*; **air display** = show of new aircraft; **display case** *or* **display unit** = glass case for showing goods for sale
(b) on display = shown in an exhibition or for sale; *the store has several automobile models on display*
2 *verb*
(a) to put something on show; *she is displaying her collection of Persian carpets at the antique fair*
(b) to show; *he displayed considerable courage in meeting the rebel troops*; *make sure your parking ticket is clearly displayed on the windshield*

③ **disposable**
[dɪˈspəʊzəbl] *adjective*
which can be used and then thrown away; *burgers are sold in disposable boxes*

② **disposal**
[dɪˈspəʊzəl] *noun*
(a) getting rid of something; *the disposal of garbage is a problem for large cities*
(b) my car is at your disposal = you can use my car if you want to

② **dispose**
[dɪˈspəʊz] *verb*
to dispose of something = to get rid of something; *how are we going to dispose of all this wastepaper?*; *his objections are easily disposed of*

③ **dispute**
[dɪˈspjuːt]
1 *noun*
argument; *he tried to mediate in the dispute*; *there was a little dispute over who would pay*

the check; **industrial dispute** *or* **labor dispute** = argument between management and workers; **in dispute** = not agreed; *the ownership of the land is in dispute*
2 *verb*
to argue that something is not correct; *I dispute her version of what happened*; *there is no disputing the fact that Sarah is the best qualified of the candidates*

④ **disregard**
[dɪsrɪˈɡɑrd]
1 *noun*
disregard for something = not paying any attention to something; *he showed a complete disregard for the safety of the passengers*
2 *verb*
to take no notice of; *she disregarded the warning signs*

③ **disrupt**
[dɪsˈrʌpt] *verb*
(a) to stop a service running normally; *the snowstorm has disrupted bus services throughout the country*
(b) to break up or to interrupt a meeting; *we are not used to having our meetings disrupted by protesters*

④ **disruptive**
[dɪsˈrʌptɪv] *adjective*
which disrupts; *their disruptive behavior spoiled the game for the rest of us*

③ **dissolve**
[dɪˈzɒlv] *verb*
(a) to put a solid substance into a liquid so that it becomes part of the liquid; *dissolve the sugar in half a cup of boiling water*; *the powder should be completely dissolved in warm water*
(b) to become part of a liquid; *the sugar dissolved very quickly*; *stir the mixture until the sugar dissolves*
(c) to bring to an end; *to dissolve a partnership or a company or a marriage*

② **distance**
[ˈdɪstəns]
1 *noun*
(a) space from one point to another; *what is the distance from Los Angeles to San Diego?*; *the farthest distance I have traveled by train is 600 miles*; *the railroad goes underground for a short distance*; **within walking distance** = near enough to walk to; *the hotel is within walking distance of the convention center*
(b) in the distance = a long way away; *I caught sight of the mountain in the distance*; *we could hear guns firing in the distance*
(c) distance learning = studying in your own time away from the place where the course is organized, using radio or TV; *the government is putting a lot of resources into distance learning projects*
2 *verb*
to distance yourself from = to show that you are some distance away from; *the police chief*

took pains to distance himself from the remarks made by the president

② **distant**
['dɪstənt] *adjective*
(a) far away; *we could hear the sound of distant guns*; **a distant relative** = not a member of the close family; *she's a very distant relative - her grandfather was my grandmother's cousin*; **in the not too distant future** = quite soon; *we expect to move in the not too distant future*
(b) not very friendly; *the manager was quite helpful but distant*

④ **distinct**
[dɪ'stɪŋkt] *adjective*
(a) separate; *there are two distinct varieties of this plant*; *their businesses are distinct from each other*
(b) clear; *I got the distinct impression that he was carrying a gun*; *did you notice the distinct tone of anger in his voice?*

③ **distinction**
[dɪ'stɪŋkʃn] *noun*
(a) difference; *there is a distinction between being interested in politics and joining a political party*; **to make a distinction between two things** = to recognize that two things are different; *you must try to make a distinction between the police and the armed forces*
(b) highest mark; *she received a diploma with distinction*
(c) especially excellent quality; *he served in the war with distinction*; *she had the distinction of being the first woman to earn a degree at the university*

④ **distinctive**
[dɪ'stɪŋktɪv] *adjective*
very noticeable, which makes one thing different from others; *the zebra has distinctive black and white stripes*; *what is so distinctive about this plant is that it flowers in winter*

③ **distinctly**
[dɪ'stɪŋktli] *adverb*
clearly; *I distinctly heard him say that she was his sister*; *she looked distinctly upset*

④ **distinguish**
[dɪ'stɪŋgwɪʃ] *verb*
(a) to see clearly; to make out details; *with the glasses we could easily distinguish the houses on the other side of the lake*
(b) **to distinguish between two things** = to recognize the difference between two things; *children must be taught to distinguish between right and wrong*; *it's difficult to distinguish between salt and refined sugar by sight*
(c) **to distinguish yourself** = to do something that makes people notice you; *he distinguished himself on the football field*

④ **distinguished**
[dɪ'stɪŋgwɪʃt] *adjective*
important and well-known (writer, painter, etc.); *a concert by a distinguished Czech musician*

④ **distort**
[dɪ'stɔrt] *verb*
(a) to twist into a different shape; *his face was distorted with pain*
(b) to give a false impression of; *he distorted the meaning of my speech*

② **distract**
[dɪ'strækt] *verb*
to attract someone's attention when they should be doing something else; *walking past the school in a bathing suit is bound to distract the students*; **to distract someone's attention** = to make someone look away; *if you distract her attention, I'll try to snatch her purse*

② **distress**
[dɪ'stres]
1 *noun*
(a) great sad or painful feeling; *I don't want to cause the family any distress*; *the whole family was in distress at Grandmother's death*
(b) difficulty; *we knew the ship was in distress when we saw the rocket signals*; **distress signal** = signal sent when you are in difficulties; *the ship sent out distress signals before she sank*
2 *verb*
to make someone very sad and worried; *the news of her grandmother's death distressed her very much*

③ **distribute**
[dɪ'strɪbjut] *verb*
(a) to share out, to give to several people; *she distributed part of her money to the poor*; *the stewardesses came around, distributing declaration forms to passengers*; *I'll distribute the list to all the committee members*
(b) to send out goods from a warehouse to retail stores; **we distribute Japanese cars** = we are the agents for Japanese cars

③ **distribution**
[dɪstrɪ'bjuʃn] *noun*
(a) giving to several people; *the newspaper has a wide distribution*; *the staff will organize the distribution of the timetable to the students*
(b) sending of goods from a warehouse to stores; *our distribution center is in New Jersey*

③ **distributor**
[dɪ'strɪbjutər] *noun*
(a) company that sells goods for another company which makes them; *who is the local distributor for this make of washing machine?*
(b) *(in an automobile engine)* mechanism that passes the electric spark to each spark plug in turn; *the distributor head needs cleaning*

③ **district**
['dɪstrɪkt] *noun*
(a) area or region; *it's a district of the town well-known for its Italian restaurants*; **the commercial district** *or* **the business district** = part of a town where offices and stores are located; *the store is well located right in the heart of the financial district of downtown*

(b) official administrative area of a town or country; **district attorney (DA)** = lawyer representing the government in a certain area

③ **disturb**
[dɪˈstɜrb] *verb*
(a) to worry someone; *it disturbed me to see that the plane's wing was shaking*
(b) to interrupt someone; *sorry to disturb you but there's an urgent e-mail message that's just come in; don't disturb your mother - she's resting;* **"do not disturb"** = notice placed on a hotel room door, to ask the hotel staff not to come into the room

③ **disturbance**
[dɪˈstɜrbəns] *noun*
(a) action of disturbing someone; *I need to work somewhere where there won't be any disturbance*
(b) noisy riot; *the students caused a disturbance in the hotel bar; there were several instances of shop windows being broken during the disturbances*

③ **disturbed**
[dɪsˈtɜrbd] *adjective*
(a) worried; *we are disturbed to hear that the company may be forced to close*
(b) ill in the mind; *in her disturbed state, she may do anything; highly disturbed children are taught in this special school*

③ **disturbing**
[dɪˈstɜrbɪŋ] *adjective*
worrying; *a disturbing number of students failed the exam; it is a disturbing fact that many children leave school without being able to read*

② **ditch**
[dɪtʃ]
1 *noun*
long hole in the ground for taking away water; *after the storm, the ditches were full of rainwater; he fell into the ditch beside the road* (NOTE: plural is **ditches**)
2 *verb (informal)*
(a) to leave something behind; *when we ran out of gas, we ditched the truck and walked to the next town*
(b) to get rid of a person; *she ditched her boyfriend*
(c) to land a plane in the sea; *the pilot ran out of fuel and decided to ditch the plane*

① **dive**
[daɪv]
1 *noun*
(a) plunge downwards head first into water; *he made a beautiful dive into the pool*
(b) *(informal)* bar or club with a bad reputation; *he met her in some dive in Milwaukee*
2 *verb*
to plunge into water head first; *he dove in and swam across the pool under water* (NOTE: **diving - dove** [dəʊv])

② **diver**
[ˈdaɪvər] *noun*
(a) swimmer who plunges head first into water; *an Australian Olympic diver*
(b) person who swims and works under water; *police divers searched the canal; the divers carried oxygen cylinders on their backs*

④ **diverse**
[daɪˈvɜrs] *adjective*
varied; *his reasons for quitting were diverse*

④ **diversion**
[daɪˈvɜrʃn] *noun*
(a) amusement; *fishing is one of the most popular diversions for people at weekends; it's a quiet rural town with very few diversions for teenagers*
(b) to create a diversion = to distract attention, for example so that someone else can commit a crime; *she created a diversion by screaming, while he put the watches into his pocket*

④ **diversity**
[daɪˈvɜrsɪti] *noun*
great variety; *various medical journals show a great diversity of opinion among specialists on the subject*

④ **divert**
[daɪˈvɜrt] *verb*
(a) to send to another place or in another direction; *because of fog in San Francisco, flights have been diverted to Oakland; traffic has been diverted to avoid the town center*
(b) to divert someone's attention = to make someone look away; *try and divert his attention while I steal his keys*

① **divide**
[dɪˈvaɪd] *verb*
(a) to cut into parts; *the cake was divided among the children; how can you divide a cake into thirteen pieces?; the two companies agreed to divide the market between them; our office is one large room divided up with low shelves*
(b) to calculate how many of one number there are in another; *ten divided by two equals five* (NOTE: **divide** is usually shown by the sign ÷ : **10 ÷ 2 = 5**: say "ten divided by two equals five")

③ **dividend**
[ˈdɪvɪdend] *noun*
part of a company's profits shared out among shareholders; *the company had a loss and there will be no dividend for the shareholders this year;* **to raise** *or* **to increase the dividend** = to pay out a higher dividend than in the previous year

③ **divine**
[dɪˈvaɪn] *adjective*
(a) referring to God; *he prayed for divine help*
(b) wonderful, excellent; *her singing was absolutely divine!*

② **division**
[dɪˈvɪʒn] *noun*
(a) important part of a large organization; *the*

sales division employs twenty people; she is the head of the production division
(b) splitting into parts; *after his death, the family argued over the division of their father's money* (NOTE: no plural in this meaning)
(c) calculation, where one figure is divided by another; *my little sister is just learning how to do division*; **long division** = complicated division sum, worked out on paper; **division sign** = printed or written sign (÷) showing that one figure is divided by another
(d) difference of opinion between groups of people; *the dispute has widened the divisions between the two sections of the party*
(e) large part of an army; *they have three divisions stationed along the border*; *the general ordered an armored division to stand by*

② **divorce**
[dɪ'vɔrs]
1 *noun*
legal separation of husband and wife where each is free to marry again; *her parents are getting a divorce*; *since their divorce, they have both married again*
2 *verb*
(a) to break off a marriage legally; *they divorced last year*
(b) to separate from your husband or wife; *she divorced her husband and married the man next door*; *he got divorced after only three years' of marriage*
(c) to separate (two ideas, etc.); *it is difficult to divorce their financial problems from the problems they are having with the house*

② **divorced**
[dɪ'vɔrst] *adjective*
no longer married; *they're both divorced, with children from their previous marriages*

① **dizzy**
['dɪzɪ] *adjective*
(a) feeling when everything seems to turn round; *can we stop the car, please, I feel dizzy*; *after standing in the sun, he became dizzy and had to lie down*; *she has started having dizzy spells*
(b) *(informal)* wild, exciting; *a dizzy round of parties and TV shows* (NOTE: **dizzier - dizziest**)

④ **DJ**
['dɪdʒeɪ] *abbreviation for* DISK JOCKEY
person who plays recorded music at a nightclub; *the DJ played another track from the album*

① **do**
[du]
1 *verb*
(a) *(used with other verbs to make questions)* *does this bus go to Miami?*; *did the doctor give you any medicine for your cough?*; *where do they live?*; *what did you find there?*
(b) *(used with other verbs and "not" to make the negative)* *they didn't laugh at the movie*; *it*

doesn't matter anymore; *his parents don't live in Detroit*
(c) *(used to make a verb stronger)* *can I sit down? - please do!*; *why don't you work harder? - I do work hard!*; *why didn't you tell me? - I did tell you!*
(d) *(used instead of another verb with* **so**; *and* **neither**); *we don't smoke - neither do I*; *he likes jam sandwiches and so does she*
(e) *(used instead of another verb in short answers to questions using the word "do")* *do you live in Phoenix? - yes, I do*; *but your parents don't live there, do they? - no, they don't*; *does the green color suit me? - yes, it does*; *did you go to the concert after all? - yes, I did*
(f) *(used instead of another verb at the end of a question or statement)* *the Russians live here, don't they?*; *it looks very nice, doesn't it?*; *it doesn't rain a lot in Spain, does it?*
(g) *(used instead of another verb)* *can you run as fast as he does?*; *he speaks Spanish better than I do*; *she asked me to close the door but I'd already done so*; *they got to the restaurant before we did*
(h) *(telling someone not to do something)* *don't throw away that letter!*; *don't put your coffee cups on the computer!*
(i) *(with nouns ending in* -ing; *)* *she's doing the shopping*; *she was doing the ironing*
(j) *(used when greeting someone)* *how do you do?* (NOTE: this does not normally expect an answer)
(k) *(followed by a noun)* to work at something or to arrange something or to clean something; *she's doing her hair*; *have you done the dishes yet?*; *what have you been doing all day?*; *they're a difficult company to do business with*; *what do you do for a living?* = what is your job?
(l) to succeed, to continue; *she's doing very well in her new job*; *he did badly in the interview*; *how's your business doing?*; *well done!* = congratulations; *I passed my driver's test - well done!*
(m) to finish being cooked; *the carrots aren't done yet*; *the chicken is done* = the chicken is cooked and ready to eat
(n) to be satisfactory; *will this size do?*; *that will do* = that's enough; *that won't do at all* = that's not at all satisfactory
(o) **to make do with** = to accept something that is not as good as you wanted; *the ordinary plates are all dirty, so we will have to make do with paper ones*
(p) to travel at a certain speed; *the automobile was doing 100 miles per hour when it hit the tree* (NOTE: **I do; you do; he/she/it does** [dʌz] ; **they do; doing - did** [dɪd] **- has done** [dʌn] ; negative: **do not** usually **don't** [dəʊnt] ; **does not** usually **doesn't** ['dʌznt] ; **did not** usually **didn't** ['dɪdnt])
2 *noun*

the dos and the don'ts = things you should do and things you should not do; *she told him all the dos and don'ts about working in the office* (NOTE: plural is **dos or do's** [duz])

② **do away with**
['du ə'wei wiθ] *verb*

to get rid of something; *the government did away with customs inspections*

① **dock**
[dɒk]
1 *noun*

(a) the docks = a harbor where cargo is put on or taken off ships; *cars should arrive at the docks 45 minutes before sailing time; we used to go down to the docks to watch the ships come in*; **dry dock** = section of a harbor from which the water can be removed, so that the bottom of a ship can be repaired; **the ship is in dock** = (i) the ship is in the harbor; (ii) the ship is being repaired

(b) box in a law court, where the prisoner sits; *she was in the dock, facing charges of theft*
2 *verb*

(a) *(of ship)* to arrive in harbor; *the ship docked at 5:00 P.M.; the cruise liner will dock in Bermuda*

(b) to remove (money from wages); *I will have to dock your pay if you are late for work again; they've docked $50 from my pay!*

① **doctor**
['dɒktər]
1 *noun*

(a) person who looks after people who are ill; *I have a ten o'clock appointment to see the doctor; if you have pains in your chest, you should see a doctor; he went to the doctor's last Friday*; **ship's doctor** = doctor who travels on a ship and so is ready to treat passengers who become sick

(b) person with one of the highest degrees from a university; *she has a doctor's degree in physics* (NOTE: **doctor** is written **Dr.** with names: **Dr. Thorne**)
2 *verb*

to change something, so that it is false; *we suspect that he had been doctoring his expenses; she was accused of doctoring the test samples*

③ **document**
['dɒkjʊmənt]
1 *noun*

(a) piece of paper with written text; *file all the documents away carefully as we may need them again; please read this document carefully and sign at the bottom of page two*
(b) separate text in a computer; *the letter was saved as a Word document*
2 *verb*

to note something in official writing; *cases of this disease are well documented in Africa; she sent in a fully documented claim for insurance*

④ **documentary**
[dɒkjʊ'mentəri]
1 *noun*

movie or TV program giving facts about a real subject sleeping; *did you see the documentary about elephants last night?; the TV documentary had an strong impact on viewers* (NOTE: plural is **documentaries**)
2 *adjective*

referring to documents; **documentary evidence** = evidence in the form of documents; *they are searching in the garbage for any documentary evidence that the meeting took place*

② **dodge**
[dɒdʒ]
1 *noun*

(informal) clever trick; *he told me a dodge to avoid paying tax*
2 *verb*

(a) to avoid, to get out of the way; *he ran across the street, dodging the traffic; she dodged behind a tree hoping he wouldn't see her*

(b) to dodge the issue = to avoid answering questions about a problem or trying to do anything about a problem; *we were very disappointed because the city council simply dodged the issue*

① **does, doesn't**
[dʌz or 'dʌznt]
see DO

① **dog**
[dɒg]
1 *noun*

animal kept as a pet, which barks, and moves its tail from side to side when it is pleased; *can you take the dog out for a walk?; police with dogs were hunting the gang of escaped prisoners*; **to let sleeping dogs lie** = not to disturb things; *I wouldn't investigate any further if I were you - better let sleeping dogs lie*; *(informal)* **to go to the dogs** = to get into a bad condition; *the whole place has gone to the dogs*; **it's a dog's life** = life is difficult, with too much work and no play (NOTE: the young are called **puppies**)
2 *verb*

to follow; *all his life he has been dogged by poor health*; **to dog someone's footsteps** = to follow behind someone closely; *failure seems to dog his footsteps* (NOTE: **dogging - dogged**)

② **doggy**
['dɒgi] *noun*

(informal) (children's word) dog; *she's brought her little doggy with her*; **doggy bag** = bag in which you can put food that you didn't eat in a restaurant to take home, supposedly for your dog

③ **do in**
['du 'ɪn] *verb (informal)*

(a) to kill; *what happened to the gang boss? - he was done in and his body was thrown into the river*

(b) to hurt *or* to exhaust; *I think I did my back in by digging the garden*

① **doll**
[dɒl] *noun*
child's toy that looks like a baby; *Susie is upstairs playing with her dolls and teddy bears*; *we bought little wooden dolls for the children at the store*; **doll's house** = very small house made as a toy

① **dollar**
['dɒlər] *noun*
(a) money used in the U.S.A.; *a 5-dollar bill*; *the country spends millions of dollars on defense*; *there are two dollars to the pound*
(b) similar currency used in many other countries; *what is the price in Australian dollars?* (NOTE: when used with a figure, usually written $ before the figure: **$250**) Note also that with the words **bill, money order,** etc., **dollar** is singular: **twenty dollars** but **a twenty-dollar bill, a fifty-dollar traveler's check**)

④ **dolphin**
['dɒlfɪn] *noun*
sea animal like a small whale; *dolphins followed the boat as it crossed the bay* (NOTE: a group of them is a **school of dolphins**)

② **dome**
[dəʊm] *noun*
round roof shaped like half of a ball; *we stopped to admire the dome of the Capitol*

④ **domestic**
[də'mestɪk] *adjective*
(a) referring to the home; *she hated having to do all the domestic work while her husband was at his job*; **domestic animals** = farm animals and pets
(b) inside a country; *sales in the domestic market have risen*; **domestic flights** = flights between airports inside the same country

④ **dominant**
['dɒmɪnənt] *adjective*
(a) most important; *the dominant color in the room is dark red*; *safety will be the dominant theme of the discussion*
(b) very powerful; *he has a very dominant personality and his wife and children have to do what he says*; *the president's party is the dominant force in the country's political system*

④ **dominate**
['dɒmɪneɪt] *verb*
(a) to rule; *he is dominated by his wife*; *the Union Party dominates the country's political system*
(b) to be very obviously seen; *the volcano dominates the town*

② **donate**
[dəʊ'neɪt] *verb*
to give; *he has donated a lot of money to charity*

② **donation**
[dəʊ'neɪʃn] *noun*
gift, especially of money; *all donations will be gratefully received*; *I can't afford to make any donations to charity this year*

① **done**
[dʌn] *verb*
see DO

① **donkey**
['dɒŋkɪ] *noun*
gray farm animal with long ears, used for riding or pulling carts; *donkeys have long ears*

④ **donor**
['dəʊnər] *noun*
person who gives; *the donor of the kidney lives in Arkansas*; *the list of the museum's donors is on a board by the entrance*; **blood donor** = person who gives blood regularly for medical use

① **don't**
[dəʊnt]
see DO

② **donut**
['dəʊnʌt]
= DOUGHNUT

① **door**
[dɔr] *noun*
(a) piece of wood, metal, etc., which closes an entrance; *he went into his office and locked the door behind him*; *she opened the car door and hit a passing cyclist*; **front door** = main door to a building; *she gave him a key to the front door or a front door key*; **back door** = door at the back of a building; *the back door leads out into the yard*
(b) used to show where a building is in a street; *he lives three doors down the street* = he lives three houses further along the street; *they live a few doors away from us*

① **doorway**
['dɔrweɪ] *noun*
space where there is a door; *she stood in the doorway, sheltering herself from the rain*

④ **dormant**
['dɔrmənt] *adjective*
not active; **to lie dormant** = to remain hidden and not active; *some viruses lie dormant for years*; **dormant volcano** = a volcano which is not erupting at the moment

③ **dose**
[dəʊs] *noun*
quantity of medicine; *normal daily dose: three tablets*; *it is dangerous to exceed the recommended dose*

① **dot**
[dɒt] *noun*
(a) small round spot; *a blue necktie with white dots*
(b) **on the dot** = exactly at a time; *the train left at four on the dot*; *see also* YEAR

④ **dotted line**
['dɒtɪd 'laɪn] *noun*
line made of a series of dots; *please sign on the dotted line*; *do not write anything below the dotted line*

① **double**
['dʌbl]
1 *adjective*
(a) twice the size; *she asked for a double portion of ice cream*
(b) **in double figures** = with two figures, the numbers from 10 to 99; *inflation is expected to reach double figures next month*
(c) with two parts, for two people; **double bed** = bed for two people; *do you want a double bed or two single beds?*; **double room** = room for two people
2 *adverb*
twice the amount; *it takes double the time*; *her salary is double mine*; **to see double** = to see two things when there is only one there
3 *noun*
(a) *(in the army)* **on the double** = running fast; *the soldiers crossed the square on the double*
(b) person who looks exactly like someone else; *it was either him or his double we saw at the movies*
(c) **doubles** = tennis game for two people on either side; **men's doubles** *or* **women's doubles** = two men against two other men *or* two women against two other women; **mixed doubles** = man and woman against another man and woman
4 *verb*
(a) to multiply by two; *think of a number and then double it*
(b) **to double back** = to turn around and go back along the same way; *the escaped prisoner doubled back toward the town*

③ **double up**
['dʌbl 'ʌp] *verb*
to bend forward; *she was doubled up in pain*

② **doubt**
[daʊt]
1 *noun*
(a) not being sure; **to have doubts about** = to say that you are doubtful about; *I have my doubts about how accurate his figures are*; **to cast doubt on** = to be unsure about; *he cast doubt on the whole proposal*; **to give someone the benefit of the doubt** = to allow someone to continue doing something, because you are not sure that accusations made against him are correct; *the referee gave him the benefit of the doubt*
(b) **no doubt** *or* **without doubt** = certainly; *no doubt they will be suing for damages*; **there's no doubt about** = it is a certain fact; *there's no doubt about it - Florida is the best place for a vacation*; *there's no doubt that he is guilty*; **in doubt** = not sure; *the result of the game was in doubt until the last minute*
2 *verb*

not to be sure of something; *I doubt whether he will want to go to the meeting*; *I doubt her honesty*; *did you ever doubt that we would win?*

② **doubtful**
['daʊtfəl] *adjective*
not sure; *I am doubtful about whether we should go*; *she had a doubtful expression on her face*; *his future with the company looks increasingly doubtful*; *it is doubtful whether the race will take place because of the snow*

② **dough**
[dəʊ] *noun*
mixture of water and flour for making bread, etc.; *the chef was making the dough for the pizza*

② **doughnut** *or* **donut**
['dəʊnʌt] *noun*
small round or ring-shaped cake cooked by frying in oil; *as soon as you have made them, dip the doughnuts in sugar*; *we ordered doughnuts and coffee for breakfast*

③ **do up**
['du 'ʌp] *verb*
(a) to attach; *he's still a baby and he can't do his buttons up properly*; *can you do up the zipper at the back of my dress?*
(b) to repair and make like new; *they bought an old house and did it up*; *he's looking for an old sports car to do up*

① **do with**
['du 'wɪθ] *verb*
(a) to concern; *it has nothing to do with us*; *it is something to do with my new book*
(b) to put somewhere; *what have you done with the newspaper?*
(c) *(informal)* to need; *after that long walk I could do with a glass of water*; *your car could sure do with a wash*

① **do without**
['du wɪð'aʊt] *verb*
not to have something, to manage without something; *if you live in the country can you do without a car?*; *plants can't do without water*

① **down**
[daʊn]
1 *preposition*
(a) toward the bottom of; *he fell down the stairs and broke his leg*; *the ball rolled down the hill*
(b) away from where the person speaking is standing; *he went down the road to the post office*; *the police station is just down the street*
2 *adverb*
(a) toward the bottom, toward a lower position; *put the box down in the corner*; *he sat down on the carpet*; *she lay down on the bed*; *I looked in the basement, but there's no one down there*
(b) at a lower level; *inflation is down again*
(c) (put) on paper; *did you write down the number of the car?*; *the police officer took down her address*
(d) as an advance payment; *I put $50 down on the TV set*

(e) toward the south; *I'm going down to Florida tomorrow (from New Jersey) they live down on the south coast*

(f) sick; *she is down with the flu*

(g) *(informal)* gloomy; *he's feeling a bit down*

(h) *(showing criticism) down with the government!*; *down with exams!* (NOTE: **down** is often used with verbs: **to go down; to break down; to fall down**, etc.)

3 *noun*

soft feathers (of a duck); *the duck lined its nest with down* (NOTE: no plural in this meaning)

4 *verb*

to swallow quickly; *he downed three bottles of beer*

① **downhill**
[daʊn'hɪl] *adverb*

toward the bottom of a hill; *the road goes downhill for a bit and then crosses the river*

② **downstairs**
[daʊn'steərz]

1 *adverb*

on or to the lower part of a building; *he heard a noise in the kitchen and went downstairs to see what it was*; *I left my cup of coffee downstairs*

2 *adjective*

on the ground floor of a building; *the house has a downstairs bedroom*; *you can use the downstairs toilet*

3 *noun*

the ground floor of a building; *the downstairs has three rooms*; *the downstairs of the house is larger than the upstairs*; *compare* UPSTAIRS

② **downtown**
['daʊntaʊn]

1 *adverb*

to the center of town; *you can take the bus to go downtown*

2 *adjective*

in the town's center; *the downtown department stores*; *her office is in downtown New York*

3 *noun*

the central district of a town; *downtown will be very crowded at this time of day*

① **downward**
['daʊnwəd]

1 *adjective*

toward the bottom; *a downward trend in the unemployment figures*

2 *adverb*

toward the bottom; *the path slopes downward to the stream*; *he went to sleep face downward on the floor*

③ **doz**
['dʌzən]
= DOZEN

② **doze**
[dəʊz] *verb*

to sleep a little, to sleep but not deeply; *she dozed off for a while after lunch*

① **dozen**
['dʌzən] *noun*

(a) twelve; *we ordered two dozen chairs*; **they're cheaper by the dozen** = they are cheaper if you buy twelve at a time; **half a dozen** = six; *half a dozen apples*

(b) dozens of = a lot of; *dozens of people visited the exhibition*; *I've been to New York dozens of times* (NOTE: **dozen** does not become plural after a number: **dozens of chairs,** but **two dozen chairs**)

① **Dr.**
see DOCTOR

④ **drab**
[dræb] *adjective*

lacking bright colours; brown, grey; *on a rainy November morning the streets look cold and drab*; *she wears drab clothes* (NOTE: **drabber - drabbest**)

② **draft**
[dræft]

1 *noun*

(a) flow of cool air into a room; *he sat in a draft and got a stiff neck*

(b) rough plan of a document; *he quickly wrote out a draft of the agreement*; *it's not the final version, it's just a draft*

(c) formerly, military service that most young men had to do; *he left the U.S.A. to avoid the draft*

(d) draft beer *or* **beer on draft** = beer that is served from a barrel, and not in a bottle or can; *I'll have the beer that's on draft, please*

2 *adjective*

(a) rough (plan, document); *they brought the draft treaty with them*; *she drew up the draft agreement on the back of an envelope*; *the lawyers were working on the draft contract*

(b) draft animals = animals that are used to pull vehicles or carry heavy loads; *in India cattle are often used as draft animals because they are easy to train*

3 *verb*

(a) to draw up a rough plan of; *we drafted the details of the agreement on a piece of paper*

(b) to call someone for military service; *at the age of eighteen he was drafted into the Marines*

(c) to ask someone to do something; *the police were drafted to control the crowds*

② **drafty**
['dræfti] *adjective*

with cool air flowing into it; *sitting in that drafty balcony has given me a cold* (NOTE: **draftier - draftiest**)

② **drag**
[dræg]

1 *verb*

(a) to pull something heavy along; *she dragged her suitcase across the platform*; *the police dragged the protesters away from the gate*

(b) to hang back, to stay behind; *Tom was dragging along at the end of the line*

(c) to pull a net along the bottom of (a lake) to try to find something; *the police dragged the lake to try to find the body of the missing boy* (NOTE: **dragging - dragged**)

2 *noun*

(a) boring thing, which stops you from doing things you really want to do; *it's a drag, having to write all the Christmas cards*

(b) *(of a man)* **in drag** = wearing women's clothes

① **dragon**
['drægən] *noun*
large animal in children's stories and old tales, which flies through the air and breathes fire; *the knight slew the dragon*; **dragon boat** = long narrow Chinese boat, with a dragon's head on the bow, rowed by a crew of twenty-two to the beat of a drummer

③ **drag on**
['dræg 'ɒn] *verb*
to go slowly; *the dinner party seemed to drag on for hours*

① **drain**
[dreɪn]
1 *noun*

(a) pipe for carrying wastewater away; *in the fall the drains get blocked by leaves*; *someone will have to come and clear the blocked drain*; *(informal)* **it's just like pouring money down the drain** = it's a waste of money

(b) gradual loss; *the office in San Francisco is a continual drain on our resources*

2 *verb*

(a) to remove a liquid; *boil the potatoes for ten minutes, drain and leave to cool*

(b) to drink the contents of (a glass); *he drained his glass and called for another round*

② **drainpipe**
['dreɪnpaɪp] *noun*
pipe on the outside of a house which takes water down to the drains; *the burglar got into the house by climbing up a drainpipe*

② **drama**
['drɑːmə] *noun*

(a) serious performance in a theater; *the theater has put on an unknown Elizabethan drama*; *I'm reading a book on 19th-century French drama*; *a new TV drama series about life in Idaho*; *she's a drama student or she's studying drama*; **drama department** = department in a college which teaches serious theater

(b) series of serious and exciting events; *he always makes a drama out of everything*; *a day of high drama in the court*; *the drama of the rescue of the children by helicopter*

③ **dramatic**
[drə'mætɪk] *adjective*

(a) giving a shock; *the door flew open and she made a dramatic entrance*; *the dramatic moment in the movie, when the pirates start to attack the children*

(b) referring to drama; *his latest dramatic work for radio*

④ **dramatically**
[drə'mætɪkli] *adverb*
in a very dramatic way; *her appearance has altered dramatically since her illness*; *the national birth rate rose dramatically in the second half of the 20th century*

① **drank**
[dræŋk]
see DRINK

② **drapes**
[dreɪps] *noun*
thick curtains; *they have new drapes in the living room*

① **draw**
[drɔː]
1 *noun*

(a) game where there is no winner; *the game ended in a draw, 2 - 2*

(b) attraction; *the zoo is a great draw for children*; *the new Disneyland will be the biggest draw in the area*

2 *verb*

(a) to make a picture with a pen or pencil; *he drew a picture of the house*; *she's drawing a pot of flowers*

(b) not to have a winner in a game; *the teams drew 2 - 2*; **the match was drawn** = neither side won

(c) to pull open or to close; *can you draw the curtains - it's getting dark*; *she drew the curtains and let in the sun*

(d) *(formal)* to pull out; *he drew a gun out of his pocket*; *she was drawing water from a well*; **to draw lots** = to take pieces of paper from a box to decide something (the person who has the marked piece wins); *we drew lots to decide who would go first*; *they drew lots for the bottle of wine*

(e) to receive money; *he doesn't draw a salary, but charges us for his expenses*; *in two years' time I'll be drawing my pension* (NOTE: **drawing - drew** [druː] **- has drawn** [drɔːn])

② **drawer**
['drɔːər] *noun*

(a) part of a desk or cupboard like an open box which slides in and out and which you pull with a handle; *I keep my checkbook in the top drawer of my desk*; **a chest of drawers** = piece of bedroom furniture with several drawers for clothes

(b) person who writes a check asking for money to be paid to someone

① **drawing**
['drɔːɪŋ] *noun*

(a) picture done with a pen or pencil; *I've bought an old drawing of the church*; **drawing board** = large board used by designers to work on

(b) selecting the winner in a lottery; *the drawing is held on Saturdays*; *we are holding a drawing to raise money for the local hospital*

③ **drawn**
[drɔn] *adjective*
(a) tired and sick; *she looked drawn after spending all night with her sick baby*
(b) *see* DRAW

④ **draw up**
['drɔ 'ʌp] *verb*
(a) to come or bring to a stop; *as I was standing at the bus stop, an automobile drew up and asked if I wanted a lift*
(b) to write down a plan, etc.; *they have drawn up a plan to save money*; *have you drawn up a list of people you want to invite to the party?*

② **dread**
[dred]
1 *noun*
great fear; *the sound of his voice filled her with dread*; *she has a dread of being touched*; **in dread of** = being very afraid of; *they lived in constant dread of being arrested by the secret police*
2 *verb*
to fear greatly; *I'm dreading taking my driver's test*; *she dreads her annual visit to the dentist*

② **dreadful**
['dredfəl] *adjective*
awful, very bad or unpleasant; *the weather has been dreadful all week*; *what a dreadful color for a hat!*

③ **dreadfully**
['dredfəli] *adverb*
awfully, extremely; *we're dreadfully busy this morning*; *I'm dreadfully sorry, but we seem to have lost your ticket*

① **dream**
[drim]
1 *noun*
(a) things that you think you see happening when you are asleep; *she had a dream about big pink elephants*
(b) things that you imagine and hope will happen in the future; *all his dreams of wealth collapsed when he lost his job*; *never in your wildest dreams did you imagine you would end up in such an important job*
(c) something you would really like to do or to see happen; *his dream is to appear on Broadway*; *they finally realized their dream of owning a cottage by a lake*
(d) *(informal)* something very pleasant or delicious; *that chocolate pudding was a dream*
2 *verb*
(a) to think you see things happening while you are asleep; *he was dreaming of white sand and a blue tropical sea*; *I dreamt about you last night*; *last night I dreamt I was drowning*
(b) to think about something; **not to dream of doing something** = not to consider doing

something; *she wouldn't dream of wearing a big hat like that*
(c) to imagine something which does not exist; *I never said that - you must have been dreaming!*
(NOTE: **he dreamed** *or* **he dreamt** [dremt])
3 *adjective*
best possible, what you really want; *they found their dream house in a small town by the sea*; *select your dream team for the Super Bowl*

① **dress**
[dres]
1 *noun*
(a) piece of a woman's or girl's clothing, covering more or less all the body; *she was wearing a blue dress* (NOTE: plural is **dresses**)
(b) special clothes; **evening dress** = formal clothes worn to an evening party (long dresses for women and dinner jacket and bow tie for men); *he was wearing evening dress* (NOTE: no plural in this meaning)
2 *verb*
(a) to put clothes on; *he got up, dressed and then had breakfast*; *she dressed her little girl all in red*
(b) to clean and put a bandage on a wound; *the nurse will dress the cut on your knee*
(c) to prepare food; *she dressed the salad with French dressing*

① **dressed**
[drest] *adjective*
(a) wearing clothes; *I can't come down to see the visitors - I'm not dressed yet*; *he got up, got dressed and then had breakfast*; *she was dressed all in black*
(b) **dressed (up) as** = wearing the costume of; *he went to the party dressed (up) as a police officer*; **dressed (up) to the nines** = wearing your very best clothes; *I saw her going out all dressed to the nines*

② **dressing**
['dresɪŋ] *noun*
(a) putting on clothes; *dressing the baby takes ages*
(b) sauce (for salad); *a bottle of Italian salad dressing*; **Thousand Island dressing** = sauce with mayonnaise, olives, onion, green peppers, etc.
(c) bandage for a wound; *the patient's dressings need to be changed every two hours*

① **drew**
[dru]
see DRAW

③ **dribble**
['drɪbl] *verb*
(a) to let liquid flow slowly out of your mouth; *the baby dribbled over her dress*
(b) to bounce a basketball along as you are running; *he dribbled the ball down the court and scored a goal*

② **dried, drier, dries, driest**
[draɪd *or* 'draɪə *or* draɪz *or* 'draɪəst]
see DRY

② **drift**
[drɪft]
1 *noun*
(a) general meaning; *did you follow the drift of the conversation?*; *my Italian isn't very good, but I got the drift of what they were saying*; *I think she got the general drift of my argument*
(b) pile of snow blown by the wind; *snow lay in drifts around the farmhouse*
(c) North Atlantic Drift = the current of warm water moving east across the North Atlantic (NOTE: also called the **Gulf Stream**)
2 *verb*
(a) to move with the flow of water, without steering; *the boat drifted down the river for two miles*
(b) to move in no particular direction; *after the match, the spectators drifted toward the exits*
(c) *(of snow)* to pile up; *the snow began to drift in the high wind*
(d) not to make any decisions; *the government has lost its sense of direction and is starting to drift*

① **drill**
[drɪl]
1 *noun*
(a) tool for making holes in wood, metal, etc.; *he used an electric drill to make the holes in the wall*
(b) military practice in marching, etc.; *new recruits spend hours practicing their drill*; **boat drill** = practice to escape from a sinking ship by getting into small boats; **fire drill** = practice to escape from a burning building
2 *verb*
(a) to make holes; *he drilled two holes for the screws*; *they are drilling for oil*
(b) to do military practice; *recruits were drilling on the parade ground*

① **drink**
[drɪŋk]
1 *noun*
(a) liquid which you swallow; *if you're thirsty, have a drink of water*; *she always has a hot drink before she goes to bed*; **soft drinks** = drinks like colas that have no alcohol in them
(b) alcoholic drink; *would you like a drink?*; *come and have a drink*; *I'll order some drinks from the bar*
2 *verb*
(a) to swallow liquid; *he drank two glasses of water*; *what would you like to drink?*; *do you want something to drink with your meal?*
(b) to drink alcoholic drinks; *she doesn't drink* or *she never drinks*; *he drinks like a fish* = he drinks a lot of alcohol
(c) to drink a toast to someone = to drink and wish someone well; *we all drank a toast to the future success of the company* (NOTE: **drinking - drank** [dræŋk] **- has drunk** [drʌŋk])

② **drip**
[drɪp]
1 *noun*
(a) small drop of water; *there's a hole in the tent - a drip just fell on my nose*
(b) giving a patient a liquid directly into the body; *she's on a drip*
2 *verb*
to fall in drops; to let a liquid fall in drops; *the faucet is dripping*; *his nose is dripping because he has a cold*; *water dripped from the roof* (NOTE: **dripping - dripped**)

① **drive**
[draɪv]
1 *verb*
(a) to make an automobile, truck, etc., travel in a certain direction; *he can swim, but he can't drive*; *he was driving a truck when the accident happened*; *she was driving to work when she heard the news on the car radio*; **I'll drive your aunt to the airport** = I'll take her to the airport in my car
(b) to force; *he drove the nail into the wall*
(c) he drives a hard bargain = he is a tough person to negotiate with (NOTE: **driving - drove** [drəʊv] **- has driven** [ˈdrɪvn])
2 *noun*
(a) journey, especially in a car; *let's go for a drive into the country*; *the baby gets carsick on long drives*; *it's a four-hour drive to the coast*
(b) the way in which power gets from the engine to a car's wheels; *a vehicle with front-wheel drive*; *a four-wheel-drive car*
(c) part of a computer that works a disk; *the computer has a CD-ROM drive*
(d) energetic way of working; *we need someone with plenty of drive to run the sales department*; **economy drive** = vigorous effort to save money or materials; **sales drive** = vigorous effort to increase sales
(e) little road leading to a house; *visitors can park in the drive*

③ **drive away**
[ˈdraɪv əˈweɪ] *verb*
(a) to ride away in a motor vehicle; *the bank robbers leapt into a van and drove away at top speed*
(b) to take someone away in a motor vehicle; *the children were driven away in a police car*
(c) to force something or someone to go away; *the smell of the sewer drives away our customers*

③ **drive back**
[ˈdraɪv ˈbæk] *verb*
(a) to go back or to come back in a motor vehicle; *we were driving back to Seattle after a weekend in the country when we heard the news on the car radio*
(b) to force someone or something back; *the police drove the demonstrators back into Main Street*

③ **driven**
['drɪvn]
see DRIVE

② **drive off**
['draɪv 'ɒf] *verb*
(a) to ride away in a motor vehicle; *the bank robbers leapt into an automobile and drove off at top speed*
(b) to force someone or something to go away; *they drove off the attackers with sticks and stones*

① **driver**
['draɪvər] *noun*
person who drives a car, bus, etc.; *he got a job as a bus driver*; *the drivers of both cars were injured in the accident*

① **driver's license**
['draɪvərz 'laɪsəns] *noun*
permit that allows someone to drive a car, truck, etc.; *applicants should hold a valid driver's license*

① **driver's test**
['draɪvərz 'test] *noun*
test that you have to pass to get a driver's license; *he's taken his driver's test three times and still hasn't passed*

③ **driving**
['draɪvɪŋ]
1 *noun*
action of driving a motor vehicle; *driving in Los Angeles can be very tiring*; *she's taking driving lessons*; **careless driving** = driving in such a way that other people or vehicles may be harmed; *he was charged with careless driving*; **driving school** = school where you can learn to drive a car, truck, etc.
2 *adjective*
(rain or snow) blown hard by the wind; *they were forced to turn back because of the driving rain*

② **drizzle**
['drɪzl] *verb*
to rain a little; *it's drizzling outside, so you'd better wear a raincoat*

① **drop**
[drɒp]
1 *noun*
(a) small amount of liquid that falls; *the roof leaks and we placed a bucket to catch the drops*; *drops of rain ran down the windows*
(b) small amount of liquid; **would you like a drop of whiskey?** = a small glass of whiskey
(c) distance that you might fall; *there is a drop of five feet from the bathroom window to the ground*
(d) decrease; *sales show a drop of 10%*
2 *verb*
(a) to let something fall; *he dropped the glass and it broke*
(b) to decrease; *prices are dropping*; *take a warm pullover, because at night the temperature can drop quite sharply*

(c) to let someone get off a bus or automobile at a place; *I'll drop you at your house*; *the bus dropped her at the school*
(d) *(informal)* to drop someone a line = to send someone a note; *drop me a line when you are back from Canada*
(e) to give up; *they have dropped the idea of moving to Block Island*; *the whole plan has been dropped because of the cost* (NOTE: dropping - dropped)

③ **drop off**
['drɒp 'ɒf] *verb*
(a) to fall asleep; *she dropped off in front of the TV*; *it took me ages to drop off*
(b) to drop someone off = to let someone who is a passenger in an automobile get out somewhere; *can you drop me off at the post office?*

④ **drought**
[draʊt] *noun*
long period when there is no rain and when the land is dry; *relief workers are bringing food to areas affected by drought*

① **drove**
[drəʊv]
see DRIVE

① **drown**
[draʊn] *verb*
(a) to die by being unable to breathe in water; *he drowned in a shallow pool*
(b) to cover up a sound; *the shouting drowned out his speech*

② **drug**
[drʌg]
1 *noun*
(a) medicine; *they have found a new drug for people with cancer*
(b) substance that affects the nerves, and which can become a habit; *the enforcement agency is looking for such things as drugs or alcohol*; **drug addict** = person who takes drugs as a habit; **drug dealer** = person who sells illegal drugs to other people
2 *verb*
to give someone a drug; *they drugged him and took him away in a car* (NOTE: drugging - drugged)

② **druggist**
['drʌgɪst] *noun*
pharmacist, the person who sells medicines and also prepares them; *ask the druggist to give you something for your stomach pains*

① **drugstore**
['drʌgstɔr] *noun*
store where medicines can be bought, as well as many other goods such as soap, paper, etc.; *you can buy some toothpaste at the drugstore on the corner*

① **drum**
[drʌm]
1 *noun*

(a) large round musical instrument that is hit with a stick; *he plays the drums in the band*
(b) large barrel or container shaped like a cylinder; *oil drums were piled up in the corner of the yard*
2 *verb*
to hit frequently; *he drummed his fingers on the table*; **to drum something into someone** = to make someone learn something; *my grandfather drummed it into me that I had to be polite to customers* (NOTE: **drumming - drummed**)

① **drummer**
['drʌmər] *noun*
person who plays the drums; *the band is looking for a new drummer*

① **drunk**
[drʌŋk] *adjective*
excited or sick because of drinking too much alcohol; *when he's drunk, he shouts at his children*; *see also* DRINK

① **drunken**
['drʌŋkən] *adjective*
who has drunk too much alcohol; *nurses had to call the police to help control the drunken patient*; *people complained about drunken teenagers breaking windows on the street*

① **dry**
[draɪ]
1 *adjective*
(a) not wet; *don't touch the door - the paint isn't dry yet*; *the soil is dry because it hasn't rained for weeks*; *this cream will help make your skin less dry*; **at the end of the movie there wasn't a dry eye in the house** = the movie made all the audience cry
(b) with no rain; *they are forecasting dry sunny periods*; **dry season** = period of the year when it does not rain much (as opposed to the rainy season)
(c) not sweet (wine); *a dry white wine is served with fish*
(d) **to have a dry sense of humor** = to make jokes without seeming to know they are funny; *he has a wonderfully dry sense of humor* (NOTE: **drier - driest**)
2 *verb*
(a) to stop being wet; *the clothes are drying in the sun*; *leave the dishes by the sink to dry*
(b) to wipe something until it is dry; *if I wash, can you dry (the dishes)?*

① **dryer**
['draɪər] *noun*
machine that dries wet things; *I dried my hair with the hair dryer*; *she bought a new washer and dryer*

③ **dry up**
['draɪ 'ʌp] *verb*
to stop flowing; *the heat wave has made the rivers dry up*; *the government grants have dried up and it looks as though the agency will have to close*

④ **dual**
['djʊəl] *adjective*
double, existing as a pair; *driving school cars have dual controls*; **she has dual citizenship** = she is a citizen of two countries

④ **dubious**
['djubiəs] *adjective*
(a) suspicious; *there were some dubious characters hanging around outside the store*; *have you heard about his dubious past in South America?*
(b) doubtful, hesitating; *I'm dubious about getting involved*; *everyone else seems to believe her story, but personally I'm dubious about it*

① **duck**
[dʌk]
1 *noun*
(a) common waterbird; *let's go and feed the ducks in Golden Gate Park*; *see also* WATER
(b) meat from this bird; *we're having roast duck for dinner*; *would you like another slice of duck?*
2 *verb*
to lower your head quickly to avoid hitting something; *she didn't duck in time and the ball hit her on the head*; *he ducked as he went through the low doorway*

② **due**
[dju]
1 *adjective*
(a) expected; *when is the baby due?*; *we are due to leave the airport at 5 o'clock*; *the plane is due to arrive at 10:30 or is due at 10:30*
(b) **due to** = because of; *the trains are late due to ice*
(c) **in due course** = later; *in due course you will have to pass an exam*
(d) owed; **to fall due** *or* **to become due** = to be ready for payment; **balance due to us** = amount owed to us which should be paid
(e) **due for** = likely to get; *we're due for a thunderstorm after all this hot weather*; *she must be due for retirement this year*
2 *adverb*
straight; *the plane flew due west*; *go due east for ten miles and you will see the church on your left*

② **dug**
[dʌg]
see DIG

② **dull**
[dʌl] *adjective*
(a) not exciting, not interesting; *the story is kind of dull*; *what's so interesting about old churches? - I find them dull*
(b) *(weather)* gray and gloomy; *a dull cloudy day*
(c) *(colors)* gloomy, not bright; *they painted the living room a dull green* (NOTE: **duller - dullest**)

② **dumb**
[dʌm] *adjective*
(a) unable to speak; *she was born deaf and dumb or she is deaf and dumb from birth*; **to be**

struck dumb = to be so surprised that you cannot say anything; *he was struck dumb by the news*

(b) *(informal)* stupid; *that was a dumb thing to do*; *how can anyone be so dumb?*

① **dump**
[dʌmp]
1 *noun*
(a) place for garbage; *take your garbage to the local dump*
(b) what a dump! = what an awful place!; *his house is a dump*
2 *verb*
(a) to put something heavily on the ground; *she just dumped her suitcases in the hall*
(b) to throw away, to get rid of; *someone has dumped an old shopping cart in the parking lot*; **to dump goods on a market** = to sell surplus goods at a very cheap price (usually overseas); *old medicines are being dumped in Africa*
(c) *(informal)* **to dump someone** = to get rid of someone; *she's been dumped by her boyfriend*

② **dungeon**
['dʌndʒən] *noun*
dark and unpleasant underground prison; *the prisoners were kept for years in the dungeons of the Tower of London*

④ **duplex**
['djupleks] *noun*
house or apartment for two families, each with a separate entrance; *I bought a duplex, with the intention of living on one side and renting the other*; *they live in a duplex on E 56th Street* (NOTE: plural is **duplexes**)

② **duplicate**
1 *adjective* ['djuplɪkət]
which is a copy; *put the duplicate invoices in the file*
2 *noun* ['djuplɪkət]
copy; *she sent the invoice and filed the duplicate*
3 *verb* ['djuplɪkeɪt]
to make a copy of a letter, etc.; *she duplicated the letter and put a copy into the file*; **you are just duplicating his work** = you are just doing the same work as he did earlier

③ **durable**
['djuərəbl]
1 *adjective*
which lasts, which does not wear away; *you need a really durable floor covering in a kitchen*; *they've signed a peace agreement but will it be more durable than the last one?*; **durable effects** = effects that will be felt for a long time; *the strike will have durable effects on the economy*
2 *noun*
consumer durables = goods bought by the public which will be used for a long time (such as washing machines or refrigerators); durable goods

④ **duration**
[djʊ'reɪʃn] *noun*
(formal) period of time for which something lasts; *they stayed in the country for the duration of the war*; *luckily the power outage was of short duration*

① **during**
['djuərɪŋ] *preposition*
while something lasts; *he went to sleep during the concert*; *conditions were bad during the war*

① **dust**
[dʌst]
1 *noun*
thin layer of dry dirt; *the room had never been cleaned - there was dust everywhere*; *a tiny bit of dust got in my eye* (NOTE: no plural)
2 *verb*
(a) to remove dust from something; *don't forget to dust the Chinese bowls carefully*
(b) to sprinkle a powder on something; *she dusted the cake with powdered sugar*

② **duster**
['dʌstər] *noun*
(a) cloth used to remove dust; *rub the surface down with a duster*
(b) long coat

① **dusty**
['dʌsti] *adjective*
covered with dust; *his room is full of dusty old books* (NOTE: **dustier - dustiest**)

② **duty**
['djuti] *noun*
(a) work that you have to do; *one of his duties is to see that the main doors are locked at night*; **to be duty-bound to do something** = to be obliged to do something; *if you have any information relating to this case, you are duty-bound to pass it to the police*
(b) on duty = doing official work which you have to do in a job; *he's on duty from 9:00 to 6:00*; *she's been on duty all day* (NOTE: no plural in this meaning)
(c) tax that has to be paid to take goods into a country; *you may have to pay duty on goods you are bringing into the U.S.A.*

③ **dwarf**
[dwɔrf] *noun*
(in fairy stories) very small person, smaller than other people; *Snow White and the Seven Dwarfs* (NOTE: plural is **dwarfs** *or* **dwarves**)

③ **dwelling**
['dwelɪŋ] *noun*
(formal) place to live; *they have had permission to build a dwelling on the site*

② **dye**
[daɪ]
1 *noun*
substance used to change the color of something; *she used a green dye to change the color of her hair*; **fast dye** = color that will not fade when washed

2 *verb*

to stain with a color; *she dyed her hair green* (NOTE: do not confuse with **die**)

② **dying**

['daɪɪŋ] *adjective*

dying for *or* **to** = wanting something very much; *we're dying for a cold drink*; *I'm dying to read his book*

④ **dynamic**

[daɪ'næmɪk] *adjective*

very energetic and with a strong personality; *a young and dynamic president*

Ee

③ **E, e**

[i]

fifth letter of the alphabet, between D and F; *which is it - "been" with two Es or "bean" spelled EA?*

② **each**

[itʃ]

1 *adjective*

every person or thing; *each ten-dollar bill has a different number*; *he was holding a towel in each hand*; *each one of us has a separate office*

2 *pronoun*

(a) every person; *they have two houses each or each of them has two houses*; *she gave them each ten dollars or she gave them ten dollars each or she gave each of them ten dollars*

(b) every thing; *each of the books has three hundred pages or the books have three hundred pages each*

② **each other**

['itʃ 'ʌðər] *pronoun*

the other one of two people or of two things; *they were shouting at each other*; *we always send each other presents on our birthdays*; *the boxes fit into each other*

① **eager**

['igər] *adjective*

wanting to do something very much; *they are eager to see the exhibition*; *I am not very eager for Sam to come to live with us*

② **eagerly**

['igəli] *adverb*

in a way that shows that you want something very much; *the children were eagerly waiting for the beginning of summer vacation*; *he reads the job advertisements eagerly every morning*

① **eagle**

['igl] *noun*

large bird of prey; **bald eagle** = large eagle with a white head, the symbol of the U.S.; *the bald eagle is a national symbol*

① **ear**

[ɪər] *noun*

(a) part of your head that you hear with; *rabbits have long ears*; *have you washed behind your ears?*; *(informal)* **to be up to your ears in** = to be very busy with; *he's up to his ears in work*; **to have** *or* **keep your ear to the ground** = to follow what is happening and know all about something

(b) ability to sense sound; *he has a good ear for music*; **to play an instrument by ear** = to play without reading the printed notes of music; *she can play the piano by ear*; *(informal)* **to play it by ear** = to do what you think is right at the time; *we won't make a plan, we'll just play it by ear and see how it goes*

① **early**

['ɜrli]

1 *adverb*

(a) before the usual time; *the plane arrived five minutes early*; *we must get up early tomorrow morning if we want to catch the first ferry across the lake*; *can you come an hour earlier tomorrow?*

(b) at the beginning of a period of time; *we went out early in the evening*; *the snow came early in the year*

2 *adjective*

(a) which happens at the beginning of a period of time or which happens before the proper time; *we picked some early vegetables*; *I caught an early flight to Vancouver*; *these flowers bloom in early summer*; **at an early date** = soon; *the meeting must be held at the earliest date possible*; **to take early retirement** = to leave a job with a pension before the usual age for retirement

(b) *(informal)* **an early bird** = someone who likes to get up early and work before breakfast, and who does not stay up late at night; *he's an early bird - he's up at 6:00 every morning*;

compare NIGHT OWL (NOTE: **earlier - earliest**)

② **earn**
[ɜrn] *verb*
(a) to be paid money for working; *he earns $30,000 a year*; *how much does a bus driver earn?*
(b) to deserve something or to be given something; *you can all take a rest now - you've earned it!*; *his joke earned him a bad mark from the teacher*

② **earnest**
['ɜrnɪst]
1 *adjective*
serious; *they were engaged in some earnest conversation*
2 *noun*
in earnest = seriously; *after lunch the discussions began in earnest*

② **earnings**
['ɜrnɪŋz] *noun*
salary, the money that you earn from work; *his earnings are not enough to pay the rent*

③ **earplug**
['ɪərplʌg] *noun*
piece of soft wax that you put in your ears to stop you from hearing loud sounds

① **earring**
['ɪərɪŋ] *noun*
ornament attached to the lobe of your ear; *he has a gold earring in his left ear*; **a pair of earrings** = two similar rings, one worn in each ear; *she was wearing a pair of old earrings that belonged to her mother*

① **earth**
[ɜrθ] *noun*
(a) the planet on which we live; *the Earth goes around the Sun once in twenty-four hours*; *the space shuttle came back to earth safely*
(b) soil, soft material made up of minerals and rotten vegetable matter, which plants grow in; *put some earth in the plant pot and then sow your cucumber seeds*

◇ **on earth**
[ɒn 'ɜrθ]
(used to make questions stronger) *why on earth did you do that?*; *who on earth is going to pay that much for a bottle of wine?*; *how on earth are we going to afford a vacation in Paris?*; *what on earth are they doing digging up the road?*

① **earthquake**
['ɜrθkweɪk] *noun*
shaking of the surface of the Earth caused by movements of the Earth's outer crust; *there have been many earthquakes in or near San Francisco*; *only a few houses were still standing after the earthquake*; *the Richter scale is used to measure earthquakes*

① **earthworm**
['ɜrθwɜrm] *noun*
little animal that looks like a very small snake and lives in soil; *the earthworms come to the surface when it rains* (NOTE: usually just called a **worm**)

② **ease**
[iz]
1 *noun*
(a) to put someone at their ease = to make someone feel relaxed and confident; *the police officer offered the children candy to put them at their ease*; **ill at ease** = nervous, uncomfortable; *she was definitely ill at ease during the interview with the manager*
(b) lack of difficulty; *he won the first round with the greatest of ease*; *the bottle has a wide mouth for ease of use* (NOTE: no plural)
2 *verb*
(a) to make less painful; *a couple of aspirins should ease the pain*
(b) to make easy; *an introduction from his uncle eased his entry into the firm*

② **easier, easiest**
['iziər 'iziəst]
see EASY

① **easily**
['izɪli] *adverb*
(a) without any difficulty; *I passed my driver's test easily*; *I can get there easily by 9 o'clock*
(b) *(for emphasis before comparatives or superlatives)* a lot (compared to something else); *he is easily the tallest man in the team*; *our store is easily the biggest on Main Street*

① **east**
[ist]
1 *noun*
(a) direction of where the sun rises; *the sun rises in the east and sets in the west*; *Colorado is to the east of Utah*; *the wind is blowing from the east*
(b) part of a country which is to the east of the rest; *the east of the country is drier than the west*; *see also* FAR EAST, MIDDLE EAST, NEAR EAST
(c) the East = (i) Asia, particularly eastern and southern Asia; (ii) area of the U.S. east of the Mississippi River
2 *adjective*
referring to the east; *we live on the east bank of the river*; **East Coast** = the part of the U.S.A. near the Atlantic; **east wind** = wind that blows from the east
3 *adverb*
toward the east; *the kitchen windows face east, so we get the morning sun*; *drive east along the freeway for twenty miles*

① **Easter**
['istər] *noun*
important Christian festival (in March or April) celebrating Christ's death and rising again; *we have two weeks' vacation at Easter*; *what are you doing during the Easter vacation?*; *we plan to go walking in the woods on Easter Monday*;

Easter Day *or* **Easter Sunday** = Sunday celebrating Christ's rising from the dead; **Easter egg** = chocolate or colored egg eaten at Easter

① **eastern**
['istən] *adjective*
from, of or in the east; *Bulgaria is part of Eastern Europe; the best snow is in the eastern part of the mountains*

① **easy**
['izi]
1 *adjective*
not difficult, not needing a lot of effort; *the driver's test isn't very easy - lots of people fail it; it's easy to see why the store closed - a big supermarket has opened next door; the office is within easy reach of the airport; my boss is very easy to get along with*; **easy terms** = conditions which mean that you do not have to pay a lot of money; *the store is leased on very easy terms*
2 *adverb*
to take things easy = to rest, not to do any hard work; *the doctor told him to take things easy for a time after his operation*; **easy now!** *or* **easy does it!** = be careful!; **go easy on the jam!** = don't take too much jam!; **it's easier said than done** = it's more difficult than you think (NOTE: **easier - easiest**)

① **eat**
[it] *verb*
(a) to chew and swallow food; *I'm hungry - is there anything to eat?; we haven't eaten anything since breakfast; the children ate all the sandwiches; eat as much as you like for $9.95!; you'll get thin if you don't eat*; **eating apple** = sweet apple that you can eat raw (as opposed to a sour apple which has to be cooked)
(b) to have a meal; *he was still eating his breakfast when I arrived; we are eating at home tonight; have you eaten yet?* (NOTE: **eating - ate** [et] **- has eaten** ['itn])

④ **eccentric**
[ik'sentrik]
1 *adjective*
strange, odd; *an eccentric old lady who wears boots all the year round*
2 *noun*
strange or odd person; *in his old age, he became something of an eccentric*

①⓪ **echo**
['ekəʊ]
1 *noun*
sound that is repeated (as when you shout in a cave, etc.); *we could hear the echo of voices in the tunnel; I heard an echo of my footsteps in the empty apartment* (NOTE: plural is **echoes**)
2 *verb*
(a) *(of sound)* to make an echo; *their voices echoed down the tunnel*
(b) to repeat; *the newspaper article echoed the opinions put forward in the mayor's speech*

③ **eclipse**
[i'klips] *noun*
time when part of the Sun or Moon disappears, because either the Earth's shadow passes over the Moon, or the Moon passes between the Earth and the Sun; *there will be an eclipse of the Moon tonight*

④ **ecological**
[ikə'lɒdʒɪkl] *adjective*
referring to ecology; *the oil installation will affect the area's ecological balance*; **ecological disaster** = disaster that seriously disturbs the balance of the environment; *the oil from the wrecked tanker caused an ecological disaster*

④ **ecology**
[i'kɒlədʒi] *noun*
study of the relationship between plants and animals and their environment; *books on ecology are in the environmental studies section of the library*

③ **economic**
[ikə'nɒmik] *adjective*
(a) referring to the economy; *I don't agree with the government's economic policy; the government has introduced controls to solve the current economic crisis; the country enjoyed a period of economic growth in the 1990s*; **economic measure** = action of measuring the effect of something on the economy
(b) not expensive; *let's take an economic vacation*

④ **economical**
[ikə'nɒmikl] *adjective*
which saves money or resources; *it's more economical to heat water by gas; the apartment has an economical rent; it is hardly economical for us to run two cars*

③ **economics**
[ikə'nɒmiks] *noun*
(a) scientific study of how money works in trade, society and politics; *she is studying for an economics degree*
(b) the way money is used in a particular activity; *we're considering the economics of closing one of the factories; have you worked out the economics of starting your own business?*

③ **economist**
[i'kɒnəmist] *noun*
person who specializes in the study of money and its uses; *the university has several famous economists on its teaching staff*

④ **economy**
[i'kɒnəmi] *noun*
(a) way in which a country makes and uses money; the financial state of a country; *the country's economy is in ruins; when will the economy start to grow again?*
(b) something you do to save and not to waste money or materials; *she tried to economize by buying cheaper brands*; **economy car rental** =

cheap rental of cars; **economy class** = air fare that is cheaper than first class or business class; **economy pack** *or* **economy size** = pack that is cheaper than the regular size; **economies of scale** = making a product more profitable by manufacturing it in larger quantities

① **edge**
[edʒ]
1 *noun*
(a) side of something flat; *he put his plate down on the edge of the table*; *she lay down on the roof and looked over the edge*; *you can stand this coin on its edge*; *the knife has a very sharp edge*
(b) line between two quite different things; *he lived in a house at the edge of the forest*; *the factory is built right on the edge of the town by the freeway*
(c) advantage; **to have the edge on a rival company** = to have a slightly larger share of the market than a rival
2 *verb*
to move in a slow, careful way; *he started edging toward the door*

④ **edible**
['edɪbl] *adjective*
which can be safely eaten; *how do you know which wild mushrooms are edible and which are poisonous?*

④ **edit**
['edɪt] *verb*
(a) to be in charge of a newspaper or magazine; *he edited the "New York Times" for two years*
(b) to make notes on a text; to change a text to make it better; *the edited text is now ready*; *it took me two hours to edit the first chapter*
(c) to get a text ready for publication; *I am editing a volume of 20th-century poetry*
(d) to cut up a film or tape and stick it together in correct order to make it ready to be shown or played; *once the film has been edited it will run for about 90 minutes*

④ **edition**
[ɪ'dɪʃn] *noun*
(a) number of copies of a book or newspaper printed at the same time; *the book of poems was published in an edition of one thousand copies*
(b) form in which a book is published; *she bought the paperback edition for her father*; **a first edition** = a copy of the first printing of a book

② **editor**
['edɪtər] *noun*
(a) journalist in charge of a newspaper or part of a newspaper; *he wrote to the editor of the "Washington Post" asking for a job*; *she is the sports editor of the local paper*
(b) person who makes notes on a text; person who gets a text, a radio or TV program, etc., ready for publication; *he worked as a dictionary editor all his life*; *the editor of a TV series on Mexican cooking*

(c) computer program for editing text; *the software contains a basic text editor*

④ **editorial**
[edɪ'tɔriəl]
1 *adjective*
referring to editors or to editing; *he has general editorial control of the series*; **editorial board** = group of editors (on a newspaper, etc.)
2 *noun*
main article written by the editor of a newspaper; *did you read today's editorial?*

② **educate**
['edjukeɪt] *verb*
to teach someone; *she was educated privately in Switzerland*; *we need to educate young people about the dangers of alcohol*

② **education**
[edju'keɪʃn] *noun*
system of teaching, or of being taught; *our children deserve the best education we can give them*; *we spent a lot of money on his education, and he's gotten a job as a garbage collector!*; **adult education** = teaching people over the age of 18; **higher education** = teaching at colleges and universities; **elementary education** = teaching small children

② **educational**
[edju'keɪʃnl] *adjective*
referring to learning and teaching, schools, etc.; *this game for 3- to 5-year-olds is very educational*; *a campaign to improve educational standards*; **educational publisher** = company that publishes school books

① **eel**
[il] *noun*
long thin fish that looks like a snake; *she ordered some smoked eel*

③ **effect**
[ɪ'fekt]
1 *noun*
(a) result or influence; *the cuts in spending will have a serious effect on the hospital*; *the cream has had no effect on her rash*; *the effects of the drug took some time to wear off*; **the order takes effect** *or* **comes into effect from January 1** = the order starts to have to be obeyed on January 1
(b) approximate meaning; *the notice said something to the effect that the store had closed*; **or words to that effect** = or something with that meaning; *she said she wouldn't pay, or words to that effect*
(c) **sound effects** = artificial sounds in theater, TV, movies; **special effects** = ghosts, cartoon characters appearing with regular actors, etc., which are used in movies or on stage
(d) *(formal)* **personal effects** = personal belongings
2 *verb*
(formal) to make, to carry out; *she was able to effect a number of changes during her time in*

charge; **to effect a payment** = to make a payment

③ **effective**
['ɪ'fektɪv] *adjective*
(a) which produces the required result; *it's a very effective remedy against colds*; *his method of keeping the children quiet is very effective*; *advertising on TV is a very effective way of selling*
(b) which takes effect; *this order is effective from January 1*

③ **effectively**
[ɪ'fektɪvli] *adverb*
in a way which produces a good result; *the stage lighting worked very effectively*

④ **efficiency**
[ɪ'fɪʃnsi] *noun*
being able to produce a good result without wasting time, money or effort; *how can we improve the efficiency of our working methods?*; *she is known for her extreme efficiency*; **business efficiency** = making a business work in an efficient way

④ **efficient**
[ɪ'fɪʃənt] *adjective*
able to work well and do what is necessary without wasting time, money or effort; *he needs an efficient assistant to look after him*; *the system of printing invoices is very efficient*; **fuel-efficient automobile** = an automobile that does not use much gas

④ **efficiently**
[ɪ'fɪʃəntli] *adverb*
in an efficient way; *the waitresses served the 250 wedding guests very efficiently*; *the new system of dealing with complaints is working very efficiently*

② **effort**
['efət] *noun*
use of the mind or body to do something; *he's made great efforts to learn Spanish*; *thanks to her efforts, we have collected more than $15,000 for the children's home*; *if we make one more effort, we should get all that junk cleared away*

③ **e.g.**
['i'dʒi *or* fər ɪg'zæmpl] *abbreviation meaning "for example"*; *some animals, e.g. polar bears, live in cold climates* (NOTE: it is short for the Latin phrase **exempli gratia**)

① **egg**
[eg] *noun*
(a) oval object with a hard shell, produced by a female bird or reptile, from which a baby bird or reptile comes; *the owl laid three eggs in the nest*; *snakes lay their eggs in the sand*
(b) a chicken's egg, used as food; *you need three eggs to make this cake*; **boiled egg** = egg that has been cooked by boiling in water; **hard-boiled egg** = egg that has been boiled until it is hard inside; **fried egg** = egg that is fried in fat or butter in a frying pan; **scrambled eggs** =

eggs that are mixed up with a fork and then cooked in butter; *I had fried eggs and bacon for breakfast*; *do you want sausages with your scrambled eggs?*

④ **egg on**
['eg 'ɒn] *verb*
to encourage someone to do something, especially something naughty; *stop egging him on - he's bad enough as it is*

③ **eh**
[eɪ] *interjection used when asking questions*; *what about a drink, eh?*; *eh? what did he say?*

① **eight**
[eɪt]
number 8; *he ate eight chocolates*; *the little girl is eight (years old)*; *I usually have breakfast before eight (o'clock)* (NOTE: plural in this meaning is **eights**)

① **eighteen**
[eɪ'tin] *number* 18; *there are eighteen people in our dance class*; *he will be eighteen (years old) next week*; **the eighteen hundreds** = the years between 1800 and 1899 (NOTE: compare with **the eighteenth century**)

① **eighteenth (18th)**
[eɪ'tinθ] *adjective & noun*
April eighteenth (April 18) today's the seventeenth, so tomorrow must be the eighteenth; *that's the eighteenth invoice we've sent out today*; *it's his eighteenth birthday next week*; **the eighteenth century** = the years from 1700 to 1799 (NOTE: compare with **the eighteen hundreds**; note also that with dates **eighteenth** is usually written **18: April 18, 2001; September 18, 1866** (say "September eighteenth"); with names of kings and queens, **eighteenth** is usually written **XVIII: King Louis XVIII** (say: "King Louis the Eighteenth"))

① **eighth (8th)**
[eɪtθ] *adjective & noun*
February eighth (February 8) King Henry the Eighth (Henry VIII) had six wives; *his eighth birthday is next Monday* (NOTE: with dates **eighth** is usually written **8: April 8, 2000; September 8, 1866** (say "September eighth"); with names of kings and queens, **eighth** is usually written **VIII: King Henry VIII** (say "King Henry the Eighth")

① **eightieth (80th)**
['eɪtiəθ] *adjective & noun*
four and a half days is about an eightieth of a year; *Granny's eightieth birthday is next week*

① **eighty**
['eɪti]
number 80; *it's about eighty miles to my parents' house*; *she's eighty (years old)* **she's in her eighties** = she is between 80 and 89 years old; **the eighties** *or* **nineteen eighties (1980s)** = the period from 1980 to 1989 (NOTE: **eighty-one** (81), **eighty-two** (82) but **eighty-first** (81st), **eighty-second** (82nd), etc.)

② **either**
['iðər or 'aɪðər]
1 *adjective & pronoun*
(a) one or the other; *you can use either computer - it doesn't matter which*; *I don't like either of them*
(b) each of two; both; *there are trees on either side of the road*; *some people don't take sugar in their coffee, some don't take milk, and some don't take either*; *they sat on either side of him* = one sat on each side of him
2 *conjunction*
(showing one of two possibilities) either ... or; *either you come here or I'll come to see you*; *what's that awful noise? - it's either a motorcycle or a noisy car*; *you must do it either today or tomorrow*
3 *adverb*
(with a negative, or to make a statement stronger) *he isn't English and he isn't Irish either*; *she doesn't want to go, and I don't want to go either*; *the report wasn't on the TV news, and it wasn't on the radio either*

④ **elaborate**
1 *adjective* [ɪ'læbərət]
very detailed, very complicated; *an elaborate dessert of cream, fruit and cake*
2 *verb* [ɪ'læbəreɪt]
to go into details; *it's a very complicated plan so I won't elaborate*; *the manager refused to elaborate any further on the salesman's reasons for leaving*

① **elastic**
[ɪ'læstɪk]
1 *adjective*
which can stretch and contract
2 *noun*
rubber band which holds cards, papers, etc., together; *put an elastic round those papers*

① **elbow**
['elbəʊ]
1 *noun*
joint in the middle of your arm; *he sat with his elbows on the table*; *she nudged him with her elbow*
2 *verb*
to push with your elbows; *he elbowed his way to the front of the crowd*

③ **elbowroom**
['elbəʊrʊm] *noun*
space to move about; *the seats in tourist class don't give you much elbowroom*

② **elder**
['eldər]
1 *adjective*
older than another person; *I have two elder brothers*; *she brought her elder sister*; **elder statesman** = older and wiser politician (NOTE: **elder** is a comparative, used mainly of brothers or sisters, but is never followed by **than**)
2 *noun*

(a) older person; *Mary is the elder of the two*; *which brother is the elder?*; *the town elders met to discuss the plan*
(b) = ELDERBERRY TREE

④ **elderberry**
['eldərberi] *noun*
common tree with white flowers and bunches of small purple berries; *there's an elderberry tree growing in the hedge by the field*

② **elderly**
['eldəlɪ]
1 *adjective*
old; *an elderly man sat down beside her*; *my mother is now rather elderly and doesn't drive anymore* (NOTE: used as a polite way of saying old)
2 *noun*
the elderly = old people

② **eldest**
['eldəst]
1 *adjective*
oldest of a series of people; *this is John, my eldest son*
2 *noun*
oldest person of a series of people; *he is the eldest of the three brothers*

② **elect**
[ɪ'lekt] *verb*
(a) to choose by voting; *she was elected senator*; *the president is elected for a term of four years*; *the chairman is elected by the members of the committee*
(b) to elect to do something = to choose to do something; *we all went to the neighborhood bar, but she elected to stay at home and watch TV*

① **election**
[ɪ'lekʃən] *noun*
process of choosing by voting; *after the election, the crowds were dancing on the streets*; *local elections are being held next week*; *the next item on the agenda is the election of a new secretary for the club*; **general election** = election where everyone in the country over a certain age can vote

> COMMENT: in the U.S.A., a presidential election is held every four years, always in November. The members of Congress are also elected in November elections, each for a two-year term, while Senators are elected for six years, one-third of the Senate coming up for election every two years

④ **electoral**
[ɪ'lektərəl] *adjective*
referring to an election; *the party suffered a terrible electoral defeat*; **electoral college** = group chosen to elect the president and vice president of the U.S.

① **electric**
[ɪ'lektrɪk] *adjective*
(a) worked by electricity; *he plays an electric guitar*; *he cut the wood with an electric chainsaw*; *she gave me an electric toothbrush for Christmas*
(b) making or carrying electricity; *don't touch those electric wires*; *electric plugs in Europe differ from those in the U.S.A.*
(c) full of excitement; *the atmosphere was electric as the votes were being counted*

② **electrical**
[ɪ'lektrɪkl] *adjective*
referring to electricity; *the college offers courses in electrical engineering*; *they are trying to repair an electrical fault*

① **electricity**
[ɪlek'trɪsɪti] *noun*
energy used to make light, heat, or power; *the electricity was cut off this morning*; *the heating is run by electricity*; *the cottage is in the mountains and doesn't have any electricity* (NOTE: no plural)

③ **electron**
[ɪ'lektrɒn] *noun*
basic negative particle in an atom

② **electronic**
[ɪlek'trɒnɪk] *adjective*
using devices which affect the electric current that passes through them; **electronic engineer** = engineer who specializes in electronic devices; **electronic mail** = e-mail, the system of sending messages from one computer to another, via telephone lines

③ **electronics**
[ɪlek'trɒnɪks] *noun*
science of the movement of electricity in electronic devices; *he is studying electronics at college*; *she works for a major electronics company*; **electronics industry** = the industry that makes TV sets, radios, calculators, etc. (NOTE: takes a singular verb)

③ **elegant**
['elɪgənt] *adjective*
very fashionable and stylish; *you look very elegant in that dress*; *who is that elegant woman in black at the back of the church?*; *she led us into her elegant dining room*

② **element**
['elɪmənt] *noun*
(a) **chemical element** = basic chemical substance; *see also* TRACE ELEMENT
(b) basic part of something; *I think we have all the elements of an agreement*
(c) natural environment; *the coach is in his element when he's talking about football*; **the elements** = the weather, usually bad weather; *you don't want to expose your new coat to the elements*
(d) wire which heats in an electric heater, stove, etc.; *I think the element has burned out*

② **elementary**
[elɪ'mentri] *adjective*
basic or simple; *elementary physics*; **elementary school** = school for small children between the ages of about 5 and 11 (grades 1 through 6 or 8) (NOTE: also called a **grade school**)

① **elephant**
['elɪfənt] *noun*
very large African or Indian animal, with large ears, a trunk and two long teeth; *if you go to the zoo, you can have a ride on an elephant*; *in some countries elephants are used for work in the jungle*

COMMENT: there are two types of elephants, the African, which is larger and wilder, and the Indian which is found in India and Southeast Asia, and is used as a working animal in forests

③ **elevate**
['elɪveɪt] *verb*
(formal) to lift up; *he was elevated to the post of chairman*; **elevated railway** = form of local railway system which runs along rails placed high above the street

① **elevator**
['elɪveɪtər] *noun*
(a) device for lifting people from floor to floor inside a building; *take the elevator to the 26th floor*; **freight elevator** = device for lifting goods from floor to floor inside a building
(b) **grain elevator** = tall building for storing grain

① **eleven**
[ɪ'levn] *number* 11; *when you're eleven (years old) you will soon go to junior high school*; *come and see me at eleven (o'clock)* **the eleven hundreds** = the years from 1100 to 1199 (NOTE: compare with **the eleventh century**)

① **eleventh (11th)**
[ɪ'levənθ] *adjective & noun*
June eleventh (June 11) his name was eleventh on the list; *it's her eleventh birthday tomorrow*; **at the eleventh hour** = at the last minute; *the contract was finally signed at the eleventh hour*; *his eleventh-hour decision to stand for election*; **the eleventh century** = the years from 1000 to 1099 (NOTE: compare with **the eleven hundreds**; note also that with dates **eleventh** is usually written **11: April 11, 2002; December 11, 1866** (say "December eleventh"); with names of kings and queens, **eleventh** is usually written **XI: King Louis XI** (say: "King Louis the Eleventh"))

④ **elicit**
[ɪ'lɪsɪt] *verb*
to obtain; *I was unable to elicit any useful information about him*

④ **eligible**
['elɪdʒɪbl] *adjective*
(a) **eligible to do something** = able to do something because you are old enough or have

the right qualifications; *you aren't eligible to vote until you are eighteen*; *she's not eligible to enter the competition because she works for the company running it*
(b) eligible for something = entitled to do something or qualified for something; *the previous president is eligible for reelection*; *she is not eligible for a grant*

③ **eliminate**
[ɪˈlɪmɪneɪt] *verb*
(a) to remove mistakes, waste, etc.; *using a computer should eliminate all possibility of error*; *the disease has been eliminated in most parts of the world*
(b) to remove someone from a competition; *he came in last and so was eliminated from the next round of the contest*

④ **elite**
[erˈliːt] *noun*
group of the best socially ranked or educated people; *only the elite can afford private education for their children*

① **else**
[els] *adverb*
(a) *(used after pronouns)* other; *what else can I say?*; *everyone else had already left*; *who else was at the meeting?*; **anyone else** = any other person; *is there anyone else who can't see the screen?*; **anything else** = any other thing; *is there anything else you don't like eating?*; *did you hear anything else?*; **somebody else** *or* **someone else** = some other person, a different person; *she was sick so someone else had to take her place*; **nobody else** *or* **no one else** = no other person; *nobody else's daughter behaved as badly as ours*; **nothing else** = no other thing; *I need one small gold ring - nothing else will do*; **nowhere else** = no other place; *there's nowhere else to go*; **somewhere else** *or* **someplace else** = in some other place, in a different place; *can we go someplace else?*
(b) or else = or if not; *don't miss the bus, or else you'll have a long wait for the next one*; *put a coat on to go out, or else you'll catch cold*; *we'd better get up early or else we'll miss the train*; *you must have a ticket, or else you will be thrown off the train by the inspector*
(c) *(as informal threat)* **you'd better pay, or else** = if you don't pay, I'll hit you

② **elsewhere**
[elsˈweər] *adverb*
somewhere else, in another place; *this store doesn't carry maps, so you'll have to try elsewhere*

④ **elude**
[ɪˈluːd] *verb*
(formal) to escape, to avoid capture; *he eluded the police by leaping over a wall*

② **e-mail** *or* **email**
[ˈiːmeɪl]
1 *noun*

(a) electronic mail, a system of sending messages from one computer to another, using telephone lines; *you can contact me by phone or e-mail if you want*; *I'll give you my e-mail address*
(b) message sent by e-mail; *I had two e-mails from him this morning*
2 *verb*
to send a message using electronic mail; *I e-mailed him about the meeting*

④ **embargo**
[ɪmˈbɑːrɡəʊ]
1 *verb*
to forbid officially the trade in something; *the government has embargoed the sale of arms to Middle Eastern countries*
2 *noun*
official ban on trade; *the oil embargo is still in place*; **to place** *or* **put an embargo on** = to forbid something officially; *they placed an embargo on trade with our country*; **to lift an embargo** = to allow trade to start again; *the government has lifted the embargo on the export of computers*; **to be under an embargo** = to be forbidden (NOTE: plural is **embargoes**)

③ **embarrass**
[ɪmˈbærəs] *verb*
to make someone feel uncomfortable by being rude, etc.; *she wanted to embarrass me in front of my friends*; *it embarrasses me to have to talk about it in public*

③ **embarrassed**
[ɪmˈbærəst] *adjective*
uncomfortable or ashamed, because you have done something wrong; *she gave an embarrassed laugh, and said she had forgotten to bring the present*; *he was so embarrassed that he turned bright red*

③ **embarrassing**
[ɪmˈbærəsɪŋ] *adjective*
that makes you feel embarrassed; *it was very embarrassing to find that the bride's mother was wearing exactly the same dress*

④ **embassy**
[ˈembəsi] *noun*
home or offices of an ambassador; *there was a party at the U.S. Embassy in Paris* (NOTE: plural is **embassies**)

③ **embrace**
[ɪmˈbreɪs]
1 *verb*
to hold and kiss someone to show affection; *they embraced for several minutes before he got on the train*
2 *noun*
(literary) holding someone tightly and kissing them; *they lay on the grass in a close embrace*

④ **embryo**
[ˈembriəʊ] *noun*
(a) first state of a living organism; *a human embryo*

(b) in embryo = in its early stages; *the plan was presented to us in embryo* (NOTE: plural is **embryos**)

④ **emerge**
[ɪˈmɜrdʒ] *verb*
(a) to emerge from inside something = to come out from inside; *they blinked as they emerged into the sunshine from the tunnel*
(b) to appear, to come into existence; *it was only after the election that he emerged as party leader*
(c) to become known; *it soon emerged that the president knew nothing about what was happening*

② **emergency**
[ɪˈmɜrdʒənsɪ] *noun*
dangerous situation where decisions have to be made quickly (such as a fire, accident, breakdown of law and order, etc.); *call for an ambulance - this is an emergency!*; **state of emergency** = time when the police or armed forces are in control of a country; *the government has declared a state of emergency*; **emergency exit** = door in a movie theater, etc., used in case of fire; **emergency operation** = operation done immediately on a seriously ill patient; **emergency room** = department in a hospital for people who are injured in accidents or suddenly become sick; **emergency services** = the police, fire service and ambulance service; **in case of an emergency** *or* **in an emergency** = if a dangerous situation develops; *in an emergency or in case of an emergency press the red button* (NOTE: plural is **emergencies**)

③ **emigrant**
[ˈemɪɡrənt] *noun*
person who emigrates; *Russian emigrants to Israel*; compare IMMIGRANT

③ **emigrate**
[ˈemɪɡreɪt] *verb*
to leave your country to live in another; *my daughter and her family have emigrated to Australia*

④ **emission**
[ɪˈmɪʃn] *noun*
(a) process of sending out; *we are trying to reduce the emission of toxic gases from the power station* (NOTE: no plural in this meaning)
(b) substance which is sent out; *gas emissions can cause acid rain*

③ **emotion**
[ɪˈmoʊʃn] *noun*
strong feeling; *jealousy and love are two of the most powerful emotions*; *he tried to hide his emotions when he made his speech*

③ **emotional**
[ɪˈmoʊʃənl] *adjective*
which shows emotion; *we said an emotional farewell to our son and his family*; *the music made her feel very emotional and she started to cry*

③ **emperor**
[ˈemprər] *noun*
ruler of an empire; *Napoleon declared himself emperor*; *the Chinese emperors lived in the Forbidden City*

④ **emphasis**
[ˈemfəsɪs] *noun*
(a) showing the importance of something, usually in speech; *don't put too much emphasis on his age*; *she banged the table for emphasis as she spoke*
(b) strength of your voice when you pronounce a word or phrase; *everyone noticed the emphasis he put on the word "peace"* (NOTE: plural is **emphases**)

④ **emphasize**
[ˈemfəsaɪz] *verb*
to show that you feel something is important, by saying it more loudly, slowly, etc.; *please emphasize that the meeting must start on time*; *he emphasized the importance of everyone working together*; *she kept on emphasizing the same point over and over again*

② **empire**
[ˈempaɪər] *noun*
several separate territories ruled by a central government; *we're studying the history of the British Empire*; *Russia's empire covered a huge area from the Pacific Ocean to the middle of Europe*

② **employ**
[ɪmˈplɔɪ] *verb*
(a) to give someone regular paid work; *he is employed as a gardener by the city*; *she is employed in the automobile industry*
(b) *(formal)* to use; *if we were to employ more up-to-date methods, would we make more money?*; *how can we best employ our free time on Sunday?*

② **employee**
[emplɔɪˈiː] *noun*
person who is employed; *the company has decided to take on twenty new employees*

③ **employer**
[ɪmˈplɔɪər] *noun*
person or organization that gives work to people and pays them; *her employer was a Hong Kong businessman*; *the automobile factory is the biggest employer in the area*

③ **employment**
[ɪmˈplɔɪmənt] *noun*
regular paid work; *everyone in paid employment has to pay tax*; **full-time employment** = work for all of a working day; *he is looking for full-time employment*; **part-time employment** = work for part of a working day; *she is in part-time employment*; **seasonal employment** = work that is available at certain times of the year only (such as in a ski resort); **temporary employment** = work that does not last for more than a few months; **contract of employment** *or* **employment contract** =

contract between management and an employee showing all the conditions of work; **employment agency** = office that finds jobs for people

① **empty**
['emtı]
1 *adjective*
with nothing inside; *when we opened it, the box was empty*; *take an empty pot and fill it with soil*; *the fridge is empty - we'll have to go out to eat*; *the ski resorts are empty because there is no snow* (NOTE: **emptier - emptiest**)
2 *noun*
something, usually a bottle, that has nothing in it; *you can take the empties back to the store* (NOTE: plural is **empties**)
3 *verb*
to make something empty; *she emptied the clothes out of the suitcase*; *he emptied the bottle into the sink*; *they emptied the contents of the cash register into a bag*

④ **enable**
[ı'neıbl] *verb*
(formal) to make it possible for someone to do something; *the dictionary should enable you to understand English better*

④ **enact**
[ı'nækt] *verb*
(formal) to make a law; *once a bill has been enacted, it becomes law*

④ **encircle**
[ın'sɜrkl] *verb*
to surround completely; *she was encircled by journalists*

② **enclose**
[ıŋ'kləuz] *verb*
(a) to put something inside an envelope with a letter; *I am enclosing a copy of our current catalog*; *please find your tickets enclosed with this letter*
(b) to put a wall or fence around an area of land; *the yard is enclosed with high brick walls*

④ **encompass**
[ın'kʌmpəs] *verb (formal)*
(a) to include; *my talk will encompass all aspects of Shakespeare's plays*
(b) to surround; *a flower garden encompassed by high walls*

④ **encounter**
[ın'kauntər]
1 *noun*
(a) meeting; *I had an unexpected encounter with my former boss at the Chicago Book Fair*; *she told him about her encounter with the cows*
(b) short fight; *the encounter only lasted a few minutes, but it seemed longer to the soldiers taking part*
2 *verb*
to meet; *on the journey we encountered several amusing people*; *I have never encountered such jealousy in anyone else*

② **encourage**
[ın'kʌrıdʒ] *verb*
(a) to make it easier for something to happen; *leaving your credit cards on your desk encourages people to steal* or *encourages stealing*
(b) to help someone to do something by giving them confidence; *he encouraged me to apply for the job*; *I always felt encouraged by his interest in what I was doing*

② **encouragement**
[ın'kʌrıdʒmənt] *noun*
giving someone the confidence to do something; *a few words of encouragement and everyone will work better*; *all he needs is a little encouragement and he will do really well*

② **encouraging**
[ın'kʌrıdʒıŋ] *adjective*
which encourages; *the math teacher was very encouraging*; *it's an encouraging sign that so many students have applied to take the course*

① **end**
[end]
1 *noun*
(a) last part of something; *she tied the two ends of the ribbon together*; *the telephone rang and I missed the end of the TV program*; *go down to the end of the road and then make a right*; **in the end** = finally, at last; *in the end the teacher let him go home*; *in the end the store had to call in the police*; **on end** = with no breaks; *he worked for hours on end*; **to come to an end** = to be finished; *the work should come to an end next month*; **to be at loose ends** = to have nothing to do; *I was at loose ends so I decided to go to the movie theater*; **to make ends meet** = to have enough money to live on; *after paying taxes, we can just make ends meet*
(b) final part of a period of time; *can you wait until the end of the week?*; **year-end accounts** = accounts prepared at the end of a financial year
(c) aim, result intended; **the end justifies the means** = if your final aim is good or honorable, you are right to do anything that is necessary to achieve it
2 *verb*
to be finished, to come to an end; *the movie ends with a wedding*; *the meeting ended with everyone fighting on the floor*; *the concert should end at about 10 o'clock*; *the game ended in a draw*

② **endanger**
[ın'deındʒər] *verb*
to put in danger; *pollution from the factory is endangering the fish in the lake*; **endangered species** = any species at risk of becoming extinct; *this little spider is an endangered species*

① **ending**
['endıŋ] *noun*
the way a story, film, etc., finishes; *I like films which have happy endings*

① **endless**
['endləs] *adjective*
with no apparent end; *the afternoon seemed endless, with one boring speech after another*; *we had an endless string of meetings with our suppliers*

③ **endorse**
[ɪn'dɔrs] *verb*
(a) to officially mark or sign the back of a document; **to endorse a check** = to sign a check on the back to show that you accept it; *the bank clerk asked him to endorse the check before depositing it*
(b) to show approval of; *I endorse what has just been said*; *they asked us to endorse Mrs. Martin as the local candidate*

④ **end up**
['end 'ʌp] *verb*
to finish; *we ended up with a bill for $15,000*; *after the movie we all ended up at my girlfriend's apartment*; *they went to several clubs, and ended up getting arrested by the police in downtown San Francisco*

③ **endure**
[ɪn'djuər] *verb*
(a) to bear; *the prisoners had to endure great hardship*; *the pain was more than she could endure*
(b) *(formal)* to last; *the memory of that day will endure forever in my mind*

② **enemy**
['enəmi] *noun*
(a) person who hates you; *did your husband have many enemies?*
(b) country or people fighting against you in a war; *they attacked enemy targets with bombs*; *the enemy has or have advanced to two miles from the city* (NOTE: plural is **enemies**, but in meaning (b) **enemy** can take a singular or plural verb)

③ **energetic**
[enər'dʒetɪk] *adjective*
active and lively; *at 82, my grandmother is still astonishingly energetic*; *she's an energetic campaigner for animal rights*

② **energy**
['enərdʒi] *noun*
(a) force or strength of a person; *he used up a lot of energy rushing around doing the Christmas shopping*
(b) power that makes something work; *the use of atomic energy or nuclear energy to make electricity*; *we try to save energy by switching off the lights when we aren't using the rooms*; *if you reduce the room temperature to sixty-eight degrees, you will save energy*; *electric buses are an energy-efficient method of public transportation*

③ **enforce**
[ɪn'fɔrs] *verb*
to make sure a rule is obeyed; *the police are there to enforce the law; this is a regulation that is very difficult to enforce*

③ **enforcement**
[ɪn'fɔrsmənt] *noun*
act of enforcing a rule; *the enforcement agency is looking for such things as drugs or alcohol*

② **engage**
[ɪn'geɪdʒ] *verb*
(a) to obtain the services of someone; *we have engaged a caterer for my daughter's party*
(b) to make parts of a machine fit into each other; *the gears aren't properly engaged*; **to engage a low gear** = to put your automobile into a low gear
(c) to be engaged in = to be busy with; *the whole family was engaged in cleaning the motor home*; *the general is engaged in important negotiations*

② **engaged**
[ɪn'geɪdʒd] *adjective*
(a) having officially stated your intention to marry; *she was engaged to Tom and then broke it off*; *John and Sue are engaged: they got engaged last week*
(b) busy, occupied; *you can't speak to the manager - she's otherwise engaged*

② **engagement**
[ɪn'geɪdʒmənt] *noun*
(a) statement that you intend to get married; *my son has announced his engagement to Pam*; *their engagement was announced in the local paper*; **engagement ring** = ring given by a man to a woman at their engagement
(b) appointment; *I have no engagements for the rest of the day*; *she noted the appointment in her engagements diary*; *I can't meet you tonight - I have a prior engagement*
(c) agreement to do something; **to break an engagement to do something** = not to do what you have legally agreed to do

① **engine**
['endʒɪn] *noun*
(a) machine that powers or drives something; *the elevator engine has broken down again - we shall just have to walk up to the 4th floor*; *early industrial equipment was powered by steam engines*
(b) vehicle that pulls a train; *the engine broke down and the train was stuck in the tunnel* (NOTE: also called a **locomotive**)

① **engineer**
[endʒɪ'niər]
1 *noun*
(a) person who looks after technical equipment, especially engines; *there are comparatively few women telephone engineers*; *the photocopier's broken down again - we'll have to call the engineer*
(b) person whose profession is designing mechanical, electrical or industrial equipment; **civil engineer** = person who specializes in the construction of roads, bridges, etc.

(c) person who drives an engine that pulls a train
2 *verb*
to arrange something secretly; *she engineered the dismissal of her husband's secretary*

③ **engineering**
[endʒɪ'nɪərɪŋ] *noun*
science or study of the design of technical equipment; *the college offers courses in electrical engineering*; civil engineering = science of building, especially of roads, bridges, etc. (NOTE: no plural)

① **England**
['ɪŋlənd] *noun*
country in the southern part of the island of Great Britain, the largest country in the United Kingdom; *how long does it take to cross from England to France?*; *our cousins live in England* (NOTE: the word **England** is often used instead of Britain, and this is a mistake, as England is only one part of Great Britain; note also the capital: **London**; people: **the English**; language: **English**; currency: **pound sterling**)

① **English**
['ɪŋlɪʃ]
1 *adjective*
(a) referring to England; *the beautiful English countryside*; *is the English weather really as bad as it is made out to be?*; *I think she is English although she speaks with an Australian accent*
(b) English breakfast = cooked breakfast with bacon, eggs, sausages, etc.; *compare* CONTINENTAL BREAKFAST; the English Channel = the sea between England and France; *the boat only takes 50 minutes to cross the English Channel* (NOTE: the word **English** is often used instead of British, and this is a mistake, as England is only one part of Great Britain; do not say **the English Prime Minister** but **the British Prime Minister**)
2 *noun*
(a) language of the United Kingdom, the U.S.A., Australia, and many other countries; *can she speak English?*; *what's the English word for "Autobahn"?*; *English is not my first language*; *we managed to make ourselves understood, even though no one in the hotel spoke English*; *several of her books have been translated into English*
(b) English language as a subject taught in school or college; *she's good at math but not so good at English*; *as well as teaching English, he also teaches drama*; *Mr. Smith is our English teacher*; *she gives English lessons at home in the evenings*; *there are twenty students in my English class*
(c) the English = the people of England; *the English on the whole are not a very emotional people*

COMMENT: English is spoken as a first language by 415 million people worldwide,

and by a further 800 million people as a second language. It was originally a German type of language, derived from the language of the Angles and Saxons who invaded England in the 4th century AD. However, over the centuries it has borrowed heavily from Latin, French and many other languages, and is nowadays a highly mixed language

③ **Englishman, Englishwoman**
['ɪŋlɪʃmən or 'ɪŋlɪʃwʊmən] *noun*
person from England; *"an Englishman's home is his castle"*; *a group of young Englishwomen were helping in the relief effort in Africa* (NOTE: plural is **Englishmen, Englishwomen**)

④ **enhance**
[ɪn'hæns] *verb*
(a) to increase the beauty or value of something; *her makeup enhanced the beauty of her dark brown eyes*
(b) to increase the value or power of something; *slot in this new memory board to enhance your computer memory*; *he took drugs to enhance his performance as a runner*

① **enjoy**
[ɪn'dʒɔɪ] *verb*
to take pleasure in something; *have you enjoyed your vacation so far?*; *when he asked them if they had enjoyed the movie they all answered "no"*; *she didn't enjoy the boat trip because she felt seasick all the time*; to enjoy yourself = to have a good time; *is everyone enjoying themselves?*; *we enjoyed ourselves so much that we're going to the same place for our vacation next year*

② **enjoyable**
[ɪn'dʒɔɪəbl] *adjective*
which pleases; *did you have a good vacation? - yes, thank you, it was most enjoyable*; *we spent an enjoyable evening playing cards*

③ **enjoyment**
[ɪn'dʒɔɪmənt] *noun*
pleasure; *the man next to me had a cough and this spoiled my enjoyment of the concert*

① **enlarge**
[ɪn'lɑrdʒ] *verb*
(a) to make a bigger photograph; *I like this photo best: I'll get it enlarged*
(b) to make bigger; *we could enlarge the vegetable garden and grow more potatoes*
(c) *(formal)* to enlarge on *or* upon = to give details of; *even though we asked him twice, he refused to enlarge upon his meeting with the principal*

② **enlist**
['enlɪst] *verb*
(a) to join the armed forces; *he left school and enlisted as a soldier for five years*
(b) to enlist someone's help = to get help from someone; *we enlisted our neighbor's help to cut down the tree*

② **enormous**
[ɪˈnɔrməs] *adjective*
very large; *their dining room is absolutely enormous*; *he ate an enormous lunch*

③ **enormously**
[ɪˈnɔrməsli] *adverb*
very much; *his refusal upset her enormously*; *we were enormously relieved to see her again*; *thefts in supermarkets have increased enormously*

① **enough**
[ɪˈnʌf]
1 *adjective*
as much as is needed; *do you have enough money for your fare or to pay your fare?*; *there isn't enough light to take photographs*
2 *pronoun*
as much of something as is needed; *I had $30 in my purse to pay the taxi, but it wasn't enough*; *have you all had enough to eat?*
3 *adverb*
as much as is needed; *this box isn't big enough for all these books*; *he doesn't work fast enough and so gets behind the others*

② **enquire** *or* **enquiry**
[ɪnˈkwaɪər *or* ɪnˈkwaɪri]
see INQUIRE, INQUIRY

④ **enrich**
[ɪnˈrɪtʃ] *verb*
(a) to make richer, better; *learning French has enriched his life*
(b) to benefit, to make more fertile; *some crops, such as beans, enrich the soil*

③ **en suite**
[ˈɒn ˈswit] *adjective*
attached to another room; *bedroom with an en suite shower room*; *is the bathroom en suite?*

② **ensure**
[ɪnˈʃʊər] *verb*
to make sure of; *when taking a shower, please ensure that the shower curtain is inside the bath* (NOTE: do not confuse with **insure**)

① **enter**
[ˈentər]
1 *verb*
(a) to go in, to come in; *he took off his hat as he entered the church*; *did they stamp your passport when you entered the country?*
(b) to write something in a record; *to enter a name on a list*
(c) to type information on a keyboard, and put it into a computer system; *we will just enter your name and address on the computer*
(d) to enter into = to begin; *to enter into negotiations with a company*; *to enter into an agreement or a contract*; *see also* COMMUNICATION, ENTRANCE, ENTRY
2 *noun*
key on a keyboard that you press when you have finished keying something, or when you want to start a new line; *to change directory, type cd and press ENTER*

④ **enterprise**
[ˈentəpraɪz] *noun*
(a) business venture, especially something that involves some risk; *his latest enterprise is importing carpets from Turkey*
(b) method of organizing business; *the state should not interfere with free enterprise*; **private enterprise** = all businesses that are not owned by the state
(c) commercial firm, business organization; *they have merged with another huge industrial enterprise*

③ **entertain**
[entəˈteɪn] *verb*
(a) to amuse; *he entertained us with stories of his life in the army*; *we hired a funny man to entertain the children*; *the tourists were entertained by the local dancers*
(b) to offer meals, accommodation, a visit to the theater, etc., to a visitor; *they're entertaining some Canadian friends this evening*
(c) *(formal)* to be ready to consider a proposal; *they said they would entertain any suggestions we might like to make*

③ **entertaining**
[entəˈteɪnɪŋ] *adjective*
amusing; *he gave a very entertaining talk about his life in Lebanon*

② **entertainment**
[entəˈteɪnmənt] *noun*
(a) amusement; *she sang for their entertainment*; *there's not much entertainment around here - the nearest movie theater is 20 miles away*
(b) offering someone meals, visits to the theater, etc.; *the entertainment of our visitors from Mexico cost us a fortune*; **entertainment allowance** = allowance given to a businessman for entertaining guests

② **enthusiasm**
[ɪnˈθjuziæzəm] *noun*
great interest and liking; *we succeeded thanks to the enthusiasm and hard work of a small group of members*; *she showed a lot of enthusiasm for our new project*

③ **enthusiastic**
[ɪnθjuziˈæstɪk] *adjective*
showing great interest and approval; *the editor was very enthusiastic about my book*; *there were enthusiastic cheers at the end of the performance*

② **entire**
[ɪnˈtaɪər] *adjective*
whole; *we spent the entire day gardening*; *the entire cast came on the stage and bowed to the audience*

④ **entirely**
[ɪnˈtaɪəli] *adverb*
completely; *I agree with you entirely*; *this is an entirely separate problem*

③ **entitle**
[ɪnˈtaɪtl] *verb*
(a) to give the right to; *I am entitled to two weeks' vacation a year*
(b) to give a title to; *Tolstoy wrote a book entitled "War and Peace"*

② **entrance**
1 [ˈentrəns] *noun*
(a) door for going in; *she was sitting at the entrance to the museum*; *we will meet at the Main Street entrance of the department store*; **back entrance** = back doorway; **main entrance** = main doorway; *the cab will drop you at the main entrance*
(b) **entrance (charge)** *or* **entrance fee** = money that you have to pay to go in; *entrance is $10 for adults and $7.50 for children*
2 [ɪnˈtræns] *verb*
to make someone very happy; *the audience was entranced by his singing*

④ **entrepreneur**
[ɒntrəprəˈnɜr] *noun*
person who directs a company and takes risks commercially; *the company was bought by a couple of young entrepreneurs*

② **entry**
[ˈentri] *noun*
(a) going in; *the sign on the door said "no entry"*; **entry charge** *or* **entry fee** = price to be paid before going into an exhibition, etc.; *the entry charge is $8* (NOTE: no plural in this sense)
(b) written information in a reference book, an accounting or computer system; *she looked up the entry on "roses" in the gardening book*; **to make an entry in something** = to write details in a book; *the police looked at the entries in the hotel's register* (NOTE: plural is **entries**)

① **envelope**
[ˈenvəloʊp] *noun*
folded paper cover for sending letters; *she wrote the address on the envelope and sealed it*; *the storekeeper wrote down all the information on the back of an envelope*; **airmail envelope** = very light envelope for airmail letters; **self-addressed stamped envelope** = an envelope with your own address written on it and a stamp stuck on it to pay for return postage; *please send a self-addressed stamped envelope for further details and our latest catalog*

④ **envious**
[ˈenviəs] *adjective*
feeling or showing envy; *we're all envious of his new car*

③ **environment**
[ɪnˈvaɪərənmənt] *noun*
(a) the earth, its natural features and resources, seen as the place where man lives; *they are trying to protect the environment*
(b) surroundings in which any organism lives, but especially where people live; *the environment in the office is not good for concentrated work*; **working environment** = the general surroundings in which a person works

③ **environmental**
[ɪnvaɪərənˈmentl] *adjective*
referring to the environment; *measures taken to protect against environmental pollution*; *she's joined an environmental group*; **environmental protection** = act of protecting the environment against pollution

④ **environmentalist**
[ɪnvaɪərənˈmentlɪst] *noun*
person who is concerned with protecting the environment; *a group of environmentalists is trying to prevent the trees being cut down*; *environmentalists want to ban the dumping of waste in the sea*

④ **envisage** *or* **envision**
[enˈvɪzɪʒ or enˈvɪʒn] *verb*
to picture to yourself; *somehow, I can't envision him as a doctor*

③ **envy**
[ˈenvi]
1 *noun*
feeling that you would like to have something which someone else has; *her beautiful long blond hair filled us all with envy*
2 *verb*
to feel you would like to be someone else; *I don't envy him with a job like the one he has*; **to envy someone something** = to want to have something that someone else has; *we all envy him his new sports car*

③ **epidemic**
[epɪˈdemɪk] *noun*
infectious disease which spreads quickly through a large number of people; *the authorities are taking steps to prevent an epidemic of influenza or a flu epidemic*; *the disease rapidly reached epidemic proportions*

④ **episode**
[ˈepɪsoʊd] *noun*
(a) short section of a longer story, one part of a TV series; *do you remember the episode where the ghost appears?*; *the hero's father gets out of prison in the third episode*
(b) short period of your life; *it's an episode in his marriage that he would rather forget*

① **equal**
[ˈikwəl]
1 *adjective*
with exactly the same amount as; *his share is equal to mine*; *male and female workers must have equal pay*; *the two sticks are of equal length or are equal in length*; **all things being equal** = assuming nothing else has changed; *all things being equal, I'd prefer to go on vacation in June*; **to be equal to the task** = to be strong enough or brave enough to do something; *he was put in charge of the prison, but was quickly found not to be equal to the task*; **equal opportunity** = employing people on their

merits, treating them with equal respect, regardless of age, race, sex, etc.

2 *verb*

(a) to be exactly the same as; *his time for the 100 meters equals the existing record*

(b) to give a result; *two plus two equals four*; *ten take away four equals six*

3 *noun*

person who is on the same level as someone else; *I don't consider him your equal*; *we're all equals here*

> COMMENT: many businesses and organizations in the U.S.A. operate a policy of **equal opportunity**, that is, they employ people on their merits and treat them with equal respect, regardless of age, race, sex, disability, etc. (**equal opportunity employer**)

③ **equality**
[ɪˈkwɒlɪti] *noun*

situation where you are equal; *the company has policies to ensure equality in the factory*; **equality of opportunity** = situation where everyone, regardless of sex, race, class, etc., has the same opportunity to get a job; *our education policy is designed to promote equality of opportunity* (NOTE: no plural)

① **equally**
[ˈikwəli] *adverb*

in exactly the same way; *they are all equally guilty*; *here men and women are paid equally badly*; *they were both equally responsible for the mistake*

④ **equation**
[ɪˈkweɪʒn] *noun*

(a) formula in mathematics or science showing that two parts are equal; *let me show you how this equation can be solved*; *he drew up the equation for converting mass to energy*

(b) balancing of various factors in a situation; *making a profit is difficult enough, but when higher interest rates are brought into the equation it becomes impossible*

② **equator**
[ɪˈkweɪtər] *noun*

imaginary line running round the Earth halfway between the North and South Poles; *Quito, the capital of Ecuador, lies very close to the equator*

② **equip**
[ɪˈkwɪp] *verb*

to equip someone *or* **something with something** = to provide someone or something with something; *an apartment equipped with a washing machine and dishwasher*; **well-equipped** = with all necessary equipment; *a well-equipped hospital*; *the hotel has a fully-equipped sports center* (NOTE: equipping - equipped)

② **equipment**
[ɪˈkwɪpmənt] *noun*

all the tools, arms, machinery, etc., that are needed; *he brought all his camera equipment with him*; *do you really need all this safety equipment on a ship?* (NOTE: no plural: for one item say **a piece of equipment**)

④ **equity**
[ˈekwɪti] *noun*

(a) fair system of justice; *she complained about the lack of equity in the company's pay structure*; **in equity** = being fair (NOTE: no plural in this meaning)

(b) value of a property, after any money owed on it has been deducted; *the equity of my home has risen over the last four years*

③ **equivalent**
[ɪˈkwɪvələnt]

1 *noun*

thing which has the same value or the same strength as something else; *what is the British equivalent of the Secretary of the Treasury?*; *I gave him $2000 and he paid me the equivalent in Mexican pesos*

2 *adjective*

having the same value or the same strength as something else; *two pints and a liter are roughly equivalent*; *she handed me the equivalent amount in Swiss francs*; **to be equivalent to** = to have the same value as, to be the same as; *a liter is roughly equivalent to two pints*

④ **era**
[ˈɪrə] *noun*

long period of history; *the colonial era*

② **erase**
[ɪˈreɪz] *verb*

to rub out writing or to remove recorded material from a tape or data from a disk; *he erased the pencil marks*; *I've erased your recording of the concert by mistake*

② **eraser**
[ɪˈreɪzər] *noun*

piece of rubber for removing writing in pencil; *he used an eraser to try to take out what he had written*

③ **erect**
[ɪˈrekt]

1 *adjective*

straight upright; *she held herself erect as she walked into the courtroom*

2 *verb*

to put up something vertical, such as a street light or a building; *they are planning to erect a monument to the princess*; *civilians rushed to hide in hastily erected bomb shelters*

④ **erode**
[ɪˈroʊd] *verb*

to wear away gradually; *the cliffs have been eroded by the sea*

④ **erotic**
[ɪˈrɒtɪk] *adjective*
strongly sexual; *she paints erotic pictures of naked men and women*

④ **erratic**
[ɪˈrætɪk] *adjective*
irregular or wild; *his erratic behavior made his neighbors suspicious; her work was erratic*

③ **error**
[ˈerər] *noun*
mistake; *the waiter made an error in calculating the total; she must have made a typing error; there isn't a single error in the whole document; I must have made an error because the screen went blank;* **computer error** = mistake made by a computer; **in error** = by mistake; *the package was sent to our Trenton office in error*

③ **erupt**
[ɪˈrʌpt] *verb*
(a) *(of volcano)* to throw out red hot rocks, ash, etc.; *the volcano last erupted in 1986*
(b) to start to become violent suddenly; *a row erupted over the closing of the train station*
(c) *(of person)* to become suddenly angry; *he listened to the discussion for a while and then erupted angrily*

③ **eruption**
[ɪˈrʌpʃn] *noun*
(of volcano) throwing out red hot rocks, ash, etc.; *several towns were destroyed in the volcanic eruption of 1978*

④ **escalate**
[ˈeskəleɪt] *verb*
(a) to get worse or more violent; *our financial problems have escalated; the border conflict escalated into an full-scale war*
(b) to increase steadily; *prices escalated during the year*

② **escalator**
[ˈeskəleɪtər] *noun*
moving stairs; *they played a game, trying to run down the up escalator; one of the escalators at the subway station is being repaired*

① **escape**
[ɪˈskeɪp]
1 *noun*
(a) action of getting away from prison or from an awkward situation; *there were three escapes from this jail last year; a weekend by the sea was a wonderful escape from the office;* **we had a narrow escape** = we were almost killed
(b) ESCAPE key (ESC) = key that stops what is happening on a computer and returns to the main program; *press ESCAPE to get back to the original screen*
2 *verb*
(a) to get away from prison or from an awkward situation; *he escaped from the prison by sawing through the bars; the police are looking for the escaped prisoners; a lion has escaped from the wildlife park*

(b) to miss; **the name of the restaurant escapes me** = I can't remember the name of the restaurant

② **escort**
1 *noun* [ˈeskɔrt]
person or group of people who are accompanying someone; *she wore red silk and her escort wore a dark suit; the president had a police escort to the airport*
2 *verb* [esˈkɔrt]
to accompany someone; *the police escorted the group into the hotel; I was escorted around by our camp counselor*

③ **especially**
[ɪˈspeʃəli] *adverb*
particularly, very; *her suitcase is especially heavy; do you want to go out? - not especially*

③ **essay**
[ˈeseɪ] *noun*
piece of writing on a particular subject; *a collection of the journalist's most famous essays; for our homework, we have to write an essay on pollution*

④ **essence**
[ˈesəns] *noun*
(a) central part of an argument; *the essence of what she had to say was very clear* (NOTE: no plural in this meaning)
(b) pure extract taken from something; *dessert flavored with essence of licorice*

③ **essential**
[ɪˈsenʃl]
1 *adjective*
which is very important or which you cannot do without; *the refugees lack essential winter clothing; you can survive without food for some time, but water is essential; it is essential that we get the delivery on time*
2 *noun*
thing which is very important or which you cannot do without; *sunscreen is an essential in Florida; we've got all the basic essentials - food, water and fuel;* **the bare essentials** = the absolute necessities of life

④ **essentially**
[ɪˈsenʃəli] *adverb*
basically, for the most part; *my new job is essentially not so very different from my old one; although he's essentially a kind man, he does lose his temper sometimes*

③ **establish**
[ɪˈstæblɪʃ] *verb*
(a) to create, to set up; *the business was established in New York in 1923; we need to establish a good working relationship with our colleagues*
(b) to show something to be true; *the police are trying to establish where the vehicle was parked that evening; it's difficult to establish what her reasons are for resigning*

③ **established**
[ɪˈstæblɪʃt] *adjective*
which has been shown to be true; *it is an established fact*

③ **establishment**
[ɪˈstæblɪʃmənt] *noun*
(a) creation, setting up; *she helped them with the establishment of the local drama society* (NOTE: no plural in this meaning)
(b) business; organization; *it's an establishment that imports radios from China*; *he runs an important teaching establishment*
(c) the Establishment = people who occupy influential positions in society or who are in authority; *they appointed several Establishment figures to the board of trustees of the museum*

② **estate**
[ɪˈsteɪt] *noun*
(a) large area of land belonging to one owner; *he owns a 250-acre estate in Illinois*
(b) real estate = property (land or buildings); real estate agent = person who sells houses, apartments, land for customers
(c) property owned by a person at the time of death; *the attorney announced the value of grandfather's estate*; the estate tax = the tax on property left by a dead person

④ **esteem**
[ɪˈstim] *noun*
(formal) respect; *the staff seem to have very little esteem for the managers*; to hold someone in (high) esteem = to respect someone; *she is someone whose work we hold in the highest esteem* (NOTE: no plural)

③ **estimate**
1 *noun* [ˈestɪmət]
(a) calculation that shows the approximate amount of something, or its worth or cost; *I wasn't in when the man came to read the electric meter, so this bill is only an estimate*; *your estimate of two dozen visitors proved to be correct*; *can you give me an estimate of how much time was spent on the job?*; rough estimate = approximate calculation
(b) price quoted by a supplier for work to be done; *three firms put in estimates for the job* (NOTE: often simply called a **quote**)
2 *verb* [ˈestɪmeɪt]
(a) to calculate approximately the cost or worth, etc., of something; *I estimate that it will cost $150,000*; *he estimated costs at $75,000*
(b) to calculate a price before supplying an item or doing a job; to estimate a job = to state in writing the probable costs of carrying out a job

② **etc.** *or* **etcetera**
[etˈsetərə]
Latin phrase meaning and so on, and other things like this; *fruit such as oranges, bananas, etc.*

③ **eternal**
[ɪˈtɜrnəl] *adjective*
which lasts for ever; *she is searching for eternal happiness*; *his eternal complaints really annoy me*

④ **ethic**
[ˈeθɪk] *noun*
good and moral behavior; work ethic = belief that working hard is the best way to live your life

④ **ethical**
[ˈeθɪkl] *adjective*
right, from a moral point of view; *is it ethical for the newspaper to publish the private phone numbers of government officials?*

④ **ethics**
[ˈeθɪks] *noun*
moral principles; *he doesn't care about the ethics of selling arms, provided he can make some money*

④ **ethnic**
[ˈeθnɪk] *adjective*
relating to race; *the census shows the ethnic makeup of the population*; ethnic food = food (such as Chinese or Indian food) from a particular country that is not European; ethnic minority = minority of the population which is of different racial origin to the majority

③ **EU**
[ˈiˈju]
= EUROPEAN UNION; *EU ministers met today in Brussels*; *the U.S.A. is increasing its trade with the EU*

② **euro**
[ˈjuərəu] *noun*
monetary unit of the EU; *many articles are priced in euros*; *what's the exchange rate for the euro?* (NOTE: written € before numbers: €250: say: "two hundred and fifty euros")

① **Europe**
[ˈjuərəp] *proper noun*
(a) the continent of Europe, the part of the world to the west of Asia, from Russia to Ireland; *most of the countries of Western Europe are members of the EU*; *Poland is in eastern Europe, and Greece, Spain and Portugal are in southern Europe*
(b) the European Union (including the UK); *Canadian exports to Europe have risen by 25%*

① **European**
[juərəˈpiən] *adjective*
referring to Europe; *they do business with several European countries*; *at home we always eat Asian food, not European*; the European Parliament = the parliament with members from each country of the EU

③ **European Union (EU)**
[juərəˈpiən ˈjuniən] *noun*
an organization that links several European countries together based on the four freedoms of movement: movement of goods, of capital, of people and of services

④ **evaluate**
[ɪ'væljʊeɪt] *verb*
(formal) to calculate the value of; *I'm trying to evaluate how useful our visit was*; *the teacher's performance in the classroom will be carefully evaluated*

④ **evaluation**
[ɪvælju'eɪʃn] *noun*
(formal) act of calculating a value; *I agreed with everything he said in his evaluation of the problem*; *the inspectors will carry out a careful evaluation of the teacher's performance* (NOTE: no plural)

① **evaporate**
[ɪ'væpəreɪt] *verb*
(of liquid) to be changed into gas; *water gradually evaporates from the soil*

② **eve**
[iv] *noun*
(a) the night or day before; *on the eve of the election the candidates prepared to celebrate*; **Christmas Eve** = December 24; **New Year's Eve** = December 31
(b) a short time before; **on the eve of our departure** = just before we left

① **even**
['ivn]
1 *adjective*
(a) even numbers = numbers that can be divided by 2; *on the right-hand side of the street all the houses have even numbers*
(b) equal (in a competition); *at the end of the competition three teams were even with 96 points*
(c) flat, level; *the road has a smooth even surface*
(d) which does not change; *they kept up an even pace for miles*; *the temperature is an even 85° all through the day*
(e) to break even = to make no profit, but no loss either; *the company is just breaking even*
2 *adverb*
(showing surprise or making an expression stronger) *he doesn't even like strawberries*; *even the cleverest businesspeople can make mistakes*; *she's fat, but her sister is even fatter*; **even now** = at this very moment; *even now, he won't admit he was wrong*; **even worse** = worse than before; *that movie was bad, but this one is even worse*

◇ **even if**
['ivn 'ɪf] *conjunction*
it doesn't matter if; *we'll try and drive there, even if it's snowing*

◇ **even so**
['ivn 'səʊ] *adverb*
in spite of what has happened; *it was pouring, but even so they decided to go ahead with the county fair*

◇ **even though**
['ivn 'ðəʊ] *conjunction*

although, in spite of the fact that; *he didn't take an umbrella, even though it was raining quite hard*

① **evening**
['ivnɪŋ] *noun*
(a) late part of the day, when it is getting dark; *I saw her yesterday evening*; *the accident took place at 8:30 in the evening*; *we arrived in London at breakfast time, having left New York the previous evening*; *we always go to a restaurant on Sunday evenings*; *they took an evening flight to Seattle*; *the evening meal is served from 7:30 to 10:30*; **this evening** = today in the evening; *we'll all meet this evening after work*
(b) evening dress = clothes worn at formal occasions in the evening

② **event**
[ɪ'vent] *noun*
(a) thing which happens; *the events leading up to the war*; *a baby's first birthday is always a happy event*
(b) in the event of = if something should happen; *in the event of his refusing the job then we will advertise it again*; **in any event** = whatever may happen; *I don't know exactly what happened - in any event it doesn't matter*; *even if he doesn't like the job, in any event he's very well paid*; **in the normal course of events** = as things usually happen; *in the normal course of events, the winner should get a silver cup*
(c) sporting competition; *the last event was the 100 meters hurdles*; **field events** = jumping and throwing competitions; **track events** = running races

④ **eventual**
[ɪ'ventjuəl] *adjective*
in the end; *his eventual aim is to become world champion*

④ **eventually**
[ɪ'ventjuəlɪ] *adverb*
in the end; *after weeks of hesitation he eventually decided to sell the cottage*

① **even up**
['ivn 'ʌp] *verb*
to make something balanced; *we've invited three girls and six boys, so we must invite three more girls to even things up*

① **ever**
['evər] *adverb*
(a) *(used with negatives, questions)* at any time; *nothing ever happens here*; *did you ever meet my brother?*; *have you ever been to North Dakota?*; **hardly ever** = almost never; *I hardly ever go to the theater*
(b) *(for emphasis after comparatives)* *she is singing better than ever*; *he went on playing the drums louder than ever*
(c) always; *ever the optimist, he suggested we try once again*; **ever since** *or* **ever since then** = from that time on; *she was knocked down by an*

automobile and ever since has been afraid to go out onto the main road; *see also* HOWEVER, WHATEVER, WHENEVER, WHEREVER, WHOEVER

② **evergreen**
['evəgriːn] *noun*
tree which keeps its leaves all winter; *holly and other evergreens can be used as decorations in winter*

① **every**
['evri] *adjective*
(a) each; *it rained every day during our vacation*; *we have a party every New Year's Day*; *every Wednesday, he goes for a swim in the local swimming pool*; *every house on the street has a garden*
(b) *(showing regular periods of time or distance)* **every two hours** = with a period of two hours in between; *the medicine is to be taken every four hours*; *have your automobile checked every 10,000 miles*; **every other day** = on one day, not on the next, but on the one after that (e.g. on Monday, Wednesday and Friday, etc.)

① **everybody** *or* **everyone**
['evribɒdi or 'evriwʌn] *pronoun*
all people, or all people involved in a particular situation; *everyone has to die some day*; *if everybody is here, we can start*; *I sent a Christmas card to everybody at work*; *everyone must show their passport* (NOTE: **everybody** and **everyone** are followed by **they, their, themselves,** etc., but the verb stays singular: **is everybody enjoying themselves?** not **everybody likes pop music, do they?**)

① **everyone**
['evriwʌn] *pronoun*
see EVERYBODY

④ **everyplace**
['evripleis] *adverb*
everywhere, in all places; *we looked everyplace for that key*

① **everything**
['evriθɪŋ] *pronoun*
(a) all things; *did you bring everything you need?*; *the burglars stole everything of value*; *everything he says annoys me*
(b) things in general; *everything was dark on the street*; *everything is under control*

① **everywhere**
['evriweər] *adverb*
in all places; *there were papers lying about everywhere*; *everywhere was white after the first snow fell*; *we've looked everywhere for the key and can't find it*

② **evidence**
['evidəns] *noun*
(a) fact which indicates that something really exists or has happened; *the spots of blood on his coat were evidence of the crime*; *scientists are looking for evidence of life on Mars*; *there is no evidence that he was ever there*; **documentary evidence** = evidence in the form of documents
(b) written or spoken report given by a witness at a trial; *the victim gave evidence in court this morning*; **to give evidence for someone** = to be a witness, and suggest that someone is not guilty; **to give evidence against someone** = to be a witness, and suggest that someone is guilty; **to turn state's evidence** = to give information against criminals who worked with you; *he hoped to get a reduced sentence by turning state's evidence*
(c) **in evidence** = very visible; *her love of Italy was nowhere more in evidence than in her kitchen* (NOTE: no plural)

④ **evident**
['evidənt] *adjective*
obvious; *his disgust was evident in his tone of voice*; *her evident delight at Tom's arrival*; *it was quite evident that they didn't want to sign the agreement*

① **evil**
['iːvl]
1 *adjective*
very wicked; *she's an evil old woman*; *his evil intentions were evident as soon as he locked the door*; **evil spirit** = wicked thing which harms people
2 *noun*
(a) very wicked acts; *the struggle between the government and the rebels was seen as a fight between good and evil* (NOTE: no plural in this meaning)
(b) bad thing; *we are committed to fighting social evils such as juvenile crime*; *see also* LESSER

④ **evolution**
[iːvə'luːʃn] *noun*
gradual development; *by a slow process of evolution, modern railway engines developed from Stephenson's "Rocket"*; **the theory of evolution** = theory, explained by Charles Darwin, that species develop by a process of natural selection; *see also* SURVIVAL OF THE FITTEST

④ **evolve**
[ɪ'vɒlv] *verb*
(a) to develop gradually; *modern dance evolved from classical ballet*; *birds originally evolved from little dinosaurs*
(b) to work out gradually a scientific theory or a way of working; *the research team has evolved its own methods of testing*

④ **ex-**
[eks]
prefix meaning who used to be; *Tom's my ex-boyfriend*

② **exact**
[ɪg'zækt]
1 *adjective*
completely accurate, not differing at all from what is expected, what has been written, etc.;

what is the exact time of arrival?; *could you repeat the exact words of the contract?*; *the girl asked me if I had the exact amount, since she had no change*

2 *verb*

(formal) **to exact something from someone** = to force someone to give something; *they stopped all vehicles on the road and exacted payment from the drivers*

① **exactly**

[ɪgˈzæktli] *adverb*

(a) not more, not less, not differing at all from an amount; *that comes to exactly ten dollars and fifty cents*; *the time is exactly 4:24 P.M.*

(b) completely; *he looks exactly like his father*

(c) *(used as an answer)* absolutely right, I agree; *it's a pity the buses don't run more frequently - exactly!*

◇ **not exactly**

[ˈnɒt ɪgˈzæktli] *phrase*

(a) not really; *was it a disaster? - not exactly a disaster, but it didn't go very well*; *it's not exactly the color I wanted*

(b) not at all; *he's not exactly pleased at having to pay out so much money*

② **exaggerate**

[ɪgˈzædʒəreɪt] *verb*

to make things seem worse, better, bigger, etc., than they really are; *the wide black belt exaggerates her small waist*; *she exaggerated the importance of my mistake*

② **exam**

[ɪgˈzæm] *noun*

= EXAMINATION; *the exam was very difficult - half the students failed*; *she passed all her exams*

② **examination**

[ɪgzæmɪˈneɪʃn] *noun*

(a) inspection of something to see if it works properly, or if something is wrong; *he had to have an X-ray and thorough examination*; *the examination of the automobile showed that its brakes were faulty*; **customs examination** = looking at goods or baggage by customs officials; **on examination** = when it was examined; *on further examination, the newspaper report was shown to be full of mistakes*

(b) written or spoken test; *the examination was very difficult - half the students failed*; *he did badly in his English examination*; *she came first in the final examination for the course* (NOTE: often shortened to **exam** in this meaning)

② **examine**

[ɪgˈzæmɪn] *verb*

(a) to inspect something to see if it is correct or healthy, that it works properly, etc.; *the doctor examined her throat*; *we will have to examine the store's scales to see if they give the correct weight*; *customs officials wanted to examine the inside of the truck*; *the water samples were examined by chemists*

(b) to test a student; *they examined everyone for mathematics and computer skills*

① **example**

[ɪgˈzæmpl] *noun*

(a) something chosen to show something; *this is a good example of French architecture of the seventeenth century*; **to set an example** = to do things yourself, so that other people can copy you; *he sets a good example by getting into the office before 8 every morning*; *she sets a bad example by talking for hours to her boyfriend on the phone*; **to make an example of someone** = to punish someone so that others will learn not to do what he did; *the magistrates made an example of him by sending him to prison for two weeks*

(b) **for example** = as a typical case; *she is keen on getting her weight down - for example, she's stopped eating bread*; *why don't we sell anything to Eastern Europe, to Poland for example?* (NOTE: **for example** can often be replaced by **e.g.**: countries in Eastern Europe, **e.g.** Poland)

③ **exceed**

[ɪkˈsid] *verb*

to go beyond; *the automobile was exceeding the speed limit*; *our expenses have exceeded our income for the first time*; *did the UN troops exceed their instructions?*

④ **exceedingly**

[ɪkˈsidɪŋli] *adverb*

very, extremely; *it is exceedingly difficult work*

② **excellent**

[ˈeksələnt] *adjective*

very good; *we had an excellent meal in a Mexican restaurant*; *her handwriting is excellent - it is much clearer than mine*

① **except**

[ɪkˈsept]

1 *preposition*

other than; *she's allowed to eat anything except milk products*; *everyone was sick on the boat, except (for) me*; *sales tax is generally levied by the state* (NOTE: do not confuse with **accept**)

2 *conjunction*

other than, apart from; *he doesn't do anything except sit and watch baseball on the TV*; *everything went well, except that James was sick*; *everyone enjoyed the birthday party, except (that) there wasn't enough to eat*

③ **exception**

[ɪkˈsepʃn] *noun*

(a) thing not included; *all the students failed, with one exception*; *are there any exceptions to the rule?*

(b) **to take exception to** = to be annoyed by something; *he took exception to what she said*

③ **exceptional**

[ɪkˈsepʃənəl] *adjective*

(a) outstanding, very good; *she's an exceptional runner*

(b) being an exception, not being included; *in exceptional cases, the entrance fee may be reduced*

④ **excerpt**
['eksɜrpt] *noun*
small part (of a larger piece of music or writing); *they played an excerpt from a Mozart symphony*; *he read excerpts from his latest novel*

③ **excess**
[ɪk'ses]
1 *noun*
(a) too much of something; *he had an excess of alcohol in his blood*; **in excess of** = more than; *quantities in excess of twenty-five pounds*; **to excess** = too much; *he drinks to excess* (NOTE: no plural in this meaning)
(b) **excesses** = bad things that you have done; *on Monday mornings he always feels guilty about the weekend's excesses*
2 ['ekses] *adjective*
too much, not needed; *the factory has excess capacity and may sell off some of its machines*; **excess baggage** = cases that weigh more than you are allowed when traveling by air, and for which you must pay extra

④ **excessive**
[ɪk'sesɪv] *adjective*
more than is usual; *the committee questioned the excessive cost of the wallpaper*

④ **excessively**
[ɪk'sesɪvli] *adverb*
too much; *the pattern of the curtains is excessively brilliant*; *she is excessively modest about her achievements*

② **exchange**
[ɪks'tʃeɪndʒ]
1 *noun*
(a) giving one thing for another; *the exchange of rings during the wedding ceremony*
(b) **foreign exchange** = changing money of different countries; **exchange rate** = rate at which one currency is exchanged for another; *the current rate of exchange is seven francs to the dollar*
(c) **telephone exchange** = central telephone switchboard, which organizes phone calls over a wide area; **stock exchange** = place where stocks and shares are bought and sold; *he works on the New York Stock Exchange*
2 *verb*
(a) to give something and get something similar back; *during the meeting we exchanged ideas on new developments in international law*; **they exchanged addresses** = they each gave the other their address
(b) **to exchange something for something else** = to give one thing and get another in return; *if the pants are too small, you can take them back and exchange them for a larger pair*; *goods can be exchanged only with proof of purchase*

(c) to change money of one country for money of another; *to exchange dollars for pounds*

② **excite**
[ɪk'saɪt] *verb*
(a) to make someone lively and happy; *his playing during the second half of the match excited the crowd*
(b) to make someone have a particular feeling; *the thought of going to work in Kuala Lumpur excited his imagination*; *the case has excited a lot of interest in the press*

② **excitement**
[ɪk'saɪtmənt] *noun*
being excited; *what's all the excitement about?*; *the kids are always in a state of excitement when we go on vacation*

② **exciting**
[ɪk'saɪtɪŋ] *adjective*
which gives you a particular feeling; *I couldn't sleep after watching an exciting movie on TV*; *the news about the house is really exciting*

③ **exclaim**
[ɪk'skleɪm] *verb*
to say something loudly and suddenly; *"here it is!" she exclaimed*

② **exclamation point** *or* **mark**
[eksklə'meɪʃn 'pɔɪnt] *noun*
written sign (!) which shows surprise; *she was obviously excited, her letter was full of exclamation points*

④ **exclude**
[ɪk'sklud] *verb*
(a) not to include; *damage by fire is excluded from the insurance policy*; *don't exclude his name from your list*
(b) **to exclude something** *or* **someone from a place** = to shut something or someone out; *small children are excluded from the club*

④ **exclusion**
[ɪk'skluʒn] *noun*
act of being shut out, of not being included; *the exclusion of some students from college* ; *see also* EXCLUDE

④ **exclusive**
[ɪk'sklusɪv] *adjective*
(a) open to selected rich customers, not open to everyone; *an exclusive ski resort*; *the new health club is very exclusive*
(b) **exclusive right** = right which belongs to one person or organization
(c) **exclusive of** = not including; *the bill was exclusive of service*; **exclusive of tax** = not including tax

④ **exclusively**
[ɪk'sklusɪvli] *adverb*
solely, only; *the parking lot is exclusively for the use of residents*

② **excuse**
1 *noun* [ɪkˈskjuːs]
reason given for doing something wrong or not as expected; *his excuse for not coming was that he forgot the date*
2 *verb* [ɪkˈskjuːz]
to forgive someone for making a small mistake; *please excuse my arriving late like this*

② **excuse me**
[ɪkˈskjuːz ˈmiː]
(a) *(to attract someone's attention) excuse me, how do I get to the bookstore?*
(b) please forgive me; *he said "Excuse me" when he bumped into her; excuse me for interrupting, but could you repeat what you have just said?*

② **execute**
[ˈeksɪkjuːt] *verb*
(a) to carry out instructions or wishes; *press ENTER to execute the program; they did their best to execute his orders*
(b) to do; *as part of the test, drivers are asked to execute an emergency stop*
(c) to kill someone who has been condemned to death; *murderers are no longer executed in this state*

③ **executive**
[ɪɡˈzekjʊtɪv]
1 *noun*
businessman who makes decisions; *you can't leave a decision like that to the junior executives; top executives usually earn very high salaries*
2 *adjective*
which carries out plans and puts things into practice; *he has an executive position on the board of directors*; **executive committee** = committee that runs an organization; **chief executive officer (CEO)** = main director who runs a company; **executive branch** = the part of government which runs the state (as opposed to the judges who apply the law, and the legislature which creates laws); *people are beginning to question the executive branch's ability to govern*

④ **exemplify**
[ɪɡˈzemplɪfaɪ] *verb*
to show as an example, to be an example; *his lack of concentration is exemplified by his poor goal scoring record*

④ **exempt**
[ɪɡˈzempt]
1 *adjective*
not forced to obey tax, laws, etc.; **exempt from tax** *or* **tax-exempt** = not required to pay tax; *drugs are exempt from sales tax; we all have to pay for medical prescriptions but senior citizens are exempt*
2 *verb*
to exempt someone from something *or* **from doing something** = to free someone from

something; *senior citizens are exempted from paying for most of their medical prescriptions*

④ **exemption**
[ɪɡˈzempʃn] *noun*
act of exempting; **exemption from tax** *or* **tax exemption** = being free from having to pay tax; *you can claim a tax exemption in this case*

② **exercise**
[ˈeksəsaɪz]
1 *noun*
practice in using physical or mental powers; *she does her piano exercises every morning*; **exercise book** = book for writing out school work; **to take exercise** = to do physical things, like walking or jogging, to keep fit; *you should do some exercise every day if you want to lose weight; exercise is good for the body and mind*
2 *verb*
(a) to use a power or right; *the U.S. exercised the right of veto*
(b) to give an animal or person exercise; *she exercised her pony on the racetrack; you must do something to exercise your stomach muscles*

③ **exhaust**
[ɪɡˈzɔːst]
1 *noun*
(a) gas that is produced by an automobile engine and is released into the air through the tailpipe; *we live downtown and the children are breathing automobile exhaust all day*
(b) tailpipe, the tube at the back of a motor vehicle from which gases produced by the engine are sent out into the air; *clouds of white smoke were coming out of the exhaust*
2 *verb*
(a) to wear out; *climbing the mountain had exhausted him*
(b) to finish; *we've exhausted our supplies of food*

③ **exhausted**
[ɪɡˈzɔːstɪd] *adjective*
tired out; *I'm exhausted after running three miles*

③ **exhaust fan**
[ɪɡˈzɔːst ˈfæn] *noun*
fan which sucks air out (as in a kitchen); *when you switch on the light in the bathroom, the exhaust fan comes on automatically*

② **exhibit**
[ɪɡˈzɪbɪt]
1 *verb*
to display; *the company is exhibiting at the Motor Show; she has rows of bowls exhibited on the shelves of her store; he is exhibiting three paintings in the local art show*
2 *noun*
object displayed in court, at an exhibition, etc.; *Exhibit A is the murder weapon; the museum has several exhibits that relate to local history*

③ **exhibition**
['eksɪ'bɪʃn] *noun*

(a) display (of works of art, flowers, etc.); *the exhibition is open from 10 A.M. to 5 P.M.*; *opening time for the exhibition is 10 A.M.*; *we stood in line for half an hour waiting to get into the Picasso exhibition*

(b) show of goods so that buyers can look at them and decide what to buy; **exhibition room** *or* **hall** = place where goods are shown so that buyers can look at them and decide what to buy

④ **exile**
['egzaɪl]
1 *noun*

(a) state of being sent away from your home country; *the ex-president went into exile in Switzerland* (NOTE: no plural in this meaning)

(b) person who is sent away from his own country; *the former king is now an exile in New York*; *the coup was mounted by exiles living across the border*

2 *verb*

to send someone away from his home country as a punishment; *the new government exiled the former dictator*

③ **exist**
[ɪgˈzɪst] *verb*

(a) to be; *when I was a child, color TV didn't exist*; *I don't believe the document exists - I think it has been burned*

(b) to live, to survive; *butterflies have existed on Earth for a very long time*; *they got lost in the jungle and managed to exist on berries and roots*

③ **existence**
[ɪgˈzɪstəns] *noun*

(a) life, being; *is there anything that proves the existence of life on Mars?*; *they lived a miserable existence in a little provincial town*

(b) **in existence** = which exists, which is actually here; *the original painting is no longer in existence*; *only one version of this automobile is still in existence in a museum in Geneva*

③ **existing**
[ɪgˈzɪstɪŋ] *adjective*

actual, which is in operation at this moment; *can we modify the existing structure in some way?*; *existing regulations do not allow the sale of food on the street*

① **exit**
['egzɪt]
1 *noun*

(a) way out of a building, an aircraft, etc.; *the customers all rushed toward the exits when the fire alarm rang*; **No Exit!** = sign showing that you must not go out this way; **emergency exit** = door used in emergency; **fire exit** = door used in case of fire

(b) **to make your exit** = to go out of a place, a room; *I apologized to my host and made my exit*; **exit visa** = visa allowing someone to leave a country

2 *verb*

(a) to leave a computer system; *press ESC to exit the system*

(b) *(informal)* to leave; *he exited the room as fast as he could*

④ **exotic**
[ɪgˈzɒtɪk] *adjective*

unusual, referring to a strange, foreign, often tropical, place; *the silk dresses of the dancers give the show an exotic air*; *spices make Indian food taste more exotic*

② **expand**
[ɪkˈspænd] *verb*

(a) to make something increase in size; *we have had to expand our sales force*

(b) to become larger; *water expands when it freezes*; *heat caused the metal pipes to expand*; *his waist is expanding fast*

③ **expansion**
[ɪkˈspænʃn] *noun*

increase in size; *the heat of the fire caused the expansion of the metal pipes*; *we are preparing for the company's forthcoming expansion into the European market* (NOTE: no plural)

② **expect**
[ɪkˈspekt] *verb*

(a) to think, to hope that something is going to happen; *I expect you are tired after your long train journey*; *he expects me to do all the housework*; *I can't talk for long, we're expecting visitors*; *we expect him to arrive at any moment* *or* *he is expected at any moment*; *the weather proved to be even worse than (they) expected*

(b) *(informal)* **to be expecting** = to be pregnant with; *my sister's expecting twins*

③ **expectation**
[ekspek'teɪʃn] *noun*

hope, feeling that something will happen; *she lived up to all our expectations*; *we thought our team would do well, but in the end they exceeded all our expectations*

② **expected**
[ɪkˈspektɪd] *adjective*

which is thought will happen, or hoped will happen; *the expected tax cuts didn't take place*

③ **expedition**
[ekspɪˈdɪʃn] *noun*

(a) journey to explore; *he set off on an expedition to the South Pole*

(b) short trip; *they went on a shopping expedition*

③ **expel**
[ɪkˈspel] *verb*

to send a child away from school, a student away from college; *he was expelled for taking drugs*; *see also* EXPULSION (NOTE: **expelling - expelled**)

③ **expenditure**
[ɪkˈspendɪtʃər] *noun*

amount of money spent; *the government's heavy expenditures on arms*; *the group objects to the expenditure of public funds on this project*

② **expense**
[ɪk'spens] *noun*
(a) amount of money or cost; *I can't afford the expense of a vacation just now*; *the expense of having a family seems to increase every week*; *he furnished the office regardless of expense* = without thinking how much it cost; **expense account** = money that someone is allowed to spend on personal expenses and entertaining guests, which will be paid for by his or her employer; **at great expense** = having spent a lot of money; *top designers had been hired at great expense*; *the house has been decorated at great expense*
(b) **at the expense of something** = in preference to something, giving something up; *she brought up her three children at the expense of her career in banking*

◇ **at someone's expense**
phrase
(a) with someone else paying the cost; *they were flown to Frankfurt at the company's expense*
(b) making fun of someone; *we all had a good laugh at his expense*

② **expenses**
[ɪk'spensɪz] *noun*
money spent in doing something; *we are making every effort to cut down on expenses*; **the salary offered is $30,000 plus expenses** = the company offers a salary of $30,000 and will repay any money spent by the employee in the course of his or her work; **all expenses paid** = with all costs paid by the company; *the company sent him to San Francisco all expenses paid or he went on an all-expenses-paid trip to San Francisco*; **business expenses** = money spent on running a business, not on stock or assets; **entertainment expenses** = money spent on giving meals, theater tickets, etc., to business visitors; **legal expenses** = money spent on fees paid to lawyers; **overhead expenses** *or* **general expenses** = money spent on the daily costs of a business; **travel expenses** = money spent on traveling and hotels for business purposes

② **expensive**
[ɪk'spensɪv] *adjective*
which costs a lot of money; *don't ask her out - she always orders the most expensive things on the menu*; *fresh vegetables are more expensive in winter*; *send your furniture to Australia by sea - it would be much too expensive by air*

② **experience**
[ɪk'spɪəriəns]
1 *noun*
(a) knowledge got by working or living in various situations; *I have no experience of traveling in the desert*; *you must write down the full details of your past experience on your*

résumé; *some experience of selling is required for this job* (NOTE: no plural in this meaning)
(b) event, incident that happens to someone; *going to the top of the Empire State Building was a wonderful experience*; *you must write a book about your experiences in the Arctic*
2 *verb*
to live through something; *I'm surprised she's so cheerful after all she experienced in prison*; *I have experienced a great deal of pleasure in my career*; *he is experiencing sharp pains in his left arm*

② **experienced**
[ɪk'spɪəriənst] *adjective*
wise from plenty of practice; *she's a very experienced doctor*; *he's the most experienced member of our staff*; *the police are experienced in crowd control*

② **experiment**
[ɪk'sperɪmənt]
1 *noun*
scientific test; *to carry out experiments on live animals*; *we're offering our customers free samples as an experiment*
2 *verb*
to carry out a scientific test; *they are experimenting with a new treatment for asthma*; *the laboratory experiments on live animals*

③ **experimental**
[ɪksperɪ'mentl] *adjective*
used in experiments; still being tested, still on trial; *this process is still at the experimental stage*; *the experimental fighter plane crashed*

① **expert**
['ekspərt]
1 *adjective*
(a) knowing a lot about a subject; *she can give you expert advice on design issues*; **expert system** = computer program that has been devised for a particular purpose
(b) **expert at doing something** = good at doing something; *he has expert knowledge of computers*
2 *noun*
(a) person who knows a great deal about a subject; *a rose expert was the judge at the flower show*; *he's a leading expert in tropical medicine or on tropical diseases*
(b) person who is very good at doing something; *she's an expert at getting the children to go to bed*; *he's an expert plumber*

④ **expertise**
[ekspə'tiz] *noun*
specialist knowledge; *we asked Mr. Smith to advise us because of his legal expertise*; *her expertise in business administration will be of great use to us* (NOTE: no plural)

③ **expire**
[ɪk'spaɪər] *verb*
to come to an end; *the lease expires in 2010*; **his passport has expired** = his passport is no longer valid

① **explain**
[ɪkˈspleɪn] *verb*
(a) to give your reasons for something; *can you explain why the weather is cold in winter and warm in summer?*
(b) to make something clear; *he tried to explain the new retirement plan to the staff*; *she explained what had happened, but the manager still thought she had tried to steal the watch*; *he explained to the customs officials that the drugs were presents for friends*

② **explanation**
[ekspləˈneɪʃn] *noun*
reason for something; *the police officer asked him for an explanation of why the stolen car was in his garage*; *the government has given no explanation for the change of plan*

② **explode**
[ɪkˈspləʊd] *verb*
(a) *(of bombs, etc.)* to blow up; *a bomb exploded on a crowded train*
(b) to make a bomb go off; *the army cleared the area and then exploded the bomb*

④ **exploit**
1 *verb* [ɪkˈsplɔɪt]
(a) to take commercial advantage of something; *we are hoping to exploit the mineral resources of Alaska*
(b) to make unfair use of someone, usually by paying them very low wages; *the company was accused of exploiting children by employing them in its shoe factories*
2 *noun* [ˈeksplɔɪt]
great or daring achievement; *he told us of his exploits during the war*

① **explore**
[ɪkˈsplɔːr] *verb*
(a) to travel and discover, especially you have not visited before; *it is a part of the jungle that has never been explored*; *we spent our vacation exploring Washington State*
(b) to investigate carefully; *we are exploring the possibility of moving the office to London*; *the president has set up a group to explore this and other issues*

① **explorer**
[ɪkˈsplɔːrər] *noun*
person who explores unknown parts of the world; *a famous Antarctic explorer*

② **explosion**
[ɪkˈspləʊʒn] *noun*
(a) blowing up of bombs, gas tanks, etc.; *several explosions were heard during the night as the army occupied the city*
(b) sudden increase; *this summer there has been an explosion in the numbers of mosquitoes*; **population explosion** = rapid increase in population

① **explosive**
[ɪkˈspləʊsɪv]
1 *noun*

material that can blow up; *tests revealed traces of explosive on his hands*; *the box contained explosives*; *police explosives experts made the bomb safe*
2 *adjective*
(a) liable to blow up; *the police found an explosive device in the car*
(b) tense, likely to be embarrassing; *the situation in the office was explosive, with the whole staff demanding to see the manager*; *the paper is running an explosive story about the senator*

③ **export**
1 *noun* [ˈekspɔːt]
export(s) = goods sent to a foreign country to be sold; *the country's major export is tea*; *exports to Africa have increased by 25%*; **export manager** = person in charge of sales to foreign countries (NOTE: usually used in the plural, but the singular form must be used before a noun)
2 *verb* [ɪkˈspɔːt]
to send goods to a foreign country for sale; *half of our production is exported*; *the company exports half of what it produces*

③ **expose**
[ɪkˈspəʊz] *verb*
(a) to show something which was hidden; *he pulled off his shirt, exposing a huge scar across his chest*; *the plastic coating had rubbed off to expose the metal underneath*
(b) to let light go onto a photographic film; *you didn't expose the film long enough*
(c) to reveal a scandal; *he was exposed as the person who wrote the letters*; *the newspaper has exposed several government scandals*
(d) to expose something *or* **someone to** = to place something or someone under the influence of something; *don't expose these plants to direct sunlight*; *he had exposed his children to serious danger*

③ **exposed**
[ɪkˈspəʊzd] *adjective*
open and not protected; *a stretch of exposed cliff*; *the cottages on the cliff are very exposed*; **a very exposed position** = a position that is not sheltered from the wind

④ **exposure**
[ɪkˈspəʊʒər] *noun*
(a) placing someone under the influence of something; *the exposure of young children to violence on television*
(b) state of not being sheltered from cold, etc.; *the survivors of the crash were all suffering from exposure after spending a night in the snow*
(c) time and amount of light needed for a picture to be taken on film; *you need a short exposure to photograph a racing automobile*; **exposure meter** = device for calculating the exposure for a photograph
(d) revealing of corruption, etc.; *the newspaper's exposure of the minister's*

involvement in the scandal; the council was embarrassed by a string of exposures of irregular financial transactions

① **express**
[ɪkˈspres]
1 *adjective*
(a) rapid (train or postal service); *we have an express delivery service to all parts of the country*
(b) done on purpose; *he did it with the express intention of killing me*
2 *verb*
to put into words or diagrams; *he expressed his thanks in a short speech*; *the chart shows visitors to our booth expressed as a percentage of all visitors to the exhibition*; **I expressed myself badly** = I did not make clear what I wanted to say

② **expression**
[ɪkˈspreʃn] *noun*
(a) word or group of words; *"until the cows come home" is an expression which means "for a very long time"*
(b) look on a person's face which shows feeling; *his expression showed how miserable he was*; *everyone noticed the expression of surprise on her face*

① **expressway**
[ɪkˈspresweɪ] *noun*
major highway for high-speed travel; *we took the expressway to Washington*

④ **expulsion**
[ɪkˈspʌlʃn] *noun*
act of being thrown out or sent away (from school, etc.); *the attorney general ordered the expulsion of the illegal immigrants*; *the school will only consider expulsion as a last resort*; *see also* EXPEL

② **extend**
[ɪkˈstend] *verb*
(a) to stretch out; *she extended both arms in welcome*; *the grounds of the house extend over two acres*
(b) to make longer or bigger; *we are planning to extend our garden*; *we have asked our landlord to extend the lease for another two years*; **extended family** = family in which relatives outside the central family group, such as aunts and uncles, are included
(c) to give; *I want to extend a warm welcome to our guests from China*

② **extension**
[ɪkˈstenʃn] *noun*
(a) act of extending; *my visa has expired, so I have applied for an extension*
(b) thing added on; *I need an extension cord for the electric saw*; *they are planning a further extension of the subway*
(c) office telephone; *can you get me extension 21?*; *the manager is on extension 23*

④ **extensive**
[ɪkˈstensɪv] *adjective*
very widespread, vast; *the grounds of the house are very extensive*; *the church roof needs extensive repair work*

③ **extent**
[ɪkˈstent] *noun*
degree, size, area; *the extent of the storm damage was only revealed later*; *he opened up the map to its full extent*; **to some extent** *or* **to a certain extent** = partly, in some way; *to some extent, the weather was the cause of the failure of the county fair* (NOTE: no plural)

③ **exterior**
[ɪkˈstɪəriər]
1 *adjective*
outside; *the exterior walls are of stone*
2 *noun*
the outside parts; *the exterior of the house is painted pink*

④ **external**
[ɪkˈstɜːrnl] *adjective*
outside; *the external walls of the house are quite solid*; *her injuries were all external*; **medicine for external use only** = medicine that is used on the skin and must not be drunk or eaten (NOTE: the opposite, referring to the inside, is **internal**)

④ **extinct**
[ɪkˈstɪŋkt] *adjective*
(a) of which all specimens are dead; *several species of birds have become extinct since rats were introduced to the island*
(b) (volcano) which doesn't erupt anymore; *this mountain is an extinct volcano*

② **extra**
[ˈekstrə]
1 *adjective*
more than normal; additional; *we need an extra four teachers or four extra teachers for this course*; *the charge for delivery is extra*; *there is no extra charge for heating*; *staff get extra pay for working on Sundays*
2 *adverb*
more than normal; in addition; *I need some extra strong string to tie the package*; *they charge extra for heavy items*; *if you pay $75 extra, you can travel first class*
3 *noun*
(a) something more than usual; *the price covers the hotels and transport but not extras like drinks and special trips*; *air-conditioning is an extra on this automobile*
(b) actor or actress who appears in a crowd scene in a movie or play, but is not a star; *the studio hired thousands of extras to make "Cleopatra"*

④ **extract**
1 *verb* [ɪkˈstrækt]
(a) to pull something out; *the dentist extracted two teeth*; *we managed to extract $15 from him*

(b) to produce something from something else; *it is no longer viable to extract tin from these mines*

2 *noun* ['ekstrækt]

(a) thing reduced from something larger; *he will be reading extracts from his latest novel*

(b) something which is reduced to a concentrated form; *she made a soup from meat extract*

② **extraordinarily**
[ɪk'strɔːdnrəli] *adverb*
extremely, very; *her action was extraordinarily brave*

② **extraordinary**
[ɪk'strɔːdnri] *adjective*
(a) marvelous, strange and unusual; *seeing her again gave him an extraordinary thrill; look at that bird's feathers - they are quite extraordinary; it's extraordinary weather for June*

(b) quite different from everything else; *these are extraordinary costs which will not be charged again*

③ **extreme**
[ɪk'striːm]
1 *adjective*
very great; *this engine is made to work well even in extreme cold*; **at the extreme end** = right at the end

2 *noun*
something very unusual, very extraordinary; *you get extremes of temperature here - very hot summers and very cold winters*; **to go to extremes** = to do everything in an extraordinary way; **to go from one extreme to the other** = to change to something completely different; *she can go from one extreme to the other - from being happy and excited one minute to being gloomy and depressed the next*

③ **extremely**
[ɪk'striːmli] *adverb*
very; *it was extremely hot in August; the movie is extremely long, and some people walked out before the end; it is extremely difficult to spend less than $50.00 a day on meals in New York*

① **eye**
[aɪ]
1 *noun*
(a) part of your head, used for seeing; *he has brown eyes; close your eyes and count to ten while we all hide; I've got a bit of dust in my eye*; **as far as the eye can see** = for a very long distance; *the plains stretch as far as the eye can see*; **to catch someone's eye** = to look at someone who is looking at you; *she caught his eye and nodded toward the door*; **keep your eyes open for!** *or* **keep an eye out for!** = watch out for!; *keep your eyes open for burglars!*; **to**

keep an eye on something = to watch something carefully to see that it is safe; *can you keep an eye on the house while we are away?*; **to keep an eye out for something** = to watch to see if something is near; *I must keep an eye out for Seville oranges to make some marmalade; can you keep an eye out for the parking attendant while I go into the bank?* *(informal)* **I'm up to my eyes in work** = I have a lot of work to do; **they don't see eye to eye** = they do not agree; *he doesn't see eye to eye with the boss*; **to have your eye on someone** = to think someone is very good, very attractive, very suspicious; *she has her eye on her best friend's brother; the police have had their eye on him for ages*

(b) small hole in the end of a needle, through which the thread goes

2 *verb*
to look at something carefully; *she sat in a corner of the café, eyeing the cakes in the window*

③ **eyeball**
['aɪbɔːl] *noun*
ball which forms your eye; *(informal)* **I'm up to my eyeballs in work** = I have a lot of work to do

② **eyebrow**
['aɪbraʊ] *noun*
small line of hair above your eye; *she has fine black eyebrows; use an eyebrow pencil to make your eyebrows clearer*; **he raised his eyebrows** = he looked surprised

③ **eyeglasses**
['aɪɡlæsɪz] *noun*
two pieces of plastic or glass in a frame which you wear in front of your eyes to help you see better; *have you seen my eyeglasses anywhere?; she has to wear eyeglasses to read*

① **eyelash**
['aɪlæʃ] *noun*
one of the hairs growing around the edge of the eyelids; *one of my eyelashes has got into my eye; she wore false eyelashes in the movie* (NOTE: plural is **eyelashes**)

① **eyelid**
['aɪlɪd] *noun*
piece of skin that covers the eye; *her eyelids began to close and soon she was fast asleep*

④ **eyeliner**
['aɪlaɪnər] *noun*
makeup for putting around your eyes

① **eyesight**
['aɪsaɪt] *noun*
ability to see; *he has got very good eyesight; my eyesight is getting so bad, I can't even thread a needle*; **her eyesight is failing** = she can't see as well as she used to (NOTE: no plural)

Ff

③ **F, f**
[ef]
sixth letter of the alphabet, between E and G;
"raffle" is spelled with a double F or with two
Fs

② **fabric**
['fæbrɪk] *noun*
(a) cloth, material; *the curtains are made of*
some expensive fabric; we need a strong fabric
for the chairs
(b) basic structure (of society); *during the*
revolution, the basic fabric of society collapsed

④ **fabricate**
['fæbrɪkeɪt] *verb*
to invent an untrue story; *the police said that she*
had fabricated the whole story

① **fabulous**
['fæbjʊləs] *adjective*
(informal) marvelous, wonderful; *it was a*
fabulous party

① **face**
[feɪs]
1 *noun*
(a) front part of your head; *don't forget to wash*
your face before you go to the party; she bought
a tube of face cream; **face-to-face** = looking at
each other; *he turned a corner and came*
face-to-face with a police officer; I don't like
doing business on the phone - I prefer to make
deals face-to-face; **to lose face** = to feel
humiliated; *she can't bear being told off in*
front of the class - it makes her lose face; **to**
make a face = to make a strange expression; *he*
made funny faces and all the children laughed;
he tried to keep a straight face = he tried not to
laugh; **to show your face** = to come to a place;
after what he said about my mother he doesn't
dare show his face here
(b) front part of something; *a clock face; she put*
the photograph face down on the desk; **he has**
vanished from the face of the earth = he has
disappeared completely
2 *verb*
(a) to have the face or front toward; *can*
everyone please face the camera?; the house
faces north
(b) to meet someone in an unpleasant situation;
the thought of facing all those journalists
frightens me; she didn't want to face the
committee yet again
(c) **to face something** *or* **be faced with**
something = to be likely to have to deal with an

unpleasant situation; *she faces a life of poverty;*
will they be able to cope with the problems
facing them?; **not to be able to face something**
= not to want to do something that you expect
will be unpleasant; *he couldn't face another*
meeting; **to face the facts** = to look at things in a
realistic way; *you really ought to face the facts:*
you'll never get a job if you don't have any
qualifications; **let's face it** = we must accept it;
let's face it, she's failed her test five times and
will probably never pass; see also MUSIC

④ **facet**
['fæsɪt] *noun*
(a) one of the flat sides on a cut gem; *a diamond*
with forty-four facets
(b) one of many aspects of a problem, etc.; *the*
problem presents many different facets

① **face up to**
['feɪs ʌp tu] *verb*
to accept an unpleasant state of affairs and try to
deal with it; *he had to face up to the fact that he*
was never going to be rich; the problems won't
go away - you must try to face up to them

④ **facial**
['feɪʃl]
1 *adjective*
referring to a face; *her facial expression*
reflected her feeling of happiness
2 *noun*
treatment in which your face is cleaned and
made more beautiful; *she went to the beauty*
salon to have a facial

④ **facility**
[fə'sɪlɪti] *noun*
(a) ability to do something easily; *she has a*
facility for languages; we offer facilities for
payment
(b) **facilities** = equipment that can be used; *the*
center provides facilities for a wide range of
sports; we have free use of all the club
facilities; **the museum has facilities for the**
disabled *or* **for the handicapped** = the museum
has special sloping paths, elevators, etc., to
allow disabled or handicapped people to visit it
(c) large commercial building; *we have opened*
our new warehouse facility (NOTE: plural is
facilities)

① **fact**
[fækt] *noun*
(a) thing that is true; *he faced up to the fact that*
he wasn't fit enough for the race; did you check
all the facts before you wrote the article?; it's a

well-known fact that it rains more often in the west of the country
(b) in fact = really; *he told the police he had seen a man steal an automobile but in fact he made the whole story up*; *it rained a lot last month, in fact it rained every day*
(c) the fact of the matter is = what is true is that; *the fact of the matter is that she is too slow to join the team*; **as a matter of fact** = actually; *have you seen John recently? - as a matter of fact I met him yesterday*

④ **faction**
['fækʃn] *noun*
group of people linked together in opposition to a leader or to a government; *three factions are fighting for control of the political party*; *trying to unite the different factions is an impossible task*

④ **factor**
['fæktər] *noun*
(a) one of the numbers which produce a certain other number when multiplied; *4 and 2 are factors of 8*; **by a factor of** = multiplied by; *reported cases of the disease have fallen by a factor of 3*
(b) number that indicates the strength of something; **factor 20 sunscreen** = lotion that gives twenty times protection against the sun's rays
(c) thing which has influence or importance; *the key factor is the price*; *the crucial factor for the success of the county fair is the weather*; **deciding factor** = most important factor which influences a decision

① **factory**
['fæktri] *noun*
building where things are made; *she works in a shoe factory*; *he owns a furniture factory*; *the factory makes computer terminals*; **factory hand** *or* **factory worker** = person who works in a factory (NOTE: plural is **factories**)

③ **faculty**
['fækəlti] *noun*
(a) ability; **mental faculties** = being able to think clearly; *in spite of being over ninety, she is still in possession of all her faculties*
(b) main division of a university; *the Faculty of Arts or the Arts Faculty*
(c) teaching staff (of a school, university, college, etc.); *there is a faculty meeting tomorrow* (NOTE: plural is **faculties**)

① **fade**
[feɪd] *verb*
(a) to lose color; *the more you wash your jeans, the more they'll fade*; *this T-shirt has faded*
(b) to become less bright or light; *as the light faded, an owl came into the garden*; *the light from the flashlight began to fade as the batteries ran out*; *the islands faded away into the distance*
(c) to become less noisy; *the sound of the music faded away*

③ **Fahrenheit**
['færənhaɪt] *noun*
scale of temperatures where the freezing and boiling points of water are 32° and 212°; *what is 75° Fahrenheit in centigrade?*; *the temperature outside was 56°F (say "fifty-six degrees Fahrenheit") do you use Celsius or Fahrenheit in the weather forecasts?*; *compare* CELSIUS, CENTIGRADE (NOTE: normally written as an **F** after the degree sign: **32°F**: say: "thirty-two degrees Fahrenheit")

COMMENT: to convert Fahrenheit to Celsius, subtract 32 and divide by 1.8. To convert Celsius temperatures to Fahrenheit, multiply by 1.8 and add 32. So 68°F is equal to 20°C.

② **fail**
[feɪl]
1 *noun*
(formal) **without fail** = definitely; *I will be there without fail tomorrow morning*
2 *verb*
(a) not to do something which you were trying to do; *the examination was very difficult - half the students failed*; *he passed in math, but failed his English exam*; *she failed in her attempt to become a senator*
(b) not to pass a candidate in an examination; *she has failed her driver's test twice*
(c) not to do something; *the automobile failed to stop at the red light*; *she failed to notify the tax office of her change of address*
(d) not to be able to do something; *I fail to see why she can't come the meeting when everyone else can*
(e) not to work properly; *the brakes failed and he couldn't stop the car*; **if all else fails** = if you can't do anything else; *if all else fails you can always borrow my car*
(f) to become weaker; *her eyesight is beginning to fail*

② **failure**
['feɪljər] *noun*
(a) breakdown or stopping; *the accident was caused by brake failure*; *the failure of the plane's engine caused the crash*; **heart failure** = dangerous condition when the heart has stopped beating; **power failure** = breakdown in electricity supplies
(b) person or thing which does not work in a satisfactory way; *his attempts to play the piano were a complete failure*; *I'm no good at anything - I'm a failure*
(c) failure to do something = not having done something; *his failure to reach the final disappointed his fans*; *failure to pay the bill will mean we will have to take legal action*

① **faint**
[feɪnt]
1 *adjective*

difficult to see or hear; *we could just see the faint outline of a man in the fog*; *the rescue team could hear a faint tapping sound coming from the ruins* (NOTE: **fainter- faintest**)

2 *verb*

to become unconscious for a short time; *she fainted at the sight of the blood*

① **fair**
['feər]

1 *adjective*

(a) light-colored (hair, skin); *her hair is quite fair*; *she's dark, but her brother is fair*

(b) not very good; *her work is only fair*

(c) right, giving someone what they deserve; *it isn't fair to go on vacation when we have so much work to do*; *that's not fair - you have to let other children play with the ball too*

(d) bright and warm (weather); *according to the TV it will be fair tomorrow* (NOTE: do not confuse with **fare**; note also: **fairer - fairest**)

2 *noun*

(a) public event held in a town, state or county; *farm animals are shown and sold at the county fair*

(b) exhibition for selling and advertising goods; *we are going to the arts fair tomorrow*

3 *adverb*

in a fair way; *you play fair with me, and I'll play fair with you*

② **fairly**
['feəli] *adverb*

quite; *I'm fairly certain I have seen this movie before*; *she had been working there a fairly short time*; *the hotel is fairly close to the train station* (NOTE: the order of words: **he's a fairly good worker** but **he's quite a good worker**)

① **fairy**
['feəri] *noun*

little creature who can work magic; *I believed in fairies when I was little*; **tooth fairy** = imaginary creature who is said to take a child's first teeth as they fall out and replace them with money; **fairy godmother** = kind person who gives you magic presents; *Cinderella's fairy godmother helped her go to the ball*; *what we need is a fairy godmother to get us out of trouble*; **fairy story** *or* **fairy tale** = children's story about fairies, princesses, giants, etc.; **fairy-tale castle** = romantic castle like those in fairy stories; **a fairy-tale wedding** = romantic wedding (like that of a prince and princess) (NOTE: plural is **fairies**)

① **faith**
[feiθ] *noun*

(a) belief, trust; **to have faith in someone** = to believe that someone is good and strong, or will protect you; *I have no faith in advice columns in newspapers*; *you must have faith in the leader of the party*; *I don't have any faith in this new treatment*; **blind faith** = absolute trust in someone, however wrong they may seem to be to other people

(b) religious belief; *we must respect people of other faiths*

(c) **in good faith** = in an honorable way, even though perhaps wrongly; *I sold him the car in good faith - I didn't know it would break down the next day*

③ **faithful**
['feiθfəl] *adjective*

(a) *(person)* trusting or loyal; *his faithful old dog sat by his bed*; *we must be faithful to our father's last wishes*

(b) *(of husband, wife)* **to be faithful** = not to have love affairs with someone else

(c) completely correct; *a faithful copy of a document*

③ **faithfully**
['feiθfəli] *adverb*

loyally, in a trusting way; *her cleaning lady had worked faithfully for her for years*; *he faithfully did what the instructor told him to do*

② **fake**
[feik]

1 *noun*

imitation; not the real thing; *that picture isn't by Picasso, it's a fake*

2 *adjective*

not real; *she was wearing a fake fur coat*

3 *verb*

to make an imitation of something, or to imitate something that isn't real; *he faked mental illness to avoid appearing in court*; *they think the laboratory faked the results of the test*

① **fall**
[fɔl]

1 *noun*

(a) amount of something which has come down; *there was a heavy fall of snow during the night*

(b) going to a lower level; *a welcome fall in the price of oil*; *the fall in the exchange rate*

(c) losing your balance; *he had a fall and hurt his back*; *she had a bad fall while skiing*

(d) **the fall** = the season of the year between summer and winter; *we go to New England in the fall to see the trees*; *fall colors are at their best in the first week of October*

2 *verb*

(a) to drop down to a lower level; *snow fell all night*; *the Canadian dollar has fallen against the American dollar*; *she fell down the stairs*; *he fell off the ladder*; *did he fall into the river or did someone push him?*; *don't put the bottle on the cushion - it may fall over*

(b) **his face fell** = he looked sad and disappointed

(c) **to fall on** = to happen or to take place; *my birthday falls on a Tuesday this year* (NOTE: **falling - fell** [fel] **- has fallen**)

④ **fallacy**
['fæləsi] *noun*

false argument; mistake; *it's a common fallacy to assume that money always brings happiness* (NOTE: plural is **fallacies**)

③ **fall asleep**
['fɔl ə'slip] *phrase*
to go to sleep; *we all fell asleep after dinner in front of the TV*

③ **fall back on**
['fɔl 'bæk ɒn] *verb*
to use something which you were keeping as a reserve; *the taxi broke down, so we had to fall back on public transportation*

③ **fall behind**
['fɔl bɪ'haɪnd] *verb*
to be late in doing something; *he fell behind in his mortgage payments*

③ **fall down**
['fɔl 'daʊn] *verb*
(a) to drop to the ground; *she fell down and hurt her knee*
(b) to become a ruin; *the house has been empty for so long it's falling down*

③ **fall for**
['fɔl 'fɔr] *verb*
(a) to fall in love with someone; *she always falls for men twice her age*
(b) to be tricked by something; *don't fall for his sales talk*

③ **fall off**
['fɔl 'ɒf] *verb*
to become fewer; *the number of visitors to the library has fallen off this year*

③ **fall out**
['fɔl 'aʊt] *verb*
to have an argument; *they fell out over the check for drinks*

③ **fall over**
['fɔl 'əʊvər] *verb*
to fall down from being vertical; *don't put the jug on the cushion - it may fall over*

③ **fall through**
['fɔl 'θru] *verb*
not to take place as was planned; *our planned vacation to Barbados fell through because we had too much work at the office*

① **false**
[fɔls] *adjective*
(a) not true; *the story he told was quite false*
(b) not real; **false teeth** = artificial teeth; **false alarm** = signal for an emergency when there isn't one; *the fire department has answered two false alarms today; she was rushed to the hospital, but it turned out to be a false alarm*

② **fame**
[feɪm] *noun*
being famous or a well-known person; *he went to Broadway to seek fame and fortune; fame hasn't spoiled her at all*

③ **familiar**
[fə'mɪljər] *adjective*
(a) heard or seen before; *the dog barked as it heard its master's familiar voice at the door; he looked around the room, and saw a couple of familiar faces*; is he familiar with that type of engine? = does he know that type of engine well?
(b) very informal, (too) friendly; *don't try to get familiar with me!; she is getting too familiar with the customers*

① **family**
['fæmɪli] *noun*
(a) group of people who are related to each other, especially mother, father and children; *the Ware family is going on vacation to Jamaica; they have a big family - three sons and two daughters*; **family pack** *or* **family size** = larger-than-normal pack of goods which is cheaper to buy; **family room** = large living area for family recreation
(b) group of animals or plants, etc., which are closely related; *lions are members of the cat family* (NOTE: plural is **families** but **family** can be used to mean a group and in this case takes on a singular verb: **the family has agreed to go on vacation in June**; if it is used to refer to the individual members in the group, it takes the plural: **the family have been fighting about politics ever since the last election**)

④ **famine**
['fæmɪn] *noun*
very serious shortage of food; *famine is widespread in some parts of Africa*

② **famous**
['feɪməs] *adjective*
well-known; *he's a famous football player; this café is famous for its milkshakes; he owns a famous department store in New York*

① **fan**
[fæn]
1 *noun*
(a) device for moving air to make things cooler; *we put electric fans in the office to try to keep cool*; **fan belt** = loop of rubber which turns a fan to cool the engine of an automobile; **exhaust fan** = fan that sucks air out; *when you switch on the light in the bathroom, the exhaust fan comes on automatically*
(b) enthusiastic supporter of a team, pop group, etc.; *there was a crowd of fans waiting for him outside the theater*
2 *verb*
to fan yourself = to make yourself cool by making the air move; *he fanned himself with his program* (NOTE: **fanning - fanned**)

② **fancy**
['fænsi]
1 *noun*
desire, something you want; **it took his fancy** = he suddenly wanted it; *the watch took her fancy, so she walked into the store and bought it*
2 *adjective*
(a) pretty, decorated; *he wore a fancy vest to the wedding*

(b) fancy prices = high prices (as charged to tourists); *I don't want to pay the fancy prices they ask in New York stores*
(c) fancy dress = dress-up costume worn to a party
3 *verb*
(a) to imagine, to believe; *she fancied she saw a dark figure in the yard*
(b) to like, to want to have; *I fancy an ice cream - any one else want one?*; *do you fancy sharing a taxi to the airport?*; *(informal)* **I think she fancies you** = I think she is attracted to you
4 *interjection showing surprise; fancy meeting you here!*

② **fantastic**
[fæn'tæstɪk] *adjective*
(a) strange, like a dream; *his stories are full of fantastic creatures*
(b) *(informal)* wonderful, amazing; *a vacation in Australia - that's fantastic!*; *it's fantastic working in TV!*

④ **fantasy**
['fæntəsi] *noun*
(a) invented story; *her story of meeting a rich man in Dallas was just a fantasy*
(b) something you hope for but which cannot come true; *he's living in a fantasy world - one day he'll wake up in the real world and it will be a shock* (NOTE: plural is **fantasies**)

① **far**
[fɑr]
1 *adverb*
(a) a certain distance away; *the supermarket is not far from here*; *how far is it from San Francisco to Los Angeles?*; *the road was blocked by traffic as far as we could see*; **as far as I know** *or* **can tell** = I think, but I'm not absolutely sure; *as far as I know, the train is on time*; *as far as I can tell, the engine is working normally*
(b) a long time ago; *as far back as 1985, he was making a lot of money*
(c) much; *it is far cheaper to go by bus than by train*; *restaurant food is far nicer than the food at school*
2 *adjective*
which is a long way away; *the store is at the far end of the Main Street* (NOTE: **far - farther** *or* **further** ['fɑrðər *or* 'fɜrðər] - **farthest** *or* **furthest** ['fɑrðəst *or* 'fɜrðəst])

◇ **far from**
['fɑr frɒm] *adverb*
not at all; *the food here is far from cheap*

◇ **by far**
['baɪ 'fɑr] *adverb*
very much; *a bike is by far the cheapest way to travel around Seattle*; *of all small automobiles, this one uses by far the least amount of gas*

◇ **so far**
['sou 'fɑr]
up till now; *so far the weather has been very cold*; *so far this winter I have managed not to*

catch the flu; *have you enjoyed your stay in New Jersey so far?*; *see also* INSOFAR AS

② **fare**
[feər]
1 *noun*
(a) price that you have to pay for a journey; *subway fares have been increased by 10%*; *the tourist class fare is much less than the first class one*; *if you walk to work, you will save $7 a week on bus fares*; *children over 12 must pay the full fare* = they must pay the same price as adults; **one-way fare** = fare for a journey from one place to another; **round-trip fare** = fare for a journey from one place to another and back again
(b) passenger in a taxicab; *he picked up a fare at the train station*
(c) *(especially in publicity)* food; *the diner serves good country fare*
2 *verb*
to do, to perform; *how did he fare on his driver's test?* (NOTE: do not confuse with **fair**)

③ **Far East**
['fɑr 'ist] *noun*
countries to the east of Pakistan and India; *when he was twenty he sailed to the Far East to work in Hong Kong*; *our trade with the Far East has suffered because of exchange problems*

① **farewell**
[feər'wel]
1 *interjection & noun*
(formal) goodbye; *it's time to say farewell*; **to bid someone farewell** = to say goodbye to someone; *he left without bidding us farewell*
2 *adjective*
at which you say farewell; *we gave a farewell party for our neighbors who were going to live in Canada*

② **farm**
[fɑrm]
1 *noun*
land used for growing crops and raising animals; *he runs a pig farm*; *we're going to work on a farm during the vacation*
2 *verb*
to grow crops, raise animals, etc., on a farm; *he farms 2500 acres in Oklahoma*

① **farmer**
['fɑrmər] *noun*
person who manages or owns a farm; *farmers are worried that the good weather won't last until harvest time*; *he is one of the biggest cattle farmers in the county*; **farmers' market** = market in a town, where local farmers bring their produce for sale; *you can buy eggs and vegetables at the farmers' market*

① **farmhouse**
['fɑrmhaus] *noun*
house where a farmer and his family live; *the pig ran out of the barn, straight into the farmhouse*

① **farming**
['fɑrmɪŋ] *noun*
work of managing a farm, of growing crops, of keeping animals for sale; *sheep farming is important in New Zealand*

④ **farm out**
['fɑrm 'aʊt] *verb*
to hand over work to another person to do; *we farm out our typing to people working from home*

① **far off**
['fɑr 'ɒf] *adverb*
(a) a long way away; *we could see the house from far off*
(b) **not far off** = almost correct; *you weren't far off in your estimate*

③ **far out**
['fɑr 'aʊt] *adverb*
(a) a long way away; *we could see the ships far out at sea*
(b) **not far out** = almost correct; *the figure he suggested wasn't very far out*

① **farther** *or* **farthest**
['fɑrðər *or* 'fɑrðəst]
see FAR; *you're too close to the camera - move farther back*; *how much farther is it to the seaside?*; *which is farther south - New York or Rome?*; *Kansas City is the farthest west you can go in Missouri*

③ **fascinate**
['fæsɪneɪt] *verb*
to interest greatly; *anything to do with stars and space travel fascinates him*

② **fascinating**
['fæsɪneɪtɪŋ] *adjective*
very interesting; *the film gives you a fascinating glimpse of life on a lake*; *the book gives a fascinating description of New York in the 1930s*; *it was fascinating to hear her talk about her travels in India*

② **fashion**
['fæʃn] *noun*
(a) most admired style at a particular moment; *it's the fashion today to wear your hair very short*; *she always follows the current fashion*; **in fashion** = popular, following the current style; *high heels are in fashion this year*; **out of fashion** = unpopular, not the current style; *red automobiles are out of fashion at the moment*; **fashion victim** = person who follows the current fashion all the time
(b) manner or way; *she was treated in a most kindly fashion*
(c) **after a fashion** = not very well; *he can speak French after a fashion*

② **fashionable**
['fæʃnəbl] *adjective*
in fashion; *she lives in the fashionable part of town*; *it's a fashionable restaurant for movie stars and journalists*

① **fast**
[fæst]
1 *adjective*
(a) quick; *this is the fast train to Philadelphia - it doesn't stop anywhere on the way*; *she was driving in the fast lane of the freeway*
(b) *(of clock)* to show a time that is later than the correct time; *your clock is fast*; **my watch is five minutes fast** = is showing a time that is five minutes later than it really is (e.g. 6:15 instead of 6:10)
(c) tightly fixed; **fast colors** = colors in clothing which do not run when washed; *you will have to wash this shirt by hand as the color isn't fast*
2 *adverb*
(a) quickly; *walk faster if you want to catch up with the children in front*; *don't go so fast - you almost hit that man on the crosswalk*
(b) **fast asleep** = sleeping so that it is difficult to wake up; *she must have been tired - she's fast asleep already*
(c) tightly fixed; *the window was stuck fast and I couldn't open it* (NOTE: **faster - fastest**)
3 *noun*
period during which you stop eating for religious or health reasons; *he started a 24-hour fast*
4 *verb*
to eat nothing for religious or health reasons; *many people fast during the period before Easter*

② **fasten**
['fæsən] *verb*
to close or attach securely; *please fasten your seat belts*; *these shoes fasten with a button*

② **fastener**
['fæsnər] *noun*
device which fastens; *I must have put on weight - I can't do the fastener up*

① **fat**
[fæt]
1 *adjective*
(a) *(person)* round and weighing too much; *two fat men got out of the little white sports car*; *you'll have to eat less - you're getting too fat*; *he's fatter than me*
(b) thick; *he pulled a fat wad of money out of his pocket* (NOTE: **fatter - fattest**)
2 *noun*
(a) part of meat that is yellowish-white; *if you don't like fat, cut it off*
(b) **cooking fat** = white substance from animals or plants, used for cooking; *fry the onions in hot fat*; **vegetable fat** = fat obtained from nuts, etc., used for cooking

③ **fatal**
['feɪtəl] *adjective*
(a) which causes death; *there were three fatal accidents on this stretch of road last year*
(b) which has bad results; *it is fatal to ask him to help with the cooking*; *she made the fatal*

mistake of asking her grandfather what he thought of the Democratic candidate

③ **fate**
[feɪt] *noun*
(a) what is certain to happen to you; *they met by chance in a bar in New Zealand, and got married - it must have been fate!*; **to tempt fate** = to do something which could have bad results; *it's tempting fate to ask him to look after your girlfriend while you are away*; *it would be tempting fate to buy that automobile without having had it checked by a mechanic*
(b) what happens to someone, especially in the end; *the people of the country have the right to decide their own fate* (NOTE: do not confuse with **fete**)

① **father**
['fɑðər] *noun*
(a) man who has a son or daughter; *ask your father if he will lend you his car*; *she is coming to dinner with her father and mother*
(b) title given to a priest; *Father Thomas is our parish priest*

④ **fatigue**
[fə'tig]
1 *noun*
(a) being tired; *after a long day walking in the mountains, the group were showing signs of fatigue*
(b) fatigues = army overalls worn when doing cleaning duty or serving in the field; *a group of G.I.s wearing fatigues*
2 *verb*
(formal) to tire someone out; *if you are sick, any physical work is fatiguing*

② **faucet**
['fɔsət] *noun*
device with a knob which, when you twist it, lets liquid come out; *the faucet in the bathroom is leaking*

② **fault**
[fɔlt]
1 *noun*
(a) making a mistake; being to blame for something going wrong; *it isn't my fault if there's nothing in the fridge*; *it's all your fault - if you hadn't stayed in bed all morning we would be at the beach by now*; **at fault** = having made a mistake; *the store is at fault if they sent you the wrong table*
(b) to find fault with something = to criticize something, to find something wrong; *she's always finding fault with my work*
(c) the fact that something is not working properly; *the invoice was wrong because of a computer fault*; *the engineers are trying to mend an electrical fault*
(d) *(in tennis)* mistake in serving; *he served two double faults*
(e) line of a crack in the Earth's crust along which movements can take place that lead to

major earthquakes; *San Francisco is built near the San Andreas Fault*
2 *verb*
to find something wrong with; *you can't fault her work*

③ **faulty**
['fɔlti] *adjective*
with mistakes, with something which doesn't work; *the lights keep going on and off - there must be a faulty connection somewhere*; *the electrician says that the wiring is faulty*; *the problem was caused by a faulty valve*

① **favor**
['feɪvər]
1 *noun*
(a) friendly act, act of kindness; *can I ask a favor? will you look after my bike while I'm in the post office?*; **to do someone a favor** = to do something to help someone; *he won't charge for it - he did it as a favor*; *will you do me a favor and look after my cat when I'm away?*
(b) approval or popularity; *she tried to win the favor of the committee*; **out of favor** = disliked
(c) preference or liking; **to be in favor of** = to prefer; *the meeting voted in favor of the resolution*; **the score is 4-1 in our favor** = we are leading 4-1
2 *verb*
(a) to like or to prefer; *the managers favor moving to a bigger office*
(b) to make things easier for someone; *the windy conditions favor the visiting team*

④ **favorable**
['feɪvrəbl] *adjective*
good, which is in your favor; *she made a favorable impression at the interview*

② **favorite**
['feɪvrɪt]
1 *adjective*
which you like best; *which is your favorite TV show?*
2 *noun*
(a) thing or person which you like best; *which ice cream is your favorite?*; *this chocolate bar is a favorite with the children*
(b) person, horse, etc., which most people think is likely to win; *he's the favorite to win the election*; *that horse is the favorite in the three o'clock race*

③ **fax**
[fæks]
1 *noun*
copy of a text or picture sent by telephone; *mail it to me, or send a fax*; *can you confirm the booking by fax?*; **fax machine** = machine attached to the telephone line which sends faxes (NOTE: plural is **faxes**)
2 *verb*
to send a letter or picture by telephone; *I will fax the design to you or I will fax you the design as soon as it is ready*

② **FBI**
['ef 'bi 'aɪ]
= FEDERAL BUREAU OF INVESTIGATION

① **fear**
['fɪər]
1 *noun*
feeling of being afraid; *fear of the dark is common in small children*; *she has no fear of heights*
2 *verb*
(a) to be afraid of something; *what do you fear most?*
(b) to be afraid that something bad will happen; *I fear we are going to get wet - look at those dark clouds*; *when the little girl had not come back home three days later, everyone began to fear the worst*; **to fear for** = to worry that something might happen; *most parents fear for their children's safety*

④ **feasible**
['fizəbl] *adjective*
which can be done; *he says it is not feasible to produce draft plans immediately*

① **feast**
[fist]
1 *noun*
(a) very large meal; *that wasn't a regular lunch - it was a feast!*
(b) special religious day; *today is the Feast of St. Nicholas*

③ **feat**
[fit] *noun*
action that is difficult to do; *building our house so quickly was quite a feat*; **no mean feat** = a great achievement; *getting the job done in record time was no mean feat*

① **feather**
['feðər] *noun*
one of many light soft parts that cover a bird's body; *a bird with green and red feathers in its tail*; *he stuck a feather in his hat*; **as light as a feather** = very light

② **feature**
['fitʃər]
1 *noun*
(a) part of the face, such as the nose or mouth, etc.; *his distinctive features mean that we should find him quite quickly*
(b) important part or aspect; *the main feature of the castle is its huge tower*; *deep valleys are a feature of Norway*
(c) important item in a TV news program; important article on a special subject in a newspaper; *did you see the feature on St. Petersburg?*
(d) full-length movie
2 *verb*
(a) to have as the main performer, especially in a movie, on TV, or in a play; *the movie featured Charlie Chaplin as a factory worker*; *the circus features Russian bears*

(b) to show as the most important item; *the tour features a visit to the Valley of the Kings*; *the next program will feature a discussion between environmental experts*
(c) to appear as the main actor or subject in a movie or on TV; *she has been featured on many TV series*

① **February**
['februəri] *noun*
second month of the year, between January and March; *my birthday is in February*; *he died on February 17*; *we are moving to new offices next February* (NOTE: February 17: say "February seventeenth")

① **fed**
[fed]
see FEED

③ **federal**
['fedərəl] *adjective*
(a) referring to the central government of the United States; *most federal offices are in Washington, DC*; *federal law is more important than state law*; **Federal Bureau of Investigation (FBI)** = main police agency for fighting crime in the U.S.A.
(b) referring to a system where a group of provinces or states exist under a central government; *the Federal Republic of Germany*

④ **federation**
[fedə'reɪʃn] *noun*
group of states or organizations which have joined together; *the employers' federation*

② **fed up**
['fed 'ʌp] *adjective*
(informal) **fed up (with)** = tired of, unhappy because you have had enough of something; *I'm fed up with watching TV every evening, why can't we go out for a change?*; *she went back to school last Tuesday and she's already fed up*

③ **fee**
[fi] *noun*
money paid to doctors, schools and lawyers, etc., for work done; *private school fees are very high*; *the lawyer's fee for two days' work was more than I earn in a month!*; **entrance fee** *or* **admission fee** = fee paid to go in

① **feed**
[fid]
1 *noun*
(a) food given to animals; *a bag of cattle feed*
(b) meal, especially given to a baby or animal; *our baby always wants a feed during the night*
(c) means of putting material into a machine; **paper feed** *or* **sheet feed** = device on a printer for inserting single sheets of paper; *the paper feed has jammed*
2 *verb*
(a) to give food to someone, to an animal; *let's go to the park and feed the ducks*; *how can you feed your family when you haven't any money?*
(b) to eat; *the lambs are feeding*

(c) to feed something into a machine = to put something in again and again; *he fed the paper into the printer*; *the grain is fed into the mill through a special door* (NOTE: **feeding - fed** [fed] **- has fed**)

④ **feedback**
['fidbæk] *noun*
(a) information or comments about something which has been done; *I don't know what the sales are like because we haven't had any feedback from our salespeople*
(b) return of a signal in an electronic circuit causing a loud high noise

① **feel**
[fil]
1 *noun*
how something seems when touched; *silk has a soft feel*; *the rough feel of the wooden floor*
2 *verb*
(a) to touch (usually with your fingers); *feel how soft the bed is*; **to feel your way** = (i) to try to find the way forward in the dark by putting out your hands; (ii) to act cautiously until you have more experience; *when the lights went out we had to feel our way out of the movie theater*; *the new boss hasn't made any decisions yet - he's still feeling his way*
(b) to seem soft, cold, etc., when touched; *the bed feels hard*; *the stone floor felt cold*
(c) to sense something with your body or mind; *did you feel the table move?*; *I felt the elevator go down suddenly*; *do you feel warmer now that you've had a cup of tea?*; *they felt happy when they saw that all was well*; *by twelve o'clock she was feeling hungry*
(d) not to feel yourself = not to feel very well; *she's not coming to the office, she's not feeling herself today*
(e) to think; *he feels it would be wrong to leave the children alone in the house*; *the police felt that the accident was due to fog* (NOTE: **feeling - felt** [felt] **- has felt**)

③ **feel for**
['fil 'fɔr] *verb*
to be sympathetic toward; *I feel for him, he's lost his job and now his wife has been taken to the hospital*

② **feeling**
['filɪŋ] *noun*
(a) something which you feel; *I had a feeling that this strange man knew who I was*; *I didn't want to hurt her feelings*
(b) ability to sense something by touching; *my hands were so cold that I lost all feeling in my fingers*

① **feel like**
['fil 'laɪk] *verb*
(a) to want to do something; *I feel like going for a swim*; *do you feel like a cup of coffee?*
(b) to seem like, when touched; *it feels like plastic, not wood*

(c) *(of weather)* to seem as if it is going to do something; *it feels like snow*

③ **feel up to**
['fil 'ʌp tu] *verb*
to be strong enough to do something; *do you feel up to walking around the park?*

① **feet**
[fit]
see FOOT

④ **feign**
[feɪn] *verb*
(formal) to pretend; *she feigned surprise*

③ **fell**
[fel] *verb*
to cut down a tree; *they felled hundreds of trees to build the new highway*; *see also* FALL

② **fellow**
['feloʊ] *noun*
(a) man; *a young fellow came up to me and asked me the time*; *who's that fellow with a beard who's watching us?*
(b) person who belongs to the same group; *I was OK on the boat, but several of my fellow passengers were sick*; **fellow sufferer** = someone who has the same illness as you; *I get back pains, and I sympathize with all fellow sufferers*
(c) member of a research institute or academic society; *he's a fellow of the art institute*
(d) a graduate student who receives a grant for further study; *he's a fellow at Harvard*

② **felt**
[felt]
1 *noun*
thick material made of wool fibers pressed together; **felt pen** *or* **felt tipped pen** = pen whose writing end is made of hard felt
2 *verb*
see FEEL

② **female**
['fimeɪl]
1 *adjective*
referring to women, girls; referring to the sex which has young; *a female tennis player*; *a female kitten*
2 *noun*
(a) *(informal)* woman or girl; *three females went into the bar*
(b) animal, insect, bird that gives birth to young or lays eggs; flower that produces seeds; *in some spiders, the female of the species is larger than the male*

③ **feminine**
['femənɪn] *adjective*
(a) like a woman, suitable for a woman; *her long white silk dress was very feminine*
(b) *(in grammar)* referring to words which have a particular form or behave in a different way, to show the female gender; *is the French word "table" masculine or feminine?*; *"actress" is the feminine form of "actor"* (NOTE: the opposite is **masculine**)

④ **feminist**
['femɪnɪst] *noun*
woman who actively supports the right of women to equal status with men

① **fence**
[fens]
1 *noun*
barrier of wood or wire, used to keep people or animals in or out of a place; *the fence was blown down*; *the boys looked through the hole in the fence*; *the builders put up a fence around the construction site*; **to stay on the fence** = to avoid giving a definite answer to a question or giving support to one particular side; *he never takes sides - he just stays on the fence*
2 *verb*
(a) to put a fence around something; *the police fenced off the accident site*
(b) to fight with swords as a sport

② **fender**
['fendər] *noun*
body panel over the wheel of an automobile, which protects against splashing water and mud; *the front fender was dented in the crash*

④ **ferocious**
[fə'rəʊʃəs] *adjective*
fierce and angry; *a couple of ferocious dogs leapt at him*

① **ferry**
['feri]
1 *noun*
boat that carries vehicles, people or goods across a stretch of water; *the little boat rocked as the ferry passed*; *we are going to take the night ferry to the island* (NOTE: plural is **ferries**)
2 *verb*
to take across by boat; *small boats ferried the refugees across the lake*

② **fertile**
['fɜrtl] *adjective*
(a) *(soil)* rich enough to produce good crops; *the farm has rich black fertile soil*; *along the river valley the soil is very fertile*
(b) *(of female, or egg)* able to produce young; *the zoo hopes the female elephant is fertile, so that she can have young*; *the swans laid several eggs but only two were fertile*
(c) which produces ideas; **he has a fertile imagination** = he imagines things very easily

② **fertilize**
['fɜrtɪlaɪz] *verb*
to spread fertilizer on land; *the soil is poor and needs to be heavily fertilized*

② **fertilizer**
['fɜrtɪlaɪzər] *noun*
chemical or natural material spread over the soil to make it richer and more able to produce crops; *farmers are being encouraged to use organic fertilizers*; *she spread fertilizer around her carrots*; **liquid fertilizer** = fertilizer in the form of a liquid which is added to water

COMMENT: fertilizers are either "organic", such as rotted plants, seaweed, powdered fish bones, or made from mixtures of chemicals

① **festival**
['festɪvl] *noun*
(a) religious celebration which comes at the same time each year and usually is a public holiday; *the tour will visit Hong Kong for the Moon Festival*
(b) artistic celebration or entertainment which is put on at regular intervals; *we saw some excellent plays at the New Haven Festival this year*; **arts festival** = competitions in music, drama, painting, etc.; **beer festival** = competition, tasting and exhibition of different types of beer; **cheese festival** = competition, tasting and exhibition of cheeses; **film festival** = competition where different films are shown; *the film won a prize at the Cannes Film Festival*

④ **fetch**
[fetʃ] *verb*
(a) to go and bring someone or something; *it's your turn to fetch the children from school*; *can you fetch me the dictionary from the library?*
(b) to be sold for a certain price; *that car won't fetch more than $300*; *these CDs fetch very high prices on the black market*

④ **fete** *or* **fête**
[feɪt]
1 *noun*
small public festival, usually in the open air, with stalls, shows of interesting things, and competitions; *I hope it doesn't rain for the village fête*
2 *verb*
to celebrate someone's achievement; *the winner of the gold medal was feted when he returned home*

① **fever**
['fivər] *noun*
(a) state when the body's temperature is higher than normal; *you must stay in bed until the fever goes down*
(b) excited state; **at fever pitch** = in a great state of excitement; *the crowd waited at fever pitch for the pop group to arrive*

① **few**
[fju] *adjective & noun*
(a) not many; *she has very few friends at work*; *we go to fewer concerts than last year*; *I wonder why few of the staff stay with us more than six months*; **few and far between** = not very frequent; *trains are few and far between on Sundays*
(b) **a few** = some, not very many; *I only took a few photographs because it rained all the time*; *I'll call you in a few minutes*; *a few of the*

wedding guests were sitting playing cards (NOTE: **fewer - fewest**)

③ **fiber**
['faɪbər] *noun*
(a) small thread of material; *from the pieces of fiber left at the scene of the murder, the police could work out what the murderer had been wearing*
(b) thin threads in food, which cannot be digested; **high-fiber diet** = diet that contains a large amount of cereals, nuts, fruit and vegetables

② **fiction**
['fɪkʃn] *noun*
(a) novels; *fiction writers such as John Steinbeck; to find the latest novels you must look in the fiction section of the library*
(b) story that is not true; *his account of the accident was pure fiction* (NOTE: no plural)

① **field**
[fild]
1 *noun*
(a) piece of ground on a farm, with a fence or hedge around it; *the sheep are in the field; a field of potatoes*
(b) **playing field** = piece of ground for playing a game; *the two teams ran onto the field;* **field events** = jumping and throwing competitions; *athletics is made up of both track and field events*
(c) special area of interest or study; *what's your field?; his field is English language teaching*
(d) **field of vision** = area which you can see over clearly
(e) fighting area in a war; *these young soldiers have no experience of combat in the field*
(f) **field day** = busy and exciting time; *the police had a field day stopping motorists speeding on the freeway*
2 *verb*
(a) to send out a team to play or to negotiate; *the university is fielding its strongest team in some years; the union fielded a strong negotiating team*
(b) *(in sports)* to catch; *he fielded a long ball*
(c) **to field questions** = to deal with questions; *he fielded questions from the journalists about his private life*

③ **fierce**
['fɪəs] *adjective*
(a) very angry and likely to attack; *watch out - that dog looks fierce*
(b) violent, very strong; *a fierce storm broke out as they were leaving the harbor; the mountains were the scene of fierce fighting; he got into a fierce argument about working conditions*

③ **fiercely**
['fɪəsli] *adverb*
strongly, violently; *she is fiercely independent; the store was blazing fiercely when the fire engines arrived*

① **fifteen**
[fɪf'tin]
number 15; *she's fifteen (years old) come and see me in fifteen minutes; the train leaves at nine fifteen (9:15)* **the fifteen hundreds (1500s)** = the years from 1500 to 1599 (NOTE: compare **the fifteenth century**)

① **fifteenth (15th)**
[fɪf'tinθ] *adjective & noun*
today is July fifteenth (July 15) that's the fifteenth phone call I've made this morning; it will be her fifteenth birthday next week; **the fifteenth century** = the years from 1400 to 1499 (NOTE: compare **the fifteen hundreds;** Note also that with dates **fifteenth** is usually written **15: July 15, 1935; October 15, 1991** (say "October fifteenth"); with names of kings and queens **fifteenth** is usually written **XV: King Louis XV** (say: "King Louis the Fifteenth")

① **fifth (5th)**
[fɪfθ]
1 *adjective*
we got married on May fifth (May 5) it's his fifth birthday tomorrow; **the fifth century** = period from 400 to 499 AD
2 *noun*
a fifth
(a) 20%; *he spends a fifth of the year traveling*
(b) four-fifths of a quart of liquor; *a fifth of scotch* (NOTE: with dates **fifth** is usually written **5: July 5, 1935; October 5, 1991** (say "October fifth"); with names of kings and queens **fifth** is usually written **V: King Henry V** (say: "King Henry the Fifth")

② **Fifth Amendment**
['fɪfθ ə'mendmənt] *noun*
the Amendment to the Constitution of the U.S.A. which allows citizens not to give evidence which might be used against them in court; *he took the Fifth and refused to answer any questions*

① **fiftieth (50th)**
['fɪftɪəθ]
1 *adjective*
she came in fiftieth and last in the race; it's her fiftieth birthday on Monday
2 *noun*
a fiftieth = 2%

① **fifty**
['fɪfti]
number 50; *my mother made fifty pots of jam; she's fifty (years old) she's in her fifties* = she's between 50 and 59 years old; **the (nineteen) fifties (1950s)** = the period from 1950 to 1959 (NOTE: **fifty-one** (51), **fifty-two** (52), but **fifty-first** (51st), **fifty-second** (52nd), etc.)

① **fifty-fifty**
['fɪfti'fɪfti]
divided into two equal amounts; **to go fifty-fifty** = with each paying half of the cost; *we'll go fifty-fifty on the check*

① **fight**
[faɪt]
1 *noun*
(a) struggle against someone or something; *he got into a fight with boys who were bigger than him*; *fights broke out between the demonstrators and the police*; *to pick a fight with someone* = to start a fight with someone
(b) boxing match; *the fight only lasted three rounds*
2 *verb*
(a) to struggle against someone or something using force; *the two boys were fighting over a book*; *rival gangs fought on the street*; *we are committed to fighting crime*; *doctors are fighting to control the disease*
(b) *to fight for something* = to struggle on behalf of something; *they are fighting for the right to vote* (NOTE: **fighting - fought** [fɔt] **- has fought**)

① **fighter**
[ˈfaɪtər] *noun*
(a) person who fights; *the referee stopped the fight when one of the fighters had a cut eye*
(b) fast attacking aircraft; *two fighters went up to attack the enemy bombers*

② **figure**
[ˈfɪgjər]
1 *noun*
(a) written number (such as 35); *I can't read the figure on the order - is it 250?*; *he added up the figures on the bill*; *checks have to be made out in both words and figures*; *see also* DOUBLE, SINGLE
(b) shape such as a square or circle; *a four-sided figure is a square*
(c) drawing or diagram in a book; *see Figure 2 on page 23*
(d) shape of a person; *we could see some figures through the mist*; *the figures in the foreground of the painting*
(e) attractive shape of a woman's body; *she still has a great figure*
(f) important person; *he's one of the important figures in the opposition movement*
(g) *figure of speech* = colorful expression; *a "tempest in a teacup" is a figure of speech meaning a lot of fuss about nothing*
2 *verb*
(a) *to figure out* = to try to think of an answer or to understand something; *try to figure out the answer yourself instead of asking someone else*; *I'm trying to figure out if we've sold more this year than last*; *he's a good salesman, but he can't figure out discounts correctly*
(b) *(informal)* to consider, to think; *I figure the costs will be high*; *we figured you'd be late because of the show*; *had you figured on being there before two o'clock?*; *that figures* = that makes sense
(c) to appear (in a novel, painting, etc.); *blond girls figure in many of his paintings*

② **file**
[faɪl]
1 *noun*
(a) metal tool used for smoothing rough surfaces; *use a file to round off the edges of the metal*; *see also* NAIL FILE
(b) holder for papers and documents; *when you have finished with the papers, put them back in the file*; *the police have a file on him*
(c) section of data on a computer; *type the name of the file and then press ENTER*
(d) line of people; *in single file* = one behind the other; *the children entered the hall in single file*
2 *verb*
(a) to smooth a surface with a file; *file down the rough edges*
(b) to put papers away in a holder or case; *file that letter under SALES*; *filing cabinet* = piece of office furniture, a tall box with drawers for putting files in; *someone broke open my filing cabinet and removed some documents*
(c) to walk in a line; *they filed past the place where the boy had been killed*
(d) to make an official request or statement; *he filed for divorce*; *to file an income tax return* = to send a statement of income to the tax office

② **fill**
[fɪl] *verb*
(a) to make something full; *he filled the bottle with water*; *she was filling the boxes with presents*
(b) *to fill a tooth* = to put something into a hole in a tooth to stop it going bad; *I hate having my teeth filled but it has to be done*
(c) *to fill a gap* = to provide something which is needed, but which no one has provided before; *the new range of small cars fills a gap in the market*
(d) *to fill a post or a vacancy* = to find someone to do a job; *your application arrived too late - the position has already been filled*

② **fill in**
[ˈfɪl ˈɪn] *verb*
(a) to fill up a hole; *he dug a hole in the garden, put the box inside, and then filled it in*
(b) to write in the empty spaces on a form; *just fill in your name and address*; *to win the prize you have to fill in the missing words*
(c) *to fill in for someone* = to do something which someone else normally does but cannot do; *I'm filling in for the manager who is on vacation*
(d) *to fill someone in* = to give someone complete information about something

② **filling**
[ˈfɪlɪŋ]
1 *adjective*
which fills (your stomach); *a meal of salad and a glass of water is not very filling*
2 *noun*
(a) something put into a hole in your tooth by a dentist; *I had to go to the dentist because one of*

my fillings came out

(b) food used to put into a sandwich, pie, cake, etc.; *a cake with a cream filling*

(c) filling station = gas station, place where you can buy gas; *let's stop at the next filling station to see if we can get a map*

② **fill out**

['fɪl 'aʊt] *verb*

to write in all the empty spaces on a form; *fill out the form and send it back to this address*; *when you have filled out the application form, send it to us in the envelope provided*

② **fill up**

['fɪl 'ʌp] *verb*

to make something completely full; *he filled the bottle up with fresh water*; **fill her up** = please fill the tank with gas

① **film**

[fɪlm]

1 *noun*

(a) roll of material that you put into a camera to take photographs or moving pictures; *I must buy more film before the wedding*; *do you want color film or black and white?*

(b) thin layer of something; *a film of moisture formed on the cold metal surface*; *everywhere was covered with a film of dust*

(c) movie, moving pictures shown at a cinema or on TV; *have you seen this old Charlie Chaplin film?*; *we've seen the film already on TV*; **film rights** = the legal right to make a film from a book

2 *verb*

to take pictures of something with a camera; *security cameras filmed him robbing the bank*; *"Star Wars" was filmed in 1977*

③ **filter**

['fɪltər]

1 *noun*

(a) device or material for straining liquids or air, for stopping any solids from passing through; *the filters in the swimming pool have to be cleaned regularly*; **filter paper** = paper used for filtering liquids; *don't forget to put a filter in before you put in the coffee*

(b) glass on a camera which allows only certain colors to pass through; *I use an orange filter to give a warm color to the picture*

(c) material at the end of a cigarette, used to remove dangerous substances in tobacco

2 *verb*

(a) to remove dirt by passing through a filter; *kidneys filter the blood*

(b) to go or to come slowly through, down, out, etc.; *sunlight filtered through the leaves*; *rumors began to filter out about an attack on the president's plane*

② **filthy**

['fɪlθi] *adjective*

very dirty; *where have you been playing - you're filthy!*; *don't touch that filthy old carpet*; *filthy children followed the tourists,*

asking for money wherever they went (NOTE: **filthier - filthiest**)

① **fin**

[fɪn] *noun*

(a) thin part on the body of a fish which helps it to swim; *from the beach they could see a black fin in the sea*

(b) similar piece on an aircraft; *the tail fin broke off when the plane crashed*

② **final**

['faɪnəl]

1 *adjective*

last, coming at the end; *this is your final warning - if you don't work harder you will be fired*; *the competition is in its final stages*; **my decision is final** = I cannot change my decision; **final date for payment** = last date by which payment should be made

2 *noun*

(a) last competition in a series between several teams or competitors; *I thought they would win a couple of rounds, but I never imagined they would get to the final*

(b) last examination at the end of a university course; *after his final he's planning to have a nice relaxing weekend*; *everybody's at home studying for their final*

① **finally**

['faɪnəli] *adverb*

at last, in the end; *the police finally cleared up the mystery*; *the little boy finally turned up in Cincinnati*

③ **finance**

['faɪnæns]

1 *noun*

(a) finances = money, especially money which belongs to the public or to a company; *my finances are in a poor state at the moment*

(b) management of money, banking, investments, credit, etc.; **Minister of Finance** = government minister in charge of a country's finances (NOTE: in the U.S.A. this minister is called **the Secretary of the Treasury**)

2 *verb*

to provide money for; *how are you going to finance your college tuition?*; *my friends are going to finance the whole operation*

② **financial**

[fɪ'nænʃl] *adjective*

referring to money; *what is our financial position?*; *the company has gotten into financial difficulties*; **financial year** = 12-month period for which accounts are calculated

③ **financially**

[fɪ'nænʃli] *adverb*

referring to money; with money; *our long-term objective is to make the company financially sound*; *we try to help our daughter financially while she is at college*

① **find**

[faɪnd]

1 *noun*

thing which you discover; *what a lucky find! a cheap hotel in the center of Paris*

2 *verb*

(a) to discover (something hidden or lost); *I found a $5 bill behind the sofa*; *did she find the book she was looking for?*

(b) to discover something which was not known before; *no one has found a cure for the common cold yet*

(c) to have an opinion about something; *I found the book very dull*; *she finds her work too easy*

(d) to make a legal decision in court; *the tribunal found that both parties were at fault*; *he was found guilty of murder*; **the judge found for the defendant** = the judge decided that the defendant was right or wrong

(e) **to be found** = to exist; *wild mushrooms are found in fields in the fall* (NOTE: finding - found [faʊnd])

③ **finding** *or* **findings**
['faɪndɪŋz] *noun*

(a) facts discovered; *the two companies signed an agreement to share their research findings*

(b) actions which are recommended, recommendations; *the finding of the committee of inquiry will be published next week*

① **find out**
['faɪnd 'aʊt] *verb*

to discover information; *your job is to find out if the competition is planning a new model*; *she needs to find out everything she can about Napoleon*; *the police are trying to find out why she went to New Mexico*

③ **find time**
['faɪnd 'taɪm] *phrase*

to do something even though you are short of time; *in the middle of the meeting he still found time to phone his girlfriend*; *we must find time to visit the new shopping center*

② **fine**
[faɪn]

1 *adjective*

(a) good; *they're forecasting fine weather for the county fair next week*

(b) well, healthy; *I was in bed with the flu yesterday, but today I'm feeling fine*

(c) good; *how are things at home? - fine!*; *it's fine to wear a short skirt when you're young and slim, but not when you're old and fat*

(d) very thin or very small; *use a sharp pencil if you want to draw fine lines*; *I can't read the notice - the print is too fine*; **the fine print** = the conditions on a contract, usually printed in very small letters; *don't forget to check the fine print before you sign the contract* (NOTE: finer - finest)

2 *adverb*

in very small pieces; *chop up the orange peel very fine*

3 *noun*

money which you have to pay for having done something wrong; *I had to pay a $40 fine for*

parking in a no-parking zone; *he was found guilty of theft and got off with a fine*

4 *verb*

to make someone pay money for having done something wrong; *he was fined $40 for parking there*

5 *interjection*

all right, agreed; *Fine! We'll all go to the beach tomorrow!*

④ **finely**
['faɪnli] *adverb*

(a) in very small pieces; *cook some finely chopped mushrooms in a little butter*

(b) in a beautiful way; *she bought some finely carved ivory figures*

① **finger**
['fɪŋgər]

1 *noun*

(a) one of the parts at the end of your hand, but usually not including the thumb; *he wears a ring on his little finger*; *he pressed the button with his finger*; **to keep your fingers crossed** = to hope that something will happen as you want it to happen; *have you seen the exam results yet? - no, but I'm keeping my fingers crossed*; **not to lay** *or* **put your finger on something** = not to remember or see something correctly; *I can't put my finger on it at the moment*; **on the fingers of one hand** = five (or less); *the number of times she's offered to buy me a drink can be counted on the fingers of one hand*; **not to lift** *or* **raise a (little) finger to help** = not to do anything to help; *we were trying to move the piano and he didn't raise a finger to help*; *it's unfair to expect her to do all the housework while her sisters don't lift a finger to help*

(b) part of a glove into which a finger goes; *I must mend my glove - there's a hole in one of the fingers*

2 *verb*

(a) to touch with your fingers; *don't finger the apples*

(b) *(informal)* to point out a criminal to the police; *he was fingered by someone else in the gang*

① **fingernail**
['fɪŋgərneɪl] *noun*

hard thin part covering the end of each finger; *she painted her fingernails green*; *don't bite your fingernails!*

① **finish**
['fɪnɪʃ]

1 *noun*

(a) final appearance; *the table has an attractive finish*

(b) final appearance which is not real, which is only on the surface; *kitchen cupboards with an oak finish*

(c) end (of a race); *he ran well and came in second at the finish*

2 *verb*

to do something completely; to come to an end; *haven't you finished your homework yet?*; *tell me when you've finished reading the paper*; *you can't go out until you've finished washing the dishes*; *the game will finish at about four o'clock*

④ **finite**
['faɪnaɪt] *adjective*
with an end, with a limit; *the world's oil resources are finite*

③ **fir**
[fɜr] *noun*
evergreen tree with leaves shaped like needles; *fir trees are often used as Christmas trees* (NOTE: do not confuse with **fur**)

① **fire**
['faɪər]
1 *noun*
(a) something which is burning, something which heats; *they burned the dead leaves on a fire in the garden*; **to catch fire** = to start to burn because of something else which is burning; *the office block caught fire*; *take those papers away - they might catch fire*; **to set fire to** = to make something start burning; *his cigarette set fire to the carpet*; **on fire** = burning; *call the emergency services - the house is on fire!*
(b) shooting with guns; *the soldiers came under fire from the guerrillas*
2 *verb*
(a) to shoot a gun; *the gunmen fired at the squad car*; *we could hear guns firing in the distance*
(b) to dismiss someone from a job; *she was fired for being late*
(c) to make excited; *he was fired with the desire to make his fortune*

② **firecracker**
['faɪərkrækər] *noun*
small paper or cardboard container filled with an explosive that makes a loud noise; *we set off lots of firecrackers on the Fourth of July*

① **fire engine**
['faɪər'endʒɪn] *noun*
large red van used by the fire services, with pumps, ladders, etc., to fight fires; *six fire engines were at the blaze*

② **fire fighter**
['faɪər'faɪtər] *noun*
person who tries to put out fires; *dozens of fire fighters tried to put out the forest fire*

① **fireman**
['faɪərmən] *noun*
man who tries to put out fires; *the firemen were fighting the blaze in the old school building* (NOTE: plural is **firemen**)

① **fireplace**
['faɪərpleɪs] *noun*
hole in the wall of a room where you can light a fire for heating; *the dog likes to lie on the carpet in front of the fireplace*

① **fire station**
['faɪər'steɪʃn] *noun*
center where fire engines are based; *the fire engines came racing out of the station*

② **fireworks**
['faɪərwɜrks] *noun*
small cardboard tubes holding chemicals which will explode when lit; *there was a big display of fireworks on the Fourth of July*

② **firm**
[fɜrm]
1 *adjective*
(a) solid or fixed; *make sure that the ladder is firm before you climb up*; *my back hurts - I think I need a firmer bed*
(b) not going to change; *there is no firm evidence that he stole the money*; **to stand firm** = not to give in; *in spite of the offers from the highway construction crew; he stood firm and refused to leave his house*
(c) which cannot be changed; *to place a firm order for two trucks*; *they are quoting a firm price of $1.83 per unit* (NOTE: **firmer - firmest**)
2 *noun*
business or company; *when he retired, the firm presented him with a watch*; *the law firm I work for was taken over last year*

② **firmly**
['fɜrmli] *adverb*
in a firm way; *he held the rail firmly*; *she said firmly that she did not want to go*

① **first**
[fɜrst]
1 *adjective & noun*
(as a number can be written **1st**) referring to the thing that comes before all other things; *King Charles the First (Charles I)* *it's our baby's first birthday on Tuesday*; *the bank is the first building on the left past the post office*; **the first century** = the period from the year 1 to 99 AD; **first name** = a person's Christian name or given name, as opposed to the surname or family name (NOTE: with dates **first** is usually written **1**: **February 1, 1992**; **December 1, 1670** (say "December first"); with names of kings and queens **first** is usually written **I**: **King Charles I** (say "King Charles the First")
2 *adverb*
(a) at the beginning; *first of all, we need to look at the plan*; **first come, first served** = dealing with orders, etc., in the order in which they are received; *applications will be dealt with on a first come, first served basis*
(b) before doing anything else; *wash your hands first, and then you can eat*
(c) for the first time; *when did you first meet your girlfriend?*

◇ **at first**
[æt 'fɜrst]
at the beginning; *at first he didn't like the work but later he got used to it*

① **first aid**
['fɜrst 'eɪd] *noun*
help given to a person who is hurt, before a doctor or ambulance arrives; *the police gave first aid to the accident victims*; **first aid kit** = box with bandages and dressings kept to be used in an emergency; *we keep a first aid kit in the automobile*

③ **first-class**
['fɜrst'klæs] *adjective*
very good; *he is a first-class tennis player*

② **first floor**
['fɜrst 'flɔ] *noun*
floor (in a store, block of apartments, etc.) that is level with the street; *the men's department is on the first floor*; *he has a first-floor office*

③ **First Lady**
['fɜrst 'leɪdi] *noun*
wife of a president, especially the wife of the president of the U.S.A.; *the First Lady has been invited to lunch at Buckingham Palace*; *the new First Lady is planning to carry out decorations to only a few rooms in the White House*

① **firstly**
['fɜrstli] *adverb*
in the first place, to start with; *why are they getting married? - firstly, they're in love, and secondly, her father has offered to buy them a condo*

③ **first-rate**
['fɜrstreɪt] *adjective*
excellent; *the food here is absolutely first-rate*; *he's a first-rate tennis player*

④ **fiscal**
['fɪskl] *adjective*
referring to tax or to government revenues; *the government's fiscal policy*; **fiscal year** = 12-month period for which accounts are calculated for tax purposes (not always the same as the calendar year)

① **fish**
[fɪʃ]
1 *noun*
animal with no legs, which lives in water and which you can usually eat; *I sat by the river all day and only caught two little fish*; **fish tank** = big container of water for keeping fish; *(informal)* **not the only fish in the sea** = one of many (NOTE: plural is usually **fish: some fish, three fish,** but also sometimes **fishes**)
2 *verb*
(a) to try to catch a fish; *we often go fishing in the lake*; *they fished all day but didn't catch anything*
(b) to try to find something; *he fished around in his suitcase and after some delay produced his passport*

① **fisherman**
['fɪʃəmən] *noun*
man who catches fish, either as his job or for sport; *fishermen are complaining that pollution is wiping out fish stocks* (NOTE: plural is **fishermen**)

③ **fish stick**
['fɪʃ 'stɪk] *noun*
frozen piece of fish, shaped like a finger and covered in breadcrumbs; *the children don't like fresh fish, but they do like fish sticks*

① **fishing**
['fɪʃɪŋ] *noun*
sport or business where you try to catch fish; *the sign said "no fishing"*; **fishing boat** = boat used for fishing; **fishing line** = long string used with a hook to catch fish; **fishing rod** = long piece of wood to which a line and hook are attached

② **fist**
[fɪst] *noun*
tightly closed hand; *he punched her with his fist*; *she banged on the table with her fist*

① **fit**
[fɪt]
1 *noun*
sudden sharp attack of illness, etc.; *she had a coughing fit or a fit of coughing*; *in a fit of anger he threw the plate across the kitchen*; **by** *or* **in fits and starts** = at odd moments, stopping often; *something has gone wrong with the printer - it only prints out by fits and starts*
2 *adjective*
(a) healthy; *he isn't fit enough to go back to work*; *you'll have to get fit if you're going to run a long-distance race*; *see also* SURVIVAL OF THE FITTEST
(b) **fit to do something** = in good enough condition to do something; *is he fit to drive?*; *that automobile isn't fit to be driven - its brakes don't work and the tires are worn*
(c) suitable; *is she a fit person to look after small children?* (NOTE: **fitter - fittest**)
3 *verb*
(a) to be the right size or shape; *he's grown so tall that his jackets don't fit him anymore*; *these shoes don't fit me - they're a size too small*
(b) to put in place; *I want to fit a new fridge in the kitchen*; *fitting the furniture into the new house was quite a problem* (NOTE: **fitting - fitted**)

③ **fit in**
['fɪt 'ɪn] *verb*
(a) to find room or time for someone or something; *we can't fit in a vacation this year as we have too much work*; *how can you fit six people into that little car?*
(b) to be able to go into a space; *how will the bed fit into that room?*
(c) to be comfortable as part of a group; *he joined the firm two years ago but has never really fit in*

③ **fitted**
['fɪtɪd] *adjective*
made to fit into a certain space; **fitted sheet** = sheet made to fit around a mattress

② **fitting**
['fɪtɪŋ]
1 *adjective*
suitable, right; *it's fitting that grandmother should sit at the head of the table - it's her birthday party, after all*
2 *noun*
(a) action of making something fit; action of trying on a new piece of clothing; *she's having the first fitting of her wedding dress this afternoon*
(b) size and shape (of shoe, etc.); *do you take a wide or narrow fitting?*
(c) thing which is fixed in a building but which could be removed; *an electric light fitting; the store is being sold with all its fixtures and fittings*

① **five**
[faɪv]
number 5; *she drank five cups of coffee; he's five (years old) next week; the meeting has been arranged for five (o'clock)*

① **fix**
[fiks]
1 *noun*
difficult position; *he's in a bit of a fix - he has no cash and can't pay for the taxi; well, you've gotten us into a nice fix, haven't you!* (NOTE: plural is **fixes**)
2 *verb*
(a) to fasten or to attach; *fix one end of the rope to the tree and the other to the fence*
(b) to arrange; *we'll try to fix a time for the meeting*
(c) to mend; *the telephone people are coming to fix the telephone; do you know how to fix the printer?*
(d) to make or to prepare a drink, meal, etc.; *let me fix you something to drink; she fixed them some chicken sandwiches*

① **fixed**
[fikst] *adjective*
(a) attached firmly; *the sign is fixed to the post with big nails*
(b) *(price, etc.)* arranged or agreed upon, which cannot be changed; *we have a fixed charge for the boardinghouse;* **fixed rate** = charge or interest that cannot be changed; *they chose a fixed-rate mortgage*

③ **fixture**
['fikstʃər] *noun*
fixtures = objects permanently fixed in a building, like radiators, which are sold with the building; *the store is for sale with all fixtures and fittings*

① **flag**
[flæg]
1 *noun*
piece of brightly colored material with the design of a country or club, etc., on it; *the French flag has blue, red and white stripes; the ship was flying the American flag; the flags*
were blowing in the wind; **white flag** = symbol showing that someone is surrendering
2 *verb*
(a) to grow tired; *we've been traveling all day - no wonder the children are starting to flag*
(b) to flag down = to wave to make a taxi stop; *he stepped out into the street and flagged down a passing taxi*
(c) to put a marker in a computer file; *don't forget to flag the addresses so that we can find them again easily* (NOTE: **flagging - flagged**)

③ **Flag Day**
['flæg 'deɪ] *noun*
day to commemorate the official U.S. flag (June 14); *tomorrow is Flag Day in various states across the country*

② **flake**
[fleɪk] *noun*
(a) small piece of snow which falls from the sky; *snow fell in large soft flakes all night*
(b) tiny, thin piece; *the paint came off in little flakes*

① **flame**
[fleɪm]
1 *noun*
bright part of fire; *flames could be seen coming out of the upstairs windows;* **in flames** = burning; *the building was already in flames when the fire engine arrived*
2 *verb*
to burn brightly; *they carried flaming torches as they walked through the town*

① **flap**
[flæp]
1 *noun*
(a) flat part which is attached to a main structure and which can move up and down; *the pilot tested the wing flaps before taking off*
(b) *(informal)* state of worried excitement; *they got into a flap about the new neighbors' dog*
(c) movement of a bird's wing; *with a flap of its wings, the bird flew off*
2 *verb*
to move up and down like a bird's wing; *flags were flapping in the breeze; the swans stood by the edge of the water, flapping their wings* (NOTE: **flapping - flapped**)

① **flash**
[flæʃ]
1 *noun*
(a) short sudden burst of light; *flashes of lightning lit up the sky with thunder in the distance;* **in a flash** = very quickly; *in a flash, she said "yes"*
(b) device for making a bright light, allowing you to take photographs in the dark; *people sometimes have red eyes in photos taken with a flash*
(c) bright light from a camera; *the scene at the entrance to the movie theater was lit up with flashes from photographers' cameras*

(d) news flash = short item of news, broadcast at an unexpected time; *there was a news flash about an earthquake in California; we interrupt the program for a news flash* (NOTE: plural is **flashes**)

2 *verb*

(a) to light up quickly and suddenly; *lightning flashed all around us*

(b) to flash by *or* **to flash past** = to move or to pass by quickly; *the champion flashed past to win in record time*

① **flashlight**
['flæʃlaɪt] *noun*
small portable usually battery-operated lamp; *take a flashlight if you're going to explore the caves*

④ **flask**
[flæsk] *noun*
bottle for keeping liquids hot or cold; *we've brought a flask of coffee*

② **flat**
[flæt]
1 *adjective*

(a) level, not sloping or curved; *a house with a flat roof*; **flat rate** = fixed charge that never changes; *taxi drivers charge a flat rate of $30 for driving you to the airport; he is paid a flat rate of $3 per thousand*

(b) *(of drink)* no longer bubbly; *my soda is flat*

(c) *(in music)* playing at a lower pitch than it should be; *that piano sounds flat to me* (NOTE: **flatter - flattest**)

2 *adverb*

(a) level, not sloping or curved; *lay your clothes out flat on the bed*; *he tripped over and fell flat on his face*

(b) completely; in a blunt way; *he turned down the offer flat*; **flat broke** = with no money at all; *I can't pay the rent - I'm flat broke*

(c) exactly; *he ran the mile in four minutes flat*

3 *noun*

(a) tire that has lost its air; *I asked the garage to fix the flat*

(b) *GB* apartment, a set of rooms for one family, on one floor, usually in a building with several similar sets of rooms; *we have rented a flat in St. Louis*

(c) *(in music)* pitch that is lower; *they played a piece in E-flat*; *he played D-sharp instead of D-flat*

④ **flatly**
['flætli] *adverb*
in a firm way; *he flatly denied having anything to do with it*

③ **flat out**
['flæt 'aʊt] *adverb*

(a) at full speed; *you'll have to drive flat out to get to the airport in time to catch the plane*

(b) very hard; *he worked flat out to finish his work on time*

① **flatten**
['flætən] *verb*
to make flat; *the rain flattened the corn in the fields*; *thousands of buildings were flattened in the San Francisco earthquake of 1906*

③ **flatter**
['flætər] *verb*
to praise someone too much; *just flatter the boss a bit and he'll give you a raise*

① **flavor**
['fleɪvər]
1 *noun*
particular taste; *the tomato soup had a strange flavor*
2 *verb*
to add things such as spices and seasoning in cooking something, to give it a special taste; *use pepper to flavor the meat*; *soup flavored with herbs*

④ **flaw**
[flɔ] *noun*

(a) defect; *the expert examined the Chinese vase, looking for flaws*; *there must be a flaw in the computer program*

(b) mistake in an argument; *there was a flaw in their calculations*

② **flea**
[fli] *noun*

(a) tiny insect that jumps and sucks blood; *if your cat has fleas, buy a special collar that will get rid of them* (NOTE: do not confuse with **flee**)

(b) flea market = open-air market for secondhand goods; *I bought this painting in the flea market last Saturday*

② **fled**
[fled]
see FLEE

③ **flee**
[fli] *verb*
to flee (from something) = to run away (from something); *as the fighting spread, the locals fled into the woods*; *she tried to flee but her foot was caught in the rope* (NOTE: **fleeing - fled** [fled])

② **fleet**
[flit] *noun*

(a) group of ships belonging together; *when the fleet is in port, the bars are full of sailors*

(b) collection of vehicles; *the company replaces its taxi fleet or fleet of taxis every two years*; *the airline's fleet of Boeing 747s*

② **flesh**
[fleʃ] *noun*

(a) soft part of the body covering the bones; **flesh wound** = wound that goes into the flesh but not very deep; **in the flesh** = in real life (not on TV or in photographs); *it was strange to see the TV news broadcaster in the flesh*

(b) soft part of fruit; *some grapefruit have pink flesh* (NOTE: no plural)

① **flew**
[flu]
see FLY (NOTE: do not confuse with **flu**)

② **flexible**
['fleksɪbl] *adjective*
(a) easy to bend; *shoes with soft rubber soles are flexible*
(b) able to adapt easily; *my timetable is very flexible - we can meet whenever you want*

② **flick**
[flɪk]
1 *noun*
(a) little sharp blow or movement; *he shook off the wasp with a flick of his hand*
(b) movie; *we went to see some old cowboy flick*
2 *verb*
to hit or move lightly and sharply; *the horse flicked its tail to get rid of flies*

① **flies**
[flaɪz]
see FLY

① **flight**
[flaɪt] *noun*
(a) travel in a plane; *go to gate 25 for flight 198*; *all flights to Paris have been canceled*; *she sat next to me on a flight to Montreal*; see also ATTENDANT, CHECK IN
(b) flying, travel through the air; *young birds stay in the nest until they are ready for flight*
(c) **flight of stairs** = set of stairs going in one direction; *go up two flights and the bathroom is the first door on the left*
(d) *(literary)* **to take flight** = to run away; **to put to flight** = to chase away

③ **fling**
[flɪŋ]
1 *noun*
to have your fling = to relax, letting out your high spirits; *now the students have had their fling, perhaps they can get back to work*; **to take a fling at something** = to try to do something
2 *verb*
to throw wildly; *he flung the empty bottle into the sea*; *she flung herself into an armchair* (NOTE: **flinging - flung** [flʌŋ])

② **flip**
[flɪp] *verb*
(a) to hit lightly; *she flipped a switch and the lights went off*
(b) to turn something over; *everyone looked on in admiration as she showed how to flip pancakes*; **to flip over** = to turn over quickly; *before he could do anything the boat had flipped over*
(c) *(informal)* to get very excited; *she flipped when she heard the result of her test*; **to flip out** = to get very angry; *he flipped out when they told him how much the check came to* (NOTE: flipping - flipped)

② **flipper**
['flɪpər] *noun*
(a) long flat piece of rubber which you can attach to your foot to help you swim faster; *she put on her flippers and mask and dove in*
(b) flat arm or leg of a sea animal used for swimming; *the seal walked across the rock on its flippers*

① **float**
[fləʊt]
1 *noun*
(a) piece of cork, etc., attached to a fishing line, which floats on the surface of the water, allowing the line and hook to hang down into the water below; *if the float goes up and down in the water it means you have caught a fish*
(b) decorated truck in a procession; *the long line of parade floats went down Main Street*
(c) soft drink with ice cream floating in it; *she ordered a root beer float*
2 *verb*
(a) to lie or put on the top of a liquid; *dead fish were floating in the river*; *he floated a paper boat on the lake*
(b) to start selling shares in a new company; *the company is to be floated on the stock exchange next week*
(c) to let a currency find its own exchange rate on the international markets, and not fix it at a certain amount; *the government decided that the best course would be to let the dollar float*

① **flock**
[flɒk]
1 *noun*
group of similar animals together, such as sheep, goats, or birds; *a flock of sheep was grazing on the hillside* (NOTE: **flock** is usually used with sheep, goats, and birds such as hens or geese; for cattle, the word to use is **herd**)
2 *verb*
to move in large numbers; *tourists flocked to see the Berlin Wall come down*; *families with children have been flocking to the beaches on the east coast*

① **flood**
[flʌd]
1 *noun*
(a) large amount of water over land that is usually dry; *the floods were caused by heavy rain*
(b) large amount of tears, letters, etc.; *the TV station received floods of complaints after the ad was shown*; *she was in floods of tears when they told her that she had to leave her house*
(c) **the Flood** = story in the Bible of the time when the earth was covered with water and only Noah and his family and animals were saved
2 *verb*
(a) to cover with water; *they are going to build a dam and flood the valley*; *fields were flooded after the river burst its banks*; *he forgot to turn the faucet off and flooded the bathroom*
(b) to flow outside the normal area; *the Nile floods each year*

(c) to come in large numbers; *the office was flooded with complaints* or *complaints came flooding into the office*

① **floor**
[flɔr]
1 *noun*
(a) part of a room on which you walk; *he put the books in a pile on the floor*; *if there are no empty chairs left, you'll have to sit on the floor*
(b) all the rooms on one level in a building; *the bathroom is on the first floor*; *his office is on the fifth floor*; *there is a good view of the town from the top floor*
2 *verb*
to be floored = not to be able to answer from astonishment; *he was floored by one of the questions on the test*

② **flop**
[flɒp]
1 *noun*
(informal) failure; *his new play was a complete flop and closed after only ten performances*; *the movie was a big hit in the U.S.A. but was a flop everywhere else*
2 *verb*
(a) to fall or sit heavily; *the lions lay flopped out in the shade of the trees*; *she got back from the sales and flopped down on the sofa*
(b) *(informal)* to be unsuccessful; *the play was a big hit on Broadway but flopped in London* (NOTE: **flopping - flopped**)

① **floppy**
['flɒpi]
1 *adjective*
(a) which hangs limp; *a white rabbit with long floppy ears*
(b) **floppy disk** = small disk that can be inserted into a computer and removed; *we sent a floppy disk of the data by mail*
2 *noun*
floppy disk; *the data is available on 3.5 inch floppies* (NOTE: plural is **floppies**)

④ **flounder**
['flaʊndər]
1 *verb*
(a) to move with difficulty in water; *he saw her floundering around in the water and realized she couldn't swim*
(b) to be uncertain of an answer to a question; *she started to flounder as soon as the questions got more difficult*
2 *noun*
species of small flat fish

① **flour**
['flaʊər] *noun*
grain crushed to powder, used for making bread, cookies, etc.; *she made the cake by mixing eggs, sugar and flour*

④ **flourish**
['flʌrɪʃ] *verb*
(a) to grow well; to do well; *palm trees flourish in hot countries*

(b) to wave something in the air; *she came in with a big smile, flourishing a check*

④ **flourishing**
['flʌrɪʃɪŋ] *adjective*
which is doing well; *the company is flourishing*; *there is a flourishing black market in spare parts for automobiles*

② **flow**
[flaʊ]
1 *noun*
movement of liquid, air, etc.; *she tried to stop the flow of blood with a tight bandage*; *there was a steady flow of visitors to the exhibition*
2 *verb*
to move along in a smooth way; *the river flows into the sea*; *traffic on the freeway is flowing at 50 miles per hour*

① **flower**
['flaʊər]
1 *noun*
(a) colorful part of a plant which attracts bees and then produces fruit or seeds; *a plant with bright yellow flowers*; **flower shop** = shop that sells flowers; **flower show** = exhibition of flowers; **in flower** = (plant) which is covered with flowers; *you must visit Washington, DC when the cherry trees are in flower*
(b) **flower girl** = girl who is one of the bride's attendants at a wedding; *two little flower girls followed the bride into the church* (NOTE: a boy who does the same is a **page**)
2 *verb*
to produce flowers; *the cherry trees flowered very late this year*; *I want a plant that flowers in early summer*

② **flown**
[fləʊn]
see FLY

② **flu**
[flu] *noun*
common illness like a bad cold, often with a high temperature; *half of the team are down with the flu*; *scores of people have got the flu*; *we all caught the flu, as well as the teacher* (NOTE: do not confuse with **flew**)

③ **fluid**
['fluɪd]
1 *noun*
liquid; *you need to drink plenty of fluids in hot weather*
2 *adjective*
which is not settled; *the situation is still fluid - nothing has been agreed yet*

② **flung**
[flʌŋ] *verb*
see FLING

③ **flush**
[flʌʃ]
1 *noun*
red color on the face; *a flush of anger covered her face* (NOTE: plural is **flushes**)
2 *verb*

(a) to go red in the face; *she flushed with pleasure when she heard the results*

(b) to flush out = to drive out of hiding; *the army brought in helicopters to flush the guerrillas out of their mountain bases*

(c) to flush a lavatory = to wash it out by moving a handle which makes water rush through; *she told the children not to forget to flush the toilet*

3 *adjective*

(a) flush with = level with; *the door must be flush with the wall*

(b) *(informal)* having plenty of money to spend; *I've just been paid, so I'm feeling very flush at the moment*

① **flute**

[flut] *noun*

wind instrument held sideways, and played by blowing across a small hole near the end; *she plays the flute in the local orchestra*

① **fly**

[flaɪ]

1 *noun*

(a) small insect that lays its eggs on food; *he tried to kill the fly with a newspaper*; *waiter, there's a fly in my soup!* (NOTE: plural is **flies**)

(b) trouser front fastened by a zipper or buttons; *look out - your fly's undone*

(c) on the fly = in a hurry; *I had a snack on the fly*

2 *verb*

(a) to move through the air (with wings, in a plane, etc.); *when the cat came into the garden, the birds flew away*; *I'm flying to China next week*; *some birds fly to Mexico for the winter*; *he flies across the Atlantic twice a month*

(b) to make (a plane) move through the air; *the doctor was flying his own plane*

(c) to move fast; *the door flew open and two men rushed in*; *I've got to fly if I want to get home by 6 o'clock*; *his daughter is already two - how time flies!*

(d) to have a flag up; *the ship was flying the Russian flag* (NOTE: **flying - flew** [flu] **- has flown** [fləʊn])

④ **FM**

['ef 'em]

= FREQUENCY MODULATION; *KMXX is at 93.5 FM*

② **foam**

[fəʊm] *noun*

mass of little bubbles; *this soap powder makes a huge amount of foam*; **foam rubber** = rubber in blocks with many little holes in it, used for chair cushions, etc.; *the sofa has foam rubber cushions*

② **focus**

['fəʊkəs]

1 *noun*

(a) point where rays of light from an object meet; *the focus of the beam is a point 20 yards from the spotlight*

(b) *(of a photograph)* point where the details of the photograph are clear and sharp; *adjust the focus so as to get a clear picture*; **in focus** = clear; **out of focus** = not clear

(c) center of attention; *the director brought the star actress to the front of the stage, so that the focus of the audience's attention would be on her* (NOTE: plural is **focuses** *or* **foci** ['fəʊsaɪ])

2 *verb*

(a) to adjust so as to be able to see clearly; *he focused his telescope on a ship in the distance*

(b) to focus on something = to look particularly at something, to concentrate on something; *the paper is focusing on the problems of the TV star's marriage*

② **fog**

[fɒg] *noun*

thick mist made up of millions of drops of water; *all flights out of JFK Airport have been delayed by fog*; *the fog is so thick that you can hardly see twenty feet in front of you*

② **foil**

[fɔɪl]

1 *noun*

thin metal sheet; **tin foil** *or* **aluminum foil** *or* **silver foil** = foil used for wrapping food before cooking; *wrap the fish in foil before putting it on the barbecue grill*

2 *verb*

to prevent a plan from being put into effect; *the bank robbery was foiled by the police*

② **fold**

[fəʊld]

1 *noun*

place where paper, cloth, etc., is bent over on itself; *she wanted the plastic surgeon to remove the folds of skin under her chin*

2 *verb*

(a) to bend something so that one part is on top of another; *fold the piece of paper in half*; *he folded the newspaper and put it into his pocket*

(b) to fold your arms = to cross your arms in front of your body; *he sat on the stage with his arms folded, looking furious*

(c) *(of a business)* to stop trading; *his business folded last December*; *the company folded with debts of over $1.5 m*

② **folder**

['fəʊldər] *noun*

cardboard envelope for holding papers; *she took a folder from the drawer*

② **folk**

[fəʊk] *noun*

(a) people; *we are just ordinary folk* (NOTE: **folk** is plural and takes a plural verb; but the plural form **folks** is also used)

(b) folk dance = traditional country dance; *everyone wears the national costume for the folk dances*; **folk song** = traditional country song

① **follow**
['fɒləʊ] *verb*
(a) to come after or behind; *the group followed the guide around the town*; *what follows B in the alphabet?*; *the dog followed the man across the field*; *I had the impression I was being followed*
(b) to do what someone tells you to do; *she followed the instructions on the can of paint*; *he made the cake following a recipe in the newspaper*
(c) to be certain because of something; *because I lent you money last week, it doesn't follow that I will lend you some every time you ask*; *if the owner of the store is arrested by the police, it follows that his business is likely to close*
(d) to understand; *I don't quite follow you - you want me to drive you all the way to Boston?*

② **follower**
['fɒləʊwər] *noun*
supporter; *the president's followers came into the capital to rally*

① **following**
['fɒləʊwɪŋ] *adjective*
which comes next; *they arrived on Friday and the following day she got sick*; *look at the following picture*

① **fond (of)**
['fɒnd 'ɒv] *adjective*
to be fond of something = to like something; *I am fond of music*; *she's very fond of chocolate*

① **food**
['fud] *noun*
things which you eat; *this hotel is famous for its food*; *do you like Italian food?*; *we arrived at the beach and found that we had forgotten to bring the food*; **food poisoning** = poisoning caused by bacteria in food; *the hotel was closed after an outbreak of food poisoning*; *half the guests at the wedding were ill with food poisoning* (NOTE: **food** is usually used in the singular)

④ **foodstuffs**
['fudstʌfs] *noun*
things which can be used as food; *on some islands, most foodstuffs have to be imported*

② **fool**
[ful]
1 *noun*
stupid person; *you fool! why didn't you step on the brake?*; *I was a fool to think that I could make her change her mind*
2 *verb*
(a) **to fool around** = to play around in a silly way; *stop fooling around with that knife - you're going to have an accident*
(b) to trick someone; *they fooled the old lady into letting them into her house*; *you can't fool me - I know you're not really sick*; **you could have fooled me** = I find it hard to believe; *she says she did her best - well, you could have fooled me!*

① **foolish**
['fulɪʃ] *adjective*
silly or stupid; *don't be so foolish - you can't go to Alaska all alone*; *playing with matches in a lumberyard is a foolish thing to do*

① **foot**
[fʊt]
1 *noun*
(a) end part of your leg on which you stand; *she has very small feet*; *watch out, you stepped on my foot!*; **to put your foot down** = to say firmly that something is not allowed; *you must put your foot down and stop this habit of everyone arriving late*; **to put your foot in it** = to say something embarrassing; *he really put his foot in it when he said that the boss's wife was fat*; *see also* WRONG
(b) bottom part, end; *there is a door at the foot of the stairs*; *there is a traffic light at the foot of the hill*; *put your robe at the foot of the bed*
(c) measurement of how long something is (= 12 inches or approximately 30 cm); *the table is four feet long*; *she's almost six feet tall*; *an eight-foot pole*; *see also* INCH (NOTE: plural is **feet**. Note also that as a measurement **foot** often has no plural: **six foot tall; three foot wide**. **Foot** is used between a number and a noun; **foot** *or* **feet** are used between a number and an adjective. With numbers **foot** is also often written ' **a 6' ladder; he is 5' 6"**: say "he's five foot six inches")
2 *verb*
to foot the bill = to pay the bill; *I found I had to foot the bill for the Christmas party*

◇ **on foot**
['ɒn 'fʊt] *phrase*
walking; *we left the car in the parking lot and went to the church on foot*; *don't wait for the bus - it's quicker to go on foot*

① **football**
['fʊtbɒl] *noun*
(a) ball used for kicking; ball used in the various games of football; *they were kicking a football around in the empty lot*
(b) a game played between two teams of eleven players on a field with a goal at each end, using a ball; *Michael played football in college*; *he spends all his time watching football on TV*; **football player** = person who plays football; *he's a famous football player*

① **footstep**
['fʊtstep] *noun*
(a) sound made by a foot touching the ground; *we heard soft footsteps along the corridor*
(b) **to follow in someone's footsteps** = to do what someone did before; *he's following in his father's footsteps and is going for a legal career*

① **for**
[fɔr] *preposition*
(a) *(showing the purpose or use of something)* *this plastic bag is for old papers*; *what's that*

key for?; **what did she say that for?** = why did she say that?

(b) *(showing why something is given)* **what did you get for your birthday?**; *what shall we buy her for Christmas?*

(c) *(showing person who gets something)* **there was no mail for you this morning**; *I'm making a cup of tea for my mother*

(d) *(showing how long something happens)* **he went to France for two days**; *we've been waiting here for hours*

(e) *(showing distance)* **you can see for miles from the top of the hill**; *the highway goes for miles without any service stations*

(f) *(showing destination)* **is this the plane for Chicago?**; *when is the next bus for LA?*

(g) in exchange; **she gave me $30 for the silver spoon**; *that old computer is no use - I wouldn't give you anything for it*

(h) in support of, in order to get; *we're striking for higher pay*

(i) in the place of someone; *can you write this letter for me?*

(j) with the purpose of; *to go for a walk*; *he was running for the bus*; *all these items are for sale*; see also AS FOR

◇ **for example** *or* **for instance**

['fɔr ɪg'zæmpl or fər 'ɪnstəns] *phrase*

to mention one thing among many; *some animals, for example polar bears, are not used to hot weather* (NOTE: **for example** can also be written as **e.g.**)

◇ **for good**

[fɔr 'gʊd]

forever; *she left school for good when she was 16*

② **forbid**

[fə'bɪd] *verb*

to tell someone not to do something; *she forbade her children to go near the bar*; *we're going to forbid smoking in this restaurant*; *swimming in the reservoir is strictly forbidden* (NOTE: **forbidding - forbade** [fə'bæd] - **forbidden** [fə'bɪdn])

② **forbidden**

[fə'bɪdn] *adjective*

which is not allowed; *the staff is forbidden to use the front entrance*; *Father's new flower garden is forbidden territory to the children*

② **force**

[fɔrs]

1 *noun*

(a) strength or power; *the force of the wind blew tiles off the roof*; *the police had to use force to push back the demonstrators*

(b) organized group of people; *he served in the police force for twenty years*; **the armed forces** = the army, navy and air force; **sales force** = a group of salespeople

2 *verb*

to make someone do something; *he was forced to stop smoking*; *you can't force me to go if I don't want to*

◇ **in force**

['ɪn 'fɔrs] *phrase*

(a) in large numbers; *the police were there in force*

(b) to be in force = to be operating or working; *the rules have been in force since 1996*; **to come into force** = to start to operate or work; *the new regulations will come into force on January 1*

② **forecast**

['fɔrkæst]

1 *noun*

description of what you think will happen in the future; *his forecast of sales turned out to be completely accurate*; **economic forecast** = description of how you expect the economy will perform in the future; **population forecast** = calculation of how many people will be living in a country or in a town at some point in the future; **weather forecast** = report on what kind of weather there will be in the next few days

2 *verb*

to say what will happen in the future; *they are forecasting storms for the south coast*; *they forecast a rise in the number of tourists* (NOTE: forecasting - forecast)

③ **foreground**

['fɔrgraʊnd] *noun*

part of a picture that seems nearest to the viewer; *there is a boat in the foreground against a background of mountains*; compare BACKGROUND

② **forehead**

['fɔrhed] *noun*

part of the front of the head between the eyes and the hair; *his hair was falling down over his forehead*

② **foreign**

['fɒrɪn] *adjective*

(a) not from your own country; *there are lots of foreign medical students at our college*; **foreign exchange** = exchanging the money of one country for money of another; *the dollar was firm on the foreign exchange markets*; **foreign language** = language spoken by people in another country; *she speaks several foreign languages, such as German and Chinese*; **foreign minister** = government minister in charge of a foreign ministry; *the Russian foreign minister chaired the meeting* (NOTE: in the U.S.A. this is the **Secretary of State** and in Great Britain the **Foreign Secretary**); **foreign ministry** = the government department dealing with relations with other countries (NOTE: in the U.S.A. this is the **State Department**)

(b) foreign body = something which should not be there, such as a piece of dust in your eye; *some foreign body seems to have gotten into the test samples*

(c) not something which you are used to or can understand; *the concept of grammar is completely foreign to her*

② **foreigner**
[ˈfɒrɪnər] *noun*

person who does not come from the same country as you; *there are crowds of foreigners in Seattle in the summer; you can tell he's a foreigner when you hear him speak*

② **forest**
[ˈfɒrɪst] *noun*

large area covered with trees; *the country is covered with thick forests; in dry weather there's a danger of forest fires; in winter bears come out of the forest to search for food*

① **forever**
[fərˈevər] *phrase*

always; *I will love you forever and ever; he's forever making a noise; the good times have gone forever;* **to take forever to do something** = to take a very long time to do something; *she took forever to get ready for the party*

④ **forfeit**
[ˈfɔrfɪt]
1 *noun*

thing taken away as a punishment; *the game was a forfeit because there were not enough players*
2 *verb*

to lose something, especially as a punishment; *they forfeited the game because not enough players showed up*

③ **forgave**
[fərˈgeɪv]
see FORGIVE

③ **forge**
[fɔrdʒ] *verb*

(a) to copy something illegally; *he forged the signature on the check; the new design of the bills makes them difficult to forge*
(b) **to forge ahead** = to go forward quickly; *the wind blew harder and the yacht forged ahead; we are forging ahead with our new project*

③ **forgery**
[ˈfɔrdʒəri] *noun*

(a) action of making an illegal copy; *he was sent to prison for forgery* (NOTE: no plural in this meaning)
(b) illegal copy; *the signature proved to be a forgery* (NOTE: plural in this meaning is **forgeries**)

① **forget**
[fərˈget] *verb*

(a) not to remember; *he's forgotten the name of the restaurant; I've forgotten how to play chess; she forgot all about her doctor's appointment; don't forget we're having lunch together tomorrow; great scenes at home - I forgot my wife's birthday!*
(b) to leave something behind; *when he left the office he forgot his car keys* (NOTE: **forgetting - forgot** [fərˈgɒt] **- has forgotten** [fərˈgɒtən])

② **forgive**
[fərˈgɪv] *verb*

to stop being angry with someone; *don't worry about it - I forgive you!; will she ever forgive me for forgetting her birthday?* (NOTE: **forgiving - forgave** [fərˈgeɪv] **- has forgiven**)

① **forgot** *or* **forgotten**
[fərˈgɒt or fərˈgɒtən]
see FORGET

① **fork**
[fɔrk]
1 *noun*

(a) small object with a handle at one end and several sharp points at the other, used for picking food up when eating; *don't try to eat Chinese food with a knife and fork; it's polite to use a fork to eat cake - don't use your fingers;* **garden fork** = very large fork used for digging
(b) Y-shaped road junction, or one of the roads leading from it; *take the left fork toward the red barn and our house is on the right*
2 *verb*

(a) to turn off a road; *fork left at the next intersection*
(b) to split into two parts; *the railway line forks at San Luis Obispo and one branch goes to the coast*
(c) *(informal)* **to fork over** = to turn over to someone; *he forked over his paycheck;* **to fork out** *or* **fork over** = to pay for something, usually without wanting to; *she didn't bring any money, so I had to fork out for the whole meal*

① **form**
[fɔrm]
1 *noun*

(a) paper with blank spaces which you have to write in; **application form** = form that has to be filled out to apply for something; *don't forget to fill out the declaration form*
(b) state or condition; *their team wasn't in top form and lost;* **in good form** = in a good mood, very amusing; *she's in good form today*
(c) shape; *a decoration in the form of a ring*
2 *verb*

(a) to make; *the children formed a circle; form a line here, please*
(b) **formed of** = made of; *the committee is formed of retired schoolteachers*
(c) to organize; *they got together and formed a club*
(d) to start to exist; *ice formed on the windows*

② **formal**
[ˈfɔrml] *adjective*

(a) done according to certain rules; *the formal opening ceremony was performed by the senator;* **formal dress** = clothes for special occasions, black coats and bow ties for men, long dresses for women; *the guests were all in formal dress*
(b) official (agreement); *we made a formal offer for the house yesterday*

(c) (language) which is serious, which is used on special occasions

④ **formally**
['fɔːməlɪ] *adverb*
according to rules, done with ceremony; *the exhibition will be opened formally by the mayor*

④ **format**
['fɔːmæt]
1 *noun*
(a) measurements of a page or book; *printers can handle all sorts of book formats*
(b) shape or size (in which something is made); *what format do you want your invitations printed in?*
(c) style of a computer disk; *my computer can't read that disk - it's the wrong format*
2 *verb*
(a) to arrange text on a computer, so that it is ready for final printing; *style sheets are used to format documents*
(b) to set a computer disk so that it is ready to receive data; *you have to format the disk before you can save data on it* (NOTE: formatting - formatted)

② **formation**
[fɔːˈmeɪʃn] *noun*
(a) shape, forming of something; *a beautiful cloud formation*; *the formation of ice occurs at temperatures below zero*
(b) in formation = in a set pattern; *the birds flew past in a V formation*

② **former**
['fɔːmər]
1 *adjective*
who was at an earlier time; *a former army officer*; *the former champion came in last in the race*
2 *noun*
the former = first person *or* thing mentioned (of two); *Mr. Smith and Mr. Jones are both directors, but the former has been with the company longer* (NOTE: the second of two is called the **latter**)

③ **formerly**
['fɔːməlɪ] *adverb*
at an earlier time; *her house was formerly a post office*; *he was formerly head of our department*

④ **formidable**
['fɔːːmɪdəbl] *adjective*
(a) frighteningly difficult; *climbing Everest is a formidable challenge*
(b) very strong; *the enemy camp is protected by formidable walls and gates*
(c) very impressive (person); *the college president is a formidable woman*

② **formula**
['fɔːmjʊlə] *noun*
(a) statement of a scientific fact, often shown by means of symbols; *the chemical formula of water is H_2O; the drug is made from a secret formula*

(b) Formula I race = automobile race where the automobiles all have engines of the largest classification
(c) milk food for babies; *don't forget to make up some formula* (NOTE: plural is formulas or formulae ['fɔːmjʊliː])

② **fort**
[fɔːt] *noun*
(a) strong army building that can be defended against enemy attacks; *the soldiers rode out of the fort*; *he was posted to a fort in the desert*
(b) to hold the fort = to be in charge while someone is away; *everyone is away on vacation so I've been left holding the fort*

② **forth**
[fɔːθ] *adverb (formal)*
(a) forward; **back and forth** = backward and forward; *I'm fed up with commuting back and forth across town every day*
(b) to set forth = to go out and forward; *the expedition set forth in May*; **to hold forth about something** = to talk without stopping about something; *my father was holding forth about the government* (NOTE: do not confuse with **fourth**)

◇ **and so forth**
[nd ˈsəʊ ˈfɔːθ] *adverb*
with other things; *he talked about plants: flowers, vegetables, and so forth*

② **forthcoming**
[fɔːθˈkʌmɪŋ] *adjective*
(a) soon to come; *his forthcoming novel will be set in Alabama*
(b) *(informal)* full of information, talking a lot; *she wasn't very forthcoming about her wedding*

① **fortieth (40th)**
['fɔːtɪəθ] *adjective & noun*
he came in fortieth in the race; *it's her fortieth birthday tomorrow*

③ **fortress**
['fɔːtrəs] *noun*
strong castle; *the king built a row of fortresses along the border* (NOTE: plural is **fortresses**)

② **fortunate**
['fɔːtʃənət] *adjective*
lucky; *you are very fortunate to have such a lovely family*; *we've been fortunate with the weather this year*

② **fortunately**
['fɔːtʃənətlɪ] *adverb*
by good luck; *fortunately, he had remembered to take an umbrella*; *he was late getting to the airport, but fortunately his flight had been delayed*

③ **fortune**
['fɔːtʃun] *noun*
(a) large amount of money; *he won a fortune from the lottery*; *he made a fortune on the stock market*; *she left her fortune to her three children*; **to cost a fortune** = to cost a lot of

money; *that store has shoes that won't cost a fortune*; *see also* SMALL

(b) what will happen in the future; **to tell someone's fortune** = to say what will happen to someone in the future; *she tells fortunes from cards*

(c) luck, chance; *she had the good fortune to be picked for the U.S. team*

① **forty**
['fɔrti]
number 40; *she's forty (years old)* *he has more than forty pairs of shoes*; *he's in his forties* = between 40 and 49 years old; **the (nineteen) forties (1940s)** = the period from 1940 to 1949 (NOTE: **forty-one** (41), **forty-two** (42), but **forty-first** (41st), **forty-second** (42nd), etc.)

① **forward**
['fɔrwəd]
1 *adjective*
moving in the direction that someone or something is facing; *she made a forward pass across the field to the wide receiver*
2 *adverb*
(a) in the direction that someone or something is facing; *she bent forward to hear what he had to say*; *he took two steps forward*; *the police officer made a sign with his hand and the cars began to go forward*
(b) advanced; *thanks to government red tape we're no further forward with our project*
(c) **to look forward to something** = to think happily about something that is going to happen; *I'm looking forward to my vacation*; *he isn't looking forward to his exams*; *I'm looking forward to seeing her again*
(d) **from that day forward** = from that time on
3 *verb*
to send on a letter to another address; *the bank forwarded the check to his house in the country*; **forwarding address** = address to which mail can be sent; *they moved and forgot to leave a forwarding address so we can't forward their mail*
4 *noun*
player in a team whose job is to attack the other side; *the team's defense came under attack from the opposing team's forwards*

③ **fossil**
['fɒsl] *noun*
remains of an ancient animal or plant left in rock; *they found some fossil shells in the cliffs*; **fossil fuels** = fuels such as coal, which are in fact remains of plants

② **foster**
['fɒstər] *verb*
(a) to be paid to bring up a child who is not your own; *they have fostered several children*
(b) to encourage an idea, etc.; *tourism fosters interest in other countries*

② **fosterparents**
['fɒstər'peərənts] *noun*
parents who bring up a child who is not their own; *her fosterparents brought her up as one of the family*

③ **fought**
[fɔt]
see FIGHT

④ **foul**
[faʊl]
1 *adjective*
(a) bad, unpleasant (taste, language, air, etc.); *what foul weather we're having!*; *the boss has been in a foul mood all day*; *a foul-smelling drain ran down the center of the street*
(b) **foul play** = murder; *the body was hanging upside down and the police suspected foul play* (NOTE: **fouler - foulest**)
2 *noun*
action which is against the rules of a game; *the referee gave a free kick for a foul on the goalkeeper*; *look at the instant replay to see if it really was a foul*
3 *verb*
(a) to make something dirty; *the smoke from the factories fouls the air here*
(b) *(in sport)* to do something to another player which is against the rules of a game; *he fouled four times during that basketball game*
(c) *(informal)* **to foul something up** = to make a mess of something or to create problems; *don't ask John to do it - he's sure to foul it up*

① **found**
[faʊnd] *verb*
(a) to establish, to begin something; *the business was founded in 1900*
(b) **to be founded on something** = to be based on something; *the charges against her are not founded on any facts*
(c) *see also* FIND

② **foundation**
[faʊn'deɪʃn] *noun*
(a) **foundations** = stone or concrete base below the ground on which a building is built; *the foundations of the building need strengthening*; **foundation stone** = stone in a wall which records the start of work on a building; *the mayor laid the foundation stone of the new library*
(b) establishing, setting up; *ever since its foundation in 1892, the company has been a great success*
(c) charity that provides money for certain projects; *a foundation for educational research*

④ **founder**
['faʊndər]
1 *noun*
person who establishes or sets up something; *he was one of the founders of Stanford University*; **founder member** = one of the first to establish a club, etc.; *the U.S.A. and the UK are both founder members of the United Nations*
2 *verb*
(a) to collapse, to fail; *the project foundered for lack of money*

(b) *(formal)* to sink; *the ship foundered in heavy seas*

④ **fountain**
['faʊntɪn] *noun*
street or garden construction which sends a jet of water into the air; *there is a statue and a fountain in the middle of the lake*; *we went for a walk by the fountain in Central Park*

① **four**
[fɔr]
number 4; *he's four (years old) I have an appointment with the doctor at four (o'clock) a square has four corners*; **on all fours** = on hands and knees; *he was crawling around under the desk on all fours*

③ **fourteen**
[fɔr'tin]
number 14; *there are fourteen houses on our block*; *he's fourteen (years old) next week*; **the fourteen hundreds (1400s)** = the period from 1400 to 1499 (NOTE: compare **the fourteenth century**)

① **fourteenth, 14th**
[fɔr'tinθ] *adjective & noun*
she came in fourteenth in the race; *the letter is dated July fourteenth (July 14) it was her fourteenth birthday yesterday*; **the fourteenth century** = the period from 1300 to 1399 (NOTE: compare **the fourteen hundreds**); (NOTE: that with dates **fourteenth** is usually written **14:** **October 14, 1999**: say "October fourteenth")

① **fourth, 4th**
[fɔrθ]
1 *adjective*
this is the fourth time he's had to go to the hospital this year; *it's her fourth birthday tomorrow*; *October fourth (October 4)* **the fourth century** = the period from 300 to 399 AD
2 *noun*
one fourth = 25% (NOTE: do not confuse with **forth**; note that instead of **a fourth** or **a fourth part,** you usually say **a quarter.** Note also that with dates **fourth** is usually written **4: January 4, 1985; October 4, 1991** (say "October fourth"); with names of kings and queens **fourth** is usually written **IV: King Charles IV** (say "King Charles the Fourth"))

① **Fourth of July**
['fɔrθ əv dʒʊ'laɪ] *noun*
the national day of the United States when people celebrate independence; *we're having a Fourth of July party*; *see also* INDEPENDENCE DAY

① **fox**
[fɒks] *noun*
clever wild animal with red fur and a thick tail; *foxes attack lambs in this part of the world*; *we traced the fox back to its hole*

② **fraction**
['frækʃn] *noun*
(a) very small amount; *sales are up a fraction*

this month; *if you move a fraction to the right, you'll all get in the picture*
(b) *(in mathematics)* part of a whole number shown in figures; *¼ and ½ are fractions*
(c) small part of something; *only a fraction of the stolen money was ever found*

② **fracture**
['fræktʃər]
1 *noun*
break (especially in bones); *the X-ray showed the fracture clearly*
2 *verb*
to break a bone; *he fractured his leg in the accident*; *they put her fractured leg in a cast*

② **fragile**
['frædʒaɪl] *adjective*
(a) easily broken, delicate; *be careful when packing the glasses - they're very fragile*
(b) *(informal)* feeling weak and sick after an illness or operation; *she's still very fragile after her recent operation*

④ **fragment**
1 *noun* ['frægmənt]
small piece; *when digging on the site of the old house they found fragments of glass*
2 *verb* [fræg'ment or 'frægmənt]
to break into small pieces; *the organization fragmented as soon as the founder died*

③ **fragrance**
['freɪgrəns] *noun*
pleasant smell; *the fragrance of the roses outside our bedroom windows*

③ **fragrant**
['freɪgrənt] *adjective*
with a sweet smell; *the roses are particularly fragrant when the sun is on them*

④ **frail**
[freɪl] *adjective*
physically weak; *her health is frail*

① **frame**
[freɪm]
1 *noun*
(a) border around glasses, a picture, mirror, window, etc.; *he has glasses with gold frames*; *I think the frame is worth more than the painting*
(b) one picture in a movie; *the book is illustrated with frames from some of his movies*
2 *verb*
(a) to put a frame around a picture; *the photograph has been framed in wood*
(b) to make someone seem to be guilty; *he says he was framed by the police*; *it wasn't me - I've been framed!*
(c) to put words together to make a sentence; *he had some difficulty in framing his reply*; *the note was framed in very formal language*

① **frame of mind**
['freɪm əv 'maɪnd] *noun*
way of thinking or feeling, general mood; *you must wait until he's in the right frame of mind before you ask the boss for a raise*

④ **framework**
['freɪmwɜrk] *noun*

(a) structure supporting a building, etc.; *the framework of the shed is sound - it just needs some paint*

(b) basis of a plan; *they are negotiating the framework of the agreement*

① **France**
[fræns] *noun*

country in Europe, south of Britain and west of Belgium and Germany; *in 1814 Britain was at war with France*; *last year we went to France for vacation*; *he's visiting friends in France* (NOTE: capital: **Paris**; people: **the French**; language: **French**; currency: **euro**)

① **frank**
[fræŋk]

1 *adjective*

saying what you think; *he gave her some frank advice*; *to be really frank with you - I think your plan is awful*

2 *verb*

to stamp a letter with a special machine (instead of using a postage stamp); *the letters were all franked before they left the office*

② **frankly**
['fræŋkli] *adverb*

telling the truth; *frankly, I don't care what you do*; *she spoke frankly about her childhood in Indiana*

② **frantic**
['fræntɪk] *adjective*

wild and very worried; doing things fast; *where have you been? we were getting frantic*; *we had frantic phone calls from your mother*; *it was a frantic race against time to save the children before the tide came in*

③ **fraud**
[frɔd] *noun*

(a) making money by making people believe something that is not true; *he is facing trial for fraud*

(b) person pretending to be something he is not; *she's a fraud - she says she's a movie star, but she's only been in TV commercials*; *he's a fraud - he didn't build that engine himself*

④ **fray**
[freɪ]

1 *noun*

fight; **to join the fray** = to join the battle or argument; *shareholders and management argued over the problem, and then the unions joined the fray*; **ready for the fray** = ready to fight; *are we all ready for the fray?*

2 *verb*

(of material) to become worn so that threads are loose; *the carpet is fraying at the edges*; *you could see the frayed collar on his shirt*; *she stitched tape along the bottom of his pants to stop them from fraying*

② **freak**
[frik]

1 *noun*

(a) unusual type of person, animal or plant; *the white whale is a freak*

(b) person who is mad about something; *my brother's a computer freak*

2 *adjective*

extraordinary (weather); *the walkers were caught in freak weather conditions on the mountain*; *the vineyards were hit by a freak snowstorm in June*

① **free**
[fri]

1 *adjective*

(a) not busy, not occupied; *will you be free next Tuesday?*; *there is a table free in the corner of the restaurant*

(b) not costing any money; *send in four box tops from cereal boxes and you can get a free toy*; *I got a free ticket for the exhibition*; *children are admitted free*; **free gift** = present given by a store to a customer who buys a certain amount of goods; *there is a free gift worth $35 to any customer buying a washing machine*

(c) able to do what you want, not forced to do anything; *he's free to do what he wants*; *it's a free country*

(d) **to be free from** *or* **of something** = to be without something unpleasant; *the country has been declared free of disease*; **free of charge** = with no payment to be made

(e) not in prison, not in a cage; *after six years in prison he's a free man again*; *lions wander free in the park*; **to set free** = to allow someone to leave prison, to let an animal out of a cage; *the young birds were raised in the zoo and then set free in the wild*; **free-range chickens** = chickens that are allowed to run about freely; *she always buys free-range chickens, even though they are more expensive* (NOTE: **freer - freest**)

2 *verb*

(a) to release someone who is trapped; *it took the fire fighters some time to free the passengers on the bus*

(b) to let someone out of prison, an animal out of a cage; *the crowd stormed the jail and freed the prisoners*

② **freedom**
['fridəm] *noun*

(a) state of being free, not trapped, not in prison; *she felt a sense of freedom being in the country after working all week in the city*; *his lawyer pleaded for his client's freedom*

(b) being free to do what you want; *the four freedoms of movement on which the EU is based are the freedom of movement of goods, of capital, of people and of services*; **freedom of information** = making official information held by government departments available to everyone; **freedom of the press** = being able to write and publish in a newspaper what you want, without fear of prosecution, provided that you do not break the law; **freedom of speech** = being able to say what you like without fear of prosecution, provided that you do not break the law

④ **freelance**

['friːlæns]

1 *adjective & noun*

independent (worker), not employed by one particular company; *she is a freelance journalist*; *he works as a freelance*

2 *adverb*

to work freelance = to work for yourself, not being employed by someone else

3 *verb*

to work for yourself; *she freelances for several newspapers*

④ **freelancer**

['friːlænsər] *noun*

independent worker, who is not employed by one particular company; *he works as a freelancer*

① **freely**

['friːli] *adverb*

in an open manner, without being forced; *he freely admitted he had been in the house where the murder took place*; *he gave himself up to the police and freely confessed to the theft of the car*

② **freeway**

['friːweɪ] *noun*

fast highway with few junctions; *we took the freeway to San Diego*

① **freeze**

[friːz]

1 *verb*

(a) to change from liquid to solid because of the cold; *the winter was mild and for the first time ever the river did not freeze over*; *it's so cold that the lake has frozen solid*

(b) to become very cold; *the forecast is that it will freeze tonight*

(c) to make food very cold so that it keeps; *we picked the peas and froze them immediately*

(d) **to freeze to death** = to die of cold; *she went out into the snow and froze to death*

(e) to keep money or costs, etc., at their present level and not allow them to rise; *we have frozen salaries at last year's scale*

(f) to stay very still; *when they heard the squad car coming, they froze* (NOTE: **froze** [frəʊz] - **has frozen**)

2 *noun*

(a) period when it is very cold; *do you remember the great freeze in the winter of 1980?*

(b) **wages and prices freeze** *or* **freeze on wages and prices** = period when wages and prices are not allowed to be increased

① **freezer**

['friːzər] *noun*

refrigerator that freezes food and keeps it frozen;

put the ice cream back into the freezer before it starts to melt; **freezer compartment** = part of a refrigerator where food is put to freeze or to be kept frozen; *we've got some frozen pizzas in the freezer compartment in case of emergencies*

① **freezing**

['friːzɪŋ] *adjective*

very cold; *guests don't appreciate sleeping in freezing bedrooms*; *close the door - it's freezing in here*

② **freight**

[freɪt]

1 *noun*

(a) action of transporting goods by air, sea or land; *we sent the order (by) air freight*

(b) goods transported; *the government is encouraging firms to send freight by rail*; **freight train** = train used for transporting goods

(c) charge for transporting goods; *we had to pay a bill for freight*

2 *verb*

to transport goods; *we freight goods to all parts of the world*

① **French**

[frentʃ]

1 *adjective*

(a) referring to France; *the French railways have a system of high speed trains covering the whole country*

(b) **to take French leave** = to go away without permission

2 *noun*

(a) language spoken in France; *he speaks French very well*; *they are learning French at school*

(b) **the French** = the people of France; *the French are famous for their wines and their cooking*

② **French fries**

['frentʃ 'fraɪz] *noun*

thin stick-shaped pieces of potato, fried in deep oil or fat; *she ordered a hamburger and French fries* (NOTE: often simply called **fries: hamburger and fries**)

④ **frequency**

['friːkwənsi] *noun*

(a) rate at which something happens; *the government is becoming alarmed at the frequency of accidents in the construction industry*

(b) number of movements per second made by a radio wave; *what frequency is National Public Radio on?*; **frequency modulation (FM)** = radio system where the number of waves per second varies; *you can pick up National Public Radio on FM* (NOTE: plural is **frequencies**)

② **frequent**

1 *adjective* ['friːkwənt]

happening often; often seen; *he was a frequent visitor to the library*; *skin cancer is becoming more frequent*; *how frequent are the planes to Atlanta?*

2 *verb* [frɪˈkwent]
(formal) to go somewhere very often; *he frequents the bar at the corner of the block*

② **frequently**
[ˈfriːkwəntli] *adverb*
often; *the ferries don't run as frequently in the winter; she could frequently be seen walking her dog in the park*

① **fresh**
[freʃ] *adjective*
(a) not used or not dirty; *I'll get you a fresh plate*; **fresh air** = open air; *after ten hours, they came out of the coal mine into the fresh air*
(b) made quite recently; *a basket of fresh rolls; let's ask for a fresh pot of coffee*
(c) fresh water = water in rivers and lakes which contains no salt (as opposed to salt water in the sea)
(d) new; *the police produced some fresh evidence*
(e) not canned or frozen; *you can buy fresh fish at the fish counter; fresh fruit salad is better than canned; fresh vegetables are difficult to get in winter*
(f) bright and attractive; *she has a fresh complexion; the kitchen is painted a fresh green color* (NOTE: **fresher - freshest**)

② **freshly**
[ˈfreʃli] *adverb*
newly, recently; *I love the smell of freshly baked bread; I've some freshly made coffee*

② **freshman**
[ˈfreʃmən] *noun*
student in the first year of study at a high school, college or university; *next year my sister will be a freshman at Harvard*

④ **freshwater**
[ˈfreʃwɔːtər] *adjective*
(water in rivers and lakes) which contains no salt; *we have a cottage on a freshwater lake*

① **Friday**
[ˈfraɪdeɪ] *noun*
the fifth day of the week, the day between Thursday and Saturday; *we all had a meal together last Friday; we always go to the movie theater on Friday evenings; we normally have our meetings on Fridays; Friday is a day of rest for Muslims; today is Friday, June 20*; **Good Friday** = the Friday before Easter Day; **man Friday** *or* **girl Friday** = general helper in an office

④ **fridge**
[frɪdʒ] *noun*
(informal) refrigerator, kitchen machine for keeping things cold; *the fridge is empty - we must buy some more food; shall I put the milk back in the fridge?*

① **fried**
[fraɪd] *adjective*
which is cooked in a little oil or fat; *would you like a fried egg for breakfast?; add the fried*

onions to the meat; we had fried rice with our sweet and sour pork; see also FRY

① **friend**
[frend] *noun*
person whom you know well and like; *she's my best friend; we're going on vacation with some friends from work*; **to make friends with someone** = to get to know and like someone; *we made friends with some French people on vacation*

② **friendly**
[ˈfrendli] *adjective*
like a friend, wanting to make friends; *don't be frightened of the dog - he's very friendly; we're not on friendly terms with the people who live next door* (NOTE: **friendlier - friendliest**)

① **friendship**
[ˈfrendʃɪp] *noun*
state of being friends; *he formed several lasting friendships at school*

① **fries**
[fraɪz]
see FRENCH FRIES

① **frighten**
[ˈfraɪtn] *verb*
to make someone afraid; *take off that horrible mask - you'll frighten the children; the cat has frightened all the birds away*

① **frightened**
[ˈfraɪtənd] *adjective*
full of fear, scared; *the frightened children ran out of the building*; **frightened of something** *or* **someone** = afraid of someone or something; *don't be frightened of the dog - he won't hurt you*

① **frightening**
[ˈfraɪtnɪŋ] *adjective*
which causes fear; *a frightening sound of footsteps in the corridor; he had a frightening thought - what if no one heard his cries for help?*

③ **fringe**
[frɪndʒ] *noun*
(a) edging of a scarf, carpet, etc., consisting of loose threads hanging down; *a lampshade with a yellow fringe*
(b) outer edge of an area; *around the fringe of the crowd people were selling souvenirs*; **fringe benefits** = extra benefits on top of a salary (such as a free car, etc.)

① **frog**
[frɒg] *noun*
(a) small animal with long legs, which lives both on land and water; *can you hear the frogs calling around the pond?; the wicked queen turned the prince into a frog*
(b) *(informal)* **to have a frog in your throat** = to have something in your throat which stops you speaking clearly; *he said "excuse me, I've a frog in my throat" and coughed several times*

① **from**
[frɒm] *preposition*
(a) away; *take three from four and you get one*
(b) *(showing the place where something starts or started)* *he comes from Germany; the bees went from flower to flower; we've had a letter from the bank; he read the book from beginning to end or from cover to cover*
(c) *(showing the time when something starts or started)* *I'll be at home from 8 o'clock for the rest of the evening; the hours of work are 9:30 to 5:30, from Monday to Friday; from now on I'm going to get up early*
(d) *(showing distance)* *it is more than 15 miles from here to the airport*
(e) *(showing difference)* *can you tell butter from margarine?; his job is totally different from mine*
(f) *(showing a cause)* *he died from the results of the accident; she suffers from coughs every winter*

① **front**
[frʌnt]
1 *noun*
(a) part of something which is furthest forward; *the front of the house is on Lincoln Street; there is a picture of the White House on the front of the book; she spilled coffee down the front of her dress*
(b) road or pedestrian walk along the edge of the sea; *we went for a walk along the front; a hotel on the seafront or a seafront hotel*
(c) line marking the point where two masses of air meet; **cold front** = edge of a mass of cold air, bringing clouds and rain; **warm front** = moving mass of warm air which pushes away a mass of cold air and also brings rain
2 *adjective*
which is in front; *she sat in the front seat, next to the driver*

◇ **in front of**
[ɪn ˈfrʌnt ɒv] *phrase*
before something; *don't stand in front of the truck - it may start suddenly; there are six people in front of me in the line; you can park your car in front of the store*

② **front door**
[ˈfrʌnt ˈdɔr] *noun*
main door to a house or building; *he came to the front door and rang the bell*

② **frontier**
[ˈfrʌntiər] *noun*
(a) furthest part of settled land; *the frontier of the Wild West*
(b) border between two countries; *she was stopped at the frontier because her passport was invalid*

① **frost**
[frɒst] *noun*
(a) white icy covering on the ground, trees, etc., when the temperature is below freezing; *the garden was white with frost*

(b) cold weather, when the temperature is below freezing; *there was a hard frost last night; a late frost can damage young plants*

① **frown**
[fraʊn]
1 *noun*
pulling your eyebrows together as a sign that you are angry, disapprove of something, or are worried; *take that frown off your face - everything's going to be all right*
2 *verb*
to pull your eyebrows together because you are concentrating or worried; *he frowned as he tried to do the calculation;* **to frown on** *or* **upon something** = to disapprove of something; *the teachers frown on singing in the halls; the company frowns on people who bring food into the office; this type of behavior is frowned upon by the municipal authorities*

① **froze**
[frəʊz]
see FREEZE

② **frozen**
[ˈfrəʊzn] *adjective*
(a) very cold; *come inside - you must be frozen out there*
(b) at a temperature below freezing point; *we went skating on the frozen lake;* **frozen food** = food stored at a temperature below freezing point; *use frozen peas if you can't get fresh ones*
(c) not allowed to be changed or used; **frozen account** = bank account where the money cannot be taken out or used because of a court order; *see also* FREEZE

① **fruit**
[frut]
1 *noun*
part of a plant which has seeds and which is often eaten raw and is usually sweet; *I must remember to buy some fruit at the store before we go on our picnic; he has six fruit trees in his orchard;* **fruit salad** = pieces of different fruit, cut up and mixed together; *for dessert we had fruit salad and yogurt* (NOTE: no plural: **some fruit, a piece of fruit**)
2 *verb*
to produce fruit; *the strawberries have finished fruiting; some pears fruit quite late in the season*

② **fruit juice**
[ˈfrut dʒus] *noun*
juice from fruit; *she started breakfast with a glass of fruit juice*

④ **frustrate**
[frʌˈstreɪt] *verb*
to prevent someone doing what he wants to do; *the weather frustrated the efforts of the rescue team*

① **fry**
[fraɪ] *verb*
to cook in oil or fat in a shallow pan; *fry the onions on a low heat so that they don't burn;*

fry the eggs in some fat (NOTE: **fries** [fraɪz] - **frying** - **fried** [fraɪd])

② **frying pan**
['fraɪɪŋ pæn] *noun*
shallow, open pan used for frying; *she burned her hand on the hot frying pan*; *put some butter in the frying pan and fry the mushrooms*

③ **ft**
= FOOT, FEET

① **fuel**
['fjʊəl]
1 *noun*
substance (coal, gas, oil, gas, wood, etc.) that can be burned to give heat or power; *what fuel do you use to heat the house?*; *what's the fuel consumption of your automobile?*; *we ran out of fuel on the freeway*
2 *verb*
(a) to provide fuel for; *the power station is fueled by coal*
(b) to increase; *our money worries were fueled by news of an increase in the mortgage rate*

④ **fulfill**
[fʊl'fil] *verb*
to complete something in a satisfactory way; *did he fulfill his promise and take you to the theater?*; *he died before he could fulfill his ambition to climb Everest*; *we are so busy that we cannot fulfill any more orders before Christmas*

① **full**
[fʊl] *adjective*
(a) with as much inside as is possible; *is the box full?*; *the bag is full of potatoes*; *we couldn't get on the first bus because it was full*; *all the hotels were full*; **I'm full up** = I've eaten so much that I can't eat anymore
(b) complete; *you must give the police full details of the accident*; *write your full name and address at the top of the paper*; **full fare** = price of a ticket for an adult, without any reduction; *children over 12 must pay full fare*; **full moon** = time when the moon appears as a complete circle (NOTE: **fuller - fullest**)

③ **full-scale**
[fʊl'skeɪl] *adjective*
(a) the same size as in real life; *a full-scale model of a Roman house*
(b) complete; *it started as a dispute over a few islands and soon developed into a full-scale war*

③ **full-time**
[fʊl'taɪm] *adjective & adverb*
working all the normal working time (i.e. about seven hours a day, five days a week); *she has full-time work or she works full-time*; *we have eight full-time and two part-time teachers at our school*; *compare* PART-TIME

② **fully**
['fʊli] *adverb*
completely or entirely; *he was fully aware that he had made a mistake*; *she still hasn't fully recovered from her accident*; *the hotel is fully booked for the Christmas week*; *when fully grown, an elephant can weigh several tons*

③ **fume**
[fjum]
1 *noun*
fumes = smoke or gas; *the children died from breathing in the fumes from the gas stove*
2 *verb*
to be angry; *after he had read the report he was absolutely fuming*

① **fun**
[fʌn]
1 *noun*
amusement; *swimming and playing around on the beach is great fun*; **to have fun** = to enjoy yourself; *we had a lot of fun on the river*; **to make fun of someone** = to laugh at someone; *don't make fun of her - she's trying her best*; *he made fun of the president*; **for fun** = as a joke; *she poured water down his neck for fun*; *just for fun, he drove the automobile through town dressed as a monkey*; *why did you do that? - just for the fun of it!*
2 *adjective*
amusing; *sitting on the grass in Central Park is a fun way of passing a Sunday afternoon*

③ **function**
['fʌŋkʃn]
1 *noun*
(a) party, gathering of people; *the college function was scheduled for next weekend*; *the president is tied up with official functions all week*; **function room** = room in a restaurant or hotel where private parties are held
(b) work done by something; *what's the function of that red switch?*
2 *verb*
(a) to work; *the computer is still functioning well after months of constant use*
(b) **to function as** = to serve as; *the sofa functions as a bed if we have visitors*

② **fund**
[fʌnd]
1 *noun*
(a) sum of money set aside for a special purpose; *she contributes to a retirement fund*
(b) collection; *he has a fund of stories about his time at sea*
2 *verb*
to provide money for a special purpose; *we have asked the government to fund the building of the new library*; *the company is funding her manager's course*

③ **fundamental**
[fʌndə'mentl] *adjective*
basic, essential; *the fundamental difference between us is that I apologize for my mistakes and you don't*; *good air quality is fundamental for children's health*

③ **funding**
['fʌndɪŋ] *noun*
money for something; *who is providing the funding for the famine relief mission?*; *where is the funding for the new library coming from?*

② **funds**
[fʌndz] *noun*
money that is available for spending; *he started college and then ran out of funds*; *the company has the funds to set up the research program*; *funds are available to get the project off the ground*

② **funeral**
['fjunərəl] *noun*
ceremony when a dead person is buried; *the church was packed for her funeral*; *the funeral will take place on Friday morning*

④ **fungus**
['fʌŋgəs] *noun*
plant which has no green leaves or flowers and which lives on rotting stuff in damp places; *some fungi, such as mushrooms, can be eaten, but others are poisonous* (NOTE: plural is **fungi** ['fʌŋgaɪ])

② **funnel**
['fʌnl] *noun*
(a) tube with a wide mouth and narrow bottom used when pouring liquids from one container into another; *using a funnel, she poured the oil from the pan into a bottle*
(b) chimney on a ship from which the smoke comes; *the liner sailed away, with smoke pouring out of her funnel*

① **funny**
['fʌni] *adjective*
(a) which makes you laugh; *we watched a funny program on children's TV*; *he made funny faces and all the children laughed*; **funny bone** = part of the elbow which gives a painful sensation when you hit it by accident
(b) strange or odd; *she's been behaving in a funny way recently*; *there's a funny smell in the bathroom* (NOTE: **funnier - funniest**)

① **fur**
[fɜr] *noun*
soft coat of an animal; *this type of cat has very short fur*; *she was wearing a fur coat* (NOTE: do not confuse with **fir**)

② **furious**
['fjʊəriəs] *adjective*
very angry; *he's furious because someone has scratched his new car*; *the passengers were furious at having to wait four hours*; *she had a furious argument with her brother*

② **furnish**
['fɜrnɪʃ] *verb*
(a) to put furniture into a house, office, etc.; *we rented a furnished apartment for a year*; *his house is furnished with antiques*
(b) *(formal)* to provide; *he furnished the police with a complete list of addresses*; *the city council furnished details of the improvement plan*

① **furniture**
['fɜrnɪtʃər] *noun*
tables, chairs, beds, cupboards, etc.; *the burglars stole all our office furniture*; *you should cover up all the furniture before you start painting the ceiling* (NOTE: there is no plural: **some furniture; a lot of furniture; a piece of furniture**)

② **furry**
['fɜri] *adjective*
covered with fur; *a little furry caterpillar*

① **further**
['fɜrðər]
1 *adverb*
a greater distance; or in addition; *can you all move further back, I can't get you in the picture*; *the police station is quite close, but the post office is further away*; *I was further disgusted by his table manners*
2 *adjective*
more; *the bank needs further information about your salary*; *please send me further details of vacations in Virginia*

③ **furthermore**
[fɜrðə'mɔr] *adverb*
also, in addition; *the party was good fun, and furthermore it didn't end too early*

① **furthest**
['fɜrðəst] *adverb & adjective*
the greatest distance; *some of the staff live quite close to the office, but James lives furthest away*; *the furthest distance I have ever flown is to Hong Kong*; *see also* FARTHEST

③ **fury**
['fjʊəri] *noun*
fierce anger; *he turned to us in fury and shouted at us to get out*; *in a fit of fury he threw the plate across the kitchen*

③ **fuse**
[fjuz]
1 *noun*
small piece of wire in an electric circuit which prevents damage; *the plug has a 13-amp fuse*; *if the lights go out, the first thing to do is to check the fuses*
2 *verb*
to become mixed by melting together

① **fuss**
[fʌs]
1 *noun*
unnecessary excitement or complaints; **to make a fuss** *or* **to kick up a fuss about something** = to complain for a long time about something which is not important; *what's all the fuss about?*; *don't make such a fuss - it's only a little scratch* (NOTE: no plural)
2 *verb*
to fuss over something = to worry about something, or to pay too much attention to

something; *don't fuss - it will be all right*; *stop fussing over your hair, you look fine*

② **future**
['fjutʃər]
1 *noun*
(a) time which has not yet happened; *what are his plans for the future?*; *you never know what the future will bring*; *can you imagine what Boston will be like in the future?*
(b) in the future = from now on; *try to get to the office on time in the future*

(c) future (tense) = form of a verb which shows that something will happen; *"he will eat" and "he is going to eat" are future forms of the verb "to eat"*

2 *adjective*
which is coming, which has not happened yet; *they are spending all their time preparing for their future retirement*; *I try to save something each week for future expenses*

Gg

③ **G, g**
[dʒɪ]
seventh letter of the alphabet, between F and H; *"jogging" is spelled with two Gs*

③ **g**
= GRAM

③ **gadget**
['gædʒɪt] *noun*
useful tool; *I bought a gadget for taking the tops off bottles*

② **gain**
[geɪn]
1 *noun*
(a) profit; **capital gains** = profit made by selling assets
(b) increase in weight, quantity, size; *there was no gain in weight*; **gain in experience** = getting more experience
2 *verb*
(a) to get; *the army gained control of the country*; *she gained some useful experience working on a farm*
(b) to increase in value; *the dollar gained six cents on the foreign exchange markets*
(c) *(of a clock, watch)* to move ahead of the correct time; *my watch gains five minutes a day*
(d) to gain on someone *or* **something** = to get closer to a person or thing you are chasing; *with each lap he was gaining on the race leader*

② **galaxy**
['gæləksi] *noun*
(a) huge group of stars; *there are vast numbers of galaxies*; *the speed of stars near the center of a galaxy may indicate the presence of black holes*
(b) mass of movie stars, etc.; *there is a galaxy of singers on our show tonight* (NOTE: plural is **galaxies**)

④ **gale**
[geɪl] *noun*
very strong wind; *several trees were blown down in the gale*

④ **galleon**
['gælɪən] *noun*
large 16th century sailing ship; *divers found the wreck of a Spanish galleon*

③ **gallery**
['gæləri] *noun*
(a) (art) gallery = place where pictures and sculptures are shown to the public ; *the new gallery has a collection of modern paintings*
(b) (art) gallery = store selling pictures, antiques; *she runs an art gallery selling pictures by local artists*
(c) balcony inside a church, hall or theater; *a group of musicians played in the gallery*; **public gallery** = place in a court, council chamber, etc., where the public can sit to listen to what is being said (NOTE: plural is **galleries**)

① **gallon**
['gælən] *noun*
measure of quantity of liquid, equal to 3.78 liters; *the car's gas tank was empty and I had to put in seven gallons of gasoline*; *an economy car gets 40 miles to the gallon* (NOTE: **gallon** is written **gal(l)** with figures: **80 gal(l)**)

① **gallop**
['gæləp]
1 *noun*
fast ride on a horse; *let's go for a gallop along the beach*
2 *verb*
to go fast; *the soldiers galloped through the woods*

① **gamble**
['gæmbl]
1 *noun*

risk; *this investment is a bit of a gamble; he took a gamble with the weather in planning his picnic for the beginning of March*

2 *verb*

to bet money on cards, horses, etc.; *he lost all his money gambling on dog races*; **to gamble on something happening** = to do something, hoping that something will happen; *we're gambling on good weather for the town's fall festival*

① **game**
['geɪm]
1 *noun*

(a) sport which can be won with skill, strength or luck; *she's not very good at games*

(b) single match between two opponents or two opposing teams; *everyone wanted to watch the basketball game; do you want a game of billiards?; our team have won all their games this year*

(c) single round in tennis, bridge, etc.; *game, set and match to Sampras; she's winning by six games to three*

(d) **to give the game away** = to reveal a secret plan; **so that's his little game!** = now we know what his plans are; **the game's up** = you've been found out

(e) **games** = large organized sports competition; *the Olympic Games*

(f) wild animals and birds (deer, rabbits, etc.) which are killed for sport or food; *our cookbook has several recipes for game*; **big game** = large wild animals, such as lions, elephants, etc.; **game reserve** *or* **game park** = park where wild animals are preserved (NOTE: no plural in this meaning)

2 *adjective*

ready and willing; *I'm game to have a go; she's always game for anything*

① **gang**
[gæŋ]
1 *noun*

(a) band of criminals, youths, etc.; *an important South American drug gang*

(b) group of workers; *gangs of men worked to repair the train tracks*

2 *verb*

to gang up (with someone) = to join up with someone to do something; *the different unions are ganging up to negotiate a hike in pay*; **to gang up on someone** = to form a group to attack one person; *she felt as if the office staff was ganging up on her*

① **gangster**
['gæŋstər] *noun*

member of a gang of criminals; *gangsters have taken over all the bars in the town*

② **gap**
[gæp] *noun*

(a) space between two things; *the sheep all rushed through the gap in the hedge; his retirement will leave a gap in the committee; we*

need someone to fill a gap in our sales force; **gap in the market** = place where you may be able to sell; *we think we've found a gap in the market*

(b) difference; *the gap is widening between rich and poor*; **age gap** = difference between people of different age groups; **generation gap** = difference between people of different generations; **trade gap** = difference between the value of a country's exports and the value of its imports

④ **gape**
['geɪp] *verb*

to open your mouth wide in surprise or shock; *he gaped when he saw the bill*

① **garage**
['gærɪdʒ or 'gærɑʒ]
1 *noun*

(a) small building where you can keep a car; *he put the car into the garage overnight; she drove the car out of the garage; don't forget to lock the garage door; the hotel has garage space for thirty cars*; **garage sale** = private sale of household goods that you don't want, held inside or outside your garage

(b) business where gas is sold and automobiles, etc., are repaired or sold; *where's the nearest garage? - I need some gas; I can't drive you to the airport - my car is in the garage; you can hire cars from the garage near the post office* (NOTE: this type of garage is also called a **service station**)

2 *verb*

to keep a vehicle in a garage; *the car was garaged overnight in the hotel underground parking lot*

① **garbage**
['gɑrbɪdʒ] *noun*

(a) household waste; *don't forget to take out the garbage*

(b) *(informal)* rubbish; *I don't believe a word of what he said - it's just garbage* (NOTE: no plural)

① **garbage can**
['gɑrbɪdʒ 'kæn] *noun*

large plastic or metal container for household garbage; *they come to empty the garbage cans once a week; she put the rest of the dinner in the garbage can* (NOTE: also called a **trash can**)

① **garbage collector**
['gɑrbɪdʒ kə'lektər] *noun*

person employed by a town to remove household garbage; *the garbage collectors are supposed to come and empty our garbage cans once a week*

① **garden**
['gɑrdən] *noun*

(a) yard, a piece of ground near a house, used for growing vegetables, flowers, etc.; *we grow all the vegetables we need in the garden; your sister's outside, sitting in the garden*

(b) **gardens** = large area of garden, usually in several sections; *the hotel is surrounded by* *flower gardens*; **botanical gardens** = gardens with a wide variety of plants which are classified and labeled

② **gardener**
['gɑrdnər] *noun*
person who looks after a garden; *she's a great gardener*; *I was just looking through the want ads when I saw that they wanted a gardener*

② **gardening**
['gɑrdnɪŋ] *noun*
looking after a garden; *he reads his gardening magazine every week*; *she does some gardening every Saturday*

③ **garlic**
['gɑrlɪk] *noun*
bulb of a plant with a strong smell, a little like an onion; *his breath smelled of garlic*; **garlic bread** = French bread heated with butter and garlic

② **garment**
['gɑrmənt] *noun*
piece of clothing; *she was dressed in a long loose garment with wide sleeves*

① **gas**
[gæs]
1 *noun*
(a) chemical substance which has no form and that becomes liquid if it is cooled; *air is formed of several gases, mainly nitrogen and oxygen*; **gas attack** = attack on the enemy using poison gas (NOTE: plural in this meaning is **gases**)
(b) chemical substance used for cooking or heating; *there is a smell of gas or it smells of gas in the kitchen*; *turn up the gas or turn the gas up - the teakettle hasn't boiled yet*; *the hotel is heated by gas*
(c) = GASOLINE; *we ran out of gas on the freeway*; *(informal)* **to step on the gas** = to drive faster; *step on the gas - we'll miss the train!* (NOTE: no plural in meanings (b) and (c))
2 *verb*
to poison or kill someone using gas; *thousands of people were gassed during the war* (NOTE: **gassing - gassed**)

① **gasoline**
['gæsəlin] *noun*
liquid used to drive an automobile engine (NOTE: usually shortened to **gas**)

② **gasp**
[gæsp]
1 *noun*
(a) taking in your breath suddenly, showing surprise or pain; *she gave a gasp when she saw the face at the window*
(b) last gasp = final action, which marks the end of something; *the killings were the last gasp of the army regime*; **he's at his last gasp** = it is almost the end of his life, reign, etc.; *the poor car is at its last gasp - we really must replace it*
2 *verb*
(a) to take a short deep breath; *he gasped when he saw the bill*

(b) to have difficulty in breathing; *after the race he lay on the ground gasping for breath*

① **gas station**
['gæs 'steɪʃn] *noun*
place where you can buy gasoline; *where's the nearest gas station?*

① **gas tank**
['gæs 'tæŋk] *noun*
tank in a vehicle in which the fuel is stored; *I put water into my gas tank by mistake*; *the reason your car won't start is that the gas tank is empty*

① **gate**
[geɪt] *noun*
(a) low door made of bars of wood or metal, in a wall or fence, not in a building; *shut the gate - if you leave it open the sheep will get out of the field*; *there is a white gate leading into the farm*
(b) door that leads to an aircraft at an airport; *flight 270 is now boarding at Gate 23*
(c) number of people attending an event such as a sports match; *there was a gate of 20,000 people*

① **gather**
['gæðər] *verb*
(a) to bring together; *he gathered his papers together after the lecture*; *she has been gathering information on the history of the local school*
(b) to come together; *groups of people gathered outside the White House*
(c) to understand; *I gather that his father is in the hospital*; *we gather he has left the office*
(d) to pick plants, flowers, fruit, etc.; *the children were gathering blackberries*; *the grape harvest has been gathered*
(e) to gather speed = to go faster; *the bus gathered speed as it ran down the hill*

③ **gathering**
['gæðərɪŋ]
1 *noun*
group of people who have come together; *a speaker from another association will address the gathering*
2 *adjective*
which is coming together; *the gathering crowds did not realize that the president had already left the country*; **the gathering storm** = the storm which is coming

① **gauge**
[geɪdʒ]
1 *noun*
instrument to measure depth, pressure, etc.; **fuel gauge** = instrument that shows how much gas there is in a gas tank; *I don't know how much gas I have left, because the gauge is stuck*; **tire gauge** *or* **pressure gauge** = instrument for measuring the amount of air in a tire
2 *verb*
to measure or to calculate; *this is an instrument which gauges the speed of the wind*; *the chairman tried to gauge the tone of the meeting*

① **gave**
[geɪv]
see GIVE

① **gay**
[geɪ]
1 *adjective*
(a) homosexual; *did you know her brother is gay?*; *it's a club where gay men and women meet*; *they met in a gay bar in San Francisco*
(b) bright, lively colors; *the houses along the street are all painted in gay colors* (NOTE: **gayer - gayest**)
2 *noun*
homosexual man (or woman); *a club for gays*

② **gaze**
[geɪz]
1 *noun*
steady look; *she refused to meet his gaze*
2 *verb*
to look in a steady way; *she gazed into his eyes*; *he stood on the cliff, gazing out to sea*

③ **G.B.**
[ˈdʒi ˈbi]
= GREAT BRITAIN

④ **GDP**
[dʒidiˈpi]
= GROSS DOMESTIC PRODUCT

③ **gear**
[gɪər]
1 *noun*
(a) equipment; *he took all his climbing gear with him*; *she was carrying her painting gear in a bag*; **landing gear** = wheels of an aircraft and their supports
(b) *(informal)* clothes; *she was putting on her tennis gear*
(c) *(of automobile, bicycle, etc.)* **gears** = arrangement of wheels of different sizes with teeth which link together, controlling the rate at which the machine moves; **to shift gears** = to move from one gear into another; *there was a loud noise as he tried to shift gears*; **bottom gear** *or* **first gear** *or* **low gear** = the lowest gear, used when going slowly, or when climbing hills; **top gear** *or* **high gear** = the highest gear, used for fast speeds; *the automobile is most economical in high gear*; *always use a low gear when going down steep hills*; **in gear** = with the gears engaged (as opposed to "in neutral")
2 *verb*
to gear something to = to fit something to; *the ferry services are geared to the tourist season*; *lessons must be geared to the students' ability*

② **gearshift lever**
[ˈgɪərʃɪft] *noun*
handle in an automobile that changes the gears; *you push the gearshift lever down and toward you to get into reverse*

② **gee (whiz)**
[ˈdʒi ˈwɪz] *interjection showing surprise*; *gee! that's some automobile!*

① **geese**
[gis] *see* GOOSE

④ **gel**
[dʒel]
1 *noun*
thick substance, especially one spread on your hair to keep it tidy; *he smoothed the gel over his hair*
2 *verb*
to become more certain or more clear; *the details of the plan began to gel* (NOTE: **gelling - gelled**)

④ **gender**
[ˈdʒendər] *noun*
(a) being male or female; *everyone has the same rights, regardless of race, religion or gender*
(b) *(in grammar)* system where nouns and adjectives have different forms to indicate if they are masculine or feminine; *what's the gender of "Tisch" in German?*

④ **gene**
[dʒin] *noun*
element in the body which carries characteristics from parent to children; *all the children have red hair like their mother - it must be in their genes*

① **general**
[ˈdʒenərəl]
1 *adjective*
(a) ordinary, not special; *he had a good general education, but didn't specialize in any particular field*; **in general** = normally; *in general, the weather is warmer in the south*
(b) referring to everything, everybody; *they issued a general instruction to all the staff*; **the General Assembly of the United Nations** = meeting of the representatives of all countries that are members of the UN; **general election** = election where all voters can vote for candidates; *which party won the last general election?*; **general store** = small country store that sells a large range of goods
(c) general anesthetic = substance given to make a patient lose consciousness so that a major operation can be carried out; *you will have to be given a general anesthetic for this operation*; *this operation can be carried out under local rather than general anesthetic* (NOTE: an anesthetic for one part of the body is a **local anesthetic**)
2 *noun*
army officer of high rank; *he has only recently been promoted to general*

② **generally**
[ˈdʒenərəli] *adverb*
normally; *the office is generally closed between Christmas and New Year*

③ **general practitioner (G.P.)**
[ˈdʒenərəl prækˈtɪʃənər] *noun*
family doctor who does not specialize in any particular branch of medicine; *Dr Smith is a*

general practitioner; *our son wants to be a general practitioner when he graduates from medical school*

③ **generate**
['dʒenəreɪt] *verb*
to produce power, etc.; *we use wind to generate electricity*

③ **generation**
[dʒenə'reɪʃn] *noun*
(a) production of power, etc.; *the generation of electricity from waves*
(b) all people born at about the same time; *the 1960s generation had an easier life than we did*; *people of my father's generation cannot understand computer technology*; **generation gap** = lack of understanding between generations
(c) members of a family born about the same time; **younger generation** = the younger members of a family; **older generation** = the older members of a family
(d) series of machines made at about the same time; *they are developing a new type of engine for the next generation of aircraft*

③ **generator**
['dʒenəreɪtər] *noun*
machine that makes electricity; *the hospital had to use the generator because there was a power outage*

③ **generous**
['dʒenərəs] *adjective*
(a) giving money or presents gladly; *a generous birthday present*
(b) very willing to give your time, etc., to help someone; *he's been very generous with his time*
(c) large; *a generous helping of pudding*

④ **genetic**
[dʒə'netɪk] *adjective*
referring to genes; **genetic code** = information which makes up a cell, and which is passed on as the cell divides

④ **genetically**
[dʒə'netɪkli] *adverb*
in a way which involves changes to genes; **genetically modified crops** = plants where the genes have been changed to make them resist diseases

④ **genetics**
[dʒə'netɪks] *noun*
the science and study of genes; *he wrote an article on the latest advances in genetics*

② **genius**
['dʒiniəs] *noun*
(a) very intelligent person; person who has great ability; *she's a chess genius*; *Napoleon was a military genius*; *she is at the top of her class - she's a real genius* (NOTE: plural in this meaning is **geniuses**)
(b) **evil genius** = wicked person who influences others; *Rasputin was the evil genius of the Russian court*

(c) great ability; *he has a genius for keeping people amused*

④ **genre**
['ʒɑnrər] *noun*
type of art, writing, etc.; *he is one of best writers in this genre*; **genre painting** = painting of scenes of everyday life; *Pieter de Hoogh is a master of Dutch genre painting*

① **gentle**
['dʒentl] *adjective*
(a) soft and kind; *the nurse has gentle hands*
(b) not very strong; *with a little gentle persuading she agreed to the plan*; *he gave the door a gentle push*
(c) not very steep; *there is a gentle slope down to the lake* (NOTE: **gentler - gentlest**)

① **gentleman**
noun
(a) man, especially an educated man from a good family; *he's such a gentleman, he always opens the door for me*
(b) *(polite way of referring to a man)* *this gentleman is waiting to be served*; *well, gentlemen, if everyone is here, the meeting can start*; **"ladies and gentlemen"** = way of starting to talk to a group of men and women (NOTE: plural is **gentlemen**)

① **gently**
['dʒentli] *adverb*
(a) softly; *he gently put the blanket over her*; *she rocked the baby gently*; **gently does it!** = be careful!
(b) not strongly; *the wind blew gently through the bushes*
(c) not very steep; *the path rises gently to the top of the hill*

③ **genuine**
['dʒenjuɪn] *adjective*
real, true; *the painting was not a genuine Picasso*; *a genuine leather purse will cost a lot more than that*

③ **geographic** *or* **geographical**
[dʒiə'græfɪk or dʒiə'græfɪkl] *adjective*
referring to geography

① **geography**
[dʒi'ɒɡrəfi] *noun*
study of the Earth's surface; *we're studying the geography of the Grand Canyon*; *I'm worse at math than at geography*

③ **geranium**
[dʒə'reɪniəm] *noun*
brightly coloured summer flower, usually red or pink; *they put pots of geraniums outside the front door*

② **germ**
[dʒɜrm] *noun*
(a) something which causes disease; *wash your hands after emptying the garbage can so you don't spread any germs*
(b) the beginning of something; *he had the germ of an idea*

② **German**
['dʒɜrmən]
1 *adjective*
referring to Germany; *there are three German players in the team*; *do you like German food?*; *see also* MEASLES
2 *noun*
(a) language spoken in Germany, Austria and parts of Switzerland and Italy; *do you know the German for "one - two - three"?*; *you must brush up your German if you are going to work in Germany*; *he took a crash course in German*; *he works all day in the office, and then goes to German classes in the evening*
(b) person from Germany; *our next-door neighbors are Germans*

① **Germany**
['dʒɜrməni] *proper noun*
large west European country, to the east of France, and west of Poland; *they used to live in Germany*; *Germany is an important member of the EU* (NOTE: capital: **Berlin**; people: **Germans**; language: **German**; currency: **euro**)

④ **gesture**
['dʒestʃər]
1 *noun*
(a) movement of hands, etc., to show feeling; *she made an impatient gesture with her hand*
(b) action that shows feeling; *the gift of fruit was a kind gesture on her part*; *as a gesture to the staff, the management has had the restrooms decorated*; **token gesture** = small action done to show that you intend to deal with a problem; *the motion criticizing the government was simply a token gesture by the opposition parties*
2 *verb*
to make a movement with your hands; *he gestured to the audience to sit down*

① **get**
[get] *verb*
(a) to receive; *we got a letter from the bank this morning*; *he will get $25 for washing the car*; *she gets more money than I do*
(b) to become; *I'm getting too old for football*; *she's getting deaf*; *he's gotten much fatter over the last year or so*; *the sun got hotter and hotter*; *the carpet's getting dirty*
(c) to have something done; *I must get my suit cleaned*; *we got the automobile repaired in time to go on vacation*
(d) to persuade someone to do something; *can you get the garage to repair the brakes?*; *I'll try and get her to bring some CDs*
(e) to catch (an illness); *I think I'm getting a cold*; *he got the measles just before the vacation started*
(f) to make something become; *he always gets his clothes dirty*; *she's busy getting the meal ready*
(g) to understand; *do you think he got my meaning?*; **got it!** = I've solved the problem! (NOTE: **getting - got** [gɒt] **- has gotten**)

③ **get across**
['get ə'krɒs] *verb*
(a) to manage to cross; *they got across the river in little boats*
(b) to make someone understand; *I'm trying to get across to the people in the office that they all have to work harder*; *we just can't seem to get our message across*

③ **get along**
['get ə'lɒŋ] *verb*
(a) to manage; *she got along quite well when her mother was away on vacation*; *we seem to get along very happily without the telephone*; *how are you getting along?*
(b) **to get along (with someone)** = to be friendly with someone, to work well with someone; *I don't think they get along*

③ **get at**
['get 'æt] *verb*
(a) to reach; *you'll need to stand on a chair to get at the box on the top shelf*
(b) to mean; *what was he really getting at when he said that some people were not working hard enough?*

② **get away**
['get ə'weɪ] *verb*
(a) to escape; *the robbers got away in a stolen automobile*
(b) **to get away with something** = not to be punished for having done something; *he was rude to the judge, but got away with it somehow*; *(formal)* **to get away with murder** = to do something really bad and still not be punished for it; *he's the teacher's favorite and she lets him get away with murder*

① **get back**
['get 'bæk] *verb*
(a) to return; *they got back home very late*; *when did they get back from the movie theater?*
(b) to get something again which you had before; *I got my money back after I had complained to the manager*; **to get your breath back** = to breathe normally after having been out of breath; *at my age, I can't walk uphill very far without stopping to get my breath back*
(c) to phone back or reply by mail; *I'll find out what the situation is and get back to you as soon as I can*

① **get by**
['get 'baɪ] *verb (informal)*
(a) to manage to do something with difficulty; *I can just get by in Portuguese*; *how are you going to get by without a car?*
(b) to manage to live; *it is difficult for them to get by in New York on only $30 a day*; *they get by somehow on only $100 a week*

③ **get down**
['get 'daʊn] *verb*
(a) to go back down onto the ground; *the cat climbed up the tree and couldn't get down*; *he got down off the ladder*

(b) to bring down; *can you get my suitcase down for me?*
(c) to make someone sad; *rainy weather always gets me down*

③ **get down to**
['get 'daun tu] *verb*
to get down to some hard work = to start working hard; *he will have to get down to work if he wants to pass the test*

③ **get going**
['get 'gəuɪŋ] *verb*
(informal) to start; *come on, let's get going!*

① **get in**
['get 'ɪn] *verb*
(a) to go inside (an automobile, etc.); *get in - the train's going to leave*; *the burglars must have got in through the bathroom window*
(b) to arrive at home, at the office, etc.; *what time did you get in last night?*; *because of the train strike, we didn't get in until eleven o'clock*; *the plane got in at 11 P.M.*
(c) to ask someone to come to do a job; *we'll get a plumber in to fix the leak*

① **get into**
['get 'ɪntu] *verb*
(a) to go inside (an automobile, etc.); *they got into the back of the automobile*; *I was just getting into bed when the phone rang*; *the burglars got into the building through a window on the ground floor*
(b) **to get into the habit of** = to start to do something regularly; *he got into the habit of calling his father "Boss"*; **to get into trouble** *or* **into difficulties** = to start to have problems; *he got into trouble with the police*

③ **get lost**
['get 'lɒst] *verb*
(a) not to know where you are; *he got lost walking from Times Square to here*; *they should be back by now - do you think they've got lost?*
(b) *(slang)* **get lost!** = go away!; *when she asked him for money he told her to get lost*

① **get off**
['get 'ɒf] *verb*
(a) to come down from or out of (a vehicle, etc.); *she got off her bicycle at the red light*; *if you want the post office, you should get off at the next stop*; *to go to the science museum, you have to get off the subway here*
(b) not to be punished, or only receive a light punishment; *she was lucky to get off so lightly*; *he was found guilty of theft and got off with a fine*

① **get on**
['get 'ɒn] *verb*
(a) to go inside or onto (a vehicle, etc.); *they got on the bus at the bank*; *the police officer got on his bike and rode away*
(b) to become old; *he's getting on and can't work as hard as he used to*

(c) **to get on (well)** = to do well; *she's getting on well at college*; *my son is getting on well in his new job - he has just been promoted*
(d) to manage; *how is the new secretary getting on?*
(e) to be friendly with someone; *they don't get on well at all*

① **get on with**
['get ɒn 'wɪð]
(a) to be friendly with someone; *he gets on very well with everyone*; *she doesn't get on with her new boss*; *they don't get on with one another*
(b) to continue to do some work; *he got on with his work and finished the job early*

① **get out**
['get 'aut] *verb*
(a) to take out; *I'll get the book out of the library*; *she was getting the car out of the garage and backed into a man on the sidewalk*
(b) to go out of something; *the bus stopped and the driver got out*; *the burglars got in through a window, but got out through the front door*
(c) **to get out of the habit of doing something** = not to do something anymore; *I've gotten out of the habit of eating meat*
(d) **to get out of (doing) something** = to avoid doing something; *I want to get out of going to the office party*

③ **get over**
['get 'əuvər] *verb*
(a) to climb over; *they got over the wall into the yard*
(b) to become better; *he's gotten over his flu*
(c) to recover from a shock; *she never got over the death of her father*

② **get ready**
['get 'redɪ] *phrase*
(a) to prepare yourself for something; *how long will it take you to get ready for the wedding?*
(b) to get something prepared; *we need to get the dinner ready - the guests will be arriving in 30 minutes*

① **get through**
['get 'θru] *verb*
(a) to go through; *the cows got through the hole in the fence*
(b) to be successful; *he got through his examinations, so he is now a qualified engineer*

③ **get through to**
['get 'θru tu] *verb*
(a) to make someone understand; *I could not get through to her that I had to be at the airport by 2:15*
(b) to manage to speak to someone on the phone; *I tried to get through to the complaints department but the line was always busy*

③ **get to**
['get tu] *verb*
(a) to arrive, to reach (a place); *we only got to the hotel at midnight*; *the plane gets to New York at 4 P.M.*; *when you get to my age you'll*

see why I'm suggesting you should plan for the future
(b) to have got to = must, to be obliged to; *you've got to come* = you must come; *he has to be at the station at 8 o'clock; do you really have to work all night?*

① **get up**
['get 'ʌp] *verb*
(a) to get out of bed; *he went to bed so late that he didn't get up until 11 o'clock; it is 9:30 and John still hasn't got up*
(b) to make someone get out of bed; *you need to get everyone up by 7:30 if we are going to leave on time*
(c) to stand up; *when he had finished his meal, he got up from the table and walked out of the room*

① **get up to**
['get 'ʌp tu] *verb*
to reach; *stop reading when you get up to page 23*

② **ghost**
[gəʊst] *noun*
(a) image of a dead person which appears; *they say the house is haunted by the ghost of its former owner; his face is white - he looks as if he has seen a ghost; **ghost story** = frightening story about ghosts*
(b) not to have a ghost of a chance = to have no chance at all; *she's trying out for the competition, but she doesn't have a ghost of a chance of winning*

③ **G.I.**
['dʒi 'aɪ]
1 *noun*
soldier in the U.S. army; *he's a G.I.* (NOTE: plural is **G.I.s**)
2 *adjective*
relating to a G.I.; *a G.I. uniform*

① **giant**
['dʒaɪənt]
1 *noun*
(a) *(in children's stories)* very large man; *a story about a giant who lived in a castle at the top of a mountain*
(b) any very large person, company, plant or building; *he's a giant of a man; stocks in the computer giant have soared*
2 *adjective*
very large; *he's grown a giant cabbage; they are planning a giant automobile factory in Detroit*

④ **giddy**
['gɪdi] *adjective*
dizzy, feeling that everything is turning round; *she felt giddy and had to sit down*

① **gift**
[gɪft] *noun*
(a) present, something given to someone; *the wedding gifts were displayed on a table; she was wrapping up gifts to put under the Christmas tree; **gift shop** = store that sells things which are often given as presents; **gift*

certificate = card or coupon given as a present, which you can exchange for goods to a certain value; *I couldn't think of what to buy her, so I gave her a gift certificate for her birthday; see also* LOOK
(b) special ability for something; *he has a gift for foreign languages; she has a gift for saying things that annoy her father*

③ **gigantic**
[dʒaɪ'gæntɪk] *adjective*
very large, huge; *he was eating a gigantic sandwich*

① **giggle**
['gɪgl]
1 *noun*
little laugh, often showing you are embarrassed; **to get the giggles** = to have an attack of laughter which you cannot stop; *when the singer came onto the stage, I got the giggles*
2 *verb*
to make a little laugh; *when she saw her mother's hat she started giggling; the class giggled at his way of walking*

② **ginger**
['dʒɪndʒər]
1 *noun*
(a) plant whose root has a sharp taste and is used in cooking; *fry the meat with onions and slices of ginger; add a pinch of powdered ginger to the cake mixture*
(b) ginger ale = carbonated non-alcoholic drink flavored with ginger
2 *adjective*
(of hair) bright orange in color; *she has ginger hair and green eyes; a ginger cat sat on the doorstep in the sun*

① **gingerbread**
['dʒɪndʒəbred] *noun*
dark cake or cookie flavored with ginger and molasses; **gingerbread man** = children's cake, made of gingerbread in the shape of a man

① **girl**
[gɜrl] *noun*
female child; *they have four children - two boys and two girls; a crowd of girls waiting at the bus stop; my sister goes to a private girls' school*

③ **girlfriend**
['gɜrlfrend] *noun*
girl or woman, usually young, that someone is very friendly with; *he broke up with his girlfriend; on Saturdays she always has lunch with a group of girlfriends; see also* BOYFRIEND

① **give**
[gɪv]
1 *verb*
(a) to send or pass something to someone as a present; *we gave her flowers for her birthday; what are you going to give him when he gets married?; we gave fifteen dollars to the Red Cross*

(b) to pass something to someone; *give me another piece of cake*; *can you give me some information about vacations in Greece?*

(c) to do something (to someone); *she gave a deep sigh*; *he gave me a broad smile*; *he gave her a kiss*; *she gave the ball a kick*

(d) to organize; *they gave a dinner for the visiting foreign minister*; *we gave a party to celebrate her twenty-first birthday*

(e) to do something in public; *she gave a concert in aid of the Red Cross*; *he will be giving the opening speech at the conference*; *she has been asked to give a lecture on Shakespeare*

(f) to bend; *the piece of wood gave as he stepped on it* (NOTE: **giving - gave** [geɪv] **- has given** [ˈɡɪvn])

2 *noun*

give and take = agreement between two people to make concessions; *what we need is a little give and take on both sides*

② **give away**
[ˈɡɪv əˈweɪ] *verb*

(a) to give as a present; *we are giving away a pocket calculator with each $15 of purchases*

(b) to reveal something which you are trying to keep secret; *his accent gave him away*; *she gave herself away by saying that she had never been to France*

(c) to lead the bride to the bridegroom at a wedding; *she was given away by her father*

② **give back**
[ˈɡɪv ˈbæk] *verb*

to hand something back to someone; *give me back my watch* or *give me my watch back*; *the burglars gave back everything they had taken*; *she borrowed my book and hasn't given it back*

③ **give in**
[ˈɡɪv ˈɪn] *verb*

to stop objecting to something, even if you didn't want to do it; *the children kept on asking him if they could go to the movies and in the end he gave in*; *in the end, father gave in and let us go camping by ourselves*

② **given**
[ˈɡɪvn]

1 *adjective*

(a) having the habit of; *he is given to sitting at home drinking all by himself*

(b) particular; **at a given point in time** = at a particular moment

(c) **given name** = first name or Christian name of a person, as opposed to the surname or family name

2 *conjunction*

given (that) = because; *given (that) it's his birthday, it's a shame he couldn't have the day off*

④ **give out**
[ˈɡɪv ˈaʊt] *verb*

(a) to give to everyone; *she gave out presents to all the children*

(b) to come to an end; *the battery has given out so I can't use my watch*

① **give up**
[ˈɡɪv ˈʌp] *verb*

(a) to stop doing something; *she's trying to give up smoking*

(b) **I give up** = I don't know the answer

(c) **to give yourself up** = to surrender to an enemy, the police, etc.; *he gave himself up to the police*; *they shouted to the gang to come out of the bank and give themselves up*

④ **give way**
[ˈɡɪv ˈweɪ] *phrase*

(a) to let someone go first; *give way (yield) to traffic coming from the right*

(b) to collapse; *the chair gave way when he sat on it*

(c) to stop objecting to something; *in the end, father gave way and let us go camping by ourselves*

① **glad**
[ɡlæd] *adjective*

pleased; *Aunt Jane was glad to get your postcard*; *the bank manager is glad you paid*; *after shopping all day, she was glad to find somewhere to sit down*; *(informal)* **glad rags** = party clothes

② **gladly**
[ˈɡlædli] *adverb*

in a pleased way, with great pleasure; *I'll gladly look after your dog while you're away*

① **glamorous**
[ˈɡlæmərəs] *adjective*

attractive; *your grandmother looks very glamorous for her age*; *he came to dinner with a glamorous blonde*; *she wants to lead the glamorous life of a movie star*

① **glance**
[ɡlɑːns]

1 *noun*

quick look; *she gave him an admiring glance*; *she took a quick glance over her shoulder*

2 *verb*

(a) to look quickly; *he glanced over his shoulder to see who was following him*; *she glanced round to attract the waiter's attention*

(b) **to glance off something** = to slide off something instead of hitting it straight on; *the ball glanced off the edge of her racket*

③ **gland**
[ɡlænd] *noun*

organ in the body which produces a chemical substance; *sweat comes from the sweat glands*; *hormones are produced by glands*

① **glare**
[ˈɡleər]

1 *noun*

(a) very bright light; *the glare of the sun on the wet road blinded me*; *pop stars live their lives in the glare of publicity*

(b) fierce look; *he gave her a glare and walked on*

2 *verb*

(a) to shine very brightly; *the sun was glaring down on the square*
(b) to look angrily; *she glared at me and went on reading her book*

① **glass**
[glæs] *noun*
(a) material that you can see through, used to make windows, etc.; *a bowl made of glass or a glass bowl; the roof of the house is made of glass or the house has a glass roof; an automobile with windows made of tinted glass* (NOTE: no plural: **some glass, a piece of glass**)
(b) thing to drink out of, usually made of glass; *we took plastic wine glasses on the picnic; she put the dirty glasses in the sink*
(c) liquid contained in a glass; *she asked for a glass of water; he was so thirsty he drank three glasses of lemonade; add a glass of red wine to my order* (NOTE: plural is **glasses** for meanings (b) and (c))

① **glasses**
[ˈglæsɪz] *noun*
two pieces of plastic or glass in a frame which you wear in front of your eyes to help you see better; *have you seen my glasses anywhere?; she has to wear glasses to read; dark glasses =* eyeglasses made of dark glass, for wearing in sunshine; *he noticed he was being followed by two men wearing dark glasses* (NOTE: **glasses** are also called **eyelglasses**. Dark glasses are also called **sunglasses**)

② **gleam**
[glim]
1 *noun*
(a) small light; *he saw the gleam of a flashlight in the distance*
(b) slight sign of feeling shown by your eyes; *he saw a gleam of recognition in the boy's eyes; there was a wild gleam in her eyes*
2 *verb*
to shine as if polished; *a line of gleaming black automobiles*

② **glide**
[glaɪd] *verb*
to move in a smooth way; *young people were gliding across the ice in time to the music*

② **glider**
[ˈglaɪdər] *noun*
aircraft which flies without a motor; *the glider rose slowly up above the clouds*

② **glimpse**
[glɪmps]
1 *noun*
brief sight; *we caught a glimpse of the princess as she drove past; there was a brief glimpse of the sun during the afternoon*
2 *verb*
to catch sight of; *we only glimpsed the back of her head as she was leaving*

② **glitter**
[ˈglɪtər]
1 *noun*

bright sparkle of light; *the glitter of the sun on the sea; she was attracted by the glitter of the Broadway theaters*
2 *verb*
to sparkle; *the jewels in the king's crown were glittering in the light of the candles; her eyes glittered hopefully as she spoke; all that glitters is not gold =* things that look very attractive on the surface often turn out not to be attractive really

② **global**
[ˈgloʊbl] *adjective*
(a) referring to the whole world; *we offer a global parcel delivery service; global warming =* warming of the Earth's atmosphere, caused by pollution
(b) referring to the whole of something; *we are carrying out a global review of salaries*

① **globe**
[gloʊb] *noun*
(a) **the globe =** the Earth; *he is trying to be the first person to fly around the globe in a balloon*
(b) map of the world on a ball; *he spun the globe around and pointed to Canada*

② **gloom**
[glum] *noun*
(a) darkness; *it was difficult to see anything in the gathering gloom*
(b) deep despair; *a feeling of deep gloom came down on the family; when the exam results came out everyone sank into gloom*

② **gloomy**
[ˈglumi] *adjective*
(a) miserable, unhappy; *she was gloomy about her chances of passing the exam; he's very gloomy about his job prospects*
(b) dark; *a gloomy Sunday afternoon in November* (NOTE: **gloomier - gloomiest**)

③ **glorious**
[ˈglɔriəs] *adjective*
splendid; *a glorious June afternoon*

② **glory**
[ˈglɔri]
1 *noun*
(a) fame; *I did it for the glory of the school, not for myself; the team covered themselves with glory =* the team had a marvelous win
(b) wonderful sight; *it is one of the glories of ancient Rome*
2 *verb*
to glory in = to take great pride in; *she glories in beating her brother at chess*

② **glossy**
[ˈglɒsi] *adjective*
shiny; **glossy magazines =** expensive colour magazines, printed on shiny paper (NOTE: **glossier - glossiest**)

① **glove**
[glʌv] *noun*
piece of clothing worn on your hand; *she gave him a pair of gloves for his birthday; you might*

have left one of your gloves on the train; *see also* HAND

① **glow**
[gləʊ]
1 *noun*
(a) soft bright light; *the warm glow of the fire*
(b) bright red color of your cheeks; *the glow of the children's cheeks showed as they came back into the house*
2 *verb*
to shine red; *the logs glowed in the fireplace*; *her face glowed with pride*

① **glue**
[glu]
1 *noun*
substance that sticks; *she spread the glue carefully onto the back of the poster*; *the glue on the envelope doesn't stick very well*; **glue sniffing** = form of drug abuse where addicts breathe in the gas from a strong glue
2 *verb*
(a) to stick things together; *he glued the label to the box*
(b) **to be glued to** = to sit in front of without moving; *the children sat glued to the TV set*

② **gnaw**
[nɔ] *verb*
to chew, to bite something again and again; *the dog was gnawing a bone*

④ **gnome**
[nəʊm] *noun*
(in children's fairy stories) little man with a beard and a pointed hat; **garden gnome** = little coloured statue of a gnome, used as a garden decoration

④ **GNP**
[dʒienˈpi]
= GROSS NATIONAL PRODUCT

① **go**
[gəʊ]
1 *verb*
(a) to move from one place to another; *the plane goes to Frankfurt, then to Rome*; *she is going to Denver for the weekend*; *he has gone to work in Washington*; *they are going on a tour of southern Europe*; *she was going downstairs when she fell*; *the automobile was carrying so much baggage that it had difficulty going up hills*; *they went on board at 8 o'clock*; *how do you go to school - by bike or by bus?*; *she has gone shopping*
(b) **food to go** = food that you take away from the counter to eat; *can I have a cheeseburger to go, please?*
(c) to work; *can you call the garage? - the automobile won't go*; *he's trying to get his motorbike to go*
(d) to leave; *get your coat, it's time to go*; *the last bus goes at half past two*
(e) to fit; *it's too big to go into the box*; *this case won't go into the back of the automobile*

(f) to be placed; *the date should go at the top of the letter*; *that book goes on the top shelf*
(g) to become; *her face went red from sitting in the sun*; *he went pale and rushed out of the room*; *you have to shout, my father's going deaf*; *she's going gray, but it suits her*
(h) to happen (successfully or not); *the party went very well*; *things are not going badly at the office*
(i) to make a sound; *the balloon landed on a candle and went "pop"*; *do you remember the song that goes: "there's no place like home"?*
(j) *(informal)* to fail to work; *as we were going down the hill, the brakes went* (NOTE: **going - went** [went] - **has gone** [gɒn])
2 *noun*
(a) **on the go** = always busy; *the store is so busy before Christmas that we're on the go from morning till night*; **to make a go of something** = to make something work successfully; *they're struggling to make a go of their business*; **she's always full of go** = she always has plenty of energy
(b) try, attempt; *he won the lottery at the first go*; *she had three goes at the test and still didn't pass*; *we'll give it one more go, and if the car doesn't start I'll call the garage*

◇ **to be going to**
[bi ˈgəʊɪŋ tu] *phrase*
(a) *(showing future)* *we're going to win*; *I hope it's going to be fine tomorrow*; *when are you going to wash your hair?*; *he's going to be a great tennis player when he's older*; *is she going to sing at the concert?*
(b) **to be going to do something** = to be about to do something; *I'm going to be late for the meeting*; *watch out - that tree is going to fall down!*; *I am going to sit in bed and read my newspaper*

③ **go about**
[ˈgəʊ əˈbaʊt] *verb*
to arrange to do something; *how do you go about getting a new passport?*; *we'd like to set up a company, but I'm not sure how to go about it*

③ **go ahead**
[ˈgəʊ əˈhed] *verb*
to start; *the project went ahead even though there was not enough staff*

② **go-ahead**
[ˈgəʊəhed] *noun*
to give something the go-ahead = to give permission for something to start; *we got the city's go-ahead to build the new supermarket*

② **goal**
[gəʊl] *noun*
(a) *(in games)* two posts between which you have to send the ball to score a point; *he was unlucky to miss the goal with that shot*
(b) *(in games)* point scored by sending the ball between the posts; *he scored a goal before being sent off*; *our team scored three goals*

(c) aim; *our goal is to open a new pizza restaurant every month*; *he achieved his goal of becoming a millionaire before he was thirty*

④ **goalkeeper**
['gəʊlkipər] *noun*
player who stands in front of the goal to stop the ball going in; *the goalkeeper dropped the ball and the other team scored*

③ **go around**
['gəʊ ə'raʊnd] *verb*
(a) to turn round something; *we went around the traffic circle and took the third road on the left*
(b) to visit; *you'll need at least two hours to go around the museum*
(c) to be enough for; *there wasn't enough ice cream to go around all twelve of us*

① **goat**
[gəʊt] *noun*
small farm animal with horns and a beard, giving milk and wool; *they keep a herd of goats*; **goat's cheese** = cheese made from goat's milk; **to separate the sheep from the goats** = to divide the good from the bad (NOTE: males are called **billy goats,** and females are called **nanny goats,** and the young are called **kids**)

① **go away**
['gəʊ ə'weɪ] *verb*
to leave; *he went away and we never saw him again*

① **go back**
['gəʊ 'bæk] *verb*
to return; *she went back to the store and asked if she could exchange the gloves*; *she worked for two years and then went back to college*

③ **go back on**
['gəʊ 'bæk ɒn] *verb*
not to do what has been promised; *he promised faithfully to lend me his car, and then went back on his promise*

① **God**
[gɒd]
1 *noun*
(a) **God** = the most important being, the being to whom people pray; *do you believe in God?*; *we pray to God that the children will be found alive*
(b) superior being, not a human being; *Bacchus was the Roman god of wine*
2 *interjection*
(a) *(showing surprise, etc.)* *God, what awful weather!*; *my God, have you seen how late it is?*
(b) *(showing thanks)* *Thank God no one was hurt in the crash!*; *Thank God the ambulance arrived in time!*

③ **goddess**
['gɒdes] *noun*
female god; *Diana was the goddess of hunting* (NOTE: plural is **goddesses**)

③ **go down**
['gəʊ daʊn] *verb*
to go to a lower level; *there are thirty-nine steps which go down to the beach*; *be careful when going down the hill*; *after having a rest in her bedroom, she went down to the hotel bar*

① **goes**
[gəʊz]
see GO

① **go in**
['gəʊ 'ɪn] *verb*
to enter; *she opened the door and went in*; *did you see anyone go in?*

③ **go in for**
['gəʊ 'ɪn fɔr] *verb*
(a) to take (an examination); *she went in for her swimming test*
(b) to take up as a career; *he's going in for medicine*

① **going**
['gəʊɪŋ]
1 *adjective*
(a) working well; *the business is being sold as a going concern*
(b) normal, usual; **the going rate** = the usual rate, the current rate of payment; *what is the current going rate for a 1998 model?*; *he was happy to pay the going rate*; *the going rate for caterers is $15.00 per hour*
2 *noun*
(a) surface of the ground; *the going is soft after last night's rain*; **do it while the going is good** = do it while it is still possible
(b) **goings-on** = strange things that happen; *you would never believe the goings-on in the apartment upstairs*

① **go into**
['gəʊ 'ɪntu] *verb*
(a) to enter; *she went into the bedroom (she said she's thinking about going into medicine)*
(b) to examine, to look at something carefully; *the bank wants to go into the details of his account*
(c) to explain in detail; *she said she had a job offer but wouldn't go into any details*
(d) *(in math)* to be able to divide a number to give a figure; *seven into three won't go*

① **gold**
[gəʊld] *noun*
(a) very valuable yellow-colored metal; *that ring isn't made of gold*; *gold is worth more than silver*; *he wears a gold ring on his little finger* (NOTE: no plural: **some gold, a bar of gold.** Note also that gold is a chemical element: chemical symbol: **Au;** atomic number: **79**)
(b) **gold (medal)** = medal given to someone who finishes first in a race or competition; *the U.S.A. won twelve golds at the Olympics*; *see also* BRONZE, SILVER

③ **gold card**
['gəʊld 'kɑrd] *noun*
special credit card for people with high salaries; *after I was promoted, the bank offered me a gold card*

golden
['gəʊldən] *adjective*
colored like gold; *she has beautiful golden hair*; **golden boy** = young man who is popular and a great success; *he's the golden boy of American football*; *(in World Cup soccer)* **golden goal** = the first goal to be scored in extra time which decides the winner of a match; **golden opportunity** = marvelous chance that will not happen again; *he had a golden opportunity to make his fortune and he didn't take it*; **golden wedding (anniversary)** = celebration when two people have been married for fifty years

golf
[gɒlf] *noun*
a game played on a large open course, by hitting a small ball into 9 or 18 separate holes with a variety of clubs, using as few strokes as possible; *he plays golf every Saturday*; *how about a game of golf?*; **golf cart** = little motor buggy for driving around a golf course; **golf course** = area of land specially designed for playing golf

COMMENT: the game is for two people, or two couples; a small hard ball is struck with a thin club with a long handle, into a series of little holes (either 9 or 18), the object being to use as few strokes as possible

golf club
['gɒlf 'klʌb] *noun*
(a) stick used to hit the ball in golf; *she put her golf clubs into the back of the golf cart*
(b) organization for people who play golf together; *he's joined his local golf club*

golfer
['gɒlfər] *noun*
person who plays golf

gone
[gɒn]
see GO

good
[gʊd]
1 *adjective*
(a) not bad; *we had a good breakfast and then started work*; *did you have a good time at the party?*; *it would be a good idea to invest in these shares*; *her Spanish is better than his*
(b) clever; *he's good at making things out of wood*; *she's good with her hands*; *he is good at football*
(c) who behaves well; *be a good girl and I'll give you a treat*; *have you been good while we've been away?*; **as good as gold** = not at all naughty; *the children were as good as gold*
(d) **a good deal of** *or* **a good many** = a lot of; *he won a good deal of money on the lottery*; *a good many people saw the accident*
(e) **good for** = making better or healthy; *running a mile before breakfast is good for you*; *they say that eating carrots is good for your sight* (NOTE: **good - better** ['betər] - **best** [best])
2 *noun*
(a) advantage, making better; *the medicine didn't do me any good*; *he decided to give up smoking for the good of his health*; *what's the good of having a big garden if you don't like gardening?*; *governments should work for the good of the people*
(b) **for good** = for ever; *he's left the town for good*
(c) **no good** = useless, not working; *this computer's no good*

good afternoon
['gʊd æftər'nun] *interjection*; *(formal, used when meeting or leaving someone in the afternoon)* *I just want to say good afternoon to the teacher*

good-bye *or* good-by
[gʊd'baɪ] *noun & interjection*
(used when leaving someone) *say good-bye to your teacher*; *good-bye! we'll see you again on Thursday* (NOTE: often shortened to **bye**)

good evening
['gʊd 'ivnɪŋ] *interjection*; *(formal, used when meeting or leaving someone in the evening)* *good evening, Mrs. Smith!*

Good Friday
['gʊd 'fraɪdeɪ] *noun*
the Friday before Easter Day

good-looking
['gʊd'lʊkɪŋ] *adjective*
(of a person) pleasant to look at; *she's a very good-looking girl*; *he's very good-looking, with lots of girlfriends*; *he's far better-looking than his brother*

good morning
['gʊd 'mɔrnɪŋ] *interjection*
(used when meeting someone in the morning) *good morning, Mr. Smith!*

goodness
['gʊdnəs] *noun*
(a) being good; *she did it out of the pure goodness of her heart*
(b) **thank goodness!** = phrase which shows relief; *thank goodness the ambulance arrived quickly!*
(c) **for goodness' sake** = expression showing you are annoyed, or that something is important; *what are you screaming for? - it's only a little mouse, for goodness' sake*; *for goodness' sake try to be quiet, we don't want the guards to hear us!*

goodnight
[gʊd'naɪt] *interjection*
(used when leaving someone late in the evening) *goodnight, everyone! sleep well!*

goods
[gʊdz] *noun*
(a) things that are produced for sale; *the company sells goods from various European countries*

(b) possessions, things which you own; *she carried all the goods she possessed in a bag*

④ **goodwill**
[gʊd'wɪl] *noun*
(a) kind feeling; *the charity relies on the goodwill of people who give money regularly*
(b) *(of a business)* value of the customers, reputation, site, etc.; *he paid $15,000 for the goodwill of the restaurant and $60,000 for the fittings*

COMMENT: goodwill can include the reputation of the business, the trade names it uses, the value of a "good site", etc.; all this is very difficult to calculate accurately

① **goof**
[guf] *(informal)*
1 *noun*
(a) mistake; *forgetting to invite the mayor was a major goof*
(b) stupid person; *he is such a goof*
2 *verb*
to make a careless mistake; *I must have goofed when I wrote the address*; **to goof off** = to avoid work; *she goofed off all morning*

② **go off**
['gəʊ 'ɒf] *verb*
(a) to go to another place; *he went off to look for a parking space; she went off saying something about buying cheese*
(b) to start working suddenly; *the burglar alarm went off in the middle of the night*
(c) to explode; *the bomb went off when there were still lots of people in the building*

③ **go on**
['gəʊ 'ɒn] *verb*
(a) to continue; *please go on, I like hearing you sing; they went on working in spite of the fire; she went on speaking for two hours; don't ask questions, just go on with your work*; **to go on about something** = to talk all the time about something; *she keeps going on about how poor she is*
(b) to happen; *what's been going on here?*
(c) to base your opinion and actions on; *the police investigating the murder don't have much to go on; we have to go on the assumption that the concert will start on time*

① **goose**
[gus] *noun*
(a) large bird, living near water, both wild and bred on farms; *a flock of wild geese landed on the runway; they keep a flock of geese in the warehouse to ward off thieves* (NOTE: plural is **geese** [gis])
(b) meat from this bird; *we're having roast goose for Christmas lunch*

④ **go out**
['gəʊ 'aʊt] *verb*
(a) to leave a building; *I don't go out often at night; he forgot to lock the door when he went out*

(b) not to be burning anymore; *the fire went out and the room got cold; all the lights in the building suddenly went out; chaos reigned when the town's electricity supply went out*
(c) to go out of business = to stop trading; *the company went out of business last week*

③ **gorgeous**
['gɔːdʒəs] *adjective*
magnificent; *the bird spread out its gorgeous tail; he came to the party with a gorgeous blonde*

③ **gorilla**
[gə'rɪlə] *noun*
large black African ape; *we are trying to protect the gorillas' natural habitat* (NOTE: do not confuse with **guerrilla**)

② **gospel**
['gɒspl] *noun*
(a) part of the Bible which tells the life of Jesus Christ; **it's the gospel truth** = it's absolutely true
(b) gospel music = religious music which first became popular in the U.S.A.

② **gossip**
['gɒsɪp]
1 *noun*
(a) stories or news about someone, which may or may not be true; *have you heard the latest gossip about Sue?*; **to spread gossip about someone** = to tell stories about someone (which may or may not be true); **gossip column** = column in a newspaper which tells stories about famous people; **gossip columnist** = person who writes a gossip column
(b) person who spreads gossip; *be careful what you say to him - he's a great gossip*
2 *verb*
to talk about people; *they spent hours gossiping about the people working in the office*

① **got**
[gɒt]
see GET

④ **go through**
['gəʊ 'θru] *verb*
to go through with something = to continue with something; *they decided not to go through with their planned pig farm because of the objections from their neighbors*

① **gotten**
['gɒtn]
see GET

④ **go under**
['gəʊ 'ʌndər] *verb*
to fail, to go bankrupt; *the company went under during the recession*

① **go up**
['gəʊ 'ʌp] *verb*
(a) to go to a higher place; *take the elevator and go up to the fourth floor*
(b) to increase, to rise to a higher level; *the price of bread has gone up*

② **govern**
['gʌvərn] *verb*
(a) to rule a country; *the country is governed by three generals*
(b) to influence, to have an effect on; *inflation is governed by interest rates and exchange rates*

① **government**
['gʌvərnmənt] *noun*
(a) system of ruling a country; *the country is aiming to achieve democratic government* (NOTE: no plural in this meaning)
(b) **central government** = main organization, dealing with the affairs of the whole country; **local government** = organizations dealing with the affairs of small areas of the country, such as towns and counties; **state government** *or* **provincial government** = government of a state or province
(c) people or political party which governs; *the president asked the leader of the largest party in parliament to form a new government; everything was working very well until the government stepped in; the government controls the price of gas; he has an important job in the government;* **a government department** = a section of the government with a particular responsibility

① **governor**
['gʌvərnər] *noun*
person who runs a state, institution, etc.; *the governor of Alabama*

② **go with**
['gəʊ 'wɪθ] *verb*
(a) to match; *blue shoes won't go with a green dress; red wine goes best with meat*
(b) to be linked to; *that remote control goes with the TV; he has a big house that goes with his job*
(c) to date; *she went with Danny, the boy down the street*

② **go without**
['gəʊ wɪ'ðaʊt] *verb*
not to have something which you usually have; *after getting lost in the mountains, they went without food for three days; she got up late and had to go without breakfast; we have too much work, so we'll have to go without a vacation this year*

③ **gown**
[gaʊn] *noun*
(a) long black coat worn by a judge, person with degree, etc., over normal clothes; *she wore her new gown to the degree ceremony*
(b) *(formal)* woman's long formal dress; *a ball gown; an evening gown*

③ **go wrong**
['gəʊ 'rɒŋ] *phrase*
to stop working properly; *what's gone wrong with the station clock?; something has gone wrong with the central heating*

③ **G.P.**
['dʒi 'pi] *noun*
= GENERAL PRACTITIONER; *our son wants to be a G.P. when he graduates from medical school*

① **grab**
[græb]
1 *noun*
to make a grab for something = to try to seize something; *he made a grab for her wallet;* *(informal)* **up for grabs** = available to anyone who wants to get it; *the company is up for grabs; now the champion has retired the world title is up for grabs*
2 *verb*
(a) to pick something up suddenly; *he grabbed his suitcase and ran to the train*
(b) to get something quickly; *let's grab some lunch before the meeting starts* (NOTE: **grabbing - grabbed**)

① **grace**
[greɪs] *noun*
(a) being elegant and attractive; *the grace of the deer as they ran off into the woods;* **with good grace** = to approve favorably; *he accepted the criticisms with good grace*
(b) prayer before a meal; *father always says grace before dinner*
(c) extra time to pay; *to give a creditor a two week grace period to pay*

③ **graceful**
['greɪsfəl] *adjective*
moving in a smooth and beautiful way; *she crossed the stage with graceful steps*

① **grade**
[greɪd]
1 *noun*
(a) exam mark; *she got top grades in math*
(b) class in school; *students in fifth grade; she's a fifth grade student*
(c) level of quality; *I always buy grade A eggs; what grade of vegetables do you sell most of?;* **to make the grade** = to succeed, to do well; **high-grade** *or* **top-grade** = best quality; **low-grade** = worst quality
2 *verb*
(a) to judge and give a mark to (a student, an essay, etc.); *the English teacher graded the essays*
(b) to sort according to size or quality; *a machine for grading fruit; hotels are graded with two, three, four or five stars*

③ **grade crossing**
['greɪd 'krɒsɪŋ] *noun*
place where a road crosses a railroad line; *the bus was held up at a grade crossing while a train passed*

① **grade school**
['greɪd 'skul] *noun*
school for small children between the ages of about 5 and 11 (grades 1 through 6 or 8) (NOTE: also called **elementary school**)

② **gradual**
['grædjʊəl] adjective
which changes a little at a time; *we're forecasting a gradual improvement in the weather*

② **gradually**
['grædjʊəli] adverb
little by little; *his condition improved gradually day by day*; *she gradually learned how to deal with customers' complaints*

② **graduate**
1 noun ['grædjʊət]
person with a degree from a university or college; *he's a Harvard graduate*; *she's a physics graduate*
2 verb ['grædjʊeit]
to get a degree; *she graduated from Harvard last year*

④ **graffiti**
[grə'fiti] noun
writing on walls in public places; *they're trying to remove the graffiti from subway cars*

① **grain**
[grein] noun
(a) cereal crop; *a field of grain*; *the grain harvest*; *see also* ELEVATOR
(b) a very small piece; *a grain of sand*
(c) patterns of lines in wood; *this old oak table has a beautiful grain*; **to go against the grain** = to go against your natural feelings; *it goes against the grain to throw away all that good food*

③ **gram**
[græm] noun
weight equal to one thousandth of a kilogram; *you will need 250 g of sugar*; *this piece of fish weighs 500 grams* (NOTE: when used with numbers, **gram** is usually written **g** *or* **gm: 50 g**)

② **grammar**
['græmər] noun
(a) rules of a language; *Russian grammar is very difficult*; *he's been learning English for years, and still makes grammar mistakes*
(b) book of rules of a language; *there's a new German grammar coming out in the fall*

① **grand**
[grænd]
1 adjective
(a) big and important; *his grand plan for making a lot of money*
(b) imposing; *we went to a very grand wedding*; *for the grand final scene everyone wore gold dresses*
(c) final; **grand total** = the total of all the figures (NOTE: **grander - grandest**)
2 noun
(informal) one thousand dollars; *they offered him fifty grand for the information*

① **grandchild**
['græntʃaild] noun
child of a son or daughter; *all her grandchildren came to the old lady's eightieth birthday party* (NOTE: plural is **grandchildren** ['græntʃildrən])

② **granddaughter**
['grændɔtər] noun
daughter of a son or daughter; *my granddaughter is nineteen now, and at college*; *our little granddaughter is just starting to talk*

① **grandfather**
['grænfæðər] noun
father of your mother or father; *tomorrow is my grandfather's hundredth birthday*; *my grandfather can remember seeing the first planes flying*; **a grandfather clock** = a tall clock (NOTE: often called **granddad** *or* **grandpa** by children)

③ **grand jury**
['grænd 'dʒuri] noun
group of people who decide whether an accused person should be given a court trial or released; *his case comes before the grand jury tomorrow*

① **grandmother**
['grænmʌðər] noun
mother of your mother or father; *it will be my grandmother's ninetieth birthday next month*; *Grandmother showed me how to make bread* (NOTE: often called **granny** *or* **grandma** by children)

① **grandparents**
['grænpeərənts] noun
parents of your mother or father; *my grandparents are all dead*

① **grandson**
['grænsʌn] noun
son of a son or daughter; *her grandson is nearly eighteen, and will be leaving school soon*; *our grandson is called Nicholas*

③ **grant**
[grænt]
1 noun
sum of money to help; *not many students get a full grant*; *my grant only pays for a few books*; *we have applied for a grant to plant trees by the side of the road*
2 verb
(a) to agree to give something; *the government has granted them a loan or a subsidy*; **to take something for granted** = to assume that you will get something, or will keep something, and so not to appreciate it; *the children seem to take it for granted that I will give them big presents every birthday*
(b) *(formal)* to admit; *I grant you it's going to be difficult, but I'm sure you'll do it well*

① **grape**
[greip] noun
fruit of the vine, eaten as dessert or used to make wine; *he bought a bunch of grapes*; *see also* SOUR

② **grapefruit**
['greɪpfruːt] *noun*
large yellow fruit, like an orange but not as sweet; *a glass of grapefruit juice*; *I'll start my breakfast with half a grapefruit, please* (NOTE: plural is **grapefruit**)

① **grapevine**
['greɪpvaɪn] *noun*
plant on which grapes grow; **I heard it from the grapevine** = someone told me about it when gossiping (NOTE: as a plant, the word **vine** is more usual)

③ **graph**
[græf] *noun*
chart showing figures in the form of a line; *the sales graph is going up*; *he drew a graph to show the fall in the number of fatal accidents over the last ten years*; *he plotted the rise in house prices on a graph*; **graph paper** = paper with little squares, for drawing graphs

④ **graphic**
['græfɪk] *adjective*
(a) drawn; *the results are shown in graphic form*
(b) vivid; *he gave a graphic description of the accident*

③ **graphics**
['græfɪks] *noun*
pictures on a computer screen or designed on a computer; *the graphics on this CD-ROM are excellent*

② **grasp**
[græsp]
1 *noun*
(a) tight hold; *she pulled his hair, and forced him to loosen his grasp on her arm*
(b) understanding; *she has a good grasp of physics*
2 *verb*
(a) to hold tightly; *she grasped the branch of the tree with both hands*
(b) to understand; *they didn't seem to grasp my meaning*

① **grass**
[græs] *noun*
(a) low green plant, which is eaten by sheep and cows in fields, or used in gardens to make lawns; *the grass is getting too long - it needs cutting*; *the cows are eating the fresh green grass*
(b) lawn; *keep off the grass!*; *we'll sit on the grass and have our picnic*; *(informal)* **not to let the grass grow under your feet** = to waste no time in doing something; *they don't let the grass grow under their feet - they phoned the minute they saw the ad*

③ **grate**
[greɪt]
1 *noun*
metal frame for holding logs in a fireplace; *he put another log onto the grate*
2 *verb*

(a) to make into small pieces by rubbing against a rough surface; *sprinkle grated cheese over your pasta*; *we made a salad of grated carrots and spring onions*
(b) to make a rough irritating noise; *the sound of metal grating on stone makes my teeth hurt*
(c) to make someone annoyed; *the way he sings while he works is beginning to grate on my nerves* (NOTE: do not confuse with **great**)

② **grateful**
['greɪtfəl] *adjective*
showing thanks for something that someone has done for you; *we are very grateful to you for your help*

④ **gratefully**
['greɪtfəli] *adverb*
in a grateful way; *she took the money gratefully*

④ **gratifying**
['grætɪfaɪɪŋ] *adjective*
which satisfies; *a gratifying response to our advertising campaign*

① **grave**
[greɪv]
1 *noun*
hole in the ground where a dead person is buried; *the whole family put flowers on the grave*; *(informal)* **to have one foot in the grave** = to be old; *(of dead person)* **to make someone turn in their grave** = to do something which would annoy a certain dead person; *Father would turn in his grave if he saw what they have done to his house*
2 *adjective*
(a) important, worrying; *it is a very grave offense*; *he is in court facing grave charges*
(b) quietly serious; *she looked at him with a grave expression* (NOTE: **graver - gravest**)

② **gravity**
['grævɪti] *noun*
(a) force that pulls things toward the ground; *apples fall to the ground because of the Earth's gravity*; **center of gravity** = the point in an object at which it will balance; *a bus has a very low center of gravity*
(b) *(formal)* being very serious; *no one seems to realize the gravity of the situation*

① **gravy**
['greɪvi] *noun*
brown sauce from meat during cooking, served with meat; *can I have some more gravy with my meat?*

① **gray**
[greɪ]
1 *noun*
color like a mixture of black and white; *he was dressed all in gray*
2 *adjective*
of a color like a mixture of black and white; *her hair has turned quite gray*; *a gray-haired old lady*; *she was wearing a light gray suit*; *look at the gray clouds - I think it is going to rain* (NOTE: **grayer - grayest**)

② **graze**
[greɪz]
1 *noun*
slight wound; *he had a graze on his knee*
2 *verb*
(a) to hurt the skin slightly; *he fell off his bicycle and grazed his knee*
(b) to feed on grass; *the sheep were grazing on the hillside*

① **great**
[greɪt]
1 *adjective*
(a) large; *we visited the Great Wall of China; she was carrying a great big pile of sandwiches;* **a great deal of** *or* **a great many** = a lot of; *there's a great deal of work to be done; she earns a great deal of money; a great many people will lose their jobs*
(b) important or famous; *New York is a great city; Picasso was a great artist; the greatest tennis player of all time*
(c) *(informal)* wonderful, very good; *we had a great time at the party; what did you think of the movie? - it was great!; it was great of you to help; it was great that they could all get to the picnic*
(d) *(humorous)* **the great and the good** = people who occupy influential positions in society; *the government looked through the ranks of the great and the good to find someone to be chairman of the board of the museum*
2 *interjection; (showing pleasure or annoyance)* *great! Let's all go to the beach!; the car's run out of gas - great!* (NOTE: do not confuse with **grate**. Note also: **greater - greatest**)

② **Great Britain (GB)**
[greɪt ˈbrɪtən] *noun*
country formed of England, Scotland and Wales (which with Northern Ireland makes up the United Kingdom); *they came to live in Great Britain some time ago; in Great Britain cars drive on the left-hand side of the road* (NOTE: capital: **London**; people: **British**; language: **English**; currency: **pound sterling (£)**)

④ **greatly**
[ˈgreɪtlɪ] *adverb*
very much; *they greatly enjoyed the birthday party*

① **Greece**
[gris] *noun*
country in southern Europe; *we go to Greece on vacation every year; Greece exports olive oil and wine* (NOTE: capital: **Athens**; people: **Greeks**; language: **Greek**; currency: **euro**)

② **Greek**
[grik]
1 *adjective*
referring to Greece; *she married the son of a Greek businessman; he's opened a Greek restaurant near us; the letters of the Greek alphabet are used in science*
2 *noun*

(a) person from Greece; *the ancient Greeks lived many years before the Romans*
(b) language spoken in Greece; *he reads Plato in the original Greek; she bought a Greek phrase book before going on vacation*

① **green**
[grin]
1 *adjective*
(a) of a color like the color of grass; *he was wearing a bright green shirt; they painted the door dark green; go on - the traffic light is green*
(b) to give the green light to = to give permission to; *the Transport Department gave the project the green light*
(c) relating to, interested in, or concerned about the environment; *she's very worried about green issues; he's a leading figure in the Green movement* (NOTE: **greener - greenest**)
2 *noun*
(a) color like grass; *the door was painted a very dark green; do you have any paint of a darker green than this?*
(b) piece of public land covered with grass in the middle of a village; *the jazz band was playing on the village green*
(c) piece of smooth short grass for playing golf; *the grass on the greens is cut very short; his ball landed about two feet from the hole on the tenth green*
(d) greens = green vegetables, especially salad, spinach and kale; *eat up your greens - they're good for you*

③ **greenhouse**
[ˈgrinhaʊs] *noun*
glass building for growing plants; *we grow tomatoes in our greenhouse in winter;* **greenhouse effect** = effect of gases in the Earth's atmosphere which prevent loss of heat and so make the climate hotter; **greenhouse gases** = gases which are produced by burning oil, gas and coal, and which rise into the atmosphere, forming a barrier which prevents loss of heat and creates the greenhouse effect (NOTE: plural is **greenhouses** [ˈgrinhaʊzɪz])

① **greet**
[grit] *verb*
to meet someone and say hi; *she greeted him with a kiss*

① **greeting**
[ˈgritɪŋ] *noun*
(a) words said when meeting or welcoming someone; *he said a few words of greeting to the guests and disappeared into the kitchen*
(b) greetings = good wishes; *we send you birthday greetings; Christmas greetings from all our family!*

① **grew**
[gru] *see* GROW

② **grief**
[grif] *noun*
very sad feeling; *she couldn't hide her grief as she watched the pictures on TV;* **to come to**

grief = to meet with a disaster; *the project came to grief when the municipal government refused to renew their grant*; *(informal)* **to give someone grief** = to make trouble or bother

① **grill**
[grɪl]
1 *noun*
(a) grid of metal bars set over a fire; *cook the chops on the grill*
(b) restaurant serving grilled food; *we'll meet up at the Mexican Grill*
(c) mixed grill = dish of different sorts of food grilled together, usually chops, sausages, bacon and vegetables
2 *verb*
(a) to cook on a grill; *we're having grilled sardines for dinner*
(b) *(informal)* to ask someone questions; *the police grilled him about the missing money*

② **grim**
[grɪm] *adjective*
(a) stern and not smiling; *his expression was grim*; *he gave a grim laugh and went on working*
(b) unpleasant, worrying; *there is some grim news about the war*
(c) gray and unpleasant; *downtown is really grim* (NOTE: grimmer - grimmest)

① **grin**
[grɪn]
1 *noun*
broad smile; *she gave me a big grin*
2 *verb*
to give a broad smile; *he grinned when we asked him if he liked his job*; **to grin and bear it** = to accept a difficult situation; *no one likes doing all these rehearsals, but we've just got to grin and bear it* (NOTE: grinning - grinned)

① **grind**
[graɪnd]
1 *noun*
the daily grind = dull work done every day
2 *verb*
(a) to crush to powder; *to grind corn or coffee*; *a cup of freshly ground coffee*
(b) to rub surfaces together; **to grind your teeth** = to rub your teeth together and make a noise (usually because you are annoyed); **to grind to a halt** = to stop working gradually; *the men went on strike, and the production line ground to a halt*; *the driver put on the brakes and the train ground to a halt* (NOTE: grinding - ground)

① **grip**
[grɪp]
1 *noun*
(a) firm hold; *he has a strong firm grip*; *these new tires give a better grip on the road surface*; **to lose your grip** = not to be as much in control as before; *she simply doesn't make any decisions - I think she's losing her grip*

(b) *(informal)* **to come to grips with something** = to start to deal with something; *the president is having to come to grips with the failing economy*; **to get a grip on yourself** = to try to control yourself, to try to be less worried about everything; *get a grip on yourself - you've got an interview in half an hour*
2 *verb*
(a) to hold tight; *she gripped the rail with both hands*
(b) to be very interesting; *the story gripped me from the first page* (NOTE: gripping - gripped)

① **groan**
[grəʊn]
1 *noun*
deep moan; *he uttered a groan and closed his eyes*
2 *verb*
(a) to moan deeply; *she groaned when she saw how much work had to be done*
(b) to groan under a weight = to carry a heavy weight; *the floor groaned under the weight of the gold bars*

③ **groove**
[gruv] *noun*
wide line cut into a surface; *the door slides along a groove in the floor*; *the ridges on the nut have to fit into the grooves on the screw*; **to be stuck in a groove** = to be in a routine job, leading a dull life with no excitement

③ **gross**
[grəʊs]
1 *adjective*
(a) total, with nothing taken away; **gross domestic product (GDP)** = value of goods and services paid for inside a country; **gross income** *or* **gross salary** = salary that is paid without taking away any tax, insurance, etc.; **gross national product (GNP)** = value of goods and services paid for in a country, including income earned in other countries; **gross profit** = profit before overheads, tax, etc., are taken away; **gross weight** = full weight, including the container and packing material (NOTE: the opposite in this meaning is **net**)
(b) very great and bad; *it was a gross error on the part of the referee* (NOTE: grosser - grossest)
2 *adverb*
with nothing taken away; *his salary is paid gross*
3 *verb*
to make a gross turnover; *the company grossed $25 m last year*
4 *noun*
twelve dozen (i.e. 144); *we ordered two gross of the chocolate bars* (NOTE: plural is **gross**)

① **ground**
[graʊnd]
1 *noun*
(a) soil or earth; *you should dig the ground in the fall*; *the house is built on solid ground*; *it*

has been so dry that the ground is hard
(b) surface of the earth; *the factory was burned to the ground*; *there were no seats, so we had to sit on the ground*; *she lay down on the ground and went to sleep*; **to get a project off the ground** = to get a project started; *he played an important role in getting the project off the ground*
(c) space between competitors in a race; **to lose ground to someone** = to fall behind someone; **to gain ground** = to catch up with someone
2 *verb*
(a) to put or keep on the ground; *after the mechanical failure was discovered, the fleet of aircraft was grounded*
(b) to base; *our teaching system is grounded on years of practice*
(c) to connect an electrical device to the earth; *machines you use in the home should be properly grounded*
(d) *see also* GRIND

① **groundhog**
['graʊndhɒg] *noun*
a woodchuck; **Groundhog Day** = February 2, believed to be the day the groundhog wakes up after sleeping through winter and if it sees its shadow, there will be six more weeks of winter, but if it does not, then spring will start early

① **group**
[grup] *noun*
(a) a number of people or things taken together; *a group of houses in the valley*; *groups of people gathered on the street*; *she is leading a group of businessmen on a tour of Italian factories*; *there are reduced entrance prices for groups of 30 and over*
(b) way of classifying things; *this drug belongs to the same group*; **age group** = people of the same age; *children in the 5 to 10 age group*; **blood group** = people with the same type of blood
(c) people playing music together; *he plays in a jazz group*; *she's the lead singer in a pop group*
(d) several different companies linked together; *the Shell group of companies*; *a major travel group*

④ **grouping**
['grupɪŋ] *noun*
putting together in a group

② **grove**
[grəʊv] *noun*
small group of trees; *an olive grove or a grove of olive trees*

① **grow**
[grəʊ] *verb*
(a) to live (as a plant); *there was grass growing in the middle of the road*; *roses grow well in our garden*
(b) to make plants grow; *he grows all his vegetables in his garden*; *we are going to grow some carrots this year*

(c) to become taller or bigger; *he's grown a lot since I last saw him*; *rubbing with oil will encourage your hair to grow*; *the profit has grown to $1.5 m*; *the town's population is growing very fast*
(d) to become gradually; *she grew weak with lack of food*; *the nights are growing colder now*; *all the time he grew richer and richer* (NOTE: **growing - grew** [gru] **- grown** [grəʊn])

② **grower**
['grəʊər] *noun*
farmer who grows a certain type of plant; *an apple grower*; *a tomato grower*

① **grown**
[grəʊn] *adjective*
(person) full size; *a grown man like you shouldn't be afraid of a little spider* (NOTE: do not confuse with **groan**)

① **grownup**
['grəʊnʌp] *noun*
adult; *the family consists of three grownups and ten children*; *she has a grownup daughter*; *the grown-ups had wine with their meal*

① **growth**
[grəʊθ] *noun*
increase in size; *the rapid growth of the population since 1980*; *they measured the tree's growth over the last fifty years*; **the country's economic growth** = rate at which a country's national income grows

① **grow up**
['grəʊ ˈʌp] *verb*
to become an adult; *what does your son want to do when he grows up or when he's grown up?*

② **grumble**
['grʌmbl]
1 *noun*
complaint about something; *do you have any grumbles about the food?*; *she's full of grumbles* = she is always complaining
2 *verb*
to grumble about something = to complain about something; *he's always grumbling about the noise from the apartment above*

③ **guarantee**
[gærən'ti]
1 *noun*
(a) legal document in which someone states that something is going to happen; *the travel agent could not give a guarantee that the accommodation would be in the hotel shown in the brochure*
(b) legal document that promises that a machine is in good condition and will work without problems for a certain length of time; *the fridge is sold with a twelve-month guarantee*; **under guarantee** = covered by a guarantee; *the station wagon is still under guarantee, so the manufacturers will pay for the repairs* (NOTE: also called a **warranty**)
(c) firm promise that something will happen; *we can't give you a guarantee that the weather will*

be fine; *there is no guarantee that he will get a job even if he gets through the training course successfully*

2 *verb*

(a) to give a legal assurance that something will work, that something will be done; *the product is guaranteed for twelve months*

(b) to make a firm promise that something will happen; *I can guarantee that the car will give you no trouble*; *we can almost guarantee good weather in the Caribbean area at this time of year*

③ **guaranteed**

[ˈgærənˈtid] *adjective*

which has been promised legally; *guaranteed delivery within 24 hours*

① **guard**

[gɑrd]

1 *noun*

(a) to be on guard *or* **to keep guard** = to be looking out for danger; *you must be on your guard against burglars at all times*; **to catch someone off guard** = to catch someone by surprise, when they are not expecting it

(b) person who protects, often a soldier; *security guards patrol the factory at night*; *our squad is on guard duty tonight*; **changing of the guard** = military ceremony, where one group of soldiers is replaced by another on guard duty at a palace, etc.; *when we were in London we watched the changing of the guard at Buckingham Palace*; **guard dog** = dog used to guard a house or other buildings; *German shepherds are often used as guard dogs*; *when we arrived at the hotel we were welcomed by a couple of barking guard dogs*

2 *verb*

to protect; *the prison is guarded at all times*

② **guardian**

[ˈgɑrdiən] *noun*

person who protects, especially someone who has been legally appointed to look after a child; *when his parents died, his uncle became his guardian*

④ **gubernatorial**

[gubərnəˈtɔriəl] *noun*

relating to a governor of a U.S. state; *there are three gubernatorial candidates*

④ **guerrilla** *or* **guerilla**

[gəˈrɪlə] *noun*

soldier who is not part of a regular national army; *the guerrillas fought their way to the capital*; **guerrilla warfare** = type of warfare fought by guerrillas, who attack in small groups in unexpected places (NOTE: do not confuse with **gorilla**)

① **guess**

[ges]

1 *noun*

trying to give the right answer or figure; *go on - make a guess!*; *at a guess, I'd say it weighs about 10 pounds*; **it is anyone's guess** = no one

really knows what is the right answer (NOTE: plural is **guesses**)

2 *verb*

(a) to try to give the right answer or figure; *I would guess it's about six o'clock*; *neither of them guessed the right answer*; *he guessed right*; *I've bought you a present - shut your eyes and guess what it is*

(b) to think; *I guess the plane's going to be late*

① **guest**

[gest] *noun*

(a) person who is asked to your home or to an event; *we had a very lively party with dozens of guests*; *none of the guests left the party early*; **be my guest** = help yourself, go ahead

(b) person staying in a hotel; **guest lounge** = special lounge for guests in a hotel

③ **guidance**

[ˈgaɪdəns] *noun*

advice; *an instructor will be on hand to give you guidance*; *he asked the bank manager for guidance about how to fill out his tax form*; **moral guidance** = advice as to what is right or wrong behavior; *part of a teacher's job is to give the students moral guidance*

① **guide**

[gaɪd]

1 *noun*

(a) person who shows the way; *they used local farmers as guides through the forest*; **guide dog** = dog which has been trained to lead a blind person; *the only dogs allowed into the restaurant are guide dogs*

(b) person who shows tourists around a place; *the guide showed us around the castle*; *the museum guide spoke so fast that we couldn't understand what she was saying*

(c) book that gives information; *a guide to Athens*; *a guide to the butterflies of Europe*

2 *verb*

to show the way; to show tourists around a place; *she guided us up the steps in the dark*; *he guided us around the castle*

② **guidebook**

[ˈgaɪdbʊk] *noun*

book with information about a place; *the guidebook lists three hotels by the beach*

④ **guidelines**

[ˈgaɪdlaɪnz] *noun*

general advice on what to do; *if you follow the government guidelines, you should not have any trouble*; *the minister has issued a new set of guidelines about city planning*

③ **guilt**

[gɪlt] *noun*

(a) state of having committed a crime; *the prisoner admitted his guilt*

(b) being or feeling responsible for something wrong which has happened; *the whole group bears the guilt for his tragic death*

② **guilty**
['gɪltɪ] *adjective*
(a) who has committed a crime; *he was found guilty of murder*; *the jury decided she was not guilty*
(b) feeling unhappy because you have done something wrong; *I feel very guilty about not having written to you* (NOTE: guiltier - guiltiest)

④ **guinea pig**
['gɪnɪ 'pɪg] *noun*
(a) little furry animal kept as a pet; *she keeps guinea pigs in a hutch in the garden*
(b) person used in an experiment; *twenty people were used as guinea pigs to test the new drug*

② **guitar**
[gɪ'tɑr] *noun*
musical instrument, usually with six strings, played with the fingers; *he plays the guitar in a band*

④ **guitarist**
[gɪ'tɑrɪst] *noun*
person who plays a guitar; *he's the lead guitarist with a pop group*; *the band had two guitarists*

② **gulf**
[gʌlf] *noun*
(a) area of sea partly surrounded by land; *the Gulf of Mexico*
(b) *(especially)* **the Gulf** = (i) the Gulf of Mexico; (ii) the Persian Gulf (the sea near Iran, Iraq, Saudi Arabia, etc.); *the tanker was carrying crude oil from the Gulf*
(c) *(formal)* great distance between two points of view; *the gulf that separates the two parties will be difficult to bridge*

④ **Gulf Stream**
['gʌlf 'strim] *noun*
warm current that crosses the North Atlantic from west to east (NOTE: also called the **North Atlantic Drift**)

② **gum**
[gʌm] *noun*
(a) flesh around the base of your teeth; *brushing your teeth every day is good for your gums*
(b) (chewing) gum = sweet substance that you chew but do not swallow; *he slowly took a piece of gum out of his mouth and put it in the ashtray*; *I've got some gum stuck to my shoe*

④ **gumdrop**
['gʌmdrɒp] *noun*
small sugar-coated candy which you can chew; *the yellow gumdrops taste like lemons*

① **gun**
[gʌn]
1 *noun*
(a) weapon that shoots bullets; *the robber pulled out a gun*; *she grabbed his gun and shot him dead*; **starting gun** = gun fired to start a race; *(informal)* **to jump the gun** = to start too quickly; *they are lifting the ban on smoking in restaurants next month but some establishments are already jumping the gun*; **to**

stick to your guns = to keep to your point of view even if everyone says you are wrong
(b) large weapon that shoots shells; *we heard the guns firing all night*; *the ship trained its guns on the town*
(c) small device that you hold in your hand to spray paint, glue, etc.; *a spray gun gives an even coating of paint*
2 *verb*
(a) to gun someone down = to shoot and kill someone; *the police officer was gunned down on the street*
(b) *(informal)* **to be gunning for someone** = to go after; *the papers are gunning for the minister for tax evasion; she is gunning for a raise* (NOTE: gunning - gunned)

② **gunfire**
['gʌnfaɪər] *noun*
the shooting of guns; *we could hear gunfire in the distance*

② **gunman**
['gʌnmən] *noun*
armed robber; *the gunman pulled out his gun and started shooting* (NOTE: plural is **gunmen**)

③ **gut**
[gʌt]
1 *noun*
(a) *(informal)* the tube inside your body which passes down from the stomach and in which food is digested as it passes through; *he complained of pain in the gut*; **gut reaction** = instinctive reaction; *my gut reaction is to vote for the woman candidate*; **I hate his guts** = I dislike him a lot
(b) *(informal)* **guts** = courage; *he had the guts to tell the boss what he should do*
2 *verb*
(a) to remove the insides of an animal or fish before cooking; *women stood in the market gutting fish*
(b) to destroy the inside of a building totally; *the house was gutted by fire* (NOTE: gutting - gutted)

② **gutter**
['gʌtər] *noun*
(a) channel by the side of a road to take away rain water; *pieces of paper and leaves were blowing about in the gutter*
(b) open pipe along the edge of a roof to catch rain water; *it rained so hard the gutters overflowed*

② **guy**
[gaɪ] *noun*
(a) *(informal)* man; *she married a guy from Texas*; *the boss is a very friendly guy*; *(in a story or movie)* **bad guy** = wicked character; *the bad guy is the one with the black hat and the five o'clock shadow*; **good guy** = hero; *the good guys always win*
(b) *(way of calling to men, women or children)* *hey, you guys, come and look at this!*

(c) rope that holds a tent; *make sure the guys are tight before the storm comes*

① **gym** *or* **gymnasium**
[dʒɪm *or* dʒɪmˈneɪzɪəm] *noun*
hall for indoor sports; *because it rained, we had to hold the school festival in the gym*; *the room in the basement has been equipped as a gymnasium*

③ **gypsy**
[ˈdʒɪpsi] *noun*
member of a people who wander from place to place, perhaps originally coming from India; *a large group of gypsies came up to us to ask for money* (NOTE: plural is **gypsies**)

Hh

③ **H, h**
[eɪtʃ]
eighth letter of the alphabet, between G and I; *the sign for a hospital is a white H on a blue background*

② **ha**
[hɑ] *interjection showing surprise or delight; ha! there's a mistake on page one of the book!*

② **habit** [ˈhæbɪt] *noun*
regular way of doing things; *he has the habit of going to bed at 9 o'clock and reading until midnight*; **to develop the habit** *or* **to get into the habit of doing something** = to start to do something regularly; *he's getting into the habit of exercising twice a week*; **to break the habit** = to stop doing something which you used to do regularly; *I haven't had a cigarette for six months - I think I've broken the habit!*; **bad habit** *or* **nasty habit** = regular way of doing something which is not nice; *she has the bad habit of biting her nails*; **from force of habit** = because this is what you do normally; *he switched off all the lights from force of habit*

④ **habitat** [ˈhæbɪtæt] *noun*
place where an animal or plant lives; *this is an ideal habitat for butterflies*

② **hack** [hæk]
1 *noun*
journalist, or writer who writes for money
2 *verb*
(a) to chop roughly; *he hacked the tree with an ax*
(b) to enter a computer system illegally; *he hacked into the bank's computer*

① **had, hadn't** [hæd *or* ˈhædənt]
see HAVE

① **hail** [heɪl]
1 *noun*

frozen rain; *I thought the hail was going to break the windshield*
2 *verb*
(a) to fall as frozen rain; *it hailed for ten minutes and then the sun came out*
(b) to wave, call, etc., to make a cab stop; *he whistled to hail a cab*
(c) to hail from = to come from; *he hails from Montana*

② **hair**
[heər] *noun*
(a) mass of long threads growing on your head; *she has long brown hair* or *her hair is long and brown*; *she always brushes her hair before washing it*; *you must get your hair cut*; *he's had his hair cut short*; *use some hair spray to keep your hair in place*; **to let your hair down** = to relax and enjoy yourself; *when the final is finished we're all going to let our hair down* (NOTE: no plural in this meaning)
(b) one of the long threads growing on the body of a human or animal; *waiter, there's a hair in my soup!*; *the cat has left hairs all over the cushion*; *he's beginning to get some gray hairs*; **to split hairs** = to try to find minute differences between things when arguing; *stop splitting hairs, you know you're in the wrong* (NOTE: the plural in this meaning is **hairs**)

① **haircut**
[ˈheəkʌt] *noun*
cutting of the hair on your head; *he needs a haircut*; *I went to get a haircut*

② **hairdresser**
[ˈheədresər] *noun*
person who cuts and washes your hair; *he's the First Lady's hairdresser*; **hairdresser's** = shop where you have your hair cut, washed, etc.; *I must go to the hairdresser's*

④ **hairstyle**
[ˈheəstaɪl] *noun*
way of cutting and styling hair; *I have decided to change my hairstyle*; *what do you think of my new hairstyle?*

① **half**
[hæf]
1 *noun*
(a) one of two parts which are the same in size; *she cut the orange in half; one half of the apple fell on the carpet; half of six is three*
(b) *(in sport)* one of two parts of a match; *our team scored a touchdown in the first half; we thought we were going to win, and then they scored in the final minutes of the second half*
(c) part of a financial year; *the sales in the first half were down from last year* (NOTE: plural is **halves** [hævz])
2 *adjective*
divided into two equal parts; **half a bottle of wine** = half of a bottle of wine; *we drank half a bottle of wine each;* **half bottle of wine** = a small bottle of wine, containing half the amount of a normal bottle; *he ordered his meal and a half bottle of Bordeaux;* **half an hour** *or* **a half hour** = 30 minutes; *I'll be back in half an hour; the journey takes two and a half hours or two hours and a half*
3 *adverb*
half as big = only 50 percent of the size; *this book is half as big or half the size of that one;* **half as big again** = 50 percent bigger

④ **half-dozen** *or* **half a dozen**
[hæf'dʌzn or 'hæf ə 'dʌzn] *noun*
six; *I bought half a dozen eggs*

② **half hour**
['hæf'aʊər] *noun*
period of thirty minutes; *there's a bus to town every half hour*

② **half past**
['hæf 'pæst] *phrase*
30 minutes after an hour; *I have an appointment with the doctor at half past five (= 5:30)*

② **half price**
['hæf 'praɪs] *noun & adjective*
50 percent of the price; *tours at half price or half-price tours; to sell goods off at half price;* **half-price sale** = sale of all goods at 50% of the usual price; *the store is holding a half-price sale*

① **halfway**
[hæf'weɪ] *adverb*
in the middle; *come on, we're more than halfway there!; the post office is about halfway between the station and our house;* **to meet someone halfway** *or* **to go halfway to meet someone** = to compromise; *I'll meet you halfway: I write the report and you present it at the meeting*

① **hall**
[hɔl] *noun*
(a) passage at the entrance to a house, where you can leave your coat; *don't wait in the hall, come straight into the dining room; she left her umbrella in the hall*
(b) large room for meetings; *the children have their dinner in the school hall;* **concert hall** =

large building where concerts are given; **sports hall of fame** = building housing memorials to star athletes
(c) college or university building where students live, sleep, study or have class; *how many students live in Ellis Hall?*

① **Halloween**
[hæləʊ'in] *noun*
October 31, when there is trick-or-treating and children wear costumes

> COMMENT: traditionally, there are parties with pumpkins hollowed out with faces cut into them and candles put inside them; children go from house to house to trick-or-treat

② **halt**
[hɔlt]
1 *noun*
complete stop; **to come to a halt** = to come to a dead stop; *the truck came to a halt just before the wall;* **to call a halt to something** = to make something stop; *he tried to call a halt to arguments inside the party;* **to grind to a halt** = to stop working gradually; *the whole plan ground to a halt for lack of funds*
2 *verb*
to stop; *the cars halted when the traffic light turned red; we are trying to halt experiments on live animals*

② **halve**
[hæv] *verb*
(a) to cut into two equal parts; *she halved the cake*
(b) to reduce by half; *because we have been on vacation, our telephone bill has been halved*

② **halves**
[hævz]
see HALF

① **ham**
[hæm]
1 *noun*
(a) salted or smoked pork; *she cut three slices of ham; we had a ham and tomato salad; she had a ham sandwich for lunch;* **ham and eggs** = fried ham with fried eggs
(b) **(radio) ham** = person who sends and receives radio messages unofficially; *a radio ham picked up the signals*
(c) *(old)* bad actor who uses too many gestures and speaks too loudly
2 *verb*
(informal) **to ham it up** = to overact on purpose

① **hamburger**
['hæmbɜrgər] *noun*
chopped beef grilled and served in a toasted roll; *the children want hamburgers and fries for lunch*

① **hammer**
['hæmər]
1 *noun*

tool with a heavy head for knocking nails; *she hit the nail hard with the hammer*

2 *verb*

(a) to knock something into something with a hammer; *it took him a few minutes to hammer the tent pegs into the ground*

(b) to hit hard, as with a hammer; *he hammered the table with his fist*; *she hammered on the door with her stick*

(c) to hammer it into someone = to try to make someone understand by repeating; *they're trying to hammer it into schoolchildren that drugs are dangerous*

Ⓢ **hammock**

['hæmək] *noun*

bed made from a piece of strong cloth hanging between two hooks; *she spent the afternoon lying in a hammock in the shade, drinking lemonade*

Ⓢ **hamper**

['hæmpər]

1 *noun*

large basket; *we packed the hamper with food for the picnic*

2 *verb*

to get in the way; *lack of funds is hampering our development project*

Ⓢ **hand**

[hænd]

1 *noun*

(a) part of the body at the end of each arm, which you use for holding things; *she was carrying a cup of tea in each hand*; *she held out her hand, asking for money*; **to shake hands** = to hold someone's hand to show you are pleased to meet them or to show that an agreement has been reached; *the visitors shook hands and the meeting started*; **to shake hands on a deal** = to shake hands to show that a deal has been agreed; **to give someone a hand** *or* **lend a hand with something** = to help with something; *can you lend a hand with moving the furniture?* ; **the store has changed hands** = the store has a new owner; **they walked along hand in hand** = holding each other by the hand

(b) to have your hands full = to be very busy, totally occupied; *with three little children to look after she has her hands full*; **hand over fist** = quickly and in large quantities; *they were making money hand over fist*; *see also* WASH

(c) one of the two pieces on a clock (the minute hand and the hour hand) that turn round and show the time; *the minute hand is longer than the hour hand*

(d) at hand = near; *the emergency exit is close at hand*; **by hand** = using your hands and tools but not using large machines; *he made the table by hand*; **in hand** = in your possession; *we have his paycheck in hand*; **on hand** = ready; *there's a doctor on hand if accidents occur*; **on the one hand** = showing the first part of a comparison; **on the other hand** = as the second part of a

comparison; but; *on the one hand he's a good salesman, on the other hand he can't figure out discounts correctly*; **out of hand** = not controlled; *our expenses have got out of hand*

(e) worker; *to take on ten more hands*; **factory hand** = worker in a factory; **old hand** = someone who has had a lot of experience in doing something; *he's an old hand at selling to Japan*

(f) action of clapping your hands together; *he did very well - give him a big hand, everyone*

2 *verb*

to pass something to someone; *can you hand me that box?*; *she handed me all her money*; *(informal)* **you've got to hand it to him** = he has to be admired for; *you've got to hand it to her, she's a great cook!*

Ⓢ **hand back**

['hænd 'bæk] *verb*

to give something back; *the customs officer handed me back my passport*

Ⓢ **handbook**

['hænbuk] *noun*

book that gives instructions on how to use or repair something; *look in the handbook to see if it tells you how to clean the photocopier*; **service handbook** = book that shows how a machine should be serviced

Ⓢ **handful**

['hænfəl] *noun*

(a) as much as you can hold in your hand; *she paid with a handful of $50 bills*

(b) very few; *only a handful of people came to the wedding*

(c) difficult child; *their son is a bit of a handful*

Ⓢ **handicap**

['hændıkæp]

1 *noun*

(a) physical or mental disability; *she was born with a physical handicap*

(b) something which puts you at a disadvantage; *not being able to drive is a handicap for this job*

(c) penalty imposed on a player to make it harder for him to win; *he has a golf handicap of 7*

2 *verb*

to put someone at a disadvantage; *she was handicapped by not being able to speak Russian* (NOTE: **handicapping - handicapped**)

Ⓢ **handicapped**

['hændıkæpt]

1 *adjective*

with a mental or physical disability; *a school for handicapped children*

2 *noun*

the handicapped = people with disabilities; *the movie theater has facilities for the handicapped*; *there is a restroom for the handicapped on the ground floor*

Ⓢ **hand in**

['hænd 'ın] *verb*

to give in something by hand; *please have the completed form ready to hand in at the reception desk*; **he handed in his notice** *or* **his resignation** = he resigned

① **handkerchief**
['hæŋkətʃif] *noun*
piece of cloth for wiping your nose; *she carries a handkerchief in her bag*; *he wiped his eyes on his handkerchief* (NOTE: often called a **hankie** or **hanky,** especially by children)

① **handle**
['hændl]
1 *noun*
(a) part of something which you hold in your hand to carry or to use the object held; *I turned the handle but the door didn't open*; *be careful, the handle of the frying pan may be hot*; *the handle has come off my suitcase*; *he broke the handle off the cup*
(b) *(informal)* **to fly off the handle** = to lose your temper; *stop telling him what to do or he'll fly off the handle*
2 *verb*
(a) to move by hand; *be careful when you handle the bottles of acid*
(b) to deal with something; *his company handles most of the traffic through the port*; *leave it to me - I'll handle it*; **handling charge** = charge made for dealing with something
(c) to sell or to trade in (a sort of service or product); *we do not handle washing machines*

① **hand over**
['hænd 'əʊvər] *verb*
to give something to someone; *she handed over the keys to the condo to the new owner*

① **handsome**
['hænsəm] *adjective*
(a) good-looking; *her boyfriend is very handsome - I'm jealous!* (NOTE: used of men, rather than women)
(b) large; *we made a handsome profit on the deal*

② **handwriting**
['hændraɪtɪŋ] *noun*
way of writing by hand; *his handwriting's so bad I can't read it*

② **handwritten**
[hænd'rɪtn] *adjective*
written by hand, not typed or printed; *she sent a handwritten letter to her aunt*

① **handy**
['hændi] *adjective*
practical and useful; *this small case is handy when traveling*; *it's handy having the post office next door*; **to come in handy** = to be useful; *the knife will come in handy when we are camping* (NOTE: **handier - handiest**)

① **hang**
[hæŋ]
1 *verb*
(a) to attach something to something so that it does not touch the ground; *hang your coat on the hook behind the door*; *he hung his umbrella over the back of his chair*; *he hung*

the painting in the hall; *the boys were hanging upside down from a tree* (NOTE: **hanging - hung** [hʌŋ])
(b) to kill someone by tying a rope around his neck and hanging him off the ground; *he was sentenced to be hanged for murder*; **to hang yourself** = to commit suicide by hanging; *he hanged himself in his prison cell* (NOTE: in this meaning, **hanging - hanged**)
2 *noun*
to get the hang of something = to understand how something works; *I don't think I'll ever get the hang of this software package*

③ **hang around**
['hæŋ ə'raʊnd] *verb*
(informal) to wait in a certain place without doing anything much; *groups of teenagers were hanging around the mall*

③ **hang back**
['hæŋ 'bæk] *verb*
to stay behind when others go on; *they all ran forward but she hung back*; *they want him to put money into their new project, but he's hanging back to see if it works properly*

③ **hang down**
['hæŋ 'daʊn] *verb*
to hang in a long piece; *her hair hung down to her waist*; *plants were hanging down from the rocks*

② **hanger**
['hæŋər] *noun*
coat hanger = piece of wood, wire or plastic on which you can hang a coat, a shirt, etc.; *keep your clothes on coat hangers - they won't need ironing twice*

③ **hang on**
['hæŋ 'ɒn] *verb*
(a) to wait; *if you hang on a few minutes you will be able to see her*
(b) *(while phoning)* to wait; *if you can hang on a moment, Mr. Smith will be off the other line soon*
(c) *(when thinking again)* **hang on!** *do you mean you're not coming with us?*
(d) **to hang on to something** = to hold something tight; *hang on to the ladder and don't look down*
(e) to keep; *I've decided to hang on to my shares until the price goes up*

③ **hang out**
['hæŋ 'aʊt] *verb*
(a) to hang things outside on a string; *they hung out flags all around the square*; *mother's hanging out her laundry to dry*
(b) *(informal)* to wait in a certain place without doing anything much; *teenagers like to hang out at the Internet café*

③ **hang up**
['hæŋ 'ʌp] *verb*
(a) to put something on a hanger or on a hook; *don't leave your jacket on the back of your chair, hang it up!*

(b) to stop a telephone conversation by putting the telephone back on its rest; *when I asked him when he was going to pay, he hung up*; *see also* HUNG UP

③ **hankie** *or* **hanky**
['hæŋki] *noun*
(informal) = HANDKERCHIEF; *don't sniff, use your hankie*

④ **haphazard**
[hæp'hæzərd] *adjective*
done at random, without any plan; *his haphazard approach to saving money*

④ **haphazardly**
[hæp'hæzərdli] *adverb*
at random, without any plan; *the books were put on the shelves quite haphazardly*

① **happen**
['hæpən] *verb*
(a) to take place; *the accident happened at the traffic light*; *how did the accident happen?*; *something happened to make all the buses late*; *he's late - something must have happened to him*
(b) *what's happened to his brother?* = what is his brother doing now?
(c) to be somewhere by chance; *the fire engine happened to be there when the fire started*; *the store happened to be empty at the time*; *we happened to meet at the library*; *do you happen to have change for $20?*; *it so happens that or it just happened that or as it happens or as it happened* = quite by chance; *as it happens I have the car today and can give you a lift*; *it just happened that my wife bumped into her boss at the supermarket*

② **happening**
['hæpnɪŋ] *noun*
event, something that happens; *tell me about all the happenings in sports while I've been away*

① **happily**
['hæpɪli] *adverb*
in a happy way; *the children played happily in the sand for hours*; *we waited for her for hours in the rain, and in the meantime, she was happily sitting at home watching TV*; *they seem to get along very happily without the telephone*

① **happiness**
['hæpinəs] *noun*
feeling of being happy; *her expression reflected her feeling of happiness*

① **happy**
['hæpi] *adjective*
(a) *(of people)* very pleased; *I'm happy to say we're getting married next month*; *I'm so happy to hear that you are better*; *she's very happy in her job*
(b) *(of event)* pleasant; *it was the happiest day of my life*; *by a happy coincidence, we both like Dutch painters and met at the exhibition*; **happy hour** = period when drinks are cheaper in a bar; *there's a happy hour every day from 6 to 7*

(c) **to be happy to do something** = to do something very willingly; *I'd be happy to lend you my truck*; **to be happy with something** = to be satisfied with something; *are you happy with your new car?*; *no one is happy with the plans for the new city hall*
(d) *(greetings)* **Happy birthday** *or* **many Happy Returns of the Day** = greeting said to someone on their birthday; **Happy Easter** = greeting said to someone at Easter; **Happy New Year** = greeting said to someone at the New Year (NOTE: **happier - happiest**)

④ **harass**
[hə'ræs] *verb*
to keep on bothering someone and worrying them; *she was harassed by a man at work*; *they harassed him by calling every day until he finally paid the bill*

④ **harassment**
[hə'ræsmənt] *noun*
action of keeping on talking to someone and worrying them; *he complained of police harassment*; **sexual harassment** = worrying someone by making sexual approaches which they do not want; *she complained of sexual harassment by her manager*

① **harbor**
['hɑrbər]
1 *noun*
port, place where boats can come and tie up; *the yacht moved away from the harbor*; *the ship came into harbor last night*; **fishing harbor** = harbor that is used by fishing boats
2 *verb*
to protect a criminal; *he was arrested and charged with harboring illegal immigrants*

① **hard**
[hɑrd]
1 *adjective*
(a) not soft; *if you have back trouble, you ought to get a hard bed*; *the ice cream is rock hard or hard as a rock*; *the cake she made is so hard I can't bite into it*
(b) difficult; *the test is too hard - I can't even begin to do it*; *the test was very hard, and most students failed*; *she finds it hard to cope without any money*
(c) severe; *there was a hard winter in 1962*
(d) *he's rather hard of hearing* = he's quite deaf
(e) *(of water)* containing calcium, which makes it difficult to wash with; *the water in this area is very hard* (NOTE: **harder - hardest**)
2 *adverb*
strongly; *he hit the nail hard*; *it's snowing very hard*; *they worked hard to finish the order on time*; *they tried hard, but couldn't score enough goals*

② **harden**
['hɑrdn] *verb*
(a) to become hard; *leave the cement for a couple of days to harden*

(b) to make harder; *we use specially hardened steel in the building of the boat*

(c) to make more experienced; *he's a hardened criminal*

② **hardly**
['hɑrdli] *adverb*

(a) almost not; *I hardly know her*; *we hardly slept last night*; *she hardly eats anything at all*

(b) hardly ever = almost never; *I hardly ever see her these days*; *it hardly ever rains in September*

(c) hardly anyone = almost no one; *hardly anyone came to the party*

② **hardship**
['hɑrdʃɪp] *noun*

difficult conditions, suffering; *she faced hardship when her husband died and left her in debt*

③ **hard up**
['hɑrd 'ʌp] *adjective*

with very little money; *I can't lend you anything because I'm kind of hard up right now*

④ **hardware**
['hɑrdweər] *noun*

(a) tools used in the home; *I bought the paint in a hardware store*

(b) military hardware = guns, shells, tanks, etc.; **computer hardware** = computers, printers, keyboards, etc.; *if I had the money I would buy the latest computer hardware*; *compare* SOFTWARE (NOTE: no plural)

④ **hardy**
['hɑrdi] *adjective*

able to survive in cold weather; *plants need to be hardy to grow high up in the mountains*; *the Finns are a hardy people* (NOTE: **hardier - hardiest**)

① **harm**
[hɑrm]

1 *noun*

damage; *he didn't mean to do any harm or he meant no harm*; *there's no harm in having a little drink before you go to bed*; **to do more harm than good** = not to be helpful at all; *talking to him now about the project will do more harm than good* (NOTE: no plural)

2 *verb*

to damage; *luckily, the little girl was not harmed*; *the bad publicity has harmed our reputation*

① **harmful**
['hɑrmfəl] *adjective*

which causes damage; *harmful sprays are banned on our farm*; *smoking is harmful to your health*

① **harmless**
['hɑrmləs] *adjective*

which does not hurt; *are you sure this spray is harmless to animals?*; *our dog barks a lot, but really he's quite harmless*; **harmless fun** = jokes,

etc., which are not supposed to harm anyone; *we were just having a bit of harmless fun*

② **harmony**
['hɑrməni] *noun*

(a) pleasant musical sounds; *the group sang in harmony*

(b) general peace; *they want to live in harmony with their neighbors*

③ **harsh**
[hɑrʃ] *adjective*

(a) severe, cruel; *the prosecutor asked for a harsh sentence to fit the crime*

(b) rough; *he shouted in a harsh voice* (NOTE: **harsher - harshest**)

① **harvest**
['hɑrvɪst]

1 *noun*

(a) picking ripe crops; *the corn harvest is in August*

(b) ripe crops that have been picked; *the best corn harvest for years*

2 *verb*

to pick ripe crops; *the corn will be ready to harvest next week*; *they have started harvesting the grapes in the vineyard*

① **has, hasn't**
[hæz or 'hæzənt]

see HAVE

② **hash**
[hæʃ] *noun*

(a) dish prepared from chopped meat and vegetables; **corned beef hash** = dish made of corned beef, onions and mashed potatoes, cooked in the oven; **hash brown potatoes** or **hash browns** = boiled potatoes, diced or mashed and fried till crisp and brown

(b) hash sign = printed sign (# which means "number"; *#32 is apartment number 32*

④ **hasten**
['heɪsn] *verb*

(a) *(formal)* to go fast; *the chief fire officer hastened into the room*

(b) to do something fast; **to hasten to add** = to add something as an explanation; *'someone must have left the keys on the table, and it wasn't me', she hastened to add*

(c) to make something go faster; *several weeks' rest will hasten your recovery*

③ **hastily**
['heɪstɪli] *adverb*

carelessly and rapidly; *he hastily jotted down the license number*

③ **hasty**
['heɪsti] *adjective*

careless and too fast; *it was a hasty decision, which he regretted afterwards*; *he went into the ladies' toilet by mistake and had to beat a hasty retreat* (NOTE: **hastier - hastiest**)

① **hat**
[hæt] *noun*

(a) piece of clothing that you wear on your head;

take your hat off when you go into a church; *he's bought a Russian hat for the winter*; **hard hat** = solid hat worn by building workers, etc.; *visitors to the building site must wear hard hats*
(b) *(informal)* **keep it under your hat** = keep it secret; **to take your hat off to someone** = (i) to greet someone, by lifting your hat up a little; (ii) to say that you admire someone; *those helicopter pilots were very brave - I take my hat off to them*; *she's made a great success of her business - I take my hat off to her*; **to be talking through your hat** = to be talking nonsense; *that's garbage - you're talking through your hat*; *see also* PASS

② **hatch**
[hætʃ]
1 *noun*
opening in the deck of a ship; cover for this opening; *he opened the hatch and went down into the cabin* (NOTE: plural is **hatches**)
2 *verb*
(a) *(of a baby bird)* to break out of the egg; *all the chicks hatched on the same day*; *(informal)* **don't count your chickens before they're hatched** = don't be too sure that everything will be all right; *he's a very cautious man, he never counts his chickens before they're hatched*
(b) to plan; *they hatched a plot to kidnap the president's daughter*

① **hate**
[heɪt]
1 *verb*
to dislike very strongly; *I think she hates me, but I don't know why*; *I hate going to the dentist*; **hate mail** = letters showing that the writer hates someone; *he received a lot of hate mail after his speech*
2 *noun*
intense dislike; *having to stand in line is one of my pet hates*

③ **hatred**
['heɪtrəd] *noun*
feelings of great dislike; *he has a hatred of exams*; **racial hatred** = dislike of people of other races

② **haul**
[hɔl]
1 *verb*
to pull with difficulty; *they hauled the boat up onto the beach*; *the police hauled the body out of the water*
2 *noun*
(a) large quantity of things which have been stolen; *the burglars made off with their haul*
(b) distance traveled with difficulty; *it's a long haul up the hill*; **long-haul flight** = long-distance flight (for example, across the Atlantic)

④ **haunt**
[hɔnt]
1 *noun*

place that you visit frequently; *I went back to some of my old haunts*; *the café is a favorite haunt of actors*
2 *verb*
(of ghosts) to visit frequently; *the castle is supposed to be haunted by the ghost of its former owner*

② **haunted**
['hɔntɪd] *adjective*
visited by ghosts; *they live in a haunted house*

① **have**
[hæv] *verb*
(a) *(also* **to have got**) to own or possess; *she has a lot of money*; *they have got a new green car*; *she has long dark hair*; *the house has no telephone*; *have you got or do you have a table for three, please?*
(b) to take, to eat, to play, etc.; *have you had any tea?*; *she has sugar in her coffee*; *they had a meal of bread and cheese*; *she had her breakfast in bed*; *they had a game of tennis*; *I had a long walk*
(c) to pay someone to do something for you; *I must have my hair cut*; *she's having the house painted*
(d) *(used to form the past of verbs)* *have they finished their work?*; *she has never been to New York*; *they had finished supper when we arrived*; *I haven't seen him for two days*; *if she had asked me I would have said no*
(e) *(greetings)* *have a nice day!*; *have a good trip!*
(f) **had better** = it would be a good thing if; *you had better stay here instead of going to the hotel*; *hadn't you better answer the phone?*
(NOTE: **have** *or* **has - having - had - has had**)

② **haven't**
['hævənt]
= HAVE NOT

③ **have on**
['hæv 'ɒn] *verb*
to wear; *what did she have on when she left the party?*; *I can't answer the door - I've got nothing on*

① **have to**
['hæv 'tʊ] *verb*
used *with other verbs to mean* "must"; *in America everyone has to drive on the right*; *he had to walk to work because he missed the bus*; *do we have to get up early?*; *you have to go through customs*

① **hawk**
[hɔk]
1 *noun*
large bird that catches and eats other birds or small animals; *the hawk was hovering over the freeway*; *she has eyes like a hawk* = she notices everything
2 *verb*
to sell goods from door to door or on the street

② **hay fever**

['heɪ 'fiːvər] *noun*

running nose and eyes caused by an allergy to flowers, scent or dust; *when I have hay fever I prefer to stay indoors; the hay fever season starts in May*

③ **hazard**

['hæzəd]

1 *noun*

dangerous situation; *don't leave those cardboard boxes in the passage - they're a fire hazard;* **at hazard** = at risk; **hazard warning lights** = warning lights on an automobile; *he pulled over to the shoulder of the road and turned on his hazard warning lights*

2 *verb*

to risk; **to hazard a guess** = to risk making a guess; *I wouldn't hazard a guess at how many people will come to the concert*

④ **hazardous**

['hæzərdəs] *adjective*

risky or dangerous; *people in hazardous occupations often get paid danger money;* **hazardous to health** = which can harm your health; **hazardous waste** = rubbish which can pose a risk to people's health

① **he**

[hi] *pronoun referring to a man or boy, and some animals*

he's my brother; he and I met in Baltimore; he's eaten all my pudding; don't be frightened of the dog - he won't hurt you; (see also HIM, HIS) (NOTE: when it is the object **he** becomes **him: he hit the ball** *or* **the ball hit him;** when it follows the verb **to be, he** usually becomes **him: who's that? - it's him, the man who borrowed my knife)**

① **head**

[hed]

1 *noun*

(a) top part of the body, which contains the eyes, nose, mouth, brain, etc.; *he says he can relax by standing on his head; she hit her head on the cupboard door;* **head over heels** = over and over; *she rolled head over heels down the hill;* **to be head over heels in love** = to be madly in love; *he's head over heels in love with my sister;* **to shake your head** = to move your head from side to side to mean "no"; *she asked him if he wanted any more coffee and he shook his head; (informal)* **head and shoulders above** = much better than; *she's head and shoulders above all the others in the class*

(b) brain, intelligence; *she has a good head for numbers; he tried to do the sum in his head; if we all put our heads together we might come up with a solution;* **to get it into your head to do something** = to decide to do something suddenly; *he got it into his head to join the army*

(c) first place, top part; *an old lady was*

standing at the head of the line; his name comes at the head of the list*

(d) most important person; *she's the head of the sales department; the headwaiter showed us to our table*

(e) top side of a coin, usually with the head of a person on it; **to play heads or tails** = to spin a coin to see which side comes out on top, and so decide something; **heads I win** = if the coin falls with the top side up, then I will win (NOTE: the opposite side is **tails**)

(f) one person, when counting; *she counted heads as the party got onto the bus;* **a head** *or* **per head** = for each person; *the trip costs $25 a head or per head*

(g) to come to a head = to reach a crisis point; *things came to a head when all the family met to discuss Grandfather's will*

2 *verb*

(a) to be the first, to lead; *he heads the list of champions*

(b) to go toward; *she headed immediately for the manager's office; the automobile headed east along the highway; he's heading toward the Texas border; she's heading for trouble*

(c) to be the manager, the most important person; *he heads our research department*

② **headache**

['hedeɪk] *noun*

(a) pain in your head, caused by changes in pressure in the blood vessels; *I must lie down, I've got a terrible headache; take an aspirin if you have a headache*

(b) problem; *the lack of resources in the education system is one of the government's biggest headaches*

③ **headfirst**

['hed'fɜrst] *adverb*

(a) with your head first; *he tripped and fell headfirst down the stairs*

(b) hastily; *don't rush headfirst into a deal with someone you hardly know*

② **heading**

['hedɪŋ] *noun*

words at the top of a piece of text; *items are listed under several headings; look under the heading "Hotels and Restaurants"*

② **headlights**

['hedlaɪts] *noun*

main white lights on the front of a vehicle; *turn on your headlights when going through the tunnel*

① **headline**

['hedlaɪn] *noun*

(a) words in large letters on the front page of a newspaper; *did you see the headlines about the accident?; the newspaper headline says TAXES TO GO UP*

(b) news headlines = summary of the news on TV or radio; *we will have an interview with the senator following the headlines*

③ **head-on**
['hedɒn] *adjective & adverb*
(a) with the front first, direct; *we had a head-on confrontation with the police*; **a head-on collision** = collision where two vehicles run into each other front to front
(b) directly; *he decided to meet objections head-on*

① **headphones**
['hedfəʊnz] *noun*
devices which you put on your ears to listen to music tapes, etc.; *please use your headphones if you want to listen to the music*

① **headquarters (HQ)**
[hed'kwɔrtərz] *noun*
main offices; *several people were arrested and taken to police headquarters downtown*; **the headquarters staff** = the staff working in a headquarters

② **heal**
[hil] *verb*
to mend, to become healthy again; *after six weeks, his wound has still not healed* (NOTE: do not confuse with **heel**)

① **health**
[helθ] *noun*
(a) being well, being free from any illness; *he has enjoyed the best of health for years*; *smoking is bad for your health*; **health care** = provision of medical services; **health maintenance organization (HMO)** = organization that provides health care to members who pay a fixed amount to the organization rather than an amount based on each service they get
(b) to your health! = greeting said to someone when drinking

① **healthy**
['helθi] *adjective*
(a) not ill; *he's healthier than he has ever been*
(b) which makes you well; *she's keeping to a healthy diet*; *baked potatoes are healthier than French fries*
(c) good, strong; *he has a healthy dislike of politicians*; *the company's bank account is looking very healthy* (NOTE: **healthier - healthiest**)

② **heap**
[hip]
1 *noun*
pile; *a heap of dirty laundry lay in the middle of the room*; *step over that heap of garbage*
2 *verb*
to pile up; *a pile of presents were heaped under the Christmas tree*; *boxes were heaped up on the station platform*

① **hear**
[hɪər] *verb*
(a) to catch sounds with your ears; *he heard footsteps behind him*; *you could hear the sound of church bells in the distance*; *I heard her*

drive up in the car; *can you hear him singing in the bath?*
(b) to listen to something; *did you hear the talk on the radio?*
(c) to get information; *I heard it on the TV news*; *I hear you're going on vacation next week*; *we have not heard from them for some time* (NOTE: **hearing - heard** [hɜrd])

② **hearing**
['hɪərɪŋ] *noun*
(a) being able to hear; *bats have a very sharp sense of hearing*; *she has hearing difficulties* (NOTE: no plural in this meaning)
(b) hearing aid = electric device put in the ear to make you hear better; *she wears a little hearing aid which you can hardly see*
(c) session of a tribunal or court; *the hearing is expected to last three days*

① **hear of**
['hɪər'ɒv] *verb*
(a) to know about something; *I've heard of a new restaurant on Main Street*; *she's never heard of the Rolling Stones*
(b) *(formal)* **not to hear of it** = not to accept an offer; *I said I would pay for the glass I broke, but she wouldn't hear of it*

① **heart**
[hɑrt] *noun*
(a) main organ in the body, which pumps blood around the body; *she isn't dead - her heart's still beating*; *the doctor listened to his heart*; *he has had heart trouble for years*
(b) center of feelings; *my heart sank when I realized that he hadn't read my letter*; **with all my heart** = with all my love; **to know something by heart** = to know and remember something; *I don't know his phone number by heart, so I'll just look it up for you*; **to learn something by heart** = to learn and remember something; *she learned the poem by heart*; **to lose heart** = to stop being interested in something; *after all the delays she lost heart in the project*; **don't take it to heart** = don't be too sad about it; **his heart isn't in it** = he has lost interest in it; **to have your heart set on something** = to want something very much; *he has his heart set on buying a little sailboat*
(c) center, middle; *the restaurant is in the heart of the old town*
(d) one of the red suits in a game of cards, shaped like a heart; *my last two cards were the ten and the queen of hearts* (NOTE: the other red suit is **diamonds; clubs** and **spades** are the black suits)

① **heart attack**
['hɑrt ə'tæk] *noun*
condition where the heart suffers because of bad blood supply; *she had a heart attack but is recovering well*

① **heat**
[hit]
1 *noun*

(a) being hot; *the heat of the sun made the ice cream melt*; *cook the vegetables over a low heat*; **heat wave** = sudden period of high temperature; *the heat wave has made rivers dry up* (NOTE: no plural)
(b) one part of a sports competition; *there are two heats before the final race*; **dead heat** = race where two competitors finish equal; *the race finished in a dead heat*
2 *verb*
to make hot; *can you heat the soup while I'm getting the table ready?*; *the room was heated by a small electric stove*; *heat the milk to room temperature*

③ **heated**
['hitɪd] *adjective*
(a) made warm; *the car has a heated windshield*; **heated swimming pool** = pool where the water is kept warm; *the school has a heated swimming pool*
(b) angry; *there was a heated discussion after the meeting*; *the representatives became very heated during the debate*

① **heater**
['hitər] *noun*
device for heating; *there is an electric heater in the bathroom*; *I'm cold - I'll to put the heater on*; **water heater** = device for heating water in a house; **electric heater** = heating device that runs on electricity; *the island can be cool in the winter, so the apartment has several portable electric heaters*

④ **heather**
['heðər] *noun*
low plant with mainly purple or pink flowers, found on hills and mountains; *the mountains of Scotland are beautiful in autumn when the heather is in flower*

② **heating**
['hitɪŋ] *noun*
way of warming a house, an office, etc.; *we turn the heating off on May 1*; *I'm cold - I'm going to switch the heating on*; **central heating** = heating of a whole house from one main heater and several radiators; *our central heating comes on at 6:30*; *the central heating broke down again*

① **heaven**
['hevn] *noun*
(a) paradise, place where good people are believed to go after they die; *she believes that when she dies she will go to heaven*
(b) **the heavens** = the sky above; **the heavens opened** = it started to pour down
(c) *(phrase showing surprise)* **good heavens! it's almost ten o'clock!**; **for heaven's sake** = expression showing you are annoyed, or that something is important; *what are you screaming for? - it's only a little mouse, for heaven's sake*; *for heaven's sake try to be quiet, we don't want the guards to hear us!*

① **heavily**
['hevɪlɪ] *adverb*
(a) as if you are heavy; *he sat down heavily on the little chair*
(b) to a great extent, very much; *the company was heavily criticized in the press*; *she is heavily in debt*; *it rained heavily during the night*
(c) **to sleep heavily** = to sleep without waking

① **heavy**
['hevɪ] *adjective*
(a) which weighs a lot; *this suitcase is so heavy I can hardly lift it*; *she's heavier than I am*
(b) **a heavy meal** = a meal that is filling and uncomfortable in your stomach; *don't go to bed just after you've had a heavy meal*
(c) in large amounts; *there has been a heavy demand for the book*; *there was a heavy fall of snow during the night*; *the radio says there is heavy traffic downtown*; **heavy smoker** = person who smokes a lot of cigarettes; *he was a heavy smoker and died of lung cancer* (NOTE: **heavier - heaviest**)

① **he'd**
[hid]
= HE HAD, HE WOULD

② **hedge**
[hedʒ]
1 *noun*
(a) row of bushes planted and kept trimmed to form a screen around a field or garden; *there is a thick hedge around the yard*
(b) financial protection; *a hedge against inflation*
2 *verb*
to hedge your bets = to invest in several areas so as to be protected against loss in one of them

① **heel**
[hil]
1 *noun*
(a) the back part of the foot; *after walking all day in the mountains, her heel hurt*; *she rolled head over heels down the hill* = she rolled over and over like a ball; **to take to your heels** = to run away; *when they heard the squad car, they took to their heels and disappeared round the corner*; **on the heels of someone** *or* **something** = following immediately behind someone or something; *with the police hot on his heels he fled to Argentina*; **to turn on your heel** = to turn suddenly and go in the opposite direction; *she turned on her heel and walked out of the room*
(b) back part of a sock, stocking or shoe; *he has a hole in the heel of his sock*; *she always wear shoes with high heels* *or* *high-heeled shoes*
2 *verb*
to put a new heel on a shoe; *I want these shoes soled and heeled, please* (NOTE: do not confuse with **heal**)

① **height**
[haɪt] *noun*
(a) measurement of how high something is; *the*

height of the bridge is only 50 feet; **he is of above average height** = he is taller than most men

(b) highest point; *looking down on the city from the heights around*; *it is difficult to find hotel rooms at the height of the tourist season*; **I don't like heights** *or* **I haven't got a head for heights** = my head goes round and round when I am high up on a building

② **heighten**
['haɪtn] *verb*
to increase; *the TV show has helped to heighten public awareness of the drug problem*

③ **heir, heiress**
['eər *or* eə'res] *noun*
(a) man or woman who will receive property from someone after that person dies; *he's the heir to the banking fortune*; *you've heard of Barbara, the tobacco heiress?*; *his heirs divided the estate between them* (NOTE: the plural of **heiress** is **heiresses**)
(b) the heir to the throne = the man or woman who will be king or queen when the present king or queen dies (NOTE: do not confuse with **hair, air**)

① **held**
[held]
see HOLD

① **helicopter**
['helɪkɒptər] *noun*
aircraft which can rise straight up in the air; *you can take a helicopter from the airport to downtown*; *it is only a short helicopter flight from downtown to the factory site*

① **he'll**
[hil]
= HE WILL

① **hell**
[hel] *noun*
(a) bad place where wicked people are sent after they die; *old pictures show hell as a burning place where wicked people are pushed into the fires* (NOTE: does not take the articles **a** *or* **the**)
(b) *(informal)* miserable place; *it's hell working in the office these days*; **to give someone hell** = to treat someone very badly
(c) a hell of a *or* **one hell of a** = (i) a dreadful thing; (ii) a marvelous thing; *the car's making a hell of a noise*; *that was one hell of a party last night!*
(d) *(informal word used to make a phrase stronger)* *what the hell's been going on here?*; *am I going to lend you $75? Hell I am!*

① **hello**
[hə'ləʊ] *interjection showing a greeting* hi; *hello! Mary, I'm glad to see you*; *when you see her, say hello to her from me*; *she called hello from the other side of the street* (NOTE: also spelled **hullo**)

① **helmet**
['helmət] *noun*
solid hat used as a protection; *soldiers wear helmets when they are on patrol*; *you must*
wear a helmet when riding a motorcycle or bicycle; **crash helmet** = solid hat worn by motorcyclists, etc.; **safety helmet** = solid hat worn by building workers, etc.; *visitors to the building site must wear safety helmets* (NOTE: also called **hard hats**)

② **help**
[help]
1 *noun*
(a) something which makes it easier for you to do something; *she was washing the floor with the help of a big brush*; *do you need any help with moving the furniture?*; *she finds the computer a great help in writing her book*; *her assistant is not much help in the office - he can't type or file*
(b) providing aid and assistance to someone; *people were calling for help from the ruins of the house*; *the nurses offered help to people injured in the accident*
(c) financial assistance; *the government provides help to areas with high unemployment*
(d) person who helps; *she has help come in twice a week to do the housework*
2 *verb*
(a) to make it easier for someone to do something; *he helped the old lady up the steps*; *the government wants to help small businesses*; *your father can help you with your homework*; *one of my friends helped me move the piano into the bedroom*
(b) *(with* **cannot***)* not to be able to stop doing something; *he couldn't help laughing*; *she can't help stealing clothes from stores*; **it can't be helped** = nothing can be done to improve the situation; **he can't help it** = it's not his fault; *she can't help it if she has a bad back*
(c) to help yourself = to serve yourself with food, etc.; *she helped herself to some cake*; *if you feel thirsty just help yourself*; *(informal)* **to help yourself to** = to steal; *she helped herself to my wallet*
3 *interjection meaning that you are in difficulties;* *help! help! call the police!*; *help! I can't stop the car!*

① **helper**
['helpər] *noun*
person who helps; *she works two mornings a week as a helper in a day care*; *I need two willing helpers to wash the car*

① **helpful**
['helpfəl] *adjective*
which helps; *she made some helpful suggestions*; *they were very helpful when we moved*

① **helping**
['helpɪŋ] *noun*
1 amount of food given to someone; *the helpings are very small in this restaurant*; *children's helpings are not as large as those for adults*; **second helping** = more of the same

food; *can I have a second helping of mashed potatoes, please?*
2 *adjective*
which helps; **to give someone a helping hand** = to help someone with work; *he gave me a helping hand with the cleaning*

① **helpless**
['helpləs] *adjective*
not able to do anything; *the house was burning and I couldn't do anything - I felt so helpless!*; *he's helpless when his car breaks down*

② **hem**
[hem] *noun*
the sewn edge of a skirt, tablecloth, etc.; *she was wearing a long skirt, with the hem touching the floor*

① **hen**
[hen] *noun*
adult female chicken; *the hens were scared by the neighbor's dog*; *look, one of the hens has laid an egg!*

④ **hence**
[hens] *adverb*
(a) this is why; *he has the flu, hence his not coming to work*
(b) *(formal)* from now; *five months hence, the situation should be better*

① **her**
[hɜr]
1 *object pronoun referring to a female*
did you see her?; *he told her to go away*; *there's a package for her in reception*
2 *adjective*
(belonging to a female, a ship, a country)
someone has stolen all her baggage; *have you seen her father?*; *the dog doesn't want to eat her food*; *France is helping her businesses to sell more abroad*

③ **herb**
[ɜrb] *noun*
plant used to give flavor to food, or as a medicine; *add some herbs to the sauce*

① **herd**
[hɜrd] *noun*
a group of animals, especially cows; *herds of cattle were grazing on the hillside* (NOTE: do not confuse with **heard**; the word **herd** is usually used with cows; for sheep, goats, and birds such as hens or geese, the word to use is **flock**)

① **here**
[hɪər] *adverb*
(a) in this place; *I'll sit here in the shade and wait for you*; *here are the keys you lost*; *I'll put the book down here next to your computer*; *they have been living here in the States for a long time*; **here you are** = take this; *here you are, today's newspaper!*
(b) to this place; *come here at once!*; *can you bring the chairs here, please?*; *here comes the bus!* (NOTE: when **here** comes at the beginning of a sentence, the following subject comes after the

verb if the subject is a noun and not a pronoun: **here comes the bus** but **here it comes**)

④ **heritage**
['herɪtɪdʒ] *noun*
important national treasures passed from one generation to the next; *the flag is part of our national heritage*

① **hero**
['hɪərəʊ] *noun*
(a) brave man; *the hero of the fire was the fireman who managed to rescue the children from an upstairs room*
(b) main male character in a book, play, movie, etc.; *the hero of the story is a little boy* (NOTE: plural is **heroes**)

④ **heroine**
['herəʊɪn] *noun*
(a) brave woman; *the heroine of the accident was a passing cyclist who pulled the children out of the burning car*
(b) main female character in a book, play, movie, etc.; *the heroine of the movie is a schoolteacher*

① **hers**
[hɜrz] *pronoun*
belonging to her; *that watch is hers, not mine*; **she introduced me to a friend of hers** = to one of her friends

① **herself**
[hɜr'self] *pronoun referring to a female subject*; *the boss' wife wrote to me herself*; *did your sister enjoy herself?*; *she's too young to be able to dress herself*; **she lives all by herself** = she lives all alone; **she did it all by herself** = she did it with no one to help her; *now she's eight, we let her walk to school all by herself*

① **he's**
[hiz]
= HE HAS, HE IS

③ **hesitate**
['hezɪteɪt] *verb*
to be slow to act, because you can't decide; *she's hesitating about whether to accept the job*; *he hesitated for a moment and then said "no"*

④ **hesitation**
[hezɪ'teɪʃn] *noun*
waiting and not deciding; *after a moment's hesitation he jumped into the water*; *I have no hesitation in recommending him for the job*

② **hey!**
[heɪ] *interjection showing a greeting or surprise*
hey! you!, what are you doing there?; *hey! that's my chair!* (NOTE: do not confuse with **hay**)

① **hi!**
[haɪ] *interjection showing a greeting*
Hi! I'm your tour leader; *Hi! Mary, how are you today?*; *say hi to her from me* (NOTE: do not confuse with **high**)

③ **hibernate**
['haɪbəneɪt] *verb*
(of animals) to rest during the winter, being more or less completely unconscious; *bears hibernate during the Canadian winter*

① **hid**
[hɪd]
see HIDE

① **hidden**
['hɪdn] *adjective*
which cannot be seen; *there's a hidden safe in the wall behind his desk; they're digging in the castle, looking for hidden treasure; see also* HIDE

① **hide**
[haɪd]
1 *verb*
(a) to put something where no one can see or find it; *she hid the presents in the attic; they kept some gold coins hidden under the bed; someone has hidden my car keys*
(b) to put yourself where no one can see or find you; *they hid in the bushes until the squad car had gone past; quick! hide behind the door!* (NOTE: hiding - hid [hɪd] - has hidden ['hɪdn])
2 *noun*
(a) thick skin of a large animal, treated to make leather; *how many hides are needed to make that leather sofa?; a hide armchair*
(b) place where people can sit to watch birds without being seen by them; *they set up hides all around the lake*

① **hide-and-seek**
['haɪdn'sik] *noun*
children's game in which a person counts until all the others have hidden and then goes and finds them

② **hiding**
['haɪdɪŋ] *noun*
action of putting yourself where no one can find you; *he stayed in hiding for three days until the soldiers left town; they decided to go into hiding for a time until the police called off their search;* **hiding place** = place where you can hide

① **high**
[haɪ]
1 *adjective*
(a) reaching far above other things; *Everest is the highest mountain in the world; the new building is 20 stories high; they are planning a 10-story-high hotel next to the beach; the kitchen has a high ceiling; the door is not high enough to let us get the tall pieces of furniture into the room* (NOTE: it is used with figures: **the mountain is 10,000 feet high; high** also refers to things that are a long way above the ground: **a high mountain, high clouds;** for people and thin things like trees use **tall: a tall man**)
(b) large in quantity; *he earns a high income; the high level of unemployment in the country; high prices put customers off; the truck shakes*

when going at high speeds; the price of gas is higher every year
(c) important; *she occupies a high post in the ministry; he was quite high up in the police force when he retired*
(d) *(informal)* **high on drugs** = influenced by drugs; *some of the teenagers were high on drugs when they were arrested*
2 *adverb*
above; up in the air; *the sun rose high in the sky; the bird flew higher and higher* (NOTE: **higher - highest**)
3 *noun*
high point; **sales have reached an all-time high** = sales are higher than they have ever been before

③ **higher education**
['haɪər edju'keɪʃn] *noun*
education in universities and colleges; *the government aims to encourage more young people to go into higher education*

④ **highlight**
['haɪlaɪt]
1 *noun*
(a) most important or interesting event; *the highlight of our tour of Greece was our visit to the Parthenon*
(b) **highlights** = characters which stand out from the text on a screen by being brighter than the rest
2 *verb*
(a) to draw attention to; *the report highlights the problems of inner city housing*
(b) to make part of the text stand out from the rest; *the headings are highlighted in bold; she highlighted the important parts of the text in bright green*

④ **highlighter**
['haɪlaɪtər] *noun*
marker pen, a colored felt pen used to highlight text; *use a highlighter to show where corrections need to be made*

④ **highly**
['haɪli] *adverb*
greatly; *the restaurant has been highly recommended; their employees are not very highly paid;* **highly-priced** = with a very high price; *he thinks highly of her* = he admires her very much

③ **high-pitched**
[haɪ'pɪtʃt] *adjective*
making a shrill sound; *he speaks in a very high-pitched voice*

① **high school**
['haɪ 'skul] *noun*
secondary school for children between the ages of 15 and 18, from g0rades 9 or 10 through grade 12; *he's in tenth grade at high school;* **junior high school** = school for children between the ages of about 12 and 15 (grades 7 through 9) (NOTE: also sometimes called **middle school**)

④ **high-speed**
['haɪspiːd] *adjective*
which runs or operates at a very high speed; *we took the high-speed train to Paris*

③ **high-tech**
['haɪ 'tek] *adjective*
referring to high technology; *high-tech industries*

① **highway**
['haɪweɪ] *noun*
main public road; *a little bridge crosses the highway*

④ **hijack**
['haɪdʒæk] *verb*
to take control of a vehicle by force; *the robbers hijacked the taxi and killed the driver; they hijacked an aircraft and ordered the pilot to fly to Moscow*

① **hike**
[haɪk]
1 *noun*
(a) long vigorous walk in the country; *we went for a 10-mile hike in the mountains*
(b) increase; *the gas company has announced another price hike*
2 *verb*
(a) to go for a long vigorous walk; *they were hiking in the Pyrenees when the accident happened*
(b) to increase prices, etc.; *oil companies have hiked up their prices*

① **hill**
[hɪl] *noun*
piece of high land, but lower than a mountain; *the hills are covered with spring flowers; their house is on top of a hill; if you climb to the top of the hill you will get a good view of the valley*

② **hillside**
['hɪlsaɪd] *noun*
sloping side of a hill; *their house is halfway up the hillside; a flock of sheep were grazing on the hillside*

① **him**
[hɪm] *object pronoun referring to a male*
have you spoken to him today?; tell him there's a letter waiting for him; that's him! - the man with the beard

① **himself**
[hɪm'self] *pronoun referring to a male subject*
the manager served me himself; the doctor has got the flu himself; did your brother enjoy himself?; he lives all by himself = he lives all alone; he did it all by himself = he did it with no one to help him; now he's eight, we let him walk to school all by himself

③ **hinge**
[hɪndʒ] *noun*
piece of metal used to hold a door, window, lid, etc., so that it can swing open and shut; *that hinge squeaks and needs some oil*

② **hint**
[hɪnt]
1 *noun*
(a) hidden suggestion, clue; *he didn't give a hint as to where he was going on vacation; I don't know what to give her for her birthday - can you give me any hints?;* **to drop a hint** = to make a suggestion; *she's been dropping hints about what she wants for her birthday;* **to take a hint** = to accept a suggestion; *he took the hint and offered to pay for the lamp he broke*
(b) very small quantity; *there's just a hint of garlic in the soup*
(c) piece of advice; *she gave me some useful hints about painting furniture*
2 *verb*
to say something in a way that makes people guess what you mean; *she hinted that her sister was pregnant*

② **hip**
[hɪp]
1 *noun*
(a) part of the body at the top of your legs; *the tailor measured him around the hips*
(b) joint at the top of the leg bone; **hip replacement** = operation to replace the whole hip joint with an artificial one; *old people sometimes need to have hip replacements*
2 *adjective*
very up-to-date; *that's a very hip shirt she's wearing*

② **hippopotamus** *(informal)* **hippo**
[hɪpə'pɒtəməs or 'hɪpəʊ] *noun*
large heavy African animal which spends most of its time in water, but comes onto dry land to feed (NOTE: plurals are **hippopotamuses** *or* **hippopotami** [hɪpə'pɒtəmaɪ] and **hippos** ['hɪpəʊz])

③ **hire**
['haɪər]
1 *noun*
(b) "for hire" = sign on a taxi showing it is empty and available for hire
2 *verb*
(a) to engage someone to work for you; *we've hired three more sales assistants; they hired a small company to paint their offices*
(b) *(of business)* **to hire out** = to provide a service for someone, against payment of a fee; *he hires out accounting staff to small firms*
(c) *(of borrower)* to pay money to use a car, boat, piece of equipment, etc., for a time; *she hired a car for the weekend; he was driving a hired car when the accident happened*

① **his**
[hɪz]
1 *adjective*
belonging to him; *he's lost all his money; have you met his mother?; our dog wants his food*
2 *pronoun*

belonging to him; *that watch is his, not mine*; **he introduced me to a friend of his** = to one of his friends

③ **Hispanic**
[hɪsˈpænɪk]
1 *adjective*
referring to countries where Spanish is spoken, especially South American countries; *Hispanic communities in the southern United States*
2 *noun*
person whose native language is Spanish, especially one living in the United States; *Hispanics form an important community in Florida*

③ **historian**
[hɪˈstɔːriən] *noun*
person who studies or writes history; *a historian who specializes in the Chinese Empire*; *the book was written by a French historian*

② **historic**
[hɪˈstɒrɪk] *adjective*
famous in history; *a historic agreement has been signed* (NOTE: can be preceded by **an** in formal style: **it is an historic day for the town**)

② **historical**
[hɪˈstɒrɪkl] *adjective*
referring to history; *Independence Day is a historical day for the whole country*; **historical novel** = story set in a particular period in the past

① **history**
[ˈhɪstəri] *noun*
(a) study of the past, of past events; *he is studying Greek history*; *she failed her history exam*; *she teaches history at the University of Michigan*
(b) book that tells the story of what happened in the past; *he wrote a history of the French Revolution*
(c) **natural history** = the study of plants and animals

① **hit**
[hɪt]
1 *noun*
(a) very popular song, movie, performer, etc.; *the song rapidly became a hit*; *the play was a Broadway hit*; *she was a hit with the senior citizen's club*
(b) blow or knock; *just one more hit on the nail and that will be enough*
(c) action of visiting a site on the Internet; *how many hits did we have on our site last week?*
2 *verb*
(a) to knock; *the automobile hit the tree*; *she hit him on the head with a bottle*; *she hit the ball so hard that we can't find it*; *I hit my head on the cupboard door*
(b) to damage, to affect badly; *the company has been hit by falling sales*
(c) to realize; *it suddenly hit her that now she was divorced she would have to live alone*

(d) to reach a figure or target; *our sales hit a record high last month*; *new cases of the flu hit two thousand last week* (NOTE: **hitting - hit**)

③ **hit back**
[ˈhɪt ˈbæk] *verb*
(a) to hit someone who has hit you; *the muggers hit him so hard that he collapsed before he could hit them back*
(b) to do something as a reaction to something; *when the supermarket chain lowered their prices, the other chains hit back by lowering prices too*; *he hit back at the inspectors, saying that their report was unfair*

① **hitch**
[hɪtʃ]
1 *noun*
unexpected temporary problem; *there's a hitch, and the wedding has been postponed*; **without a hitch** = with no trouble or problems; *the party went off without a hitch*
2 *verb*
(a) **to hitch up** = to pull up; *he hitched up his pants*
(b) **to hitch (a ride)** = to ask a driver to take you as a passenger, usually by signaling with the thumb or by holding a sign with your destination written on it; *he hitched a ride to Memphis*; *her car broke down and she hitched a lift from a passing motorist*
(c) to attach; *the trailer was hitched to the back of the car*

③ **hitchhiker**
[ˈhɪtʃhaɪkər] *noun*
person who hitches a lift; *he picked up two hitchhikers who were going to Montana*; *the hitchhiker grabbed the steering wheel and tried to send the truck into the ditch*

③ **hit on**
[ˈhɪt ˈɒn] *verb*
to discover, to get a good idea; *we hit on the idea of taking him to a concert as a birthday present*

④ **HMO**
= HEALTH MAINTENANCE ORGANIZATION

④ **hoard**
[hɔrd]
1 *noun*
store of food, money, etc., which has been collected; *they discovered a hoard of gold coins in the field*
2 *verb*
to buy and store supplies in case of need; *squirrels hoard nuts for the winter*; *everyone has started hoarding fuel in case supplies run out*

① **hobby**
[ˈhɒbi] *noun*
favorite thing which you do in your spare time; *his hobby is making model planes* (NOTE: plural is **hobbies**)

① **hockey**
['hɒki] *noun*
(a) game played on ice where skaters try to hit a hard rubber disk called a puck into their opponents' goal using a long stick which is curved at the end; *the hockey gold medal will be fought out between Canada and Russia*
(b) **field hockey** = team game played on grass where you try to hit a small ball into your opponents' goal using a long stick which is curved at the end; *he played on the field hockey team at school*

> COMMENT: hockey is played between two teams of six players, each game being made up of three 20-minute periods; field hockey is played between two teams of 11 players, each game having two 35-minute halves

④ **hodgepodge**
['hɒdʒpɒdʒ] *noun*
mixture or mess; *there is a hodgepodge of items on the table*

① **hold**
[həʊld]
1 *verb*
(a) to keep tight, especially in your hand; *she was holding the baby in her arms*; *she held her ticket between her teeth as she was carrying suitcases in both hands*; *hold tight - the machine is going to start*; *he held the bag close to his chest*
(b) to contain, to be large enough for something to fit inside; *the bottle holds two gallons*; *the box will hold four pairs of shoes*; *will the automobile hold eight people?*; *the plane holds 250 passengers*
(c) to make something happen; *they are holding a party for their wedding anniversary*; *the meeting will be held next Tuesday in the town hall*; *we are holding the school festival next week*
(d) to stay the same; *will the nice weather hold until Saturday?*
(e) to possess; *she holds a valid driver's license*; *he holds the record for the 2000 meters*
(f) *(on telephone)* **hold the line please** = please wait; *the chairman is on the other line - will you hold?*
(g) to keep inside; *the prisoners were held in the embassy*; **to hold water** = to be valid, to be true; *his argument doesn't hold water*; **to hold your breath** = to keep air in your lungs to go under water, as a test or because you are afraid that something will happen; *she held her breath under water for a minute*; *we're all holding our breath to see if he wins a gold medal*
(h) to capture and control a place; *the rebels are holding the airport*; *government forces still hold about half the country* (NOTE: **holding - held** [held])
2 *noun*
(a) bottom part of a ship or an aircraft, in which cargo is stored; *you can't take all that baggage with you, it has to go in the hold*
(b) action of gripping something; *he lost his hold on the ladder*; *keep tight hold of the bag, we don't want it stolen*; **to get hold of someone** = to find someone you need by telephone; *I tried to get hold of the doctor but he was out*; **to get hold of something** = to find something which you want to use; *do you know where I can get hold of a ladder?*; **to take hold of something** = to grip something, to take control of something; *the fire took hold rapidly*
(c) action of having a strong influence over someone; *she has some kind of hold over her husband*

③ **hold back**
['həʊld 'bæk] *verb*
(a) not to tell; *she held back important information from the police*
(b) not to go forward; *most of the crowd held back until they saw it was safe*

③ **hold down**
['həʊld 'daʊn] *verb*
(a) to keep at a low level; *we are holding our prices down*
(b) **to hold down a job** = to manage to do a job

② **holder**
['həʊldər] *noun*
(a) thing which holds; *put the pen back into its holder*
(b) person who holds; *she is an American passport holder or she is the holder of an American passport*; *he is the world record holder in the 1000 meters*

③ **holding**
['həʊldɪŋ] *noun*
investments owned; *she has holdings in several South American companies*; **holding company** = company which owns shares in other companies

① **hold on**
['həʊld 'ɒn] *verb*
(a) to hold something tightly; *she held on to the rope with both hands*; *hold on to your purse in the crowd*; *hold on tight, we're turning!*
(b) to wait; *hold on a second, I'll get my umbrella*; *do you want to speak to the manager? - hold on, I'll find him for you*

③ **hold out**
['həʊld 'aʊt] *verb*
to resist against; *the guerrillas held out for ten weeks against a huge enemy army*

③ **hold out for**
['həʊld 'aʊt fɔr] *verb*
to wait and ask for more; *you should hold out for a 10% pay raise*

① **hold up**
['həʊld 'ʌp] *verb*
(a) to lift; *he held up his hand*; *he held the little boy up so that he could see the procession*; *the roof is held up by those pillars*

(b) to make late; *the planes were held up by fog*; *government red tape is holding up the deal*; *the strike will hold up deliveries*

(c) to attack and rob; *six gunmen held up the security van*

③ **holdup**
[ˈhəʊldʌp] *noun*
(a) delay, time when something is later than planned; *long hold-ups are expected because of construction crews on the freeway*; *there's been a holdup and the shipment won't arrive till next week*

(b) armed attack; *the gang carried out three holdups on the same day*

① **hole**
[həʊl] *noun*
opening, space in something; *you've got a hole in your sock*; *we all looked through the hole in the fence*; *rabbits live in holes in the ground*

① **holiday**
[ˈhɒlɪdeɪ] *noun*
(a) day on which no work is done because of laws or religious rules; *the office is closed for the Christmas holiday* ; **public holiday** = day when all workers rest and enjoy themselves instead of working; **legal holiday** = holiday which is fixed by law

(b) *GB* vacation, a period when you don't work, but rest, go away and enjoy yourself; *he's going to Spain on holiday*; *the manager isn't in the office - he's on holiday*

COMMENT: In the U.S.A., New Year's Day, the third Monday in January (Martin Luther King Day), February 12 (Lincoln's Birthday), the third Monday in February (Washington's birthday) also called President's Day, the last Monday in May (Memorial Day), July 4 (Independence Day), the first Monday in September (Labor Day), the second Monday in October (Columbus Day), November 11 (Veterans' Day), the fourth Thursday in November (Thanksgiving) and Christmas Day are public holidays throughout most states, although there are other local holidays

③ **Holland**
[ˈhɒlənd] *noun*
another name for the Netherlands (NOTE: strictly speaking, **Holland** is only one of the provinces of the Netherlands (the province to the north of Amsterdam), but the word is frequently used in English to mean the whole country)

① **hollow**
[ˈhɒləʊ]
1 *noun*
lower part on a flat surface; *they made a hollow in the ground for a campfire*
2 *adjective*
with a hole inside; *a hollow log*; *if you tap the box it sounds hollow*

③ **holly**
[ˈhɒli] *noun*
small evergreen tree with shiny dark green leaves with sharp spines, and bright red berries; *for Christmas, we decorate the house with holly*

② **holy**
[ˈhəʊli] *adjective*
(a) sacred; *they went to ask a holy man his advice*

(b) **the Holy Father** = the Pope; **the Holy See** = the office of Pope (NOTE: do not confuse with **wholly**; note: **holier - holiest**)

① **home**
[həʊm]
1 *noun*
(a) place where you live; *their home is an apartment in downtown Santa Fe*; *will you be at home tomorrow morning?*; *when do you leave home for work in the morning?*; **make yourself at home** = do as if you were in your own home; *he lay down on the sofa, opened a bottle of beer, and made himself at home*; **home away from home** = comfortable and welcoming place, just like your home; *the hotel is a real home away from home*; *(informal)* **nothing to write home about** = nothing very exciting or special; *his new job is nothing to write home about*

(b) area where you come from; *she lives in California but her home is still Ohio*; *his home is in the Midwest*

(c) house; *they are building fifty new homes on the outskirts of town*

(d) house where people are looked after; *my aunt has moved to a nursing home*; **children's home** = a home for children who have no parents or who come from broken homes

(e) *(in sports)* **at home** = on the local sports ground; *our team is playing at home next Saturday* (NOTE: the opposite is **away**)

(f) family, household; *she comes from a broken home*

2 *adverb*
toward or in the place where you usually live; *we're going home now*; *he usually gets home by 7 o'clock*; *I'm tired - I just want to stay home*; *don't send it - I'll take it home with me*; *if you don't want to walk, you can always take the bus home* (NOTE: used without a preposition: **he went home, she's coming home,** etc.)

3 *adjective*
(a) referring to where you live or where you were born; *my home town is Pierre*; *send the letter to my home address, not to my office*; **home cooking** = style of food as cooked at home, not in restaurants; *I like good home cooking*

(b) *(in sports)* local; *the home side won*; *our team beat the home team 3 - 0*; *we have a home game next Saturday*

(c) in this country, not abroad; *home sales were better than exports last month*; *they find it difficult selling into the home market*

② **homeland**
['həʊmlænd] *noun*
home of a people; *the refugees tried to return to their homeland after the war*

① **homeless**
['həʊmləs]
1 *adjective*
with nowhere to live; *the homeless woman sleeps on the street*
2 *noun*
the homeless = people with nowhere to live; *the homeless sleep in parks or doorways*

② **home plate**
['həʊm 'pleɪt] *noun*
(in baseball) base that a batter stands at when hitting the ball and that a runner must touch to score a run; *the catcher stood behind the home plate*

① **home run**
['həʊm 'rʌn] *noun*
(in baseball) hit which is hard enough for a player to touch all the bases and score a run; *the crowd cheered as the player hit a home run*

② **homestead**
['həʊmsted] *noun*
house and surrounding land, especially land given by the government, which is used for farming

① **homework**
['həʊmwɜrk] *noun*
work that you take home from school to do in the evening; *have you finished your math homework?*; *I haven't any homework today, so I can watch TV* (NOTE: no plural)

④ **homosexual**
[həʊməʊ'seksjʊəl] *adjective & noun*
(person) who is attracted to people of the same sex; *did you know her brother is a homosexual?*

② **honest**
['ɒnɪst] *adjective*
(a) who tells the truth; *he was honest with the police and told them what he had done*
(b) (person) who can be trusted; *I wouldn't buy a car from that dealer - I'm not sure they're completely honest*

② **honestly**
['ɒnɪstli] *adverb*
telling the truth; *honestly, it was John who took the cookies, not me*; *I honestly don't think she will ever come back to live here*

② **honesty**
['ɒnəsti] *noun*
telling the truth; *I admire him for his honesty in saying the job was too difficult for him*; *in all honesty* = saying what is true; *in all honesty I don't think we'll be able to get to the station in time*

① **honey**
['hʌni] *noun*
(a) sweet substance produced by bees; *I like honey on toast; Greek cakes are often made with honey*
(b) *(calling a person you love)* hey, honey, come and look at this!*; *honey, don't get mad at me!*

② **honeymoon**
['hʌnimun]
1 *noun*
(a) vacation taken immediately after a wedding; *for their honeymoon they went to Peru*; **honeymoon couple** = two people on honeymoon
(b) period after an election when the new government is popular; *the president's honeymoon period has come to an end*
2 *verb*
to go on a honeymoon; *they plan to honeymoon in Florida*

① **honor**
['ɒnər]
1 *noun*
(a) acting according to what you think is right; *he's a man of honor*; **code of honor** = rules of right and wrong which are applied to what people do
(b) mark of respect; *it is an honor for me to be invited here today*
(c) **with honors** = showing a high level of study; *she graduated in math with honors*
(d) Your Honor = way of addressing a judge
2 *verb*
(a) to respect, to pay respect to; *to honor the dead*
(b) to give an award as a mark of respect; *he was honored by the university*
(c) to do what you promised; *he honored his promise and gave a party for the winners of the prize*
(d) *(of a bank)* **to honor a check** = to pay the sum written on the check

③ **honorable**
['ɒnrəbl] *adjective*
who or which can be respected; *after years in government he lived the rest of his life in honorable retirement*

① **hood**
[hʊd] *noun*
(a) loose piece of clothing to cover your head; *he has a blue anorak with a hood*
(b) folding roof on a car, pram, etc.; *let's put down the hood, it's very hot*
(c) metal cover for the front part of a car, covering the engine; *he lifted the hood to see what was wrong with the motor*

① **hoof**
[huf] *noun*
hard part of the foot of a horse, cow, and many other animals (NOTE: plural is **hooves** [huvz])

① **hook**
[hʊk]
1 *noun*
(a) bent piece of metal for hanging things on; *hang your coat on the hook behind the door*

(b) very small piece of bent metal, attached to a line for catching fish; *the fish ate the worm but didn't swallow the hook*; **to get someone off the hook** = to get someone out of a difficult situation; *she got him off the hook by lying to his boss*
2 *verb*
to hang on a hook; to attach with a hook; *she hooked the curtains back to let in more light*

① **hop**
['hɒp]
1 *noun*
(a) little jump; *some birds walk in a series of little hops*
(b) short flight; *it's only a short hop from Miami to Orlando*
(c) bitter dead flower of a climbing plant, used in making beer; *hops are used to give the bitter flavor to some malt liquors*
2 *verb*
(a) to jump on one leg; *he hurt his toe and had to hop around on one foot*; **hopping mad** = very angry; *he was hopping mad when they told him his new car had been stolen*
(b) *(of birds, animals, etc.)* to jump with both feet together; *the bird hopped across the grass*; *the frog hopped onto the lily leaf*
(c) *(informal)* to jump aboard a plane, train, or bus; *I'll hop the next bus*; **to hop in** = to get in; *I stopped the car and told him to hop in*; **to hop on** *or* **to hop off** = to get on or off; *with the old trolleys, you can hop on and off anywhere along the street, although it can be dangerous* (NOTE: **hopping - hopped**)

① **hope**
['həʊp]
1 *noun*
wanting and expecting something to happen; *our only hope is that she will get better soon*; *they have given up all hope of rescuing any more victims from the floods*; **in the hope that** = wanting something to happen; *I called in the hope that you might have a table free for tonight*; *I called in hopes of getting an appointment*
2 *verb*
(a) to want and expect something to happen; *we all hope our team wins*; *she's hoping she will soon be able to drive an automobile*; *I hope it doesn't rain*; **I hope so** = I want it to happen; *are you coming to the party? - yes, I hope so*; **I hope not** = I don't want it to happen; *it's going to rain tomorrow, isn't it? - I hope not!*; **to hope for something** = to want something to happen; *we are hoping for a change in the weather, it's rained every day this week so far*
(b) to expect to do something; *the chairman hopes to be at the meeting tomorrow*; *they said they hoped to be back home by 6 o'clock*; *I had hoped to go to the party but in the end I couldn't*

② **hopeful**
['həʊpfəl]
1 *adjective*
confident that something will happen; *we are hopeful that the company will accept our offer*
2 *noun*
(informal) person who hopes to get a job, a place in a team, etc.; *we are looking at six young hopefuls for the job*

② **hopefully**
['həʊpfəlɪ] *adverb*
(a) confidently; *he looked hopefully at the list of lottery numbers*
(b) let us hope; *hopefully the rain will stop*

② **hopeless**
['həʊpləs] *adjective*
(a) with no hope; *the invoices are in a hopeless mess*; **he's a hopeless case** = he will never get any better
(b) no good; *she's hopeless at tennis*; *he's hopeless when it comes to fixing automobiles*

② **horizon**
[hə'raɪzn] *noun*
line where the earth and the sky meet; *two ships could be seen on the horizon*

④ **horizontal**
[hɒrɪ'zɒntl] *adjective*
flat, level with the ground; *he drew a horizontal line under the text*

④ **hormone**
['hɔrməʊn] *noun*
substance produced by glands in the body and carried to other parts of the body by the bloodstream to stimulate certain cells into action; **growth hormone** = hormone that stimulates the growth of the long bones in the body; **hormone replacement therapy (HRT)** = treatment for women as they age

① **horn**
[hɔrn] *noun*
(a) sharp pointed bone growing out of an animal's head; *I don't like the look of that bull's horns*
(b) warning device on a car; **to sound a horn** = to make a warning noise with a horn; *honk your horn when you come to the corner*
(c) metal musical instrument that is blown into to make a note; *they played a piece for horn and orchestra*

① **horrible**
['hɒrəbl] *adjective*
awful, terrible; *the victims of the fire had horrible injuries*; *he's a horrible little boy*; *we had a horrible meal at the restaurant*

③ **horrific**
[hə'rɪfik] *adjective*
which makes you shocked; *the victims of the crash suffered horrific injuries*; *the police discovered a horrific murder*

③ **horrified**
['hɒrɪfaɪd] *adjective*
frightened or shocked; *she was horrified at the pictures*; *the horrified spectators watched the two planes collide*

③ **horrify**
['hɒrɪfaɪ] *verb*
to frighten, to shock; *the pictures of accident victims are meant to horrify*; *he was horrified by the bill from the builders*

③ **horrifying**
['hɒrɪfaɪɪŋ] *adjective*
frightening, shocking; *they told horrifying tales of their escape from the war zone*

③ **horror**
['hɒrər] *noun*
feeling of being very frightened; *he couldn't hide his horror at hearing the news*; *she has a horror of spiders*; *everyone watched in horror as the planes collided*; **horror movie** *or* **horror film** = frightening movie, with ghosts, dead bodies, etc.

① **horse**
[hɔrs] *noun*
large animal used for riding or pulling; *she was riding a black horse*; *the coach was pulled by six white horses*; *he's out on his horse every morning*; **dark horse** = person you know nothing about and who may win; *the third candidate is something of a dark horse*; *(informal)* **straight from the horse's mouth** = from a very reliable source; *it's straight from the horse's mouth - the manager told me so himself*; *see also* LOOK

① **hose**
[həʊz] *noun*
long tube, either rubber or plastic, for sending water; *the firemen used their hoses to put out the fire*; *that hose isn't long enough to reach to the end of the garden*

① **hospital**
['hɒspɪtəl] *noun*
place where sick or hurt people are looked after; *she was taken ill at work and sent to the hospital*; *when is she due to go into the hospital?*; *he was in the hospital for several days after the accident*; **general hospital** = hospital which deals with all types of injuries and illnesses

① **host**
[həʊst]
1 *noun*
(a) person who has invited guests; *the host asked his guests what they wanted to drink*
(b) *(on a TV, radio show)* the person who introduces and talks to the guests; *she's the host of a popular talk show*; *the best hosts on Saturday night TV are those that make jokes*
(c) a host of = large number of; *we face a host of problems*
2 *verb*

(a) to act as host; *the company hosted a party for two hundred guests*; *she hosted a dinner for the visiting diplomats*
(b) to be the center where something takes place; *Barcelona hosted the Olympic Games in 1992*

③ **hostage**
['hɒstɪdʒ] *noun*
person who is captured and held by someone or an organization, which threatens to kill him unless certain demands are met; *three of the hostages will be freed tomorrow*; *he was held hostage for more than a year by the rebels*

④ **hostile**
['hɒstl] *adjective*
(a) referring to an enemy; *hostile forces are moving toward the airport*
(b) showing a dislike of someone; *the crowd seemed hostile, so the president decided to stay inside the White House*; **hostile questioning** = asking questions which attack the person being asked; **hostile takeover** = takeover where the board of the company being bought do not recommend the sale and try to fight it

① **hot**
[hɒt] *adjective*
(a) very warm; with a high temperature; *the weather is very hot in June but August is the hottest month*; *if you're too hot, take your coat off*; *plates should be kept hot before serving the meal* (NOTE: the opposite is **cold**)
(b) very highly spiced (food); *this curry is really hot*; *he chose the hottest dish on the menu* (NOTE: the opposite is **mild**)
(c) good; *here's a really hot tip*; *I'm not feeling very hot this morning*; **to get into hot water** = to get into trouble; *he got into hot water with his boss after he failed to turn up for the meeting*; **in the hot seat** = having to make decisions; *I pity the club chairman - he's really in the hot seat*
(d) vigorous and energetic; **in hot pursuit** = chasing someone actively; *the rebels retreated into the mountains with the government forces in hot pursuit* (NOTE: **hotter - hottest**)

① **hot dog**
['hɒt 'dɒg] *noun*
snack made of a long hot German sausage eaten in a roll of bread; *you can buy hot dogs at this stand*

① **hotel**
[həʊ'tel] *noun*
building where travelers can rent a room for the night, eat in a restaurant, drink in a bar, etc.; *they are staying at the Grand Hotel, which is the only five-star hotel in town*; *I'll meet you in the hotel lobby*; *all the hotel rooms in the town are booked*; *see also* CHECK IN, CHECK OUT

① **hour**
['aʊər] *noun*
(a) period of time that lasts sixty minutes; *the train journey takes two hours*; *it's a three-hour*

flight to Haiti; the train travels at over 150 miles per hour; he is paid by the hour = he is paid for each hour he works; *the pay is $15 per hour; the hours of work are from 9:30 to 5:30; the lunch hour is from 12:30 to 1:30; she works a thirty-five hour week;* **a quarter of an hour** = 15 minutes; **half an hour** = 30 minutes; *I'll be ready in a quarter of an hour; the next train will be in half an hour's time;* **hour hand** = short hand on a clock or watch which shows the hours

(b) on the hour = at an exact hour, and not before or after that hour; *flights to Las Vegas leave every hour on the hour*

(c) banking hours = time when a bank is open for its customers; *you cannot get money from a bank outside banking hours;* **office hours** = time when an office is open; *staff are not allowed to make private calls during office hours;* **outside hours** *or* **off-hours** = when the office is not open; *there is a special number you can call outside office hours; see also* SMALL

② **hourly**
['auəlɪ] *adjective*
happening every hour; *there are hourly news updates on that channel;* **hourly rate** = amount of money paid for an hour worked; *her hourly rate is $14.00;* **hourly workers** = workers paid at a fixed rate for each hour worked

① **house**
1 *noun* [haus]
(a) building in which someone lives; *he has bought a house in San Francisco; he has a small apartment in town and a large house in the country; all the houses on our block look the same*
(b) business; *she runs a publishing house; an important finance house has backed the deal*
(c) part of an assembly; *the American Congress is formed by the House of Representatives and the Senate*
(d) bar or restaurant, etc.; *drinks are on the house* = drinks are free to customers; **house wine** = special cheap wine selected by a restaurant; *we'll have a bottle of your house red, please*
(e) showing of a movie, play, etc.; **full house** = notice showing that a cinema or theater is full; *the play has played to full houses all week* (NOTE: plural is **houses** ['hauzɪz])
2 *verb* [hauz]
to provide accommodation for someone or something; *his collection of old automobiles is housed in a barn; we have been asked if we can house three students for the summer term; the city is responsible for housing homeless people*

③ **household**
['haushəuld] *noun*
people living together in a house; *this free newspaper is distributed to every household in the town;* **household goods** = goods that are used in a house; *the household goods department is on the ground floor;* **household name** = a well-known brand

② **House of Representatives**
['haus əv reprɪ'zentətɪvz] *noun*
lower house of the U.S. Congress; *he's been elected to the House of Representatives* (NOTE: members of the House of Representatives are called **Congressmen** and **Congresswomen**)

① **housework**
['hauswɜrk] *noun*
cleaning work in a house or apartment; *his wife does all the housework* (NOTE: no plural)

③ **housing**
['hauzɪŋ] *noun*
providing places where people can live; **housing project** = group of publicly funded houses and apartments, usually for people with low incomes; *permission has been given for several new housing projects on the south side of Chicago*

④ **hover**
['hɒvər] *verb*
(a) to hang in the air without moving forward; *flies hovering over the surface of a pool*
(b) to hover around = to stay near; *he hovered around her for the whole evening; he was hovering around the bar, hoping that someone would offer him a drink*

① **how**
[hau] *adverb*
(a) *(showing or asking the way in which something is done)* *how do you turn off the stove?; can you tell me how to get to the train station from here?; I don't know how he does it*
(b) *(showing or asking to what extent)* *how big is their house?; how many people are there in your family?; she showed us how good she was at skiing; how old is your little boy?; how far is it to the church?*
(c) *(showing surprise)* *how cold it is outside!; how different it is from what I remember!*
(d) *(informal)* **how about?** = would you like?; *how about a swim before breakfast?; how about a cup of coffee?;* **how do you mean?** = what do you mean?

① **how are you?** *or* **how do you do?**
[hau 'ɑr ju *or* 'hau djə 'du]
(a) *(showing a general greeting)* *how do you do, sir?; hi Robert! how are you?* (NOTE: in this meaning a detailed reply is not expected)
(b) *(asking the state of your health)* *how are you today?; the doctor asked me how I was*

① **how are you doing?**
['hau ju 'duɪŋ]
(general greeting) *hi Kate! how are you doing?*

① **how come?**
['hau 'kʌm]
(informal) why; *how come you're late?; how come the front door was left open?* (NOTE: the word order: **how come you're late?** but **why are you late?**)

③ **however**
['haʊ'evər]
1 adverb
(a) to whatever extent; *however many times she tried, she couldn't pass the driving test*; *I must have the house painted, however expensive it's going to be*; *however hard he tried, he still couldn't swim*
(b) *(form of "how" which emphasizes)* *however did you manage to get in?*
(c) in this case; *we never go out on Saturdays - however, this Saturday we're going to a wedding*
2 conjunction
in whatever way; *do it however you like*

④ **howl**
[haʊl]
1 verb
to make a long loud cry; *the wild dogs howled outside the cabin*; *the wind howled in the chimney*
2 noun
long loud cry; *howls of disappointment came from the fans*

③ **HRT**
= HORMONE REPLACEMENT THERAPY

① **huckleberry**
['hʌkəlberi] noun
common shrub with a dark blue fruit

① **hug**
[hʌg]
1 noun
throwing your arms around someone; *she ran to the little girl and gave her a hug*
2 verb
(a) to throw your arms around someone; *the players hugged each other when the goal was scored*
(b) to hold something very tightly; *the little girl was hugging a blue blanket*
(c) to keep very close to something; *the road hugs the foot of the mountain*; *she drove along slowly, hugging the shoulder* (NOTE: hugging - hugged)

① **huge**
[hjudʒ] adjective
very large; *huge waves hit the ship*; *the concert was a huge success*; *failing the test was a huge disappointment for him*

④ **hue**
[hju] noun
(formal) color; *the garden is filled with flowers of every hue*

① **hum**
[hʌm]
1 verb
(a) to make a low buzz; *bees were humming around the pots of jam*
(b) to sing without words; *if you don't know the words of the song, you can always hum the tune* (NOTE: humming - hummed)
2 noun

low buzz; *a loud hum came out of the loudspeaker*

① **human**
['hjumən]
1 adjective
referring to people; **human error** = mistake made by a person, and not by a machine; *they concluded that the accident was due to human error*; *he's only human* = he can make mistakes like anyone else; *I know there's a mistake in the exam question, teachers are only human, after all!*; **human resources** = the workers in a company, seen as a group; **human resources manager** = manager who deals with pay, sick leave, administration, etc., for all the staff (NOTE: also called a **personnel manager**)
2 noun
person, a human being; *the animals in the park don't seem to be afraid of humans*; *humans have only existed on Earth for a short time compared to fish*

① **human being**
['hjumən 'biːŋ] noun
a person; *the first human beings lived many thousands of years ago*; *I've been walking all day in the forest and you're the first human being I've met*

③ **humanity**
[hju'mæniti] noun
(a) all people; *a crime against humanity*
(b) *(formal)* great kindness; *she showed great humanity to the refugees*
(c) **humanities** = the arts subjects at university, such as English, History, Philosophy, as opposed to the sciences; *they don't offer many scholarships for majors in the humanities*

① **human rights**
['hjumən 'raɪts] noun
rights which each member of society should enjoy, such as freedom of speech, freedom of movement, etc.; *demonstrators are protesting abuses of human rights in various parts of the world*

③ **humble**
['hʌmbl] adjective
(a) modest, feeling you are not important; *seeing how much work she does for charity makes me feel very humble*
(b) poor, ordinary; *he comes from a humble family*; *they live in a humble little house in the mountains* (NOTE: humbler - humblest)

③ **humid**
['hjumɪd] adjective
damp, (air) which contains moisture; *I don't like humid weather - I much prefer a hot dry climate*

③ **humidity**
[hju'mɪdɪti] noun
measurement of how much moisture is contained in the air; *the temperature is 88° with 90% humidity*; *flowers are sensitive to changes in temperature and humidity*

② **humiliate**
[hjʊˈmɪlɪeɪt] *verb*
to make someone feel unimportant or stupid;
*our team was completely humiliated - they lost
10 - 2!*; *she is supposed to be his best friend but
she humiliated him in front of everyone*

③ **humiliation**
[hjumɪlɪˈeɪʃn] *noun*
making someone feel stupid or not important;
the humiliation of failing his test once again

① **humor**
[ˈhjumər]
1 *noun*
(a) seeing what is funny; *he has a good sense of
humor*; *she has absolutely no sense of humor*;
*"female wants to meet male, aged 30 - 35, with
a good sense of humor"*
(b) *(formal)* general feeling; *I am in no humor
to talk about vacations just now*; *he was not in
a humor to discuss what happened during their
vacation in Hawaii*; *his good humor lasted
until the end of the party*
2 *verb*
to humor someone = to say you agree with
what someone wants; *when he starts shouting
and cursing, you to have to try to humor him to
keep him happy*

② **humorous**
[ˈhjumərəs] *adjective*
(formal) funny; *our host made some humorous
remarks to try to make everyone relax*

③ **hump**
[hʌmp] *noun*
(a) raised part on the back of a person or animal;
*Arabian camels have only one hump, while
Bactrian camels have two*
(b) small raised part in the ground; *they have
built speed humps in the road to slow down the
traffic*

① **hundred**
[ˈhʌndrəd]
(a) number 100; *the church is over a hundred
years old*; *my grandfather will be 100 next
month*; *they came in the hundreds to visit the
grave*; *do I have to tell you a hundred times to
stop that noise?*
(b) one hundred percent = 100%; one
hundred percent happy with = totally satisfied
with; *I'm not one hundred percent happy with
his work*
(c) hundreds of = very many; *hundreds of
birds were killed by the cold weather*; *hundreds
of people caught the flu last winter* (NOTE: in
numbers **hundred** does not change and is followed
by **and** when reading: **491 =** four hundred and
ninety-one; **102 =** a hundred and two. Note also: **a
hundred and one** (101), **three hundred and six**
(306) but **the hundred and first** (101st), **the three
hundred and sixth** (306th), etc.)

① **hundredth (100th)**
[ˈhʌndrədθ] *adjective & noun*
the clock is correct to one hundredth of a
*second (100th of a second); tomorrow is his
hundredth birthday; a cent is one hundredth of
a dollar*

① **hung**
[hʌŋ]
see HANG

② **Hungarian**
[hʌŋˈgeəriən]
1 *adjective*
referring to Hungary; *Franz Liszt was a famous
Hungarian composer*
2 *noun*
(a) person from Hungary; *it has been 3 years
since a Hungarian last won a gold medal*
(b) language spoken in Hungary; *I am going to
study in Budapest and want to take a course in
Hungarian*

① **Hungary**
[ˈhʌŋgəri] *noun*
country in central Europe, east of Austria and
west of Romania; *the river Danube flows
north-south through the center of Hungary*
(NOTE: capital: **Budapest**; people: **the
Hungarians**; language: **Hungarian**; currency:
forint)

① **hunger**
[ˈhʌŋgər] *noun*
state of wanting to eat, of needing to eat; **to die
of hunger** = to die because you do not have
enough to eat; *there are children dying of
hunger in some countries in Africa*; **hunger
strike** = refusing to eat, as a form of protest; *the
prisoner went on a hunger strike*

① **hungry**
[ˈhʌŋgri] *adjective*
wanting to eat; *you must be hungry after that
game of football*; *I'm not very hungry - I had a
big lunch*; *hurry up with the food - we're
getting hungry*; **to go hungry** = not to have
enough to eat; *students had to go hungry when
their room and board was not paid* (NOTE:
hungrier - hungriest)

③ **hung up**
[ˈhʌŋ ˈʌp] *adjective*
(informal) worried or bothered about something;
*he's really hung up about his promotion
prospects*

① **hunt**
[hʌnt]
1 *verb*
(a) to hunt for something = to search for
something; *we're hunting for a cheap
apartment*; *they came to New York the week
after Christmas, hunting for bargains*
(b) to chase wild animals for food or sport; *we
took the dogs out hunting rabbits*; *our cat is not
very good at hunting mice*; *they go there to
hunt deer* (NOTE: you hunt animals, but you hunt
for things)
2 *noun*
search; *the hunt for new offices has just started*

① **hunter**
['hʌntər] *noun*
person who hunts; *a tiger hunter*; **bargain hunter** = person who looks for bargains; *bargain hunters were lining up outside the store on the first day of the sales*

④ **hurdle**
['hɜrdl] *noun*
(a) small fence that you have to jump over in a race; *she fell at the first hurdle*
(b) **hurdles** = race where you jump over fences; *the last event was the 100 meter hurdles*
(c) obstacle in the way of something; *only one more hurdle to clear and then we will have bought the house*

① **hurricane**
['hʌrɪkən] *noun*
tropical storm with strong winds and rain; *the hurricane damaged properties all along the coast* (NOTE: used in the Caribbean Sea or Eastern Pacific Ocean; in the Far East this is called a **typhoon**; in the Indian Ocean it is called a **cyclone**)

① **hurried**
['hʌrɪd] *adjective*
done in a rush, too quickly; *we just had time for a hurried lunch before running to catch the train*

① **hurry**
['hʌri]
1 *noun*
in a hurry = doing things fast; *the waiters are always in a hurry*; *can't you drive any faster? - we're in a hurry to catch our plane!*; *he wants the report in a hurry*; **what's the hurry?** = why are you going so fast?; *what's the hurry? it's only two o'clock and the plane doesn't leave until nine*; **there's no hurry** = you need not do it fast; *there's no hurry for the figures, we do not need them until next week* (NOTE: no plural)
2 *verb*
(a) to go, do or make something fast; *she hurried across the room*; *you'll have to hurry if you want to catch the last mail collection*; *there's no need to hurry - we've got plenty of time*
(b) to make someone go faster; *don't hurry me, I like to take my time*

① **hurry up**
['hʌri 'ʌp] *verb*
(a) to go or do something faster; *hurry up - we'll be late for the movie*; *can't you get the cook to hurry up, I'm getting hungry?*
(b) to make someone do something faster; *can you hurry up that order, the customer wants it tomorrow?*

① **hurt**
[hɜrt]
1 *verb*
(a) to have pain; to give pain; *my tooth hurts*; *no one was badly hurt in the accident*; *where did you hurt yourself?*; *is he badly hurt?*; *two players got hurt in the game*
(b) to harm, to damage; *the bad publicity did not hurt our sales*; *the news report will certainly hurt his reputation*; **it won't hurt to** *or* **it never hurts to** = it would be a good thing to; *it wouldn't hurt to complain to the manager*; *it never hurts to be polite to customers* (NOTE: **hurting - hurt**)
2 *noun*
(a) place where you have a pain; *he has a hurt on his toe*
(b) feeling of sadness because you have been badly treated; *she feels upset because of the hurt to her pride*

① **husband**
['hʌzbənd]
1 *noun*
man to whom a woman is married; *her husband is Cuban*; *he's the doctor's husband*; **to live as husband and wife** = to live together as if you were married without being married; *they lived together as husband and wife for twenty years*; *compare* WIFE
2 *verb*
(formal) not to waste money, supplies, etc.; *we must learn to husband our resources*

④ **hush puppies**
['hʌʃ 'pʌpiz] *noun*
corn cakes, fried and usually served with fish; *a meal of fish cakes and hush puppies*

② **hut**
[hʌt] *noun*
small rough wooden house; *they found a beach hut where they spent the night*

④ **hybrid**
['haɪbrɪd] *adjective & noun*
cross between two varieties of plant or animal; *she is well known for growing hybrid roses*

④ **hydrogen**
['haɪdrədʒən] *noun*
a common gas which combines with oxygen to form water (NOTE: Chemical element: chemical symbol: **H**; atomic number: **1**)

④ **hygiene**
['haɪdʒin] *noun*
being clean and keeping healthy conditions; *for reasons of hygiene, dogs are not allowed into the shop*

④ **hyphen**
['haɪfn] *noun*
printing sign (-) used to show that two words are joined or that a word has been split; *there is a hyphen in the word forty-five*

Ii

③ **I, i**

[aɪ]

ninth letter of the alphabet, between H and J; *she said "I" for "Italian"*; **to dot one's i's and cross one's t's** = to be very careful to get the final details right

② **I**

[aɪ] *pronoun used by a speaker when talking about himself or herself*; *she said, "I can do it", and she did it*; *she and I come from the same town*; *he told me that I could go home early*; *I said I was going to be late* (NOTE: when it is the object of a verb, **I** becomes **me: I gave it to him - he gave it to me; I hit him - he hit me;** when it follows the verb **be, I** usually becomes **me: who is it? - it's me!**)

① **ice**

[aɪs]

1 *noun*

(a) water which is frozen and has become solid; *when water freezes, it turns into ice*; *the ice on the lake is dangerous, it isn't thick enough to walk on*; *would you like ice in your drink?*; *her hands are like ice* = her hands are very cold

(b) to break the ice = to start to talk when everyone has been silent; *the party started quietly, but the drinks soon broke the ice*; **to keep something on ice** = not to do anything about something for the moment; **to put something on ice** = to file a plan or document as the best way of forgetting about it; *we can't afford the expense at the moment, so we'll put the project on ice until next year*

(c) ice bucket = bucket of ice in which a wine bottle is placed to keep cool

(d) ice dessert other than cream; *we had ices during the intermission*; *two coffee ices, please*

(e) ice water = water that has been made very cold, often by putting ice in it (NOTE: no plural for meaning (a): **some ice, a lump of ice;** the plural **ices** means **ice creams**)

2 *verb*

to put icing on a cake; *a cake iced with chocolate*

① **iceberg**

[ˈaɪsbɜrg] *noun*

huge block of ice floating on the sea; *the Titanic hit an iceberg and sank*

① **ice cream**

[ˈaɪs ˈkrim] *noun*

frozen sweet made from cream and flavored with fruit juice or other sweet substance; *a vanilla ice cream*; *what kind of ice cream do you want - strawberry or chocolate?*; *can you help me - I can't carry six ice creams at the same time?*

③ **ice over** *or* **ice up**

[ˈaɪs ˈoʊvər or ˈʌp] *verb*

to become covered with ice; *the wings of the plane had iced up*

② **icicle**

[ˈaɪsɪkl] *noun*

long piece of ice hanging from a roof, etc., formed by water dripping in freezing weather; *icicles hung down from the edge of the roof*

② **icing**

[ˈaɪsɪŋ] *noun*

covering of sugar and flavors, spread over a cake or cookies; *she made some chocolate icing for the cake*

① **I'd**

[aɪd] *short for* I HAD, I WOULD

③ **ID**

[ˈaɪ ˈdi] *noun*

card or other document which shows a photograph of the holder, with the name, date of birth and other details, carried by citizens of a country or members of a group to prove who they are; *the cat has a collar with an ID tag*; *show your ID when entering the premises*; *in some European countries you are legally required to carry an ID around with you*; *do you have any ID on you?*

① **idea**

[aɪˈdɪə] *noun*

(a) something which you think of; **to have an idea that** = to think that; *I have an idea that the buses don't run on Sundays*; **to have no idea** *or* **not to have the faintest idea** = not to know; *where's your brother? - I have no idea or I don't have the faintest idea*; *I had no idea it was as late as that*

(b) plan that you make in your mind; *some of his ideas were really original*; *I've had an idea - let's all go for a picnic!*; *that's a good idea!*; **a bright idea** = a good plan; *he had the bright idea of painting the bathroom red*

② **ideal**

[aɪˈdɪəl]

1 *noun*

highest point of good life which people try to reach; *my ideal would be to work hard and get rich*; **man of ideals** = person who has high moral standards

2 *adjective*

perfect, extremely suitable; *this is the ideal site for a factory*; *the cottage is an ideal place for watching birds*

④ **ideally**

[aɪ'dɪəli] *adverb*

if everything were perfect; *ideally, I'd take three weeks off, but there's too much work at the office*

③ **identical**

[aɪ'dentɪkl] *adjective*

exactly the same; *the twins wore identical clothes for the party*; *their political opinions are identical*; **identical to** = exactly the same as; *her political opinions are identical to mine*; **identical twins** = twins who look exactly alike

② **identification**

[aɪdentɪfɪ'keɪʃn] *noun*

(a) saying who someone is, giving his or her name, personal details, etc.; *the identification of the body was made by the victim's sister*; **identification lineup** = line of people at a police station from whom a witness is asked to identify a suspected criminal; *she was asked to pick out the mugger at an identification lineup*

(b) document which shows who someone is; *the bank teller asked him for identification*; *see also* PIN NUMBER

② **identify**

[aɪ'dentɪfaɪ] *verb*

(a) to say who someone is or what something is; *can you identify what kind of rock this is?*; *she was able to identify her attacker*

(b) to state that something belongs to you; *each person was asked to identify his or her baggage*

(c) to identify with = to feel you have the same feelings as someone or to have a feeling of sympathy for someone or something; *I can identify with the hero who spends his life trapped in a small provincial town*

② **identity**

[aɪ'dentɪti] *noun*

someone's name, personal details, etc.; *he changed his identity when he went to work for the secret service*; **identity card (ID)** = a card which shows a photograph of the holder, with the name, date of birth and other details, carried by citizens of a country or members of a group to prove who they are; *show your identity card when entering the Ministry*; *in some European countries you are legally required to carry an identity card with you at all times*; **proof of identity** = proof in the form of a document, such as a driver's license, that a person is who he or she claims to be; *the police asked her for proof of identity*

④ **ideology**

[aɪdɪ'ɒlədʒi] *noun*

theory of life based not on religious belief, but on political or economic philosophy; *her socialist ideology led her to join the party*; *he wrote a study of Communist ideology*

② **idle**

['aɪdl]

1 *adjective*

(a) lazy (person); *he's the idlest man I know - he never does any work at all*; **he's bone idle** = he never does any work

(b) not working; *the machines stood idle during the strike*; *2000 employees were made idle by the recession* (NOTE: **idler - idlest**)

2 *verb*

(of machine) to run at a low speed; *he waited for her in the car with the engine idling*

④ **i.e.**

['aɪ 'i] *abbreviation meaning "that is"*

it's best to study Russian in a country where they speak it - i.e. Russia; *the import restrictions apply to expensive items, i.e. items costing more than $3,750* (NOTE: it is short for the Latin phrase **id est**)

① **if**

[ɪf]

1 *conjunction*

(a) *(showing what might happen)* *if it freezes tonight, the sidewalks will be dangerous tomorrow*; *if I'm in Boston, I'll come and see you*; *if he had told me you were ill, I'd have come to see you in the hospital*; *if I won the lottery, I would take a long vacation*; *if he's going to be late, he'll phone to tell me*

(b) *(asking questions)* *do you know if the plane is late?*; *I was wondering if you would like to have some tea*

(c) although; *he is nice, if kind of lazy*

2 *noun*

question which is not certain; *he'll catch the plane if he gets up in time, and that's a very big if*

◇ **if only**

['ɪf 'əʊnli]

(exclamation showing regret) *if only I had some money!*; *if only she'd told me, I could have advised her what to do*

④ **ignorance**

['ɪgnərəns] *noun*

not knowing; *ignorance of the law is no excuse*; **to keep someone in ignorance of something** = not to tell someone about something; *the soldiers were deliberately kept in ignorance of the dangers facing them* (NOTE: no plural)

④ **ignorant**

['ɪgnərənt] *adjective*

not knowing anything; stupid; *he left school completely ignorant of the rules of English spelling*

② **ignore**

[ɪg'nɔr] *verb*

not to notice someone or something on purpose; *she ignored the red light and just drove straight through*; *when we met he just ignored me*

① **ill**

[ɪl] *adjective*

(a) sick, not well; *stress can make you ill*; *if you're feeling ill you ought to see a doctor*; **to fall ill** = to become ill; *she fell seriously ill and we thought she was going to die*; **to be taken ill** = to become ill suddenly; *he was taken ill while on vacation in Mexico*

(b) **ill at ease** = embarrassed, not comfortable; *she seemed ill at ease when we started talking about the missing money*; *he felt ill at ease in his new suit at a party where he knew nobody* (NOTE: ill - **worse** [wɜrs] - **worst** [wɜrst])

① **I'll**

[aɪl] *short for* I WILL, I SHALL

② **illegal**

[ɪˈliɡl] *adjective*

against the law; *it is illegal to serve alcohol to people under 21*; *illegal immigrants will be deported*

③ **illegally**

[ɪˈliɡəli] *adverb*

against the law; *he was accused of entering the country illegally*; *the car was illegally parked*

③ **illness**

[ˈɪlnəs] *noun*

not being well; *she developed a serious illness*; *a lot of the staff are absent because of illness* (NOTE: plural is **illnesses**)

④ **illusion**

[ɪˈluʒn] *noun*

impression which is not true; **optical illusion** = thing which seems real when you see it, but which is not; *the sword seemed to go right through his body, but it was just an optical illusion*; *the lines are not different lengths - it's just an optical illusion*; **to have no illusions about something** = to know the real unpleasant facts about something; *she has no illusions about her husband being faithful*

② **illustrate**

[ˈɪləstreɪt] *verb*

(a) to put pictures into a book; *the book is illustrated with color photographs of birds*

(b) to show as an example; *the article illustrates his views on the way the company should develop*

(c) to be an example of; *this poem illustrates the kind of style I prefer*

③ **illustration**

[ɪləˈstreɪʃn] *noun*

(a) picture in a book; *the book has 25 color illustrations*

(b) example; *his daughter's birthday party is a good illustration of the way he likes to spend money*

① **I'm**

[aɪm] *short for* I AM

② **image**

[ˈɪmɪdʒ] *noun*

(a) portrait; *I want the portrait to be a faithful image of my mother*; *(informal)* **he's the spitting image of his father** = he looks exactly like his father

(b) idea which other people have of a person or of an organization; *the children are so badly behaved that it gives a bad image of the family*; *in an attempt to change his image he bought a lot of new clothes*; *they are spending a lot of money to improve the company's image*

(c) picture produced by a lens, mirror or computer; *the mirror throws an image onto the paper*; *can this software handle images in that format?*; *can you adjust the camera, the image on the screen is out of focus?*

② **imaginary**

[ɪˈmædʒɪnəri] *adjective*

not real, which is imagined; *all his novels are set in an imaginary town in the Midwest*

② **imagination**

[ɪmædʒɪˈneɪʃn] *noun*

ability to picture things in your mind; *she let her imagination run wild in her stories for children*; **to use your imagination** = to imagine what is possible; *try and use your imagination - think of the money we could make*; **to let your imagination get the better of you** *or* **run away with you** = to think things are possible when they are not; *he let his imagination get the better of him and saw himself as a future president*

① **imagine**

[ɪˈmædʒɪn] *verb*

to picture something in your mind; *imagine yourself sitting on a beach in the hot sun*; *she thought she had heard footsteps, and then decided she had imagined it*

③ **imitate**

[ˈɪmɪteɪt] *verb*

to copy something or someone; to do as someone does; *he made us all laugh by imitating the teacher*

③ **imitation**

[ɪmɪˈteɪʃn]

1 *noun*

(a) act of imitating; *he does a very good imitation of the president*

(b) copy made of something; **beware of imitations** = be careful not to buy low quality goods which are made to look like other more expensive items

2 *adjective*

copied, not genuine; *it's not real leather, just imitation*; *the bag is made of imitation leather*

③ **immediate**

[ɪˈmidjət] *adjective*

(a) very soon; *he wrote an immediate letter of complaint*; *you didn't expect an immediate reply, did you?*; *your order will receive immediate attention*

(b) closest, (sitting) next to you; *he had to share his program with the person to his immediate left*

③ **immediately**
['ɪ'miːdɪətli] *adverb*
straightaway; *he got my letter, and wrote back immediately*; *as soon as he heard the news he immediately phoned his wife*

③ **immense**
[ɪ'mens] *adjective*
huge; very big; enormous; *he has an immense black beard*; *the bill was immense, and we all complained*; *the dictator decided to build an immense palace in the mountains*

③ **immigrant**
['ɪmɪɡrənt] *noun*
person who comes to a country to settle; *immigrants make up a very important part of the economy of California*; *immigrants are rushing to Germany because the economy is booming*; **illegal immigrant** = person who has entered a country illegally and wants to settle there; *compare* EMIGRANT

② **immigration**
[ɪmɪ'ɡreɪʃn] *noun*
(a) settling in a new country; *the government is encouraging immigration because of the shortage of workers in key industries*; **immigration controls** = restrictions placed by a country on the numbers of immigrants who can come into the country; *many countries have imposed immigration controls*
(b) **Immigration** = section of an airport where new arrivals have to show their passports; *he was stopped at Immigration*; *you will need to show all these documents when you go through Immigration*

④ **immune**
[ɪ'mjuːn] *adjective*
(a) *(person)* protected against infection; *I seem to be immune to colds - I just never have any*; *this injection should make you immune to yellow fever*; **immune system** = complex network of cells which protects the body from disease; *in people with this disease, the immune system gradually fails to work*
(b) legally protected against, not liable to; *she believed she would be immune from prosecution* (NOTE: you are immune **to** a disease, and **from** prosecution)

④ **immunity**
[ɪ'mjuːnɪti] *noun*
(a) **immunity to a disease** = being able to resist attacks of a disease; *the injection will give immunity to the disease for six months*
(b) **immunity from** *or* **against arrest** = protection against being arrested; *when he offered to give information to the police, he was granted immunity from prosecution*; **diplomatic immunity** = freedom from the control of the laws of the country you are living in because of being a diplomat; *the ambassador refused to pay his parking fines and claimed diplomatic immunity*

④ **impact**
['ɪmpækt]
1 *noun*
(a) strong effect; *the TV documentary had an strong impact on the viewers*
(b) shock; *the automobile was totally crushed by the impact of the collision*; **on impact** = as soon as it hit; *the plane burst into flames on impact with the ground*
2 *verb*
to impact (on) something = to have a strong effect on something; *the fall in the value of the currency will impact strongly on the stock market*; *the accident will impact his future as a racing driver*

② **impatient**
[ɪm'peɪʃnt] *adjective*
unable to wait for something, always in a hurry to do something; *we were all impatient for the movie to start*; *he's very impatient with anyone who works slowly*

③ **impatiently**
[ɪm'peɪʃntli] *adverb*
in a hurried way, not patiently; *"can't you go any faster?" she said impatiently*; *we are all waiting impatiently for the new book to come out*; *she looked at her watch impatiently*

④ **implement**
1 *noun* ['ɪmplɪmənt]
tool or instrument; *the builder brought an implement for bending pipes*; **garden implements** = tools such as forks and spades which are used in the garden
2 *verb* ['ɪmplɪment]
to put into effect; *the changes must be implemented immediately*

④ **implication**
[ɪmplɪ'keɪʃn] *noun*
(a) suggestion that someone is connected with a crime; *the newspaper revealed his implication in the affair of the stolen diamonds*
(b) **implications** = possible effects of an action; *what will be the implications of the election results for public spending?*

④ **imply**
[ɪm'plaɪ] *verb*
to suggest; *he implied that he knew where the papers had been hidden*; *the lawyer implied that the witness had not in fact seen the accident take place*

② **import**
1 *noun* ['ɪmpɔrt]
imports = goods which are brought into a country for sale; *imports from Poland have risen to $1 million a year*; *all imports must be declared to customs*; **import controls** = rules limiting goods that can be brought into a country; *import controls on foreign makes of automobiles have been lifted*; **import duty** = tax paid on goods brought into a country; *the government charges an import duty on some items coming into the country*; **import license**

or **import permit** = official document that allows goods to be imported; *don't try to import guns if you don't have an import license*; **import quota** = fixed quantity of a particular type of goods which the government allows to be imported; *the government has imposed an import quota on automobiles* (NOTE: usually in the plural, **imports**, but always **import** before another noun)

2 *verb* [ɪm'pɔrt]

to bring goods into a country; *the company imports television sets from Japan*; *this automobile was imported from France*

① **importance**
[ɪm'pɔrtəns] *noun*

serious effect or influence; *do not attach too much importance to what he says*; *the bank attaches great importance to the deal*

① **important**
[ɪm'pɔrtənt] *adjective*

(a) which matters a great deal; *it's important to be in time for your interview*; *I have to go to New York for an important meeting*; *he left a file containing important papers in the taxi*
(b) (person) in a high position; *he has an important government job*; *she's an important government official*; *he was promoted to a more important position*

④ **impose**
[ɪm'pəʊz] *verb*

(a) to ask someone to pay a fine, a tax; *the judge imposed a fine on the shoplifter*; *the government imposed a 10% tax increase on electrical items*
(b) to put something into action; *they have tried to impose a ban on smoking*
(c) to impose on someone = to cause someone trouble; *I hope it's not imposing on you too much, but I need to have the report today*

④ **imposing**
[ɪm'pəʊzɪŋ] *adjective*

grand or solemn; *the cathedral is an imposing brick building*

① **impossible**
[ɪm'pɒsəbl] *adjective*

(a) which cannot be done; *it's impossible to do all this work in two hours*; *getting skilled staff is becoming impossible*
(b) (person or situation) awkward and difficult; *the new secretary is completely impossible*

② **impress**
[ɪm'pres] *verb*

(a) to make someone admire or respect someone or something; *her rapid response to the request impressed her boss*; *she was impressed by his skill with oil paints*; *the military government organized the display to impress the neighboring states*
(b) to impress something on someone = to make someone understand; *I must impress on you just how urgent this is*

② **impressed**
[ɪm'prest] *adjective*

admiring the effect; *what a beautiful garden - I'm really impressed!*

② **impression**
[ɪm'preʃn] *noun*

(a) effect on someone's mind; *blue walls create an impression of coldness*; *the exhibition made a strong impression on her*
(b) to be under *or* **to labor under an impression** = to have a wrong impression, to assume something which is quite wrong; *he was laboring under the impression that air fares were cheaper in Europe than in the U.S.A.*; **to get the impression that** = to sense that, to have a feeling that; *I got the impression that she wanted us to leave*

② **impressive**
[ɪm'presɪv] *adjective*

which impresses; *he had a series of impressive wins in the chess tournament*; *the government staged an impressive display of military hardware*

② **imprison**
[ɪm'prɪzn] *verb*

to put or to keep someone in prison; *he was imprisoned by the state for six months*

③ **imprisonment**
[ɪm'prɪzənmənt] *noun*

putting or keeping someone in prison; *the penalty for the first offense is a fine of $200 or six weeks' imprisonment*; **a term of imprisonment** = time which a prisoner has to spend in prison; *he was sentenced to the maximum term of imprisonment*; **life imprisonment** = being put in prison for your whole life (the penalty for murder); *the murderer was sentenced to life imprisonment*

④ **improper**
[ɪm'prɒpər] *adjective*

(a) not according to the normal rules; *it was a quite improper use of our registered name*
(b) used in a wrong way; *the improper use of a drug can cause serious damage to health*

④ **improperly**
[ɪm'prɒpərlɪ] *adverb*

not done in the correct way; *the medicine was improperly prepared*

② **improve**
[ɪm'pruv] *verb*

(a) to make something better; *we are trying to improve our image with a series of TV commercials*; **to improve on something** = to try to do better than something; *she tried to improve on her previous best time*
(b) to get better; *the general manager has promised that the bus service will improve*; *it poured down all morning, but in the afternoon the weather improved a little*

② **improvement**
[ɪm'pruvmənt] *noun*

(a) making or becoming better; *there has been*

no improvement in the bus service since we complained; the new software is a great improvement on the old version
(b) thing which is better; *they carried out some improvements to the house; we are planning some home improvements such as a new kitchen*

④ **impulse**
['ImpʌIs] *noun*
sudden feeling or decision; *he had a sudden impulse to take the car and drive to Mexico;* **to do something on impulse** = to do something because you have just thought of it, not because it was planned; **impulse buying** = buying goods which you have just seen, not because you had planned to buy them

④ **impulsive**
[Im'pʌlsIv] *adjective*
acting because of a sudden decision, without thinking; *his impulsive action cost several lives; he is too impulsive - he never thinks about the consequences of his actions*

④ **impulsively**
[Im'pʌlsIvli] *adverb*
without thinking; *she impulsively called the fire department*

① **in**
[In]
1 *preposition & adverb*
(a) *(showing place) he lives in the country; in Michigan it snows a lot during the winter; she's in the kitchen; he's still in bed; don't stand outside in the pouring rain*
(b) at home, in an office, at a station; *is the boss in?; he isn't in yet; my husband usually gets in from work about now; the bus from Cheyenne is due in at 6:30*
(c) *(showing time) in the fall the leaves turn brown; on vacation there was nothing to do in the evenings; she was born in 1996; he ate his meal in five minutes; we went skiing in January*
(d) *(showing time in the future) I'll be back home in about two hours; she should arrive in twenty minutes' time*
(e) in fashion; *this year, short skirts are in*
(f) *(showing a state or appearance) he was dressed in black; she ran outside in her pajamas; we're in a hurry; the words in a dictionary are set out in order of their first letters*
(g) *(showing a proportion or ratio) one in ten of the children wears eyeglasses*
2 *noun*
the ins and outs of something = the complicated details; *he knows all the ins and outs of trading on the Internet*
3 *adjective*
(informal) fashionable; *round dark glasses are the in thing this summer*

◇ **in for**
['In 'fɔr] *adverb*

to be in for something = to be about to get something; *I think we're in for some bad weather; she's in for a nasty shock*

◇ **in front**
['In 'frʌnt]
1 *adverb*
further forward; *my mother sat in the backseat and I sat in front*
2 *preposition*
in front of = placed further forward than something; *a tall man came and sat in front of me and I couldn't see the screen*

◇ **in on**
['In 'ɒn] *adverb*
to be in on a secret = to know a secret; *who else was in on the secret?;* **to let someone in on a secret** = to tell someone a secret; *the gang let the driver in on the secret*

③ **inability**
[Inə'bIlIti] *noun*
not being able to do something; *his inability to write English correctly is a handicap*

④ **inaccessible**
[Inək'sesIbl] *adjective*
impossible to reach or to get to; *the explorers were lost in an inaccessible mountain region*

④ **inactive**
[In'æktIv] *adjective*
not active or not doing anything; *the sales team seems to have been totally inactive*

④ **inadequate**
[In'ædIkwət] *adjective*
(a) not enough; *the island has inadequate supplies of water in the summer months*
(b) not competent, not good enough for a job; *being compared to his brother, the congressman, made him feel quite inadequate*

④ **inadvertently**
[Inəd'vɜrtəntli] *adverb*
said or done by mistake and not on purpose; *she inadvertently put a plastic dish in the oven*

④ **inappropriate**
[Inə'prəuprIət] *adjective*
not suitable, not fitting the circumstances; *wearing jeans to the wedding was considered inappropriate*

③ **Inc.**
[In'kɔrpəreItId] *abbreviation for* INCORPORATED; *we're dealing with a company called John Doe, Inc.*

④ **incentive**
[In'sentIv] *noun*
thing which encourages; *the possibility of extra pay is an incentive to the sales force;* **incentive bonus** = extra money paid when production is increased; **incentive scheme** = plan to encourage better work by paying higher commissions or bonuses; *we are setting up an incentive plan which we hope will increase sales*

① **inch**
[ɪnʃ]
1 *noun*
measure of length (= 2.54cm); *snow lay six inches deep on the ground*; *she is five foot six inches tall (5' 6" a three and a half inch floppy disk*; *see also* FOOT (NOTE: plural is **inches.** Note also that with numbers **inch** is usually written " : a 3½" disk; he is 5' 9": say: "a three and a half inch disk; he's five foot nine")
2 *verb*
to inch forward = to go forward little by little; *the line inched forward slowly*; *the project is inching forward, but it's hard work getting things moving*

② **incident**
[ˈɪnsɪdənt] *noun*
(a) something which happens; *last year six hundred incidents of oil pollution were reported*
(b) usually violent action or disturbance; *there were several incidents during the demonstration*

③ **incidentally**
[ɪnsɪˈdentəli] *adverb*
by the way; *incidentally, you didn't see my watch anywhere in the office, did you?*

④ **inclined**
[ɪnˈklaɪnd] *adjective*
(a) sloping; *the roadway is inclined to give easy access to the warehouse*
(b) likely to do something; *she is inclined to get very annoyed when anyone criticizes her golf*

② **include**
[ɪnˈklud] *verb*
to count someone or something along with others; *the waiter did not include service in the bill*; *the total is $260, not including insurance and handling charges*; *there were 120 people at the wedding if you include the children*

② **included**
[ɪnˈkludɪd] *adjective*
taken together with something else; *the vacation costs $750, everything included*; *the service is not included in the check*

② **including**
[ɪnˈkludɪŋ] *preposition*
taking something together with something else; *the total comes to $35.00 including sales tax*; *not including* = not counting; *there were thirty people at the lunch, not including the children*

④ **inclusive**
[ɪnˈklusɪv] *adjective*
(a) which counts something in with other things; *inclusive of tax* = including tax; *the bill is not inclusive of sales tax*; *inclusive charge* = charge which includes all costs; *the charge is not inclusive, you will have to pay extra for postage*
(b) *(giving figures or dates)* **the conference runs from April 12 to 16 inclusive** = it starts on the morning of April 12 and ends on the evening of April 16; *we'll be away from Monday to Friday inclusive*

② **income**
[ˈɪŋkʌm] *noun*
money which you receive, especially as pay for your work, or as interest on savings; *their weekly income is not really enough to live on*; **income tax** = tax on money earned as wages or salary, or on money earned by a business; *income tax is deducted from his salary each month*; *she pays income tax at the lowest rate*

④ **incorporate**
[ɪnˈkɔrpəreɪt] *verb*
(a) to bring something into something else to make one main whole; *we are trying to incorporate the suggestions from the committees into the main proposal*
(b) to form an official body or a registered company; *the company was incorporated three years ago*; *J. Doe Incorporated* (NOTE: usually shortened to **Inc.** after names: **J. Doe Inc.**)

③ **increase**
1 *noun* [ˈɪŋkris]
(a) growth, process of becoming larger; *an increase in tax or a tax increase*; *an increase in the cost of living*
(b) salary raise; *she went to her boss and asked for an increase*; **cost-of-living increase** = increase in pension to allow it to keep up with higher cost of living
(c) **on the increase** = becoming more frequent; *shoplifting is on the increase*
2 *verb* [ɪŋˈkris]
(a) to rise, to grow, to expand; *the price of oil has increased twice in the past year*; **to increase in price** = to become more expensive; **to increase in size** *or* **in value** = to become larger or more valuable
(b) to make something become bigger; *the boss increased her salary*; *subway fares have been increased by 10%*

③ **increased**
[ɪŋˈkrist] *adjective*
which has become bigger; *these increased plane fares mean that we cannot afford to travel so much*

② **increasingly**
[ɪŋˈkrisɪŋli] *adverb*
more and more; *he found it increasingly difficult to keep up with all the work he had to do at the office*; *his future with the company looks increasingly doubtful*

② **incredible**
[ɪnˈkredɪbl] *adjective*
(a) which you find difficult to believe; *it is absolutely incredible that anyone as rich as he is can avoid paying tax*
(b) of remarkable size, quantity, etc.; *over the years he has made an incredible fortune from selling antique cars*; *you should go to see "Jaws" - it's an incredible movie*

③ **incredibly**
[ɪnˈkredɪblɪ] *adverb*
(a) difficult to believe; *incredibly, he passed his driver's test the first time*
(b) very, extremely; *she's incredibly tall*; *it is incredibly difficult to find a parking space near my office in the middle of the day*

② **indeed**
[ɪnˈdiːd]
1 *adverb*
(a) *(for emphasis)* greatly, really; *thank you very much indeed for inviting me to stay*; *they have been very kind indeed to their daughter*
(b) in fact; *they are very poor - indeed they have no money at all*
2 *interjection showing indignation*
she called me stupid - indeed! how rude!; *are you the person who scratched my car? - indeed not!*

③ **indefinite**
[ɪnˈdefɪnɪt] *adjective*
(a) without a definite end; *he has been suspended for an indefinite period, pending an inquiry*
(b) **the indefinite article** = "a" or "an" (as opposed to the definite article "the")

② **independence**
[ɪndɪˈpendəns] *noun*
(a) freedom; *the country achieved independence in 1994*; **Independence Day** = U.S. national holiday on July 4 that celebrates the adoption of the Declaration of Independence; *see also* FOURTH OF JULY; **the American War of Independence** = war by the American colonies against Britain (1775-1786) by which the United States of America was formed; **Declaration of Independence** = document written by Thomas Jefferson (1776) by which the American states declared their independence from Britain
(b) not needing or not relying on anyone else; *she's eighteen and is looking forward to a life of independence from her family*

② **independent**
[ɪndɪˈpendənt]
1 *adjective*
(a) free, not ruled by anyone else; *Slovenia has been independent since 1991*
(b) not owned by a group, not run by the state; *the big chains are squeezing the independent bookstores out of the market*
(c) with enough income from investments, etc., to be able to live without working; *he has a considerable independent income*
(d) not needing or not relying on anyone else; *she's eighteen and wants to be independent of her family*
2 *noun*
(a) candidate who does not belong to a political party; *he ran in the presidential primaries as an independent*

(b) store that is owned by a person and is not part of a chain; *supermarkets have a bad effect on the small independents*

② **index**
[ˈɪndeks]
1 *noun*
(a) list showing the references in a book; *look up the references to Hollywood in the index* (NOTE: plural in this meaning is **indexes**)
(b) regular report that shows rises and falls in prices, unemployment, etc.; *the economic indices look very promising at the moment*; **cost-of-living index** = way of measuring the cost of living, shown as a percentage increase on the figure for the previous year; *some retirement pensions are linked to the cost-of-living index* (NOTE: plural in this meaning is **indexes** *or* **indices** [ˈɪndɪsiz])
2 *verb*
to relate pensions, wages, etc., to the cost-of-living index; *the government is considering indexing retirement pensions*

① **India**
[ˈɪndjə] *noun*
large country in southern Asia, south of China and east of Pakistan; *India is bounded to the north by the Himalayas*; *India is the largest democracy in the world* (NOTE: capital: **New Delhi**; people: **Indians**; official languages: **Hindi, English, Gujarati, Tamil, etc.**; currency: **rupee**)

② **Indian**
[ˈɪndjən]
1 *adjective*
(a) referring to India; *Indian cooking is famous for its curries*; **Indian elephant** = elephant found in India and Southeast Asia, slightly smaller than the African elephant, and used as a working animal in forests
(b) referring to one of the original peoples of America; *the traditional Indian skills of hunting and tracking*; **in Indian file** = in line, one behind the other; *the children walked into the assembly in Indian file*; **Indian summer** = period of hot weather in the fall; *why not take advantage of the Indian summer and go to LA for the long weekend*
2 *noun*
(a) person from India; *many Indians went to live in Britain in the 1960s*
(b) person from one of the original American peoples; *the train of pioneers' wagons was attacked by Indians* (NOTE: now usually called **Native Americans**)

② **indicate**
[ˈɪndɪkeɪt] *verb*
to show; *can you indicate the position of the enemy camp on this map?*; *the latest figures indicate a fall in the number of unemployed*

③ **indication**
[ɪndɪˈkeɪʃn] *noun*
sign; *he gave absolutely no indication that he was thinking of leaving the company*

④ **indicator**
['ɪndɪkeɪtər] *noun*
(a) something which indicates; *the inflation rate is a good indicator of the strength of the economy*
(b) flashing light on an automobile that shows which way the driver is going to turn; *his left indicator was flashing and then he turned right!*

④ **indignant**
[ɪn'dɪgnənt] *adjective*
feeling offended or angry; *he was very indignant when the inspector asked him for his ticket*; *the manager came out to speak to the indignant shoppers who had been standing in line for hours in the rain*

④ **indignation**
[ɪndɪg'neɪʃn] *noun*
being indignant; *much to her indignation, she was asked to come for a medical test*; *the crowd showed their indignation at the referee's decision by throwing bottles*

④ **indirect**
[ɪndə'rekt or ɪndaɪ'rekt] *adjective*
not direct; *the taxi took us to the airport by a very indirect route*

④ **indiscriminate**
[ɪndɪ'skrɪmənət] *adjective*
(a) not selective; *the indiscriminate use of pesticides*
(b) not in order; *an indiscriminate heap of documents*

③ **individual**
[ɪndɪ'vɪdjuəl]
1 *noun*
(a) one single person; *we cater for private individuals as well as for groups*
(b) *(informal)* person; *the police would like to talk to the individual who was responsible for this*
2 *adjective*
(a) single, for a particular person; *we treat each individual case on its merits*; *we provide each member of the tour group with an individual map of the town*
(b) enough for one person; *I want three individual portions of ice cream, please*

② **indoor**
['ɪndɔr] *adjective*
inside a building; *if it's raining we can play indoor games*; *our school has an indoor swimming pool*

① **indoors**
[ɪn'dɔrz] *adverb*
inside a building; *if it's cold and wet, you should stay indoors*; *in view of the weather, we had the party indoors*; *everyone ran indoors when it started to rain*

④ **indulge**
[ɪn'dʌldʒ] *verb*
(a) **to indulge in** = to enjoy yourself doing something; *I like to indulge in a hot bath and massage once in a while*
(b) to give someone little luxuries; *she always indulges her little grandson with chocolates and presents*; **to indulge yourself** = to give yourself a little luxury; *I love coffee cakes, but I don't often get the chance to indulge myself*

② **industrial**
[ɪn'dʌstriəl] *adjective*
referring to manufacturing work; *the Midwest is the main industrial region in the U.S.*; **industrial action** = strike or protest by workers; *the union members have voted in favor of industrial action*; **industrial park** = group of factories built together; *we are moving to a new industrial park near the highway*

② **industrialize**
[ɪn'dʌstriəlaɪz] *verb*
to set up industries in a country where there were none before; *the government set out to industrialize the agricultural region in the north of the country*; *Southeast Asian countries industrialized very rapidly*

② **industry**
['ɪndʌstri] *noun*
manufacturing companies, or other types of commercial activity; *oil is a key industry*; *the automobile industry has had a good year*; *the government is helping industry to sell more products abroad*; *the tourist industry brings in a lot of foreign currency* (NOTE: plural is **industries**)

④ **inefficient**
[ɪnɪ'fɪʃnt] *adjective*
not efficient; *this model is very inefficient - its fuel consumption is much higher than it should be*

③ **inevitable**
[ɪn'evɪtəbl] *adjective*
which must happen, which cannot be avoided; *it was inevitable that the younger children would want to leave home*

③ **inevitably**
[ɪn'evɪtəbli] *adverb*
naturally, of course; *inevitably after walking all day in the mountains they came back hungry and tired*

④ **infancy**
['ɪnfənsi] *noun*
(a) young childhood; *two of her children died in infancy*
(b) **in its infancy** = in the very early stages of development; *in 1910, the aircraft industry was still in its infancy*

③ **infant**
['ɪnfənt] *noun*
(formal) very young child; *infants need feeding every few hours*

③ **infantry**
['ɪnfəntri] *noun*
soldiers who fight on foot, not in tanks, or on

horses, etc.; *the infantry was advancing to the front line* (NOTE: no plural)

③ **infect**
[ɪn'fekt] *verb*
to pass a disease on to someone, or to a part of the body; *she claimed she had been infected by her boyfriend; the disease infected his liver; his whole arm soon became infected*

② **infection**
[ɪn'fekʃn] *noun*
disease that spreads from one person to another; *her throat infection keeps coming back; he was sneezing and spreading infection to other people in the office; she seems to catch every little infection there is*

③ **infectious**
[ɪn'fekʃəs] *adjective*
(a) (disease) which can be passed from one person to another; *this strain of flu is highly infectious; German measles are infectious, so children who have it must be kept away from others* (NOTE: compare **contagious**)
(b) which can be passed on to someone else; *he's a great music teacher and his enthusiasm for church music is very infectious*

④ **inferior**
[ɪn'fɪəriər]
1 *adjective*
(a) not as large as; *the enemy's inferior numbers meant they could not attack the castle*
(b) **inferior to** = not as good as something or someone else; *this camera is inferior to that one, although they are both the same price; the store was accused of selling cheap inferior goods at high prices*
2 *noun*
person of a lower rank; *he always speaks to his inferiors in a very superior way* (NOTE: the opposite is **superior**)

② **infield**
['ɪnfiːld] *noun*
(in baseball) the area inside the bases and home plate; *Joe plays in the infield for the Tigers*

④ **infinite**
['ɪnfɪnət] *adjective*
with no end, which will never end; *she has infinite patience with little children*

④ **inflation**
[ɪn'fleɪʃn] *noun*
state of the economy where prices and wages are rising to keep pace with each other; *the government is trying to keep inflation down below 3%; we have 15% inflation or inflation is running at 15%*; **rate of inflation** *or* **inflation rate** = percentage increase in prices over a twelve-month period

③ **inflict**
[ɪn'flɪkt] *verb*
to inflict pain or damage on someone = to cause pain or damage to someone; *drugs can inflict serious harm on young people; the bombs inflicted heavy damage on the capital*

③ **influence**
['ɪnfluəns]
1 *noun*
being able to change someone or something; *he has had a good influence on the other staff in the department; the influence of the moon on the tides; he was charged with driving under the influence of alcohol*
2 *verb*
to make someone or something change; *she was deeply influenced by her old teacher; the moon influences the tides; the price of oil has influenced the price of industrial goods*

④ **influential**
[ɪnflu'enʃl] *adjective*
(a) which causes change; *her speech was influential in changing the opinion of the other members of the committee*
(b) powerful; *she has influential friends who got the police to drop the charges*

④ **influenza**
[ɪnflu'enzə] *noun*
infectious disease like a bad cold, with fever and pains in the muscles, transmitted by a virus; *she is in bed with influenza; half the staff in the office are off with influenza* (NOTE: usually shortened to **flu**)

> COMMENT: influenza is spread by little drops of moisture in the air, transmitted by coughs or sneezes. It can be quite mild, but there are violent strains like Hong Kong flu, which weaken patients a lot

② **inform**
[ɪn'fɔːm] *verb*
(a) to tell someone officially; *have you informed the police that your watch has been stolen?; I regret to inform you that your father has died; we are pleased to inform you that your offer has been accepted*
(b) **to inform on someone** = to tell the authorities that someone has done something wrong; *he met the police secretly and informed on his colleagues*

④ **informal**
[ɪn'fɔːml] *adjective*
(a) relaxed, not formal; *dress casually - the party will be informal; the guide gave us an informal talk on the history of the building*
(b) (type of language) used when talking to friends, but not used on formal occasions

③ **information**
[ɪnfər'meɪʃn] *noun*
facts about something; *can you send me information about vacations in Arizona?; she couldn't give the police any information about how the accident happened; she gave me a very useful piece or bit of information; for further information, please write to Department 27*; **information office** = office that gives information to tourists and visitors (NOTE: no

plural: **some information**; for one item say **a piece of information**)

③ **information technology (IT)**
[infəˈmeɪʃn tekˈnɒlədʒi] *noun*
computers, and forms of technology that depend on computers; *the government is determined to increase the resources for information technology in schools*

> COMMENT: information technology covers everything involved in the acquiring, storing, processing and distributing of information by electronic means, including e-mail, the Internet, radio, television, telephone as well as computers

④ **infrequent**
[ɪnˈfrikwənt] *adjective*
not frequent, not happening very often; *their visits became more and more infrequent*

④ **infrequently**
[ɪnˈfrikwəntli] *adverb*
not happening very often; *very infrequently, he is late for work*

④ **infuriate**
[ɪnˈfjʊəriert] *verb*
to make someone very angry; *slow service in restaurants always infuriates him*

④ **ingenious**
[ɪnˈdʒiniəs] *adjective*
very clever; *she has an ingenious scheme for winning money on the lottery*

④ **ingredient**
[ɪnˈɡridiənt] *noun*
material that goes to make something; *the ingredients are listed on the pack*; *all the ingredients for the cake can be bought at the local supermarket*

④ **inhabit**
[ɪnˈhæbɪt] *verb*
to live in a place; *nobody inhabits the island*; *the area is mainly inhabited by wild goats*

④ **inhabitant**
[ɪnˈhæbɪtənt] *noun*
person who lives in a place; *the local inhabitants do not like the noisy summer tourists*; *the inhabitants of the island were warned that they should boil their drinking water*

② **inherit**
[ɪnˈherɪt] *verb*
(a) to receive money, etc., from a person who has died; *she inherited a small fortune from her father*; *when her grandfather died she inherited the store*
(b) to have characteristics passed on from a parent; *I think she has inherited her father's gloomy character*
(c) to take over a client or a problem from someone who had the job before you; *when they bought the store they inherited a lot of old*

equipment; *the new manager had inherited a lot of financial problems*

② **initial**
[ɪˈnɪʃl]
1 *adjective*
first; *the initial stage of the project went off very well*; *my initial reaction was to say "no"*; *he started the business with an initial investment of $750*
2 *noun*
initials = the first letters of a person's names; *John Smith has a bag with his initials JS on it*
3 *verb*
to write your initials on a document to show you have read and approved it; *can you initial each page of the contract to show that you have approved it?*; *please initial the agreement at the place marked with an X*

④ **initially**
[ɪˈnɪʃəli] *adverb*
at the beginning; *initially we didn't like our new apartment, but we have gotten used to it now*

④ **initiate**
[ɪˈnɪʃiert] *verb*
(a) to start something; *he initiated the new project last year*
(b) to introduce someone into something secret, to show someone the basic information about something; *she was initiated into the club*

④ **initiative**
[ɪˈnɪʃətɪv] *noun*
decision that you hope will get something moving; *the government has proposed various initiatives to get the negotiations moving again*; **to take the initiative** = to decide to do something that other people don't want to do; *the manager decided to take the initiative and ask for a meeting with the boss*; *the president took the initiative in asking the rebel leader to come for talks*

③ **inject**
[ɪnˈdʒekt] *verb*
(a) to force a liquid into something under pressure; *the nurse injected him with the vaccine*; *he injected himself with a drug*
(b) to put something new into something; *come on, let's try to inject some life into these rehearsals!*

③ **injection**
[ɪnˈdʒekʃn] *noun*
(a) act of injecting a liquid into the body; *the doctor gave him injections against tropical diseases*
(b) liquid that is to be injected; *the clinic has ordered another batch of flu injections*

② **injure**
[ˈɪndʒər] *verb*
to hurt; *he injured his spine playing hockey*; *two people were injured in the bank hold-up*; *he was badly injured in a freeway accident*

③ **injured**
['ɪndʒəd] *noun*
the injured = people who have been wounded; *the badly injured were taken to the hospital by helicopter* (NOTE: plural; for one person say **the injured man, the injured girl,** etc.)

② **injury**
['ɪndʒəri] *noun*
hurt, wound; *he never really recovered from his football injury*; *she received severe back injuries in the accident* (NOTE: plural is injuries)

③ **injustice**
[ɪn'dʒʌstɪs] *noun*
lack of justice; *the injustice of the court's decision caused a storm of protest in the newspapers*; *we all believe that an injustice has been done*

① **ink**
[ɪŋk]
1 *noun*
liquid for writing with a pen; *he has ink marks on his shirt*; *the ink won't come off the tablecloth*; *she wrote comments on his work in red ink*
2 *verb*
to ink in = to write or draw using ink on top of something which was written or drawn in pencil

② **inland**
['ɪnlænd] *adverb*
toward the interior of a country; *if you go inland from the port, you soon get into the forest*

④ **in-line skates**
['ɪnlaɪn 'skeɪts] *noun*
type of roller skates, with a series of little wheels in line; *two girls on in-line skates zoomed past us at great speed*

④ **inmate**
['ɪnmeɪt] *noun*
person living in a home or in a prison; *five inmates escaped last week*

① **inn**
[ɪn] *noun*
small hotel; *we stayed at a country inn in the mountains*

② **inner**
['ɪnər] *adjective*
inside; *go through that arch and you will come to the inner garden*; *heat is conducted from the inner to the outer layer of the material*; **inner tube** = thin rubber tube containing air inside a tire (NOTE: the opposite is **outer**)

③ **inner city**
['ɪnər 'sɪti] *noun*
the central part of a city; *inner-city problems* or *problems of the inner city*; *there are always traffic jams in the inner city at rush hour*; *inner-city hotels are most convenient, but can be noisy*

③ **innocence**
['ɪnəsəns] *noun*
(a) not being guilty; *the lawyers tried to prove his innocence*
(b) not having any experience or particular knowledge; *in my innocence, I believed them when they said they were police officers*

② **innocent**
['ɪnəsənt]
1 *adjective*
(a) not guilty; *he was found to be innocent of the crime*; *in U.S. law, the accused is always presumed to be innocent until he is proved to be guilty*
(b) not having any experience or knowledge; *she's totally innocent when it comes to dealing with car salesmen*
2 *noun*
person who has no experience or knowledge; *he's a total innocent when it comes to dealing with car salesmen*

④ **innovation**
[ɪnə'veɪʃn] *noun*
new invention, new way of doing something; *the computer is an innovation that has changed everyone's lives*; *it was something of an innovation to have a wedding in the local fire station*

④ **innovative**
['ɪnəveɪtɪv] *adjective*
which is a new way of doing something; *he has many innovative ideas*

④ **inordinate**
[ɪn'ɔrdɪnət] *adjective*
excessive, more than is usual; *we spend an inordinate amount of time discussing minor problems*

④ **inordinately**
[ɪn'ɔrdɪnətli] *adverb*
excessively; *he was inordinately pleased with himself*

④ **input**
['ɪnpʊt] *noun*
(a) electric current that goes into an apparatus; *plug the input cable into the computer*
(b) data fed into a computer; *the input from the various branches is fed automatically into the corporate office computer*
(c) contribution to a discussion; *thank you very much for your useful input during the meeting*

③ **inquire**
[ɪn'kwaɪər] *verb*
(a) to ask questions about something; *the cook inquired if anything was wrong with the meal*; *she phoned the travel agent to inquire about air fares to Australia*; *she inquired about my mother's health*; **"inquire within"** = ask for more details inside the office or store
(b) to conduct an official investigation into a problem; to investigate, to try to find out about something; *the police are inquiring into his background*; *social services are inquiring*

about the missing girl (NOTE: also spelled **enquire**)

③ **inquiry**
[ɪŋˈkwaɪri] *noun*
(a) formal investigation into a problem; *a government inquiry into corruption in the police force*; *a public inquiry will be held about plans to build another airport*
(b) question about something; *I refer to your inquiry of May 25*; *all inquiries should be addressed to this department*; *he made an inquiry about buses to Harrisburg* (NOTE: plural is **inquiries**; also spelled **enquiry**)

① **insect**
[ˈɪnsekt] *noun*
small animal with six legs and a body in three parts; *a butterfly is a kind of insect*; *insects have eaten the leaves of the cabbages*; *she was stung by an insect*; **insect bite** = sting caused by an insect which goes through the skin and hurts

② **insecure**
[ɪnsɪˈkjʊər] *adjective*
(a) not safe; *she felt insecure when walking downtown alone at night*
(b) not firmly fixed; *be careful! that ladder looks insecure*

③ **insert**
1 *verb* [ɪnˈsɜrt]
to put something inside; *he inserted each leaflet into an envelope*; *insert a coin into the slot and press the button to select the drink you want*
2 *noun* [ˈɪnsɜrt]
paper that is put inside something; *the wedding invitation had an insert with a map showing how to get to the church*

① **inside**
[ɪnˈsaɪd]
1 *adverb*
indoors; *come on inside - it's cold on the street*; *it rained all afternoon, so we just sat inside and watched TV*; *is there anyone there? - the house seems quite dark inside*
2 *preposition*
(a) in; *there was nothing inside the bottle*; *she was sitting inside the car, reading a book*; *I've never been inside his office*
(b) within; **inside of two hours** = in less than two hours
3 *noun*
part that is in something; *I know their office from the outside, but what is the inside like?*; *the meat isn't cooked - the inside is still quite red*
4 *adjective*
(a) which is inside; *he put his wallet into his inside pocket*
(b) which is indoors; *the office has an inside garage*
(c) **inside information** = information that is only known by people working in a certain organization; *she said she had inside information about the company's plans*

◇ **inside out**
[ˈɪnsaɪd ˈaʊt] *phrase*
(a) turned with the inner part facing out; *he put his pajamas on inside out*
(b) **to know something inside out** = to know something very well; *she knows California inside out*

② **insides**
[ɪnˈsaɪdz] *noun*
(informal) the interior of something, especially your stomach; *my insides are upset after last night's meal*

④ **insight**
[ˈɪnsaɪt] *noun*
clear ideas or knowledge; *we appreciated the insight into the workings of the State Department he was able to bring us*

④ **insignificant**
[ɪnsɪgˈnɪfɪkənt] *adjective*
very small and unimportant; *the numbers involved are really insignificant*; *an insignificant little man with a black moustache*

② **insist**
[ɪnˈsɪst] *verb*
to state in a firm way; *he insisted that he had never touched the car*; **to insist on something** = to state in a firm way that something must be done or given; *she insisted on being given a refund*; *I insist on an immediate explanation*

④ **insofar as** *or* **in so far as**
[ˈɪnsoʊfɑr ˈæz]
(formal) to the extent that, to a certain extent, partly; *we found the assembly instructions, insofar as they applied to our model, quite easy to understand*

② **inspect**
[ɪnˈspekt] *verb*
to look at something closely; *the kitchens are regularly inspected by the health department*; *she inspected the room to see if it had been cleaned properly*; *the customs officers were inspecting the baggage of all travelers coming from Lima*

① **inspection**
[ɪnˈspekʃn] *noun*
examining something closely; *they carried out an inspection of the kitchen*

③ **inspector**
[ɪnˈspektər] *noun*
(a) senior official who examines something closely; *inspectors came to examine the condition of the house*
(b) police officer of high rank; *the inspector made a statement to the TV reporters*

③ **inspiration**
[ɪnspɪˈreɪʃn] *noun*
(a) sudden urge to write poems, to compose music, etc.; *her inspiration comes from the countryside of her native Canada*

(b) sudden good idea; *we had run out of sugar and all the stores were closed, but she had an inspiration and tried the local diner*

② **install**
[ɪn'stɔl] *verb*
to put a person into a job, a machine into a workshop, etc.; *it took the builder a week to install the new central heating system*

④ **installation**
[ɪnstə'leɪʃn] *noun*
(a) putting a machine in place; *the installation of the central heating took six days*
(b) group of machines which have been put in place; *the harbor installations are very modern; the fire seriously damaged the oil installations*

③ **installment**
[ɪn'stɔlmənt] *noun*
(a) payment of part of a total sum which is made regularly; *they are paying for the kitchen by monthly installments; you pay $40 down and twelve monthly installments of $30;* **installment plan** = system of buying something by paying a sum regularly each month until the purchase is completed; *they bought the car on the installment plan*
(b) part of something which is being shown or delivered in parts; *the next installment of the series will be shown on Monday evening*

④ **instance**
['ɪnstəns] *noun*
case, example; *there have been several instances of theft in our local school; in this instance, we will pay for the damage;* **for instance** = as an example; *some animals, for instance penguins, don't mind cold water*

② **instant**
['ɪnstənt]
1 *noun*
moment or second; *for an instant, he stood still and watched the police officers*
2 *adjective*
immediate; *a savings account can give you instant access to your money;* **instant coffee** = coffee powder to which you add hot water to make a fast cup of coffee; *she made a cup of instant coffee; do you mind if it's instant coffee, we've run out of fresh?*

① **instantly**
['ɪnstəntlɪ] *adverb*
immediately, at once; *he got my letter, and instantly wrote me back; all the passengers must have died instantly*

① **instead (of)**
[ɪn'sted] *adverb*
in place of; *since he's sick, I'm going instead of him; instead of stopping when the police officer shouted, he ran away; why don't you help me with the housework, instead of sitting and watching TV all day?; we don't have any coffee - would you like some tea instead?; if you can't go, can I go instead?*

④ **instinct**
['ɪnstɪŋkt] *noun*
something which you have from birth and have not learned; *many animals have a hunting instinct;* **by instinct** = from a feeling that you have inside you; *our little daughter seems to know by instinct if we have bought any chocolates; he seemed to feel by instinct that the plane was dangerous*

④ **instinctive**
[ɪn'stɪŋktɪv] *adjective*
natural (reaction); *my instinctive reaction was to call the police*

③ **institute**
['ɪnstɪtjut]
1 *noun*
organization set up for a special purpose; *they are proposing to set up a new institute of education; she goes to the research institute's library every week*
2 *verb*
(formal) to set up or to start; *to institute a lawsuit against someone*

③ **institution**
[ɪnstɪ'tjuʃn] *noun*
(a) organization, a society set up for a special purpose; *a prison is an institution that houses criminals;* **financial institution** = bank or other company whose work involves lending or investing large sums of money
(b) permanent custom; *to move to the suburbs has rapidly become a national institution; he spoke about the institution of marriage*
(c) *(formal)* setting up, starting; *the institution of legal proceedings against the president*

③ **instruct**
[ɪn'strʌkt] *verb*
(a) to instruct someone to do something = to tell someone officially to do something; *the inspectors instructed the restaurant to replace its kitchen equipment; the firemen instructed us to leave the building*
(b) to show someone how to do something; *my assistant will instruct you in various ways of coping with a fire*

③ **instruction**
[ɪn'strʌkʃən] *noun*
(a) orders; *he gave instructions to the driver;* **shipping instructions** = details of how goods are to be shipped and delivered; **to await instructions** = to wait for someone to tell you what to do; **according to instructions** = as the instructions show; *we assembled the machine according to the manufacturer's instructions;* **failing instructions to the contrary** = unless someone tells you to do the opposite; *failing instructions to the contrary, everyone should meet at the bus station at 9:00*
(b) indication of how something is to be done or used; *I can't read the instructions on the medicine bottle - the letters are too small; she gave us detailed instructions how to get to the*

church; **instruction manual** = book that tells you how something should be used

② **instructor**
[ɪnˈstrʌktər] *noun*
teacher, especially of a sport; **driving instructor** = person who teaches people how to drive; **ski instructor** = person who teaches people how to ski; **swimming instructor** = person who teaches people how to swim

② **instrument**
[ˈɪnstrəmənt] *noun*
piece of equipment; *the technical staff have instruments which measure the output of electricity*; **musical instrument** = device that is blown or hit, etc., to make a musical note; *he doesn't play the piano, the drums or any other musical instrument*; **wind instruments** = musical instruments which you have to blow to make a note; *she plays several wind instruments*; *see also* STRING INSTRUMENTS

② **insult**
1 *noun* [ˈɪnsʌlt]
rude word said to or about a person; *that is an insult to the government*; *the crowd shouted insults at the police*; **an insult to someone's intelligence** = something which is so obvious or easy that anyone could understand it; *that TV quiz is an insult to the intelligence of the viewers*
2 *verb* [ɪnˈsʌlt]
to say rude things about someone; *he was accused of insulting the president's wife*

② **insulting**
[ɪnˈsʌltɪŋ] *adjective*
rude; *he made some insulting remarks about the teachers*; *don't be insulting - it's a very beautiful hat*

② **insurance**
[ɪnˈʃʊrəns] *noun*
agreement with a company by which you are paid compensation for loss or damage in return for regular payments of money; *do you have travel insurance?*; **to take out an insurance against fire** = to pay money, so that if a fire happens, compensation will be paid to you; **insurance company** = company that provides insurance; *we contacted the insurance company as soon as the break-in was discovered*; **insurance policy** = document with the details of an insurance; *the insurance policy will be sent to you by mail*; **auto insurance** or **car insurance** = insuring a car, the driver and passengers in case of accident; *my auto insurance only covers drivers named in the policy*; **home insurance** = insuring a home and its contents against damage; *home insurance can be arranged by your bank*; **life insurance** = insurance paying a sum of money when someone dies; *the mortgage company requires you to take out a life insurance policy*

③ **insure**
[ɪnˈʃʊər] *verb*
to agree with a company that if you pay them a regular sum, they will pay you compensation for loss or damage to property or persons; *she insured her watch for $15,000*; *they forgot to insure the building against fire*; *have you insured the contents of the house?* (NOTE: do not confuse with **ensure**)

④ **insurer**
[ɪnˈʃʊrər] *noun*
person or company which insures; *we contacted the insurer as soon as the break-in was discovered*

④ **intact**
[ɪnˈtækt] *adjective*
in one piece, not broken; *the cups arrived intact, but several plates were broken during the move*

② **intake**
[ˈɪnteɪk] *noun*
(a) thing or things which are absorbed or taken in; *she is trying to reduce her calorie intake* or *her intake of calories*
(b) group of new students, soldiers, etc.; *we are increasing our intake of foreign students again this year*; *this year's intake of recruits has more potential officers than usual*

④ **integer**
[ˈɪntɪdʒər] *noun*
whole number, not a fraction; *integers are numbers such as 25, 1755 or -161, but not 3¾*

③ **integrate**
[ˈɪntɪgreɪt] *verb*
to link up to form a whole; *to integrate immigrants into the community*

③ **integration**
[ɪntɪˈgreɪʃn] *noun*
act of integrating; *the integration of the two schools will allow for better use of our resources*

④ **integrity**
[ɪnˈtegrɪti] *noun*
(a) honesty, strong moral principles; *his integrity is in doubt since the report on the company loan scandal*
(b) existence as a single thing or group; *we must try to maintain the integrity of the association by avoiding a split among the members*

④ **intellectual**
[ɪntəˈlektʃuəl]
1 *adjective*
(a) referring to the way you use your brain; *the puzzle requires considerable intellectual effort*; *she has great intellectual capacity*
(b) *(person)* who is good at using his or her brain; *she is more intellectual than her husband*
2 *noun*
person who believes that the brain is very important, who uses his or her brain to make a living; *left-wing intellectuals have criticized the president*

② **intelligence**
[ɪnˈtelɪdʒəns] *noun*
(a) ability to think and understand; *his intelligence is well above average*; **intelligence quotient (IQ)** = number believed to show how intelligent a person is compared to others; *she has an IQ of 110*
(b) information provided by the secret services; *intelligence gathered by our network of agents is very useful to us in planning future strategy*; **the intelligence services** = the government departments involved in spying

③ **intelligent**
[ɪnˈtelɪdʒənt] *adjective*
(a) clever, able to understand things very well; *she is more intelligent than her brother*; *he's the most intelligent child in his class*
(b) able to think and reason; *is there intelligent life on Mars?*; *an intelligent computer terminal*

③ **intend**
[ɪnˈtend] *verb*
to intend to do something = to plan to do something; *I intended to get up early but I didn't wake up till 9*; *the company intends to sue for damages*; **I intended no insult** = I did not mean my words to be taken as an insult

④ **intended**
[ɪnˈtendɪd] *adjective*
(a) which is aimed at; *they never reached their intended destination*; *the murderer followed his intended victim*
(b) provided for a special purpose; *the big plate is intended to be used for serving meat*

④ **intense**
[ɪnˈtens] *adjective*
(a) very strong or vigorous; *there was a period of intense diplomatic activity to try to get the hostages released*; *he had an intense period of study before the exams*
(b) extremely serious (person); *she is a very intense young woman*

④ **intensify**
[ɪnˈtensɪfaɪ] *verb*
(a) to become stronger; *the rain intensified and continued all night*
(b) to make something stronger; *he intensified his attacks on the government*

④ **intensive**
[ɪnˈtensɪv] *adjective*
(a) with a lot of effort; *he took a two-week intensive course in Spanish*
(b) intensive care (unit) = section of a hospital dealing with seriously sick patients who need a lot of attention; *two of the accident victims are still in intensive care*

④ **intent**
[ɪnˈtent]
1 *adjective*
determined; *she's intent on becoming a manager*
2 *noun*

aim, intention; **for** *or* **to all intents and purposes** = virtually, in almost every way; *he is for all intents and purposes the boss of the business*

③ **intention**
[ɪnˈtenʃn] *noun*
aim or plan to do something; *I can assure you that I have no intention of going to the party*; *the fans came with the deliberate intention of stirring up trouble*

④ **intentionally**
[ɪnˈtenʃnəli] *adverb*
on purpose; *the computer was left on intentionally*

④ **interact**
[ɪntəˈrækt] *verb*
to interact with someone *or* **something** = to have a sympathetic effect on someone or something; *the students are interacting well with the teachers*

④ **intercollegiate**
[ɪntərkəˈlidʒɪət] *adjective*
involving two or more colleges; *we like watching intercollegiate football*

③ **intercourse**
[ˈɪntərkɔrs] *noun*
sex act between a man and a woman; *they had intercourse on the first night they met*

② **interest**
[ˈɪntrəst]
1 *noun*
(a) special attention to something; *she takes a lot of interest in politics*; *he has no interest in what his sister is doing*; *why doesn't he take more interest in local affairs?*
(b) thing which you pay attention to; *her main interest is sailing*; *list your special interests on your résumé*
(c) percentage that is paid to someone who lends money; *if you put your money in a savings account you should get 6% interest on it*; *savings accounts pay more interest*; *how much interest do I have to pay if I borrow $1500?*; **simple interest** = interest calculated on the capital only, and not added to it; **compound interest** = interest that is added to the capital and then itself earns interest; **interest rate** *or* **rate of interest** = percentage charged for borrowing money; *the Federal Reserve Bank has raised interest rates*; *savings accounts offer a good interest rate* *or* *a good rate of interest*
(d) financial share in something; **he has a controlling interest in the company** = he owns more than 50% of the shares and so can direct how the company is run; **majority interest** = situation where someone owns a majority of the shares in a company; *he has a majority interest in a supermarket chain*; **minority interest** = situation where someone owns less than 50% of the shares in a company; **conflict of interest** = situation where a person may profit personally

from decisions which he makes in his official capacity

2 *verb*

to attract someone; *he's particularly interested in classic cars*; *nothing seems to interest him very much*; *the book didn't interest me at all*; *he tried to interest several companies in his new invention*

① **interested**

['ɪntrəstɪd] *adjective*

with a personal interest in something; *he's interested in old churches*; *she's interested in science fiction*

① **interesting**

['ɪntrəstɪŋ] *adjective*

which attracts your attention; *there's an interesting article in the newspaper about the U.S.-Mexico border*; *she didn't find the TV program very interesting*; *what's so interesting about old cars? - I find them dull*

① **interfere**

[ɪntər'fiər] *verb*

to interfere in *or* with something = to get in the way of something, to be involved in something in such a way that it doesn't work well; *her mother is always interfering in her life*; *stop interfering with my plans*

④ **interim**

['ɪntərɪm]

1 *adjective*

(report) given halfway through a period, before the final result is known; *please send us an interim report on the first year of your research project*; **interim dividend** = dividend paid at the end of six months

2 *noun*

in the interim = meanwhile; *we are still painting the office building: in the interim you will have to share an office with your boss*

③ **interior**

[ɪn'tiəriər]

1 *adjective*

inside; **interior decorating** = arranging and decorating the inside of a house (curtains, paint, wallpaper, carpets, etc.)

2 *noun*

(a) inner part (of a building, car, etc.); *she cautiously walked into the interior of the cave*; *the interior of the building is fine, but the exterior needs painting*

(b) Department of the Interior = U.S. government department dealing with the conservation and development of natural resources; **Secretary of the Interior** = U.S. government minister in charge of the Department of the Interior

③ **interior decorator** *or* **designer**

[ɪn'tiriər 'dekəreɪtər or dɪ'zaɪnər] *noun*

person who designs the inside of a building, including wallpaper, paint colors, furniture, curtains, carpets, etc.; *we have asked an interior*

designer to advise us on the design of the restaurant

④ **interjection**

[ɪntər'dʒekʃn] *noun*

exclamation, a word used to show surprise; *interjections like "ooh" are usually followed by an exclamation mark*

② **intermission**

[ɪntər'mɪʃən] *noun*

period of time between parts of a play, concert or other performance; *latecomers won't be allowed in until the first intermission*

④ **internal**

[ɪn'tɜrnl] *adjective*

inside; *the heart, lungs and other internal organs* (NOTE: the opposite, referring to the outside, is **external**)

③ **Internal Revenue Service (IRS)**

[ɪn'tɜrnl 'revənju 'sɜrvɪs] *noun*

federal government department which deals with tax; *the Internal Revenue Service wrote claiming we owe some tax from last year*; *the IRS called in a tax auditor to go over the company's books*

④ **international**

[ɪntər'næʃənəl] *adjective*

between countries; *an international conference on the environment*; *an important international company*; **international call** = telephone call to another country

② **Internet**

['ɪntərnet] *noun*

international network linking thousands of computers using telephone links; *we send messages over the Internet to hundreds of users of our products*; *he searched the Internet for information on cheap tickets to Alaska* (NOTE: also called simply **the Net**)

> COMMENT: Internet addresses of companies and other organizations are made up of two or three parts. The first part is the name of the organization (often written in a short form); the second can be .com (for a company), .co (for companies based outside the U.S.A.), .edu (for educational establishments), .net (for Internet suppliers), .gov for government organizations and .mil (for military). With the exception of the U.S.A., all countries add a further two-character country of origin name, such as .au for Australia, .cn for China, .uk for the United Kingdom, or .de for Germany

③ **interpret**

[ɪn'tɜrprət] *verb*

(a) to translate aloud what is spoken in one language into another; *the guide knows Greek, so he will interpret for us*

(b) to explain the meaning of something; *his letter was interpreted as meaning that he* refused the offer; her fit of giggles was interpreted as "yes"

④ **interpretation**
[ɪntɜrprɪ'teɪʃn] noun
(a) meaning; *a poem can have many interpretations*; *the book puts quite a different interpretation on the meaning of the rule*
(b) translating aloud what is being said in one language into another; *she is taking a course in German interpretation*
(c) way of playing a piece of music; *two of the young musicians were praised for their interpretations of Bach*

③ **interpreter**
[ɪn'tɜrprətər] noun
person who translates aloud from one language to another; *the hotel secretary will act as interpreter*; *we need an Italian interpreter*

② **interrupt**
[ɪntə'rʌpt] verb
to start talking when someone else is talking; to do something to stop something working; *excuse me for interrupting, but have you seen the office keys anywhere?*; *the strike interrupted the flow of spare parts to our factory*

③ **intersection**
[ɪntər'sekʃn] noun
place where roads cross; *Times Square is a busy New York intersection*; *the accident occurred at one of the busiest intersections in the city*

④ **interstate**
['ɪntərsteɪt]
1 adjective
involving two or more states; *we took the interstate highway to San Diego*
2 noun
main road between two states; *they took Interstate 80 to Nevada*

④ **interval**
['ɪntərvl] noun
(a) period of time between two points; *there will be bright intervals during the morning, but it will rain in the afternoon*; *there will be a short interval during which the table will be cleared*
(b) the distance between two points in a series of points; *the apple trees were planted at intervals of 10 feet*
(c) **at intervals** = from time to time; *at intervals, he almost seems normal*; **at regular intervals** = quite often; *at regular intervals during my interview, the phone would ring and the man interviewing me would take down messages*
(d) (in music) difference in pitch; *the interval between D and A is a fifth*

④ **intervention**
[ɪntər'venʃn] noun
coming between two things; acting to make a change in a system; *the Federal Reserve Bank's intervention in the banking crisis; the*

intervention of the army ended the fighting between the two political parties

② **interview**
['ɪntərvju]
1 noun
(a) questioning by one or more people of a person applying for a job; *we asked six candidates for an interview; he's had six interviews, but still no job offers; when will you attend your first interview?*
(b) discussion (on radio, TV, in a newspaper) between an important or interesting person and a journalist; *she gave an interview to the Sunday magazine*
2 verb
(a) to talk to a person applying for a job to see if he or she is suitable; *we interviewed ten candidates, but did not find anyone we liked*
(b) to ask a famous or interesting person questions and publish them afterwards; *the journalist interviewed the vice president*

④ **intimate**
1 adjective ['ɪntɪmət]
(a) very close; *she is an intimate friend from my school days*
(b) sexual; *they have had an intimate relationship for some months*
(c) very detailed; *the burglars must have had intimate knowledge of the layout of the house*
2 verb ['ɪntɪmeɪt]
to announce or to suggest, but not very clearly; *he intimated that he was going to resign and go to work in Australia*

④ **intimidate**
[ɪn'tɪmɪdeɪt] verb
to frighten someone by threatening them or appearing to threaten them; *witnesses had been intimidated by local criminals; the professor intimidated his students*

① **into**
['ɪntu] preposition
(a) (showing movement toward the inside) *she went into the store; he fell into the lake; put the cards back into their box; you can't get ten people into a taxi; we all stopped talking when he came into the room*
(b) against, colliding with; *the bus drove into a tree*
(c) (showing a change) *water turns into steam when it is heated; she changed into an evening dress for the party*; **to burst into tears** = to start crying suddenly; *when she opened the box she burst into tears*
(d) (showing that you are dividing) *try to cut the cake into ten equal pieces*; **six into four won't go** = you can't divide four by six
(e) (informal) liking something very much; *he's into ethnic music*

④ **intolerable**
[ɪn'tɒlərəbl] adjective
which you cannot bear; *the pain had become intolerable*

④ **intricate**
['ɪntrɪkət] *adjective*
very complicated, made of many different parts; *an intricate design of circles and triangles*

④ **intrigue**
[ɪn'triːg]
1 *noun*
secret plot; *she was a victim of the intrigues in the department*
2 *verb*
(a) to plot; *they intrigued to have the president removed from office*
(b) to make someone interested; *the girl's story intrigued him*

④ **intrinsic**
[ɪn'trɪnzɪk] *adjective*
forming a basic part of something; *parades are an intrinsic part of the celebrations on July 4*

② **introduce**
[ɪntrə'djuːs] *verb*
(a) to present someone to another person or to people who did not know him or her previously; *he introduced me to a friend of his called Anne*; *she introduced me to her new teacher*
(b) to announce a TV or radio program, etc.; *he introduced the start of the baseball commentary*
(c) to bring something to a new place; *several species of plant now common in the U.S. were introduced by the Europeans*

② **introduction**
[ɪntrə'dʌkʃn] *noun*
(a) letter making someone known to other people who did not know him previously; *I'm going to Moscow next week - can you give me an introduction to anyone there?*; *I'll give you an introduction to Mike Smith - he is an old friend of mine*
(b) act of presenting something for the first time; *the World Fair in Chicago was his introduction to the American business scene*
(c) piece at the beginning of a book which explains the rest of the book; *read the introduction, which gives an explanation of the book's layout*
(d) basic book about a subject; *he's the author of an introduction to mathematics*
(e) bringing into use; **the introduction of new technology** = putting new computers into a business or industry

④ **intrude**
[ɪn'truːd] *verb*
to go in with force, or to become involved where you are not wanted; *TV reporters who intrude on a film star's private life*

④ **inundate**
['ɪnʌndeɪt] *verb*
(a) to overwhelm with a lot of things or people; *we have been inundated with requests for tickets*

(b) *(formal)* to flood; *huge areas of farmland were inundated when the banks of the river gave way*

③ **invade**
[ɪn'veɪd] *verb*
(a) to attack and enter a country with an army; *William the Conqueror invaded England in 1066*
(b) *(of the press, official inspectors, etc.)* **to invade someone's privacy** = to disturb someone's private life; *she claimed that the photographers had invaded her privacy by climbing over the garden wall*

④ **invalid**
1 *adjective*
(a) ['ɪnvəlɪd] sick or disabled; *her invalid mother lives in a nursing home*
(b) [ɪn'vælɪd] not valid, not legal ; *his permit is invalid*; *the claim has been declared invalid*
2 *noun* ['ɪnvəlɪd]
sick or disabled person; *she's been an invalid since her operation*

② **invasion**
[ɪn'veɪʒn] *noun*
(a) entering a country by force with an army; *the invasion took place in early June*
(b) **invasion of privacy** = behavior of the press, official inspectors, etc., which disturbs someone's private life; *the photographers climbing over the wall was an invasion of my privacy*

① **invent**
[ɪn'vent] *verb*
(a) to create a new process or a new machine; *she invented a new type of computer terminal*; *who invented the electric car?*
(b) to think up an excuse; *when she asked him why he was late he invented some excuse*

② **invention**
[ɪn'venʃn] *noun*
(a) act of creating a new process or a new machine; *the invention of computers was made possible by developments in electronics*
(b) new device; *he tried to sell his latest invention to a Japanese automobile manufacturer*

① **inventor**
[ɪn'ventər] *noun*
person who invents new processes or new machines; *he's the inventor of the clock radio*

④ **inventory**
['ɪnvəntri] *noun*
(a) list of contents (of a house, etc.); *the landlord checked the inventory when the tenants left* (NOTE: plural in this meaning is **inventories**)
(b) stock of goods held in a warehouse; *the whole inventory was destroyed by fire*; **inventory control** = system of checking that there is not too much stock in a warehouse, but just enough to satisfy orders

② **invert**
[ɪnˈvɜrt] *verb*
to turn something upside down or back to front;
invert the mold and ease the jelly onto the dish;
*in some languages you invert the subject and
verb to form a question*

③ **inverted commas**
[ɪnˈvɜrtɪd ˈkɒməz] *noun*
printed or written marks (" ") showing that a
quotation starts or finishes; *that part of the
sentence should be in inverted commas*

② **invest**
[ɪnˈvest] *verb*
(a) to put (money) into savings, property, etc., so
that it will increase in value; *she was advised to
invest in municipal bonds; he invested all his
money in a restaurant*
(b) to spend money on something which you
believe will be useful; *we have invested in a
new fridge*

② **investigate**
[ɪnˈvestɪgeɪt] *verb*
to study or to examine something closely; *the
detective is investigating the details of the case*;
*we are investigating the possibility of going to
live in Vermont*

② **investigation**
[ɪnvestɪˈgeɪʃn] *noun*
close examination; *a police investigation into
the causes of the crash*

② **investment**
[ɪnˈvesmənt] *noun*
(a) money in the form of shares or deposits that
are expected to increase in value; *he has been
very successful with his investments*;
long-term investments *or* **short-term
investments** = shares, etc., which are likely to
increase in value over a long or short period;
*buying a house is considered a good long-term
investment*
(b) money spent by a government or a company
to improve its resources; *the economy is
suffering from a lack of investment in training*;
investment always falls during a recession

③ **investor**
[ɪnˈvestər] *noun*
person who puts money into savings or property;
a wise investor has to be cautious sometimes

② **invisible**
[ɪnˈvɪzəbl] *adjective*
which cannot be seen; *the message was written
in invisible ink and hidden inside the pages of
the telephone directory*; *compare* VISIBLE

② **invitation**
[ɪnvɪˈteɪʃn] *noun*
letter or card, asking someone to do something;
*he received an invitation to his sister's
wedding*; *she had an invitation to dinner*; **at
someone's invitation** = invited by someone; *she
spoke to the meeting at the invitation of the
committee*

② **invite**
[ɪnˈvaɪt] *verb*
to ask someone to do something, especially to
come to a party, etc.; *we invited two hundred
people to the party*; *she invited us to come in*;
she's been invited to talk to the club

③ **inviting**
[ɪnˈvaɪtɪŋ] *adjective*
which looks attractive; *the empty restaurant
didn't look very inviting*; *after the long, hot,
dusty walk the water in the lake looked inviting*

④ **invoice**
[ˈɪnvɔɪs]
1 *noun*
note sent to ask for payment for services or
goods; *our invoice dated November 10 has still
not been paid*; *they sent in their invoice six
weeks late*; *ask the salesman to make out an
invoice for $375*
2 *verb*
to send a note asking for payment for services or
goods; **we invoiced you on November 10** = we
sent you an invoice on November 10

④ **involuntarily**
[ɪnˈvɒləntrəli] *adverb*
unconsciously; *he involuntarily gave away the
secret*

④ **involuntary**
[ɪnˈvɒləntri] *adjective*
(a) done unconsciously; *his leg gave an
involuntary jerk*; *an involuntary reaction to the
news*
(b) not done willingly; *the tourists found
themselves to be involuntary hostages*

② **involve**
[ɪnˈvɒlv] *verb*
(a) to bring someone or something into an
activity, situation, dispute or crime, etc.; *we
want to involve the local community in the
decision about the new airport*; *a competition
involving teams from ten different countries*
(b) to make necessary; *going to Central Park
from here involves taking a bus and then the
subway*

② **involved**
[ɪnˈvɒlvd] *adjective*
complicated; *even his accountant said that the
tax forms were very involved*; *the whole process
of getting a visa was really involved*

③ **involvement**
[ɪnˈvɒlvmənt] *noun*
contact with someone, taking part in something;
*did she have any involvement with the music
festival?*; *the police were unable to prove his
involvement in the crime*

③ **IQ**
[ˈaɪ ˈkju] = INTELLIGENCE QUOTIENT; *she
has an IQ of 110*

① **Ireland**
[ˈaɪələnd] *noun*
large island forming the western part of the
British Isles, containing the Republic of Ireland

and Northern Ireland; *these birds are found all over Ireland*; **Northern Ireland** = the northern part of the island of Ireland, which is part of the United Kingdom

① **Ireland (the Republic of Ireland)**
['aɪələnd] *noun*
country to the west of the United Kingdom, forming the largest part of the island of Ireland, a member of the EU; *Ireland was declared a republic in 1949* (NOTE: capital: **Dublin**; people: **the Irish**; languages: **Irish, English**; currency: **euro**)

② **Irish**
['aɪrɪʃ]
1 *adjective*
referring to Ireland; *the Irish Sea lies between Ireland and Britain*; **Irish coffee** = hot coffee, served in a glass, with Irish whiskey added to it and whipped cream poured on top
2 *noun*
(a) Celtic language still spoken in parts of Ireland; *Eire is the Irish name for the Republic of Ireland*
(b) the Irish = people who live in Ireland; *the Irish are famous for their folk music*

① **iron**
['aɪən]
1 *noun*
(a) common gray metal; *the old gates are made of iron* (NOTE: Chemical element: chemical symbol: **Fe**; atomic number: **26**; note also, no plural in this meaning: **some iron, lumps of iron, pieces of iron**)
(b) electric device that is heated to make clothes smooth after washing; *don't leave the iron plugged in, it will burn the clothes*; *if your iron is not hot enough it won't make the shirts smooth*
(c) golf club with a metal head
2 *verb*
(a) to make cloth smooth, using an iron; *he was ironing his shirt when he got a phone call*; *her skirt doesn't look as though it has been ironed*
(b) to iron out = to sort out, to solve a problem; *we had a very productive meeting - all the remaining problems were ironed out*

② **ironing**
['aɪənɪŋ] *noun*
clothes that have been washed and are ready to be ironed; *she was doing the ironing*; *there's a lot of ironing waiting to be done*

② **ironing board**
['aɪənɪŋ 'bɔːd] *noun*
special narrow table used when ironing clothes

④ **irony**
['aɪrəni] *noun*
(a) way of referring to something where you say the opposite of what you mean; *do I detect a note of irony in his letter?*
(b) situation when something happens at the wrong moment, as if on purpose; *the irony of it*

was that the rain finally stopped on the last day of our vacation

② **irregular**
[ɪ'regjʊlər] *adjective*
(a) not regular; *an irregular pattern of lines and circles*; *his heart had an irregular beat*
(b) not level; *an irregular stone path leads across the garden*
(c) not happening always at the same time; *his payments are very irregular*; *he makes irregular visits to his mother in the hospital*
(d) not according to the rules; *this procedure is highly irregular*

④ **irrelevant**
[ɪ'reləvənt] *adjective*
not relevant, with no connection to the subject; *his comments about the weather were irrelevant to the subject being discussed*; *whether he's rich or not is irrelevant - I love him!*

③ **irritable**
['ɪrɪtəbl] *adjective*
easily annoyed; *he was tired and irritable, and snapped at the children*

③ **irritate**
['ɪrɪteɪt] *verb*
(a) to annoy; *it irritates me when flights are delayed*
(b) to make a burning feeling; *some plant oils irritate the skin*

③ **irritated**
['ɪrɪteɪtɪd] *adjective*
annoyed; *"leave me alone," she said in an irritated voice*

③ **irritating**
['ɪrɪteɪtɪŋ] *adjective*
which annoys; *it's irritating to see how badly the work has been done*; *he has the irritating habit of scratching the top of his head*

③ **IRS**
['aɪɑr'es] = INTERNAL REVENUE SERVICE

① **is**
[ɪz]
see BE

④ **Islam**
['ɪzlæm] *noun*
the religion of the Muslims, founded by Muhammad

① **island**
['aɪlənd] *noun*
piece of land with water all around it; *they live on a little island in the middle of the river*; *the Caribbean islands are favorite vacation destinations*

① **isn't**
['ɪznt] = IS NOT

④ **isolated**
['aɪsəleɪtɪd] *adjective*
(a) separated from others; *they live in an isolated village in the hills*

(b) one only; **isolated attack** = single attack, which has not been repeated; *an isolated case of mugging*

② **issue**
['ɪʃu]
1 *noun*
(a) problem; *the main issues will be discussed at the meeting*; **to make an issue of something** = to have a big discussion about something; *she's apologized so don't try to make an issue of it*; **the point at issue** = the question which is being discussed; *the point at issue is whether the government is prepared to compromise*; **to take issue with someone** = to disagree with someone
(b) publication of a book; putting new stamps on sale; putting new coins or notes into circulation; *there will be a new issue of stamps this month*
(c) giving out of permits, licenses, uniforms, etc.; *the issue of hunting licenses has been delayed*
(d) one copy of a newspaper or magazine; *we bought the January issue of the magazine*
(e) giving out new shares; **rights issue** = giving stockholders the right to buy more shares more cheaply
2 *verb*
(a) to put (new stamps) on sale; to publish (books); to put (new coins or notes) into circulation; *the new set of stamps will be issued next week*; *initially the euro will be issued alongside national currencies*
(b) to give out or to hand out permits, licenses, uniforms, etc.; *the government issued a report*; *the secretary of state issued guidelines for expenditure*
(c) to come out; *smoke began to issue from the hole in the ground*

① **it**
[ɪt] *pronoun referring to a thing*
(a) *(used to show something which has just been mentioned)* *what do you want me to do with the box? - put it down*; *where's the box? - it's here*; *she picked up a potato and then dropped it on the ground*; *I put my book down somewhere and now I can't find it*; *where's the newspaper? - it's on the chair*; *the dog's thirsty, give it something to drink*
(b) *(referring to no particular thing)* *look! - it's snowing*; *it's miles from here to the train station*; *it's almost impossible to get a ticket at this time of year*; *what time is it? - it's ten o'clock*; *it's dangerous to use an electric saw when it's wet* (NOTE: **it's = it is** or **it has**; do not confuse with **its**)

③ **IT**
['aɪ 'ti] = INFORMATION TECHNOLOGY

② **Italian**
[ɪ'tæljən]
1 *adjective*
referring to Italy; *my wife loves Italian food*; *we bought some Italian wine last week*

2 *noun*
(a) person from Italy; *the Italians have a passion for soccer*
(b) language spoken in Italy; *Italian is one of the languages that are derived from Latin*; *we go to Italy on vacation every year, and the children speak good Italian*

③ **italic**
[ɪ'tælɪk]
1 *adjective*
sloping (of letters); *the text under the illustrations is printed in italic type*
2 *noun*
italics = sloping letters; *this example is printed in italics* (NOTE: the other two main styles of print are **roman** and **bold**)

> COMMENT: as the word suggests, italics were invented in Italy (in the fifteenth century). Italics are used to show words that you want to highlight in some way, but are not used for whole paragraphs

① **Italy**
['ɪtəli] *noun*
country in southern Europe, south of France, Switzerland and Austria; *Italy is the home of great sixteenth century painters like Michelangelo and Raphael* (NOTE: capital: **Rome**; people: **Italians**; language: **Italian**; currency: **euro**)

① **itch**
[ɪtʃ]
1 *noun*
place on the skin where you want to scratch; *I've got an itch in the middle of my back which I just can't reach* (NOTE: plural is **itches**)
2 *verb*
to make someone want to scratch; *the cream made my skin itch more than before*

② **item**
['aɪtəm] *noun*
(a) thing (in a list); *we are discussing item four on the agenda*; *do you have any items of jewelry in your baggage?*; *please find enclosed an order for the following items from your catalog*; *I couldn't buy several items on the shopping list because the store had run out*
(b) piece of information, for example on a news program; *here is a summary of the main items of news or the main news items*

① **it'll**
[ɪtl] *short for* IT WILL

② **its**
[ɪts] *adjective referring to "it"*
I can't use the tractor - one of its tires is flat; *the company pays its staff very badly* (NOTE: do not confuse with **it's**)

① **it's**
[ɪts] *short for* IT IS, IT HAS

② **itself**
[ɪt'self] *pronoun referring to a thing*
(a) *(referring to an object) the dog seems to have hurt itself; the screw had worked itself loose*; **all by itself** = alone, with no one helping; *the church stands all by itself in the middle of the street; the bus started to move all by itself*
(b) *(for emphasis) if the plug is all right there must be something wrong with the computer itself*

① **I've**
[aɪv] = I HAVE

② **ivory**
['aɪvəri] *noun*
(a) hard white substance from an elephant's tooth; *she bought some finely carved ivory figures; trade in ivory has been banned*
(b) **ivory tower** = imaginary place where an intellectual can live, isolated from the ordinary world; *he thinks he lives in an ivory tower, but he still has to pay his rent each month*

② **ivy**
['aɪvi] *noun*
plant which climbs up walls and trees; *the building is covered with ivy*; **Ivy League** = group of colleges in the Eastern U.S. with a good reputation; *Yale and Harvard are both Ivy League schools*

Jj

② **jab**
[dʒæb] *verb*
to poke with something sharp; *he jabbed the piece of meat with his fork; she jabbed me in the back with her umbrella* (NOTE: **jabbing - jabbed**)

② **jack**
[dʒæk] *noun*
(a) device for raising something heavy, especially an automobile; *I used the jack to lift up the car and take the wheel off*
(b) *(in playing cards)* the card with the face of a young man, with a value between the queen and the ten; *I won because I had the jack of hearts*
(c) electric or telephone plug with a single pin; *when he had plugged the jack in he could use the telephone*

① **jacket**
['dʒækɪt] *noun*
(a) short coat worn with pants; *he was wearing a blue jacket and brown pants; this orange jacket shows up in the dark when I ride my bike; take your jacket off if you are hot; see also* DINNER JACKET, LIFE JACKET, YELLOW JACKET
(b) paper cover wrapped around a book; *the design of a book jacket has to be very attractive to make people want to buy the book*

① **jackrabbit**
['dʒækræbɪt] *noun*
large North American hare with long ears and long back legs; *we saw a jackrabbit in the woods*

① **jail**
[dʒeɪl]
1 *noun*
prison; *she was sent to jail for three months*
2 *verb*
to put someone in prison; *he was jailed for six years*

② **jalopy**
[dʒæ'lɒpi] *noun*
(informal) an old car in bad condition; *he was driving a jalopy*

① **jam**
[dʒæm]
1 *noun*
(a) sweet food made by boiling fruit and sugar together; *a pot of strawberry jam; do you want jam or honey on your bread?; we made jam with the fruit in the garden; do you have any more jam - the jar is empty?* (NOTE: no plural in this meaning: **some jam, a pot of jam**; note also the difference with **marmalade** which is made from sour fruit like oranges and lemons)
(b) block which happens when there are too many things in too small a space; *there is a paper jam in the printer*; **traffic jam** = too much traffic on the roads, so that automobiles and trucks can't move; *the accident on the bridge caused a traffic jam; there are rush hour jams every evening between 5:00 and 6:30*
(c) *(informal)* awkward situation; *he's gotten himself in a jam*
2 *verb*
(a) *(of machine)* to stick and not to be able to

move; *hold on - the paper has jammed in the printer*
(b) to force things into a small space; *don't try to jam all those boxes into the back of the car*; *the telephone system was jammed with calls* (NOTE: jamming - jammed)

① **Jamaica**
[dʒəˈmeɪkə] *noun*
country consisting of an island in the Caribbean Sea, one of the islands that make up the West Indies (NOTE: capital: **Kingston**; people: **Jamaicans**; language: **English**; currency: **Jamaican dollar**)

② **Jamaican**
[dʒəˈmeɪkən]
1 *adjective*
referring to Jamaica; *a bottle of Jamaican rum*
2 *noun*
person from Jamaica; *Jamaicans are passionate about soccer*

② **jamboree**
[dʒæmbəˈri] *noun*
large party or social gathering; *we went to a country music jamboree*

② **janitor**
[ˈdʒænɪtər] *noun*
person who looks after a building; *go and ask the janitor to replace the lightbulb in the entrance hall*

① **January**
[ˈdʒænjuəri] *noun*
first month of the year, followed by February; *he was born on January 26*; *we never go on vacation in January because it's too cold*; *we all went skiing last January* (NOTE: **January 26**: say "January twenty-sixth")

① **Japan**
[dʒəˈpæn] *noun*
country in the Far East, formed of several islands to the east of China and south of Korea; *Japan hosted the 1998 Winter Olympics* (NOTE: capital: **Tokyo**; people: **the Japanese**; language: **Japanese**; currency: **yen**)

② **Japanese**
[dʒæpəˈniz]
1 *adjective*
referring to Japan; *a typical Japanese meal can include rice and raw fish*
2 *noun*
(a) the Japanese = people from Japan; *the Japanese are very formal*
(b) language spoken in Japan; *he has lived in Japan for some time and speaks quite good Japanese*; *we bought a Japanese phrase book before we went to Japan*

① **jar**
[dʒɑr]
1 *noun*
container for jam, etc., usually made of glass; *there was some honey left in the bottom of the jar*; *open another jar of jam - this one is empty*;

cookie jar = special jar for putting cookies in; *he kept the money in an empty cookie jar*
2 *verb*
to produce an unpleasant effect; *the sound of the drill jarred my ears*; *those orange curtains jar with the purple cushions* (NOTE: jarring - jarred)

① **jaw**
[dʒɔ] *noun*
bones in the face which hold the teeth and form the mouth; **upper jaw** = part of the skull holding the top set of teeth; **bottom jaw** *or* **lower jaw** = bone holding the lower teeth, which moves to make the mouth open or shut; *she hit him so hard that she broke his lower jaw*

② **jaywalk**
[ˈdʒeɪwɒk] *verb*
to walk across a street at a place where it is not allowed; *the police officer saw her jaywalking and wrote her a ticket*

① **jaywalker**
[ˈdʒeɪwɒkər] *noun*
someone who jaywalks; *the jaywalker was given a ticket by the police officer*

② **jazz**
[dʒæz] *noun*
type of music with a strong rhythm, first played in the southern United States; *I'm a real jazz fan*; *Louis Armstrong was one of the kings of jazz*

② **jealous**
[ˈdʒeləs] *adjective*
feeling annoyed because you want something which belongs to someone else; *John was jealous of Mark because all the girls crowded around him*; *she was jealous of his new automobile*; *her new boyfriend is real handsome - I'm jealous!*

② **jealousy**
[ˈdʒeləsi] *noun*
feeling of being annoyed because someone has something which you don't have; *his jealousy of his wife's success broke their marriage*

① **jeans**
[dʒinz] *noun*
pants made of a type of strong cotton, often blue; *I like wearing jeans better than wearing a skirt*; *she came into the restaurant in her jeans*; *he bought a new pair of jeans*; **designer jeans** = fashionable jeans designed by a famous designer (NOTE: sometimes also called **blue jeans**)

① **Jell-O**™
[ˈdʒeləʊ] *noun*
trademark for a fruit jelly dessert

① **jelly**
[ˈdʒeli] *noun*
(a) type of jam made of fruit juice boiled with sugar; *she loves peanut butter and jelly sandwiches*; *see also* ROLL

(c) to turn to jelly = to tremble and become soft; *when he heard the sound of the bell his legs turned to jelly*

④ **jelly bean**
['dʒeli 'biːn] *noun*
sugar-coated candy, shaped like a bean

① **jerk**
[dʒɜːrk]
1 *noun*
(a) sudden sharp pull; *he felt a jerk on the fishing line*
(b) *(slang)* stupid person; *don't ask that jerk anything!*
2 *verb*
to pull something sharply; *he jerked the rope*

③ **jersey**
['dʒɜːrzi] *noun*
(a) woolen pullover which fits close to your body; *she was knitting a pink jersey for the new baby*
(b) special shirt worn by a member of a soccer team, etc.; *after the game the players swapped jerseys with the other team*

① **jet**
[dʒet]
1 *noun*
(a) long narrow stream of liquid or gas; *a jet of water put out the flames*
(b) aircraft with jet engines; *jets flew low overhead*; **jet lag** = being tired after flying by jet aircraft across several time zones; *she had terrible jet lag after flying home from Europe*
(c) jet black = very black and shiny; *a new jet black car*
2 *verb*
(informal) to travel by jet aircraft; *she jetted off to Los Angeles for a short vacation; Nice airport was busy with stars jetting in for the Cannes Film Festival* (NOTE: **jetting - jetted**)

③ **jet engine**
['dʒet 'endʒɪn] *noun*
engine which is worked by a jet of gas; *the two jet engines are located on either side of the plane*

① **jewel**
['dʒuːəl] *noun*
precious stone, such as a diamond; *I'll just lock up these jewels in the safe; she admitted having stolen the jewels*

① **jewelry**
['dʒuːəlri] *noun*
pretty decorations to be worn, made from precious stones, gold, silver, etc.; *the burglar stole all her jewelry* (NOTE: no plural)

② **jingle**
['dʒɪŋgl]
1 *noun*
(a) sound made when little pieces of metal knock together; *the jingle of little bells round the horses' necks*
(b) song with a simple rhythm; **advertising jingle** = tune that advertises a product

2 *verb*
to make a sound like little pieces of metal knocking together; *the bell jingled as he went into the store*

① **job**
[dʒɒb] *noun*
(a) regular work which you get paid for; *he applied for a job as a bus driver; he's finding it difficult getting a job because he can't drive; when the factory closed, hundreds of people lost their jobs*; **to be out of a job** = to lose your regular paid work; *if they introduce that new computer system, the secretary will be out of her job*
(b) piece of work; *don't sit down, there are a couple of jobs I want you to do; he does all sorts of little electrical jobs around the house;* **to make a good job of something** = to do something well; *they made a very good job of mending the table;* **odd jobs** = small items of work, especially repairs, done in the house; *he does odd jobs for us around the house*

② **jobless**
['dʒɒbləs]
1 *adjective*
with no job; *jobless teenagers pose a problem for the government*
2 *noun*
the jobless = people who have no jobs (NOTE: takes a plural verb)

② **jock**
[dʒɒk] *noun*
(informal) college athlete

② **jockey**
['dʒɒki] *noun*
(a) person who rides horses in races; *he's the youngest jockey to ride in the race*
(b) disk jockey (DJ) = person who plays music disks at a disco or on radio; *who's your favorite radio DJ?*

② **jog**
[dʒɒg]
1 *noun*
(a) slow run, especially when taken for exercise; *she goes for a jog every morning*
(b) quite slow running pace; *he ran at a jog around the park*
2 *verb*
(a) to run at an easy pace, for exercise; *he jogged along the river bank for two miles; she was listening to her portable radio as she was jogging*
(b) to move at a steady, but rather slow pace; *the train jogged through the suburbs, stopping at every station*
(c) to push lightly; *someone jogged my elbow and I spilled my drink;* **it jogged his memory** = it made him remember; *the police are hoping that the film from the security camera will jog people's memories* (NOTE: **jogging - jogged**)

② jogging

['dʒɒɡɪŋ] *noun*

running at an easy pace for exercise; *jogging every morning is good for you*; **to go jogging** = to run at an easy pace for exercise; *they went jogging along the sidewalks near their home*

① join

[dʒɔɪn] *verb*

(a) to put things together; *you have to join the two pieces of wood together*; *the rooms were joined together by making a door in the wall*

(b) to come together; *go on for about two hundred yards, until a road joins this one*; *the two rivers join about four miles beyond the town*

(c) to become a member of a club, group, etc.; *after college, he is going to join the police*; *she joined the army because she wanted to travel*

(d) **to join a firm** = to start work with a company; *he joined on January 1* = he started work on January 1

(e) to do something with someone; *we're going to have a cup of coffee - would you like to join us?*

② join in

['dʒɔɪn 'ɪn] *verb*

to take part in something done as a group; *he started to sing and everyone else joined in*

② joint

[dʒɔɪnt]

1 *noun*

(a) place where several pieces are attached, especially in building; *the joints of the drawer have come loose*

(b) place where bones come together and can move, such as the knee or elbow; *her elbow joint hurt after her game of tennis*

(c) *(informal)* club or restaurant; *let's go to Rick's joint*

(d) *(slang)* cigarette with marijuana; *he smoked a couple of joints during the evening*

2 *adjective*

combined, with two or more things linked together; **joint account** = bank account for two people, such as husband and wife; **joint authors** = two authors who have written a book together; **joint ownership** = owning of a property by several owners

④ jointly

['dʒɔɪntlɪ] *adverb*

together with one or more other people; *this law applies when two or more people own a property jointly*; *the prize was awarded jointly to the British and Russian teams*

② join up

['dʒɔɪn 'ʌp] *verb*

(a) to link things together; *they joined up several loops to make a chain*

(b) to join the military; *he joined up when he was 18 and soon rose to become an officer*

① joke

[dʒəʊk]

1 *noun*

thing said or done to make people laugh; *she poured water down his neck as a joke*; *they all laughed at his jokes*; *he told jokes all evening*; **practical joke** = trick played on someone to make other people laugh; *he's fond of practical jokes - once he tied a can to the back of his father's automobile*

2 *verb*

to tell jokes; to say or do something to make people laugh; *he used to joke about always being late for the office*; **he was only joking** = he did not mean it seriously; **you're joking!** *or* **you must be joking!** = you are not being serious, are you?; *he's just bought a limo - you must be joking, he's only the office boy!*

① jolly

['dʒɒli] *adjective*

happy, pleasant, enjoyable; *it was marvelous to see all the jolly faces of the children*; *her birthday party was a very jolly affair* (NOTE: jollier - jolliest)

② journal

['dʒɜrnl] *noun*

(a) *(formal)* diary; *he kept a journal during his visit to China*; *she wrote a journal of the gradual progress of her illness*

(b) magazine which comes out every month or three months, especially one on a learned subject; *she edits the journal of the Historical Society*

(c) book for recording each day's business; *she wrote the day's sales in the sales journal*

③ journalism

['dʒɜrnəlɪzm] *noun*

profession of writing for newspapers or reporting on events for radio or TV; *she took a journalism course to help her chances of getting a job on a newspaper*

③ journalist

['dʒɜrnəlɪst] *noun*

person who writes for newspapers or reports on events for radio or TV; *journalists asked the police officer some very awkward questions*; *the movie stars were greeted by journalists from around the world on the first night of the new movie*

① journey

['dʒɜrnɪ]

1 *noun*

traveling, usually a long distance; *it's at least two days' journey from here*; *they went on a train journey across China*; *she has a difficult journey to work every day - she has to change buses twice*

2 *verb*

(formal) to travel; *they journeyed many miles to find the treasure*; *the book tells the story of a man who journeyed from Italy to China in the 13th century*

① **joy**
[dʒɔɪ] *noun*
state of being very happy; *we all wished them great joy on their wedding day; they were full of joy at seeing their son again*

③ **Jr.**
['dʒuniər] = JUNIOR

① **judge**
[dʒʌdʒ]
1 *noun*
(a) person appointed to make legal decisions in a court of law; *he was convicted for stealing, but the judge let him off with a small fine*
(b) person who decides which is the best entry in a competition; *the three judges of the beauty contest couldn't agree*
(c) person with good sense; *he's a good judge of character*
2 *verb*
(a) to make decisions in a court of law or competition, etc.; *he was judged guilty; her painting was judged the best and she won first prize*
(b) to estimate a value, to decide on the quality of a situation; *to be a good driver you need to be able to judge distances well; the senator judged it would be impossible for him to win the election so he dropped out of the race*

② **judgment** *or* **judgement**
['dʒʌdʒmənt] *noun*
(a) legal decision by a judge or court; *the judgment of the tribunal was fair; the defendant will appeal the judgment*
(b) ability to see things clearly and to make good decisions; *he trusted his wife's judgment in everything;* **against your better judgment** = although you feel it is not the right thing to do; *he accepted the money against his better judgment; against her better judgment, she reported her son to the police*

④ **jug**
[dʒʌg] *noun*
container with a handle, used for pouring liquids; *could we have another jug of water, please?*

① **juice**
[dʒus] *noun*
liquid from fruit, vegetables, meat, etc.; *they charged me $3 for two glasses of orange juice; she had a glass of grapefruit juice for breakfast*

① **juicy**
['dʒusi] *adjective*
full of juice; *juicy peaches taste wonderful; these are the juiciest oranges we've had this year* (NOTE: **juicier - juiciest**)

① **July**
[dʒu'laɪ] *noun*
seventh month of the year, between June and August; *she was born in July - her birthday is July 23; we went to Spain last July; July is always one of the busiest months for vacations* (NOTE: **July 23:** say "July twenty-third")

① **jump**
[dʒʌmp]
1 *noun*
sudden movement into the air; *the jump was higher than she thought and she hurt her leg; (in sports)* **long jump** *or* **high jump** = sport where you see who can jump the furthest or highest; *she won a gold medal in the high jump*
2 *verb*
(a) to go suddenly into the air off the ground; *quick, jump on that bus - it's going downtown!; the horse jumped over the fence; she jumped down from the chair*
(b) to jump the gun = to start before it is your turn, before it is the right time
(c) to move upwards suddenly; *the price of oil has jumped from $15.50 to $30.00*
(d) to make a sudden movement because you are frightened; *she jumped when I came up behind her quietly and said "Boo!"; when they fired the gun, it made me jump*
(e) to miss something; *the typewriter jumped a line; I think I jumped a page in my book*

② **jump at**
['dʒʌmp 'æt] *verb*
to accept eagerly; *she jumped at the chance to work in Australia*

③ **junction**
['dʒʌŋkʃn] *noun*
place where railroads or roads meet; *our motel is at the junction of the two highways*

① **June**
[dʒun] *noun*
sixth month of the year, between May and July; *she was born in June: her birthday is June 17; last June we had a vacation in Canada* (NOTE: **June 17:** say "June seventeenth")

① **jungle**
['dʒʌngl] *noun*
thick tropical forest which is difficult to travel through; *they explored the jungle, hoping to find rare birds*

② **junior**
['dʒuniər]
1 *adjective*
(a) younger, less important; *he was the junior member of the team*
(b) junior college = community college, a two-year college at which students can learn a technical subject or prepare to enter a college or university; **junior high (school)** = school for children between the ages of about 12 and 15 (grades 7 through 9)
2 *noun*
(a) student in the third year at a high school or college; *my son is currently a junior at UCLA*
(b) son in a family who has the same name as his father; *John Smith, Junior (Jr)*

① **junk**
[dʒʌŋk] *noun*
(a) useless articles, rubbish; *don't keep that - it's junk; you should throw away all that junk*

under your bed; **junk food** = bad commercially prepared food which is less nutritious than food made at home; *they just watch TV and live off junk food* (NOTE: no plural in this meaning)

(b) large Chinese sailboat; *Hong Kong harbor was full of junks*

④ **jurisdiction**
[dʒuərɪs'dɪkʃn] *noun*
legal power over someone or something; *the judge has no jurisdiction over the case*; **within the jurisdiction of the court** = in the legal power of the court; **outside the jurisdiction of the court** = not covered by the legal power of the court; *the matter is outside the jurisdiction of the court*

② **jury**
['dʒuəri] *noun*
(a) group of citizens who are sworn to decide whether someone is guilty or innocent on the basis of the evidence given in a court of law; *the jury brought in a verdict of not guilty*; **jury duty** = service which all citizens may be asked to perform, to sit on a jury
(b) the jury is still out on this = no one is sure what the result will be
(c) group of judges in a competition; *he's been chosen to serve on the jury for the literary prize*

① **just**
[dʒʌst]
1 *adverb*
(a) exactly; *thank you, that's just what I was looking for*; *just how many of students have got computers?*; *what time is it? - it's just seven o'clock*; *he's just fifteen - his birthday was yesterday*
(b) just enough = scarcely, almost not enough; *she had just enough money to pay the check*; *he had just enough time to get dressed before the police arrived*
(c) *(showing a very small quantity in space or time)* *your umbrella is just by the door*; *don't come in just yet - we're not ready*; *can you wait just a minute?*
(d) *(showing the immediate past or future)* *the bus has just arrived from Little Rock*; *she had just got into her bath when the phone rang*; *I don't want any coffee, thank you, I'm just going out*; *thanks for calling - I was just going to phone you*
(e) only; *we're just good friends, nothing more*; *I've been to Mexico City just once*
2 *adjective*
fair, without favoring anyone; *the decision of the court was just*

◇ **just about**
['dʒʌst ə'baut]
(a) nearly, more or less; *I've just about finished my homework*; *the meal's just about ready*
(b) just about to do something = going to do something very soon; *we were just about to leave*; *they were just about to go to bed when someone knocked on the door*

◇ **just as**
['dʒʌst 'æz]
(a) at the same time; *just as I got into the car there was a loud bang*
(b) in exactly the same way; *the movie is just as good as the book*; *it is just as hot inside the house as it is outside*; *she loves her cats just as other people love their children*

◇ **just now**
['dʒʌst 'nau]
(a) at the present time; *we're very busy in the office just now*
(b) a short time ago; *I saw her just now in the post office*

② **justice**
['dʒʌstɪs] *noun*
(a) fair treatment in law; *justice must always be seen to be done*
(b) to bring someone to justice = to start legal action against someone; **rough justice** = judging someone in a rough and unfair way
(c) to do justice to = to treat something as it deserves; *I wasn't very hungry so I couldn't do justice to your marvelous meal*; *his rather dull description doesn't do justice to the garden*
(d) magistrate; **Justice of the Peace** = magistrate or local judge

③ **justification**
[dʒʌstɪfɪ'keɪʃn] *noun*
(a) reason which shows that something has been done correctly; *what was his justification for doing that?*; *they tried to find some justification for what they had done*
(b) *(in typing and printing)* spacing out the words in the lines so that the right margin is straight; *we use an automatic justification program*

③ **justify**
['dʒʌstɪfaɪ] *verb*
(a) to show that something is fair, to prove that something is right; *how can you justify spending all that money?*
(b) the end justifies the means = if your final aim is good or honorable, you are right to do anything that is necessary to achieve it
(c) *(in printing)* to space letters and figures on the page so that the ends of lines are neat and straight; *the text should be fully justified*

③ **juvenile**
['dʒuvənaɪl]
1 *adjective*
(a) referring to young people; *young offenders are tried before a juvenile court*
(b) silly, like a young person; *the new comedy series on TV is really juvenile*
2 *noun*
(formal) young person; *the police entered the club and arrested four people, two of them juveniles*

Kk

K, k
[keɪ]
eleventh letter of the alphabet, between J and L; *K is the eleventh letter of the alphabet; in words like "know" and "knock" the K ist not pronounced*

K
[keɪ] *abbreviation*
one thousand dollars; **$30K** = thirty thousand dollars (NOTE: say "thirty K": "the salary is around thirty K")

kangaroo
[kæŋgə'ru] *noun*
large Australian animal, which carries the young animals in a pouch

keel
[kil] *noun*
long beam in the bottom of a ship; *the dolphins swam under the keel and came up on the other side of the ship*

keen
[kin] *adjective*
(a) **keen on something** *or* **someone** = liking something or someone, enthusiastic about something; *he's keen on keeping fit - he goes running every morning; I am not very keen on classical music; I don't think she's very keen on her new math teacher*
(b) **keen competition** = strong competition; *we are facing some keen competition from European manufacturers*
(c) very sensitive; *bats have a keen sense of hearing* (NOTE: **keener - keenest**)

keep
[kip] *verb*
(a) to have for a long time or for ever; *can I keep the newspaper I borrowed?; I don't want that book anymore, you can keep it; the police kept my gun and won't give it back*
(b) to continue to do something; *the clock kept going even after I dropped it on the floor; he had to keep smiling so that people would think he was pleased; keep quiet or they'll hear you ; the food will keep warm in the oven*
(c) to have or put something in a particular place; *I keep my car keys in my pocket; where do you keep the paper for the laser printer?*
(d) to make someone stay in a place or state; *it's cruel to keep animals in cages; I was kept late at the office; they kept us waiting for half an hour; we put the plates in the oven to keep them warm*
(e) to prevent someone from doing something or from going somewhere; *she kept him from going out and playing baseball; he kept her from seeing her friends*
(f) to stay; **let's keep in touch** = we mustn't lose contact with each other; **she kept him company** = she stayed with him; **to keep an eye on** = to watch carefully; *he's keeping an eye on the store while I'm away*; **to keep your ear to the ground** = to follow what is happening and know all about something
(g) **to keep a diary** = to write notes every day about what has happened; *she kept a diary of her vacation in Oregon*
(h) to stay in good condition and not to go rotten; *strawberries don't keep* (NOTE: **keeps - keeping - kept** [kept])

keep back
['kip 'bæk] *verb*
(a) to hold on to something which you should give to someone; *they kept back $30 from the deposit to cover damage to the carpet*
(b) **to keep something back from someone** = not to tell someone information which you could give to them; *I have the feeling that she's keeping something back from us*

keep down
['kip 'daʊn] *verb*
(a) to keep at a low level; *keep your voice down, the police will hear us!*
(b) to keep from getting ahead; *nothing's going to keep me down*

keeper
['kipər] *noun*
(a) person in charge of a certain type of animal in a zoo; *an elephant keeper*
(b) person in charge of a section of a museum; *the keeper of Roman coins in the museum*

keep off
['kip 'ɒf] *verb*
not to walk on; *keep off the grass!*

keep on
['kip 'ɒn] *verb*
to continue to do something; *my computer keeps on breaking down; the automobiles kept on moving even though the road was covered with snow*

keep out
['kip 'aʊt] *verb*
(a) to stop someone going in; *there were "Keep Out!" notices around the building site; we have*

put up notices telling people to keep their dogs out of the field where the lambs are
(b) not to get involved; *he kept out of the quarrel*; *try to keep out of trouble with the police*

③ **keep to**
['kɪp 'tu] *verb*
(a) to stay in a position; *when you drive in England, remember to keep to the left*
(b) not to move away from a subject; *let's keep to the subject of the new interstate*
(c) to keep something to yourself = to keep something secret, not to talk about something; *he doesn't want to talk about his illness, he'd rather keep it to himself*

② **keep up**
['kɪp 'ʌp] *verb*
to make something stay at the same high level; *he finds it very difficult to keep up his German*; *they won't be able to keep up that speed for very long*; **keep it up!** = continue doing what you doing!; *you're doing very well - keep it up!*

② **keep up with**
['kɪp 'ʌp wɪð] *verb*
(a) to go at the same speed as; *my foot hurts, that's why I can't keep up with the others*; *his salary hasn't kept up with the cost of living*; **to keep up with the Joneses** = to try to do the same things as your neighbors or friends to show that you have as much money as they have
(b) to keep yourself informed about; *have you kept up with the news from Russia?*

① **kept**
[kept]
see KEEP

① **ketchup**
['ketʃʌp] *noun*
spiced tomato sauce, available in bottles; *do you want some ketchup with your hamburgers?*

① **kettle**
['ketl] *noun*
a container with a lid and spout, used for boiling water; *turn the gas up, the kettle hasn't boiled yet*; **the kettle's boiling** = the water in the kettle is boiling

① **key**
[kɪ]
1 *noun*
(a) piece of metal used to open a lock; *I can't start the car, I lost the key*; *where did you put the front door key?*; **key ring** = ring on which you can put several keys to keep them together; *the garage gave me a key ring with their phone number on it*
(b) part of a computer, piano, etc., which you push down with your fingers; *the "F" key always sticks*; *there are sixty-four keys on the keyboard*; **control key** = key on a computer that works part of a program; **shift key** = key on a typewriter or computer keyboard that makes capital letters or switches to another function;

hold down the shift key while you click on "help"
(c) explanation of a problem; *the key to the signs is written under the diagram*
(d) system of musical tones; *the symphony is written in the key of F major*
2 *adjective*
most important; *the key person in the company is the head of the sales department*; *oil is a key industry*
3 *verb*
to type letters or figures on a keyboard; *she keyed in the data*

② **keyboard**
['kɪbɔrd]
1 *noun*
set of keys on a computer, piano, etc.; *she spilled her coffee on the computer keyboard*; *he practices on the keyboard every day*
2 *verb*
to put data into a computer, using a keyboard; *she was keyboarding the figures*

③ **kg**
= KILOGRAM

① **kick**
[kɪk]
1 *noun*
(a) hitting with your foot; *the goalkeeper gave the ball a kick*; *(in soccer, rugby)* **free kick** = kick that a player is allowed to make without anyone opposing him, to punish the other side for something that they have done; *the referee awarded a free kick*
(b) *(informal)* thrill, feeling of excitement; *he gets a kick out of watching football on TV*; **he did it for kicks** = he did it to give himself some excitement
(c) *(informal)* strong effect; *my! this drink has a kick in it!*
2 *verb*
(a) to hit something with your foot; *he kicked the ball into the net*; *she kicked her little brother*
(b) *(informal)* **to kick the habit** = the get rid of a bad habit; *I wish he'd kick the habit of whistling while he works*; *he doesn't smoke anymore - he kicked cigarettes a couple of months ago*; *see also* BUCKET
(c) to kick yourself = to be annoyed with yourself because of doing something silly, forgetting something, etc.; *I could have kicked myself as soon as I said it*; *they must be kicking themselves now for not having bought the house when they had the chance*

③ **kick off**
['kɪk 'ɒf] *verb*
to start; *let's kick off with a discussion about modern painters*

③ **kick out**
['kɪk 'aut] *verb*
to get rid of someone; *he was kicked out of the club for not paying his subscription*; *they*

kicked him out of the school because he had started to take drugs

③ **kick up**
['kɪk 'ʌp] *verb*
(informal) to kick up a fuss = to make a fuss, a row; *the kids are only messing about - there's no need to kick up a fuss by calling the police*

① **kid**
[kɪd]
1 *noun*
(a) *(informal)* child; *there were a few school kids on their bicycles; I saw your kids going off on the bus this morning; they've been married a few years, and have got a couple of kids; kid brother* = younger brother; *I have to stay in to baby-sit my kid brother*
(b) young goat; *a mother goat and two little kids*
2 *verb*
(informal) to make someone believe something which is not true; **I was only kidding** = I didn't mean it; **no kidding?** = is it really true? (NOTE: **kidding - kidded**)

② **kidnap**
['kɪdnæp] *verb*
to steal soemone and take them away; *the millionaire's son was kidnapped and held for two weeks* (NOTE: **kidnapping - kidnapped**)

② **kidney**
['kɪdnɪ] *noun*
(a) one of a pair of organs in animals that clean the blood; **kidney machine** = apparatus through which a patient's blood is passed to be cleaned when his kidneys have failed; *he has to be linked to the kidney machine for several hours each week;* **kidney stone** = hard mass like a little piece of stone, which forms inside a kidney; **kidney transplant** = operation to transplant a kidney; *the kidney transplant was a success*
(b) this organ from a lamb, pig, etc., used as food; *steak and kidney pie*

① **kill**
[kɪl] *verb*
(a) to make someone or something die; *he was sentenced to death for killing his wife; the drought has killed the entire crop; the automobile hit a cat and killed it; six people were killed in the plane crash*
(b) **to kill time** = to spend time while waiting for something important; *I killed some time waiting for the train by having a cup of coffee;* **to kill two birds with one stone** = to get two successful results from one action; *while I'm in Chicago for the conference I could kill two birds with one stone and visit my parents; (informal)* **my feet are killing me** = my feet are hurting

① **killer**
['kɪlər] *noun*
(a) person who kills; *the police are still hunting for the killer;* **serial killer** = person who has

committed several murders, one after the other; *because there are similarities between the murders, the police think they are dealing with a serial killer*
(b) which kills; *a killer flu virus;* **killer whale** = black and white whale that eats fish and seals

④ **killing**
['kɪlɪŋ] *noun*
(a) murder, putting a person or animal to death; *the police are investigating the killing of the tourists; there have been reports of killings in the nearby towns; the killing of elephants has been banned*
(b) **to make a killing** = to make a very large profit; *he made a killing on the stock market*

④ **kilo** *or* **kilogram**
['kiloʊ or 'kiləgræm] *noun*
measure of weight (= one thousand grams); *the crate weighs 78 kilos; the police found two kilos of drugs in the back of the car* (NOTE: plural is **kilos.** Note also that it is written **kg** after figures: **20 kg**)

③ **kilometer**
[kɪ'lɒmɪtər] *noun*
measure of length (one thousand meters); *the two roads join about three kilometers from here; the town is about ten kilometers from the sea* (NOTE: written **km** after figures: **70km**)

③ **kilt**
[kɪlt] *noun*
skirt worn by men in Scotland, and also by women; *she wore a red kilt; Scottish soldiers wear kilts*

① **kind**
[kaɪnd]
1 *adjective*
friendly, helpful, thinking about other people; *it's very kind of you to offer to help; how kind of you to invite him to your party!; you should always be kind to little children; he's a kind old gentleman* (NOTE: **kinder - kindest**)
2 *noun*
(a) sort, type; *a butterfly is a kind of insect; we have several kinds of apples in the garden; we discussed all kinds of things*
(b) *(informal)* **kind of** = in a certain way; *I was kind of annoyed when she told me that*
(c) **of a kind** = similar; *the three sisters are three of a kind; it's nothing of the kind* = that's not correct at all

① **kindergarten**
['kɪndərgɑrtən] *noun*
class for young children, usually for five year olds, to prepare them for first grade; *our youngest son attends kindergarten*

① **kindly**
['kaɪndli]
1 *adjective*
thoughtful and pleasant; *a kindly neighbor brought him soup when he was sick*
2 *adverb*

(a) in a thoughtful or pleasant way; *he behaved very kindly toward me*; **not to take kindly to =** not to like; *she doesn't take kindly to being told she's fat*

(b) *(formal)* please, if you don't mind; *kindly shut the door*; *customers are kindly requested to pay at the cash register*

② **kindness**
['kaɪndnəs] *noun*
being kind; *she was touched by his kindness*

① **king**
[kɪŋ] *noun*
(a) man who reigns over a country by right of his birth; *the king and queen came to visit the town* (NOTE: **king** is spelled with a capital letter when used with a name or when referring to a particular person: **King Henry VIII**)

(b) main piece in chess; *she moved her knight to threaten his king*

(c) *(in cards)* the card with the face of a man with a beard; *he knew he could win when he drew the king of spades*

(d) champion, top person; *he's king of the pop music scene*; *the lion is king of the jungle*

③ **kingdom**
['kɪŋdʌm] *noun*
(a) land ruled over by a king or queen; *England is part of the United Kingdom*; *he gave her a book of old stories about a magic kingdom*

(b) part of the world of nature; *the animal kingdom*

④ **kingfisher**
['kɪŋfɪʃər] *noun*
small bright blue bird that dives for fish; *we saw a kingfisher down by the pond*

① **kiss**
[kɪs]
1 *noun*
(a) touching someone with your lips to show love; *she gave the baby a kiss*; **to blow someone a kiss =** to show your love for someone by touching your lips with your hands and making a gesture to the person at a distance; *as the train left, she blew him a kiss*

(b) **kiss of death =** something which ruins a business, etc.; *the new supermarket is the kiss of death to small businesses in the town* (NOTE: plural is **kisses**)

2 *verb*
to touch someone with your lips to show that you love them; *she kissed her daughter and walked away*; *they kissed each other goodbye*; *the politicians are in town, shaking hands with voters and kissing babies*

① **kit**
[kɪt] *noun*
(a) **first aid kit =** box with bandages kept to be used in an emergency; *the doctor rushed to the scene with his first aid kit*

(b) box containing pieces which can be put together to make a piece of furniture, a model,

etc.; *he spent the afternoon building a model airplane from a kit*

① **kitchen**
['kɪtʃən] *noun*
room where you cook food; *she put the meat down on the kitchen table*; *if you're hungry, have a look in the kitchen to see if there's anything to eat*; *don't come in with dirty shoes on - I've just mopped the kitchen floor*

② **kite**
[kaɪt] *noun*
(a) toy made of light wood and paper or cloth which is flown in a strong wind on the end of a string; *the wind nearly blew the kite away*

(b) shape in mathematics like a kite, with two short sides and two long sides, and no right angles

① **kitten**
['kɪtn] *noun*
(a) baby cat; *the kittens are playing in their basket*; *the cat carefully picked up her kitten by the back of its neck*

(b) *(informal)* **to have kittens =** to be very nervous; *she was having kittens, waiting for her interview*

④ **kiwi**
['kiwi] *noun*
bird which cannot fly, found in New Zealand; **kiwi fruit =** small tropical fruit, with a rough skin and green flesh; *kiwi fruit are full of vitamins*

③ **km**
[kɪ'lɒmɪtərz] = KILOMETERS

① **knee**
[ni] *noun*
(a) joint in the middle of your leg, where it bends; *she sat the child on her knee*; *he went down on one knee and asked her to marry him*; *he was on his knees looking under the bed*; **knee socks =** long socks which go up to your knees

(b) part of a pair of pants that covers the knee; *my jeans have holes in both knees*

① **kneel**
[nil] *verb*
to go down on your knees; *everyone knelt down and the priest said a prayer*; *she knelt beside his bed and listened to his breathing* (NOTE: **kneeling - kneeled** *or* **knelt** [nelt])

② **knew**
[nju] *see* KNOW

③ **knickers**
['nɪkərz] *noun*
woman's or girl's underwear; *she bought a pair of blue knickers*

① **knife**
[naɪf]
1 *noun*
instrument used for cutting, with a sharp metal blade fixed in a handle; *put out a knife, fork and*

spoon for each person; *you need a sharp knife to cut meat*; **bread knife** = special large knife for cutting bread (NOTE: plural is **knives** [naɪvz])

2 *verb*

to stab someone with a knife; *he was knifed in the back during the fight* (NOTE: **knifes - knifing - knifed**)

① **knight**
[naɪt] *noun*

(a) man honored by a king for services to his country (and taking the title "Sir"); *he was made a knight*

(b) *(in medieval times)* brave soldier; *King Arthur and his knights*

(c) one of two pieces in a chess set with a horse's head; *with a clever move she took his knight*

① **knit**
[nɪt] *verb*

(a) to make a piece of clothing out of wool by linking threads together with the aid of two long needles; *my mother is knitting me a sweater*; *she was wearing a blue knitted hat* (NOTE: **knitting - knitted**)

(b) **to knit your brow** = to make folds of skin on your forehead as you try to do something difficult; *she knit her brow as she tried to understand the guidebook* (NOTE: **knitting - knit**)

① **knives**
[naɪvz]
see KNIFE

① **knob**
[nɒb] *noun*

(a) round handle on a door, a chest of drawers, etc.; *in some old houses, the doorknobs are made of china*

(b) round button that you turn on a radio, TV, etc.; *turn the knob to increase the volume*

① **knock**
[nɒk]

1 *noun*

(a) sound made by hitting something; *suddenly, there was a knock at the door*

(b) hitting something; *she received a knock on the head with a brick*

2 *verb*

(a) to hit something; *knock twice before going in*; *you'll need a heavy hammer to knock that nail in*

(b) to criticize; *she wrote an article knocking the vice president*

③ **knock about** *or* **around**
['nɒk ə'baut or ə'raund] *verb*

(a) to wander about doing nothing; *he spent several years knocking about the back streets of New Orleans*

(b) **to knock someone around** = to beat someone; *he was badly knocked around in the fight*; **to knock something about** = to damage something; *the town was badly knocked about in the war*

③ **knock back**
['nɒk 'bæk] *verb*

(a) to drink a drink quickly; *he knocked back his drink and ran outside*

(b) **to knock someone back a sum** = to cost someone a sum; *it will knock me back a few hundred dollars*

③ **knock down**
['nɒk 'daun] *verb*

(a) to make something fall down; *they are going to knock down the old house to build an apartment block*

(b) to hit; *she was knocked down by an automobile*

(c) to reduce a price; *they knocked the price down to $75*

③ **knock off**
['nɒk 'ɒf] *verb*

(a) to make something fall off by hitting it; *the cat knocked the glass off the shelf*

(b) *(informal)* to stop work; *the workmen all knocked off at 4:30*

(c) to reduce the price of something (by an amount); *he knocked $1500 off the price of the car*

③ **knock out**
['nɒk 'aut] *verb*

(a) to hit someone so hard that he is no longer conscious; *she was knocked out by a blow on the head*; *the boxer was knocked out in the third round*

(b) to make someone go to sleep; *the doctor gave her something that knocked her out*

① **knot**
[nɒt]

1 *noun*

(a) the ends of a piece of string, rope, etc., fastened together; *he's too small to be able to tie knots properly*; *is the knot of my necktie straight?*; **to tie the knot** = to get married

(b) small group; *knots of people stood and watched the firefighters*

(c) measure of speed used to show the speed of a ship or of the wind; *the ship was doing 22 knots when she hit the rocks*; *there's a wind speed of 60 knots*

(d) round place on a piece of wood where a branch was originally growing; *this piece of wood is no good - it is full of knots*

2 *verb*

to tie a knot in something; *he knotted the end of the rope* (NOTE: **knotting - knotted**)

① **know**
[nəʊ]

1 *verb*

(a) to have learned something, to have information about something; *do you know how to start the computer?*; *he didn't know she had died*; *how was I to know she wasn't his wife?*; *you knew it would be expensive*; *do you know the Spanish for "one - two - three"?*; *his secretary doesn't know where he is*; *he is* known to have right-wing views; is she in trouble? - not that I know of

(b) to have met someone; *I know your sister - we were at school together*; *I used to know a man called Jones who worked in your company*; **to know someone by sight** = to know who someone is, even though you have never spoken to him or her

(c) to have been to a place often; *I know Texas very well*; *she doesn't know Japan at all*

(d) to experience; *she knew years of poverty before she became famous*; *he knows what it is like to be out of work* (NOTE: **knowing - knew** [nju] **- has known**)

2 *noun*

(informal) **in the know** = knowing something that most people do not know; *those in the know say that's the best restaurant in town*; *someone in the know gave me the tip*

② **know-how**
['nəʊhaʊ] *noun*

(informal) knowledge about how something is made or is done; *this book gives you all the know-how you'll need about fixing a sink*

② **knowledge**
['nɒlɪdʒ] *noun*

(a) what a particular person knows about something; *to my knowledge, he left the house at 10 P.M.*; *the police have no knowledge of the accident*; **to the best of my knowledge** = as far as I know; *to the best of my knowledge, no one else has seen this document*; **it is common knowledge that** = everyone knows that; *it is common knowledge that his wife wants to go to live in Maine*

(b) general facts or information that people know; *this book is supposed to list all human knowledge*

① **known**
[nəʊn] *adjective*

which is known; **a known quantity** = something, a fact or a situation, which you know about; *when trading with Canadian companies, at least you are dealing with a known quantity* (NOTE: the opposite is an **unknown quantity**)

② **knuckle**
['nʌkl] *noun*

joint in your fingers; *she hurt her knuckles when she fell*

Ll

③ **L, l**
[el]

twelfth letter of the alphabet, between K and M; *Louise wrote her initial "L" on the back of the letter*

③ **l**
= LITER

① **lab**
[læb] *noun*

short for LABORATORY

② **label**
['leɪbl]

1 *noun*

(a) piece of paper, plastic, etc., attached to something to show price, contents, someone's name and address, etc.; **address label** = label with an address on it; *put a baggage label on your bag if you don't want it to get lost*; *she stuck a label on the package*; *the price on the label is $35.00*

(b) especially, the name of a recording company on a record or CD; *the group has made their first single on the Virgin label*

2 *verb*

to put a label on something; *all the goods are labeled with the correct price*

② **labor**
['leɪbər]

1 *noun*

(a) (hard) work; *after digging the garden, it is good to lie on the grass and rest from your labors*; **to charge for materials and labor** = to charge for both the materials used in a job and also the hours of work involved; **hard labor** = prison sentence where the prisoner has to do hard work with his hands (NOTE: plural can be **labors** in this meaning)

(b) all workers; *cheap labor is difficult to find*; **labor dispute** = argument between management and workers

(c) the process of giving birth to a baby; *she went into labor at home, and her husband drove her to the hospital*; *she was in labor for 12 hours*

2 *verb*

(a) to work very hard; *they labored night and day to finish the project in time*

(b) **to labor under an impression** = to have a wrong impression, to assume something which is quite wrong; *he was laboring under the impression that airfares were cheaper in Europe than in the U.S.A.*; **to labor the point** = to discuss something too long; *I don't want to* *labor the point, but may I raise the question for the third time?*

② **laboratory**
['læbrətɔri] *noun*
place where scientific experiments, testing and research are carried out; *she's a chemist working in the university laboratories*; *all our products are tested in our own laboratories* (NOTE: plural is **laboratories**)

② **Labor Day**
['leɪbər 'deɪ] *noun*
U.S. holiday held to celebrate workers on the first Monday in September

② **labor union**
['leɪbər'junɪən] *noun*
organization that represents workers who are its members in discussions with employers about wages and conditions of employment; *the labor union has many members*

② **lace**
[leɪs]
1 *noun*
(a) thin strip of leather, cord, etc., for tying up a shoe, etc.; *his laces kept coming undone*; *she's too little to be able to tie her laces herself*
(b) decorative fabric with open patterns of threads like a net; *a lace tablecloth*; *her wedding dress was trimmed with lace* (NOTE: no plural in this meaning)
2 *verb*
to fasten with laces; *he laced up his boots*

② **lack**
[læk]
1 *noun*
not having enough of something; *the children are suffering from a lack of food*; *the project was canceled because of a lack of funds* (NOTE: no plural)
2 *verb*
not to have enough of something; *the sales staff lack interest*; *he doesn't lack style - he puts on his sunglasses the moment the sun comes out*

② **lacking**
['lækɪŋ] *adjective*
lacking in = without any; *she's completely lacking in business sense*

① **lad**
[læd] *noun*
boy or young man; *don't expect too much - he's just a young lad*

① **ladder**
['lædər] *noun*
(a) device made of horizontal bars between two uprights, used for climbing; *the ladder was leaning against the wall*; *he was climbing up a ladder*; *she got down off the ladder*
(b) the corporate ladder = series of steps by which people are promoted; *by being appointed director of sales, he moved several steps up the corporate ladder*

① **ladies' room**
['leɪdɪz 'rum] *noun*
women's toilet; *can you tell me where the ladies' room is, please?*; *the ladies' room is down the corridor on the right*

① **lady**
['leɪdi] *noun*
(polite way of referring to a woman) *there are two ladies waiting to see you*; **the First Lady** = the wife of the president (NOTE: plural is **ladies**)

① **ladybug**
['leɪdibʌg] *noun*
small beetle, usually red with black spots; *I found a ladybird with six spots in the garden*

② **lag**
[læg]
1 *noun*
interval of time between two things that happen; *there's often a long time lag between setting up in business and seeing any results*; *see also* JET LAG
2 *verb*
to be behind, to fall behind; *she was lagging 10 m behind the leaders in the race* (NOTE: lagging - lagged)

① **laid**
[leɪd] *see* LAY

③ **laid up**
['leɪd 'ʌp] *adjective*
unable to work because of illness; *half the staff are laid up with the flu*

③ **lain**
[leɪn] *see* LIE

① **lake**
[leɪk] *noun*
area of fresh water surrounded by land; *let's take a boat out on the lake*; *we can sail across the lake*; *the hotel stands on the shores of Lake Michigan*

① **lamb**
[læm] *noun*
(a) young sheep; *in spring, the fields are full of sheep and their tiny lambs*
(b) meat from a lamb or sheep; *a leg of lamb*; *we had roast lamb and potatoes* (NOTE: no plural in this meaning)

① **lamp**
[læmp] *noun*
device that makes light; *the campsite is lit by large electric lamps*; **street lamp** = large light in a street; **table lamp** = lamp on a table; **floor lamp** = floor lamp, a room lamp on a tall pole standing on the floor

② **lampshade**
['læmpʃeɪd] *noun*
decorative cover put over a lamp; *I don't like the bright orange lampshade you bought*

① **land**
[lænd]
1 *noun*
(a) earth (as opposed to water); *they were glad*

to be back on (dry) land again after two weeks at sea

(b) piece of ground; *she owns some land in the north of the country; we bought a piece of land to build a house*

(c) country; *people from many lands visited the exhibition; he wants to see his native land again before he is too old to travel* (NOTE: usually no plural in meanings (a) and (b): **some land; a piece of land**)

2 *verb*

(a) to arrive on the ground, or on another surface; *the flight from Houston has landed; we will be landing at Newark in five minutes; the ducks tried to land on the ice; (informal)* **to land on one's feet** = to be successful; *after being made redundant he joined the police force and has really landed on his feet*

(b) to end in a place or position; *he tried to break into a school and landed in prison*

(c) to be successful in hitting someone; *he landed several punches on his opponent's head*

(d) to put goods or passengers on to land after a voyage by sea or by air; *the ship was landing goods at the port; we landed several passengers at JFK Airport*

(e) to catch a big fish; *we landed three salmon*

(f) to manage to get something; *he landed a contract with a Chinese company*

② **landing**
['lændɪŋ] *noun*

(a) *(especially of aircraft)* arriving on the ground or on a surface; *the plane made a smooth landing; strong winds meant that landing on the aircraft carrier was difficult*

(b) flat place at the top of stairs; *she was waiting for me on the landing*

③ **landlady**
['lændleɪdi] *noun*

woman from whom you rent a house, room, etc.; *you must pay your rent to the landlady every month* (NOTE: plural is **landladies**)

③ **landlord**
['lændlɔrd] *noun*

man or company from whom you rent a house, room, office, etc.; *tell the landlord if your roof leaks; the landlord refused to make any repairs to the roof*

③ **landmark**
['lændmɑrk] *noun*

(a) building or large object on land which you can see easily; *the Statue of Liberty is a famous New York landmark*

(b) outstanding or important event, etc.; *the day when power was handed over to China was a landmark in the history of Hong Kong*

② **landscape**
['lændskeɪp]

1 *noun*

(a) scenery, appearance of the country; *go to Arizona if you want to see beautiful landscapes;* **landscape gardening** = making a

garden more beautiful by making artificial lakes, planting trees, etc.

(b) painting of a country scene; *he collects 18th-century English landscapes*

2 *verb*

to improve the appearance of a garden by making artificial lakes, planting trees, etc.; *he spent years landscaping his garden*

① **lane**
[leɪn] *noun*

(a) narrow road, often in the country; *a lane with hedges on both sides*

(b) way for traffic going in a particular direction or at a certain speed; *this freeway has three lanes on either side; one lane of the interstate has been closed for repairs;* **truck lane** = part of a road where only trucks and buses may go; **inside lane** *or* **slow lane** = track nearest the side of the road, used by vehicles which are moving slowly, or those which are planning to turn off the road; **center lane** *or* **middle lane** = track in the center of the three lanes on a freeway; **outside lane** *or* **fast lane** = track nearest the center of a road, used by vehicles which are moving fast

(c) way for one runner in a race; *she is coming up fast on the inside lane*

① **language**
['læŋgwɪdʒ] *noun*

(a) way of speaking or writing used in a country or by a group of people; *Chinese is a very difficult language to learn, but it is the language spoken by most people in the world; we go to English language classes twice a week; I don't like traveling in places where I don't know the language; his first language is German, but he speaks several other languages very well;* **sign language** = way of communicating with deaf people, making signs with your fingers

(b) **bad language** = swearing and rude words; *you should have heard the bad language when he ran into her new car*

(c) **programming language** = system of signs and words used to program a computer

② **lap**
[læp]

1 *noun*

(a) your body from your waist to your knees, when you are sitting; *she listened to the story, sitting in her father's lap*

(b) circuit, one trip around a racetrack; *he finished lap 23 - only two laps to go!*

(c) part of a long journey; *the last lap of the tour was from Bangkok to Singapore*

(d) **it's in the lap of the gods** = no one knows what will happen; *I can't predict the result of the election - it's all in the lap of the gods;* **in the lap of luxury** = in great luxury; *they live in the lap of luxury*

2 *verb*

(a) *(of animal)* to drink with its tongue; *the dog*

lapped the water in the pond

(b) *(of waves)* to wash against something; *little waves lapped against rocks; the water was lapping around his ankles*

(c) to go so fast that you are one whole lap ahead of another competitor in a race; *the winner had lapped three other runners* (NOTE: lapping - lapped)

③ **laptop**
['læptɒp] *noun*
small computer that can be held on your knees; *I take my laptop with me onto the plane so that I can write my reports*

③ **lap up**
['læp 'ʌp] *verb*
(a) *(of animals)* to drink fast with the tongue; *the cat was lapping up the milk*

(b) *(informal)* to accept something in an eager way; *she told him how good his book was, and he just sat there lapping it up*

① **large**
[lɑrdʒ] *adjective*
(a) big; *she ordered a large cup of coffee; our house has one large bedroom and two very small ones; how large is your garden?; why has she got an office that is larger than mine?*

(b) by and large = generally speaking; *by and large, it is cheaper living in LA than in San Francisco* (NOTE: larger - largest)

◇ **at large**
['æt 'lɑrdʒ] *phrase*
(a) not in prison; *two prisoners escaped and one is still at large*

(b) in general; *the advertising campaign is aimed at the public at large*

④ **largely**
['lɑrdʒli] *adverb*
mainly, mostly; *the strange weather is largely due to El Niño; his farm is largely fields of grass*

④ **large-scale**
['lɑrdʒskeɪl] *adjective*
involving large numbers of people or large sums of money; *the police are launching a large-scale campaign against automobile thefts; compare* SMALL-SCALE

④ **larva**
['lɑrvə] *noun*
early stage in the life of an insect, like a fat worm; *caterpillars are the larvae of butterflies* (NOTE: plural is larvae ['lɑrviː])

④ **laser**
['leɪzər] *noun*
instrument that produces a concentrated beam of light; **laser printer** = office printing machine that prints using a laser beam

② **lash**
[læʃ]
1 *verb*
(a) to hit something with a whip; *she lashed at the horse to make it go faster*

(b) to hit against something, as if with a whip; *the rain was lashing against the windows*

(c) to fasten or tie down tightly with rope; *containers carried on the deck of a ship must be securely lashed down*

2 *noun*
(a) stroke with a whip; *he was sentenced to six lashes*

(b) flexible part of a whip; *he hit the horse with the tip of his lash*

(c) eyelash; *she has lovely long lashes* (NOTE: plural is lashes)

② **lasso**
[lə'suː]
1 *noun*
rope with a loop at the end for catching cows, horses, etc.; *he caught the horse with a lasso* (NOTE: plural is lassoes)

2 *verb*
to catch an animal with a lasso; *he lassoed the horse* (NOTE: lassoes - lassoing - lassoed)

① **last**
[læst]
1 *adjective*
(a) which comes at the end of a list, line or period of time; *the post office is the last building on the right; the invoice must be paid by the last day of the month; she's the last person I would want to take to a classy restaurant* = I would never go to a classy restaurant with her; **last thing at night** = at the very end of the day; *we always have a drink of hot milk last thing at night;* **last but not least** = the last in a list, but by no means the least important; *last but not least, mother topped the cake with chocolate icing;* **the last straw** = the final problem which makes everything seem hopeless; *there was one problem after another with our move, and the last straw was when the new house caught fire*

(b) most recent; *she's been sick for the last ten days; the last three books I read were garbage;* **second to last** = the one before the last one; *my second to last car was a sports car*

(c) *(time)* **last night** = the evening and night of yesterday; *we had dinner together last night;* **last Tuesday** = the Tuesday before today; *I saw her last Tuesday; do you still have last Tuesday's newspaper?;* **last week** = the week before this one; *the fair was in town last week - you missed it!;* **last month** = the month before this one; *last month it rained almost every day;* **last year** = the year before this one; *where did you go on vacation last year?*

2 *noun*
(a) thing or person coming at the end; *she was the last to arrive; that's the last of the apples* = we have finished all the apples

(b) final words; *that's not the last they've heard from me*

(c) *(time)* **before last** = the one before the most recent; **the Tuesday before last** = two Tuesdays

ago; **the week before last** = two weeks ago; **the year before last** = two years ago; *he changed his vehicle the year before last*
3 *adverb*
(a) at the end; *she came last in the competition; out of a line of twenty people, I was served last*
(b) most recently; *when did you see her last?; she was looking sick when I saw her last or when I last saw her*
4 *verb*
to stay; to go on; *the nice weather won't last; our vacations never seem to last very long; the storm lasted all night; the meeting lasted for three hours*

◇ **at last** *or* **at long last**
[æt 'læst or æt 'lɒŋ læst]
in the end, after a long time; *we walked for hours and got home at last at six o'clock; I waited for half an hour, and at long last two buses came together*

① **lasting**
['læstɪŋ] *adjective*
which lasts for a long time; *his visit to China made a lasting impression on him; I've had these batteries for months - they're very long-lasting*

③ **last-minute**
['læst 'mɪnɪt] *adjective*
very late; *she made some last-minute changes to the wedding dress; people making last-minute bookings can get tours at half price*

① **late**
[leɪt]
1 *adjective*
(a) after the usual time; after the time when it was expected; *the plane is thirty minutes late; it's too late to change your ticket; hurry or you'll be late for the show; we apologize for the late arrival of the plane from Amsterdam;* **at the latest** = no later than; *I'll call back before 7 o'clock at the latest*
(b) at the end of a period of time; *the traffic was bad in the late afternoon; he moved to Des Moines in the late 1980s*
(c) toward the end of the day; *it's late - I'm going to bed*
(d) latest = most recent; *have you seen his latest movie?; he always drives the latest model car; the latest snow reports are published each day in the papers*
(e) dead; *his late father was a director of the company; the late president was working on this book when he died* (NOTE: only used before a noun in this meaning)
2 *adverb*
(a) after the usual time; *the plane arrived late; I went to bed later than usual last night; our visitors got up late this morning*
(b) later = at a time after the present; after a time which has been mentioned; *the family came to live in New Hampshire and she was born a month later; can we meet later this*

evening?; **see you later!** = I hope to see you again later today; **later (on)** = afterwards, at a later time; *I'll do it later on; we were only told later that she was very sick* (NOTE: later - latest)

② **lately**
['leɪtli] *adverb*
during recent days or weeks; *have you seen her father lately?; we've been very busy at the office lately*

④ **Latin America**
['lætɪn ə'merɪkə] *noun*
countries in South and Central America where Spanish and Portuguese are spoken

③ **latter**
['lætər]
1 *adjective*
(formal) coming at the end of a list; *I'm busy on Monday and Tuesday, but I'll be free during the latter part of the week*
2 *noun*
the latter = second person or thing mentioned of two things; *which do you prefer, apples or pears? - I prefer the latter* (NOTE: the first of two is called the **former**)

① **laugh**
[læf]
1 *noun*
(a) sound you make when you think something is funny; *he has a lovely deep laugh; "that's right," he said with a laugh;* **to do something for a laugh** = to do something as a joke or for fun; *don't be angry - they only did it for a laugh*
(b) to have the last laugh = to be successful in the end, after people have laughed at you earlier on; *everyone told him that his new type of vacuum cleaner wouldn't work, but he had the last laugh when it sold in millions*
2 *verb*
(a) to make a sound to show you think something is funny; *he was very good last night - he had everyone laughing at his jokes; she fell off the ladder and everyone laughed*
(b) to laugh at someone = to make fun of someone; *don't laugh at her because she's so fat; you mustn't laugh at his hat - he's very proud of it*

③ **laughter**
['læftər] *noun*
sound or act of laughing; *laughter greeted his appearance on the stage; as soon as he opened his mouth, the audience burst into laughter* (NOTE: no plural)

② **launch**
[lɔntʃ]
1 *noun*
(a) act of starting off a boat, a rocket, a new product, etc.; *the launch of the new automobile went off successfully; the rocket launch has been delayed by two weeks;* **launch party** = party held to advertise the launching of a new product

(b) type of small motor boat; *he took the launch out on the lake* (NOTE: plural is **launches**)

2 *verb*

(a) to put a boat into the water, especially for the first time and with a lot of ceremony; *the Queen launched the new ship*

(b) to put a new product on the market; *they are launching their new automobile at the auto show*

(c) to give something or someone a start; *the TV ad helped to launch her movie career*

(d) to begin; *the enemy launched an attack on our headquarters*

② **Laundromat**
['lɔndrəmæt] *noun*
trademark for a shop with washing machines which anyone can pay to use; *I take my washing to the Laundromat once a week*

① **laundry**
['lɔndri] *noun*
(a) clothes, bed sheets, etc., that have been washed, or that are ready to be washed; *put the dirty laundry in the washing machine*; *please put any laundry into the bag provided*

(b) place where clothes, bed sheets, etc. are washed; *the hotel's sheets and towels are sent to the laundry each day*

② **lava**
['lɑvə] *noun*
hot liquid rock flowing from a volcano; *the flow of lava came down the side of the mountain toward our house*

③ **lavatory**
['lævətri] *noun*
bathroom, a room with a sink and a toilet; *where's the lavatory, please?* (NOTE: plural is **lavatories**)

① **law**
[lɔ] *noun*
(a) the law = the set of rules by which a country is governed; *everyone is supposed to do what the law says*; **within the law** = according to the laws of a country; **against the law** = not according to the laws of a country; *it is against the law to drive at night without lights*; **to break the law** = to do something which is not allowed by law; *he is breaking the law by selling cigarettes to little children*

(b) to lay down the law = to tell someone to do something; *he insists on laying down the law, which makes the office staff unhappy*; **to take the law into your own hands** = to do things which are illegal, because you want to punish someone; *they took the law into their own hands and burned down his house*; **law and order** = situation where the laws of the country are followed by most people; *the government reacted quickly to impose law and order again*

(c) one single part of the rules governing a country, usually in the form of an act of Congress; *Congress has passed a law against the ownership of assault rifles*

(d) all the laws of a country taken together; **civil law** = laws relating to people's rights and agreements between individuals; **commercial law** = laws regarding business; **contract law** *or* **the law of contract** = laws relating to private agreements; **corporation law** = laws which refer to the way corporations work; **criminal law** = laws that deal with crimes against the law of the land, which are punished by the state; **international law** = laws referring to the way countries deal with each other; **the law of the sea** = laws referring to ships, ports, etc. (NOTE: no plural in this meaning)

(e) general scientific rule; *the law of gravity can be demonstrated by showing how an apple falls to the ground and not up into the air*; **the law of supply and demand** = general rule that the amount of a product which is available is related to what possible customers need

① **lawn**
[lɔn] *noun*
part of a garden covered with short grass; *he lay on his back on the lawn*; *your lawn needs mowing*; *we need to water the lawn every day during the summer*

③ **lawn bowls**
[lɔn bəulz] *noun*
game played on grass, where teams of players roll large balls toward a small ball thrown as a target; *their team is the lawn bowls champion*

② **lawnmower**
['lɔnməuər] *noun*
machine for cutting grass; *the quiet of the Sunday morning was broken by the sound of electric lawnmowers in all the gardens*

③ **lawsuit**
['lɔsut] *noun*
legal case brought to a court; **to bring a lawsuit against someone** = to tell someone to appear in court because you think they have acted wrongly toward you; *the parents of the victims brought a lawsuit against the tour company*

② **lawyer**
['lɔjər] *noun*
person who has studied law and can advise you on legal matters; *if you are arrested you have the right to speak to your lawyer*

② **lay**
[leɪ]
1 *verb*
(a) to put something down flat; *he laid the papers on the table*; *a new carpet has been laid in the dining room*

(b) to lay the table = to put knives, forks, spoons, etc., on the table ready for a meal; *the table is laid for four people*

(c) to produce an egg; *the hens laid three eggs* (NOTE: **laying - laid**)

2 *adjective*
not trained for a profession or to be a member of a religious group; *lay people often cannot understand doctors' language*; *lay members of*

the church helped the priest to organize the Christmas party

③ **layer**
['leɪər] *noun*

flat, usually horizontal, covering of something; *she put a layer of chocolate on the cake, then one of cream*

③ **lay off**
['leɪ 'ɒf] *verb*

to dismiss a worker, sometimes only temporarily; *unfortunately, the best way to save money is to lay off staff*

③ **layoff**
['leɪɒf] *noun*

person who has been dismissed from his or her job; *there have been layoffs, even at middle management level; it's a shame about the layoffs, but if the firm goes bust we'll all be in the same boat*

② **layout**
['leɪaʊt] *noun*

design, especially of a building, a garden, a book, etc.; *they have altered the layout of the offices; the burglars must have had a plan of the layout of the house*

① **lazy**
['leɪzi] *adjective*

not wanting to do any work; *she's just lazy - that's why the work never gets done on time; he is so lazy he does not even bother to open his mail* (NOTE: lazier - laziest)

③ **lb**
[paʊndz] = POUND(S) *it weighs 26 lb; take 6 lb of sugar*

① **lead**
1 [led] *noun*
(a) very heavy soft metal; *tie a piece of lead to your fishing line to make it sink* (NOTE: Chemical element: chemical symbol: **Pb**; atomic number: **82**)
(b) black part in the middle of a pencil; *if your lead's broken then you need to sharpen the pencil*
2 [lid] *noun*
(a) electric wire, etc., which joins a machine to the electricity supply; *the lead is too short to go across the room*
(b) first place (in a race); *he went into the lead or he took the lead; who's in the lead at the halfway stage?; she has a lead of 20 m over her nearest rival*
(c) string or thin piece of leather to hold a dog; *all dogs must be kept on a lead in the park*
(d) main part in a play, opera, ballet, etc.; *the male lead fell and broke his arm*
(e) lead editorial = one of the main articles in a newspaper, giving the newspaper's views on a topic of current interest; *the rail disaster was featured in the lead editorial*
3 [lid] *verb*
(a) to be in first place, to have the most

important place; *our side was leading at half time; they were leading by three yards*
(b) to go in front to show the way; *she led us to the secret box; the road leads you to the top of the hill*
(c) to be in charge of; to be the main person in a group; *she is leading a group of businesswomen on a tour of Chinese factories*
(d) to lead to = to make something happen; *the discussions led to an international treaty; it led me to think she was lying* = it made me think she was lying (NOTE: **leading - led** [led])
4 [lid] *adjective*
(person) who sings or plays the main tunes in a pop group; *she's the lead singer of the group*

① **leader**
['lidər] *noun*
(a) person who leads; *he is the leader of the Democratic Party; the leader of the construction workers' union*
(b) leading article, one of the main articles in a newspaper, giving the newspaper's views on a topic of current interest; *the rail disaster was featured in the leader*

① **leadership**
['lidəʃɪp] *noun*
(a) ability to be the person who manages or directs others; *we think he has certain leadership qualities*
(b) position of a leader; *under his leadership the party became stronger and stronger*
(c) group of leaders of an organization; *the leadership was weaker after the president's resignation;* **collective leadership** = group of leaders who make decisions together (NOTE: no plural)

③ **leading**
['lidɪŋ] *adjective*
most important; **leading article** = leader, one of the main articles in a newspaper, giving the newspaper's views on a topic of current interest; **leading lady** = actress who plays the main part in a play or movie; **leading light** = person who plays an important part in a group; *she's one of the leading lights of the women's movement;* **leading question** = question that is put in such a way as to get a particular answer; *he prepared a few leading questions to use in the interview*

③ **lead on**
['lid 'ɒn] *verb*
(a) to go first; *lead on, we will all follow you!*
(b) to lead someone on = to promise someone something, and then not do it; *they promised him a new car, but they were just leading him on*

③ **lead up to**
['lid 'ʌp tu] *verb*
to prepare the way for something to happen; *the events which led up to the war*

① **leaf**
[lif]
1 *noun*

(a) one of many flat green parts of a plant; *the leaves of the trees turn brown or red in the fall; insects have eaten the leaves of the roses*
(b) sheet of paper, especially a page of a book; **to turn over a new leaf** = to make a new start; *after years of wild living he decided to turn over a new leaf and join the family firm*
(c) very thin sheet of metal, etc.; *the ceiling is covered in gold leaf* (NOTE: plural is **leaves** [livz])
2 *verb*

to leaf through = to turn the pages of a book rapidly without reading it properly; *he leafed through the book, looking at the illustrations*

③ **leaflet**
['liflət] *noun*
sheet of paper, often folded, giving information; *opposition groups handed out leaflets at the beginning of the rally; they did a leaflet mailing to 20,000 addresses*

③ **league**
[lig] *noun*
(a) association of sports clubs which play against each other; *he plays for one of the minor league teams;* **not in the same league as** = not as good or as successful as; *you can't compare our little corner store to the supermarket, they're not in the same league*
(b) group joined together for a particular purpose; **to be in league with someone** = to work with someone against someone else

① **leak**
[lik]
1 *noun*
(a) escape of liquid or gas, etc., through a hole; *I can smell gas - there must be a gas leak in the kitchen*
(b) escape of secret information; *the leak of the report led to the official's resignation*
2 *verb*
(a) *(of liquid or gas, etc.)* to flow away, to escape; *water must have been leaking through the ceiling for days*
(b) to pass on secret information; *governments don't like their plans to be leaked to the press; we found that the salesman was leaking information to a rival company*

① **lean**
[lin]
1 *adjective*
(a) *(of person)* thin; *he's a tall lean man*
(b) *(of meat)* with little fat; *a slice of lean ham* (NOTE: **leaner - leanest**)
2 *verb*
to be in or to put into a sloping position; *the ladder was leaning against the shed; she leaned her bike against the wall; he leaned over and picked up the cushion; it's dangerous to lean out of car windows* (NOTE: **leaning - leaned** *or* [lent])

③ **lean on**
['lin 'ɒn] *verb*

(a) to try to influence someone; *someone must have leaned on the committee to get them to agree*
(b) to depend on someone; *if things get difficult she always has her father to lean on*

③ **leant**
[lent]
see LEAN

① **leap**
[lip]
1 *noun*
(a) jump; *she took a leap forward and fell into the water*
(b) great improvement or progress; **by leaps and bounds** = making rapid progress; *his Spanish has improved by leaps and bounds*
(c) a leap in the dark = an action where you are not sure of what the result will be; *the deal is something of a leap in the dark, but we hope it will pay off*
2 *verb*
(a) to jump; *she leapt with joy when she heard the news*
(b) to go up suddenly; *sales leaped during March* (NOTE: **leaping - leaped** *or* **leapt** [lept])

③ **leap at**
['lip 'æt] *verb*
to accept eagerly something which is suggested; *she leapt at the offer of a part in the play*

② **leapt**
[lept]
see LEAP

② **leap year**
['lip 'jɜr] *noun*
every fourth year, in which February has 29 days; *the years 2004 and 2008 are both leap years*

① **learn**
[lɜrn] *verb*
(a) to find out about something, or how to do something; *he's learning to ride a bicycle; we learn French and German at school;* **to learn something by heart** = to learn and remember something; *she learned the poem by heart;* **to learn from your mistakes** = to make mistakes and because of them learn how something should be done; *he doesn't want to ask advice, so I only hope he learns from his mistakes*
(b) to hear (news); *her boss learned that she was planning to leave the company; how did you come to learn about the product?* (NOTE: **learning - learned**)

① **learner**
['lɜrnər] *noun*
person who is learning; *she's in the learners' class at the swimming pool;* **learner's permit** = temporary license allowing someone to learn how to drive

② **learning**
['lɜrnɪŋ] *noun*
getting knowledge about something or of how to do something; *learning how to run the machine*

will take up most of his first week at work; **learning curve** = gradual process of learning; **a steep learning curve** = having to learn new skills fast; *being promoted from being a secretary to sales director involved a steep learning curve*

④ **lease**
[lis]
1 *noun*
(a) written contract, allowing someone to use a building, piece of land, etc., for a specified period; *we're renting our offices on a twenty-year lease*; **the lease expires** *or* **runs out in 2020** = the lease comes to an end in 2020
(b) to give someone a new lease on life = to make someone want to make a fresh start or to live life in a better way; *Alan's retirement has given him a new lease on life*
2 *verb*
(a) to lease (out) = to give on a lease; *he leased the store to a company from South Carolina*; *my landlord leases out six other apartments*
(b) to take or hold on a lease; *we're leasing our offices at a good rate*; *we lease our printer as it's cheaper than buying one*

③ **least**
[list]
1 *adjective*
smallest; *this car uses by far the least amount of gas*
2 *pronoun*
the least = the smallest amount; *she was the one who spent the least during their trip around Missouri*; **to say the least** = which was more than I expected; *I thought he was in the office so when I saw him in the supermarket I was surprised to say the least*; **not in the least** = not at all; *it doesn't bother me in the least to have to work on Sundays*
3 *adverb*
less than everyone or everything else; *I liked that part of the book least*; *he was the least proud man she had ever met*; **least of all** = absolutely less than everyone else; *no one was interested in what I said, least of all my son*; *see also* AT LEAST

② **leather**
[ˈleðər] *noun*
skin of certain animals used to make shoes, bags, etc.; *a leather bag*; *my shoes have leather soles*

① **leave**
[liv]
1 *noun*
permission to be away from work; *he has six weeks' annual leave*; **leave of absence** = being allowed to be away from work; **sick leave** = period when a worker is away from work because of illness; **to go on leave** *or* **to be on leave** = to go or be away from work; *she is away on two months' sick leave*
2 *verb*

(a) to go away from somewhere; *when they couldn't find what they wanted, they left the store*; *the train leaves every day at 8:25A.M.*; *when does the next bus leave for Cheyenne?*
(b) to forget to do something; to forget to take something with you; *I packed in a rush and left my toothbrush at home*
(c) to allow something to stay in a certain condition; *did you leave the light on when you locked up?*; *yesterday she left the iron on and burned a hole in the ironing board*; *someone left the door open, and the dog got out*; *the coffee left a stain on the cloth*
(d) not to take something; *leave some pizza for your brother*
(e) to go away from someone; *she's left her husband*; **leave me alone** = don't bother me
(f) not to do something, so that someone else has to do it; *she went out, leaving me all the dishes to wash*
(g) to give (something) to someone in your will; *he left all his property to his grandson*
(h) leave it to me = let me do it; *leave it to me, I'll find out the address for you*; **I leave it to you to decide** = you are the one who has to decide, not me (NOTE: **leaving - left** [left])

③ **leave behind**
[ˈliv bɪˈhaɪnd] *verb*
to forget to take something with you; not to take something with you; *he left his car keys behind in the post office*; *the car was too full, so we had to leave Aunt Mary behind at home*

④ **leave off**
[ˈliv ˈɒf] *verb*
(a) to stop doing something; *he's left off writing home so we don't know where he is*
(b) to forget to include; *she left the ZIP code off the address*; *the waitress left the drinks off the check*

① **leave out**
[ˈliv ˈaʊt] *verb*
to forget something; not to put something in; *she left out the date on the check*; *she described the accident, but left out the most important detail*; *he was left out of the football game because he had hurt his leg*

① **leaves**
[livz]
see LEAF, LEAVE

② **lecture**
[ˈlektʃər]
1 *noun*
talk to students or any other group of people on a particular subject; *she gave a lecture on Chinese art*; *are you going to the lecture this evening?*; *the lecture lasted thirty minutes, and then there was time for questions*; **lecture tour** = tour with lectures on the places visited, paintings or other objects seen, etc.; *the museum has a program of lecture tours on 20th-century art*
2 *verb*

(a) to give a lecture on something; *he will lecture on Roman history next Thursday*
(b) to teach a subject, by giving lectures; *she lectures on history at Harvard University*

② **lecturer**
['lektʃərər] *noun*
(a) person who gives a talk on a particular subject; *this week's lecturer is from England*
(b) regular teacher in a university or college; *he has been a lecturer for five years; many of the students knew the lecturer when he was a student himself*

② **led**
[led]
see LEAD

② **ledge**
[ledʒ] *noun*
narrow flat part that sticks out from a cliff or building; *every little ledge on the cliff is occupied by a nesting bird; he climbed up 150 feet and stopped on a narrow ledge just wide enough to stand on*; **window ledge** = flat part that sticks out under a window; *the cat was sunning herself on the window ledge*

④ **lee**
[li] *noun*
side of a building, hill, ship, etc., sheltered from the wind; *they picnicked on the lee of the hill, so as to be out of the wind*

④ **leek**
[lik] *noun*
vegetable of the onion family, with a white stem and long green leaves; *a bowl of leek and potato soup* (NOTE: do not confuse with **leak**)

① **left**
[left]
1 *adjective*
(a) not right, referring to the side of the body that usually has the hand you use less often; *I can't write with my left hand; the post office is on the left side of the street as you go toward the church*
(b) *(in politics)* referring to the socialists; *his politics are left of center*; *compare* RIGHT
(c) still there, not used up; *after paying for the food and drink, I've still got $5 left; if you eat three of the candies, there will be only two left for everyone else; there was nobody left in the building*; *see also* LEAVE
2 *noun*
(a) the side toward the left; *the school is on the left as you go toward the town center; she was sitting at the chairman's left*
(b) turn toward the left; *go straight ahead and make a left at the traffic light*
(c) *(in politics)* **the Left** = the socialists, the group supporting the rights of the workers; *we support the Left on social issues*; **swing to the Left** = movement of votes toward the left-wing candidates
3 *adverb*
toward the left; *turn left at the next street*

② **left-hand**
['left'hænd] *adjective*
on the left side; *the checkbook is in the left-hand drawer of his desk; the post office is on the left-hand side as you go toward the station*

① **left-handed**
['left'hændɪd] *adjective*
using the left hand more often than the right for doing things; *she's left-handed, so we got her a left-handed cup for her birthday*

① **leftover**
['leftəuvər]
1 *noun*
leftovers = food not eaten at a meal; *she threw the leftovers into the garbage*
2 *adjective*
not eaten at a meal; *you can use the leftover rice to make risotto*

④ **left-wing**
['leftwɪŋ] *adjective*
in politics, on the left; *he has very left-wing views; a left-wing government was formed; left-wing intellectuals have criticized the President*

① **leg**
[leg] *noun*
(a) part of the body with which a person or animal walks; *the bird was standing on one leg, asleep; some animals can't stand on their back legs; she fell down the steps and broke her leg*; *see also* ARM
(b) **to pull someone's leg** = to tease someone, to try to make someone believe something that isn't true; *don't worry, she will get here on time - I was only pulling your leg*; **on its last legs** = almost worn out; *the poor old truck is on its last legs*; **not to have a leg to stand on** = to be in an awkward situation because you cannot prove what you say; *the children produced a later will, so the claimants to the estate didn't have a leg to stand on*
(c) one of the parts of a chair, etc., which touch the floor; *the table has four legs*
(d) stage (of a journey, tour, bicycle race, etc.); *the last leg of the trip goes from Paris to Amsterdam; the first leg of the tour takes in the Lincoln Memorial, the Washington Monument and the White House*

④ **legacy**
['legəsi] *noun*
(a) what is left to a person according to the instructions in someone's will; *he received a large legacy from his uncle; the legacy can be paid only to a claimant who can prove his or her right to it*
(b) what is left behind by someone; *the rundown subway system is a legacy of the previous administration* (NOTE: plural is **legacies**)

② **legal**
['ligl] *adjective*
(a) according to the law, allowed by the law; *it's legal to drive at 16 if you have a learner's permit*; **legal tender** = money that must legally be accepted if you give it in payment; *foreign currency isn't legal tender, but some stores accept it*
(b) referring to the law; **to take legal action** = to sue someone, to take someone to court; **to take legal advice** = to ask a lawyer to advise about a legal problem; **legal aid** = free legal work done for people without enough money to pay lawyers' fees; *you can apply for legal aid if you want to take the case further*

② **legally**
['ligəli] *adverb*
in accordance with the law; *you must be over 21 to legally drink alcoholic beverages*

③ **legend**
['ledʒənd] *noun*
story from the past which may not be based on fact; *the legend of Jason and the Golden Fleece*

④ **legendary**
['ledʒəndri] *adjective*
(a) famous, often talked about; *his liking for money is legendary*; *her legendary dislike of men with beards*
(b) referring to legends; *a legendary tale of witches and good fairies*

③ **legislation**
[ledʒɪ'sleɪʃn] *noun*
laws, written rules which are passed by Congress and applied in the courts; *Congress has voted on the new legislation*; **labor legislation** = laws concerning the employment of workers (NOTE: no plural)

③ **legislative**
['ledʒɪslətɪv] *adjective*
referring to laws or to the making of laws; *Congress is the legislative body in the U.S.*

③ **legislature**
['ledʒɪslətʃər] *noun*
(a) body that makes laws; *members of the legislature voted against the proposal*
(b) building where a parliament body meets; *the protesters marched toward the state legislature*

> COMMENT: the Legislature in the U.S.A. is Congress. The Legislature is one of the three arms of Government, the others being the Executive and the Judicial

④ **legitimate**
[lɪ'dʒɪtəmət] *adjective*
(a) according to the law; *he acted in legitimate defense of his rights*
(b) born to married parents; *the old king had no legitimate children, so the title passed to his brother*
(c) **legitimate concern** = reasonable concern which is justified; *if you think it's a subject of legitimate concern you should tell your manager*

③ **leisure**
['liʒər] *noun*
(a) **leisure (time)** = free time when you can do what you want
(b) **do it at your leisure** = do it when there is an opportunity, without any hurry; *please send in your report at your leisure* (NOTE: no plural)

① **lemon**
['lemən] *noun*
(a) pale yellow fruit with a sour taste; *oranges are much sweeter than lemons*; **lemon tea** = tea served with a slice of lemon and sugar, and not with milk
(b) tree that produces these fruit; *lemons grow best in hot dry climates*

① **lemonade**
[lemə'neɪd] *noun*
drink flavored with lemons; *can I have a glass of lemonade with ice, please?*

② **lend**
[lend] *verb*
(a) to let someone use something for a certain period of time; *he asked me if I would lend him $10 till Monday*; *I lent her my dictionary and now she won't give it back*; *compare* BORROW
(b) **to lend a hand** = to help; *can you lend a hand with the cooking?*; **to lend an ear to someone** = to listen to what someone has to say; **to lend itself to** = to be able to be used for something special; *the garden lends itself to landscaping*; *the room lends itself to playing chamber music*
(c) to make a certain effect; *the Christmas decorations lend a seasonal air to the shopping center*; *her new suit lends her an air of authority* (NOTE: **lending - lent** [lent])

② **lender**
['lendər] *noun*
person who lends money; *the interest on the loan must be paid to the lender every month*

② **length**
[leŋθ] *noun*
(a) measurement of how long something is from end to end; *the table is at least twelve feet in length*
(b) **length of time** = amount of time something takes or lasts; *can you estimate the length of time you need to do this?*; *she was a bit vague about the length of her visit* = she was not certain how long she was going to stay
(c) long piece of something; *she bought a length of curtain material in the sale*; *we need two 3-yard lengths of copper pipe for the central heating system*
(d) distance from one end to the other of a swimming pool; *he swam two lengths of the swimming pool*

② **lengthy**
['leŋθi] *adjective*
(very) long; *she wrote a lengthy note, detailing all the problems involved* (NOTE: **lengthier - lengthiest**)

① **lens**
[lenz] *noun*
piece of curved glass or plastic, etc., used in eyeglasses, cameras, etc.; *my eyesight is not very good, and I have to have glasses with strong lenses*; *if the sun is strong enough you can set fire to a piece of paper using a lens*; **contact lenses** = tiny lenses worn directly on your eyes instead of eyeglasses

③ **lent**
[lent]
see LEND

① **less**
[les]
1 *adjective & pronoun*
a smaller amount (of); *you will get thinner if you eat less food*; *the check came to less than $15*; *she finished her homework in less than an hour*; *he sold it for less than he had paid for it*
2 *adverb*
(a) not as much; *I like that one less than this one*; *the second movie was less interesting than the first*; *I want a car that is less difficult to drive*; **less and less** = getting smaller all the time; *I enjoy my work less and less*; *he's less and less able to look after his garden*; **more or less** = almost, not completely; *the rain has more or less stopped*; *I've more or less finished painting the kitchen*
(b) **in less than no time** = very quickly; *they repaired the automobile in less than no time*; **nothing less than** = absolutely no less than; *she'll be satisfied with nothing less than a husband who is a millionaire*
3 *preposition*
minus, with a certain amount taken away; *we pay $15 an hour, less 75 cents for insurance*

③ **lessen**
['lesən] *verb*
to become less; to make something become less; *wearing a seat belt lessens the risk of injury* (NOTE: do not confuse with **lesson**)

③ **lesser**
['lesər] *adjective*
smaller, not as large or important; *the pieces of pottery found on the site were of lesser importance than the sword found with them*; **the lesser of two evils** = one of two things that is not quite as bad as the other; *faced with the choice of taking a taxi or waiting in the rain for a bus, we chose the lesser of two evils and decided to take the taxi*

② **lesson**
['lesən] *noun*
(a) period of time in school, etc., when you are taught something; *he went to sleep during the Spanish lesson*; *we have six lessons of history a week*; *she's taking driving lessons*; *he gives piano lessons at home in the evenings*
(b) something which you learn from experience and which makes you wiser; *he learned his lesson, he knows you shouldn't be rude to police officers*; **to teach someone a lesson** = to punish someone for doing something wrong; *I locked up her bike - that will teach her a lesson*

② **let**
[let] *verb*
(a) to allow someone to do something; *he let her borrow his car*; *will you let me see the papers?*; *let me see what I can do for you*
(b) **to let someone know something** = to tell someone about something, to give someone information about something; *please let me know the result as soon as you can*; *can you let me know when the package arrives?*
(c) to allow someone to borrow a house or office for a while and pay for it; *we're letting our cottage to some friends for the weekend*; **the apartment is to let at $1500 a month** = the apartment can be rented for $1500 per month; *see also* LET'S (NOTE: **letting - has let**)

① **let down**
['let 'daʊn] *verb*
(a) not to help when someone expects you to help; *I asked three people to speak at the meeting but they all let me down*
(b) to lower something or someone; *they let him down into the old mine on a rope*

② **let go**
['let 'gəʊ] *verb*
to stop holding on to something; *don't let go of the driving wheel*; *she was holding on to a branch, but then had to let go*

④ **lethal**
['liːθl] *adjective*
which kills; *she took a lethal dose of the tablets*

③ **let in**
['let 'ɪn] *verb*
to allow to come in; *don't let the dog in if she's wet*; *my boots let in water*

③ **let yourself in for**
['let jə'self 'ɪn fɔr] *verb*
to allow yourself to get involved in something difficult or unpleasant; *you're letting yourself in for all sorts of problems*; *she didn't realize what she was letting herself in for when she said she would look after six little children*

③ **let off**
['let 'ɒf] *verb*
(a) not to punish someone severely; *he was charged with stealing, but the judge let him off with a fine*
(b) to agree that someone need not do something; *she let the class off from having homework*

④ **let on**
['let 'ɒn] *verb*
to tell a secret; *they didn't let on to the police that I was there*

② **let out**
['let 'aut] *verb*
(a) to allow to go out; *the boys let the pigs out of the field*; *we let the dogs out into the garden in the evening*; *she let the air out of my front tire*
(b) to make a piece of clothing bigger; *can you let out these pants, they're getting too tight?* (NOTE: in this meaning the opposite is to **take in**)

① **let's**
[lets] = LET US *(making a suggestion that you and someone else should do something together)* *let's go to the movies*; *don't let's leave yet or let's not leave yet*

① **letter**
['letər] *noun*
(a) piece of writing sent from one person or organization to another to pass on information; *there were two letters for you in this morning's mail*; *don't forget to write a letter to your mother to tell her how we all are*; *we've had a letter from the bank manager*
(b) one of the signs that make up the alphabet, a sign used in writing which means a certain sound; *Z is the last letter of the alphabet*; *I'm trying to think of a word with ten letters beginning with A and ending with R*; **to the letter** = exactly as written; *they followed his instructions to the letter*; *the referee makes sure that the rules of the game are followed to the letter*; *see also* CAPITAL

① **lettuce**
['letɪs] *noun*
plant with large green leaves which are used in salads; *he made a salad with lettuce, tomatoes, and cucumber with an oil dressing* (NOTE: no plural except when referring to several plants: **a row of lettuces**)

② **let up**
['let 'ʌp] *verb*
to do less, to become less; *the rain didn't let up all day*; *she's working too hard - she ought to let up a bit*

① **level**
['levəl]
1 *noun*
(a) position relating to height or amount; *I want to lower the level of our borrowings*; *the floods had reached a level of 5 feet above normal*; **decisions made at top level** = decisions made by the head of an organization
(b) floor in a building; *go up to the next level*; *the restrooms are at street level*
(c) *(informal)* **on the level** = honest, not trying to deceive; *I don't think the salesman is being on the level with us*
(d) equal, the same; *at half-time the scores were level*
2 *adjective*
(a) flat, even; *are these shelves level, or do they slope to the left?*
(b) **level with** = at the same level as; *the floor that is level with the street is the first floor*

3 *verb*
(a) to make level; *they leveled the house* = they destroyed the house completely
(b) **to level off** *or* **to level out** = to stop going up or down; *price increases are starting to level off*; *the road climbs for about two miles and then levels out*; *(informal)* **to level with** = to be frank with (somebody); *level with me and tell me what you thought of my painting*

② **lever**
['livər] *noun*
instrument like a metal rod, which helps to lift a heavy object, or to move part of a machine, etc.; *we used a pole as a lever to lift up the block of stone*; **gearshift lever** = handle in an automobile that changes the gears; *you push the gearshift lever down and toward you to get into reverse*

④ **levy**
['levi]
1 *noun*
tax or other payment demanded and collected; *I think the import levies on luxury goods are too high*; *we paid the levy on time* (NOTE: plural is **levies**)
2 *verb*
to demand or to collect a tax or other payment; *customs levied a large fine on the company*

④ **liability**
[laɪə'bɪlɪti] *noun*
(a) legal responsibility; *make sure you understand your legal liabilities before you sign the contract*; **to accept liability for something** = to agree that you are responsible for something; **to refuse liability for something** = to refuse to agree that you are responsible for something; **they couldn't meet their financial liabilities** = they couldn't pay their debts (NOTE: plural in this meaning is **liabilities**)
(b) tendency to do something; *he has an unfortunate liability to burst into tears when anyone criticizes him*
(c) disadvantage; *bad eyesight is a liability if you want to be a pilot*

④ **liable**
['laɪəbl] *adjective*
(a) **liable for** = legally responsible for something; *you will be liable for the payment of the fine*; *parents can be made liable for their children's debts*
(b) **liable to** = likely to do something; *the weather's liable to be stormy*; *she is liable to burst into tears at the slightest criticism*

④ **libel**
['laɪbl]
1 *noun*
written statement which is not true and which can damage someone's reputation; *I will sue you for libel*
2 *verb*
to libel someone = to damage someone's reputation in writing; *he accused the newspaper of libeling him*; *compare* SLANDER

④ **liberal**
['lɪbrəl] *adjective*
(a) not strict, happy to accept other people's views; *the liberal view would be to let the teenagers run the club themselves*
(b) generous; *he left a very liberal tip*
(c) liberal arts = college studies such as philosophy, history, social sciences or languages

④ **liberate**
['lɪbəreɪt] *verb*
(formal) to set someone or something free from something; *the hostages were finally liberated by the security forces; the capital was liberated by government troops*

② **liberty**
['lɪbətɪ] *noun*
(a) freedom; *when he was in prison he wrote poems about his lost liberty; the new legislation is a restriction of the liberty of the individual*
(b) at liberty = free; not in prison; *six of the escaped prisoners are still at liberty; to be at liberty to do something* = to be free to do something; *you are at liberty to go now*
(c) to take liberties = to do something without permission; **to take liberties with something** *or* **someone** = to treat something or someone as if they belong to you; *she borrowed my cell phone without asking - she's always taking liberties with other people's property; the boss felt she was taking liberties by using the office phone to ask about getting another job;* **civil liberties** = freedom of people to act within the law (liberty of the press, liberty of the individual, etc.); *outside security cameras can be seen as a restriction on civil liberties*

① **librarian**
[laɪ'breərɪən] *noun*
trained person who works in a library; *the librarian helped us find what we wanted in the card catalog; she is starting her career as a librarian*

① **library**
['laɪbrɪ] *noun*
(a) place where books are kept which can be borrowed; *he forgot to take his books back to the library; you can't sell it, it's a library book;* **reference library** = library with reference books, where readers can search for information but not take the books away from the library
(b) collection of books, records, etc.; *he has a big record library* (NOTE: plural is **libraries**)

① **license**
['laɪsəns]
1 *verb*
to give someone official permission to do something; *the restaurant is licensed to serve beer, wine and spirits; she is licensed to run an employment agency*
2 *noun*
(a) document that gives official permission to own something or to do something; *she has applied for an export license for these paintings;* **driver's license** = permit that allows someone to drive an automobile, truck, etc.; *applicants should hold a valid driver's license;* **license plate** = plate (one on the front and one on the back of an automobile) that shows a number that identifies the vehicle
(b) under license = with a permit from someone who has a right to something; *the automobiles are made in South America under license from the U.S. firm*

① **lick**
[lɪk]
1 *noun*
a stroke with the tongue; *the dog gave him a friendly lick; I like to lick ice cream cones*
2 *verb*
(a) to stroke with your tongue; *you shouldn't lick the plate when you've finished your pudding; they licked their lips when they saw the cookies*
(b) to beat, to hit; *we licked the visiting team*

③ **licorice**
['lɪkərɪs] *noun*
black substance from the root of a plant, used to make candy and also in medicine; *she bought a bag of licorice; dessert flavored with essence of licorice*

② **lid**
[lɪd] *noun*
covering for a container, sometimes with a handle; *where's the lid of the black saucepan?; he managed to get the lid off the jam jar*

② **lie**
[laɪ]
1 *verb*
(a) to say something which is not true; *she was lying when she said she had been at home all evening; he lied to the police about the accident* (NOTE: in this meaning: **lying - lied**)
(b) to be in a flat position; to be situated; *six soldiers lay dead on the ground; the dog spends the evening lying in front of the fire; there were bits of paper lying all over the sidewalk; the capital lies near the center of the country;* **to lie in wait for someone** = to hide and wait for someone to come so as to attack him (NOTE: in this meaning: **lying - lay** [leɪ] - **has lain** [leɪn])
2 *noun*
something which is not true; *someone has been telling lies about her; that's a lie! - don't believe what he says*

③ **lie down**
['laɪ 'daʊn] *verb*
to put yourself in a flat position, especially on a bed; *I'll just go and lie down for five minutes; the burglars told him to lie down on the floor*

③ **lie in**
['laɪ 'ɪn] *verb*
to stay in bed late in the morning; *I think I'll lie in this morning*

③ **lie low**
['laɪ 'ləʊ] *verb*
to keep hidden and quiet; *you'd better lie low until the police go away*; *after the robbery, they lay low for a few months*

③ **lieutenant**
[lu'tenənt] *noun*
(a) rank in the armed forces below a captain; *the lieutenant has to report to his captain*
(b) main helper; *the mayor came into the room with two of his lieutenants*

① **life**
[laɪf] *noun*
(a) time when you are alive; *he spent his whole life working on the farm*; *in early life* = when you are a child; *in early life he lived in the country*; *for life* = for as long as someone is alive; *his pension gives him a comfortable income for life*; *(informal) not on your life!* = certainly not!; *don't you want to go camping? - not on your life!*
(b) being a living person; *to lose your life* = to die; *several lives were lost when the ship sank*; *she saved my life* = she saved me from dying; *to take your (own) life* = to commit suicide; *in a fit of despair she took her life*; *between life and death* = in danger of dying; *her daughter lay in the hospital between life and death* (NOTE: plural is **lives** in meanings (a) and (b))
(c) experience; *life can be hard when you don't have much money*; *being a miner is a hard life*
(d) living things; *is there life on Mars?*; *there's no sign of life in the house* = it looks as though there is no one in it; *pond life* = animals and plants which live in ponds
(e) being lively and energetic; *the young actors injected some life into the old play*; *the movie comes to life when she appears on the screen*
(f) biography, the written story of someone's life; *she has written a life of Henry VIII*

④ **life jacket**
['laɪf 'dʒækɪt] *noun*
light coat filled with air or cork, to keep you from drowning; *children must all wear life jackets on the river*; *instructions for putting on the life jacket are in the pocket in front of your seat*

② **life preserver**
['laɪf prɪ'zɜrvər] *noun*
thing worn to prevent you from drowning, such as a belt or life jacket

③ **life span**
['laɪfspæn] *noun*
length of time something or someone exists; *some artificial elements have a life span of a few millionths of a second*

③ **lifestyle**
['laɪfstaɪl] *noun*
way in which someone or a group of people live their daily lives; *I don't want to be a movie star, I don't envy their lifestyle at all*; *we live in New York City and enjoy an urban lifestyle*

② **lifetime**
['laɪftaɪm] *noun*
time when you are alive; *I hope to see men on Mars in my lifetime*; *he finally won the lottery after a lifetime of poverty*; *the chance of a lifetime* = the best chance you are ever likely to get; *take the offer - it's the chance of a lifetime*

① **lift**
[lɪft]
1 *noun*
(a) ride in an automobile offered to someone; *she gave me a lift to the station*; *to hitch a lift* = to ask a driver to take you as a passenger, usually by signaling with the thumb or by holding a sign with your destination written on it; *he hitched a lift to the party*; *her car broke down and she hitched a lift from a passing motorist*
(b) **chair lift** *or* **ski lift** = chairs which take people up to the top of a mountain slope; *the chair lift takes about ten minutes to reach the top*
2 *verb*
(a) to pick something up or move it to a higher position; *my briefcase is so heavy I can hardly lift it off the floor*; *he lifted up the little girl so that she could see the soldiers*; *he hurt his back lifting the box down from the shelf*
(b) to remove; *the government has lifted the ban on selling guns*
(c) to go away; *the fog had lifted by lunchtime*
(d) *(informal)* to copy; *whole sections of his book were lifted from one I wrote two years ago*

① **light**
[laɪt]
1 *noun*
(a) being bright, the opposite of darkness; *I can't read the map by the light of the moon*; *there's not enough light to take a photo*; *to stand in someone's light* = to stand between someone and a source of light
(b) electric bulb that gives light; *turn the light on - I can't see to read*; *it's dangerous to ride a bicycle with no lights*; *in the fog, I could just see the red lights of the car in front of me*; *(informal) there's light at the end of the tunnel* = there is some hope that everything will be all right in the end
(c) way of making a cigarette, etc., catch fire; *can you give me a light? or have you got a light?*
(d) *to cast light or to throw light on something* = to make something easier to understand; *the papers throw light on how the detective reached his decision*; *to come to light* = to be discovered; *documents have come to light that could help the police in their investigations*; *in (the) light of something* = when something is considered; *in the light of the reports in the press, can you explain the president's decision?*
2 *verb*
(a) to start to burn, to make something start to burn; *can you light the oven for me?*; *he couldn't get the fire to light*; *light a candle - it's*

dark in the shed; *can you light the candles on the birthday cake?*
(b) to give light to something; *the full moon lit the village, so we could see the church clearly*; *the police used flashlights to light the accident site* (NOTE: **lighting - lit** [lɪt])

3 *adjective*
(a) not heavy; *I can lift this box easily - it's quite light* or *it's as light as a feather*; *you need light clothing for tropical countries*; *she's just been ill, and can only do light work*
(b) *(color)* pale; *he was wearing a light green shirt*; *I prefer a light carpet to a dark one*
(c) having a lot of light so that you can see well; *the big windows make the kitchen very light*; *it was six o'clock in the morning and just getting light*
(d) not very serious; *I like to listen to light music when I am doing the cooking*; *she took some detective novels as light reading on the train* (NOTE: **lighter - lightest**)

4 *adverb*
to travel light = to travel with very little baggage; *if you're hitchhiking across Australia, it's best to travel light*

③ **lightbulb**
['laɪtbʌlb] *noun*
glass ball which gives electric light; *you'll need a ladder to change the lightbulb*

② **lighten**
['laɪtən] *verb*
(a) to make brighter, not so dark; *you can lighten the room by painting it white*
(b) to make lighter, not so heavy; *I'll have to lighten my suitcase - it's much too heavy to carry*

① **lighthouse**
['laɪthaʊs] *noun*
tall building near the sea containing a bright light to guide ships away from rocks; *most of the lighthouses on Scottish islands are worked automatically*

② **lighting**
['laɪtɪŋ] *noun*
the light in a place; *the lighting is very bad in this restaurant - I can't see what I'm eating*

① **lightly**
['laɪtlɪ] *adverb*
(a) not heavily; *she touched my arm lightly*; *I always sleep lightly and wake up several times each night*
(b) not severely; *she was lucky to get off so lightly* = she was lucky not to be punished
(c) not very much; *some lightly cooked vegetables*

② **lightning**
['laɪtnɪŋ] *noun*
(a) flash of electricity in the sky, followed by thunder; *the storm approached with thunder and lightning*
(b) **like lightning** = very fast; *leopards can run like lightning*

③ **lights**
[laɪts] *noun*
red, green and yellow lights for making traffic stop and start; *make a left at the next set of lights*; *he drove straight across the junction when the lights were red* (NOTE: short for **traffic lights**)

③ **light up**
['laɪt 'ʌp] *verb*
(a) to make something bright; *the flames from the burning gas store lit up the night sky*; *the firework display lit up the beach*
(b) to become bright and cheerful; *her face lit up when she saw the presents under the Christmas tree*

④ **light-year**
['laɪt 'jɜr] *noun*
(a) distance traveled by light during one year (about 5.88 trillion miles); *stars are light-years from Earth*
(b) **light-years apart** = very different; *the new model is light-years in advance of its competitors*

① **like**
[laɪk]
1 *preposition*
(a) similar to, in the same way as; *he's like his mother in many ways, but he has his father's nose*; *like you, I don't get along with the new boss*; *the picture doesn't look like him at all*; *he can swim like a fish*; *it tastes like strawberries*; *what's that record? - it sounds like Copland*; *it feels like snow* = it feels as if it is going to snow; *do you feel like a cup of coffee?* = do you want a cup of coffee?
(b) *(asking someone to describe something)* *what was the weather like when you were on vacation?*; *what's he like, her new boyfriend?*
2 *adverb*
(as) like as not = probably; *as like as not, Dan will arrive late*
3 *conjunction*
in the same way as; *she looks just like I did at her age*
4 *verb*
(a) to have pleasant feelings about something or someone; *do you like the new manager?*; *she doesn't like eating meat*; *how does he like his new job?*; *no one likes driving in rush hour traffic*; *in the evening, I like to sit quietly and read the newspaper*
(b) to want; *I'd like you to meet one of our sales executives*; *I'd like to go to Baton Rouge next week*; *take as many apples as you like*
5 *noun*
(a) thing which you like; *we try to take account of the likes and dislikes of individual customers*
(b) **the likes of** = someone like; *the likes of him should not be allowed in*

④ **likelihood**
['laɪlihʊd] *noun*
being likely to happen; *there's every likelihood that he will be late*; *it's cloudy so the likelihood*

of rain is high; the likelihood is that no party will be the outright winner in the elections

③ **likely**
['laɪkli]
1 *adjective*
which you think is going to happen; *it's likely to snow this weekend; he's not likely to come to the party; is that at all likely?* (NOTE: **likelier - likeliest**)
2 *adverb*
probably; *most likely he's gone home*; **not likely!** = certainly not; *Are you going to the office party? - Not likely!*

③ **likewise**
['laɪkwaɪz] *adverb*
in the same way, similarly; *John passed the math test - likewise his sister Penny*

② **liking**
['laɪkɪŋ] *noun*
pleasant feeling toward someone or something; *she has a liking for chocolate; this drink is too sweet for my liking*; **to take a liking to someone** = to start to like someone; *the manager has taken a liking to her*

① **lily**
['lɪli] *noun*
type of flower shaped like a trumpet, which grows from a bulb; *the church was decorated with arrangements of white lilies* (NOTE: plural is **lilies**)

② **lily of the valley**
['lɪli əv ðə 'væli] *noun*
spring plant with small white flowers and a strong scent; *we picked some lily of the valley yesterday* (NOTE: plural is **lilies of the valley** *or* **lily of the valley**)

② **limb**
[lɪm] *noun*
(a) leg or arm; *he was lucky not to break a limb in the accident*; **danger** *or* **risk to life and limb** = danger that someone may be hurt; *when he's on his motorcycle he's a danger to life and limb*
(b) branch of a tree; **out on a limb** = in a difficult or exposed situation; *he feels out on a limb, with no one to share responsibility for running the company*

④ **limber**
['lɪmbər]
1 *adjective*
supple, which bends easily; *dancers have limber muscles*
2 *verb*
to limber up = to do exercises to make your muscles more supple before playing a sport; *the athletes were limbering up before the race*

② **lime**
[laɪm] *noun*
(a) white substance containing calcium, used in making cement; *the builder ordered some bags of lime* (NOTE: no plural in this meaning)

(b) small green tropical fruit, similar to a lemon; tree that bears such fruit; *you need the juice of two limes to make this recipe*

② **limit**
['lɪmɪt]
1 *noun*
furthest point beyond which you cannot go; **age limit** = youngest or oldest age at which you are allowed to do something; *we put an age limit of thirty-five on new employees*; **speed limit** = highest speed at which you are allowed to drive; *the speed limit in residential areas is 25 miles per hour; the police hope that the new speed limits will cut down the number of accidents*; **weight limit** = heaviest weight which something can stand; *the bridge has a weight limit of 3 tons*; **over the limit** = with more alcohol in your blood than is allowed by law; *the breath test showed he was way over the limit*; **within limits** = in a modest way, not excessively; *we're prepared to help you within limits*
2 *verb*
not to allow something to go beyond a certain point; *her parents limited the number of evenings she could go out; the boss wants to limit expenditures on entertainment*

③ **limitation**
[lɪmɪ'teɪʃn] *noun*
(a) act of limiting
(b) thing which stops you going further; **to know your limitations** = to know what you are capable of doing; *he knows his limitations but still keeps trying to be a race car driver*

② **limp**
[lɪmp]
1 *noun*
way of walking, when one leg hurts or is shorter than the other; *his limp has improved since his operation*
2 *verb*
to walk with a limp; *after the accident she limped badly*
3 *adjective*
soft, not stiff; *all we had as a salad was two limp lettuce leaves; he gave me a limp wave of the hand*

① **line**
[laɪn]
1 *noun*
(a) long thin mark; *she drew a straight line across the sheet of paper; parking isn't allowed on yellow lines; the tennis ball went over the line*; **to draw the line at** = to refuse to do; *I don't mind having a cup of coffee with the boss, but I draw the line at having to invite him for a meal at home*
(b) long string; *she hung her laundry on the clothesline; he sat with his fishing line in the river, waiting for a fish*
(c) wire along which telephone messages are sent; *the snow brought down the telephone lines; can you speak louder - the line is bad;*

crossed line = when two telephone conversations are mixed together; **to be on the line** = to be talking to someone on the telephone; *don't interrupt - I'm on the line to New York*; *do you want to speak to Charles while he's on the line?*

(d) row of people, etc.; *we had to stand in line for half an hour to get into the exhibition*; *the line of trucks and buses stretched for miles at the border*

(e) row of written or printed words; *he printed the first two lines and showed them to me*; *can you read the bottom line on the chart?*; *(informal)* **to drop someone a line** = to send someone a short letter; *I'll drop you a line when I get to New York*

(f) **lines** = words learned and then spoken by an actor; *he forgot his lines and had to be prompted*

(g) way of doing things; **in line with** = according to, following (a decision); *we acted in line with the decision made at the meeting*; **to take a hard line** = not to be weak; *the principal takes a hard line with boys who sell drugs on the playground*

(h) type of work; *what's his line of business?*

(i) series of different products, all sold or made by the same company; *we sell several lines of refrigerators*; *I'm afraid we don't stock that line anymore*

2 *verb*

(a) to stand side by side in a line; *soldiers were lining the streets*

(b) to put a lining inside something, especially a piece of clothing; *his jacket is lined in red silk*; *you'll need thick lined boots in Canada*

③ **lined**
['laɪnd] *adjective*

(a) with lines on it; **lined paper** = paper with lines printed on it; *a pad of lined paper*

(b) with people or things standing side by side; **an avenue lined with trees** *or* **a tree-lined avenue** = an avenue with trees along both sides

① **linen**
['lɪnɪn] *noun*

(a) cloth made from fibers from a plant; *he bought a white linen suit*

(b) **(household) linen** = sheets, pillowcases, tablecloths, etc.; *put clean linens on the bed for the visitors* (NOTE: no plural in meaning (a))

② **liner**
['laɪnər] *noun*

(a) large passenger ship; *they went on a cruise round the Caribbean Sea on an American liner*

(b) thing used for lining; *you'll need a coat with a warm liner if you're going to Canada in winter*

① **line up**
['laɪn ʌp] *verb*
to stand in a line; *line up over there if you want to take the next boat*

① **lineup**
['laɪnʌp] *noun*
identification lineup = line of people at a police station from whom a witness is asked to identify a suspected criminal; *she was asked to pick out the mugger at an identification lineup*

④ **linguistic**
[lɪŋˈgwɪstɪk] *adjective*
referring to language(s); *translating this letter into Slovenian is going to test her linguistic skills*

② **lining**
['laɪnɪŋ] *noun*
material put on the inside of something, especially a piece of clothing; *you'll need a coat with a warm lining if you're going to Canada in winter*; **every cloud has a silver lining** = however gloomy things may seem, there is always something that is good

③ **link**
[lɪŋk]
1 *noun*

(a) thing which connects two things or places; *the Channel Tunnel provides a fast rail link between England and France*; **telephone link** = direct line from one telephone to another

(b) one of the rings in a chain; *a chain with solid gold links*

2 *verb*
to join together; *they linked arms and walked down the street*; *his salary is linked to the cost of living*; *all the departments are linked to the main computer*; *the train links New York and Washington*

③ **link up**
['lɪŋk ʌp] *verb*
to join two or more things together; *we have been able to link up all our computers to form a network*

① **lion**
['laɪən] *noun*

(a) large wild animal of the cat family; *lions can be seen in African nature reserves*; **mountain lion** = large brown wild cat of North and South America

(b) **the lion's share** = the biggest part; *Pat took $1000, the lion's share of the $1500 prize*

① **lip**
[lɪp] *noun*

(a) one of the two parts forming the outside of the mouth; *put some balm on your lips to stop them from burning*; **to lick your lips** = to show that you expect you are going to enjoy something; *they licked their lips when they saw the cookies*; **my lips are sealed** = I have promised not to say anything

(b) edge of something round and deep, such as a cup, bowl, etc.; *there's a chip on the lip of that cup*

① **lipstick**
['lɪpstɪk] *noun*

substance for coloring the lips; *she was wearing red lipstick*; *she bought a stick of pink lipstick*

② **liquid**
['lɪkwɪd]
1 *noun*
substance such as water, which flows easily and which is neither a gas nor a solid; *you will need to drink more liquids in hot weather*
2 *adjective*
(a) which is neither gas nor solid, and which flows easily; *a bottle of liquid soap*
(b) liquid assets = cash, or items which can easily be changed into cash

① **liquor**
['lɪkər] *noun*
alcoholic beverage, especially one that has been distilled; *she never drinks hard liquor*

① **list**
[lɪst]
1 *noun*
(a) number of items, names, addresses, etc., written or said one after another; *we've drawn up a list of people to invite to the party*; *he was sick, so we crossed his name off the list*; *the things on the list are in order of importance*; **address list** *or* **mailing list** = list of names and addresses of people and companies; **shopping list** = list of things which you need to buy; **to be on the sick list** = to be reported sick; **to be on the danger list** *or* **on the critical list** = to be dangerously ill; *after the accident, she was on the critical list for some hours*
(b) catalog; **list price** = price of something as shown in a catalog; *he asked for a discount on the list price*; **wine list** = list of wines available in a restaurant; *he asked to see the wine list*
(c) situation where a boat leans to one side; *the ship had taken in water and had developed a 5° list*
2 *verb*
(a) to say or to write a number of items one after the other; *she listed the ingredients on the back of an envelope*; *the catalog lists twenty-three models of washing machines*
(b) *(of a ship)* to lean to one side; *the ship was listing badly and the crew had to be taken off by helicopter*

① **listen**
['lɪsən] *verb*
to pay attention to someone who is talking or to something which you can hear; *don't make a noise - I'm trying to listen to a music program*; *why don't you listen to what I tell you?*; **to listen for** = to wait to see if something makes a noise; *can you listen for the telephone while I'm in the backyard?*

③ **listener**
['lɪsnər] *noun*
person who listens; *the radio station has thousands of listeners*; *Cathy is a good listener - I often go to talk over my problems with her*

④ **listing**
['lɪstɪŋ] *noun*
published list of information; *movie listings are found on the back page of the local paper*; **computer listing** = printout of a list of items taken from the data stored in a computer

② **lit**
[lɪt] *see* LIGHT

④ **liter**
['litər] *noun*
measurement for liquids (almost 2 pints); *I need a 2-liter can of blue paint*; *this bottle holds two liters* (NOTE: usually written l after figures: **25 l** say "twenty-five liters")

④ **literacy**
['lɪtərəsi] *noun*
being able to read and write; *the school is concentrating on improving literacy*

④ **literal**
['lɪtrəl] *adjective*
keeping to the exact meaning of the original words; *a literal translation usually sounds odd*

④ **literally**
['lɪtəli] *adverb*
(a) word for word, in a literal way; *she translated the text literally*
(b) *(to emphasize)* *she was literally made speechless by the interviewer's questions*

④ **literary**
['lɪtrəri] *adjective*
referring to literature; *her style of writing is very literary*; **literary critic** = person who writes reviews of books; **literary prize** = prize given to the writer of a novel, poems, etc.

② **literature**
['lɪtrɪtʃər] *noun*
(a) books or writing, especially novels, poetry, drama, etc.; *she's studying English and American literature*
(b) what has been written on a particular subject; *he knows the literature on Einstein's theories very well*
(c) written publicity material about something; *do you have any literature on travel packages for Montana?* (NOTE: no plural)

② **litter**
['lɪtər]
1 *noun*
(a) garbage left on streets or in public places; *the city tries to keep the main streets clear of litter* (NOTE: no plural in this meaning)
(b) group of young animals born at one time; *she had a litter of eight puppies*
2 *verb*
to drop garbage about; *the street was littered with pieces of paper*

① **little**
['lɪtl]
1 *adjective*
(a) small, not big; *they have two children - a baby boy and a little girl* (NOTE: no comparative or superlative forms in this sense)

(b) not much; *we drink very little milk*; *a TV uses very little electricity* (NOTE: **little - less - least** [list])

2 *pronoun*

a little = a small quantity; *I'm not hungry - just give me a little of that soup*; *can I have a little more coffee please?*

3 *adverb*

not much; not often; *it's little more than two miles from the beach*; *we go to the movie theater very little these days*

◇ **little by little**
['lɪtɪlbaɪ'lɪtl] *adverb*
gradually, not all at once; *they planted trees here and there, until little by little the garden became like a jungle*; *she's getting better little by little*

① **live**
1 *adjective* [laɪv]
(a) living, not dead; *there are strict rules about transporting live animals*; *guess who's moved to the house next door? - a real live TV star*
(b) not recorded; *a live radio show*
(c) carrying electricity; *don't touch the live wires*; *the boys were killed trying to jump over the live line*
2 *adverb* [laɪv]
not recorded; *the show was broadcast live*
3 *verb* [lɪv]
(a) to have your home in a place; *they have gone to live in Canada*; *do you prefer living in the country to the city?*; *he lives next door to a movie star*; *where does your daughter live?*
(b) to be alive; *King Henry VIII lived in the 16th century*; *the doctor doesn't think my mother will live much longer*

③ **live in**
['lɪv 'ɪn] *verb*
to live in the building where you work; *we want a nurse to live in*

④ **live-in**
['lɪv'ɪn] *adjective*
who lives in the place of work; *we have a live-in nurse for my grandfather*

① **lively**
['laɪvli] *adjective*
very active; *the boss is still a lively old man*; *it was a very lively party with a dance band and dozens of young people*; *it's the liveliest nightclub in town* (NOTE: **livelier - liveliest**)

④ **live off**
['lɪv 'ɒf] *verb*
to earn money from; *the whole population of the town lives off tourism*

① **live on**
['lɪv 'ɒn] *verb*
to use food or money to stay alive; *they seem to live on cans of tuna*; *a family can't live on $75 a week*; *our son is staying with us until he earns enough to live on*

② **liver**
['lɪvər] *noun*
(a) large organ in the body which helps to digest food and cleans the blood; *her liver was damaged in the car crash*
(b) animal's liver used as food; *I'll start with chicken livers and salad*; *he looked at the menu and ordered liver and onions*

① **lives**
[lɪvz]
see LIVE

① **lives**
[laɪvz]
see LIFE

③ **live through**
['lɪv 'θru] *verb*
to experience something dangerous; *we lived through two world wars*

③ **live together**
['lɪv tə'geðər] *verb*
(of two people) to live in the same house and have a sexual relationship; *they lived together for two years before they got married*

③ **live up**
['lɪv 'ʌp] *verb*
(a) to live up to expectations = to succeed as was expected; *the movie didn't live up to the publicity that preceded it*
(b) *(informal)* **to live it up** = to lead a life in which you spend a lot of money on wild parties, etc.; *she won a cash prize and immediately started to live it up*

③ **live with**
['lɪv 'wɪθ] *verb*
(a) to put up with something; *we can't do anything about the noise of the aircraft - you'll just have to live with it*
(b) to live with someone = to live in the same house and have a sexual relationship with someone; *he lives with a writer of children's books*

② **living**
['lɪvɪŋ]
1 *adjective*
alive; *does she have any living relatives?*
2 *noun*
(a) money that you need for your daily life; *he earns his living by selling postcards to tourists*; **what do you do for a living?** = what job do you do?; *he doesn't earn a living wage* = he does not earn enough to pay for food, heating, rent, etc.
(b) cost of living = money which a person has to pay for food, heating, rent, etc.; *higher interest rates increase the cost of living*; *see also* COST OF LIVING

① **living room**
['lɪvɪŋ 'rum] *noun*
(in a house or apartment) comfortable room for sitting in; *they were sitting in the living room watching TV*; *why is the living room door*

shut?; *she does her homework on the sofa in the living room*

① **lizard**
['lɪzərd] *noun*
type of small reptile with four legs and a long tail; *little lizards were running around on the walls*

③ **llama**
['lɑmə] *noun*
animal like a camel, with thick hair, found in South America; *Dan went for a ride on a llama when he was in Peru*

① **load**
[ləud]
1 *noun*
(a) heavy objects that are carried in a truck, wagon, etc.; *the truck delivered a load of bricks*; **truckload** *or* **vanload** = amount of goods carried on a truck or van; *they delivered six truckloads of wood*; *when we moved we had three vanloads of books*
(b) responsibility, thing which is difficult to live with; *that's a load off my mind* = I feel much less worried; *I've finished my midterms - that's a load off my mind*
(c) *(informal)* **loads of** = plenty, lots of; *it was a wonderful party - there was loads to eat*; *you don't need to rush - there's loads of time before the train leaves*; *John always has loads of good ideas*
2 *verb*
(a) to put something, especially something heavy, into or onto a truck, van, etc.; *they loaded the furniture into the van*
(b) to put film into a camera
(c) to put a program into a computer; *load the program before you start keyboarding*

① **loaf**
[ləuf]
1 *noun*
(a) large single piece of bread made separately, which you cut into slices before eating it; *he bought a loaf of bread at the corner store*; *we eat about 10 loaves of bread per week*; **sliced loaf** = loaf of bread which has already been sliced in a machine before it is sold (NOTE: plural is **loaves** [ləuvz])
(b) piece of food cooked in an oven; *we had meat loaf for supper*
2 *verb*
to loaf around = to hang around, doing nothing; *he doesn't have a real job and just loafs around downtown all day*

② **loan**
[ləun]
1 *noun*
(a) act of lending; *I had the loan of his car for three weeks*; **on loan** = being lent; *the picture is on loan to the museum*
(b) thing lent, especially a sum of money; *he bought the house with a $150,000 loan from the bank* (NOTE: do not confuse with **lone**)

2 *verb*
to lend; *the furniture for the exhibition has been loaned by the museum*

① **loaves**
[ləuvz]
see LOAF

② **lobby**
['lɒbɪ]
1 *noun*
(a) entrance hall; *I'll meet you in the hotel lobby in half an hour*
(b) group of people who try to influence important people, especially members of Congress; *the senators met members of the green lobby* (NOTE: plural is **lobbies**)
2 *verb*
to try to influence someone; *she lobbied her senator with a detailed letter and other documents* (NOTE: **lobbying - lobbied**)

① **lobster**
['lɒbstər] *noun*
shellfish with a long body, two large claws, and eight legs, used as food; *we had a bowl of lobster soup*

③ **local**
['ləukəl]
1 *adjective*
(a) referring to a place or district near where you are; *she works as a nurse in the local hospital*; *the local paper comes out on Fridays*; *she was formerly the head of the local school*; **local government** = section of elected government which runs a town or district; *we complained to the local authority about the bus service*; **local call** = telephone call to a number in the same area as the person making the call; **local time** = time of day in a particular place; *it will be 1 A.M. local time when we land*
(b) **local anesthetic** = substance which removes the feeling in a certain part of the body only; *she had the operation under local anesthetic*; *this operation can be carried out under local rather than general anesthetic* (NOTE: an anesthetic for the whole of the body is a **general anesthetic**)
2 *noun*
locals = people who live in the area; *the locals don't like all the rich people who take a vacation in their town*; *the restaurant caters to the tourist trade rather than to the locals*

③ **locally**
['ləukəlɪ] *adverb*
in the district near where you are; *when we go camping we usually try to buy everything locally*

② **locate**
[ləu'keɪt] *verb*
(a) to find the position of something; *divers are trying to locate the old Spanish ship*
(b) **to be located** = to be in a particular position; *the heart is located in the left side of the body*; *the warehouse is located near to the highway*

② **location**
[ləʊˈkeɪʃn] *noun*
(a) place or position; *the hotel is in a very central location*
(b) *(filming)* **on location** = in a real setting, not in a studio; *the movie was shot on location in North Africa*
(c) finding the position of something; *the company specializes in the location of underwater wrecks*

① **lock**
[lɒk]
1 *noun*
(a) device which closes a door, safe, box, etc., so that you can only open it with a key; *she left the key in the lock, so the burglars got in easily; we changed the locks on the doors after a set of keys were stolen*
(b) amount by which the wheels of a car can turn left or right; *the wheels have an excellent lock - they turn easily on a narrow road*
(c) section of a river with gates which can be opened or closed to control the flow of water, and so allow boats to move up or down to different levels; *they passed through dozens of locks on their trip down the Mississippi*
2 *verb*
(a) to close a door, safe, box, etc., so that it has to be opened with a key; *I forgot to lock the safe; we always lock the front door before we go to bed*
(b) to fix or to become fixed in a certain position; *the wheels suddenly locked as he went round the corner*

① **locked**
[lɒkt] *adjective*
which has been shut with a key; *the burglars managed to break into a locked safe; the cash box wasn't locked*

③ **locker**
[ˈlɒkər] *noun*
small cupboard for personal belongings which you can close with a key; *luggage lockers can be rented at the railway station*

③ **locker-room**
[ˈlɒkər ˈruːm] *noun*
room where people can change clothes before going to play a game; *the coach gave us a talk in the locker-room just before play started; the referee sent several players to the locker room*

② **lock in**
[ˈlɒk ˈɪn] *verb*
to make someone stay inside a place by locking the door; *I think we've been locked in*

② **lock out**
[ˈlɒk ˈaʊt] *verb*
to make someone stay outside a place by locking the door; *she took the key and locked her husband out; he came back late at night and found he was locked out of the hotel; I've left the keys inside the car and locked myself out*

② **lock up**
[ˈlɒk ˈʌp] *verb*
(a) to close a building by locking the doors; *he always locks up before he goes home; she was locking up the store when a man walked in*
(b) to keep a person or thing inside a place or container by locking the door or lid; *lock up the jewels in the safe or lock the jewels up in the safe*
(c) to put someone in prison; *they locked him up for a week*

② **locomotive**
[ləʊkəˈməʊtɪv] *noun*
engine of a train; *they got rid of the old steam locomotives*

② **lodge**
[lɒdʒ] *verb*
(a) to rent a room in a house; *he lodges with Mrs. Bishop on Pennsylvania Avenue*
(b) *(formal)* **to lodge a complaint against someone** = to make an official complaint about someone; *they lodged a complaint with the local utility company;* **to lodge something with someone** = to deposit something with someone to look after for you; *they lodged all the documents with the attorney*
(c) to become stuck; *a piece of bread was lodged in her throat; the bullet was lodged in his spine*

① **log**
[lɒg]
1 *noun*
(a) thick piece of a tree; *he brought in a load of logs for the fire;* **to sleep like a log** = to sleep very deeply; *after his 12-mile walk he slept like a log*
(b) daily detailed record of speed, position, etc., especially on a ship or plane; *the ship's log gave details of their position when the fire broke out*
2 *verb*
(a) to write down details of something which has happened in a book as a record; *have you logged your day's activities into the book?*
(b) *(computing)* **to log in** *or* **log on** = to enter a special code and start to access a computer system; **to log off** *or* **log out** = to exit a computer system by entering an instruction (NOTE: **logging - logged**)

④ **logic**
[ˈlɒdʒɪk] *noun*
(a) power of formal reasoning; *your logic is faulty - just because she has an MA doesn't mean she's a good teacher*
(b) sense, good reason; *I don't see the logic of owning two cars and not being able to drive*

③ **logical**
[ˈlɒdʒɪkl] *adjective*
(a) clearly reasoned; *a logical conclusion*
(b) *(of person)* able to reason clearly; *she's a very logical person and thinks everything through carefully*

① **lone**
[ləʊn] *adjective*
single, one alone; *she was the lone American in a crowd of Germans; a lone house on the edge of the forest; a lone rider on the beach* (NOTE: do not confuse with **loan**)

① **lonely**
['ləʊnli] *adjective*
(a) feeling sad because of being alone; *it's odd how lonely you can be in a big city full of people*
(b) (place) with few or no people; *the top of the mountain is a lonely place at night; we spent the weekend in a lonely cabin in the forest* (NOTE: **lonelier - loneliest**)

① **long**
[lɒŋ]
1 *adjective*
(a) not short in length; *a long piece of string; the Nile is the longest river in the world; my hair needs cutting - it's getting too long*
(b) not short in time; *what a long program - it lasted almost three hours; they've been waiting for the bus for a long time; we don't approve of long vacations in this job*
(c) (indicating measurement in time) *how long is it before your vacation starts?;* (said when meeting someone) **long time no see!** = I haven't seen you for a long time (NOTE: the use with figures: **the road is six miles long; a piece of string a yard long**)
2 *adverb*
(a) for a long time; *have you been waiting long?; I didn't want to wait any longer; long ago, before the war, this was a wealthy farming area;* **so long!** = see you soon!
(b) **as long as** = provided that; *I like going on picnics as long as it doesn't rain* (NOTE: **longer - longest**)
3 *verb*
to want something very much; *I'm longing for a cup of coffee; everyone was longing to be back home*

④ **long-distance**
[lɒŋ'dɪstəns] *adjective*
(a) (in sport) (race) between two places that are far apart; *she was over fifty when she took up long-distance running; you'll have to get fit if you're going to run a long-distance race*
(b) made over a long distance; *we spent three days walking along one of the long-distance paths in the hills; long-distance telephone calls cost less after 6 P.M.*

③ **longing**
['lɒŋɪŋ] *noun*
great desire for something; *after three months traveling in South America, he had a longing to be back home in Vancouver*

③ **long-lasting**
['lɒŋ'læstɪŋ] *adjective*
which lasts a long time; *long-lasting batteries can run for a much longer time than regular*
batteries; the effects of exposure to sunlight can be very long-lasting

④ **long-range**
[lɒŋ'reɪndʒ] *adjective*
which covers a long distance or a long time; *the long-range weather forecast is not very reliable; they stationed long-range missiles along the border*

④ **long-term**
[lɒŋ'tɜrm] *adjective*
planned to last for a long time; *he asked the bank for a long-term loan; they never make any long-term plans; see also* SHORT-TERM

④ **longtime**
['lɒŋtaɪm] *adjective*
who has existed for a long time; *his longtime partner*

③ **long wave**
['lɒŋ 'weɪv] *noun*
radio wave longer than 1000 meters; *we listened to NPR on long wave; see also* MEDIUM WAVE, SHORTWAVE

① **look**
[lʊk]
1 *noun*
(a) seeing something with your eyes; *take a good look at this photograph and tell me if you recognize anyone in it; we only had time for a quick look around the town*
(b) searching for something; *we had a good look for the ring and couldn't find it anywhere*
(c) the way someone or something appears; *there is a modern look about her clothes;* **good looks** = pleasing and beautiful appearance; *his good looks and charm attracted many women*
2 *verb*
(a) to turn your eyes toward something; *I want you to look carefully at this photograph; look in the restaurant and see if there are any tables free; if you look out of the office window you can see our house; he opened the lid of the box and looked inside*
(b) **to look someone in the eye** = to look straight at someone in a confident way; *he didn't dare look me in the eye;* **don't look a gift horse in the mouth** = don't criticize something that someone has given you for free
(c) to appear to be; *I went to see her in the hospital and she looks worse; is he only forty? - he looks much older than that; those pies look good; it looks as if it might snow*

① **look after**
['lʊk 'æftər] *verb*
to take care of; *nurses look after patients in hospital; who's going to look after your dog when you're away?*

③ **look ahead**
['lʊk ə'hed] *verb*
to make plans for the future; *I'm looking ahead to the summer and hoping to get a part-time job*

③ **look around**
['lʊk ə'raʊnd] *verb*
(a) to turn to see what is behind you; *she heard footsteps behind her and quickly looked around*
(b) to go around looking at something; *did you have time to look around the town?; can I help you? - no, I'm just looking around to see what is available*

③ **look back**
['lʊk 'bæk] *verb*
(a) to turn your head to see what is behind you; *he looked back and saw a police car was following him*
(b) **he never looked back** = he was very successful; *the first year after starting the business was difficult, but after that they never looked back*

③ **look back on**
['lʊk 'bæk ɒn] *verb*
to think about something which happened in the past; *he looked back on his time with the company with satisfaction; looking back on the events of last week, I think we could have handled the problems better*

① **look down**
['lʊk 'daʊn] *verb*
to look down on someone = to think you are better than someone; *he looks down on anyone who hasn't been to college*

① **look for**
['lʊk 'fɔr] *verb*
to search for, to try to find; *we looked for the watch everywhere but couldn't find it; the police are looking for three escaped prisoners*

① **look forward to**
['lʊk 'fɔrwəd 'tu] *phrase*
to think happily about something which is going to happen; *the whole family is looking forward to going on vacation; she isn't looking forward to taking her driver's test; I'm looking forward to seeing my parents again*

④ **look in (on)**
['lʊk 'ɪn ɒn] *verb*
to pay a short visit; *I'll look in on my aunt to see how she is; they didn't stay long - they just looked in on us*

② **look into**
['lʊk 'ɪntʊ] *verb*
to try to find out about a matter or problem; *I asked the manager to look into the question of staff sick days*

① **look like**
['lʊk 'laɪk] *phrase*
(a) to be similar to; *he looks just like his father*
(b) *(asking someone to describe something)* *what's he look like, her new boyfriend?; tell me what she looks like so that I can recognize her when she gets off the train*
(c) to seem to be going to happen; *take an umbrella, it looks like rain; the sky is dark, it looks like snow*

① **look out**
['lʊk 'aʊt] *verb*
(a) to be careful; *look out! - the car is going backwards!*
(b) **to look out on** *or* **over** = to have a view toward; *the windows of the office look out over a park*

② **lookout**
['lʊkaʊt] *noun*
(a) careful watch; *keep a sharp lookout for pickpockets; from their lookout post they could see across the forest;* **to be on the lookout for** = to watch carefully for; *she's always on the lookout for bargains; the police are on the lookout for car thieves; the club is always on the lookout for fresh talent*
(b) business, affair; **that's his lookout** = that is something he must deal with himself

② **look out for**
['lʊk 'aʊt fɔr] *verb*
(a) to keep looking to try to find; *we're looking out for new offices because ours are too small; I'll look out for his sister at the party*
(b) to be careful about; *look out for ice on the sidewalk*
(c) **to look out for someone** = to protect someone; *the falling rock missed us by inches - someone was obviously looking out for us!*

② **look over**
['lʊk 'əʊvər] *verb*
(a) to examine briefly; *she looked over the figures and said they seemed to be OK*
(b) to have a view over something; *the office looks out over an old railroad track*

① **look up**
['lʊk 'ʌp] *verb*
(a) to turn your eyes upwards; *she looked up and saw clouds in the sky*
(b) to try to find some information in a book; *I'll look up his address in the telephone book; look up the word in the dictionary if you don't know what it means*
(c) to get in contact with; *look me up the next time you're in New York*
(d) to get better; *things are looking up*

③ **look up to**
['lʊk 'ʌp tu] *verb*
to admire, to respect someone; *she looks up to her professor and copies everything he does*

③ **loom**
[lum]
1 *verb*
to appear in a threatening way; *a storm loomed on the horizon; a bus suddenly loomed out of the fog*
2 *noun*
machine on which cloth is woven; *she weaves cloth on a hand loom at home*

① **loop**
[lup]
1 *noun*

circle made by a piece of thread or ribbon, etc., which crosses over itself; *to tie your laces, start by making a loop*

2 *verb*

to attach with a loop; *she looped the cord over the tent pole*

① **loose**

[lus] *adjective*

(a) not attached; *watch out! - the sail is loose and swinging toward you!*; *the front wheel is loose and needs to be tightened*; *the boat came loose and started to drift away*

(b) loose ends = things which need to be finished; *I'll take care of any loose ends before I go*; **to be at loose ends** = not to be sure what to do; *we're at loose ends with the car being repaired*

(c) loose change = money in coins only; *can you spare some loose change for the charity?* (NOTE: **looser - loosest**)

④ **loosely**

['lusli] *adverb*

not tightly; *the skirt fits loosely around her waist*; *he tied the boat loosely to the post*

③ **loosen**

['lusən] *verb*

(a) to make something less tight; *he loosened his belt and relaxed*

(b) to loosen your grip on something = to hold something less tightly than before; *the Senate forced the president to loosen his grip on the army*

③ **loot**

[lut]

1 *verb*

to steal, especially from stores and houses, during a riot or other emergency; *some houses were looted after the floods*

2 *noun*

(a) things that have been stolen; *the police discovered the rest of the loot under his bed*

(b) *(slang)* money; *he's got plenty of loot* (NOTE: no plural)

② **lord**

[lɔrd]

1 *noun*

(a) person who rules or is above other people in society; *powerful lords forced King John to sign the Magna Carta*

(b) the Lord = God or Jesus Christ; *praise the Lord for his mercy*

(c) *(expression of surprise or shock)* **good lord!** *I didn't realize it was so late!*

2 *verb*

to lord it over someone = to treat someone like a servant; *she lords it over the junior staff in the office*

④ **lore**

[lɔr] *noun*

traditional beliefs and knowledge; *it's part of children's lore that it is unlucky to walk under a ladder* (NOTE: no plural)

② **lose**

[luz] *verb*

(a) to put or drop something somewhere and not to know where it is; *I can't find my purse - I think I lost it on the train*; *if you lose your ticket you'll have to buy another one*

(b) not to have something any longer; *we lost money on the lottery*; **to lose weight** = to get thinner; *she doesn't eat potatoes since she's trying to lose weight*; **the clock loses 10 minutes every day** = it falls 10 minutes behind the correct time every day; **to lose sight of** = not to see something any longer; *we lost sight of her in the crowd*; **to lose your cool** *or* **your temper** = to become angry; *he lost his temper when they told him there were no tables free*; **to lose time** = to waste time, not to do something quickly enough; *don't lose any time in mailing the letter*; **to lose your way** = to end up not knowing where you are; *they lost their way in the fog on the mountain*; *see also* HEART

(c) not to win; *we lost the game 10 - 0*; *did you win? - no, we lost* (NOTE: **losing - lost** [lɒst])

② **loss**

[lɒs] *noun*

(a) no longer having something; *he was very sad at the loss of his house*

(b) money that you have spent and have not got back; *companies often make losses in their first year of operation*; **they sold it at a loss** = they sold it for less than they paid for it

(c) to be at a loss what to do = not to know what to do; *we are at a loss to know what to do next*; *I'm at a loss for something to do now that the party has been canceled* (NOTE: plural is **losses**)

① **lost**

[lɒst] *adjective*

to be lost = to end up not knowing where you are; *did you bring a map? I think we're lost!*; **lost and found office** = place where articles which people have left on trains, buses, etc., are kept, and where they can be claimed by their owners; *go to the lost and found office tomorrow and ask if anyone has found the hat*; *have you asked the lost and found office if they've got your bag?*; *we found an umbrella on the train and handed it in at the lost and found office*; *see also* GET LOST

① **lot**

[lɒt] *noun*

(a) a lot of *or* **lots of** = a large number or a large quantity; *there's lots of time before the train leaves*; *what a lot of cars there are in the parking lot!*; *I've been to the movie theater quite a lot recently*; *she's feeling a lot better now*; *lots of people are looking for jobs*

(b) the lot = everything; *that's the lot - there's nothing left*; *there were old pots and books and newspapers - we sold the lot for $75*; *we picked pounds of beans and ate the lot for dinner*

(c) piece of land, especially one to be used for

development; **parking lot** = place where you can park automobiles; *you can park in the visitors' parking lot*
(d) item or group of items sold at an auction; *lot 23 is a collection of books and pictures* /(draw names, straws, etc.)

④ **lottery**
['lɒtri] *noun*
(a) game of chance in which numbered tickets are sold with prizes given for certain numbers; *she won over $3 million on the lottery*; *there were three winners on this week's lottery*; *he buys a lottery ticket every week*
(b) situation where anyone may win; *getting a government contract is something of a lottery* (NOTE: plural is **lotteries**)

① **loud**
[laʊd]
1 *adjective*
(a) which is very easily heard; *can't you stop your watch making such a loud noise?*; *turn down the radio - it's too loud*
(b) *(of colors)* too bright; *he was wearing a particularly loud necktie which didn't go with his jacket at all*
2 *adverb*
loudly; *I can't sing any louder*; *she laughed out loud in church* (NOTE: **louder - loudest**)

② **loudspeaker**
[laʊd'spikər] *noun*
part of a radio, TV, public address system, etc., which allows sound to be heard; *he set up two loudspeakers in opposite corners of the room*; *the captain called the passengers over the loudspeaker and asked them to go on deck*

③ **lounge**
[laʊnʒ]
1 *noun*
(a) comfortable room for sitting in; *let's go and watch TV in the lounge*
(b) **departure lounge** = room at an airport where passengers wait to board their planes; *as more flights were delayed, the departure lounge filled up with angry travelers*
2 *verb*
to lounge around = to sit or lie doing nothing or very little; *he doesn't do anything on Saturdays, he just lounges around*; *it rained all the time, so we had to spend the day lounging around in the hotel*

① **love**
[lʌv]
1 *noun*
(a) great liking for someone or something; *give my love to your wife*; *his great love is baseball*; **to be in love** = to love each other; *they seem to be very much in love*; **to fall in love with someone** = to start to like them very much; *they fell in love at first sight*
(b) **to make love (to someone)** = to have sex with someone; *she swore that he had never*

made love to her *or* that they had never made love
(c) **there's no love lost between them** = they hate each other; *the partners got on well to begin with, but now there's no love lost between them*
(d) *(in games such as tennis)* score of zero points; *she lost the first set six - love (6-0)*
(e) person whom you love; *she's the love of his life*
2 *verb*
(a) to have strong feelings for someone or something; *she loves little children*; *the children love their teacher*; *his wife thinks he loves someone else*
(b) to like something very much; *we love going to the beach*; *I'd love to come with you, but I've got too much work to do*

① **lovely**
['lʌvli] *adjective*
very pleasant; *it's a lovely warm day*; *she was wearing a lovely pink hat* (NOTE: **lovelier - loveliest**)

① **lover**
['lʌvər] *noun*
(a) person, especially a man, who is having a sexual relationship with someone; *her lover was arrested when the woman's body was found on the beach*
(b) person who loves something; *a lover of French food*

① **low**
[loʊ]
1 *adjective*
(a) not high; *she hit her head on the low branch*; *the town is surrounded by low hills*; *we shop around to find the lowest prices*; *the engine works best at low speeds*; *the temperature here is too low for oranges to grow*; *sales were lower in December than in November*
(b) sad and depressed; *she was very low when I saw her last* (NOTE: **lower - lowest**)
2 *adverb*
toward the bottom; not high up; *the plane was flying too low - it hit the trees*; **supplies are running low** = supplies are becoming scarce; *see also* LIE LOW
3 *noun*
point where something is very small; *the exchange rate has reached a new low*
4 *prefix meaning* "with not much of"; **low-fat** = containing very little fat; *do you have any low-fat yogurt?*

① **lower**
['loʊər]
1 *adjective*
which is below something else of the same sort; **lower deck** = bottom deck on a ship or bus; *they booked a cabin on the lower deck*; **lower jaw** = bottom jaw, the bone holding the lower teeth, which moves to make the mouth open or shut;

she hit him so hard that she broke his lower jaw
(NOTE: the opposite is **upper**)

2 *verb*

(a) to make something go down; *they lowered the boats into the water*; *the crane lowered the machine into the building*

(b) to make smaller; *all the stores have lowered their prices to attract customers*; **to lower your voice** = to speak more quietly

② **loyal**
['lɔɪəl] *adjective*

faithful, who supports someone or something; *dogs are usually very loyal to their owners*; *she's a loyal member of the Republican Party*

② **loyalty**
['lɔɪəltɪ] *noun*

being loyal; *all the staff should show their loyalty by coming to the meeting*

① **luck**
[lʌk]

1 *noun*

something, usually good, which happens to you; *their winning the championship was pure luck*; **good luck with your driver's test!** = I hope you do well in your driver's test; **I wear this ring for luck** = because I hope it will bring me good luck; **to be down on your luck** = to be going through a period of bad luck; *he was down on his luck and thought of trying to find work in Canada*

2 *verb*

to luck out = to have something good happen through chance

① **luckily**
['lʌkɪlɪ] *adverb*

which is a good thing; *it started to rain but luckily I had taken my umbrella*; *luckily I was at home when the telephone repairman called*

① **lucky**
['lʌkɪ] *adjective*

(a) having good things happening to you; *he's lucky not to have been sent to prison*; *how lucky you are to be going to Hawaii!*

(b) which brings luck; *15 is my lucky number*
(NOTE: **luckier - luckiest**)

④ **ludicrous**
['ludɪkrəs] *adjective*

ridiculous, which makes you laugh; *it's ludicrous that we have to carry our bags from the train up three flights of stairs*

① **luggage**
['lʌgɪdʒ] *noun*

baggage, the suitcases, bags, etc., for carrying your belongings when traveling; *check that you haven't left any luggage behind on the bus*; **luggage rack** = space for bags, etc., above the seats in a plane, train, etc.; *she put her suitcase on the luggage rack* (NOTE: **luggage** has no plural; to show one suitcase, etc., say **an item of luggage, a piece of luggage**)

② **lumberjack**
['lʌmbərdʒæk] *noun*

person who cuts down trees and transports the logs; *the lumberjack cut down the tree*

② **lump**
[lʌmp]

1 *noun*

(a) piece of something, often with no particular shape; *a lump of sugar*

(b) **lump sum** = money paid in one amount; *he received a lump sum from an insurance policy*

(c) hard or swollen part on the body; *she went to the doctor because she had found a lump in her throat*

2 *verb*

to lump together = to bring several different things together; *we lump all the cash purchases together under "other items" in the account book*

① **lunch**
[lʌnʃ]

1 *noun*

meal eaten in the middle of the day; *come on - lunch will be ready soon*; *we always eat lunch at 12:30*; *we are having burgers and chips for lunch*; *I'm not hungry so I don't want a big lunch*; *the restaurant serves 150 lunches a day*; **business lunch** *or* **working lunch** = lunch where you discuss business (NOTE: plural is **lunches**)

2 *verb*

to have lunch; *I'm lunching with my sister today*; *don't forget we're lunching with the agents tomorrow*

③ **lunchtime**
['lʌnʃtaɪm] *noun*

time when you usually have lunch; *it's half past twelve - almost lunchtime*; *the office is closed at lunchtime*

① **lung**
[lʌŋ] *noun*

one of two organs in the chest with which you breathe; *the doctor listened to his chest to see if his lungs were all right*

> COMMENT: the two lungs are situated in the chest, with the heart between them. Air goes down into the lungs and the oxygen in it is deposited in the blood

③ **luxurious**
[lʌkˈʒʊəriəs] *adjective*

very comfortable; *the apartment is furnished with luxurious carpets and fittings*; *business class is not as luxurious as first class*

① **luxury**
['lʌkʃəri] *noun*

(a) great comfort; *he lived a life of great luxury*; *a hot bath is a real luxury after two weeks camping in the mountains*; **luxury hotel** = a five-star hotel, a very good hotel, with luxurious rooms and higher prices

(b) thing which is pleasant to have but not necessary; *she often buys little luxuries for dessert on Friday nights* (NOTE: plural in this meaning is **luxuries**)

② **lying**
['laɪɪŋ] *see* LIE

④ **lynch**
[lɪnʃ] *verb*
(of a mob) to catch an accused person and kill him, especially by hanging, without a trial; *the crowd lynched one man, but the actual murderer escaped*

④ **lyrical**
['lɪrɪkl] *adjective*
(poem, etc.) concerned with feeling; *a lyrical description of the countryside in spring*

③ **lyrics**
['lɪrɪks] *noun*
words of a song; *he wrote the lyrics for the musical*

Mm

③ **M, m**
[em]
thirteenth letter of the alphabet, between L and N; *"accommodation" is spelled with two Ms*

① **machine**
[mə'ʃin] *noun*
(a) thing which works with a motor; *we have bought a machine for putting leaflets in envelopes*; *there is a message on my answering machine*; *she made her dress on her sewing machine*; *the washing machine has broken and flooded the kitchen*
(b) organization; *the party machine moved into action to prepare for the general election*

① **machine gun**
[mə'ʃin 'gʌn] *noun*
gun which automatically fires many bullets rapidly, one after the other; *the rapid fire of a machine gun could be heard in the distance*; *from their lookout post they were able to cover the whole square with machine-gun fire*

② **machinery**
[mə'ʃinəri] *noun*
(a) many machines, taken as a group; *the factory has got rid of a lot of old machinery*
(b) way of organizing; *the machinery for awarding government contracts* (NOTE: no plural: **some machinery, a piece of machinery**)

① **mad**
[mæd] *adjective*
(a) having a serious mental disorder; *he's quite mad*; *she became mad and had to be put in a special hospital*
(b) silly, crazy; *everyone thought he was mad to try to cross the Atlantic in a rowboat*; *(informal)* **mad about** = very keen on; *he's mad about doing crossword puzzles in newspapers*; **mad as a hatter** = totally crazy; *don't ask him for advice - he's mad as a hatter*
(c) wildly frantic; *the noise is driving her mad*; *(informal)* **like mad** = very fast; with a lot of enthusiasm; *he drove like mad and managed to get to the station in time to catch the train*; *they worked like mad to finish the job on time*
(d) very angry; *she's mad at him for borrowing her car*; *he was hopping mad when they told him his automobile had been stolen* (NOTE: **madder - maddest**)

④ **madam**
['mædəm] *noun*
(polite way of referring to a lady) *Madam Chairman*; *would madam like some more tea?*

① **made**
[meɪd] *see* MAKE

③ **made-to-order**
['meɪd tə 'ɔrdər] *adjective*
(clothes, etc.) which are made specially according to the measurements of one particular person; *I've bought a made-to-measure suit*

③ **made-up**
['meɪdʌp] *adjective*
(a) wearing makeup; *she was heavily made-up to try to hide the mark on her cheek*
(b) invented; *it was a made-up story - none of the report was true*

④ **madly**
['mædli] *adverb*
in a wild way; *they were madly in love*; *as soon as we came through the gate, the dogs rushed across the yard, barking madly*

③ **Mafia**
['mæfiə] *noun*
secret Italian organization dealing in crime or group of people similar to the Mafia; *the drug mafia*

② **magazine**
[mægə'zin] *noun*
(a) illustrated paper which comes out regularly; *the computing magazine comes out on Fridays*
(b) radio or TV program made up from various items on the same theme, broadcast regularly; *following the news, this week's science magazine has features on space telescopes and global warming*

(c) container for bullets which can be attached to a gun; *he clipped the magazine to the gun*

① **magic**
['mædʒɪk] *noun*
spells, tricks, etc., that do not appear to follow normal scientific rules; *he made a rabbit appear in his hat, and the children all thought it was magic*; **as if by magic** = suddenly, without any possible explanation; *he pushed a button and, as if by magic, lights came on all over the garden*

② **magician**
[mə'dʒɪʃn] *noun*
(a) wizard; *Merlin was the great magician in old stories*
(b) conjuror; *they hired a magician to entertain the children at the party*

④ **magistrate**
['mædʒɪstreɪt] *noun*
judge who hears cases in a minor court; *she appeared before the magistrate*; *he was fined $750 by the magistrate*

① **magnet**
['mægnət] *noun*
(a) piece of metal that attracts iron and steel and will point roughly north and south when balanced on a point; *you can move little pieces of iron around on a piece of paper by holding a magnet underneath*; *she has a figure of Mickey Mouse that sticks to the fridge door with a magnet*
(b) anything which attracts; *butterflies were attracted to the flowers like a magnet*; *the big city is a magnet for teenagers running away from home*

③ **magnetic**
[mæg'netik] *adjective*
(a) which attracts metal; *iron and steel can be made magnetic, but wood and paper cannot*; **magnetic field** = area around a magnet which is under its influence; **magnetic north** *or* **Magnetic North Pole** = the point near the North Pole to which a floating magnet will point; *see also* STRIP, TAPE
(b) having a power of attraction; *she has a magnetic personality - everyone looks at her when she enters a room*

③ **magnificent**
[mæg'nɪfɪsənt] *adjective*
very fine, very splendid, very luxurious; *he lives in a magnificent 20-bedroom mansion by the lake*; *she gave a magnificent performance as Cleopatra*

② **magnifying glass**
['mægnɪfaɪɪŋ 'glɑs] *noun*
lens which makes small objects appear larger; *she used a magnifying glass to read the instructions on the bottle*

④ **magnitude**
['mægnɪtjud] *noun*
(a) *(formal)* importance; *they did not underestimate the magnitude of the task*

(b) measure of the brightness of any object in the sky; *a star of the third magnitude*
(c) scale of an earthquake; *the earthquake registered a magnitude of 5.4*

③ **magpie**
['mægpaɪ] *noun*
common large black and white bird; *magpies sometimes steal bright objects like bits of glass*

② **maid**
[meɪd] *noun*
female servant; *the maid forgot to change the towels* (NOTE: do not confuse with **made**)

① **mail**
[meɪl] *noun*
1 *noun*
(a) letters that are delivered; *the mail hasn't come yet*; *my secretary opens my mail as soon as it arrives*; *the receipt was in this morning's mail*
(b) service provided by the post office; *the check was lost in the mail*; *we sent the package by first-class mail*; *it's cheaper to send the order by surface mail than by air*; **mail merge** = computer program that allows the same letter to be written to many different addresses; *see also* AIRMAIL, EMAIL
2 *verb*
to send something by the postal services; *we mailed the catalog to addresses all over Massachusetts*; *he mailed the order last Wednesday* (NOTE: do not confuse with **male**)

① **mailbox**
['meɪlbɒks] *noun*
(a) a box into which you can put letters, which will then be collected and sent on by the postal service; *she dropped the letters in the mailbox*
(b) a private box into which a mail carrier delivers mail; *I always check my mailbox before I go to work*
(c) electronic system by which e-mails are received; *you need to clear out the advertising messages from your mailbox*

② **mail carrier**
['meɪl 'kæriər] *noun*
person who delivers letters to houses or collects them from mailboxes; *the mail carrier comes very early - before eight o'clock*

③ **mailing list**
['meɪlɪŋ 'lɪst] *noun*
list of names and addresses of people to whom information can be sent; *his name is on our mailing list*; *we are building up a mailing list of possible customers*

② **mailman**
['meɪlmæn] *noun*
= MAIL CARRIER

③ **mail order**
[meɪl 'ɔrdər] *noun*
ordering and buying by mail; *I bought the sofa by mail order or from a mail-order catalog*

② **main**

[meɪn]

1 *adjective*

most important; *the main thing is to get to work on time*; *their main factory is in Detroit*; *January is the main month for skiing vacations*; *an automobile will meet you at the main entrance*; **Main Street** = most important street in a small town, where the stores and banks are

2 *noun*

(a) large pipe for water, gas, etc.; *a water main burst and flooded the street*; *workmen hit a gas main when they were digging a hole in the road*

(b) in the main = generally speaking; *in the main, English speakers have difficulty in learning other languages*

④ **mainland**

['meɪnlənd] *noun*

large solid mass of land, as opposed to an island; *the ferry takes 15 minutes to reach the mainland*

② **mainly**

['meɪnli] *adverb*

(a) most often; *we sell mainly to businesses*; *people mainly go on vacation in the summer*

(b) chiefly; *she is mainly interested in old churches*

④ **mainstream**

['meɪnstrim]

1 *adjective*

(group, trend, etc.) most important; *it took him more than ten years to become a mainstream Hollywood director*; *she wants to get into mainstream politics*

2 *noun*

the most important part of a group, etc.; *the opinion of the mainstream of the party is very important*

③ **maintain**

[meɪn'teɪn] *verb*

(a) to keep something going; *we like to maintain good relations with our customers*

(b) to keep something in good working order; *the boiler needs to be regularly maintained*

(c) to state as a fact; *throughout the trial he maintained that the vehicle was not his*

④ **maintenance**

['meɪntənəns] *noun*

(a) keeping in working order; *we offer a full maintenance service*

(b) keeping things going or working; *the maintenance of contacts with government officials*

(c) money for upkeep, especially paid by a divorced or separated person to help pay for living expenses for children; *he refused to pay maintenance for their children*

② **majesty**

['mædʒəsti] *noun*

(a) beautiful or impressive sight; *the majesty of*

the range of white mountains took his breath away

(b) *(formal)* (used as a form of address to a king or queen) *Her Majesty, Queen Elizabeth II* (NOTE: when speaking formally to a king or queen, say **Your Majesty**)

② **major**

['meɪdʒər]

1 *adjective*

(a) important; *cigarettes are a major cause of lung cancer*; *computers are a major influence on modern industrial society*; *many small roads are blocked by snow, but the major roads are open*; **the major part of** = most of; *the major part of the movie takes place in Seattle*; **major league** = highest-ranking league in professional sports, especially baseball; *he's playing in the major leagues now*

(b) musical key; *she played a piece by Bach in B major*; *compare* MINOR

2 *noun*

rank of an officer in the army below colonel; *a major came up in a truck with six soldiers* (NOTE: used as a title with a surname: **Major Smith**)

3 *verb*

to specialize in a subject at college; *she majored in English literature*

③ **majority**

[mə'dʒɒrɪti] *noun*

(a) larger part of a group; *the majority of the members of the club doesn't want to change the rules*; **in the majority** = being more than half of the members; *women are in a majority on the committee*; *see also* SILENT

(b) number of votes by which a candidate or party wins; *she won by a majority of 3300 votes*; *the Democrats won by a small majority* (NOTE: plural is **majorities**)

② **make**

[meɪk]

1 *noun*

the country or the company which makes something; *Japanese makes of automobiles*; *what is the make of your refrigerator?*

2 *verb*

(a) to put together, to build; *he made a boat out of old pieces of wood*; *these knives are made of steel*

(b) to get ready; *do you want me to make some tea?*; *she is making a cake*; **to make a bed** = to make a bed tidy after someone has slept in it; *when we got to the hotel, the beds hadn't been made*

(c) to add up to a total; *six and four make ten*

(d) to earn (money); *he made millions of dollars by buying and selling property*

(e) to give someone a feeling; *the smell of coffee makes me hungry*; *the rough sea made him feel sick*; *looking at old photographs made her sad*; *he made himself comfortable in the armchair*

(f) to reach a place; *Ireland made the quarterfinals of the World Cup*

(g) to force someone to do something; *his mother made him clean his room*; *the teacher made us all stay after school*; *I can't make the car go any faster*; *what on earth made you do that?* (NOTE: making - made [meɪd])

③ **make do with**
['meɪk 'du 'wɪθ] *verb*
to use something because there is nothing else available; *she forgot her pajamas, and had to make do with a T-shirt*; *the store has no wheat bread left so we'll have to make do with white*; *all the glasses are broken, so we'll have to make do with plastic cups*

② **make for**
['meɪk 'fɔr] *verb*
(a) to go toward; *the army was making for the capital*; *as soon as the movie started, she made straight for the exit*
(b) to help something to happen; *frozen food makes for easier meals*

③ **make of**
['meɪk ɒv] *verb*
to have an impression or opinion about something; *what did you make of the news on TV?*; *we don't know what to make of this letter*

③ **make off with**
['meɪk 'ɒf wɪð] *verb*
to steal something; *the burglar made off with all their silver*

② **make out**
['meɪk 'aʊt] *verb*
(a) to be able to see clearly; *can you make out the house in the dark?*
(b) to be able to understand; *I can't make out why he doesn't want to come*
(c) to claim something which is probably not true; *the weather in Alaska isn't really as bad as it is made out to be*; *she tries to make out that she's very poor*
(d) to write something, such as a name; *the check is made out to James Smith*
(e) *(informal)* to be successful; *he tried opening a seafood restaurant but it didn't make out*; *how is Bobby making out at school?*

① **maker**
['meɪkər] *noun*
person who makes something; *the makers of vitamins must have made a lot of money over the years*; *the company is the world's biggest maker of ice cream*

① **make up**
['meɪk 'ʌp] *verb*
(a) to invent a story; *he said he had seen a man climbing into the house, but in fact he made the whole story up*
(b) to make yourself up = to put on powder, lipstick, etc.
(c) to form; *the staff is made up of secretaries and drivers*

(d) to make up your mind = to decide; *they can't make up their minds on where to go for their vacation*; *his mind is made up* = nothing will make him change his mind; *it's no use talking to him - his mind is made up*
(e) to make up lost time = to act quickly because you did not act earlier; *it's June already - we'll have to plant our beans now to make up lost time*

② **makeup**
['meɪkʌp] *noun*
(a) face powder, lipstick, etc., which are put on your face to make it more beautiful or to change its appearance; *she wears no makeup apart from a little lipstick*; *he spent hours over his makeup for the part of the old grandfather*
(b) way in which something is formed or arranged; *by bringing in new managers, he's altered the whole makeup of the company*; *the census shows the ethnic makeup of the population*

② **male**
[meɪl]
1 *adjective*
(a) referring to the sex which does not give birth to young; *a male deer crossed the road in front of our truck*
(b) referring to men or boys; *the male population is more likely to get the flu than the female*
2 *noun*
(a) man or boy; *the wreckage contained the bodies of two males and two females*
(b) animal or insect of the sex which does not give birth to young or lay eggs; *with spiders, the female is usually bigger than the male* (NOTE: do not confuse with **mail**)

④ **mall**
noun [mɔl]
shopping mall = enclosed covered shopping area with stores, restaurants, banks and other facilities; *the new shopping mall is taking customers away from the stores downtown*

④ **mammal**
['mæml] *noun*
type of animal which gives birth to live young and feeds them with milk; *human beings, cats, dolphins and bats are all mammals*

① **man**
[mæn]
1 *noun*
(a) male human being; *that tall man is my brother*; *there's a young man at the reception desk asking for Mr. Smith*
(b) any human being; *Stone Age men existed several thousand years ago*
(c) the man in the street = an ordinary person; *the man in the street isn't interested in world politics* (NOTE: plural is **men** [men])
2 *verb*
to provide staff to work something; *the switchboard is manned all day*; *the booth was*

manned by three saleswomen; she sometimes mans the front desk when everyone else is at lunch (NOTE: mans - manning - manned)

① **manage**
['mænɪdʒ] *verb*
(a) to be in charge of something; *she manages all our offices in Europe; we want to appoint someone to manage the new store*
(b) **to manage to do something** = to do something successfully; *did you manage to call the office?; the burglars managed to open the door of the safe*
(c) to be able to work properly or cope with a situation; *can you manage all by yourself?; how are we going to manage without a driver?*

② **management**
['mænɪdʒmənt] *noun*
(a) group of people who direct workers; *the management has decided to move to new offices*; **under new management** = with a new owner or manager; *the store is under new management*; **senior management** = senior managers or directors; **middle management** = managers of departments who are not as important as directors; *there have been layoffs, even at middle management level*
(b) directing and control of work; *he's taking a course in management; if anything goes wrong now it's just a case of bad management*

② **manager**
['mænɪdʒər] *noun*
(a) person in charge of a department in a store or in a business; *the bank manager wants to talk about your account; the sales manager organized a publicity campaign; she's the manager of the shoe department*
(b) organizer of a sports team; *the club have just laid off their manager*
(c) person who is employed to organize the work of a singer, sportsman, actor, etc.; *her manager is organizing her tour of North America*

① **mane**
[meɪn] *noun*
long hair on the neck of a lion or horse; *he clung onto the horse's mane as it raced along the edge of the sea* (NOTE: do not confuse with **main**)

③ **maneuver**
[mə'nuvər]
1 *noun*
(a) **maneuvers** = military exercises; *the fleet is on maneuvers in the Mediterranean*
(b) planned action to avoid something; *the captain had to make a sudden maneuver to avoid hitting the smaller ship; the company has carried out various maneuvers to avoid bankruptcy*
2 *verb*
(a) to move something heavy or difficult to handle; *we maneuvered the piano into position on the stage*

(b) to work to put yourself in a good position; *she managed to maneuver herself onto the board of the company*

④ **mango**
['mæŋgəʊ] *noun*
large tropical fruit with yellow flesh and a big stone; *we ate fresh mangoes after our Indian meal* (NOTE: plural is **mangoes**)

④ **manipulate**
[mə'nɪpjuleɪt] *verb*
(a) to handle; *she found it difficult to manipulate the steering wheel while wearing gloves*
(b) to influence people or situations so that you get what you want; *by manipulating the media, the government made sure its message got across to the people*
(c) to produce false accounts to make a company seem more profitable than it really is; *he was accused of manipulating the sales figures to protect the share price*

② **manner**
['mænər] *noun*
(a) way of behaving; *she has a very unpleasant manner; the staff doesn't like the new assistant's manner*
(b) **manners** = way of behaving in public; *it's bad manners to speak with your mouth full; those boys need to be taught some manners*
(c) sort; **in a manner of speaking** = in some kind of way; *in a manner of speaking, I'm glad to have got fired, as I won't have to work in that dreadful office again*

④ **manslaughter**
['mænslɔtər] *noun*
offense of killing someone without having intended to do so; *he was acquitted of murder but found guilty of manslaughter; compare* MURDER

② **mantelpiece**
['mæntlpis] *noun*
shelf above a fireplace; *the clock on the mantelpiece struck twelve*

③ **manual**
['mænjuəl]
1 *adjective*
(a) done by hand; **manual work** = work done with your hands; *he has no qualifications, so he does some manual work while studying*; **manual worker** = worker who works with his hands
(b) (car) where the gears are changed by hand; *I prefer a manual model to an automatic*
2 *noun*
book of instructions; *look in the manual to see if it tells you how to clean the printer*

② **manufacture**
[mænju'fæktʃər]
1 *noun*
making of a commercially produced product; *most of the automobiles are of foreign manufacture*

2 *verb*

to make products commercially; *we no longer manufacture buses here*

② **manufacturer**

[mænjʊˈfæktʃərər] *noun*

person or company producing industrial products; *an aircraft manufacturer; a shoe manufacturer*

③ **manufacturing**

[mænjʊˈfæktʃərɪŋ]

1 *noun*

the business of making things in large quantities for sale; *only 25% of the nation's workforce is now engaged in manufacturing*

2 *adjective*

that manufactures things; **manufacturing industries** = industries that take raw materials and make them into finished products; **manufacturing town** = a town that has many industries based in it; *this used to be a prosperous manufacturing town before the factories closed*

③ **manuscript**

[ˈmænjʊskrɪpt] *noun*

(a) document, letter, poem, etc., which has been written by hand or typed; *one of the original manuscripts of the book is on display in the library; several manuscripts by George Washington are being sold*

(b) handwritten or typed version of a book that has not been printed or published; *he sent his manuscript to several publishers, but no one wanted to publish it* (NOTE: often written **MS**, plural **MSS**, say "manuscripts")

① **many**

[ˈmeni]

1 *adjective*

(a) a large number of things or people; *many old people retire to live in Florida; so many people wanted rooms that the hotel was booked up; she ate twice as many cookies as her sister did*

(b) *(asking a question)* how many times have you been to California?; how many passengers were there on the plane?*

(c) a great many *or* **a good many** = quite a lot; *a good many people think we should build a new highway;* **too many** = more than necessary; *there were too many people waiting and not enough room on the bus for all of them;* **one too many** = one more than enough (NOTE: **many - more** [mɔr] **- most** [mʊst]. Note also that **many** is used with nouns that you can count: **not many apples** but **not much bread**)

2 *pronoun*

a large number of people; *many of the students knew the lecturer when he was a student himself; many would say that smoking should be banned in all public places*

① **map**

[mæp]

1 *noun*

drawing which shows a place, such as a town, a country or the world as if it is seen from the air; *here's a map of Canada; the town where they live is so small I can't find it on the map; show me on the map where the mountains are; they lost their way because they'd forgotten to take a map;* **street map** = plan showing streets with their names; *if you're going to New York City, you'll need a street map*

2 *verb*

(a) to make a map of a country, etc.; *the explorers mapped the whole of the south of the country*

(b) to map out = to plan in advance; *we met yesterday to map out our publicity program; he mapped out a plan to buy the company* (NOTE: **mapping - mapped**)

② **maple**

[ˈmeɪpl] *noun*

northern tree, growing mainly in the U.S.A. and Canada, with sweet sap; *maples are particularly beautiful in fall when their leaves turn red;* **maple syrup** = syrup made from the sap of the maple tree; *we had pancakes with maple syrup*

④ **marathon**

[ˈmærəθən] *noun*

(a) long distance race; *a marathon is run over 26 miles; she's training for the New York marathon*

(b) anything which lasts a long time and is very tiring; *the marathon meeting of club members lasted for over five hours; after a marathon negotiating session, we finally reached agreement*

① **marble**

[ˈmɑrbl] *noun*

(a) very hard type of stone which can be polished so that it shines brilliantly; *the entrance hall has a marble floor; the tabletop is made from a single piece of green marble*

(b) marbles = set of small glass balls for playing with; *children were playing marbles on the school playground; I found a marble under the sofa*

① **march**

[mɑrtʃ]

1 *noun*

(a) walking in step by soldiers, sailors, etc.; *the soldiers were tired after their long march through the mountains;* **march past** = ceremony where soldiers march in step in front of someone important; *all sections of the armed forces took part in the march past at which the president took the salute;* **quick march** = rapid walking pace; **slow march** = slow walking pace

(b) mass of people walking to protest something; *the police estimate that around 5000 people took part in the march*

(c) music with a regular beat for marching; *at the end of the ceremony the band played a slow march;* **wedding march** = music that is played after a wedding; *as the bride and bridegroom*

came out of the church the organ played the wedding march (NOTE: plural is **marches**)
2 *verb*
(a) to walk in step; *the guards marched after the band*; *we were just in time to see the soldiers march past*
(b) **the police marched him off to prison** = they took him away quickly to prison
(c) to walk quickly and with a particular purpose; *she marched into the store and asked to speak to the manager*
(d) to walk in a protest march; *thousands of workers marched to the capitol building*

① **March**
[mɑrtʃ] *noun*
third month of the year, between February and April; *her birthday is in March*; *today is March 6*; *we moved to Chicago last March*; *we often have storms in March* (NOTE: **March 6**: say: "March sixth")

② **mare**
['meər] *noun*
female horse; *the mares were running in the field*

② **margarine**
['mɑrdʒərɪn] *noun*
mixture of animal or vegetable oil which is used instead of butter; *can you tell the difference between butter and margarine?*; *I prefer butter to margarine*

③ **margin**
['mɑrdʒɪn] *noun*
(a) white space at the edge of a page of writing; *write your comments in the margin*; *we left a wide margin so that you can write notes in it*
(b) extra space, time, etc.; **leave a margin for error** = allow extra space or time in case you have made a mistake; **safety margin** = space or time left to allow for safety; **by a wide margin** = by a big distance, by a large number of votes, etc.; *the Democratic candidate won by a wide margin*
(c) money received which is more than money paid; *small businesses operate on very narrow margins*; *we have to cut our margins to remain competitive*; **gross margin** = difference between the price received and the cost of manufacture; **net margin** = difference between the price received and all costs, including overheads

③ **marine**
[mə'rin]
1 *adjective*
referring to the sea; *she studied marine biology*
2 *noun*
(a) **the merchant marine** = the merchant navy
(b) soldier serving in the navy; *he decided not to join the Marines, but to become a pilot instead*; *the Marines attacked the enemy air base*

① **mark**
[mɑrk]
1 *noun*

(a) small spot of a different color; *the red wine has made a mark on the tablecloth*; *she has a mark on her forehead where she hit her head*
(b) points given to a student; *she got top marks in English*; *what kind of mark did you get for your homework?*
(c) line showing a certain point; *his income has reached the $150,000 mark*; **high-water mark** = line showing where the high tide reaches
(d) target; **wide of the mark** = not at all correct; *his estimate of the costs was wide of the mark*
(e) printed sign; **exclamation mark** = written sign (!) which shows surprise; **question mark** = written sign (?) which shows that a question is being asked
(f) *(order given to runners at the beginning of a race)* **on your marks, get set, go!**
2 *verb*
(a) to make a mark; **the box is marked "dangerous"** = it has the word "dangerous" written on it
(b) to correct and give points to work; *the teacher hasn't finished marking our homework*; *has the English exam been marked yet?*
(c) *(in games)* **to mark an opponent** = to follow an opposing player closely, so as to prevent him getting the ball
(d) **to mark time** = to stay on one spot, not to move forward; *sales are simply marking time*

③ **mark down**
['mɑrk 'daʊn] *verb*
to reduce the price of something; *we have marked all prices down by 30% for the sale*

③ **marked**
[mɑrkt] *adjective*
(a) very obvious, definite; *this month's sales showed a marked improvement*; *his performance was first class - in marked contrast to his game last week*
(b) **a marked man** = man who has been selected by an enemy as a probable target; *he informed on the leader of the gang, and since has become a marked man*

① **marker**
['mɑrkər] *noun*
(a) thing which marks; colored felt pen that makes a wide mark
(b) person who gives a mark to a piece of work, an examination, an entry in a competition, etc.; *our teacher is a very hard marker - nobody gets more than seven out of ten*

① **market**
['mɑrkɪt]
1 *noun*
(a) place where fruit and vegetables, etc., are sold from small tables, often in the open air; *we buy all our vegetables and fish at the market*; *there is a market every Saturday, so parking will be difficult*
(b) **on the market** = for sale; *their house has been on the market for three months*; **to put on**

the market = to offer for sale; *we put our house on the market three months ago and no one has even been to look at it*; **in the market for** = wanting to buy; *we are in the market for good quality antiques*
(c) place where a product is required, where a product could be sold; *the market for Russian automobiles has almost disappeared*; *the potential global market for this product is enormous*; **market research** = examining the possible sales of a product and the possible customers before it is put on the market; *if we had done proper market research we would have discovered that there were several products that are cheaper than ours*; *before you launch the product, you must do thorough market research*; **market share** *or* **share of the market** = percentage of possible sales which a company or product has; *they started an advertising campaign aimed at increasing their market share*; **domestic market** *or* **home market** = the market in the country where you live; *sales in the domestic market have not increased*; **export markets** *or* **overseas markets** = markets outside the country where you live
(d) black market = illegal selling at high prices; *there is a flourishing black market in spare parts for automobiles*; *we had to pay black market prices*; *you can buy whiskey on the black market*
2 *verb*
to sell products using marketing techniques; *this product is being marketed in all European countries*

③ **marketing**
['mɑrkɪtɪŋ] *noun*
techniques of publicity, design, etc., used to sell a product; *our marketing strategy needs to be revised totally*; *they used aggressive marketing to boost sales*; **marketing department** = department in a company which specializes in ways of selling a product; **marketing director** = person in charge of a marketing department

③ **mark up**
['mɑrk 'ʌp] *verb*
to increase the price of something; *these prices have been marked up by 10%*; *if retailers find the discount too low they mark the prices up to make a better profit*

④ **marmalade**
['mɑrməleɪd] *noun*
jam made from oranges, lemons, grapefruit, etc.; *I've made fifty jars of lemon marmalade*; *compare* JAM

② **maroon**
[mə'run]
1 *adjective*
deep purple red; *he was wearing a maroon tie*
2 *verb*
to leave someone in a place from which there is

no escape; *the bus broke down, leaving us all marooned miles from anywhere*

① **marriage**
['mærɪdʒ] *noun*
(a) being legally joined as husband and wife; *a large number of marriages end in divorce*; *she has two sons by her first marriage*
(b) wedding, the ceremony of being married; *they had a simple marriage, with just ten guests*; *the marriage took place in the city hall*

① **married**
['mærɪd] *adjective*
joined as husband and wife; *are you married or single?*; *married life must suit him - he's put on weight*; **married name** = name taken by a woman when she gets married; *after the divorce she stopped using her married name*

② **marry**
['mæri] *verb*
(a) to make two people husband and wife; *they were married in the village church*
(b) to become the husband or wife of someone; *she married the boy next door*; *how long have you been married?*; *she's married to a police officer*; *they're getting married next Saturday*

② **marsh**
[mɑrʃ] *noun*
area of wet land; *ducks and geese come to the marshes during winter*; *the developers want to drain the marsh and build on it*; **salt marsh** = wet land covered by the sea at high tide (NOTE: plural is **marshes**)

③ **marshal**
['mɑrʃl]
1 *noun*
(a) organizer of a race or a show; *marshals directed the crowds to the stands*; *some marshals rushed to the scene of the crash and others waved flags to try to stop the race*
(b) officer of a court; *federal marshals raided several houses looking for a prisoner who had escaped from jail*
(c) chief of police or chief of the fire department in an area
2 *verb*
to organize people, things, etc., into order; *extra police were brought in to marshal the crowds of fans*; *he tried to marshal the facts but was too sleepy to think clearly*

④ **marsupial**
[mɑr'supiəl] *noun*
type of animal found mainly in Australia, which carries its young in a pocket of skin in the front of its body; *kangaroos are marsupials; the opossum is the only American marsupial*

④ **marvel**
['mɑrvl]
1 *noun*
thing which you think is wonderful; *the building is one of the marvels of the modern age*
2 *verb*

to marvel at someone or something = to show wonder or surprise at someone *or* something; *everyone marveled at the sheer size of the building*

① marvelous
['mɑrvələs] *adjective*
wonderful; *the children had a marvelous time at the circus*; *I've got some marvelous news - Mary is pregnant!*; *soft music is marvelous for getting babies to sleep*

③ masculine
['mæskjulɪn] *adjective*
(a) male, referring to men; *she has a very masculine way of walking*
(b) with qualities that are typical of men; *the boy answered in a deep masculine voice*
(c) *(in grammar)* referring to words which have a particular form to show the male gender; *is the French word "table" masculine or feminine?*
(NOTE: the opposite is **feminine**)

① mashed potatoes
['mæʃd pə'teɪtəuz] *noun*
potatoes that have been boiled until they are soft and then crushed smooth and mixed with butter and milk; *our children prefer fries to mashed potatoes*

① mask
[mæsk]
1 *noun*
something which covers or protects your face; *the burglars wore black masks*; *he wore a mask to go diving*; **gas mask** = mask that covers the face and allows you to breathe when there is poisonous gas about; *the soldiers were told to put on their gas masks*; **oxygen mask** = mask that appears from a panel above your head if there is a drop in pressure in a plane; *if there is an emergency an oxygen mask will automatically drop down in front of you*
2 *verb*
to cover up or to hide; *she masked her face with her scarf*; *too much curry will mask the flavor of the other spices*

③ mass
[mæs]
1 *noun*
(a) large number or large quantity of things; *masses of people went to the exhibition*; *a mass of leaves blew onto the sidewalk*; *I have a mass of letters or masses of letters to write*
(b) **Mass** = main Catholic religious service; *she's a strict Catholic and goes to Mass every week*; **high mass** = mass with full ceremony; **low mass** = mass without much ceremony
(NOTE: plural is **masses**)
2 *verb*
to gather in large numbers; *the rebel army is massing on the border*
3 *adjective*
involving a large number of people; *they found a mass grave on the hillside*; *the group is organizing a mass protest in Washington, D.C.*;

mass media = communications such as TV, radio or newspapers, which reach a large number of people; *politicians use the mass media to try to influence the way people think*; **mass meeting** = meeting attended by a lot of people; *the union has called a mass meeting of all workers*; **mass murderer** = killer of a large number of people at one time; **mass transit** = system of public transportation in a city; *buses and trains and other forms of mass transit*

③ massacre
['mæsəkər]
1 *noun*
killing of a large number of people or animals; *witnesses to the massacre led reporters to a mass grave on the hillside*
2 *verb*
to kill many people or animals; *the soldiers massacred hundreds of innocent civilians*

④ massage
[mə'sɑʒ]
1 *noun*
rubbing of the body to relieve pain or to get someone to relax; *she gave me a massage*; *I like to indulge in a hot bath and massage once in a while*
2 *verb*
to rub someone's body to relieve pain or to get them to relax; *he asked the nurse to massage his back*

③ massive
['mæsɪv] *adjective*
(a) very large; *the company has massive losses*; *a massive rock came rolling down the mountain toward the climbers*
(b) very severe; *he had a massive heart attack*

③ mast
[mɑst] *noun*
(a) tall pole on a ship which carries the sails; *the gale was so strong that it snapped the yacht's mast*
(b) tall metal construction to carry an antenna; *they have put up a television mast on top of the hill*

② master
['mæstər]
1 *noun*
(a) **ship master** = person in control of a ship; *the ship's doctor asked the master to radio for a helicopter*
(b) skilled person; *a master potter*; *he's a master of disguise*; **an old master** = painting by a great painter of the past; *the collection of old masters in this gallery is priceless*
2 *adjective*
(a) controlling; *details of the master plan are known to only a few people*; **master disk** = main disk from which copies are made; *keep the master disk in a safe place*; **master key** = main key; *the director has a master key which opens all the doors in the building*; **master switch** = switch which controls all other switches; *the*

burglars turned off the master switch and all the lights went out
(b) master bedroom = main bedroom in a house; *the master bedroom has a bathroom attached*
3 *verb*
to become skilled at something; *she has mastered the art of reading the news on TV; although he passed his driver's test some time ago, he still hasn't mastered freeway driving*

② **masterpiece**
['mæstəpis] *noun*
very fine painting, book, piece of music, etc.; *some people think that "War and Peace" is a masterpiece, but others think it's much too long; the "Mona Lisa" is a masterpiece, but what about Warhol's picture of Marilyn Monroe?*

① **mat**
[mæt] *noun*
(a) small piece of carpet, etc., used as a floor covering; *wipe your shoes on the mat before you come in*; **bath mat** = small carpet to step on to when getting out of a bath
(b) place mat = small piece of cloth, wood, etc., put under a plate on a table; *the table was laid with glasses, knives and forks, and place mats; she placed little cork mats on the table to stop the wine glasses from marking it*

② **match**
[mætʃ] **1** *noun*
(a) game between two teams, etc.; *we watched the tennis match on TV; he won the last two table tennis matches he played*
(b) small piece of wood or cardboard with a tip which catches fire when you rub it against a rough surface; *he bought a pack of cigarettes and a box of matches; she struck a match and lit a candle*
(c) thing or person which is equal; **she's met her match** = she has met someone who is as strong, powerful, etc., as she is
(d) thing which goes together with another; **they make a good match** = they go well together (NOTE: plural is **matches**)
2 *verb*
(a) to be equal to; *our sales match those of our rivals in the export market*
(b) to fit or to go with; *the yellow wallpaper doesn't match the bright green carpet*

③ **matching**
['mætʃɪŋ] *adjective*
which fits or goes with something; *she wore a yellow coat with matching hat and shoes*

② **mate**
[meɪt] **1** *noun*
(a) one of a pair of people or animals, male or female, husband or wife; *some birds sing and others show off their feathers to attract a mate*

(b) friend, companion; *they're classmates*; **running mate** = person who stands for election as number two to the main candidate; *if the candidate for president wins, then his running mate becomes vice president*
(c) *(in the merchant navy)* **first mate** = second officer after the captain
(d) *(in chess)* position where the king cannot move, and the game ends; *mate in three moves!*
2 *verb*
(a) *(of animals)* to breed; *the zoo staff are hoping the old bear will mate with the new female*
(b) *(in chess)* to put your opponent's king in a position where he cannot move*

① **material**
[mə'tɪəriəl]
1 *noun*
(a) substance that can be used to make something; *you can buy all the materials you need in the hardware store*; **building materials** = cement, wood, bricks, etc.; *the bill for building materials alone came to over $3000*; **raw materials** = materials like wool or iron which have not been made into anything; *the country exports raw materials such as copper, and imports finished products*
(b) cloth; *I bought three yards of material to make a curtain; what material is your coat made of?*
(c) facts, information; *she's gathering material for a TV program on drugs* (NOTE: no plural in meanings (b) and (c))
2 *adjective*
(a) referring to physical things or to money; *the explosion caused a lot of material damage; his success on TV has improved his material life*
(b) important or relevant; *if you have any material evidence please contact the police*

② **math**
['mæθ] *noun*
science of numbers and measurements; *I'm taking a course in math; he passed in math, but failed in English*

② **matter**
['mætər]
1 *noun*
(a) problem, difficulty; *what's the matter?*; **there's something the matter with the engine** = there is something that makes the engine not work properly
(b) concern, business; **it's a matter for the police** = it is something, which we should tell the police about
(c) as a matter of fact = to tell you the truth; *I know Toronto quite well, as a matter of fact I go there every month on business*; **as a matter of course** = in the usual way; *the police checked his driver's license as a matter of course*
(d) material; *we put rotting vegetable matter on the garden as fertilizer*
(e) no matter what = whatever; *no matter what*

time it is, call the doctor immediately the symptoms appear; **no matter how** = however; *no matter how hard he tried he couldn't ride a bike*

2 *verb*

to be important; *it doesn't matter if you're late; his job matters a lot to him; does it matter if we sit by the window?*

① **mattress**

['mætrəs] *noun*

thick pad forming the part of a bed that you lie on; *those who didn't have beds slept on mattresses on the floor; the children jumped up and down on our mattress and ruined it;* **spring mattress** = mattress with springs inside (NOTE: plural is **mattresses**)

③ **mature**

[mə'tjʊər]

1 *adjective*

(a) older, adult; *the park has many mature trees;* **mature student** = student who is older than the usual age for students; *the college is trying to encourage more mature students to take courses*

(b) ripe; *mature cheese is normally quite strong*

(c) which is reasonable, like an adult; *she's very mature for her age; that's not a very mature way to behave*

2 *verb*

(a) to become older, riper or wiser; *whiskey is left to mature for years; he matured a lot during his year in Canada; girls are supposed to mature faster than boys*

(b) to become due for payment; *the policy will mature in 20 years' time*

④ **maturity**

[mə'tjʊrɪti] *noun*

(a) state of being an adult, or of doing things like an adult; *he's only twelve, yet his painting already shows signs of considerable maturity*

(b) time when a bond becomes due to be paid; *the bonds have reached maturity;* **maturity date** = date when an insurance policy matures (NOTE: no plural)

③ **maximum**

['mæksɪməm]

1 *adjective*

largest possible; *what is the maximum number of guests the hotel can take?*

2 *noun*

the greatest possible number or amount; *the management is aiming to increase profits to the maximum;* **fifteen at a maximum** = at most fifteen, not more than fifteen (NOTE: plural is **maximums** *or* **maxima**)

① **May**

[meɪ] *noun*

fifth month of the year, after April and before June; *her birthday's in May; today is May 15 ; we went on vacation last May* (NOTE: **May 15:** say "May fifteenth")

① **may**

[meɪ] *verb used with other verbs*

(a) *(to mean it is possible) if you don't hurry you may miss the train; take your umbrella, they say it may rain; here we are sitting in the bar, and he may be waiting for us outside*

(b) *(to mean "can", "it is allowed")* **guests may park in the hotel parking lot free of charge; you may sit down if you want**

(c) *(asking questions politely)* **may I ask you a question?; may we have breakfast early tomorrow as we need to leave the hotel before 8 o'clock?** (NOTE: present: **I may, you may, he may, we may, they may.** Note also that **may** is always used with other verbs and is not followed by **to**)

① **maybe**

['meɪbi] *adverb*

possibly, perhaps; *maybe the next bus will be the one we want; maybe you should ask a police officer; maybe the weather forecast was right after all;* **maybe not** = possibly not; *are you coming? - maybe not*

③ **mayonnaise**

[meɪə'neɪz] *noun*

sauce made of eggs, oil and vinegar, served with cold food; *mayonnaise is used for salads and sandwiches*

② **mayor**

['meər] *noun*

person who is chosen as the official head of a town or city; *the new recreation center was opened by the mayor; after his election, the mayor led the procession to a reception in the town hall*

COMMENT: in the U.S.A., mayors are all elected by popular vote, and appoint their team to run the various departments in a city. Note also that "Mayor" is used in English to apply to persons holding similar positions in other countries: **the Mayor of Berlin; the Mayor of Paris**

① **me**

[mi] *object pronoun used by the person who is speaking to talk about himself or herself;* **give me that book; I'm shouting as loud as I can - can't you hear me?; she's much taller than me; who is it? - it's me!**

① **meadow**

['medoʊ] *noun*

large field of grass; *the path through the meadow leads to a little bridge over the river*

① **meal**

[mil] *noun*

occasion when people eat food at a special time; *most people have three meals a day - breakfast, lunch and dinner; you sleep better if you only eat a light meal in the evening; when they had finished their evening meal they watched TV; you can have your meals in your room at a small extra charge*

① **mean**
[min]
1 *adjective*
(a) nasty or unpleasant; *he played a mean trick on his mother; that was a mean thing to say*
(b) not liking to spend money or to give something; *don't be mean - let me borrow your car; she's very mean with her money*
(c) average; *the mean temperature in summer is 70°*
(d) *(slang)* very good; *she cooks a mean pizza* (NOTE: **meaner - meanest**)
2 *noun*
middle or average figure; *sales are higher than the mean for the first quarter*
3 *verb*
(a) to talk about, to refer to; *did he mean me when he was talking about fat old men?; what do you mean when you when you say she's old-fashioned?*
(b) to show, to represent; *when a red light comes on it means that you have to stop; "Zimmer" means "room" in German; what does that sign mean with two people with sticks? - it means that elderly people may be crossing the road*
(c) to be meant to; *see* MEANT (NOTE: **meaning - meant** [ment])

① **meaning**
['minɪŋ] *noun*
what something represents; *if you want to find the meaning of the word, look it up in a dictionary; the meaning of a red light is pretty clear to me*

④ **means**
[minz] *noun*
(a) way of doing something; *is there any means of sending the message to New York this afternoon?; do we have any means of copying all these documents quickly?; the bus is the cheapest means of getting around town*
(b) **by all means** = of course; *by all means use my phone if you want to;* **by no means** = not at all; *she's by no means sure of getting the job*
(c) money; *they don't have the means to buy another store;* **it is beyond my means** = I don't have enough money to buy it

② **meant**
[ment] *verb*
to be meant to = should, ought to; *we're meant to be at the station at 11 o'clock; this medicine is not meant to be used by children; trains are meant to leave every half hour; see also* MEAN

② **meantime**
['mintaɪm]
1 *noun*
in the meantime = meanwhile, during this time; *we waited for her for hours in the rain, and in the meantime, she was happily sitting at home watching TV; the new stadium will be finished by Easter but in the meantime matches are still being played in the old one*

2 *adverb*
during this time; *the little girl hid under the table - meantime, we were all looking for her in the garden*

② **meanwhile**
['minwaɪl] *adverb*
during this time; *she hid under the table - meanwhile, the sound of boots on the stairs was coming nearer*

② **measles**
['mizlz] *noun*
children's disease which gives a red rash and a high temperature; *one of our children has got the measles; children can have injections against measles;* **German measles** = usually mild disease which gives a red rash but which can affect the unborn baby if caught by a pregnant woman

④ **measurable**
['meʒərəbl] *adjective*
which can be measured; *the difference between the two is barely measurable*

① **measure**
['meʒər]
1 *noun*
(a) certain amount or size; *there was a measure of truth in what she said; we have no accurate measure of the pressure inside the volcano*
(b) thing which shows the size or quantity of something; **tape measure** = long strip of plastic marked in centimeters or inches, etc., used for measuring; *he took out a tape measure and measured the length of the table*
(c) action; *the government has taken measures to reform the welfare system; what measures are you planning to fight air pollution?*
(d) type of action, especially a law passed by Congress; *a new measure to combat crime*
2 *verb*
(a) to be of a certain size, length, quantity, etc.; *how much do you measure around your waist?; the table measures four foot long by three foot wide; a package which measures 10 in by 25 in or a package measuring 10 in by 25 in*
(b) to find out the length or quantity of something; *she measured the window for curtains; he measured the size of the garden*

② **measurement**
['meʒəmənt] *noun*
(a) quantity or size, etc., found out when you measure; *he took the measurements of the room; the piano won't go through the door - are you sure you took the right measurements?; the measurements of the box are 25 in x 20 in x 5 in*
(b) the action of measuring; *the measurement of pollution levels is being carried out by satellites*

② **meat**
[mit] *noun*
food from an animal or bird, not from a fish; *can I have some more meat, please?; would you like*

meat or fish for your main course?; *I like my meat very well cooked* (NOTE: no plural: **some meat, a piece** *or* **a slice of meat**)

> COMMENT: the names of different types of meat are different from the names of the animal from which they come. Fully grown cows give "beef"; young cows give "veal"; pigs give "pork", or if salted, "bacon" and "ham". Only lambs and birds (chicken, duck, turkey, etc.), give meat with the same name as the animal

② **mechanic**
[mɪˈkænɪk] *noun*
person who works on engines; *the mechanics managed to repair the engine and we went on with the race*

② **mechanical**
[meˈkænɪkl] *adjective*
referring to a machine; *engineers are trying to fix a mechanical fault*

④ **mechanism**
[ˈmekənɪzm] *noun*
(a) working parts of a machine; *if you take the back off the watch you can see the delicate mechanism inside*
(b) way in which something works; *the mechanism for awarding government contracts*

② **medal**
[ˈmedl] *noun*
metal disc, usually attached to a ribbon, made to remember an important occasion or battle, and given to people who have performed well; *the old soldiers put on all their medals for the parade*; **gold medal** *or* **silver medal** *or* **bronze medal** = medal for first, second, third place in sporting competitions; *she won a silver medal at the 2000 Olympics*

③ **media**
[ˈmidiə] *noun*
(a) **the (mass) media** = means of passing information to a large number of people, such as newspapers, TV, radio; *the book attracted a lot of interest in the media* or *a lot of media interest*
(b) *see also* MEDIUM

④ **median (strip)**
[ˈmɪdjən ˈstrɪp] *noun*
the section of road or grass, bushes, etc., between the two opposing lanes of a major road; *the automobile had crossed the median strip and hit a vehicle traveling in the opposite direction*

④ **mediate**
[ˈmidɪeɪt] *verb*
to intervene to try to make two opponents agree; *he was asked to mediate between the two sides*; *I don't want to get involved in mediating the dispute*

④ **Medicaid**
[ˈmedɪkeɪd] *noun*
government program that helps pay medical

costs for people with a low or no income; *his surgery was paid for by Medicaid*

② **medical**
[ˈmedɪkl]
1 *adjective*
referring to medicine; *she's a medical student*; *the Red Cross provided medical help*; **medical excuse** = document signed by a doctor to show that a worker has been ill; **medical insurance** = insurance that pays the cost of treatment by a doctor, surgeon, etc.

④ **Medicare**
[ˈmedɪkeər] *noun*
government program that provides health insurance for older citizens; *my grandpa is eligible for Medicare*

④ **medication**
[medɪˈkeɪʃn] *noun*
(a) drugs taken by a patient; *are you taking any medication?*; *this medication should not be given to children below the age of twelve*
(b) treatment by giving drugs; *the doctor prescribed a course of medication*

① **medicine**
[ˈmedsɪn] *noun*
(a) drug taken to treat a disease; *if you have a cough you should take some cough medicine*; *the pharmacist told me to take the medicine four times a day*; *some cough medicines make you feel sleepy*; *(informal)* **to have a taste of your own medicine** = to be treated in the same way as you have treated others; *he made us fill out all those forms, let's give him a taste of his own medicine*
(b) study of diseases and how to cure or prevent them; *he went to college to study medicine* (NOTE: no plural in this meaning)

④ **medieval**
[medɪˈivl] *adjective*
referring to the Middle Ages; *the ruins of a medieval castle stand high above the town*

④ **mediocre**
[miːdɪˈoʊkər] *adjective*
ordinary, not particularly good; *it was a very mediocre performance*

④ **Mediterranean**
[medɪtəˈreɪniən]
1 *noun*
the Mediterranean (Sea) = the sea between Europe and Africa; *we went for a cruise around the Mediterranean*
2 *adjective*
referring to the Mediterranean Sea; *the Mediterranean climate is good for olives*; *she has bought a villa on one of the Mediterranean islands*

② **medium**
[ˈmidiəm]
1 *adjective*
(a) middle, average; *he is of medium height*
(b) **medium wave** = radio frequency range between 200 and 1000 meters

2 *noun*

(a) middle point; **happy medium** = satisfactory compromise; *finding a happy medium between the demands of work and the family is not easy*

(b) type of paint or other materials used by an artist; *he started to experiment with different mediums, such as watercolors*

(c) means of doing something, of communicating something; *television is the most popular medium of communication*; *deaf people can communicate through the medium of sign language* (NOTE: plural is **media** *or* **mediums**)

① **meet**
[mit]
1 *verb*

(a) to come together with someone; *he met her at the train station*; *we'll meet for lunch before we go to the movie theater*; *if you don't know how to get to our office, I'll meet you at the bus stop*

(b) to come together; *several streets meet at Times Square in New York*; *if you draw a line from each corner of a square to the opposite corner, the two lines will meet in the center*

(c) to get to know someone; *I've never met your sister - come and meet her then!*; *have you met our sales manager?*; *yes, we have already met*

(d) to pay for; *the company will meet your expenses*; *he was unable to meet his mortgage payments*

(e) to be suitable for; *does the car now meet the standards set by the auto racing authorities?* (NOTE: **meeting - met** [met])

2 *noun*

sports event where several teams or people compete; *we went to the swim meet*

① **meeting**
['mitɪŋ] *noun*

(a) action of coming together in a group; *the next meeting of the club will be on Tuesday*; *there were only four people at the committee meeting*; **to address a meeting** = to speak to a meeting; **to conduct a meeting** = to be chairman of a meeting; *as he was going away on business, he asked his deputy to conduct the meeting*; **to close a meeting** = to end a meeting; **to hold a meeting** = to organize a meeting of a group of people; *the meeting will be held in the committee room*; **to open a meeting** = to start a meeting

(b) point where two things come together; *the meeting of the two railroad lines is marked on the map*

③ **meet up**
['mit 'ʌp] *verb*

(of several people) to come together; *we all met up in the local restaurant*

① **meet with**
['mit 'wɪθ] *verb*

(a) to find, to come up against (a problem); to have (an accident); *the advancing soldiers met with stiff resistance*; *she met with an accident in the elevator*

(b) to meet someone; *he met with the salespeople in New York*

② **melody**
['melədi] *noun*

tune; *the melody of the song is easy to remember*; *according to my grandfather, folk melodies are still the best* (NOTE: plural is **melodies**)

① **melon**
['melən] *noun*

large round fruit that grows on a low plant; *we had melon and ham as a starter*; *see also* WATERMELON

① **melt**
[melt] *verb*

to change from solid to liquid by heating; *if the sun comes out the snow will start to melt*; *the heat of the sun made the road surface melt*; *at very high temperatures glass will melt*

① **member**
['membər] *noun*

(a) person who belongs to a group; *the two boys went swimming while the other members of the family sat on the beach*; *three members of the staff are away sick*

(b) organization that belongs to a society; *the member states of the EU*; *the members of the United Nations*

① **membership**
['membəʃɪp] *noun*

(a) belonging to a group; *I must remember to renew my membership*; *membership costs $75 a year*; **membership card** = card that shows you belong to a club or to a political party; *bring your membership card with you*

(b) all the members of a group; *the membership voted to reject the proposal*; *the club has a membership of five hundred*

③ **memo**
['meməʊ] *noun*

note or short message between people working in the same organization; *did you see the memo from the head office?*; *he sent a memo to all heads of department*; **memo pad** = pad of paper for writing short notes; *he wrote the number down on a memo pad* (NOTE: plural is **memos**)

④ **memorable**
['memrəbl] *adjective*

which you cannot forget easily; *we didn't have a very memorable vacation as it rained all the time*; *I can still remember that memorable afternoon in 1987 when his horse won the gold cup*

② **memorial**
[mɪˈmɔːriəl]
1 *adjective*

which reminds you of something or someone; **memorial service** = church service to remember someone who has died

2 *noun*

monument to remind you of something or someone; *the mayor unveiled the memorial to the dead poet*; **war memorial** = monument to soldiers who died in a war

② **Memorial Day**
['mɪ'mɔrɪəl 'deɪ] *noun*
May 30, holiday in memory of war dead, now generally observed the last Monday in May in the U.S.

① **memory**
['memri] *noun*
(a) *(in people)* being able to remember; *he repeated the poem from memory*; **if my memory serves me right** = if I can remember it correctly; *see also* PHOTOGRAPHIC
(b) *(in computers)* capacity for storing information; *this computer has a much larger memory than the old one*
(c) **memories** = things which you remember; *we have many happy memories of our vacations in Michigan*; **in memory of** = to remind you of; *we are holding this church service in memory of the sailors who died* (NOTE: the plural, only in this meaning, is **memories**)

① **men**
[men]
see MAN; **men's toilet** *or* **men's room** = public lavatory for men

① **mend**
[mend]
1 *verb*
I tore my coat on the fence - can you mend it for me?
2 *noun*
on the mend = getting better; *she has been quite sick, but she's on the mend now*

③ **menswear**
['menzweər] *noun*
clothes for men; *the menswear department is on the first floor* (NOTE: no plural)

③ **mental**
['mentl] *adjective*
(a) referring to the mind; **mental age** = method of showing a person's mental development by giving the age when such a stage of development is normally reached; *she is 19 with a mental age of 8*; **mental cruelty** = being cruel to someone by what you say, rather than by what you do; **mental illness** = illness that affects the mind
(b) **mental hospital** = hospital for patients with mental illnesses

② **mentality**
[men'tælɪti] *noun*
way of thinking which is typical of someone or of a group; *I don't understand the mentality of people who are cruel to animals*; *see also* SIEGE

② **mention**
['mentʃən]
1 *noun*

act of referring to something; *there was no mention of the explosion in the morning papers*; *just the mention of his name made her furious*
2 *verb*
(a) to refer to something; *the press has not mentioned the accident*; *can you mention to the secretary that the date of the next meeting has been changed?*
(b) *(said when someone has thanked you)* **don't mention it** = it was a pleasure; **not to mention** = as well as, not forgetting; *it cost us $30 just to get into the exhibition, not to mention the expensive meal we had in the museum restaurant*

① **menu**
['menju] *noun*
(a) list of food available in a restaurant; *what's on the menu today?*; *the lunch menu changes every week*; *some dishes are not on the menu, but are written on a blackboard*
(b) list of options available on a computer program; **menu bar** = series of little pictures on a computer screen which are the options you can choose; **pull-down menu** = menu which appears as a list on part of the screen; *the pull-down menu is displayed by clicking on the menu bar at the top of the screen*

③ **merchandise**
1 *noun* ['mɜrtʃəndaɪs]
goods for sale; *we have a wide range of merchandise for sale* (NOTE: no plural)
2 *verb* ['mɜrtʃəndaɪz]
to sell goods by a wide variety of means; *her children's books make more money through merchandising than through sales in bookstores*

② **merchant**
['mɜrtʃənt] *noun*
(a) businessman; person who buys and sells a particular product; *a tobacco merchant*; *a wine merchant*
(b) **merchant bank** = bank which lends money to companies, not to people; **merchant marine** = a country's commercial ships; *at sixteen he ran away from school to join the merchant marine*; **merchant seaman** = seaman on a commercial ship; **merchant ship** = commercial ship; *he's serving on a merchant ship running between the Caribbean Sea and Europe*

③ **mercy**
['mɜrsi] *noun*
(a) kindness toward unfortunate people; *the parents of the little boy pleaded for mercy with the gang who had kidnapped him*; **to have mercy on** = not to want to punish or harm someone; **mercy killing** = killing of someone who is very sick, in pain, and not likely to get better
(b) gift of fate; **at the mercy of** = which depends entirely on; *the success of the flower show is very much at the mercy of the weather*; **we**

must be thankful for small mercies = we must be grateful that everything has turned out relatively well so far; *despite lots of things going wrong, at least it didn't rain - we must be thankful for small mercies*; left to the tender mercies of someone = left to someone to deal with as he likes; *the tour guide went back to the hotel, leaving us to the tender mercies of the local taxi drivers*

④ **mere**
['mɪər] *adjective*
(a) simply, only ; *he's a mere boy* = he's only a boy; **the mere sight of grass makes me sneeze** = simply seeing grass makes me sneeze
(b) **the merest** = the smallest or least important; *the merest hint of garlic makes her sick*

③ **merely**
['mɪəli] *adverb*
simply, only; *I'm not criticizing you - I merely said I would have done it in a different way*

④ **merge**
[mɜrdʒ] *verb*
to join together with something; *the two freeways merge here*; *the firm has merged with its main competitor*

④ **merger**
['mɜrdʒər] *noun*
joining together of two companies; *he has a proposed a merger between his manufacturing company and our retail company*; *as a result of the merger, the company is the largest in the field*

④ **meringue**
[məˈræŋ] *noun*
sweet baked dessert made of egg whites and sugar; **lemon meringue pie** = pie with lemon cream inside and meringue on top

④ **merit**
['merɪt]
1 *noun*
being good, or excellent; *there is some merit in what he says, but I can't agree with all of it*; *this movie has no merit whatsoever*; **to go into the merits of** = to examine the good and bad points of; *the committee spent hours going into the merits of the various development plans*; **merit bonus** = extra pay given because of good work
2 *verb*
to be worthy of or to deserve something; *the plan merits further discussion*; *her essay only merited a "B+"*

① **merry**
['meri] *adjective*
happy and cheerful; *to wish somebody a Merry Christmas*; **the more the merrier** = the more there are the happier everyone is; *invite anyone you like, the more the merrier!* (NOTE: merrier - merriest)

① **mess**
[mes] *noun*
(a) dirt or disorder; *the milk boiled over and made a mess on the floor; we had to clear up the mess after the party*
(b) **to be in a mess** = to be in a difficult situation; **to make a mess of something** = to do something badly; *they made a mess of the repair job*

① **message**
['mesɪdʒ] *noun*
(a) information that is sent; *I will leave a message with his secretary*; *can you give the director a message from his wife?*; *we got his message by e-mail*; **message board** = board on which messages can be left for anyone to see (such as at a conference, or in a hotel lobby)
(b) political or religious idea which a group is trying to pass on to the public; *their message is one of universal peace*; *his message of hard work and simple living did not always attract the voters*
(c) *(informal)* **to get the message** = to understand; *she finally got the message when he stood up and handed her her coat*; **to get the message across to someone** = to make someone understand something; *we managed to get the message across, even though no one spoke English*

③ **mess around**
['mes əˈraʊnd] *verb*
to spend your spare time doing something without having planned what to do; *he spends his weekends messing around in the yard*

① **messenger**
['mesəndʒər] *noun*
person who brings a message; *we sent the package by special messenger*

① **mess up**
['mes 'ʌp] *verb*
(informal) to ruin or to spoil; *I'm sorry we can't come - I hope it doesn't mess up your arrangements*

① **messy**
['mesi] *adjective*
(a) dirty; *painting a ceiling is a messy business*; *little children are always messy*
(b) unpleasant and full of problems; *it was a long messy divorce case* (NOTE: messier - messiest)

② **met**
[met]
see MEET

② **metal**
['metl] *noun*
material, such as iron, copper, etc., that can carry heat and electricity and is used for making things; *a heavy metal skillet*; *these spoons are plastic but the knives are metal*; *these chairs are very heavy - they must be made of metal*

④ **metaphor**
['metəfər] *noun*
way of describing something by giving it the qualities of something else, as in "our hawk-eyed readers soon spotted the mistake";

he uses an ant's nest as a metaphor for downtown on a busy day

③ **meter**
['mitər]
1 *noun*
(a) device for counting how much time, water, gas, etc., has been used; *he came to read the gas meter*; **parking meter** = device into which you put money to pay for parking for a certain time
(b) standard measurement of length (approximately 39.4 inches); *the room is about three meters square*; *the river is 50 meters across*; *the table is more than two meters long*; *the walls are two meters thick*; **ten square meters** = area of 5 meters x 2 meters (NOTE: **ten square meters** is usually written **10m²**)
(c) race over a certain distance; *he holds the world record for the 1000 meters*
2 *verb*
to measure with a meter; *the quantity of water used is metered by the water company*

② **method**
['meθəd] *noun*
way of doing something; *we use the most up-to-date manufacturing methods*; *what is the best method of payment?*

③ **metric**
['metrɪk] *adjective*
using the meter as a basic measurement; **the metric system** = system of measuring, using meters, liters and grams

> COMMENT: the metric system is a decimal system, using various basic units multiplied or divided by hundreds, thousands, etc. The basic measurements are: **length:** meter; **weight:** gram; **area:** acre; **capacity:** liter. Each of these basic units can be divided into hundredths (prefix centi-) or thousandths (prefix milli-), or can be multiplied by one thousand (prefix kilo-). So the basic measurements of length are: millimeter, centimeter, meter and kilometer, and of weight: milligram, gram, kilogram)

③ **metropolitan**
[metrə'pɒlɪtən] *adjective*
referring to a large city; *it's within the Boston metropolitan area*

② **Mexican**
['meksɪkən]
1 *adjective*
referring to Mexico; *Mexican cooking is hot and spicy*; *the Mexican soccer team looks like a winning team*; *have you seen the photos from our Mexican vacation?*
2 *noun*
person from Mexico; *many Mexicans have emigrated to California*

① **Mexico**
['meksɪkəʊ] *noun*
large country in Latin America, south of the United States; *there is a long border between the U.S.A. and Mexico* (NOTE: capital: **Mexico City**; people: **Mexicans**; language: **Spanish**; currency: **Mexican peso**)

① **mice**
[maɪs]
see MOUSE

② **microchip**
['maɪkrəʊtʃɪp] *noun*
very small piece of a chemical substance with printed circuits on it; *smart cards have microchips in them*

② **microphone**
['maɪkrəfəʊn] *noun*
(a) device which you speak into to send sound through the radio or TV, or to record on disk or tape; *he had difficulty in making himself heard without a microphone*
(b) device for capturing sound and passing it to a secret listening device; *there was a microphone hidden in the bedside light*; *see also* MIKE

② **microscope**
['maɪkrəskəʊp] *noun*
instrument with lenses which makes things that are very small appear much larger; *he examined the blood sample under the microscope*

③ **microscopic**
[maɪkrə'skɒpɪk] *adjective*
so small as to be visible only through a microscope; *microscopic forms of life are visible in the oldest rocks*

④ **microwave**
['maɪkrəweɪv]
1 *noun*
small oven that cooks very rapidly using very short electric waves; *put the dish in the microwave for three minutes*
2 *verb*
to cook something in a microwave; *you can microwave those potatoes*

② **midday**
['mɪddeɪ] *noun*
twelve o'clock in the middle of the day; *he won't be back home before midday*; *we were having our midday meal when the builders arrived*

① **middle**
['mɪdl]
1 *adjective*
in the center; halfway between two ends; *they live in the middle house on the block, the one with the green door*
2 *noun*
(a) center; *she was standing in the middle of the road, trying to cross*; *Chad is a country in the middle of Africa*
(b) *(referring to time)* halfway through a period; *we were woken in the middle of the night by a dog barking*; *we were just in the middle of eating our supper when they called*; *his cellular phone rang in the middle of the meeting*; *the house was built in the middle of the nineteenth century*

(c) waist; *it's quite deep - the water comes up to my middle; how much does he measure around his middle?*

② **middle-aged**
['mɪdl'eɪdʒd] *adjective*
no longer very young, but not very old (between 40 and 60 years old); *her brother is much older than she is, he's quite middle-aged; there were two middle-aged women in the seats next to ours*

③ **Middle Ages**
['mɪdl 'eɪdʒɪz] *noun*
historical period from about AD 500 to 1500; *parts of the castle date back to the Middle Ages* (NOTE: the adjective from **Middle Ages** is **medieval**)

① **middle class**
['mɪdl 'klæs] *noun & adjective*
professional class between the upper class and the lower or working class; *as people become more wealthy, so the middle class expands; they live in a middle-class suburb*

① **Middle East**
['mɪdl 'ist] *noun*
area between Egypt and Pakistan; *tensions are running high in the Middle East; the U.S.A. has made peace in the Middle East one of its top priorities*

① **middle school**
['mɪdl 'skul] *noun*
school for children between the ages of about 11 and 15 (usually grades 6-8, 6-9 or 7-8) (NOTE: sometimes called **junior high school**)

① **midnight**
['mɪdnaɪt] *noun*
twelve o'clock at night; *I must go to bed - it's after midnight; we only reached the hotel at midnight*

③ **midterm**
['mɪdtɜrm] *noun*
examination held in the middle of a school term; *I've finished my midterms - that's a load off my mind*

② **might**
[maɪt]
1 *noun*
(formal) force; *she pulled at it with all her might, and still could not move it; all the might of the armed forces is displayed during the Memorial Day parade*
2 *verb used with other verbs*
(a) *(to mean it is possible)* *take an umbrella, it might rain; if he isn't here, he might be waiting outside; I might call in to see you tomorrow if I have time; that was a stupid thing to do - you might have been killed!; they might win, but I wouldn't bet on it*
(b) *(to mean something should have been)* *you might try and stay awake next time;* **he might have done something to help** = it would have been better if he had done something to help; **you might have told me** = I wish you had told

me; *you might have told me you'd invited her as well*
(c) *(asking a question politely)* *might I have another soda?* (NOTE: negative: **might not is** usually **mightn't**. Note also that **might** is always used with other verbs and is not followed by **to**)

① **mighty**
['maɪti]
1 *adjective*
strong, powerful; *with one mighty swing he lifted the sack onto the truck; all she could remember was getting a mighty blow on the head, and then everything went black* (NOTE: **mightier - mightiest**)
2 *adverb*
very; *that's mighty kind of you;* (informal) **he's in a mighty hurry** = he's very impatient

③ **migrant**
['maɪgrənt]
1 *noun*
(a) worker who moves from one job to another or from one country to another to look for work; *the government is trying to prevent migrants from coming into the country;* **economic migrant** = person who moves to live in another country where living conditions are better
(b) bird which moves from one place to another with the seasons; *the marshes are an ideal place to see the winter migrants*
2 *adjective*
who moves from one job to another or from one country to another; *migrant workers often do the jobs no one wants to do; migrant farm workers are exploited by rich land owners*

② **migrate**
[maɪ'greɪt] *verb*
to move from one place to another with the seasons; *herds of animals migrate across the desert in search of water; the marshes are an ideal place to see migrating geese*

② **migration**
[maɪ'greɪʃn] *noun*
movement of animals and birds from one country to another; *the swallows are starting to gather in groups, ready for their long migration south for the winter; we tag birds so that we can study their migration routes*

② **mike**
[maɪk] *noun*
= MICROPHONE

① **mild**
[maɪld] *adjective*
(a) not harsh, not too bad; *there was some mild criticism, but generally the plan was welcomed; he had a mild heart attack and was soon back to work again*
(b) not severe (weather); *winters in the south of the country are usually milder than in the north*
(c) not strong-tasting; *we'll choose the mildest curry on the menu* (NOTE: in this meaning the opposite is **hot**. Note also: **milder - mildest**)

① **mile**
[maɪl] *noun*
(a) measure of length (= 1,760 yards or 5,280 feet or 1.61 kilometers); *he thinks nothing of cycling ten miles to work every day*; *the car can't go any faster than sixty miles per hour*; *the line of automobiles stretched for three miles from the road works*; **the speedboat was doing 100 miles per hour** = it was traveling at 100 miles per hour
(b) **miles** = long distance; *there are no stores for miles around*; *we walked for miles and came back to the point where we started from*

④ **militant**
[ˈmɪlɪtənt]
1 *adjective*
very active in supporting a cause or political party; *he is on the militant wing of the party*
2 *noun*
(a) person who is very active in supporting a cause or a political party; *the party must keep its militants under control*
(b) person who supports a policy of using violence to achieve aims; *a few militants in the march started throwing stones at the police*

② **military**
[ˈmɪlɪtri]
1 *adjective*
referring to the armed forces; *the two leaders discussed the possibility of military intervention*; *military spending has fallen over the past three years*; **military service** = period of time served in the armed forces; *in some countries there is still compulsory military service for all young men*
2 *noun*
the military = the armed forces; *faced with riots all over the country, the government called in the military*

① **milk**
[mɪlk]
1 *noun*
white liquid produced by female animals to feed their young, especially the liquid produced by cows; *do you want milk with your coffee?*; *can we have two glasses of milk, please?*; *don't forget to buy some milk, there's none in the fridge*; **milk chocolate** = pale brown chocolate made with milk; *see also* CRY (NOTE: no plural: some milk, a bottle of milk, a glass of milk)
2 *verb*
(a) to take milk from an animal; *the cows are waiting to be milked*
(b) (*informal*) to get as much advantage as possible from a situation; *the newspapers milked the story for all it was worth*

① **mill**
[mɪl] *noun*
(a) small machine for grinding seeds into powder; *there is a pepper mill on the table*
(b) large machine for grinding corn into flour; *corn is fed into the mill through a little door*

(c) (*informal*) **to go through the mill** *or* **to be put through the mill** = (i) to be fully trained; (ii) to suffer a great deal; *her divorce has really put her through the mill*
(d) large factory, building which contains machines for grinding or making materials; *after lunch the visitors were shown around the mill*; **paper mill** = factory producing paper; **steel mill** = factory producing steel

④ **millimeter**
[ˈmɪlimitər] *noun*
one thousandth of a meter; *one inch equals roughly 25 millimeters* (NOTE: usually written **mm** after figures: **35 mm**)

② **million**
[ˈmɪljən]
(a) number 1,000,000; *the population of California is over 29 million*
(b) **millions of** = a very large number of; *millions of trees are chopped down to make paper*; *the country spends millions of dollars on imports of oil*; *millions of people spend their vacations in California* (NOTE: no plural with figures: **sixty million**)

① **millionaire**
[mɪljəˈneər] *noun*
person who has more than a million dollars; *if you win the lottery you will become an instant millionaire*; *only a millionaire could afford a yacht like his* (NOTE: to show the currency in which a person is a millionaire, say **a dollar millionaire, a sterling millionaire**, etc.)

② **millionth (1,000,000th)**
[ˈmɪljənθ] *adjective & noun*
referring to a million; *a millionth of a second*; *the museum gave a prize to their millionth visitor*

③ **mince**
[mɪns] *verb*
(a) to dice vegetables or fruit until they are in very small pieces; *mince the onion for the recipe*
(b) **he didn't mince his words** = he said exactly what he thought; *I didn't mince my words - I told them exactly what I thought of their plan*

④ **mincemeat**
[ˈmɪnsmiːt] *noun*
mixture of suet, apples, spices, dried fruit, etc., used to make mince pies; **to make mincemeat (out) of someone** = to defeat someone, to destroy someone completely; *he made mincemeat of his opponent* (NOTE: no plural)

① **mind**
[maɪnd]
1 *noun*
part of the body which controls memory and thought; *his mind always seems to be on other things*; *I've forgotten her name - it just slipped my mind*; *I think of her night and day - I just can't get her out of my mind*; *my mind went blank as soon as I saw the exam paper*; **what do you have in mind?** = what are you thinking

of?; *let's do something unusual this weekend - what do you have in mind?*; **she has something on her mind** = she's worrying about something; *she's not her usual happy self today - I think she has something on her mind*; *let's try to take his mind off his midterms* = let's try to stop him worrying about the midterms; **state of mind** = general feeling; *she was in a very gloomy state of mind*; **to make up your mind (to do something)** = to decide (to do something); *I can't make up my mind whether to take the afternoon off to do some shopping or stay in the office and work*; *she couldn't make up her mind what clothes to wear to the wedding*; **to change your mind** = to decide to do something different; *he was going to go by automobile but then changed his mind and went by bus*; *he has decided to go on vacation next week and nothing will make him change his mind*; **to be of two minds about something** = not to be sure about something, not to have decided yet about something; *I'm of two minds about his proposal*

2 *verb*

(a) to be careful, to watch out; *mind the steps - they're very steep!*; *mind you get back early*; *mind the plate - it's hot!*

(b) to worry about; *don't mind me, I'm used to working with children*; **never mind** = don't worry; *never mind - you'll get another chance to enter the competition next year*

(c) to look after something for someone, or while the owner is away; *who will be minding the house while you're on vacation?*; **mind your own business!** = don't interfere with other people's problems

(d) to be bothered or annoyed by; *nobody will mind if you're late*; *there aren't enough chairs, but I don't mind standing up*

(e) *(asking politely)* do you mind if I open the window?

(f) **wouldn't mind** = would rather like; *I wouldn't mind a cup of coffee*

(g) to obey; *children should mind their parents*

① **mine**
[maɪn]

1 *pronoun*

belonging to me; *that book is mine*; *can I borrow your bike, mine's been stolen*; *she's a great friend of mine*

2 *noun*

(a) deep hole in the ground from which coal, etc., is taken out; *the coal mine has stopped working after fifty years*; *he has shares in an African gold mine*

(b) sort of bomb which is hidden under the ground or under water; *the tank went over a mine and two soldiers were killed*; *it will take years to clear all the mines left by the rebel army*

3 *verb*

(a) to dig coal, etc., out of the ground; *they mine gold in the south of the country*

(b) to place explosive mines in land or water; *the entrance to the harbor has been mined*

② **miner**
[ˈmaɪnər] *noun*

person who works in a mine; *twelve miners were trapped when the roof of a coal mine collapsed yesterday* (NOTE: do not confuse with minor)

④ **mineral**
[ˈmɪnərəl] *noun*

(a) substance, such as rock, which is dug out of the earth, or which is found in food, etc.; *what is the mineral content of cabbage?*; *the company hopes to discover valuable minerals in the mountains*

(b) **mineral water** = water from a spring; *pure mineral water was bubbling up out of the ground*; *do you want orange juice or mineral water?*

③ **miniature**
[ˈmɪnɪtʃər]

1 *noun*

(a) very small model, portrait, painting, bottle of alcohol, etc.; *we went to an exhibition and saw a miniature of the new building*

(b) **in miniature** = reproduced on a very small scale ; *in the model town, everything is in miniature*

2 *adjective*

very small; *he has a miniature camera*

④ **minimal**
[ˈmɪnɪməl] *adjective*

very low or small, the smallest possible; *there is a minimal charge to cover some of our expenses*; *the cars were moving very slowly when they hit each other, so damage was minimal*

③ **minimum**
[ˈmɪnɪməm]

1 *adjective*

smallest possible; *the minimum amount you can save is $35 per month*; *the minimum age for drivers is 16*; **minimum wage** = minimum hourly wage that all employers must pay

2 *noun*

smallest possible amount; *we try to keep expenditures to a minimum*; *she does the bare minimum of work, just enough to pass her classes*

① **mining**
[ˈmaɪnɪŋ] *noun*

action of taking coal and other minerals out of the land; *mining is an important industry here*; *the company is engaged in mining for diamonds or in diamond mining*

① **minister**
[ˈmɪnɪstər]

1 *noun*

(a) member of a government in charge of a department; *the inquiry is to be headed by a former government minister*; *he was the minister of trade in the previous government*

(NOTE: in the U.S.A., ministers are also called **secretaries: the Secretary for Commerce**)

(b) leader in a Christian church; *the couple were married by a minister*

2 *verb*

to minister to someone's needs = to take care of someone; *nurses went to the country to minister to the needs of the refugees*

② **ministry**
['mɪnɪstri] *noun*

(a) government department; offices of a government department; *he works in the Ministry of Defense* (NOTE: plural is **ministries**; in the U.S.A., important ministries are also called **departments: the Commerce Department**)

(b) duties of being a priest in a Christian church; *he wanted to enter the ministry*

③ **minor**
['maɪnər]

1 *adjective*

(a) not very important; *it was just a minor injury*; *she has a minor role in the movie*; *he played a minor part in the revolution*; **minor league** = league in professional sports which is not the highest ranking

(b) musical key; *she played a Mozart piece in B minor*; *compare* MAJOR

2 *noun*

(a) young person under the age of 18; *we are forbidden to serve alcohol to minors*

(b) second most important subject taken by a student; *he has a minor in history*

3 *verb*

to minor in = to take as a secondary subject; *she is minoring in philosophy* (NOTE: do not confuse with **miner**)

③ **minority**
[maɪ'nɒriti] *noun*

number or quantity that is less than half of a total; *a minority of members voted against the proposal*; **the men are in the minority** = there are more women than men

① **mint**
[mɪnt]

1 *noun*

(a) factory where coins are made; *the mint is preparing to make the new coins*; **in mint condition** = perfect, in exactly the same condition as when it was made; *he is offering a camera for sale in mint condition*

(b) common herb used as flavoring; **mint sauce** = sauce made of chopped mint, served with lamb

(c) small white sweet, tasting of peppermint; *he always keeps a pack of mints in his pocket to suck when traveling*

2 *verb*

to make coins; *new coins are minted by the government*

① **minus**
['maɪnəs]

1 *preposition*

less, take away; *ten minus eight equals two (10 - 8 = 2)* *her monthly wages minus taxes are $2000*

2 *noun*

sign (-) meaning less; *minus 10 degrees (-10°)*

④ **minuscule**
['mɪnəskjul] *adjective*

very small; *she was carrying a minuscule amount of the drug*

① **minute**

1 ['mɪnɪt] *noun*

(a) one sixtieth part of an hour; *there are sixty minutes in an hour, and sixty seconds in a minute*; *the doctor can see you for ten minutes only*; *if you don't mind waiting, Mr. Smith will be free in about twenty minutes' time*; *the house is about ten minutes' walk* or *is a ten-minute walk from the office*; **six minutes to four** = 3:54; **eight minutes past three** = 3:08; **minute hand** = long hand on a clock or watch which shows the minutes

(b) very short space of time; *I'll be ready in a minute*; *why don't you wait for a minute and see if the dentist is free?*; **I won't be a minute** = I'll be very quick; *I'm just going to pop into the bank - I won't be a minute*; **at any minute** or **any minute now** = very soon; *I expect the train to arrive at any minute*

(c) **minutes** = notes taken of what has been said at a meeting; *the secretary will take the minutes of the meeting*; *copies of the minutes of the last meeting will be sent to all members of the committee*

2 [maɪ'njut] *adjective*

very small; *a minute piece of dust must have got into the watch*; **in minute detail** = with all details carefully drawn or explained; *I explained it all to you in the minutest detail, and you still got it wrong* (NOTE: superlative is **minutest**)

① **miracle**
['mɪrəkl] *noun*

(a) very lucky happening; *it was a miracle she was not killed in the accident*

(b) marvelous event which happens apparently by the power of God; *she went to the church and was cured - it must have been a miracle*

④ **miraculously**
[mɪ'rækjələsli] *adverb*

wonderfully, in a way which cannot be explained; *miraculously no one was killed when the two trains collided*

① **mirror**
['mɪrər]

1 *noun*

piece of glass with a metal backing which reflects an image; *they looked at themselves in the mirror*; **bathroom mirror** = mirror in a bathroom; **rearview mirror** = mirror inside an automobile which allows the driver to see what is behind without turning his head

2 *verb*

to be very similar to; to be the same as; *the report mirrors the information given to the committee by local doctors*; *her astonishment at the news mirrored mine*

④ **miscarriage**
['miskærɪdʒ] *noun*
(a) **miscarriage of justice** = wrong decision by a court, which can be changed on appeal; *the papers think there has been a gross miscarriage of justice*
(b) loss of a baby during pregnancy; *she had two miscarriages before having her first child*

② **mischief**
['mistʃif] *noun*
naughty or wicked action; *the children were full of mischief last night - they just wouldn't go to bed*; **he is always getting into mischief** = he's always doing something naughty

③ **mischievous**
['mistʃivəs] *adjective*
wicked or naughty; *he's a mischievous little boy - whatever is he doing now?*

② **miserable**
['mizrəbl] *adjective*
(a) sad, unhappy; *he's in a very miserable state of mind*; *can't you do something to cheer her up? - she's very miserable since her boyfriend left her*
(b) bad or unpleasant (weather); *what miserable weather - will it ever stop raining?*
(c) very low (salary); *she earns a miserable wage as a library assistant*

① **misery**
['mizəri] *noun*
being very unhappy; *there were terrible scenes of human misery in the refugee camps*; *his life in the home was sheer misery*; **to put someone out of his misery** = not to keep someone waiting any longer, but tell them the result of the exam, etc.; *let's go and put the candidates out of their misery*

④ **mishmash**
['miʃmæʃ] *noun*
badly organized mixture; *the meal was a mishmash of sweet and savory foods*

③ **misleading**
[mis'lidɪŋ] *adjective*
quite wrong; likely to cause a mistake; *the map he gave us was very misleading*; *she gave misleading information to the press*

① **Miss**
[mis] *noun*
(a) title given to a girl or woman who is not married; *have you met Miss Jones, our new sales manager?*; *the letter is addressed to Miss Anne Smith*
(b) way of addressing a young woman; *Excuse me, Miss, you dropped a glove* (NOTE: with a name, **Miss** can be followed by the surname, or by the Christian name and surname)

① **miss**
[mis]
1 *noun*
not having hit something; *he hit the target twice and then had two misses*; **a near miss** = situation where you almost hit something; *that was a near miss - we missed the other vehicle by inches* (NOTE: plural is **misses**)
2 *verb*
(a) not to hit; *he missed the target*; *she tried to shoot the rabbit but missed*
(b) not to see, hear, notice, etc.; *we missed the road in the dark*; *I missed the article about books in yesterday's evening paper*; *I arrived late, so missed most of the discussion*; **you didn't miss much** = there wasn't much to see, the movie, etc., wasn't very good; **he just missed being knocked down** = he was almost knocked down
(c) not to catch; *he tried to catch the ball but he missed it*; *she missed the last bus and had to walk home*
(d) to be sad because you don't do something anymore, because someone is not there anymore; *do you miss living by the sea?*; *I miss going on those long country walks*; *you'll be missed if you go to work in another office*; *we'll all miss Jack when he retires*

② **missile**
['misl] *noun*
(a) rocket with a bomb inside, which can be guided to its target; *they think the plane was brought down by an enemy missile*
(b) thing which is thrown to try to hit someone; *the students threw missiles at the police*

① **missing**
['misɪŋ] *adjective*
lost, which is not there; *I'm looking for my missing car keys*; *they found there was a lot of money missing*; *the police searched everywhere for the missing children*

③ **mission**
['miʃn] *noun*
(a) aim or purpose for which someone is sent; *the students were sent on a mission to find the best place for a picnic*; **her mission in life is to help refugee children** = her chosen task is to help refugee children; **mission statement** = statement that gives the aims of an organization
(b) group of people sent somewhere with a particular aim; *several firms took part in a trade mission to Japan*; *a United Nations peace mission*; *a rescue mission was sent out into the mountains*
(c) place where diplomats work, an embassy; *there were riots outside several diplomatic missions in the capital*

③ **miss out on**
['mis 'aut ɒn] *verb*
(informal) not to enjoy something because you are not there; *I missed out on the skiing trip because I had measles*

② **mist**
[mɪst]
1 *noun*
thin fog; *early morning mist covered the fields*
2 *verb*
to mist up *or* **over** = to become covered with a fine layer of drops of water; *the steam in the bathroom had misted up the mirror; switch on the heating for the rear window to stop it from misting over*

① **mistake**
[mɪs'teɪk]
1 *noun*
act or thought that is wrong; *she made a mistake in typing the address; there are lots of mistakes in this book;* **by mistake** = wrongly; *they sent the wrong items by mistake; by mistake she put my letter into an envelope for the chairman; we took the wrong bus by mistake*
2 *verb*
to think wrongly; *I mistook him for his brother* = I thought he was his brother; *he is mistaken in thinking I am your brother; there's no mistaking him, with his red hair and purple tie* (NOTE: **mistakes - mistaking - mistook** [mɪs'tʊk] - **has mistaken** [mɪs'teɪkən])

① **mistaken**
[mɪs'teɪkən] *adjective*
wrong; *I am afraid you are mistaken - I was in Springfield on that date; it must be a case of mistaken identity - it can't have been me she saw because I wasn't there; unless I am very much mistaken, that's an owl up there on top of the tree; if I'm not mistaken, Dr. James is your brother*

② **mistletoe**
['mɪzəltəʊ] *noun*
green plant with small white berries, which grows on other plants, especially trees; *at Christmas, we decorated the house with holly and mistletoe*

① **mistook**
[mɪs'tʊk]
see MISTAKE

② **mistress**
['mɪstrəs] *noun*
(a) woman who has a sexual relationship with a man without being married to him; *she had engaged a detective to follow her husband and photograph him with his mistress*
(b) woman in charge; *the dog chased after a rabbit but came back when his mistress whistled;* **she's her own mistress** = she is independent (NOTE: plural is **mistresses**)

② **misunderstand**
[mɪsʌndər'stænd] *verb*
not to understand correctly; *sorry, I misunderstood the question* (NOTE: **misunderstanding - misunderstood** [mɪsʌndər'stʊd])

② **misunderstanding**
[mɪsʌndər'stændɪŋ] *noun*
not understanding something correctly; *there was a misunderstanding over my tickets*

① **mitt**
[mɪt] *noun*
padded glove that has a section for the thumb and a separate, wider section for the fingers and is worn to protect the hand; *a catcher's mitt; an oven mitt*

① **mix**
[mɪks]
1 *noun*
mixture of things together; *there was an odd mix of people at the party;* **cake mix** = main ingredients for a cake that are bought ready mixed in a pack
2 *verb*
(a) to blend different things together; *she made the cake by mixing eggs and flour; oil and water do not mix*
(b) to get along with other people; *he finds it hard to mix with the other staff in the office*

② **mixed**
[mɪkst] *adjective*
made up of different things put together; *the reaction to the proposal has been rather mixed - some people like it, but others don't;* **I have very mixed feelings about the project** = I like some things about the project but not others; **in mixed company** = when both men and women are together; *that's not the kind of joke you can tell in mixed company; (in tennis)* **mixed doubles** = doubles match where a man and woman play against another man and woman; **mixed marriage** = marriage between two people of different races; **mixed school** = school with both boys and girls

① **mixture**
['mɪkstʃər] *noun*
different things mixed together; *if the mixture is too thick, add some more water; his latest paintings are a strange mixture of shapes and colors;* **cough mixture** = liquid medicine to cure a cough

③ **mix up**
['mɪks 'ʌp] *verb*
(a) to think someone or something is someone or something else; *I always mix her up with her sister; she must have got the addresses mixed up; his papers got all mixed up* = the papers were out of order, upside down, etc.
(b) **to be mixed up in** *or* **with** = to be part of, involved in; *he was mixed up in the bank scandal; how did she get mixed up with those awful people*

③ **mm**
abbreviation for MILLIMETER

① **moan**
[məʊn]
1 *noun*

(a) low sound from someone who is hurt; *the rescue team could hear moans from inside the wrecked aircraft*; *when she read the news she gave a loud moan*

(b) *(informal)* complaining about various things; *the staff is having a moan about their pay*

2 *verb*

(a) to make a low sound as if you are hurt; *they could hear someone moaning in the bathroom*

(b) to complain about something; *they are moaning about working conditions*; *stop moaning, it will be your turn soon*

① **mob**

[mɒb]

1 *noun*

crowd of people who are out of control; *mobs of soccer fans ran through the streets*; *an angry mob surged toward the gates*

2 *verb*

to surround with a wild crowd; *as the stars arrived they were mobbed by teenage fans* (NOTE: **mobbing - mobbed**)

② **mobile**

['məʊbl]

1 *adjective*

which can move; **she is not very mobile** = she can't walk easily; **mobile home** = a home that has wheels to move it to a permanent site (NOTE: also called a **trailer**)

2 *noun*

artistic construction using small pieces of metal, card, etc. which when hung up move in the slightest draft; *they bought a mobile of colored fish to hang over the baby's bed*

② **mockingbird**

['mɒkɪŋbɜrd] *noun*

North American bird that copies sounds made by other birds

④ **mode**

[məʊd] *noun*

way of doing something; *she will have to change her mode of life when she goes to college*; **mode of payment** = way in which payment is made (such as cash or check)

① **model**

['mɒdl]

1 *noun*

(a) small version of something larger; *the exhibition has a model of the new town hall*; *he spends his time making model planes*

(b) person who wears new clothes to show them to customers; *he used only top models to show his designs on the catwalk*

(c) particular type of automobile, etc., produced at a particular time; *this is this year's model*; *he bought a 1999 model Ford*; **demonstration model** = automobile, or other piece of equipment, which has been used by a store to show how it works, and is then sold at a lower price

2 *verb*

(a) to make shapes in a soft material; *he modeled a statue of the little girl*

(b) to copy; **she modeled her way of working on that of her father** = she imitated her father's way of working

(c) to wear newly designed clothes to show to customers; *she is modeling the fall collection by Dior*

② **modem**

['məʊdem] *noun*

device which links a computer to the telephone lines, so as to send data; *you'll need a modem to connect to the Internet*

④ **moderate**

1 *adjective* ['mɒdərət]

not excessive; *she had moderate success with her examination*; *the economy has ended a period of steady moderate growth*; *the union's wage demands are really quite moderate*

2 *noun* ['mɒdərət]

person whose political ideas are not very violent; *after years of struggle the moderates have gained control of the party*

3 *verb* ['mɒdəreɪt]

to make or become less strong; *they moderated their demands*; *as the wind moderated, the waves became smaller*; **to moderate your language** = to be less rude or violent in what you say; *she asked him to moderate his language because there were children present*

① **modern**

['mɒdən] *adjective*

referring to the present time; *it is a fairly modern invention - it dates back to the 1980s*; *her parents have a very modern attitude toward boyfriends*; *you expect really modern offices to have automatic windows and central heating systems*; **modern languages** = languages which are spoken today; *she's studying Spanish and Italian in the modern languages department*

② **modernize**

['mɒdənaɪz] *verb*

to make something up to date; *it took a lot of effort to modernize the curriculum*; *if we want to modernize the kitchen, we'll have to throw out all the old cupboards*

④ **modest**

['mɒdɪst] *adjective*

(a) not boasting; *he was very modest about his gold medal*

(b) not very expensive; *the union's demands were really quite modest*; *we had a modest meal in a local restaurant*; **a modest apartment** = an apartment that does not look expensive

④ **modify**

['mɒdɪfaɪ] *verb*

to change or to alter something to fit a different use; *the management modified its wage proposals in the light of the court's ruling*; *the automobile will have to be modified if we want to sell it here*

④ **module**
['mɒdjul] *noun*
part of a larger thing made up of various sections; *the science course is made up of a series of modules*

② **moist**
[mɔɪst] *adjective*
slightly wet; *mushrooms grow well in moist soil*; *to clean the oven, just wipe with a moist cloth* (NOTE: **moister - moistest**)

① **moisture**
['mɔɪstʃər] *noun*
small drops of water in the air or on a surface; *there's a lot of moisture in the air*; *this soil is too dry - it lacks moisture* (NOTE: no plural)

② **mold**
[məʊld]
1 *noun*
(a) soft earth; **leaf mold** = soft earth formed from dead leaves; *plant the bulbs in pots of leaf mold*
(b) hollow shape into which a liquid is poured, so that when the liquid becomes hard it takes that shape; *gold bars are made by pouring liquid gold into molds*; *pour the gelatin into the mold and put it in the fridge to set*
(c) gray plant growth which looks like powder; *throw that bread away - it has mold on it*
2 *verb*
to shape something; *she molded a little dog out of wax*

② **mole**
[məʊl] *noun*
(a) small mammal with soft dark gray fur, which lives under the ground; *moles made little hills of soil all over the lawn*
(b) small dark raised spot on the skin; *the doctor removed a mole from the back of her hand*

③ **molecule**
['mɒlɪkjul] *noun*
smallest unit in a substance that can exist by itself; *a molecule of water has one oxygen atom and two hydrogen atoms*

① **mom**
[mɒm] *noun*
child's name for mother; *his mom always waits for him outside school*

① **moment**
['məʊmənt] *noun*
(a) very short time; *can you please wait a moment - the doctor is on the phone?*; *I only saw her for a moment*; **a moment ago** = just now; *we only heard of it a moment ago*
(b) **at any moment** = very soon; *I expect it to rain at any moment*; **at the moment** = now; *I'm kind of busy at the moment*; **at this moment in time** = at this particular point; *at this moment in time, it is not possible for me to answer reporters' questions*; **for the moment** = for a little while; *we won't take any action for the moment*

④ **momentum**
[mə'mentəm] *noun*
forward movement; *he stopped rowing a few yards from the end of the race but his momentum carried him over the finishing line*; **to gain momentum** *or* **to gather momentum** = to go forward faster; *the protest movement is gathering momentum*; **to lose momentum** = to go more slowly; *when a spinning top loses momentum it falls over*

① **mommy**
['mʌmi] *noun*
child's name for mother; *Mommy! can I have some candy?* (NOTE: also often shortened to **mom**)

③ **monarch**
['mɒnərk] *noun*
king or queen; *France used to have a monarch but is now a republic*

④ **monarchy**
['mɒnərki] *noun*
system of government with a ruler such as a king or queen; *there's a big debate about whether they should get rid of the monarchy and become a republic* (NOTE: plural is **monarchies**)

① **Monday**
['mʌndeɪ] *noun*
first day of the week, the day between Sunday and Tuesday; *some supermarkets are shut on Mondays*; *she had to go to the doctor last Monday*; *next Monday is a holiday*

④ **monetary**
['mʌnɪtəri] *adjective*
referring to money or currency; *the government's monetary policy is in ruins*

① **money**
['mʌni] *noun*
(a) coins or notes that are used for buying things; *how much money do you have in the bank?*; *he doesn't earn very much money*; *we spent more money last week than in the previous month*; *we ran out of money in Spain and had to come home early*; *(informal)* **to have money to burn** = to have more money than you know what to do with; *they spent thousands on their house - they simply have money to burn*; *see also* SENSE
(b) currency used in a country; *I want to change my U.S. dollars into Mexican money* (NOTE: no plural)

③ **monitor**
['mɒnɪtər]
1 *noun*
screen of a computer or a small television screen used for checking what is happening; *the larger the monitor, the less strain it will be on your eyes*; *my computer has a color monitor*; *a bank of monitors allows the police to see everything that happens in the shopping center*; *details of flight arrivals and departures are displayed on monitors around the airport*
2 *verb*

to check, to watch over (the progress of something); *doctors are monitoring her heart condition*; *how do you monitor the performance of the sales staff?*

③ **monk**
[mʌŋk] *noun*
man who is a member of a religious group; *the monks lived on a little island off the north coast* (NOTE: the equivalent women are **nuns**)

① **monkey**
['mʌŋki]
1 *noun*
a tropical animal which lives in trees and normally has a long tail; *monkeys ran up the trees looking for fruit*
2 *verb*
to monkey around with something = to play with something; *stop monkeying around with that saw!*

③ **monopoly**
[mə'nɒpəli] *noun*
system where one person or company supplies all of a product in one area without any competition; *the state has a monopoly of the tobacco trade*; *the company has a monopoly of French wine imports* (NOTE: plural is **monopolies**)

① **monster**
['mɒnstər]
1 *noun*
(a) large, horrible, strange and frightening animal ; *the kids dressed up as monsters for Halloween*; *she drew a picture of a green monster with purple horns and huge teeth*
(b) cruel or wicked person; *her father was a monster who used to beat her with his belt*
2 *adjective*
(informal) very large; *look at the monster cabbage Pa's grown in the garden*; *what a monster burger!*

② **month**
[mʌnθ] *noun*
(a) one of the twelve parts that a year is divided into; *December is the last month of the year*; *what day of the month is it today?*; *there was a lot of hot weather last month, in fact it was hot all month (long)* *she's taken a month's vacation to visit her parents in Chicago*
(b) **months** = a long time; *it's months since we went to the movie theater*; **for months** = for a very long time; *we haven't had any homework for months*

② **monthly**
['mʌnθli]
1 *adjective & adverb*
happening every month; *he is paying for his truck by monthly installments*; *my monthly paycheck is late*; *she gets paid monthly*
2 *noun*
magazine which is published each month; *I buy all the computer monthlies* (NOTE: plural is **monthlies**)

② **monument**
['mɒnjʊmənt] *noun*
building, statue, etc., erected in memory of someone who is dead; *they put up a monument to the people from the town who died in the war*

④ **mooch**
[mutʃ] *verb*
to beg, to take something and not pay it back; *she's always mooching cigarettes*

④ **moocher**
['mutʃər] *noun*
person who begs, who lives off others

③ **mood**
[mud] *noun*
(a) feeling in general; *wait until she's in a good mood and then ask her*; *the boss is in a terrible mood this morning*; *her mood changed as soon as she opened the letter*; *a mood of gloom fell over the office*
(b) fit of bad temper; *don't talk to the boss - he's in one of his moods*

① **moon**
[mun] *noun*
thing in the sky which goes around the Earth and shines at night; *the first man walked on the Moon in 1969*; *the moon is shining very brightly tonight*; *there's no moon because it's cloudy*; **full moon** = time when the moon is a full circle; *by the light of the full moon they could clearly make out people moving on the hills*; **new moon** = time when the moon is visible as only a thin curved line; *the guerrillas waited for the new moon to make their attack*; *(informal)* **once in a blue moon** = very rarely; *we only go to the theater once in a blue moon*

① **moonlight**
['munlaɪt] *noun*
light from the moon; *we could see the path clearly in the moonlight*

④ **moor**
['mʊər or mɔr]
1 *noun*
poor land covered with heather and grass and small bushes; *the north of the state is wild country, full of moors and forests*
2 *verb*
to attach a boat to something; *the boat was moored to the river bank*

① **moose**
[mus] *noun*
North American animal, similar to a large deer; *we saw several moose when we were hiking*; *a herd of moose crossed the river* (NOTE: plural is **moose**)

① **mop**
[mɒp]
1 *noun*
soft brush with a head made of soft string or foam rubber, used for washing floors; *I'll just pass the mop over the kitchen floor*
2 *verb*

to wash with a mop; *she was mopping the kitchen floor* (NOTE: mopping - mopped)

③ **mop up**
['mɒp 'ʌp] *verb*
(a) to clear up spilled liquid; *use a cloth to mop up the water on the floor*; *we spent days mopping up after the floods*
(b) to overcome small groups of enemy fighters; *it took our soldiers several days to mop up the last pockets of enemy resistance in the mountains*

③ **moral**
['mɒrəl]
1 *adjective*
(a) referring to right and wrong behavior; *judges have a moral obligation to be fair*; *he refused to join the army on moral grounds*
(b) referring to good behavior; *she's a very moral person*; **to give someone moral support** = to encourage someone without active help
2 *noun*
(a) lesson which you can find in a story; *there must be a moral in this somewhere*; *the moral of the story is that if you always tell lies, no one will believe you when you tell the truth*
(b) **morals** = way of behaving of society as a whole or of each individual; *some people blame TV for the corruption of public morals*

④ **morale**
[mə'ræl] *noun*
feeling of confidence; *the manager gave us a little talk to try to raise staff morale*; *low morale has made everyone gloomy*; *after his interview, his morale was low*

④ **morality**
[mə'ræliti] *noun*
sense of moral standards; *where is the morality in a Hollywood actress spending millions on her wedding and not doing anything to help the poor and disabled?* (NOTE: no plural)

① **more**
[mɔr]
1 *adjective*
extra, which is added; *do you want any more tea?*; *there are many more trains on weekdays than on Sundays*
2 *pronoun*
extra thing; *is there any more of that soup?*; *$450 for that suit - that's more than I can afford!*; *we've only got nine men, we need two more to make a soccer team*
3 *adverb*
(a) *(used with adjectives to make the comparative)* *the dog was more frightened than I was*; *she is much more intelligent than her sister*; *the dinner was even more unpleasant than I had thought it would be*
(b) **more or less** = almost, not completely; *the rain has more or less stopped*; *I've more or less finished my homework*
(c) **once more** = one more time; *he played the song once more before the show ended* (NOTE:

more is used to make the comparative of adjectives that do not take the ending **-er**)

④ **moreover**
[mɔ'rəʊvər] *adverb*
(formal) in addition; *we all felt cold, wet and hungry, and moreover, we were lost*; *if you do that again I will report you to the principal and moreover tell your parents*

② **Mormon**
['mɔrmən]
1 *noun*
member of a religious group called the Church of Jesus Christ of Latter-day Saints; *Mormons do not consume caffeine*
2 *adjective*
relating to the Mormons; *there are many Mormon people in Salt Lake City*

① **morning**
['mɔrnɪŋ] *noun*
(a) first part of the day before 12 o'clock; *every morning he took his packed lunch and went to the office*; *tomorrow morning we will be meeting our Japanese agents*; *have you read the morning paper?*; *if we want to be in Boston for lunch you have to catch the early morning train*
(b) *(showing times)* **I woke up at four in the morning** = at 4:00 A.M. (NOTE: **in the morning** is often written and said as **A.M.: we were woken at four A.M.**)

④ **mortal**
['mɔrtl]
1 *adjective*
(a) which causes death; *he suffered a mortal blow in the fight*; **mortal enemy** = enemy who wants to kill you
(b) referring to death; **we are all mortal** = we are all going to die eventually
2 *noun*
a human being; *remember that every mortal will die someday*

④ **mortar**
['mɔrtər] *noun*
cement mixture for holding together the bricks or stones used in building; *the wall is dangerous - you can see how the mortar is falling away*

③ **mortgage**
['mɔrgɪdʒ]
1 *noun*
(a) agreement by which someone lends money on the security of a property; *he took out a mortgage on the house*; *she bought a house with a $350,000 mortgage*
(b) money lent on the security of a property; **mortgage payments** = the installments paid back on a mortgage; *he fell behind with his mortgage payments*; *my mortgage payments have increased this month*; **second mortgage** = second loan obtained using a property that is already mortgaged as a security
2 *verb*

to give a property as security for a loan; *he mortgaged his house to set up his business*; *because his house was already mortgaged, he had to take out a second mortgage to pay for his car*

③ **Moslem**
['mɒzləm]
see MUSLIM

④ **mosque**
[mɒsk] *noun*
building where Muslims meet for prayer; *everyone must take off their shoes before entering a mosque*; *Muslims are called to prayer from the tower of the mosque*

② **mosquito**
[məs'kiːtəʊ] *noun*
small flying insect which sucks blood and stings; *her arms were covered with mosquito bites*; *I was woken up by a mosquito buzzing around my head*; **mosquito net** = thin net spread over a bed to prevent mosquitoes biting at night; *your mosquito net won't do much good - it has a big hole in it* (NOTE: plural is **mosquitoes**)

① **most**
[məʊst]
1 *adjective*
the largest number of; *most people go on vacation in the summer*; *he spends most evenings watching TV*; *most apples are sweet*
2 *pronoun*
very large number or amount; *most of the work was done by my wife*; *she spent most of the evening on the phone to her sister*; *it rained for most of our vacation*; *most of the children in the group can ride bikes*
3 *adverb*
(a) *(making the superlative)* *she's the most intelligent child in the class*; *the most important thing if you are a salesman is to be able to drive a car*
(b) very; *I find it most frustrating that the bus service is so slow*; *most probably the plane will be held up by the fog*; *thank you, you are most kind* (NOTE: **most** is used to form the superlative of adjectives that do not take the ending **-est**)

② **mostly**
['məʊstli] *adverb*
usually, most often; *we sometimes go to Washington for our vacations, but mostly we stay in Idaho*; *the staff consists mostly of women*

① **motel**
['məʊtel] *noun*
hotel for people traveling by car, often with all the rooms on one floor and with parking spaces near the rooms; *it was getting late, so he started looking for an inexpensive motel by the highway*

① **moth**
[mɒθ] *noun*
flying insect with large wings like a butterfly, but which flies mainly at night; *moths were*

flying around the streetlight; *she screamed as a moth flew into her face*

COMMENT: a moth's wings fold flat covering its back when it is not flying, while a butterfly's wings stand upright, or open out on each side of its body

① **mother**
['mʌðər]
1 *noun*
(a) woman who has children; *he's twenty-two but still lives with his mother*; *her mother's a dentist*; *Mother! there's someone asking for you on the telephone!*
(b) **mother tongue** = language which you spoke when you were a little child; *she speaks English very well, but Spanish is her mother tongue* (NOTE: **Mother** is sometimes used as a name for a **mother**, but **Mom** *or* **Mommy** are more usual)
2 *verb*
to look after someone or something very carefully; *the new recruits will have to be mothered along until they get some experience*

① **motion**
['məʊʃn]
1 *noun*
(a) act of moving; *the motion of the ship made him feel sick*; **motion sickness** = sickness caused by the movement of an automobile, aircraft, bus or train, etc.; **in motion** = moving; *do not try to get on or off while the train is in motion*; *now that we have planning permission for the new sports hall, we can set things in motion to get the foundations laid*
(b) movement of part of the body; *a slight motion of his head indicated that he was making a bid at the auction*; *she made a motion as if to get up, but in the end stayed in her seat*
(c) **to go through the motions** = to do something for the sake of appearances without believing in it; *he's lost all interest in his job - he's just going through the motions*
(d) proposal which is to be put to the vote at a meeting; *the motion was carried by 220 votes to 196*; **to second a motion** = to support the person who proposed the motion; **to table a motion** = to put forward a proposal for discussion by putting details of it on the table at a meeting
2 *verb*
to make a movement with your hands which means something; *he motioned us to our chairs*; *she motioned to me to open the window*

④ **motivate**
['məʊtɪveɪt] *verb*
to encourage someone to do something; *it's the job of the coach to motivate his team*; *we need some extra incentives to motivate the sales force*; **highly motivated** = eager; *the staff are all highly motivated to tackle the new job*; *she's a hard-working, highly-motivated individual*; **racially motivated** = done because of racial

hatred; *the attack on the house was racially motivated*

④ **motivation**
[məʊtɪ'veɪʃn] *noun*
encouragement to do something; *the staff lack motivation - hence the poor sales*; *his only motivation is money*

③ **motive**
['məʊtɪv]
1 *noun*
reason for doing something; *the police are trying to find a motive for the murder*
2 *adjective*
motive force = force which makes something move; *wind is the motive force that makes a yacht move forward*

① **motor**
['məʊtər]
1 *noun*
the part of a machine that makes it work; *the model plane has a tiny electric motor*
2 *adjective*
(a) referring to automobiles
(b) **motor nerve** = nerve that makes part of the body move
3 *verb*
to travel in a motor vehicle; *we motored through Pennsylvania*

② **motorbike**
['məʊtəbaɪk] *noun*
light motorcycle, a two-wheeled cycle driven by a motor; *motorbike accidents are quite common*; *my brother let me sit on his new motorbike*; *I'm learning to ride a motorbike*

① **motorcycle**
['məʊtəsaɪkl] *noun*
two-wheeled cycle driven by a motor; *he fell off his motorcycle as he went around the corner*; *he learned to ride a motorcycle when he was 65*

③ **motorcyclist**
['məʊtəsaɪklɪst] *noun*
person who rides a motorcycle; *all motorcyclists have to wear crash helmets*; *the police officer watched as the motorcyclist raced away up the hill*

③ **motorist**
['məʊtərɪst] *noun*
person who drives an automobile; *the government is trying to persuade motorists to use their cars less*; *motorists are warned of long delays on all roads leading to the coast*

② **mount**
[maʊnt]
1 *noun*
(a) frame for a picture; *he stuck the photograph into a mount and put it on his desk*
(b) support for something; *put the telescope onto its mount*
(c) *(formal)* horse, etc., on which a rider sits; *his mount was not successful in the competition*
(d) *(usually in names)* mountain; *Mount Kilimanjaro*; *Mount Saint Helens*

2 *verb*
(a) to climb on to something; to climb up something; *they mounted their horses and rode off*; *he mounted the stairs two at a time*; *the automobile turned, mounted the sidewalk, and hit a wall*
(b) to increase; *tension is mounting as the time for the tennis final approaches*
(c) to set something in a frame or in a metal holder, etc.; *mount the photograph in a black frame*; *the diamonds were mounted in silver*
(d) to organize something; *the unions are mounting a campaign to get the government to back down*; *our forces mounted a surprise attack on the enemy*; *the museum is mounting an exhibition of drawings*; *the coup was mounted by exiles living across the border*

② **mountain**
['maʊntən] *noun*
(a) very high piece of land, rising much higher than the land that surrounds it; *Everest is the highest mountain in the world*; *every weekend we go climbing in the mountains*; *how far is it to the top of the mountain?*; **mountain railway** = special railway that climbs steep mountains
(b) large amount; *there is a mountain of letters on the manager's desk*; **mountains of** = a large quantity of; *I have mountains of work to do*

④ **mounting**
['maʊntɪŋ] *adjective*
increasing; *the crowd waited with mounting excitement*; *the committee was horrified at the mounting cost of the exhibition*

③ **mount up**
['maʊnt 'ʌp] *verb*
to increase; *during his absence the bills mounted up*

① **mouse**
[maʊs] *noun*
(a) small animal with a long tail, often living in holes in the walls of houses; *I saw a mouse sitting in the middle of the kitchen floor*; *our cat is good at catching mice* (NOTE: plural is **mice** [maɪs])
(b) device that is held in the hand and moved across a flat surface, used to control a computer; *you can copy text to another file using the mouse*; *click twice on the mouse to start the program*

① **mouth**
1 [maʊθ] *noun*
(a) opening in your face through which you take in food and drink, and which has your teeth and tongue inside; *it's not polite to talk with your mouth full*; *he sleeps with his mouth open*; *the cat was carrying a mouse in its mouth*; **to make your mouth water** = to look so good that you want to eat it or own it; *those cakes make my mouth water*; *his new automobile made her mouth water*
(b) wide or round entrance; *the mouth of the cave is hidden by bushes*; *the train came out of*

the mouth of the tunnel; New York City is built at the mouth of the Hudson river (NOTE: plural is **mouths** [maʊðz])

2 [maʊð] *verb*

to speak without making any sound; *I could see her mouthing something on the other side of the window*

④ **mouthful**
['maʊθfəl] *noun*

(a) amount which you can hold in your mouth; *he took a mouthful of meat and chewed hard; the baby took a mouthful and immediately spat it out; she dove into the waves and got a mouthful of salt water*

(b) *(informal)* complicated word or phrase; *I'll spell the name of the town for you - it's a bit of a mouthful*

① **move**
[muv]

1 *noun*

(a) change from one place to another; *the police were watching every move he made; it's time to make a move* = we must leave; **on the move** = moving; *after I've been on the move all day I just want to get home and go to bed;* **get a move on!** = hurry up!

(b) action done to achieve something; *it was a clever move to get here early before the crowds arrive;* **what's the next move?** = what do we have to do next?; **who will make the first move?** = who will act first?

(c) change of house or office; *luckily, nothing got broken during our move*

(d) changing the place of a piece in chess, etc.; *it's your move - I've just moved my queen*

2 *verb*

(a) to change the place of something; *move the chairs to the side of the room; who's moved my drink? - I left it on the table; he moved his hand to show he had heard*

(b) to change your position; *I could hear some animal moving about outside the tent; the only thing moving was the tip of the cat's tail;* **don't move!** = stand still

(c) to leave one house, apartment or office to go to another; *he got a new job and they had to move from Georgia to Alabama; they didn't like living in the country, so they moved back to New York City; the company is moving its office, from Houston Road to Maple Avenue*

(d) to propose formally that a motion be accepted by a meeting; *I move that the committee should meet again next week*

(e) to make someone feel sad; *the sad Irish songs moved her to tears; we were all deeply moved by the ceremony*

③ **move about**
['muv ə'baʊt] *verb*

(a) to change the place of something often; *he keeps on moving the chairs about*

(b) to change position often; *I can hear someone moving about downstairs; crowds of people were moving about in the square*

③ **move away**
['muv ə'weɪ] *verb*

to change place to somewhere further away; *the ship gradually moved away from the dock;* **we're moving away from Hartford** = we are going to live in another town away from Hartford

③ **move back**
['muv 'bæk] *verb*

(a) to go back; *after the meeting, please move the chairs back to where they were before*

(b) to change house or office to where you were before; *after three years in Manhattan they decided to move back to the country*

③ **move in**
['muv 'ɪn] *verb*

(a) to put your furniture into a new house and start to live there; *they only moved in last week; they got married and moved in with her parents*

(b) to come together as a group; *when everything is ready the police will move in on the gang*

④ **movement**
['muvmənt] *noun*

(a) moving, not being still; *there was hardly any movement in the trees; all you could see was a slight movement of the cat's tail*

(b) group of people who are working toward the same aims; *the movement for equal pay for women; he's a leading figure in the Green movement*

(c) mechanism; *a clock movement*

③ **move on**
['muv 'ɒn] *verb*

(a) to go forward; *we stopped for a quick visit to the cathedral and then moved on to the next town*

(b) to make people move; *the police moved the crowd on*

(c) to deal with the next item; *we will now move on to item 10 on the agenda*

① **movie**
['muvi] *noun*

cinema film; *we go to the movies most weekends;* **movie theater** = place where films are shown; **movie star** = well-known movie actor or actress; *there are pictures of famous movie stars in the entrance to the theater*

④ **moving**
['muvɪŋ] *adjective*

(a) which is changing position; *make sure all the moving parts are clean*

(b) which makes you feel sad; *a moving ceremony; his final speech was very moving*

② **mow**
[məʊ] *verb*

to cut grass, hay, etc.; *I must mow the lawn while it is dry* (NOTE: **mowing - mowed - has mown** [məʊn])

① **Mr.**
['mɪstər] *noun*
title given to a man; *Mr. Jones is our new sales manager*; *here are Mr. and Mrs. Smith*; *(at the beginning of a letter) Dear Mr. Smith* (NOTE: **Mr.** is always used with a surname, sometimes with both the Christian name and surname)

① **Mrs.**
['mɪsɪz] *noun*
title given to a married woman; *Mrs. Jones is our manager*; *(at the beginning of a letter) Dear Mrs. Jones* (NOTE: **Mrs.** is always used with a surname, sometimes with both the Christian name and surname)

③ **Ms.**
[mʌz or mɪz] *noun*
way of referring to a woman (without showing if she is married or not); *(at the beginning of a letter) Dear Ms. Jones* (NOTE: **Ms.** is always used with a surname, sometimes with both the Christian name and surname)

④ **MS** = MANUSCRIPT (NOTE: plural is **MSS**)

① **much**
[mʌtʃ]
1 *adjective*
(a) a lot of; *with much love from Aunt Mary*; *how much sugar do you need?*; *I never take much money with me when I go on vacation*; *she eats too much meat*; **as much as** = the same quantity; *you haven't eaten as much fruit as she has*; *he spends twice as much money as I do* **(b)** *(asking the price)* *how much does it cost to go to Columbia?*; *how much is that book?* (NOTE: **much** is used with nouns you cannot count: **not much money** but **not many boys**)
2 *adverb*
very; a lot; *he's feeling much better today*; *it's much less cold in the south of the country*; *does it matter very much?*; *much as I like her, I don't want to share an office with her*; *much to my surprise, he arrived on time*; **as much as** = the same amount as; *you haven't eaten as much as she has* (NOTE: **much - more** [mɔr] **- most** [məʊst])
3 *pronoun*
a lot; *he didn't write much in his exam*; *much of the work has already been done*; **do you see much of him?** = do you see him often?

① **mud**
[mʌd] *noun*
very wet earth; *you need a stiff brush to get the mud off your shoes*; *the pigs were lying in the mud*; *the boat got stuck in the mud as the tide went out*

④ **muddle**
['mʌdl]
1 *noun*
confused mess; *the papers were lying all over the floor in a muddle*; *she tried to put up the tent on her own but she got into a muddle*; *there was some muddle over the tickets*
2 *verb*

to muddle (up) = to confuse, to mix up; *don't muddle the papers - I've just put them in order*; *Granny is 96 so she often muddles up our names*; *I always muddle him up with his brother - they are very alike*

① **muddy**
['mʌdɪ] *adjective*
full of mud; covered with mud; *don't come into the kitchen with your muddy boots on*; *the truck stopped in the middle of a muddy field* (NOTE: **muddier - muddiest**)

① **muffin**
['mʌfɪn] *noun*
small cake with a flat bottom and a rounded top; *I usually order a blueberry muffin and coffee for breakfast*

③ **muffled**
['mʌfəld] *adjective*
not as loud or clear as usual because the sound has been made quieter; *muffled cries were coming from inside the cupboard*

② **mug**
[mʌg]
1 *noun*
large china cup with a handle; *she passed round mugs of coffee*
2 *verb*
to attack and rob someone on the street; *she was mugged as she was looking for her car keys*; *she's afraid of going out at night for fear of being mugged*; *the gang specializes in mugging tourists* (NOTE: **mugging - mugged**)

③ **mugger**
['mʌgər] *noun*
person who attacks and robs someone on the street; *the muggers were caught on the next street*

④ **multiple**
['mʌltɪpl]
1 *adjective*
involving many people or things; *she was taken to the hospital suffering from multiple injuries*; **multiple crash** = crash involving several automobiles or trucks; **multiple ownership** = situation where something is owned by several people jointly
2 *noun*
(a) number which contains another number several times exactly; *nine is a multiple of three* **(b)** repeated groups of the same number of something; **sold in multiples of five** = you can buy five, ten, fifteen, etc.; *these bonds are available in multiples of $200*

② **multiplication**
[mʌltɪplɪ'keɪʃn] *noun*
action of multiplying; *the children are taught addition, subtraction and multiplication*; **multiplication sign** = sign (x) used to show that one number is to be multiplied by another

① **multiply**
['mʌltɪplaɪ] *verb*
to calculate the result when several numbers are added together a certain number of times;

square measurements are calculated by multiplying length by width; *ten multiplied by five gives fifty* (NOTE: **multiply** is usually shown by the sign x : **10 x 4 = 40**: say "ten multiplied by four equals forty" or "ten times four is forty")

② **mumble**
['mʌmbl] *verb*
to speak in a low voice which is not clear; *she mumbled something about the telephone and went to the back of the shop*

② **mummy**
['mʌmi] *noun*
ancient dead body which has been treated with chemicals to stop it from going rotten; *we went to see the Egyptian mummies in the museum* (NOTE: plural is **mummies**)

① **mumps**
[mʌmps] *noun*
infectious disease of children, where you get swellings on the sides of your neck; *she caught mumps from the children next door*; *he can't go to school - he's got the mumps*

② **munch**
[mʌnʃ] *verb*
to chew something that is crisp or dry (and make a noise while chewing); *he was munching a biscuit when he answered the phone*

④ **municipal**
[mju'nɪsɪpl] *adjective*
referring to a town; *the municipal offices are closed today*

① **murder**
['mɜrdər]
1 *noun*
(a) act of deliberately killing someone; *the murder was committed during the night*; *she was accused of murder*; *they denied the murder charge*; *compare* MANSLAUGHTER
(b) (*informal*) difficult situation; *it was sheer murder getting to work this morning*
2 *verb*
to kill someone deliberately; *he was accused of murdering a police officer*

① **murderer**
['mɜrdərər] *noun*
person who has committed a murder; *the murderer was sentenced to life imprisonment*; **mass murderer** = killer of a large number of people at one time; *see also* SERIAL

② **murmur**
['mɜrmər]
1 *noun*
low sound of people talking, of water flowing, etc.; *there was a murmur of voices in the hall*
2 *verb*
to speak very quietly; *she murmured something and closed her eyes*

② **muscle**
['mʌsl]
1 *noun*
part of the body which makes other parts move; *he has very powerful arm muscles*; **to strain a muscle** *or* **to pull a muscle** = to injure a muscle by using it too much; *she strained a muscle in her back*
2 *verb*
(*informal*) **to muscle in on something** = to try to interfere with something; *he's always trying to muscle in on our projects and get all the credit for them*

② **muscular**
['mʌskjʊlər] *adjective*
referring to muscles; *she suffered from muscular pain after working in the garden*; *he has very muscular arms*

① **museum**
[mju'ziəm] *noun*
building which you can visit to see a collection of valuable or rare objects; *the museum has a rich collection of Italian paintings*; *this museum is always very popular with school parties*

① **mushroom**
['mʌʃrum] *noun*
round white plant which can be eaten; *do you want fried mushrooms with your steak?*

① **music**
['mjuzɪk] *noun*
(a) sound made when you sing or play an instrument; *do you like Russian music?*; *she's taking music lessons*; *her music teacher says she plays the piano very well*
(b) written signs which you read to play an instrument; *here's some music, see if you can play it on the piano*; *he can play the piano by ear - he doesn't need any music*
(c) (*informal*) **to face the music** = to receive punishment; *the manager went abroad when the bank collapsed, but came back to face the music* (NOTE: no plural: **some music**; **a piece of music**)

① **musical**
['mjuzɪkl]
1 *adjective*
(a) referring to music; *do you play any musical instrument?*
(b) loving music, being able to play musical instruments; *his whole family is very musical - they all either sing or play in orchestras*
2 *noun*
play with songs and popular music; *musicals such as "Cats" and "My Fair Lady" have been playing for years*

① **musician**
[mju'zɪʃn] *noun*
person who plays music as a profession; *a group of young musicians playing the street*; *the actors applauded the group of musicians who had played during "Twelfth Night"*

③ **Muslim**
['mʊzləm]
1 *adjective*
following the religion of Muhammad; *he comes from a strict Muslim family*

2 *noun*

person who follows the religion of Muhammad; *Islam is the religion of Muslims or the Muslim religion*; *he comes from a family of strict Muslims*

① **must**

[mʌst]

1 *verb used with other verbs*

(a) *(meaning it is necessary) you must go to bed before eleven*; *we mustn't be late or we'll miss the bus*; *you must hurry up if you want to see the TV program*; *must you really go so soon?* (NOTE: the negative: **mustn't, needn't** Note also the meanings: **mustn't** = not allowed; **needn't** = not necessary: **we mustn't be late; you needn't hurry**)

(b) *(meaning it is very likely) I must have left my umbrella on the train*; *there is someone knocking at the door - it must be the mail carrier*; *you must be wet through after walking in the rain* (NOTE: negative: **can't**; **it can't be the doctor**; past is **had to**; **I must go to the dentist: yesterday I had to go to the dentist**; negative: is **didn't have to**; perfect: **must have**; **I must have left it on the train**; negative: **can't have**; **I can't have left it on the train**. Note also that **must** is only used with other verbs and is not followed by **to**)

2 *noun*

something important; *when in Florida, a trip to the Everglades is a must*

② **mustache**

['mʌstæʃ] *noun*

hair grown on the upper lip; *he looks quite different now he's shaved off his mustache*

① **mustard**

['mʌstərd] *noun*

yellow paste with a hot taste, made from mixing powdered seeds and water, eaten with meat, especially ham and beef; *would you like some mustard on your roast beef sandwich?*; *dijon mustard is yellow and quite strong*; **mustard powder** = sharp-tasting yellow powder made from crushed mustard seeds; **mustard yellow** = dull yellow color

① **mustn't**

['mʌsnt] = MUST NOT

④ **mutual**

['mjutʃʊəl] *adjective*

referring to what is done by two people, countries, companies, etc., to each other; *they have a lot of mutual respect*; *if we work together, it could prove to be to our mutual advantage*; *she doesn't like him and the feeling is entirely mutual*; **our mutual friend** = the friend of both of us; **by mutual agreement** *or* **by mutual consent** = with the agreement of both parties; *by mutual agreement they have decided to sell the apartment and split the money between them*

① **my**

[maɪ] *adjective*

belonging to me; *is that my pen you're using?*; *have you seen my glasses anywhere?*; *we went skiing and I broke my leg*

① **myself**

[maɪˈself] *pronoun*

referring to me; *I hurt myself climbing down the ladder*; *it's true - I saw it myself*; *I enjoyed myself a lot at the party*; **all by myself** = all alone, with no one else; *I built the house all by myself*; *I don't like being all by myself in the house at night*

② **mysterious**

[mɪˈstɪəriəs] *adjective*

which cannot be explained; *who is the mysterious stranger at the back of the hall?*; *she died in mysterious circumstances, but the police are not sure it was murder*

① **mystery**

['mɪstri] *noun*

thing which cannot be explained; *the police finally cleared up the mystery of the missing body*; *it's a mystery how the box came to be hidden under her bed* (NOTE: plural is **mysteries**)

④ **myth**

[mɪθ] *noun*

(a) ancient story about gods; *poems based on the myths of Greece and Rome*

(b) idea which is not true, but which many people believe; *it was many years before people stopped believing the myth that the Earth was flat*; *the sales figures showed up the myth of their so-called super sales force*

Nn

① **N, n**
[en]
fourteenth letter of the alphabet, between M and O; *can you think of a five-letter word beginning with N and ending in R?*

① **nail**
[neɪl]
1 *noun*
(a) little metal rod use to hold two things together; *hit the nail hard with the hammer*; *you need a hammer to knock that nail in*; *(informal)* **to hit the nail on the head** = to judge something accurately
(b) as **hard as nails** = very hard; *she's as hard as nails - she'll never agree to what you want*
(c) hard part at the end of your fingers and toes; *she painted her nails red*; *he was cutting his nails*; **nail file** = flat stick covered with rough paper, used to smooth your nails; *do you have a nail file? - I've broken a nail*; **nail scissors** = special small scissors for cutting nails
2 *verb*
to attach with nails; *he nailed the notice to the door*

④ **naive**
[naɪˈiːv] *adjective*
innocent, lacking experience; *he is very naive for his age*; *it was naive of her to think he was interested in her work*

② **naked**
[ˈneɪkɪd] *adjective*
(a) with no clothes on; *crowds of naked children were playing around in the river*; *a naked man stood on the balcony*
(b) without any covering; *a naked electric bulb hung from the ceiling*; **naked flame** = flame that is burning without any protection around it

① **name**
[neɪm]
1 *noun*
(a) special way of calling someone or something; *hi! my name's James*; *what's the name of the store next to the post office?*; **I know him by name** = I have never met him, but I know who he is; **in the name of someone** = using someone's name; *the table is booked in the name of "Green"*; **to put your name down for** = to apply for; *she put her name down to join the club*; **under the name of** = using the name of; *he wrote his novels under the name "Saki"*; *they checked into the hotel under the name of "Smith"*; **to make a name for yourself**
= to do something that makes you famous; *he made a name for himself as a criminal lawyer*
(b) **Christian name** *or* **first name** = a person's first name, the special name given to someone as a child; *I know his surname's Smith, but what's his Christian name?*; *her first name is Natasha, but I don't know her surname*; **family name** = surname, the name of someone's family, shared by all people in the family; *Smith is the commonest family name in this town*
(c) **to call someone names** = to be rude to someone; *don't call the teacher names*; **to give something a bad name** = to give something a bad reputation; *employing waiters who are rude to customers is going to give the restaurant a bad name*
2 *verb*
to call someone or something by a name; *can you name three U.S. presidents?* ; *they named the cat Jonah*; **to name someone after someone** = to give someone the same name as someone else; *they named their son Peter after his grandfather*

④ **namely**
[ˈneɪmlɪ] *adverb*
that is to say; *only one student failed the exam, namely poor Bruce*

① **nanny**
[ˈnænɪ] *noun*
(a) girl who looks after small children in a family; *she's training to be a nanny*; *our new nanny starts work tomorrow* (NOTE: plural is **nannies**)
(b) *(children's word)* **nanny goat** = female goat; *a nanny goat and her two kids* (NOTE: a male goat is a **billy goat**)

① **nap**
[næp] *noun*
short sleep; *after lunch he always takes a little nap*

④ **narrate**
[nəˈreɪt] *verb*
(a) to tell a story; *the story is narrated by the hero's wife*
(b) to speak the commentary to a documentary film; *he narrated the film about whales*

④ **narrative**
[ˈnærətɪv]
1 *noun*
written story; *he's writing a narrative about their journeys in South America*
2 *adjective*

describing an action; *he wrote a narrative poem about the war against Troy*

① **narrow**
['nærəʊ]
1 *adjective*
(a) not wide; *why is your bicycle seat so narrow?*; *we went down a narrow passage to the store*
(b) narrow escape = near miss, situation where you almost hit something; *she had a narrow escape when her bike was hit by a truck*; **narrow majority** = majority of only a few votes (NOTE: **narrower - narrowest**)
2 *verb*
(a) to make less wide; *he narrowed his eyes*
(b) to become less wide; *the road narrows suddenly, and there is hardly enough room for two cars to pass*
(c) to narrow something down to = to reduce something to; *we have narrowed down our choice of candidates to two*

② **nasty**
['næsti] *adjective*
unpleasant; *what a nasty smell!*; *he's in for a nasty shock*; *it was nasty of her to report you to the teacher*; **to turn nasty** = to become unpleasant suddenly; *when she couldn't pay, the manager turned quite nasty* (NOTE: **nastier - nastiest**)

② **nation**
['neɪʃən] *noun*
(a) country; *a great nation such as the U.S.A. has a duty to protect smaller countries from attack*; *see also* UNITED NATIONS
(b) people living in a country; *the president spoke to the nation about the declaration of war*

③ **national**
['næʃənl]
1 *adjective*
(a) belonging to a country; *this is in our national interest*; *the story even appeared in the national newspapers*; *they sing the national anthem before the baseball game*
(b) national park = area of land protected by the government for people to enjoy
2 *noun*
person from a certain country; *two German nationals were arrested at the scene of the crime*

④ **nationalism**
['næʃnəlɪzm] *noun*
feeling of great pride in your country, feeling that your country is better than others; *Brazilian nationalism as shown by their soccer supporters*

④ **nationalist**
['næʃənəlɪst]
1 *noun*
person who wants his country to be independent; *the nationalists have not been invited to the negotiations*

2 *adjective*
wanting your country to be independent; *there is a lot of nationalist feeling in the country*

③ **nationality**
[næʃə'næləti] *noun*
being a citizen of a state; *what is your nationality?*; **she has dual nationality** = she is a citizen of two countries at the same time (NOTE: plural is **nationalities**)

③ **native**
['neɪtɪv]
1 *noun*
(a) person born in a place; *he's a native Texan*
(b) original inhabitant; *the sailors were killed by natives as they came onto the beach*
2 *adjective*
belonging to a country; *the elephant is native to Africa*; **native language** *or* **native tongue** = language that you spoke when you were a little child; *she speaks English very well, but Spanish is her native language*; *her native language is Italian*

③ **Native American**
['neɪtɪv ə'merɪkən] *noun*
person from one of the original American peoples

② **natural**
['nætʃərəl] *adjective*
(a) ordinary, not unusual; *her behavior at the meeting was quite natural*; *it's only natural if you can't sleep the night before finals*; *it's natural to worry about your first baby*; *it was natural for small storekeepers to feel annoyed when the supermarket opened*
(b) coming from nature, and not made by man; *do you think the color of her hair is natural?*; *yes, she's a natural blonde*; *the inquest decided that he died from natural causes*; **natural gas** = gas that is found in the earth and not made by men; **natural history** = study of plants, animals, etc.

② **naturally**
['nætʃərəli] *adverb*
(a) of course; *naturally the top team beat the bottom team*; *do you want to watch the game? - naturally!*
(b) because of nature, not made by man; *she has naturally fair hair*
(c) in a normal way; *he behaved quite naturally at the office, so we were surprised when he was arrested for murder*

① **nature**
['neɪtʃər] *noun*
(a) plants and animals; *we must try to protect nature and the environment*; **nature study** = school lessons where you learn about plants and animals
(b) character of a person, thing, animal; *he has a very violent nature*; **human nature** = the general character of people; *it's only human nature to want to get on and do better than others*; **better nature** = feelings of kindness that

you have inside you; *they appealed to the president's better nature to release the prisoners*

① **naughty**
['nɔti] *adjective*
(usually of a child) behaving badly, not doing what you are told to do; *the children are very quiet - they must be doing something naughty*; *that boy is very naughty - but his sister is worse*; *it was very naughty of you to put glue on your daddy's chair* (NOTE: **naughtier - naughtiest**)

② **naval**
['neɪvl] *adjective*
referring to the navy; *he comes from a naval family*; *we are very interested in naval history*; **naval base** = base for ships of the navy; **naval academy** = college where students study before entering the navy

③ **navigate**
['nævɪgeɪt] *verb*
(a) to guide a ship or aircraft; *the pilot navigated the boat into the harbor*
(b) to give directions to the driver of a car; *can you navigate as far as Oxford? - I know my way from there*

① **navy**
['neɪvi]
1 *noun*
(a) military force that fights battles at sea; *he left school and joined the navy*; *the navy has many ships*
(b) dark blue color; *she was dressed in navy*
2 *adjective*; **navy (blue)** = of a dark blue color; *she was wearing a navy skirt*; *he's bought a navy blue pullover*

① **near**
[nɪər] *adverb, preposition & adjective*
(a) close to, not far away from; *our house is near the post office*; *bring your chair nearer to the table*; *he lives quite near (here) which is the nearest drugstore?*; **near miss** = situation where you almost hit something; *that was a near miss - we missed the other automobile by inches!*; *(in an automobile)* **near side** = the side closer to the side of the road; *someone has scratched the near-side door* (NOTE: the other side, the side where the driver sits, is the **off side**)
(b) soon, not far off in time; *her birthday is on December 21 - it's quite near to Christmas*; *can you phone again nearer the day and I'll see if I can find a few minutes to see you?* (NOTE: **nearer - nearest**)

② **nearby**
[nɪər'baɪ] *adverb & adjective*
not far away; *he lives just nearby*; *they met in a nearby restaurant*

③ **Near East**
['nɪər'ist] *noun*
countries at the eastern end of the Mediterranean; *flights to the Near East have been stopped because of fighting in the area*

① **nearly**
['nɪərli] *adverb*
almost; *he's nearly 18 - he'll be going to college next year*; *the movie lasted nearly three hours*; *the book isn't nearly as good as the last one I read*; *hurry up, it's nearly time for breakfast*

① **neat**
[nit] *adjective*
(a) tidy, without any mess; *leave your bedroom neat and tidy*; *a shirt with a neat white collar*
(b) straight, alcohol without any water added; *I prefer my whiskey neat*
(c) **a neat idea** = a good idea (NOTE: **neater - neatest**)

④ **necessarily**
[nesə'serəli] *adverb*
which cannot be avoided; *going to Chicago from here necessarily means taking two flights*; **not necessarily** = possibly sometimes but not always; *taking the train isn't necessarily slower than going by plane*

① **necessary**
['nesesri] *adjective*
which has to be done; *it's absolutely necessary for taxes to be paid on time*; *it is necessary to have a current passport if you are going abroad*; *are you sure all this equipment is really necessary?*; *does she have the necessary qualifications for the job?*

② **necessity**
[nə'sesɪti] *noun*
what is needed; essential thing; *an automobile is a necessity if you live in the country*; *can they afford the simple necessities of life?* (NOTE: plural is **necessities**)

③ **neck**
[nek] *noun*
(a) part that joins your head to your body; *she was sitting in a draft and got a stiff neck*; *he wore a gold chain around his neck*
(b) *(informal)* **pain in the neck** = an annoying person; *he's a real pain in the neck*; **to breathe down someone's neck** = to watch what someone is doing and be ready to criticize; *I wish he would stop breathing down my neck all the time*; **to stick your neck out** = to do something risky; *I'll stick my neck out and say that the government will lose the next election*
(c) **neck and neck** = equal (in a race, in an election); *the two boats finished neck and neck*; *the result is still not clear - the two parties are neck and neck*
(d) part of a piece of clothing which goes around your neck; *he takes size 16 neck in shirts*
(e) narrow part; *the neck of a bottle*; **neck of land** = narrow piece of land between two pieces of water; *(informal)* **in this neck of the woods** = in this part of the country; *not many people live in this neck of the woods*

② **necktie**
['nektaɪ] *noun*
a tie, a long piece of colored cloth which men

wear around their necks under the collar of their shirts; *is it the sort of party for which you have to wear a necktie?*

① **need**
[nid]
1 *noun*
what is necessary or wanted; *there's no need for you to wait - I can find my own way home*; **in need** = requiring food and help; *the Red Cross is bringing supplies to families in need*; **to be in need of** = to want something; *they're in urgent need of medical supplies*
2 *verb*
(a) *(meaning to be necessary)* *we shall need Mexican pesos for our vacation*; *painting needs a lot of skill*; *I need someone to help me with the cooking*
(b) *(meaning to want to use)* *does anyone need any more coffee?*; *we don't need all these chairs*; *do you need this hammer anymore or can I use it?*; *do you need any help?*
(c) *(used with other verbs meaning to be necessary)* *need you make so much noise in the bath?*; *need you go now?*; *the living room needs painting or needs to be painted*; *you don't need to come if you have a cold*; *the police need to know who saw the accident*

① **needle**
['nidl] *noun*
(a) metal tool for sewing, like a long pin, with a hole at one end for the thread to go through; *this needle hasn't got a very sharp point*; *you must try to pull the piece of wool through the hole in the needle*; **knitting needle** = thin pointed plastic or metal stick used for knitting
(b) hollow metal tool used for injections; *it is a serious disease transmitted by infected blood or needles*
(c) hand on a dial; *he looked at the dial and saw the needle was pointing to zero*
(d) thin leaf of a pine tree

② **needn't**
['nidnt] *verb (used with other verbs to mean "it isn't necessary")*
she needn't come if she has a cold; *you needn't have made a cake - I'm not hungry*; *she needn't make such a fuss about a little spider* (NOTE: **needn't** is only used with other verbs and is not followed by **to**. Note also the difference in meanings: **mustn't** = not allowed; **needn't** = not necessary: **we mustn't be late; you needn't hurry**)

② **negative**
['negətɪv]
1 *noun*
(a) meaning "no"; *the answer was in the negative*
(b) developed film with an image where the light parts are dark and dark parts light; *don't touch the negatives with your dirty fingers*
2 *adjective*

(a) showing the absence of something; *her blood test was negative*; **a negative response** = saying "no"
(b) **negative pole** = the end of a magnet which points to the south
(c) **negative film** = film where the light parts are dark and the dark parts are light (as opposed to positive film)
(d) **negative terminal** = one of the terminals in a battery, shown by a minus (-) sign; *the brown wire should be attached to the negative terminal* (NOTE: the opposite is **positive**)

③ **neglect**
[nɪ'glekt]
1 *noun*
lack of care; *the building has suffered from years of neglect* (NOTE: no plural)
2 *verb*
(a) to fail to look after someone or something properly; *he neglected his three children*; *the building had been neglected by its owners*
(b) not to do something; *he neglected to tell the police that he had been involved in an accident*

④ **negligible**
['neglɪdʒəbl] *adjective*
very small, not worth bothering about; *the effect of the strike was negligible*

④ **negotiate**
[nɪ'gəʊʃɪeɪt] *verb*
(a) to discuss with someone; *we are negotiating with the travel agent for a refund*
(b) to make a commercial arrangement; *the two parties negotiated the terms of the contract*
(c) to go around something which is in the way; *we had to negotiate several large rocks in the road*; *the burglars managed to negotiate the alarm system successfully*

④ **negotiation**
[nɪgəʊʃɪ'eɪʃn] *noun*
(a) discussing; *the only answer to this conflict is peaceful negotiation*; **it is open to negotiation** = the terms can be negotiated (NOTE: no plural in this meaning)
(b) **negotiations** = discussions; *we have started negotiations with the management over new contracts of employment*

④ **negotiator**
[nɪ'gəʊʃɪeɪtər] *noun*
person who discusses; *union negotiators discussed terms with the directors*; *the negotiators shook hands and sat down at the conference table*

① **neighbor**
['neɪbər] *noun*
person who lives near you, who is sitting next to you, etc.; *help yourself and then pass the plate on to your neighbor*; *he doesn't get along with his neighbors*; **next-door neighbors** = people who live in the house next to yours; **the Colombians and the Venezuelans are neighbors** = their countries are close together

① **neighborhood**
['neɪbərhʊd] *noun*
(a) small area and the people who live in it; *this is a quiet neighborhood, we don't like noisy parties*; *the doctor knows everyone in the neighborhood*
(b) **in the neighborhood of** = (i) near; (ii) approximately; *there are three hotels in the neighborhood of the Conference Center*; *the sum involved is in the neighborhood of $150,000*

③ **neighboring**
['neɪbərɪŋ] *adjective*
which is close to you; *there are no stores where we live, so we go to the neighboring town to do our shopping*; *Colombia and Venezuela are neighboring countries*

① **neither**
['niːðər or 'naɪðər]
1 *adjective & pronoun*
not either of two (people, etc.); *neither automobile or neither of the automobiles passed the test*; *neither sister is dark or neither of the sisters is dark*
2 *adverb*
not either; *he doesn't eat meat and neither does his wife*; *she isn't fat but neither is she really very thin*
3 *conjunction*
(a) **neither...nor** = not one...and not the other; *the water is neither too hot nor too cold - it's just right*; *she's neither Chinese nor Japanese - she comes from Korea*; *neither his mother nor his father is coming to the wedding*
(b) **neither here nor there** = not important; *whether you go by bus or subway is neither here nor there, provided you get to the meeting on time*

③ **nephew**
['nefjuː] *noun*
son of a sister or brother; *my nephew has just finished college*

② **nerve**
[nɜrv] *noun*
(a) thread in the body which takes messages to and from the brain; *nerves are very delicate and easily damaged*
(b) **to be in a state of nerves** = to be tense and worried; **to get on someone's nerves** = to annoy someone; *that buzzing noise is really getting on my nerves*
(c) *(informal)* being too confident; *he has a lot of nerve to ask for a day off, when he was away all last week*
(d) being brave; *he wanted to try jumping with a parachute but at the last minute he lost his nerve*

② **nervous**
['nɜrvəs] *adjective*
(a) referring to the nerves; *the nervous system*; **nervous energy** = excited tense energy; *see also* BREAKDOWN
(b) worried; *she gets nervous if she is alone in the house at night*; *he's nervous about driving to New York*

④ **nervously**
['nɜrvəsli] *adverb*
in a nervous way; *the bridegroom and best man waited nervously in the church*

① **nest**
[nest]
1 *noun*
construction built by birds to lay their eggs in; *the birds built their nests among the trees*; *the owls have laid three eggs in their nest*
2 *verb*
(of birds) to build a nest and lay eggs; *the ducks are nesting by the river bank*; **nesting site** = place where a bird may build a nest

④ **nest egg**
['nest 'eg] *noun*
money that you have saved; *we've saved up a nice little nest egg for our retirement*

③ **nestle**
['nesl] *verb*
to settle in comfort; *the cat nestled down quietly in the cushions*

① **net**
[net]
1 *noun*
(a) woven material with large holes
(b) piece of this material used for a special purpose; **butterfly net** = bag of very light net with which you can catch butterflies; **fishing net** = a large net used by fishermen to catch fish; **tennis net** = a net stretched across the middle of a tennis court; *he hit the ball into the net*
(c) **the Net** = INTERNET
2 *verb*
to make a profit; *we netted $4500 on the deal* (NOTE: **netting - netted**)
3 *adjective*
after deductions; *that figure is net, not gross*; **net earnings** *or* **net income** *or* **net salary** = money earned after tax has been deducted; **net price** = final price that is paid by the buyer; **net profit** = profit calculated after deducting all expenses; **net weight** = weight after deducting the weight of packaging material (NOTE: the opposite is **gross**)

① **Netherlands**
['neðərlændz] *noun*
European country, to the west of Germany and north of Belgium; *Amsterdam is the largest city in the Netherlands*; *see also* DUTCH, HOLLAND (NOTE: capital: **Amsterdam**; people: **the Dutch**; language: **Dutch**; currency: **guilder, euro**)

④ **nettle**
['netl] *noun*
stinging nettle = type of common weed that stings when you touch it; *he walked with bare legs through the wood and got stung by nettles*; **to grasp the nettle** = to deal with a problem

quickly and firmly to settle it before it causes you any more trouble; *no politician has dared grasp the nettle of corruption in sport*

② **network**
['netwɜrk]
1 *noun*
(a) system of linked roads, railways, etc.; *there is a network of tunnels under the university; the rail network; a satellite TV network*
(b) linked computer system; *how does this network operate?; you can make reservations at any of our hotels throughout the country using our computer network*
(c) group of people linked together; *his rapidly developing network of contacts in government*
2 *verb*
to link up two or more computers to allow them to exchange information; *desk PCs are usually networked and share resources*

③ **neutral**
['njutrəl]
1 *adjective*
(a) not in favor of one side or the other in a dispute; *the UN sent in neutral observers; the referee has to stay neutral*
(b) refusing to take part in a war; *during the war, Switzerland remained neutral*
(c) with a light color, such as pale brown or pale gray; *red walls, green furniture and a neutral carpet*
2 *noun*
(a) country that does not take part in a war
(b) citizen of a neutral country; *only neutrals were admitted to the talks*
(c) *(automobiles, trucks, etc.)* not in gear; *the truck is in neutral*

① **never**
['nevər] *adverb*
not at any time; not ever; *we'll never forget that restaurant; I've never bought anything in that store although I've often been inside it; he never eats meat; never mind!* = don't worry, don't bother about it; *well I never!* = how surprising!; *well I never - it's James!*

③ **nevertheless**
[nevəðə'les] *adverb*
in spite of all that; *I know it is raining, but nevertheless I'd like to go for a walk along the beach; she had a cold, but went to the meeting nevertheless*

① **new**
[nju] *adjective*
(a) made quite recently, never used before; *this is the new model - it's just come out; are your shoes new?*
(b) which arrived recently, fresh; *there are two new secretaries in the office; new potatoes* = first young potatoes of a year's harvest
(c) which has just been bought; *she bought herself a new motorcycle; he's trying to get his new computer to work*
(d) quite different from what was before; *we*

need someone with new ideas; they put some new wallpaper in the bedroom* (NOTE: newer - newest)

① **newcomer**
['njukʌmər] *noun*
person who has just come to a place; *the family are newcomers to the town; could all newcomers to the meeting please sign the register?*

④ **newly**
['njuli] *adverb*
recently; *he was showing off his newly purchased automobile; the house has been bought by a newly married couple*

① **news**
[njuz] *noun*
spoken or written information about what has happened; *what's the news of your sister?; she told me all the latest news about the office; he was watching the 7 o'clock news on TV; I don't want to hear any bad news;* **have you heard the news?** = have you heard what has happened?; *have you had any news about your pay raise?;* **to break the news to someone** = to tell someone the bad news; *he broke the news to his daughters;* **no news is good news** = if there is nothing new to mention, things must be going well (NOTE: **news** is singular, not plural)

④ **news agency**
['njuz 'eɪdʒənsi] *noun*
office which distributes information to newspapers and TV; *he works for an international news agency*

② **newscaster** *or* **news broadcaster**
['njuzkæstər or 'njuz 'brɔdkæstər] *noun*
person who reads the news on radio or TV; *the newscaster read the latest report on the war; you don't often hear news broadcasters pronouncing names wrongly*

② **news conference**
['njuz 'kɒnfərəns] *noun*
meeting with journalists to give information about something and answer questions; *the climbers held a news conference at the airport on their return from Everest*

① **newspaper**
['njuzpeɪpər] *noun*
publication consisting of loose folded sheets of paper, which usually comes out each day, with news of what has happened; *he was so absorbed in his newspaper that he didn't notice that the toast had burned; we saw your picture in the local newspaper; the newspapers are full of news of the election; there's an interesting article on fishing in the newspaper;* **daily newspaper** = newspaper that is published every weekday (NOTE: **a newspaper** is often simply called a **paper**)

① **newsstand**
['njuzstænd] *noun*
small store, often outdoors, selling newspapers, magazines, candy, etc.; *he stopped at a*

newsstand on the way home to buy a newspaper

② **new year**
['nju 'jɜr] *noun*
the first few days of the year; *I started my new job in the new year*; **Happy New Year!** = good wishes for the New Year; **New Year's resolution** = plan to improve your way of living, decided on at the New Year, and usually abandoned shortly afterwards; *each New Year I make the same resolutions, but never manage to keep them*; **to stay up to see the New Year in** = to stay up until after midnight on December 31 to celebrate the beginning of the New Year

② **New Year's Day**
[nju jɜrz 'deɪ] *noun*
1 January; *it's a shame you have to work on New Year's Day*

② **New Year's Eve**
[nju jɜrz 'iv] *noun*
31 December; *the only time we drink champagne is on New Year's Eve*

① **New York (City)**
['nju 'jɔrk] *noun*
large city on the Eastern coast of the U.S.A.; *we are due to arrive in New York City at 5 o'clock*; *she's the manager of our New York office*; *New York City seems to get busier and busier each time I visit*; *yesterday New York City had three inches of snow*

① **New Zealand**
['nju 'zilənd] *noun*
country in the Pacific Ocean, to the east of Australia; *the sheep trade is important to the New Zealand economy* (NOTE: capital: **Wellington**; people: **New Zealanders**; language: **English**; currency: **New Zealand dollar**)

② **New Zealander**
['nju 'ziləndər] *noun*
person from New Zealand; *my sister recently married a New Zealander*

① **next**
[nekst]
1 *adjective & adverb*
(a) coming after in time; *on Wednesday we go to Paris, and the next day we travel to Italy*; *first you put the eggs into a bowl and next you add some sugar*; *don't forget to give me a call the next time you're in town*; *next week is the start of our vacation*; *the next time you go to the supermarket, can you get some coffee?*
(b) nearest in place; *the ball went over the fence into the next garden*; *she took the seat next to mine*; **it costs next to nothing** = it doesn't cost very much
2 *pronoun*
the thing or person following; *after two buses went past full, the next was almost empty*; *I'll be back from vacation the week after next*; *(asking the next person in the line to come)* **next, please!**

① **next door**
['nekst 'dɔr] *adjective & adverb*
in the house next to this one; *who lives next door to your mother?*; *the store is next door to a bank*; *our next-door neighbors have gone on vacation, and we are looking after their cat*

① **nice**
[naɪs] *adjective*
(a) pleasant, fine; *we had a nice time at the seaside*; *if the weather's nice let's have a picnic*; *the nicest thing about the town is that it is on the sea*
(b) pleasant, polite; *that wasn't a very nice thing to say*; *try and be nice to your grandfather* (NOTE: **nicer - nicest**)

③ **nicely**
['naɪsli] *adverb*
(a) very well; *that will do nicely, thank you*
(b) politely; *you can have a cookie if you ask for it nicely*

① **nickel**
['nɪkl] *noun*
five cent coin; *two nickels equal a dime*

① **nickname**
['nɪkneɪm]
1 *noun*
short or informal name given to someone; *her real name's Henrietta, but everyone calls her by her nickname "Bobbles"*
2 *verb*
to give a nickname to; *he was nicknamed "Camel" because of his big nose*

③ **niece**
[nis] *noun*
daughter of a brother or sister; *my niece gave me a tie for my birthday*

① **night**
[naɪt] *noun*
(a) part of the day when it is dark; *it's dangerous to walk alone on the streets at night*; *burglars got into the office during the night*; *he is on night duty three days a week*; *they're planning to have a night out tomorrow*
(b) *(informal)* **a night owl** = someone who likes to work, eat, etc., until late at night, and does not get up early in the morning; *she's a night owl and finds it difficult to get up in time for work*; *compare* EARLY BIRD (NOTE: do not confuse with **knight**)

② **nightclub**
['naɪtklʌb] *noun*
club which is only open at night; *our daughter will only come with us on vacation if we go to a resort with lots of nightclubs*

① **nightmare**
['naɪtmeər] *noun*
(a) very frightening dream; *I had a nightmare that I was drowning*
(b) horrible experience; *the dinner party was a nightmare*; *a nightmare journey across the desert*

④ **nil**

[nɪl] *noun*

nothing; *our advertising budget has been cut to nil*

① **nine**

[naɪn]

number 9; *she's nine (years old) tomorrow*; *the store opens at 9 o'clock*; **nine times out of ten** = very often; *see also* DRESSED

① **nineteen**

[naɪn'tiːn]

number 19; *he's nineteen (years old) tomorrow*; **in the 1950s** = during the years 1950 to 1959; **the nineteen hundreds (1900s)** = the years from 1900 to 1999 (NOTE: compare with **the nineteenth century**)

① **nineteenth (19th)**

[naɪn'tiːnθ] *adjective & noun*

referring to nineteen; *it's his nineteenth birthday tomorrow*; *August nineteenth (August 19)*; **the nineteenth century** = the period from 1800 to 1899 (NOTE: compare with **the nineteen hundreds**; note also that with dates **nineteenth** is usually written **19 July 19, 1935; October 19, 1991**: (say "October nineteenth")

④ **ninetieth (90th)**

[ˈnaɪntiəθ] *adjective & noun*

referring to ninety; *a ninetieth of a second*; *it will be my grandfather's ninetieth birthday next month*

① **ninety**

[ˈnaɪnti] number 90; *my old aunt will be ninety (years old) next week and her husband is ninety-two: they are both in their nineties*; **the nineteen nineties (1990s)** = the years from 1990 to 1999 (NOTE: **ninety-one** (91), **ninety-two** (92), etc., but **ninety-first** (91st), **ninety-second** (92nd), etc.)

① **ninth (9th)**

[naɪnθ] *adjective & noun*

referring to nine; *tomorrow is his ninth birthday*; *today is June ninth (June 9) he missed the record by a ninth of a second*; **the ninth century** = the period from 800 to 899 AD (NOTE: with dates **ninth** is usually written **9 July 9, 1935; October 9, 1991**: (say "October ninth"); with names of kings and queens **ninth** is usually written **IX: King Charles IX** (say: "King Charles the Ninth")

② **nip**

[nɪp]

1 *noun*

short sharp bite; *the little dog gave him a nasty nip*

2 *verb*

(a) to pinch sharply; *he nipped off the end of the stalk to stop the plant growing any taller*; *see also* BUD

(b) to bite sharply; *the dog nipped the letter carrier in the leg* (NOTE: **nipping - nipped**)

④ **nitrogen**

[ˈnaɪtrədʒən] *noun*

important gas which is essential for life, and which forms most of the atmosphere; *nitrogen is absorbed into the body from protein* (NOTE: Chemical element: chemical symbol: **N**; atomic number: **7**)

① **no**

[nəʊ] *adjective & adverb*

(a) *(showing the opposite of "yes")* *I asked my mother if we could borrow her car but she said "no"*; *do you want another cup of coffee? - no, thank you*

(b) not any; *there's no milk left in the fridge*; *we live in a small town, and there's no post office for miles around*; *we had no reply to our fax*

(c) *(signs)* **no entry** = do not go in this way; **no exit** = do not go out this way; **no parking** = do not park; **no smoking** = do not smoke

(d) *(informal)* **no way** = certainly not; *will you lend me $3000? - no way!*

(e) not at all; *my new kitchen knife is no sharper than the old one*; *she no longer works here*; *I'm no good at math*

③ **no.**

[ˈnʌmbər]

abbreviation for NUMBER

④ **noble**

[ˈnəʊbl]

1 *noun*

person of high rank; *the nobles forced the king to sign the treaty*

2 *adjective*

(a) with a fine character; *it was very noble of him to lend her his umbrella*; *she did it for the noblest of reasons*

(b) of high rank in society; *she comes from a noble family* (NOTE: **nobler - noblest**)

① **nobody**

[ˈnəʊbədi] *pronoun*

no one or no person; *there was nobody in the café*; *we met nobody on our way here*; *nobody wants to do her job*; *you'll have to drive the bus - nobody else has a driver's license*

④ **nocturnal**

[nɒkˈtɜːnl] *adjective*

referring to the night; **nocturnal animals** = animals which are active at night, and sleep during the daytime

① **nod**

[nɒd]

1 *noun*

little movement of the head up and down, meaning "yes"; *he gave me a nod as I came in*; *(informal)* **to give the nod to** = to accept without any discussion

2 *verb*

(a) to move the head slightly up and down, meaning "yes"; *when he asked her if she understood the question, she nodded or nodded her head*; *he nodded to show his agreement* (NOTE: the opposite is to **shake** your head, meaning "no")

(b) to move the head slightly up and down, to mean "hello" or "goodbye"; *she nodded at me as I went past*

(c) to nod off = to go to sleep; *she was nodding off in front of the television* (NOTE: nodding - nodded)

① **noise**
[nɔɪz] *noun*
(a) loud or unpleasant sound; *don't make any noise - the guards might hear you*; *the workmen are making so much noise that we can't use the telephone*
(b) sound in general; *the baby made a little sucking noise*; *is there anything the matter with the washing machine? - it's making a funny noise*; *there was a noise of running water in the bathroom*; *he woke up when he heard a noise in the kitchen*

③ **noisily**
[ˈnɔɪzɪli] *adverb*
making a lot of noise; *he drank his coffee noisily*

① **noisy**
[ˈnɔɪzi] *adjective*
which makes a lot of noise; *a crowd of noisy little boys*; *unfortunately, the hotel overlooks a noisy road junction*; *the new electric drill is even noisier than our old one* (NOTE: noisier - noisiest)

④ **nominal**
[ˈnɒmɪnl] *adjective*
(a) in name, not in fact; *he's the nominal head of the company*
(b) involving a small amount of money; *we pay a nominal fee*

③ **nominate**
[ˈnɒmɪneɪt] *verb*
to propose someone for an office; *he's been nominated to the committee*; *she was nominated as a candidate for the next election*

② **nomination**
[nɒmɪˈneɪʃn] *noun*
(a) action of nominating; *her nomination to the board of directors*
(b) name which has been proposed; *there are three nominations for the post of secretary*

① **none**
[nʌn]
1 *pronoun*
(a) not any; *how many dogs do you have? - none*; *can you buy some milk, we've none left in the fridge?*; *a little money is better than none at all*; *her health is none too good* = it is not very good
(b) not one; *none of my friends smoke*; *none of the group can speak Chinese*
2 *adverb*
(used with "the" and comparative) not at all; *she seems none the better for her vacation*; *he was none the worse for his accident* = he was not at all hurt in the accident; *to be none the wiser* = to know no more about it than you did

before; *I read his report, and I'm still none the wiser*; *his lengthy explanation left us none the wiser about how the system would work*

④ **nonetheless**
[nʌnðəˈles] *adverb*
in spite of all that; *I know it is raining, but nonetheless I'd like to go for a swim before breakfast*; *he had a cold, but went to the meeting nonetheless*

② **nonsense**
[ˈnɒnsəns] *noun*
silly ideas; *I'm too fat - nonsense, you're have a nice shape!*; *he talked a lot of nonsense*; *it's nonsense to expect people to pay money for that* (NOTE: no plural)

① **noon**
[nun] *noun*
twelve o'clock in the middle of the day; *we'll stop for lunch at noon*

① **no one**
[ˈnəʊwʌn] *pronoun*
nobody, no person; *you can go to the bathroom - there's no one there*; *we met no one we knew*; *no one here takes sugar in their tea*; *no one else has a driver's license so you'll have to be the driver*

③ **nor**
[nɔr] *conjunction* and not; *I did not meet him that year nor in subsequent years*; *I never went there again, nor did my wife*; *I don't want to go - nor me!*; *see also* NEITHER

① **normal**
[ˈnɔrməl] *adjective*
usual, what usually happens; *we hope to resume normal service as soon as possible* ; *what's the size of a normal swimming pool?*; *at her age, it's only normal for her to want to go to parties*

② **normally**
[ˈnɔrməli] *adverb*
usually; *the bus is normally late*; *she doesn't normally drink wine*

① **north**
[nɔrθ]
1 *noun*
direction to your left when you are facing the direction where the sun rises; *there will be snow in the north of the country*; *it's cold when the wind blows from the north*
2 *adjective*
referring to the north; *we went on vacation to the north coast of Maine*; *the north side of our house never gets any sun*; *when the north wind blows, you can expect snow*
3 *adverb*
toward the north; *they were traveling north at the time*; *go north for three miles and then you'll see the freeway to Boston*; *our office windows face north*

② **North America**
[ˈnɔrθ əˈmerɪkə] *noun*
part of the American continent to the north of Mexico, formed of the U.S.A. and Canada; *he*

has traveled widely in North America from Alaska to Florida

① **northeast**
[nɔrˈθiist]
1 *adverb*
direction between north and east; *they were traveling northeast at the time*; *go northeast for three miles and then you'll come to our farm*; *our office windows face northeast*
2 *noun*
part of country to the north and east; *the Northeast of the U.S.A. will have snow showers*; *it's cold when the wind blows from the northeast*

① **northern**
[ˈnɔrðən] *adjective*
referring to the north; *northern countries have more rain*; *they live in the northern part of the country*

① **North Pole**
[ˈnɔrθ ˈpəʊl] *noun*
furthest point at the north of the Earth; *an explorer who has been to the North Pole*

① **northwest**
[nɔrθˈwest]
1 *adverb*
direction between west and north; *they were traveling northwest at the time*; *go northwest for a few miles and then you'll come to our house*
2 *adjective*
coming from the north and west; *the northwest wind blows cold Arctic air*
3 *noun*
part of the country to the north and west; *in the U.S.A., the population in the Northwest is lower than in the Northeast*; *the old castle stood to the northwest of the cathedral*

① **Norway**
[ˈnɔrweɪ] *noun*
country in northern Europe, to the west of Sweden; *in northern Norway it is light almost all day long in summer* (NOTE: capital: **Oslo**; people: **Norwegians**; language: **Norwegian**; currency: **Norwegian krone**)

② **Norwegian**
[nɔrˈwidʒən]
1 *adjective*
referring to Norway; *Ibsen is the most famous Norwegian author*
2 *noun*
(a) person from Norway; *the Norwegians have a very large fishing fleet*
(b) language spoken in Norway; *Norwegian is similar in many ways to Swedish*

① **nose**
[nəʊz]
1 *noun*
part of the head which you breathe through and smell with; *he has a cold, and his nose is red*; *dogs have wet noses*; *she has the flu - her nose is running*; *don't wipe your nose on your sleeve, use a tissue*; **to blow your nose** = to blow air through your nose into a handkerchief to remove liquid from your nose; **to speak through your nose** = to talk as if your nose is blocked, so that you say "b" instead of "m" and "d" instead of "n"; **to look down your nose at something** = to look at something as if you don't think it is very good; *she has a degree and looks down her nose at the other secretaries*; **to do something under someone's nose** = to do something right in front of someone who doesn't notice; *the prisoners walked out of the prison under the noses of the guards*; **to pay through the nose for something** = to pay far more for something than you should; *he paid through the nose for his ticket to New York because it was the only seat left*; **to turn your nose up at something** = to show that you don't feel something is good enough for you; *it's a marvelous deal, I don't see why you should turn your nose up at it*
2 *verb*
(informal) **to nose about** *or* **to nose around** = to look or to search in a place; *what are you doing nosing around in my papers?*; *I don't like people nosing about in the office safe*

② **nostril**
[ˈnɒstrl] *noun*
one of two holes in your nose, which you breathe through; *my left nostril's blocked*

① **not**
[nɒt] *adverb (often shortened to* **n't***)*
(a) *(used with verbs to show the negative)* *she can't come*; *it isn't there*; *he didn't want any meat*; *we couldn't go home because of the fog*; *don't you like coffee?*; *a service charge is not included*
(b) **not...either** = and not...also; *she doesn't eat meat, and she doesn't eat fish either*; *it wasn't hot, but it wasn't very cold either*
(c) **not only...but also** = not just this...but this as well; *she isn't only blind, but she's deaf also*; *the movie wasn't only very long, but it was also very bad*
(d) *(used to make a strong negative - not shortened in this sense)* *is it going to rain? - I hope not*; *I don't like bananas - why on earth not?*; *he begged her not to leave him alone*; *there was not one single store open*; *everyone was invited, not forgetting the bus driver*; **not a few** = many

④ **notable**
[ˈnəʊtəbl] *adjective*
which is worth noticing; *it was a notable achievement*; *she was notable by her absence*; *the town is notable for its fish restaurants*

④ **notably**
[ˈnəʊtəbli] *adverb*
(a) especially; *some Western countries, notably Canada and the United States, have a very high standard of living*

(b) in a way that is easily noticed; *the food was notably better than the last time we ate there*

① **note**

[nəʊt]

1 *noun*

(a) a few words in writing to remind yourself of something; *she made a few notes before she gave her speech*; *she made a note of what she needed to buy before she went to the supermarket*; **to take note of** = to pay attention to; *we have to take note of public opinion*

(b) short message; *she left a note for the lawyer with his secretary*; *he wrote me a note to say he couldn't come*

(c) musical sound or a written sign meaning a musical sound; *he can't sing high notes*

(d) key on a piano; *she played a tune, using only the black notes on the piano*

(e) further explanations about a text; *the notes are at the back of the book*

2 *verb*

(a) to write down something in a few words; *the police officer noted on his pad all the details of the accident*

(b) to take notice of; *please note that our prices were raised on January 1*

③ **notebook**

['nəʊtbʊk] *noun*

(a) small book for making notes; *the police officer wrote down the details in his notebook*

(b) very small computer which you can carry around with you

③ **noted**

['nəʊtɪd] *adjective*

famous; *the town is noted for its botanical gardens*; *Mr. Smith, the noted local artist*

① **nothing**

['nʌθɪŋ] *pronoun*

(a) not anything; *there's nothing interesting on TV*; *she said nothing about what she had seen*; *there's nothing more we can do*; **nothing much happened** = not very much happened; *he has nothing left in the bank* = no money left; **for nothing** = free, without having to pay; *we're friends of the woman organizing the show and she got us into the exhibition for nothing*

(b) **to think nothing of doing something** = to do something easily; *he thinks nothing of cycling ten miles to work*; **it's nothing to do with you** = it doesn't concern you

① **notice**

['nəʊtɪs]

1 *noun*

(a) piece of writing giving information, usually put in a place where everyone can see it; *he pinned up a notice about the staff tennis match*

(b) official warning that something has to be done, that something is going to happen; *they gave us five minutes' notice to leave the office*; *if you want to resign, you have to give a month's notice*; *the train times were changed without notice*; **until further notice** = until

different instructions are given; *you must pay $300 on the last day of each month until further notice*; **at** *or* **on short notice** = with very little warning; *it had to be done on short notice*; *the bank manager will not see anyone at such short notice*

(c) attention; *it has been brought to my notice that students have been going into town at lunchtime*; **take no notice of what the police officer says** = pay no attention to what he says, don't worry about what he says

2 *verb*

to see; to take note of; *I wore one blue and one white sock all day and nobody noticed*; *I didn't notice you had come in*; *did you notice if John was sitting next to Sarah?*

② **noticeable**

['nəʊtɪsəbl] *adjective*

which is easily noticed; *the mark on your necktie is hardly noticeable*; *I can't see any noticeable difference between them*

② **notification**

[nəʊtɪfɪ'keɪʃn] *noun*

(formal) act of informing someone; *have they received any notification of the date of the court case?*; *we have had no notification that the sale has taken place*; *on receipt of the notification, they decided to appeal*

③ **notify**

['nəʊtɪfaɪ] *verb*

to notify someone of something = to tell someone something formally; *customs were notified that the shipment had arrived*; *the local doctor notified the health department of the case of tropical fever*

② **notion**

['nəʊʃn] *noun*

(a) idea; *she has this strange notion that she ought to be a TV star*

(b) **notions** = small articles used in sewing, like needles, ribbon, etc.

④ **notorious**

[nəʊ'tɔːriəs] *adjective*

well known for something bad; *he comes from a notorious gangster family*; *this road junction is notorious for accidents*

② **noun**

[naʊn] *noun*

(in grammar) word which can be the subject of a verb and is used to refer to a person or thing; *nouns are words such as "brick" and "elephant"*; **proper noun** = word which is the name of a place, a person, a building, etc.; *proper nouns such as 'The Statue of Liberty", "the Mona Lisa", etc.* (NOTE: proper nouns are almost always written with a capital letter)

③ **novel**

['nɒvl]

1 *noun*

long story with invented characters and plot; *"Pickwick Papers" was Dickens' first major novel*

2 *adjective*

new; *being in New York is a novel experience for me*

③ **novelist**

['nɒvəlɪst] *noun*

person who writes novels; *John Steinbeck is one of the most important American novelists*

① **November**

[nə'vembər] *noun*

eleventh month of the year, the month after October and before December; *today is November 5* ; *she was born in November*; *we never go on vacation in November* (NOTE: **November 5:** say "November fifth")

① **now**

[naʊ]

1 *adverb*

at this point in time; *I can hear a train coming now*; *please can we go home now?*; *the flight is only two hours - he ought to be in Atlanta by now*; *now's the best time for going skiing*; *a week from now we'll be sitting on the beach*; **until now** *or* **up to now** = until this point in time; *until now, I've never had to see a doctor*

2 *conjunction*

now that = since, because; *now that I know how to drive I can take more vacations by myself*; *now you've mentioned it, I do remember having a phone call from him last week*

3 *interjection*

(a) *(showing a warning)* **now then**, *don't be rude to the teacher!*; *come on now, work hard!*; *now, now! nobody wants to hear you crying*

(b) *(attracting someone's attention)* *now, everyone, let's begin the meeting*

② **nowadays**

['naʊədeɪz] *adverb*

at the present time; *nowadays lots of people go to Hawaii on vacation*; *the traffic is so bad nowadays that it takes us an hour to drive across town*

② **nowhere**

['nəʊweər] *adverb*

(a) not in or to any place; *my purse was nowhere to be found*; *where are you going? - nowhere*; *there is nowhere else for them to live*; **to get nowhere** = to be unsuccessful; *I called six stores to try and find a part for the washing machine, but got nowhere*; **to be getting nowhere** = not to have any success; *I'm getting nowhere with my research*

(b) **nowhere near** = not at all; *the work is nowhere near finished*; *he has nowhere near done all his homework*

③ **nuclear**

['njuklɪər] *adjective*

(a) referring to energy from atoms; *a nuclear power station*; **nuclear power** = electricity produced by a nuclear power station; **nuclear weapons** = weapons made from energy from

atoms, as opposed to conventional weapons such as guns

(b) **nuclear family** = family consisting simply of parents and children; *see also* EXTENDED FAMILY

③ **nudge**

[nʌdʒ]

1 *noun*

little push, usually with your elbow; *she gave me a nudge to wake me up*

2 *verb*

to give a little push, usually with the elbow; *he nudged me when it was my turn to speak*

③ **nuisance**

['njusəns] *noun*

thing which annoys; *the dog's a nuisance because she always wants attention*; *it's a nuisance the bus doesn't run on Sundays*

② **numb**

[nʌm] *adjective*

which has no feeling; *the tips of his fingers went numb*

① **number**

['nʌmbər]

1 *noun*

(a) figure; *13 is not a lucky number*; *they live on the opposite side of the road at number 49*; *can you give me your telephone number?*; *a number 6 bus goes downtown*; *please quote your account number*; **box number** = reference number used when asking for mail to be sent to a post office or to a newspaper's offices; *please address your reply to Box No. 209*

(b) quantity of people or things; *the number of tickets sold was disappointing*; *a large number of children or large numbers of children will be sitting the exam*; *there were only a small number of people at the meeting*; **a number of times** = often; *I've seen that movie a number of times*; **any number of times** = very often; *I've been to Europe any number of times*; *she could take her driver's test any number of times but she still wouldn't pass it* (NOTE: when **a number** refers to a plural noun it is followed by a plural verb: **a number of houses were damaged**)

(c) piece of music, song; *she played a selection of numbers by Cole Porter*

2 *verb*

(a) to give something a number; *the raffle tickets are numbered 1 to 1000*; *I refer to our invoices numbered 234 and 235*; *all the seats are clearly numbered*

(b) to count; *visitors to the exhibition numbered several thousand*; *he numbers among the most important writers of the 20th century*

④ **numeracy**

['njuːmərəsi] *noun*

being able to work with numbers; *staff are trying to improve the children's numeracy skills*

③ **numeral**
['njumərəl] *noun*
written sign representing a number; *a computer file name can be made up of letters or numerals*; **Arabic numerals** = figures such as 3, 4 and 20; **Roman numerals** = figures such as III, IV and XX

③ **numerous**
['njumərəs] *adjective*
very many; *he has been fined for speeding on numerous occasions*

② **nun**
[nʌn] *noun*
woman member of a religious order; *a Tibetan nun*; *nuns served hot soup to the refugees* (NOTE: do not confuse with **none**; note: the equivalent men are **monks**)

① **nurse**
[nɜrs]
1 *noun*
(woman or man) person who looks after sick people; *she has a job as a nurse in the local hospital*; *he's training to be a nurse*
2 *verb*
(a) to look after people who are sick; *when she fell sick her daughter nursed her until she was better*
(b) to be sick with something; *he's sitting in bed nursing his cold*; *she came back from her vacation nursing a broken arm*
(c) to nurse a feeling = to have a secret feeling against someone; *he has been nursing feelings of jealousy about his brother for years*

① **nursery**
['nɜrsəri] *noun*
(a) place where babies or young children are looked after; *my sister went to a nursery every day from the age of 18 months*; **day nursery** = nursery which is open during the day; **nursery school** = first school for very small children; **nursery rhyme** = children's traditional song
(b) place where young plants are grown and sold; *buy some plants from the nursery* (NOTE: plural is **nurseries**)

④ **nursing**
['nɜrsɪŋ]
1 *noun*
profession of being a nurse; *she decided to go to school for nursing*; *have you considered nursing as a career?*
2 *adjective*
referring to the job of looking after sick people; **nursing home** = small private hospital, especially one looking after old people

① **nut**
[nʌt] *noun*
(a) fruit of a tree, with a hard shell; **to crack nuts** = to break the shells of nuts to get at the fruit inside; *he cracked the nuts with his teeth*
(b) metal ring which screws onto a metal rod to hold it tight; *screw the nut on tightly*; *(informal)* **nuts and bolts of something** = the main details of something; *you'll need to master the nuts and bolts of the stock market before going to work in a broker's office*; *see also* NUTS

④ **nutrient**
['njutriənt] *noun*
(formal) substance in food which encourages the growth of living things; *plants take nutrients from rain*

> COMMENT: proteins, fats, vitamins are all nutrients needed to make animals grow; carbon, hydrogen, etc., are nutrients needed by plants

④ **nutrition**
[nju'trɪʃn] *noun*
(a) study of food; *we are studying nutrition as part of the food science course*
(b) receiving food; *a scheme to improve nutrition in the poorer areas*

④ **nutritious**
[nju'trɪʃəs] *adjective*
valuable as food because it provides nutrients which are needed by the body; *ice cream is not a very nutritious food*

① **nuts**
[nʌts] *adjective*
(informal) mad; **nuts about someone** *or* **something** = very keen on someone or something; *he's nuts about old automobiles*; **to drive someone nuts** = to make someone crazy; *I wish they'd turn the music down - it's driving me nuts*

Oo

O, o
[əʊ]
fifteenth letter of the alphabet, between N and P; *"cooperate" can be spelled with a hyphen between the Os*

oak
[əʊk] *noun*
(a) type of large tree which loses its leaves in winter; *oaks grow to be very old*; *a forest of oak trees*
(b) wood from this tree; *an oak table*

oar
[ɔr] *noun*
long wooden pole with a flat part at the end, used for moving a boat along; *his oar got stuck in the weeds of the river*

oasis
[əʊˈeɪsɪs] *noun*
(a) place in the desert where there is water, and where plants grow; *after crossing the desert for days they finally arrived at an oasis*
(b) quiet pleasant place which is different from everything else around it; *Gramercy Park is a peaceful oasis in the middle of downtown Manhattan* (NOTE: plural is **oases** [əʊˈeɪsiːz])

oath
[əʊθ] *noun*
(a) solemn legal promise that someone will say or write only what is true; *all the members of the jury have to take an oath*; *the lords swore an oath to serve the king*; **he was under oath** = he had promised in court to say what was true; *he was accused of lying to the court when he was under oath*
(b) swear word; *as the police grabbed him, he let out a long string of oaths* (NOTE: plural is **oaths** [əʊðz])

oats
[əʊts] *noun*
(a) cereal plant of which the grain is used as food; *the farmer has decided to grow oats in this field this year*
(b) to sow your wild oats = to behave in a wild way when young

obedient
[əˈbidiənt] *adjective*
doing what your are told to do; *our old dog is very obedient - he always comes when you call him*

obey
[əʊˈbeɪ] *verb*
to do what someone tells you to do; *if you can't obey orders you shouldn't be a police officer; everyone must obey the law*

object
1 *noun* [ˈɒbdʒekt]
(a) thing; *they thought they saw a strange object in the sky*
(b) aim; *their object is to take control of the radio station*
(c) *(in grammar)* noun or pronoun, etc., which follows directly from a verb or preposition; *in the phrase "the cat caught the mouse", the word "mouse" is the object of the verb "caught"*
(d) money is no object = money is not a problem; *money is no object to them - they're very wealthy*
2 *verb* [əbˈdʒekt]
(a) to object (to) = to refuse to agree to; *she objected to the plans to widen the road*; *I object most strongly to paying extra for my little suitcase*
(b) to say why you refuse to agree; *he objected that the pay was too low*

objection
[əbˈdʒekʃn] *noun*
reason for refusing to agree to something; *do you have any objection to me smoking?*; *any objections to the plan?*; **to raise an objection to something** = to object to something; *she raised several objections to the proposal*

objective
[əbˈdʒektɪv]
1 *adjective*
considering things from a general point of view and not from your own; *you must be objective when planning the future of your business* (NOTE: the opposite is **subjective**)
2 *noun*
aim, object which you are aiming at; *our long-term objective is to make the company financially sound*; *the company has achieved its main objectives*

obligation
[ɒblɪˈgeɪʃn] *noun*
(a) duty; legal debt; **to meet your obligations** = to pay your debts; *he cannot meet his obligations*
(b) duty to do something; *you have an obligation to attend the meeting*; **to be under an obligation to someone** = to feel it is your duty to help someone; *she felt under an obligation to look after her friend's cat*; *two*

weeks' free trial without obligation to buy = the customer can try the item at home for two weeks without having to buy it at the end of the trial

③ **oblige**
[ə'blaɪdʒ] *verb*
(a) to force someone to do something; *he was obliged to hand the money back*
(b) to feel obliged to do something = to feel it is your duty to do something; *he felt obliged to study medicine at school because his father was a doctor*
(c) to do something useful or helpful; *he wanted to oblige you by weeding your garden for you*
(d) *(formal)* **to be obliged to someone** = to be grateful to someone for having done something; *thank you - I'm much obliged to you for your help; I'd be obliged if you could shut the window*

③ **oblong**
['ɒblɒŋ] *noun*
shape with two pairs of equal sides, one pair being longer than the other; *the screen is an oblong, approximately 30 cm by 40 cm*

④ **obscure**
[əb'skjʊər]
1 *adjective*
(a) not clear; *there are several obscure points in his letter*
(b) not well-known; *they always stay in some obscure place in the Rockies which no one has ever heard of*
2 *verb*
to hide, especially by covering; *the view from the top of the mountain was obscured by low clouds*

③ **observation**
[ɒbzə'veɪʃn] *noun*
(a) action of observing; *by careful observation, the police found out where the thieves had hidden the money;* **under observation** = being carefully watched; *the patient will be kept under observation for a few days*
(b) remark; *he made several observations about the government*

② **observe**
[əb'zɜrv] *verb*
(a) to follow or to obey (a law, rule, custom, etc.); *his family observes all the Jewish festivals; the local laws must be observed*
(b) to watch or to look at; *they observed the sunset from the top of the mountain*
(c) to notice; *the police observed the van coming out of the garage*
(d) to make a remark; *I merely observed that the bus was late as usual*

② **observer**
[əb'zɜrvər] *noun*
person who attends an event and watches (especially without taking part); *the UN sent observers to the elections*

④ **obsess**
[əb'ses] *verb*
to occupy someone's mind all the time; *he is obsessed by wanting to make money; she is obsessed with wanting everything to be tidy*

④ **obsession**
[əb'seʃn] *noun*
(a) fixed idea which occupies your mind all the time; *making money is an obsession with him*
(b) idea or problem which worries you all the time, often associated with mental illness; *she has an obsession with washing her hair*

③ **obstacle**
['ɒbstəkl] *noun*
thing which is in the way, which prevents someone going forward; *the truck had to negotiate rocks and other obstacles to cross the mountain pass; their computer system is not compatible with ours, which is an obstacle to any joint projects*

④ **obstruct**
[əb'strʌkt] *verb*
(a) to block, to stop something going through; *a large black car was obstructing the entrance*
(b) to stop someone from doing something; *he was fined for obstructing the referee*

③ **obtain**
[əb'teɪn] *verb*
to get; *she obtained a copy of the will; he obtained control of the business*

③ **obvious**
['ɒbviəs] *adjective*
clear; easily seen; *it's obvious that we will have to pay for the damage; it was obvious to everyone that the store was not making any money*

③ **obviously**
['ɒbviəsli] *adverb*
clearly; *obviously we will need to borrow various pieces of equipment*

③ **occasion**
[ə'keɪʒən] *noun*
(a) a special occasion = a special event (such as a wedding, etc.); *the baby's first birthday was a special occasion; it's an extra-special occasion - she's one hundred years old today!*
(b) happening, time when something happens; *it is an occasion for celebrations;* **on occasion** = from time to time; *on occasion, we spend a weekend in the country*

③ **occasional**
[ə'keɪʒnəl] *adjective*
happening now and then, not very often; *he was an occasional visitor to my parents' house; we make the occasional trip to New York;* **occasional table** = small table used from time to time

③ **occasionally**
[ə'keɪʒnəli] *adverb*
sometimes, not very often; *occasionally he has to work late; we occasionally go to the movie theater*

③ **occupation**
['ɒkjuˈpeɪʃn] *noun*
(a) act of occupying, of being occupied; *the occupation of the country by enemy soldiers; the occupation of the TV station by protesters*
(b) job, position, employment; *what is her occupation?; his main occupation is running a small engineering firm*

③ **occupational**
['ɒkjuˈpeɪʃnl] *adjective*
referring to a job; *stress is an occupational hazard, I'm afraid*; **occupational therapist** = person who treats patients by making them do certain activities and exercises; **occupational therapy** = treating patients by using activities to help them deal with problems or disabilities, used especially for handicapped patients or patients suffering from mental illness

③ **occupied**
['ɒkjupaɪd] *adjective*
(a) being used; *all the rooms in the hotel are occupied; the bathroom is occupied, so you'll have to wait*
(b) **occupied with** = busy with; *she is always occupied with her family; he is occupied with sorting out the mail*

③ **occupy**
['ɒkjupaɪ] *verb*
(a) to live in or work in; *they occupy the apartment on the second floor; the firm occupies offices in downtown Manhattan*
(b) to be busy with; *dealing with the office occupies most of my time*
(c) to take control of a place by being inside it; *protesters occupied the TV station*

② **occur**
[əˈkɜr] *verb*
(a) to happen; *when did the accident occur?*
(b) to come to your mind; *it has just occurred to me* = I have just thought that; *did it never occur to you that she was lying?*
(c) to exist; *coal deposits occur in several parts of the country* (NOTE: **occurring - occurred**)

① **ocean**
['əʊʃn] *noun*
very large area of sea surrounding the continents; *ocean currents can be very dangerous; ocean liners used to dock here*

COMMENT: the oceans are: the Atlantic, the Pacific, the Indian, the Antarctic (or Southern) and the Arctic

② **o'clock**
[əˈklɒk] *phrase*
(used with numbers to show the time) get up - it's 7 o'clock; we never open the store before 10 o'clock; by 2 o'clock in the morning everyone was asleep (NOTE: **o'clock** is only used for the exact hour, not for times which include minutes. It can also be omitted: **we got home before eight** or **we got home before eight o'clock**)

① **October**
[ɒkˈtəʊbər] *noun*
tenth month of the year, between September and November; *do you ever go on vacation in October?; today is October 18; last October we moved to Santa Fe* (NOTE: **October 18:** say "October eighteenth")

① **octopus**
['ɒktəpəs] *noun*
sea animal with eight long arms; *there's a huge octopus in the aquarium* (NOTE: plural is **octopuses**)

① **odd**
[ɒd] *adjective*
(a) strange, peculiar; *it's odd that she can never remember how to get to their house; he doesn't like chocolate - really, how odd!*
(b) **odd numbers** = numbers (like 17 or 33) which cannot be divided by two; *the odd-numbered buildings or the buildings with odd numbers are on the opposite side of the street*
(c) roughly, approximately; *she had twenty odd pairs of shoes in cardboard boxes*
(d) one forming part of a group; **odd shoe** = one shoe of a pair; **we have a few odd boxes left** = we have a few boxes left out of all the boxes we had (NOTE: **odder - oddest**)

④ **odds**
[ɒdz] *noun*
(a) difference between the amount which can be won and the amount which has been bet; *odds of 10 to 1*
(b) the possibility that something will happen; *the odds are against it; the odds are that she'll get the job*
(c) **it makes no odds** = it makes no difference; **to be at odds with someone** = to quarrel with someone all the time
(d) **odds and ends** = group of various things that have no connection with each other; *he used odds and ends found on the beach to make a sculpture; we made a meal from various odds and ends we found in the fridge*

② **odor**
['əʊdər] *noun*
(formal) smell, scent; *I think I can smell a faint odor of cheese*

① **of**
[ɒv] *preposition*
(a) *(showing a connection) she's the sister of the girl who you met at the party; where's the top of the jam jar?; what are the names of his children?*
(b) *(showing a part or a quantity) how much of the cloth do you need?; there are four boys and two girls - six of them altogether; half of the staff are on vacation; a quart of orange juice*
(c) *(making a description) the school takes children of ten and over; the city of New Orleans is important for its jazz*

(d) *(showing position, material, cause) he lives in the north of the town; the sweater is made of cotton; she died of cancer*

(e) *(in time) it's five minutes of six* = it's five minutes before six (NOTE: **of** is often used after verbs or adjectives **to think of, to be fond of, to be tired of, to smell of, to be afraid of,** etc.)

① **of course**
['ɒv 'kɔrs]
(a) *(used to make "yes" or "no" stronger) are you coming with us? - of course I am!; do you want to lose all your money? - of course not!*
(b) naturally; *he is rich, so of course he lives in a big house*

① **off**
[ɒf]
1 *adverb & preposition*
(a) *(showing movement or position away from a place) we're off to the stores; the office is just off the main road; they spent their vacation on an island off the coast of California; the children got off the bus; take your boots off before you come into the house*
(b) away from work; *she took the week off; it's my secretary's day off today*
(c) not switched on; *switch the light off before you leave the office; is the TV off?* (NOTE: **off** is often used after verbs **to keep off, to break off, to fall off, to take off,** etc.)
2 *adjective*
(a) switched off; *make sure the switch is in the OFF position*
(b) spoiled; *I think this meat's a bit off*
(c) canceled; *she phoned to say the deal was off*
(d) not liking food; not taking food or drink; *I'm off alcohol for six months; she's off shellfish because it gives her a rash*

◇ **off and on**
['ɒf ənd 'ɒn] *adverb*
not all the time, with breaks in between; *it's been raining off and on all afternoon* (NOTE: also **on and off**)

④ **off-color**
[ɒf'kʌlər] *adjective*
slightly indecent; *he made an off-color remark*

④ **offend**
[ə'fend] *verb*
(a) to be or to go against public opinion, someone's feelings; *he offended the whole town by the article he wrote in the local paper*
(b) to commit a crime; *he was released from prison and immediately offended again*

④ **offender**
[ə'fendər] *noun*
person who commits an offense against the law; *the job of the police is to bring offenders to justice*; **first offender** = someone who commits an offense for the first time; *since he was a first offender, he was let off with a warning*; **young offender** = young person who commits a crime

③ **offense**
[ə'fens] *noun*
(a) state of being offended; **to take offense at** = to be offended by; *he took offense at being called lazy; don't take offense - I didn't really mean it*
(b) crime, act which is against the law; *he was charged with committing an offense; since it was his first offense, he was let off with a fine*
(c) ['ɒfens] *(in sport)* the team or section of a team that attacks

④ **offensive**
[ə'fensɪv]
1 *adjective*
(a) unpleasant, which offends; *what an offensive smell!; the waiter was quite offensive*
(b) *(in army)* **offensive weapons** = weapons that are used in an attack; *it is against the law to carry offensive weapons*
2 *noun*
(a) (military) attack; *the offensive was successful, and the enemy retreated*
(b) **to take the offensive** *or* **to go on the offensive** = to start to do something against someone; *he took the offensive and demanded an explanation*

① **offer**
['ɒfər] *verb*
1 *noun*
(a) thing which is proposed; *she accepted his offer of a job in Paris*
(b) **bargain offer** *or* **special offer** = goods that are put on sale at a reduced price; *this week's bargain offer - 30% off all vacations in Egypt; oranges are on special offer today; this supermarket always has special offers*
2 *verb*
to say that you will give something or do something; *she offered to drive him to the station*; **to offer someone a job** = to tell someone that he can have a job in your company; *if they offer you the job, take it; he was offered a job, but he turned it down*

② **offering**
['ɒfrɪŋ] *noun*
thing which is offered; a present; *it's only a small offering, I'm afraid; all offerings will be gratefully received!*

① **office**
['ɒfɪs] *noun*
(a) room or building where you carry on a business or where you organize something; *I'll be working late at the office this evening; why is Miss Jones's office bigger than mine?; we bought some new office furniture*; **doctor's office** = room where a doctor sees his patients
(b) position, job; *she holds the office of secretary*; **term of office** = period of time when someone has a position; *during his term of office as president*
(c) government department; *the office of the state treasurer; see also* POST OFFICE

② **officer**
['ɒfɪsər] *noun*
(a) person who holds an official position; *the customs officer asked me to open my suitcase*
(b) person who is in charge of others in the army, navy, air force, etc.; *regular soldiers must always salute officers*
(c) police officer = policeman or policewoman; *there are two police officers at the door*

③ **official**
[ə'fɪʃl]
1 *adjective*
(a) referring to any organization, especially one which is recognized as part of a government, etc.; *he left official papers in the cab; we had an official order from the local authority; he represents an official body*
(b) done or approved by someone in authority; *she received an official letter of explanation; the strike was made official by the union headquarters*
2 *noun*
person holding a recognized position; *they were met by an official from the embassy; airport officials inspected the shipment*

③ **officially**
[ə'fɪʃəli] *adverb*
(a) in an official way; *she has been officially named as a member of the Canadian team*
(b) according to what is said in public; *officially, you are not supposed to go in through this door, but everyone does*

③ **offshore**
[ɒf'ʃɔr] *adjective*
(a) at a distance from the shore; *we went to visit an offshore oil installation*
(b) offshore wind = wind that blows from the coast toward the sea
(c) on an island which is a foreign country or tax haven; *offshore investments have produced a good rate of return*

③ **offside**
['ɒf'saɪd] *adjective & adverb*
(in sports) between the ball and the opposing team's goal; *he was offside, so the goal did not count*

① **often**
['ɒfən] *adverb*
many times, frequently; *I often have to go to town on business; do you eat beef often?; how often is there a bus to Richmond?; every so often* = from time to time; *we go to the movie theater every so often*

② **oh**
[əʊ] *interjection*
(showing surprise, interest, excitement) Oh look, there's an elephant!; Oh can't you stop making that noise?; Oh, Mike, someone phoned for you while you were out; you must write to the bank manager - oh no I won't

① **oil**
[ɔɪl]
1 *noun*
(a) thick mineral liquid found mainly underground and used as a fuel or to make something move easily; *the door squeaks - it needs some oil; some of the beaches are covered with oil; the company is drilling for oil in the desert*
(b) liquid of various kinds which flows easily, produced from plants and used in cooking; *cook the vegetables in hot oil; olive oil* = oil made from olives
(c) oil (paint) = paint made with colors and oil; *I used to paint in oils but now I prefer watercolors; oil painting* = picture painted in oils, not in watercolor
2 *verb*
to put oil on or into (especially to make a machine run more easily); *you should oil your bicycle chain; that door needs oiling*

② **oily**
['ɔɪli] *adjective*
(a) containing oil; *oily food makes me feel sick; the tank was full of some oily liquid*
(b) covered with oil; *he used an old oily rag to clean his motorcycle* (NOTE: **oilier - oiliest**)

③ **ointment**
['ɔɪntmənt] *noun*
smooth healing cream which you spread on the skin; *rub the ointment onto your knee*

① **OK** *or* **okay**
['əʊ'keɪ]
1 *interjection*
all right, yes; *would you like a coffee? - OK!; it's ten o'clock - OK, let's get going*
2 *adjective*
all right; *he was off sick yesterday, but he seems to be OK now; it is OK for me to bring the dogs?*
3 *noun*
to give something the OK = to approve something; *the committee gave our plan the OK*
4 *verb*
to approve something; *the committee OK'd or okayed our plan* (NOTE: **OK'd** ['əʊ'keɪd])

① **old**
[əʊld] *adjective*
(a) not young; *my uncle is an old man - he's eighty-four*
(b) having existed for a long time; *he collects old automobiles; play some old music, I don't like this modern stuff*
(c) not new; which has been used for a long time; *put on an old shirt if you're going to wash the car; he got rid of his old truck and bought a new one*
(d) with a certain age; *he's six years old today; how old are you?*
(e) *(used as a pleasant way of talking about someone) he's a sweet old man; come on, old thing, it's time to go home* (NOTE: **older - oldest**)

② **old-fashioned**
[əʊldˈfæʃənd] *adjective*
not in fashion; out of date; *she wore old-fashioned clothes*; *call me old-fashioned, but I don't approve of the way young people behave*

② **olive**
[ˈɒlɪv] *noun*
(a) small black or green fruit from which oil is made for use in cooking; *olives are grown in Mediterranean countries like Spain, Greece and Italy*; **black olives** = ripe olives; **green olives** = olives which are eaten before they are ripe; *which do you prefer - green or black olives?*; **olive oil** = oil made from olives; *add a little olive oil to the pan*
(b) tree which produces this fruit; **olive branch** = sign of peace; *the negotiators held out the olive branch*
(c) olive (green) = dull green color like that of olives which are not yet ripe; *he wore an olive green coat*

② **Olympics** *or* **Olympic Games**
[əˈlɪmpɪks or əˈlɪmpɪk ˈɡeɪmz] *noun*
international athletic competition held every four years; *he's an Olympic sportsman*; *she broke the world record or she set up a new world record in the last Olympics*; *the Olympic Games were held in Sydney in 2000*

③ **omelet**
[ˈɒmlət] *noun*
dish made of beaten eggs, cooked in a frying pan and folded over before serving, with various other things inside; *I had a cheese omelet and fries for lunch*

③ **omit**
[əˈmɪt] *verb*
(a) to leave something out; *she omitted the date when typing the contract*
(b) to omit to do something = not to do something; *he omitted to tell the police that he had lost the documents* (NOTE: **omitting - omitted**)

① **on**
[ɒn]
1 *preposition*
(a) on the top or surface of something; *put the box down on the floor*; *flies can walk on the ceiling*
(b) hanging from; *hang your coat on the hook*
(c) *(showing movement or place)* a crowd of children got on the train; *the picture's on page three*; *the post office is on the left-hand side of the street*
(d) part of; *she's on the staff of the bank*; *he's been on the committee for six years*
(e) doing something; *I have to go to Vancouver on business*; *we're off on vacation tomorrow*
(f) *(showing time, date, day)* the store is open on Sundays; *we went to see my mother on her birthday*; **on his arrival** = when he arrived
(g) *(means of travel)* you can go there on foot - it only takes five minutes; *she came on her new bike*

(h) about; *the committee produced a report on Japanese industry*; *she wrote a book on wild flowers*
(i) *(showing an instrument or machine)* he played some music on the piano; *the song is available on CD*; *he was on the telephone for most of the morning*; *the movie was on TV last night*
2 *adverb*
(a) being worn; *do you all have your boots on?*; *the central heating was off, so he kept his coat on in the house*
(b) working; *is the iron still on?*; *the heating is on*; *she left all the lights on*; *she turned the engine on*; *he switched the TV on*
(c) being shown or played; *what's on at the movie theater this week?*
(d) continuing, not stopping; *he didn't stop to say hi, but just walked on*; *he went on playing the drums even though we asked him to stop*; *go on - I like to hear you play the piano*
(e) *(showing time has passed)* later on that evening, the phone rang; *he almost drowned, and from that time on refused to go near water* (NOTE: **on** is often used after verbs: **to sit on, to jump on, to put on, to lie on,** etc.)

◇ **on and off**
[ˈɒn ənd ˈɒf] *adverb*
not all the time, with breaks in between; *it's been raining on and off all afternoon* (NOTE: also **off and on**)

◇ **on and on**
[ˈɒn ənd ˈɒn] *adverb*
without stopping; *we drove on and on through the night*

① **once**
[wʌns]
1 *adverb*
(a) one time; *take the tablets once a day*; *the magazine comes out once a month*; *how many times did you go to the movie theater last year? - only once*; **once in a while** = from time to time, but not often; *it's nice to go to have an Indian meal once in a while*
(b) formerly, at a time in the past; *once, when it was snowing, the automobile slid off the road*; *he's a man I knew once when I worked in Alaska*; *(beginning children's stories)* **once upon a time** = at a certain time in the past; *once upon a time, there was a wicked old woman who lived in a house in the forest*; see also AT ONCE
2 *conjunction*
as soon as (in the future); *once he starts talking you can't get him to stop*; *once we've moved I'll give you a phone call*

① **one**
[wʌn]
1 number 1; *one plus one makes two*; *our grandson is one year old today*; *his grandmother is a hundred and one*
2 *noun*

single item; *have a chocolate - oh dear, there's only one left!*; **one by one** = one after another; *he ate all the chocolates one by one*; *they came in one by one and sat in a row at the back of the hall*

3 *adjective & pronoun*
(a) single (thing); *which hat do you like best - the black one or the red one?*; *one of the staff will help you carry the box to your car*; *I've lost my map - do you have one?*; *small automobiles use less gas than big ones*; *all the china plates were dirty so we made do with paper ones*
(b) *(formal)* you; *one can't spend all the morning waiting to see the doctor, can one?*; *at his age, one isn't allowed to drive an automobile*
(c) one another = each other; *we write to one another every week* (NOTE: **one** (1) but **first** (1st))

① **oneself**
[wɒnˈself] *pronoun*
referring to the person speaking as an indefinite subject; *it's important to be able to look after oneself*; *it's not easy to do it oneself*

① **one-way**
[ˈwɒn ˈweɪ]
going in one direction only; **one-way ticket** = ticket for one journey from one place to another; **one-way street** = street where the traffic only goes in one direction; *don't make a left here - it's a one-way street*

④ **ongoing**
[ˈɒngəʊɪŋ] *adjective*
which is continuing; *it is part of our ongoing curriculum development*

① **onion**
[ˈʌnjən] *noun*
strong-smelling vegetable with a round white bulb; *fry the onions in butter*; *I don't like onion soup*

② **on-line**
[ˈɒnlaɪn] *adjective & adverb*
directly connected to a computer; *you need to have the right software to access the data on-line*

② **only**
[ˈəʊnli]
1 *adjective*
one single (thing or person), when there are no more; *don't break it - it's the only one I've got*; **only child** = son or daughter who has no other brothers or sisters; *she's an only child*
2 *adverb*
(a) with no one or nothing else; *we've only got ten dollars between us*; *only an accountant can deal with this problem*; *this elevator is for staff only*
(b) as recently as; *we saw her only last week*; *only yesterday the bank phoned for information*
3 *conjunction*

(a) but, except; *I like my mother-in-law very much, only I don't want to see her every day of the week*
(b) *(phrase showing a strong wish)* **if only** *we had known you were in town!*; *she's late - if only she'd phone to let us know where she is!*

◇ **only just**
[ˈəʊnli ˈdʒʌst]
almost not; *we only just had enough money to pay the check*; *he had to run and only just caught the last bus*

◇ **only too**
[ˈəʊnli ˈtu]
very much; *we would be only too glad to help you if we can*

② **onto**
[ˈɒntu] *preposition* upon, on the top of; *the speaker went up onto the platform*; *the door opens directly onto the yard*; *turn the box onto its side* (NOTE: also spelled **on to**)

① **oops!**
[ʊps] *interjection*
(showing surprise or that you are sorry) *oops! I didn't mean to step on your toe*

① **open**
[ˈəʊpən]
1 *adjective*
(a) not shut; *the safe door is open*; *leave the window open - it's very hot in here*
(b) working, which you can go into; *is the supermarket open on Sundays?*; *the show is open from 9 A.M. to 6 P.M.*; *the competition is open to anyone over the age of fifteen*
(c) without anything to protect you; *we like walking in the open air*; **the yard is open on three sides** = there is a fence or wall on one side of the yard only; **open space** = area of land that has no buildings or trees on it; *the parks provide welcome open space in the center of the city*
(d) with an open mind = with no particular opinions; *I'd like to keep an open mind until the investigation is completed*
2 *noun*
(a) place outside that is not covered or hidden; *keep the plants in the greenhouse during the winter, but bring them out into the open in the summer*; *the police investigation brought all sorts of offenses out into the open*
(b) competition that anyone can enter provided he or she is good enough; *he has qualified for the U.S. Open*
3 *verb*
(a) to make something open; *can you open the door for me, I'm trying to carry these heavy boxes?*; *don't open the envelope until I tell you to*
(b) to start doing something, to start a business; *a new restaurant is going to open next door to us*; *most stores open early in the morning*
(c) to make something begin officially; *the new hotel was opened by the mayor*; *the exhibition*

will be formally opened by the queen; the chairman opened the meeting at 10:30

① **opener**
['əupnər] *noun*
device that opens; *see also* CAN OPENER

① **opening**
['əupnɪŋ] *noun*
(a) action of becoming open; *the opening of the exhibition has been postponed; the office opening times are 9:30 to 5:30*
(b) hole or space; *the cows got out through an opening in the wall*
(c) opportunity, such as a job vacancy; *we have openings for telephone sales staff*

① **openly**
['əupənli] *adverb*
in a frank and open way; *they discussed the plan quite openly; can I talk openly to you about my sister?*

④ **open onto**
['əupən 'ɒntu] *verb*
to lead out on to or to look out on to; *the door opens straight onto the street; the windows open onto the garden*

② **opera**
['ɒprə] *noun*
performance on the stage with music, in which the words are sung and not spoken; *"the Marriage of Figaro" is one of Mozart's best-known operas; we have tickets for the opera tomorrow; we are going to see the new production of an opera by Britten*

② **operate**
['ɒpəreɪt] *verb*
(a) to make something work; *he knows how to operate the machine; she is learning how to operate the new telephone switchboard*
(b) to function, to work; *small businesses operate on very narrow margins; how does this network operate?*
(c) **to operate on a patient** = to treat a patient by cutting open the body; *she was operated on by Mr. Jones; operating room* = special room in a hospital where surgeons carry out operations; *they rushed him straight into the operating room*

② **operation**
[ɒpə'reɪʃn] *noun*
(a) action of operating; *the rescue operation was successful;* **to come into operation** = to begin to be applied; *the new schedules came into operation on June 1*
(b) treatment when a surgeon cuts open the body; *she's had three operations on her leg; the operation lasted almost two hours*

① **operator**
['ɒpəreɪtər] *noun*
(a) person who works instruments, etc.; *he's a computer operator; she's a machine operator*
(b) person who works a central telephone system; *dial 0 for the operator; you can place a call through or via the operator*

(c) person who organizes things; **tour operator** = travel agent who organizes package vacations or tours; *(informal)* **smooth operator** = a clever but possibly dishonest businessperson

② **opinion**
[ə'pɪnjən] *noun*
(a) what someone thinks about something; *ask the lawyer for his opinion about the letter;* **he has a very high opinion of his assistant** = he thinks his assistant is very good; **he has a very low opinion of his assistant** = he thinks his assistant is very bad
(b) **in my opinion** = as I think; *in my opinion, we should wait until the weather gets warmer before we go on vacation; tell me what in your opinion we should do*

③ **opinion poll**
[ə'pɪnjən 'pəul] *noun*
asking a sample group of people questions, so as to get the probable opinion of the whole population; *the opinion poll taken before the election did not reflect the final result; opinion polls showed that people preferred butter to margarine*

① **opossum**
[ə'pɒsʌm] *noun*
small animal, the only American marsupial; *opossums play "dead" when they are frightened*

③ **opponent**
[ə'pəunənt] *noun*
(a) person or group which is against something; *opponents of the planned freeway have occupied the site*
(b) *(in boxing, an election, etc.)* person who fights someone else; *his opponent in the election will be Lorna Smith; he knocked out his last three opponents*

② **opportunity**
[ɒpər'tjunɪti] *noun*
chance or circumstances which allow you to do something; *when you were in London, did you have an opportunity to visit St. Paul's Cathedral?; I'd like to take this opportunity to thank all members of staff for the work they have done over the past year;* **a good opportunity for doing something** = a good time for doing something; *it is an excellent opportunity to buy the business;* **equal opportunity program** = employing people on their merits, treating them with equal respect, regardless of age, race, sex, etc.; *see also* WINDOW

③ **oppose**
[ə'pəuz] *verb*
(a) to put yourself against someone in an election; *she is opposing him in the election*
(b) to try to prevent something happening; *several groups oppose the new law*

③ **opposed to**
[ə'pəʊzd 'tu] *adjective*
(a) not in favor of; *he is opposed to the government's policy on education*
(b) in contrast to; *if you paint the kitchen a light color as opposed to dark red, you will find it will look bigger*

② **opposite**
['ɒpəzɪt]
1 *preposition*
on the other side of, facing; *I work in the offices opposite the train station*; *she sat down opposite me*
2 *adjective*
which is on the other side; *the store's not on this side of the street - it's on the opposite side*; *her van was hit by a truck going in the opposite direction*
3 *noun*
something which is completely different; *"black" is the opposite of "white"*; *she's just the opposite of her brother - he's tall and thin, she's short and fat*; *he likes to say one thing, and then do the opposite*

③ **opposition**
[ɒpə'zɪʃn] *noun*
(a) action of opposing; *there was a lot of opposition to the company's plans to knock down the town hall and build a supermarket*
(b) *(in politics)* the party or group that opposes the government; *the leader of the opposition rose to speak*; *the party lost the election and is now in opposition*

④ **opt**
[ɒpt] *verb*
to choose; **to opt for something** *or* **to do something** = to choose something, to decide in favor of something; *in the end, she opted for a little black dress*; *we couldn't decide where to go on vacation, and in the end opted to go to Florida*; *see also* OPT OUT

④ **optical**
['ɒptɪkl] *adjective*
(a) referring to the eyes or to eyesight; **optical illusion** = thing which seems real when you see it, but is not; *the sword seemed to go right through his body, but it was just an optical illusion*; **optical telescope** = telescope that uses mirrors and lenses to make the image and light coming from stars very much larger (as opposed to a radio telescope)
(b) referring to the science of light; **optical fibers** = fine threads of glass used for transmitting light signals; *metal telephone cables are being replaced by optical fibers*

③ **optician**
[ɒp'tɪʃn] *noun*
person who sells glasses or contact lenses, etc.; **optician's** = the store and offices of an optician; *I must go to the optician's to get some new eyeglasses*

④ **optimism**
['ɒptɪmɪzm] *noun*
belief that everything is as good as it can be or will work out for the best in the future; cheerful attitude; *he showed considerable optimism for the future of the company*; *I like your brother - he's always full of optimism*

④ **optimist**
['ɒptɪmɪst] *noun*
person who believes everything will work out for the best in the end; *he's an optimist - he always thinks everything will turn out fine*

④ **optimistic**
[ɒptɪ'mɪstɪk] *adjective*
feeling that everything will work out for the best; *we are optimistic about the plan or that the plan will succeed*

③ **option**
['ɒpʃn] *noun*
(a) choice, other possible action; *one option would be to sell the house*; *the tour offers several options as visits to churches and museums*
(b) **to hold an option on something** = to have the opportunity to buy or sell something within a certain time or at a certain price

③ **optometrist**
[ɒp'tɒmətrɪst] *noun*
person who tests your eyesight, prescribes and sells glasses or contact lenses, etc.; *the optometrist prescribed some reading glasses*

④ **opt out**
['ɒpt 'aʊt] *verb*
to opt out of something = to decide not to take part in something; *he opted out of the trip because he couldn't afford the price of a ticket*

② **or**
[ɔr] *conjunction*
(a) *(linking alternatives, showing other things that can be done)* *you can come with us in the van or just take the bus*; *do you prefer tea or coffee?*; *was he killed in an accident or was he murdered?*; *the movie starts at 6:30 or 6:45, I can't remember which*
(b) *(approximately)* *five or six people came into the store*; *it costs three or four dollars*

◇ **or else**
['ɔr 'els]
(a) or if not; *don't miss the bus, or else you'll have a long wait for the next one*; *put a coat on to go out, or else you'll catch cold*; *we'd better get up early or else we'll miss the train*; *you must have a ticket, or else you will be thrown off the bus by the driver*
(b) *(as informal threat)* **you'd better pay, or else** = if you don't pay, I'll hit you

③ **oral**
['ɔrəl]
1 *adjective*
(a) spoken, by speaking; *there is an oral test as well as a written one*

(b) **oral medicine** = medicine taken by the mouth

2 *noun*

examination where you answer questions by speaking, not writing; *he passed the written examination but failed the oral*

① **orange**
['ɒrɪnʒ]

1 *noun*

(a) sweet tropical fruit, colored between red and yellow; *she had a glass of orange juice and a cup of coffee for breakfast; we had roast duck and orange sauce for dinner;* **orange marmalade** = marmalade made from oranges (usually bitter oranges)

(b) **orange (tree)** = tree which bears this fruit; *a grove of oranges and lemons; we have a little orange tree in a pot*

(c) the color of an orange, a color between yellow and red; *he painted the bathroom a very bright orange*

2 *adjective*

of the color of an orange; *that orange necktie is awful*

① **orbit**
['ɔrbɪt]

1 *noun*

curved path of something moving through space; *the rocket will put the satellite into orbit round the Earth*

2 *verb*

to move in an orbit round something; *the satellite orbits the Earth once every five hours*

③ **orchestra**
['ɔrkəstrə] *noun*

(a) large group of musicians who play together; *the New York Philharmonic Orchestra*

(b) **orchestra pit** = part of a theater, usually next to the stage and just below it, where the musicians sit; *you can see into the orchestra pit from where we're sitting*

(c) seats on the main floor of a theater nearest the orchestra and the stage; *we got seats in the orchestra*

① **order**
['ɔrdər]

1 *noun*

(a) instruction to someone to do something; *he shouted orders to the workmen; if you can't obey orders you can't be a soldier*

(b) *(from a customer)* asking for something to be served or to be sent; *we've had a large order for books from Russia; she gave the waitress her order*

(c) things ordered in a restaurant; goods ordered by a customer; *the waiter brought him the wrong order; our order has been lost in the mail*

(d) special way of putting things; *put the invoices in order of their dates; the stock in the warehouse is all in the wrong order or all out of order* = it is not in the right place

(e) functioning correctly; **out of order** = not working; *you'll have to use the stairs, the elevator is out of order;* **in order** = correct; *are his papers in order?*

(f) **in order that** = so that; *cyclists should wear orange coats in order that drivers can see them in the dark;* **in order to** = so as to; *she ran as fast as she could in order to catch the bus; he looked under the car in order to see if there was an oil leak*

2 *verb*

(a) to tell someone to do something; *they ordered the protesters out of the building; the doctor ordered him to take four weeks' vacation*

(b) *(of a customer)* to ask for something to be served or to be sent; *they ordered chicken, salad and some wine; I've ordered a new computer for the office*

② **order about** *or* **around**
['ɔrdərə'baʊt *or* ə'raʊnd] *verb*

(informal) to tell someone what to do all the time; *I don't like being ordered around*

① **ordinary**
['ɔrdənri] *adjective*

not special; *I'll wear my ordinary suit to the wedding; they lead a very ordinary life;* **out of the ordinary** = not usual, very different; *their apartment is quite out of the ordinary;* **nothing out of the ordinary** = normal; *the weather in June was nothing out of the ordinary*

① **organ**
['ɔrgən] *noun*

(a) part of the body with a special function, such as the heart, liver, etc.; *he was very ill and some of his organs had stopped functioning*

(b) musical instrument with a keyboard and many pipes through which air is pumped to make a sound; *she played the organ at our wedding; the organ played the "Wedding March" as the bride and bridegroom walked out of the church*

(c) *(formal)* journal; *it is the organ of the book trade*

③ **organic**
[ɔr'gænɪk] *adjective*

(a) referring to living things; **organic chemistry** = chemistry of carbon compounds

(b) grown using natural fertilizers without any chemicals; *organic vegetables are more expensive but are better for you;* **organic farming** = farming using only natural fertilizers

④ **organism**
['ɔrgənɪzm] *noun*

living thing; *with a microscope you can see millions of tiny organisms in ordinary water*

③ **organization**
[ɔrgənaɪ'zeɪʃn] *noun*

(a) action of arranging something; *the organization of the meeting was done by the secretary*

(b) organized group or institution; *he's chairman of an organization that looks after blind people*; *international relief organizations are sending supplies*

③ **organize**
['ɔrgənaɪz] *verb*
(a) to arrange; *she is responsible for organizing the meeting*; *we organized ourselves into two groups*; *the company is organized in three sections*
(b) to put into good order; *we have put her in charge of organizing the historical documents relating to the town*

② **organizer**
['ɔrgənaɪzər] *noun*
(a) person who arranges things; **tour organizer** = company or person who arranges a tour
(b) **personal organizer** = little computer or book in which you enter your appointments, addresses, etc.; *I'll put the dates in my personal organizer*; *he was lost when someone stole his organizer*

③ **origin**
['ɒrɪdʒɪn] *noun*
beginning, where something or someone comes from; *his family has Cuban origins*; **country of origin** = country where a product is manufactured or where food comes from; *there should be a label saying which is the country of origin*

③ **original**
[ə'rɪdʒɪnl]
1 *adjective*
(a) from the beginning; *the original ideas for his paintings came from his own garden*
(b) new and different, made for the first time; with ideas not based on those of other people; *they solved the problem by using a very original method*; *the planners have produced some very original designs for a downtown square*
(c) not a copy; *they sent a copy of the original invoice*; *he kept the original receipt for reference*
2 *noun*
thing from which other things are copied, translated, etc.; *send a copy of the will but keep the original*; *the original was lost in the mail but luckily I kept a copy*; *she found that the old painting she had bought in a sale was an original and not a copy*

③ **originally**
[ə'rɪdʒɪnəli] *adverb*
in the beginning; *originally it was mine, but I gave it to my brother*; *the family originally came from Ireland in the 19th century*

④ **originate**
[ə'rɪdʒɪneɪt] *verb*
(a) to begin, to start from, to have a beginning; *this strain of flu originated in Hong Kong*; *his problems at work originated in his home life*

(b) to make for the first time; *we have originated a new style of computer keyboard*

② **ornament**
['ɔnərmənt] *noun*
small thing used as decoration; *there's a row of china ornaments on the mantelpiece*; *the Christmas ornaments are fragile*

④ **orthodox**
['ɔrθədɒks] *adjective*
(a) holding the generally accepted beliefs of a religion, a philosophy, etc.; *the state treasury is following orthodox financial principles*
(b) (people) who observe traditional religious practices very strictly; *he was brought up in an orthodox Jewish family*
(c) **Orthodox Church** = the Christian Church of Eastern Europe

① **ostrich**
['ɒstrɪtʃ] *noun*
very large bird which cannot fly but which can run fast, and is found in Africa; *ostrich feathers used to be popular as decoration for hats*
(NOTE: plural is **ostriches**)

① **other**
['ʌðər] *adjective & pronoun*
(a) different (person or thing), not the same; *we went swimming while the other members of the group sat and watched*; *I don't like chocolate cupcakes - can I have one of the other ones or one of the others?*; *I'm fed up with Florida - can't we go some other place next year?*
(b) second one of two; *he has two automobiles - one is red, and the other (one) is blue*; *one of their daughters is fat, but the other (one) is quite thin*
(c) *(showing something which is not clear)* *she went to stay in some hotel or other in Baltimore*; *he met some girl or other at the party*
(d) **the other day** or **the other week** = a day or two ago, a week or two ago; *I'm surprised to hear he's in the hospital - I saw him only the other day and he looked perfectly well*; **every other** = every second one; *he wrote home every other day* = on Monday, Wednesday, Friday, etc.
(e) **one after the other** = following in line; *the trees were cut down one after the other*; *all the family got colds one after the other*

② **otherwise**
['ʌðərwaɪz] *adverb*
(a) in other ways; *your little boy can be noisy sometimes, but otherwise he's an excellent pupil*
(b) if not, or else; *are you sure you can't come on Tuesday? - otherwise I'll have to cancel my visit to the doctor*

② **ought**
[ɔt] *verb used with other verbs*
(a) *(to mean it would be a good thing)* *you ought to go swimming more often*; *you ought to see the doctor if your cough doesn't get better*;

he oughtn't to eat so much - he'll get fat; the travel agent ought to have told you the hotel was full before you went on vacation
(b) *(to mean it is probable that)* *she ought to pass her driver's test easily; he left his office at six, so he ought to be home by now* (NOTE: negative is **ought not**, shortened to **oughtn't**. Note also that **ought** is always followed by **to** and a verb)

① **ounce**
[aʊns] *noun*
measure of weight (= 28 grams); *the baby weighed six pounds three ounces; mix four ounces of cream with two eggs*

① **our**
[aʊər] *adjective*
which belongs to us; *our office is near the station; our cat is missing again; two of our children caught the flu* (NOTE: do not confuse with **hour**)

① **ours**
[aʊərz] *pronoun*
thing or person that belongs to us; *that house over there is ours; friends of ours told us that the restaurant was good; can we borrow your car, because ours is being repaired?* (NOTE: do not confuse with **hours**)

② **ourselves**
[aʊər'selvz] *pronoun*
(a) referring to us; *we organized ourselves into two teams; we were enjoying ourselves when the police came*
(b) all by ourselves = with no one else; *we built the house all by ourselves; we don't like being all by ourselves in the dark house*

① **out**
[aʊt]
1 *adverb*
(a) away from inside; *how did the rabbit get out of its cage?; she pulled out a box of matches; take the computer out of its packing case; see also* OUT OF
(b) not at home; *no one answered the phone - they must all be out; school is out* = school is over for the day or year
(c) away from here; *the tide is out; the fishing boats left the harbor and are now out at sea*
(d) *(in baseball)* no longer permitted to play in a turn; *the pitcher struck the batter out*
(e) wrong (in calculating); *the cash in the till was $15 out*
(f) just appeared; *the roses are all out* = the roses are all in flower; *her book is just out* = her book has just been published (NOTE: **out** is often used with verbs: **to jump out, to come out, to get out,** etc.)
2 *noun*
(a) *(in baseball)* action of making someone stop playing; *the catcher caught the ball - that's the last out of this inning*
(b) means of escape; *our lawyers are looking for an out for us*

3 *adjective*
(a) not in fashion; *long hair is out this year*
(b) no longer burning; *the fire is out*
(c) not switched on; *make sure the lights are out when you leave*
(d) *(in baseball)* no longer permitted to play in a turn; *you're out after three strikes*

③ **outage**
['aʊtɪdʒ] *noun*
losing the supply of electricity, etc.; *the outage was caused by a snowstorm*

③ **outbreak**
['aʊtbreɪk] *noun*
sudden series of cases of an illness or disturbance; *there has been an outbreak of measles at the school; there was an outbreak of violence at the prison yesterday*

④ **outcome**
['aʊtkʌm] *noun*
result; *the outcome of the match was in doubt until the final few minutes; what was the outcome of the appeal?*

③ **outdoor**
['aʊt'dɔr] *adjective*
in the open air; *the club has an outdoor swimming pool; the hotel offers all sorts of outdoor activities* (NOTE: the opposite is **indoor**)

① **outdoors**
[aʊt'dɔrz]
1 *adverb*
in the open air, not inside a building; *the ceremony is usually held outdoors; why don't we have our coffee outdoors and sit in the sun?; the concert will be held outdoors if the weather is good;* NOTE: you can also say **out of doors**. The opposite is **indoors**)
2 *noun*
the open air, the open countryside; *the pictures of the Rocky Mountains covered in snow are a typical scene of the great American outdoors*

① **outer**
['aʊtər] *adjective*
on the outside; *though the outer surface of the pie was hot, the inside was still cold;* **outer space** = space beyond the Earth's atmosphere

① **outfield**
['aʊtfild] *noun*
(in baseball) area beyond the infield, inside the baselines; *the players in the outfield looked so far away from where we were sitting*

① **outfielder**
['aʊtfildər] *noun*
baseball player occupying a position in the outfield; *the outfielder caught the ball and threw it all the way to home plate*

② **outfit**
['aʊtfit] *noun*
(a) set of clothes, especially those needed for a particular purpose; *she bought a new outfit for the wedding; for the costume ball she wore a nurse's outfit*

(b) organization; *we called in a public relations outfit; I want some really professional builders, not an outfit like my brother's*

② **outgoing**
['aʊtgəʊɪŋ] *adjective*
(a) **outgoing call** = phone call going out of a building to someone outside; **outgoing mail** = mail which is sent out
(b) lively, who likes to be with others; *he has a very outgoing personality*
(c) (person) who is leaving a job; *they gave a round of applause to the outgoing chairman*

③ **outing**
['aʊtɪŋ] *noun*
short trip; *the children went on an outing to the beach*

④ **outlandish**
[aʊt'lændɪʃ] *adjective*
strange or different from the usual; *many of these clothes are too outlandish for me to wear*

② **outlet**
['aʊtlət] *noun*
(a) place where something can be sold or distributed; *he owns a small number of clothing outlets across the state*; **retail outlets** = retail stores
(b) means by which an idea or feeling can get out; *he ran the marathon as an outlet for his stress at work*
(c) device in a wall with holes into which a plug can be fitted, to allow electricity to flow; *the outlet needs to be covered when small children are around*; *there's only one outlet for the entire room!*

③ **outline**
['aʊtlaɪn]
1 *noun*
(a) line showing the outer edge of something; *he drew the outline of an automobile on the paper*
(b) broad description without giving much detail; *she gave the meeting an outline of her proposals; I don't have much time - just give me the outline of the story*
2 *verb*
to make a broad description of a plan, etc.; *he outlined the plan to the bank manager; she outlined her proposals to the meeting*

③ **outlook**
['aʊtlʊk] *noun*
(a) view of the world in general; *his gloomy outlook can be seen in his novels*
(b) view of what will happen in the future; *we think the outlook for the company is excellent; the economic outlook is not good; the outlook for tomorrow's weather is mainly sunny with some rain*

① **out of**
['aʊt 'ɒv] *preposition*
(a) outside of, away from; *get out of my way!; they went out of the room*; **out of your mind** = mad; *are you out of your mind?*

(b) from among a total; *she got 60 points out of 100 on her exam; the report states that one out of ten police officers takes bribes*; **nine times out of ten** = nearly all the time; *nine times out of ten it's the other driver who is wrong*
(c) from; *her dress is made out of a piece of old silk; he made a fortune out of buying and selling antiques*
(d) no longer available; *we're out of carrots today; I'm out of change - can I borrow a quarter?*; **out of print** = with no printed copies left; *all his books are now out of print*

③ **out-of-date**
['aʊt əv 'deɪt] *adjective*
(a) no longer in fashion; *wide pants are out-of-date*
(b) no longer valid; *I'm afraid your pass is out-of-date; she tried to travel with an out-of-date ticket*

③ **out of touch**
['aʊt əv 'tʌtʃ] *adjective*
(a) not having the most recent information about something; *he seems out of touch with what's been happening in his department*
(b) not communicating with somebody by letter, telephone, etc.; *we've been out of touch with our relatives in Canada for several years* (NOTE: the opposite is **in touch**)

③ **out of work**
['aʊt əv 'wɜrk]
1 *adverb*
with no job, unemployed; *the recession has put millions out of work*
2 *adjective*
with no job, unemployed; *the company was set up by three out-of-work engineers*

④ **output**
['aʊtpʌt] *noun*
amount which a firm, machine or person produces; *the factory has doubled its output in the last six months*

④ **outrage**
['aʊtreɪdʒ]
1 *noun*
offense; vigorous attack against moral standards; *the terrorist attack was an outrage; I think the new tax on food is an outrage*
2 *verb*
to shock, to be a cause of great indignation; *his behavior outraged his parents*

④ **outrageous**
[aʊt'reɪdʒəs] *adjective*
annoying and shocking; *it is outrageous that they can charge these prices*

④ **outright**
['aʊtraɪt]
1 *adjective*
complete; *she's the outright winner of the competition*
2 *adverb*
straight out, openly; *he told me outright that he didn't like me*

① **outside**
['aʊtsaɪd]
1 *noun*
part which is not inside; *he polished the outside of his automobile*; *the apple was red and shiny on the outside, but rotten inside*
2 *adjective*
which is on the outer surface; *the outside walls of the house are brick*; **outside lane** = fast lane, the track nearest the center of a road, used by vehicles which are moving fast; **outside line** = line from an internal telephone to the main telephone system; *you dial 9 to get an outside line*; *see also* BROADCAST
3 *adverb*
not inside a building; *it's beautiful and warm outside in the garden*; *the dog's all wet - it must be raining outside*
4 *preposition*
in a position not inside; *I left my umbrella outside the front door*

③ **outsider**
[aʊt'saɪdər] *noun*
person who does not belong to a group, etc.; *she has always been a bit of an outsider*

② **outskirts**
['aʊtskɜrts] *noun*
outer edges of a town, etc.; *most of the workers live in blocks of apartments around the outskirts of the city*

② **outstanding**
[aʊt'stændɪŋ] *adjective*
(a) excellent; of very high quality, of a very high standard; *her performance was outstanding*; *an antique Chinese bowl of outstanding quality*
(b) not yet paid; *the invoice from the accountant is still outstanding*; *I have some outstanding bills to settle*

④ **oval**
['əʊvl]
1 *noun*
long rounded shape like an egg; *he drew an oval on the paper*
2 *adjective*
with a long rounded shape like an egg; *the pie was cooked in an oval bowl*; *our table is oval, not circular*; **Oval Office** = room in the White House which is the personal office of the President of the U.S.

① **oven**
['ʌvən] *noun*
metal box with a door, which is heated for cooking; *don't put that plate in the oven - it's made of plastic*; *supper is cooking in the oven*; *can you look in the oven and see if the meat is cooked?*

① **over**
['əʊvər]
1 *preposition*
(a) above or higher than; *he put a blanket over the bed*; *planes fly over our house every minute*; *the river rose over its banks*

(b) on the other side, to the other side; *he threw the ball over the wall*; *the children ran over the bridge*
(c) from the top of; *he fell over the cliff*; *she looked over the edge of the roof*
(d) during; *over the last few weeks the government has taken several measures*; *let's discuss the problem over lunch*
(e) more than; *children over 16 years old have to pay full price*; *the car costs over $60,000*; *we had to wait for over two hours*
2 *adverb*
(a) several times; *he plays the same CD over and over again*; *she did it ten times over*
(b) down from being upright; *the bottle fell over and all the contents poured out*; *she knocked over the potted plant*; *he leaned over and picked up a pin from the floor*; *see also* ALL OVER
(c) more than; *children of 16 and over pay full price*; *there are special prices for groups of 30 and over*
(d) not used, left behind; *any food left over after the meal can be given to the dog* (NOTE: **over** is used after many verbs: **to run over, to fall over, to come over, to look over,** etc.)
3 *adjective*
finished; *is the match over yet?*; *when the war was over everyone had more food to eat*

② **overall**
1 [əʊvər'ɔl] *adjective*
covering or taking in everything; *the overall outlook for the country is good*; *the overall impression was favorable*
2 [əʊvər'ɔl] *adverb*
taking in everything; *overall, her work has improved considerably*

① **overalls**
['əʊvərɔlz] *noun*
suit of working clothes (pants and top) worn over normal clothes to keep them clean when you are working; *all the workers wear white overalls*

① **overboard**
['əʊvərbɔrd] *adverb*
into the water from the edge of a ship, etc.; *he fell overboard and was drowned*; **man overboard!** = someone has fallen into the water!

③ **overcome**
[əʊvər'kʌm] *verb*
to gain victory over an enemy, a problem, etc.; *the army quickly overcame the rebels*; *do you think the drugs problem can ever be overcome?* (NOTE: **overcame** [əʊvə'keɪm] **- has overcome**)

④ **overdraft**
['əʊvərdræft] *noun*
amount of money which you withdraw from your bank account, which is more than there is in the account, i.e. you are borrowing money from the bank; *he has an overdraft of $750 on his checking account*

overflow

1 [əʊvər'fləʊ] *verb*
to flow over the top; *the river overflowed its banks*

2 ['əʊvərfləʊ] *noun*
pipe to take away a liquid when there is too much of it; *the overflow was blocked and water started coming through the ceiling*

overgrown

[əʊvər'grəʊn] *adjective*
covered with plants and weeds because it has not been looked after; *the garden is completely overgrown*

overhead

1 [əʊvər'hed] *adverb*
above you, above your head; *look at that plane overhead*

2 [əʊvər'hed] *adjective*
(a) above (your head); *please put your hand baggage in the overhead racks*; **overhead reading light** = a small light directly over your head

(b) overhead expenses = general expenses involved in a business as a whole, such as salaries, heating, rent, etc.; *the accounting department is calculating the overhead expenses for next year's budget*

3 ['əʊvərhed] *noun*
overhead expenses; *by cutting back on the overhead we should make a profit*

overhear

[əʊvər'hiər] *verb*
to hear accidentally something which you are not meant to hear; *I couldn't help overhearing what you said just then* (NOTE: **overheard** [əʊvər'hɜːd])

overlap

[əʊvər'læp] *verb*
to cover part of something else; *try not to let the pieces of wallpaper overlap*; *the two meetings are likely to overlap, so I will ask for one to be put back* (NOTE: **overlapping - overlapped**)

overlook

[əʊvər'lʊk] *verb*
(a) not to notice; *she overlooked several mistakes when she was grading the exam papers*

(b) to pretend not to notice; *in this instance we will overlook the delay in making payment*

(c) to look out on to; *my office overlooks the factory*; *I want a room overlooking the hotel gardens, not the parking lot*

overnight

[əʊvər'naɪt]
1 *adverb*
for the whole night; *we will stay overnight in France on our way to Italy*; *will the food stay fresh overnight?*

2 *adjective*
lasting all night; *they took an overnight flight back from China*; *there are three sleeping cars on the overnight express*

overseas

[əʊvər'siːz]
1 *adverb*
in a foreign country, across the sea; *he went to work overseas for some years*

2 *adjective*
referring to foreign countries, across the sea; *overseas sales are important for our company*

overt

[əʊ'vɜrt] *adjective*
open, not hidden; *an overt attempt to bribe government officials*

overtake

[əʊvər'teɪk] *verb*
to go past someone traveling in front of you; *she overtook three trucks on the freeway*; *we were going so slowly that we were overtaken by cyclists* (NOTE: **overtaking - overtook - has overtaken**)

overthrow

1 ['əʊvərθrəʊ] *noun*
removal of a government or ruler from power; *the revolution led to the overthrow of the military ruler*

2 [əʊvər'θrəʊ] *verb*
to defeat; *do you think the rebels can overthrow the military government?*; *the former regime was overthrown and the President fled* (NOTE: **overthrew** [əʊvər'θru] **- overthrown**)

overtime

['əʊvərtaɪm]
1 *noun*
hours worked more than normal working time; *he worked six hours' overtime*; *the overtime rate is one and a half times normal pay*; *the basic wage is $160 a week, but you can expect to earn more than that with overtime*; **overtime pay** = money paid for working beyond normal hours; *overtime pay is calculated at one and a half times the standard rate*

2 *adverb*
more than normal hours of work; *the staff had to work overtime when the hotel was full*; *how much extra do I get for working overtime?*

overtly

[əʊ'vɜrtli] *adjective*
openly; *he overtly said he intended to fight for the enemy*

overturn

[əʊvər'tɜrn] *verb*
(a) to make something fall over; to turn upside down; *the baby accidentally overturned the bowl of fish*; *the fishing boat overturned in the storm*

(b) to vote against a previous decision; *the verdict was overturned on appeal*; *the decision to raise taxes was overturned by the legislature*

overwhelming

[əʊvər'welmɪŋ] *adjective*
enormous; *there was an overwhelming response to their appeal for money*; *they got an overwhelming "yes" vote*

① **owe**
['əʊ] *verb*

(a) to owe money to someone = to be due to pay someone money; *he still owes me the $75 he borrowed last month*

(b) to owe something to something = to have something because of something else; *he owes his good health to taking a lot of exercise*

③ **owing to**
['əʊɪŋ 'tu] *preposition*

because of; *the plane was late owing to fog; I am sorry that owing to staff shortages, we cannot supply your order on time*

① **owl**
[aʊl] *noun*

bird which is mainly active at night; *owls hunt mice and other small animals*; see also NIGHT

① **own**
[əʊn]
1 *adjective*

belonging to you alone; *I don't need to borrow a car - I have my own vehicle; he has his own hair salon*

2 *noun*

(a) of my own *or* **of his own, etc.** = belonging to me or to him alone; *he has an office of his own; I have an automobile of my own; they got married and now have a house of their own*

(b) on my own *or* **on his own, etc.** = alone; *I'm on my own this evening - my wife's playing bridge; he built the house all on his own*

3 *verb*

to have, to possess; *there's no sense in owning two automobiles, since my wife doesn't drive; who owns this store?*

① **owner**
['əʊnər] *noun*

person who owns something; *the police are trying to find the owner of the stolen van; insurance is necessary for all house owners*

① **ownership**
['əʊnərʃɪp] *noun*

situation where someone owns something; *the ownership of the land is in dispute; the barbershop has been sold and is under new ownership*; **home ownership** = situation where people own their own homes; *the government is encouraging more home ownership*; **private ownership** = situation where a company is owned by private shareholders; *the company is being sold into private ownership*; **public ownership** = situation where an industry is owned by the state

③ **own up (to)**
['əʊn 'ʌp tu] *verb*

to say that you have done something wrong; *she owned up to having tried to steal the jewels; the teacher asked who had thrown spitballs but no one would own up*

③ **oxygen**
['ɒksɪdʒən] *noun*

common gas which is present in the air and is essential for plant and animal life; *hydrogen combines with oxygen to form water; the divers ran out of oxygen and had to end their dive early*; **oxygen mask** = mask that appears from a panel above your head if there is a drop in pressure in a plane; *if there is an emergency an oxygen mask will automatically drop down in front of you* (NOTE: Chemical element: chemical symbol: **O**; atomic number: **8**)

② **oyster**
['ɔɪstər] *noun*

type of expensive fish with two flat shells; *you eat oysters with lemon juice, straight out of their shells*

④ **ozone**
['əʊzəʊn] *noun*

harmful form of oxygen, which is found in the atmosphere and which is poisonous to humans; **ozone hole** = gap that forms in the ozone layer, allowing harmful radiation from the sun to reach the Earth; *the ozone hole is getting larger every year*; **ozone layer** = layer of ozone in the upper atmosphere, formed by the action of sunlight on oxygen, which protects the Earth from harmful rays from the sun

Pp

③ **P, p**
[pi]

sixteenth letter of the alphabet, between O and Q; *you spell "photo" with a PH and not an F*

③ **pace**
[peɪs]
1 *noun*

(a) distance covered by one step; *walk thirty paces to the north of the stone; step three paces back*

(b) speed; **to keep pace with** = to keep up with; *she kept pace with the leaders for the first three laps; wages haven't kept pace with inflation; (of a runner, driver, horse, etc.)* **to set the pace** = to

go fast, showing how fast a race should be run; *the German driver set the pace in his Ferrari*
2 *verb*
(a) to walk; *he paced back and forth in front of the door*
(b) to measure by walking; *he paced out the distance between the tree and the house*
(c) to set the pace for a runner, etc.; *to help him train for the marathon she paced him on her bicycle*

② **pacific**
[pə'sıfık] *adjective*
preferring peace and calm; **the Pacific Ocean** *or* **the Pacific** = huge ocean between North America and Asia and South America and New Zealand; *they set out to cross the Pacific in a small boat*; **the Pacific Rim** = the countries around the edge of the Pacific Ocean, including Southeast Asia, Japan, the western states of the U.S.A., South America, Australia and New Zealand

① **pack**
[pæk]
1 *noun*
(a) set of things put together in a box; *he bought a pack of chewing gum*
(b) group of wild animals together; *a pack of wild dogs*
(c) bag that you can carry on your back; *he carried his pack over his shoulder*
(d) face pack = thick substance that you put on your face to improve your skin; *don't come in, I've still got my face pack on*
2 *verb*
(a) to put things into a suitcase ready for traveling; *the taxi's arrived and she hasn't packed her suitcase yet*; *I've finished packing, so we can start*; *he packed his toothbrush at the bottom of the bag*
(b) to put things in containers ready for sending; *the books are packed in boxes of twenty*; *fish are packed in ice*
(c) to put a lot of people or things into something; *how can you pack ten adults into one tent?*; *the streets are packed with Christmas shoppers*; *the supermarket shelves are packed with fruit and vegetables*

① **package**
['pækıdʒ]
1 *noun*
(a) parcel that has been wrapped up for sending; *there was a package for you in the mail*; *we mailed the package to you yesterday*
(b) box or bag in which goods are sold; *instructions for use are printed on the package*
(c) group of different items joined together in one deal; *it was an all-inclusive vacation package*; *we discussed a retirement package*; **pay package** *or* **salary package** *or* **compensation package** = salary and other benefits offered with a job; *the job carries an attractive salary package*

2 *verb*
to put into packages; *the chocolates are attractively packaged in silver foil*

① **packaging**
['pækıdʒıŋ] *noun*
paper, cardboard, etc., used to wrap goods; *the boxes are sent in plastic packaging*

② **packed**
[pækt] *adjective*
full of people; *the restaurant was packed and there were no free tables*

② **packet**
['pækıt] *noun*
small package or pack; *a packet of tobacco*

② **pack in**
['pæk 'ın] *verb*
(informal) to pack it in = to stop whatever you are doing; *it's getting dark, let's pack it in for the day*; *he packed in his job and bought a farm*

② **packing**
['pækıŋ] *noun*
(a) putting things into suitcases, etc.; *my wife's in the hotel room doing our packing*
(b) packing case = special wooden box for sending goods; **packing list** *or* **packing slip** = list of goods that have been packed, sent with the goods to show they have been checked
(c) material used to protect goods that are being packed; *the goods are sealed in clear plastic packing*

③ **pack off**
['pæk 'ɒf] *verb*
to send someone away; *as soon as they were old enough, she packed her children off to Quebec to learn French*; *we've packed the children off to their grandparents' for the summer vacations*

③ **pack up**
['pæk 'ʌp] *verb*
(a) to put things into a box before going away; *they packed up all their equipment and left*
(b) to stop working; *I'll pack up now and finish the job tomorrow morning*

④ **pact**
[pækt] *noun*
agreement, treaty; *the two countries signed a defense pact*

② **pad**
[pæd]
1 *noun*
(a) soft cushion that protects; *put your knee pads on before skating*; **shoulder pads** = thick pads put inside the shoulders of a coat, to make it look bigger
(b) set of sheets of paper attached together; **desk pad** = pad of paper kept on a desk for writing notes; **memo pad** *or* **note pad** = pad of paper for writing memos or notes; **phone pad** = pad of paper kept by a telephone for writing messages; *I wrote down his address on the phone pad*
2 *verb*

(a) to walk with heavy soft feet; *the lion was padding up and down in its cage*
(b) to soften something hard by using soft material; *the chairs should be padded to make them more comfortable*
(c) to pad out = to add text to a speech or article, just to make it longer; *he padded out his talk to last half an hour* (NOTE: **padding - padded**)

① **padlock**
['pædlɒk]
1 *noun*
small portable lock with a hook for locking things together; *the gate is fastened with a padlock*
2 *verb*
to lock with a padlock; *he padlocked his bicycle to the lamppost*

① **page**
[peɪdʒ]
1 *noun*
(a) a side of a sheet of paper used in a book, newspaper, etc.; *it's a short book, it only has 64 pages*; *the photograph of the author is on the back page*; *start reading at page 34*; *look at the picture on page 6* (NOTE: with numbers the word **the** is left out: **on the next page** but **on page 50**)
(b) boy who is one of the bride's attendants at a wedding; *two little pages followed the bride into the church* (NOTE: a girl who does the same is a **flower girl**)
2 *verb*
to call someone by radio, over a loudspeaker, etc.; *Mr. Smith isn't in his office right now - I'll page him for you*

① **paid**
[peɪd]
see PAY

① **pain**
[peɪn]
1 *noun*
(a) feeling of being hurt; *if you have a pain in your chest, you ought to see a doctor*; *she had to take drugs because she could not stand the pain*; *I get pains in my teeth when I eat ice cream*
(b) to take pains over something *or* **to do something** = to take care to do something well; *they took great pains over the organization of the conference*; *she took pains to make everyone feel at home*
(c) *(informal)* **a pain (in the neck)** = annoying person; *he's a real pain in the neck*; *she's a pain - she always gets good grades*
2 *verb*
(formal) to hurt; *it pains me to have to do this, but we must report you to the police*

① **painful**
['peɪnfəl] *adjective*
which hurts, which causes pain; *she got a painful blow on the back of the head*; *I have very painful memories of my first school*

① **paint**
[peɪnt]
1 *noun*
colored liquid that you use to give something a color or to make a picture; *we gave the ceiling two coats of paint*; *I need a two-gallon can of green paint*; *the paint's coming off the front door*; *see also* PAINTS
2 *verb*
(a) to cover something with paint; *we hired a man to paint the house*; *they painted their front door blue*; *she painted her nails bright red*
(b) *(informal)* **to paint the town red** = to have a wild party on the town; *after the test results come out we are all going to paint the town red*
(c) to cover with a liquid; *the nurse painted his knee with antiseptic*
(d) to make a picture of something using paint; *she painted a picture of the town*; *the sky is not easy to paint*

① **paintbrush**
['peɪntbrʌʃ] *noun*
brush used to put paint on something; *I dropped my paintbrush in the can of paint*; *he used a very fine paintbrush to do the branches of the trees* (NOTE: plural is **paintbrushes**)

① **painter**
['peɪntər] *noun*
(a) person who paints (a house, etc.); *the painters are coming next week to paint the kitchen*
(b) artist, a person who paints pictures; *he collects pictures by 19th-century French painters*

① **painting**
['peɪntɪŋ] *noun*
(a) action of putting on paint; *painting the kitchen always takes a long time*
(b) picture done with paints; *do you like this painting of the old church?*

② **paints**
[peɪnts] *noun*
set of tubes of paint or cubes of watercolor paint, in a box; *she bought me a box of paints for my birthday*

① **pair**
[peər]
1 *noun*
(a) two things taken together; *a pair of socks*; *a pair of gloves*; *she's bought a new pair of boots*; *these socks are a pair* = they go together
(b) two things joined together to make a single one; *I'm looking for a clean pair of pants*; *where's my pair of green shorts?*; *this pair of scissors is blunt*
2 *verb*
to pair off *or* **up** = to join with another person to do something; *everyone paired off for the treasure hunt*

① **pajamas**

[pə'dʒæməz] *noun*

light shirt and pants that you wear in bed; *I bought two pairs of pajamas at the sale*; *when fire broke out in the hotel, the guests ran into the street in their pajamas* (NOTE: **a pair of pajamas** means one shirt and one pair of pants)

① **palace**

['pæləs] *noun*

large building where a king, queen, president, etc., lives; *the presidential palace is in the center of the city*; *the queen of England lives in Buckingham Palace*

③ **pale**

[peɪl] *adjective*

(a) with a light color; *what color is your hat? - it's a pale blue color*

(b) not looking healthy, with a white face; *she's always pale and that worries me*; *when she read the letter she went pale* (NOTE: **paler - palest**)

② **palm**

[pɑm] *noun*

(a) soft inside surface of your hand; *she held out some bits of bread in the palm of her hand and the birds came and ate them*

(b) tall tropical tree with long leaves; *date palms grow in the desert*; *the boy climbed a coconut palm and brought down a nut*

① **pan**

[pæn]

1 *noun*

metal container with a handle, used for cooking; *she burned her hand on the hot pan*; *see also* FRYING PAN, SAUCEPAN

2 *verb*

(a) *(informal)* to criticize; *his latest movie has been panned by the critics*

(b) **to pan for gold** = to wash mud in a stream hoping to find gold in it (NOTE: **panning - panned**)

① **pancake**

['pænkeɪk] *noun*

(a) thin soft flat cake made of flour, milk, and eggs, cooked in a frying pan; *we had pancakes with maple syrup for breakfast*

(b) **as flat as a pancake** = very flat; *the country around Cambridge is as flat as a pancake*

① **panda**

['pændə] *noun*

(giant) panda = large black and white animal found in China, which looks like a bear

② **pane**

[peɪn] *noun*

sheet of glass in a window, etc.; *they threw some stones and broke three panes of the window* (NOTE: do not confuse with **pain**)

② **panel**

['pænl]

1 *noun*

(a) flat piece that forms part of something; *take off the panel at the back of the washing machine*; **instrument panel** = flat part of an automobile in front of the driver, with dials that show speed, etc.

(b) group of people who answer questions or who judge a competition; *she's on the panel that will interview candidates for the post*; **panel of experts** = group of people who give advice on a problem

2 *verb*

to cover with sheets of wood; *he decided to panel the study in oak*; *the room is paneled in oak*

② **panic**

['pænɪk]

1 *noun*

terror, great fear; *the forecast of flooding caused panic in towns near the river*; **panic buying** = rush to buy something at any price because stocks may run out or because the price may rise

2 *verb*

to become frightened; *don't panic, the fire engine is on its way* (NOTE: **panicking - panicked**)

② **pant**

[pænt] *verb*

to breathe fast; *he was red in the face and panting as he crossed the finishing line*

① **pants**

[pænts] *noun*

(informal) trousers, clothes that cover your body from the waist down, split in two parts, one for each leg; *the waiter was wearing a black jacket and a pair of striped pants*; *I need a belt to keep my pants up*

① **paper**

['peɪpər]

1 *noun*

(a) piece of thin material which you write on, and which is used for wrapping or to make books, newspapers, etc.; *he got a letter written on pink paper*; *I need another piece of paper or another sheet of paper to finish my letter*; *there was a box of paper tissues by the bed* (NOTE: no plural for this meaning: **some paper, a piece of paper, a sheet of paper**)

(b) newspaper; *I buy the paper to read on the train every morning*; *my photo was on the front page of today's paper*; *our local paper comes out on Fridays*; *the Sunday papers are so big that it takes me all day to read them*

(c) **papers** = documents; *she sent me the relevant papers*; *he has lost the customs papers*

(d) **on paper** = in theory; *on paper the system is ideal, but no one has ever seen it working*

(e) exam; *the English paper was very difficult*; *she wrote a good history paper*

(f) scientific essay; *he wrote a paper on economics which was published in one of the learned journals*

2 *verb*

to cover the walls of a room with wallpaper; *they papered the room in a pattern of red and blue flowers*

② **paperback**
['peɪpərbæk] *noun*
cheap book with a paper cover; *I took a couple of paperbacks to read on the plane*; *the novel will come out in paperback in the spring*

④ **par**
[pɑr] *noun*
(a) being equal; **to be on a par with** = to be equal to; *it isn't really on a par with their previous performances*
(b) **below par** = not very well; *he's feeling a bit below par after his illness*
(c) *(in golf)* number of strokes usually needed by a good player to hit the ball into the hole; *he went five under par*; *(informal)* **par for the course** = what usually happens; *Jack forgot my birthday again, but that's par for the course*

① **parade**
[pə'reɪd]
1 *noun*
(a) display of soldiers; *an officer inspects the men before they go on parade*; **parade ground** = square area on a military camp where parades are held
(b) series of bands, decorated cars, etc., passing in a street; *the parade was led by a children's band*; *Independence Day is always celebrated with a military parade through the center of the capital*; **fashion parade** = display of new clothes by models
2 *verb*
to march past in rows; *the soldiers paraded up the street*

② **paradise**
['pærədaɪs] *noun*
(a) wonderful place where good people are supposed to live after death; *for a moment, I thought I must have died and gone to paradise*
(b) any beautiful place or a place where you feel very happy; *their grandparents' farm was a paradise for the children*

② **paragraph**
['pærəgræf] *noun*
section of several lines of writing, which can be made up of several sentences; *to answer the first paragraph of your letter* or *paragraph one of your letter*; *please refer to the paragraph headed "shipping instructions"*

COMMENT: a paragraph always starts a new line, often with a small blank space at the beginning. A blank line is usually left between paragraphs

③ **parallel**
['pærələl]
1 *adjective*
(lines) which are side by side and remain the same distance apart without ever touching; *draw two parallel lines three millimeters apart*; *the road runs parallel to* or *with the railroad*
2 *noun*
line running around the Earth at a certain distance from the poles; *the 49th parallel forms the border between the United States and Canada*

② **paralyzed**
['pærəlaɪzd] *adjective*
with muscles made so weak that they cannot work properly; *his arm was paralyzed after his stroke*

③ **parcel**
['pɑrsəl]
1 *noun*
package (to be sent by mail, etc.); *the mailman has brought a parcel for you*; *the parcel was wrapped up in brown paper*; *if you're going to the post office, can you mail this parcel for me?*
2 *verb*
to wrap and tie something up to send by mail; *I parceled the books up yesterday but I haven't mailed them yet*

① **pardon**
['pɑrdən]
1 *noun*
(a) forgiving someone; **I beg your pardon!** = excuse me, forgive me; *I beg your pardon, I didn't hear what you said*; *I do beg your pardon - I didn't know you were busy*
(b) act of legally forgiving an offense which someone has committed; *the prisoners received a pardon from the president*
2 *verb*
(a) to forgive someone for having done something wrong; *pardon me for interrupting, but you're wanted on the phone*; *please pardon my late reply to your letter*
(b) to forgive an offense which someone has committed, and allow him or her to leave prison; *some political prisoners were pardoned and set free*
3 *interjection*
pardon me! = excuse me, forgive me

① **parent**
['peərənt] *noun*
(a) **parents** = mother and father; *his parents live in Olympia*; *did your parents tell you I had met them in St. John's?*
(b) father or mother; **single parent** = one parent (mother or father) who is bringing up a child or children alone; *single parent families are more and more common*

④ **parish**
['pærɪʃ] *noun*
(a) area served by a church; *he's the minister of this parish*
(b) *(in Louisiana)* administrative district like a county in other states; *there are 64 parishes in Louisiana* (NOTE: plural is **parishes**)

① **park**
[park]
1 *noun*
(a) open space with grass and trees; *Central Park is in New York; you can ride a bicycle across the park but vehicles are not allowed in*
(b) **national park** = area of land protected by the government for people to enjoy; *we went camping in Yellowstone National Park*
(c) closed place where you can play a sport; *we all went to the baseball park*
2 *verb*
(a) to leave your automobile in a place while you are not using it; *you can park your car on the street next to the hotel*
(b) *(informal)* **to park yourself** = to put yourself in a place, especially where you are not wanted; *he came and parked himself next to me*

② **parked**
[parkt] *adjective*
(of vehicle) left in a parking lot, standing at the side of the road, etc.; *the bus crashed into two parked cars*

② **parking**
['parkɪŋ] *noun*
action of leaving an automobile in a place; *parking downtown is difficult*; **no parking** = sign showing that you must not park your automobile in a certain place; **parking meter** = device into which you put money to pay for parking; **parking lot** = area where you can leave an automobile when you are not using it

④ **parkway**
['parkweɪ] *noun*
broad road divided in two, planted with trees down the center; *she drove along the parkway to the church*

③ **parliament**
['parləmənt] *noun*
group of elected representatives who vote the laws of a country; *the British Parliament is made up of the House of Commons and the House of Lords*

③ **parliamentary**
[parlə'mentəri] *adjective*
referring to parliament; **parliamentary elections** = elections to parliament (as opposed to local elections)

② **parlor**
['parlər] *noun*
(a) room in a house or building used for meeting and talking; *they all sat down in the front parlor*
(b) special shop where people meet; *we went to the ice-cream parlor; she met her sister in the beauty parlor*

① **parrot**
['pærət] *noun*
bright coloured tropical bird with a large curved beak; *he keeps a green parrot in a cage in his sitting room*

③ **parsley**
['parsli] *noun*
green herb used in cooking; *sprinkle some chopped parsley on top of the fish*

④ **parsnip**
['parsnɪp] *noun*
plant with a long white root which is eaten as a vegetable; *roast parsnips are served with beef and potatoes*

① **part**
[part]
1 *noun*
(a) piece; *parts of the movie were very good; they live in the downstairs part of a large house; they spend part of the year in Florida*; **spare parts** = pieces used to put in place of broken parts of a machine, automobile, etc.; *see also* PARTS OF SPEECH
(b) **in part** = not completely; *to contribute in part to the costs or to pay the costs in part*
(c) character in a play, movie, etc.; *he played the part of Hamlet*; **to play a part** = to be one of several people or things which do something; *the guests played an important part in putting out the hotel fire*; **to take part in** = to join in; *they all took part in the game; did he take part in the concert?*
2 *verb*
(a) to divide into sections; *he parts his hair on the right side*
(b) **to part company** = to leave, to split up; *we all set off together, but we parted company when we got to Denver; see also* PART WITH

② **partial**
['parʃl] *adjective*
(a) not complete; *he got partial compensation for the damage to his house; the treatment was only a partial success*
(b) **partial to** = with a liking for; *everyone knows he is partial to chocolate*
(c) in a way which is not fair; *the judge was accused of being partial*

② **partially**
['parʃəli] *adverb*
not completely; *he is partially deaf; I partially agree with what they are proposing*

④ **participant**
[par'tɪsɪpənt] *noun*
person who takes part; *all participants should register with the organizers before the race starts; conference participants are asked to meet in the entrance hall*

④ **participate**
[par'tɪsɪpeɪt] *verb*
to take part in something; *he refused to participate in the TV discussion*

④ **participation**
[partɪsɪ'peɪʃn] *noun*
taking part in something; *their participation is vital to the success of the talks; his participation in the show will ensure that we get a good audience*

③ **particle**
['pɑrtɪkl] *noun*
very small piece; *they found tiny particles of glass in the yogurt*; *an electron is a basic negative particle in an atom*

③ **particular**
[pər'tɪkjulər]
1 *adjective*
(a) special, referring to one thing or person and to no one else; *the printer works best with one particular type of paper*
(b) in particular = especially; *fragile goods, in particular glasses, need careful packing*
(c) having special likes and dislikes; *she's very particular about her food*; *give me any room you have available - I'm not particular*
2 *noun*
particulars = details; *the sheet that gives particulars of the house for sale*; *the officer asked for particulars of the missing automobile*

② **particularly**
[pər'tɪkjulərli] *adverb*
especially; *I particularly asked them not to walk on the lawn*; *it's a particularly difficult problem*; *he isn't particularly worried about the result*

④ **partisan**
['pɑrtɪzæn]
1 *adjective*
strongly supporting a certain point of view; *his partisan views are obvious*
2 *noun*
(a) person who supports a policy forcefully; *she's a partisan of women's rights*
(b) member of a local armed resistance movement, fighting against an occupying army; *the town was captured by partisans*

② **partly**
['pɑrtli] *adverb*
not completely; *the house is partly built, but still needs to be decorated*; *I'm only partly satisfied with the result*; *we're selling our house in Albany, partly because we need the money, but also because we want to move nearer to the sea*

① **partner**
['pɑrtnər]
1 *noun*
(a) person who works in a business and has a share in it with others; *he became a partner in a firm of lawyers*; **silent partner** = partner who has a share in a business but does not work in it
(b) person you live with, without necessarily being married; *we invited him and his partner for drinks*
(c) person who plays games or dances with someone; *take your partners for the next dance*; *Sally is my usual tennis partner*
2 *verb*
to be the partner of someone; *she was partnered by her sister in the doubles*

① **partnership**
['pɑrtnəʃɪp] *noun*
business association between two or more people where the risks and profits are shared according to an agreement between the partners; **to go into partnership with someone** = to join with someone to form a partnership; *they went into partnership to market his new invention*

④ **part of speech**
['pɑrts əv 'spitʃ] *noun*
different types of words, such as nouns, verbs, etc., which are classified according to their use in grammar; *nouns, adjectives and verbs are different parts of speech*; *what part of speech is "this"?*

② **part-time**
[pɑrt'taɪm] *adjective & adverb*
not for the whole working day; *he is trying to find part-time work when the children are in school*; *we are looking for part-time staff to keyboard data*; *she works part-time in the local supermarket*

③ **part with**
['pɑrt 'wɪθ] *verb*
to give or sell something to someone; *he refused to part with his old bicycle*; *I'm reluctant to part with the keys to the house*

① **party**
['pɑrti] *noun*
(a) special occasion when several people meet, usually in someone's house; *we're having a party on New Year's Eve*; *our family Christmas party was a disaster as usual*; *she invited twenty friends to her birthday party*
(b) group of people doing something together; *parties of tourists walking around the gardens*; *see also* WORKING PARTY
(c) political party = organization of people with similar political opinions and aims; *which party does he belong to?*; *she's a member of the Republican Party*
(d) person or organization which is involved in a legal dispute, a contract, or a crime; **third party** = any third person, in addition to the two main parties involved in a contract; *see also* THIRD (NOTE: plural is **parties**)

① **pass**
[pæs]
1 *noun*
(a) *(in football, etc.)* sending the ball to another player; *he sent a long pass across the field to Johnson, who made a touchdown*
(b) low area where a road can cross between two mountain peaks; *the Loveland Pass is closed by snow*; *the road winds up a steep pass to the border*
(c) ticket showing a person is allowed to go somewhere; *I left my bus pass at home, so I had to pay for a ticket*
(d) permit to go in or out regularly; *you need a pass to enter the White House offices*; *all members of staff must show a pass* (NOTE: plural is **passes**)

2 *verb*

(a) to go past; *if you walk toward the bank you will pass the office on your right*; *I passed her on the stairs*; *if you're passing the bookstore, can you pick up the book I ordered?*

(b) to move something toward someone; *can you pass me the salt, please?*; *he passed the ball to one of the halfbacks*; **to pass the hat** = to ask for money

(c) to be successful in a test or examination; *he passed in English, but failed in Spanish*; *she passed her driver's test the first time!*

(d) to vote to approve something; *the House has passed a law against the ownership of guns*; *the proposal was passed by 10 votes to 3*

② **passage**
['pæsɪdʒ] *noun*

(a) corridor or narrow way; *she hurried along the passage*; *there's an underground passage between the two train stations*

(b) section of a text; *she quoted passages from the Bible*; *I photocopied a particularly interesting passage from the book*

(c) *(formal)* action of moving from one place to another; *the attackers promised the soldiers safe passage if they surrendered* (NOTE: no plural in this meaning)

③ **pass around**
['pæs raʊnd] *verb*

to hand something to various people; *she passed the box of chocolates around the table*; *the steward passed around immigration forms*

③ **pass away**
['pæs ə'weɪ] *verb*

to die; *mother passed away during the night* (NOTE: also **pass on**)

② **passenger**
['pæsɪndʒər] *noun*

person who is traveling in an automobile, bus, train, plane, etc. but who is not the driver or one of the crew; *his car's quite big - it can take three passengers in the back seat*; *the plane was carrying 104 passengers and a crew of ten*; **passenger side** = the side of the automobile opposite the driver; **passenger train** = train which carries passengers but not freight

② **passerby**
['pæsə'baɪ] *noun*

person who is walking past; *a passerby saw what happened and called the police*; *she was looked after by passersby until the ambulance came* (NOTE: plural is **passersby**)

① **passing**
['pæsɪŋ] *adjective*

(a) which is going past; *the driver of a passing automobile saw the accident and called the police on his cell phone*

(b) not permanent; *it's just a passing fashion*

④ **passion**
['pæʃn] *noun*

very strong emotion or enthusiasm; *she has a passion for auto racing*; *he didn't put enough passion into the love scene*

④ **passionate**
['pæʃənət] *adjective*

strongly emotional; *he's passionate about promoting honesty in the police force*; *she has a passionate love for Italian art*

④ **passive**
['pæsɪv]

1 *adjective*

allowing things to happen to you and not taking any action yourself; **passive resistance** = protesting something by refusing to do it, but not by using violence; *the protesters organized a program of passive resistance*; **passive smoking** = breathing in smoke from other people's cigarettes, when you do not smoke yourself; *passive smoking is believed to be one of the causes of lung cancer*

2 *noun*

form of a verb which shows that the subject is being acted upon (NOTE: if you say "the automobile hit him" the verb is active, but "he was hit by the automobile" is passive)

③ **pass off**
[pæs 'ɒf] *verb*

to pass something off as something else = to pretend that it is another thing in order to cheat; *he passed the wine off as Californian*; **to pass yourself off as** = to pretend to be; *he passed himself off as a rich banker from South America*

③ **pass on**
['pæs 'ɒn] *verb*

(a) to move something on to someone else; *she passed on the information to her boss*

(b) to die; *my father passed on two years ago* (NOTE: also **pass away** in the same meaning)

③ **pass out**
['pæs 'aʊt] *verb*

to become unconscious for a short time; *he passed out when he saw the blood*; *when he told her that her mother was seriously ill in the hospital, she passed out*

① **passport**
['pæspɔrt] *noun*

official document allowing you to pass from one country to another; *if you are going abroad you need to have a valid passport*; *we had to show our passports at customs*; *his passport has expired*

③ **pass up**
['pæs 'ʌp] *verb*

(informal) not to make use of a chance or opportunity which is offered; *he passed up the chance of going to work in our office in Indianapolis*

① **password**
['pɑswɜrd] *noun*

secret word which you need to know to be allowed to go into a military camp or to use a computer system; *the soldiers stopped him at the gate and asked for the password*; *you need to know the password to get into the system*

① **past**
[pæst]
1 *preposition*
(a) later than, after; *it's past lunchtime, and Mother's still not come back from the stores*; *it's ten past nine (9:10) - we've missed the TV game show*
(b) from one side to the other in front of something; *if you go past the bank, you'll see the store on your left*; *she walked past me without saying anything*; *the car went past at least 60 miles per hour* (NOTE: **past** is used for times between o'clock and the half hour: **3:05 =** five past three; **3:15 =** a quarter past three; **3:25 =** twenty-five past three; **3:30 =** three-thirty. For times after **half past** see **to**. **Past** is also used with many verbs: **to go past, to drive past, to fly past,** etc.)
2 *adjective*
which has passed; *he has spent the past year working in Oregon*; *the time for talking is past - what we need is action*
3 *noun*
(a) time before now; *in the past we always had an office party just before Christmas*
(b) **past (tense)** = form of a verb which shows that it happened before the present time; *"sang" is the past (tense) of the verb "to sing"*

④ **pasta**
['pæstə] *noun*
Italian food made of flour and water, cooked by boiling and eaten with oil or sauce; *spaghetti is a type of pasta*; *I'll just have some pasta and a glass of wine* (NOTE: no plural: **some pasta, a bowl of pasta**; note that **pasta** takes a singular verb: **the pasta is very good here**)

① **paste**
[peɪst]
1 *noun*
(a) thin liquid glue; *spread the paste evenly over the back of the wallpaper*
(b) soft food; *mix the flour, eggs and milk to a smooth paste*; *add tomato paste to the soup*; **curry paste** = hot spicy paste, used to make Indian dishes; *see also* TOOTHPASTE
2 *verb*
to glue paper, etc.; *she pasted a sheet of colored paper over the front of the box*; *he pasted the articles from the newspaper into a big book*; *see also* CUT

③ **pastry**
['peɪstri] *noun*
(a) mixture of flour, fat and water, used to make pies; *she was in the kitchen making pastry*
(b) **pastries** = sweet cakes made of pastry filled with cream or fruit, etc.; **Danish pastries** = sweet pastry cakes with jam or fruit folded inside

① **pat**
[pæt]
1 *noun*
(a) little tap with the hand; *I didn't hit her - I just gave her a little pat*; **a pat on the back** = praise; *the committee got a pat on the back for having organized the show so well*
(b) **pat of butter** = small usually square piece of butter
2 *verb*
to give someone or something a pat; *he patted his pocket to make sure that his money was still there*; **to pat someone on the back** = to praise someone (NOTE: **patting - patted**)

① **patch**
[pætʃ]
1 *noun*
(a) small piece of material used for covering up a hole; *his mother sewed a patch over the hole in his pants*
(b) small area; *they planted some vegetables on a patch of ground by the old railroad tracks*; **cabbage patch** = small piece of ground where you grow cabbages (NOTE: plural is **patches**)
2 *verb*
to repair by attaching a piece of material over a hole; *her jeans are all mended and patched*; *we patched the curtains with some material we had left over*

① **patch up**
['pætʃ 'ʌp] *verb*
(a) to mend with difficulty; *the garage managed to patch up the engine*; *the surgeon patched him up but warned him not to fight with knives again*
(b) **to patch up a quarrel** = to become more friendly again after quarreling; *they had a bitter argument, but patched up their quarrel in time for the party*

③ **patent**
['pætənt]
1 *noun*
official confirmation that you have the sole right to make or sell a new invention; *to take out a patent for a new type of lightbulb*; *they have applied for a patent for their new invention*
2 *adjective (also* ['peɪtənt]*)*
(a) covered by an official patent; **patent medicine** = medicine made under a trade name by one company
(b) **patent leather** = leather with an extremely shiny surface
3 *verb*
to patent an invention = to register an invention with a government department to prevent other people from copying it

① **path**
[pæθ] *noun*
(a) narrow track for walking; *there's a path across the field*; *follow the path until you get to the sea*

(b) bicycle path = narrow lane for bicycles by the side of a road

(c) direction in which something is moving or coming; *people in villages in the path of the tropical storm were advised to get away as fast as possible; the school stands right in the path of the new freeway*

④ **pathetic**
[pə'θetɪk] *adjective*
(a) which makes you feel pity; *he made a pathetic attempt at a joke; she looked so pathetic I hadn't the heart to tell her off*
(b) *(informal)* extremely bad; *their performance in the final game was absolutely pathetic*

③ **patience**
['peɪʃns] *noun*
being patient; *with a little patience, you'll soon learn how to ride a bike; I don't have the patience to wait that long;* **to try someone's patience** = to make someone impatient; *looking after a class of thirty little children would try anyone's patience*

② **patient**
['peɪʃənt]
1 *adjective*
(a) being able to wait a long time without getting annoyed; *you must be patient - you will get served in time*
(b) careful and thorough; *weeks of patient investigation by the police resulted in his arrest*
2 *noun*
sick person who is in a hospital or who is being treated by a doctor, dentist, etc.; *there are three other patients in the ward; the nurse is trying to take the patient's temperature*

② **patiently**
['peɪʃəntli] *adverb*
without getting annoyed; *they waited patiently for the bus to arrive*

③ **patriot**
['peɪtriət] *noun*
person who is proud of his country and is willing to defend it; *he's a real patriot; all true patriots must fight to save their country*

③ **patriotic**
[pætri'ɒtɪk] *adjective*
proud of your country and willing to defend it; *they sang patriotic songs before the international game; I'm not ashamed of being patriotic - I think this is a wonderful country*

② **patrol**
[pə'trəʊl]
1 *noun*
(a) keeping guard by walking or driving up and down; *they make regular patrols around the walls of the prison; he was on patrol downtown when he saw some men wearing masks running away from a bank;* **patrol car** = police car
(b) group of people keeping guard; *each time a patrol went past we hid behind a wall*

2 *verb*
to keep guard by walking or driving up and down; *armed security guards are patrolling the warehouse* (NOTE: **patrolling - patrolled**)

② **pattern**
['pætərn] *noun*
(a) instructions which you follow to make something; *she followed a pattern from a magazine to knit her son a sweater*
(b) design of lines, flowers, etc., repeated again and again on cloth, wallpaper, etc.; *she was wearing a coat with a pattern of black and white spots; do you like the pattern on our new carpet?*
(c) general way in which something usually happens; *a change in the usual weather pattern*

③ **pause**
[pɔz]
1 *noun*
short stop during a period of work, etc.; *the exercise consists of running in place for ten minutes, with a short pause after each 100 steps; he read his speech slowly, with plenty of pauses*
2 *verb*
to rest for a short time; to stop doing something for a short time; *she ran along the road, only pausing for a second to look at her watch*

① **pave**
[peɪv] *verb*
(a) to cover a road or path, etc., with a hard surface; *in the old town, the streets are paved with round stones; there is a paved driveway behind the restaurant*
(b) to pave the way for something = to prepare the way for something to happen; *the election of the new president paves the way for a change of government*

② **pavement**
['peɪvmənt] *noun*
hard road surface; *she fell off her bike and hit her head on the pavement*

① **paw**
[pɔ] *noun*
foot of an animal with claws; *the bear held the fish in its paws*

③ **pawn**
[pɔn]
1 *noun*
smallest piece in chess; *he took two of my pawns*
2 *verb*
to leave an object in exchange for borrowing money: you take back the object when you pay back the money; *I was so desperate that I pawned my grandfather's watch; he was in a bad state, even his shoes had been pawned*

① **pay**
[peɪ]
1 *noun*
wages or salary; *they're on strike for more pay; I can't afford luxuries on my miserable pay;*

basic pay = normal salary without extra payments; **take-home pay** = pay left after tax and insurance have been deducted; **vacation with pay** = vacation which a worker can take by contract and for which he or she is paid; **unemployment pay** = money given by the government to someone who is unemployed; *see also* RAISE

2 *verb*

(a) to give money for something; *how much did you pay for your car?*; *how much rent do you pay?*; *please pay the waiter for your drinks*; *she paid him $15 for his old bike*

(b) to give money to someone for doing something; *we pay secretaries $15 an hour*; *I paid them $3 each for washing the car*; *I'll pay you $3 to wash my truck* (NOTE: you **pay someone to wash the automobile** before he washes it, but you **pay someone for washing the automobile** after he has washed it)

(c) **to pay attention to** = to note and think about something carefully; *pay attention to the following instructions*; **to pay a visit** = to visit; *we'll pay my mother a visit when we're in town* (NOTE: **paying - paid** [peɪd])

④ **payable**
['peɪəbl] *adjective*
which must be paid; *this invoice is payable at 30 days*; *no tax is payable on these items*; *the first quarter's rent is payable in advance*

③ **pay back**
['peɪ 'bæk] *verb*
(a) to give someone money which you owe; *he borrowed ten dollars last week and hasn't paid me back*

(b) **to pay someone back for** = to take revenge on someone for having done something; *"that will pay them back for ruining our party," he said as he smashed their car window*

③ **paycheck**
['peɪtʃək] *noun*
regular check by which an employee is paid; *we get computerized paychecks*; *my monthly paycheck is late*

② **payment**
['peɪmənt] *noun*
(a) giving money for something; *I make regular monthly payments into her account*; *she made a payment of $15,000 to the attorney*

(b) money paid; *did you receive any payment for the work?*; *if you fall behind with your payments, they will take the automobile back*; **mortgage payments** = the installments paid back on a mortgage; *he fell behind with his mortgage payments*; *my mortgage payments have increased this month*

③ **pay off**
['peɪ 'ɒf] *verb*
(a) to finish paying money that is owed; *he's aiming to pay off his mortgage in ten years*; *she said she couldn't pay off the loan*

(b) to pay all the money owed to someone and terminate his or her employment; *when the company was taken over, the factory was closed and all the workers were paid off*

(c) *(informal)* to be successful; *their more cautious approach paid off in the end*; *all that hard work paid off when she graduated with honors*

③ **pay out**
['peɪ 'aʊt] *verb*
(a) to give money to someone; *the insurance company paid out thousands of dollars after the storm*; *we have paid out half our profits in dividends*

(b) to let a rope go out bit by bit; *they paid out the rope as I climbed down the cliff*

③ **pay up**
['peɪ 'ʌp] *verb*
to pay all the money that you owe; *the tourist paid up quickly when the taxi driver called the police*

③ **PC**
['piː'siː]
= PERSONAL COMPUTER

① **pea**
[piː] *noun*
climbing plant of which the round green seeds are eaten as vegetables; *what vegetables do you want with your meat? - peas and carrots, please*; **pea soup** = green soup, made with peas; **sweet peas** = plant of the pea family with scented flowers

① **peace**
[piːs] *noun*
(a) state of not being at war; *the UN troops are trying to keep the peace in the area*; *both sides are hoping to reach a peace settlement*; **peace process** = negotiations, concessions, discussions, etc., which take place over a long time, with the aim of ending a war

(b) calm, quiet state; *noisy motorcycles ruin the peace and quiet of the area*

① **peaceful**
['piːsfəl] *adjective*
(a) calm; *we spent a peaceful afternoon by the river*

(b) liking peace; *the Swiss seem to be a very peaceful nation*

④ **peacekeeping**
['piːskiːpɪŋ] *adjective & noun*
trying to keep peace in a region where there is a war; *the army is mainly involved in peacekeeping rather than in fighting*; *UN peacekeeping forces are in the area*

① **peach**
[piːtʃ] *noun*
(a) sweet fruit, with a large stone and soft skin; *we had peaches and cream for dessert*

(b) **peach (tree)** = tree that bears peaches; *he's planted two peach trees in his back garden*; *the peach trees were all in flower* (NOTE: plural is **peaches**)

(c) pink and yellow color; *they painted the bathroom a light peach color*

① **peacock**
['pikɒk] *noun*
large bird, which has an enormous tail with brilliant blue and green feathers; *peacocks were wandering about the palace garden*

② **peak**
[pik]
1 *noun*
(a) top of a mountain; *can you see that white peak in the distance? - it's Everest*
(b) highest point; *the team reached a peak during training and have fallen back since*; *the graph shows the peaks of pollution over the last month*; **peak period** = period of the day when most electricity is used, when most traffic is on the roads, etc.
2 *verb*
to reach the highest point; *sales peaked in January*

① **peanut**
['pinʌt] *noun*
(a) nut that grows in the ground in seed cases like a pea; *I bought a pack of peanuts to eat with my beer*; **peanut butter** = paste made from crushed peanuts; *she made peanut butter and jelly sandwiches for the kids*
(b) *(informal)* very small amount of money; *why does he stay in that job, when he only earns peanuts?*; *she worked for peanuts in the family store*

① **pear**
[peər] *noun*
(a) fruit like a long apple, with one end fatter than the other; *when are pears in season?*
(b) **pear (tree)** = tree that bears pears; *we've planted a pear and an apple tree in the garden* (NOTE: do not confuse with **pair**)

② **pearl**
[pɜrl] *noun*
precious little round white ball formed inside an oyster; *she wore a string of pearls which her grandmother had given her*

② **peasant**
['pezənt] *noun*
farm worker or farmer who works the land as a small landowner or worker; *the peasants still use traditional farming methods*

② **pebble**
['pebl] *noun*
small round stone; *the boys were throwing pebbles into the water*

① **pecan**
['pikæn] *noun*
(a) edible nut of the pecan tree; *we sprinkled some chopped pecans on the cake*
(b) tree native to the southern U.S.; *he is cutting down the pecan tree*

② **peculiar**
[pɪ'kjuliər] *adjective*

(a) odd, strange; *it's peculiar that she refuses to have a TV in the house*; *there's a peculiar smell coming from the kitchen*
(b) *(formal)* **peculiar to** = only found in one particular place or person; *fish and chips is a dish that is peculiar to Britain*

① **pedal**
['pedəl]
1 *noun*
(a) lever worked by the foot; *if you want to stop the car, put your foot down on the brake pedal*
(b) flat part that you press down on with your foot to make a bicycle go forward; *he stood up on the pedals of his bike to go up the hill*
2 *verb*
to make a bicycle go by pushing on the pedals; *he had to pedal hard to get up the hill*

③ **pedestrian**
[pə'destriən]
1 *noun*
person who walks on a sidewalk, or along a road; *two pedestrians were also injured in the accident*
2 *adjective*
(a) referring to pedestrians; *the street is open to pedestrian traffic only*; **pedestrian crossing** = place where pedestrians can cross a road
(b) common or ordinary; *she gave a terribly pedestrian performance as Juliet*

① **peel**
[pil]
1 *noun*
outer skin of a fruit, etc.; *throw the banana peel into the trash can*; *this orange has a very thick peel* (NOTE: no plural)
2 *verb*
(a) to take the outer skin off a fruit or a vegetable; *he was peeling a banana*; *if the potatoes are very small you can boil them without peeling them*
(b) to come off in layers; *I went into the sun yesterday and now my back is peeling*

② **peer**
['pɪər]
1 *noun*
person of the same rank or class as another; *he's always trying to compete with his peers*; **peer group** = group of people of equal status
2 *verb*
to look at something hard when you cannot see very well; *she peered at the screen to see if she could read the figures*

③ **peg**
[peg]
1 *noun*
small wooden or metal stake or pin; *the children hang their coats on pegs in the hall*; *they used no nails in building the roof - it is all held together with wooden pegs*; **tent peg** = metal peg driven into the ground, to which ropes are attached to keep a tent firm; *the ground was so hard that we had to hammer the tent pegs in*

2 *verb*
(a) *(informal)* to identify; *she pegged him as being a health nut*
(b) to hold prices, etc., stable; *prices will be pegged at the current rate for another year* (NOTE: **pegging - pegged**)

① **pen**
[pen]
1 *noun*
(a) object for writing with, using ink; *I've lost my red pen - can I borrow yours?*; *if you haven't got a pen you can always write in pencil*; **felt-tip pen** = pen with a point made of hard cloth
(b) place with a fence around it where animals, such as sheep, can be kept; *they put the sheep in a pen overnight*; *somehow the lambs managed to get out of their pen*
2 *verb*
(a) to put in a pen; *the sheep were penned while waiting to be taken to the market*
(b) **to feel penned in** = to be in a small space, closely surrounded by other things; *she felt penned in, living in the same house as her husband's parents* (NOTE: **penning - penned**)

② **penalty**
['penəlti] *noun*
(a) punishment; *the maximum penalty for this offense is two years imprisonment*; **to pay the penalty** = to be punished for something; *the coup failed and the leaders had to pay the penalty*; **death penalty** = punishment by death; *he was given the death penalty for his crimes*
(b) punishment in sport for something which is against the rules; *he was awarded a penalty kick*; *they scored after a penalty*
(c) disadvantage; *being chased by photographers is one of the penalties of being rich and famous* (NOTE: plural is **penalties**)

① **pencil**
['pensəl]
1 *noun*
object for writing with, made of a tube of wood, with a strip of colored material in the middle; *examination answers must be written in ink, not in pencil*
2 *verb*
to write with a pencil; **to pencil in** = to write something with a pencil, which you rub out later if it isn't correct; *I'll pencil in the meeting for next Wednesday*

④ **pending**
['pendɪŋ]
1 *adjective*
which has not happened or been dealt with; which will happen or be dealt with soon; *an official announcement is pending*
2 *preposition*
pending advice from our lawyers = while waiting for advice from our lawyers; *he has been suspended with full pay, pending an inquiry*

③ **penetrate**
['penɪtreɪt] *verb*
to go into or through something; *the knife penetrated his lung*; *a bullet which can penetrate three inches of solid wood*

① **penguin**
['peŋgwɪn] *noun*
black and white bird found in the regions near the South Pole, which swims well but cannot fly

② **peninsula**
[pə'nɪnsjʊlə] *noun*
large piece of land that goes out into the sea; *Singapore is situated at the tip of the Malay Peninsula*; *the state of Michigan comprises two peninsulas*

① **penny**
['peni] *noun*
small coin, one cent, of which one hundred equal a dollar (NOTE: usually written ¢ after a figure: 26¢; the plural is **pennies** for the coin, **cents** for the amount)

③ **pension**
['penʃn]
1 *noun*
money paid regularly to someone who has retired from work, to a widow, etc.; *he has a good pension from his firm*; *she finds a teacher's pension quite enough to live on*
2 *verb*
to pension someone off = to make someone stop working and live on a pension; *they pensioned him off at the age of 55*

④ **pensioner**
['penʃnər] *noun*
person who gets a pension; *we offer special discounts for pensioners*; *he's a pensioner, so he has to be careful with his money*

① **people**
['pipl]
1 *noun*
(a) men, women or children taken as a group; *there were at least twenty people waiting to see the doctor*; *so many people wanted to see the movie that there was a line every night*; *a group of people from our office went to Nova Scotia*
(b) inhabitants of a country; *the people of China work very hard*; *government by the people, for the people*
2 *verb*
peopled by = filled with inhabitants; *the island was peopled by natives who had sailed across the Pacific*

① **pepper**
['pepər] *noun*
(a) sharp spice used in cooking, made from the seeds of a tropical climbing plant; *add salt and pepper to taste* (NOTE: no plural in this meaning)
(b) a green or red fruit used as a vegetable; *we had stuffed green peppers for lunch*

COMMENT: there are basically two types of

the spice: black pepper from whole seeds and white pepper from seeds that have had their outer layer removed. You can buy pepper in the form of seeds or already ground. There is no connection between the spice and the plants which give green and red peppers

① **peppermint**
['pepərmɪnt] *noun*
(a) herb which produces an oil used in sweets, drinks and toothpaste; *I always use peppermint-flavored toothpaste*
(b) a candy flavored with peppermint; *a bag of peppermints*

③ **per**
[pɜr] *preposition*
(a) out of each; **twenty per thousand** = twenty out of every thousand; *there are about six mistakes per thousand words*; *see also* PERCENT
(b) for each; *I can't bicycle any faster than fifteen miles per hour*; *these potatoes cost 20 cents per pound*; *we paid our secretaries $11 per hour*

④ **perceive**
[pər'siv] *verb*
to notice through the senses; to become aware of something; *the changes are so slight that they're almost impossible to perceive with the naked eye*; *doctors perceived an improvement in his condition during the night*; *some drugs are perceived as being a danger to health*

① **percent**
[pər'sent]
1 *noun*
out of each hundred; **twenty-five percent (25%)** = one quarter, twenty-five parts out of a total of one hundred; **fifty percent (50%)** = half, fifty parts out of a total of one hundred; *sixty-two percent (62%) of the people voted*; *eighty percent (80%) of the automobiles on the road are less than five years old*
2 *adjective*
showing a quantity out of a hundred; *they are proposing a 5% increase in fares*
3 *adverb*
one hundred percent happy with = totally satisfied with; *I'm not one hundred percent happy with his work* (NOTE: **percent** is written **%** when used with figures: **30%** (say "thirty percent"))

③ **percentage**
[pər'sentɪdʒ] *noun*
figure shown as a proportion of a hundred; *a low percentage of the population voted*; *what percentage of businesses are likely to be affected?*; **percentage point** = 1 percent; **half a percentage point** = 0.5 percent

④ **perception**
[pər'sepʃn] *noun*
ability to notice or realize; *he doesn't have a very clear perception of what he is supposed to do*

③ **perch**
[pɜrtʃ]
1 *noun*
branch or ledge on which a bird can sit; *the bird flew down from his perch and landed on the back of my chair* (NOTE: plural is **perches**)
2 *verb*
(a) *(of bird)* to sit; *the bird was perched on a high branch*
(b) *(of person, building)* to be placed high up; *she was sitting perched on a stool at the bar*; *a castle perched high on the side of a mountain*

① **perfect**
1 ['pɜrfəkt] *adjective*
(a) which is good in every way; *your coat is a perfect fit*; *don't change anything - the room is perfect as it is*
(b) ideal; *she's the perfect secretary*; *George would be perfect for the job of salesman*; *I was in a perfect position to see what happened*
(c) **perfect (tense)** = past tense of a verb which shows that the action has been completed; *in English the perfect is formed using the verb "to have"*
2 [pər'fekt] *verb*
to make something new and perfect; *she perfected a process for speeding up the invoicing system*

④ **perfection**
[pər'fekʃn] *noun*
state of being perfect; *perfection is not always easy to achieve*; **to perfection** = perfectly; *he timed his kick to perfection*

② **perfectly**
['pɜrfɪktli] *adverb*
extremely well; *she typed the letter perfectly*; *the suit fits you perfectly*; *I'm perfectly capable of finding my own way home*; *she's perfectly willing to take the test*

① **perform**
[pər'fɔrm] *verb*
(a) to carry out an action; *she performed a perfect dive*; *it's the sort of task that can be performed by any computer*
(b) to act in public; *the group will perform at the outdoor theater next week*; *the play will be performed in the town hall*

① **performance**
[pər'fɔrməns] *noun*
(a) how well a machine works, a sportsman runs, etc.; *we're looking for ways to improve our performance*; *after last night's miserable performance I don't think the team is likely to reach the finals*
(b) public show; *the next performance will start at 8 o'clock*; *there are three performances a day during the summer*

performer
[pər'fɔrmər] *noun*
person who gives a public show; *a crowd gathered where the street performers were entertaining the tourists*

perfume
['pɜrfjum] *noun*
scent, a liquid which smells nice, and which is put on the skin; *do you like my new perfume?*

perhaps
[pər'hæps] *adverb*
possibly; *perhaps the train is late; they're late - perhaps the snow's very deep; is it going to be fine? - perhaps not, I can see clouds over there*

perilous
['perıləs] *adjective*
(formal) very dangerous; *without a helicopter there was no way we could rescue them from their perilous position*

period
['pıəriəd]
1 *noun*
(a) length of time; *she swam under water for a short period; the offer is open for a limited period only; it was an unhappy period in her life*
(b) time during which a lesson is given in school; *we have three periods of English on Thursdays*
(c) printed mark like a small dot, showing the end of a sentence or an abbreviation; *when reading, you can take a breath at a period*
2 *interjection*
meaning "and that's all"; *she doesn't like Chinese food, period*

periodical
[piri'ɒdıkl] *noun*
magazine which appears regularly; *he writes for several monthly periodicals*

periodically
[piri'ɒdıkli] *adverb*
from time to time; *you need to check the gas level periodically*

permanent
['pɜrmənənt] *adjective*
lasting for ever; supposed to last for ever; *he has found a permanent job; she is in permanent employment; they are living with her parents for a few weeks - it's not a permanent arrangement*

permanently
['pɜrmənəntli] *adverb*
for ever; always; *the store seems to be permanently closed; you can never speak to him on the phone - he's permanently in meetings; the car crash left him permanently disabled*

permission
[pər'mıʃn] *noun*
freedom which you are given to do something; *you need permission from the boss to go into the warehouse; he asked the manager's permission to take a day off*

permit
1 ['pɜrmıt] *noun*
paper which allows you to do something; *you have to have a permit to sell hamburgers from a van*; **learner's permit** = temporary license allowing someone to learn how to drive; **parking permit** = paper which allows you to park an automobile
2 [pər'mıt] *verb*
to allow; *this ticket permits three people to go into the exhibition; smoking is not permitted on the subway* (NOTE: **permitting - permitted**)

persist
[pər'sıst] *verb*
to continue to exist; *the fog persisted all day*; **to persist in doing something** = to continue doing something, in spite of problems; *he will persist in singing while he works although we've told him many times to stop; she persists in refusing to see a doctor*

persistent
[pər'sıstənt] *adjective*
continuing to do something, even though people want you to stop; *he can be very persistent if he wants something badly enough; she broke down under persistent questioning by the police*

person
['pɜrsən] *noun*
man or woman; *the police say a person or persons entered the house by the window; his father's a very interesting person*; **the manager was there in person** = he was there himself; **missing person** = someone who has disappeared, and no one knows where he is; *her name is on the police Missing Persons list*

personal
['pɜrsənl] *adjective*
(a) belonging or referring to a particular person or people; *they lost all their personal property in the fire*; **personal best** = best time, speed, etc., that a sportsman has achieved, though not necessarily a record; **personal computer (PC)** = small computer used by a person at home; **personal organizer** = little computer or book in which you enter your appointments, addresses, etc.; *I'll put the dates in my personal organizer*
(b) referring to someone's private life in an offensive way; *the attacks on the senator became increasingly personal*

personality
[pɜrsə'nælıti] *noun*
(a) character; *he has a strange personality*; **she has lots of personality** = she's a lively and interesting person; *see also* SPLIT
(b) famous person, especially a TV or radio star; *the new supermarket is going to be opened by a famous sports personality*

② **personally**
['pɜrsnəli] *adverb*
(a) from your own point of view; *personally, I think you're making a mistake*
(b) in person; *he is sorry that he can't be here to accept the prize personally*
(c) don't take it personally = don't think it was meant to criticize you

④ **personnel**
[pɜrsə'nel] *noun*
staff, the people employed by a company; *we've made some changes to the personnel in the last few weeks*; **personnel manager** = manager who deals with pay, sick leave, administration, etc., for all the staff (NOTE: now often called a **human resources manager**)

④ **perspective**
[pər'spektɪv] *noun*
(a) *(in art)* way of drawing objects or scenes, so that they appear to have depth or distance; *he has the perspective wrong - that's why the picture looks so odd*
(b) way of looking at something; *a French politician's perspective on the problem will be completely different from mine*; *she was looking at the situation from the perspective of a parent with two young children*; **to put things into perspective** = to show things in an objective way; *you must put the sales figures into perspective - they look bad, but they're much better than last year*

③ **persuade**
[pər'sweɪd] *verb*
to get someone to do what you want by explaining or asking; *she managed to persuade the bank manager to give her a loan*; *after hours of discussion, they persuaded him to hand over his gun*

① **Peru**
[pə'ru] *noun*
country in South America, along the Pacific coast; *Lima is the capital of Peru* (NOTE: capital: **Lima;** people: **Peruvians;** language: **Spanish;** currency: **inti**)

② **Peruvian**
[pə'ruviən]
1 *adjective*
referring to Peru; *they visited ancient temples in the Peruvian mountains*
2 *noun*
person from Peru; *the Peruvians are sending a delegation to the conference*

④ **pessimism**
['pesɪmɪzm] *noun*
state of believing that only bad things will happen; *he sits alone in his bedroom all day, full of pessimism at his prospects of finding another job*; *her pessimism is starting to affect the other members of the team*

④ **pessimist**
['pesɪmɪst] *noun*
person who thinks only bad things will happen; *pessimists thought the policy was bound to fail*

④ **pessimistic**
[pesɪ'mɪstɪk] *adjective*
believing that only bad things will happen; *I'm pessimistic about our chances of success*

① **pest**
[pest] *noun*
(a) plant, animal, or insect that harms other plants or animals; *many farmers look on rabbits as a pest*
(b) *(informal)* person who annoys; *that little boy is an absolute pest - he won't stop whistling*

① **pet**
[pet]
1 *noun*
(a) animal kept in the home to give pleasure; *the family has several pets - two cats, a dog and a white rabbit*
(b) teacher's pet = school child who is the favorite of the teacher and so is disliked by the other children
2 *adjective*
(a) favorite; *the weather is his pet topic of conversation*; **pet name** = special name given to someone you are fond of; *ever since he was a baby he's been called by his pet name "Bootsie"*
(b) (animal) kept at home; *you can't keep your pet snake in the bathtub!*

③ **petal**
['petl] *noun*
colourful part of a flower; *daffodils have bright yellow petals*

④ **petition**
[pə'tɪʃn]
1 *noun*
(a) official request, signed by many people; *she wanted me to sign a petition against the building of the new road*; *we went to the town hall to hand the petition to the mayor*
(b) legal request; *a divorce petition*
2 *verb*
to ask someone for something officially, to make an official request; *they petitioned the town council for a new library*; *he petitioned the government to provide a special pension*; *she is petitioning for divorce*

③ **pharmacist**
['fɑrməsɪst] *noun*
person who prepares and sells medicines; *ask the pharmacist for advice on which sunscreen to use* (NOTE: also called a **druggist**)

③ **pharmacy**
['fɑrməsi] *noun*
(a) store which makes and sells medicines; *he runs the pharmacy on Main Street* (NOTE: plural in this meaning is **pharmacies;** also called a **drugstore**)
(b) study of medicines; *she's studying pharmacy*; *he has a diploma in pharmacy* (NOTE: no plural in this meaning)

④ **phase**
['feɪz]
1 *noun*
period or stage in the development of something; *the project is now in its final phase*; *it's a phase she's going through and hopefully she will grow out of it*; *I'm sure dyeing his hair green is just a phase*; **critical phase** = important point where things may go wrong; *negotiations have reached a critical phase*
2 *verb*
to phase something in *or* **to phase something out** = to introduce or to remove something gradually; *the new telephone system will be phased in over the next two months*

④ **phenomenon**
[fe'nɒmɪnən] *noun*
very remarkable thing which happens; *a strange phenomenon which only occurs on the highest mountains*; *scientists have not yet found an explanation for this phenomenon*; **natural phenomenon** *or* **phenomenon of nature** = remarkable thing which happens naturally; *volcanoes are natural phenomena* (NOTE: plural is **phenomena**)

④ **philanthropic**
[filən'θrɒpɪk] *noun*
showing love of human beings, shown by giving money to charity; *she spent her life in philanthropic work*

④ **philanthropist**
[fɪ'lænθrəpɪst] *noun*
person who does good work to help people; *he was a philanthropist who often helped poor people find jobs*

④ **philanthropy**
[fɪ'lænθrəpɪ] *noun*
love of human beings, shown especially by giving money to charity

④ **philosopher**
[fɪ'lɒsəfər] *noun*
person who studies the meaning of human existence; person who teaches philosophy; *as a famous philosopher once said: "I think, therefore I am"*

④ **philosophical**
[filə'sɒfɪkl] *adjective*
(a) thoughtful; calm in the face of problems; *to take a philosophical attitude*; *it's best to be philosophical about it and not get too upset*
(b) referring to philosophy; *she was involved in a philosophical argument*

④ **philosophy**
[fɪ'lɒsəfɪ] *noun*
(a) study of the meaning of human existence; *he's studying philosophy*
(b) general way of thinking; *my philosophy is that you should treat people as you want them to treat you*

① **phone**
[fəʊn]
1 *noun*
telephone, a machine which you use to speak to someone who is some distance away; *can't someone answer the phone - it's been ringing and ringing*; *I was in the garden when you called, but by the time I got to the house the phone had stopped ringing*; *if someone calls, can you answer the phone for me?*; *she ran to the phone and called the ambulance*; **by phone** *or* **over the phone** = using the telephone; *she reserved a table by phone*; *he placed the order over the phone*
2 *verb*
to call someone using a telephone; *your wife phoned when you were out*; *can you phone me at ten o'clock tomorrow evening?*; *I need to phone our office in New York*; **to phone for something** = to make a phone call to ask for something; *he phoned for a taxi*; **to phone about something** = to make a phone call to speak about something; *he phoned about the message he had received* (NOTE: **phone** is often used in place of **telephone: phone call, phone book**, etc., but not in the expressions **telephone switchboard, telephone operator, telephone exchange**)

◇ **on the phone**
['ɒn ðə 'fəʊn]
(a) speaking by telephone; *don't make such a noise - the boss is on the phone*; *she has been on the phone all morning*
(b) with a telephone in the house; *don't look for their address in the phone book - they're not listed*

① **phone book**
['fəʊn 'bʊk] *noun*
book that gives the names of people and businesses in a town, with their addresses and phone numbers; *the restaurant must be new - it isn't in the phone book* (NOTE: also called a **phone directory**)

① **phone booth**
['fəʊn 'buð] *noun*
public box with a telephone; *call me from the phone booth outside the station, and I'll come and pick you up*; *there was a line of people waiting to use the phone booth*

① **phone call**
['fəʊn 'kɔl] *noun*
telephone call, speaking to someone by telephone; *I had a phone call from an old friend today*; *I need to make a quick phone call before we leave*

④ **phonecard**
['fəʊnkɑrd] *noun*
plastic card that you use in a telephone; *you can use a phonecard to operate a public telephone*

① **phone number**
['fəʊn 'nʌmbər] *noun*
number of one particular phone; *what's the phone number of the garage?*; *if I give you my phone number promise you won't forget it*; *see note at* TELEPHONE NUMBER

photo 429 pick

① **photo**
['fəʊtəʊ] *noun*
photograph, a picture taken with a camera; *here's a photo of the house in the snow*; *I've brought some family photos to show you* (NOTE: plural is **photos**)

③ **photocopier**
['fəʊtəʊkɒpiər] *noun*
machine that makes photocopies; *I'll just take this down to the photocopier and make some copies*; *the paper has jammed in the photocopier*; *you can make color copies on this photocopier*

③ **photocopy**
['fəʊtəʊkɒpi]
1 *noun*
copy of a document made by photographing it; *she made six photocopies of the contract*
2 *verb*
to copy something and make a print of it; *can you photocopy this letter, please?*

② **photograph**
['fəʊtəgræf]
1 *noun*
picture taken with a camera; *I've found an old black and white photograph of my parents' wedding*; *she's trying to take a photograph of the cat*; *he kept her photograph on his desk*; *you'll need two passport photographs to get your visa*
2 *verb*
to take a picture with a camera; *she was photographing the flowers in the botanical gardens*

② **photographer**
[fə'tɒgrəfər] *noun*
person who takes photographs; *the photographer asked us to stand closer together*; *she's a photographer for a local newspaper*; *a photographer was at the scene to record the ceremony*

④ **photographic**
[fəʊtəʊ'græfik] *adjective*
(a) referring to photography; *all your photographic gear is still in the back of my van*
(b) photographic memory = being able to remember things in exact detail, as if you were still seeing them

② **photography**
[fə'tɒgrəfi] *noun*
taking pictures on sensitive film with a camera; *she bought a camera and took up photography*; *an exhibition of 19th-century photography*; *photography is part of the art and design course*; *photography is one of the visual arts*

③ **phrase**
[freɪz]
1 *noun*
short sentence or group of words; *try to translate the whole phrase, not just one word at a time*; *I'm trying to remember a phrase from "Hamlet"*; **phrase book** = book of translations

of common expressions; *we bought a Japanese phrase book before we went to Japan*; *(informal)* **to coin a phrase** = to emphasize that you are saying something which everyone says; *"when it rains it pours" - to coin a phrase*
2 *verb*
to put into words; *I try and phrase my letter as politely as I can*

② **physical**
['fɪzɪkl] *adjective*
(a) referring to the human body; *the illness is mental rather than physical*; *he has a strong physical attraction for her*; **physical exercise** = exercise of the body; *you should do some physical exercise every day*
(b) referring to matter, energy, etc.; **physical geography** = study of rocks and earth, etc.; **physical chemistry** = study of chemical substances

② **physically**
['fɪzɪkli] *adverb*
(a) referring to the body; *she is physically handicapped, but manages to look after herself*; *I find him physically very attractive*
(b) referring to the laws of nature; *it is physically impossible for a lump of lead to float*

② **physician**
[fɪ'zɪʃn] *noun*
(formal) doctor; *consult your physician before taking this medicine*

④ **physicist**
['fɪzɪsɪst] *noun*
person who studies physics; *an atomic physicist*

③ **physics**
['fɪzɪks] *noun*
study of matter, energy, etc.; *she teaches physics at the local college*; *it's a law of physics that things fall down to the ground and not up into the sky*

① **piano**
['pjænəʊ] *noun*
large musical instrument with black and white keys that you press to make music; *she's taking piano lessons*; *she played the piano while her brother sang*; **grand piano** = large horizontal piano; **upright piano** = smaller piano with a vertical body

① **pick**
[pɪk]
1 *noun*
(a) something which you choose; **take your pick** = choose which one you want; *we've got green, red and blue balloons - just take your pick!*
(b) a large heavy tool with a curved metal head with a sharp end that you lift up and bring down to break things; *they started breaking up the concrete path with picks and spades*
2 *verb*
(a) to choose; *the captain picks the football team*; *she was picked to play the part of*

Hamlet's mother; *the Association has picked Indianapolis for its next meeting*

(b) to take fruit or flowers from plants; *they've picked all the strawberries*; *don't pick the flowers in the botanical gardens*

(c) to take away small pieces of something; *she picked the bits of grass off her skirt*; **to pick your teeth** = to push something between your teeth to remove little bits of food; *he was picking his teeth with a match*; **to pick at your food** = to eat little bits as if you have no appetite; *she's lost her appetite - she just picks at her food*

(d) **to pick someone's brains** = to ask someone for advice or information; **to pick someone's pocket** = to take something from someone's pocket without them noticing; *I lost my wallet - someone picked my pocket on the train!*; **to pick a lock** = to open a lock with a piece of wire; *he picked the lock of the car and drove off before I could stop him*

① **pickle**
['pɪkl] *noun*
pickle(s) = cucumber prepared in a vinegar sauce; *a cheese and pickle sandwich*; *do you want pickles with your hamburger?*

① **pick on**
['pɪk 'ɒn] *verb*
to choose someone to attack or criticize; *why do you always pick on children who are younger than you?*; *the manager is picking on me all the time*

① **pick out**
['pɪk 'aʊt] *verb*
to choose; *he picked out all the best fruit*

② **pickpocket**
['pɪkpɒkɪt] *noun*
person who steals things from people's pockets; *"Watch out! Pickpockets are operating in this area!"*; *tourists should be on the watch for pickpockets*

② **pick up**
['pɪk 'ʌp] *verb*
(a) to lift something up which is lying on the surface of something; *she dropped her handkerchief and he picked it up*; *he bent down to pick up a coin that he saw on the sidewalk*
(b) to learn something easily without being taught; *she never took any piano lessons, she just picked it up*; *he picked up some Chinese when he was working in Hong Kong*
(c) to give someone a lift in a vehicle; *the limousine will pick you up from the hotel*; *can you send a taxi to pick us up at seven o'clock?*
(d) to meet someone by chance and start a relationship with them; *she's a girl he picked up in a bar*
(e) to arrest; *he was picked up by the police at the airport*
(f) to improve, to get better; *she's been in bed for weeks, but is beginning to pick up*; *business is picking up after the Christmas vacation*

(g) **to pick up speed** = to go faster; *the truck began to pick up speed as it went down the hill*

① **pickup**
['pɪkʌp] *noun*
(a) light van with an open back; *they loaded all their gear into the back of a pickup*
(b) act of collecting someone or something; *the customer pickup point is behind the store*; *I've got several pickups to do before I can go home*

① **picnic**
['pɪknɪk]
1 *noun*
meal eaten in the open air; *if it's fine, let's go for a picnic*; *they stopped by the woods, and had a picnic lunch*
2 *verb*
to eat a picnic; *people were picnicking on the bank of the river* (NOTE: **picnicking - picnicked**)

① **picture**
['pɪktʃər]
1 *noun*
(a) drawing, painting, photo, etc.; *she drew a picture of the house*; *the book has pages of pictures of wild animals*; *she cut out the picture of the president from the magazine*
(b) **to get the picture** = to understand the problem; *I get the picture - you want me to arrange to get rid of her*
2 *verb*
to imagine; *it takes quite an effort to picture him in a skirt*

① **pie**
[paɪ] *noun*
(a) meat or fruit cooked in a pastry case; *for dessert, there's pumpkin pie and ice cream*; *if we're going on a picnic, I'll buy a big apple pie*; *(informal)* **pie in the sky** = ideal situation which you can never reach
(b) **shepherd's pie** = cooked meat in a dish with potatoes on top

① **piece**
[pis]
1 *noun*
(a) (small) bit of something; *would you like another piece of cake?*; *I need two pieces of black cloth*; *she played a piece of music by Chopin*
(b) *(informal)* **to be a piece of cake** = to be very easy; *that test was simple - a piece of cake!*
(c) **pieces** = broken bits of something; *the watch came to pieces in my hand*; *the plate was in pieces on the floor*; *you will have to take the clock to pieces to mend it* (NOTE: **piece** is often used to show one item of something which has no plural: **equipment: a piece of equipment**; **concrete: a piece of concrete**; **cheese: a piece of cheese**; **news: a piece of news**; **advice: a piece of advice**)
2 *verb*
to piece together = to put things together to form a whole; *the police are trying to piece*

together the events which took place during the evening of the murder

④ **pier**
['pɪər] *noun*
construction built from the shore out into the sea, where boats can tie up to load or unload; *we went for a stroll along the pier*

③ **pierce**
[pɪəs] *verb*
to make a hole in something; *she decided to have her ears pierced*; *he pierced the metal cap on the jar with the point of a kitchen knife*

① **pig**
[pɪg] *noun*
pink or black farm animal with short legs, which gives meat; *the farmer next door keeps pigs* (NOTE: fresh meat from a **pig** is called **pork**; **bacon** and **ham** are types of smoked or cured meat from a pig)

① **pigeon**
['pɪdʒn] *noun*
fat grayish bird which is common in towns; *let's go and feed the pigeons in the park*

① **pile**
[paɪl]
1 *noun*
(a) heap; *look at that pile of laundry*; *the pile of plates crashed onto the floor*; *the wind blew piles of dead leaves into the road*; *he was carrying a great pile of books*
(b) thick wooden or concrete post, driven into the ground; *they drove piles into the bed of the river to support the bridge*
(c) soft surface of cloth; *just feel the pile on these cushions*; *we have put a thick pile carpet in the sitting room*
2 *verb*
to pile (up) = to heap up; *all the Christmas presents are piled (up) under the tree*; *complaints are piling up about the service*

① **pilgrim**
['pɪlgrɪm] *noun*
person who goes to visit a holy place; *pilgrims came to Rome from all over the world*; **the Pilgrims** *or* **Pilgrim Fathers** = emigrants who left England to settle in America in 1620

① **pill**
[pɪl] *noun*
(a) small round tablet of medicine; *take two pills before breakfast*
(b) *(informal)* **on the Pill** = taking a course of contraceptive tablets; *she went on the Pill when she was seventeen*

④ **pillar**
['pɪlər] *noun*
column which supports part of a building; *the roof is supported by a row of wooden pillars*; *one of the pillars supporting the bridge collapsed*

① **pillow**
['pɪləʊ] *noun*
bag full of soft material which you put your head on in bed; *I like to sleep with two pillows*; *she sat up in bed, surrounded by pillows*

① **pillowcase** *or* **pillow slip**
['pɪləʊkeɪs or 'pɪləʊslɪp] *noun*
cloth bag to cover a pillow with; *the maids change the room and put clean sheets and pillowcases on the beds every morning*

① **pilot**
['paɪlət]
1 *noun*
(a) person who flies a plane; *he's training to be an airline pilot*; *he's a helicopter pilot for an oil company*
(b) person who guides boats into or out of a harbor; *ships are not allowed into the harbor without a pilot*
(c) made or used as a test; *a pilot for a new TV series*; **pilot study** = small plan or operation used as a test before starting a full-scale plan; *he is running a pilot study for training unemployed young people*
(d) **pilot light** = little gas flame, which burns all the time, and which lights the main gas jets automatically when a heater or oven is switched on; *there's a smell of gas in the kitchen - the pilot light has gone out*
2 *verb*
(a) to guide a boat, aircraft, etc.; *he safely piloted the ship into harbor*
(b) to guide someone; *he piloted her through a series of underground passages to the meeting room*

① **pimple**
['pɪmpl] *noun*
small red bump on the surface of your skin; *you've got a pimple on your chin*

① **pin**
[pɪn]
1 *noun*
(a) small thin sharp metal stick with a round head, used for attaching clothes, papers, etc., together; *she fastened the ribbons to her dress with a pin*; **safety pin** = pin whose point fits into a cover when it is fastened, and so can't hurt anyone
(b) **pins and needles** = sharp tickling feeling in your hand or foot after it has lost feeling for a time; *wait a bit - I've got pins and needles in my foot*
2 *verb*
(a) to attach with a pin; *she pinned up a notice about the meeting*; *he pinned her photograph on the wall*; *he pinned the calendar to the wall by his desk*
(b) to trap someone so that they cannot move; *several people were pinned under the fallen roof*; *the automobile pinned her against the wall* (NOTE: **pinning - pinned**)

② **pincers**
['pɪnsərz] *noun*
claws of a crab or lobster; *a crab can pinch you with its pincers*

② **pinch**
[pɪnʃ]
1 *noun*
(a) squeezing tightly between finger and thumb; *he gave her arm a pinch*
(b) small quantity of something held between finger and thumb; *add a pinch of salt to the boiling water*
(c) in a pinch = if really necessary; *in a pinch, we can manage with only one sales assistant*; **to feel the pinch** = to find you have less money than you need; *we really started to feel the pinch when my father lost his job* (NOTE: plural is **pinches**)
2 *verb*
(a) to squeeze tightly, using the finger and thumb; *Ow! you're pinching me!*
(b) *(informal)* to steal; *someone's pinched my pen!*

④ **pinch-hit**
['pɪnʃ'hɪt] *verb*
(a) *(in baseball)* to bat in place of another player
(b) to take someone's place; *he's pinch-hitting for the regular electrician today*

③ **pin down**
['pɪn 'daʊn] *verb*
to pin someone down = to get someone to say what he or she really thinks, to get someone to make his or her mind up; *I'm trying to pin the chairman down to make a decision*; *she's very vague about dates - it's difficult to pin her down*

① **pine**
[paɪn]
1 *noun*
(a) pine (tree) = type of tree with needle-shaped leaves which stay on the tree all year round; *they planted a row of pines along the edge of the field*
(b) wood from a pine tree; *we've bought a pine table for the kitchen*; *there are pine closets in the kids' bedroom*
2 *verb*
to pine for something = to feel sad because you do not have something anymore; *she's miserable because she's pining for her cat*

② **pineapple**
['paɪnæpl] *noun*
large sweet tropical fruit, with stiff leaves on top; *she cut up a pineapple to add to the fruit salad*

① **ping-pong**
['pɪŋpɒŋ] *noun*
(informal) trademark for table tennis; *let's have a game of ping-pong*; *he was playing ping-pong with the children*

① **pink**
[pɪŋk]
1 *adjective*
(a) pale red or flesh color; *she uses pink paper when she writes to her friends*; **shocking pink** = very bright pink, which seems to glow; *he wore a pair of shocking pink socks*
(b) *(informal)* **tickled pink** = very much amused; *we were tickled pink to get our first letter from our little granddaughter*
(c) pink slip = note saying that you have been fired
2 *noun*
(a) pale red color; *the bright pink of the flowers shows clearly across the garden*
(b) small scented garden flower; *there was bunch of pinks on the table*

④ **pin money**
['pɪn 'mʌni] *noun*
(informal) small amount of money used for buying personal things; *she earns some pin money typing at home*

③ **PIN number**
['pɪn 'nʌmbər] *noun*
(= PERSONAL IDENTIFICATION NUMBER) special number which is allocated to the holder of a credit card or debit card; *I can never remember my PIN number*

② **pint**
[paɪnt] *noun*
liquid measure (= 0.473 of a liter); *he drinks a pint of milk a day*

② **pioneer**
[paɪə'nɪər]
1 *noun*
(a) person who is among the first to try to do something; *he was one of the pioneers of radar*; *the pioneers in the field of laser surgery*
(b) person who is among the first to explore or settle in a new land; *the first pioneers settled in this valley in about 1860*
2 *verb*
to be first to do something; *the company pioneered developments in the field of electronics*; *she pioneered a new route across the Andes*

① **pipe**
[paɪp] *noun*
(a) tube; *he's clearing a blocked pipe in the kitchen*; *the water came out of the hole in the pipe*
(b) tube for smoking tobacco, with a bowl at one end in which the tobacco burns; *he only smokes a pipe, never cigarettes*

④ **pipeline**
['paɪplaɪn] *noun*
(a) very large tube for carrying oil, natural gas, water, etc., over long distances; *an oil pipeline crosses the desert*
(b) in the pipeline = being worked on, coming; *the company has a series of new products in the pipeline*; *she has two new novels in the pipeline*

② **pirate**
['paɪərət]
1 *noun*

(a) sailor who attacks and robs ships; *pirates buried treasure on the island hundreds of years ago*
(b) person who copies a patented invention or a copyright work; **pirate radio** = illegal radio station; **video pirates** = people who organize the copying of videos to make a profit
2 *verb*
to copy a book, disk, design, etc., which is copyright; *the designs for the new dress collection were pirated in the Far East; I found a pirated copy of my book on sale in a street market*

① **pistol**
['pɪstl] *noun*
small gun that is held in the hand; *he pointed a pistol at the storekeeper and asked for money;* **starting pistol** = small gun that you fire to start a race

① **pit**
[pɪt]
1 *noun*
(a) deep, dark hole in the ground; *they dug a pit to bury the garbage*
(b) mine where coal is dug; *my grandfather spent his whole life working down in a pit*
(c) hard stone inside a fruit; *a date pit*
2 *verb*
to pit your strength against someone = to try to fight someone; *the little country pitted her strength against her much larger neighbor* (NOTE: **pitting - pitted**)

① **pitch**
[pɪtʃ]
1 *noun*
(a) *(in baseball)* action of throwing the ball to the batter by the pitcher; *the pitch was wide*
(b) *(music)* being able to sing or play notes correctly; *he has perfect pitch*
(c) high point (of anger or excitement); *excitement was at fever pitch*
(d) **sales pitch** = smooth talking, aimed at selling something; *she was completely taken in by his sales pitch*
2 *verb*
(a) to put up a tent; *they pitched their tent in a field by the beach;* **pitched battle** = battle where the opposing sides stand and face each other
(b) to throw a ball; *I pitched him a high ball to see if he could catch it*
(c) *(of boat)* to rock with the front and back going up and down; *the little boat was pitching up and down on the waves* (NOTE: the other movement of a boat, from side to side, is to **roll**)

① **pitcher**
['pɪtʃər] *noun*
(a) baseball player who throws the ball to the other team's batters; *the ball was thrown back to the pitcher*
(b) large jug for water or wine; *she brought us a pitcher of red wine*

② **pity**
['pɪti]
1 *noun*
(a) feeling of sympathy for someone who is in an unfortunate situation; *have you no pity for the homeless?;* **to take pity on someone** = to feel sorry for someone; *at last someone took pity on her and showed her how to work the machine*
(b) **it's a pity that** = it is sad that; *it's a pity you weren't there to see it; it's such a pity that the rain spoiled the picnic;* **it would be a pity to** = it would be unfortunate to; *it would be a pity not to eat all this beautiful food*
2 *verb*
to feel sympathy for someone; *I pity his children*

① **pizza**
['pitsə] *noun*
Italian dish, consisting of a flat round pie base cooked with tomatoes, onions, etc., on top; *we can pick up a pizza for supper tonight*

① **place**
[pleɪs]
1 *noun*
(a) where something is, or where something happens; *here's the place where we saw the cows; make sure you put the file back in the right place;* **all over the place** = everywhere; *there were dead leaves lying all over the place*
(b) *(informal)* home; *would you like to come back to my place for a cup of coffee?; he has an apartment in New York and a little place in the country*
(c) seat; *I'm keeping this place for my sister; I'm sorry, but this place has been taken;* **to change places with someone** = to take each other's seat; *if you can't see the screen, change places with me*
(d) space for one person at a table; *please set two places for lunch;* **place setting** = set of knife, fork and spoon, etc., for one person; *we need an extra place setting - Frank's bringing his girlfriend*
(e) position (in a race); *the U.S. runners are in the first three places*
(f) page where you have stopped reading a book; *I left a piece of paper in the book to mark my place; I've lost my place and can't remember where I got to*
(g) **to take place** = to happen; *the fight took place outside the football stadium; the movie takes place in China*
(h) name given to a smart street in a town; *they live in Regent Place*
2 *verb*
to put; *the waitress placed the bottle on the table; please place the envelope in the box*

④ **placid**
['plæsɪd] *adjective*
calm; *the normally placid life of the town was suddenly disrupted*

plague
[pleɪg]
1 *noun*

(a) fatal infectious disease transmitted by fleas from rats; *thousands of people died in the Great Plague of London in 1665*; **to avoid someone like the plague** = to try not to meet someone; *I avoid him like the plague because he's always asking if he can borrow money*

(b) great quantity of pests; *we've had a plague of ants in the yard*

2 *verb*

to annoy or to bother someone; *we were plagued with wasps last summer; she keeps plaguing me with silly questions*

plain
[pleɪn]
1 *adjective*

(a) easy to understand; *the instructions are written in plain English*

(b) obvious; *it's perfectly plain what he wants; we made it plain to them that this was our final offer*

(c) simple, not decorated; *we put plain wallpaper in the dining room; the outside is covered with leaves and flowers, but the inside is quite plain*; **plain cover** = envelope without any company name on it

(d) not pretty; *his two daughters are rather plain*

(e) **plain yogurt** = yogurt without any flavoring (NOTE: do not confuse with **plane**; note: **plainer - plainest**)

2 *noun*

flat area of country; *a broad plain bordered by mountains*

plainly
[ˈpleɪnli] *adverb*

(a) in an obvious way; *he's plainly bored by the French lesson*

(b) clearly; *it is plainly visible from here*

plaintiff
[ˈpleɪntɪf] *noun*

person who starts a legal action against someone in the civil courts; *she's the plaintiff in a libel action; the court decided in favor of the plaintiff* (NOTE: the other party in an action is the **defendant**)

plan
[plæn]
1 *noun*

(a) organized way of doing things; *he made a plan to get up earlier in the future; she drew up plans for the school trip to Montana*; **according to plan** = in the way it was arranged; *the party went off according to plan*

(b) drawing of the way something is arranged; *here are the plans for the kitchen; the fire exits are shown on the plan of the office*; **town plan** *or* **street plan** = map of a town; *can you find Harrisburg Road on the town plan?*

2 *verb*

(a) to arrange how you are going to do something; *she's busy planning her vacation in Wyoming*

(b) to intend to do something; *they are planning to move to Dallas next month; we weren't planning to go on vacation this year; I plan to take the 5 o'clock flight to New York*

(c) to arrange how to build something; *she planned the bathroom herself; a new town is being planned next to the airport* (NOTE: **planning - planned**)

plane
[pleɪn]
1 *noun*

(a) aircraft, machine which flies; *when is the next plane for Salt Lake City?; how are you getting to Atlanta? - we're going by plane; don't panic, you've got plenty of time to catch your plane; he was stuck in a traffic jam and missed his plane*

(b) tool with a sharp blade for making wood smooth; *he smoothed off the rough edges with a plane* (NOTE: do not confuse with **plain**)

2 *verb*

to make wood smooth with a plane; *he planed the top of the table*

planet
[ˈplænɪt] *noun*

(a) one of the bodies that turn around the sun; *is there life on any of the planets?; Earth is the third planet from the Sun*

(b) the planet Earth; *an environmental disaster could affect the whole planet*

> COMMENT: the planets in our system are in order of their distance from the Sun: Mercury, Venus, Earth, Mars, Jupiter, Saturn, Uranus, Neptune, and Pluto

plank
[plæŋk] *noun*

long flat piece of wood used in building; *hold the plank steady while I saw it in half*

planner
[ˈplænər] *noun*

person who draws up plans; *the planners made the parking lot too small*; **the government's economic planners** = people who plan the future economy of the country for the government

planning
[ˈplænɪŋ] *noun*

making plans; *the trip will need very careful planning; the project is still in the planning stage*; **family planning** = decision by parents on how many children to have; *a family planning clinic; the clinic gives advice on family planning*; **planning department** = section of a local government office which deals with building development and how property in different areas of the city should be used; *you will need to consult the city's planning department*

① **plant**
[plænt]
1 *noun*
(a) living thing which grows in the ground and has leaves, a stem and roots; *he has several rows of cabbage plants in his garden*; *some plants grow very tall*; **houseplants** = plants that you grow in pots in the house; *will you water my houseplants for me while I'm on vacation?*; **plant pot** = special pot for growing plants in
(b) machinery; *investment in buildings and plant accounts for 90% of our costs* (NOTE: no plural in this meaning)
(c) large factory; *they are planning to build an automobile plant near the river*
2 *verb*
(a) to put a plant in the ground; *we've planted two pear trees and a peach tree in the garden*
(b) to put in a place; *someone phoned to say that a bomb had been planted on Main Street*
(c) to put goods secretly in a place in order to make it look as if they were placed there illegally; *the police were accused of planting the drugs in her car*

① **plantation**
[plæn'teɪʃn] *noun*
tropical estate growing a particular crop; *a coffee plantation*; *a rubber plantation*

① **plaster**
['plæstər]
1 *noun*
mixture of fine sand and lime which is mixed with water and is used for covering the walls of houses; *the apartment hasn't been decorated yet and there is still bare plaster in most of the rooms*
2 *verb*
(a) to cover with plaster; *they had to take off the old plaster and plaster the walls again*
(b) to cover with a thick layer, as if with plaster; *she plastered her face with makeup*

③ **plastic**
['plæstɪk]
1 *noun*
(a) material made in factories, used to make all sorts of things; *we take plastic plates when we go to the beach*; *the supermarket gives you plastic bags to put your shopping in*; *we cover our garden furniture with plastic sheets when it rains* (NOTE: no plural: **a bowl made of plastic**)
(b) *(informal)* **plastic (money)** = credit cards and charge cards; *I don't have any cash with me, do you take plastic?*
2 *adjective*
plastic surgery = surgery to repair parts of the body which do not look as they should

> COMMENT: plastic surgery is used especially to treat accident victims or people who have suffered burns

① **plate**
[pleɪt]
1 *noun*
(a) flat round dish for putting food on; *put one pie on each plate*; *pass all the plates down to the end of the table*; **dinner plate** = large plate for serving a main course on
(b) food which is served on a plate; *they passed round plates of sandwiches*; *she ate two plates of cold meat*
(c) flat piece of metal, glass, etc.; *the dentist has a shiny plate on his door*; *see also* LICENSE PLATE
(d) picture in a book; *the book is illustrated with twenty color plates*
(e) objects made of copper covered with a thin layer of gold or silver; *the spoons aren't sterling silver - they're just plate*
2 *verb*
to cover a metal object with a thin layer of gold or silver; *the metal cross is plated with gold*

② **platform**
['plætfɔrm] *noun*
(a) high flat structure by the side of the railway lines at a station, to help passengers get on or off the trains easily; *crowds of people were waiting on the platform*; *the train for Berlin will leave from platform 3*
(b) high wooden floor for speakers to speak from; *the main speakers sat in a row on the platform*
(c) **platform shoes** = shoes with very thick soles; *I can't imagine how she can walk in those platform shoes*
(d) program of action outlined by a political party at an election

① **play**
[pleɪ]
1 *noun*
(a) written text which is acted in a theater or on TV; *did you see the play on TV last night?*; *we went to the theater to see the new play*; *two of Shakespeare's plays are on the list for the English exam*
(b) movement or action in a game; *the catcher made a good play*; **out of play** = not on the field; *the ball was kicked out of play*
(c) way of amusing yourself; *they watched the children at play*; *all right, you children, it's time for play*
(d) **it's child's play** = it is very easy; *it's child's play if you've got the right tools for the job*
2 *verb*
(a) to take part in a game; *he plays hockey for his college*; *do you play tennis?*
(b) *(of a game)* to be held; *the tennis match was played on the center court*; *baseball isn't played in the winter*
(c) to amuse yourself; *the boys were playing in the garden*; *when you've finished your lesson you can go out to play*; *he doesn't like playing with other children*

(d) to make music on a musical instrument or to put on a disk; *he can't play the piano very well*; *let me play you my new Bach CD*

(e) to act the part of a person in a movie or play; *Orson Welles played Harry Lime in "The Third Man"*

③ **play back**
['pleɪ 'bæk] *verb*
to listen to something which you have just recorded on tape; *he played back the messages left on his answering machine*

① **player**
['pleɪər] *noun*
(a) person who plays a game; *you only need two players for chess*; *tennis players have to be fit*; *four of the players in the opposing team are sick*
(b) person who plays a musical instrument; *a famous horn player*

① **playground**
['pleɪgraʊnd] *noun*
place, at a school or in a public area, where children can play; *the little girls were playing quietly in a corner of the playground*

③ **playing cards**
['pleɪɪŋ 'kɑrdz] *noun*
set of 52 pieces of card with pictures or patterns on them, used for playing various games; *a deck of playing cards*; *he can do tricks with playing cards*; *see also* CARD

④ **plea**
[pli] *noun*
(a) answer to a charge in court; *he entered a plea of "not guilty"*
(b) *(formal)* request; *her pleas for help were rejected*

② **plead**
[plid] *verb*
(a) to answer a charge in a law court; *he pleaded guilty to the charge of murder*
(b) to give an excuse; *she said she couldn't come, pleading pressure of work*
(c) to plead with someone = to try to change someone's mind by asking again and again; *I pleaded with her not to go*

① **pleasant**
['plezənt] *adjective*
which pleases; *what a pleasant garden!*; *how pleasant it is to sit here under the trees!*; *he didn't bring the pleasantest of news* = he brought bad news (NOTE: **pleasanter - pleasantest**)

② **pleasantly**
['plezəntli] *adverb*
in a pleasant way; *he smiled at me pleasantly*; *I was pleasantly surprised that she had remembered my birthday*

② **please**
[pliz]
1 *interjection*

(used to ask politely) *can you close the window, please?*; *please sit down*; *can I have a ham sandwich, please?*; *do you want some more tea? - yes, please!*; *compare* THANK YOU
2 *verb*
to make someone happy or satisfied; *she's not difficult to please*; *please yourself* = do as you like; *shall I take the red one or the green one? - please yourself*

② **pleased**
[plizd] *adjective*
happy; *we're very pleased with our new house*; *I'm pleased to hear you're feeling better*; *he wasn't pleased when he heard his test results*

② **pleasing**
['plizɪŋ] *adjective*
which pleases; *she's made very pleasing progress this year*; *the whole design of the garden is very pleasing*

① **pleasure**
['pleʒər] *noun*
pleasant feeling; *his greatest pleasure is sitting by the river*; *it gives me great pleasure to be able to visit you today*; *with pleasure* = gladly; *I'll do the job with pleasure*

④ **pleat**
[plit] *noun*
ironed fold in a skirt, etc.; *her skirt has pleats*

② **pledge**
[pledʒ]
1 *noun*
(a) promise; *they made a pledge to meet again next year, same time, same place*; *the government never fulfilled its pledge to cut taxes*
(b) to take the pledge = to swear never to drink alcohol again
(c) object given to a lender when borrowing money, and which will be returned to the borrower when the money is paid back; *any pledges which have not been claimed after six months will be sold*
2 *verb*
(a) to promise formally; *she pledged $75 to the charity*; *thousands of people have pledged their support for the project*
(b) to give something as a pledge when borrowing money; *she had to pledge her wedding ring to buy food for the children*

④ **plentiful**
['plentɪfəl] *adjective*
abundant; in large quantities; *apples are plentiful and cheap this year*

② **plenty**
['plenti] *noun*
large quantity; *you've got plenty of time to catch the train*; *plenty of people complain about the bus service*; *do you have enough bread? - yes, we've got plenty* (NOTE: no plural)

② **pliers**
['plaɪərz] *noun*
(pair of) pliers = tool shaped like scissors for

pinching, pulling, or cutting wire; *I need a pair of pliers to pull out these rusty nails*

③ **plot**
[plɒt]
1 *noun*
(a) small area of land for building, for growing vegetables, etc.; *they own a plot of land next to the river*; *the plot isn't big enough to build a house on*
(b) basic story of a book, play, movie; *the novel has a complicated plot*; *I won't tell you the plot of the movie so as not to spoil it for you*
(c) wicked plan; *they discussed a plot to hold up the security van*
2 *verb*
(a) to mark on a map; *we plotted a course to take us to the island*
(b) to draw a graph; *they plotted the rise in house prices on a graph*
(c) to draw up a wicked plan; *they plotted to assassinate the president* (NOTE: plotting - plotted)

① **plow**
[plaʊ]
1 *noun*
(a) farm machine for turning over soil; *the plow is pulled by a tractor*
(b) snowplow = powerful machine with a large blade in front, used for clearing snow from streets, railroads, etc.; *the snowplows were out all night clearing the main roads*
2 *verb*
to turn over the soil; *some farmers still use horses to plow the fields*

② **plow on**
[ˈplaʊ ˈɒn] *verb*
to continue with something difficult; *in spite of the shouting from the audience, the minister plowed on with his speech*; *it's a difficult job, but we'll just have to plow through until it's finished*

② **pluck**
[plʌk] *verb*
(a) to pull out feathers; *to pluck a chicken*
(b) to pull and release the strings of a guitar or other musical instrument to make a sound; *he was plucking the strings of his guitar*

① **plug**
[plʌg]
1 *noun*
(a) device with pins which go into holes and allow electric current to pass through; *the vacuum cleaner is supplied with a two-pronged plug*
(b) flat rubber disk that covers the hole for wastewater in a bath or sink; *can you call reception and tell them there's no bath plug in the bathtub*; *she pulled out the plug and let the dirty water drain away*
(c) earplug, a piece of soft wax that you put in your ear to stop you from hearing loud sounds

(d) *(in an automobile)* spark plug = device that passes the electric spark through the gas; *if the spark plugs are dirty, the engine won't start*; *the garage put in a new set of spark plugs*
(e) *(informal)* piece of publicity; to give a plug to a new product = to publicize a new product; *during the radio interview, she got in a plug for her new movie*
2 *verb*
(a) to block up (a hole); *we plugged the leak in the bathroom*; *he plugged his ears with absorbent cotton because he couldn't stand the noise*
(b) *(informal)* to publicize; *they ran six commercials plugging vacations in Florida*; *they paid the radio station to plug their new album* (NOTE: plugging - plugged)

③ **plug in**
[ˈplʌg ˈɪn] *verb*
to push an electric plug into holes and so attach a device to the electricity supply; *the computer wasn't plugged in - that's why it wouldn't work*

① **plum**
[plʌm] *noun*
sweet gold, red or purple fruit with a smooth skin and a large stone; *she bought a pound of plums to make a pie*

① **plumber**
[ˈplʌmər] *noun*
person who installs or repairs water pipes, radiators, etc.; *there's water dripping through the kitchen ceiling, we'll have to call a plumber*

② **plunge**
[plʌnʒ]
1 *noun*
to take the plunge = to decide suddenly to do something; *I've decided to take the plunge and buy a satellite dish*
2 *verb*
(a) to throw yourself into water; *he plunged into the river to rescue the little boy*
(b) to fall sharply; *share prices plunged at the news of the change of government*

② **plural**
[ˈplʊrəl] *adjective & noun*
(in grammar) form of a word showing that there are more than one; *does "government" take a singular or plural verb?*; *what's the plural of "mouse"?*; *the verb should be in the plural after "programs"*

④ **plurality**
[plʊˈrælɪti] *noun*
(in an election) (i) number of votes which the candidate with most votes receives; (ii) having more votes than another candidate; *the candidate with a simple plurality wins the seat*

① **plus**
[plʌs]
1 *preposition*
(a) added to; *his salary plus commission comes to more than $35,000* (NOTE: in calculations plus

is usually shown by the sign + : **10 + 4 = 14**: say "ten plus four equals fourteen")

(b) more than; **houses valued at $300,000 plus** = houses valued at over $300,000

2 *adjective*

favorable, good and profitable; *being able to drive is certainly a plus factor*; **on the plus side** = this is a favorable point; *the weather wasn't very good, but on the plus side, it didn't actually rain*

3 *noun*

(a) plus (sign) = sign (+) meaning more than; *she put in a plus instead of a minus*

(b) *(informal)* favorable sign, a good or favorable point; *it's a definite plus that the hotel has room service*

① **P.M.** *or* **p.m.**
['pi 'em] *adverb*

in the afternoon, after 12:00; *the exhibition is open from 10 A.M. to 5:30 P.M.*; *if you telephone after 6 P.M. the calls are at a cheaper rate*

③ **PO**
['pi'əʊ] = POST OFFICE; **PO Box number** = reference number given for delivering mail to a post office, so as not to give the actual address of the person who will receive it

③ **poach**
[pəʊtʃ] *verb*

(a) to cook eggs without their shells, or fish, etc., in gently boiling water; *would you like your eggs boiled or poached?*; *they served poached salmon as a first course*

(b) to catch animals, birds or fish on someone else's land without permission; *the farmer suspected that someone was poaching his rabbits*

① **pocket**
['pɒkɪt]

1 *noun*

(a) one of several little bags sewn into the inside of a coat, etc., in which you can keep your money, handkerchief, keys, etc.; *she looked in all her pockets but couldn't find her keys*; *he was leaning against a fence with his hands in his pockets*; **breast pocket** = pocket on the inside of a jacket; **hip pocket** *or* **back pocket** = pocket at the back of a pair of pants; **pocket calculator** = small calculator that you can put in your pocket; **pocket dictionary** = small dictionary that you can put in your pocket

(b) to be $35 in pocket = to have made a profit of $35; *when we counted the takings we found we were over $150 in pocket*; **to be out of pocket** = having lost money which you paid personally; **to be $35 out of pocket** = to have lost $35; *the lunch left him $50 out of pocket*; *if you are out of pocket you can always get some cash from the accounting department*; *nobody paid my expenses, so I was $150 out of pocket at the end of the day*

(c) hole with a small bag at each corner and side of a billiard table; *the black ball stopped at the edge of the pocket*

2 *verb*

to put in your pocket, to keep; *at the end of the sale, she pocketed all the money*

③ **pocket money**
['pɒkɪt 'mʌni] *noun*

money for small individual expenses; *do you need some pocket money?*

② **pod**
[pɒd] *noun*

(a) long green tube in which peas or beans, etc., grow; *some peas can be eaten in their pods*

(b) glass container with seats for travelers; *we all got into a pod on the London Eye*

① **poem**
['pəʊɪm] *noun*

piece of writing, with words carefully chosen to sound attractive, set out in lines usually of a regular length; *he wrote a long poem about an old sailor*; *the poem about the Civil War was set to music by Spalding*

② **poet**
['pəʊɪt] *noun*

person who writes poems; *Lord Byron, the famous English poet*; *the poet gives a wonderful description of a summer morning*

② **poetry**
['pəʊɪtri] *noun*

poems taken as a type of literature; *reading poetry makes me cry*; *this is a good example of German poetry* (NOTE: no plural)

① **point**
[pɔɪnt]

1 *noun*

(a) sharp end of something long; *the point of my pencil has broken*; *the stick has a very sharp point*

(b) decimal point = dot used to show the division between whole numbers and parts of numbers (NOTE: three and a half is written: **3.5** (say "three point five"). Note also that in many other languages, this is a comma)

(c) particular place; *the path led us for miles through the woods and in the end we came back to the point where we started from*; *we had reached a point 2000 ft above sea level*; **starting point** = place where something starts

(d) particular moment in time; *from that point on, things began to change*; *at what point did you decide to resign?*; **at that point** = at that moment; *all the lights went off at that point*; **at this point in time** = at this particular moment; *at this point in time, it is not possible for me to answer reporters' questions*; **on the point of doing something** = just about to do something; *I was on the point of phoning you*

(e) meaning or reason; *there's no point in asking them to pay - they haven't any money*; *the main point of the meeting is to see how we can continue to run the center without a grant*;

what's the point of doing the same thing all over again?; **I see your point** = I see what you mean; *I see your point, but there are other factors to be considered; I can't see the point of doing that*

(f) score in a game; *their team scored three points; in football, a touchdown counts as six points*

(g) temperature; *what's the boiling point of water?*

2 *verb*

(a) to aim a gun or your finger at something; to show with your finger; *the teacher is pointing at you; it's rude to point at people; don't point that gun at me - it might go off; the guide pointed to the map to show where we were*

(b) to put mortar between bricks in a completed wall, so as to make the surface smooth; *after the wall was built they pointed it with gray mortar*

② **pointed**
['pɔɪntɪd] *adjective*
(a) with a sharp point at one end; *a pointed stick*
(b) sharp and critical; *he made some very pointed remarks about the waitress*

③ **point of view**
['pɔɪnt əv 'vju] *noun*
particular way of thinking about something; *from our point of view, it's been a great success; try to see things from your parents' point of view*

① **point out**
['pɔɪnt 'aʊt] *verb*
(a) to show; *the tour guide will point out the main things to see in the town; the report points out the mistakes made by the agency over the last few years*
(b) to give a point of view; *she pointed out that the children in her class were better behaved than in previous years*

② **poison**
['pɔɪzn]
1 *noun*
substance that kills or makes you sick if it is swallowed or if it gets into the blood; *there's enough poison in this bottle to kill the whole town; don't drink that - it's poison*
2 *verb*
(a) to kill with poison; *she was accused of poisoning her husband*
(b) to put poison in; *he didn't know the wine was poisoned; chemicals from the factory are poisoning the river*

③ **poisoning**
['pɔɪznɪŋ] *noun*
(a) taking poison into your system; **blood poisoning** = condition caused by bacteria in the blood; *wash the wound carefully or you might get blood poisoning*; **food poisoning** = poisoning caused by bacteria in food; *the hotel was closed after an outbreak of food poisoning; half the guests at the wedding were ill with food poisoning*

(b) using poison to kill or harm people; *he was accused of the poisoning of several old ladies*

③ **poisonous**
['pɔɪzənəs] *adjective*
which can kill or harm with poison; *it is dangerous to try to catch poisonous snakes; these plants are deadly poisonous*

② **poke**
[pəʊk] *verb*
to push with your finger or with a stick; *he poked the pig with his stick*

① **Poland**
['pəʊlənd] *noun*
large country in Eastern Europe, between Germany and Russia; *Poland is an important industrial country* (NOTE: capital: **Warsaw;** people: **the Poles;** language: **Polish;** currency: **zloty**)

③ **polar**
['pəʊlər] *adjective*
referring to the North Pole or South Pole; *he went to explore the polar regions*; **polar bear** = big white bear found in areas near the North Pole

① **pole**
[pəʊl] *noun*
(a) long rod of wood or metal; **tent pole** = pole that holds up a tent; *one of the tent poles snapped in the wind*
(b) one of the points at each end of the line around which the Earth turns; **magnetic pole** = one of the two poles which are the centers of the Earth's magnetic field; **North Pole** = furthest point at the north of the Earth; **South Pole** = furthest point at the south of the Earth

② **Pole**
[pəʊl] *noun*
person from Poland; *Pope John Paul II is a Pole*

③ **pole position**
['pəʊl pə'zɪʃn] *noun*
position of the first automobile in a race; *he was in pole position at the start of the Grand Prix*

① **police**
[pə'lis]
1 *noun*
organization that controls traffic, tries to stop crime and tries to catch criminals; *the police are looking for the driver of the automobile; call the police - I've just seen someone drive off in my car* (NOTE: takes a plural verb: **the police are looking for him**)
2 *verb*
to make sure that rules or laws are obeyed; *we need more officers to police the area; the problem is how to police the UN resolutions*

③ **police force**
['plis 'fɔrs] *noun*
group of police in a certain area; *he joined the police force after graduating from college; the*

local police force is trying to cope with drug dealers coming from the city

① **policeman, policewoman**
['plɪsmən or 'plɪswʊmən] *noun*
ordinary member of the police; *three armed policemen went into the building*; *if you don't know the way, ask a policeman* (NOTE: plurals are **policemen, policewomen**)

③ **police officer**
['plɪs 'ɒfɪsər] *noun*
member of the police force; *I'm a police officer, madam, please get out of the automobile*; *a passing police officer chased the robbers as they tried to escape from the bank*

③ **police station**
['plɪs 'steɪʃn] *noun*
building with the offices of a particular local police force; *three men were arrested and taken to the police station*

③ **policy**
['pɒlɪsi] *noun*
(a) decisions on the general way of doing something; *the government's policy on wages or the government's wages policy*; *it is not our policy to give details of employees over the phone*; *people voted for the Democrats because they liked their policies*
(b) insurance policy = document that shows the conditions of an insurance contract; **accident policy** = an insurance contract against accidents; **comprehensive policy** = an insurance that covers all risks; **to take out a policy** = to sign the contract for an insurance and start paying the premiums; *she took out a house insurance policy* (NOTE: plural is **policies**)

② **polish**
['pɒlɪʃ]
1 *noun*
substance used to make things shiny; *give the car a good wash before you put the polish on*; **floor polish** = polish used to make wooden floors shiny; **furniture polish** = wax used to make furniture shiny; **shoe polish** = wax used to make shoes shiny (NOTE: plural is **polishes**)
2 *verb*
to rub something to make it shiny; *he polished his shoes until they shone*

① **Polish**
['pəʊlɪʃ]
1 *adjective*
referring to Poland; *the Polish Army joined in the military exercises*
2 *noun*
language spoken in Poland; *I know three words of Polish*; *you will need an English-Polish dictionary if you're visiting Warsaw*

④ **polish off**
['pɒlɪʃ 'ɒf] *verb*
(a) to finish off a job quickly; *he polished off his essay in half an hour*

(b) to eat a meal quickly; *they polished off a plate of fried eggs and sausages and then asked for waffles and syrup*

③ **polish up**
['pɒlɪʃ 'ʌp] *verb*
to improve a skill; *she spent a term in Mexico polishing up her Spanish*

① **polite**
[pə'laɪt] *adjective*
not rude; *sales staff should always be polite to customers* (NOTE: **politer - politest**)

② **politely**
[pə'laɪtli] *adverb*
in a polite way; *she politely answered the tourists' questions*

③ **political**
[pə'lɪtɪkl] *adjective*
referring to government or to party politics; *I don't want to get involved in a political argument*; *she gave up her political career when she had the children*; **political refugee** = person who has left his country because he is afraid of being put in prison for his political beliefs; *these political refugees are afraid that they will be jailed if they go back to their country*

③ **politician**
[pɒlɪ'tɪʃn] *noun*
person who works in politics; *politicians from all parties have welcomed the report*

③ **politics**
['pɒlɪtɪks] *noun*
(a) ideas and methods used in governing a country
(b) study of how countries are governed; *he studied politics and economics at college*

④ **poll**
[pəʊl]
1 *noun*
(a) vote, voting; *we are still waiting for the results of yesterday's poll*; *a poll of factory workers showed that more than 50% supported the union's demands*
(b) number of votes cast in an election; *the poll was lower than usual - only 35% of the voters bothered to vote*
(c) the polls = places where people vote in an election; *the polls close at 9 o'clock*; **to go to the polls** = to vote in an election; *the people of France go to the polls next Sunday to elect a new president*; *see also* OPINION POLL
2 *verb*
(a) to get a number of votes in an election; *she polled more than ten thousand votes*
(b) to poll a sample of the population = to ask a sample group of people what they feel about something

③ **pollen**
['pɒlən] *noun*
yellow powder in a flower which touches part of a female flower and so creates seeds; *bees carry pollen from one flower to the next*; **pollen**

count = number showing the amount of pollen in the air, which can cause hayfever

③ **pollute**
[pə'lut] *verb*
to make the environment dirty by putting harmful substances into it; *the company was fined for polluting the lake with chemicals*

③ **pollution**
[pə'luʃn] *noun*
(a) action of making the environment dirty; *pollution of the atmosphere has increased over the last 50 years*
(b) dirty or harmful materials that are put into the environment; *it took six months to clean up the oil pollution on the beaches*; *the pollution in the center of town is so bad that people have started wearing face masks*; **air pollution** = dirt and gas in the air; **noise pollution** = spoiling people's pleasure by making a lot of noise

③ **polyester**
[pɒlɪ'estər] *noun*
type of artificial fibre used especially to make clothes; *he bought two polyester shirts in the sale*

② **pond**
[pɒnd] *noun*
small lake; *there's a duck pond in the middle of the town*; *children sail their boats on the pond in the park*

① **pony**
['pəʊni] *noun*
small horse; *my best friend lets me ride her pony sometimes* (NOTE: plural is **ponies**)

④ **ponytail**
['pəʊnɪteɪl] *noun*
hairstyle where your hair is tied at the back and falls loosely; *she usually wears her hair in a ponytail*; *our new mail carrier has a ponytail*

① **pool**
[pul]
1 *noun*
(a) **(swimming) pool** = large bath of water for swimming in; *we have a little swimming pool in the backyard*; *he swam two lengths of the pool*; **indoor pool** = swimming pool inside a building; *our school has an indoor swimming pool*; **outdoor pool** = swimming pool in the open air; **heated pool** = pool where the water is kept warm
(b) small lake; *he dove in and swam across the mountain pool*
(c) group where people share facilities; *we belong to a pool of people who baby-sit for one another*; **car pool** = arrangement where several people travel to work in one automobile
(d) supply of something ready to be used; *we can draw on a pool of unemployed teenagers*
(e) game rather like billiards, where you hit balls into pockets using a cue; *we were playing pool in the bar*
2 *verb*

to pool resources = to group resources together; *the only way we can afford it will be to pool our resources*

① **poor**
[pɔr] *adjective*
(a) with little or no money; *the family is very poor now that the father has no work*; *the poorer students find it difficult to get through college without grants*; *this is one of the poorest countries in Africa*
(b) **poor in** = with very little of something; *the soil in my garden is very poor in vegetable matter*
(c) not very good; *vines can grow even in poor soil*; *they were selling off poor-quality vegetables at a cheap price*; *she's been in poor health for some months*
(d) *(showing you are sorry)* **poor old you!** - having to stay at home and finish your homework while we go to the movies; *my poor legs - after climbing up the mountain!* (NOTE: **poorer - poorest**)

④ **poorly**
['pɔrli] *adverb*
not in a very good way; *the offices are poorly laid out*; *the job is very poorly paid*

① **pop**
[pɒp]
1 *noun*
(a) noise like a cork coming out of a bottle; *there was a pop as she lit the gas*; **to go pop** = to make a noise like a cork; *the automobile engine went pop and we stopped suddenly*; *the balloon landed on the candles and went pop*
(b) *(informal)* **pop (music)** = modern popular music; *she prefers jazz to pop*; *he spends all day listening to pop records*; *we went to a pop concert last night*; **pop chart** = list showing the most popular songs at a certain time; *the record is at number ten in the pop charts*; **pop group** = group of singers and musicians who play pop songs; *he was lead singer in a 1980s pop group*
(c) *(informal)* name for a father; *I'll ask my pop if we can borrow his ladder*
(d) **(soda) pop** = sweet soft drink containing soda water; *would you like pop with your meal?*
2 *verb*
(a) *(informal)* to go quickly; *I'll just pop down to the town*; *he popped into the drugstore*; *I'm just popping around to Jane's*; *I'd only popped out for a moment*
(b) to put quickly; *pop the pie in the oven for ten minutes*
(c) to make a noise like "pop"; *champagne corks were popping as the result was announced* (NOTE: **popping - popped**)

① **popcorn**
['pɒpkɔrn] *noun*
type of corn with kernels that burst when heated to form light, white balls; *the children behind me ate popcorn continuously during the movie*

② **Pope**
['pəʊp] *noun*
the head of the Roman Catholic Church; *the Pope said mass in a stadium before 50,000 people*; *security was very tight for the Pope's visit*

① **poppy**
['pɒpɪ] *noun*
common red wild flower which often grows in fields; *she picked a bunch of poppies on her way home through the fields* (NOTE: plural is poppies)

② **popular**
['pɒpjʊlər] *adjective*
(a) liked by a lot of people; *the department store is popular with young mothers*; *the West Coast is a popular area for vacations*
(b) referring to the mass of ordinary people; *he was elected by popular vote*; *it is a popular belief that walking under a ladder brings bad luck*

③ **popularity**
[pɒpjuˈlærɪti] *noun*
being liked by a lot of people; *the scandal doesn't seem to have affected the president's popularity*

③ **population**
[pɒpjuˈleɪʃn] *noun*
number of people who live in a place; *the population of the country is 60 million*; *this city has a population of over three million*

① **pork**
[pɔrk] *noun*
fresh meat from a pig, eaten cooked; *we're having pork for dinner tonight* (NOTE: no plural; note also that salted or smoked meat from a pig is ham or bacon)

> COMMENT: roast pork is traditionally seasoned with herbs and onions, and served with apple sauce

② **porpoise**
['pɔrpəs] *noun*
sea animal similar to a dolphin, which swims in groups; *a school of porpoises followed the ship*

② **port**
[pɔrt] *noun*
(a) harbor, or town with a harbor; *the ship is due in port on Tuesday*; *we left port at midday*; *to call at a port* = to stop at a port to pick up or drop off cargo; *port of call* = port at which a ship stops; *our next port of call is San Diego*; *fishing port* = port which is used mainly by fishing boats
(b) left side (when looking forward on board a ship or aircraft); *passengers sitting on the port side of the plane can see the bridge*; *the ship turned to port to avoid the yacht*
(c) opening in a computer for plugging in a piece of equipment; *a mouse port*

(d) strong sweet wine from Portugal or similar drink made elsewhere; *at the end of the meal the port was passed round*

② **portable**
['pɔrtəbl]
1 *adjective*
which can be carried; *he used his portable computer on the plane*
2 *noun*
small computer which can be carried; *I keyboard all my orders on my portable*

③ **porter**
['pɔrtər] *noun*
(a) person who carries baggage for travelers at hotels or train stations; *find a porter to help us with all this baggage*
(b) person who does general work in a hospital, including moving the patients around; *the nurse asked a porter to fetch a wheelchair*

② **portion**
['pɔrʃn]
1 *noun*
(a) small part of something larger; *this is only a small portion of the material we collected*; *our car was in the rear portion of the train*
(b) serving of food, usually for one person; *the portions in that French restaurant are tiny*; *ask the waitress if they serve children's portions*
2 *verb*
to portion out = to share out; *we portioned out the money between the four of us*

② **portrait**
['pɔrtreɪt] *noun*
painting or photograph of a person's face; *he has painted a portrait of the mayor*; *old portraits of members of the family lined the walls of the dining room*

④ **portray**
[pɔrˈtreɪ] *verb*
(formal) to paint or to describe a scene or a person; *in the biography he is portrayed as gloomy and miserable, while in real life he was nothing like that at all*

① **Portugal**
['pɔrtjʊgəl] *noun*
country is Southern Europe, to the west of Spain; *Portugal is a country of great travelers* (NOTE: capital: **Lisbon**; people: **the Portuguese**; language: **Portuguese**; currency: **Portuguese escudo, euro**)

② **Portuguese**
[pɔrtjuˈgiz]
1 *adjective*
referring to Portugal; *a Portuguese sailor*
2 *noun*
(a) person from Portugal; *she married a Portuguese*; *the Portuguese* = people from Portugal
(b) language spoken in Portugal, Brazil, etc.; *I don't know the word for it in Portuguese*

① **pose**
[pəʊz]
1 *noun*

(a) way of standing, sitting, etc.; *she is painted standing in an elegant pose*; *he struck a funny pose as I was taking the photo*

(b) way of behaving which is just pretending; *he'd like you to think he's an expert but it's just a pose*

2 *verb*

(a) to pose for someone = to stand or sit still while someone paints or photographs you; *he posed for her in his uniform*

(b) to pretend to be; *he got into the prison by posing as a doctor*

(c) to set a problem; to put a question; *what to do with illegal immigrants poses a problem for the immigration services*

④ **posh**
[pɒʃ] *adjective*

(informal) very smart; *I decided I had better wear my poshest dress to the wedding*; *we ate in a really posh restaurant* (NOTE: **posher - poshest**)

② **position**
[pə'zɪʃən]
1 *noun*

(a) place where someone or something is; *from his position on the roof he can see the whole of the street*; *the ship's last known position was 200 miles east of Bermuda*

(b) job; *the sales manager has a key position in the firm*; *he's going to apply for a position as manager*; *we have several positions vacant*

(c) situation or state of affairs; *what is the company's cash position?*

(d) to be in a position to do something = to be able to do something; *I am not in a position to answer your question at this point in time*

2 *verb*

to put, to place in a position; *she positioned herself near the exit*

③ **positive**
['pɒzɪtɪv]
1 *adjective*

(a) meaning "yes"; *she gave a positive answer*

(b) certain, sure; *I'm positive I put the key in my pocket*; *are you positive he said six o'clock?*

(c) plus, more than zero; *a positive quantity*

(d) *(in a test)* showing that something is there; *the pregnancy test was positive*

(e) positive film = film where the light parts are light and the dark are dark (as opposed to negative film)

(f) positive terminal = one of the terminals in a battery, shown by a plus (+) sign; *the wire should be attached to the positive terminal*

2 *noun*

photograph printed from a negative, where the light and dark appear as they are in real life (NOTE: the opposite is **negative**)

③ **possess**
[pə'zes] *verb*

(a) to own; *he possesses several farms in the south of the country*; *he lost all he possessed in the fire*

(b) to occupy someone's mind and influence their behavior; *terror possessed her as she saw the door slowly open*; **what possessed him to do it?** = why on earth did he do it?

(c) *(of an evil spirit)* to control someone in mind and body

③ **possession**
[pə'zeʃn] *noun*

(a) ownership; **in someone's possession** = being held by someone; *the jewelry came into my possession when my mother died*; *when he couldn't keep up the mortgage payments the bank took possession of the house*

(b) possessions = things which you own; *they lost all their possessions in the flood*

② **possibility**
[pɒsə'bɪlɪti] *noun*

being likely to happen; *is there any possibility of getting a ticket to the show?*; *there is always the possibility that the plane will be early*; *there is no possibility of the bank lending us any more money*

② **possible**
['pɒsəbl] *adjective*

which can be; *that field is a possible site for the factory*; *it is possible that the plane has been delayed*; *a bicycle is the cheapest possible way of getting round the town*

◇ **as possible**

[æz 'pɒsəbl] *(used to make a superlative)* *I want to go as far away as possible for my vacation*; *please do it as quickly as possible*; *they will need as much time as possible to finish the job*

② **possibly**
['pɒsəblɪ] *adverb*

(a) perhaps; *the meeting will possibly finish late*; *January had possibly the most snow we have ever seen*

(b) *(used with "can" or "can't" to make a phrase stronger)* *you can't possibly eat twenty-two cookies!*; *how can you possibly expect me to do all that work in one day?*

① **post**
[pəʊst]
1 *noun*

(a) long piece of wood, metal, etc., put in the ground; *the fence is attached to concrete posts*; *his shot hit the post*

(b) job; *he applied for a post in the sales department*; *we have three posts vacant*; *they advertised the post in the newspaper*

2 *verb*

(a) to send someone to another place, often overseas, to work; *he was posted to an air base in Germany*; *she has been posted overseas*

(b) to keep someone posted = to keep someone informed; *please keep us posted about your vacation arrangements*

① postage
['pəʊstɪdʒ] *noun*

money which you pay to send something by mail; *what is the postage for an airmail letter to Australia?*; **postage stamp** = piece of paper which you buy and stick on a letter, etc., to pay for it to be sent on by the postal service

② postal
['pəʊstəl] *adjective*

referring to the mail services; *postal charges are going up by 10% in September*; **postal ballot** = ballot where the votes are sent by mail

① postcard
['pəʊstkɑrd] *noun*

flat piece of card (often with a picture on one side) which you send to someone with a short message on it; *send us a postcard when you arrive in China*; *they sent me a postcard of the town where they were staying*

① poster
['pəʊstər] *noun*

large notice, picture or advertisement stuck on a wall; *they put up posters advertising the concert*; *the wall was covered with election posters*; **poster paints, poster color** = water paints in bright colors, often used by children

① post office (PO)
['pəʊst 'ɒfɪs] *noun*

building where you can buy stamps, send letters and parcels, pay bills; *the main post office is on Main Street*; *there are two parcels to be taken to the post office*; *post offices are shut on Sundays*; **Post Office box number** *or* **PO box number** = reference number given for delivering mail to a post office, so as not to give the actual address of the person who will receive it (NOTE: the official name of the post office is the U.S. Postal Service (USPS))

① postpone
[pəs'pəʊn] *verb*

to put back to a later date or time; *the meeting has been postponed until next week*; *he asked if the meeting could be postponed to tomorrow*

③ posture
['pɒstʃər] *noun*

way of sitting, standing, etc.; *she does exercises to improve her posture*

① pot
[pɒt]
1 *noun*

(a) rounded container; *the plant is too big - it needs a bigger pot*; *she made a big pot of soup*; *can we have a pot of tea for two, please?*
(b) *(informal)* **to go to pot** = to become ruined, useless; *my service has gone to pot since I stopped playing tennis regularly*
2 *verb*

to put a plant into a pot; *she potted her tomatoes* (NOTE: **potting - potted**)

① potato
[pə'teɪtəʊ] *noun*

(a) common white root vegetable which grows under the ground; *do you want any more potatoes?*; *we're having roast lamb and potatoes for Sunday lunch*; **baked potatoes** = potatoes baked with the skin left on; **boiled potatoes** = potatoes cooked in boiling water; **mashed potatoes** = potatoes which have been boiled until they are soft and are then mashed and mixed with butter and milk; **roast potatoes** = potatoes cooked in the oven with fat; **potato chips** = thin slices of potato fried until they are hard
(b) **sweet potato** = a tropical vegetable like a long red potato with sweet yellow flesh inside (NOTE: plural is **potatoes**)

④ potent
['pəʊtənt] *adjective*

(a) which has a strong effect; *people don't realize how potent these drugs are*
(b) powerful; *this is a potent argument in favour of the proposed ban*

④ potential
[pə'tenʃl]
1 *adjective*

possible; *he's a potential world champion*; *the potential profits from the deal are enormous*; **potential customers** = people who could be customers; **potential market** = market that could be exploited
2 *noun*

possibility of developing into something useful or valuable; *the discovery has enormous potential*; *she doesn't have much experience, but she has a lot of potential*; *the whole area has great potential for economic growth*

② potter
['pɒtər]
1 *noun*

person who makes pots; *the potter makes cups and bowls to sell to tourists*
2 *verb*

to potter about = not to do anything in particular, to do little jobs here and there; *he spent Saturday morning pottering about in the garden*

② pottery
['pɒtri] *noun*

(a) pots, plates, etc., made of clay; *there's a man in the market who sells local pottery*
(b) workshop or factory where pots are made; *I bought this vase from the pottery where it was made* (NOTE: plural in this meaning is **potteries**)

② pouch
[paʊtʃ] *noun*

(a) small bag for carrying coins, etc.; *she carried the ring in a small leather pouch round her neck*
(b) bag in the skin in front of animals such as kangaroos, where the young are carried; *the kangaroo carries its young in its pouch* (NOTE: plural is **pouches**)

③ **pounce**
[paʊns] *verb*

to pounce on something = to jump on something; *the cat was waiting in the bushes, ready to pounce on any bird that came by*

① **pound**
[paʊnd]
1 *noun*

(a) measure of weight (about 450 grams); *she bought a pound of onions and five pounds of carrots; the baby was tiny - she only weighed three pounds when she was born; how much is tea? - it's 75 cents a pound* (NOTE: with numbers the word **pound** can be written **lb** after the figure: **it weighs 26 lb; take 6 lb of sugar**: say "twenty-six pounds, six pounds")

(b) pound sign = the symbol # (as on a telephone)

(c) money used in Britain and several other countries; *the cheapest lunch will cost you £25 (twenty-five pounds) at that restaurant; he tried to pay for his bus ticket with a £20 note (twenty pound note)* (NOTE: with numbers **pound** is usually written **£** before figures: **£20, £6000**, etc. (say "twenty pounds, six thousand pounds"). Note also that with the words **note, money order**, etc., **pound** is singular: **twenty pounds** but **a twenty pound note, a fifty-pound traveler's check**)

(d) place where automobiles are taken when they have been parked in places where parking is forbidden; *he had to go to the police pound to get his automobile back*

2 *verb*

(a) to hit hard; *he pounded the table with his fist*

(b) to smash into little pieces; *the ship was pounded to pieces by heavy waves*

(c) to run or walk heavily; *the man pounded the pavement searching for work; he pounded up the stairs*

(d) *(of heart)* to beat fast; *her heart was pounding as she opened the door*

① **pour**
[pɔr] *verb*

(a) to make a liquid flow; *the waiter poured water all over the table; he poured the wine into the glasses; she poured water down his neck as a joke*

(b) to flow out or down; *clouds of smoke poured out of the house; there was a sudden bang and smoke poured out of the engine*

(c) to rain very hard; *it poured all afternoon; (informal)* **when it rains it pours** = troubles, problems, etc., never come one at a time, but several together

③ **pour down**
[ˈpɔr ˈdaʊn] *verb*

to rain very hard; *don't go out without an umbrella - it's pouring down*

④ **poverty**
[ˈpɒvərti] *noun*

(a) being poor; *he lost all his money and died in poverty; poverty can drive people to crime; the*

poverty line = amount of money that you need to buy the basic things to live on; *thousands of families are living below the poverty line*

(b) *(formal)* **the poverty of** = the very small amount of; *the poverty of our resources means that we are dependent on outside funds* (NOTE: no plural)

④ **POW**
[ˈpiəʊˈdʌblju]
= PRISONER OF WAR

② **powder**
[ˈpaʊdər] *noun*

1 very fine dry grains (like flour); *to grind something to powder; the drug is available in the form of a white powder*; **face powder** = scented powder for putting on your face

2 *verb*

to put powder on something; *she was powdering her cheeks*

② **power**
[paʊwər]
1 *noun*

(a) being able to control people or happenings; *he is the official leader of the party, but his wife has all the real power; I haven't the power or it isn't in my power to ban the demonstration;* **the full power of the law** = the full force of the law

(b) driving force; *they use the power of the waves to generate electricity; the engine is driven by steam power;* **wind power** = force of the wind (used to make sails go round, make a yacht go forward, etc.)

(c) (electric) power = electricity used to drive machines or devices; *turn off the power before you try to repair the TV set;* **power station** *or* **power plant** = factory where electricity is produced; *this power station burns coal; they are planning to scrap their nuclear power stations*

(d) political control; *the socialists came to power in 1997; during the period when he was in power the country's economy was ruined*

(e) important, powerful country; *China is one of the great world powers*

(f) *(in mathematics)* number of times one number is multiplied by another; *3 to the power 4* (NOTE: written 3^4)

2 *verb*

(a) to be powered by = to be driven by; *powered by two Olympic champions, the boat raced across the lake; the aircraft is powered by four jet engines*

(b) to move fast; *with its huge engine the boat powered through the water*

① **powerful**
[ˈpaʊwərfəl] *adjective*

very strong; *this model has a more powerful engine; the chairman is the most powerful person in the organization; she was swept away by the powerful current; this is the most powerful personal computer on the market*

③ **PR**
[piˈɑr] *noun*
= PUBLIC RELATIONS

④ **practical**
[ˈpræktɪkl]
1 *adjective*
(a) referring to practice and action rather than ideas; *she needs some practical experience*; *he passed the practical exam but failed the written part*; *I need some practical advice on how to build a wall*
(b) practical joke = trick played on someone to make other people laugh; *he's fond of practical jokes - once he tied a can to the back of his father's automobile*
(c) possible or sensible; *it isn't practical to attach two computers to the same lead*; *has anyone got a more practical suggestion to make?*; *we must be practical and not try anything too difficult*
2 *noun*
examination or test to show how well someone can work in practice; *she passed the written test but failed the practical*

④ **practically**
[ˈpræktɪkli] *adverb*
(a) almost; *practically all the students passed the test*; *the summer is practically over*; *his suit is such a dark gray it is practically black*
(b) in a practical way; *we must try to solve the problem practically*

② **practice**
[ˈpræktɪs]
1 *noun*
(a) actually applying something; **to put something into practice** = to apply something, to use something; *I hope soon to be able to put some of my ideas into practice*; **in practice** = when actually done; *the plan seems very interesting, but what will it cost in practice?*
(b) repeated exercise; *you need more practice before you're ready to enter the competition*; *he's at football practice this evening*; *the automobiles make several practice runs before the race*; **out of practice** = not able to do something because of not having done it recently; *I used to be able to play quite well, but I'm a bit out of practice*
(c) medical practice, dental practice, legal practice = business of a doctor, dentist, lawyer, etc.; *there are three doctors in this practice*
(d) practices = ways of doing things; *he has written a study of marriage practices on the Pacific islands*; **code of practice** = rules drawn up which people must follow when doing business
2 *verb*
(a) to do repeated exercises; *he's practicing catching and throwing*
(b) to carry on a job as a doctor or lawyer; *he's officially retired but still practices part-time*

④ **practitioner**
[prækˈtɪʃənər] *noun*
person who does a skilled job; *she's a practitioner of the ancient Japanese art of flower arranging*; *see also* GENERAL PRACTITIONER

① **prairie**
[ˈpreəri] *noun*
plains in North America, mainly without trees and covered in grass, where most of the world's grain is produced; *their family had farmed the prairie for decades*; *the road crosses the prairie, going straight for hundreds of miles*

③ **praise**
[preɪz]
1 *noun*
admiration, showing approval; *the rescue team earned the praise of the people they had saved*; **to sing the praises of someone** = to praise someone all the time; *she's always singing the praises of the new doctor*
2 *verb*
to express strong approval of something; *the mayor praised the firemen for their efforts to put out the fire*

④ **prawn**
[prɔn] *noun*
sea animal like a large shrimp; *for lunch we had grilled prawns and salad*

① **pray**
[preɪ] *verb*
(a) to speak to God, asking God for something; *farmers prayed for rain*; **to pray for someone** = to ask God to protect someone; *we pray for the children from the town, missing in the mountains*
(b) *(old)* please; **pray be seated** = please sit down

① **prayer**
[preər] *noun*
speaking to God; *she says her prayers every night before going to bed*; *they said prayers for the sick*

② **preach**
[pritʃ] *verb*
to speak in church about religious matters; *she preached to a crowded church about the need for tolerance*; **to preach to the converted** = to try to convince people of something when they already know about it; *it's a waste of time telling us about the advantages of using computers - you're just preaching to the converted*

④ **precarious**
[prɪˈkeəriəs] *adjective*
not safe, likely to fall off; *the house is in a precarious position on the edge of the cliff*; *their financial future is looking very precarious*

③ **precautions**
[prɪˈkɔʃnz] *noun*
care taken in advance to avoid something unpleasant; *the company has taken precautions*

to avoid fire in the warehouse; the restaurant did not take proper fire precautions; what safety precautions must be taken before we can open the swimming pool to the public?

④ **precede**
[prɪˈsid] *verb*
to take place before something; *a period of calm often precedes a storm; the concert was preceded by a short talk given by the musician*

③ **preceding**
[prɪˈsidɪŋ] *adjective*
which comes before; *the three weeks preceding the school play were taken up with constant rehearsals; they spent the preceding two weeks interviewing candidates*

④ **precinct**
[ˈprisɪŋkt] *noun*
administrative district in a town; *they live in the 16th precinct*

② **precious**
[ˈpreʃəs] *adjective*
(a) worth a lot of money; **precious metal** = metal, such as gold, which is worth a lot of money; **precious stones** = stones, such as diamonds, which are rare and very valuable
(b) of great value to someone; *all her precious photographs were saved from the fire; the memories of that vacation are very precious to me*
(c) very; *he earns precious little money*

④ **precipice**
[ˈpresɪpɪs] *noun*
steep side of a mountain; *she was hanging on a rope over the edge of the precipice*

④ **precise**
[prɪˈsaɪs] *adjective*
exact; *we need to know the precise measurements of the box; at that precise moment my father walked in; can you be more precise about what the men looked like?*

③ **precisely**
[prɪˈsaɪsli] *adverb*
exactly; *the train arrived at 12:00 P.M. precisely; I don't know precisely when it was, but it was about three months ago; how, precisely, do you expect me to cope with all this work?*

④ **precision**
[prɪˈsɪʒn] *noun*
accuracy; *her instructions were carried out with the greatest precision;* **precision drawing** = very accurate drawing; **precision instrument** = instrument for very accurate work

④ **preconception**
[prikənˈsepʃn] *noun*
idea which is formed in advance, without the benefit of information or experience; *I want you to forget any preconceptions you may have when you start working for us*

③ **predict**
[prɪˈdɪkt] *verb*

to tell what you think will happen in the future; *the weather forecast predicted rain; he predicted correctly that the deal would not last; everything happened exactly as I had predicted*

④ **predictable**
[prɪˈdɪktəbl] *adjective*
which could be predicted; *his reaction was totally predictable*

④ **predictably**
[prɪˈdɪktəbli] *adverb*
in a way which could have been predicted; *her reaction was predictably furious*

③ **prediction**
[prɪˈdɪkʃn] *noun*
telling what you think will happen in the future; *here are my predictions for the year 2010; most of her predictions turned out to be correct*

④ **predominant**
[prɪˈdɒmɪnənt] *adjective*
most striking or obvious; *red is the predominant colour in the design*

② **prefer**
[prɪˈfɜr] *verb*
to prefer something to something = to like (to do) something better than something else; *I prefer butter to margarine; she prefers walking to going on the subway; we went to the bar, but she preferred to stay at home and watch TV; I'd prefer not to go to New Mexico this summer* (NOTE: **preferring - preferred**)

③ **preferable**
[ˈprefrəbl] *adjective*
which you would prefer; *any exercise is preferable to sitting around doing nothing*

③ **preference**
[ˈprefrəns] *noun*
liking for one thing more than another; *the girl at the reception desk asked him if he had any preference for a room with a view; the kids all showed a marked preference for ice cream as dessert*

① **prefix**
[ˈprifɪks] *noun*
part of a word put in front of another to form a new word; *the prefix "anti-" is very common* (NOTE: plural is **prefixes;** the opposite, letters which are added at the end of a word, is a **suffix**)

③ **pregnancy**
[ˈpregnənsi] *noun*
state of being pregnant; *smoking during pregnancy can harm your child; her second pregnancy was easier than the first;* **pregnancy test** = test to see if a woman is pregnant

③ **pregnant**
[ˈpregnənt] *adjective*
(a) carrying a child inside your body before it is born; *don't carry heavy weights when you're pregnant; she hasn't told her family yet that she's pregnant; we have a pregnant girl in our class*

(b) pregnant pause = pause while everyone waits for someone to say something; *Martha's extraordinary announcement was followed by a pregnant pause*

② **prehistoric**
[prihɪˈstɒrɪk] *adjective*
referring to the time before there was a written history; *prehistoric people used sharp stones as knives*

④ **prejudice**
[ˈpredʒədɪs]
1 *noun*
feeling against someone or preference for one person or thing over another; *the committee seems to have a prejudice against women candidates*; **color prejudice** = prejudice against someone whose skin is not white; **racial prejudice** = prejudice against someone because of race; *he accused his former boss of racial prejudice; she was a victim of racial prejudice*
2 *verb*
to make someone have less friendly feelings toward someone or something; *the newspaper reports prejudiced the jury against the accused*

④ **preliminary**
[prɪˈlɪmɪnəri] *adjective*
which goes before something; *the committee will hold a preliminary meeting the day before the conference opens*; *this is only the preliminary report - the main report will be published later*

④ **premier**
[ˈpremiər]
1 *noun*
prime minister; *the French premier is visiting Canada*
2 *adjective*
first, most important; *the town advertises itself as Vermont's premier ski resort*

④ **premise**
[ˈpremɪs] *noun*
(formal) assumption, thing which you assume to be true; *her argument is based on false premises*; *he argued from the premise that all wars are evil*

④ **premises**
[ˈpremɪsɪz] *noun*
building and the land it stands on; *smoking is not allowed on the premises*; *there is a doctor on the premises at all times*; **business premises** *or* **commercial premises** = building used for commercial use; **office premises** *or* **store premises** = building which houses an office or store (NOTE: the word is plural, even if it only applies to one building)

④ **premium**
[ˈpremiəm] *noun*
(a) amount paid for an insurance policy; *the house insurance premium has to be paid this month*; *we pay a monthly premium of $10*
(b) **at a premium** = scarce, and therefore valuable; *fresh vegetables were at a premium*

during the winter months; **to put a premium on something** = to show that something is useful or valuable; *employers put a premium on staff who can speak good English*
(c) bonus; *they pay a premium for work completed ahead of schedule*; **premium offer** = offer for sale at a specially attractive price

② **preparation**
[prepəˈreɪʃn] *noun*
(a) action of getting ready; *the preparations for the wedding went on for months*; *we've completed our preparations and now we're ready to start*; **in preparation for** = to get ready for; *she bought a hat in preparation for the wedding*
(b) substance which has been mixed; *a chemical preparation*

① **prepare**
[prɪˈpeər] *verb*
(a) to get something ready; *I have some friends coming to dinner and I haven't prepared the meal*; *you'd better prepare yourself for some bad news*
(b) to get ready for something; *he is preparing for his exam*

① **prepared**
[prɪˈpeəd] *adjective*
(a) ready; *be prepared, you may get quite a shock*; *six people are coming to dinner and I've got nothing prepared*
(b) **prepared to do something** = willing to do something; *they are prepared to sell the house if necessary*; **prepared for something** = ready for something; *she wasn't really prepared for her test*; *the country is prepared for an attack*

④ **preposition**
[prepəˈzɪʃn] *noun*
word used with a noun or pronoun as its object to show place or time; *prepositions like "by" and "near" are very common, as in "he was knocked down by a motorcycle" or "she was sitting near me"*

④ **preschool**
[ˈpriskul] *noun*
school for children under the age of five; *my daughter goes to preschool in the mornings*

③ **prescribe**
[prɪˈskraɪb] *verb*
(of a doctor) to tell someone to use something; *he prescribed a course of injections*; *she prescribed some antibiotics*

② **prescription**
[prɪˈskrɪpʃn] *noun*
order written by a doctor to a pharmacist asking for a drug to be prepared and sold to a patient; *she took the prescription to the drugstore*; **available by prescription** = available from a pharmacist only when prescribed by a doctor; *this medicine is only available by prescription*

② **presence**
['prezns] *noun*
(a) being present; *the presence of both his wives in court was noted*; *your presence is requested at a meeting of the committee on June 23*; **in someone's presence** = when someone is near; *she actually said that in my presence*; *he slapped her face in the presence of witnesses*
(b) **presence of mind** = being calm and sensible, and able to act quickly; *the hotel staff showed great presence of mind in getting the guests out quickly*
(c) effect you have on other people; *the general has a commanding presence*

① **present**
1 *noun* ['prezənt]
(a) thing which you give to someone as a gift; *I got a watch as a Christmas present*; *how many birthday presents did you get?*; *the office gave her a present when she got married*
(b) the time we are in now; *the novel is set in the present*; **at present** = now; *the hotel still has some vacancies at present*; **for the present** = for now; *that will be enough for the present*
(c) form of a verb showing that the action is happening now; *the present of the verb "to go" is "he goes" or "he is going"*
2 *adjective* ['prezənt]
(a) being there when something happens; *how many people were present at the meeting?*
(b) at the time we are in now; *what is his present address?*; **present tense** = form of a verb showing that the action is happening now; *the present tense of "to stand" is "he stands" or "he is standing"*
3 *verb* [prɪ'zent]
(a) to give formally (as a present); *when he retired after thirty years, the firm presented him with a large clock*
(b) to introduce a show on TV, etc.; *she's presenting a program on gardening*
(c) **to present yourself** = to go to a place; *he was asked to present himself at the police station the next morning*

③ **presentation**
[prezən'teɪʃn] *noun*
(a) act of giving a present; *the chairman will make the presentation to the retiring sales manager*
(b) demonstration of a proposed plan; *the distribution company made a presentation of the services they could offer*

④ **present-day**
[prezənt'deɪ] *adjective*
modern; *by present-day standards his old car uses far too much gas*

③ **presently**
['prezəntlɪ] *adverb*
(a) now, at the present time; *he's presently working for a chemical company*
(b) soon; *he'll be making a speech presently*

③ **preserve**
[prɪ'zɜrv]
1 *verb*
(a) *(formal)* to look after and keep in the same state; *our committee aims to preserve the wildflowers in our area*; *the doctors' aim is to preserve the life of the child*
(b) to treat food so that it keeps for a long time; *freezing is a common method of preserving meat*
2 *noun*
(a) **nature preserve** = area of land where animals and plants are protected; *we often go to the nature preserve to watch birds*
(b) **preserves** = jams, fruit cooked for keeping, etc.; *she has a stall in the market where she sells her preserves*

④ **preside (over)**
[prɪ'zaɪd 'əʊvər] *verb*
(a) to be president or chairman of something; *she presided over the university appointments committee for several years*
(b) to be in charge when something happens; *he presided over a radical reorganization of the party's structure*

③ **presidency**
['prezɪdnsɪ] *noun*
(a) job of being president; *he has been proposed as a candidate for the presidency*
(b) time when someone is president; *during Britain's presidency of the European Union*; *the Second World War ended during the Truman presidency*

① **president**
['prezɪdənt] *noun*
(a) head of a republic; *during his term of office as president*; *the French President came to Washington on an official visit* (NOTE: usually used as a title followed by the surname: **President Wilson**)
(b) chief member of a club; *we're wondering who'll be the next president of the honor society*; *A. B. Smith was elected president of the sports club*

③ **presidential**
[prezɪ'denʃl] *adjective*
referring to a president; *the presidential residence is in the center of the city*

① **press**
[pres]
1 *noun*
(a) newspapers taken as a group; *the election wasn't reported in the American press*; *there has been no mention of the problem in the press*; **freedom of the press** = being able to write and publish in a newspaper what you want, without being afraid of prosecution unless you break the law
(b) journalists and other people who work for newspapers, or on radio and TV; *everywhere she went she was followed by the press*; *press*

photographers were standing outside the White House (NOTE: no plural in meanings (a) and (b))
(c) machine that presses; *the automobile body is formed from a metal sheet in a press*; **printing press** = machine for printing books, newspapers, etc. (NOTE: plural is **presses**)
2 *verb*
(a) to push, to squeeze, to get very close to someone; *everyone pressed around the movie stars*
(b) to push a button to call something; *press 12 for room service*; *press the top button for the sixth floor*
(c) to iron; *his jacket needs pressing*
(d) to press on *or* **to press forward** = to continue, to go ahead; *in spite of the weather they pressed on with the preparations for the county fair*

③ **press conference**
['pres 'kɒnfərəns] *noun*
meeting where newspaper, radio and TV reporters are invited to hear news of a new product, a takeover bid or to talk to a famous person; *the White House gave a press conference*

③ **pressed**
[prest] *adjective*
we're pressed for time = we are in a hurry; **I'd be hard pressed to do it** = it would be difficult for me to find time to do it

③ **pressing**
['presɪŋ] *adjective*
urgent, that needs to be done quickly; *he had to leave because of a pressing engagement in Los Angeles*

③ **press release**
['pres rɪ'liːs] *noun*
sheet giving news about something which is sent to newspapers and TV and radio stations; *the company sent out a press release about the launch of the new automobile*

② **pressure**
['preʃər] *noun*
(a) something which forces you to do something; *pressure from farmers forced the senator to change his mind*; **to put pressure on someone to do something** = to try to force someone to do something; *they put pressure on the government to build a new highway*; **under pressure** = being forced (to do something); *he did it under pressure*; *we're under pressure to agree to changes to the contract*
(b) force of something which is pushing or squeezing; *there is not enough pressure in your tires*; **blood pressure** = pressure at which the heart pumps blood; *he has to take pills for his high blood pressure*
(c) stress caused by having a lot of responsibility; *he gave up his job in the bank because he couldn't stand the pressure*

③ **pressure group**
['preʃər'gruːp] *noun*

group of people who try to influence the government, the city council, etc.; *they formed a pressure group to fight for animal welfare*

④ **prestige**
[pre'stiːʒ] *noun*
importance because of high quality, high value, etc.; *there's a lot of prestige attached to working for the State Department*

④ **prestigious**
[pre'stɪdʒəs] *adjective*
which makes you seem very important; *they are based at a prestigious address in Park Lane*

④ **presumably**
[prɪ'zjuːməbli] *adverb*
probably; as you think is true; *presumably this is what she wanted us to do*; *they've presumably forgotten the date of the meeting*

③ **presume**
[prɪ'zjuːm] *verb*
(a) to suppose, to assume; *I presume this little bridge is safe for automobiles?*; *the jury has to presume he is innocent until he is proved guilty*; *she is presumed to have fled to South America*
(b) *(formal)* **not to presume to do something** = not to do something because it would be rude to do it; *I wouldn't presume to contradict her - she's the expert*

② **pretend**
[prɪ'tend] *verb*
to make someone believe you are something else, so as to trick them; *he got into the house by pretending to be a telephone engineer*; *she pretended she had the flu and phoned to say she was taking the day off*

① **pretty**
['prɪti]
1 *adjective*
pleasant to look at; *her daughters are very pretty*; *she is prettier than her mother*; *what a pretty little house!* (NOTE: **prettier** - **prettiest**. Note also that **pretty** is used of things or girls, but not of boys or men)
2 *adverb*
(informal) quite; *the patient's condition is pretty much the same as it was yesterday*; *I'm pretty sure I'm right*; *you did pretty well, considering it's was the first time you had played billiards*

④ **prevalent**
['prevələnt] *adjective*
common, occurring frequently; *the disease is prevalent in some African countries*

① **prevent**
[prɪ'vent] *verb*
(a) to stop something happening; *we must try to prevent any more flooding*
(b) to prevent someone from doing something = to stop someone doing something; *we can't do much to prevent the river from flooding*; *the police prevented anyone from leaving the building*

③ **previous**
['priviəs]
1 *adjective*
former, earlier; *the letter was sent to my previous address*; *the group of workers arrived the previous night and started work first thing in the morning*; *I had spent the previous day getting to know my way around the town*; *he could not accept the invitation because he had a previous engagement* = because he had earlier accepted another invitation to go somewhere
2 *adverb*
previous to = before; *what job were you in, previous to this one?*

① **previously**
['priviəsli] *adverb*
before; *this is my first visit to Chicago by car - previously I've always gone by plane*; *the arrangements had been made six weeks previously*; *at that time they were living in New York, and previously had lived in Chicago*

③ **prey**
[preɪ]
1 *noun*
animal eaten by another animal; *mice and small birds are the favorite prey of owls*; **birds of prey** = birds that eat other birds or small animals (NOTE: no plural)
2 *verb*
(a) to prey on *or* **upon** = to attack animals and eat them; *lions mainly prey on deer and zebra*
(b) something is preying on her *or* **on her mind** = something is worrying her (NOTE: do not confuse with **pray**)

① **price**
[praɪs]
1 *noun*
money that you have to pay to buy something; *the price of gas is going up*; *I don't want to pay such a high price for a hotel room*; *there has been a sharp increase in house prices during the first six months of the year*; **net price** = price that cannot be reduced by a discount; **retail price** = price at which the storekeeper sells to a customer; **price list** = sheet giving prices of goods for sale; **price war** = sales battle between companies, where each lowers prices to get more customers; **to increase in price** = to become more expensive
2 *verb*
to give something a price; *the book is priced at $15.95*; *that house won't sell - it is too highly priced*; **the company has priced itself out of the market** = the company has raised its prices so high that its products do not sell

④ **priceless**
['praɪsləs] *adjective*
extremely valuable; *his priceless collection of paintings was destroyed in the fire*

③ **price tag**
['praɪs 'tæg] *noun*

(a) ticket with a price written on it; *how much is this shirt? - the price tag has come off it*
(b) price at which something is for sale; *automobile with a $75,000 price tag*

④ **prickle**
['prɪkl] *noun*
sharp point on a plant or animal; *be careful of the prickles when you're picking blackberries*

② **pride**
[praɪd]
1 *noun*
(a) pleasure in your own ability or possessions; *he takes great pride in his garden*
(b) very high opinion of yourself; *his pride would not let him admit that he had made a mistake*
2 *verb*
to pride yourself on = to be extremely proud of; *she prides herself on her cookies*

③ **priest**
[prist] *noun*
person who has been blessed to serve God, to carry out formal religious duties, etc.; *they were married by the local priest*

③ **primarily**
['praɪmrəli] *adverb*
mainly, mostly; *this is primarily a business trip*; *we're examining primarily the financial aspects of the case*

① **primary**
['praɪməri]
1 *adjective*
main, basic; *our primary concern is the safety of our passengers*; **primary colors** = basic colors (red, yellow and blue) which can combine to make up all the other colors; **primary election** = first election to choose a candidate to represent a political party in a main election; *a candidate who does not win the primary election in his own state is certain to fail in the national vote*
2 *noun*
primary election; *he won the New Hampshire primary* (NOTE: plural is **primaries**)

③ **prime**
[praɪm]
1 *adjective*
(a) most important; *the prime suspect in the case is the dead woman's husband*; *she is a prime target for any kidnap gang*; *this is a prime example of what is wrong with this country*; **prime position** *or* **prime site** = good position for a commercial property; *the restaurant is in a prime position on Main Street*; **prime-time television** = TV programs shown at the time when most people watch television; *the interview is being shown on prime-time TV*
(b) of best quality; *prime Argentinian beef*
(c) **prime number** = number (such as 2, 5, 11, etc.) which can only be divided by itself or by 1
2 *noun*

period when you are at your best; *he was at his prime when he won the championship*; *past your prime* = no longer at your best; *at 35, she's past her prime as a tennis player*

3 *verb*

(a) to give wood or metal a first coat of special paint, before giving the top coat; *the paint is coming off because the wood hadn't been primed properly*

(b) to get something prepared; *the bomb had been primed and would have exploded in ten minutes*

(c) to put water into a water pump or oil into a machine, so as to start it working

(d) **to prime someone to do something** = to prepare someone in advance by giving information, advice, etc.; *she came primed with a few questions which would embarrass the speaker*

④ **prime minister (PM)**
['praɪm 'mɪnɪstər] *noun*
head of the government in Britain and other countries; *the Australian prime minister or the prime minister of Australia*; *she cut out the picture of the prime minister from the newspaper*; *the prime minister will address the nation at 6 o'clock tonight*

③ **primitive**
['prɪmɪtɪv] *adjective*
(a) referring to very early times; *a primitive people who flourished in the Stone Age*
(b) rough, crude; *they live in a primitive hut in the woods*; *our accounts system is a bit primitive but it works*

④ **primrose**
['prɪmrəʊz] *noun*
small pale yellow spring flower; *primroses flower in early spring*

① **prince**
[prɪns] *noun*
son of a king or queen (NOTE: used as a title with a name: **Prince Edward**)

① **princess**
[prɪn'ses] *noun*
(a) daughter of a king or queen; *once upon a time a beautiful princess lived in a castle by the edge of the forest*
(b) wife of a prince (NOTE: used as a title with a name: **Princess Sophia**; note also that the plural is **princesses**)

② **principal**
['prɪnsɪpl]
1 *adjective*
main, most important; *the country's principal products are paper and wood*; *she played a principal role in setting up the organization*
2 *noun*
(a) head of an elementary school or high school; *the principal wants to see you in her office*
(b) main performer (actor, dancer, singer, etc.); *the principals were quite good but the rest of the dancers were awful*

(c) money on which interest is paid, capital which has been invested; *up to now you've been paying interest, but now you can start repaying some of the principal* (NOTE: do not confuse with **principle**)

④ **principle**
['prɪnsɪpl] *noun*
(a) law; general rule; *the principles of nuclear physics*; *it is a principle in our system of justice that a person is innocent until he is proved guilty*; **in principle** = in agreement with the general rule; *I agree in principle, but we need to discuss some of the details very carefully*; *in principle, the results should be the same every time you do the experiment*
(b) personal sense of what is right; *she's a woman of very strong principles*; *it's against my principles to work on a Sunday*; **on principle** = because of what you believe; *she refuses to eat meat on principle* (NOTE: do not confuse with **principal**)

① **print**
[prɪnt]
1 *noun*
(a) letters printed on a page; *I can't read this book - the print is too small*; **the small print** *or* **the fine print** = the conditions on a contract, usually printed in very small letters; *don't forget to check the small print before you sign the contract*
(b) mark made on something; *the print of an animal's foot has been preserved in this rock*; *the police examined the tire prints left by the vehicle*
(c) picture or photograph that has been printed; *the print is very blurred*; *I'm going to have some more prints made of this photo*
2 *verb*
(a) to mark letters or pictures on paper by a machine, and so produce a book, poster, newspaper, etc.; *the book is printed directly from a computer disk*; *we had five hundred copies of the leaflet printed*
(b) to write capital letters or letters which are not joined together; *print your name in the space below*

③ **printed**
['prɪntɪd] *adjective*
produced on paper using a printing press; **printed matter** = paper with printing on it, such as posters, books, newspapers, magazines, etc.; *printed matter can be sent through the mail at a lower rate*; **printed word** = information in a printed form; *people rely more on television and radio for news and less on the printed word*

③ **printer**
['prɪntər] *noun*
(a) person or company that prints books, newspapers, etc.; *the book has gone to the printer, and we should have copies next week*
(b) machine that prints; **laser printer** = office printing machine that prints using a laser beam

③ **print out**
['prɪnt 'aʊt] *verb*
to print information from a computer through a printer; *she printed out three copies of the letter*

④ **printout**
['prɪntaʊt] *noun*
printed information from a computer; *the travel agent gave me a printout of flight details and hotel reservations*

④ **prior**
['praɪər] *adjective*
(a) before; previous; *the house can be visited by prior arrangement with the owner*; *I had to refuse her invitation because I had a prior engagement in Vancouver*; **without prior agreement** = without any agreement in advance
(b) *(formal)* **prior to** = before; *they had left prior to my arrival*

④ **priority**
[praɪ'ɒrɪti] *noun*
(a) right to be first; **to have priority over** *or* **to take priority over something** = to be more important than something, to need to be done first; *people with serious injuries have priority over those with only minor cuts*; **to give something top priority** = to make something the most important item; *we should give top priority to solving our financial problems*; *the president wants us to give the problem top priority*
(b) thing which has to be done first; *finding somewhere to stay the night was our main priority*

① **prison**
['prɪzn] *noun*
building where people are kept when they are being punished for a crime; *the judge sent him to prison for five years*; *his father's in prison for theft*; *the criminals managed to escape from prison by digging a tunnel* (NOTE: **prison** is often used without the article **the**)

② **prisoner**
['prɪznər] *noun*
person who is in prison; *the prisoners were taken away in a police van*; **prisoner of war (POW)** = member of the armed forces captured by the enemy in time of war

③ **privacy**
['prɪvəsi] *noun*
not being disturbed by other people; *she read the letter in the privacy of her bedroom*

② **private**
['praɪvət]
1 *adjective*
(a) which belongs to one person, not to everyone; *he flew there in his private jet*; *(informal)* **private investigator** = a detective who is not a member of the police force and is employed by an ordinary person; **private property** = property that belongs to a private person, not to the public; *you can't park here - this is private property*; **the private sector** = companies that are listed on the stock exchange

or owned by individuals, and not by the government; *the research is financed by money from the private sector*; **private showing** = viewing of an exhibition, etc., to specially invited guests, before it is open to the public; *we've been invited to a private showing of her latest exhibition*
(b) which refers to one particular person and should kept secret from others; *you have no right to interfere in my private affairs*; *this is a private discussion between me and my son*; **in private** = away from other people; *she asked to see the teacher in private*
2 *noun*
ordinary soldier of the lowest rank (NOTE: can be used with the surname: **Private Jones**)

③ **privilege**
['prɪvɪlɪdʒ] *noun*
favor or right granted to some people but not to everyone; *it is a great privilege being asked to speak to you tonight*; *I once had the privilege of meeting the Pope*

③ **privileged**
['prɪvɪlɪdʒd] *adjective*
who has a special advantage; *you must think yourselves privileged to have her as your colleague*; *only a privileged few will be able to see the exhibition*

① **prize**
[praɪz]
1 *noun*
something given to a winner; *he won first prize in the music competition*; *he answered all the questions correctly and claimed the prize*; *the prize was awarded to the young Russian competitors*; **prize money** = money given to the person who wins a competition; *there is $15,000 in prize money at stake*
2 *adjective*
which has won a prize because of being of good quality; *he showed a prize sheep at the agricultural show*
3 *verb*
to value something highly; *I prize his friendship particularly*

④ **probable**
['prɒbəbl] *adjective*
likely; *it's probable that she left her bag on the train*; *the police think it is probable that she knew her murderer*

③ **probably**
['prɒbəbli] *adverb*
likely to happen; *we're probably going to Nebraska for our vacation*; *my father is probably going to retire next year*; *are you going to Jamaica as usual this year? - probably*

② **problem**
['prɒbləm] *noun*
(a) something which is difficult to answer; *half the students couldn't do all the problems on the math test*; **to pose a problem** = to be a difficult question; *what to do with illegal immigrants*

poses a problem for the immigration services; **to solve a problem** = to find an answer to a problem; *the police are trying to solve the problem of how the thieves got into the house*; *we have called in an expert to solve our computer problem*
(b) no problem! = don't worry, it isn't difficult

④ **procedure**
['prə'sidʒər] *noun*
(a) way in which something ought to be carried out; *to obtain permission to build a new house you need to follow the correct procedure*
(b) medical treatment; *a new procedure for treating cases of drug addiction*

② **proceed**
[prə'sid] *verb*
(a) to go further; *he proceeded down Main Street toward the river*
(b) to do something after something else; *the students then proceeded to shout and throw bottles at passing cars*
(c) to proceed with something = to go on doing something; *shall we proceed with the committee meeting?*

③ **proceed against**
[prə'sid ə'geinst] *verb*
to start a lawsuit against someone; *the police can't proceed against her without more evidence*

④ **proceedings**
[prə'sidiŋz] *noun*
(a) legal proceedings = lawsuit or legal action; *if payment is not made within two days, we shall start proceedings against you*; *the proceedings are expected to last three days*
(b) report of what takes place at a meeting; *the proceedings of the Historical Society*

③ **proceeds**
['prəusidz] *noun*
money that you receive when you sell something; *she sold her house and invested the proceeds in a little store*; *all the proceeds of the bake sale go to charity*

③ **process**
['prəuses]
1 *noun*
(a) method of making something; *a new process for extracting oil from coal*; *see also* PEACE (NOTE: plural is **processes**)
(b) in the process of doing something = while doing something; *she interrupted me while I was in the process of writing my report*; *we were in the process of moving to Vermont when I had the offer of a job in Australia*
2 *verb*
(a) to manufacture goods from raw materials; *the iron is processed to make steel*; **processed cheese** = cheese that has been treated so that it will keep for a long time
(b) to deal with a claim, bill, etc., in the usual routine way; *to process an insurance claim*; *orders are processed in our warehouse*

(c) to sort out information, especially using a computer; *the computer processes the data and then prints it out*

④ **processing**
['prəusesiŋ] *noun*
data processing *or* **information processing** = selecting and examining data in a computer to produce information in a special form; **word processing** *or* **text processing** = working with words, using a computer to produce, check and print letters, texts, reports, etc.; *she did a course in word processing before taking a job as a secretary*; *what word processing software do you use?*; *the word processing package is bundled with the computer*

④ **procession**
[prə'seʃn] *noun*
group of people (with a band, etc.) walking in line; *he carried the little boy on his shoulders so that he could see the procession*; *the funeral procession will arrive at the church at 11:00*; **in procession** = in a line as part of a ceremony; *the people who have received their degrees will walk in procession through the university grounds*

④ **processor**
['prəusesər] *noun*
(a) machine that processes; *mix the ingredients in a food processor*
(b) computer that processes information; **word processor** = computer that is used for working with words, to produce texts, reports, letters, etc.; *she offered to write the letter for me on her word processor*

② **produce**
1 *noun* ['prɒdjus]
things grown on the land; *vegetables and other garden produce* (NOTE: do not confuse with **product**)
2 *verb* [prə'djus]
(a) to show or bring out; *the tax office asked him to produce the relevant documents*; *he produced a pile of notes from his inside pocket*
(b) to make; *the factory produces automobiles and trucks*
(c) to put on a play, a movie, etc.; *she is producing "Hamlet" for the local drama club*
(d) to grow crops, to give birth to young, etc.; *the region produces enough rice to supply the needs of the whole country*; *our cat has produced six kittens*

④ **producer**
[prə'djusər] *noun*
(a) company or country that makes or grows something; *an important producer of steel*; *the company is a major automobile producer*
(b) person who puts on a play or a movie; *she's the producer of the play now showing at the local theater*; *the producers weren't happy with the director's choice of cast*

COMMENT: a producer of a movie is the person who has general control of the making of the movie, especially of its finances, but does not deal with the technical details. The director organizes the actual making of the movie, giving instructions to the actors, dealing with the lighting, sound, etc.

② **product**
['prɒdʌkt] *noun*
(a) thing which is manufactured or made; *Germany is helping her industry to sell more products abroad*; *how did you come to learn about our product?*; **dairy products** = milk, butter, cream, etc. (NOTE: do not confuse with **produce**)
(b) **gross domestic product (GDP)** = annual value of goods sold and services paid for inside a country; **gross national product (GNP)** = annual value of goods and services in a country, including income from other countries
(c) *(in mathematics)* number that is the result when numbers are multiplied; *the product of 4 times 10 is 40*

③ **production**
[prə'dʌkʃn] *noun*
(a) manufacturing; *we are trying to step up production*; *production will probably be held up by the strike*
(b) putting on a play or movie; *the movie is currently in production in Hollywood*
(c) particular version of a play; *have you seen the production of "Henry V" at the Lincoln Center?*
(d) showing something; **on production of** = when something is shown; *goods bought can be exchanged only on production of the sales slip*

③ **productive**
[prə'dʌktɪv] *adjective*
which produces; *they own some very productive farmland*; *how can we make our workforce more productive?*; **productive meeting** = a useful meeting which should lead to an agreement; *we had a very productive morning - all the remaining problems were ironed out*

④ **productivity**
[prɒdʌk'tɪvɪti] *noun*
rate of output, rate of production in a factory; *bonus payments are linked to productivity*; *productivity has fallen since the company was taken over*; **productivity bonus** = bonus paid for increased rate of production

② **profession**
[prə'feʃn] *noun*
(a) work that needs special training, skill or knowledge; *the legal profession*; *the medical profession*; *the teaching profession*; *she is an accountant by profession*
(b) declaration of belief in something; *a profession of faith*

② **professional**
[prə'feʃnəl]
1 *adjective*
(a) referring to a profession; *he keeps his professional life and his private life completely separate*; **professional qualifications** = documents showing that someone has successfully finished a course of study which allows him to work in one of the professions; *he got a job as an accountant even though he had no professional qualifications*
(b) expert or skilled; *they did a very professional job in designing the new office*
(c) *(sportsman)* who is paid to play; *a professional football player*
2 *noun*
(a) expert; *don't try to deal with the problem yourself - get a professional*
(b) sportsman who is paid to play; *for many years, professionals were not allowed to compete in the Olympics; he ran as an amateur for several years, then turned professional*
(c) sportsman who coaches others; *a golf professional*

② **professor**
[prə'fesər] *noun*
(a) most senior teacher in a subject at a university; *a professor of English*; *an economics professor*
(b) title taken by some teachers of music, art, etc.; *she goes to Professor Smith for piano lessons* (NOTE: **professor** is written with a capital letter when used as a title: **Professor Smith**)

③ **profile**
['prəʊfaɪl] *noun*
(a) view of someone's head, seen from the side; *a photograph showing her in profile*
(b) **to keep a low profile** = to be quiet, not to be obvious; *it would be better if you kept a low profile until all the fuss has died down*; **to keep** *or* **maintain a high profile** = to keep yourself in the view of the public; *a politician needs to keep a high profile*; *advertising helps to maintain the company's profile*
(c) short biography of a famous person in a newspaper; *there's a profile of the politician in the Sunday paper*

② **profit**
['prɒfit]
1 *noun*
money you gain from selling something which is more than the money you paid for it; *the sale produced a good profit or a handsome profit*; **gross profit** = profit calculated as income from sales less the cost of the goods sold (i.e., without deducting any other expenses); **net profit** = profit calculated as income from sales less all expenditures; **profit and loss account** = statement of company expenditures and income over a period of time, showing whether the company has made a profit or loss; **profit margin** = percentage of money gained against

money paid out; **to make a profit** = to have more money as a result of a deal; *we aim to make a quick profit*; *we made a large profit when we sold our house*; *it you don't make a profit you will soon be out of business*; **to show a profit** = to make a profit and put it in the company accounts; *we are showing a small profit for the first quarter*; **profit sharing** = workers who share in the profits of a company

2 *verb*

to profit from = to gain from; *I profited from her advice*

③ **profitable**
['prɒfitəbl] *adjective*
likely to produce a profit; *he signed a profitable deal with a Polish company*; *I am sure he will find a profitable use for his talents as a salesman*

④ **profound**
[prə'faund] *adjective*
very serious, very deep; *he showed a profound understanding of the problems of the unemployed*; *we gave profound thanks for our rescue*

④ **profoundly**
[prə'faundli] *adverb*
very seriously, completely; *we were profoundly shocked by the pictures on TV*

① **program**
['prəugrəm]
1 *noun*
(a) TV or radio show; *we watched a program on life in the 17th century*; *there's a sports program after the news*; *I want to listen to the program at 9:15*; *there are no good TV programs tonight*
(b) paper in a theater or at a football game, etc., which gives information about the show; *the program gives a list of the actors*; *the performance's program costs $8*
(c) instructions given to a computer; *to load a program*; *to run a program*; *a graphics program*; *a text editing program*
2 *verb*
(a) to give instructions to a computer; *the computer is programmed to print labels*; **programming language** = system of signs and words used to program a computer
(b) to arrange programs on TV or radio; *the new chat show is programmed to compete with the news on the other channel* (NOTE: **programming - programmed**)

② **progress**
1 *noun* ['prəugres]
(a) movement forward; *we are making good progress toward finishing the house* (NOTE: no plural)
(b) in progress = which is happening or being done; *the meeting is still in progress*; *we still have a lot of work in progress*
2 *verb* [prə'gres]

to advance; *work on the new road is progressing slowly*

④ **progressive**
[prə'gresɪv] *adjective*
(a) (movement) in stages; *I have noticed a progressive improvement in your work*
(b) advanced (ideas); *they elected a leader with progressive views on education*

③ **prohibit**
[prə'hɪbɪt] *verb*
to say that something must not be done; *the rules prohibit singing in the dining room*

③ **project**
1 ['prɒdʒekt] *noun*
(a) plan, scheme; *we are working on a building project*; **housing project** = group of publicly funded houses and apartments, usually for people with low incomes; *planning permission has been given for several new housing projects in the south side of Chicago*
(b) work planned by students on their own; *her project is to write the history of her town*; *she asked her teacher for some help with her project*
2 [prə'dʒekt] *verb*
(a) to plan something, to expect to do something; *they are projecting to build a new science park near the university*
(b) to send a picture onto a screen; *the lecturer projected slides of his visit to Africa*

④ **projection**
[prə'dʒekʃn] *noun*
(a) calculation of something which is forecast for the future; *we have made a projection of the additional housing needed in this area by the year 2010*; *computer projections forecast an easy win for the government*
(b) *(formal)* thing which sticks out; *she cut her arm on a sharp projection of rock*
(c) action of sending a picture onto a screen; **projection room** = room in a cinema, with the projector, where the film is sent onto the screen

② **projector**
[prə'dʒektər] *noun*
machine which sends pictures onto a screen; *the projector broke down so we couldn't see the end of the film*

④ **prolonged**
[prə'lɒŋd] *adjective*
lasting for a long time; *his prolonged absence worried his family*; *she died after a prolonged illness*

② **prom**
[prɒm] *noun*
formal dance held for a high school class, often held at the end of the school year; *my daughter wants a new dress for her high school prom*

④ **prominent**
['prɒmɪnənt] *adjective*
(a) standing out, easily seen; *she has a very prominent nose*

(b) famous or important; *a prominent labor union leader*; *terrorists shot a prominent member of the ruling party*

① **promise**
['prɒmɪs]
1 *noun*
(a) act of saying that you will definitely do something; *but you made a promise not to tell anyone else and now you've told my mother!*; *I'll pay you back on Friday - that's a promise*; **to go back on a promise** *or* **to break a promise** = not to do what you said you would do; *the management went back on its promise to increase salaries*; *he broke his promise to take her to Mexico for vacation*; **to keep a promise** = to do what you said you would do; *he says he will pay next week, but he never keeps his promises*; *she kept her promise to write to him every day*
(b) to show promise = to make people feel that you will do well in the future; *this year's students certainly show promise*
2 *verb*
(a) to give your word that you will definitely do something; *they promised to be back for supper*; *you must promise to bring the computer back when you have finished with it*; *he promised he would look into the problem*; *she promised the staff an extra week's vacation but they never got it*
(b) to look as if something will happen; *the meeting promises to be very interesting*

④ **promising**
['prɒmɪsɪŋ] *adjective*
(a) who is likely to succeed; *she's the most promising candidate we have interviewed so far*
(b) good, and likely to become much better; *the results of the antibiotic have been very promising*; *the economic situation looks much more promising than it did a year ago*

② **promote**
[prə'məʊt] *verb*
(a) to give someone a better job; *he was promoted from salesman to sales manager*
(b) to make sure that people know about a product or service, by advertising it; *there are posters all over the place promoting the new supermarket*
(c) to encourage; *the club's aim is to promote gardening*

③ **promotion**
[prə'məʊʃn] *noun*
(a) move to a better job; *he ruined his chances of promotion when he argued with the boss*
(b) advertising of a new product; *we're giving away small bottles of shampoo as a promotion*

③ **prompt**
[prɒmpt]
1 *adjective*
done immediately; *thank you for your prompt reply* (NOTE: **prompter - promptest**)
2 *verb*

(a) to suggest to someone that he should do something; *it prompted him to write to the local paper*
(b) to tell an actor words which he has forgotten; *he had to be prompted in the middle of a long speech*
3 *noun*
message to a computer user, telling him to do something; *the prompt came up on the screen telling me to insert the disk in drive A*

③ **promptly**
['prɒmptlɪ] *adverb*
immediately; rapidly; *he replied to my letter very promptly*

④ **prone**
[prəʊn] *adjective*
(a) prone to = likely to do something, likely to suffer from something; *when you're tired you are prone to make mistakes*; *he's prone to chest infections*; **accident-prone** = likely to have accidents often; *the new waitress seems to be accident-prone*
(b) (lying) flat; *they found her lying prone on the floor*

② **pronoun**
['prəʊnaʊn] *noun*
word used instead of a noun, such as "I", "you", "he", "she" and "it"; *there are three pronouns in the sentence "she gave it to me"*

③ **pronounce**
[prə'naʊns] *verb*
(a) to speak sounds which form a word; *how do you pronounce "Paris" in French?*
(b) to state officially; *he was pronounced dead on arrival at the hospital*; *the priest pronounced them man and wife*

③ **pronunciation**
[prənʌnsɪ'eɪʃn] *noun*
way of speaking words; *what's the correct pronunciation of "controversy"?*; *you should try to improve your pronunciation by taking lessons from native speakers*

① **proof**
[pruf]
1 *noun*
(a) thing which proves or which shows that something is true; *the police have no proof that he committed the murder*; **proof of identity** = proof in the form of a document, such as a driver's license, that a person is who he or she claims to be; *the police asked her for proof of identity*
(b) sheet with text or pictures printed on it, for the publisher, author or designer to look at and make corrections; *she has a pile of proofs to check*; *he was looking at the first proofs of his latest cartoon*
2 *adjective*
proof against = safe from, not affected by; *after it has been treated, the wood is proof against insects and rot*; *no one was proof against her charms*

③ **prop**
[prɒp]
1 *noun*
support, something which holds something up; *I used a piece of wood as a prop to keep the window open*
2 *verb*
to support; *he propped up the table with a pile of books; she propped the door open with a brick* (NOTE: **propping - propped**)

③ **propaganda**
[prɒpə'gændə] *noun*
spreading of (usually false) information about something which you want the public to believe; *they conducted a propaganda campaign against the mayor*

③ **proper**
['prɒpər] *adjective*
right and correct; *she didn't put the sugar back into its proper place in the cupboard; this is the proper way to use a knife and fork; the package wasn't delivered because it didn't have the proper address*

④ **properly**
['prɒpərli] *adverb*
correctly; *the accident happened because the garage hadn't fitted the tire properly; the package wasn't properly addressed*

③ **proper noun**
['prɒpər 'naʊn] *noun*
noun which is the name of a person, a country, the title of a book, movie, etc.; *most proper nouns begin with a capital letter*

② **property**
['prɒpərti] *noun*
(a) thing that belongs to someone; *the furniture is the property of the landlord; the hotel guests lost all their property in the fire; the management is not responsible for property left in the restaurant*
(b) buildings and land; *the family owns property in Tennessee; a lot of industrial property was damaged in the war;* **commercial property** = buildings used as offices or stores
(c) a building; *we have several downtown properties for sale* (NOTE: no plural for meanings (a) and (b); plural for (c) is **properties**)

④ **prophetic**
[prə'fetɪk] *adjective*
which says what will happen in the future; *his speech proved to be prophetic*

④ **proportion**
[prə'pɔrʃn] *noun*
(a) part of a whole; *only a small proportion of his income comes from his TV appearances*
(b) relationship between the amount of something and the amount of something else; *mix equal proportions of sugar and flour; what is the proportion of men to women on the committee?*
(c) in proportion to = showing how something is related to something else; *our sales in Europe are tiny in proportion to those in the U.S.A.; the payment is very high in proportion to the time worked;* **out of proportion** = not in a proper relationship; *his salary is totally out of proportion to the work he does*
(d) proportions = the relative height, length of a building, picture, etc.; *they proposed building a library of huge proportions; the picture looks odd, the artist seems to have got the proportions of the people wrong*

③ **proposal**
[prə'pəʊzl] *noun*
(a) suggestion, plan which has been suggested; *the committee made a proposal to rebuild the clubhouse; his proposal was accepted by the committee; she put forward a proposal but it was rejected*
(b) proposal (of marriage) = asking someone to marry you; *she thought he liked her, but she didn't expect a proposal*

② **propose**
[prə'pəʊz] *verb*
(a) to suggest, to make a suggestion; *I propose that we all go for a swim*
(b) to propose to do something = to say that you intend to do something; *they propose to repay the loan at $30 a month*
(c) to propose to someone = to ask someone to marry you; *he proposed to me in a restaurant*

② **proposed**
[prə'pəʊzd] *adjective*
which has been suggested; *the proposed route of the freeway*

③ **proposition**
[prɒpə'zɪʃn] *noun*
(a) thing which has been proposed; *their proposition is not very attractive;* **it will never be a commercial proposition** = it is not likely to make a profit
(b) tough proposition = problem that is difficult to solve

④ **prose**
[prəʊz] *noun*
writing which is not poetry; *his letters are examples of classical English prose*

④ **prosecute**
['prɒsɪkjut] *verb*
to bring someone to court to answer a criminal charge; *he was prosecuted for a traffic offense; people found stealing from the store will be prosecuted*

④ **prosecution**
[prɒsɪ'kjuʃn] *noun*
(a) bringing someone to court to answer a charge; *he faces prosecution for fraud*
(b) lawyers who represent the party who brings a charge against someone; *the costs of the case will be borne by the prosecution; the prosecution argued that the money had been stolen;* **prosecution counsel** *or* **counsel for the prosecution** = lawyer acting for the prosecution (NOTE: the opposing side in a court is the **defense**)

④ **prosecutor**
['prɒsɪkjutər] *noun*
lawyer who prosecutes; *it was the prosecutor's turn to question the witness*; **public prosecutor** = government lawyer who brings charges against a criminal in a law court on behalf of the state

③ **prospect**
1 *noun* ['prɒspekt]
(a) future possibility; *there is no prospect of getting her to change her mind; faced with the grim prospect of two weeks at home he decided to go on vacation*; **to have something in prospect** = to expect something to happen
(b) prospects = future possibilities in a job; *his prospects are very good; what are her job prospects?; he's very gloomy about his job prospects*
2 *verb* [prə'spekt]
to search for minerals; *the team went into the desert to prospect for oil*

④ **prospective**
[prə'spektɪv] *adjective*
who may do something in the future; *he's been nominated as a prospective candidate for the school board*; **prospective buyer** = someone who may buy in the future; *there is no shortage of prospective buyers for the house - I'm sure we'll sell it easily*

④ **prosperity**
[prɒs'periti] *noun*
being rich; *they owe their prosperity to the discovery of oil on their land*; **in times of prosperity** = when people are rich (NOTE: no plural)

④ **prosperous**
['prɒspərəs] *adjective*
wealthy, rich; *it's a very prosperous town*

① **protect**
[prə'tekt] *verb*
to keep someone or something safe from dirt, germs, etc.; *the cover protects the machine against dust; the vaccine is supposed to protect you against the flu*

① **protection**
[prə'tekʃn] *noun*
shelter, being protected; *the trees give some protection from the rain; the legislation offers no protection to part-time workers; the injection gives some protection against the flu*; **police protection** = being protected by the police

③ **protective**
[prə'tektɪv] *adjective*
who or which protects; *visitors to the factory must wear protective clothing; she's very protective toward her little brother; he put a protective arm around her*

③ **protein**
['prəutin] *noun*
compound which is an essential part of living cells, one of the elements in food which you need to keep your body working properly; *the doctor told her she needed more protein in her diet*

COMMENT: meat, eggs, soy beans and fish contain a lot of protein. Compare with carbohydrates, which provide the body with energy

③ **protest**
1 *noun* ['prəutest]
(a) statement that you object or disapprove of something; *the new highway went ahead despite the protests of the local people; she resigned as a protest against the change in government policy*; **protest march** = march through streets to show that you protest something; *we're organizing a protest march to the town hall*
(b) in protest of = showing that you do not approve of something; *the staff occupied the offices in protest of their low pay*; **to do something under protest** = to do something, but say that you do not approve of it
2 *verb* [prə'test]
(a) to protest something = to say that you do not approve of something, to raise a violent objection to; *everyone has protested the increase in bus fares*
(b) to insist that something is true, when others think it isn't; *she went to prison still protesting her innocence*

③ **Protestant**
['prɒtestənt]
1 *adjective*
referring to the Christian Church which separated from the Catholic Church in the 16th century; *the Church of England is a Protestant Church*
2 *noun*
member of a Christian Church which separated from the Catholic Church in the 16th century

③ **protester**
[prə'testər] *noun*
person who protests; *several protesters lay down in the street and were arrested*

③ **proud**
[praud] *adjective*
(a) proud of something = full of pride about something; *you must be very proud of your children; he is proud to have served in the navy*
(b) *(informal)* **to do someone proud** = to do well by someone; *the restaurant did us proud*; **to do yourself proud** = to give yourself an expensive treat?; *he did himself proud and bought himself a bottle of wine* (NOTE: **prouder - proudest**)

④ **proudly**
['praudli] *adverb*
with pride; *she proudly showed me her new automobile*

prove
[pruv] *verb*
(a) to show that something is true; *the police think he stole the car but they can't prove it*; *I was determined to prove him wrong or to prove that he was wrong*
(b) to prove to be something = to actually be something when it happens; *the weather for the weekend proved to be even hotter than was expected*; *it's proving very difficult to persuade him to sell his house*

provide
[prə'vaɪd] *verb*
to supply; *medical help was provided by the Red Cross*; *our hosts provided us with an automobile and driver*

provided (that) *or* **providing**
[prə'vaɪdɪd ðæt or prə'vaɪdɪŋ] *conjunction*
on condition that; as long as, so long as; *it's nice to go on a picnic provided it doesn't rain*; *you can all come to watch the rehearsal providing you don't interrupt*

provide for
[prə'vaɪd 'fɔr] *verb*
(a) to provide for someone = to give enough money to buy food and clothes for someone; *he earns very little and finds it difficult to provide for a family of six children*; *will your family be provided for when you die?*
(b) to provide for something = to allow for something which may happen in the future; *the lease provides for an annual increase in the rent*

province
['prɒvɪns] *noun*
(a) large administrative division of a country; *the provinces of Canada*
(b) the provinces = parts of a country away from the capital; *there are fewer stores in the provinces than in the capital*
(c) area of knowledge or of responsibility; *that's not my province - you'll have to ask the finance manager*

provincial
[prə'vɪnʃl]
1 *adjective*
(a) referring to a province, to the provinces; *a provincial government*
(b) not very sophisticated; *they're very provincial down in that part of the world*; *he's too provincial to appreciate this kind of music*
2 *noun*
person from the provinces; *you provincials are out of touch with New York fashion*

provision
[prə'vɪʒn] *noun*
(a) providing something; *the provision of medical services is the responsibility of local government*; **to make provision for** = to see that something is allowed for in the future; *we've made provision for the computer network to be expanded*; *there is no provision for or no provision has been made for car parking in the plans for the office block*
(b) provisions = food; *people in remote areas need to stock up with provisions for the winter*
(c) condition in a contract; *it's a provision of the contract that the goods should be sent by air*

provisional
[prə'vɪʒnəl] *adjective*
(a) temporary; *a provisional government was set up by the army*
(b) not final; *they faxed their provisional acceptance*; *we made a provisional reservation over the phone*

provoke
[prə'vəʊk] *verb*
(a) to make someone angry, so that he does something violent; *she provoked him into throwing a brick through her front window*
(b) to make a reaction take place; *his reply provoked an angry response from the crowd*

prune
[prun]
1 *noun*
dried plum; *he had a bowl of cooked prunes for breakfast*
2 *verb*
to cut back a tree or bush, to keep it in good shape; *that bush is blocking the window - it needs pruning*

psychiatrist
[saɪ'kaɪətrɪst] *noun*
person who studies and treats mental disease; *I think she should see a psychiatrist not a medical doctor*

psychiatry
[saɪ'kaɪətri] *noun*
study of mental disease; *when he finished his basic medical training he chose to specialize in psychiatry*

psychological
[saɪkə'lɒdʒɪkl] *adjective*
referring to psychology; *her problems are mainly psychological*; *this could have a very bad effect on the child's psychological development*

psychologist
[saɪ'kɒlədʒɪst] *noun*
person who studies the human mind; *psychologists have developed a new theory to explain why some people get depressed*

psychology
[saɪ'kɒlədʒi] *noun*
study of the human mind; *she's taking a psychology course*; *the psychology department at the university*

pt
[paɪnt]
= PINT

PTO
[pitiˈəʊ]
(a) = PARENT-TEACHER ORGANIZATION

(b) *short for* "please turn over", letters written at the bottom of a page, showing that there is something written on the other side

④ **pub**
['pʌb] *noun*
(informal) place where you can buy beer and other alcoholic drinks; *I love to go to the pubs when I'm in Ireland*

② **public**
['pʌblɪk]
1 *adjective*
(a) referring to the people in general; *the jewels are on public display in a museum*; *it's in the public interest that the facts should be known*; **public gardens** = place in a town where there are flowers and trees and grass, where people can walk around and enjoy themselves; **public holiday** = holiday for everyone, when everyone can rest and enjoy themselves instead of working; *most of the stores are closed today because it's a public holiday*; **public opinion** = general feeling held by most of the public; **public sector** = state-owned companies; **public telephone** = telephone which can be used by anyone; **public transportation** = transport (such as buses, trains) that can be used by anyone; *it's quicker to go by public transportation*
(b) to go public = (i) to tell something to everyone; (ii) to sell shares in a company on the stock exchange; *after the leaks to the press, the government finally went public on the proposal*; *the plan is for the company to go public next year*
2 *noun*
(a) people in general; *the public have the right to know what is going on*; **the traveling public** = people who travel frequently (NOTE: **public** can take either a singular or plural verb)
(b) in public = in the open; in front of everyone; *this is the first time he has appeared in public since his accident*; *I dared him to repeat his remarks in public*

③ **publication**
[pʌblɪˈkeɪʃn] *noun*
(a) action of making public, publishing; *the publication of the official figures has been delayed*
(b) book or newspaper that has been published; *he asked the library for a list of gardening publications*

③ **publicity**
[pʌbˈlɪsɪti] *noun*
advertising, attracting people's attention to a product; *we're trying to get publicity for our school play*; *the failure of the show was blamed on bad publicity*; **publicity campaign** = period when planned publicity takes place

④ **publicize**
['pʌblɪsaɪz] *verb*
to attract people's attention to something; to make publicity for something; *the advertising campaign is intended to publicize the services of the tourist board*

② **public relations (PR)**
['pʌblɪk rɪˈleɪʃnz] *noun*
maintaining good connections with the public, especially to put across a point of view or to publicize a product; *the company does not have a public relations department*; *the city council needs better public relations to improve its image*; *our public relations department organized the launch of the new model*

③ **public school**
['pʌblɪk 'skul] *noun*
school that is funded by public taxes; *the state has decided to spend more money on its public school system*

③ **publish**
['pʌblɪʃ] *verb*
to make known to the public; to bring out a book, a newspaper for sale; *the government has not published the figures yet*; *the company publishes six magazines for the business market*; *we publish dictionaries for students*

④ **publisher**
['pʌblɪʃər] *noun*
person who produces books or newspapers for sale; *I'm trying to find a publisher for my novel*; *he's a publisher who specializes in reference works*

③ **publishing**
['pʌblɪʃɪŋ] *noun*
producing books or newspapers for sale; *she works in publishing or she has a job in publishing*; *if you're interested in books, have you thought of publishing as a career?*; **publishing house** = firm that publishes books

② **pudding**
['pʊdɪŋ] *noun*
sweet food that has been cooked or boiled; *there's too much sugar in this pudding*; *he helped himself to some more pudding*; *see also* RICE

① **puddle**
['pʌdl] *noun*
small pool of water, such as a pool on the pavement left after rain; *I stepped into a puddle and got my shoes wet*

① **pull**
[pʊl]
1 *verb*
(a) to move something toward you or after you; *pull the door to open it, don't push*; *the truck was pulling a trailer*; *she pulled some envelopes out of her bag*; *these little boys spend their time pulling girls' hair*; **to pull someone's leg** = to make someone believe something as a joke; *don't believe anything he says - he's just pulling your leg*
(b) to pull a muscle = to injure a muscle by using it too much; *she's pulled a muscle in her back*
2 *noun*

(informal) influence; *she must have some pull over him*

④ **pulley**
['pulɪ] *noun*
apparatus for lifting heavy weights with a rope that runs round several wheels; *we arranged a pulley to raise the beams to roof level*

① **pull in(to)**
['pul 'ɪn] *verb*
to drive into an area, especailly a parking place; *pull into that place over there*

① **pull off**
['pul 'ɒf] *verb*
(a) to take off a piece of clothing by pulling; *he sat down and pulled off his dirty boots*
(b) to do something successfully; *he pulled off a big financial deal*; *it will be marvelous if we can pull it off*

① **pull out**
['pul 'aut] *verb*
(a) to pull something out of something; *they used a rope to pull the automobile out of the river*; *see also* FINGER
(b) to drive an automobile out of an area, especially a parking place; *he forgot to signal as he was pulling out*; *don't pull out into the main road until you can see that there is nothing coming*
(c) to stop being part of a deal or agreement; *our Australian partners pulled out at the last moment*

① **pull over**
['pul 'əuvər] *verb*
to drive an automobile toward the side of the road; *the patrol car signaled to him to pull over*

③ **pullover**
['puləuvər] *noun*
piece of clothing made of wool which covers the top part of your body, and that you pull over your head to put it on(as a sweater); *he's wearing a new red pullover; my girlfriend's knitting me another pullover, this time with a V neck*

① **pull through**
['pul 'θru] *verb*
to recover from an illness; *she pulled through, thanks to the expert work of the specialists*

① **pull together**
['pul tə'geðər] *verb*
to pull yourself together = to become more calm; *although he was shocked by the news he soon pulled himself together*

① **pull up**
['pul 'ʌp] *verb*
(a) to bring something closer; *pull your chair up to the window*
(b) to stop an automobile, etc.; *an automobile pulled up and the driver asked me if I wanted a ride; he didn't manage to pull up in time and ran into the back of the car in front*

③ **pulse**
[pʌls] *noun*
(a) regular beat of your heart; *the doctor took his pulse; her pulse is very weak*
(b) dried seed of peas or beans; *pulses are used a lot in Mexican cooking*

① **pump**
[pʌmp]
1 *noun*
machine for forcing liquid or air; **bicycle or tire pump** = small hand pump for blowing up bicycle tires; **gas pump** = machine which supplies gas at a gas station
2 *verb*
(a) to force in something, such as liquid or air, with a pump; *your back tire needs pumping up; the banks have been pumping money into the company; the heart pumps blood around the body*
(b) *(informal)* **to pump someone** = to ask someone a lot of questions to try to get information; *we pumped her after the interview to find out the kind of questions she had been asked*

① **pumpkin**
['pʌŋkɪn] *noun*
large round orange-colored fruit; *we always have pumpkin pie for Thanksgiving dessert*

② **punch**
[pʌnʃ]
1 *noun*
(a) blow with the fist; *she landed two punches on his head*
(b) metal tool for making holes; *the holes in the belt are made with a punch* (NOTE: plural is **punches**)
2 *verb*
(a) to hit someone with your fist; *he punched me in the nose*
(b) to make holes in something with a punch; *the conductor punched my ticket*

④ **punctual**
['pʌŋktʃuəl] *adjective*
on time; *he was punctual for his appointment with the dentist*

③ **punctuation**
[pʌŋktʃu'eɪʃn] *noun*
dividing up groups of words using special printed signs; **punctuation marks** = symbols used in writing, such as period, comma, dash, etc., to show how a sentence is split up; *the sentence reads "Charles I walked and talked half an hour after he was dead" - there must be some punctuation missing*

② **puncture**
['pʌŋktʃər]
1 *noun*
flat, a hole in a tire; *I've got a puncture in my back tire*
2 *verb*
to make a small hole in something; *a nail had punctured the tire*

② **punish**
['pʌnɪʃ] *verb*
to make someone suffer because of something he has done; *the children must be punished for stealing apples*; *the simplest way to punish them will be to make them pay for the damage they caused*

② **punishment**
['pʌnɪʃmənt] *noun*
treatment given to punish someone; *as a punishment, you'll mop the kitchen floor*; **capital punishment** = killing someone as a punishment for a crime; *capital punishment will never be restored in this state*

③ **punt**
[pʌnt] *(in football)*
1 *noun*
kick in which the ball is dropped and kicked before it reaches the ground; *he caught the punt and then started running*
2 *verb*
to kick a dropped ball before it reaches the ground; *he punted the football about 25 yards*

① **pupil**
['pjupl] *noun*
(a) child at a school; *there are twenty-five pupils in the class*; *the piano teacher thinks he is her best pupil*
(b) black hole in the central part of the eye, through which the light passes; *the pupil of the eye grows larger when there is less light*

① **puppy**
['pʌpi] *noun*
baby dog; *our dog has had six puppies* (NOTE: plural is **puppies**)

② **purchase**
['pɜrtʃəs]
1 *noun*
(formal) thing bought; *she had difficulty getting all her purchases into the car*; **to make a purchase** = to buy something; *we didn't make many purchases on our trip to New York*; **purchase price** = price paid for something; *we offer a discount of 10% off the normal purchase price*
2 *verb*
(formal) to buy; *they purchased their automobile in California*; **purchasing power** = quantity that can be bought with a certain amount of money; *the fall in the purchasing power of the dollar*

② **purchaser**
['pɜrtʃəsər] *noun*
(formal) person who buys something; *he has found a purchaser for his house*

② **pure**
['pjuər] *adjective*
(a) very clean; not mixed with other things; *a bottle of pure water*; *a pure silk shirt*; *a pure mountain stream*
(b) innocent; with no faults; *she led a pure life*

(c) total, complete; *this is pure nonsense*; *it is pure spite on his part*; *it was by pure luck that I happened to find it* (NOTE: **purer - purest**)

② **purely**
['pjuərli] *adverb*
only, solely; *he's doing it purely for the money*; *this is a purely educational visit*

① **purple**
['pɜrpl]
1 *adjective*
(color) mixing red and blue; *the sky turned purple as night approached*
2 *noun*
color like a mixture of red and blue; *they painted their living room a deep purple*

② **purpose**
['pɜrpəs] *noun*
(a) aim or plan; *the purpose of the meeting is to plan the school festival*; **I need the invoice for tax purposes** = I need the invoice so that I can declare it to the tax
(b) **on purpose** = in a way which was planned; *don't be cross - he didn't do it on purpose*; *she pushed him off the chair on purpose*

④ **purposefully**
['pɜrpəsfəli] *adjective*
with a specific aim; *he strode purposefully down the corridor*

① **purse**
[pɜrs]
1 *noun*
(a) small bag for carrying money; *I know I had my purse in my pocket when I left home*; *she put her ticket in her purse so that she wouldn't forget where it was*; **to control** *or* **hold the purse strings** = to control the money; *as she's the only person in the family earning any money, she controls the purse strings*
(b) small bag which a woman carries to hold her money, pens, handkerchief, etc.; *a robber snatched her purse on the street*
2 *verb*
to purse your lips = to press your lips together to show you are annoyed

④ **pursue**
[pər'sju] *verb*
(a) to chase someone or something; *the police pursued the stolen car across the state*; *the guerrillas fled, pursued by government troops*
(b) to carry on a career, an activity; *he pursued a career in law*; *we intend to pursue a policy of reducing taxation*

③ **pursuit**
[pər'sjut] *noun*
(a) chase after someone; *the pursuit lasted until the thieves were caught*; **in pursuit of** = looking for; *we set off in pursuit of our friends who had just left the hotel*; *the robbers left in a stolen car with the police in pursuit*; **in hot pursuit** = chasing someone actively; *the rebels retreated into the mountains with the government forces in hot pursuit*

(b) trying to find something, to do something; *her aim in life is the pursuit of pleasure*

(c) activity that someone does regularly; *he spends his time in outdoor pursuits*

① **push**
['pʊʃ]
1 *noun*

(a) action of making something move forward; *he gave the shopping cart a little push and sent it out into the road*; *can you give the car a push? - it won't start*

(b) action of attacking, of moving forward against someone; *our troops made a sudden push into enemy territory*; *the company made a big push to get into European markets*

2 *verb*

(a) to make something move away from you or in front of you; *we'll have to push the automobile to get it to start*; *the piano is too heavy to lift, so we'll have to push it into the next room*; *did she fall down the stairs or was she pushed?*

(b) to press with your finger; *push the right-hand button to start the computer*; *(in an elevator) he pushed fourth floor*

(c) *(informal)* **I am pushed for time** = I haven't much time to spare; *let's have a snack because I'm pushed for time*

③ **push off**
['pʊʃ 'ɒf] *verb*

(informal) to start (on a journey); **we really ought to push off now** = it's time for us to go

① **puss** *or* **pussy** *or* **pussycat**
[pʊs *or* 'pʊsi *or* 'pʊsikæt] *noun*

children's names for a cat; *a big black pussy came to meet us*; *you mustn't pull the pussy's tail* (NOTE: plural is **pussies**)

① **put**
[pʊt] *verb*

(a) to place; *did you remember to put the milk in the fridge?*; *where do you want me to put this book?*

(b) to say in words; *if you put it like that, the proposal seems attractive*; *can I put a question to the speaker?*

(c) **to put the shot** = to throw a heavy ball as a sport; *he has put the shot further than anyone else in our team* (NOTE: **putting - put - has put**)

② **put away**
['pʊt ə'weɪ] *verb*

to clear things away; *put your football things away before you go to bed*

① **put back**
['pʊt 'bæk] *verb*

to put something where it was before; *go and put that can of beans back on the shelf*; *did you put the milk back in the fridge?*

④ **put by**
['pʊt 'baɪ] *verb*

to save (money); *she has some money put by to live on when she retires*

④ **put down**
['pʊt 'daʊn] *verb*

(a) to place something lower down onto a surface; *he put his suitcase down on the floor beside him*

(b) to list or to note; *put me down for one order*

(c) to let passengers get off; *the taxi driver put me down outside the hotel*

(d) **to put your foot down** = (i) to insist that something is done; (ii) to make an automobile go faster; *she put her foot down and told them to stop playing music all night*; *he put his foot down and we soon left the squad car behind*

(e) to make a deposit; *to put down money on a house*; *she had to put down a deposit on the watch*

(f) to kill a sick animal; *the cat is very old, she'll have to be put down*

① **put forward**
['pʊt 'fɔrwərd] *verb*

(a) to suggest; *I put forward several suggestions for plays we might go to see*

(b) to change an appointment to a earlier time; *can we put forward the meeting from Thursday to Wednesday?*

(c) to change the time on a clock to a later one; *when crossing from San Francisco to New York, you need to put your watch forward three hours*; *remember to put your watch forward five hours when you go to London*

① **put in**
['pʊt 'ɪn] *verb*

(a) to place inside; *I forgot to put in my pajamas when I packed the case*

(b) to install; *the first thing we have to do with the cottage is to put in central heating*

(c) to do work; *she put in three hours' extra work yesterday evening*

(d) **to put in for** = to apply; *she put in for a job in the accounting department*; *he has put in for a grant to study in Italy*

② **put off**
['pʊt 'ɒf] *verb*

(a) to arrange for something to take place later; *we have put the meeting off until next month*

(b) to bother someone so that he can't do things properly; *stop making that strange noise, it's putting me off my work*

(c) to say something to make someone decide not to do something; *he told a story about cows that put me off my food*; *I was going to see the movie, but my brother said something that put me off*

② **put on**
['pʊt 'ɒn] *verb*

(a) to place something on top of something, on a surface; *put the lid on the saucepan*; *he put his hand on my arm*; *put the suitcases down on the floor*

(b) to dress yourself in a certain piece of clothing; *I put a clean shirt on before I went to*

the party; *put your gloves on, it's cold outside*; *put on your boots if you're going out in the rain*
(c) to switch on; *can you put the light on, it's getting dark?*; *he put the heat on in the car*
(d) to add; *she has put on a lot of weight since I saw her last*
(e) *(informal)* to tease or joke; *he's just putting you on*

① **put out**
['pʊt 'aʊt] *verb*
(a) to place outside; *did you remember to put the cat out?*
(b) to stretch out your hand, etc.; *she put out her hand to stop herself from falling*
(c) to switch off; *he put the light out and went to bed*
(d) *(informal)* **to be put out** = to be annoyed; *he was very put out because you didn't ask him to stay for dinner*

② **put up**
['pʊt 'ʌp] *verb*
(a) to attach to a wall, to attach high up; *I've put up the photos of my family over my desk*; *they are putting up Christmas decorations all along Main Street*
(b) to build something so that it is upright; *they put up a wooden shed in their yard*
(c) to lift up; *the gunman told us to put our hands up*

(d) to give someone a place to sleep in your house; *they've missed the last train, can you put them up for the night?*

② **put up with**
['pʊt 'ʌp wɪθ] *verb*
to tolerate someone or something unpleasant; *living near the airport means that you have to put up with a lot of aircraft noise*; *how can you put up with the noise of all those barking dogs?*

① **puzzle**
['pʌzl]
1 *noun*
(a) game where you have to find the answer to a problem; *I can't do the puzzle in today's paper*
(b) something you can't understand; *it's a puzzle to me why they don't go to live in the country*
2 *verb*
(a) to be difficult to understand; *it puzzles me how the robbers managed to get away*
(b) to find something difficult to understand; *she puzzled over the problem for hours*

④ **pyramid**
['pɪrəmɪd] *noun*
shape with a square base and four sides rising to meet at a point; **Pyramids** = huge stone buildings, built as temples or places for the dead by the Ancient Egyptians and Central Americans; *we went to Egypt mainly to see the Pyramids*

Qq

③ **Q, q**
[kju]
seventeenth letter of the alphabet, between P and R; *a "q" is always followed by the letter "u"*

② **qualification**
[kwɒlɪfɪ'keɪʃn] *noun*
(a) proof that you have completed a specialized course of study; *does she have the right qualifications for the job?*; **professional qualifications** = proof that you have studied for and obtained a diploma for a particular type of skilled work; **what are his qualifications?** = what sort of degree or certificate does he have?
(b) something which limits the meaning of a statement, or shows that you do not agree with something entirely; *I want to add one qualification to the agreement: if the goods are not delivered by June 30, then the order will be canceled*
(c) being successful in a test or competition

which takes you on to the next stage; *she didn't reach the necessary standard for qualification*

② **qualified**
['kwɒlɪfaɪd] *adjective*
(a) with the right qualifications; *she's a qualified doctor*; **highly qualified** = with very good results in school; *all our staff are highly qualified*
(b) not complete, with conditions attached; *the committee gave its qualified approval*; *the school fair was only a qualified success*

④ **qualifier**
['kwɒlɪfaɪər] *noun*
(a) person who qualifies in a sporting competition; *how many qualifiers were there from the first round?*
(b) round of a sporting competition which qualifies a team to go to the next round; *they won their qualifier and went through to the second round*

③ **qualify**
['kwɒlɪfaɪ] *verb*
(a) to qualify as = to study for and obtain a certificate that allows you to do a certain type of work; *he has qualified as an engineer*; *when I first qualified I worked as an attorney-at-law*
(b) to qualify for = (i) to be in the right position for, to be entitled to; (ii) to pass a test or one section of a competition and so go on to the next stage; *the project does not qualify for a government grant*; *she qualified for round two of the competition*
(c) to attach conditions to; *I must qualify the offer by saying that your proposals still have to be approved by the chairman*; **the auditors have qualified the accounts** = the auditors have found something in the accounts of the company which they do not agree with

② **quality**
['kwɒlɪti]
1 *noun*
(a) how good something is; *we want to measure the downtown air quality*; *there are several high-quality restaurants around here*; **quality control** = checking a product to make sure that it is of the right standard; *quality control is important for making sure all goods leaving the factory are of the right standard*; **quality of life** = how good it is to live in a certain town or country, including low pollution and crime levels, good stores, restaurants, schools, etc.
(b) of quality = of good quality; *they served a meal of real quality*; *the carpet is expensive because it is of very good quality*
(c) something characteristic of a person; *she has many qualities, but unfortunately is extremely lazy*; *what qualities do you expect in a good salesman?* (NOTE: plural is **qualities**)
2 *adjective*
of good quality; *we aim to provide a quality service at low cost*

③ **quantity**
['kwɒntɪti] *noun*
(a) amount; **a quantity of** = (i) a lot of; (ii) a certain amount of; *the police found a quantity of stolen jewels*; *a small quantity of illegal drugs was found in the automobile*; **quantities of** = a large amount of; *quantities of stolen goods were found in the garage*
(b) unknown quantity = person or thing you know nothing about; *the new boss is something of an unknown quantity* (NOTE: plural is **quantities**)

④ **quantum**
['kwɒntəm] *noun*
(formal) amount(small amounts into which many forms of energy are divided into many parts); **quantum leap** = great movement forward; *his discovery was a quantum leap forward in the fight against cancer*; **quantum theory** = theory in physics that energy exists in amounts which cannot be divided

② **quarrel**
['kwɒrəl]
1 *noun*
argument; *they have had a quarrel and aren't speaking to each other*; *I think the quarrel was over who was in charge of the cash register*; **to pick a quarrel with someone** = to start an argument with someone; *it was very embarrassing when my father picked a quarrel with the waiter over the check*; **to patch up a quarrel** = to settle an argument; *after several months of arguing they finally patched up their quarrel*; **to have no quarrel with someone** *or* **something** = not to have any reason to complain about someone or something; *I have no quarrel with the idea of women priests*
2 *verb*
to quarrel about *or* **over something** = to argue about something; *they're always quarreling over money*

④ **quarry**
['kwɒri] *noun*
place where stone, etc., is dug out of the ground; *if you hear an explosion, it is because they're working in the quarry* (NOTE: plural is **quarries**)

③ **quart**
[kwɔrt] *noun*
measure of liquid, equal to two pints; *a quart of orange juice*

① **quarter**
['kwɔrtər] *noun*
(a) one of four parts, a fourth, 25%; *she cut the pear into quarters*; *the jar is only a quarter empty*; *he paid only a quarter of the normal fare because he works for the airline*
(b) three quarters = three out of four parts, 75%; *three quarters of the offices are empty*; *the bus was three quarters full* (NOTE: **a quarter** and **three quarters** are often written **1/4** and **3/4**)
(c) a quarter of an hour = 15 minutes; **it's (a) quarter to three** = it's 2:45; **at a quarter past eight** = at 8:15
(d) 25 cent coin; *do you have a quarter for the machine?*
(e) period of three months; *the payments are due at the end of each quarter*; *the first quarter's rent is payable in advance*; **first quarter** = period of three months from January to the end of March; **second quarter** = period of three months from April to the end of June; **third quarter** = period of three months from July to the end of September; **fourth quarter or last quarter** = period of three months from October to the end of the year

① **quarterback**
['kwɔrtərbæk] *noun*
football player who gives the signals at the start of each play; *the quarterback passed the football to the receiver*

③ **quarterfinal**
['kwɔrtər'faɪnəl] *noun*

(in sport) one of four matches in a competition, the winners of which go into the semifinals; *Ireland made the quarterfinals of the World Cup*

③ **quarterly**
['kwɔrtərli]
1 *adjective & adverb*
which happens every three months; *a quarterly payment*; *there is a quarterly charge for electricity*; *we pay the rent quarterly or on a quarterly basis*
2 *noun*
magazine that appears every three months; *he writes for one of the political quarterlies* (NOTE: plural is **quarterlies**)

② **quarters**
['kwɔrtərz] *noun*
(a) accommodation for people in the armed forces or for servants; *when they come off duty the staff go back to their quarters*; **married quarters** = accommodation for families in the armed forces
(b) at close quarters = close to, very near; *I had seen her often on TV, but this was the first time I had seen her at close quarters*

② **quartet**
[kwɔr'tet] *noun*
(a) four musicians playing together; *she plays the cello in a string quartet*
(b) piece of music for four musicians; *a Beethoven string quartet*
(c) four people or four things; *a quartet of U.S. scientists discovered the cancer cure*; *have you read his quartet of novels about Egypt?*

④ **quay**
[ki] *noun*
place where ships tie up to load or unload; *we went down to the quay to watch the fishing boats unload* (NOTE: do not confuse with **key**)

① **queen**
[kwin] *noun*
(a) wife of a king; *King Charles I's queen was the daughter of the King of France*
(b) woman ruler of a country; *Elizabeth II is the queen of England*
(c) queen bee = the main bee in a group, which can lay eggs
(d) second most important piece in chess, after the king; *in three moves he had captured my queen*
(e) *(in playing cards)* the card with the face of a woman; *he had the queen of spades* (NOTE: **queen** is spelled with a capital letter when used with a name or when referring to a particular person: **Queen Elizabeth I**)

① **queer**
['kwɪər] *adjective*
odd or strange; *there's something very queer about the message*; *isn't it queer that she hasn't phoned back?* (NOTE: **queerer - queerest**)

④ **query**
['kwɪəri]
1 *noun*

question; *she had to answer a mass of queries about the tax form* (NOTE: plural is **queries**)
2 *verb*
to doubt whether something is true; to ask a question about something; *I would query whether these figures are correct*; *the committee members queried the cost of the Christmas party*

① **question**
['kwestʃən]
1 *noun*
(a) sentence that needs an answer; *the teacher couldn't answer the children's questions*; *some of the questions on the exam were too difficult*; *the manager refused to answer questions from journalists about the fire*
(b) problem or matter; *the question is, who do we appoint to run the store when we're on vacation?*; *the main question is that of cost*; *he raised the question of moving to a less expensive part of town*; **it is out of the question** = it cannot possibly be done; *you cannot borrow any more money - it's out of the question*; *it's out of the question for her to have any more time off*
2 *verb*
(a) to ask questions; *the police questioned the driver for four hours*
(b) to query, to suggest that something may be wrong; *we all question how accurate the computer printout is*

④ **questionnaire**
[kwestʃə'neər] *noun*
printed list of questions given to people to answer; *we sent out a questionnaire to ask people what they thought of the new toothpaste*

① **question mark**
['kwestʃən 'mark] *noun*
sign (?) used in writing to show that a question is being asked; *there should be a question mark at the end of that sentence*; **there's a question mark over something** = it is doubtful if something will happen or will be good enough; *there's still a question mark over whether or not he can come*; *there's a big question mark over the captain*

④ **queue**
[kju] *GB noun*
(a) line of people, automobiles, etc., waiting one behind the other for something; *there was a queue of people waiting to get into the exhibition*; **to form a queue** = to stand in line; *please form a queue to the left of the door*
(b) series of documents (such as orders, application forms) or telephone calls which are dealt with in order; *your call is being held in a queue and will be dealt with as soon as a member of staff is free*; **his order went to the end of the queue** = his order was dealt with last (NOTE: do not confuse with **cue**)

① **quick**
[kwɪk] *adjective*
rapid or fast; *I'm trying to work out the quickest way to get to the office; we had a quick lunch and then went off for a walk; he is much quicker at calculating than I am; I am not sure that going by taxi is quicker than taking the subway;* **quick as a flash** = very quickly; *I dropped my purse and quick as a flash a little boy picked it up* (NOTE: **quicker - quickest**)

① **quickly**
['kwɪklɪ] *adverb*
rapidly, without taking much time; *he ate his supper very quickly because he wanted to watch the match on TV; the police came quickly when we called 911*

① **quiet**
['kwaɪət]
1 *adjective*
(a) without any noise; *can't you make the children keep quiet? - I'm trying to work; the hotel leaflet said that the rooms were quiet, but ours looked out over a busy main road;* **quiet as a mouse** = very quiet; *she sat in the corner, as quiet as a mouse, watching what was going on*
(b) with no great excitement; *we had a quiet vacation by the sea; it's a quiet little town; the hotel is in the quietest part of the town* (NOTE: **quieter - quietest**)
2 *noun*
(a) calm and peace; *all I want is a bit of peace and quiet and then he starts playing drums; the quiet of the Sunday afternoon was spoiled by aircraft noise*
(b) **on the quiet** = in secret; *they got married last weekend on the quiet*
3 *verb*
to make calm; *she tried to quiet the screaming child*

① **quietly**
['kwaɪətli] *adverb*
without making any noise; *the burglar climbed quietly up to the window; she shut the door quietly behind her*

② **quit**
[kwɪt] *verb*
(a) *(informal)* to leave a job, a house, etc.; *when the boss criticized her, she quit; I'm fed up with the office, I'm thinking of quitting*
(b) *(informal)* to stop doing something; *will you quit bothering me!; he quit smoking; see also* QUITS (NOTE: **quitting - quit** *or* **quitted**)

① **quite**
[kwaɪt] *adverb*

(a) more or less; *it's quite a long play; she's quite a good secretary; the book is quite amusing but I liked the TV play better*
(b) completely; *you're quite mad to go walking in that snow; I don't quite understand why you want to go China;* **not quite** = not completely; *the work is not quite finished yet; have you eaten all the bread? - not quite*
(c) **quite a few** *or* **quite a lot** = several or many; *quite a few people on the boat were sick; quite a lot of staff drive to work*

③ **quits**
[kwɪts] *adjective*
even; *if you pay the check and I pay you half, then we'll be quits; (informal)* **to call it quits** = (i) to say that you are even; (ii) to decide to stop doing something; *give me $4 and we'll call it quits; it's getting late, let's call it quits and start again tomorrow morning*

④ **quota**
['kwəʊtə] *noun*
fixed amount of goods which can be supplied; *the government has set quotas for milk production;* **import quota** = fixed quantity of a particular type of goods which the government allows to be imported; *the government has set an import quota on automobiles*

② **quotation**
[kwəʊ'teɪʃn] *noun*
(a) words quoted; *the article ended with a quotation from one of Churchill's speeches*
(b) **quotation marks** = printed or written marks showing that a quotation starts or finishes; *that part of the sentence should be in quotation marks* (NOTE: the marks " " are **double quotation marks** and the marks ' ' are **single quotation marks**)

② **quote**
[kwəʊt]
1 *noun*
(a) quotation, words quoted; *I need some good quotes from his speech to put into my report*
(b) *(informal)* **quotes** = quotation marks; *that part of the sentence should be in quotes*
2 *verb*
(a) to repeat a number as a reference; *in reply please quote this number; he replied, quoting the number of the invoice*
(b) to repeat what someone has said or written; *he started his speech by quoting lines from Shakespeare's "Hamlet";* **can I quote you on that?** = can I repeat what you have just said?; *I think the fee will be $25,000, but don't quote me on that*
(c) to give an estimate for work to be done; *he quoted $15,000 for the job; their prices are always quoted in dollars*

Rr

③ **R, r**
[ɑr]
eighteenth letter of the alphabet, between Q and S

① **rabbit**
['ræbɪt] *noun*
common wild animal with gray fur, long ears and a short tail; *the rabbit ran down its hole*; *he tried to shoot the rabbit but missed*; *she keeps a pet rabbit in a cage*

① **race**
[reɪs]
1 *noun*
(a) contest to see which person, horse, automobile, etc., is the fastest; *she was second in the 200 meters race*; *the bicycle race goes around the whole country*; **race against time** = struggle to get something finished on time; *they tried to block the hole in the seawall but with the high tide rising it was a race against time*
(b) contest to be elected to a position in politics; *the governor of Texas will enter the presidential race*
(c) large group of people with similar skin color, hair, etc.; *the government is trying to stamp out discrimination on grounds of race*; *they are prejudiced against people of mixed race*; **race relations** = relations between different groups of races in the same country; *race relations officers have been appointed in some police forces*
2 *verb*
(a) to run, ride, etc., to see who is the fastest; *I'll race you to see who gets to school first*
(b) to run fast; *they saw the bus coming and raced to the bus stop*; *he snatched some watches from the shop window and then raced away down the street*

③ **racecourse**
['reɪskɔrs] *noun*
track where horse races are run

① **racetrack**
['reɪstræk] *noun*
track where races are run; *we're also going to the races - we'll meet you at the racetrack at 2:00 P.M.*; *his car ran off the racetrack into the crowd*

④ **racial**
['reɪʃl] *adjective*
referring to different races; *the election was fought on racial issues*; **racial discrimination** = bad treatment of someone because of his or her race; **racial prejudice** = prejudice against someone because of race; *he accused his ex-boss of racial discrimination or of racial prejudice*

④ **racially**
['reɪʃəlɪ] *adverb*
in a racial way; **racially motivated** = done because of racial hatred; *the attack on the house was racially motivated*

③ **racing**
['reɪsɪŋ] *noun*
contests to see who is fastest; *we enjoy watching the racing at weekends*; *he was a famous auto racing driver*

④ **racism**
['reɪsɪzm] *noun*
believing that a group of people are not as good as others because they are of a different race, and treating them differently; *there was no question of racism in this instance, it was more just bad temper on the part of the manager*

④ **racist**
['reɪsɪst]
1 *adjective*
believing that some people are not as good as others because of race and treating them differently; *the family live in constant terror of racist attacks*; *the murder was thought to have been a racist attack*
2 *noun*
person who treats someone differently because of race; *the manager's a racist and you won't change his views*

① **rack**
[ræk]
1 *noun*
frame which holds things such as baggage, or letters; *he put the envelope in the letter rack on his desk*; **luggage rack** = space for bags above the seats in a plane, train, etc.; *the luggage rack was full so she kept her bag on her lap*; *please place all hand luggage in the overhead luggage racks*; **wine rack** = frame in which bottles of wine can be kept flat; *see also* ROOF RACK
2 *verb*
(a) to rack your brains = to think very hard; *I'm racking my brains, trying to remember the name of the store*
(b) racked with = suffering continuously from; *she was racked with pain*

② **racket**
['rækɪt] *noun*
(a) light frame with a handle and tight strings, used for hitting the ball in games; **tennis racket** = racket used to play tennis; *she bought a new tennis racket at the start of the summer season*; *she asked if she could borrow his racket for the tournament*
(b) *(informal)* loud noise; *stop that racket at once!*; *the people next door make a terrible racket when they're having a party*
(c) *(informal)* illegal deal that makes a lot of money; *don't get involved in that racket, you'll go to prison if you get caught*; *he runs a cut-rate ticket racket*

② **radar**
['reɪdɑr] *noun*
(a) system for finding objects such as ships or aircraft, and working out where they are from radio signals which are reflected back from them as dots on a monitor; *the plane's radar picked up another plane coming too close*
(b) **radar trap** = small radar device by the side of a road which senses and notes details of automobiles which are traveling too fast

④ **radiant**
['reɪdiənt] *adjective*
(a) bright; *she came out of the church with a radiant smile*
(b) which is sent out in the form of rays; **radiant heat** = heat which is transmitted by infrared rays from something hot

② **radiation**
[reɪdɪ'eɪʃn] *noun*
sending out rays or heat; *local residents were concerned about the effects of radiation from the nearby nuclear power station*; *any person exposed to radiation is more likely to develop certain types of cancer*

② **radiator**
['reɪdɪeɪtər] *noun*
(a) metal panel filled with hot water for heating; *turn the radiator down - it's boiling in here*; *when we arrived at the hotel our room was cold, so we switched the radiators on*
(b) metal panel filled with cold water for cooling a car engine; *the radiator froze, causing the car to break down*

④ **radical**
['rædɪkl]
1 *adjective*
(a) complete; basic (difference); *the government has had a radical change of mind about press freedom*; *he pointed out the radical difference between the two parties' policies on education*
(b) new and totally different; *his more radical proposals were turned down by the committee*; **radical party** = a party which is in favor of great and rapid change in the way a country is governed; *he's not a radical and doesn't belong to the radical party*

2 *noun*
member of a radical party; *two Radicals voted against the government*

④ **radically**
['rædɪkli] *adverb*
in a completely different, radical way; *the U.S. political scene has changed radically over the last twelve months*

① **radio**
['reɪdiəʊ]
1 *noun*
(a) method of sending out and receiving messages using airwaves; *they got the news by radio*; *we always listen to the radio when we're on vacation*; **radio telescope** = telescope that uses radio waves to find or see stars and other objects in the sky; *astronomers used a new advanced radio telescope to observe the planet*; **radio waves** = way in which radio signals move through the atmosphere; *the transmission and reception of sound and data by radio waves is called radio communications*
(b) device that sends out and receives messages using airwaves; *turn on the radio - it's time for the weather forecast*; *I heard the news on the car radio*; *please, turn the radio down - I'm on the phone*
2 *verb*
to send a message using a radio; *they radioed for assistance*

② **radioactive**
[reɪdiəʊ'æktɪv] *adjective*
(substance) which gives off energy in the form of radiation which can pass through other substances; *after the accident, part of the nuclear plant remained radioactive for 20 years*; *the problems of disposal of radioactive waste*

① **radish**
['rædɪʃ] *noun*
small red root vegetable, eaten raw in salads; *we started with a bowl of radishes and butter* (NOTE: plural is **radishes**)

④ **radius**
['reɪdiəs] *noun*
(a) line from the centre of a circle to the outside edge; *we were asked to measure the radius of the circle*
(b) distance in any direction from a particular central point; *people within a radius of twenty miles heard the explosion* (NOTE: the plural is **radii** ['reɪdɪaɪ])

③ **raffle**
['ræfl]
1 *noun*
lottery where you buy a ticket with a number on it, in the hope of winning a prize; *she won a bottle of perfume in a raffle*
2 *verb*
to give a prize in a lottery; *they raffled a sports car for charity*

② **raft**
['ræft] *noun*
boat made of pieces of wood tied together to form a flat surface; *they took their raft all the way down the Amazon*

① **rag**
['ræg]
1 *noun*
(a) piece of torn cloth; *he used an old oily rag to clean his motorcycle*
(b) rags = old torn clothes; *the children were dressed in rags*
2 *verb*
to tease; *he was ragged a lot at school about his mustache; the other girls ragged her about her rich boyfriend*

② **rage**
['reɪdʒ]
1 *noun*
violent anger; *he rushed up to the driver of the other automobile in a terrible rage;* **to fly into a rage** = to get very angry suddenly; *when he phoned her she flew into a rage; see also* ROAD RAGE
2 *verb*
to be violent; *the storm raged all night*

② **raid**
['reɪd]
1 *noun*
sudden attack; *robbers carried out six raids on post offices during the night; police carried out a series of raids on addresses in New York;* **air raid** = sudden attack by planes
2 *verb*
to make a sudden attack on a place; *the police raided the club; we caught the boys raiding the fridge*

① **rail**
['reɪl]
1 *noun*
(a) straight metal or wooden bar; *the pictures all hang from a picture rail; hold on to the rail as you go down the stairs; there is a heated towel rail in the bathroom*
(b) one of two parallel metal bars on which trains run; *don't try to cross the rails - it's dangerous*
(c) the railway, a system of travel using trains; *six million commuters travel to work by rail each day; we ship all our goods by rail; rail travelers are complaining about rising fares*
2 *verb*
(a) **to rail off** = to close an area with fences; *police railed off the entrance to the court*
(b) **to rail against** = to speak violently against; *he railed against the actions of the authorities*

② **railings**
['reɪlɪŋz] *noun*
metal bars used as a fence; *don't put your hand through the railings around the lion's cage; he leaned over the railings and looked down at the street below*

① **railroad**
['reɪlrəʊd] *noun*
way of traveling which uses trains to carry passengers and goods; *by the end of the 19th century, the railroad stretched from the east to the west coast of America*

① **rain**
['reɪn]
1 *noun*
(a) drops of water which fall from the clouds; *the ground is very dry - we've had no rain for days; yesterday we had 0.5 inches of rain or 0.5 inches of rain fell here yesterday; if you have to go out in the rain take an umbrella; all this rain will help the plants grow;* **driving rain** = rain that is blown by the wind; *they were forced to turn back because of the driving rain* (NOTE: no plural in this meaning: **some rain, a drop of rain**)
(b) *(in tropical countries)* **rains** = the season when it rains a lot; *the rains came late last year*
2 *verb*
to fall as drops of water from the clouds; *as soon as we sat down and took out the sandwiches, it started to rain; it rained all day, so we couldn't visit the gardens;* *(informal)* **to be raining cats and dogs** = to rain a lot; *it rained hard all morning, but had cleared up by early afternoon;* **the game was rained out** = the game was stopped because of rain (NOTE: **rain** is only used with the subject **it**; do not confuse with **reign, rein**)

① **rainbow**
['reɪnbəʊ] *noun*
arch of color which shines in the sky when it is sunny and raining at the same time; *a rainbow shone across the valley when the sun came out*

COMMENT: the colors of the rainbow are: red, orange, yellow, green, blue, indigo (dark blue) and violet

② **raincoat**
['reɪnkəʊt] *noun*
coat which keeps off water, which you wear when it is raining; *take a raincoat with you if you think it's going to rain; she took off her raincoat in the hall*

③ **rain forest**
['reɪn 'fɒrɪst] *noun*
thick forest which grows in tropical regions where there is a lot of rain; *tropical rain forests contain over half of all the world's animals and plants*

① **rainy**
['reɪni] *adjective*
when it rains; *our vacation was spoiled by the rainy weather;* **rainy season** = period of the year when it rains a lot (as opposed to the dry season); *the rainy season lasts from April to August; don't go there in October - that's the beginning of the rainy season* (NOTE: **rainier - rainiest**)

COMMENT: the phrase "rainy season" is only used of areas where there is a very marked difference between the seasons

① **raise**
[reɪz]
1 *noun*
increase in salary; *she asked the boss for a raise*
2 *verb*
(a) to make something higher; *he picked up the flag and raised it over his head*; *the newspaper headline says TAXES TO BE RAISED*; *airfares will be raised on June 1*; *when the store raised its prices, it lost half of its customers*; *he raised his eyebrows* = he looked surprised
(b) to mention a subject which could be discussed; *no one raised the subject of politics*; *the chairman tried to prevent the question of layoffs being raised*
(c) to obtain money; *the hospital is trying to raise $3 million to finance its expansion program*; *where will he raise the money from to start up his business?*
(d) to grow plants from seed; *the new varieties are raised in controlled conditions*

② **raisin**
['reɪzn] *noun*
dried grape; *can you buy some raisins for the Christmas pudding?*

① **rake**
[reɪk]
1 *noun*
garden tool with a long handle and metal teeth, used for smoothing earth or for pulling dead leaves together
2 *verb*
(a) to smooth loose soil; *she raked the vegetable bed before sowing her carrots*
(b) to pull dead leaves together with a rake; *he raked the leaves from under the trees*

③ **rally**
['ræli]
1 *noun*
(a) large meeting of members of an association or political party; *we are holding a rally to protest the job cuts*
(b) competition where automobiles have to go through difficult country in a certain time; *he won the Monte Carlo rally by 55 minutes*; *the passenger has to deal with the maps, signs and timing for a rally driver*
(c) series of shots in tennis; *it was a great final - full of powerful serves and exciting rallies*
(d) rise in price when the trend has been downward; *shares staged a rally on the New York Stock Exchange* (NOTE: plural is **rallies**)
2 *verb*
(a) to gather together; **to rally around** = to group together to support someone; *when her husband was sent to prison her friends rallied around*

(b) to recover for a time from an illness, or from a setback; *he was very poorly on Monday, but by the end of the week he had rallied a little*
(c) to rise in price, when the trend has been downwards; *shares rallied on the news of the latest government figures*

① **ram**
[ræm]
1 *noun*
male sheep; *we keep the rams separate from the females*
2 *verb*
(a) to hit another ship, car, etc., hard; *the car rammed into the side of the truck*
(b) to push something hard; *he rammed the envelope into his pocket* (NOTE: **ramming - rammed**)

③ **Ramadan**
['ræmədæn] *noun*
Muslim religious festival, the ninth month of the Muslim year, during which you are not allowed to eat or drink during the daytime

③ **ramp**
[ræmp] *noun*
slightly sloping surface joining two different levels; *they have built a ramp so that wheelchairs can get into the library*

① **ran**
[ræn] *see* RUN

① **ranch**
[rænt∫] *noun*
very large farm on which cattle or other animals are kept; *he works on a cattle ranch in Montana*; *the cowboys returned to the ranch each evening* (NOTE: plural is **ranches**)

④ **random**
['rændəm]
1 *adjective*
done without any planning; **random check** = check on items taken from a group without choosing them in any particular order; *the customs officer carried out a random check for drugs*; **random sample** = sample for testing which has not been specially selected; *a random blood sample proved that he had been taking drugs*
2 *noun*
done without any planning; **at random** = without choosing; *pick any card at random*

① **rang**
[ræŋ] *see* RING

① **range**
[reɪndʒ]
1 *noun*
(a) series of buildings or mountains in line; *there is a range of small buildings next to the farm which can be converted into vacation cottages*; *they looked out at the vast mountain range from the plane window*
(b) wide open fields for animals to graze; *the cattle were left to feed on the range during the summer*

(c) choice or series of colors, etc., available; *we offer a wide range of sizes*; *we have a range of vacations at all prices*; *I am looking for something in the $30 - $45 price range*; *he's in the $75,000 - $100,000 salary range*

(d) distance which you can go; distance over which you can see or hear; *the missile only has a range of 65 miles*; *the police said the man had been shot at close range*; *the optician told her that her range of vision would be limited*

2 *verb*

to range from = to spread; *the sizes range from small to extra large*; *vacations range in price from $250 to $450 per person*; *the quality of this year's essay papers ranged from excellent to very poor*

② rank
[ræŋk]

1 *noun*

(a) position in society, in the army; *what rank does he hold in the police force?*; *after ten years he had reached the rank of sergeant*; **other ranks** = ordinary soldiers; **he rose from the ranks** = from being an ordinary soldier he became an officer; *General Smith rose from the ranks*

(b) **rank and file** = ordinary people; *rank-and-file union members voted against the proposal*

(c) row of soldiers; *the soldiers kept rank as they advanced toward the enemy*

2 *verb*

to be classified in order of importance; *Shakespeare ranks among the greatest world authors*; *as an artist he doesn't rank as highly as his sister*

④ ranking
['ræŋkɪŋ] *noun*

place in order of importance; *she moved several places up the tennis rankings*; *the police commissioner is the highest ranking police officer in the district*

③ rap
[ræp]

1 *noun*

(a) sharp tap; *there was a rap on the door*

(b) *(informal)* **to take the rap** = to accept responsibility, to take the blame; *he had to take the rap for the team's bad results*

(c) form of music where the singer speaks words rapidly over a regular beat; **rap artist** = person who speaks words to rap music; *he's the greatest rap artist playing today*

2 *verb*

(a) to give a sharp tap; *he rapped on the door with a stick, but no one came to open it*

(b) to talk with someone; *we rapped about our problems all afternoon* (NOTE: **rapping - rapped**)

③ rape
[reɪp]

1 *noun*

(a) offense of forcing a person to have sexual intercourse without consent; *there's been a dramatic increase in the number of rapes in this area over the past year*; *he was in court, charged with rape*

(b) plant with yellow flowers, whose seeds are used to produce oil; *market prices for rape soared last fall*

2 *verb*

to force someone to have sexual intercourse without consent; *the girl was raped in the parking lot*; *he was in court, charged with raping the student*

② rapid
['ræpɪd]

1 *adjective*

fast; *there has been a rapid rise in real estate prices this year*; *the rapid change in the weather forced the yachts to return to the harbor*

2 *noun*

rapids = place where a river runs fast over rocks; *he took her down the rapids in a small boat*; **to shoot rapids** = to sail over rapids in a boat

② rapidly
['ræpɪdli] *adverb*

quickly; *the new store rapidly increased sales*; *she read the letter rapidly and threw it away*

③ rare
[reər] *adjective*

(a) not usual, not common; *it's very rare to meet a foreigner who speaks perfect Chinese*; *experienced salesmen are rare these days*; *these woods are the breeding ground of a rare species of frog*

(b) (meat) which is very lightly cooked; *how would you like your steak? - rare, please!* (NOTE: **rarer - rarest**)

③ rarely
['reərli] *adverb*

not often, hardly ever; *I rarely buy a Sunday newspaper*; *he is rarely in his office on Friday afternoons*

② rash
[ræʃ]

1 *noun*

mass of red spots on the skin, which stays for a time and then disappears; *he showed the rash to the doctor*; *she had a rash on her arms*; **to break out in a rash** = to suddenly get a rash; **heat rash** = spots caused by hot weather; *he suffers from heat rash every summer*; **diaper rash** = rash on a baby's bottom, caused by the baby having a wet diaper; *she puts cream on the baby's bottom to prevent diaper rash* (NOTE: plural is **rashes**)

2 *adjective*

not cautious, not careful; done without thinking; *it was a bit rash of him to suggest that he would pay for everyone* (NOTE: **rasher - rashest**)

① **rat**

[ræt] *noun*

common small gray animal with a long tail, living in basements, refuse dumps, on ships, etc.; *rats live in the drains in the city*; *plague is a disease which is transmitted to people by fleas from rats*; **like rats leaving a sinking ship** = when large numbers of people leave a company or an organization which they think is going to collapse; *employees are leaving the company like rats leaving a sinking ship*

② **rate**

[reɪt]

1 *noun*

(a) number shown as a proportion of another; **birth rate** = number of children born per 1000 of the population; *the national birth rate rose dramatically in the second half of the 20th century*; **death rate** = number of deaths per 1000 of population; *the death rate from the flu soared during the winter*

(b) how frequently something is done; *his heart was beating at a rate of only 59 per minute*

(c) level of payment; *he immediately accepted the rate offered*; *before we discuss the position further, I would like to talk about the rates of pay*; *their rate of pay is lower than ours* ; **fixed rate** = charge or interest which cannot be changed; *they chose a fixed-rate mortgage*; **flat rate** = fixed charge which never changes; *we charge a flat rate of $15.00 per visit*; *taxi drivers charge a flat rate of $30 for driving you to the airport*; **going rate** = the usual rate, the current rate of payment; *what is the going rate for a 1996 model Cougar?*; *we are happy to pay you the going rate*; **interest rate** *or* **rate of interest** = percentage charged for borrowing money; *the bank has raised interest rates again*; *savings accounts offer a good interest rate or a good rate of interest*

(d) **exchange rate** *or* **rate of exchange** = rate at which one currency is exchanged for another; *the current rate of exchange is 6.40 francs to the dollar*; *what is today's rate for the dollar?*

(e) speed; *at the rate he's going, he'll be there before us*; *if you type at a steady rate of 70 words per minute, you'll finish the text today*

(f) **first-rate** = very good; *he's a first-rate tennis player*; *the food here is absolutely first-rate*; **second-rate** = not very good; *I don't want any second-rate actor, I want the best you can find*

(g) **at any rate** = whatever happens; *I don't think he really wants to come, at any rate he won't be able to since he's sick*; *the taxi cost more than I expected, but at any rate we got to the airport on time*

2 *verb*

to give a value to something; *she's rated in the top 20 players*; *I don't rate his chances of winning very highly*

② **rather**

['ræðr] *adverb*

(a) quite; *their house is rather on the small side*; *her dress is a rather pretty shade of blue*

(b) *(used with* **would**; *to mean* **prefer**); *we'd rather stay in the office than go to the party*; *is your company going to pay for everybody? - we'd rather not*; *I'd rather we stayed with her*; *they'd rather she went with them*

(c) *(showing that something is done instead of something else)* *rather than wait for hours for a bus, we decided to walk home*; *he tried to use his credit card rather than pay cash*

(d) **or rather** = or to be more precise; *his father is a doctor, or rather a surgeon*

④ **rating**

['reɪtɪŋ] *noun*

(a) assessment, giving a score; *what rating would you give that movie?*; **credit rating** = amount of money which someone feels a customer can afford to borrow; *his credit rating was excellent so he was able to open a charge account with the store*

(b) **ratings** = estimated number of people who watch TV programs; *the show is high in the ratings, which means it will attract good publicity*

④ **ratio**

['reɪʃiəʊ] *noun*

proportion; *the ratio of successes to failures*; *our runners beat theirs by a ratio of two to one* (NOTE: plural is **ratios**)

④ **ration**

['ræʃn]

1 *noun*

amount of food or supplies allowed; *the rations allowed for the expedition were more than enough*

2 *verb*

to allow only a certain amount of food or supplies; *gas may be rationed this winter*; *during the war we were rationed to one ounce of cheese per person per week*

④ **rational**

['ræʃənl] *adjective*

sensible, based on reason; *she had made a rational decision*; *it's not being rational when you say you're going to build a house all by yourself*

① **rattle**

['rætl]

1 *noun*

toy which makes a loud noise when waved; *the baby threw its rattle out of the crib*

2 *verb*

to make a repeated banging noise; *the wind made the windows rattle*

③ **rattlesnake**

['rætlsneɪk] *noun*

poisonous snake which makes a rattling noise with its tail

② **ravine**
[rə'vin] *noun*
deep narrow valley; *the car crashed through the fence and ended up at the bottom of a ravine*

① **raw**
[rɔ] *adjective*
(a) not cooked; *don't be silly - you can't eat raw potatoes!; we had a salad of raw cabbage and tomatoes; sushi is a Japanese dish of raw fish; they served the meat almost raw*
(b) **raw materials** = substances in their natural state which have not yet been made into manufactured goods (such as wool, wood, sand, etc.); *what raw materials are needed for making soap?; a Malaysian company provides the raw materials used by the tire manufacturer*
(c) cold and damp (weather); *a very raw winter's morning; the driving wind was cold and raw*
(d) *(skin)* sensitive because the surface has been rubbed off; *her new shoes left her heel red and raw*
(e) *(informal)* **raw deal** = unfair treatment; *he got a raw deal from the government when they refused to pay him a pension*

② **ray**
[reɪ] *noun*
(a) beam of light or heat; *a ray of sunshine lit up the gloomy room*; **ray of hope** = small hopeful sign; *see also* X-RAY
(b) type of large flat sea fish; *we had a ray fish cooked in butter*

② **razor**
['reɪzər] *noun*
knife with a very sharp blade for shaving; *he was shaving with his electric razor*

③ **Rd**
[rəud] *short for* ROAD; *his address is 125 Cambridge Rd*

① **reach**
[ritʃ]
1 *noun*
(a) how far you can stretch out your hand; *keep the medicine bottle out of the reach of the children*
(b) how far you can travel easily; *the office is within easy reach of the train station*
(c) **reaches** = section of a river; *the upper reaches of the Amazon*
2 *verb*
(a) to stretch out your hand to; *she reached across the table and took some meat from my plate; he's quite tall enough to reach the tool cupboard; can you reach the suitcase from the top shelf?*
(b) to arrive at a place; *we were held up by fog and only reached home at midnight; the plane reaches Hong Kong at 4:00 P.M.; we wrote to tell her we were coming to visit, but the letter never reached her*

(c) to get to a certain level; *the amount we owe the bank has reached $150,000*
(d) to do something successfully; **to reach an agreement** = to agree; *the two parties reached an agreement over the terms of the sale*; **to reach a decision** = to decide; *the board has still not reached a decision about closing the factory*

③ **react**
[ri'ækt] *verb*
(a) to do or to say something in response to words or an action; *how will he react when we tell him the news?; when she heard the rumor she didn't react at all*; **to react against something** = to show opposition to something; *the farmers reacted against the new law by blocking the roads with their tractors*; **to react to something** = to have a particular response to something; *how did he react to news of her death?; he didn't react at all well to the injection*
(b) *(of a chemical)* **to react with something** = to change chemical composition because of a substance; *acids react with metals*

③ **reaction**
[ri'ækʃn] *noun*
(a) thing done or said in response; *his immediate reaction to the news was to burst into laughter; there was a very negative reaction to the proposed building development*; **natural reaction** = a normal way of responding; *bursting into tears is a natural reaction when you pass the bar exam; what was his reaction to the news?* = what did he say? what did he do?; *what was his reaction when you told him you were leaving him?*
(b) act of reacting; *a chemical reaction takes place when acid is added*

④ **reactor**
[ri'æktər] *noun*
plant which creates heat and energy by starting and controlling atomic processes through nuclear reactions; *a nuclear disaster could have happened if the reactor had exploded*

① **read**
[rid]
1 *verb*
(a) to look at and understand written words; *she was reading a book when I saw her; what are you reading at the moment?; we're reading about the general election*
(b) to speak aloud from something which is written; *the chairman read a message from the president during the meeting; she read a story to the children last night; can you read the instructions on the medicine bottle - the print is too small for me?*
(c) to look at and understand written music; *she can play the piano by ear, but can't read music*
(d) *(computers)* to take in and understand data from a disk or sent via a modem, etc.; *our PCs cannot read these disks because they are not*

from our system; the reader at the cash register reads the bar code on each product
(e) to read between the lines = to understand a hidden meaning which is not immediately obvious; *if you read between the lines of his letter you can tell that he is deeply unhappy* (NOTE: **reading - read** [red])

2 *noun*
(a) action of looking at and understanding the words in a book, etc.; *I like to have a read in the train on my way to work*
(b) good book for reading; *his latest novel will be a good vacation read; you can't beat that book for a fantastic read*

① **read aloud** *or* **read out**
['rid ə'laud *or* 'rid 'aut] *verb*
to speak the words you are reading; *she read the letter aloud to the family; the teacher read out all the students' grades to the whole class*

① **reader**
['ridər] *noun*
(a) person who reads books, newspapers, etc.; *a message from the editor to all our readers; she's a great reader of detective stories*
(b) school book to help children to learn to read; *the teacher handed out the new readers to the class; I remember one of my first readers - it was about two children and their dog*
(c) electronic device that understands data or symbols; *a bar code reader*

④ **readily**
['redɪlɪ] *adverb*
(a) easily and quickly; *this product is readily available in most stores*
(b) willingly, without any hesitation; *is there anyone readily available to help me this weekend?; she came readily when I asked her to help me*

① **reading**
['ridɪŋ] *noun*
(a) act of looking at and understanding written words; *reading and writing should be taught early;* **reading glasses** = glasses that help you to read things which are close; **reading lamp** = small lamp on a desk or beside a bed, for use when reading or writing; *make sure that the reading lamp on your desk is switched off; I can't read in bed at night, I haven't got a reading lamp*
(b) material (such as books, etc.) that is read; *this book is too difficult, it's not suitable reading for a child her age*
(c) speaking aloud from something that is written; *they gave a poetry reading in the bookstore*
(d) way of understanding a text; *a new reading of "Hamlet"*

① **ready**
['redɪ] *adjective*
(a) prepared for something; *hold on - I'll be ready in two minutes; are all the children ready to go to school?; why isn't the bus here? - the*

group is all ready and waiting to go; **ready for anything** = prepared to do anything; *now that I've had some food, I'm ready for anything!*
(b) fit to be used or eaten; *don't sit down yet - the meal isn't ready; is the coat I brought to be cleaned ready yet?* (NOTE: **readier - readiest**)

② **real**
['rɪəl] *adjective*
(a) not a copy, not artificial; *is that watch real gold?; that plastic apple looks very real or looks just like the real thing; he has a real leather case*
(b) *(used to emphasize)* that automobile is a **real bargain** at $450; *their little girl is going to be a real beauty; insects can be a real problem on picnics; getting all the staff to agree to move to New Jersey is a real problem*
(c) which exists; *have you ever seen a real live tiger?; there's a real danger that the store will be closed;* **real life** = everyday existence, as opposed to life in a movie or novel, etc.; *he dreams of being a pilot, but in real life he's an insurance salesman; winning the lottery is the kind of thing you read about in the newspapers, but it never happens to you in real life;* **real world** = the world as it actually exists, with all its faults, not the world of novels or TV; *it's back to the real world now after our vacation*
(d) **real estate** = land or buildings that are bought or sold; *he made his money from real estate deals in the 1990s;* **real estate agent** = person who sells property for customers

③ **realistic**
[rɪə'lɪstɪk] *adjective*
(a) which looks as if it is real; *these flowers look so realistic, I can't believe they're made of plastic*
(b) accepting life as it really is; *let's be realistic - you'll never earn enough money to buy this house; I'm just being realistic when I say that you should think again about the offer*

④ **reality**
[rɪ'ælɪtɪ] *noun*
what is real and not imaginary; *the grim realities of life in an industrial town; he worked hard, and his dreams of wealth soon became a reality*

③ **realize**
['rɪəlaɪz] *verb*
(a) to get to a point where you understand clearly; *she didn't realize what she was letting herself in for when she said she would look after the children; we soon realized we were on the wrong road; when she went into the manager's office she did not realize she was going to get fired*
(b) to get money by selling something; *the sale of his stamp collection realized $150,000*
(c) to make something become real; *after four years of hard work, the auto racing team realized their dream of winning the Grand Prix; by buying a house by the ocean he realized his greatest ambition;* **to realize a**

project *or* **a plan** = to make a project or a plan happen; *the plan took five years to realize*

② **really**
['rɪəlɪ] *adverb*
(a) in fact; *she's not really French, is she?*; *the building really belongs to my father*
(b) *(used to show surprise)* *it's really time you had your hair cut*; *she doesn't like apples - really, how strange!*; *did you really mean what you said?*; *asking all the staff to move is a really tall order*

② **rear**
['rɪər]
1 *noun*
part at the back; *the rear of the automobile was damaged in the accident*; *they sat toward the rear of the bus*; **to bring up the rear** = to walk behind the others; *the military band brought up the rear of the parade*
2 *adjective*
at the back; *the children sat in the rear seats of the car*; *he rolled down the rear window*; **rearview mirror** = mirror in the center of the front of an automobile, so that the driver can see what is behind him without turning round; *he checked in his rearview mirror before turning into the side road*
3 *verb*
(a) to breed animals; *they rear horses on their farm*; *they stopped rearing pigs because of the smell*
(b) to rise up, to lift up; *an elephant suddenly reared up out of the long grass*; *the walls of the castle reared up before them*
(c) *(of horse, etc.)* to rise on its back legs; *the terrified horse reared (up) and threw its rider*

① **reason**
['rizən]
1 *noun*
(a) thing which explains why something has happened; *the airline gave no reason for the plane's late arrival*; *the boss asked him for the reason why he was late with his work*; **for some reason** = in a way which you cannot explain; *for some reason (or other) the contractor sent us two invoices*
(b) the power of thought; *use reason to solve a problem in mathematics*
(c) ability to make sensible judgments; *she wouldn't listen to reason*; **it stands to reason** = it makes sense; *it stands to reason that he wants to join his father's firm*; **to see reason** = to see the wisdom of someone's argument; *she was going to report her neighbors to the police, but in the end we got her to see reason*; **within reason** = to a sensible degree, in a sensible way; *the children get $10 pocket money each week, and we let them spend it as they like, within reason*
2 *verb*
(a) to think or to plan carefully and in a logical way; *he reasoned that any work is better than*

no work, so he took the job; *if you take the time to reason it out, you'll find a solution to the problem*
(b) **to reason with someone** = to try to calm someone, to try to make someone change his mind; *the police officer tried to reason with the man who was holding a knife*

③ **reasonable**
['rizənəbl] *adjective*
(a) not expensive; *the hotel's charges are quite reasonable*; *the restaurant offers good food at reasonable prices*
(b) sensible, showing sense; *the manager of the store was very reasonable when she tried to explain that she had left her credit cards at home*

③ **reasonably**
['rizənəblɪ] *adverb*
in a reasonable way; *the meals are very reasonably priced*; *very reasonably, he asked to have the brakes of the truck checked before buying it*

③ **reassure**
[riə'ʃur] *verb*
to make someone less afraid or less worried; *he tried to reassure everyone that the bus service would not be cut*; *the manager wanted to reassure her that she would not lose her job*

③ **rebel**
1 *noun* ['rebəl]
person who fights against a government or against those who are in authority; *the rebels fled to the mountains after the army captured their headquarters*; *he considers himself something of a rebel because he wears his hair long*
2 *verb* [rɪ'bel]
to fight against someone or something; *the peasants are rebelling against the king's men*; *the class rebelled at the idea of doing extra homework* (NOTE: **rebelling - rebelled**)

④ **rebellion**
[rɪ'beljən] *noun*
revolt, fight against the government; *the rebellion began when some people refused to pay taxes*; *government troops crushed the student rebellion*

① **rebuild**
[ri'bɪld] *verb*
to build again; *the original house was knocked down and rebuilt*; *how long will it take to rebuild the wall?*; *rebuilding the house took longer than we expected* (NOTE: **rebuilding - rebuilt** [ri'bɪlt])

② **recall**
[rɪ'kɔl]
1 *verb*
(a) to remember; *I don't recall having met her before*; *she couldn't recall any details of the accident*
(b) *(of a manufacturer)* to ask for products to be returned because of possible faults; *they recalled 10,000 washing machines because of a*

faulty electrical connection; they have recalled all their 1999 models as there is a fault in the steering
(c) to tell an ambassador to come home from a foreign country; *the United States recalled their ambassador after the military coup*
2 *noun*
calling to come back or to be brought back; *the recall of the washing machine because of an electrical fault caused the manufacturers some serious problems; the recall of the ambassador is expected anytime now*; **beyond recall** = gone and will never come back; *those days beyond recall when we were young!*

① **receipt**
[rɪ'siːt] *noun*
(a) act of receiving; **to acknowledge receipt of a letter** = to write to say that you have received a letter; *we acknowledge receipt of your letter of the January 15; we would like you to confirm receipt of the goods; invoices are payable within 30 days of receipt*; **on receipt of** = when you receive; *on receipt of the notification, they decided to appeal*
(b) paper showing that you have paid, that you have received something; *goods cannot be exchanged unless a sales receipt is shown; would you like a receipt for that shirt?*
(c) **receipts** = money taken in sales; *our receipts are down against the same period last year*

① **receive**
[rɪ'siːv] *verb*
(a) to get something which has been sent; *we received a package from the supplier this morning; we only received our tickets the day before we were due to leave; the staff have not received any wages for six months*; **"received with thanks"** = words put on an invoice to show that a sum has been paid; *(informal)* **to be on the receiving end of** = to have to suffer; *he was on the receiving end of a lot of criticism*
(b) to greet or to welcome a visitor; *the group was received by the minister*

③ **receiver**
[rɪ'siːvər] *noun*
(a) football player who catches the ball; *the quarterback passed the football to the receiver*
(b) radio apparatus that receives signals; **shortwave receiver** = radio receiver able to pick up broadcasts on the short wave bands

③ **recent**
['riːsənt] *adjective*
new, which took place not very long ago; *we will mail you our most recent catalog; the building is very recent - it was finished only last year*

② **recently**
['riːsəntlɪ] *adverb*
only a short time ago; *I've seen him quite a lot recently; they recently decided to move to Maine*

④ **reception**
[rɪ'sepʃn] *noun*

(a) welcome; *the committee gave the proposal a favorable reception; the critics gave the play a warm reception; the mayor had a rowdy reception at the meeting*
(b) *(at a hotel)* place where guests register; *let's meet at reception at 9:00 A.M. tomorrow*; **reception clerk** = person who works at the reception desk; **reception desk** = desk where visitors check in; *please leave your key at the reception desk when you go out*
(c) *(at an office)* place where visitors register and say who they have come to see; *there's a parcel waiting for you in reception*
(d) big party held to welcome special guests; *he hosted a reception for the prince*; **wedding reception** = party held after a wedding, including drinks, toasts, etc.; *only the members of the two families will be at the church, but we've been invited to the reception afterwards; will you be attending Anne and John's wedding reception?*
(e) quality of the sound on a radio or the sound and picture on a TV broadcast; *perhaps you'd get better reception if you moved the TV to another room*

② **recess**
['riːses] *noun*
(in schools) short period for rest and play; *we couldn't go out during recess because it was raining*

④ **recession**
[rɪ'seʃn] *noun*
situation when a country's economy is doing badly; *many businesses failed during the recession*

> COMMENT: the general way of deciding if a recession is taking place is when the country's GNP falls for three quarters in a row

② **recipe**
['resɪpɪ] *noun*
(a) instructions for cooking food; *I copied the recipe for onion soup from the newspaper; you can buy postcards with recipes of local dishes*; **recipe book** = cookbook; *I gave her a Thai recipe book for her birthday; if you're not sure how long to cook turkey, look it up in the recipe book*
(b) effective way to do something; *there is no single recipe for success*; **it's a recipe for disaster** = it's certain to lead to disaster; *the way the management is approaching the problem is a recipe for disaster*

③ **recite**
[rɪ'saɪt] *verb*
to say a poem, etc., aloud in public; *the author will recite two of his poems this evening*

② **reckon**
['rekn] *verb*
(a) to calculate, to estimate; *we reckon the costs to be about $35,000*

(b) to think; *we reckon we'll be there before lunch*

(c) to reckon on = to count on or to depend on; *we can reckon on the support of the president; don't reckon on good weather for your vacations*

(d) to reckon with = to have to deal with; *he didn't realize that he still had to reckon with the bank manager; leave early, don't forget you'll have to reckon with the rush hour traffic*

③ **recognition**
[rekəg'nɪʃn] *noun*
recognizing or acknowledging; *in recognition for his services he was given a watch*; **he's changed beyond all recognition** = he has changed so much that I didn't recognize him

② **recognize**
['rekəgnaɪz] *verb*
(a) to know someone or something because you have seen him or it before; *he'd changed so much since I last saw him that I hardly recognized him; he didn't recognize his father's voice over the phone; do you recognize the handwriting on the letter?*

(b) to recognize a mistake *or* **that you have made a mistake** = to admit that you have made a mistake; *she should have recognized her mistake and said she was sorry; I recognize that we should have acted earlier*

(c) to approve of something or someone officially; *the language school has been recognized by the Department of Education; she is recognized as an expert in the field of genetics*; **to recognize a government** = to say that a new government which has taken power in a country is the legal government of that country; *Germany was one of the first countries to recognize Croatia as a new independent country*

② **recognized**
['rekəgnaɪzd] *adjective*
which has been approved officially; *he has a certificate from a recognized language school; she's a recognized expert on kidney disease*

② **recommend**
[rekə'mend] *verb*
(a) to suggest that someone should do something; *I would recommend that you talk to the bank manager; the doctor recommended seeing an eye specialist*

(b) to praise something or someone; *she was highly recommended by her boss; I certainly would not recommend Miss Smith for the job; can you recommend a good hotel in Caracas?*

④ **recommendation**
[rekəmen'deɪʃn] *noun*
(a) advice; *my recommendation is that you shouldn't sign the contract; he's staying in bed at the doctor's recommendation*

(b) praise; *we appointed her on the recommendation of her boss*

① **record**
1 *noun* ['rekɔrd]
(a) success in sport which is better than any other; *she holds the world record for the 100 meters; he broke the world record or he set up a new world record at the last Olympics; the college team is trying to set a new record for eating pizzas*; **at record speed** *or* **in record time** = very fast; *he finished the book in record time*

(b) success which is better than anything before; **record sales** = sales which are higher than ever before; *we're looking forward to record sales this month; last year was a record year for our store; sales for 1999 equaled our previous record of 1996*; **we broke our record for June** = we sold more than we have ever sold before in June

(c) written evidence of something that has happened; *we have no record of the sale*; **for the record** *or* **to keep the record straight** = so as to note something that has been done; *for the record, we will not deal with this company again*; **he is on record as saying** = he is accurately reported as saying; **off the record** = in private, not to be made public; *she spoke off the record about her marriage*

(d) description of what someone has done in the past; *he has a record of dishonest business deals*; **track record** = success or failure of someone or a business in the past; *he has a good track record as a salesman*

(e) flat, round piece of black plastic on which sound is stored; *she bought me an old Elvis Presley record for Christmas; burglars broke into his flat and stole his record collection*
2 *verb* [rɪ'kɔrd]
(a) to report; to make a note; *first, I have to record the sales, then I'll mail the parcels*

(b) to fix sounds on a film or tape; *the police recorded the whole conversation through a hidden microphone; this song has been badly recorded*

① **recorder**
[rɪ'kɔrdər] *noun*
(a) instrument that records sound; *my tape recorder doesn't work, so I can't record the concert*

(b) small wooden musical instrument that you play by blowing; *like most children, I learned to play the recorder at school*

④ **recording**
[rɪ'kɔrdɪŋ] *noun*
(a) action of fixing sounds on tape or on disc; *be on time - the recording session starts at 3 pm*

(b) music or speech that has been recorded; *did you know there was a new recording of the piece?*

② **recover**
[rɪ'kʌvər] *verb*
(a) to recover from an illness = to get well again after an illness; *she is still recovering from the flu*

(b) to recover from a shock = to get over a

shock; *it took him weeks to recover from the shock of seeing his son in court*
(c) to get back something which has been lost, stolen, invested, etc.; *she's trying to recover damages from the driver of the automobile*; *you must work much harder if you want to recover the money you invested in your business*
(d) [ri'kʌvər] to put a new cover on a piece of furniture; *instead of buying a new chair, I had the old one recovered*

③ **recovery**
[rɪ'kʌvri] *noun*
(a) getting well again; *she made a quick recovery and is now back at work*
(b) getting back something which has been lost, stolen, invested, etc.; *the TV show led to the recovery of all the stolen goods*; *we are aiming for the complete recovery of the money invested*
(c) upwards movement of the economy, of a company's shares; *the U.S. economy staged a rapid recovery*

④ **recreation**
[rekrɪ'eɪʃn] *noun*
pleasant activity for your spare time; *what is your favorite recreation?*; *doesn't he have any recreations other than sitting watching TV?*

③ **recreational vehicle (RV)**
[rekrɪ'eɪʃnəl 'viːkl] *noun*
large vehicle in which you can sleep, store equipment and cook; *we will travel in the RV*

② **recruit**
[rɪ'krut]
1 *noun*
new soldier, new member of staff, etc.; *recruits are not allowed in the officers' mess*; *the club needs new recruits*
2 *verb*
to encourage someone to join the army, a company, etc.; *they have sent teams to universities to recruit new graduates*; **to recruit new staff** = to get new staff to join a company; *we are recruiting staff for our new store*

④ **recycle**
[ri'saɪkl] *verb*
to process waste material so that it can be used again; *glass and newspapers are the main items for recycling*; *the city council is encouraging us to recycle more household garbage*; **recycled paper** = paper made from wastepaper; *she always writes to me on recycled paper*

① **red**
[red]
1 *adjective*
(a) colored like the color of blood; *she turned bright red when we asked her what had happened to the money*; *don't start yet - the traffic lights are still red*
(b) **red hair** = hair which is a red or orange color; *all their children have red hair*; *red-haired girls often wear green clothes*
(NOTE: **redder - reddest**)
2 *noun*

(a) color, like the color of blood; *I would like a darker red for the door*; *don't start yet - the traffic lights are still red*
(b) **in the red** = showing a loss; *my bank account is in the red*; *the company went into the red*

③ **red carpet**
['red 'kɑrpɪt] *noun*
carpet put down when an important visitor comes, hence an official welcome; *they rolled out the red carpet for the president's visit*; *he got the red-carpet treatment*

② **Red Cross**
['red 'krɒs] *noun*
international organization that provides emergency medical help, and also relief to victims of floods, etc.; *Red Cross officials have been sent to the refugee camps*; *we met a representative of the Red Cross*

③ **red-hot**
[red'hɒt] *adjective*
(a) *(of metal)* so hot that it is red; *the bar of steel is red-hot when it comes out of the mill*
(b) *(informal)* very hot; *watch out - that pan is red-hot!*

③ **red tape**
['red 'teɪp] *noun*
official forms that take a long time to complete; *the project has been held up by government red tape*

② **reduce**
[rɪ'djus] *verb*
to make smaller or less; *the police are fighting to reduce traffic accidents*; *prices have been reduced by 15%*; *I'd like to reduce the size of the photograph so that we can use it as a Christmas card*; **reduced prices** = lower prices; *there are reduced prices for groups of 30 and over*; **to reduce staff** = to lay off employees in order to have a smaller number of staff; *unfortunately, the best way to save money is to reduce staff*; **to reduce weight** = to get thinner; *she started a new diet in order to reduce weight*

③ **reduction**
[rɪ'dʌkʃn] *noun*
making smaller (price, speed, standards, etc.); *price reductions start on August 1*; *the company was forced to make job reductions*

② **redundant**
[rɪ'dʌndənt] *adjective*
no longer needed, more than necessary; *two of the offices are redundant - we should let them*

② **redwood**
['redwʊd] *noun*
very tall conifer which grows on the West Coast of the U.S.A.; *there are forests of redwoods in northern California*

③ **reed**
[rid] *noun*
tall thick grass growing in wet places; *reeds*

grow by the edge of rivers or lakes (NOTE: do not confuse with **read**)

③ **reef**
[rif] *noun*
long line of rocks just above or beneath the surface of the sea; *the Great Barrier Reef is off the north-east coast of Australia*

② **reel**
[ril]
1 *noun*
round object used for winding thread, wire or film round; *she put a new reel of film on the projector*
2 *verb*
to stagger; *two men came out of the bar and went reeling down the street; the punch on the face sent the boxer reeling; the company is still reeling from its losses in the Far East*

② **reelect**
[riːˈlekt] *verb*
to elect again; *she was reelected with a large majority*

② **reelection**
[riːˈlekʃn] *noun*
being reelected; *her reelection was unexpected; the previous president is eligible for reelection*

④ **reel off**
[ˈril ˈɒf] *verb*
to give a list of names or figures rapidly; *he reeled off a list of hotels and their prices; she reeled off a series of dates and invoice numbers*

② **ref**
[ref] *noun (informal)*
(a) *(in sports)* = REFEREE; *come on ref - that was a foul!*
(b) = REFERENCE

③ **refer to**
[rɪˈfɜr tʊ] *verb*
(a) to mention something; *do you think he was referring to me when he talked about clever managers?; the note refers you to page 24*
(b) to look into something for information; *he referred to his diary to see if he had a free afternoon*
(c) to pass a problem to someone to decide; *we have referred your complaint to our head office; he was referred to an ear specialist by his doctor; see your primary doctor first, and he or she will refer you to a specialist* (NOTE: referring - referred)

② **referee**
[refəˈri]
1 *noun*
(a) *(in sports)* person who supervises a game, making sure that it is played according to the rules; *when fighting broke out between the players, the referee stopped the match; the referee sent several players to the locker room* (NOTE: referees are in charge of most sports, such as basketball or boxing, but not for tennis, where the person in charge is an **umpire**)

(b) person who gives a report on your character, ability, etc.; *she gave the name of her former boss as a referee; when applying please give the names of three referees*
2 *verb*
to act as a referee in a sports match; *there's no one to referee the match this afternoon*

③ **reference**
[ˈrefrəns] *noun*
(a) **reference to something** = mention of something; *she made a reference to her brother-in-law; the report made no reference to the bank*; **with reference to** = concerning, about; *with reference to your letter of May 25*
(b) direction for further information; *there are references to various documents at the back of the book*; **reference book** = book, such as a dictionary or directory, where you can look for information; *we sell far more novels than reference books*; **reference library** = library with reference books, where readers can search for information but not take the books away from the library
(c) report on someone's character, ability, etc.; *we ask all applicants to supply references*; **to contact references** = to get in touch with referees to see what they think of the person applying for a job; *when she applied for the job we took up her references and found they were not as good as we had expected*
(d) person who gives a report on your character; *he gave my name as a reference; please use me as a reference if you wish*

④ **referendum**
[refəˈrendəm] *noun*
vote where all the people of a country or an area are asked to vote on an issue; *last year there was a referendum on the ballot to ban gambling here* (NOTE: plural is **referenda** *or* **referendums**)

① **refill**
1 *noun* [ˈrifɪl]
container with a fresh quantity of liquid; *dishwasher soap is sold in handy refill packs*
2 *verb* [riˈfɪl]
to fill again; *we stopped twice to refill the car on the way to Indiana*

④ **refine**
[rɪˈfaɪn] *verb*
(a) to make more pure; *juice from sugar cane is refined by boiling*
(b) to make something better; *the system needs to be further refined before we can introduce it nationally*

① **reflect**
[rɪˈflekt] *verb*
(a) to send back light, heat, an image, etc.; *the light reflected on the top of the car; white surfaces reflect light better than dark ones; a photograph of white mountains reflected in a clear blue lake*
(b) to reflect (on something) = to think carefully about something; *he reflected that this was the*

sixth time he had been arrested for speeding ; **to reflect badly on someone** = to show someone in a bad way; *the story reflects badly on the way the manager runs his department*

② **reflection**
[rɪ'flekʃn] *noun*
(a) sending back of light or heat; *you should wear dark glasses because of the reflection of the sun on the snow*
(b) reflected image in a mirror, in water, etc.; *she saw her reflection in the store window and smiled*
(c) thought; *a few moments' reflection convinced her that she had done the right thing*; **on reflection** = on thinking more; *on reflection, I think I'd better leave today rather than tomorrow*
(d) **to be a reflection on someone** = to show someone in a bad way; *it's no reflection on you if your father is in prison*

② **reform**
[rɪ'fɔrm]
1 *noun*
act of changing something to make it better; *they are planning a series of reforms to the health care system*
2 *verb*
(a) to change to make better, to improve; *they want to reform the educational system*
(b) to stop committing crimes, to change your habits to become good; *after his time in prison he became a reformed character*; *he used to drink a lot, but since he got married he has reformed*

③ **refreshing**
[rɪ'freʃɪŋ] *adjective*
(a) which makes you clean and fresh again; *I had a refreshing drink of cold water*; *a refreshing shower of rain cooled the air*
(b) exciting and new; *our new offices are a refreshing change from the old building*

① **refreshments**
[rɪ'freʃmənts] *noun*
food and drink; *light refreshments will be served after the concert*; *refreshments are being offered in a tent on the lawn*

① **refrigerator**
[rɪ'frɪdʒəreɪtər] *noun*
electric kitchen cabinet for keeping food and drink cold; *there's some cold orange juice in the refrigerator*; *milk will keep for several days in a refrigerator*; *each hotel bedroom has a small refrigerator with cold drinks* (NOTE: often called a **fridge**)

④ **refuge**
['refjudʒ] *noun*
place of refuge = place to shelter; **to seek refuge** = to try to find shelter; *during the fighting, they sought refuge in the U.S. embassy*; **to take refuge** = to shelter; *when the hurricane approached, they took refuge in the cellar*

② **refugee**
[refju'dʒi] *noun*
person who has left his country because of war, religious differences, etc.; *at the beginning of the war, thousands of refugees fled over the border*; **economic refugee** = person who has left his country because the economic situation is bad, and it is difficult to find work; **political refugee** = person who has left his country because he is afraid of being put in prison for his political beliefs; *these political refugees are afraid that they will be jailed if they go back to their country*

② **refund**
['rifʌnd]
1 *noun*
money paid back; *she got a refund after she complained to the manager*; **full refund** *or* **refund in full** = paying back all the money paid; *he got a full refund when he complained about the service*
2 *verb*
to pay money back; *we will refund the cost of postage*; *the tour company only refunded $150 of the $600 I had paid*

② **refusal**
[rɪ'fjuzl] *noun*
(a) saying that you do not accept something, saying no; *did you accept? - no! I sent a letter of refusal*; **to meet with a flat refusal** = to be refused completely; *his request met with a flat refusal*
(b) **to give someone first refusal of something** = to let someone have first choice when doing something; *I asked him if I could have first refusal of his apartment if ever he decided to sell it*

② **refuse**
1 *noun* ['refjus]
(formal) garbage, things which are not wanted; *please put all refuse in the bin*; *refuse collection on our block is on Thursdays* (NOTE: no plural)
2 *verb* [rɪ'fjuz]
(a) to say that you will not do something; *his father refused to lend him any more money*; *he asked for permission to see his family, but it was refused*
(b) **the automobile refused to start** = the automobile would not start; *once again this morning the car refused to start* (NOTE: you refuse **to do something** or refuse **something**)

② **regain**
[rɪ'geɪn] *verb*
to get something back which was lost; *she soon regained her strength and was able to walk*; *what can I do to regain any of the money I've lost?*; **to regain consciousness** = to become conscious again; *she never regained consciousness after the accident*

③ **regard**
[rɪ'gɑrd]

1 *noun*

(a) concern for something; **with regard to** = relating to, concerning; *with regard to your request for extra funds*

(b) opinion of someone; *he is held in high regard by his staff*

(c) regards = best wishes; *she sends her (kind) regards*; *please give my regards to your mother*

2 *verb*

(a) to regard someone *or* **something as** = to consider someone or something to be; *the police are regarding the case as attempted murder*

(b) to have an opinion about someone; *she is highly regarded by the manager*

(c) as regards = relating to, concerning; *as regards the cost of the trip, I'll let you know soon what the final figure is*

④ **regarding**
[rɪ'gɑrdɪŋ] *preposition*
relating to, concerning; *he left instructions regarding his possessions*; *regarding your offer, I think we will have to say no*

② **regardless**
[rɪ'gɑrdləs] *adverb*
without paying any attention to; **regardless of** = in spite of; *they drove through the war zone regardless of the danger*; *they furnished their house regardless of expense* = without thinking of how much it would cost; **to carry on regardless** = to continue in spite of everything; *although the temperature was well over 120°, they carried on working regardless*

④ **regime** *or* **régime**
[reɪ'ʒim] *noun*
(a) usually strict type of government or administration; *under a military régime, civil liberties may be restricted*

(b) government of a country; *the former régime was overthrown and the president fled*

③ **regiment**
['redʒɪmənt] *noun*
group of soldiers, usually commanded by a colonel; *an infantry regiment was sent to the war zone*

② **region**
['ridʒən] *noun*
(a) large administrative area; *this region is known for its wines*

(b) in the region of = about or approximately; *he is earning a salary in the region of $38,000*; *the house was sold for a price in the region of $300,000*

② **regional**
['ridʒənəl] *adjective*
referring to a region; *the recession has not affected the whole country - it is only regional*; *after the national news, here is the regional news for Cape Cod*

② **register**
['redʒɪstər]
1 *noun*

(a) list of names; *I can't find your name in the register*; *his name was struck off the register*; **register of voters** = list of the names of people who can vote in an election

(b) book in which you sign your name; *after the wedding, the bride and bridegroom and witnesses all signed the register*; *please sign the hotel register when you check in*

(c) cash register = machine that shows and adds the prices of items bought in a store, with a drawer for keeping the money received; *she opened the cash register to put in the money given by the customer*

2 *verb*

(a) to write a name officially in a list; *if you don't register, we won't be able to get in touch with you*; *babies have to be registered as soon as they are born*; **to register at a hotel** = to write your name and address when you arrive at the hotel; *they registered at the hotel under the name of Macdonald*

(b) to put a letter into the special care of the post office; *she registered the letter, but it still got lost*

(c) to record, to show a feeling, a figure; *temperatures of over 150° were registered in the desert*; *the amount of pollution was so small it didn't register on our monitor*; *his face registered anger and pain*

(d) *(informal)* to notice, to pay attention; *I told him he was getting a big pay raise, but it didn't seem to register*

② **registered**
['redʒɪstəd] *adjective*
(a) which has been noted on an official list; *a registered trademark*

(b) registered mail = system where details of a letter or parcel are noted by the post office before it is sent, so that compensation can be claimed if it is lost; *to send documents by registered mail*; **registered letter** = letter that has been officially recorded at the post office; *the registered letter that arrived this morning was not important*

④ **registrar**
['redʒɪstrar] *noun*
person who keeps official records; *all births have to be recorded with the registrar of births, marriages and deaths*; *they were married by the registrar*

② **registration**
[redʒɪ'streɪʃn] *noun*
act of registering; *registration of new students will start at 1 pm*; **registration number** = official number of something; *the insurance company needs the automobile registration number*

④ **registry**
['redʒɪstri] *noun*
place where official records are kept; *check with the Registry of Motor Vehicles*

③ **regret**
['rɪ'gret]
1 *noun*
being sorry; *I have absolutely no regrets about what we did*; *she showed no regret for having made so much mess*; **much to someone's regret** = making someone very sorry; *much to my regret I will not be able to go to Chicago*; *much to the children's regret or much to the regret of the children, the ice-cream parlor closed down*
2 *verb*
to be sorry that something has happened; *I regret to say that you were not successful*; *I regret the trouble this has caused you*; *we regret the delay in the arrival of our flight from Boston*; *we regret to inform you that the tour has been canceled* (NOTE: **regretting - regretted**)

② **regular**
['regjulər]
1 *adjective*
(a) done at the same time each day; *his regular train is the 12:45*; *the regular flight to Atlanta leaves at 6:00*; **regular customer** = customer who always buys from the same store; *he's a regular customer, you don't need to ask for proof of identity*; **regular income** = income which comes in every week or month; *it is difficult to budget if you don't have a regular income*
(b) ordinary, standard; *the regular price is $1.25, but we are offering them at 99¢*; **regular size** = ordinary size of goods (smaller than economy size, family size, etc.); *just buy a regular size pack, it will be enough for the two of us*
2 *noun*
(informal) customer who always goes to the same restaurant, store, etc.; *the waiter recognized him as a regular*

④ **regularly**
['regjulərli] *adverb*
in a regular way; *she is regularly the first person to arrive at the office each morning*

③ **regulate**
['regjuleɪt] *verb*
(a) to adjust a machine so that it works in a certain way; *the heater needs to be regulated to keep the temperature steady*; *turn this button regulate the volume*; *her heart is regulated by a tiny device in her chest*
(b) to maintain something by law; *speed on the freeway is strictly regulated*

③ **regulation**
[regju'leɪʃn] *noun*
(a) act of regulating; *the greenhouse is fitted with an automatic heat regulation system*; *the regulation of the body's temperature by sweating*
(b) **regulations** = laws, rules; *the restaurant broke the fire regulations*; *safety regulations were not being properly followed*; *the new government regulations on housing standards*

③ **regulator**
['regjuleɪtər] *noun*
(a) person whose job it is to see that regulations are followed in an industry; *the industry regulator makes sure that the rules are followed*
(b) instrument which regulates a machine; *this truck is fitted with a speed regulator*

② **rehearsal**
[rɪ'hɜrsəl] *noun*
practice of a play or concert, etc., before the first public performance; *the director insisted on extra rehearsals because some of the cast didn't know their lines*; *see also* DRESS REHEARSAL

② **rehearse**
[rɪ'hɜrs] *verb*
to practice a play, a concert, etc., before a public performance; *we're rehearsing the concert in the town hall*

③ **reign**
[reɪn]
1 *noun*
(a) period when a king or queen rules; *during the reign of Elizabeth I*
(b) **reign of terror** = period when law and order have broken down and people live in a continual state of fear
2
(a) *verb*
to rule; *Queen Victoria reigned between 1837 and 1901*; *she reigned during a period of great economic development*
(b) to be in existence; *chaos reigned when the town's electricity supply went out* (NOTE: do not confuse with **rain, rein**)

③ **rein**
[reɪn]
1 *noun*
(a) leather strap which the rider holds to control a horse; *she walked beside the horse holding the reins*; *the rider pulled hard on the reins to try to make the horse stop*
(b) **to keep something on a tight rein** = to control something strictly; *unless you keep your expenses on a tight rein, you'll have problems*
2 *verb*
to rein back or **rein in** = to keep under control; *the leader of the opposition tried to rein in his supporters who wanted to attack the president's residence* (NOTE: do not confuse with **rain, reign**)

③ **reinforce**
[riɪn'fɔrs] *verb*
to make stronger or more solid; *you must reinforce that wall before it collapses*; *this event has reinforced my decision to leave*; **reinforced concrete** = concrete strengthened with metal rods; *the new bridge was built with reinforced concrete*

② **reject**
1 noun ['ridʒekt]
person or thing which has been refused as not satisfactory; *these men are rejects from military service*; *the store specializes in selling rejects*
2 verb [rɪ'dʒekt]
(a) to refuse to accept something; *she flatly rejected his proposal*; *we rejected his offer for the house because it was too low*; *she rejected three different wallpaper designs because they were too bright*
(b) to throw something away as not satisfactory; *half the batch was rejected and sold off cheaply as seconds*
(c) *(medical)* not to accept a transplanted organ; *his body rejected the new heart*

③ **relate**
[rɪ'leɪt] verb
(a) to be concerned with; *the regulations that relate to landing passengers at the harbor*
(b) **to relate to someone** = to understand someone and be able to communicate with them; *do you find it difficult to relate to him?*
(c) to tell a story; *it took him half an hour to relate what had happened*

① **related (to)**
[rɪ'leɪtɪd 'tu] adjective
(a) belonging to the same family; *are you related to the Schmidt family on Brooklyn Road?*
(b) linked; *a disease that is related to the weakness of the heart muscle*; *he has a drug-related illness*; *there are several related items on the agenda*

③ **relating to**
[rɪ'leɪtɪŋ 'tu] adverb
referring to, connected with; *documents relating to the sale*

② **relation**
[rɪ'leɪʃn] noun
(a) member of a family; *all my relations live in Canada*; *Laura's no relation of mine, she's just a friend*
(b) link between two things; *is there any relation between his appointment as vice president and the fact that his uncle owns the business?*; **in relation to** = referring to, connected with; *documents in relation to the sale*
(c) **relations** = links (with other people); *we try to maintain good relations with our customers*; *relations between the two countries have become tense*; *see also* PUBLIC RELATIONS

② **relationship**
[rɪ'leɪʃnʃɪp] noun
(a) link or connection; *there is a relationship between smoking and lung cancer*; *we try to have a good working relationship with our staff*; **love-hate relationship** = situation where two people get along well together and then dislike each other in turn

(b) close (sexual) friendship; *she decided to end the relationship when she found he had been seeing other women*

② **relative**
['relətɪv]
1 noun
person who is related to someone; member of a family; *we have several relatives living in Canada*; *he has no living relatives*
2 adjective
(a) compared to something else; *everything is relative - if you have ten cows you are rich in some African countries*; **relative poverty** = poverty compared with really wealthy people or with the wealth someone used to have; *my old uncle lives in relative poverty*
(b) *(in grammar)* **relative pronoun** = pronoun, such as "who" or "which", which connects two clauses

④ **relatively**
['relətɪvli] adverb
more or less; *the children have been relatively free from colds this winter*; *we are dealing with a relatively new company*

① **relax**
[rɪ'læks] verb
(a) to rest from work; to be less tense; *they spent the first week of their vacation relaxing on the beach*; *guests can relax in the bar before going to eat in the restaurant*; *just lie back and relax - the injection won't hurt*
(b) to make less strict; *the club has voted to relax the rules about the admission of women members*

② **relaxation**
[rilæk'seɪʃn] noun
rest from work; *do you consider gardening a form of relaxation?*; *he plays tennis for relaxation or as relaxation*

② **relaxed**
[rɪ'lækst] adjective
calm, not upset; *even if he failed his test, he's still very relaxed about the whole thing*

② **relaxing**
[rɪ'læksɪŋ] adjective
which makes you less tense; *I always enjoy a relaxing hot bath after a game of softball*; *if you feel stressed, just close your eyes and listen to relaxing music*

② **relay**
1 noun ['rileɪ]
(a) group of people working in turn with other groups; *a shift is usually composed of groups of workers who work in relays*; *all the work had been done by the time the next relay arrived*
(b) **relay race** = running race by teams in which one runner passes a stick to another who then runs on; *they won the 400 m relay*
2 verb [rɪ'leɪ]
(a) to pass on a message; *she relayed the news to the other members of her family*; *all messages are relayed through this office*

(b) to pass on a TV or radio broadcast through a secondary station; *the programs are received in the capital and then relayed to TV stations around the country*

② **release**
[rɪ'lis]
1 *noun*
(a) setting free; *the release of prisoners from jail*; *the release of hormones into the blood*
(b) press release = sheet giving news about something which is sent to newspapers and TV and radio stations so that they can use the information in it; *we issued a press release about the opening of the new store*
(c) new releases = new records or CDs that are put on the market
(d) setting free from pain; *his death was a release*
2 *verb*
(a) to set free; *six prisoners were released from prison*; *customs released the goods after we paid a fine*; *we nursed the injured rabbit for a week and then released it in the field*; *the glands release hormones into the blood*
(b) to make public; *the government has released figures about the number of people out of work*

④ **relevant**
['relɪvənt] *adjective*
which has to do with something being mentioned; *which is the relevant government department?*; *he gave me all the relevant papers*; *is this information at all relevant?*

② **reliable**
[rɪ'laɪəbl] *adjective*
which can be relied on, which can be trusted; *it is a very reliable automobile*; *the sales manager is completely reliable*

④ **reliably**
[rɪ'laɪəbli] *adverb*
in a way which can be trusted; *I am reliably informed that he was not on the plane*; *the machine has worked reliably for months*

③ **relief**
[rɪ'lif] *noun*
(a) reducing pain or stress; *an aspirin should bring relief*; *he breathed a sigh of relief when the patrol car went past without stopping*; *it's a relief to have finished my finals!*
(b) help; *the Red Cross is organizing relief for the flood victims*
(c) person who takes over from another; *a relief nurse will take over from you at one o'clock*; *your relief will be here in half an hour*; relief shift = shift which comes to take the place of another shift; *the relief shift is due in ten minutes*
(d) carving in which the details of design stand out; in relief = standing out, prominent; relief map = map where height is shown by color, so mountains are brown and plains are green

③ **relieve**
[rɪ'liv] *verb*
(a) to make better, easier; *he took aspirins to relieve the pain*
(b) *(formal)* to relieve oneself = to pass waste matter out of the body; *he stopped by the side of the road to relieve himself*
(c) to help; *an agency that tries to relieve stress after divorce*
(d) to take over from someone; *you can go and have something to eat - I'm here to relieve you*
(e) to remove a problem from someone; *let me relieve you of some of these parcels*; *this piece of equipment will relieve you of some of your work*

③ **relieved**
[rɪ'livd] *adjective*
glad to be rid of a problem; *everyone is relieved that she has passed her driver's test*; *she was relieved to find that she did not owe him any money after all*; *how relieved I am to hear the news!*

① **religion**
[rɪ'lɪdʒən] *noun*
belief in gods or in one God; *does their religion help them to lead a good life?*; *it is against my religion to eat meat on Fridays*

② **religious**
[rɪ'lɪdʒəs] *adjective*
(a) referring to religion; *there is a period of religious study every morning*
(b) having strong belief in God; *she's very religious - she goes to church every day*

④ **relinquish**
[rɪ'lɪŋkwɪʃ] *verb*
(formal) to leave or to let go of something; *he finally relinquished control of the business*

④ **reluctant**
[rɪ'lʌktənt] *adjective*
reluctant to = not eager to, not willing to; *he was reluctant to go into the water because it looked cold*

④ **reluctantly**
[rɪ'lʌktəntli] *adverb*
not eagerly; *he reluctantly agreed to do the work*

② **rely (on)**
[rɪ'laɪ ɒn] *verb*
to depend on; *I'm relying on you to read the map*; *we rely on part-time staff for most of our mail-order business*

② **remain**
[rɪ'meɪn] *verb*
(a) to stay; *we expect it will remain fine for the rest of the week*; *she remained behind at the office to finish her work*
(b) to be left; *half the food remained on the guests' plates and had to be thrown away*; *after the accident not much remained of the vehicle*
(c) it remains to be seen = we will find out later; *how many people have survived the crash remains to be seen*; *it remains to be seen*

whether she's ever going to be able to walk again

② remainder
[rɪ'meɪndər]
1 *noun*
(a) what is left after everything else has gone; *what shall we do for the remainder of the vacations?*; *after the bride and bridegroom left, the remainder of the party stayed in the hotel to have supper*
(b) remainders = new books that are sold off cheaply because they are not selling well; *remainders are sold through special bookstores*
2 *verb*
to sell off new books cheaply; *a store full of piles of remaindered books*

② remaining
[rɪ'meɪnɪŋ] *adjective*
which is left; *the only remaining house in the village was damaged*; *she's not the only remaining member of her family - her sister is still alive*

② remains
[rɪ'meɪnz] *noun*
(a) things left over or left behind; *the remains of the evening meal were left on the table until the next morning*; *we're trying to save the Roman remains from destruction by the construction company*
(b) *(formal)* body of a dead person; *the emperor's remains were buried in the cathedral*

② remark
[rɪ'mark]
1 *noun*
comment; *I heard his remark even if he spoke in a low voice*; **to make remarks about** = to make sharp or rude comments about; *she made some remarks about the filth in the restaurant*
2 *verb*
to notice, to comment on; *she remarked on the dirty table*

② remarkable
[rɪ'markəbl] *adjective*
very unusual, which you might notice; *she's a remarkable woman*; *it's remarkable that the bank has not asked us to pay back the money*

② remarkably
[rɪ'markəbli] *adverb*
unusually; *remarkably, the bank didn't ask for the money to be paid back; he did remarkably well on his exams; apart from a minor infection, his health has been remarkably good*

③ remedy
['remədi]
1 *noun*
thing which may cure; *it's an old remedy for colds* (NOTE: plural is **remedies**)
2 *verb*
to correct something, to make something better; *tell me what's wrong and I'll try to remedy it right away*

① remember
[rɪ'membər] *verb*
(a) to bring back into your mind something which you have seen or heard before; *do you remember when we got lost in the fog?; my grandmother can remember seeing the first television programs; she remembered seeing it on the dining room table; she can't remember where she put her umbrella; I don't remember having been in this hotel before; I remember my grandmother very well; it's strange that I can never remember my father's birthday; did you remember to switch off the kitchen light?* (NOTE: you **remember doing something** which you did in the past; you **remember to do something** in the future)
(b) to ask someone to pass your good wishes to someone; *please remember me to your father when you see him next*

① remind
[rɪ'maɪnd] *verb*
(a) to make someone remember something; *now that you've reminded me, I do remember seeing him last week; remind me to book the tickets for the show; she reminded him that the meeting had to finish at 6:30 P.M.*
(b) to remind someone of = to make someone think of something; *do you know what this reminds me of?; she reminds me of her mother*

③ reminder
[rɪ'maɪndər] *noun*
(a) thing which reminds you of something; *keep this picture as a reminder of happier days*
(b) letter to remind a customer to do something; *we had a reminder from the gas company that we hadn't paid the bill*

④ reminiscent
[remɪ'nɪsənt] *adjective*
which reminds you of the past; *this landscape is reminiscent of paintings by Constable; his whole attitude is reminiscent of that of his father*

④ remote
[rɪ'məʊt] *adjective*
(a) far away; *the hotel is situated in a remote mountain village*; **remote control** = device that controls a model plane, TV, etc., by radio signals; *has anyone seen the remote control for the TV or the TV remote control?*
(b) slight, not very strong; *there's a remote chance of finding a cure for his illness; the possibility of him arriving on time is remote; look at the fog - there is not the remotest possibility of the plane taking off*
(c) *(person)* who does not communicate very much; *their daughter is difficult to get to know, she seems so remote* (NOTE: **remoter - remotest**)

③ removal
[rɪ'muvəl] *noun*
taking something away; *the removal of the ban on importing computers; garbage collectors*

are responsible for the removal of household waste

② **remove**
[rɪ'muv] *verb*
to take away; *you can remove his name from the mailing list; the waitress removed the dirty plates and brought us some tea*

③ **renew**
[rɪ'nju] *verb*
(a) to start again; *renew your efforts and don't lose hope*
(b) to replace something old with something new; *we need to renew the electric wires in the kitchen*
(c) to continue something for a further period of time; *don't forget to renew your insurance policy*; **to renew a subscription** = to pay a subscription for another year; *I don't think I'll renew my subscription to the magazine - I hardly ever read it*

③ **renewable**
[rɪ'njuəbl] *adjective*
(a) which can be renewed; *the season ticket is renewable for a further year*
(b) which can be replaced, which can renew itself; *renewable sources of energy such as solar power, and power from wind or water*

② **renewal**
[rɪ'njuəl] *noun*
act of renewing; *we noticed a renewal of interest in old paintings*; **the subscription is up for renewal** = the subscription needs to be renewed

④ **renown**
[rɪ'naʊn] *noun*
(formal) being famous; *her renown as an opera singer*

④ **renowned**
[rɪ'naʊnd] *adjective*
(a) *(formal)* very famous; *Florence is renowned as the center of Italian art*
(b) **renowned for** = famous for something; *she's renowned for being late; a store which is renowned for the quality of its products*

① **rent**
[rent]
1 *noun*
money paid to live in an apartment or house, to use an office, etc.; *rents are high in the center of the town; the landlord asked me to pay three months' rent in advance*; **rent control** = government regulation of rents
2 *verb*
(a) to pay money to use a house, apartment, automobile, etc.; *he rents an office in downtown St. Louis; they were driving a rented automobile when they were stopped by the police; he rented a cottage by the beach for three weeks*
(b) **to rent (out)** = to let someone use a house, office, apartment, etc., for money; *we rented*

(out) one floor of our building to a Japanese company

② **rental**
['rentəl] *noun*
rent, money paid to use a room, apartment, office, car, etc.; *the room rental has gone up this quarter*; **car rental firm** = company which specializes in offering cars for rent; *there are no reliable car rental firms around here*

② **reorganization**
[rɪɔrgənaɪ'zeɪʃn] *noun*
act of reorganizing; *the reorganization of the company will take a long time*

① **reorganize**
[rɪ'ɔrgənaɪz] *verb*
to organize in a new way; *do you plan to reorganize the club and accept more members?; she reorganized the library and we can't find anything anymore*

③ **rep**
[rep] *(informal)* = REPRESENTATIVE
salesman who visits clients, trying to sell them something; *they have vacancies for reps in the north of the country; we have a reps' meeting every three months*

② **repaid**
[rɪ'peɪd]
see REPAY

① **repair**
[rɪ'peər]
1 *noun*
(a) mending something which is broken or has been damaged; *his automobile is in the garage for repair; the hotel is closed while they are carrying out repairs to the heating system*
(b) **to be in a good state of repair** *or* **in good repair** = to be in good condition; *this automobile is still in a very good state of repair, I won't change it yet*
2 *verb*
to mend, to make something work which is broken or damaged; *I dropped my watch on the sidewalk, and I don't think it can be repaired; she's trying to repair the washing machine; the photocopier is being repaired*

① **repay**
[rɪ'peɪ] *verb*
to pay back; *I'll try to repay what I owe you next month; thank you for your help - I hope to be able to repay you one day*; **he repaid me in full** = he paid me back all the money he owed me (NOTE: **repaying - repaid** [rɪ'peɪd])

③ **repayment**
['rɪ'peɪmənt] *noun*
paying back; *repayment of the loan is by monthly installments*

① **repeat**
[rɪ'pit]
1 *verb*
to say something again; *could you repeat what you just said?; he repeated the address so that*

the police officer could write it down; she kept on repeating that she wanted to go home; **to repeat yourself** = to say the same thing over and over again; *he's getting old - he keeps repeating himself*

2 *adjective*

repeat performance = performance which is done a second time; *the play is being performed on Friday, and there will be a repeat performance on Saturday*

3 *noun*

performance (of a play, TV show) which is done a second time; *during the summer the TV seems to be showing only repeats*

② **replace**
[rɪ'pleɪs] *verb*

(a) to put something back where it was before; *please replace the books correctly on the shelves*

(b) to replace something with something else = to put something in the place of something else; *the washing machine needs replacing; we are replacing all our permanent staff with part-time people; see also* SEARCH

② **replacement**
[rɪ'pleɪsmənt] *noun*

(a) replacing something with something else; *the garage recommended the replacement of the hand pump with an electric model; the republican movement would like to see the replacement of the king by a president;* **hip replacement** = operation to replace the whole hip joint with an artificial one; *old people sometimes need to have hip replacements; see also* HORMONE

(b) thing which is used to replace something; *an electric motor was bought as a replacement for the old one;* **replacement parts** = spare parts of an engine used to replace parts which have worn out

(c) person who replaces someone; *my secretary leaves us next week, so we are advertising for a replacement*

④ **replay**
1 *noun* ['riːpleɪ]

(a) match that is played again because the first match was a draw; *they tied 2-2 so there will be a replay next week*

(b) instant replay = section of a sporting event that is shown again on TV at a slower speed, so that the action can be examined carefully; *look at the instant replay to see if it really was a foul*

2 *verb* [riː'pleɪ]

to play again; *he replayed the message on the answering machine several times, but still couldn't understand it; the match will be replayed next week*

② **reply**
[rɪ'plaɪ]
1 *noun*

(a) answer; *I asked him what he was doing but got no reply; we wrote last week, but haven't*

had a reply yet; send a stamped addressed envelope for a reply; we had six replies to our advertisement*

(b) in reply = as an answer; *in reply to my letter, I received a fax two days later; she just shook her head in reply and turned away* (NOTE: plural is **replies**)

2 *verb*

to answer; *he never replies to my letters; we wrote last week, but he hasn't replied yet; he refused to reply to questions until his lawyer arrived*

② **report**
[rɪ'pɔrt]
1 *noun*

(a) description of what has happened or what will happen; *we read the reports of the accident in the newspaper; can you confirm the report that the council is planning to sell the old town hall?*

(b) report card = document from a school, telling how a student has done over a period; *we discussed Jane's report card with her teacher*

2 *verb*

(a) to tell someone what happened; to write a description of what happened; *you must report the burglary to the police; she reported that her purse had been stolen from her bedroom; the press reported a plane crash in Georgia; she reported seeing the missing man in her store;* **to report back** = to send a report back to the office, etc., on what has happened; *you must report back as soon as you find out what happened; go and visit our suppliers and report back to me on the situation*

(b) to present yourself officially; *to report for work; candidates should report to the personnel office at 9:00*

(c) to report to someone = to be responsible to someone, to be under someone; *she reports directly to the chief executive officer*

④ **reportedly**
[rɪ'pɔrtɪdli] *adverb*

according to what has been reported; *he was reportedly killed before he reached the border*

① **reporter**
[rɪ'pɔrtər] *noun*

journalist who writes reports of events for a newspaper or for a TV news program; *the newspaper sent reporters to cover the floods; all the reporters gathered in a room to interview the president; he works as a reporter for a regional newspaper*

② **reporting**
[rɪ'pɔrtɪŋ] *noun*

action of reporting something in the press; *any reporting of the details of the trial has been forbidden; CNN is famous for its reporting of world events*

③ **represent**
[reprɪ'zent] *verb*

(a) to speak or act on behalf of someone or of a

group of people; *he asked his attorney to represent him at the meeting*
(b) to work for a company, showing goods or services to possible buyers; *he represents an American automobile firm in Europe*
(c) to indicate, to be a symbol of; *the dark green on the map represents woods*

④ **representation**
[reprɪzen'teɪʃn] *noun*
(a) act of selling goods for a company; *we can provide representation throughout Europe*
(b) having someone to act on your behalf; *the minority shareholders want representation on the board*
(c) way of showing; *the design on the Canadian flag is a representation of a red leaf*
(d) representations = complaints or protests; *we made representations to the manager on behalf of the junior members of staff*

③ **representative**
[reprɪ'zentətɪv]
1 *adjective*
typical; *the sample isn't representative of the whole batch*
2 *noun*
(a) person who represents, who speaks on behalf of someone else; *he asked his attorney to act as his representative*; *representatives of the workers have asked to meet the management*
(b) traveling salesman; *they have vacancies for representatives in the north of the country* (NOTE: often called simply a **rep**)
(c) *(in the United States)* **the House of Representatives** = the lower house of Congress (NOTE: the upper house of Congress is the **Senate**)

④ **reproduce**
[rɪprə'djus] *verb*
(a) to copy; *some of his letters have been reproduced in the book of his poems*; *it is very difficult to reproduce the sound of an owl accurately*
(b) to produce young; *some animals will not reproduce when kept in zoos*

③ **reptile**
['reptaɪl] *noun*
cold-blooded animal with a skin covered with scales, which lays eggs; *snakes are reptiles*

③ **republic**
[rɪ'pʌblɪk] *noun*
system of government which is governed by elected representatives headed by an elected or nominated president; *France and Germany are republics, but Spain and the UK are not*

③ **republican**
[rɪ'pʌblɪkən]
1 *adjective*
referring to a republic; *the republican movement would like to see the replacement of the king by a president*
2 *noun*

person who believes that a republic is the best form of government; *some republicans made speeches against the emperor*

③ **Republican**
[rɪ'pʌblɪkən]
1 *adjective*
referring to the Republican Party, one of the two main political parties in the U.S.A.
2 *noun*
member of the Republican Party, one of the two main political parties in the U.S.A.

③ **Republican Party**
[rɪ'pʌblɪkən 'parti] *noun*
one of the two main political parties in the U.S.A., which supports business and is against too much state intervention in industry and welfare; *the Republican Party's candidate for the presidency*; *compare* DEMOCRATIC PARTY

④ **reputation**
[repju'teɪʃn] *noun*
opinion that people have of someone; *he has a reputation for being difficult to deal with*; *the cook has a reputation for often losing his temper*; *his bad reputation won't help him find a suitable job*

③ **request**
[rɪ'kwest]
1 *noun*
asking for something; *your request will be dealt with as soon as possible*; **on request** = if asked for; *"catalog available on request"*; **request stop** = bus stop where buses stop only if you signal to them
2 *verb*
to ask for something politely; *I am enclosing the leaflets you requested*; *guests are requested to leave their keys at the reception desk*

③ **require**
[rɪ'kwaɪər] *verb*
(a) to demand that someone should do something; *we were required to go to the local police station*; *you are required to fill out the forms when you register*
(b) to need; *the disease requires careful treatment*; *writing the program requires a computer specialist*

② **requirement**
[rɪ'kwaɪərmənt] *noun*
(a) what is necessary; *it is a requirement of the job that you should be able to drive*
(b) requirements = things which are needed; *we try to meet our customers' requirements*; *if you send us a list of your requirements, we shall see if we can supply them*

④ **requisite**
['rekwɪzɪt]
1 *adjective*
(formal) necessary; *does he have the requisite credits?*
2 *noun*

(formal) thing which is necessary; *patience is a requisite for a happy marriage*

③ **rescue**
['reskju]

1 *noun*

action of saving; *mountain rescue requires teams of specially trained people*; *no one could swim well enough to go to her rescue*; **rescue party** *or* **rescue team** *or* **rescue squad** = group of people who are going to save someone; *rescue parties were sent out immediately after the plane came down in the jungle*

2 *verb*

to save someone from a dangerous situation; *the helicopter rescued the crew of the sinking ship*; *the company nearly collapsed, but was rescued by the bank*; *when the river flooded, the party of tourists had to be rescued by boat*

② **research**
[rɪ'sɜrtʃ]

1 *noun*

(a) scientific study, which tries to find out facts; *the company is carrying out research to find a cure for colds*; *the research laboratory has come up with encouraging results*; *our research proved that the letter was a forgery*

(b) market research = examining the possible sales of a product and the possible customers before it is put on the market; *if we had done proper market research we would have discovered that there were several products that are cheaper than ours*; *before you launch the product, you must do thorough market research*

2 *verb*

to study, to try to find out facts; *research your subject thoroughly before you start writing about it*

④ **resent**
[rɪ'zent] *verb*

to feel annoyed because of a real or imaginary hurt; *she resents having to look after her father-in-law*; *we bitterly resent the suggestion that the company has tricked its customers*

② **reservation**
[rezə'veɪʃn] *noun*

(a) booking of a seat, table, etc.; *I want to make a reservation on the plane to Chicago tomorrow evening*; **(room) reservations** = department in a hotel which deals with bookings for rooms; *can you put me through to reservations?*

(b) doubt; *I have no reservations whatsoever that I have made the right decision*; *if you have any reservations about the contract, please let me know as soon as possible*

(c) area of land set apart for Native Americans; *you have to have permission to enter the reservation*

② **reserve**
[rɪ'zɜrv]

1 *noun*

(a) amount kept back in case it is needed in the future; *our reserves of coal were used up during the winter*; **in reserve** = waiting to be used; *we're keeping the can of gas in reserve*

(b) nature reserve = area of land where animals and plants are protected; *we often go to the nature reserve to watch birds*

(c) being shy, not being open about your feelings; *he had to break down her reserve before he could get her to talk about her illness*

2 *verb*

(a) to book a seat or a table; *I want to reserve a table for four people*; *have you reserved a table? - if not, we have only two tables free*; *can you reserve two seats for me for the evening performance?*

(b) to keep back for a special use, or to use later; *put half the cherries into the cake mixture and reserve the rest for decoration*; *don't read this book now, reserve it for your vacation*; *I'm reserving my right to change my mind*

(c) to reserve judgment = not to make up your mind about something until later; *I'll reserve judgment until I've heard all the facts*

④ **reserved**
[rɪ'zɜrvd] *adjective*

(a) booked; *there are two reserved tables and one free one*; *is this seat reserved?*

(b) who does not reveal his or her thoughts and feelings; *Clare is very reserved and doesn't talk much*; *he's a very reserved man and does not mix with other members of staff*

③ **reservoir**
['rezəvwɑr] *noun*

(a) large, usually artificial, lake where drinking water is kept for pumping to a city; *there has been very little rain this year and the reservoirs are only half full*

(b) large collection of something kept ready; *there is a huge reservoir of skilled labor waiting to be employed*

③ **residence**
['rezɪdəns] *noun*

(a) place where you live; *Jennifer and Tom's residence was unaffected by the storm*; *they have a country residence where they spend their weekends*

(b) act of living in a place; **residence permit** = official document allowing a foreigner to live in a country; *he has applied for a residence permit*

③ **resident**
['rezɪdənt]

1 *adjective*

who lives permanently in a place; *there is a resident janitor*

2 *noun*

(a) person who lives in a place, a country, a hotel, etc.; *you need an entry permit if you're not a resident of the country*; *only residents are allowed to park their automobiles here*

(b) doctor who is getting specialized clinical training; *she is a surgical resident*

④ **residential**
[rezɪˈdenʃl] *adjective*
residential area = part of a town with houses rather than stores or factories; *the apartment is not in a residential area, it's above a shoe store*; **residential street** = street with houses, and no stores or factories; *he lives in a quiet residential street*

③ **resign**
[rɪˈzaɪn] *verb*
(a) to give up a job; *he resigned with effect from July 1*; *she has resigned (her position) as bank manager*
(b) **to resign yourself to something** = to accept something; *I have to resign myself to never being rich*; *he was still 20 yards behind his rival and resigned himself to coming in second*

④ **resignation**
[rezɪgˈneɪʃn] *noun*
(a) act of giving up a job; *his resignation was accepted by the board*; *have you written your letter of resignation?*; *he tendered* or *he handed in his resignation* = he resigned
(b) accepting an unpleasant situation; *he looked at his test results with resignation*

③ **resigned**
[rɪˈzaɪnd] *adjective*
accepting something unpleasant; *a resigned look appeared on his face*; **resigned to** = accepting that something unpleasant will happen; *I'm resigned to living by myself for the rest of my life*

④ **resilient**
[rɪˈzɪliənt] *adjective*
(a) *(person)* who is strong or able to recover easily from a shock; *she is a very resilient person, and will recover quickly*
(b) which easily returns to its original shape after being squashed; *cork is a surprisingly resilient material*

③ **resist**
[rɪˈzɪst] *verb*
to fight against something, not to give in to something; *he resisted all attempts to make him sell the house*; *bands of guerrillas resisted in the mountains*; *they resisted the enemy attacks for two weeks*

④ **resistance**
[rɪˈzɪstəns] *noun*
opposition to something, fighting against something; *bands of guerrillas put up a fierce resistance in the mountains*; *the refugees had no resistance to disease*; *there was a lot of resistance to the new plan from the local residents*; **resistance movement** = movement of ordinary people against an enemy occupying their country; *the resistance movement was very strong in their area during the war*; **passive resistance** = resisting the police by

refusing to do something, but without using violence; *the protesters organized a program of passive resistance to the new presidential decree*; **he took the line of least resistance** = he did the easiest thing

③ **resistant**
[rɪˈzɪstənt] *adjective*
which resists; *this plate is not heat-resistant and shouldn't be used in an oven*

④ **resolution**
[rezəˈluːʃn] *noun*
(a) decision to be decided at a meeting; **to put a resolution to a meeting** = to ask a meeting to vote on a proposal; *the meeting passed* or *carried* or *adopted the resolution*; *the meeting rejected the resolution* or *the resolution was defeated by ten votes to twenty*
(b) being determined to do something; *her resolution to succeed is strong, and I am sure she will get through*; **New Year's resolution** = plan to improve your way of living, decided on at the New Year, and usually abandoned shortly afterwards; *each New Year I make the same resolutions, but never manage to keep them*; *my New Year's resolution was to get more exercise, but it didn't last long*
(c) *(of a TV or computer image)* being clear; *a high-resolution screen*

③ **resolve**
[rɪˈzɒlv]
1 *noun*
determination, what you have firmly decided to do; *the teacher encouraged him in his resolve to go to college*
2 *verb*
to firmly decide to do something; *we all resolved to work harder*

③ **resort**
[rɪˈzɔrt]
1 *noun*
(a) place where people go on vacation; *they go to a famous ski resort in Colorado*; *crowds have been flocking to the resorts on the south coast*
(b) **as a last resort** or **in the last resort** = when everything else fails; *he accepted her offer of a lift as a last resort*
2 *verb*
to resort to = to use something in a difficult situation, when everything else has failed; *in the end the police had to resort to using tear gas*

③ **resource**
[rɪˈsɔrs] *noun*
source of supply for what is needed or used; *we have enough resources - financial or otherwise - to build a rocket*; **financial resources** = supply of money for something; **natural resources** = raw materials that come from nature, such as minerals, oil, wood; *the country is rich in natural resources*; *see also* HUMAN RESOURCES

② **respect**
[rɪˈspekt]
1 *noun*

(a) admiration or regard for someone; *he showed very little respect for his teacher*; *no one deserves more respect than her mother*; **to command respect** = to be admired; *her TV programs about the war commanded much respect*
(b) **with respect to** = concerning; *I have nothing to say with respect to the new treatment*; **in some respects** = in some ways; *in some respects, she doesn't act like a mature person*
(c) **respects** = polite good wishes; *my father sends you his respects*; **to pay your respects to someone** = to go to visit someone important; **to pay your last respects to someone** = to go to someone's funeral
2 *verb*
(a) to admire or to honor someone; *everyone respected her decision to quit her job*
(b) to show you care about something; *farmers have been accused of not respecting the environment*
(c) to do what is required by something; *the landlord has not respected the terms of the contract*

② **respectable**
[rɪ'spektəbl] *adjective*
(a) considered by people to be good, proper, and worthy of respect; *she's marrying a very respectable young engineer*; *I don't want to bring up my children here, it is not a respectable area*
(b) fairly large; *he made quite a respectable score*

② **respected**
[rɪ'spektɪd] *adjective*
admired by many people; *he's a highly respected professor of physics*; *the book is a very respected work of reference*

④ **respectively**
[rɪ'spektɪvli] *adverb*
in the order just mentioned; *Mr. Smith and Mr. Jones are owner and manager of the store, respectively*

② **respond**
[rɪ'spɒnd] *verb*
(a) to give a reply; *she shouted at him, but he didn't respond*
(b) to show a favorable reaction to; *I hope the public will respond to our new advertisement*; *the government has responded to pressure from industry*; **he is responding to treatment** = he is beginning to get better

② **response**
[rɪ'spɒns] *noun*
(a) answer; *there was no response to our call for help*; **in response to** = as an answer to; *in response to the United Nations' request for aid, the government has sent blankets and tents*
(b) answers given by the people attending a service in church; *a series of prayers with repeated responses*

③ **responsibility**
[rɪspɒnsɪ'bɪlɪti] *noun*
(a) being in a position where you look after or deal with something; *the management accepts no responsibility for customers' property*; *there is no responsibility on his part for the poor results*; *who should take responsibility for the students' welfare?*; *he has taken on a lot of responsibility* = he has agreed to be responsible for many things; **position of responsibility** = job where important decisions have to be made
(b) thing which you are responsible for; **responsibilities** = duties; *he finds the responsibilities of being chairman of the club too demanding*

② **responsible**
[rɪ'spɒnsɪbl] *adjective*
(a) **responsible for** = causing; *the fog was responsible for the accident*
(b) looking after something, and so open to blame if it gets lost, damaged, etc.; *he is not responsible for the restaurant next door to his hotel*; *we hold customers responsible for any items that are broken*
(c) **responsible to someone** = being under the authority of someone; *she's directly responsible to the head nurse*
(d) (person) who can be trusted; *you can rely on him, he's very responsible*; **responsible position** *or* **responsible job** = job where decisions have to be made; *he is looking for a responsible position in the post office*

① **rest**
[rest]
1 *noun*
(a) being quiet and peaceful, being asleep, doing nothing; *all you need is a good night's rest and you'll be fine again tomorrow*; *we took a few minutes' rest and started running again*; *I'm having a well-earned rest after working hard all week*
(b) not moving; *the ball finally came to rest two inches from the hole*
(c) what is left; *here are the twins, but where are the rest of the children?*; *I drank most of the milk and the cat drank the rest*; *throw the rest of the food away - it will go bad* (NOTE: **rest** takes a singular verb when it refers to a singular: **here's the rest of the milk; where's the rest of the string? the rest of the money has been lost;** it takes a plural verb when it refers to a plural: **here are the rest of the children; where are the rest of the chairs? the rest of the books have been lost**)
(d) thing which supports; *she pulled up another chair as a rest for her foot*; **headrest** = cushion on top of an automobile seat against which you can lean your head
2 *verb*
(a) to be quiet and peaceful; *don't disturb your father - he's resting*; *they ran for ten miles, rested for a few minutes, and then ran on again*

(b) to lean something against something; *she rested her bike against the wall*

(c) *(formal)* **to let something rest** = to stop discussing something; *after advice from our attorney, we decided to let the matter rest*

② **restaurant**
['restərɒnt] *noun*
place where you can buy and eat a meal; *I don't want to stay at home tonight - let's go out to the Mexican restaurant on Main Street*; *she was waiting for me at the restaurant*

③ **restful**
['restfəl] *adjective*
which makes you feel calm and relaxed; *after struggling through the crowds we were glad to get back to the restful calm of the hotel*

③ **restless**
['restləs] *adjective*
always moving about; *after five days of rain, the children were restless and really needed to go out to play*; *she's becoming restless, she's hardly been here two months and she wants to go abroad again*

③ **restore**
[rɪ'stɔr] *verb*
(a) to repair, to make something like new again; *the old house has been restored and is now open to the public*

(b) to give back; *after the war the castle was not restored to its former owners*

(c) to make something exist again; *to everyone's delight, the management decided to restore the bonus system*

④ **restrain**
[rɪ'streɪn] *verb*
to try and stop someone doing something; *it took six policemen to restrain him*; **to restrain yourself** = to keep your temper under control; *next time, I won't restrain myself: I'll tell him exactly what I think of him*

④ **restraint**
[rɪ'streɪnt] *noun*
control; *she showed remarkable restraint when he criticized her work so rudely*; **with great restraint** = without losing your temper; *with great restraint, he quietly wiped the tomato sauce off his pants and said nothing to the waitress*; **lack of restraint** = giving people too much freedom; *the lack of restraint in the school doesn't go down well with the parents*; **wage restraint** *or* **pay restraint** = keeping wage increases under control; *the government is planning to impose pay restraints*

③ **restrict**
[rɪ'strɪkt] *verb*
to limit; *you are restricted to two bottles per person*; *the government is trying to restrict the flow of foreign workers coming into the country*

③ **restricted**
[rɪ'strɪktɪd] *adjective*

limited; *there will be a restricted train service next Sunday*; *these seats are cheaper because you only have a restricted view of the stage*; **restricted area** = (i) area where automobiles must obey a speed limit; (ii) place where only certain people are allowed

② **restriction**
[rɪ'strɪkʃn] *noun*
limitation; *the police have placed restrictions on his movements*; *restrictions have been imposed on certain imports*; *there is a 50-mile-an-hour speed restriction on this highway*

② **result**
[rɪ'zʌlt]
1 *noun*
(a) something which happens because of something else; *what was the result of the police investigation?*; **as a result (of)** = because of; *there was a traffic jam and, as a result, I missed her plane*

(b) final score in a game, final marks in an exam, etc.; *she isn't pleased with her exam results*; *I enjoyed making the carpet but I'm only partly happy with the result*; *he listened to the baseball results in the radio*
2 *verb*
to result from = to happen because of something which has been done; *the increase in the company's debts resulted from the expansion program*; **to result in** = to produce as an effect; *adding new staff to the sales force resulted in increased sales*

④ **resume**
[rɪ'zjum] *verb*
to start again after stopping; *the meeting resumed after a short break*; *normal train services will resume after the track has been repaired*; *after the fire, the staff resumed work as normal*

④ **résumé**
['rezumeɪ] *noun*
(a) short piece which sums up the main points of a discussion, of a book; *a brief résumé of the contents of the book is all I need*

(b) summary of the details of a person's life, especially details of education and previous jobs; *attach a résumé to your application form*

④ **retail**
['riteɪl]
1 *noun*
selling small quantities of goods direct to the public; *the goods in stock have a retail value of $15,000*; **retail outlet** *or* **retail store** = store which sells goods direct to the customer; *he buys wholesale and then sells to various retail outlets*; *compare* WHOLESALE
2 *verb*
to sell goods direct to customers who do not sell them again; **to retail at** *or* **for** = to sell for a certain price; *these glasses retail at $9.95 for two*

3 *adverb*
he sells retail and buys wholesale = he buys goods in bulk at a wholesale discount and sells in small quantities at full price to the public

④ **retailer**
['riteɪlər] *noun*
storekeeper who sells goods directly to the public; *as a retailer, I buy either from a wholesaler or direct from the factory*; *retailers buy goods from wholesalers and then sell them on to the public*; *compare* WHOLESALER

④ **retain**
[rɪ'teɪn] *verb (formal)*
(a) to keep; *please retain this invoice for tax purposes*; *one news item especially retained my attention*; *he managed to retain his calm in spite of constant shouting from the audience*; **retaining wall** = wall which holds back earth or the water in a reservoir
(b) to retain a lawyer to act for you = to agree with a lawyer that he or she will act for you, and to pay a fee in advance

① **retire**
[rɪ'taɪər] *verb*
(a) to stop work and take a pension; *he will retire from his job as manager next April*; *when he retired, the firm presented him with a watch*; *she's retiring this year*
(b) to make a worker stop work and take a pension; *they decided to retire all staff over 50*
(c) to come to the end of an elected term of office; *the secretary retires from the committee after six years*
(d) *(literary)* **to retire for the night** = to go to bed; *it was two o'clock in the morning and all the hotel guests had retired to their bedrooms*

② **retired**
[rɪ'taɪərd] *adjective*
who has stopped work and draws a pension; *the club is run by a retired teacher*

④ **retiree**
[rɪ'taɪəri] *noun*
person who has retired; *the club was made up of retirees from all walks of life*

② **retirement**
[rɪ'taɪəmənt] *noun*
(a) act of retiring from work; *he says that the pension he'll get on his retirement won't be enough to live on*; **to take early retirement** = to retire from work before the usual age; *I enjoy my work and I don't want to take early retirement*; **retirement age** = age at which people retire (usually 65); *she reached retirement age last week*
(b) period of life when you are retired; *he spent his retirement in his house in New Hampshire*; *most people look forward to their retirement*

③ **retreat**
[rɪ'trit]
1 *noun*
(a) pulling back an army from a battle; *the army's retreat was swift and unexpected*; **in**

retreat = going back from a battle; **in full retreat** = going back fast; *the army is in full retreat*
(b) quiet place; *they spent the weekend at their mountain retreat*
2 *verb*
(a) to pull back from a battle; *Napoleon retreated from Moscow in 1812*
(b) to go to a quiet place; *our dog retreats to his basket if we shout at him*

④ **retrieve**
[rɪ'triv] *verb*
(a) to get back something which was lost; *he retrieved his case from the principal's office*
(b) to bring back something which has been stored in a computer; *she retrieved the address files which she thought had been deleted*

① **return**
[rɪ'tɜrn]
1 *noun*
(a) going back, coming back to a place; *it snowed on the day of her return from Canada*; *I'll come and see you on my return*; **return ticket** *or* **a return** = ticket that allows you to go to one place and come back
(b) sending back; *he asked for the immediate return of the borrowed tools*
(c) action of going back to a former condition; *the president wants to encourage a return to old family traditions*
(d) key on a keyboard that you press when you have finished keying something, or when you want to start a new line; *to change directory, type C: and press return*
(e) income from money invested; *this account should bring in a quick return on your investment*
(f) official return = official report; **to file an income tax return** = to send a statement of income to the tax office; *your income tax return should be sent no later than July 1*
(g) returns = goods which a store hasn't sold and which are sent back to the supplier
2 *verb*
(a) to come back or to go back; *when she returned from lunch she found two messages waiting for her*; *when do you plan to return to Raleigh?*
(b) to give back or to send back; *the letter was returned to the sender*
3 *adjective*
return address = address to send something back; *there was no return address on the letter so we couldn't send it back*; **return fare** = fare for a journey from one place to another and back again; *a return fare is cheaper than two one-way fares*

③ **reveal**
[rɪ'vil] *verb*
to show something which was hidden; *he revealed his total lack of knowledge of automobile engines*; *an unexpected fault was*

revealed during the test; *the X-ray revealed a broken bone*

③ **revealing**
[rɪ'vilɪŋ] *adjective*
which shows something which is usually hidden; *he made a very revealing remark*; **revealing dress** = dress which shows parts of the body that are normally kept hidden

② **revenge**
[rɪ'venʒ]
1 *noun*
punishing someone in return for harm they have caused you; *they attacked the police station in revenge for the arrest of three members of the gang*; *all the time he spent in prison, his only thought was of revenge*; *he had his revenge in the end, when her car broke down and she had to call for help*
2 *verb*
to give punishment in return for a wrong done to someone; *she revenged her murdered husband by killing the murderer*

④ **revenue**
['revənju] *noun*
(a) money that is received; *his only source of revenue is his store*
(b) money received by a government in tax; **Internal Revenue Service** = federal government department that deals with tax; *the Internal Revenue Service wrote again claiming we owe some tax from last year*

② **reverse**
[rɪ'vərs]
1 *adjective*
opposite; *the reverse side of the carpet is made of rubber*; *the conditions are printed on the reverse side of the invoice*; **in reverse order** = backwards; *they called out the names of the winners in reverse order*
2 *noun*
(a) opposite side; *didn't you read what was on the reverse of the label?*
(b) the opposite; *you're mistaken, the reverse is true*
(c) automobile gear which makes you go backwards; *put the automobile into reverse and back very slowly into the garage*; *the car's stuck in reverse!*
(d) defeat in battle or in an election; *the army suffered a disastrous reverse*; *the Republicans suffered a series of reverses*
3 *verb*
(a) to make something do the opposite; *the page order was reversed by mistake*; *just follow the trend, don't try to reverse it*
(b) to make an automobile go backwards; *reverse as far as you can, then go forward*; *be careful not to reverse into that tree*
(c) to change a legal decision to another, opposite, one; *the judge's decision was reversed by the Supreme Court*

② **review**
[rɪ'vju]
1 *noun*
(a) written comments on a book, play, movie, etc., published in a newspaper or magazine; *did you read the review of her latest movie in today's paper?*; *his book got some very good reviews*
(b) examination of several things together; *the company's annual review of each department's performance*; **salary review** = examination of salaries in a company to see if the workers should earn more; *let's hope we all get an increase at the next salary review*
(c) monthly or weekly magazine which contains articles of general interest; *his first short story appeared in a Canadian literary review*
(d) *(formal)* general inspection of the army, navy, etc.; *a naval review will be held next month*
2 *verb*
(a) to read a book, see a movie, etc., and write comments about it in a newspaper or magazine; *her exhibition was reviewed in today's paper*; *whoever reviewed her latest book, obviously didn't like it*; **review copy** = copy of new book sent to a newspaper or magazine, asking them to review it
(b) to examine in a general way; *the bank will review our overdraft position at the end of the month*; *let's review the situation in the light of the new developments*
(c) to study a lesson again; *you must review your geography before the test*
(d) *(formal)* to inspect soldiers, sailors, ships, etc.; *the general rode on his white horse to review the troops*

④ **reviewer**
[rɪ'vjuər] *noun*
person who writes comments on books, plays, movies, etc.; *there's a new movie reviewer on the Sunday paper and he didn't like this movie*; *she's the book reviewer for our local newspaper*

④ **revise**
[rɪ'vaɪz] *verb*
to change, to make something correct; *he is revising the speech he is due to give this evening*; *these figures will have to be revised, there seems to be a mistake*

④ **revision**
[rɪ'vɪʒən] *noun*
action of revising; *have you started the revision of the book yet?*

④ **revive**
[rɪ'vaɪv] *verb*
(a) to recover, to get well again; *after drinking some water he had revived enough to go on with the marathon*
(b) to bring someone back to life again; *the ambulance crew managed to revive her on the way to the hospital*

(c) to make something popular again; *it won't be easy to revive people's interest in old country crafts*

④ **revolt**
[rɪˈvəʊlt]
1 *noun*
mass protest against an authority; *the government faces a revolt from its main supporters*
2 *verb*
(a) to rise up against authority; *the prisoners revolted against the harsh treatment in the jail*
(b) to disgust; *it revolted me to see all that food being thrown away*

③ **revolting**
[rɪˈvəʊltɪŋ] *adjective*
disgusting, which makes you feel sick; *don't ask me to eat that revolting food again*; *look at the state of the kitchen - it's revolting!*

③ **revolution**
[revəˈluʃn] *noun*
(a) armed rising against a government; *the government soldiers shot the leaders of the revolution*; *he led an unsuccessful revolution against the last president*; *during the French Revolution many innocent people were executed*
(b) turning around a central point; *the engine turns at 5000 revolutions a minute*
(c) change in the way things are done; *a revolution in data processing*; **Industrial Revolution** = the development of industry during the 19th century in western Europe and the United States; **technological revolution** = the change to computers and other developments in information technology; *the twentieth century was the time of the technological revolution*

④ **revolutionary**
[revəˈluʃənəri]
1 *adjective*
(a) aiming to change things completely; very new; *there is a new revolutionary treatment for cancer*
(b) referring to a political revolution; *his revolutionary ideas upset the establishment*
2 *noun*
person who takes part in an uprising against a government; *the captured revolutionaries were shot when the army took control*

② **revolver**
[rɪˈvɒlvər] *noun*
small hand gun which turns after each shot is fired, so that another shot can be fired quickly; *some policemen are armed with revolvers*

① **reward**
[rɪˈwɔrd]
1 *noun*
money given to someone as a prize for finding something, or for information about something; *she got a $30 reward when she took the purse she had found to the police station*; *he is not*

interested in money - *the Olympic gold medal will be reward enough*
2 *verb*
to give someone money as a prize for finding something, or for doing something; *he was rewarded for finding the box of papers*; *all her efforts were rewarded when she won first prize*

③ **rheumatism**
[ˈruːmətɪzm] *noun*
disease which gives painful or stiff joints or muscles; *I get rheumatism in the winter*; *she has rheumatism in her knees*; *she is being treated for rheumatism*

③ **rhinoceros**
[raɪˈnɒsərəs] *noun*
large Asian or African animal with a thick skin and one or two horns on its head; *look out - that rhinoceros is going to charge!* (NOTE: plural is **rhinoceroses**)

② **rhubarb**
[ˈruːbɑrb] *noun*
plant of which the thick red leaf stalks are cooked and eaten as a dessert; *we're having rhubarb tart for pudding*

① **rhyme**
[raɪm]
1 *noun*
(a) way in which some words end in the same sound; *can you think of a rhyme for "taught"?*
(b) little piece of poetry; **nursery rhyme** = little piece of poetry for children; *the children sang nursery rhymes and danced in a ring*
2 *verb*
to rhyme with = to end with the same sound as another word; *"Mr." rhymes with "sister"*

③ **rhythm**
[ˈrɪðəm] *noun*
strong regular beat in music, poetry, etc.; *they stamped their feet to the rhythm of the music*; **rhythm and blues** = type of popular music that combines blues and jazz, has a strong beat and was developed by African Americans

① **rib**
[rɪb] *noun*
(a) one of twenty-four curved bones which protect your chest; *he fell down while skiing and broke two ribs*
(b) the same bones of an animal, cooked and eaten; **spareribs** = pork ribs cooked in a savory sauce; *we are having spareribs for the barbecue*

① **ribbon**
[ˈrɪbn] *noun*
long thin strip of material for tying things or used as decoration; *she had a red ribbon in her hair*; **printer ribbon** *or* **typewriter ribbon** = thin strip of material or plastic, with ink or carbon on it, used in a printer or typewriter

① **rice**
[raɪs] *noun*
(a) very common food, the seeds of a tropical plant; *she only had a bowl of rice for her evening meal*; **rice pudding** = a pudding made

of rice, milk and sugar, cooked together (NOTE: no plural: **some rice, a bowl of rice, a spoonful of rice**)

(b) common food plant, grown mainly in Asian countries; *women were planting rice in the fields*

COMMENT: rice with long grains is grown in tropical countries, such as India; rice with short grains is grown in colder countries such as Japan. There are thousands of varieties of rice, and the world's leading rice-exporting countries are the U.S.A. and Thailand. Wild rice is not rice at all, but a form of North American grass

① **rich**
[rɪtʃ]
1 *adjective*
(a) who has a lot of money; *they're so rich that they can afford to go on vacation for six months*; *if only we were rich, then we could buy a bigger house*; *he never spends anything, and so he gets richer and richer*
(b) thick and dark (color); *she painted the kitchen a rich chocolate color*
(c) with many treasures; *our local museum has an unusually rich collection of paintings by local artists*; **rich in** = containing a lot of; *the area is rich in old churches*; *the south of the country is rich in coal*; *these tablets are rich in vitamin B*
(d) made with a lot of cream, butter, etc.; *this cream cake is too rich for me* (NOTE: **richer - richest**)
2 *noun*
the rich = rich people; *at that price, the car is only for the really rich*

② **rid**
[rɪd] *phrase*
to get rid of something = to dispose of something or to throw something away; *do you want to get rid of that old chair?*; *we have been told to get rid of twenty staff*; *she doesn't seem able to get rid of her cold* (NOTE: **getting rid - got rid**)

③ **ridden**
['rɪdən]
see RIDE

① **riddle**
['rɪdl] *noun*
puzzling question to which you have to find the answer; *here's a riddle for you: "what's black and white and red all over?" (the answer is "a book" if you say "read" instead of "red")*

① **ride**
[raɪd]
1 *noun*
(a) pleasant trip on a horse, on a bike, in an automobile, etc.; *does anyone want to come for a bike ride?*; *he took us all for a ride in his new automobile*; *the train station is only a short bus ride from the college*

(b) *(informal)* **to take someone for a ride** = to trick someone; *free beer? - there's no free beer, someone's been taking you for a ride!*; *the recruit was really taken for a ride when the others told him that there was a party at the colonel's house and he believed them*
(c) action of traveling; *you will enjoy the smooth ride of the new four-wheel drive model*
2 *verb*
to go on a horse, on a bike, etc.; *he rode his bike across the road without looking*; *she's never ridden (on) an elephant*; *my little sister is learning to ride, but she's frightened of big horses* (NOTE: **rides - riding - rode** [rəʊd] **- has ridden** ['rɪdən])

② **rider**
['raɪdər] *noun*
(a) person who rides; *the rider of the black horse fell at the first fence*; *motorcycle riders must wear helmets*
(b) additional clause; *to add a rider to a contract*

③ **ridge**
[rɪdʒ] *noun*
long narrow raised part; *the mountain ridge stretches for miles*

② **ridiculous**
[rɪ'dɪkjʊləs] *adjective*
silly, which everyone should laugh at; *it's ridiculous to tell everyone to wear suits when it's so hot in the office*

② **rifle**
['raɪfl]
1 *noun*
gun with a long barrel; *gunmen with rifles were on the roofs surrounding the fort*; **rifle range** = place where you practice shooting with rifles; *she goes to the rifle range every Saturday to practice*
2 *verb*
to search for something, usually to steal it; *the burglars rifled through the drawers of her desk*

④ **rig**
[rɪg]
1 *noun*
(a) **oil rig** = construction for drilling for oil
(b) *(informal)* large truck; *he drives a 16-wheel rig*
2 *verb*
to arrange a dishonest result; *they were accused of rigging the election*; *see also* RIG UP (NOTE: **rigging - rigged**)

① **right**
[raɪt]
1 *adjective*
(a) not wrong, correct; *you're right - the number 8 bus doesn't go there*; *she gave the right answer every time*; *he says the answer is 285 - absolutely right!*; *is the station clock right?*; *she didn't put the bottles back in the right place*; *if you don't stand the jar the right*

way up it will leak; *see also* ALL RIGHT, SIDE

(b) not left, referring to the hand that most people use to write with; *in the U.S.A., cars drive on the right side of the road*; *the keys are in the top right drawer of my desk*; *he was holding the suitcase in his right hand*

(c) *(in politics)* referring to the conservatives; *he's on the right wing of the party*; *his politics are right of center*

2 *noun*

(a) what is correct, not wrong; *in the right* = correct, which should not be criticized; *she was proved to be in the right*

(b) the side opposite to the left; *when you get to the next crossroads, turn to the right*; *who was that girl sitting on the right of your father?*; *go straight ahead, and take the second road on the right*

(c) being legally entitled to do or to have something; *the accused has the right to remain silent*; *the manager has no right to read my letters*; *the staff have a right to know why the store is closing down*; *see also* RIGHTS

(d) *(in politics)* **the Right** = the political group supporting traditional values and rights; *we support the Right by campaigning for our local Republican candidate*; **swing to the right** = movement of votes toward the right-wing candidates

3 *adverb*

(a) straight; *to get to the police station, keep right on to the end of the road, and then make a left*; *go right along to the end of the hall, you'll see my office in front of you*; *instead of stopping at the crossroads, he drove right on across the main road and into a tree*

(b) **right (away)** = immediately; *they called the ambulance right after the accident*; *the ambulance came right away*; **right now** = at this particular point in time; *right now, it is not possible for me to answer reporters' questions*

(c) exactly; *the bookstore is right at the end of the road*; *the phone rang right in the middle of the TV program*; *she stood right in front of the TV and no one could see the screen*

(d) correctly; *she guessed the answer right*; *everything is going right for her*

(e) toward the right-hand side; *to get to the station, make a right at the traffic light*; *children should be taught to look left and right before crossing the road*

4 *verb*

(a) to right a wrong = to correct something that is wrong; *she campaigned to right the wrongs done to single mothers*

(b) to right itself = to turn the right way up again; *the yacht turned over and then righted itself*

5 *interjection*

agreed, OK; *right, so we all meet again at 7 o'clock?*

③ **right angle**
['raɪt 'æŋgl] *noun*
angle of 90°; *the two streets meet at a right angle*

② **right-hand**
['raɪt 'hænd] *adjective*
on the right side; *look in the right-hand drawer of my desk*; *the bar is on the right-hand side of the street*; **right-hand man** = main assistant; *he's my right-hand man, I couldn't do without him*; **right-hand drive automobile** = automobile where the driver sits on the right side of the automobile

> COMMENT: most automobiles have left-hand drives: British, New Zealand and Japanese automobiles have right-hand drives

② **right-handed**
['raɪt 'hændɪd] *adjective*
using the right hand more often than the left for things like writing and eating; *she's right-handed*

③ **rights**
[raɪts] *noun*
(a) what you should be allowed to do or to have; *they are working for women's rights or for the rights of women*; *the rights of ordinary working people are being ignored*; **human rights** = rights which each ordinary member of society should enjoy, such as freedom of speech, freedom of movement, etc.; *demonstrators are protesting abuses of human rights in various parts of the world*

(b) legal right to have something; *he has the U.S. rights to the invention*; *she sold the Spanish rights to a Spanish publisher*; **movie rights** = the legal right to make a movie from a book; **foreign rights** = legal right to sell something in another country

(c) rights issue = issue of new shares in a company which are offered to existing shareholders at a cheap price

④ **right-wing**
[raɪt'wɪŋ] *adjective*
belonging to the conservative political parties; *the defeat was a blow to the right-wing candidate*

④ **rigid**
['rɪdʒɪd] *adjective*
stiff, which doesn't bend; *this pole is too rigid, you will need something more flexible*; *the club's rules are so rigid that a lot of members are leaving*

④ **rigorous**
['rɪgərəs] *adjective*
very thorough; *the customs inspection is rigorous, they open every single case*; *these tests are too rigorous for small children*

③ **rig up**
['rɪg 'ʌp] *verb*

to arrange, to construct something quickly; *they rigged up a telescope in the garden*

② **rim**
[rɪm] *noun*
(a) edge of something round, like a wheel or a cup; *the rim of the glass is chipped*
(b) frame of eyeglasses; *he wears glasses with steel rims*

④ **rind**
[raɪnd] *noun*
skin on fruit, bacon or cheese; *add the grated rind of a lemon*; *can you eat the rind of this cheese?*

① **ring**
[rɪŋ]
1 *noun*
(a) round shape of metal, etc.; *she has a gold ring in her nose*; *he wears a ring on his little finger*; **wedding ring** = ring that is put on the finger during the wedding ceremony
(b) circle of people or things; *the teacher asked the children to sit in a ring around her*
(c) noise of an electric bell; *there was a ring at the door*
(d) space where a show takes place, where a boxing match is held, etc.; *everyone shouted when the lions ran into the ring*; **boxing ring** = square area, surrounded with a rope fence, in which boxing matches take place; *the two boxers climbed into the ring*
2 *verb*
(a) to make a sound with a bell; *the delivery man rang the bell*; *at Easter, all the church bells were ringing*; *if you ring your bicycle bell people will get out of the way*; *is that your phone ringing?*
(b) **to ring a bell** = to remind someone of something; *does the name Wade ring any bells?*; *yes, the name does ring a bell*
(e) **to ring the changes** = to try various things to see which is best, to go through the range of possibilities; *I don't always buy the same newspaper, I prefer to ring the changes between "The New York Times", "The Washington Post" and "International Herald Tribune"* (NOTE: ringing - rang [ræŋ] - has rung [rʌŋ])
3 *verb*
(a) to draw a ring around something; *I have ringed the mistakes in red*
(b) to surround; *rebel troops ringed the president's palace* (NOTE: ringing - ringed)

③ **ring up**
[ˈrɪŋ ˈʌp] *verb*
to add up; *I rang up the receipts on the register*

② **rink**
[rɪŋk] *noun*
skating rink = large enclosed area for ice skating, playing ice hockey, etc.; *in the evening we all went to the skating rink*; *there used to be an indoor skating rink here*

② **rinse**
[rɪns]
1 *noun*
washing something in clean water to get rid of soap; *give your shirt a good rinse*
2 *verb*
to put things covered with soap or dirty things into clean water to remove the soap or the dirt; *rinse the dishes before drying them*

② **riot**
[ˈraɪət]
1 *noun*
(a) wild disorder by a crowd of people; *the riot was started by some university students*; **to run riot** = to get out of control; *after the match, the supporters ran riot and the police had to be called in*; *in her stories for children she lets her imagination run riot*; **to read someone the riot act** = to warn someone to stop doing something; *I read her the riot act when I found she had been using the office telephone to call her mother in Australia*
(b) mass of colors; *the color scheme is a riot of reds and greens*
(c) very amusing movie, play, etc.; *the whole show was a riot, I never laughed so much*
2 *verb*
to take part in a riot; to get out of control; *the protestors were rioting on the streets*

① **rip**
[rɪp] *verb*
(a) to tear, to pull roughly; *I ripped my sleeve on a nail*; *she ripped open the package to see what he had given her*; *the old bathroom is being ripped out and new units put in*
(b) to go through something violently; *the tropical storm ripped through the town* (NOTE: ripping - ripped)

① **ripe**
[raɪp] *adjective*
(a) ready to eat or to be harvested; *don't eat that apple - it isn't ripe yet*
(b) **the time is ripe** = it is the right time to do something; *the time is ripe to take steps to stop imports of the drug* (NOTE: riper - ripest)

④ **rip off**
[ˈrɪp ˈɒf] *verb*
(a) to tear off; *it's the last day of the month so you can rip the page off the calendar*; *someone has ripped off the book's cover*
(b) *(slang)* **to rip someone off** = to cheat someone, to make someone pay too much; *they were ripped off by the taxi driver*

④ **rip-off**
[ˈrɪpɒf] *noun*
(slang) bad deal, something that costs too much; *what a rip-off! - it's not worth half the price*; *that car was a rip-off - it had been involved in an accident*

② **ripple**
[ˈrɪpl] *noun*

little wave; *even a little stone thrown into the water will make ripples*

② **rise**
[raɪz]
1 *noun*
(a) movement or slope upwards; *there is a gentle rise until you get to the top of the hill; salaries are increasing to keep up with the rise in the cost of living; the recent rise in interest rates has made mortgages more expensive*
(b) *(formal)* **to give rise to something** = to make something happen; *the news gave rise to rumors about a coup*
2 *verb*
(a) to go up; *the sun always rises in the east; the road rises gently for a few miles; prices have been rising steadily all year; if you open the oven door, the cake won't rise properly*
(b) *(formal)* to get up, to get out of bed or out of a chair; *he always rises early* (NOTE: **rising - rose** [rəuz] **- has risen** [ˈrɪzn])

① **risk**
[rɪsk]
1 *noun*
(a) possible bad result; *there is not much risk of rain in August; the risk of becoming blind is very remote; there is a financial risk attached to this deal; at the risk of looking silly, I'm going to ask her out for a meal*
(b) **to run the risk of** = to be in danger of; *they run the risk of being caught by customs; if you ask for a pay raise now, you run the risk of losing your job;* **to take a risk** = to do something that may make you lose money or suffer harm; *he's so careful, he never takes any risks; drive slowly, we're in no hurry and there's no need to take any risks*
(c) **owner's risk** = the owner is responsible if something happens to his property; *automobiles are parked at the owners' risk;* **fire risk** = situation or materials that could start a fire; *that room full of wastepaper is a fire risk*
2 *verb*
to do something that may possibly harm you; *the fireman risked his life to save her; he risked all his savings on buying the bookstore*

② **risky**
[ˈrɪski] *adjective*
which is dangerous; *he lost all his money in some risky ventures in South America; there is ice on the road, driving would be very risky* (NOTE: **riskier - riskiest**)

④ **ritual**
[ˈrɪtjuəl]
1 *adjective*
referring to a religious ceremony; *the people of the village performed a ritual rain dance*
2 *noun*
(a) regular ceremony; *the ritual of the mass*
(b) something which you do regularly in the same way; *every evening it's the same ritual: he puts the cat out and locks the door*

④ **rival**
[ˈraɪvl]
1 *adjective*
competing, who competes; *two rival companies are trying to win the contract; is this the rival product you were talking about?; Simon and I are friends but we play for rival teams*
2 *noun*
person who competes; company which competes; *do you know if he has any rivals?; we keep our prices low to be cheaper than our biggest rival*
3 *verb*
to compete with someone; to be of similar quality to someone; *it will not be easy to rival such a good product; our local restaurant rivals any New York seafood restaurant of the same size*

① **river**
[ˈrɪvər] *noun*
large mass of fresh water which runs across the land and goes into the sea or into a lake; *New York City is built on the mouth of the Hudson river; the river is very deep here, so it's dangerous to swim in it*

③ **roach**
[rəʊtʃ] *noun*
(informal) cockroach, big black or brown insect, a common household pest; *in hot damp climates, roaches are often found in kitchens* (NOTE: plural is **roaches**)

① **road**
[rəʊd] *noun*
(a) hard way used by automobiles, trucks, etc., to travel along ; *drivers must be careful because roads are covered with ice; children are taught to look both ways before crossing the road; what is your office address? - 265 Lonsdale Road* (NOTE: often used in names: **Lonsdale, Yew Road**, etc., and usually written **Rd: Lonsdale Rd,** etc.)
(b) **road signs** = signs put at the side of the road giving information to drivers; *if you come to a road sign saying "Kingston", turn back because you will have gone too far; there are no road signs at that junction, but that is where you have to make a left*
(c) **on the road** = traveling; *as a salesman, he's on the road thirty weeks a year; we were on the road for thirteen hours before we finally reached the motel*

④ **road rage**
[ˈrəʊd ˈreɪdʒ] *noun*
violent attack by a driver on another automobile or its driver, caused by anger at the way the other driver has been driving; *there have been several incidents of road rage lately; in the latest road rage attack, the driver jumped out of his car and knocked a cyclist to the ground*

④ **roadrunner**
[ˈrəʊdrʌnər] *noun*
bird found in southwestern U.S. that runs very

fast; *I saw a few roadrunners when I visited New Mexico*

② **roam**
[rəʊm] *verb*

to wander about without any particular destination; *angry fans roamed around the streets smashing windows*

① **roar**
[rɔr]
1 *noun*

loud noise of shouting, of an engine, etc.; *you could hear the roar of the crowd at the football game several miles away*; *the roar of the jet engines made it impossible for me to hear what she said*
2 *verb*

to make a loud noise; *he roared with laughter at the movie*; *the lion roared and then ran toward us*

③ **roaring**
['rɔrɪŋ] *adjective*

wild; **roaring fire** = big fire, with flames going up the chimney; *we sat in front of a roaring fire and drank hot cocoa*; **to do a roaring business** = to sell something very fast; *the ice cream sellers have been doing a roaring business during the hot weather*

① **roast**
[rəʊst]
1 *verb*

to cook over a fire or in an oven; *if you want the meat well-cooked, roast it for a longer period at a lower temperature*; *you can either roast the pheasant or cook it in red wine*
2 *adjective*

which has been roasted; *what a lovely smell of roast meat!*; *we had roast chicken for dinner*; **roast potato** = potato baked in fat in an oven; *serve the meat with roast potatoes and green vegetables* (NOTE: although the verb has the forms **roasting - roasted**, when referring to meat, the adjective **roast** is used: **roast meat, roast beef**, but **roasted peanuts**)
3 *noun*

meal with meat cooked in an oven; *we always have a roast on Sundays*

① **rob**
[rɒb] *verb*

to attack and steal from someone; *a gang robbed our local bank last night*; *the old lady was robbed of all her savings* (NOTE: **robbing - robbed**)

① **robber**
['rɒbər] *noun*

person who attacks and steals from someone; *the robbers attacked the bank in broad daylight*; *three of the robbers were caught*

① **robbery**
['rɒbri] *noun*

attacking and stealing; *there was a robbery on our block yesterday*; *did they ever find out who committed the bank robbery?* (NOTE: plural is **robberies**)

① **robin**
['rɒbɪn] *noun*

common North American bird with dark feathers and a red breast; *the robin lays blue eggs*

② **robot**
['rəʊbɒt] *noun*

machine which is programmed to work like a person automatically; *these cars are made by robots*

④ **robust**
[rə'bʌst] *adjective*

(a) strong, vigorous; *this young tree is very robust and should survive the winter*; *my grandmother is not very robust but she still manages to look after herself*
(b) vigorous and determined; *he gave some robust answers to the journalists' questions*; *our troops will give a robust response to any enemy attack*

① **rock**
[rɒk]
1 *noun*

(a) large stone, large piece of stone; *the ship was breaking up on the rocks*
(b) music with a strong rhythm; *rock (music) is the only music he listens to*
2 *verb*

(a) to sway from side to side; to make something sway from side to side; *the little boat rocked in the wake of the ferry*; *the explosion rocked the town*; *(informal)* **don't rock the boat** = don't do anything to disturb what has been arranged; *everything has been organized, so please don't rock the boat with any new suggestions*
(b) to move from side to side, holding something; *the baby is crying, I'll try to rock him to sleep*

◇ **on the rocks**
phrase

(a) in great difficulties; *the company is on the rocks*; *their marriage is on the rocks*
(b) served with ice; *a whiskey on the rocks*

④ **rock bottom**
['rɒk 'bɒtəm] *noun*

the lowest point; *sales have reached rock bottom*; **rock-bottom prices** = the lowest prices possible; *we can't give you a bigger discount - the prices quoted are rock-bottom*

① **rocket**
['rɒkɪt]
1 *noun*

(a) type of firework which flies up into the sky; *we stood in the square and watched the rockets lighting up the sky*
(b) type of bomb which is shot through space at an enemy; *they fired a rocket into the police station*

(c) space rocket = large device which is fired into space, carrying satellites, etc.; *we are sending a rocket to Jupiter*
(d) type of green vegetable eaten in salads
2 *verb*
to shoot upwards very fast; *prices have rocketed this summer*

① **rocky**
['rɒki] *adjective*
(a) full of rocks and large stones; *they followed a rocky path up the mountain*
(b) *(informal)* difficult; *the company has had a rocky year*
(c) the Rocky Mountains *or* **the Rockies** = range of high mountains, running south from western Canada into the western United States; *the pictures of the Rocky Mountains covered in snow are a typical postcard scene; we picked up two backpackers who were hitchhiking to the Rockies*

② **rod**
[rɒd] *noun*
long stick; *you need something like a metal rod to hold the tent upright*; **fishing rod** = long stick with a line attached, used for fishing

① **rode**
[rəʊd]
see RIDE

③ **role**
[rəʊl] *noun*
(a) part played by someone, in a play or movie; *he plays the role of the king*; **title role** = part after which a play is named; *who's playing the title role in "Hamlet"?*
(b) part played by someone in real life; *he played an important role in getting the project off the ground* (NOTE: do not confuse with **roll**)

① **roll**
[rəʊl]
1 *noun*
(a) tube of something which has been turned over and over on itself; *a roll of fax paper; a roll of toilet paper or a toilet roll*
(b) list of names; **to call the roll** = to read out the list of names to see if everyone is there; **roll of honor** or **honor roll** = list of people who have done something special, such as students who have gained academic honors, or soldiers killed in battle
(c) very small loaf of bread for one person, sometimes cut in half and used to make a sandwich; *will an egg salad and a bread roll be enough for you?*; *the airline's continental breakfast was just a roll and a cup of coffee*
(d) action of rolling; *it takes time to get used to the roll of the ship; with a roll of her eyes and a shake of her head, she left the room* (NOTE: do not confuse with **role**)
2 *verb*
(a) to make something go forward by turning it over and over; *he rolled the ball to the other player*

(b) to go forward by turning over and over; *the ball rolled down the hill; my dime has rolled under the piano*
(c) to make something move on wheels; *the table is fitted with wheels, just roll it into the room; the patient was rolled into the operating room ten minutes ago*
(d) to turn something flat over and over; *he rolled the poster into a tube*
(e) to move from side to side; *the ship rolled in the heavy seas; she rolled her eyes and pointed at the door* (NOTE: the other movement of a boat, where the front and back go up and down, is to **pitch**)

② **roller**
['rəʊlər] *noun*
(a) heavy round object which rolls, such as one used for making lawns or games pitches flat; *they used the roller just before the match started*
(b) plastic tube used for rolling your hair into curls; *she isn't ready yet - her hair is still in rollers*

① **rollerblades**
['rəʊlərbleɪdz] *noun*
trademark for a type of roller skate, with a series of little wheels in line; *the young man on rollerblades zoomed past us at great speed*

① **roller skate**
['rəʊlər 'skeɪt] *noun*
boot with wheels which you wear to glide along fast; *I have some roller skates but I'd love to have rollerblades*

③ **roll up**
['rəʊl 'ʌp] *verb*
(a) to turn something flat over and over until it is like a tube; *he rolled up the carpet or he rolled the carpet up*
(b) *(informal)* to arrive; *they just rolled up and asked if we could put them up for the night; the bridegroom finally rolled up an hour late and said he'd had a flat tire*

④ **Roman**
['rəʊmən]
1 *adjective*
referring to Rome, the capital of Italy and of the ancient Roman Empire; *a book about Roman emperors*; **Roman alphabet** = the alphabet used in many European languages (A, B, C, D, etc.), as opposed to the Greek or Russian alphabets; *the Inuit would like to preserve their own alphabet rather than use the Roman one*; **Roman numerals** = numbers written as by the Romans (I, II, III, IV, etc.) (NOTE: Roman numerals are still used for names of kings and queens, and in copyright dates on some movies and TV programs)
2 *noun*
(a) person who lives or lived in Rome; *the Romans invaded Britain in 43 AD*

(b) printing type with straight letters; *the book is set in Times Roman* (NOTE: the other two styles of print are **italic** and **bold**)

① **romance**
[rə'mæns]
1 *noun*
love affair; *she told us all about her vacation romance*; *their romance didn't last*
2 *adjective*
romance language = language that is based on Latin; *French is a romance language, can you name any others?*

③ **romantic**
[rə'mæntɪk] *adjective*
(a) full of mystery and love; *we had a romantic dinner by the beach which I'll never forget*; *the atmosphere on the ship was very romantic*; **romantic novel** = novel which is a love story
(b) *(literary or artistic style)* which is very imaginative; which is based on personal emotions; *his style is too romantic for my liking*; *the romantic period is not my favorite literary period*

① **roof**
[ruf] *noun*
(a) part of a building, etc., which covers it and protects it; *the cat walked across the roof of the greenhouse*; *she lives in a little cottage with a red roof*
(b) top of the inside of the mouth; *I burned the roof of my mouth drinking hot soup*
(c) top of an automobile, bus, truck, etc.; *we had to put the cases on the roof of the automobile*; **roof rack** = frame on the top of an automobile which holds baggage, etc.

② **room**
[rum] *noun*
(a) part of a building, divided from other parts by walls; *the apartment has six rooms, plus kitchen and bathroom*; *we want an office with at least four rooms*; **dining room** = room where you eat; *see also* BATHROOM, BEDROOM, LIVING ROOM, etc.
(b) bedroom in a hotel; *your room is 316 - here's your key*; *his room is just opposite mine*; **double room** = room for two people; *do you have a double room for three nights?*; **single room** = room for one person; *I would like to book a single room for tomorrow night*; **room service** = arrangement in a hotel where food or drink can be served in a guest's bedroom; *if we call room service, we can have food sent up to our room*
(c) space for something; *the table is too big - it takes up a lot of room*; *there isn't enough room in the car for six people*; *we can't have a piano in our apartment - there just isn't enough room*; **to make room for** = to squeeze together to make space for; *there is no way we can make room for another passenger*; **there's room for improvement** = things could be improved; *the system is better than it was, but there is still*

room for improvement (NOTE: no plural in this meaning: **some room, no room, too much room**)

③ **roost**
[rust]
1 *noun*
perch where a bird sleeps; **to rule the roost** = be in charge, to the boss; *he's the CEO, but it's his secretary who rules the roost in the firm*
2 *verb*
(a) to perch asleep; *six chickens were roosting in the shed*
(b) **to come home to roost** = to come back to have a bad effect on the person who actually did it; *his mistakes in investing on the stock market have come home to roost*

① **rooster**
['rustər] *noun*
male domestic chicken; *we were woken by the rooster on our neighbor's farm*

① **root**
[rut]
1 *noun*
(a) part of a plant which goes down into the ground, and which takes energy from the soil; *I'm not surprised the plant died, it has hardly any roots*; *(of a cutting)* **to take root** = to make roots; *the cuttings died, none of them took root*; **to put down roots** = to begin to feel at home in a place; *we have been living in Cheyenne for three months and are beginning to put down roots*; **root beer** = soft drink flavored with extracts of roots and herbs; **root crops** *or* **root vegetables** = vegetables that are grown for their roots which are eaten, such as carrots, etc.; *it is impossible to grow root vegetables in this kind of soil*
(b) part of a hair or a tooth which goes down into the skin; *he pulled her hair out by the roots* (NOTE: do not confuse with **route**)
2 *verb*
to root for = to support a person or team, especially by cheering; *we're all rooting for the college team*

④ **root out**
['rut 'aut] *verb*
(a) to pull up a plant with its roots; *I spent the morning rooting out weeds in the garden*
(b) to remove something completely; *the police are trying to root out corruption*

① **rope**
[rəup]
1 *noun*
(a) very thick string; *you'll need a rope to pull the truck out of the ditch*; *the burglar climbed down from the balcony on a rope*
(b) **to learn the ropes** = to learn how to do something; *we send new salesmen out with an experienced rep to learn the ropes*
2 *verb*
(a) to tie together with a rope; *the climbers roped themselves together*; *we roped the sofa onto the roof of the automobile*

(b) to rope someone in = to get someone to help or to join in; *rope in as many people as you can, we need all the help we can get*; *she was roped in to deal with the children's lunch*

(c) to rope off = to stop people from going into a place by putting a rope around it; *the VIP area has been roped off - you need a special ticket to get in*

① **rose**
[rəʊz]
1 *noun*
(a) common garden flower with a strong scent; *he gave her a bunch of red roses*; *these roses have a beautiful scent*
(b) common wild shrub with these strongly scented flowers; *wild roses were growing along the path*
2 *verb*
see RISE

① **rot**
[rɒt]
1 *noun*
decay; *once rot infects the roots, it will kill the plant quickly*; *dry rot* = decay in the wooden parts of a house caused by a type of mushroom; *get rid of the dry rot before you do any other repairs to the house*
2 *verb*
to decay, to go bad; *the wooden fence is not very old but it has already started to rot*; *see also* ROTTEN (NOTE: **rotting - rotted**)

③ **rotary**
['rəʊtəri] *noun*
traffic circle, place where several roads meet, and traffic has to move in a circle around a central area; *he was driving counterclockwise round the rotary when the accident took place*

① **rotate**
[rəʊ'teɪt] *verb*
to turn round like a wheel; *rotate the knob to the right to increase the volume*

② **rotation**
[rəʊ'teɪʃn] *noun*
turning; *the rotation of the Earth around the Sun*

② **rotten**
['rɒtən] *adjective*
(a) decayed; *the apple looked nice on the outside, but inside it was rotten*; *don't walk across that little bridge, I think it is rotten*
(b) *(informal)* miserable; *I had a rotten time at the party - no one would dance with me*; *we had rotten weather on vacation*; *to feel rotten* = (i) to feel sick; (ii) to feel ashamed; *yesterday I felt slightly unwell, but today I feel really rotten*; *I feel so rotten for having spoiled your birthday party*

① **rough**
[rʌf]
1 *adjective*

(a) not smooth; *the sea's rough today - I hope I won't be sick*; *we had a rough crossing to the island*
(b) with a sharp, unpleasant taste; *this wine's a bit rough - but what can you expect for $4.95?*
(c) approximate, not very accurate; *I made some rough calculations on the back of an envelope*
(d) not finished; *he made a rough draft of the new design*
(e) not gentle; *don't be rough when you're playing with the puppy* (NOTE: **rougher - roughest**)
2 *noun*
(a) design which has not been finished; *she showed me some roughs for the new gardening magazine*
(b) part of a golf course where the grass is not cut; *his ball went into the rough*
3 *verb*
(a) *(informal)* **to rough it** = to live in uncomfortable conditions; *we roughed it in the cabin in the mountains*
(b) to rough something out = to make a rough design for something; *he roughed out the plan of the house on the back of an envelope*
(c) *(informal)* **to rough someone up** = to attack someone; *when he refused to pay, the landlord sent some people round to rough him up*

③ **rough-and-ready**
['rʌf n 'redi] *adjective*
approximate; not beautifully finished; *the plan is a bit rough-and-ready, but it will give you a general idea of what we want*; *I'm not too pleased with the work he did - it is a bit too rough-and-ready*

③ **roughly**
['rʌfli] *adverb*
(a) approximately, more or less; *there were roughly one hundred people in the audience*; *the cost of building the new kitchen will be roughly $35,000*
(b) in a rough way; *don't play so roughly with the children*; *the removal men threw the boxes of china roughly into the back of their van*

① **round**
[raʊnd]
1 *adjective*
(a) with a shape like a circle; *in Chinese restaurants, you usually sit at round tables*
(b) with a shape like a globe; *soccer is played with a round ball*; *people used to believe that the Earth was flat, not round*
(c) in round figures = not totally accurate, but correct to the nearest 10 or 100; *expect to pay $5000 in round figures*
2 *adverb & preposition*
in a circular way; *the wheels of the truck went round and round*
3 *noun*
(a) rounds = usual course of places visited; *the guard made his rounds of the building*
(b) round (of drinks) = drinks bought by one

person for a group of people; *it's my turn to buy the next round*

(c) part of a competition; *those who answer all the questions correctly, go on to the next round*; *he was knocked out in the first round*

(d) playing all the holes on a golf course; *I think we have time for one more round before it gets dark*

(e) series of meetings; *a round of pay negotiations*

(f) one bullet; *the police fired several rounds into the crowd of students*

4 *verb*

to go round; *he rounded the corner and saw a crowd in front of him*; *the boat sank as it was rounding the little island*

④ **roundabout**
['raʊndəbaʊt] *adjective*

not direct; *the taxi took a very roundabout route to get to the studio*

③ **round down** *or* **round off**
['raʊnd daʊn] *verb*

to decrease to the nearest full figure; *the figures have been rounded down to the nearest dollar*

③ **rounds**
[raʊndz] *noun*

regular visits; *the doctor made his rounds of the patients*

③ **round-trip**
['raʊnd 'trɪp] *noun*

journey from one place to another and back again; *by train, the round trip will cost $25*; **round-trip ticket** = ticket for a journey from one place to another and back again; *a round-trip ticket is cheaper than two one-way tickets* (NOTE: also called a **return ticket**)

① **round up**
['raʊnd 'ʌp] *verb*

(a) to gather people or animals together; *the secret police rounded up about fifty suspects and took them off in vans*; *she rounded up the children and took them into the museum*; *the farmer is out in the fields rounding up his cattle*

(b) to increase to the nearest full figure; *the figures have been rounded up to the nearest dollar*; *I owed him $9.98 so I rounded it up to $10.00*

① **route**
[rut *or* raʊt]

1 *noun*

(a) way to be followed to get to a destination; *we still have to decide which route we will take*; **bus route** = normal way that a bus follows; *the movie theater is not on the bus route, we'll have to go there by car*

(b) en route = on the way; *the tanker sank when she was en route to the Gulf* (NOTE: do not confuse with **root**)

2 *verb*

to send someone along a route; *the demonstration was routed along Main Street to the town hall*

③ **routine**
[ru'tin]

1 *noun*

(a) normal, regular way of doing things; *children don't like their routine to be changed*; *a change of routine might do you good*; *having a cup of coffee while reading the newspaper is part of his morning routine*; **daily routine** = things that you do every day; *buying a newspaper on his way to work and a bar of chocolate on his way home is all part of his daily routine*

(b) instructions that carry out a task as part of a computer program; *the routine copies the screen display onto a printer*

(c) sequence of dance steps; *the dancers were practicing a very complicated routine*

2 *adjective*

normal or everyday; *he went to the doctor for a routine checkup*; *we're making a routine check of the central heating system*

④ **routinely**
[ru'tinli] *adverb*

in a routine way, done as a routine; *we routinely check the fire fighting equipment*

① **row**

1 *noun*

(a) [rəʊ] line of things, side by side or one after the other; *he has a row of cabbages in the garden*; *they pulled down an old house to build a row of stores*; *I want two seats in the front row*

(b) [raʊ] serious argument; *they had a row about who was responsible for the accident*

2 *verb*

(a) [rəʊ] to make a boat go forward by using long blades; *she rowed across the lake to fetch a doctor*

(b) [raʊ] *(informal)* to argue; *they were rowing about who would pay the check*

① **rowboat**
['rəʊbəʊt] *noun*

small boat for rowing; *we rented a rowboat and went down the river*

③ **rowdy**
['raʊdi] *adjective*

making a great deal of noise; *a rowdy party in the apartment next door kept us all awake*; *the mayor had a rowdy reception at the meeting* (NOTE: **rowdier - rowdiest**)

③ **rowing**
['rəʊɪŋ] *noun*

making a boat move by the use of long wooden blades; *I'm not good at rowing*; *the university has a rowing team*

① **royal**
['rɔɪəl] *adjective*

referring to a king or queen; **royal family** =

family of a king or queen; **royal blue** = dark blue

② **royalty**
['rɔɪəltɪ] *noun*
(a) members of a king's or queen's family; *please dress formally, there will be royalty present* (NOTE: no plural in this meaning)
(b) money paid to the author of a book or an actor in a movie, or the owner of land where oil is found, etc., as a percentage of sales; *do you receive royalties on the sales of your book?*; *all royalty checks are paid direct to my offshore account* (NOTE: plural is **royalties**)

③ **RSVP**
['ar es vi 'pi] *abbreviation for the French phrase répondez s'il vous plaît, meaning "please answer"* letters printed on an invitation asking the person invited to reply

② **rub**
[rʌb]
1 *verb*
to move something across the surface of something else; *he rubbed his hands together to get them warm*; *these new shoes have rubbed against my heel*; *the cat rubbed herself against my legs*; **to rub someone the wrong way** = to make someone annoyed; *she's in a bad mood, someone must have rubbed her the wrong way* (NOTE: **rubbing - rubbed**)
2 *noun*
action of rubbing; *she gave her shoes a quick rub to remove the dust*; *he hit his head on the low ceiling, and gave it a rub*

① **rubber**
['rʌbər] *noun*
elastic material made from juice from a tropical tree; *automobile tires are made of rubber*; *many years ago, we visited a rubber plantation in Malaysia*; **rubber band** = ring of rubber which holds cards, papers, etc., together; *put a rubber band round those papers*

② **rubbish**
['rʌbɪʃ] *noun*
(a) trash, things which are no use and are thrown away; *we had to step over heaps of rubbish to get to the restaurant*
(b) garbage, nonsense, something which has no value; *have you read the new best-seller? - it's rubbish!*; *he's talking rubbish, don't listen to him* (NOTE: no plural)

② **rub in**
['rʌb 'ɪn] *verb*
(a) to make a cream enter the skin by rubbing; *she rubbed sunscreen into her skin*
(b) *(informal)* **don't rub it in** = don't go on talking about my mistake; *yes, I know I made a mistake, but please, don't rub it in*

③ **rub out**
['rʌb 'aʊt] *verb*
to remove a pencil mark with a rubber; *it's written in pencil so you can rub it out easily*

④ **rucksack**
['rʌksæk] *noun*
bag carried on the back of a walker (knapsack); *he put extra clothes and a bottle of water in his rucksack*; *a group of walkers with muddy boots and rucksacks came into the diner* (NOTE: larger bags are called **backpacks**)

③ **rudder**
['rʌdər] *noun*
flat vertical part at the stern of a boat or on the tail of an aircraft, used for steering; *after the rudder broke off they had to use an oar to steer with*

② **rude**
[rud] *adjective*
not polite, likely to offend, trying to offend; *don't point at people - it's rude*; *the teacher asked who had written rude words on the board*; *he was rude to the teacher and has gotten bad grades ever since* (NOTE: **ruder - rudest**)

② **rudely**
['rudlɪ] *adverb*
in a rude way; *she told him rudely what he could do with his offer*

② **rudeness**
['rudnəs] *noun*
being rude; *he was fired for his rudeness to the customers*

④ **rudimentary**
[rudə'mentərɪ] *adjective*
basic; not fully developed; *her knowledge of French is rudimentary*

① **rug**
[rʌg] *noun*
(a) small carpet; *this beautiful rug comes from the Middle East*
(b) thick blanket, especially one used when traveling; *put a rug over your knees if you're cold*

③ **rugby**
['rʌgbɪ] *noun*
GB **rugby football** = type of ball game played with an oval ball which is thrown as well as kicked; *when and where is the next rugby match?*; **rugby ball** = type of oval ball used in rugby

② **ruin**
['ruɪn]
1 *noun*
(a) complete loss of all your money; *he faces complete ruin*
(b) remains of an old building with no roof, fallen walls, etc.; *the house was a total ruin when I bought it*; **to fall into ruin** = to become a ruin; *the house was empty for many years and gradually fell into ruin*
2 *verb*
(a) to wreck or to spoil completely; *our vacation was ruined by the weather*
(b) to bring to financial collapse; *the failure of the bank ruined a lot of businesses*

② **ruined**

['ruɪnd] *adjective*

(a) in ruins; *smoke rose from the ruined houses*

(b) not able to pay your debts; *a ruined company director*

② **ruins**

['ruɪnz] *noun*

remains of old buildings with no roofs, fallen walls, etc.; *in the afternoon we visited the castle ruins*; **in ruins** = wrecked; *the town was in ruins after the war*; *after being arrested at the nightclub, his career was in ruins*

② **rule**

[rul]

1 *noun*

(a) strict order of the way to behave; *there are no rules that forbid parking here at night*; *according to the rules, your ticket must be paid for two weeks in advance*; **against the rules** = not as the rules say; *you can't hold the ball in your hands in soccer - it's against the rules*

(b) as a rule = usually; *as a rule, we go to bed early during the week*

(c) rule of thumb = easily remembered way of doing a simple calculation; *as a rule of thumb you can calculate that a pound is half a kilo*

(d) government; *the country became prosperous under the rule of the generals*

2 *verb*

(a) to govern or to control; *the president rules the country according to military principles*; *who rules here, the CEO or his wife?*

(b) to give an official or legal decision; *the judge ruled that the documents had to be brought to the court*

(c) to draw a straight line using a ruler; **ruled paper** = paper with lines on it

② **rule out**

['rul 'aut] *verb*

to leave something out, not to consider something; *you can rule out the possibility of leaving tomorrow*; *you can rule me out - I'm much too tired to go dancing*; *only graduates should apply, so that rules me out*; *I wouldn't rule out the possibility of the voters staying at home on election day*

① **ruler**

['rulər] *noun*

(a) long narrow piece of wood or plastic with measurements marked on it, used for measuring and drawing straight lines; *you need a ruler to draw straight lines*

(b) person who governs; *he's the ruler of a small African state*

③ **ruling**

['rulɪŋ]

1 *adjective*

(a) in power, governing; **ruling party** = party that forms the government; *the ruling party is not very popular and will not succeed in winning enough votes*

(b) in operation at the moment; *we will invoice at ruling prices*

2 *noun*

legal decision made by a judge, etc.; *the judge will give a ruling on the case next week*; *according to the ruling of the court, the contract was illegal*

③ **rumor**

['rumər]

1 *noun*

story spread from one person to another but which may not be true; *there's a rumor going around that John's finally getting married*

2 *verb*

to spread a story; *it was rumored in the press that they were about to get divorced*

① **run**

[rʌn]

1 *noun*

(a) going quickly on foot as a sport; *I always go for a run before breakfast*; *you must be tired out after that long run*

(b) short trip in an automobile; *let's go for a run down to the seaside*

(c) making a machine work; **test run** = trial made on a machine; *a test run will help you to see if the machine is working properly*

(d) rush to buy something; *the store reported a run on the new computer game*

(e) regular route of a plane, bus, etc.; *on this run, the bus does not go as far as the post office*; *she's a stewardess on the New York - London run*

(f) series of little holes in stockings or tights; *I can't wear these stockings because there's a run in them*

2 *verb*

(a) to go quickly on foot; *when she heard the telephone, she ran upstairs*; *children must be taught not to run across the road*; *she's running in the 200 meter race*

(b) *(of buses, trains, etc.)* to be working; *all trains are running late because of the accident*; *this bus doesn't run on Sundays*

(c) *(of machines)* to work; *he left his automobile on the street with the engine running*; *my automobile's not running very well at the moment*

(d) to go; *the main street of the town runs north and south*; *the movie runs for three hours*

(e) to direct, to organize a business, a club, etc.; *he runs a chain of shoe stores*; *I want someone to run the sales department for me when I'm away on vacation*; *he runs the local youth club*; *the country is run by the army*

(f) to use an automobile regularly; *we can't afford to run two automobiles*

(g) to drive by automobile; *let me run you to the station*

(h) to be in force; *the lease has only six months more to run*

(i) to amount to; *the costs ran into thousands of*

dollars

(j) *(of liquid)* to flow, to move along easily; *the river runs past our house*; *this color won't run* = the color will not stain other clothes if they are all washed together

(k) to run in a family = to be an inherited feature; *red hair runs in their family*

(l) to publish a story in several editions of a newspaper; *the paper is running a shocking story about the senator's wife* (NOTE: **running - ran** [ræn] **- has run**)

② **run across**
['rʌn ə'krɒs] *verb*
(a) to cross quickly on foot; *the little boy ran across the road after his ball*
(b) to find or to meet by accident; *I ran across it in a secondhand bookstore*

① **run after**
['rʌn 'æftər] *verb*
to follow someone fast; *he ran after the mail carrier to give back the letter which was wrongly addressed*; *the dog never runs after cats, only birds*

① **run away**
['rʌn ə'weɪ] *verb*
(a) to escape, to go away fast; *they were running away from the police*; *she ran away from school when she was 16*; *the youngsters ran away to New York*
(b) to run away with someone = to go away from your family to live with someone or to marry someone; *she ran away with her Spanish teacher*
(c) to let your imagination run away with you = to think things are possible when they are not; *don't let your imagination run away with you!*

④ **run down**
['rʌn 'daʊn] *verb*
(a) to knock down with a vehicle; *she was run down by a car which did not stop*
(b) *(of clock, machine)* to stop working or go slower because of lack of power; *the clock has stopped - the battery must have run down*
(c) to chase and capture someone or something; *the border guards will run them down*
(d) to criticize someone; *it's not fair to run him down when he's not there to defend himself*

③ **run for**
['rʌn 'fɔr] *verb*
(a) to go fast to try to catch; *he ran for the bus but it left before he got to the stop*
(b) to be a candidate for an office; *he's running for president*

② **rung**
[rʌŋ]
1 *noun*
one of the bars on a ladder; *if you stand on the top rung you can climb onto the roof*; *put your foot on the bottom rung to hold the ladder steady*
2 *verb*
see RING

② **run into**
['rʌn 'ɪntʊ] *verb*
(a) to go into a place fast; *she ran out of the house shouting "Fire!"*
(b) to go fast and hit something (usually in a vehicle); *he didn't look where he was going and ran into an old lady*; *the bus turned the corner too fast and ran into a parked truck*
(c) to amount to; *costs have run into thousands of dollars*; *her income runs into five figures*
(d) to find someone by chance; *I ran into him again in a café downtown*

② **runner**
['rʌnər] *noun*
(a) person or horse running in a race; *my horse came in last of seven runners*; *there are thousands of runners in the New York Marathon*
(b) runner bean = type of climbing bean

③ **runner-up**
['rʌnə'ʌp] *noun*
person who comes after the winner in a race or competition; *Natasha won the competition and her younger brother was runner-up*; *France won the World Cup and Brazil was the runner-up* (NOTE: plural is **runners-up**)

① **running**
['rʌnɪŋ]
1 *adjective*
(a) which runs; **running battle** = battle that moves around from place to place; *the police were engaged in running battles with the protesters*; **running commentary** = commentary on an action while the action is taking place; *the reporter gave a running commentary on the riots from his hotel window*; **running total** = total that is carried from one column of figures to the next; *the running total appears at the bottom of the first column and at the top of the next one*; **running water** = water that is available in a house through water pipes and taps; *I'm not sure that all the houses here have running water*; *there is hot and cold running water in all the rooms*
(b) used when running a race; *running shorts*; *running shoes*
(c) for three days running = one day after another for three days; *the company have made a profit for the sixth year running*
(d) running mate = person who stands for election as number two to the main candidate; *if the candidate for president wins, then his running mate becomes vice president*
2 *noun*
(a) race; **to be in the running for** = to be a candidate for; *three candidates are in the running for the post of chairman*; **out of the running** = with no chance of doing something; *she's out of the running for the job in the bookstore*
(b) action of managing; *I now leave the running of the firm to my son*

③ **run off**
['rʌn 'ɒf] *verb*
(a) to go away fast; *he grabbed the watch and ran off down the street*
(b) to print using a machine; *she ran off a few copies of the leaflet*

③ **run off with**
['rʌn 'ɒf 'wɪð] *verb*
(a) to go away with someone; *he ran off with the girl next door and phoned his parents to say they had gone to Lansing*
(b) to steal something and go away; *the secretary ran off with our cash box*

④ **run-of-the-mill**
['rʌnəvðə'mɪl] *adjective*
ordinary; *it's a run-of-the-mill operation which any doctor can do*

① **run on**
['rʌn 'ɒn] *verb*
(a) to use something as a fuel; *the machine runs on electricity*
(b) to continue; *does the play run on until very late?*

① **run out**
['rʌn 'aut] *verb*
to run out of something = to have nothing left of something; *the automobile ran out of gas on the freeway; I must go to the supermarket - we're running out of peanut butter*

② **run over**
['rʌn 'əuvər] *verb*
(a) to knock someone down by hitting them with a vehicle; *she was run over by a taxi; the automobile ran over a dog*
(b) to continue; *the description of the accident runs over two pages*

③ **run through**
['rʌn 'θru] *verb*
(a) to read a list rapidly; *let's run through the agenda before the meeting starts to see if there are any problem areas; she ran through the paragraph again to make sure she understood what it meant; we must run through the list of guests to see if we have forgotten anyone*
(b) to use up; *we have run through our entire stock of wine in one weekend*
(c) to repeat; *just run through that scene again to see if you all know your lines*

① **run up**
['rʌn 'ʌp] *verb*
(a) to go up quickly on foot; *she ran up the stairs carrying a thermometer; the runners have to run up the mountain and back again*
(b) **to run up to** = to come closer quickly on foot; *he ran up to the police officer and asked him to call an ambulance*
(c) to make debts go up quickly; *the business was running up debts of thousands of dollars each week*

③ **run up against**
['rʌn 'ʌp ə'genst] *verb*
to find your way blocked by something; *whatever we try to do, we seem to run up against local regulations; we ran up against unexpected difficulties*

③ **runway**
['rʌnweɪ] *noun*
track on which planes land and take off at an airport; *the plane went out onto the runway and then stopped for half an hour*

③ **rural**
['ruərəl] *adjective*
referring to the countryside; *rural roads are usually quite narrow; we live quite close to a town but the country around us still looks very rural*

① **rush**
[rʌʃ]
1 *noun*
(a) fast movement; *there was a rush of hot air when they opened the door; there has been a rush to change dollars to pounds; when the movie ended there was a rush for the restrooms;* **rush job** = job that has to be done fast; *it is a rush job that needs to be dealt with immediately* (NOTE: no plural in this meaning)
(b) type of wild grass growing in water; *rushes grow along the shores of lakes and rivers* (NOTE: plural in this meaning is **rushes**)
(c) **rushes** = first prints of a film that are shown before being edited
2 *verb*
to hurry, to go forward fast; *the ambulance rushed to the accident; crowds of shoppers rushed to the stores on the first day of the sales;* **don't rush me** = don't keep on making me hurry; *I need time to do this work, please don't rush me*

③ **rush hour**
['rʌʃ 'auər] *noun*
time of day when traffic is bad, when trains are full, etc.; *don't travel during the rush hour if you want to avoid the traffic; his taxi was stuck in the rush hour traffic*

① **Russia**
['rʌʃə] *proper noun*
large country in Eastern Europe, covering also a large part of Asia up to the Pacific Ocean; *have you ever been to Russia?; he went on a journey across Russia* (NOTE: capital: **Moscow;** people: **Russians;** language: **Russian;** currency: **rouble**)

② **Russian**
['rʌʃn]
1 *adjective*
referring to Russia; *she speaks English with a Russian accent; Russian winters can be extremely cold*
2 *noun*
(a) person from Russia; *are there any Russians in the group?*
(b) language spoken in Russia; *we'll start the Russian lesson by learning the alphabet; he*

can speak Russian quite well; I can read Russian but I can't speak it

① **rust**
[rʌst]
1 *noun*
orange layer that forms on metal left in damp air; *there is a bit of rust on the hood of the automobile; the underneath of the automobile is showing signs of rust*
2 *verb*
to form rust; *don't leave the hammer and screwdriver outside in the rain - they'll rust*

④ **rustle**
['rʌsl] *verb*
to make a soft dry noise; *don't rustle the newspaper when the radio is on, I can't hear the news*

② **rusty**
['rʌsti] *adjective*
(a) covered with rust; *she tried to cut the string with a pair of rusty old scissors; he has a rusty old fridge in his front drive*

(b) *out of practice; my Portuguese used to be good, but it is very rusty now* (NOTE: **rustier - rustiest**)

④ **rut**
[rʌt] *noun*
deep track made in soft earth by the wheels of vehicles; *the wheels of the car were stuck in deep ruts*

③ **ruthless**
['ruːθləs] *adjective*
cruel, with no pity for anyone; *the new ruler is just as ruthless as the man he replaced; the manager has the reputation for being ruthless with employees who don't pull their weight; be ruthless, throw all those old letters away*

② **RV**
['ɑr 'viː] *abbreviation for*
RECREATIONAL VEHICLE

④ **Rx**
['ɑr'eks] *symbol for*
prescription for medicine

Ss

③ **S, s**
[es]
nineteenth letter of the alphabet, between R and T; *"she sells seashells on the seashore" - how many Ss are there in that?*

① **sack**
[sæk]
1 *noun*
(a) large bag made of strong cloth or paper, used for carrying heavy things; *he hurt his back lifting up the sack of potatoes*
(b) *(informal)* **to get** *or* **to be given the sack** = to be dismissed from a job; *you'll get the sack if you talk to the boss like that*
(c) complete destruction of a town; *the sack of Rome*
2 *verb*
(a) *(informal)* to dismiss someone from a job; *he was sacked because he was always late for work*
(b) to destroy a town completely; *the town was captured and sacked by the advancing enemy forces*
(c) *(informal)* **to sack out** = to go to sleep, not usually in a bed; *he sacked out on the couch*

③ **sacred**
['seɪkrəd] *adjective*
(a) associated with religion; *the sacred texts were kept locked away;* **sacred art** = paintings

of Christian religious scenes; **sacred music** = music to be played at Christian religious ceremonies
(b) holy; *Hindus believe that cattle are sacred*
(c) respected; *nothing is sacred to a reporter chasing a good story; she believed it was her sacred duty to look after his garden while he was away*

② **sacrifice**
['sækrɪfaɪs]
1 *noun*
(a) things which you give up to achieve something more important; *he finally won the competition, but at great personal sacrifice; she made many financial sacrifices to get her children through college*
(b) making an offering to a god by killing an animal or person; *he ordered the sacrifice of two lambs to please the gods*
(c) animal offered to a god; *chickens, sheep and lambs were all offered as sacrifices to their gods*
2 *verb*
(a) to give up; *I have sacrificed my career to be able to stay at home and bring up my children; she has sacrificed herself for the cause of animal welfare*

(b) to offer something as a sacrifice; *the priests sacrificed a sheep to the god*

① **sad**
[sæd] *adjective*
(a) not happy, miserable; *he's sad because the vacation has come to an end; what a sad movie! - everyone was crying; reading his poems makes me sad; it was sad to leave the house for the last time; he felt sad watching the boat sail away; it's sad that he can't come to see her; isn't it sad about her little boy being in the hospital?*
(b) *(slang)* boring, not in fashion; *only sad people collect stamps* (NOTE: **sadder - saddest**)

① **saddle**
['sædl]
1 *noun*
(a) rider's seat on a bicycle or motorcycle; *she threw her leg across the saddle and settled herself behind him; my old saddle was very comfortable but this new one is harder*
(b) rider's seat on a horse; *he leapt into the saddle and rode away;* **in the saddle** = in command; *she's in the saddle now - you have to do what she says*
(c) cut of meat from the back of an animal; *saddle of lamb*
2 *verb*
(a) to put a saddle on a horse; *she quickly saddled her horse and rode off*
(b) to saddle someone with = to give someone a difficult job or heavy responsibility; *he got saddled with the job of sorting out the garbage; don't saddle me with all your problems!*

② **sadly**
['sædli] *adverb*
in a sad way; *after the funeral we walked sadly back to the empty house; she stared sadly out of the window at the rain; sadly, John couldn't join us for lunch that day*

① **sadness**
['sædnəs] *noun*
feeling of being very unhappy; *her sadness at finding her cat dead*

③ **safari**
[sə'fɑri] *noun*
expedition to photograph or kill wild animals in Africa; *he went on a safari holiday in Kenya;* **safari park** = park where large wild animals are free to run about, and visitors drive around in their cars to look at them

① **safe**
[seif]
1 *adjective*
(a) not in danger, not likely to be hurt; *in this cave, we should be safe from the storm; all the children are safe, but the school was burned down; a savings account is a safe place for your money; is it safe to touch this snake?; it isn't safe for women to go downtown alone at night*
(b) in safe hands = in no danger; *the guide is very experienced, so we are in safe hands;* **safe**

and sound = without being hurt or damaged; *we all arrived at our destination, safe and sound; the present reached me safe and sound, thanks to the efficiency of the post office*
(c) to be on the safe side = just in case, to be certain; *it should only take an hour to get to the airport, but let's give ourselves an hour and a half, just to be on the safe side*
(d) *(in baseball)* having reached a base without being put out (NOTE: **safer - safest**)
2 *noun*
strongbox for keeping documents, money, jewels, etc., in; *put your valuables in the hotel safe; the burglars managed to open the safe;* **wall safe** = safe installed in a wall

② **safekeeping**
['seifkipiŋ] *noun*
keeing something safely, usually in a safe; *we put the letters in the bank for safekeeping*

① **safely**
['seifli] *adverb*
(a) without being hurt; *the rescue services succeeded in getting all the passengers safely off the burning train; we were shown how to handle bombs safely; "drive safely!" she said as she waved goodbye*
(b) without being damaged; *the cargo was safely taken off the sinking ship*
(c) without making a mistake or having problems; *can we safely say that this is a genuine Picasso?; she got safely through the first part of her exams*

① **safety**
['seifti] *noun*
(a) being safe; *the police tried to ensure the safety of the public; I am worried about the safety of air bags in automobiles;* **fire safety** = measures taken to keep a place safe for workers and visitors in case of fire ; **safety belt** = belt which you wear in a plane to stop you being hurt if there is an accident; **safety helmet** = solid hat worn by construction workers, etc.; *visitors to the building site must wear safety helmets* (NOTE: also called **hard hats**); **safety pin** = pin whose point fits into a little cover when it is fastened, and so can't hurt anyone; **to take safety precautions** *or* **safety measures** = to act to make sure something is safe; *be sure to take proper safety precautions when handling gas cylinders;* **safety regulations** = rules to make a place of work safe for the workers
(b) for safety = to make something safe, to be safe; *put the money in the office safe for safety; keep a note of the numbers of your traveler's checks for safety* (NOTE: no plural)

① **said**
[sed] *see* SAY

① **sail**
[seil]
1 *noun*
(a) piece of cloth which catches the wind and drives a boat along; *the wind dropped so they*

lowered the sail and started to row; *they pulled up the sail and set out across the sea*
(b) to set sail = to leave by boat; *they set sail for Europe*
(c) trip in a boat; *they went for a sail down the river* (NOTE: do not confuse with **sale**)
2 *verb*
(a) to travel on water; *the ship was sailing toward the rocks*; *we were sailing east*
(b) to travel in a sailboat; *he was the first person to sail alone across the Atlantic*; *she's planning to sail around the world*
(c) to leave harbor; *the ferry sails at 12:00*
(d) to go without difficulty; *the automobile just sailed along the freeway*; *it's annoying to see a bus sail past just when you're getting to the bus stop*; **to sail through** = to pass easily; *he sailed through his driver's test*

① **sailboat**
['seɪlbəʊt] *noun*
boat (such as a yacht) that uses mainly sails to travel

② **sailing**
['seɪlɪŋ] *noun*
(a) travel in a ship
(b) sport of going in a sailboat; *I plan to take up sailing when I retire*; *we have made plans to go on a sailing vacation in the Caribbean Sea*
(c) departure (of a ship); *there are no sailings to France because of the strike*; *there are three sailings every day to Martha's Vineyard*; **sailing time** = time when a boat leaves the harbor
(d) plain sailing = easy progress; *once he had passed the first semester, it was just plain sailing until he got his degree*

① **sailor**
['seɪlər] *noun*
person who works on a ship; *the sailors were washing down the deck of the ship*

② **saint**
[seɪnt] *noun*
(a) person who led a very holy life, and is recognized by the Christian church; *there are more than 50 statues of saints on the west front of the cathedral*; *St. Peter was a fisherman*; *will Mother Teresa be made a saint?*
(b) very good or devoted person; *she has the patience of a saint and never shouts at the children*; *he may be no saint in his personal life but he has the support of the voters* (NOTE: written **St.** [snt] with names: **St. Cecilia, St. Christopher**)

② **sake**
[seɪk] *noun*
(a) for the sake of something *or* **for something's sake** = for certain reasons, because of something; *he's not really hungry, he's just eating for eating's sake*; *the president decided to resign for the sake of the country*; *they gave the children sweets, just for the sake of a little peace and quiet*; *the muggers killed the old*

lady, just for the sake a few dollars; **for the sake of someone** *or* **for someone's sake** = because you want to help someone, to please someone, or because you think someone needs something; *will you come to the party for my sake?*; **for old times' sake** = to remember how good the old times were; *let's have a meal together for old times' sake*
(b) *(exclamation)* **for heaven's sake** *or* **for goodness' sake** = expressions showing you are annoyed, or that something is important; *what are you screaming for? - it's only a little mouse, for heaven's sake*; *for goodness' sake try to be quiet, we don't want the guards to hear us!*

① **salad**
['sæləd] *noun*
cold food, such as vegetables, often served raw; cold fish or meat served with cold vegetables; *we found some ham, tomatoes and lettuce in the fridge, and made ourselves a salad*; *a chicken salad sandwich*; **salad bar** = bar where customers help themselves to a wide variety of meat, fish or vegetable salads; **salad dressing** = mixture of oil, etc., used on salad; **fruit salad** = pieces of fresh fruit, mixed and served cold

③ **salaried**
['sælərɪd] *adjective*
paid a salary; *the company has 250 salaried staff members*

② **salary**
['sæləri] *noun*
payment for work, made to an employee with a contract of employment, especially in a professional or office job; *she started work at a low salary, but soon went up the salary scale*; *the company froze all salaries for a period of six months*; *I expect a salary increase as from next month*; **basic salary** = normal salary without extra payments; **gross salary** = salary before tax is deducted; **net salary** = salary that is left after deducting tax and national insurance contributions; **starting salary** = amount of pay an employee gets when starting work with a company; *he was appointed at a starting salary of $30,000*; **salary check** = regular check by which an employee is paid (NOTE: plural is **salaries**)

① **sale**
[seɪl] *noun*
(a) act of selling, act of giving an item or doing a service in exchange for money, or for the promise that money will be paid; *the sale of the house produced $300,000*; *the store only opened this morning and we've just made our first sale*; **cash sale** = transaction paid for in cash; **credit card sale** = transaction paid for by credit card
(b) occasion when things are sold at cheaper prices; *there's a sale this week in the department store on Main Street*; *I bought these plates for $2 in a sale*; *the sale price is*

50% of the normal price; **half-price sale** = sale of all goods at 50% of the usual price

(c) for sale = ready to be sold; **to offer something for sale** *or* **to put something up for sale** = to announce that something is ready to be sold; *they put the factory up for sale*; *these items are not for sale to the general public*; *the office building is for sale at $1.5 million*; *I noticed there was a "for sale" sign outside her house*

(d) on sale = ready to be sold in a store; *his latest novel is on sale in all good bookstores*; *local cheeses are on sale in the market* (NOTE: do not confuse with **sail**)

① **sales**
['seɪlz] *noun*

(a) money that a business receives from selling things; *the business has annual sales of over $375,000*; *sales have risen over the first quarter*; **sales forecast** = estimate of future sales; **sales manager** = person in charge of a sales department; **sales representative** = person who works for a company, showing goods or services for sale

(b) time when many stores sell goods at low prices; *the sales start on Saturday*; *I bought these shirts in the January sales*; *she bought the cups in the sales or at the sales*

③ **sales assistant** *or* **sakesclerk**
['seɪlz ə'sɪstənt *or* 'seɪlzklɜrk] *noun*
person who sells goods to customers in a store; *the sales assistant will help you*

① **salesgirl**
['seɪlzgɜrl] *noun*
woman who sells goods to customers in a store; *this purse hasn't got a price on it - I'll just go and ask a salesgirl how much it is*

③ **saleslady**
['seɪlzleɪdi] *noun*
woman who sells goods to customers in a store; *ask the saleslady if they have that skirt in your size* (NOTE: plural is **salesladies**)

② **salesman** *or* **salesperson**
['seɪlzmən *or* seɪlzpɜrsən] *noun*

(a) man who sells goods to customers in a store; *the salesman is going to show us the latest model*

(b) person who represents a company, selling its products or services to other companies; *we have six salesmen calling on accounts in downtown Chicago* (NOTE: plural is **salesmen**)

① **saleswoman** *or* **salesperson**
['seɪlzwʊmən *or* seɪlzpɜrsən] *noun*
woman in a store who sells goods to customers; *our saleswomen are all dressed in pale blue dresses* (NOTE: plural is **saleswomen** ['seɪlzwɪmɪn])

② **salmon**
['sæmən]
1 *noun*
large fish with silver skin and pink flesh; *in Alaska the bears love to catch salmon as they swim up the rivers*; *we had grilled salmon and new potatoes*; **salmon steak** = thick slice of salmon; **smoked salmon** = salmon which has been cured by smoking, and is served in very thin slices (NOTE: plural is **salmon**)

2 *adjective*
with a pink color like salmon; *we put a salmon-pink wallpaper in the bathroom*

COMMENT: salmon live in the sea, but swim up rivers in the winter. Nowadays, salmon are also farmed on fish farms

④ **salon**
['sælɒn] *noun*
store where people can have their hair cut or styled, or have beauty treatments; *the hairdressing salon is on the fifth floor*; *she went to the beauty salon for a facial*

① **salt**
[sɒlt]
1 *noun*

(a) white substance used to make food taste better (used especially with meat, fish and vegetables); *there's too much salt in this soup*; *you don't need to put any salt on your fish*; **to take something with a grain of salt** = not to believe something entirely; *you have to take everything she says with a grain of salt* (NOTE: no plural: **some salt**, **a spoonful** *or* **a pinch of salt**)

(b) large pieces of a chemical compound used to put on frozen streets to melt ice or snow; *trucks were out all night spreading salt on the streets*

(c) the salt of the earth = ordinary good honest person; *he's a wonderful man - the salt of the earth!*

2 *adjective*
containing salt; *the sea is made up only of salt water*

3 *verb*

(a) to spread salt on; *they were salting the streets during the night*

(b) to add salt to; *you forgot to salt the soup*

① **salt water**
['sɒlt 'wɔtər] *noun*
water that contains salt, such as sea water (as opposed to fresh water in rivers and lakes); *she dove into the waves and got a mouthful of salt water*; *you can float more easily in salt water than in a lake*

② **salute**
[sə'lut]
1 *noun*

(a) movement to express respect, recognition, etc., especially putting your right hand up to touch the peak of your cap; *the officer returned the soldier's salute*; **to take the salute** = to be the person whom soldiers on parade salute; *the general took the salute at the march past*

(b) firing guns to mark an important occasion; *the arrival of the president was marked with a 21-gun salute*

2 *verb*

(a) to give a salute to someone; *ordinary soldiers must salute their officers*

(b) to praise someone; *we salute the brave firemen who saved the children*

③ **salvage**
['sælvɪdʒ]

1 *noun*

(a) saving a ship or cargo from being destroyed; **salvage money** = payment made by the owner of a ship or cargo to the person who saved it; *were you paid any salvage money for the goods rescued from the boat?*; **salvage vessel** = ship that specializes in saving other ships and their cargoes

(b) goods saved from a wreck, fire, etc.; *a sale of flood salvage items*

(c) saving garbage for use; *a company specializing in the salvage of plastics from household waste*

2 *verb*

(a) to save from a wreck, fire, etc.; *we are selling off a warehouse full of salvaged goods*; *we managed to salvage the computer disks from the fire*

(b) to save something from loss; *the company is trying to salvage its reputation after the chief executive officer was sent to prison for fraud*; *the banks managed to salvage something from the collapse of the company*

② **salvation**
[sæl'veɪʃn] *noun*

action of saving a person's soul from sin; *he sought his salvation in working for the homeless*

③ **Salvation Army**
[sæl'veɪʃn 'ɑrmi] *noun*

Christian organization run on military lines, which does welfare work; *my sister has joined the Salvation Army*; *we tracked him down to a Salvation Army home in the city*

① **same**
[seɪm] *adjective & pronoun*

(a) being, looking, sounding, etc., exactly alike; *these two beers taste the same*; *you must get very bored doing the same work every day*; *she was wearing the same dress as me*; *this book is not the same size as that one*; **to stay the same** = not to change; *the weather is expect to stay the same for the next few days*

(b) showing that two or more things are in fact one; *they all live in the same street*; *should we all leave at the same time?*; *our children go to the same school as theirs*; *see also* ALL THE SAME

① **sample**
['sæmpl]

1 *noun*

specimen, a small part which is used to show what the whole is like; *a sample of the cloth or a cloth sample*; *try a sample of the local cheese*; *we interviewed a sample of potential*

customers; **free sample** = sample given free to advertise a product

2 *verb*

(a) to test, to try by taking a small amount; *why don't you sample the wine before placing your order?*

(b) to ask a group of people questions to find out a general reaction; *they sampled 2000 people at random to test the new soap*

④ **sanction**
['sæŋkʃn]

1 *noun*

(a) approval, permission; *you will need the sanction of the local authorities before you can knock the house down*

(b) **economic sanctions** = restrictions on trade with a country in order to try to influence its political development; *to impose sanctions on a country or to lift sanctions from a country*

2 *verb*

to approve; *the committee sanctioned expenditures of $2.4 million on the development project*

① **sand**
[sænd]

1 *noun*

mass of tiny bits of rock, found on beaches, in the desert, etc.; *a beach of fine white sand*; *the black sand beaches of the Northern coast of New Zealand*; *he kicked sand in my face*; **sand castle** = little castle of sand made by children on a beach; *the children built sand castles on the beach with their buckets*

2 *verb*

(a) *(also* **sand down***)* to rub smooth; *they sanded the floor before polishing it*

(b) to spread sand on; *trucks have been out all night sanding the roads*

④ **sands**
['sændz] *noun*

area of sandy beach; *the sands stretch for miles along the coast*

① **sandwich**
['sændwɪtʃ]

1 *noun*

(a) snack made with two slices of bread with meat, salad, etc., between them; *she ordered a cheese sandwich and a cup of coffee*; *what kind of sandwiches do you want to take for your lunch?*; *I didn't have a big meal - just a peanut butter and jelly sandwich with a soda*; **club sandwich** = sandwich made of three slices of bread, with a filling of meat, salad, fish, etc., between them; **sandwich bar** = small shop which mainly sells sandwiches (NOTE: plural is **sandwiches**)

(b) **sandwich boards** = boards carried in front of and behind a person with advertisements on them; **sandwich man** = man who carries sandwich boards

2 *verb*

to insert something between two others; *I stood all the way home on the subway, sandwiched between two fat men*

① **sandy**
['sændi] *adjective*
covered with sand; *the resort has miles of safe sandy beaches* (NOTE: **sandier - sandiest**)

① **sang**
[sæŋ]
see SING

① **sank**
[sæŋk]
see SINK

③ **Santa Claus**
['sæntə 'klɒz] *noun*
man in a long red coat, with a big white beard, who is supposed to bring presents to children on Christmas Day

③ **sarcastic**
[sɑr'kæstɪk] *adjective*
using sharp unpleasant remarks which mean the opposite of what they say; *"aren't you the clever one?" he said in a sarcastic tone*

② **sardine**
[sɑr'din] *noun*
small fish that can be eaten fresh, or is commonly bought in cans; *we had grilled sardines in a little restaurant overlooking the harbor*; **packed (together) like sardines** = standing or sitting very close together; *in the rush hour we were packed like sardines on the subway*

④ **SASE**
abbreviation for
self-addressed stamped envelope

① **sat**
[sæt]
see SIT

③ **satellite**
['sætəlaɪt] *noun*
(a) device that orbits the Earth, receiving and transmitting signals, pictures and data; *the signals are transmitted by satellite all round the world*; **communications satellite** = satellite that relays radio or TV signals from one part of the Earth to another; **satellite broadcasting** = sending radio or TV signals from one part of the Earth to another using a communications satellite; **satellite dish** = device, shaped like a large saucer, used to capture satellite broadcasts; **satellite TV** = television system, where pictures are sent via a space satellite; *we watched the program on satellite TV*
(b) body in space which goes round a planet; *the Moon is Earth's only satellite*

② **satisfaction**
[sætɪs'fækʃn] *noun*
(a) good feeling; sense of comfort or happiness; *after finishing his meal he gave a deep sigh of satisfaction*; *I get no satisfaction from telling you this - you're fired*; **job satisfaction** =

feeling which you have that you are happy in your work and pleased with the work you do
(b) *(formal)* payment of money or goods to someone, who then agrees to stop a claim against you; *they demanded satisfaction from the driver of the other car*

① **satisfactory**
[sætɪs'fæktəri] *adjective*
quite good, which satisfies; *the result of the election was very satisfactory for big business*; *a satisfactory outcome to the discussions*

② **satisfied**
['sætɪsfaɪd] *adjective*
contented; *I've finished painting the kitchen, and I hope you're satisfied with the result*; *she gave a satisfied smile*; **satisfied customer** = customer who has got what he wanted

② **satisfy**
['sætɪsfaɪ] *verb*
(a) to make someone pleased with what he has bought, with the service he has received; *the city council's decision should satisfy most people*; *our aim is to satisfy our customers*
(b) **to satisfy a demand** = to fill a demand; *we cannot produce enough to satisfy the demand for the product*; **to satisfy yourself** = to make sure; *the buyer must satisfy himself that the automobile is in good condition*
(c) to comply with conditions; *the payments received so far do not satisfy the conditions attached to the contract*

② **satisfying**
['sætɪsfaɪɪŋ] *adjective*
which satisfies; *it was very satisfying to see the two of them getting on so well*; *to grow all our own fruit and vegetables is very satisfying*

① **Saturday**
['sætədeɪ] *noun*
sixth day of the week, the day between Friday and Sunday; *he works in a store, so Saturday is a normal working day for him*; *we go shopping in Seattle most Saturdays*; *Saturday is the Jewish day of rest*; *today is Saturday, November 15*; *the 15th is a Saturday, so the 16th must be a Sunday*; *we arranged to meet up at the movie theater next Saturday evening*

② **sauce**
[sɒs] *noun*
liquid with a particular taste, poured over food; *ice cream with chocolate sauce*; *we had chicken with a curry sauce*; *the waitress put a bottle of hot sauce on the table*; *we had roast duck and orange sauce for dinner*

② **saucepan**
['sɒspæn] *noun*
deep metal cooking pan with a lid and a long handle; *where's the lid of the saucepan?*; *watch the saucepan - I don't want the milk to boil over*; *put the mixture in a saucepan and cook over a low heat*; *I never put the saucepans in the dishwasher*

① **saucer**
['sɔsər] *noun*
shallow dish which a cup stands in; *where are the cups and saucers? - they're in the cupboard*; **saucer of milk** = milk put in a saucer, usually for a cat to drink

① **sausage**
['sɒsɪdʒ] *noun*
tube full of ground seasoned meat, eaten hot; *you can't possibly eat all those sausages!*; *I'll have sausages and eggs for breakfast*

② **savage**
['sævɪdʒ]
1 *adjective*
fierce, likely to hurt; *hunger had made the dogs really savage*; *she suffered a savage beating and had to have stitches in her head*
2 *noun*
wild human being; *how could he turn into such a savage and attack her like that?*
3 *verb*
to attack with teeth; *he was savaged by a dog*

① **save**
[seɪv]
1 *verb*
(a) to stop someone from being hurt or killed; *the firemen saved six people from the burning house*; *how many passengers were saved when the ferry sank?*; **the police officer saved my life** = the police officer helped me and prevented me from being killed
(b) to stop something from being damaged; *we managed to save most of the paintings from the fire*
(c) to put things such as money to one side so that you can use them later; *I'm saving to buy a car*; *if you save $10 a week, you'll have $520 at the end of a year*; *they save old pieces of bread to give to the ducks in the park*; *he saves bits of string in case he may need them later*
(d) not to waste (time, money, etc.); *by walking to work, he saves $35 a week in bus fares*; *she took the package herself so as to save the cost of postage*; *if you have your automobile serviced regularly it will save you a lot of expense in the future*; *going to Chicago by air saves a lot of time*
(e) to store data on a computer disk; *don't forget to save your files when you are finished*
(f) *(in sports)* to stop an opponent from scoring; *the goalkeeper saved two goals*
2 *noun*
(in sports) action of stopping the ball from going into the goal; *the goalkeeper made a brilliant save, and the result was that the match was drawn*
3 *preposition & conjunction*
(formal) except for; *everyone was there, save Richard, who was sick*

① **save on**
['seɪv 'ɒn] *verb*
not to waste, to use less; *by introducing shift work we find we can save on fuel; by walking to work, you will find that you can save on bus fares*

① **save up**
['seɪv 'ʌp] *verb*
not to spend the money you get because you are keeping it for a special purpose; *I'm saving up to buy a motorcycle*; *they are saving up for a vacation in Europe*

① **saving**
['seɪvɪŋ]
1 *noun*
using less; *we are aiming for a 10% saving in fuel*
2 *suffix*
which uses less; **energy-saving** *or* **labor-saving device** = machine that saves energy *or* labor

① **savings**
['seɪvɪŋz] *noun*
(a) money that you can save; *he put all his savings into a bank account*; *she spent all her savings on a round the world trip*; **savings account** = bank account where you can put money in regularly and that pays interest, often at a higher rate than a checking account; **savings bank** = bank where you can deposit money and receive interest on it; **savings bond** = document showing you have invested money in a government savings plan
(b) money that you do not need to spend; *there are incredible savings on flights to Florida*

④ **savory**
['seɪvəri] *adjective*
(a) having a pleasant taste or smell; *she makes very savory meals*
(b) salty or spicy, and not sweet; *pancakes with maple syrup are sweet, but hash browns are savory*

① **saw**
[sɔ]
1 *noun*
tool with a long metal blade with teeth along its edge, used for cutting; *he was cutting logs with a saw*; *my old saw doesn't cut very well*; **chain saw** = saw made of a chain with teeth in it, which turns very fast when driven by a motor
2 *verb*
(a) to cut with a saw; *she was sawing wood*; *they sawed the old tree into pieces*; *you will need to saw that piece of wood in half* (NOTE: **saw - sawed - has sawed** *or* **sawn** [sɔn])
(b) *see also* SEE

① **say**
[seɪ]
1 *verb*
(a) to speak words; *what's she saying? - I don't know, I don't understand Portuguese*; *she says the fee is $5 per person*; *don't forget to say "thank you" after the party*; *the weather forecast said it was going to rain and it did*; *I was just saying that we never hear from my brother, when he phoned*

(b) to give information in writing; *the letter says that we owe the bank $300*; *the notice says that you are not allowed to walk on the grass*

(c) to suggest; *choose any number - (let's) say eighteen*; *let's have another meeting next week - shall we say Thursday?* (NOTE: **says** [sez] - **saying - said** [sed] - **has said**)

2 *noun*

right to speak about something; *the children have no say in the matter*; *she always wants to have the final say in an argument*; *they will all expect to have their say in choosing the new leader*

3 *interjection*

(to show surprise) say! haven't we met someplace before?

③ **saying**

['seɪɪŋ] *noun*

phrase which is often used ; *my mother was fond of old sayings*; **as the saying goes** = according to the old saying; *"Birds of a feather flock together" as the saying goes*

④ **scaffolding**

['skæfəldɪŋ] *noun*

construction of poles and planks which makes a series of platforms for workmen to stand on while building a house; *they put up scaffolding round the building*

① **scale**

[skeɪl]

1 *noun*

(a) proportion used to show a large object in a smaller form; *map with a scale of 1 to 100,000*; *the architect's design is drawn to scale*; *a scale model of the new downtown development*

(b) measuring system which is graded into various levels; *the Richter scale is used to measure earthquakes*; **scale of charges** *or* **scale of prices** = list showing prices for different goods or services; **scale of salaries** *or* **salary scale** = list showing the range and system of salaries in a company; *he was appointed at the top end of the salary scale*

(c) **large scale** *or* **small scale** = working with large or small amounts of investment, staff, etc.; **to start in business on a small scale** = to start in business with a small staff, few products, little capital

(d) small machine for weighing; *she put two bananas on the scale*; *the bathroom scales must be wrong - I'm heavier than I was yesterday*; **to tip the scales at** = to weigh; *he tipped the scales at 210 lb*

(e) thin plate protecting the skin of fish and snakes; *don't forget to scrape the scales off the sardines before you grill them*

(f) series of musical notes arranged in a rising or falling order; *she practices her scales every morning*

2 *verb*

(a) *(formal)* to climb up; *six climbers tried to scale the north face of the mountain*

(b) **to scale up** *or* **to scale down** = to increase or to reduce in proportion; *not enough students have passed the test, so the grades will have to be scaled up*; *the company is scaling down its operations in Thailand*

② **scan**

[skæn]

1 *verb*

(a) to look very carefully at something all over; *we scanned the horizon but no ships were to be seen*; *he scanned the map to try to find Cambridge Street*

(b) to pass a radar beam over (an area); to pass X-rays through part of the body; *first they scanned the right side of the brain*; *the hospital has decided to see again all patients who have been scanned over the last year*

(c) to examine a drawing or text and produce computer data from it; *they scanned the text of the book*

(d) to analyze a line of poetry to identify the rhythm; *some modern poetry is impossible to scan*

(e) *(of poetry)* to fit a regular rhythm; *the second line of the poem doesn't scan* (NOTE: **scanning - scanned**)

2 *noun*

(a) examination of part of the body by passing X-rays through the body and analyzing the result in a computer; *she went to have a scan after ten weeks of pregnancy*; **brain scan** = examining the inside of the brain by passing X-rays through the head

(b) picture of part of the body shown on a screen, derived by computers from X-rays

(c) examination of an image or an object to obtain data; *a heat scan will quickly show which of the components is getting too hot*

② **scandal**

['skændl] *noun*

(a) talking about wrong things someone is supposed to have done; *have you heard the latest scandal about him?*

(b) wrong action that produces a general feeling of public anger; *the government was brought down by the scandal of the president's wife's diamonds*; *the government should do something about the scandal of unemployed teenagers*; *it's a scandal that her father never allowed her to go to her school prom*

② **scar**

[skɑr]

1 *noun*

mark left on the skin after a wound has healed; *he still has the scars of his operation*

2 *verb*

(a) to leave a mark on the skin; *he was scarred for life as a result of the accident*

(b) to leave a mark on the mind of someone; *the abuse she suffered at school has scarred for ever* (NOTE: **scarring - scarred**)

② **scarce**

[skeəs] *adjective*

(a) not enough for the amount needed; *this happened at a period when food was scarce*; *good designers are getting scarce*

(b) *(informal)* **to make oneself scarce** = to hide, to keep out of someone's way (NOTE: **scarcer - scarcest**)

② **scarcely**
['skeəsli] *adverb*
almost not; *he can scarcely walk because of his bad back*; *I can scarcely believe it!*; **scarcely anyone** = almost no one; *scarcely anyone bought tickets for the show*

① **scare**
[skeər]
1 *noun*
making someone frightened; *what a scare you gave me - jumping out at me in the dark like that!*; **bomb scare** = frightening rumor or announcement that there might be a hidden bomb somewhere
2 *verb*
to frighten; *the thought of traveling alone across Africa scares me*; *she was scared by the spider in the bathroom*; *(informal)* **to scare the life out of someone** = to frighten someone completely; **to scare away** = to frighten something so that it goes away; *the cat has scared all the birds away from the garden*

① **scared**
[skeəd] *adjective*
frightened; *don't be scared - the snake is harmless*; *she was too scared to answer the door*; *I'm scared at the idea of driving in the rush hour traffic*; *she looked round with a scared expression*; **scared stiff** = so frightened that you cannot move; *I was scared stiff when I saw the children playing with the gun*

② **scarf**
[skɑrf] *noun*
(a) long piece of cloth that is worn around your neck to keep you warm; *take your scarf - it's snowing*; *the students were wearing striped scarves*; *it's cold - wrap your scarf around your neck*
(b) square piece of cloth that a woman can wear over her head; *put a scarf over your head - it's windy outside* (NOTE: plural is **scarves** [skɑrvz])

① **scatter**
['skætər] *verb*
(a) to throw in various places; *the crowd scattered flowers all over the path*
(b) to run in different directions; *when the police arrived, the children scattered*

② **scattered**
['skætəd] *adjective*
spread out over a wide area; *there are scattered farms in the hills*; *I found the photos scattered all over the floor*

② **scattering**
['skætərɪŋ] *noun*
a small quantity or number of things; *only a scattering of people turned up at the meeting*

④ **scenario**
[sɪ'nɑriəʊ] *noun*
(a) written draft of a movie with details of plot, characters, scenes, etc.; *he wrote the scenario for "Gone with the Wind"*
(b) general way in which you think something may happen; *the worst scenario would be if my wife's mother came on vacation with us* (NOTE: plural is **scenarios**)

② **scene**
[sin] *noun*
(a) short part of a play or movie; *did you like the scene where he is trying to climb up the skyscraper?*; *it was one of the funniest scenes ever*
(b) **behind the scenes** = without being obvious, without many people knowing; *she helped her mother a lot behind the scenes*
(c) place where something has happened; *the fire department were on the scene very quickly*; *it took the ambulance ten minutes to get to the scene of the accident*; *a photographer was at the scene to record the ceremony*
(d) *(informal)* general area in which something happens; *the U.S. political scene has changed radically over the last twelve months*; *he's king of the pop music scene*; **it's not my scene** = it's not the kind of thing I usually do or like
(e) view; *he took a photo of the scene from the hotel window*
(f) display of angry emotion; *she made a terrible scene when she discovered her husband with a girl*; *I can't stand it when people make scenes*

② **scenery**
['sinri] *noun*
(a) features of the countryside, such as mountains, lakes, rivers, etc.; *the beautiful scenery of New England*
(b) painted cloth background used to imitate real buildings, rooms, landscapes, etc., on the stage in a theater; *they lowered the scenery onto the stage*; *in between the acts all the scenery has to be changed* (NOTE: no plural)

④ **scenic**
['sinɪk] *adjective*
referring to beautiful scenery; *welcome to scenic Nova Scotia*; **scenic route** = road (often a longer roundabout route) running through beautiful countryside

② **scent**
[sent]
1 *noun*
(a) pleasant smell of something which you can recognize; *the scent of roses in the cottage garden*
(b) perfume, a liquid which smells nice, and which is put on the skin; *that new scent of yours makes me sneeze*

(c) smell; **on the scent of** = following a trail left by; *the dogs followed the scent of the robbers*; **to throw someone off the scent** = to give someone misleading information; *she tried to throw the reporters off the scent by saying that her husband had gone into the hospital*
2 *verb*
(a) to give something a pleasant smell; *the toilet cleaner is scented with pine*
(b) to discover something by smelling; *dogs can scent rabbits in holes in the ground*
(c) to begin to feel that something exists; *the team raced forward, scenting victory* (NOTE: do not confuse with **cent, sent**)

③ **scented**
['sentɪd] *adjective*
with a pleasant scent; *strongly scented roses*; *a slightly scented soap*

② **schedule**
['skedʒul]
1 *noun*
(a) timetable, plan of times drawn up in advance; *he has a busy schedule of appointments*; *his secretary tried to fit me into his schedule*; **to be ahead of schedule** = to be early; *the building of the hotel was completed ahead of schedule*; **to be on schedule** = to be on time; *the flight is on schedule*; **to be behind schedule** = to be late; *I am sorry to say that we are three months behind schedule*
(b) list of times of departure and arrival of trains, planes, coaches, etc.; *the summer schedules have been published*
(c) program or list of events; *the schedule of events for the music festival*
(d) list, especially of documents attached to a contract; *please find enclosed our schedule of charges*; *the schedule of territories to which an insurance policy applies*
2 *verb*
(a) to put something on an official list; *see the list of scheduled prices*; *the house has been scheduled as an ancient monument*
(b) to arrange the times for something; *the building is scheduled for completion in May*; *the flight is scheduled to arrive at six o'clock*; *we have scheduled the meeting for Tuesday morning*; **scheduled flight** = flight that is in the airline timetable (as opposed to a chartered flight); *he left for Rio de Janeiro on a scheduled flight*

③ **scheme**
[skim]
1 *noun*
plan or diagram; *the scheme shows the planets and stars' positions*; *he has thought up some scheme for making money very quickly*; *I think the opposition parties have some scheme to embarrass the government*
2 *verb*
to plan something in secret; *she spent most of her time in the office scheming against the*

finance department; they have been scheming to buy the store cheaply

③ **scholar**
['skɒlər] *noun*
(a) person who has great learning; *he is a well-known scholar of French history*
(b) student at school who has a scholarship; *because I was a scholar my parents didn't have to pay any fees*

④ **scholarship**
['skɒləʃɪp] *noun*
(a) money given to someone to help pay for the cost of his or her study; *the college offers scholarships to attract the best students*; *she got* or *won a scholarship to carry out research into causes of cancer*
(b) deep learning; *the article shows sound scholarship* (NOTE: no plural in this meaning)

① **school**
[skul]
1 *noun*
(a) place where students, usually children, are taught; *our little boy is five, so he'll be going to school this year*; *some children start school younger than that*; *what did the children do at school today?*; *when he was 16, he left school and joined the army*; *which school did you go to?*; *we moved here because there are good schools nearby*; **school year** = period that starts in September and finishes in June; **elementary** *or* **grade school** = school for small children between the ages of about 5 and 11 (grades 1 through 6 or 8); **high school** = school for children between the ages of about 15 and 18 (grades 9 or 10 through 12); **junior high school** *or* **middle school** = school for children between the ages of about 12 and 15 (grades 7 through 9); **nursery school** = school for very small children, for children under five years old; **private school** = school that is not run by the state and which the students have to pay to attend; *see also* PUBLIC SCHOOL
(b) section of a college or university; *the school of medicine is one of the largest in the country*; *she's in law school*
(c) **art school** = college where students learn to draw, paint, etc.; **music school** = college where students learn to play or write music
(d) group of similar artists; *these painters belong to the abstract school*
2 *verb*
(formal) to train; *he was schooled in the art of tapping telephones*

② **schoolbook**
['skulbʊk] *noun*
book used when learning a subject at school; *schools need more funds to purchase schoolbooks*

② **school bus**
['skul 'bʌs] *noun*
bus that collects children from home in the morning, takes them to school and brings them

back home in the afternoon; *the school bus leaves her in front of the house every afternoon*; *the school bus picks up our children every morning*

④ **schoolchildren**
['skultʃɪldrən] *noun*
children who go to school; *the schoolchildren are collected by bus every morning*; *she took a group of schoolchildren to visit the museum*

③ **schoolkid**
['skul 'kɪd] *noun*
(informal) child or teen who is at school; *at half past three the store was full of schoolkids trying to buy candy*

① **schoolroom**
['skulrum] *noun*
room in which children are taught

② **schoolteacher**
['skultitʃər] *noun*
person who teaches in a school; *she has taken her degree in history and is now training to be a schoolteacher*

② **science**
['saɪəns] *noun*
(a) study of natural physical things, based on observation and experiment; *she took a science course* or *she studied science*; *we have a new science teacher this term*; *he has a master's degree in marine science*; *see also* SOCIAL SCIENCE
(b) the sciences = the science subjects at school, such as physics, chemistry, as opposed to the arts

② **scientific**
[saɪən'tɪfɪk] *adjective*
referring to science; *we employ hundreds of people in scientific research*; *he's the director of a scientific institute*; *she loved art and music and was never very scientific*

② **scientifically**
[saɪən'tɪfɪkli] *adverb*
by using scientific experiments; *we must try to prove our theory scientifically*

② **scientist**
['saɪəntɪst] *noun*
person who specializes in a science, often doing research; *scientists have not yet found a cure for the common cold*; *space scientists are examining the photographs of Mars*

② **scissors**
['sɪzərz] *noun*
tool for cutting paper, cloth, etc., made of two blades attached in the middle, with handles with holes for the thumb and fingers; *these scissors aren't very sharp*; *do you have a pair of scissors I can borrow?*; **nail scissors** = special small curved scissors for cutting your nails; *she cut the story out of the paper with her nail scissors*
(NOTE: no singular form: for one, say **a pair of scissors**)

① **scoop**
[skup]
1 *noun*
(a) deep round spoon with a short handle, for serving ice cream, etc.; *you must wash the scoop each time you use it*
(b) portion of ice cream, etc.; *I'll have one scoop of strawberry and one scoop of chocolate, please*
(c) exciting news story which a reporter is the first to find, or which no other newspaper has reported; *he came back from the visit to the football player's girlfriend with a scoop*
2 *verb*
(a) to cut out with a scoop; *he scooped out a helping of mashed potato*; **to scoop out the inside of something** = to remove the inside of something with a spoon, etc.; *take a melon, and scoop out the seeds*
(b) to lift up, as with a scoop; *she scooped up the babies into her arms and ran upstairs*; *he scooped up all the newspapers off the floor*
(c) to scoop a newspaper = to report a news item before another paper does; *they scooped their rivals with the story of the senator's girlfriend*

④ **scope**
[skəʊp] *noun*
furthest area covered by observation or action; *these matters are beyond the scope of our investigation*

① **score**
[skɔr]
1 *noun*
(a) number of goals or points made in a match; *the final score in the baseball game was 5-1*; *I didn't see the beginning of the match - what's the score?*; *(informal)* **what's the score?** = what is the news?; **I know the score** = I know all the problems involved
(b) scores of = many; *scores of people stayed at home during the train strike*; *I must have seen that movie scores of times*
(c) written music; *he composed the score for the musical*
(d) to settle old scores = to take revenge for things that happened a long time ago
(e) on that score = as far as that is concerned; *he will eat any kind of food, so you won't have any trouble on that score*
2 *verb*
(a) to make a goal or point in a match; *they scored three goals in the first twenty minutes*; *she scored sixty-five!*
(b) to get a certain number of points on a test; *she scored a 100 on the test*
(c) *(music)* to arrange music for certain instruments; *a piece scored for piano and three drums*
(d) to scratch a flat surface; *score the surface of the wood with a sharp knife so that glue will hold better*

④ **Scot**
[skɒt] *noun*
person from Scotland; *is she English? - no, she's a Scot*

② **Scotch**
[skɒtʃ]
1 *adjective*
referring to Scotland (NOTE: "Scottish" is the more usual adjective); **Scotch whisky** = whisky made in Scotland
2 *noun*
(a) Scotch whisky; *a bottle of scotch*
(b) a glass of this drink; *a large scotch, please* (NOTE: plural is **scotches**)
(c) **Scotch tape** = trademark for a type of transparent sticky tape; *can you pass me the reel of Scotch tape, please?*; *he sealed the parcel with some Scotch tape*
3 *verb*
to prove something wrong, to put a stop to something; *by appearing in public, the president scotched rumors of his death*

① **Scotland**
[ˈskɒtlənd] *noun*
country to the north of England, forming part of the United Kingdom; *he was brought up in Scotland*; *Scotland's most famous export is whisky* (NOTE: capital: **Edinburgh**; people: **the Scots**)

② **Scottish**
[ˈskɒtɪʃ] *adjective*
referring to Scotland; *is she English? - no, she's Scottish*; *the beautiful Scottish mountains*

② **scramble**
[ˈskræmbl]
1 *noun*
rush; *there was a last-minute scramble for tickets*
2 *verb*
(a) to hurry, using your hands and knees if necessary; *he scrambled over the wall*
(b) to rush; *everyone was scrambling to get food*
(c) **scrambled eggs** = eggs mixed together and stirred as they are cooked in butter; *we had a starter of scrambled eggs with smoked salmon*
(d) to mix up a radio signal or telephone link so that it cannot be understood without a device for making it clear; *calls from the army chief of staff to the President are scrambled*

② **scrap**
[skræp]
1 *noun*
(a) little piece; *a scrap of paper*; *there isn't a scrap of evidence against him*; *she is collecting scraps of cloth to make a blanket*
(b) waste materials; *to sell an automobile for scrap*; *the scrap value of the automobile is $300*; **scrap dealer** *or* **scrap merchant** = person who deals in scrap; **scrap heap** = heap of garbage; *that automobile's good for the scrap*

heap; **scrap metal** *or* **scrap paper** = waste metal or waste paper
(c) **scraps** = bits of waste food; *they keep the scraps to feed to their pigs*
2 *verb*
(a) to throw away as useless; *they had to scrap 10,000 faulty spare parts*; *they are planning to scrap their nuclear power stations*
(b) to give up, to stop working on a plan; *we've scrapped our plans to go to the Grand Canyon*
(c) to fight; *they were scrapping over who should get the best bit of the chicken* (NOTE: **scrapping - scrapped**)

② **scrape**
[skreɪp]
1 *verb*
to scratch with a hard object which is pulled across a surface; *she scraped the paint off the door*; *he fell off his bike and scraped his knee on the sidewalk*
2 *noun*
(informal) awkward situation which you get into by mistake; *he's always getting into scrapes*

① **scratch**
[skrætʃ]
1 *noun*
(a) long wound on the skin; *put some antiseptic on the scratches on your arms*; **without a scratch** = with no injuries; *he came out of the car crash without a scratch*
(b) long mark made by a sharp point; *I will never be able to cover up the scratches on the automobile door*
(c) **to start from scratch** = to start something new without any preparation; **up to scratch** = of the right quality; *the recording was not up to scratch* (NOTE: plural is **scratches**)
2 *verb*
(a) to make a long wound on the skin; *his legs were scratched by the bushes along the path*
(b) to make a mark with a sharp point; *I must touch up the car where it has been scratched*
(c) to rub a part of the body with your fingernails; *he scratched his head as he wondered what to do next*; *stop scratching - it will make your rash worse!*
(d) to remove your name from the list of competitors; *one of the players scratched at the last minute*
3 *adjective*
collected together at the last minute; *our opponents were a scratch team from the next town*

① **scream**
[skrim]
1 *noun*
(a) loud cry of pain; *he let out a scream of pain*; *the screams of the victims of the fire*
(b) **screams of laughter** = loud laughter
(c) *(informal)* funny person; *she's an absolute scream when she starts talking about the office*
2 *verb*

(a) to make loud cries; *people on the third floor were screaming for help*; *they screamed with pain*

(b) to shout in a high voice; *she screamed at the class to stop singing*

(c) to scream with laughter = to laugh very loudly

① **screen**
[skrin]
1 *noun*

(a) flat panel that acts as protection against drafts, fire, noise, etc.; *a screen decorated with flowers and birds*; *the hedge acts as a screen against the noise from the freeway*

(b) flat glass surface on which a picture is shown; *a computer screen*; *I'll call the information up on the screen*; *our new TV has a very large screen*

(c) flat white surface for projecting films or pictures; *we'll put up the screen on the stage*; *a cinema complex with four screens*; **the small screen** = television

2 *verb*

(a) to protect from drafts, fire, noise, etc.; *they planted a row of trees to screen the farm buildings*; *part of the room was screened off*; *put the umbrella up to screen us from the sun*

(b) to show a movie in a cinema or on TV; *tonight's movie will be screened half an hour later than advertised*

(c) to consider or investigate people, such as candidates for a job, before making a final choice; *applicants will be screened before being invited to an interview*

(d) to screen people for a disease = to examine a lot of people to see if they have a disease; *all women over 40 should be screened for breast cancer*

② **screw**
[skru]
1 *noun*

metal pin with a groove winding round it, which you twist to make it go into a hard surface; *I need some longer screws to go through this thick piece of wood*; *the plate was fixed to the door with brass screws*; *(informal)* **to have a screw loose** = to be slightly mad

2 *verb*

(a) to attach with screws; *the picture was screwed to the wall*

(b) to attach by twisting; *he filled up the bottle and screwed on the top*; *screw the lid on tightly*; *(informal)* **he has his head screwed on the right way** = he's very sensible

② **screwdriver**
['skrudraɪvər] *noun*

tool with a long handle and special end that is used for turning screws; *she tightened up the screws with a screwdriver*

③ **scribble**
['skrɪbl] *verb*

(a) to make marks which don't have any

meaning; *the kids have scribbled all over their bedroom walls*

(b) to write badly in a hurry; *she scribbled a few notes in the train*

④ **scrimmage**
['skrɪmɪdʒ] *noun*

practice game; *we played against the seniors in the scrimmage*

② **script**
[skrɪpt] *noun*

(a) written text of a movie or play; *the actors settled down with their scripts for the first reading*

(b) style or system of handwriting; *the Germans used to write in medieval script*

① **scrub**
[skrʌb]
1 *noun*

area of land with a few small bushes; *they walked for miles through the scrub until they came to a river*

2 *verb*

(a) to clean by rubbing with soap and a brush; *scrub your fingernails to get rid of the dirt*; *a well-scrubbed kitchen table*

(b) *(informal)* to remove something that has been recorded on tape; *can you scrub the last five minutes of the recording?*; **scrub that** = you can forget about that (NOTE: **scrubbing - scrubbed**)

② **sculptor**
['skʌlptər] *noun*

person who makes figures or shapes out of clay, wood, metal or stone; *we visited the sculptor's studio and watched him working on his next statue*

② **sculpture**
['skʌlptʃər] *noun*

figure carved out of stone or wood, etc., or made out of metal; *there is a sculpture of Martin Luther King Jr. in the center of the square*

① **sea**
[si] *noun*

(a) area of salt water between continents or islands, but not as large as an ocean; *swimming in the sea is more exciting than swimming in a river*; *the sea's too rough for the ferries to operate*; *his friends own a house by the sea*; *the north coast of Honduras is on the Caribbean Sea*; **at sea** = traveling by ship; *we were at sea for only five days*; **by sea** = using ships as a means of transport; *when we moved to England we sent our furniture by sea*; **sea crossing** = journey across the sea; *the sea crossing between Denmark and Sweden can be quite rough*; **to run away to sea** = to leave home to work as a sailor; *when he was sixteen he ran away to sea* (NOTE: in names **Sea** is written with a capital letter: **the Caribbean Sea**, etc.)

(b) mass of things; *standing on the platform looking at the crowd, all I could see was a sea of faces*

② **seafood**
['siːfʊd] *noun*
fish or shellfish that can be eaten; *I never eat seafood - it doesn't agree with me*; **seafood restaurant** = a restaurant that specializes in seafood (NOTE: no plural)

① **seal**
[siːl]
1 *noun*
(a) large animal with short fur, which eats fish, living mainly near to or in the sea; *seals lay sunning themselves on the rocks*
(b) piece of paper, metal, or wax which is used to attach something to close it so that it cannot be opened; *customs officials attached their seal to the box*
(c) way in which something is closed; *the screw top gives a tight seal*
2 *verb*
(a) to close something tightly; *a box carefully sealed with sticky tape*; **sealed envelope** = envelope where the flap has been stuck down to close it; *the information was sent in a sealed envelope* (NOTE: an envelope left open is an **unsealed envelope**)
(b) to attach a seal; to stamp something with a seal; *customs sealed the shipment*

① **seaman**
['siːmən] *noun*
man who works on a ship; *he works as an ordinary seaman on an oil tanker* (NOTE: plural is **seamen**)

② **search**
[sɜːtʃ]
1 *noun*
(a) action of trying to find something; *our search of the apartment revealed nothing*; *they carried out a search for the missing children*; *I did a quick search on the Internet for references to Penang*; **search party** = group of people sent to look for someone; *the children haven't come back from the beach - we'll have to send out a search party*; **search warrant** = official document signed by a magistrate which allows police to go into a building and look for criminals, weapons or stolen goods
(b) *(in real estate)* examination of records to make sure that a property belongs to the person who is trying to sell it; *the lawyer's searches revealed that part of the land belonged to the neighboring farm* (NOTE: plural is **searches**)
2 *verb*
(a) to examine very carefully; *the police searched the house from top to bottom but still couldn't find any weapons*; *she was stopped and searched by customs*
(b) **to search for** = to try to find; *the police searched for the missing children*; *I searched the Internet for references to Ireland*; **to search through** = to look for something carefully; *she searched through her papers, trying to find the document*

(c) *(computing)* **search and replace** = looking for words or phrases and replacing them automatically with other words or phrases

② **seasick**
['siːsɪk] *adjective*
sick because of the movement of a ship; *she didn't enjoy the cruise because she was seasick all the time*; *I'll stay on deck because I feel seasick when I go down to my cabin*

② **seaside**
['siːsaɪd] *noun*
area at the edge of the sea; *we do not want the seaside to be heavily developed*

① **season**
['siːzən]
1 *noun*
(a) one of four parts of a year; *the four seasons are spring, summer, fall, and winter*; *spring is the season when the garden is full of flowers*
(b) part of the year when something usually happens; *the tourist season is very long here - from March to September*; *it's baseball season at the moment*; *California is very crowded during the tourist season*; **off-season** = time of year (often during the winter) when there are fewer travelers, and so fares and hotels are cheaper; *tour operators urge more people to travel in the off-season*; **dry season** = period of the year when it does not rain much (as opposed to the rainy season); **rainy season** = period of year when it rains a lot (as opposed to the dry season); *don't go there in October - that's the beginning of the rainy season*; **hunting season** = period of the year when you can shoot game; *the shooting season starts in August*
(c) *(of fruit, etc.)* **in season** = which is fresh, easily available and ready to buy; *strawberries are cheaper in season*; *pears are in season just now*; **out of season** = more expensive because the growing season is over
2 *verb*
(a) to add flavoring, spices, etc., to a dish; *the meat is seasoned with mint*
(b) to dry wood until it is ready to be used; *they made the windows with wood that had not been seasoned properly*

③ **seasonal**
['siːzənəl] *adjective*
(a) which only lasts for a season, usually the vacation season; *work on the island is only seasonal*; **seasonal demand** = demand that exists only during the peak of the season; **seasonal employment** = job that is available at certain times of the year only (such as in a ski resort); **seasonal labor** = workers who work for a season (usually the summer) only
(b) characteristic of a particular time of year; *in December the supermarket shelves are stocked with Christmas decorations and other seasonal goods*; *we can expect seasonal weather, with temperatures about average for this time of year*

② **season ticket**
['sizən 'tɪkɪt] *noun*
ticket that you can use for a certain period of time for theater performances or sporting events; *we bought season tickets for baseball*

① **seat**
[sit]
1 *noun*
chair, something that you sit on; *he was sitting in the driver's seat*; *can we have two seats in the front row?*; *please take your seats, the play is about the begin*; *all the seats on the bus were taken so I had to stand*; *our kitchen chairs have wooden seats*; *bicycle seats are narrow and not very comfortable*; **to take a seat** = to sit down; *please take a seat, the dentist will see you in a few minutes*
2 *verb*
to have room for people to sit down; *the restaurant seats 75*; *the bus seats sixty*

① **seat belt**
['sit 'belt] *noun*
belt that you wear in an automobile or plane to stop you being hurt if there is an accident; *the sole survivor of the crash had been wearing a seat belt*; *the "fasten seat belts" sign came on*

③ **seated**
['sitid] *adjective*
sitting down; *everyone stood up when the chairman came in, except John, who remained seated*

② **seaweed**
['siwid] *noun*
plant that grows in the sea; *the rocks are covered with seaweed* (NOTE: no plural: **some seaweed, a piece of seaweed**)

① **second**
['sekənd]
1 *noun*
(a) one of sixty parts that make up a minute; *I'll give you ten seconds to get out of my room*; *they say the bomb will go off in twenty seconds*
(b) very short time; *please wait a second*; *wait here - I'll be back in a second*
(c) something or someone that comes after the first thing or person; *today is March second (March 2)* (NOTE: in dates **second** is usually written **2: August 2, 1932, July 2, 1666**; (say "July second"); with names of kings and queens **second** is usually written **II: Queen Elizabeth II** (say "Queen Elizabeth the Second")
(d) person who helps a boxer during a fight; **seconds out** = instruction to the seconds to leave the ring before a round begins
2 *adjective*
(a) coming after the first and before the third; *February is the second month of the year*; *he came in second in the race*; *it's his second birthday next week*; *B is the second letter in the alphabet*; *that's the second time the telephone has rung while we're having dinner*; **the second century** = the period from AD100 to

199; **second helping** = another helping of the same dish; *after we had finished, the waiter came round with a second helping of fish*
(b) *(followed by a superlative)* only one other is more; *this is the second longest bridge in the world*; *he's the second highest paid member of staff*
3 *verb* ['sekənd]
to second a motion = to be the first person to formally support a proposal put forward by someone else in a meeting; *the motion was seconded by Mrs. Lang*

④ **secondary**
['sekəndri] *adjective*
(a) which comes after the first (or primary) ; **secondary school** = high school, a school for children between the ages of about 15 and 18 (grades 9 or 10 through 12)
(b) **of secondary importance** = not so very important; *the color of the automobile is of secondary importance*

② **second-class**
['sekənd 'klæs] *adjective & adverb*
(a) *(of travel, hotels, etc.)* less expensive and less comfortable than first class; *I find second-class hotels are perfectly adequate*; *we always travel second-class because it is cheaper*
(b) *(of postal service)* less expensive and slower than first class; *a second-class letter is cheaper than a first-class*; *send it second-class if it is not urgent*
(c) **second-class citizens** = people who have fewer rights, opportunities, etc., than others; *unemployed people are in danger of becoming second-class citizens*

③ **secondhand**
[sekənd'hænd]
1 *adjective*
not new; which someone else has owned before; *I love shopping at secondhand stores*; *we bought this sofa from a secondhand dealer*
2 *adverb*
to buy something secondhand = to buy something that someone else has owned before; *we bought this automobile secondhand*

③ **secondly**
['sekəndlɪ] *adverb*
in second place; *I'm not going to his party: firstly it's my mother's birthday, and secondly, I don't really like his family*

③ **seconds**
['sekəndz] *noun*
(a) *(informal)* another helping of the same dish; *can I have seconds of dessert, please?*
(b) items that have been turned down as not being of top quality; *the store has a sale of seconds*; *we bought our dinner service from a store selling seconds*

③ **secrecy**
['sikrəsi] *noun*

being secret; keeping something secret; *you will see that secrecy is extremely important when we're discussing the new project*; *why is there so much secrecy about the candidate's age?*

① **secret**
['sikrət]
1 *adjective*
hidden, not known by other people; *there is a secret door into the tower*; **to keep something secret** = to make sure that no one knows about it; *she kept his birth secret for twenty years*
2 *noun*
(a) thing which is not known or which is kept hidden; *if I tell you a secret will you promise not to repeat it to anyone?*; **is he in on the secret?** = does he know the secret?; **to keep a secret** = not to tell someone something which you know and no one else does; *can he keep a secret?*
(b) in secret = without anyone knowing; *they met in secret by the lake in the park*; **he makes no secret of where the money came from** = everyone knows where the money came from; **what's the secret of?** = how do you do something successfully; *what's the secret of making cole slaw?*

② **secretary**
['sekrətri] *noun*
(a) person who writes letters, answers the phone, files documents, etc., for someone; *both my daughters are training to be secretaries*; *his secretary phoned to say he would be late*
(b) official who keeps the minutes and official documents of a committee or club; *he was elected secretary of the committee or committee secretary*
(c) company secretary = person who is responsible for a company's legal and financial affairs
(d) member of the government in charge of a department; *the Secretary of Education or the Education Secretary*; **Secretary of the Treasury** *or* **Treasury Secretary** = the head of the Treasury, the government department which deals with financial affairs (NOTE: plural is **secretaries**)

② **secretary-general**
['sekrətri 'dʒenrəl] *noun*
chief administrative officer of an international organization; *the United Nations secretary-general has called a meeting of the Security Council* (NOTE: plural is **secretaries-general**)

② **secretary of state**
['sekrətri əv 'steit] *noun*
senior member of the government in charge of foreign affairs; *the U.S. secretary of state is having talks with the Israeli prime minister*

② **secretly**
['sikrətli] *adverb*
without anyone knowing; *they used to meet secretly in the park*; *he secretly photocopied the plans and took them home*

② **section**
['sekʃn] *noun*
(a) part of something which, when joined to other parts, goes to make up a whole; *the wind section of an orchestra*; *the financial section of a newspaper*; *he works in a completely different section of the organization*
(b) the cutting of tissue in a surgical operation
(c) diagram showing the inside of something as if cut open; *the drawing shows a section through the main part of the engine*

④ **sector**
['sektər] *noun*
(a) part of the economy or of the business organization of a country; *all sectors of industry suffered from the rise in the exchange rate*; *computer technology is a booming sector of the economy*; **private sector** = part of industry which is privately owned; *the recreation center is funded completely by the private sector*; **public sector** = the civil service and industries which belong to the state; *salaries in the private sector have increased faster than in the public sector*
(b) part of a circle between two lines drawn from the center to the outside edge; *the circle had been divided into five sectors*

③ **secure**
[sɪ'kjuər]
1 *adjective*
(a) safe against attack, robbers, etc.; *you need to keep your jewels secure against theft*; *he made all the doors secure by fitting bolts to them*
(b) firmly fixed; *don't step on that ladder, it's not secure*; **secure job** = job that you are sure to keep for a long time
2 *verb*
(a) to make safe, to attach firmly; *secure all the doors before the storm comes*; *she secured herself to the rock with a strong rope*
(b) to get something safely so that it cannot be taken away; *he secured the backing of a big bank*; *they secured a new lease on very favorable terms*

④ **securely**
[sɪ'kjuəli] *adverb*
in a secure way; *don't worry, all the silver is securely locked away*; *she tied the dog securely to a fence*

④ **securities**
[sɪ'kjuərətiz] *noun*
investments in stocks and shares; certificates to show that someone owns stocks or shares

② **security**
[sɪ'kjuərɪti] *noun*
(a) safety, protection against criminals; *there were worries about security during the prince's visit*; *security in this office is nil*; *security guards patrol the factory at night*; **airport security** = measures to protect aircraft against terrorists or bombs; **hotel security** = measures

taken to protect a hotel against theft or fire; **security check** = check to see that no one is carrying a bomb, etc.
(b) thing given to someone who has lent you money and which is returned when the loan is repaid; *he uses his house as security for a loan*; *the bank lent him $30,000 without security*; **to stand security for someone** = to guarantee that if the person does not repay a loan, you will repay it for him
(c) job security *or* **security of employment** = feeling which a worker has that he has a right to keep his job, that he can stay in his job until he retires (NOTE: no plural in these meanings; but compare **securities**)

② **Security Council**
['sɪ'kjʊərɪti 'kaʊnsəl] *noun*
ruling body of the United Nations; *France is a permanent member of the Security Council*

COMMENT: the Security Council has fifteen members, five of which are permanent: these are the United States, Russia, China, France and the United Kingdom. The other ten members are elected for periods of two years. The five permanent members each have a veto over the decisions of the Security Council

④ **seduce**
[sɪ'djus] *verb*
(a) to persuade someone to have sex; *she was seduced by her Spanish teacher*
(b) to persuade someone to do something which is perhaps wrong; *he was seduced by the idea of earning a huge salary*

① **see**
[si] *verb*
(a) to use your eyes to notice; *can you see that tree in the distance?*; *they say eating carrots helps you to see in the dark*; *we ran because we could see the bus coming*; *I have never seen an elephant before*
(b) to watch a movie, etc.; *I don't want to go to the cinema this week, I've seen that movie twice already*; *we saw the football game on TV*
(c) to go with someone to a place; *the little boy saw the old lady across the road*; *I'll see her home*; *my secretary will see you out*
(d) to understand; *I can't see why they need to borrow so much money*; *you must see that it's very important for everything to be ready on time*; *don't you see that they're trying to trick you?*; *I see - you want me to lend you some money*
(e) to check to make sure that something happens; *the baby-sitter will see that the children are in bed by nine o'clock*; *can you see if a check has arrived in the mail?*
(f) to meet; *we see her quite often*; *she doesn't see much of him*; *see you next week!*; *see you again soon!*

(g) to visit a lawyer, doctor, etc.; *if your tooth hurts you should see a dentist*; *he went to see his bank manager to arrange a mortgage*
(h) *(showing a possibility)* **will you be able to take a vacation this year? - we'll see!** (NOTE: **sees - seeing - saw** [sɔ] **- has seen** [sin])

① **seed**
[sid]
1 *noun*
(a) part of a plant that is formed after the flowers die and from which a new plant will grow; *sow the seed(s) in fine earth*; *a pack of parsley seed*; *can you eat melon seeds?*
(b) *(of plant)* **to go to seed** = to become tall and produce flowers and seeds; *the lettuces have gone to seed*; **he's gone to seed** = he doesn't look after himself properly, he doesn't look as well as he did before (NOTE: **seed** can be plural when it refers to a group: **a pack of lettuce seed; sow the celery seed in sand**)
(c) *(in tennis)* player ranked in comparison to other players in a tournament; *she's the top-seeded player*; *the number one seed was beaten in the first round of the tournament*
2 *verb*
(a) to seed itself = to produce seed which falls onto the ground and grows; *flowers have seeded themselves all along the side of the highway*
(b) to choose the seeds in a tennis competition; *he was seeded No. 5*

③ **see in**
['si 'ɪn] *verb*
(a) to have a midnight party to celebrate; *we stayed up late to see the New Year in*
(b) to see something in someone = to be attracted by someone; *I can't understand what she sees in him*

① **seeing**
['siɪŋ]
1 *noun*
action of sensing with the eyes; *seeing is believing*
2 *conjunction*
seeing that = since; *seeing that everyone's here, why don't we open a bottle of wine?*

② **seek**
[sik] *verb*
(a) to look for; *the police are seeking a group of teenagers who were in the area when the attack took place*; **to seek refuge** = to try to find shelter; *during the fighting, they sought refuge in the American embassy*
(b) to ask for; *they are seeking damages from the driver of the automobile*; *she sought an interview with the president* (NOTE: **seeking - sought** [sɔt] **- has sought**)

① **seem**
[sim] *verb*
to look as if; *she seems to like her new job or it seems that she likes her new job*; *everyone seemed to be having a good time at the party*; *the new boss seems very nice*; *it seems to me*

that the parcel has gone to the wrong house; it seemed strange to us that no one answered the phone

③ **seemingly**
['siːmɪŋli] *adjective & adverb*
apparently; *the seemingly endless flow of refugees; he had seemingly lost his way*

① **seen**
[siːn] *see* SEE

③ **see off**
['siː 'ɒf] *verb*
to go to the airport or station with someone who is leaving on a journey; *the whole family went to see her off at the airport*

③ **see through**
['siː 'θruː] *verb*
(a) to see from one side of something to the other; *I can't see through the windshield - it's so dirty*
(b) to understand everything, not to be tricked by something; *we quickly saw through their plan*

② **see to**
['siː 'tuː] *verb*
to arrange, to make sure that something is done; *can you see to it that the children are in bed by nine o'clock?; my wife will see to the Christmas cards*

④ **segment**
['seɡmənt] *noun*
(a) part of a circle or sphere when a line is drawn across it; **grapefruit segments** = pieces of grapefruit
(b) part of something that seems to form a natural division; *30- to 40-year-olds are the richest segment of the population*

② **seize**
[siːz] *verb*
(a) to grab something and hold it tight; *she seized the bag of money in both hands and would not let go*; **to seize the opportunity** = to take advantage of the situation to do something; *when the president's car slowed down, he seized the opportunity and threw his bomb*
(b) to take possession of something by force; *customs seized the shipment of books*

② **seize on** *or* **seize upon**
['siːz 'ɒn or ʌ'pɒn] *verb*
to take and use; *she immediately seized upon his suggestion; my idea was seized on and developed by a rival company*

② **seize up**
['siːz 'ʌp] *verb*
to stop working properly; *the automobile seized up on the hill and we had to call a garage*

② **seldom**
['seldəm] *adverb*
not often; *I seldom get invited to parties; seldom do you hear such a beautiful voice* (NOTE the word order when **seldom** is at the beginning of a phrase: **you seldom hear** *or* **seldom do you hear**)

② **select**
[sɪ'lekt]
1 *verb*
to choose carefully; *she looked carefully at the shelves before selecting a book; he was selected for the New York Yankees; selected items are reduced by 25%*
2 *adjective*
the best, chosen by or for the best people; *she went to a very select school in New Jersey; they live in a very select area; a select group of players who have scored more than 100 goals in international soccer*

① **selection**
[sɪ'lekʃn] *noun*
(a) range; *there is a huge selection of hats to choose from*
(b) thing that has (or things that have) been chosen; *a selection of our product line; a selection of French cheeses*; **selection board** *or* **selection committee** = committee that chooses a candidate for a job; **selection procedure** = general method of choosing a candidate for a job

② **selective**
[sɪ'lektɪv] *adjective*
(a) which chooses (carefully); *I'm very selective about the invitations I accept*; **selective school** = school that chooses pupils by asking them to take an entrance exam
(b) which only has a specific or certain function; *use a selective spray on the rose bushes*

② **self**
[self] *noun*
your own person or character; *she was ill for some time, but now she's her old self again; she's not her usual happy self today - I think she has something on her mind* (NOTE: plural is **selves**)

② **self-**
[self] *prefix referring to yourself*
a self-taught scientist

② **selfish**
['selfɪʃ] *adjective*
doing things only for yourself and not for other people; *don't be so selfish - pass the box of chocolates around*

① **sell**
[sel]
1 *verb*
(a) to give something to someone for money; *he sold his house to my father; she sold him her bicycle for a few dollars; we managed to sell the car for $750; the store sells vegetables but not meat*
(b) to be sold; *those packs sell for $35 a dozen; his latest book is selling very well* (NOTE: **selling - sold** [səʊld])
2 *noun*
the act of selling something; **to give a product the hard sell** = to make great efforts to persuade customers to buy it; **to give a product the soft sell** = to persuade people to buy something, by

encouraging and not forcing them to do so (NOTE: do not confuse with **cell**)

③ **seller**
['selər] *noun*
(a) person who sells something; *there were a few postcard sellers by the cathedral*; **seller's market** = market where a person selling goods or a service can ask high prices because there is a large demand for the product; *prices are high in a seller's market*; *compare* BUYER'S MARKET
(b) thing that sells; *this book is a steady seller*; **best-seller** = thing that sells very well; *her book was a best-seller*

① **sell off**
['sel 'ɒf] *verb*
to sell goods quickly and cheaply to get rid of them; *at the end of the day the market traders sell off their fruit and vegetables very cheaply*

① **sell out**
['sel 'aut] *verb*
(a) to sell your business; *he sold out to his partner and retired to the seaside*
(b) to sell all the stock of an item; *this item has sold out; do you have it in a size 10? - no, I'm afraid we're sold out*
(c) (*informal*) to give in to a group of influential people; *the environmental group has accused the government of selling out to the oil companies*; *see also* SELL OUT OF

① **sell out of**
['sel 'aut 'ɒv] *verb*
to sell out of an item = to sell all the stock of an item; *the store has sold out of bread; do you have it in a size 10? - no, I'm afraid we're sold out of all the small sizes*

② **semester**
[sə'mestər] *noun*
one of two terms in a school or college year; *they arrived at college for the fall semester; after the spring semester we look for summer jobs*

③ **semicolon**
['semikəulɒn] *noun*
punctuation mark (;) used to separate two parts of a sentence, and also used to show a pause; *you can put a semicolon when you want to show a break in a sentence*

③ **semifinal**
['semi'fainəl] *noun*
one of the last two matches in a competition, the winners of which go into the final game; *the two semifinals will be held on the same day*

④ **seminar**
['seminɑr] *noun*
meeting of a small group of university students to discuss a subject with a teacher; *the Spanish seminar is being held in the conference room*

③ **senate**
['senət] *noun*
(a) upper house of the legislative body in some countries; *she was first elected to the Senate in 1990*
(b) body which rules a university; *does the senate concern itself solely with administrative matters?*

③ **senator**
['senətər] *noun*
member of the Senate (in Congress); *she was first elected a senator in 1980* (NOTE: written with a capital letter when used as a title: **Senator Jackson**)

① **send**
[send] *verb*
(a) to make someone or something go from one place to another; *my mother sent me to the stores to buy some bread; I was sent home from school because I had a headache; he sent the ball into the net; the firm is sending him out to Australia for six months*
(b) to use the postal services; *the office sends 200 Christmas cards every year; send me a postcard when you get to Russia; send the letter airmail if you want it to arrive next week; send your gifts to the following address*
(c) (*informal*) to make someone act or feel in a certain way ; *the noise of drilling on the road outside the office sent me through the roof* (NOTE: **sending - sent** [sent])

③ **send away for**
['send ə'wei 'fɔr] *verb*
to write and ask someone to send you something, usually something which you have seen in an advertisement; *we sent away for the new catalog; I sent away for a book which was advertised in the newspaper*

③ **send back**
['send 'bæk] *verb*
to return something by mail; *if you don't like the shirt, send it back and I'll get you something different*

④ **sender**
['sendər] *noun*
person who sends; *the sender of the package did not put enough stamps, so we had to pay extra*; **"return to sender"** = words on an envelope or package to show that it is to be sent back to the person who sent it; *the letter was returned to the sender*

③ **send for**
['send 'fɔr] *verb*
to ask someone to come; *he collapsed and we sent for the doctor; the restaurant had to send for the police*

③ **send in**
['send 'in] *verb*
to send a letter to an organization; *he sent in his resignation; she sent in an application for the job*

③ **send off**
['send 'ɒf] *verb*
(a) to help someone leave; *the referee sent both players off*

(b) to mail; *he sent the postcard off without a stamp*

③ **send out for**
['send 'aʊt 'fɔr] *noun*
to ask for something to be delivered; *we sent out for pizza*

② **senior**
['sinjər]
1 *adjective*
(a) older; *the senior members of the family sat at the head table*; **senior citizen** = old retired person; **senior high school** = school for grades 10 through 12
(b) more important in rank, etc.; *a sergeant is senior to a corporal*; *my senior colleagues do not agree with me*; **senior manager** = manager who has a higher rank than others
(c) referring to the fourth (final) year of high school or college; *they went to the senior prom*
2 *noun*
(a) older person; *he must be at least ten years your senior*
(b) student in his or her fourth (final) year of high school or college
(c) the father in a family where the son has the same name; *Harry Markovitz, Senior*

② **sensation**
[sen'seɪʃn] *noun*
(a) general feeling; *I felt a curious sensation as if I had been in the room before*
(b) physical feeling; *she had a burning sensation in her arm*
(c) thing or person that causes great excitement; *the new ballet was the sensation of the season*

② **sensational**
[sen'seɪʃnl] *adjective*
(a) which causes great excitement; *his sensational discovery shocked the world of pharmacy*
(b) *(informal)* very good; *a sensational new movie - don't miss it!*; *she looks sensational in that outfit*

② **sense**
[sens]
1 *noun*
(a) one of the five ways in which you notice something (sight, hearing, smell, taste, touch); *he may be 93, but he still has all his senses*; *his senses had been affected by the drugs he was taking*; *dogs have a good sense of smell*
(b) general feeling about something; *staying in the Grand Hotel, she had a sense of being cut off from the real world*; *the police seemed to have no sense of urgency*
(c) meaning; *he was using "bear" in the sense of "to carry"*; **to make sense** = to have a meaning; *the message doesn't make sense*; **to make sense of something** = to understand something; *I can't make any sense of what she's trying to say*
(d) being sensible; *at least someone showed some sense and tried to calm the situation*; *she*

didn't have the sense to refuse; *I thought Patrick would have had more sense than that*
(e) **in one sense** *or* **in a sense** = up to a point, partly; *in a sense, he was right*; **in no sense** = in no way, not at all; *she's in no sense to blame for what happened*
2 *verb*
to be aware of, to feel; *I could sense the feeling of anger in the room*

③ **sense of direction**
['sens əv daɪ'rekʃn] *noun*
ability to know which way to go in a place which you do not know well; *she has a very good sense of direction: she managed to find her way around San Francisco with no difficulty at all*

③ **sense of humor**
['sens əv 'hjumər] *noun*
ability to see the funny side of things; *he has a good sense of humor*; *she has no sense of humor at all*

② **sensible**
['sensɪbl] *adjective*
showing good judgment and wisdom; *staying indoors was the sensible thing to do*; *try and be sensible for once!*; **sensible shoes** = shoes that are strong and comfortable for walking, rather than fashionable

④ **sensitive**
['sensɪtɪv] *adjective*
(a) with keen feelings, easily upset; *she's a very sensitive young woman*; *some actors are extremely sensitive to criticism*; **price-sensitive** = selling better or worse depending on the price
(b) controversial, which may provoke an argument; *human rights is a very sensitive issue at the moment*
(c) which measures very accurately; *we need a more sensitive thermometer*; *a very sensitive light meter*
(d) which reacts to light, etc.; *if you have very sensitive skin use plenty of sun cream*; *flowers are sensitive to changes in temperature and humidity*

② **sent**
[sent]
see SEND

② **sentence**
['sentəns]
1 *noun*
(a) words put together to make a complete statement, usually ending with a period; *I don't understand the second sentence in your letter*; *begin each sentence with a capital letter*
(b) judgment of a court; *he was given a six-month prison sentence*; *the judge passed sentence on the accused*
2 *verb*
to give someone an official legal punishment; *she was sentenced to three weeks in prison*; *he was sentenced to death for murder*

④ **sentiment**
['sentɪmənt] *noun*
(a) general feeling; *the government had to take public sentiment into account*
(b) **sentiments** = opinions; *I think it's all a waste of time - my sentiments exactly!*

③ **sentimental**
[sentɪ'mentəl] *adjective*
showing emotions of love or pity, not reason; *she gets all sentimental on her son's birthday*; *her father sang a sentimental old love song*; **sentimental value** = being valuable because of the memories attached to it, not because of its actual money value; *the stolen watch was of great sentimental value*

① **separate**
1 *adjective* ['sepərət]
not together, not attached; *they are in separate rooms*; *the house has one bathroom with a separate toilet*; *the dogs were kept separate from the other pets*; *can you give us two separate invoices?*; **to send something under separate cover** = to send something in a different envelope or parcel
2 *verb* ['sepəreɪt]
(a) to divide; *the personnel are separated into part-time and full-time staff*; *the teacher separated the class into two groups*
(b) to keep apart; *the police tried to separate the two gangs*; *is it possible to separate religion and politics?*
(c) to break away from a partner and become independent; *they are arguing all the time - it wouldn't surprise me if they were to separate*; *the Baltic states separated from Russia*

② **separately**
['sepərətli] *adverb*
in a separate way, each alone; *each of us will pay separately*

② **separation**
[sepə'reɪʃn] *noun*
(a) dividing; *he favors the separation of the students into smaller groups*; *the separation of the house into two apartments will require permission*
(b) living apart; *a six-month separation of mother and child may have long-term effects*; *after my parents' separation I lived with my father*

① **September**
[sep'tembər] *noun*
ninth month of the year, between August and October; *the weather is usually good in September*; *her birthday is in September*; *today is September 3* ; *we always try to take a short vacation in September* (NOTE: **September 3**: say "September third")

③ **sequence**
['sikwəns] *noun*
(a) series of things which happen or follow one after the other; *the sequence of events which led to the accident*

(b) **in sequence** = in order of numbers; *make sure that the invoices are all in sequence according to their dates*
(c) scene in a movie; *they showed some sequences from her latest movie*

③ **sergeant**
['sɑrdʒənt] *noun*
rank in the army or the police, above a corporal; *Sergeant Torres drilled the new recruits*; *a police sergeant arrested him* (NOTE: used as a title with a surname: **Sergeant Torres**)

③ **serial**
['sɪəriəl]
1 *adjective*
in a series; *place the cards in serial order*; **serial murderer** *or* **serial killer** = person who has committed several murders, one after the other; *because there are similarities between the murders, the police think they are dealing with a serial killer*; **serial number** = number in a series; *this batch of shoes has the serial number 25-02*
2 *noun*
radio or TV show which is presented in several installments; *an Australian police serial* (NOTE: do not confuse with **cereal**)

② **series**
['sɪriz] *noun*
(a) group of things which come one after the other in order; *we had a series of phone calls from the bank*
(b) TV or radio programs which are broadcast at the same time each week; *there's a new wildlife series starting this week* (NOTE: plural is **series**)

③ **serious**
['sɪriəs] *adjective*
(a) not funny; not joking; *we watched a very serious program on drugs*; *he's such a serious little boy*; *stop laughing - it's very serious*; *he's very serious about the proposal*; *the doctor's expression was very serious*
(b) important and possibly dangerous; *there was a serious accident on the freeway*; *the storm caused serious damage*; *there's no need to worry - it's nothing serious*
(c) carefully planned; *the management is making serious attempts to improve working conditions*

④ **seriously**
['sɪriəsli] *adverb*
(a) in a serious way; *she should laugh more - she mustn't always take things so seriously*
(b) badly; *the cargo was seriously damaged by water*; *her mother is seriously ill*
(c) with a lot of thought; *they seriously considered going to live on an island*; *we are taking the threat from our competitors very seriously*

② **servant**
['sɜrvənt] *noun*
(a) person who is paid to work for a family; *they*

employ two servants in their Los Angeles home; get it yourself - I'm not your servant!
(b) civil servant = person who works in a government department; *as a government translator I was considered a civil servant*; *the civil servants who advise officials have a tremendous influence on government policy*

① **serve**
[sɜrv]
1 *verb*
(a) to give food or drink to someone; *she served the soup in small bowls; I'll serve the potatoes; take a plate and serve yourself from the dishes on the table; has everyone been served?*
(b) to bring food or drink to someone at table; *which waitress is serving this table?; I can't serve six tables at once*
(c) to go with a dish, etc.; *fish is served with a white sauce; you should serve red wine with meat*
(d) to work as an official; *he served in the army for ten years*
(e) to help a customer in a store, etc.; *are you being served?; the manager served me himself; will you serve this lady next, please?; I waited ten minutes before being served*
(f) to provide a service; *the local bus serves the villages in the hills; the aim of our organization is to serve the local community; this hospital serves the western side of the city*
(g) to serve as = to be useful as; *the tall hedge serves as a screen to cut out the noise from the freeway*
(h) *(in games like tennis)* to start the game by hitting the ball; *she is serving to win the match; he served first*
(i) *(informal)* **it serves you right** = you deserve what has happened to you; *it serves them right if they missed the train, they shouldn't have taken so long to get ready*
2 *noun*
(in tennis) action of hitting the ball first; *she has a very powerful serve; three of his serves hit the net*

① **service**
['sɜrvɪs]
1 *noun*
(a) time when you work for a company, or organization, or in the armed forces; *did he enjoy his service in the army?; she did six years' service with the police force; he was awarded a gold watch for his long service to the company; he saw service in Africa;* **length of service** = number of years someone has worked
(b) serving or helping someone in a store or restaurant; *the food is good here, but the service is very slow; the check includes an extra 10% for service; is the service included?; the check does not include service;* to add on 10% for service; **service charge** = money which you pay for service in a restaurant; *a 10% service charge is added;* **room service** = arrangement in a hotel for food or drink to be served in your bedroom

(c) regular check of a machine; *the automobile has had its 30,000-mile service;* **service center** = office or workshop which specializes in keeping machines in good working order; **service handbook** *or* **service manual** = book which shows how to keep a machine in good working order
(d) group of people working together; **civil service** = organization and personnel which administer a country; *you have to pass an examination to get a job in the civil service or to get a civil service job;* **the health service** = doctors, nurses, hospitals, etc., all taken as a group; *do you think we have the best health service in the world?;* **the (armed) services** = the army, the navy and the air force; *have you thought about a career in the services?; service families often have to travel abroad*
(e) provision of a facility which the public needs; *the postal service is efficient; the bus service is very irregular; the hotel provides a shoe cleaning service;* **the rent includes services** = the rent includes the cost of water, gas and electricity
(f) favor, something done for someone; *you would do me a great service if you could carry my suitcases for me;* *(formal)* **to be of service to someone** = to help someone; *can I be of service to anyone?*
(g) religious ceremony; *my mother never misses the nine o'clock service on Sundays*
(h) *(in tennis)* action of hitting the ball first; *she has a very powerful service*
(i) set of china for a meal; **dinner service** = big and small plates, serving dishes, etc.; *a complete dinner service costs a lot, so I'll buy it for you bit by bit;* **tea service** = plates, cups, saucers, teapot, etc.,
2 *verb*
to keep (a machine) in good working order; *the car needs to be serviced every six months; the photocopier has gone back to the manufacturer for servicing*

① **services**
['sɜrvɪsɪz] *noun*
area with a service station, restaurants and sometimes a hotel, on a highway; *there are no services for 50 miles*

① **service station**
['sɜrvɪssteɪʃn] *noun*
garage where you can buy gas and have small repairs done to an automobile; *we need gas - I'll stop at the next service station*

② **session**
['seʃn] *noun*
(a) time when an activity is taking place; *all these long sessions in front of the computer screen are ruining my eyesight;* **practice session** = time when a tennis player, etc., practices; **recording session** = time when music is being recorded
(b) meeting of a committee, legislature, etc.; *the*

first session of the talks will be held on Monday; **closing session** = last part of a conference; **opening session** = last part of a conference; **in session** = in the process of meeting; *the committee has been in session for two hours; we have to keep quiet while court is in session*

① **set**
[set]
1 *noun*
(a) group of things which go together, which are used together, which are sold together; *he carries a set of tools in the back of his automobile; the six chairs are sold as a set;* **tea set** = cups, saucers, plates, teapot, etc.,
(b) TV set = piece of electrical equipment that shows TV pictures; *they have bought a new 20-inch color set*
(c) *(in movies)* place where a movie is shot; *she has to be on set at 7:00 A.M.; we went on a tour of the studios and watched a set being built*
(d) *(in tennis)* one part of a tennis match, consisting of several games; *she won the set 7-5; he lost the first two sets*
2 *verb*
(a) to put in a special place; *she set the plate of cookies down on the table next to her chair;* **to set the table** = to put the knives, forks, plates, glasses, cups, etc., in their right places on the table
(b) to fix; *make sure you set your alarm clock; the price of the new computer has been set at $750*
(c) *(surgery)* to fix a broken limb; *the doctor set his broken arm; (of a limb)* to heal; *the broken wrist is setting very well*
(d) to set someone to work = to give someone work to do; *the children were set to work washing the dishes*
(e) to make something happen; *he went to sleep smoking a cigarette and set the house on fire; all the prisoners were set free; I had been worried about her, but her letter set my mind at rest*
(f) to go down; *the sun rises in the east and sets in the west*
(g) to write music to go with words; *the poem about cats was set to music*
(h) *(printing)* to put a text into printed characters; *the phrases in this dictionary have been set in bold* (NOTE: **sets - setting - has set**)
3 *adjective*
(a) fixed, which cannot be changed; *visits are only allowed at set times;* **set menu** = menu that cannot be changed
(b) ready; *we're all set for a swim; my bags are packed and I'm all set to leave; the government is set to introduce new regulations against smoking; her latest novel is set to become the best-selling book of the year;* **"on your marks, get set, go!"** = orders given to runners at the beginning of a race

④ **set about**
['set ə'baʊt] *verb*

to start to do something; *they set about making a camp fire; we haven't started building the wall yet because we don't know how to set about it*

④ **set aside**
['set ə'saɪd] *verb*
(a) to dismiss, to reject; *the proposal was set aside by the committee*
(b) to save and keep for future use; *we set money aside every month for the children's vacations*

④ **set back**
['set 'bæk] *verb*
(a) to delay, to make something late; *the bad weather has set the harvest back by two weeks*
(b) to place further back; *the house is set back from the road*
(c) *(informal)* **to set someone back** = to be a cost to someone; *the meal set me back $150*

④ **setback**
['setbæk] *noun*
problem that makes something late or stops something going ahead; *the company suffered a series of setbacks in 2000; just when we thought he was better, he had a setback and had to go back to the hospital*

④ **set down**
['set 'daʊn] *verb*
(a) *(formal)* to put something in writing; *the rules are set down in this book*
(b) to let passengers get off; *the bus set down several passengers and two others got on*

③ **set in**
['set 'ɪn] *verb*
to start and become permanent; *then the bad weather set in and we couldn't climb anymore; winter has set in early this year*

① **set off**
['set 'ɒf] *verb*
(a) to begin a trip; *we're setting off for Baton Rouge tomorrow; they all set off on a long walk after lunch*
(b) to start something working; *they set off a bomb in the shopping center; if you touch the wire it will set off the alarm; being in the same room as a cat will set off my cough*

② **set out**
['set 'aʊt] *verb*
(a) to begin a journey; *the walkers set out to cross the mountains; we have to set out early tomorrow*
(b) to explain clearly; *we asked her to set out the details in her report*
(c) to aim to do something; *he set out to ruin the party*

② **setting**
['setɪŋ] *noun*
(a) background for a story; *the setting for the story is Hong Kong in 1935*
(b) place setting = set of knives, forks, spoons, etc., for one person; *we only need two place settings on table 6*

(c) silver or gold frame in which a precious stone is fixed; *a diamond in a silver setting*

② **settle**
['setl] *verb*
(a) to arrange, to agree; to end (a dispute); *well, I'm glad everything's settled at last; have you settled the title for the new movie yet?; it took six months of negotiation for the union and management to settle their differences*
(b) to settle a bill = to pay the bill; *please settle this invoice without delay; the insurance company refused to settle his claim for damages*
(c) to go to live in a new country; *they sold everything and settled in Canada; the first pioneers settled in this valley in about 1860*
(d) to place yourself in a comfortable position; *she switched on the television and settled in her favorite armchair*
(e) to settle money on someone = to arrange for money to be passed to trustees to hold for someone in the future; *they settled $3000 a year on their new grandson*
(f) to fall to the ground, to the bottom; *wait for the dust to settle; a layer of mud settled at the bottom of the pond*

③ **settle down**
['setl 'daun] *verb*
(a) to place yourself in a comfortable position; *after dinner, she likes to settle down in a comfortable chair with a good book*
(b) to change to a calmer way of life without many changes of house or much traveling; *he has worked all over the world, and doesn't seem ready to settle down; she had lots of boyfriends, and then got married and settled down in Alabama*

③ **settle for**
['setl 'for] *verb*
to choose or to decide on something which is not quite what you want; *they didn't have any white sofas, so we settled for a brown one*

③ **settle in**
['setl 'ɪn] *verb*
to become used to a new house, job, etc.; *she's enjoying her job, though she took some time to settle in; the children have all settled into their new school*

② **settlement**
['setlmənt] *noun*
(a) payment of a bill; *this invoice has not been paid - can you arrange for immediate settlement?*
(b) agreement in a dispute; *in the end a settlement was reached between management and workers*
(c) place where a group of people come to live; *they established a settlement by the railway*

② **settle on**
['setl 'ɒn] *verb*
(a) to decide on, to choose; *after a lot of hesitation we finally settled on the red one*

(b) *(of insect, etc.)* to sit on; *if only the butterfly would settle on that flower I'd be able to take a picture of it*

③ **settle up**
['setl 'ʌp] *verb*
to pay a bill, to pay the total of what is owed; *you pay the bill and I'll settle up with you later*

② **set up**
['set 'ʌp] *verb*
(a) to establish; *to set up a committee or a working party; a fund has been set up to receive donations from the public; he set himself up as a real estate agent; to set up a company* = to start a company legally; **to set up home** *or* **to set up house** = to go somewhere to live in your own apartment, house, etc.; *they don't intend to set up house yet*
(b) *(informal)* to deceive someone on purpose; *we were set up by the police*

④ **setup**
['setʌp] *noun*
(informal) organization; *he works for some public relations setup*

① **seven**
['sevən]
number 7; *there are only seven children in his class; she's seven (years old) next week; the train is supposed to leave at seven (o'clock)* **the seven hundreds** = the years from AD 700 to 799 (NOTE: compare **the seventh century**)

① **seventeen**
[sevən'tin]
number 17; *he will be seventeen (years old) next month; the train leaves at seventeen sixteen (17:16)* **the seventeen hundreds (1700s)** = the years from 1700 to 1799 (NOTE: compare **the seventeenth century**)

① **seventeenth (17th)**
[sevən'tinθ] *adjective & noun*
Q is the seventeenth letter of the alphabet; it's his seventeenth birthday next week; he came in seventeenth out of thirty; **the seventeenth century** = the years from 1600 to 1699 (NOTE: compare **the seventeen hundreds;** Note also that with dates **seventeenth** is usually written **17: July 17, 1935; October 17, 1991:** (say "October seventeenth"); with names of kings and queens **seventeenth** is usually written **XVII: King Louis XVII** (say: "King Louis the Seventeenth")

① **seventh (7th)**
['sevənθ] *adjective & noun*
his office is on the seventh floor; it's her seventh birthday on Saturday; what is the seventh letter of the alphabet?; the seventh of July or July the seventh (July 7) Henry the Seventh (Henry VII) **the seventh century** = the period from AD 600 to 699 (NOTE: in dates **seventh** is usually written **7: April 7, 1797:** (say "April seventh"); with names of kings and queens **seventh** is usually written **VII: King Henry VII** say "King Henry the seventh")

① seventieth (70th)
['sevəntiəθ] *adjective & noun*
don't forget tomorrow is your grandmother's seventieth birthday

① seventy
['sevənti]
number 70; *she will be seventy (years old) on Tuesday; that shirt cost him more than seventy dollars; she's in her seventies* = she is between 70 and 79 years old; **the (nineteen) seventies (1970s)** = the years from 1970 to 1979 (NOTE: **seventy-one (71), seventy-two (72)** etc., but **seventy-first (71st), seventy-second (72nd)** etc.)

② several
['sevrəl] *adjective & pronoun*
more than a few, but not a lot; *several buildings were damaged in the storm; we've met several times; several of the students are going to Italy; most of the guests left early but several stayed on until midnight*

③ severe
[sə'vɪər] *adjective*
(a) very strict; *he was very severe with any child who did not behave; discipline in the school was severe*
(b) *(illness, weather, etc.)* very bad; *the government imposed severe financial restrictions; the severe weather has closed several main roads; she had a severe attack of the flu* (NOTE: **severer - severest**)

② severely
[sə'vɪərli] *adverb*
(a) strictly; *she was severely punished for being late*
(b) badly; *flights have been severely affected by snow; a severely handicapped child*

④ severity
[sə'verɪti] *noun*
being severe; *he attacked the government with increasing severity; the severity of the cold has killed many small birds*

② sew
[səʊ] *verb*
to attach, make or mend by using a needle and thread; *I've taught both my sons how to sew; the button's come off my shirt - can you sew it back on?* (NOTE: do not confuse with **sow;** note also: **sewing - sewed - sewn** [səʊn])

③ sewer
['sʊər] *noun*
large pipe which takes waste water and refuse away from a building; *the main sewer runs underneath the road*

① sex
[seks] *noun*
(a) one of two groups (male and female) into which animals and plants can be divided; *they've had a baby, but I don't know what sex it is; there is no discrimination on the grounds of sex, race and religion;* **opposite sex** = people of the other sex to yours (i.e., men to women, women to men); *he's very attractive to the opposite sex*
(b) sexual relations; *a movie full of sex and violence; sex was the last thing on her mind;* **to have sex with someone** = to have sexual relations with someone; **safe sex** = having sex in a way that avoids transmission of a sexual disease

③ sexual
['sekʃʊəl] *adjective*
referring to sex; *their relationship was never sexual;* **sexual partner** = person you have sex with; *see also* DISCRIMINATION

④ sexually
['sekʃʊəli] *adverb*
in a sexual way; *do find her sexually attractive?;* **sexually transmitted disease** = disease transmitted by having sexual intercourse

② sexy
['seksi] *adjective*
(informal) attractive in a sexual way; *she was wearing a very sexy dress; you look very sexy in that suit; he's the sexiest actor in the movies today* (NOTE: **sexier - sexiest**)

② shabby
['ʃæbi] *adjective*
poor, worn (clothes); *he wore a shabby coat with two buttons missing* (NOTE: **shabbier - shabbiest**)

① shade
[ʃeɪd]
1 *noun*
(a) variation of a color; *her hat is a rather pretty shade of green*
(b) dark place that is not in the sunlight; *let's try and find some shade - it's too hot in the sun; the sun's so hot that we'll have to sit in the shade*
(c) *(informal)* **shades** = sunglasses; *you can take off your shades now we're indoors*
(d) lampshade, a decorative cover put over a lamp; *I don't like the bright orange shade you bought; a brass table lamp with a red silk shade*
2 *verb*
to protect something from sunlight; *she shaded her eyes against the sun; the old birch tree shades that corner of the garden*

① shadow
['ʃædəʊ]
1 *noun*
dark place behind an object where light is cut off by the object; *in the evening, the trees cast long shadows across the lawn; she saw his shadow move down the hall; they rested for a while, in the shadow of a large tree*
2 *verb*
to follow someone closely, but without being seen; *the drugs dealer was shadowed by two police officers*

② shaft
[ʃæft] *noun*
(a) long handle of a spade, etc.; *the shaft of the spade was so old it snapped in two*

(b) thin beam of light; *tiny particles of dust dancing in a shaft of sunlight*

(c) rod that connects parts of an engine; *the shaft transmits power from the engine to the wheels*

(d) deep hole or big tube; *the air shaft had become blocked*; **elevator shaft** = tube inside a building in which an elevator moves up and down; **mine shaft** = hole in the ground leading down to a mine

① **shake**
[ʃeɪk]
1 *verb*

(a) to move something from side to side or up and down; *shake the bottle before pouring*; *the house shakes every time a train goes past*; *his hand shook as he opened the envelope*; **to shake your head** = to move your head from side to side to mean "no"; *when I asked my dad if I could borrow the car he just shook his head* (NOTE: the opposite, meaning "yes", is to **nod**)

(b) to surprise, to shock; *his family was shaken by the news that he had been arrested*; *the sight of it really shook me* (NOTE: **shaking - shook** [ʃʊk] **- has shaken**)

2 *noun*

(a) action of moving rapidly up and down; *if the ketchup won't come out, give the bottle a shake*

(b) **milkshake** = drink made by mixing milk and sweet flavoring; *he drank two chocolate milkshakes*

(c) moving from side to side; *he indicated "no" with a shake of his head*

② **shake hands**
[ʃeɪk ˈhændz] *verb*

to shake hands *or* **to shake someone's hand** = to greet someone by holding their right hand; *he shook hands with me*; *she refused to shake my hand*; *the negotiators shook hands and sat down at the conference table*; **to shake hands on a deal** = to shake hands to show that a deal has been agreed

> COMMENT: in the U.S.A. you shake hands with someone mainly in quite formal circumstances, for example when you meet them for the first time or when you are saying goodbye to someone and do not expect to see them again soon. You do not normally shake hands with people you see every day

③ **shake off**
[ˈʃeɪk ˈɒf] *verb*

to get rid of something, usually something unpleasant; *before you leave the beach, remember to shake the sand off your towel*; *they drove at top speed but couldn't shake off the squad car*; *I don't seem able to shake off this cold*

③ **shall**
[ʃæl] *verb used with other verbs*

(a) *(to make the future) we shall be out on Saturday evening*

(b) *(to show a suggestion) shall we open the windows?*; *shall I give them a call?* (NOTE: negative: **shall not** [ʃænt]; past: **should, should not** usually **shouldn't** Note also that **shall** is mainly used with **I** and **we**)

② **shallow**
[ˈʃæləʊ]
1 *adjective*

(a) not deep, not far from top to bottom; *children were playing in the shallow end of the pool*; *the river is so shallow in summer that you can walk across it*

(b) without any serious meaning; *it's a very shallow treatment of a serious subject* (NOTE: **shallower - shallowest**)

2 *noun*

shallows = parts of a river or the sea where the water is shallow; *the children walked into the shallows looking for little fish*

② **shame**
[ʃeɪm]
1 *noun*

(a) feeling caused by having done something that you should not have done; *she went bright red with shame*; *to my shame, I did nothing to help*; **to die of shame** = to feel very ashamed; *I could have died of shame!*

(b) **what a shame!** = how sad; *what a shame you couldn't come to the party!*; *it's a shame your father isn't well - I'm sure he would have enjoyed the play*; *it's a shame to have to go to the office on such a beautiful sunny day*; **shame on you!** = you should be ashamed of yourself

2 *verb*

to make someone feel ashamed; *we hope to shame her into contributing to the party*; *see also* ASHAMED

① **shampoo**
[ʃæmˈpuː]
1 *noun*

(a) liquid soap for washing hair, carpets, automobiles, etc.; *there are bottles of shampoo in the bathroom*

(b) action of washing the hair; *she went to the hairdresser's for a shampoo*

2 *verb*

to wash your hair, a carpet, an automobile, etc., with liquid soap; *the hairdresser shampooed her hair, and then cut it*; *they have a machine for shampooing carpets* (NOTE: **shampooing - shampooed**)

② **shape**
[ʃeɪp]
1 *noun*

(a) form of how something looks; *she has a ring in the shape of a letter S*; *the old table was a funny shape*; *this sweater's beginning to lose its shape* = it is beginning to stretch

(b) in good shape = in good physical form; *he's in good shape for the race*; *she's in a very bad shape*; **to take shape** = to begin to look as it will do when finished; *after all his hard work, the new garden in beginning to take shape*; **in any shape or form** = of any type; *the boss does not tolerate criticism in any shape or form*

2 *verb*

(a) to make into a certain form; *he shaped the pastry into the form of a little boat*

(b) to shape up = to result, to end up; *things are shaping up as we expected*; *it's shaping up to be a fine day*

② **shaped**
[ʃeɪpt] *adjective*
with a certain shape; *the new art gallery is shaped like an enormous tube*; *a square-shaped hole in the floor*

② **share**
[ˈʃeər]
1 *noun*

(a) part of something that is divided between two or more people; *did he get his share of the prize?*; *take your share of the cake and leave me the rest*; *she should have paid her share of the food bill*; *there's a lot of work to do, so everyone must do their share*; **to have a share in** = to take part in, to have a part of; *all the staff should have a share in decisions about the company's future*; *she has her share of the responsibility for the accident*; **market share** *or* **share of the market** = percentage of a total market which the sales of a company cover; *their share of the market has gone up by 10%*

(b) one of the many equal parts into which a company's capital is divided; *he bought 2000 shares in the company*; *shares fell on the Tokyo market*

2 *verb*

(a) to share (out) = to divide up something among several people; *let's share the check*; *in her will, her money was shared (out) among her sons*; *they shared the pencils out amongst them*

(b) to share something with someone = to allow someone to use something which you also use; *we offered to share our information with them*; *he doesn't like sharing his toys with other children*

(c) to use something which someone else also uses; *we share an office*; *we shared a taxi to the airport*

② **shareholder**
[ˈʃeərhəʊldər] *noun*
a person who owns shares in a company; *our first duty is to our shareholders*; *he called a shareholders' meeting*; **majority** *or* **minority shareholder** = person who owns more or less than half the shares in a company; *the attorney acting on behalf of the minority shareholders*

③ **share index**
[ˈʃeərˈɪndeks] *noun*

figure based on the current market price of certain shares on a stock exchange; *all the European share indexes rose following the rise in the Dow Jones Index*

> COMMENT: all stock exchanges publish share indexes. The best known are the Dow Jones and Nasdaq in New York, the Footsie in London and the Nikkei in Tokyo

① **sharp**
[ʃɑrp]
1 *adjective*

(a) with a good edge for cutting or pushing in; *for injections, a needle has to have a very sharp point*; *the beach is covered with sharp stones*; *this knife is useless - it isn't sharp enough*

(b) sudden, great or severe; *there was a sharp drop in interest rates*; *the road makes a sharp right-hand bend*; *he received a sharp blow on the back of his head*; *we had a sharp frost last night*; *it's cold, there's a sharp north wind*

(c) bitter; *lemons have a very sharp taste*

(d) very keen and sensitive; *she has a sharp sense of justice*; *she has a sharp eye for a bargain*; *he's pretty sharp at spotting mistakes*

(e) showing criticism; *he got a very sharp reply to his fax*; **sharp tongue** = a tendency to criticize people openly; *her sharp tongue has landed her in trouble once again*

(f) *(in music)* playing at a higher pitch than it should be; *that piano sounds sharp* (NOTE: **sharper - sharpest**)

2 *adverb*

(a) exactly; *the bus will leave the hotel at 7:30 sharp*

(b) suddenly, making a tight turn; *the road turned sharp right*

3 *noun*

(in music) pitch that is higher; *they played Bach's Sonata in F-sharp major*; *he played D-sharp instead of D-flat*

② **sharpen**
[ˈʃɑrpən] *verb*
to make something sharp; *I must sharpen my pencil*; *my old saw doesn't cut very well - it needs sharpening*

③ **sharply**
[ˈʃɑrpli] *adverb*

(a) strongly; *he felt his mother's death very sharply*

(b) completely; *the two groups are sharply divided on this issue*

(c) in a way that criticizes; *she spoke quite sharply to the poor old lady*

(d) suddenly; *the temperature fell sharply during the night*; *the road turns sharply to the right*

① **shave**
[ʃeɪv]
1 *noun*
act of cutting off the hair on your face; *he went to have a shave at the men's hairdresser's next*

to the hotel; **a close shave** = situation where you almost hit something; *it was a close shave - we missed the other vehicle by inches*

2 *verb*

(a) to cut off the hair on your face; *he cut himself shaving*

(b) to cut the hair on your head or legs, etc., very short; *I didn't recognize him with his head shaved*

(c) to cut a thin piece off something; *you need to shave a bit more off to make the door fit the frame*

① **she**

[ʃi] *pronoun referring to a female person, a female animal, and sometimes to automobiles, ships and countries*; *she's my sister*; *she and I are going on vacation to New Mexico together*; *I'm angry with her - she's taken my bicycle*; *she's a sweet little cat, but she's no good at catching mice*; *the customs officers boarded the ship when she docked* (NOTE: when it is the object **she** becomes **her: she hit the ball** *or* **the ball hit her**; when it follows the verb to **be**, she usually becomes **her: who's that? - it's her, the girl we met yesterday**)

② **shears**

[ʃɪərz] *noun*

very large scissors, used for gardening, cutting wool off sheep, etc.; *he's cutting the hedge with the shears*

③ **shed**

[ʃed]

1 *noun*

small wooden building; *they keep the garden tools in a shed in the backyard*; *she's in the shed putting flowers into pots*

2 *verb*

(a) to lose something that you are carrying or wearing; *in the fall, the trees shed their leaves as soon as the weather turns cold*; *a truck has shed its load of wood at the traffic circle*; *we shed our clothes and dove into the cool water*

(b) to let blood, tears, light, etc., flow; *she shed tears of anger as she listened to the speech*; *not one drop of blood was shed*

(c) to shed light on = to make clearer; *can anyone shed any light on what actually happened?*; *the finds in the cave shed light on the history of this region*

(d) *(formal)* to lose weight, to become lighter; *he goes on a run every morning to try to shed some weight*; *by not eating potatoes, she managed to shed three pounds* (NOTE: shedding - shed)

① **she'd**

[ʃid] = SHE HAD, SHE WOULD

① **sheep**

[ʃip] *noun*

common farm animal, which gives wool and meat; *a flock of sheep*; *the sheep are in the field*; *see also* BLACK SHEEP (NOTE: no plural: **one sheep, ten sheep**. The young are

lambs. Note also that the meat from a **sheep** is also called **lamb**)

④ **sheer**

[ʃɪər]

1 *adjective*

(a) complete; *it was sheer heaven to get into a hot bath after the marathon*; *it was sheer jealousy that made him write that letter*

(b) very steep; *it was a sheer 100-foot drop to the beach below*

2 *adverb*

straight up or down; *the cliff drops sheer to the beach below*

3 *verb*

to sheer off = to move to the side at an angle; *the automobile was speeding toward the tunnel but sheered off into the crowd instead*

① **sheet**

[ʃit] *noun*

(a) large piece of thin cloth which is put over a bed (you put two of them on a bed, one to lie on, and one to cover you); *she changed the sheets on the bed*; *guests are asked to bring their own towels and sheets*

(b) large flat piece of paper, cardboard, metal, ice, etc.; *can you give me another sheet of paper?*; **sheet lightning** = lightning where you cannot see the flash, but the clouds are lit up by it; *see also* BALANCE SHEET

② **shelf**

[ʃelf] *noun*

flat piece of wood attached to a wall or in a cupboard on which things can be put; *he put up or built some shelves in the kitchen*; *the shelves were packed with books*; *put that book back on the shelf*; *can you reach the box from the top shelf?*; *the plates are on the top shelf in the kitchen cupboard*; **shelf life** = number of days or weeks when a product can be kept in a store and still be good to use (NOTE: plural is **shelves** [ʃelvz])

② **shell**

[ʃel]

1 *noun*

(a) hard outside part covering some animals; *the children spent hours collecting shells on the beach*

(b) hard outside part of an egg or a nut; *I found a big piece of shell in my scrambled eggs*

(c) hard outside part of a building; *only the shell of the building remained after the fire*

(d) metal tube like a small bomb, which is fired from a gun; *a shell landed on the ruler's palace*

2 *verb*

to attack with shells; *anti-government forces shelled the capital*

① **she'll**

[ʃil] = SHE WILL

② **shellfish**

[ˈʃelfɪʃ] *noun*

sea animals with shells; *I never eat shellfish - it*

doesn't agree with me (NOTE: no plural: **a plate of shellfish, a shellfish restaurant**)

② **shelter**
['ʃeltər]
1 *noun*
(a) protection; *we stood in the shelter of a tree waiting for the rain to stop*; *on the mountain there was no shelter from the pouring rain*; **to take shelter** = to go somewhere for protection; *when the gunmen started to shoot we all took shelter behind a wall*
(b) construction where you can go for protection; *people ran to the bomb shelters as soon as they heard the planes*; **bus shelter** = construction with a roof where you can wait for a bus
2 *verb*
(a) to give someone protection; *the school sheltered several families of refugees*
(b) to go somewhere for protection; *sheep were sheltering from the snow beside the hedge*

④ **sheltered**
['ʃeltərd] *adjective*
protected from wind, cold, danger, bad influences, etc.; *the farm is in a sheltered valley*; *they have lived a very sheltered life*

④ **shelve**
[ʃelv] *verb*
(a) to put back to a later date which is not certain; *the project was shelved for lack of money*; *discussion of the problem has been shelved*
(b) to slope down; *the beach shelves gently so it is safe for little children*

① **shelves**
[ʃelvz] *noun*
see SHELF

① **shepherd**
['ʃepərd]
1 *noun*
man who looks after sheep; *do shepherds still carry a stick with a hooked end?*
2 *verb*
to guide; *the children were shepherded into the building*; *the police were shepherding the crowds away from the scene of the accident*

① **she's**
[ʃiz] = SHE HAS, SHE IS

② **shield**
[ʃild]
1 *noun*
(a) large plate held in one hand, carried by riot police, etc., as protection; *the policemen bent down behind their plastic shields*
(b) thing which protects from danger; *you need a shield over your face when working with this equipment*
2 *verb*
(a) to protect from danger; *he tried to shield her from the wind*
(b) to protect someone who has done something wrong; *she's just shielding her father*

② **shift**
[ʃɪft]
1 *noun*
(a) change of position, of direction, etc.; *the company is taking advantage of a shift in the market toward higher priced goods*; *there has been a shift of emphasis from competition to partnership*; *I don't understand this shift in attitude*
(b) period of time during which one group of workers works before being replaced by another group; *which shift are you working today?*; *we work an eight-hour shift*; **day shift** = shift worked during the day; **night shift** = shift worked during the night; *there are 150 men on the day shift*; *he works the night shift*
(c) loose dress; *as it was so hot she wore only a light cotton shift*
2 *verb*
(a) to move; to change position or direction; *we've shifted the television from the kitchen into the dining room*; *the center of attention shifted to Washington DC*
(b) **to shift gears** = to change from one gear to the next when driving an automobile; *there was a loud noise as he tried to shift gears*; **to shift up** = to move to a higher gear when driving an automobile; *shift up to fourth gear when you get onto the freeway*; **to shift down** = to move to a lower gear when driving an automobile; *shift down when you come to the hill*

③ **shift key**
['ʃɪft ˈki] *noun*
key on a typewriter or computer keyboard which makes capital letters or switches to another function; *hold down the shift key while you click on "help"*

② **shins**
[ʃɪnz] *noun*
front part of your leg below the knee; *he scraped his shins climbing over the wall*

① **shine**
[ʃaɪn]
1 *noun*
(a) reflection of light; *the shine of polished tables*
(b) action of polishing; *give the brass bowl a shine*
2 *verb*
(a) to be bright with light; *the sun is shining and they say it'll be hot today*; *she polished the table until it shone*; *the wine glasses shone in the light of the candles*; *why do cats' eyes shine in the dark?*; *the moon shone down on the waiting crowd*
(b) to make light fall on something; *he shone his flashlight into the well* (NOTE: in these meanings **shining - shone** [ʃɒn])
(c) to polish something to make it bright; *she was shining the silver*; *don't forget to shine your shoes* (NOTE: in this meaning **shining - shined**)

② shiny

['ʃaɪni] *adjective*

which shines; *the book has a shiny cover*; *he drove up in his new and very shiny automobile* (NOTE: shinier - shiniest)

① ship

[ʃɪp]

1 *noun*

large boat for carrying passengers and cargo on the sea; *she's a fine ship*; *how many ships does the U.S. Navy have?*; *the first time they came to the United States, they came by ship*; **cargo ship** = ship that carries only goods and not passengers; **to jump ship** = (i) to leave the ship on which you are working and not come back; (ii) to leave a project or team to go to work for a rival (NOTE: a **ship** is often referred to as **she** or **her**)

2 *verb*

to send goods (or people) but not always on a ship; *we ship goods all over the country*; *the container of spare parts was shipped abroad last week*; *we've shipped the children off to my sister's for two weeks* (NOTE: shipping - shipped)

① shipment

['ʃɪpmənt] *noun*

(a) sending of goods; *we make two shipments a week to England*

(b) goods that are shipped; *two shipments were lost in the fire*; *a shipment of computers was damaged*

② shipping

['ʃɪpɪŋ] *noun*

(a) sending of goods; *shipping by rail can often work out cheaper*; **shipping company** = company that specializes in the sending of goods; **shipping instructions** = details of how goods are to be shipped and delivered (NOTE: in this meaning, **shipping** does not always mean using a ship)

(b) cost of transporting goods; *shipping is not included in the invoice*

(c) ships; *they attacked enemy shipping in the Gulf*; **shipping lanes** = routes across the sea that are regularly used by ships; **shipping line** = company that owns ships (NOTE: no plural)

① shirt

[ʃɜrt] *noun*

light piece of clothing that you wear on the top part of the body under a sweater or jacket; *the teacher wore a blue suit and a white shirt*; *when he came back from the trip he had a suitcase full of dirty shirts*; *it's so hot that the workers in the fields have taken their shirts off*; *(informal)* **keep your shirt on!** = don't lose your temper

② shiver

['ʃɪvər]

1 *noun*

action of trembling because of cold, fear, etc.; **to send shivers down someone's spine** = to make

someone very afraid; *the mere thought of my grandfather driving along the freeway at his age sends shivers down my spine*

2 *verb*

to tremble with cold, fear, etc.; *she shivered in the cold night air*; *he was coughing and shivering, so the doctor told him to stay in bed*

② shock

[ʃɒk]

1 *noun*

(a) sudden unpleasant surprise; *it gave me quite a shock when you walked in*; *he's in for a nasty shock*

(b) weakness caused by low blood pressure, after an illness or injury or having a sudden surprise; *several of the passengers were treated for shock*; *she was in a state of shock after hearing that her son had drowned*

(c) **electric shock** = sudden pain when an electric current goes through your body; *I got a shock when I touched the back of the TV set*

2 *verb*

to give someone a sudden unpleasant surprise; *the conditions in the hospital shocked the inspectors*

③ shocked

[ʃɒkt] *adjective*

having an unpleasant surprise; *we were all shocked to hear that he had been arrested*; *she said, "How could you do it?" in a shocked voice*

③ shocking

['ʃɒkɪŋ] *adjective*

very unpleasant, which gives a sudden surprise; *it is a very shocking movie*; *the shocking news of the plane crash*; *it is shocking that no one offered to help*

① shoe

[ʃu] *noun*

(a) piece of clothing that is worn on your foot; *she's bought a new pair of shoes*; *he put his shoes on and went out*; *take your shoes off if your feet hurt*; **tennis shoes** = special shoes worn to play tennis or lightweight sneaker (NOTE: two shoes are called **a pair of shoes**)

(b) **in his shoes** = in his place, in the situation he is in; *what would you do if you were in his shoes?*; *I wouldn't like to be in her shoes*

④ shone

[ʃɒn] *see* SHINE

② shook

[ʃʊk] *see* SHAKE

① shoot

[ʃut]

1 *noun*

little new growth of a plant, growing from a seed or from a branch; *one or two green shoots are already showing where I sowed my lettuces*; *the vines have made a lot of new shoots this year*; *after pruning, the roses will send out a lot of strong new shoots*

2 *verb*

(a) to fire a gun; *soldiers were shooting into the woods*

(b) to hit or kill by firing a gun; *one of the robbers was shot by a police officer when he tried to run away; we went out hunting and shot two rabbits*

(c) to go very fast; *when the bell rang she shot down the stairs; he started the engine and the automobile shot out of the garage*

(d) to make a movie; *they're shooting a gangster movie on our block* (NOTE: **shoots - shooting - shot** [ʃɒt])

③ **shoot up**
['ʃut 'ʌp] *verb*

(a) to go up fast; *prices shot up during the strike*

(b) to grow fast; *these tomatoes have shot up since I planted them; she used to be such a small child but she's really shot up in the last couple of years*

① **shop**
[ʃɒp]

1 *noun*

(a) a small store; *the candy shop is opposite the fire station*

(b) workshop, a place where goods are made or repaired; **body shop** = workshop where automobile bodies are repaired; **repair shop** = small factory where machines are repaired

(c) closed shop = system whereby a company agrees to employ only union members in certain jobs; *the union is asking the management to agree to a closed shop*

(d) to talk shop = to talk about your business; *the dinner party was dull - the men all sat in a corner talking shop*

2 *verb*

to look for and buy things in shops; *she's out shopping for his birthday present; Mom's gone shopping in town; they went shopping on Fifth Avenue; do you ever shop locally?* (NOTE: **shopping - shopped**)

③ **shop around**
['ʃɒp ə'raʊnd] *verb*

to go to various stores to find which one has the cheapest goods before you buy what you want; *if you want a cheap TV set you ought to shop around; you should shop around before getting your car serviced*

① **shopkeeper**
['ʃɒpkipər] *noun*

a person who owns a shop; *the shopkeeper is angry with the schoolchildren because they broke his window*

③ **shoplifter**
['ʃɒplɪftər] *noun*

person who steals things from stores; *we saw the shoplifter put a necklace in her bag; we have installed cameras to deter shoplifters*

① **shopper**
['ʃɒpər] *noun*

person who buys things in a shop; *the store stays open till midnight for late-night shoppers; Fifth Avenue was crowded with shoppers when the sales started*

① **shopping**
['ʃɒpɪŋ] *noun*

(a) buying things in a store; *we do all our shopping at the weekend; he's gone out to do the weekly shopping;* **window shopping** = looking at goods in shop windows, without buying anything; **shopping bag** = bag for carrying your shopping in; **shopping basket** = basket for carrying shopping; **shopping cart** = metal basket on wheels, used by shoppers to put their purchases in as they go around a supermarket;

(b) things which you have bought in a store; *put all your shopping on the table; she was carrying two baskets of shopping* (NOTE: no plural: **some shopping, a lot of shopping**)

③ **shopping center**
['ʃɒpɪŋ 'sentər] *noun*

building with several different stores and restaurants, together with a parking lot; *we must stop them from building any more shopping centers*

① **shore**
[ʃɔr]

1 *noun*

land at the edge of the sea or a lake; *she stood on the shore waving as the boat sailed away;* **to go on shore** = to go on to the land from a ship; *when we were on shore in Barbados our cruise ship sailed without us*

2 *verb*

to shore something up = to hold something up which might fall down; *they had to put in metal beams to shore up the ceiling; the press secretary is trying to shore up the president's reputation*

① **short**
[ʃɔrt]

1 *adjective*

(a) *(size, length)* not long; *do you have a short piece of wire?;* **short-sleeved shirt** = shirt with short sleeves

(b) *(distance)* not far; *she only lives a short distance away; the taxi driver wanted to take me along Main Street, but I told him there was a shorter route; the shortest way to the train station is to go through the park;* **short wave** = radio frequency below 60 meters

(c) *(period of time)* not long, small; *he phoned a short time ago; we had a short vacation in June; she managed to have a short sleep on the plane*

(d) *(height)* not tall; *he is only five feet four - much shorter than his brother*

(e) not as much as there should be; *the delivery was three items short;* **when we counted the cash we were $15 short** = we had $15 less than we should have had

(f) short of = with not enough; *I can't offer you any tea as we're short of milk*; *can I pay later as I'm kind of short of cash at the moment?*; **to run short of** = to have less and less of; *in the hot weather the bars ran short of beer*

(g) short for = written or spoken with fewer letters than usual; *Inc. is short for Incorporated*; **for short** = as a shortened version; *his name is Jonathan but everyone calls him Jonty for short* (NOTE: **shorter - shortest**)

2 *adverb*

(a) suddenly; *I stopped short when I saw her walking toward me*

(b) short of = without doing something; *short of giving her the heave-ho, I don't know what we can do*

3 *verb*

to make a bad connection in an electric circuit, making the electric current follow the wrong path; *he switched on TV and shorted out the whole house*

② **shortage**
['ʃɔrtɪdʒ] *noun*
lack of something; *a chronic shortage of skilled staff*; *what is the government going to do about the housing shortage?*; *during the war, there were food shortages*

④ **shortcake**
['ʃɔrtkeɪk] *noun*
dessert made of light cake with fruit and cream

② **short circuit**
['ʃɔrt 'sɜrkɪt] *noun*
bad connection in an electric circuit, making the electric current follow the wrong path; *the worn cable caused a short circuit*

② **short-circuit**
['ʃɔrt 'sɜrkɪt] *verb*
(a) to make a short circuit; *a faulty contact caused the system to short-circuit*
(b) to get through something complicated by using a simple shortcut; *is there any way of short-circuiting some of the administrative procedures?*

② **shortcut**
['ʃɔrtkʌt] *noun*
(a) way which is shorter than usual; *we can take a shortcut through the park*
(b) quicker way of doing something; *there are no shortcuts to learning Russian*

② **shorten**
['ʃɔrtən] *verb*
to make shorter; *smoking will shorten your life*; *I must have these pants shortened*; *"telephone" is often shortened to "phone"*

③ **shortly**
['ʃɔrtli] *adverb*
soon; *he left his office shortly before 5 o'clock*; *don't worry, she'll be here shortly*

② **shorts**
[ʃɔrts] *noun*
short pants for men or women, that come down above the knees; *he was wearing a pair of green running shorts*; *they won't let you into the church in shorts*; **boxer shorts** = men's underwear shaped like sports shorts

② **shortstop**
['ʃɔrtstɒp] *noun*
baseball player who covers the area between second and third base; *the shortstop caught the ball*

④ **short-term**
[ʃɔrt'tɜrm] *adjective*
for a short period only; *staying in a hotel is only a short-term solution*; *we have taken on more staff on a short-term basis*; *see also* LONG-TERM

② **shortwave**
['ʃɔrtweɪv] *noun*
radio communications frequency below 60 metres; **shortwave receiver** = radio receiver able to pick up broadcasts on the short wave bands

① **shot**
[ʃɒt]
1 *noun*
(a) action of shooting; the sound of shooting; *the police fired two shots at the vehicle*; *some shots were fired during the bank robbery*; *a neighbor said she'd heard a shot*
(b) like a shot = very rapidly; *he heard a noise and was off like a shot*
(c) *(informal)* attempt; *he passed the test at the first shot*; **to have a shot at something** = to try to do something; *I'd like to have a shot at driving a bus*
(d) *(slang)* injection; *the doctor gave him a yellow fever shot*
(e) *(slang)* small drink of alcohol; *he poured himself a shot of whiskey and sat down to wait*
(f) photograph; *I took several shots of the inside of the house*
(g) large heavy sphere thrown in a sporting competition; *how much does the shot weigh?*; **to throw the shot put** = to throw a heavy sphere in a competition
(h) person who shoots well or badly; *she's a first-class shot*; *he's a hopeless shot*

2 past tense and past participle of SHOOT

② **should**
[ʃʊd] *verb used with other verbs*
(a) *(used in giving advice or warnings, used to say what is the best thing to do)* *you should go to the doctor if your cough gets worse*; *I should have been more careful*; *she shouldn't eat so much if she's trying to lose weight*; *should I ask for more coffee?*; *why should I clean up the mess you've made?*
(b) *(used to say what you expect to happen)* *if you leave now you should be there by 4 o'clock*; *they should have arrived by now*; *there shouldn't be any more problems now* (NOTE: in meanings (a) and (b) **ought to** can be used instead of **should**)

(c) *(indicating a possibility)* *if the president should die in office, the vice president automatically takes over; I'll be in the next room should you need me*
(d) *(used instead of* **would***); (old) we should like to offer you our congratulations; if I had enough money I should like to buy a new car* (NOTE: negative: **should not,** usually **shouldn't**. Note also that **should** is the past of **shall: shall we go to a Mexican restaurant? - I suggested we should go to a Mexican restaurant**)

② **shoulder**
[ˈʃəʊldər]
1 *noun*
(a) part of the body at the top of the arm; *the police officer touched me on the shoulder; he fell and hurt his shoulder; look over your shoulder, he's just behind you;* **shoulder blade** = one of two large flat bones covering the top part of your back; *he fell when skiing and broke his shoulder blade;* **shoulder to shoulder** = side by side; *the three men stood shoulder to shoulder blocking the way; see also* BAG, CHIP, COLD
(b) piece of clothing which covers the part between the top of the arm and the neck; *there's an ink mark on the shoulder of your shirt; a captain has three stars on his shoulders*
(c) piece of meat from the top part of the front leg of an animal; *we had a shoulder of lamb and new potatoes*
(d) dirt or pavement running on either side of a road; *I pulled over to the shoulder because I had a flat tire*
2 *verb*
to carry responsibility, blame, etc.; *he had to shoulder all the responsibility for the company's collapse; she was left to shoulder the blame for the accident*

② **shout**
[ʃaʊt]
1 *noun*
yell, loud cry; *she gave a shout and dove into the water; people came running when they heard the shouts of the children*
2 *verb*
to make a loud cry, to speak very loudly; *they stamped on the floor and shouted; I had to shout to the waitress to get served; they were shouting greetings to one another across the street*

① **shove**
[ʃʌv]
1 *noun*
sudden push; *she gave the automobile a shove and it started to roll down the hill*
2 *verb*
(a) to push roughly; *he shoved the papers into his pocket; stop shoving - there's no more room on the bus*
(b) *(informal)* **to shove off** = to leave; *we must shove off for home*

① **shovel**
[ˈʃʌvl]
1 *noun*
wide spade; *the workmen picked up shovels and started to clear the pile of sand*
2 *verb*
(a) to lift up with a shovel; *they were shoveling sand into the truck; he collapsed after shoveling snow from the path*
(b) *(informal)* to put a large amount of food into your mouth; *it wasn't very elegant, the way he was shoveling potatoes into his mouth*

① **show**
[ʃəʊ]
1 *noun*
(a) exhibition, things which are displayed for people to look at; *the computer trade show opens tomorrow; she has entered her two cats for the local cat show;* **show apartment** *or* **show house** = new apartment or house that is decorated and filled with furniture by the builders so that people can see how other apartments or houses will look
(b) **on show** = displayed for everyone to see; *is there anything new on show in this year's exhibition?*
(c) something which is on at a theater; *"Cats" is a wonderful show; we're going to a show tonight; the show starts at 7:30, so let's have dinner early*
(d) **show of hands** = vote where people show how they vote by raising their hands; *the motion was carried on a show of hands*
(e) *(informal)* planned activity or organization; *she's running the whole show by herself*
2 *verb*
(a) to let someone see something; *he wanted to show me his photos; she proudly showed me her new automobile; you don't have to show your passport when you're traveling to Canada*
(b) to point something out to someone; *show me where the accident happened; he asked me to show him the way to the train station; the salesman showed her how to work the photocopier; my watch shows the date as well as the time*
(c) to prove; *the results show how right we were to invest in Europe*
(d) **to show signs of** = to be visible; *the wound doesn't show any signs of infection*
(e) to be seen, to be obvious; *the repairs were badly done and it shows; her rash has almost disappeared and hardly shows at all*
(f) *(informal)* **to show someone the door** = to make someone leave, to dismiss someone; *when we complained we were shown the door* (NOTE: **showing - showed - has shown** [ʃəʊn])

③ **show around**
[ˈʃəʊ əˈraʊnd] *verb*
to lead a visitor around a place; *the old guide showed us around the castle; he showed the students around his laboratory; I have to go out now but my mother will show you around*

② **shower**

['ʃaʊər]

1 *noun*

(a) slight fall of rain, snow, etc.; *in April there's usually a mixture of sunshine and showers*; *there were snow showers this morning, but it is sunny again now*

(b) device in a bathroom for sending out a spray of water to wash your whole body ; **shower curtain** = curtain around a shower to prevent the water going everywhere; **shower room** = small bathroom with a shower in it

(c) bath taken in a spray of water from over your head; *she went up to her room and had a shower*; *he has a cold shower every morning*; *you can't take a shower now, there's no hot water*; **shower cap** = plastic cap to prevent your hair getting wet when taking a shower

(d) party where presents are given to a girl about to get married or who has had a baby; *we are holding a shower for Lillian next Saturday*

2 *verb*

(a) to wash under a spray of water; *he showered and went down to greet his guests*

(b) **to shower someone with something** = to give large amounts of something to someone; *she was showered with presents*

③ **show in**

['ʃəʊ 'ɪn] *verb*

to bring someone into a room, etc.; *please show the next candidate in*; *he was shown into a comfortable room with a view over the sea*

① **shown**

[ʃəʊn] *see* SHOW

③ **show off**

['ʃəʊ 'ɒf] *verb*

(a) to show how you think you are much better than others; *don't watch her dancing about like that - she's just showing off*

(b) to display something you are proud of; *he drove past with the radio on very loud, showing off his new automobile*

③ **show out**

['ʃəʊ 'aʊt] *verb*

to take someone to the door when they are leaving; *let me show you out*

② **show up**

['ʃəʊ 'ʌp] *verb*

(a) *(informal)* to come; *we invited all our friends to the picnic but it rained and only five of them showed up*

(b) to do something which shows other people to be worse than you; *she dances so well that she shows us all up*

(c) to be seen clearly; *when I ride my bike at night I wear an orange jacket because it shows up clearly in the dark*

② **shrank**

[ʃræŋk] *see* SHRINK

② **shred**

[ʃred]

1 *noun*

(a) strip torn off something; *she tore his newspaper to shreds*; *the curtains were on the floor in shreds*

(b) small amount; *there's not a shred of evidence against him*

(c) long thin strip of fruit, vegetables, etc.; *marmalade with shreds of orange peel in it*

2 *verb*

(a) to tear (paper) into thin strips, which can then be thrown away or used as packing material; *they sent a pile of old invoices to be shredded*; *she told the police that the manager had told her to shred all the documents in the file*

(b) to cut into very thin strips; *here's an attachment for shredding vegetables*; *add a cup of shredded carrot* (NOTE: **shredding - shredded**)

② **shrimp**

[ʃrɪmp] *noun*

little sea animal with many legs and a tail; *the children spent the afternoon fishing for shrimp in the rock pools* (NOTE: no plural)

② **shrink**

[ʃrɪŋk]

1 *verb*

(a) to make smaller; *the water must have been too hot - it's shrunk my shirt*

(b) to get smaller; *my shirt has shrunk in the wash*; *the market for typewriters has shrunk almost to nothing* (NOTE: **shrank** [ʃræŋk] - **shrunk** [ʃrʌŋk])

2 *noun*

(slang) psychiatrist; *she's been to see a shrink but she's no better at all*

② **shrivel**

['ʃrɪvl] *verb*

to make or become dry and wrinkled; *you should water that plant - it's leaves are starting to shrivel*

② **shrub**

[ʃrʌb] *noun*

small plant with stiff stems; *a flowering shrub would look lovely under that window*

③ **shrug**

[ʃrʌg]

1 *verb*

to shrug your shoulders = to move your shoulders up to show you are not sure, not interested, etc.; *when I asked him what he thought about it all, he just shrugged his shoulders and walked off*

2 *noun*

moving your shoulders up to show you are not sure, not interested, etc.; *he just gave a shrug and walked on* (NOTE: **shrugging - shrugged**)

② **shrunk**

[ʃrʌŋk] *see* SHRINK

② **shuffle**

['ʃʌfl] *verb*

(a) to walk dragging your feet along the ground; *he shuffled into the room in his slippers*

(b) to mix the playing cards before starting a game; *I think he must have done something to the cards when he was shuffling them*; *he shuffled the pack and dealt three cards to each player*

② **shut**
[ʃʌt]
1 *adjective*
closed, not open; *she lay with her eyes shut*; *come in - the door isn't shut!*
2 *verb*
(a) to close something which is open; *can you please shut the window - it's getting cold in here*; *here's your present - shut your eyes and guess what it is* (NOTE: **shutting - shut**)

③ **shut down**
['ʃʌt 'daʊn] *verb*
(a) to close completely; *the factory shut down for the holiday weekend*
(b) to switch off an electrical system; *they had to shut down the power station because pollution levels were too high*

② **shut in**
['ʃʌt 'ɪn] *verb*
to lock inside; *the door closed suddenly and we were shut in*; *we shut the cat in the basement at night*

② **shut off**
['ʃʌt 'ɒf] *verb*
(a) to switch something off; *can you shut off the water while I fix the tap?*
(b) to stop access to; *we can shut off the dining room with folding doors*; *the palace is shut off from the road by a high wall*

② **shut out**
['ʃʌt 'aʊt] *verb*
(a) to lock outside; *if the dog keeps on barking you'll have to shut him out*; *I was shut out of the house because I'd left my keys inside*
(b) to stop light from getting inside; to stop people from seeing a view; *those thick curtains should shut out the light*; *a high wall shuts out the view of the factory*
(c) to stop thinking about something; *try to shut out the memory of the accident*

② **shutout**
['ʃʌtaʊt] *noun*
game in which one of the sides does not score; *the football game was almost a shutout*

① **shutter**
['ʃʌtər] *noun*
(a) folding wooden or metal cover for a window; *close the shutters if the sunlight is too bright*
(b) *(in a camera)* part which opens and closes very rapidly to allow the light to go on to the film; *he released the shutter and took the picture*

④ **shuttle**
['ʃʌtl]
1 *noun*

(a) thing which moves from one place to another; *there's a shuttle bus from the hotel to the exhibition grounds*; **shuttle service** = bus or plane that goes regularly backward and forward between two places; *the ferry operates a shuttle service between the islands*; **shuttle diplomacy** = action of a diplomat going backward and forward between two countries to try to make them reach an agreement; *see also* SPACE SHUTTLE
(b) small device holding thread which goes backward and forward under and over the vertical threads when weaving
2 *verb*
to go backward and forward regularly; *waiters were shuttling back and forth from the kitchen to the dining room*

② **shut up**
['ʃʌt 'ʌp] *verb*
(a) to close something inside; *I hate being shut up indoors on a sunny day*
(b) *(informal)* to stop making a noise; *tell those children to shut up - I'm trying to work*; *shut up! - we're tired of listening to your complaints*; *once he starts talking it's impossible to shut him up*

① **shy**
[ʃaɪ]
1 *adjective*
nervous and afraid to do something; *he's so shy he sat in the back row and didn't speak to anyone*; **once bitten twice shy** = once you have had a bad experience you will not want to do it again; *I'm not getting involved with him again - once bitten twice shy!*
2 *verb*
(of a horse) to jump in a nervous way; *his horse shied at the noise of the gun*

① **sick**
[sɪk]
1 *adjective*
(a) ill, not well; *he's been sick for months*; *we have five staff off sick*; **sick leave** = time when a worker is away from work because of illness
(b) **to be sick** = to bring up partly digested food from the stomach into the mouth; *the last time I ate mushrooms I was sick all night*; **to feel sick** = to want to bring food up from the stomach into the mouth; *when I got up this morning I felt sick and went back to bed*; *the oily food made her feel sick*; *see also* SEASICK
(c) **to be sick (and tired) of** = to have had too much of; *I'm sick of listening to all his complaints*; *she's sick and tired of doing housework all day long*; **to make someone sick** = to make someone very annoyed; *all my friends earn more than I do - it makes me sick!*
(d) referring to something sad, disgusting; *he made some sick jokes about handicapped people*
2 *noun*
the sick = people who are ill; *nurses were looking after the sick and the dying*

① **sickness**
['sɪknəs] *noun*
(a) feeling of wanting to bring up food from the stomach into the mouth; **morning sickness =** feeling of wanting to be sick, felt by pregnant women in the morning; **travel sickness =** sickness caused by the movement of an automobile, aircraft, bus or train, etc.
(b) not being well; *there is a lot of sickness during the winter months*

① **side**
[saɪd]
1 *noun*
(a) one of the four parts which with the top and bottom make a solid object such as a box; *stand the box upright - don't turn it onto its side*
(b) one of the two parts which with the front and back make a building; *the garage is attached to the side of the house*
(c) one of the surfaces of a flat object; *please write on both sides of the paper*
(d) one of two parts or two edges of something; *our office is on the opposite side of the street to the bank*; *the airport is on the west side of the city*; *the children were standing by the side of the road*; **to look on the bright side =** to be optimistic; *you should look on the bright side - you'll have plenty of free time now you've lost your job*; *see also* WRONG
(e) one of two parts separated by something; *she jumped over the fence to get to the other side*; *in England, cars drive on the left-hand side of the road*
(f) sports team; *the local side was beaten 2 - 0*
(g) part of the body between the top of the legs and the shoulder; *I can't sleep when I'm lying on my right side*; *the policemen stood by the prisoner's side*; *they all stood side by side*
(h) one of the sides of an animal, used as a piece of meat; *a side of bacon*
(i) *(informal)* **on the side =** separate from your normal work, and sometimes hidden from your employer; *her salary is very low, so the family lives on what she can make on the side*
(j) *(informal)* aspect of something; *the car runs well but it's kind of on the small side*; **the book is on the heavy side =** (i) the book is quite heavy; (ii) the book is fairly difficult to read
(k) to be on someone's side = to support someone in a battle or argument, to have the same point of view as someone; *don't attack me - I'm on your side*; *whose side is he on?*; **to take sides =** to say who you agree with; *he refused to take sides in the argument*
(l) family, ancestors; *on my mother's side everyone has blue eyes*
2 *adjective*
which is at the side; *there is a side entrance to the store*; *can you take that bucket around to the side door?*; **side plate =** small plate placed next to your dinner plate; *they served the vegetables on side plates*
3 *verb*

to side against someone = to disagree with someone in an argument; *I can't understand why they all are siding against me*; **to side with someone =** to agree with someone in an argument; *why do you always side with the boss?*

◇ **on the right side**
[ɒn ðə 'raɪt saɪd] *phrase*
(a) in the correct relationship with; *you'll be in trouble if you don't keep on the right side of the law*
(b) *(informal)* not older than; *she's still on the right side of forty*

④ **sideboard**
['saɪdbɔrd] *noun*
large piece of furniture for holding plates, glasses, etc., made like a table with a cupboard underneath; *there was a bowl of fruit on the sideboard*

④ **side effect**
['saɪd ɪ'fekt] *noun*
effect produced by a drug, treatment, etc., which is not the main effect intended; *one of the side effects of the treatment is that the patient's hair falls out*; *the drug is being withdrawn because of its unpleasant side effects*

① **sidewalk**
['saɪdwɔk] *noun*
hard path for walkers at the side of a road; *a girl was cycling along the sidewalk*; *we sat at a sidewalk café*

② **sideways**
['saɪdweɪz] *adverb*
to the side or from the side; *take a step sideways and you will be able to see the castle*; *if you look at the post sideways you'll see how bent it is*

④ **siege**
[sidʒ] *noun*
surrounding an enemy town or castle with an army to prevent supplies getting in, and so force it to surrender; *the army laid siege to the castle*; *the inhabitants almost starved during the siege of the town*; **under siege =** surrounded by an enemy; *the town has been under siege for several weeks*; *the pop star's hotel was under siege by photographers and reporters*; **siege mentality =** feeling that you are surrounded by enemies

③ **sigh**
[saɪ]
1 *noun*
long deep breath, showing sadness, etc.; *she gave a deep sigh and put the phone down*; *you could hear the sighs of relief from the audience when the heroine was saved*
2 *verb*
to breathe deeply showing you are sad, relieved, etc.; *he sighed and wrote out another check*

① **sight**
[saɪt]
1 *noun*

(a) one of the five senses, being able to see; *my grandfather's sight isn't very good anymore*; **to lose your sight** = to become blind; *he lost his sight in the accident*

(b) seeing, view; *he can't stand the sight of blood*; *we caught sight of a bear up in the mountains*; *she kept waving until the automobile disappeared from sight*; *the fog cleared and the mountains came into sight*; *they waved until the boat was out of sight*; *the house is hidden from sight behind a row of trees*; *the little boy burst into tears at the sight of the dead rabbit*; **at first sight** = when you see something for the first time; *at first sight I thought he was wearing a pair of dark blue pajamas*

(c) something (especially something famous) which you ought to see; *they went off on foot to see the sights of the town*; *the guidebook lists the main tourist sights in Beijing*; **to do the sights** = to visit the main tourist attractions; *we did the sights in London*

(d) to look a sight = to look awful; *she looks a sight in that old coat*

(e) sights = part of a gun that you look through to aim; *he spent so long adjusting the gun's sights that the deer had disappeared*; **to set your sights on** = to aim for; *she's set her sights on becoming an actress*

2 *verb*

to see something a long way away; *we often sight rare birds on the lake*; *the helicopter sighted some pieces of wood from the boat* (NOTE: do not confuse with **cite**, **site**)

① **sign**
['saɪn']
1 *noun*

(a) movement of the hand which means something; *he made a sign to us to sit down*

(b) drawing, notice, etc., which advertises something; *the store has a big sign outside it saying "for sale"*; *a "no smoking" sign hung on the wall*; **(road) sign** = panel by the side of a road, giving instructions or warnings; *go straight on until you come to a sign pointing left, marked "to the sea"*

(c) something which shows something; *there is no sign of the rain stopping*; *the economy is showing signs of improvement*; *the police can find no sign of how the burglars got into the office*; *he should have arrived by now, but there's no sign of him*

(d) printed character; *the dollar sign ($) the pound sign (£ or #)*

2 *verb*

to write your name in a special way on a document to show that you have written it or that you have approved it; *the secretary brought him all the letters to sign*; *sign on the dotted line, please*; *the letter is signed by the chief executive officer*; *a check is not valid if it has not been signed*

② **signal**
['sɪgnl]
1 *noun*

(a) sign or movement that tells someone to do something; *I'll give you a signal to start playing "Happy Birthday"*

(b) device used to tell someone to do something; *the signal had turned to red so the train had to stop*; *the turn signal is blinking*

(c) electronic sound heard on a radio receiver; *we heard a faint signal coming from the mountains*

2 *verb*

to make signs to tell someone to do something; *the driver signaled to show that he was turning right*; *she signaled to me that we were running out of time*

3 *adjective*

(formal) remarkable; *the conference was a signal success*

② **signature**
['sɪgnətʃər] *noun*

(a) name written in a special way by someone to show that a document has been authorized or accepted; *he found a pile of checks on his desk waiting for his signature*; *her signature doesn't look like her name at all*; *the storekeeper looked very closely at her signature and compared it with the one on the credit card*

(b) signature tune = tune that is used to identify a radio or TV broadcast; *that program has had the same signature tune for over 30 years*

③ **sign for**
['saɪn 'fɔr'] *verb*

to sign a document to show that you have received something; *he signed for the package*

③ **significance**
[sɪg'nɪfɪkəns] *noun*

(a) meaning; *what is the significance of your logo of a ship?*

(b) importance; *there was no significance in the fact that her temperature was higher than usual*; **of great significance** = very important; *the contents of the letter were of great significance*; *his remarks were of little significance*

④ **significant**
[sɪg'nɪfɪkənt] *adjective*

important, full of meaning; *it is highly significant that everyone else was asked to the meeting, but not the finance director*; *there has been a significant improvement in his condition*

④ **significantly**
[sɪg'nɪfɪkəntlɪ] *adverb*

in a significant way; *my home town has not altered significantly in 20 years*; *the company has employed her again but on a significantly lower salary*

④ **sign on**
['saɪn 'ɒn'] *verb*

to start work; *he signed on to the project*

① **silence**

['saɪləns]

1 *noun*

quiet, absence of noise; *I love the silence of the countryside at night*; *the crowd of tourists waited in silence*; *the chairman held up his hand and asked for silence*; *there was a sudden silence as she came in*; *there will be a minute's silence at 11 o'clock*; **wall of silence** = plot by everyone to say nothing about what has happened; *the police investigation met with a wall of silence*

2 *verb*

to stop someone saying or writing something; *he tried to silence his critics by taking them to court*; *she refused to be silenced and continued to write her articles about government corruption*

② **silent**

['saɪlənt] *adjective*

not talking, not making any noise; *he kept silent for the whole meeting*; *she seems rather silent today*; *a very silent and reserved young man*; *the house was cold and silent*; *this new washing machine is almost silent*; *they showed some old silent movies*; **the silent majority** = the majority of people who do not protest, who are not members of political parties, etc., but who vote according to their beliefs

① **silk**

[sɪlk] *noun*

cloth made from threads produced by caterpillars living in trees; *she was wearing a beautiful silk scarf*; *I bought some blue silk to make a dress*

① **silly**

['sɪli] *adjective*

stupid, not thinking; *don't be silly - you can't go to the party dressed like that!*; *she asked a lot of silly questions*; *of all the silly newspaper articles that must be the silliest* (NOTE: **sillier - silliest**)

① **silver**

['sɪlvər]

1 *noun*

(a) precious white metal; *gold is worth more than silver*; *how much is an ounce of silver worth?* (NOTE: Chemical element: chemical symbol: **Ag**; atomic number: **47**)

(b) coins made of white metal; *he held out a handful of silver*

(c) **silver foil** = thin sheet of shiny metal that looks like silver, used for wrapping food in; *chocolate bars are wrapped in silver foil*

(d) knives, forks and spoons made of silver; *she's in the kitchen, polishing the silver*; *don't worry, all the silver is securely locked away*

(e) **silver (medal)** = medal given to someone who finishes in second place in a race or competition; *the U.S.A. won ten silver medals at the Olympics*; *see also* BRONZE, GOLD

(f) shiny white color, like silver; *the automobile has been sprayed in silver*

(g) **silver wedding** = celebration when two people have been married for twenty-five years

2 *adjective*

of a shiny white color, like silver; *the automobile has been sprayed with silver paint*; *she wore silver shoes to match her purse*

② **similar**

['sɪmɪlər] *adjective*

very alike but not quite the same; *here is the old lampshade - do you have anything similar to replace it?*; *the two automobiles are very similar in appearance*; *our situation is rather similar to yours*

② **similarity**

[sɪmɪ'lærɪti] *noun*

being similar; *he bears an astonishing similarity to my uncle*; *there is no similarity whatsoever between the two cases*; *the two children are fair with blue eyes, but the similarity stops there* (NOTE: plural is **similarities**)

② **similarly**

['sɪmɪləli] *adverb*

in a similar way; *all these infections must be treated similarly*; *he always writes a nice thank-you letter, and similarly so does his sister*

③ **simmer**

['sɪmər] *verb*

(a) to cook by boiling gently; *we left the soup to simmer gently*

(b) **to simmer down** = to become calmer after being very annoyed; *will you try to simmer down and listen to me, please?*

② **simple**

['sɪmpl] *adjective*

(a) easy; *the machine is very simple to use*; *she described the accident in a few simple words*; *it turned out to be a simple job to open the door*; *they say the new tax forms are simpler than the old ones*

(b) ordinary, not very special, not complicated; *they had a simple meal of bread and soup*; *it's a very simple pattern of lines and squares* (NOTE: **simpler - simplest**)

③ **simple interest**

['sɪmpl 'ɪntrəst] *noun*

interest calculated on the capital only, and not added to it; *the loan will be cheaper because it only attracts simple interest* (NOTE: the opposite is **compound interest**)

② **simply**

['sɪmpli] *adverb*

(a) in a simple way; *he described very simply how the accident had happened*; *she always dresses very simply*

(b) only; *he did it simply to annoy everyone*; *she gave a new look to the room simply by painting one wall red*

(c) *(to emphasize)* *your garden is simply beautiful*; *it's simply terrible - what shall we do?*

④ **simultaneous**
[sɪməl'teɪnɪəs] *adjective*
happening at the same time as something else; *there will be simultaneous radio and TV broadcast of the concert*; **simultaneous translation** = translation of a speech into another language done at the same time as a person is speaking

① **sin**
[sɪn]
1 *noun*
(a) wicked action that goes against the rules of a religion; *envy is one of the seven deadly sins*; **to live in sin** = to live together without being married
(b) something bad; *it would be a sin to waste all that food*
2 *verb*
to commit a sin, to do something wicked; *the priest told him he had sinned* (NOTE: sinning - sinned)

② **since**
[sɪns]
1 *preposition* during the period after; *she's been here since Monday*; *we've been working non-stop since four o'clock - can't we have a rest?*
2 *conjunction*
(a) during the period after; *he has had trouble borrowing money ever since he was rude to the bank manager*; *since we got to the hotel, it has rained every day*
(b) because; *since he's ill, you can't ask him to help you*; *since it's such a fine day, let's go for a walk*
3 *adverb*
during the period until now; *she phoned on Sunday and we haven't heard from her since*; *he left the U.S.A. in 1995 and has lived abroad ever since*

① **sincere**
[sɪn'sɪər] *adjective*
very honest and genuine; *a politician needs to appear sincere*; *we send you our sincere best wishes for a rapid recovery*

③ **sincerely**
[sɪn'sɪəlɪ] *adverb*
really, truly; *I sincerely wanted to see her at Christmas*; *he believed most sincerely that she would come immediately*; **Sincerely yours** = used as an ending to a letter addressed to a named person

① **sing**
[sɪŋ] *verb*
to make music with your voice; *she was singing as she worked*; *please sing another song*; *he always sings in the bath*; *she sang a funny song about elephants* (NOTE: singing - sang [sæŋ] - has sung [sʌŋ])

① **singer**
['sɪŋər] *noun*
person who sings; *she's training to be a professional singer*; *I'm not a very good singer*

① **single**
['sɪŋgl]
1 *adjective*
(a) one alone; *he handed her a single sheet of paper*; *there wasn't a single person I knew at the party*; *the single most important fact about him is that he has no money*; **every single (one)** = each one; *you will need every single cent you have to pay for the house*; *every single time I asked her out, she refused*
(b) for one person only; *do you have a single room for two nights, please?*; *we prefer two single beds to a double bed*
(c) not married; *she's twenty-nine and still single*; *are there any single men on the course?*; **single parent** = one parent (mother or father) who is bringing up a child alone
(d) **in single figures** = less than ten; *inflation was over 20% but now it is down to single figures*
2 *noun*
(a) a room in a hotel for one person; *she asked for a single*
(b) *(in baseball)* play where the batter safely reaches first base and stops there; *she often gets a single the first time she bats*
(c) record with one piece of music on it; *the group's first single went into the top ten*

④ **singles**
['sɪŋglz] *noun*
(a) **singles** = tennis game played between two people; *the men's singles champion*
(b) **singles** = people who are not married; *they went to a singles bar*

② **singular**
['sɪŋgjʊlər]
1 *adjective*
(a) *(formal)* odd, strange; *we found ourselves in a really singular position*
(b) showing that there is only one thing or person; *"she" is a singular pronoun*
2 *noun*
form of a word showing that there is only one; *"child" is the singular, and "children" is the plural*; *the singular of "they have" is "he has"*; *the singular of "bacteria" is "bacterium"*

④ **sinister**
['sɪnɪstər] *adjective*
which looks evil, which suggests that something bad will happen; *there's nothing sinister about their getting together*; *the sinister atmosphere of the castle*; *his colleague is a sinister character who never smiles*

① **sink**
[sɪŋk]
1 *noun*
fixed washbowl for washing dishes, etc., in a kitchen; *the sink was piled high with dirty*

dishes; *he was washing his hands at the kitchen sink*; **sink unit** = arrangement of cupboard, sink, faucets, waste pipes, etc., forming a single piece of furniture

2 *verb*

(a) to go down to the bottom (of water, mud, etc.); *the ferry sank in 30 meters of water*; *the paper boat floated for a few minutes, then sank*; *you should tie a piece of lead to your fishing line to make it sink*

(b) to drop suddenly; *she was so upset that she just sank into an armchair and closed her eyes*; *my heart sank when I heard the news*; *inflation has sunk to the lowest point ever*

(c) to invest money in something; *he sank all his savings into a car rental business* (NOTE: sinking - sank [sæŋk] - sunk [sʌŋk])

③ **sink in**
[ˈsɪŋk ˈɪn] *verb*
to become fixed in the mind; *the speaker waited a moment for the meaning of what he had said to sink in*

① **sip**
[sɪp]
1 *noun*
little drink; *she took a sip of water, and went on with her speech*
2 *verb*
to drink taking only a small amount of liquid at a time; *the girl was sipping her drink quietly* (NOTE: sipping - sipped)

② **sir**
[sɜr] *noun*
(a) *(usually used by someone serving in a store or restaurant)* polite way of referring to a man; *would you like a drink with your lunch, sir?*; *please come this way, sir*
(b) *(in letters)* **Dear Sir** = polite way of addressing a man you do not know; **Dear Sirs** = polite way of addressing a company

② **siren**
[ˈsaɪrən] *noun*
device which makes a loud warning signal; *a police car raced past with its siren howling*

① **sister**
[ˈsɪstər]
1 *noun*
(a) girl or woman who has the same father and mother as someone else; *his three sisters all look alike*; *my younger sister Louise works in a bank*; *do you have any sisters?*
(b) nun; *Sister Mary joined the convent two years ago*
2 *adjective*
sister company = company that forms part of the same group as another company; **sister ship** = ship that is of the same design and belongs to the same company as another ship

① **sit**
[sɪt] *verb*
(a) to be resting with your behind on something; to move in into this position; *mother was sitting*

in bed eating her breakfast; *there were no seats left, so they had to sit on the floor*

(b) to take a test; *she failed her English exam and had to sit for it again*

(c) to sit for a picture = to pose, to stand or sit still while someone paints or photographs you; *she sat for her portrait*; *he sat for her in his uniform*

(d) *(of a court, congress, or other organization)* to be in session; *we have to keep quiet while court is sitting*

(e) to occupy a position; *he sits in Congress*

(f) *(of bird)* to rest; *the pigeon always comes and sits on the fence when I'm sowing seeds*

(g) to look after children, to baby-sit; *I'm looking for someone to sit for me tomorrow evening* (NOTE: sits - sitting - sat [sæt] - has sat)

① **sit back**
[ˈsɪt ˈbæk] *verb*
(a) to rest your back against the back of a chair when sitting; *just sit back and enjoy the movie*
(b) to do nothing; *he just sat back and watched everyone else do the work*

① **sit down**
[ˈsɪt ˈdaʊn] *verb*
to sit on a seat; *if everyone will sit down, the meeting can start*; *they all sat down and the movie began*; *come and sit down next to me*

④ **sit-down**
[ˈsɪtdaʊn]
1 *adjective*
(a) sit-down meal = meal where you sit at a table; *we'd rather have sandwiches in the bar than a sit-down meal*
(b) sit-down protest *or* **sit-down strike** = strike where the workers stay in their place of work and refuse to work or to leave; *the factory has been occupied by workers staging a sit-down strike*
2 *noun*
(informal) little rest; *I've been on my feet all day - I think I deserve a sit-down*

② **site**
[saɪt]
1 *noun*
(a) place where something is or will be; *this is the site for the new factory*; **building site** *or* **construction site** = place where a building is being built; *all visitors to the site must wear safety helmets*; **camping site** *or* **campsite** = place where you can camp
(b) place where something happened, where something once existed; *they're trying to find the site of the old Roman town*
(c) *(Internet)* **web site** = collection of pages on the Web which have been produced by one company and are linked together; *how many hits did we have on our web site last week?*
2 *verb*
to be sited = to be placed on a particular piece of land; *the hotel will be sited between the airport*

and the new exhibition center (NOTE: do not confuse with **cite, sight**)

② **sitting room**
['sɪtɪŋ 'rum] *noun*
lounge, comfortable room for sitting in; *we spent the evening in the sitting room watching TV*

③ **situated**
['sɪtjʊeɪtɪd] *adjective*
placed, in a certain situation; *the factory is situated next to the train station*; *the tourist information office is situated on Main Street*

③ **situation**
[sɪtjuˈeɪʃn] *noun*
(a) position, way in which something is placed; *what's your opinion of the company's present situation?*; *I wonder how she got herself into this situation*
(b) job; *I'm looking for a more permanent situation*
(c) place where something is; *the hotel is in a very pleasant situation by the sea*

① **sit up**
['sɪt 'ʌp] *verb*
(a) to sit with your back straight; *sit up straight!*
(b) to move from a lying to a sitting position; *he's too weak to sit up*; *he sat up in bed to eat his breakfast*
(c) to stay up without going to bed; *we sat up playing cards until 2 A.M.*

① **six**
[sɪks]
(a) number 6; *he's six (years old)* *we're having some people over for drinks at six (o'clock)* *there are only six chocolates left in the box - who's eaten the rest?*; **the six hundreds** = the years from AD 600 to 699 (NOTE: compare **the sixth century**)
(b) **six-pack** = pack containing six bottle or cans; *they brought a six-pack of beer to the party*

② **sixteen**
[sɪksˈtin]
number 16; *he'll be sixteen next month*; *the train leaves at seven sixteen (7:16)* **the sixteen hundreds (1600s)** = the years from 1600 to 1699 (NOTE: compare **the sixteenth century**)

② **sixteenth (16th)**
[sɪksˈtinθ] *adjective & noun*
she came in sixteenth in the race; *the sixteenth of July or July the sixteenth (July 16)* *her sixteenth birthday is on Tuesday*; **the sixteenth century** = the years from 1500 to 1599 (NOTE: compare **the sixteen hundreds**; Note also that with dates **sixteenth** is usually written **16: July 16, 1935; October 16, 1991:** (say "October sixteenth"); with names of kings and queens **sixteenth** is usually written **XVI: King Louis XVI** (say: "King Louis the Sixteenth")

② **sixth (6th)**
[sɪksθ] *adjective & noun*

his office is on the sixth floor; *what is the sixth letter of the alphabet?*; *ten minutes is a sixth of an hour*; *the sixth of August or August the sixth (August 6) tomorrow is her sixth birthday*; **the sixth century** = the period from AD 500 to 599 (NOTE: in dates **sixth** is usually written **6: January 6, 1984:** (say "January sixth"); with names of kings and queens **sixth** is usually written **VI: King Edward VI** (say "King Edward the Sixth")

③ **sixtieth (60th)**
['sɪkstɪəθ] *adjective & noun*
he was sixtieth out of 120 people who entered the race; *a minute is a sixtieth of an hour and a second is a sixtieth of a minute*; *don't forget - it's dad's sixtieth birthday tomorrow*

① **sixty**
['sɪksti]
number 60; *she's sixty (years old)* *the chair cost more than sixty dollars ($60)* *she's in her sixties* = she's between 60 and 69 years old; **the (nineteen) sixties (1960s)** = the years from 1960 to 1969 (NOTE: **sixty-one (61)**, **sixty-two (62)**, etc., but **sixty-first (61st)**, **sixty-second (62nd)**, etc.)

① **size**
[saɪz]
1 *noun*
measurements of something, how big something is, or how many there are of something; *their garage is about the same size as our house*; *the school has an Olympic size swimming pool*; *he takes size ten in shoes*; *what size collars do you take?*; *the size of the staff has doubled in the last two years*
2 *verb*
to size someone up = to judge someone's qualities; *she quickly sized him up*

② **sizzle**
['sɪzl] *verb*
to make a sound like food cooking in oil or fat; *the sausages were sizzling in the pan*

① **skate**
[skeɪt]
1 *noun*
pair of skates = a pair of boots with sharp blades attached for sliding on ice; *(informal)* **to put your skates on** = to hurry, to get going; *you'll have to put your skates on if you want to catch that train*
2 *verb*
(a) to move on ice wearing skates; *she skated across the lake*; *we're going skating tomorrow*
(b) **to skate around something** = to try to avoid mentioning something; *they skated around the subject of salaries*

① **skater**
['skeɪtər] *noun*
person who goes on skates; *there were dozens of skaters on the frozen lake*

③ **skating**
['skeɪtɪŋ] *noun*
sport of sliding on ice on skates; *skating is very popular in Canada*; **skating rink** = special area for ice skating, or for playing ice hockey, etc.; *there used to be an indoor skating rink here*

② **skeleton**
['skelɪtn] *noun*
(a) all the bones that make up a body; *they found the skeleton of a rabbit in the shed*; *he demonstrated using the skeleton in the biology lab*; *(informal)* **skeleton in the closet** = embarrassing secret that a family is trying to keep hidden; *after the newspaper report, I wonder how many more skeletons they have hidden in the closet*
(b) **skeleton staff** = a few staff left to carry on with essential work while most of the workforce is away; *only a skeleton staff will be on duty over the Christmas period*
(c) **skeleton key** = key that will fit several different doors in a building; *I've locked myself out of my office - could you let me have the skeleton key, please?*

④ **skeptical**
['skeptɪkl] *adjective*
doubtful, who doubts; *you seem skeptical about his new plan*; *I'm skeptical of the success of the experiment*; *he listened to her with a skeptical look on his face*

② **sketch**
[sketʃ]
1 *noun*
(a) rough quick drawing; *he made a sketch of the church*
(b) short comic situation on TV or radio; *the show takes the form of a series of short sketches* (NOTE: plural is **sketches**)
2 *verb*
to make a quick rough drawing of something; *she was sketching the old church*; *he sketched out his plan on the back of an envelope*

② **ski**
[ski]
1 *noun*
one of two long flat pieces of wood, etc., which are attached to your boots for sliding over snow; *we always rent skis when we get to the ski resort*; *someone stole my new pair of skis*; **ski instructor** = person who teaches people how to ski; **ski boots** = boots to wear when skiing; **ski resort** = town in the mountains where people stay when on a skiing vacation; **water skis** = larger pieces of wood for attaching under your feet for sliding over water
2 *verb*
to travel on skis; *the mountain rescue team had to ski to the site of the accident*; *we skied down to the bottom of the slope without falling*; *she broke her arm skiing*; **to go skiing** = to slide over snow on skis as a sport; *we go skiing in*

Switzerland every winter (NOTE: **skis - skiing - skied**)

③ **skid**
[skɪd]
1 *noun*
sideways slide in a vehicle; *the car went into a skid and hit a lamppost*
2 *verb*
to slide sideways in a vehicle suddenly because the wheels do not grip the surface; *if you brake too hard on ice you're likely to skid* (NOTE: **skidding - skidded**)

② **skiing**
['skiːɪŋ] *noun*
the sport of sliding on skis; *skiing is a very popular sport*; *have you ever done any skiing?*

② **skill**
[skɪl] *noun*
ability to do something well; *portrait painting needs a lot of skill*; *he acquired management skills through running his own business*; *he's a chair maker of great skill*

② **skilled**
[skɪld] *adjective*
(a) being able to do something well, using a particular skill; *she's a skilled dance instructor*; *we need skilled computer analysts*; **skilled workers** *or* **skilled labor** = workers who have special skills or who have had a long period of training
(b) needing a particular skill; *nursing and other skilled professions*

② **skillet**
['skɪlɪt] *noun*
frying pan; *a heavy metal skillet*; *we fried the fish in an iron skillet*

② **skillful**
['skɪlfəl] *adjective*
showing a lot of skill; *he's a very skillful painter*

① **skim**
[skɪm] *verb*
(a) to remove things floating on a liquid; *skim the soup to remove the fat on the surface*
(b) to dash over the surface of something; *flies skimmed across the surface of the lake*; **to skim through a book** = to read a book quickly (NOTE: **skimming - skimmed**)

① **skin**
[skɪn]
1 *noun*
(a) outer surface of the body; *the baby's skin is very smooth*; **to be just skin and bones** = to be extremely thin
(b) outer surface of a fruit or vegetable; *this orange has a very thick skin*; *you can cook these new potatoes with their skins on*
(c) thin layer on top of a liquid; *I don't like the skin on the top of chocolate pudding*
(d) *(informal)* **to have a thick skin** = to be able to stand a lot of criticism; *luckily he has a thick skin or he would get very annoyed at what the newspapers say about him*; **by the skin of your**

teeth = only just; *he escaped from the enemy by the skin of his teeth*; **to jump out of your skin** = to be very frightened or surprised; *the bang made her jump out of her skin*

2 *verb*

to remove the skin from an animal, fish, etc.; *ask the butcher to skin the rabbit for you* (NOTE: skinning - skinned)

① **skinny**

['skɪnɪ] *adjective*

(*informal*) very thin; *a tall skinny guy walked in*; *she has very skinny legs* (NOTE: skinnier - skinniest)

① **skip**

[skɪp] *verb*

(**a**) to run along partly hopping and partly jumping; *the children skipped happily down the lane*

(**b**) to jump over a rope which you turn over your head; *the girls were skipping*

(**c**) to miss part of something; *she skipped the middle chapters and went on to read the end of the story*; *I'm not hungry, I'll skip the dessert* (NOTE: skipping - skipped)

② **skipper**

['skɪpər] *noun*

captain of a ship; *we reported to the skipper that there was water in the ship's engine room*

② **skirt**

[skɜrt]

1 *noun*

piece of clothing worn by women covering the lower part of the body from the waist down; the lower part of a dress starting at the waist; *she started wearing jeans to work, but the supervisor told her to wear a skirt*

2 *verb*

(**a**) to go around; *the main road skirts (around) the town*

(**b**) not to touch; *he only skirted around the subject, and didn't deal with it in depth at all*

① **skull**

[skʌl] *noun*

the bones that form the head; *they found a human skull when they were digging*; *the scan showed a fracture of the skull or a skull fracture*

① **sky**

[skaɪ] *noun*

space above the earth which is blue during the day and where the moon and stars appear at night; *what makes the sky blue?*; *it's going to be a beautiful day - there's not a cloud in the sky*; *the wind carried the balloon high up into the sky*

① **skyscraper**

['skaɪskreɪpər] *noun*

very tall building; *did you like the scene in the movie where he is trying to climb up the skyscraper?*; *they're planning a 100-story skyscraper near the park*

③ **slab**

[slæb] *noun*

flat square block of stone, etc.; *a slab of concrete fell from the building*

③ **slack**

[slæk] *adjective*

(**a**) not tight; *the ropes are slack - pull on them to make them tight*

(**b**) not busy; *business is slack at the end of the week* (NOTE: slacker - slackest)

① **slam**

[slæm]

1 *noun*

grand slam = winning a series of competitions, such as all the main tennis competitions held in a year; *the men's grand-slam winner*; *she's aiming for the grand slam*

2 *verb*

(**a**) to bang a door shut; to shut with a bang; *when he saw me, he slammed the door in my face*; *the wind slammed the door and I was locked out*

(**b**) **to slam on the brakes** = to apply the brakes fast when driving; *he slammed on the brakes and just stopped in time to avoid an accident* (NOTE: slamming - slammed)

④ **slander**

['slændər]

1 *noun*

spoken statement which is not true and which damages a person's reputation; *what she said about me is slander*; *to sue somebody for slander*

2 *verb*

to damage someone's reputation by saying things about him or her which are not true; *they slandered him at yesterday's press conference*; *compare* LIBEL

② **slang**

[slæŋ] *noun*

popular words or phrases used by certain groups of people but which are not used in correct style; *don't use slang in your essay*; *slang expressions are sometimes difficult to understand*

② **slant**

[slænt]

1 *noun*

slope; *the garden is on a slant, which makes cutting the lawn difficult*

2 *verb*

to slope; *the path slants down the side of the hill*

① **slap**

[slæp]

1 *noun*

(**a**) blow given with your hand flat; *she gave him a slap in the face*; **a slap on the wrist** = small punishment, slight criticism; *the department had a slap on the wrist from the inspectors, but nothing serious*

(**b**) friendly gesture; *he congratulated her with a slap on the back*

2 *verb*

(a) to hit with your hand flat; *she slapped his face*

(b) to tap as a friendly gesture; *they all slapped him on the back to congratulate him*

(c) to put something down flat on a surface; *she slapped the notes down on the table*; *they just slapped some paint on the wall to cover up the dirty marks* (NOTE: **slapping - slapped**)

3 *adverb*

to run slap (bang) into something = to run right into something; *he rode his bike slap into middle of the procession*

② **slash**
[slæʃ]
1 *noun*

(a) long cut with a knife; *he had a nasty slash on his arm*; *she took a knife and made a slash across the painting*

(b) printing sign (/) used to show an alternative; *all members/visitors must sign the register* (NOTE: also called a **virgule**. Plural is **slashes**)

2 *verb*

(a) to make a long cut with a knife; *he slashed the painting with a kitchen knife*

(b) to reduce a price, the number of something, sharply; *the management has slashed the number of staff*; *prices have been slashed in all departments*

② **slate**
[sleɪt] *noun*

(a) dark blue or gray stone which splits easily into thin sheets; *slate is used for making roofs*

(b) thin piece of this stone used to cover a roof; *the slates were already piled up ready to be put on the roof*

(c) list of candidates for a position; *the Democratic slate in the state elections*

③ **slaughter**
['slɔtər]
1 *noun*

(a) killing of animals; *these lambs will be ready for slaughter in a week or so*

(b) killing of many people; *the wholesale slaughter of innocent civilians* (NOTE: no plural)

2 *verb*

(a) to kill animals (usually for meat); *here's the shed where the cattle are slaughtered*; *the infected pigs have been slaughtered*

(b) to kill many people at the same time; *thousands of civilians were slaughtered by the advancing army*

① **slave**
[sleɪv]
1 *noun*

person who belongs to someone legally and works for him; *in the old days, slaves worked on the tobacco plantations*; *(informal)* **slave driver** = boss who makes his staff work too hard

2 *verb*

to slave (away) = to work hard; *here am I slaving away over a hot stove, and you just sit and watch TV*

② **sleek**
[slik] *adjective*

smooth, shiny, which is looked after very well; *after dinner we walked across the sleek lawns to the river* (NOTE: **sleeker - sleekest**)

① **sleep**
[slip]
1 *noun*

rest (usually at night) with your eyes closed, and when you are not conscious of what is happening; *I need eight hours' sleep a night*; *try to get a good night's sleep - there's a lot of work to be done tomorrow*; *he always has a short sleep after lunch*; **to go to sleep** *or* **to get to sleep** = to start sleeping; *don't make all that noise - Daddy's trying to get to sleep*; *she put the light out and went to sleep* (NOTE: you can also say **to fall asleep**); **to put someone to sleep** = (i) to make someone go to sleep; (ii) to give someone an anesthetic; *her boring speeches would send anyone to sleep*; **to put an animal to sleep** = to kill an animal that is old or sick; **my foot has gone to sleep** = my foot has lost all feeling; **not to lose any sleep over something** = not to worry about something; *it's such a tiny sum that I won't lose any sleep over it*

2 *verb*

(a) to be asleep, to rest with your eyes closed not knowing what is happening around you; *she never sleeps for more than six hours each night*; *he slept through the whole of the TV news*; *don't make any noise - Daddy's trying to sleep*; *(informal)* **to sleep like a log** = to sleep very deeply; *after his 12-mile walk he slept like a log*

(b) **cabin that sleeps four** = a cabin with enough beds for four people

(c) *(informal)* **to sleep with someone** *or* **to sleep together** = to have sexual relations with someone; *they say he's slept with almost all the girls in the office* (NOTE: **sleeps - sleeping - slept** [slept])

③ **sleeping**
['slipɪŋ] *adjective*

(a) who is asleep; *the firemen picked up the sleeping children and carried them to safety*

(b) **sleeping bag** = warm bag for sleeping in a tent, etc.; **sleeping car** = car on a train with beds where passengers can sleep; *there are three sleeping cars on the overnight express*; **sleeping partner** = partner who has a share in a business but does not work in it; **sleeping pill** *or* **sleeping tablet** = medicine that makes you go to sleep

① **sleepy**
['slipi] *adjective*

(a) feeling ready to go to sleep; *sitting in front of the TV made him sleepier and sleepier*; *the children had a busy day - they were getting very sleepy by 8 o'clock*; *some cough medicines make you feel sleepy*; *if you feel sleepy, don't* *try to drive the car*

(b) quiet; *a sleepy little country town* (NOTE: **sleepier - sleepiest**)

② **sleet**
[sliːt] *noun*
snow mixed with rain; *the temperature fell and the rain turned to sleet*

② **sleeve**
[sliːv] *noun*
(a) part of a piece of clothing that covers your arm; *the sleeves on this shirt are too long; he was wearing a blue shirt with short sleeves*
(b) *(informal)* to keep something up your sleeve = to have a plan which you are keeping secret

① **slept**
[slept] *see* SLEEP

① **slice**
[slaɪs]
1 *noun*
(a) thin piece cut off something to eat; *can you cut some more slices of bread?; have a slice of chocolate cake; would you like another slice of ham?*
(b) *(in sports)* way of hitting a ball, which makes it go in a different direction
2 *verb*
(a) to cut into slices; *she stood at the table slicing the tomato for lunch;* **sliced bread** = loaf of bread that has already been cut into slices before you buy it; *(informal)* **the best thing since sliced bread** = the most wonderful new invention in the world
(b) to hit a ball so that it spins off to one side; *he sliced the ball into the net*

① **slid**
[slɪd] *see* SLIDE

① **slide**
[slaɪd]
1 *noun*
(a) metal or plastic structure for children to go down lying or sitting; *there are swings and a slide in the local playground*
(b) small piece of movie that can be projected on a screen; *she put the screen up and showed us the slides of her last trip; there will be a slide show in the town hall;* **slide projector** = apparatus for showing pictures from slides onto a screen
(c) steady fall; *the government must act to stop the slide in the dollar*
2 *verb*
(a) to move without difficulty over an even surface; *the drawer slides in and out easily; the automobile slid to a stop; the children were sliding on the ice when it broke; the van has a sliding door which doesn't shut properly*
(b) to move something easily; *he slid the money over the table*
(c) to move down steadily; *the dollar slid after interest rates were lowered;* **to let things slide** = to allow things to get worse, not to bother if

things get worse; *she doesn't look after herself - she's just letting things slide* (NOTE: **sliding - slid** [slɪd])

② **slight**
[slaɪt]
1 *adjective*
not very big; *their daughter's a slight young girl; all you could see was a slight movement of the cat's tail; there was a slight improvement in his condition during the night; she wasn't the slightest bit nervous* (NOTE: **slighter - slightest**)
2 *noun*
(formal) insult; *I treat that remark as a slight on our reputation*

③ **slightly**
[ˈslaɪtli] *adverb*
not very much; *he was only slightly hurt in the car crash; this bank is offering a slightly better interest rate; I only know him slightly*

① **slim**
[slɪm]
1 *adjective*
thin, not fat; *how do you manage to stay so slim?; a slim, fair-haired boy; she looks slimmer in that dress* (NOTE: **slimmer - slimmest**)
2 *verb*
to diet in order to become thin; *she started slimming down before her summer vacation* (NOTE: **slimming - slimmed**)

③ **slime**
[slaɪm] *noun*
slippery substance, which forms in ponds or on hard damp surfaces; *is there anything which will get this green slime off the path?*

③ **slimy**
[ˈslaɪmi] *adjective*
unpleasant and slippery; *what's this slimy mess at the bottom of the fridge?* (NOTE: **slimier - slimiest**)

② **sling**
[slɪŋ]
1 *noun*
(a) type of leather loop, used for throwing stones; *David threw a stone with his sling, and killed Goliath*
(b) bandage attached round your neck, used to support an injured arm; *he's going around with his arm in a sling*
2 *verb*
to hold up or to put something to hang; *he slung his jacket over the back of his chair; she slung her bag over her shoulder* (NOTE: **slinging - slung** [slʌŋ])

① **slip**
[slɪp]
1 *noun*
(a) mistake; *he made a couple of slips in adding up the bill;* **a slip of the tongue** = a mistake in speaking
(b) small piece of paper; *as she opened the book a small slip of paper fell out; he handed her the*

green slip with the reference number on it ; **deposit slip** = piece of paper stamped by the bank clerk to prove that you have paid money into your account; **pink slip** = notice that you are being dismissed from a job; **sales slip** = paper showing that an article was bought at a certain store on a certain day; *goods can be exchanged only on production of a sales slip* **(c) pillow slip** = cloth bag to cover a pillow; *the girl had forgotten to change the pillow slips* **(d)** small person; *she was just a slip of a girl* **(e)** woman's underwear like a thin dress or skirt, worn under other clothes; *she bought a black slip* **(f)** men's underwear which is very short; *he wore a white vest and slip* **2** *verb* **(a)** to slide (and fall) by mistake; *he slipped and dropped all his shopping; he was using the electric saw when it hit something hard and slipped*; **slipped disk** = painful state where one of the disks in the spine has moved out of place **(b)** to slide out of something which is holding you tight; *the dog slipped its lead and ran away* **(c)** to push something without being seen; *he slipped the keys into his pocket* **(d)** to go down to a lower level; *profits slipped badly last year; the dollar slipped on the foreign exchanges* **(e)** to go quickly; *I'll just slip out to the Post Office with this letter* (NOTE: **slipping - slipped**)

③ **slip on**
['slɪp 'ɒn] *verb*
(a) to slip because you step on something; *he slipped on the wet leaves and broke his ankle* **(b)** to put clothes on quickly; *she slipped on pants and a sweatshirt and ran into the street*

① **slippers**
['slɪpərz] *noun*
light comfortable shoes worn indoors; *he ran out into the street in his slippers; put your slippers on if your shoes hurt*

② **slit**
[slɪt]
1 *noun*
long cut or narrow opening; *she peered through a slit in the curtains* **2** *verb*
to make a slit; *he slit open the envelope with a knife* (NOTE: **slitting - slit**)

② **slogan**
['sləʊgn] *noun*
phrase that is easy to remember and is used in publicity for a product or for a political party, etc.; *we are using the slogan "Smiths can make it" on all our publicity; the walls of the factory were covered with election slogans*

① **slope**
[sləʊp]
1 *noun*
(a) surface or piece of ground that is not level, and rises or falls; *the land rises in a gentle slope*

to the church; they stopped halfway down the slope; **ski slope** = specially prepared and marked slope for skiing down a mountain **(b)** angle at which something slopes; *the hill has an slope of 1 in 10, put the car in low gear* **2** *verb*
to go upwards or downwards; *the path slopes toward the house*

② **slot**
[slɒt]
1 *noun*
(a) long thin hole; *a coin has got stuck in the slot of the parking meter; put the system disk into the left-hand slot on the front of your computer*; **slot machine** = machine for gambling, or that provides drinks, cigarettes, plays music, etc., when you put a coin into a slot **(b)** set time available for doing something; *the airline has asked for more takeoff and landing slots at the airport* **2** *verb*
to slot into = to fit into a slot; *the program has been slotted for the evening schedule* (NOTE: **slotting - slotted**)

① **slow**
[sləʊ]
1 *adjective*
(a) not fast, needing a long time to do something; *luckily, the automobile was only going at a slow speed; she is the slowest walker of the group; the company is very slow at answering my letters; sales got off to a slow start but picked up later* **(b)** showing a time that is earlier than the right time; *the office clock is four minutes slow* (NOTE: **slower - slowest**)
2 *verb*
to go slowly; *the procession slowed as it reached the cathedral* **3** *adverb*
not fast; *go slow at the intersection*

① **slow down**
['sləʊ 'daʊn] *verb*
(a) to go more slowly; *the van had to slow down as it came to the traffic light; please slow down, I can't keep up with you* **(b)** to make something go more slowly; *the snow slowed the traffic down on the freeway* **(c)** to work less hard; *you should slow down a bit - you're doing too much*

③ **slowdown**
['sləʊdaʊn] *noun*
becoming less busy, especially when employees slow down production on purpose; *there has been a recent slowdown in the company's expansion*

① **slowly**
['sləʊli] *adverb*
not fast; *luckily, the truck was going very slowly when it hit the fence; the group walked slowly round the exhibition; speak more slowly so that everyone can understand; see also* SURELY

④ **slug**
[slʌg] *noun*
common garden animal like a snail with no shell; *slugs have eaten all my lettuces*

③ **slump**
[slʌmp]
1 *noun*
(a) rapid fall; *there has been slump in sales*
(b) period of economic collapse with high unemployment and loss of trade; *economists argued about the reasons for the slump*
2 *verb*
(a) to sit or to lie down in a clumsy way; *he sat slumped on a chair doing his homework; at the end of the meal, she just slumped down onto the sofa*
(b) to fall fast; *the dollar slumped on the foreign exchange markets*

② **sly**
[slaɪ] *adjective*
cunning and slightly dishonest; *the sly old girl - she never told me she had won the lottery*

② **smack**
[smæk]
1 *noun*
hitting someone with your hand flat as a punishment; *if you pull the cat's tail you'll get a smack*
2 *verb*
(a) to punish someone by hitting them with your hand flat; *she smacked the little girl for being rude*
(b) to put something down noisily; *she smacked the report down on the table and walked out of the room*
(c) to smack your lips = to make a loud noise with your lips to show you are hungry or would like to have something; *she smacked her lips as he mentioned diamonds*
(d) to show signs of; *the whole affair smacks of fraud*
3 *adverb*
straight, directly; *the bus ran smack into a tree*

① **small**
[smɔl]
1 *adjective*
(a) little, not big; *small automobiles use less gas than large ones; the house is too big for us, so we're selling it and buying a smaller one; she only paid a small amount for that clock; the guidebook isn't small enough to carry in your pocket; these pants are already too small for him*; **small business** = little company with a low turnover and few employees; **small businessman** = man who runs a small business; **small change** = loose coins; no importance; *do you have any small change, I only have notes?; my problem is small change compared to your difficulty*
(b) young; *big farm animals can frighten small children*
(c) small fortune = a lot of money; *those shoes cost me a small fortune; she earns a small fortune selling postcards*
(d) small hours = early in the morning; *we went on talking until the small hours (of the morning)* (NOTE: **smaller - smallest**)
2 *noun*
the small of the back = the middle part of your back below and between the shoulder blades; *something is tickling me in the small of my back*

③ **small-scale**
['smɔlskeɪl] *adjective*
working in a small way, with few staff and not much money; *it is a small-scale operation with only three full-time staff*; **a small-scale enterprise** = a small business; *compare* LARGE-SCALE

① **smart**
[smɑrt]
1 *adjective*
(a) well-dressed or elegant; *a smart young man asked me if he could use my cell phone; he looked very smart in his uniform*
(b) clever; *it was smart of her to note the automobile's license plate; he's the smartest of the three brothers*; **smart card** = plastic credit card with a computer chip in it
(c) sharp (blow); *she gave a smart knock on the door*
(d) rapid; *the horse set off at a smart pace; (informal)* **look smart!** = hurry up! (NOTE: **smarter - smartest**)
2 *verb*
to hurt with a burning feeling; *the place where I burnt my hand is still smarting*
3 *noun*
sharp pain from a blow; *he remembered the smart of the slap on his cheek*

① **smash**
[smæʃ]
1 *verb*
(a) to break into pieces; *he dropped the plate and it smashed to pieces*
(b) to break something to pieces; *demonstrators smashed the windows of squad cars*
(c) to break a record, to do better than a record; *she smashed the world record; six records were smashed at the Olympics*
(d) to go violently; *the train smashed into the automobile; the crowd smashed through the railings*
(e) *(in tennis)* to play a fast stroke, sending the ball down to the ground
2 *noun*
(a) sound of something breaking into pieces; *we could hear the smash of plates being dropped in the kitchen*
(b) bad accident; *six people are feared killed in the train smash*
(c) *(in tennis)* fast stroke, sending the ball down to the ground

① **smell**
[smel]
1 *noun*
(a) one of the five senses, which you can feel through your nose; *animals have a better sense of smell than humans; these dogs have a very keen sense of smell and can sniff out even a minute quantity of drugs*
(b) something which you can sense with your nose; *I love the smell of coffee coming from the restaurant; he can't stand the smell of fried onions; there's a smell of burning or there's a burning smell coming from the kitchen; she noticed a smell of gas downstairs*
(c) unpleasant thing which you can sense with your nose; *there's a smell or a funny smell or a nasty smell in the shed*
2 *verb*
(a) to notice the smell of something; *can you smell gas?; wild animals can smell humans; my nose is blocked - I can't smell anything; just smell these roses!; Mmm! - I can smell waffles!*
(b) to make a smell; *I don't like cheese that smells too strong; what's for dinner? - it smells very good!; there's something that smells funny in the bathroom; it smelled of gas in the kitchen*
(c) to bring your nose close to something to smell it; *she bent down to smell the roses* (NOTE: **smelling - smelled** *or* **smelt** [smelt])

② **smile**
[smaɪl]
1 *noun*
way of showing that you are pleased, by turning your mouth up at the corners; *the dentist gave me a friendly smile; she had a big smile as she told them the good news*
2 *verb*
to show that you are pleased by turning your mouth up at the corners; *that girl has just smiled at me; everyone smile please - I'm taking a photo!*

① **smoke**
[sməʊk]
1 *noun*
(a) white, gray or black cloud, given off by something that is burning; *the restaurant was full of cigarette smoke; clouds of smoke were pouring out of the upstairs windows; two people died from breathing toxic smoke; smoke alarms are in all the hotel rooms*
(b) *(informal)* time when you are smoking a cigarette; *cigarettes aren't allowed in the office, so everyone goes outside for a quick smoke; I'm dying for a smoke!*
(c) to go up in smoke = (i) to be burnt; (ii) to fail, not to work; *his entire art collection went up in smoke in the fire; all her plans for buying a bigger house have gone up in smoke*
2 *verb*
(a) to give off smoke; *two days after the fire, the ruins of the factory were still smoking*

(b) to breathe in smoke (from a cigarette, pipe, etc.); *everyone was smoking even though the signs said "no smoking"; she doesn't smoke much - only one or two cigarettes a day; you shouldn't smoke if you want to play football; I've never seen her smoking a cigar before;* **he smokes like a chimney** = he smokes a lot of cigarettes
(c) *(in a house)* **the chimney smokes** = the fire sends smoke into the room instead of taking it up the chimney
(d) to preserve food (such as meat, fish, bacon, cheese) by hanging it in the smoke from a fire; *a factory where they smoke fish;* **smoked salmon** = salmon that has been cured by smoking, and is served in very thin slices; *a plate of smoked salmon sandwiches*

② **smoker**
[ˈsməʊkər] *noun*
person who smokes cigarettes; *we only have two members of staff who are smokers;* **heavy smoker** = person who smokes a lot of cigarettes; *he was a heavy smoker and died of lung cancer*

② **smoking**
[ˈsməʊkɪŋ] *noun*
action of smoking cigarettes, etc.; *smoking is bad for your health; smoking is not allowed on the subway;* **"no smoking"** = do not smoke here; *I always sit in the "no smoking" part of the restaurant*

② **smooth**
[smuð]
1 *adjective*
(a) with no bumps, with an even surface; *the smooth surface of a polished table; the baby's skin is very smooth; velvet has a smooth side and a rough side;* **to take the rough with the smooth** = to accept that there are bad times as well as good times
(b) with no sudden movements; *dirt in the fuel tank can affect the smooth running of the engine; the plane made a very smooth landing*
(c) *(person)* too polite, with manners which are too good; *that car salesman's a bit too smooth for my liking* (NOTE: **smoother - smoothest**)
2 *verb*
(a) to make something smooth with a tool or with your hand; *she smoothed the sheets and adjusted the pillows; the edge of the shelf needs smoothing, it's still quite rough;* **to smooth the way for someone** *or* **something** = to make things easy for someone or something; *the retiring president cut taxes to smooth the way for his successor;* **to smooth things over** = to settle an argument; *after the quarrel, I called round at her house to try and smooth things over*
(b) to spread something gently over a surface; *smooth the cream over your face and let it dry*

② **smother**
[ˈsmʌðər] *verb*
(a) to kill someone by stopping them from

breathing; *they took the kittens away from the cat and smothered them*
(b) to cover; *a chocolate cake simply smothered in cream*

② **smudge**
[smʌdʒ]
1 *noun*
dirty mark; *there is a smudge on the top corner of the photograph*
2 *verb*
to make a dirty mark, such as by rubbing ink which is not dry; *don't touch the paint until it's dry, otherwise you'll smudge it*

④ **smug**
[smʌg] *adjective*
happy with what you have done; *he accepted his prize with a smug look on his face*

② **smuggle**
['smʌgl] *verb*
(a) to take goods into a country without declaring them to customs; *they tried to smuggle cigarettes into the country; we had to smuggle the spare parts over the border*
(b) to take something into or out of a place illegally; *the knives were smuggled into the prison by a someone visiting a prisoner; we'll never know how they smuggled the letter out*

① **snack**
[snæk]
1 *noun*
a light meal, a small amount of food; *we didn't have time to stop for a proper lunch, so we just had a snack on the way*
2 *verb*
to eat a snack; *she never eats proper meals, she just snacks all the time*

③ **snack bar**
['snæk 'bɑr] *noun*
small simple restaurant where you can buy a light meal; *he met the girl by chance at a snack bar*

④ **snag**
[snæg] *noun*
little problem, thing which prevents you from doing something; *we've run into a snag: there are no flights to the island on Sundays*

① **snake**
[sneɪk]
1 *noun*
long animal that has no legs and moves along the ground by moving from side to side; *is this snake safe to handle?*
2 *verb*
to bend and twist; *the Great Wall of China snakes over the mountains*

② **snap**
[snæp]
1 *noun*
(a) **cold snap** = short period of sudden cold weather; *a cold snap can have disastrous effects on my tomatoes*

(b) little metal fastener for clothes, in two parts which you press to attach together; *she fastened all the snaps on her daughter's jacket*
(c) *(informal)* something very easy; *the math test was a snap*
2 *adjective*
sudden; **a snap decision** = a decision taken in a hurry; *they carried out a snap check or a snap inspection of the passengers' baggage; the government called a snap election*
3 *verb*
(a) to say something in a sharp angry tone; *he was tired after a long day in the office, and snapped at the children; the manager snapped at the store assistant, but it wasn't her fault*
(b) to break sharply with a dry noise; *the branches snapped as he walked through the wood*
(c) **to snap your fingers** = to make a clicking noise with your middle finger and thumb; *they sat snapping their fingers in time to the music;* **to snap into place** = to make a click when fitting together; *push gently on the videocassette until it snaps into place; (informal)* **to snap out of it** = to stop being depressed; *he told her to snap out of it* (NOTE: **snapping - snapped**)

② **snarl**
[snɑrl]
1 *noun*
angry sound made by a wild animal; *as she opened the door of the cage she heard a snarl*
2 *verb*
to make an angry sound; *the tiger snarled as he approached its cage*

② **snatch**
[snætʃ]
1 *noun*
little piece of something heard; *in the evening, I heard snatches of song from across the lake* (NOTE: plural is **snatches**)
2 *verb*
to grab something rapidly; *he came beside her on his bike and snatched her purse; I didn't have time for a proper meal, but I snatched a sandwich; she snatched a few hours' sleep in the break room*

① **sneak**
[snik]
1 *verb*
to go quietly without being seen; *she sneaked into the room; the burglar sneaked up to the house, hidden by the trees;* **to sneak up on someone** = to creep up behind someone without being noticed (NOTE: the past tense is **sneaked** or **snuck**)
2 *noun*
(informal) person who tells an adult what another child has done; *you promised not to say anything, you little sneak!*

② **sneakers**
['snikərz] *noun*
sport shoes with soft, flat rubber soles; *I walk to work in my sneakers*

③ **sneer**
['snɪər]
1 *noun*
unpleasant smile; *he held the axe in his hand and looked at her with a sneer*
2 *verb*
to give someone a nasty smile or to speak in a way that shows that you don't approve; *he sneered at her attempts to speak French*

① **sneeze**
[sniz]
1 *noun*
automatic action to blow air suddenly out through your mouth and nose because the inside of your nose tickles; *coughs and sneezes spread diseases*
2 *verb*
to make a sneeze; *the smell of roses makes me sneeze*; *he has hay fever and can't stop sneezing*; *(informal)* it's not to be sneezed at = you should not refuse it; *it's a good offer and not to be sneezed at*

① **sniff**
[snɪf]
1 *noun*
breathing in air through your nose; *the dog gave a sniff at the plate before licking it*; *he gave a little sniff and walked out of the store*
2 *verb*
(a) to breathe in air through your nose; *he sniffed and said "I can smell fish"*; *the customs inspection is very strict, a dog is taken round to sniff (at) each bag and suitcase*; *(informal)* it's not to be sniffed at = you should not refuse it; *a free ticket with Air Canada is not to be sniffed at*; to sniff something out = to discover something by smelling; *the dogs sniffed out drugs hidden in her bag*
(b) to breathe in air through your nose because you have a cold; *he's coughing and sniffing and should be in bed*; *don't sniff, use your hanky*
(c) to breathe in gas from glue; *the police caught them sniffing glue*; *see also* GLUE

① **snow**
[snəʊ]
1 *noun*
water which falls as light white ice crystals in cold weather; *two feet of snow fell during the night*; *the highest mountains are always covered with snow*; *children were out playing in the snow*; *we went for a skiing vacation and there was hardly any snow*; snow tires = special tires with thick treads, for use when driving on snow (NOTE: no plural: **some snow, a lot of snow**)
2 *verb*
(a) to fall as snow; *look - it's started to snow!*; *it snowed all day, and the streets were blocked*; *they say it's going to snow tomorrow*; *it hardly ever snows here in March* (NOTE: in this meaning, **to snow** is always used with the subject **it**)

(b) to trick someone by smooth talking; *she was snowed by the salesman*

① **snowball**
['snəʊbɔl]
1 *noun*
ball made with snow; *they were throwing snowballs at passing cars*; *I tried to make a snowball but the snow was too dry*
2 *verb*
to get steadily bigger; *the protests started slowly and then snowballed into mass demonstrations*

③ **snowed in**
['snəʊd 'ɪn] *adjective*
blocked by snow and not able to travel; *we were snowed in, and sat indoors playing cards*

③ **snowed under**
['snəʊd 'ʌndər] *adjective*
(informal) with too much work; *we're snowed under with orders*; *he's snowed under with work*

④ **snow job**
['snəʊ 'dʒɒb] *noun*
trying to trick someone by smooth talking; *the salesman gave us a big snow job*

① **snowman**
['snəʊmæn] *noun*
model of a man made of snow; *the children made a snowman in the school playground*; *when the sun came out the snowman melted* (NOTE: plural is **snowmen**)

② **snowmobile**
['snəʊməbil] *noun*
small motor vehicle on skis, used for traveling over snow; *he traveled into town on his snowmobile*

② **snowplow**
['snəʊplaʊ] *noun*
vehicle that has a scoop or blade in front for clearing snow from roads; *the snowplows have cleared the main highways*

② **snowstorm**
['snəʊstɔrm] *noun*
storm when the wind blows and snow falls; *all flights are delayed because of the snowstorm*

③ **snuck**
[snʌk] *see* SNEAK

① **snug**
[snʌg] *adjective*
warm, comfortable, out of the cold; *here we are, sitting by the fire, warm and snug*

② **snuggle**
['snʌgl] *verb*
to curl yourself up to be warm; *they snuggled under their blankets*

① **so**
[səʊ]
1 *adverb*
(a) *(showing how much)* *it's so cold that the lake is covered with ice*; *we liked the Grand Canyon so much that we're going there again*

on vacation next year; *the soup was so hot that I couldn't eat it*

(b) very much; *she was so kind to us when we were children*; *the movie was not so boring - some parts were very exciting*

(c) also; *she was late and so was I*; *the children all caught the flu, and so did their teacher*; *I like apples - so do I*; *he's a good cook and so is his wife*; *the teacher will be late and so will everyone else*

(d) *(showing that the answer is "yes")* *was your car completely smashed? - I'm afraid so*; *will you be coming to the party? - I hope so!*; *are they going to be at the meeting? - I suppose so*

2 *conjunction*

(a) and this is the reason why; *it was snowing hard so we couldn't go for a walk*; *she has the flu so she can't come to the office*

(b) **so that** = in order that; *people riding bikes wear yellow vests so that drivers can see them easily*; **so as to** = in order to; *they had to run to the station so as not to miss the train*

3 *adjective*

(a) *(informal)* **just so** = exactly as it should be; *she always wants everything to be just so*

(b) *(to emphasize, replacing an adjective)* *he's very rude, and his wife is even more so*; *see also* AND SO ON

◇ **so far**

['səʊ 'fɑr] *adverb*

until now; *he said he would lend me his book but so far he hasn't done so*; *how do you like your new job so far?*

◇ **so there!**

[sə 'ðeər] *phrase*

(making a decision) that's my opinion, and it's none of your business; *if you don't want to come with me, I'll go all by myself, so there!*

◇ **so what**

[səʊ 'wɒt] *phrase*

what does it matter; *he may be annoyed - so what?*; *so what if I fail my test, I can always take it again*

① **soak**

[səʊk]

1 *noun*

action of lying in a bath for a long time; *after a game of softball, it's good to have a soak in a hot bath*

2 *verb*

(a) to put something in a liquid for a time; *dry beans should be soaked in cold water overnight before cooking*

(b) to get or to make very wet; *I forgot my umbrella and got soaked*; *the rain soaked the soil*

① **soap**

[səʊp]

1 *noun*

(a) substance that you wash with, made from oils and usually with a pleasant smell; *there's no soap left in the bathroom*; *I've put a new bar of*

soap in the kitchen; *there is a liquid soap dispenser in the men's restroom* (NOTE: no plural in this meaning: **some soap, a bar** *or* **a cake** *or* **a piece of soap**)

(b) **soap (opera)** = serial story on television about the daily lives of a set of characters; *he sat in bed watching daytime soaps*

2 *verb*

to cover with soap; *there's no need to soap yourself all over, just your legs and feet*

③ **soar**

[sɔr] *verb*

(a) to fly high up into the sky; *the rocket went soaring into the night sky*

(b) *(of a bird)* to fly high in the sky without moving its wings; *we watched the big bird soaring above the mountain*

(c) to go up very quickly; *food prices soared during the cold weather* (NOTE: do not confuse with **sore**)

② **sob**

[sɒb] *verb*

to cry, taking short breaths; *she lay sobbing on the bed* (NOTE: **sobbing - sobbed**)

③ **sober**

['səʊbər] *adjective*

(a) not drunk; *I wasn't drunk after the party - I was stone cold sober*

(b) serious; *the sober truth is that we can't afford it*; *it was a very sober gathering, nobody laughed or made a joke*

(c) dark with no bright colors; *she was wearing a sober dark gray suit*

③ **so-called**

['səʊkɔld] *adjective*

word or name that is not true; *one of her so-called friends stole her watch*

④ **soccer**

['sɒkər] *noun*

football, a game played between two teams of eleven players with a round ball which can be kicked or headed, but not carried; *he played soccer at school and then joined his local team*; *they went to a soccer match last Saturday*; *let's have a game of soccer*; *he spends all his time watching soccer on TV*; *rival soccer fans fought on the street*; *they seem to play a different type of soccer from us* (NOTE: the game is called **football** in most countries, but is generally called **soccer** in the U.S.A. to distinguish it from American football)

① **social**

['səʊʃl] *adjective*

(a) referring to people as a group, to human society; *the demand for equal treatment for all classes can lead to social conflict*; *an area with very serious social problems*; **social science** = study of people and the society they live in, including history, economics, etc.; **Social Security** = system of payments made by the U.S. government to people upon retirement; *he lives on social security payments*; **social**

services = state services to help people with family problems; *the children are being looked after by social services*; **social system** = the way in which a society is organized; **social worker** = person who works to help people with family or financial problems; *the old people get a weekly visit by a social worker*; *see also* EXCLUSION
(b) referring to friendly contact with other people; *we are organizing some social events for the visiting students*; *not being able to make conversation is a terrible social handicap*; **social life** = life involving other people, going to parties, movies, etc.; *with two babies under two years old, they have no social life whatsoever*; *we don't have much social life nowadays*

④ **socialism**
['səʊʃəlɪzm] *noun*
(a) ideas and beliefs of socialists, that the means of production and distribution should belong to the people, that people should be cared for by the state and that all wealth should be shared equally; *his book explains the principles of socialism*
(b) political system where the state is run on these principles; *under socialism, this factory was owned by the state*

④ **socialist**
['səʊʃəlɪst]
1 *adjective*
believing in socialism, being in favor of social change, wider sharing of wealth and of industry and welfare run by the state; **Socialist Party** = political party that follows the principles of socialism; *the Socialist Party won the last elections*
2 *noun*
person who believes in socialism; *he's been a socialist all his life*

③ **socialize**
['səʊʃəlaɪz] *verb*
to meet people for friendly talk and activities; *the outing is an opportunity for people to socialize and get to know each other better*; *we don't socialize much with the people on our block*

③ **society**
[sə'saɪəti] *noun*
(a) a large group of people, usually all the people living in a country, considered as an organized community; *society needs to be protected against criminals*; *a free and democratic society*; *a member of society*; **consumer society** = type of society where consumers are encouraged to buy goods
(b) club or association of people who have the same interests; *he belongs to the local drama society* (NOTE: plural is **societies**)

① **sock**
[sɒk]
1 *noun*
(a) piece of clothing worn on your foot inside a shoe; *he's almost ready - he only has to put on his socks and shoes*; *I've just bought a pair of socks*; **knee socks** = long socks which go up as far as the knees; *(informal)* **to pull your socks up** = to try to do better; *he'll have to pull his socks up or he'll lose his job*
(b) *(informal)* punch; *she gave him a sock in the jaw*
2 *verb*
(informal) to hit someone hard; *she socked the mugger on the jaw*

② **socket**
['sɒkɪt] *noun*
(electric) socket = device in a wall with holes into which a plug can be fitted, to allow electricity to flow; *there is a socket on the wall that you can plug the vacuum cleaner into*; *this plug doesn't fit that socket*; **light socket** = part of a lamp where the bulb is fitted

① **soda**
['səʊdə] *noun*
(a) soda (water) = water made fizzy by adding carbon dioxide; *I like club soda mixed with fruit juice*
(b) soda (pop) = sweet soft drink containing soda water; *would you like a soda with your meal?*
(c) drink made from soda water and ice cream; *I ordered a chocolate soda*

② **sofa**
['səʊfə] *noun*
long comfortable seat with a soft back; *he was asleep on the sofa*

① **soft**
[sɒft] *adjective*
(a) not hard, which moves easily when pressed; *there are big soft armchairs in the lobby of the hotel*; *I don't like soft seats in an automobile*; *do you like soft ice cream?*
(b) not loud; *when she spoke, her voice was so soft that we could hardly hear her*; *soft music was playing in the background*
(c) not bright; *soft lighting makes a room look warm*
(d) soft on = not severe toward; *judges were accused of being soft on crime*; **to have a soft spot for** = to like very much; *she has a soft spot for her gym instructor* (NOTE: **softer - softest**)

① **softball**
['sɒftbɔl] *noun*
game similar to baseball but played with a larger, softer ball; *they play softball in high school*

② **soft drink**
['sɒft 'drɪŋk] *noun*
drink that is not alcoholic; *I'll just have a soft drink because I'm driving*; *we've got soft drinks for the children*

② **soften**
['sɒfn] *verb*
to make something soft, to become soft; *heat the chocolate gently to soften it*; *her voice softened when she spoke to the children*; **to soften someone up** = to make someone weaker before

asking for something, or before launching an attack; *can you try and soften him up a bit before I ask to borrow the car?*; *bombing raids were made to soften up the enemy defenses*

③ **softly**
['sɒflɪ] *adverb*

(a) in a gentle way; *I touched her arm softly*

(b) quietly, not loudly; *she spoke so softly that we couldn't hear what she said*; *the burglars crept softly up the stairs*

② **software**
['sɒftweər] *noun*

computer programs that are put into a computer to make it work, as opposed to the machine itself; *what word processing software do you use?*; compare HARDWARE (NOTE: no plural)

② **soggy**
['sɒgɪ] *adjective*

wet and soft; *if you put tomato sandwiches into plastic bags they will go soggy* (NOTE: **soggier - soggiest**)

① **soil**
[sɔɪl]

1 *noun*

earth in which plants grow; *put some soil in the plant pot and then sow your flower seeds*; *this soil's too poor for growing fruit trees*; *the farm has 150 acres of rich black soil*

2 *verb*

to make dirty; *his overalls were soiled by black oil and rust*; *use more laundry powder if the clothes are heavily soiled*

④ **solar**
['səʊlər] *adjective*

referring to the sun; **solar energy** *or* **solar power** = electricity produced from the radiation of the sun; *my calculator runs on solar power*; *solar power is a renewable source of energy*; **solar system** = the sun and the planets that orbit round it; *there are nine planets in the solar system*

① **sold**
[səʊld] *see* SELL

② **soldier**
['səʊldʒər]

1 *noun*

person serving in the army; *here's a photograph of my father as a soldier*; *we were just in time to see the soldiers march past*; *enemy soldiers blew up the bridge*; *the children are playing with their toy soldiers*

2 *verb*

to soldier on = to continue doing something, in spite of difficulties; *even though sales are down, we must soldier on*; *she's soldiering on, reviewing for the exam*

② **sold out**
['səʊld 'aʊt] *adjective*

no longer in stock, because all the stock has been sold; *the book was sold out within a week*

② **sole**
[səʊl]

1 *adjective*

only; belonging to one person; *their sole aim is to make money*; *she was the sole survivor from the crash*; *I have sole responsibility for what goes on in this office*; *he has the sole right to it* = he is the only person allowed to use it; **sole agency** = agreement to be the only person to represent a company or to sell a product in a certain area; *he has the sole agency for Ford automobiles*

2 *noun*

(a) the underneath side of your foot; *he tickled the soles of her feet*

(b) main underneath part of a shoe, but not the heel; *these shoes need repairing - I've got holes in both soles*

(c) small flat white sea fish; *he ordered grilled sole* (NOTE: plural in this meaning is **sole**)

3 *verb*

to put a new sole on a shoe; *I want these shoes soled and heeled, please* (NOTE: do not confuse with **soul**)

④ **solely**
['səʊlɪ] *adverb*

(a) only; *the machine was designed solely for that purpose*

(b) without other people being involved; *he was solely to blame for what happened*

④ **solemn**
['sɒləm] *adjective*

(a) serious and formal, when it would be wrong to laugh; *the doctor looked very solemn and shook his head*; *at the most solemn moment of the ceremony someone's cellular phone rang*

(b) that should be treated as very serious and not to be broken; *he made a solemn promise never to smoke again*; **solemn and binding agreement** = agreement that is not legally binding, but which all parties are supposed to obey

④ **solicitor**
[sə'lɪsɪtər] *noun*

person who comes to the door collecting for charity

① **solid**
['sɒlɪd]

1 *adjective*

(a) hard, not liquid; *the water in the tank had frozen solid*; *she is allowed some solid food*

(b) firm, strong; *is the table solid enough to stand on?*; *his wealth is built on a solid base of property and shares*

(c) made only of one material; *the box is made of solid silver*

(d) **for six hours solid** = for six hours without stopping; *negotiations went on for nine hours solid* (NOTE: **solider - solidest**)

2 *noun*

(a) hard substance that is not liquid; *many solids melt when heated, and become liquids*

(b) food, as opposed to drink; *the baby is beginning to eat solids*

② **solo**
['səʊləʊ]
1 *noun*
piece of music played or sung by one person alone; *she played a piano solo* (NOTE: plural is **solos**)
2 *adjective*
done by one person alone; *she gave a solo performance during the concert; a piece for solo trumpet; he crashed on his first solo flight*
3 *adverb*
done by one person alone; *he flew solo across the Atlantic*

③ **solution**
[sə'luːʃn] *noun*
(a) action of solving a problem; *the solution of the problem is taking longer than expected*
(b) answer to a problem; *the manager came up with a solution to the computer problem; we think we have found a solution to the problem of where to stay on vacation; the solutions to the puzzle are at the back of the book*
(c) mixture of a solid substance in a liquid; *wash your eye in a weak salt solution*

① **solve**
[sɒlv] *verb*
to find an answer to; *the loan will solve some of his financial problems; we have called in an expert to solve our computer problem; he tried to solve the puzzle*

① **some**
[sʌm]
1 *adjective & pronoun*
(a) a certain number of; *some young drivers drive much too fast; some books were damaged in the fire; some days it was so hot that we just stayed by the swimming pool all day; can you cut some more slices of bread?; she bought some oranges and bananas; we've just picked a basket of apples - would you like some?;* **some of** = a few; *some of the students are sick; some of these apples are too green*
(b) a certain amount; *can you buy some bread when you go to town?; can I have some more coffee?; to some extent it's an interesting problem; her illness is of some concern to her family*
(c) *(followed by a singular noun)* referring to a person or thing you cannot identify; *some man just knocked on the door and tried to sell me a magazine; I read it in some book I borrowed from the library; we saw it in some store or other on Fifth Avenue*
(d) *(referring to a period of time or a distance)* *don't wait for me, I may be some time; their house is some way away from the train station* (NOTE: **some** is used with plural nouns and with nouns that have no plural: **some people, some apples, some bread,** etc.)
2 *adverb*
(formal) approximately, more or less; *some fifty people came to the meeting; the house is some sixty years old*

① **somebody** *or* **someone**
['sʌmbədi or 'sʌmwɒn] *pronoun*
a certain person; *somebody is sitting on my chair; I can't talk any longer - there's someone waiting outside the telephone booth; somebody phoned about an order; I know someone who can fix your car*

② **somehow**
['sʌmhaʊ] *adverb*
by some means, although you don't know how; *somehow we must get back home by 6 o'clock; the work has to be done somehow*

① **someone**
['sʌmwɒn] *see* SOMEBODY

④ **someplace**
['sʌmpleɪs] *adverb*
somewhere; *haven't I seen you before someplace?; is there someplace else we can talk?*

② **somersault**
['sʌmərsɒlt] *noun*
rolling over and over, head first; *he did a couple of somersaults on the mat*

② **something**
['sʌmθɪŋ] *pronoun*
(a) a certain thing; *there's something soft at the bottom of the bag; something's gone wrong with the TV; can I have something to drink, please?; there's something about her that I don't like*
(b) important thing; *come in and sit down, I've got something to tell you*
(c) approximate amount; *it cost us something around fifty dollars; something like 20% of the students can't spell*
(d) approximate name; *he's called Nick or Dick, or something like that; it's a fish or shellfish or something, anyway it lives in salt water*

② **sometimes**
['sʌmtaɪmz] *adverb*
occasionally, at various times; *sometimes it gets quite cold in June; sometimes the automobile starts easily, and sometimes it won't start at all; she sometimes comes to see us when she's in town on business*

② **somewhat**
['sʌmwɒt] *adverb*
(formal) more than a little, rather; *it's a somewhat difficult question to answer; their system is somewhat old-fashioned; we were somewhat surprised to see him there*

① **somewhere**
['sʌmweər] *adverb*
(a) someplace, in or at a certain place which is not specified; *I left my umbrella somewhere when I was in Cheyenne; let's go somewhere else, this restaurant is full; his parents live somewhere in Montana*
(b) **somewhere around** *or* **somewhere between** *or* **somewhere in the region of** = approximately;

somewhere between 50 and 60 people turned up for the meeting; *he has collected somewhere in the region of 25,000 books*

① **son**

[sʌn] *noun*

male child of a father or mother; *they have a large family - two sons and four daughters*; *her son has got married at last*; *their youngest son is in the hospital*

① **song**

[sɒŋ] *noun*

(a) words which are sung; *she was singing a song in the bath*; *the group's latest song has just come out on CD*; *the soldiers marched along, singing a song*

(b) *(informal)* **for a song** = for very little money; *she bought it for a song in the local market*; **he made a great song and dance about it** = he made a great fuss about it; *they made a terrible song and dance about having to wait for a taxi*

(c) special sound made by a bird; *I'm sure that's the song of a robin - look, he's over there!*

① **soon**

[sun] *adverb*

(a) in a short time from now; *don't worry, we'll soon be in Madison*; *it will soon be time to go to bed*; *can't we meet any sooner than that?*; *the fire started soon after 11 o'clock*

(b) **as soon as** = immediately; *please phone the office as soon as you get to the hotel*; *as soon as I put the phone down it rang again*; *the boss wants to see you as soon as possible*

(c) **just as soon** = would rather, would prefer; *I'd just as soon stay at the office than go to the party*; see also RATHER, SOONER (NOTE: **sooner - soonest**)

① **sooner**

['sunər] *adverb*

(a) **sooner or later** = at some time in the future; *sooner or later, they will realize that they need to save as much money as possible*; *she drives so fast that sooner or later she'll have an accident*; **sooner rather than later** = quickly rather than taking a long time; *it would be wise to reduce the staff sooner rather than later*

(b) **the sooner the better** = it would be better to do it as soon as possible; *she should consult a lawyer, and the sooner the better*

(c) **would just as soon do something** = would prefer to do something; *do you want to come with us? - no, I'd just as soon stay at home*; *we'd just as soon live in Chicago than Detroit*; see also RATHER, SOON

③ **soothe**

[suð] *verb*

to relieve pain, to make something less painful, to calm; *the pharmacist gave me a cream to soothe the rash*; *she managed to soothe their hurt feelings*

④ **soothing**

['suðɪŋ] *adjective*

which relieves pain, which calms; *the nurse put some soothing cream on my rash*; *I find this piece by Mozart very soothing*

④ **sophisticated**

[sə'fɪstɪkeɪtɪd] *adjective*

(a) knowing a lot about the way people behave, and what is the current fashion; *they think smoking makes them look sophisticated*

(b) cleverly designed, complicated (machine); *his office is full of the latest and most sophisticated computer equipment*

① **sore**

[sɔr]

1 *adjective*

(a) rough and sensitive; painful; *he can't play tennis because he has a sore elbow*; **sore throat** = infected throat, which is red and hurts when you swallow or speak; *she has a sore throat and has lost her voice*; *(informal)* **to stick out like a sore thumb** = to be easily seen

(b) angry; *he's sore at her for telling the boss about him* (NOTE: **sorer - sorest**)

2 *noun*

small wound on the skin; *he had sores on his back from lying in bed for a long time*; **cold sore** = infected spot on the lips caused by a virus (NOTE: do not confuse with **soar**)

② **sorry**

['sɒri]

1 *adjective*

to be sorry = to be sad about; *I'm sorry I can't stay for dinner*; *he trod on my foot and didn't say he was sorry*; *everyone was sorry to hear you had been sick*; **not to be sorry** = to be quite happy; *we weren't sorry to see him go* = we were glad when he left; **to feel sorry for someone** = to be sympathetic about someone's problems; to pity someone; *we all feel sorry for her - her family is always criticizing her*; **to feel sorry for yourself** = to be miserable; *he's feeling very sorry for himself - he's just been laid off* (NOTE: **sorrier - sorriest**)

2 *interjection; used to excuse yourself*

sorry! I didn't see that table had been reserved; *can I have another chocolate, please? - sorry, I haven't any left*

② **sort**

[sɔrt]

1 *noun*

(a) type, kind; *there were all sorts of people at the meeting*; *I had an unpleasant sort of day at the office*; *what sorts of ice cream do you have?*; *do you like this sort of TV show?*

(b) *(informal)* **sort of** = rather, more or less; *she was sort of expecting your phone call*; *we're all feeling sort of upset*

(c) *(informal)* **of sorts** = not very good; *he made a speech of sorts at the ceremony*

2 *verb*

(a) to arrange in order or groups; *the apples are sorted according to size before being packed*; *the votes are sorted then counted*; **sorting**

office = department in a post office where letters are put in order according to their addresses

(b) to put things in order; *she is sorting index cards into the order of their dates*

② **sort out**
['sɔrt 'aʊt] *verb*

(a) to settle a problem; *did you sort out the hotel bill?*

(b) to put things in order or in groups; *I must sort out the papers in this drawer; until they're sorted out, we shan't know which are our files and which are theirs*

(c) to collect or select things of a particular kind from a mixed group of things; *sort out all the blue forms and bring them to me, please*

③ **sought**
[sɔt]
see SEEK

① **soul**
[soʊl] *noun*

(a) the spirit in a person, the part which is believed by some people to go on existing after a person dies; *do you believe your soul lives on when your body dies?; from the depths of his soul he longed to be free*

(b) to be the life and soul of a party = to make a party go well

(c) person; *she's a cheerful old soul; poor soul! he sits at home all day, and doesn't have anyone to go to see him* (NOTE: do not confuse with **sole**)

① **sound**
[saʊnd]
1 *noun*

noise, something which you can hear; *sounds of music came from the street; I thought I heard the sound of guns; please can you turn down the sound on the TV when I'm on the phone?; she crept out of her bedroom and we didn't hear a sound;* **speed of sound** = the rate at which sound travels; *the Concorde flies faster than the speed of sound;* **I don't like the sound of that** = I do not think that is a very good idea

2 *verb*

(a) to make a noise; *sound your horn when you come to a corner; they sounded the alarm after two prisoners escaped*

(b) to seem; *it sounds as if he's made an unfortunate choice; the book sounds interesting according to what I've heard;* **that sounds strange** = it seems strange to me; **that sounds like an automobile** = I think I can hear an automobile; **that sounds like my father** = (i) that is like the way my father talks; (ii) I think I can hear my father coming; (iii) that's typical of the way my father usually behaves

3 *adjective*

(a) in good condition, not rotten; *most of the walls of the house are sound* ; **he is of sound mind** = he is not mad

(b) sensible, which can be trusted; *he gave us some very sound advice*

(c) deep (sleep); *I was awoken from a sound sleep by the ringing of the telephone* (NOTE: **sounder - soundest**)

4 *adverb*

deeply; *the children were sound asleep when the police came*

④ **sound out**
['saʊnd 'aʊt] *verb*

to sound someone out about something = to ask someone's opinion about something; *I'll sound out the other members of the committee to see what they think*

② **soup**
[sup] *noun*

liquid food that you eat hot from a bowl at the beginning of a meal, usually made from meat, fish or vegetables; *we have onion soup or mushroom soup today; does anyone want soup?; we started the meal with chicken soup; a bowl of hot soup is always welcome on a cold day; if you're hungry, open a can of soup;* **soup bowl** *or* **soup plate** *or* **soup spoon** = special bowl, plate or spoon for eating soup (NOTE: no plural: **some soup, a bowl of soup**)

② **sour**
[saʊər]
1 *adjective*

(a) with a sharp bitter taste; *if the lemonade is too sour, add some sugar; nobody likes sour milk; (informal)* **sour grapes** = feeling bitter about something which you want but can't have; *he said that the latest model was no better than the older ones, but that was just sour grapes*

(b) **to go sour** = (i) to take on a sharp taste; (ii) to stop work and become unpleasant; *the cream has gone sour; after a few weeks, the whole deal began to go sour* (NOTE: **sourer - sourest**)

2 *verb*

to make unpleasant; *relations between the two countries have been soured by the incident*

④ **source**
[sɔrs] *noun*

(a) place where something comes from; *I think the source of the infection is in one of your teeth; the source of the river is in the mountains; you must declare income from all sources to the tax office*

(b) person or thing which is the cause of something; *the children are a constant source of worry; polluted water is a possible source of disease*

① **south**
[saʊθ]
1 *noun*

(a) direction facing toward the sun at the middle of the day, direction to your left when you are facing the direction where the sun sets; *look south from the mountain, and you will see the city in the distance; the city is to the south of the mountain range; the wind is blowing from the south*

(b) part of a country to the south of the rest; *the south of the country is warmer than the north*; *she went to live in the south of Nebraska*; **the South** = southeastern part of the U.S.

2 *adjective*

referring to the south; *the south coast is popular for vacations*; *cross to the south side of the river*; **south wind** = wind that blows from the south

3 *adverb*

toward the south; *many birds fly south for the winter*; *go due south for two miles, and you will see the town on your left*; *the river flows south into the Pacific Ocean*

③ **South America**
['sauθ ə'merikə] *noun*
southern part of the American continent containing Brazil, Argentina, Chile and several other countries; *Brazil is the largest country in South America*; *he is hiding from the police somewhere in South America*

① **southeast**
[sauθ'ist] *adjective, adverb & noun*
direction between south and east; *Southeast Asia is an important trading area*; *Atlanta is in the southeast of the U.S.A.*; *the river runs southeast from here*

① **southern**
['sʌðən] *adjective*
of the south; *the southern part of the country is warmer than the north*

② **South Pole**
['sauθ 'pəul] *noun*
furthest point at the south of the Earth; *they were trying to reach the South Pole*

③ **southwest**
[sauθ'west] *adjective, adverb & noun*
direction between south and west; *we need to head southwest for two miles*; *Arizona is in the southwest of the United States*; *the Southwest (southwest U.S.)*

③ **souvenir**
[suvə'niər] *noun*
thing bought which reminds you of the place where you bought it; *I bought a scarf as a souvenir of my vacation in Alberta*; *keep it as a souvenir of your visit*; *they were selling souvenir programs of the show*; **souvenir store** = store that sells souvenirs; *there are too many souvenir stores on the seafront*

③ **sow**
[səu]
1 *verb*
to put seeds into soil so that they send out shoots and become plants; *peas and beans should be sown in April*; *sow the seed in fine soil* (NOTE: do not confuse with **sew**; note also: **sowing - sowed - has sown** [səun])
2 *noun* [sau]
female pig; *our sow has had eight little pigs*

④ **soy**
[sɔi] *noun*

plant that produces beans which have a high protein and fat content; *meat substitutes are often made from soy*; **soy beans** = beans of the soy plant, which have a high protein and fat content and are low in carbohydrates; **soy sauce** = dark sauce with a salt flavor, made from soy beans; *Chinese dishes are often seasoned with soy sauce*

① **space**
[speis]
1 *noun*
(a) empty place between other things; *there's a space to park your automobile over there*; *write your name and reference number in the space at the top of the paper*
(b) area that is available for something; *his desk takes up too much space*; **floor space** = area of the floor in a building; **office space** = area available for offices or used by offices; *we are looking for extra office space for our new staff*
(c) **(outer) space** = area beyond the Earth's atmosphere; *the first man in space was the Russian Yuri Gagarin*; *this is a photograph of Earth taken from space*; *could someone be sending messages from outer space?*; **space shuttle** = type of plane that is launched by a rocket, then flies in space and returns eventually to Earth so that it can be used for another trip; *the space shuttle will be launched next week*; **space station** = satellite which goes round the Earth and in which people can live and carry out scientific experiments
(d) **open space** = open country, with no buildings; *Canada's wide open spaces*
(e) **in a short space of time** = in a little time; *you can't do that in a short space of time, you'll need several weeks at least*; *in a very short space of time the burglars had filled their van with furniture*
2 *verb*
to space things out = to place things at intervals, with gaps between them; *payments can be spaced out over a period of ten years*; *make sure the text is correctly spaced out on the page*

③ **space bar**
['speis 'bar] *noun*
long bar at the bottom of a typewriter or computer keyboard which inserts a single space into text; *I use my thumb on the space bar when I type*

④ **spacious**
['speiʃəs] *adjective*
very large, with plenty of space; *they live in a spacious apartment in Boston*; *the spacious landscapes of the Midwest*

② **spade**
[speid] *noun*
(a) common gardening tool with a wide square blade at the end of a long handle, used for digging; *he handed me the spade and told me to start digging*; **to call a spade a spade** = to say

exactly what you think without trying to hide your opinions by being polite; *if she's not satisfied, she's not afraid to call a spade a spade*

(b) small tool, used by children to play in sand; *the children took their buckets and spades to the beach*

(c) spades = one of the black suits in a pack of cards; *my last two cards were the ten and the ace of spades*; *she played the king of spades* (NOTE: the other black suit is **clubs; hearts** and **diamonds** are the red suits)

① **spaghetti**
[spəˈgeti] *noun*
long thin strips of pasta, cooked and eaten with a sauce; *I ordered spaghetti with a special cream sauce*

① **Spain**
[speɪn] *proper noun*
country in southern Europe, to the south of France and the east of Portugal; *lots of people go to Spain for their vacations*; *we are going to Spain next July* (NOTE: capital: **Madrid**; people: **the Spanish** *or* **the Spaniards**; language: **Spanish**; currency: **peseta, euro**)

③ **span**
[spæn]
1 *noun*
(a) width of wings, of an arch, etc.; *each section of the bridge has a span of fifty feet*
(b) length of time; *over a span of five years* or *over a five-year span*
2 *verb*
to stretch across space or time; *her career spanned thirty years*; *the bridge will span the river* (NOTE: **spanning - spanned**)

① **Spanish**
[ˈspænɪʃ]
1 *adjective*
referring to Spain; *I want to change my dollars into Spanish money*
2 *noun*
language spoken in Spain and many countries of Latin America; *he's studying French and Spanish as part of his business course*

④ **spanner**
[ˈspænər] *noun*
metal tool with an opening which fits round a nut and which can be twisted to undo the nut or tighten it; *I need a smaller spanner to tighten this little nut*

② **spare**
[speər]
1 *adjective*
extra, not being used; *I always take a spare pair of shoes when I travel*; **spare parts** = pieces used to put in place of broken parts of an automobile, etc.; *I can't get spare parts for that type of washing machine*; **spare time** = time when you are not at work; *he built himself an automobile in his spare time*; **spare tire** = fifth tire carried in an automobile to replace one that

has a puncture; *when he took it out, he found the spare tire had a puncture as well*
2 *noun*
spares = spare parts, pieces used to mend broken parts of an automobile, etc.; *we can't get spares for that make of washing machine*; *it's difficult to get spares for the automobile because they don't make this model anymore*
3 *verb*
(a) *(asking someone if they can do without something)* *can you spare your assistant to help me for a day?*; *can you spare about five minutes to talk about the problem?*; *if you have a moment to spare, can you clean the car?*; *can you spare a dollar for a cup of coffee?*
(b) not to show or give; *the driver's test was awful, but I'll spare you the details*
(c) to spare someone *or* **someone's life** = not to kill someone; *he pleaded with the soldiers to spare his life*; *no one was spared, all the people in the village were killed*

③ **spareribs**
[ˈspeərɪbz] *noun*
pork ribs cooked in a savory sauce; *we are having spareribs for the barbecue*

① **spark**
[spɑrk]
1 *noun*
little flash of fire or of light; *sparks flew as the train went over the junction*
2 *verb*
to spark (off) = to make something start; *the shooting of the teenager sparked off a riot*; *the proposal to close the station sparked anger amongst travelers*

② **sparkle**
[ˈspɑrkl]
1 *noun*
bright light; *there was a sparkle in her eyes as she answered the phone*
2 *verb*
(a) to shine brightly; *her jewels sparkled in the light of the candles*; *his eyes sparkled when he heard the salary offered*
(b) *(of person)* to be lively; *she was sparkling with enthusiasm*

④ **spark plug**
[ˈspɑrk ˈplʌg] *noun*
(in an automobile engine) device that is screwed into the top of a cylinder and produces a spark to light the fuel; *if the spark plugs are dirty the engine won't run very well*; *the garage put in a new set of spark plugs*

④ **spat**
[spæt] *see* SPIT

① **speak**
[spik] *verb*
(a) to say words, to talk; *she spoke to me when the meeting was over*; *he walked past me without speaking*; *he was speaking to the mailman when I saw him*; *the manager wants to speak to you about sales in Africa*; **to speak**

your mind = to say exactly what you think; *(informal)* **speak for yourself** = that's what you think, I don't agree; *as we are both quite fat... - speak for yourself!*
(b) to be able to say things in (a foreign language); *we need someone who can speak Russian*; *he speaks English with a British accent*; *you will have to brush up your Japanese as my mother speaks hardly any English*
(c) to make a speech; *do you know who is speaking at the conference?*
(d) so to speak = as you might say; *he's a very close friend, we're like brothers, so to speak* (NOTE: **speaking - spoke** [spǝuk] **- has spoken** [ˈspǝukn])

① **speaker**
[ˈspikǝr] *noun*
(a) person who speaks; *we need an Arabic speaker to help with the tour*; *he is a popular speaker* = many people come to hear him give speeches at meetings
(b) loudspeaker; *one of the speakers doesn't work*; *see also* LOUDSPEAKER
(c) the presiding officer of an organization which makes laws; *the Speaker of the House presides over a meeting of the House of Representatives*

> COMMENT: in the U.S. House of Representatives, the Speaker is elected by other Congressmen

② **speak up**
[ˈspik ˈʌp] *verb*
(a) to speak louder; to say what you have to say in a louder voice; *can you speak up please - we can't hear you at the back!*
(b) to make your opinions known strongly; *he's not afraid to speak up when he thinks someone has been badly treated*; **to speak up for** = to show your support for; *he was the only person who spoke up for me at the inquiry*

① **spear**
[ˈspɪǝr]
1 *noun*
long pointed throwing stick, used as a weapon; *they kill fish with spears*
2 *verb*
to push something sharp into something to catch it; *spearing fish is not easy*; *she managed to spear a sausage on the barbecue grill with her fork*

① **special**
[ˈspeʃǝl]
1 *adjective*
(a) referring to something or someone who is not ordinary but has a particular importance or use; *this is a very special day for us - it's our twenty-fifth wedding anniversary*; *a report from our special correspondent in Beijing*; *he has a special pair of scissors for cutting metal*; *this is a special news report*

(b) nothing special = very ordinary; *there is nothing special about his new automobile*; *did anything happen at the meeting? - no, nothing special*
2 *noun*
particular dish on a menu; **today's special** *or* **special of the day** = special dish prepared for the day and not listed in the printed menu; *I'll have the special, please*

② **specialist**
[ˈspeʃǝlɪst]
1 *noun*
(a) person who knows a lot about something; *you should go to a tax specialist for advice*
(b) doctor who specializes in a certain branch of medicine; *he was referred to a heart specialist*
2 *adjective*
specialized; *does he have any specialist knowledge of international currency transactions?*

③ **specialize**
[ˈspeʃǝlaɪz] *verb*
to specialize in something = to study one particular subject; to produce one thing in particular; *at college, she specialized in Roman history*; *the company specializes in electronic components*

③ **specially**
[ˈspeʃǝli] *adverb*
particularly, for a special occasion; *the cake was specially made*; *see also* ESPECIALLY

③ **species**
[ˈspiʃɪz] *noun*
group of living things, such as animals or plants, which can breed with each other; *several species of butterfly are likely to disappear as the weather becomes warmer* (NOTE: plural is **species**)

④ **specific**
[spǝˈsɪfɪk] *adjective*
referring precisely to something; *can you be more specific about what you're trying to achieve?*; *I gave specific instructions that I was not to be disturbed*; *is the money intended for a specific purpose?*

③ **specifically**
[spǝˈsɪfɪkli] *adverb*
particularly; *I specifically said I didn't want a blue door*; *the advertisement is specifically aimed at people over 60*

④ **specification**
[spesɪfɪˈkeɪʃǝn] *noun*
detailed information about what is needed; *she gave full specifications about how she wanted the kitchen to be laid out*; **the finished product is not up to specification** *or* **does not meet our specifications** = the product is not made in the way which was stated; **job specification** = very detailed description of what is involved in a job; *there was nothing about word processing in my job specification*

③ **specify** [ˈspesəfaɪ] *verb*
to give clear details of what is needed; *please specify full details of the address to which the goods must be sent*; *do not include sales tax on the invoice unless specified*

① **specimen** [ˈspesɪmən] *noun*
(a) sample of something taken as standard; *the bank asked for a specimen signature for their records*
(b) example of a particular kind of creature or thing; *he has some very rare specimens in his butterfly collection*; *this is a fine specimen of this kind of tree*

② **specs** [speks] *noun*
(informal) = SPECTACLES; *I can't see anything without my specs!*

③ **spectacle** [ˈspektəkl] *noun*
(a) something very impressive to look at; show; *the flower display is a spectacle not to be missed*; *for sheer spectacle you can't beat a military parade*
(b) **spectacles** = two pieces of plastic or glass in a frame which you wear in front of your eyes to help you see better; *have you seen my spectacles anywhere?*; *she has to wear spectacles to read*; *I can't remember where I put my spectacles*; *he's worn spectacles since he was a child* (NOTE: **spectacles** are also called **eyeglasses**)

② **spectacular** [spekˈtækjʊlər]
1 *adjective*
very impressive to see or watch; *the parade of tanks was even more spectacular than last year*; *she was very ill, but has made a spectacular recovery*
2 *noun*
impressive show; *a musical spectacular featuring over a hundred singers and dancers*

③ **spectator** [ˈspekteɪtər] *noun*
person who watches an event; *thousands of spectators watched the tennis match*

④ **speculate** [ˈspekjʊleɪt] *verb*
(a) **to speculate about** = to make guesses about; *we are all speculating about what's going to happen*
(b) to take a risk in business which you hope will bring profit; *he made a lot of money by speculating on the Stock Exchange*

③ **sped** [sped]
see SPEED

① **speech** [spiːtʃ] *noun*
(a) formal talk given to an audience; *he made some notes before giving his speech*; *he wound up his speech with a story about his father*; *who will be making the speech at the awards ceremony?* (NOTE: plural in this meaning is **speeches**)
(b) speaking, making sounds with the voice which can be understood; *teaching speech to deaf children can be a very slow process*
(c) spoken language; *this word is more often used in speech than in writing*; **freedom of speech** = being able to say what you want; *the protesters demanded freedom of speech*; **parts of speech** = different types of words, such as nouns, verbs, etc., which are classified according to their use; *nouns, adjectives and verbs are different parts of speech*

① **speed** [spiːd]
1 *noun*
rate at which something moves or is done; *the bus was traveling at a high speed when it crashed*; *your automobile will use less gas if you go at an even speed of 56 miles per hour*; *the speed with which they repaired the gas leak was incredible*; *the train travels at speeds of over 300 miles per hour*; **speed bump** = small raised part in a road; *they have built speed bumps in the road to slow down the traffic*
2 *verb*
(a) to move quickly; *the ball sped across the ice*
(b) to go too fast; *he was arrested for speeding on the freeway* (NOTE: **speeding - sped** [sped] *or* **speeded - has sped**)

② **speed limit** [ˈspiːd ˈlɪmɪt] *noun*
fastest speed at which automobiles are allowed to go legally; *the speed limit in towns is 30 miles per hour*; *what is the speed limit on this highway?*

③ **speed up** [ˈspiːd ˈʌp] *verb*
(a) to go faster; *she sped up as she came to the traffic light*
(b) to make something happen faster; *can't we speed up production?*; *we are aiming to speed up our delivery times*

② **spell** [spel]
1 *noun*
(a) short period; *there was a spell of cold weather over the holiday weekend*; *the warm spell will last until Thursday*
(b) words which the person speaking hopes will have a magic effect; *her wicked sister cast a spell on the princess*
2 *verb*
to write or say correctly the letters that make a word; *how do you spell your last name?*; *we spelled his name wrong on the envelope*; *W-O-R-R-Y spells "worry"*; **to spell out** = to explain very clearly; *let me spell out the consequences of this course of action*

① **spelling**
['spelɪŋ] *noun*
correct way in which words are spelled; *she is a good journalist, but her spelling is awful*

① **spend**
[spend] *verb*
(a) to pay money; *I went shopping and spent a fortune*; *why do we spend so much money on food?*
(b) to use time doing something; *he wants to spend more time with his family*; *she spent months arguing with the tax people*; *don't spend too long on your homework*; *why don't you come and spend the weekend with us?*
(NOTE: **spending - spent** [spent])

③ **spending**
['spendɪŋ] *noun*
paying money; *government spending on health has increased by 10%*; **consumer spending** = spending by consumers; *interest rates were increased to control consumer spending*; **spending money** = money for ordinary personal expenses; *how much spending money are you taking on vacation?*

④ **sperm**
[spɜrm] *noun*
male sex cell which fertilizes the female eggs; *out of millions of sperm only one will fertilize an egg* (NOTE: plural is **sperm**)

④ **sphere**
['sfɪər] *noun*
(a) object which is perfectly round like a ball; *the Earth is not quite a perfect sphere*
(b) general area; *it's not a sphere of activity that we know very well*; **sphere of influence** = area of the world where a strong country can influence smaller or weaker countries; *some Latin American countries fall within the U.S.A.'s sphere of influence*

② **spice**
[spaɪs]
1 *noun*
(a) substance made from the roots, flowers, seeds or leaves of plants, used to flavor food; *pepper and mustard are the main spices I use*; *you need lots of spices to cook Indian food*
(b) thing which excites interest; *I included a murder scene to add a bit of spice to the story*
2 *verb*
to spice something up = (i) to add spices to something; (ii) to make something more exciting or interesting; *a pinch of mustard will spice up the sauce*; *we need something to spice up the scene where the hero and heroine meet in the rain*

③ **spicy**
['spaɪsi] *adjective*
with a lot of spices; *he loves spicy Indian food*; *Mexican cooking is hot and spicy* (NOTE: **spicier - spiciest**)

① **spider**
['spaɪdər] *noun*
small animal with eight legs, which makes a web and eats insects; *it is fascinating to watch a spider making its web*

② **spike**
[spaɪk] *noun*
(a) sharply pointed piece of metal; *the wall was topped with a row of metal spikes*
(b) **spikes** = sharp points in the soles of shoes; *spikes give a golfer a much better grip on the terrain*

① **spill**
[spɪl]
1 *noun*
pouring of a liquid by accident; *the authorities are trying to cope with the oil spill from the tanker*
2 *verb*
(a) to pour liquid, powder, etc., out of a container by mistake; *that glass is too full - you'll spill it*; *he spilt soup down the front of his shirt*; *she dropped the bag and some of the flour spilled out onto the floor*
(b) *(informal)* **to spill the beans** = to reveal a secret (NOTE: **spilling - spilled** *or* **spilt** [spɪlt])

④ **spilt**
[spɪlt] *see* CRY, SPILL

① **spin**
[spɪn]
1 *noun*
(a) turning movement of a ball as it moves, of an automobile out of control; *he put so much spin on the ball that it bounced sideways*; *he jammed on the brakes and the vehicle went into a spin*
(b) *(informal)* **to put a spin on something** = to give something a special meaning; *the PR people have tried to put a positive spin on the sales figures*
(c) *(informal)* short ride in an automobile; *let's go for a spin in my new car*
2 *verb*
(a) to move round and round very fast; *the Earth is spinning in space*; *the plane was spinning out of control*
(b) to make something turn round and round; *the washing machine spins the clothes to get the water out of them*; *he spun the wheel to make sure it turned freely*
(c) to twist raw wool, cotton, etc., to form a thread; *a spinning wheel*
(d) *(of a spider)* to make a web; *the spider has spun a web between the two posts* (NOTE: **spinning - spun** [spʌn])

② **spinach**
['spɪnɪtʃ] *noun*
plant with green leaves eaten raw as salad or cooked as a vegetable; *we had a spinach salad*

③ **spin around**
['spɪn ə'raʊnd] *verb*
(a) to turn around and around very fast; *the Earth spins around in space*

(b) to turn round fast to face in the opposite direction; *I tapped him on the shoulder and he spun around to face me*

② **spine**
['spaɪn] *noun*
(a) a series of bones linked together to form a flexible support from the base of the skull to the hips; *he injured his spine playing hockey*
(b) sharp part like a pin, on a plant, animal, fish, etc.; *some animals have dangerous spines*; *did you know that lemon trees have spines?*
(c) back edge of a bound book, usually with the title printed on it; *the title and the author's name are printed on the front cover of the book and also on the spine*

④ **spiral**
['spaɪrəl]
1 *noun*
(a) shape that is twisted around and around like a spring; *he drew a spiral on the sheet of paper*
(b) thing which turns, getting higher or lower all the time; *smoke was rising in spirals from the top of the chimney*
2 *adjective*
which twists around and around; *a spiral staircase leads to the top of the tower*
3 *verb*
(a) to move up or down in a spiral; *the rocket spiraled up into the air*; *the leaves dropped off the tree and spiraled down to the ground*
(b) to move rapidly upwards; *prices of imported goods are spiraling*; **spiraling inflation** = inflation where price rises make workers ask for higher wages which then increase prices again

② **spirit**
['spɪrɪt]
1 *noun*
(a) energy and determination; *I like her because she has got such spirit*; *she fought her case with great spirit*
(b) feelings which are typical of a particular occasion; *a good salesman needs to have the spirit of competition*; *I don't think she approached the task in the right spirit*; **to enter into the spirit of** = to take part in something with enthusiasm; *the chief executive officer entered into the spirit of the party*; **Christmas spirit** = excitement and friendly feelings which are supposed to exist at Christmas; *laying us all off on December 24 didn't show much Christmas spirit*; **public spirit** = feeling that you belong to a certain part of society and have to do things to help others in the group
(c) ghost of someone dead; *the spirits of the dead*; **evil spirit** = wicked ghost which harms people; **Holy Spirit** = the third person of the Christian Trinity
(d) real intention of something; *that's not really in keeping with the spirit of the agreement*
(e) *see also* SPIRITS
2 *verb*

to spirit away = to remove as if by magic; *they spirited her away before the photographers could get to her*

④ **spirits**
['spɪrɪts] *noun*
(a) strong alcohol, or alcoholic drink such as whiskey, etc.; *the club is licensed to sell beers, wines and spirits*; **mineral spirits** = alcohol with an unpleasant odor, used as paint thinner
(b) mood; *the news had an excellent effect on our spirits*; *their spirits sank when they realized they had no chance of winning*; **in high spirits** = in a very excited mood; *she's been in high spirits since she passed her test*

② **spit**
[spɪt]
1 *noun*
(a) metal rod pushed through meat over a fire, which is turned so that the meat is cooked all through; *they roasted pieces of lamb on spits*; *a spit-roasted lamb*
(b) thin piece of land which goes out into the sea; *the nature reserve is sited at the end of a spit of land*
(c) liquid that forms in your mouth; *(informal)* **spit and polish** = vigorous cleaning
(d) he is the spitting image of his father = he looks like an exact copy of his father
2 *verb*
(a) to push liquid or food out of your mouth; *he took a mouthful and immediately spit it out*
(b) to spit on = to send liquid out of the mouth to show contempt; *he spat on the automobile as it drove away*
(c) to rain a little; *it isn't really raining - it's just spitting* (NOTE: **spitting - spat** [spæt])

④ **spite**
[spaɪt]
1 *noun*
(a) bad feeling; *they sprayed his truck with white paint out of spite*
(b) in spite of = although something happened or was done; *in spite of all his meetings, he still found time to call his wife*; *we all enjoyed ourselves, in spite of the awful weather*; *see also* DESPITE
2 *verb*
to annoy someone on purpose; *he did it purely to spite his sister*

④ **spiteful**
['spaɪtfəl] *adjective*
full of a nasty feelings against someone; *he made several spiteful remarks about his teacher*

① **splash**
[splæʃ]
1 *noun*
(a) sound when something falls into a liquid or when a liquid hits something hard; *she fell into the pool with a loud splash*; *listen to the splash of the waves against the rocks*

(b) sudden show; *the red flowers make a bright splash of color in the front garden*
(c) *(informal)* **to make a splash** = to do something that attracts a lot of publicity; *his new show made a splash on Broadway*
2 *verb*
(a) *(of liquid)* to make a noise when something is dropped into it or when it hits something; *I missed the ball and it splashed into the pool*; *the rain splashed against the windows*; *the little children were splashing about in the pools of water*
(b) to make someone wet by sending liquid on to him; *the automobile drove past through the rain and splashed my pants*
(c) to move through water, making a noise; *he splashed his way through the shallow water to the rocks*

② **splendid**
['splendɪd] *adjective*
magnificent, which impresses; *after a splendid lunch we all had a short nap*; *it was absolutely splendid to see your father again*

② **splinter**
['splɪntər]
1 *noun*
tiny thin piece of wood or metal which can get under your skin; *can you try and get this splinter out of my thumb for me?*
2 *verb*
to split into thin pointed pieces; *the wooden door splintered as the firemen hit it with their axes*

① **split**
[splɪt]
1 *verb*
(a) to divide something into parts; *he split the log into small pieces with an ax*; **to split the difference** = to agree on a figure which is half way between two figures suggested; *you are offering $30 and he wants $60, so why don't you split the difference and settle on $45?*; *see also* HAIR
(b) to divide or to come apart; *my pants were too tight - they split when I bent down*; *after they lost the election, the party split into various factions*; *(informal)* **my head is splitting** *or* **I have a splitting headache** = I have a very bad headache (NOTE: **splitting - split**)
2 *noun*
(a) division; *they are trying to hide the split between the two factions of the party*
(b) **banana split** = dessert made of a banana cut in half, whipped cream, ice cream, chocolate sauce and nuts
(c) *(in dancing)* **to do the splits** = to put yourself on the floor, with your legs spread in opposite directions
3 *adjective*
which has been broken in half; **split ends** = hair problem, when the end of each hair splits into different strands; *my hair needs to be cut*

because of my split ends; **split peas** = dried peas split in half; **in a split second** = very rapidly; *everything happened in a split second*; **to have a split personality** = mental condition where you react from time to time in two totally different and opposing ways

② **split up**
['splɪt 'ʌp] *verb*
(a) to divide; *we must try to split up the class into groups of three or four*
(b) to start to live apart; *they had a fight and split up*

② **spoil**
[spɔɪl]
1 *verb*
(a) to ruin something which was good; *we had such bad weather that our camping vacation was spoiled*; *half the contents of the warehouse were spoiled in the flood*; **to spoil your appetite** = to make you not want to eat; *don't eat so many chips - they'll spoil your appetite for lunch*
(b) to be too kind to someone, especially a child, so that he or she sometimes becomes badly behaved; *you'll spoil that child if you always give in to him*; *grandparents are allowed to spoil their grandchildren a little*
(c) **to be spoiling for a fight** = to be eager to get into a fight; *the socialists were spoiling for a fight with the liberals*
(d) to go bad; *if we don't eat this meat today it will spoil*
2 *noun*
spoils = goods taken by soldiers from a defeated enemy; *their spoils filled several trucks*

① **spoke**
[spəʊk]
1 *noun*
rod that connects the center of a wheel to the outside edge; *the wheel isn't turning straight because one of the spokes is bent*
2 *verb*
see also SPEAK

② **spoken**
['spəʊkən] *see* SPEAK

② **spokesman** *or* **spokeswoman** *or* **spokesperson**
['spəʊksmən *or* 'spəʊkswumən *or* 'spəʊkspɜrsən] *noun*
person who speaks on behalf of a party, group, politician, etc.; *a spokesman for the government or a government spokesman* (NOTE: plural is **spokesmen** *or* **spokeswomen**)

① **sponge**
[spʌnʒ]
1 *noun*
(a) block of soft material full of small holes, which soaks up water and is used for washing; *I use a large sponge to wash the car*
(b) **sponge cake** = light soft cake; **sponge pudding** = light soft pudding
2 *verb*

to wipe clean with a sponge; *he sponged the kitchen table*

② **sponsor**
['spɒnsər]
1 *noun*
(a) person or company that pays to help a sport, an exhibition, a music festival, etc., financially in return for the right to advertise at sporting events, on sports clothes, programs, etc.; *the company is the sponsor of our baseball league*
(b) company that pays part of the cost of making a TV or radio program by advertising on the program
(c) person who pays money to a charity when someone else walks, swims, runs, a certain distance; *he's taking part in the competition and wants sponsors*
(d) person who takes responsibility for someone; *she acted as his sponsor when he applied for membership of the club*
2 *verb*
to be a sponsor; *the company has sponsored the football game*; *will you sponsor me if I apply to join the club?*; *I sponsored her to take part in a marathon for charity*

④ **spontaneous**
[spɒn'teɪnɪəs] *adjective*
which happens of its own accord, which is not forced or prepared in advance; *in a spontaneous show of affection, she flung her arms around him and kissed him*; *what he said sounded more like a prepared statement than a spontaneous comment*

① **spoon**
[spun]
1 *noun*
object with a handle at one end and a small bowl at the other, used for eating liquids and soft food, or for stirring food which is being cooked; *use a spoon to eat your pudding*; *we need a big spoon to serve the soup*; **coffee spoon** = little spoon used for stirring coffee; **soup spoon** = special larger spoon for eating soup; *see also* DESSERT SPOON, TEASPOON
2 *verb*
to move something with a spoon; *she spooned sugar onto her plate*; **to spoon something into something** = to put something in with a spoon; *they were spooning soup out into each bowl*

② **spoonful**
['spunfəl] *noun*
amount that a spoon can hold; *she always takes her coffee with two spoonfuls of sugar*; *put a spoonful of tea into the pot and add boiling water (also spoonsful)*

④ **sporadic**
[spə'rædɪk] *adjective*
which happens at irregular intervals; *we have sporadic thunderstorms during the summer months*; *they heard sporadic bursts of gunfire at night*

② **sport**
[spɔrt]
1 *noun*
(a) any game; all games taken together; *do you like watching sports on TV?* *or* *do you like the sports programs on TV?*; *the world of sports is celebrating his record win*; **sports facilities** = equipment and buildings for playing sports, such as tennis courts, swimming pools, etc.; *the club has extensive sports facilities*
(b) game that you play; *the only sport I play is tennis*; *she doesn't play any sport at all*
(c) **good sport** = person who doesn't mind being teased; *he's a good sport*
2 *verb*
to wear something proudly; *he was sporting a red and orange necktie*

③ **sports car**
['spɔrts ˌkɑr] *noun*
fast open car; *he bought a dark green sports car to impress his girlfriend*

② **sportsman, sportswoman**
['spɔrtsmən *or* spɔrtswʊmən] *noun*
person who plays a sport; *she's an Olympic sportswoman* (NOTE: plurals are **sportsmen, sportswomen**)

② **spot**
[spɒt]
1 *noun*
(a) particular place; *this is the exact spot where the crime took place*; *this road junction is a notorious blind spot*; **on the spot** = at a particular place where something happens; *I happened to be on the spot when the incident took place*; *we had twenty policemen on the spot to make sure there was no trouble*; **to put someone on the spot** = to place someone in a position where he or she has to do something difficult; *he was put on the spot when they asked him if had ever used drugs*
(b) colored mark, usually round; *her dress has a pattern of white and red spots*; *he wore a blue necktie with white spots*; *see also* SOFT
(c) small round mark or bump on the skin; *she suddenly broke out in spots after eating fish*
(d) *(informal)* small amount; *would you like a spot of lunch?*; *we had a spot of luck*; *he's had a spot of bother with the tax people*
(e) **TV spot** = short period on TV which is used for commercials; *we are running a series of TV spots over the next three weeks*
2 *verb*
to notice; *the teacher didn't spot the mistake*; *we spotted him in the crowd* (NOTE: **spotting - spotted**)

③ **spotless**
['spɒtləs] *adjective*
very clean; *her kitchen is absolutely spotless*

③ **spotlight**
['spɒtlaɪt] *noun*
(a) bright light which shines on one small area; *she stood in the spotlights on the stage*

(b) to turn the spotlight on something = to draw attention to something; *the TV program turns the spotlight on the problem of refugees*

④ **spouse**
['spaʊz] *noun*
(formal) husband or wife; *members of the club may be accompanied by their spouses*

② **spout**
[spaʊt] *noun*
tube which sticks out of a container, shaped for pouring liquids; *you can fill the kettle through the spout*

① **sprain**
[spreɪn]
1 *verb*
to tear a joint, such as your ankle; *he sprained his ankle jumping over the fence*; *he sprained his wrist and can't play tennis tomorrow*
2 *noun*
condition where the parts of a joint which hold the bones together are torn because of a sudden movement; *he is walking with a stick because of an ankle sprain*

③ **sprang**
[spræŋ] *see* SPRING

③ **sprawl**
[sprɔl] *verb*
to lie with your arms and legs spread out; *he sprawled in his armchair and turned on the TV*

① **spray**
[spreɪ]
1 *noun*
(a) mass of tiny drops of liquid; *the waves crashed against the sea wall sending spray over the road*; *we used a spray to kill the flies*; *she uses a spray to clear her blocked nose*
(b) spray (can) = container that sends out liquid in a spray; *this paint is sold in ordinary cans or as a spray*
(c) little branch of a plant with flowers on it; *the room was decorated with sprays of orange flowers*
2 *verb*
to send out liquid in fine drops; *he sprayed water all over the beds of flowers*; *they sprayed the room to get rid of the insects*

① **spread**
[spred]
1 *noun*
(a) soft food for spreading on bread or crackers; *as snacks, they offered us crackers with cheese spread*
(b) range; *there is a wide spread of abilities in the class*; *she has a wide spread of interests*
(c) *(informal)* attractive mass of food; *you should have seen the spread at her wedding reception!*
(d) action of moving over a wide area; *doctors are trying to check the spread of the disease*
2 *verb*
(a) to arrange over a wide area; *spread the paper flat on the table*

(b) to move over a wide area; *the fire started in the top floor and soon spread to the roof*; *the disease has spread to the main towns*
(c) to cover with a layer of something; *she spread a white cloth over the table*; *he was spreading butter on a piece of bread*
(d) to spread payments over several months = to make payments over several months, not all at once (NOTE: **spreading - spread**)

③ **spread out**
['spred 'aʊt] *verb*
(a) to arrange things over a wide area; *she spread out the clothes on her bed*; *he spread out the plans on the CEO's desk*
(b) to move away from others over a wide area; *the demonstrators spread out across the square*; *the police officers spread out to search the woods*

② **spring**
[sprɪŋ]
1 *noun*
(a) season of the year between winter and summer; *in spring all the trees start to grow new leaves*; *we always go to New England in the spring*; *they started work last spring or in the spring of last year and they still haven't finished*; *you should come to Washington in April and see the beautiful spring flowers!*
(b) wire which is twisted round and round and which goes back to its original shape after you have pulled it or pushed it; *the bed is so old the springs have burst through the mattress*; *there's a spring to keep the door shut*
(c) strong pieces of special metal which absorb energy and allow a vehicle to travel easily over different surfaces; *the springs on this car are starting to squeak*
(d) place where a stream of water rushes out of the ground; *this water comes from a spring in Wisconsin*
(e) quick jump into the air; *a little spring and he had reached the window ledge*
2 *verb*
(a) to move suddenly; *everyone sprang to life when the officer shouted*; *the door sprang open without anyone touching it*
(b) to spring from = to come suddenly from; *where on earth did you spring from?*
(c) *(informal)* **to spring something on someone** = to surprise someone; *she sprang the question on him and he didn't know how to answer it* (NOTE: **springing - sprang** [spræŋ] **- has sprung** [sprʌŋ])

② **sprinkle**
['sprɪŋkl] *verb*
to scatter around; *sprinkle a little water on the shirt before you iron it*; *sprinkle the top of the pie with sugar*

④ **sprint**
[sprɪnt]
1 *noun*

fast run, especially at the end of a race; *he must save some energy for the final sprint*

2 *verb*

to run very fast over a short distance; *I had to sprint to catch the bus*; *she sprinted down the track*

② **sprout**

[spraʊt]

1 *noun*

new shoot of a plant; **bean sprouts** = little shoots of beans, eaten especially in Chinese cooking; **brussels sprouts** = shoots that look like tiny cabbages

2 *verb*

to produce new shoots; *throw those old potatoes away, they're starting to sprout*; *the bush had begun to sprout fresh green leaves*

② **sprung**

[sprʌŋ] *see* SPRING

③ **spun**

[spʌn] *see* SPIN

④ **spur**

[spɜr]

1 *noun*

(a) sharp metal point attached to the heel of a rider's boot which makes the horse go faster; *he put on his spurs and went to saddle up his horse*

(b) to win your spurs = to show your qualities for the first time; *it's a chance for this young player to win his spurs at international level*

(c) thing which stimulates; *the letter from the university was the spur that encouraged him to work harder*

(d) on the spur of the moment = without being planned in advance; *we decided on the spur of the moment to go to Phoenix*

(e) hill which leads from a higher mountain; *the hill we climbed was a spur of the Rockies*

(f) minor highway or railroad track leading off a main one; *a spur road runs off to the power station*

2 *verb*

to urge someone on; *the runners were spurred on by the shouts of the crowd* (NOTE: **spurring - spurred**)

③ **spurt**

[spɜrt]

1 *noun*

sudden rush, sudden effort; *he put on a spurt and won the race*

2 *verb*

(a) to spurt out = to come out in a strong jet; *oil spurted out of the burst pipe*

(b) to run fast suddenly; *he spurted past two runners and came in first*

① **spy**

[spaɪ]

1 *noun*

person who is paid to try to find out secret information about the enemy, a gang, a rival

firm; *he was exposed as a Russian spy* (NOTE: plural is **spies**)

2 *verb*

to spy on someone = to watch someone in secret, to find out what they are planning to do; *we discovered that our neighbors had been spying on us*; **to spy for someone** = to find out secret information and pass it back to someone; *he was accused of spying for the Germans*

③ **squad**

[skwɒd] *noun*

(a) small group of soldiers who perform duties together; *Corporal, take your squad and guard the prisoners*; **firing squad** = group of soldiers whose duty is to shoot someone who has been sentenced to death

(b) department in the police service; *he's the head of the drug squad*; **squad car** = police car on patrol duty

(c) group of players from whom a sports team will be chosen; *the football squad*

② **square**

[skweər]

1 *noun*

(a) shape with four equal sides and four corners with right angles; *boards used for playing chess are divided up into black and white squares*; *graph paper is drawn with a series of small squares*; *(informal)* **back to square one** = to start again from the point you originally started from; *the test plane crashed, so it's back to square one again*

(b) open space in a town, with big buildings all around; *the hotel is in the main square of the town, opposite the town hall*; *Red Square is in the middle of Moscow*

(c) *(mathematics)* result when a number is multiplied by itself; *9 is the square of 3*

2 *adjective*

(a) shaped like a square, with four equal sides and four corners with right angles; *you can't fit six people around a small square table*; *my notebook paper isn't square*; **a square peg (in a round hole)** = someone whose character means that he does not fit easily into a job, etc.

(b) making a 90° angle; *there's not one corner in the room that is square*

(c) honest and fair; *are you being square with me?*; **square deal** = honest treatment in business; *they didn't get a square deal from the tax office*; **square meal** = a good substantial meal; *(informal)* **now we're square** = we do not owe each other anything

(d) multiplied by itself; **square foot** = area of one foot multiplied by one foot; **ten square feet** = space of 2 feet x 5 feet; **square meter** = area of one meter multiplied by one meter; **ten square meters** = space of 2 meters x 5 meters; *the room is 5 m by 9 m, so its area is 45 square meters (45 m^2* **square yard** = area of one yard multiplied by one yard (NOTE: **ten square meters** is usually written **10 m^2**)

3 *verb*

(a) to make something square; *you will need a saw to square that piece of wood*

(b) to pay someone what is owed; to pay someone a bribe; *they had to square a couple of local officials before the deal went through*

(c) *(informal)* **to square it with someone** = to see that someone gives approval; *let me deal with it - I'll square it with the inspector*

(d) **to square your shoulders** = to straighten your shoulders

(e) *(mathematics)* to multiply a number by itself; *3 squared is 9*

① **squash**
[skwɒʃ]

1 *verb*

to crush, to squeeze; *hundreds of commuters were squashed into the train; he sat on my hat and squashed it flat*

2 *noun*

(a) fruit of the gourd family with a hard skin which grows from a vine used as a vegetable; *squashes grow well in warm climates*

(b) a situation where a lot of people are crowded in a small space; *it's rather a squash with twenty people in the room* (NOTE: no plural in this meaning)

(c) fast game for two players played in an enclosed court, with a small, soft rubber ball and light, long-handled rackets; *he plays squash every day after the office; let's play a game of squash*

② **squat**
[skwɒt] *verb*

to crouch down, sitting on your heels; *she squatted on the floor, trying to clean the carpet* (NOTE: **squatting - squatted**)

① **squeak**
[skwik]

1 *noun*

high little noise like that of a mouse or a door; *you can tell when someone comes into the backyard by the squeak of the gate*

2 *verb*

to make a squeak; *that door squeaks - it needs oiling*

① **squeal**
[skwil]

1 *noun*

loud high noise; *the children let out squeals of delight when they saw the presents under the Christmas tree*

2 *verb*

to make a loud high noise; *she squealed when she heard she had won first prize*

① **squeeze**
[skwiz]

1 *noun*

(a) act of pressing or crushing; *I gave her hand a squeeze*; **a tight squeeze** = a situation where there is very little space to get into or through; *you can get through the hole, but it's a tight squeeze*

(b) amount pushed out; *he put a squeeze of toothpaste on his brush*; **squeeze of lemon** = a few drops of lemon juice

(c) **credit squeeze** = period when lending by the banks is restricted by the government

2 *verb*

(a) to press on something; to press or crush a fruit, a tube, etc., to get something out of it; *she squeezed my arm gently; he squeezed an orange to get the juice; she squeezed some toothpaste onto her brush*

(b) to crush, to force into a small space; *you can't squeeze six people into that little automobile; more people tried to squeeze on the train even though it was full already; the cat managed to squeeze through the window*

③ **squirt**
[skwɜrt] *verb*

to send out a thin jet of liquid; *don't squirt so much dishwashing liquid into the bowl; she squeezed the tube and masses of toothpaste squirted out*

③ **St.**
see SAINT, STREET

② **stab**
[stæb]

1 *noun*

(a) deep wound made by the point of a knife; *he died of stab wounds*

(b) **stab in the back** = attack by someone who is thought to be loyal; *his speech was a stab in the back for the party leader*

(c) *(informal)* **to take** *or* **make a stab at something** = to try to do something; *I want to take a stab at driving a bus*

2 *verb*

(a) to wound by pushing with the point of a sharp knife; *he was stabbed in the chest*

(b) **to stab someone in the back** = to do something nasty to someone who thinks you are his friend; *she was stabbed in the back by people who owed their jobs to her* (NOTE: **stabbing - stabbed**)

④ **stabilize**
['steɪbɪlaɪz] *verb*

(a) to make firm; *we need more weight on this side of the boat to stabilize it; the United Nations is sending in troops to try to stabilize the situation*

(b) to become steady; *prices have stabilized*

① **stable**
['steɪbl]

1 *noun*

(a) building for keeping a horse; *my horse is not in his stable, who's riding him?*

(b) **stables** = place where horses are kept for breeding, racing, etc.; *she enjoys working in the stables because she loves horses*

2 *adjective*

(a) steady, which does not shake; *the ladder is not very stable, will you hold it for me?*; *put a book under one leg of the desk to keep it stable* **(b)** which does not change; *the hospital said his condition was stable*

① **stack**
[stæk]
1 *noun*
(a) pile of things one on top of the other; *there was a stack of replies to our advertisement*
(b) *(informal)* **stacks of** = lots of; *you can charge tourists what you like - they've got stacks of money*
2 *verb*
(a) to pile things on top of each other; *the skis are stacked outside the school*; *she stacked up the dirty plates*; *the warehouse is stacked with boxes*
(b) *(of aircraft)* to circle round waiting in turn for permission to land at a busy airport; *we have had aircraft stacking for over fifteen minutes on busy days*

② **stadium**
['steɪdiəm] *noun*
large building for sport, with seating arranged around a sports field; *our sports stadium was packed with spectators*; *they are building an Olympic stadium for the next Games* (NOTE: plural is **stadiums** *or* **stadia**)

② **staff**
[stæf]
1 *noun*
(a) all the people who work in a company, school, college, or other organization; *she's on the school staff*; *only staff can use this elevator*; *a quarter of our staff are sick*; *that firm pays its staff very badly*; *he joined the staff last Monday*; *three members of staff are away sick*; **kitchen staff** = people who work in a kitchen; **office staff** = people who work in offices; **staff room** = room for teachers in a school (NOTE: **staff** refers to a group of people and so is often followed by a verb in the plural)
(b) general staff = group of senior army officers who work in headquarters
(c) *(formal)* long stick; *the police attacked the protesters and beat them with staffs*
2 *verb*
to provide workers for an organization; *they are planning to staff the office with part-time salespeople*; *the bar is staffed by Australians*

② **stage**
[steɪdʒ]
1 *noun*
(a) raised floor in a theater where the actors perform; *the pop group came onto the stage and started to sing*
(b) the stage = the profession of acting; *she is planning to go on the stage*; *he has chosen the stage as a career*
(c) one of several points of development; *the first stage in the process is to grind the rock to powder*; *the different stages of a production process*; **the contract is still in the drafting stage** = the contract is still being drafted; **in stages** = in different steps; *the company has agreed to repay the loan in stages*
(d) section of a long journey; *stage one of the tour takes us from Tallahassee to Montgomery*; **in easy stages** = not doing anything very difficult; *we did the walk in easy stages*; *the tour will cross India by easy stages*
2 *verb*
(a) to put on, to arrange a play, a show, a musical, etc.; *the exhibition is being staged in the conference center*
(b) to show; **to stage a recovery** = to recover; *she has staged a remarkable recovery after her accident*

③ **stagger**
['stægər]
1 *noun*
movement when someone walks but is not steady on his feet; *he walked with a noticeable stagger*
2 *verb*
(a) not to walk in a steady way, to walk almost falling down; *she managed to stagger across the road and into the police station*; *three men staggered out of the club*
(b) to surprise enormously; *I was staggered at the amount they charge for service*
(c) to arrange vacations, working hours, payments, etc., so that they do not all begin and end at the same time; *staggered vacations help the tourist industry*; *we have to stagger the lunch hour so that there is always someone on the switchboard*

② **stain**
[steɪn]
1 *noun*
(a) mark which is difficult to remove, such as ink or blood; *it is difficult to remove coffee stains from the tablecloth*; *there was a round stain on the table where he had put his wine glass*
(b) liquid paint used to give a different color to wood; *we bought some dark green stain for the garden furniture*
2 *verb*
(a) to make a mark of a different color on something; *if you eat those berries they will stain your teeth*; *the tablecloth was stained with strawberry jam*; *his shirt was stained with blood*
(b) to color something with a stain; to put a stain on a surface; *the door will be stained light brown*

② **stair**
[steər] *see* STAIRS

③ **staircase**
['steərkeɪs] *noun*
set of stairs which go from one floor in a building to another; *a spiral staircase leads to*

the top of the tower; the staircase is at the back of the building

① **stairs**
[steərz] *noun*
steps which go up or down inside a building; *you have to go up three flights of stairs to get to my office; he slipped and fell down the stairs; see also* DOWNSTAIRS, UPSTAIRS (NOTE: **stair** is sometimes used in the singular meaning one step: **he was sitting on the bottom stair**)

③ **stake**
[steɪk]
1 *noun*
(a) strong pointed piece of wood or metal, pushed into the ground to mark something, or to hold something up; *they hammered stakes into the ground to put up a wire fence; the apple trees are attached to stakes*
(b) money which has been bet or invested; *with a $10 stake he won $150; the stakes are high* = a lot of money could be won or lost; *he has a stake in the company* = he has invested money in the company
(c) *at stake* = which may be lost if what you do fails; *you must reply to the story in the paper, the reputation of the family is at stake!* (NOTE: do not confuse with **steak**)
2 *verb*
(a) to put sticks in the ground to mark an area; *we staked out the area where the riding events were to take place*
(b) *to stake your claim to something* = to say in public that you have the right to take something; *as soon as we arrived at the hotel she staked her claim to the only room with a view of the sea*
(c) to risk; *he risked his reputation on the libel action; I'd stake my life on it, he's not guilty; they had staked everything on the success of this product; to stake money on something* = to risk or bet money on something; *she staked $15,000 on a throw of the dice*

① **stalk**
[stɔk]
1 *noun*
(a) stem of a plant which holds a leaf, a flower, a fruit, etc.; *roses with very long stalks are more expensive; cherries often come attached to stalks in pairs*
2 *verb*
(a) to walk in a stiff, proud or angry way; *she stalked into the committee room*
(b) to follow someone or something secretly in order to catch them; *the hunters stalked the deer; the photographers stalked the movie star; the TV presenter was being stalked by a fan*

② **stall**
[stɔl]
1 *noun*

(a) small wooden stand in a market, where a trader displays and sells his goods; *he has a stall at the fair; we wandered round the market looking at the fruit stalls*
(b) separate section for one animal in a building such as a stable; *each horse had its own stall with its name on it*
(c) small enclosed space; *have you cleaned the shower stall?*
2 *verb*
(a) *(informal)* to put off answering a question, making a decision, etc.; *have they got genuine doubts about the plan or are they simply stalling?*
(b) *(of a car engine)* to stop, often when trying to drive off; *if he takes his foot off the pedal, the engine stalls; the car stalled at the traffic light and he couldn't start it again*
(c) *(of an aircraft)* to go so slowly that the engine stops and it falls

④ **stammer**
['stæmər] *verb*
to hesitate and repeat sounds when speaking; *she rushed into the police station and stammered "he's - he's - he's after me, he's got - got - a knife"*

① **stamp**
[stæmp]
1 *noun*
(a) little piece of paper with a price printed on it which you stick on a letter, postcard, etc., to show that you have paid for it to be sent by mail; *she forgot to put a stamp on the letter before she mailed it; he wants to show me his stamp collection*
(b) machine for making a mark on something; *we have a stamp for marking invoices when they come into the office*; **date stamp** = device with rubber numbers which can be moved, used for marking the date on documents or on food for sale
(c) mark made on something; *the invoice has the stamp "received with thanks" on it; the customs officer looked at the stamps in his passport*
2 *verb*
(a) to stick a stamp on a letter or parcel; *all the envelopes need to be sealed and stamped*
(b) to mark something with a stamp; *they stamped my passport when I entered the country*
(c) to walk in a heavy way, banging your feet on the ground; *they stamped on the insects to kill them; he was so angry that he stamped out of the room*
(d) to make a noise by banging your feet on the ground; *the audience stamped on the floor in time to the music*

② **stamp out**
['stæmp 'aut] *verb*
to stop or to remove; *the police are trying to stamp out corruption*

① **stand**
[stænd]
1 *verb*
(a) to be upright on your feet, the opposite of sitting or lying down; *she stood on a chair to reach the top shelf*; *they were so tired they could hardly keep standing*; *if there are no seats left, we'll have to stand*; *don't just stand there doing nothing - come and help us*
(b) to be upright; *only a few houses were still standing after the earthquake*; *the jar was standing in the middle of the table*
(c) to get up from a seat; *she stood and rushed to the door*
(d) to put upright; *stand the lamp over in the corner*; *he stood the pot on the table*
(e) to tolerate, to put up with; *the office is filthy - I don't know how you can stand working here*; *she can't stand all this noise*; *he stopped going to history lessons because he couldn't stand the teacher* (NOTE: **standing - stood** [stʊd])
2 *noun*
(a) **stands** = seats where you sit to watch an event; *the stands were full for the race*
(b) something which holds something up; *the pot of flowers fell off its stand*
(c) booth for displaying goods for sale; *the flower stand looked very colorful*; **newsstand** = small store, often with an open side, selling newspapers, magazines, candy, etc.
(d) position; *his stand against the party leader earned him a term in prison*; *she was criticized for her stand against government policy*; **to take a stand against something** = to protest something; *they are taking a strong stand against corruption in the party*
(e) **witness stand** = place in a courtroom where the witnesses give evidence

③ **standard**
['stændərd]
1 *noun*
(a) the level of quality achieved by something; *the standard of service in this restaurant is very high*; *this piece of work is not up to your usual standard*
(b) excellent quality which is set as a target; *this product does not meet our standards*; *she has set a standard which it will be difficult to match*; **standard of living** *or* **living standards** = quality of personal home life (such as amount of food or clothes bought, size of the family car, etc.); *they can't complain about their standard of living, they're really quite well off*
(c) tree or bush grown with a tall trunk; *do you prefer an ordinary rose bush or a standard?*
(d) large official flag; *my grandson is carrying the troop's standard*
2 *adjective*
(a) usual, normal; *she joined on a standard contract*; *you will need to follow the standard procedure to join the association*; **standard pronunciation** = pronunciation of educated

speakers; **standard rate** = normal charge for something, such as a phone call or income tax; **standard work** = book that is the recognized authority on a subject; *he's the author of the standard work on mountain birds*
(b) on a tall pole; **standard lamp** = floor lamp, a room lamp on a tall pole standing on the floor; **standard rose** = rose grown with a tall stem
(c) **standard time** = time that applies everywhere within a certain area of the world

② **stand around**
['stænd ə'raʊnd] *verb*
to stand, and not do anything; *they just stood around and watched us working*

② **stand aside**
['stænd ə'saɪd] *verb*
to step to one side; *we stood aside to let the ambulance crew pass*

② **stand back**
['stænd 'bæk] *verb*
to take a step or two backwards; *stand back, the marathon runners are coming*

③ **stand by**
['stænd 'baɪ] *verb*
(a) to confirm, to refuse to change; *I stand by what I said in my statement to the police*
(b) to stand and watch, without getting involved; *several people just stood by and made no attempt to help*
(c) to be ready; *we have several fire engines standing by*
(d) to support, to give help; *she stood by him while he was in prison*

③ **stand down**
['stænd 'daʊn] *verb*
to agree not to stay in a position or not to stand for election; *the mayor decided to stand down after several years in office*

③ **stand for**
['stænd 'fɔr] *verb*
(a) to have a meaning; *what do the letters ND stand for?*
(b) to accept; *they will never stand for that*; *I won't stand for any naughty behavior from the children*

③ **stand guard**
['stænd 'gɑːd] *verb*
to be on guard to protect something; *soldiers are standing guard over the parliament building to prevent attacks*; *there were ten security men standing guard over the president as he went for a walk in the town*

③ **stand in for**
['stænd 'ɪn fɔr] *verb*
to take the place of someone; *she's standing in for the chairman who is sick*

② **standing**
['stændɪŋ]
1 *adjective*

(a) upright, not lying or sitting; *after the earthquake, the few buildings left standing needed to be repaired*
(b) permanent; *we have a standing agreement with our supplier to send back items we don't want*; **standing order** = order written by a customer asking a bank to pay money regularly to an account, or to a company to send something regularly; *I pay my subscription by standing order; we have a standing order for two dozen eggs every Friday*; **it is a standing joke with us** = it is something we always make jokes about; *his style of dancing is a bit of a standing joke with us*
2 *noun*
(a) being upright on your feet; *standing all day at the exhibition is very tiring*
(b) good reputation; *his standing in the community has never been higher; a hotel of good standing*
(c) **long-standing customer** *or* **customer of long standing** = person who has been a customer for many years

③ **stand out**
['stænd 'aʊt] *verb*
(a) to be easily seen; *their house stands out because it is painted pink; her red hair makes her stand out in a crowd*
(b) to be very clear against a background; *that picture would stand out better against a white wall*
(c) to be much better than others; *two of the young musicians stood out for their interpretations of Bach*

① **stand up**
['stænd 'ʌp] *verb*
(a) to get up from sitting; *when the president comes into the room all the children should stand up; he stood up to offer his seat to the older lady*
(b) to stand upright, to hold yourself upright; *stand up straight and face forward*
(c) to put something in an upright position; *stand the books up on the shelf; she stood her umbrella up by the door*
(d) *(informal)* **to stand someone up** = not to meet someone even though you had arranged to; *we were going to have dinner together and he stood me up*

③ **stand up for**
['stænd 'ʌp fɔr] *verb*
to try to defend someone or something in an argument; *he stood up for the rights of the small storekeepers; no one stood up for her when she was laid off*

④ **stank**
[stæŋk] *see* STINK

③ **staple**
['steɪpl]
1 *noun*
(a) piece of wire that is pushed through papers and bent over to hold them together; *he used*

some scissors to take the staples out of the papers
(b) main food in a diet; *rice is the staple of the Chinese diet*
2 *adjective*
main; **staple product** = main product of a country, town, etc.; *corn is the staple crop of several American states*; **staple diet** = main part of what you eat; *rice with fish is the staple diet of many people in the Far East*
3 *verb*
to fasten papers together with a staple or with staples; *staple the check to the order form*; **to staple papers together** = to attach various papers with a staple or with staples; *all these papers need to be stapled together and filed*

③ **stapler**
['steɪplər] *noun*
little device used to attach papers together with staples; *the stapler has run out of staples*

① **star**
[stɑr]
1 *noun*
(a) bright object that can be seen in the sky at night like a very small bright light; *on a clear night you can see thousands of stars; the pole star shows the direction of the North Pole*
(b) famous person who is very well known to the public; *who is your favorite movie star?*; *the movie has an all-star cast; the boxing star got special treatment at the hotel*
(c) **star sign** = the sign of the stars and planets which marks your birth; *(informal)* **thank your lucky stars** = consider yourself very lucky; *thank your lucky stars that you were not on that plane*
(d) shape that has several points like a star; *draw a big star and color it red*
(e) a printing symbol shaped like a star; *a star next to a word refers you to the notes at the bottom of the page*
(f) classification sign for hotels, restaurants, etc.; **three-star hotel** = hotel that has been classified with three stars, under a classification system; *we stayed in a two-star hotel and found it perfectly comfortable*
2 *verb*
(a) to appear as a main character in a movie or play; *she starred in "Gone with the Wind"; he has a starring role in the new production of "Guys and Dolls"*
(b) to mark a text with a star; *read the starred instructions carefully* (NOTE: **starring - starred**)

① **stare**
[steər]
1 *verb*
(a) to look at someone or something for a long time; *she stared sadly out of the window at the rain*
(b) *(informal)* **to stare someone in the face** = to be very obvious; *he couldn't find the answer even if it was staring him in the face*

2 *noun*

long fixed look; *he gave her a stare and walked on*

① **starfish**

['stɑːfɪʃ] *noun*

flat sea animal, with five arms branching like a star from a central body; *the children found a starfish on the beach and brought it back home in a bucket* (NOTE: plural is **starfish**)

④ **starling**

['stɑːlɪŋ] *noun*

common bird with dark feathers with a green shine on them; *a flock of starlings were pecking about on the grass*

① **start**

[stɑːt]

1 *verb*

(a) to begin to do something; *the babies all started to cry* or *all started crying at the same time*; *he started to eat* or *he started eating his dinner before the rest of the family*; *take an umbrella - it's starting to rain*; *when you learn Russian, you have to start by learning the alphabet*; *we must start packing now or we'll miss the plane*; *at what time does the match start?*; **to start with** = first of all; *we have lots to do but to start with we'll do the dishes*

(b) to leave on a journey; *we plan to start at 6 o'clock*

(c) *(of a machine)* to begin to work; *the automobile won't start - the battery must be dead*; *the engine started at my first attempt*

(d) to make something begin to work; *I can't start the car*; *it is difficult to start an automobile in cold weather*

(e) to make something begin; *he fired a gun to start the race*; *the police think that the fire was started deliberately*

(f) to jump with surprise; *she started when she heard the bang*

2 *noun*

(a) beginning of something; *building the house took only six months from start to finish*; *things went wrong from the start*; *let's forget all you've done up to now, and make a fresh start*

(b) leaving for a journey; *we're planning on a 6 o'clock start*; **let's make an early start tomorrow** = let's leave early

(c) place where a race begins; *the race cars were lined up at the start*

(d) being in advance of other competitors; *we'll never catch them, they have three hours' start on us*; *I'll give you four yards' start*

(e) sudden jump of surprise; *she gave a start when he put his hand on her shoulder*

① **starter**

['stɑːtər] *noun*

(a) *(informal)* first part of a meal; *what do you all want as starters?*; *I don't want a starter - just the main course*

(b) person who starts doing something; *there were sixty starters in the race, but only twenty*

finished

(c) person who organizes the start of something; *the starter fired a gun and the race started*

(d) **starter (motor)** = electric motor in an automobile which sets the main engine going; *your battery's OK, so maybe the starter isn't working*

① **startle**

['stɑːtl] *verb*

to make someone suddenly surprised; *I'm sorry, I didn't mean to startle you*; *she looked up startled when she heard the knock at the door*; *we were all startled to hear about his getting married*

③ **startling**

['stɑːtlɪŋ] *adjective*

suddenly surprising; *everyone was talking about the startling election results*

② **start off**

['stɑːt 'ɒf] *verb*

(a) to begin; *we'll start off with soup and then have a meat dish*

(b) to leave on a journey; *you can start off now, and I'll follow when I'm ready*

② **start out**

['stɑːt 'aut] *verb*

(a) to leave on a journey; *she started out for home two hours ago, so I am surprised she hasn't arrived*

(b) to begin; *I'd like to start out by saying how pleased I am to be here*

② **start up**

['stɑːt 'ʌp] *verb*

(a) to make a business begin to work; *she started up a restaurant, but it failed*

(b) to make an engine start to work; *he started up the truck*; *from here you can hear the noise of the racing cars starting up*

② **starvation**

[stɑːˈveɪʃn] *noun*

lack of food which results in illness; *people are dying of starvation in parts of Africa*

① **starve**

[stɑːv] *verb*

(a) not to have enough food; *many people starved to death in the desert*

(b) **to starve someone of something** = not to give enough supplies to someone; *the health agency is being starved of funds*

① **state**

[steɪt]

1 *noun*

(a) condition (often a bad condition), the way something or someone is; *the children are in a state of excitement*; *the students left the house in a terrible state*; *look at the state of your affairs*; *she's not in a fit state to receive visitors*

(b) condition where you are depressed, worried, etc.; *she's in such a state that I don't want to leave her alone*; *he was in a terrible state after the phone call*

(c) state of health = being well or sick; *his state of health has improved with treatment*; **state of mind** = a person's feelings at a particular time; *he's in a very miserable state of mind*; *in her present state of mind she's unlikely to be able to decide what to do*

(d) government of a country; *we all pay taxes to the state*; *the state should pay for the museums*; **state-owned** = owned by the country or government and not by private individuals

(e) independent country; *the member states of the European Union*; **head of state** = official leader of a country, though not necessarily the head of the government

(f) one of the parts of a federal country; *State of Arizona*; *New South Wales has the largest population of all the Australian states*; *see also* UNITED STATES OF AMERICA

2 *adjective*
referring to the state; **State Department** = part of the U.S. government that deals with relations with other countries; **state enterprise** = company run by the state

3 *verb*
to give information clearly; *please state your name and address*; *it states in the instructions that you must not open the can near a flame*; *the document states that all revenue has to be declared to the tax office*

② **statement**
['steɪtmənt] *noun*
(a) clearly written or spoken description of what happened; *she made a statement to the police*
(b) list of invoices and credits and debits sent by a supplier to a customer at the end of each month; *I want to query something in last month's statement*; **bank statement** = written document from a bank showing the balance of an account; **monthly** *or* **quarterly statement** = statement which is sent every month or every quarter

② **States**
['steɪts] *noun*
(informal) the United States of America; *we've lost touch with him now that he's gone to live in the States*; *they hitched their way across the States*

③ **statesman**
['steɪtsmən] *noun*
important political leader or representative of a country; *a meeting of world statesmen to agree to a nuclear test ban treaty* (NOTE: plural is **statesmen**)

① **station**
['steɪʃn]
1 *noun*
(a) (train) station = place where trains stop, where passengers get on or off, etc.; *the train leaves the Central Station at 4:15*; *this is a fast train - it doesn't stop at every station*; *we'll try to get something to eat at the station sandwich bar*

(b) bus station = place where buses begin or end their journeys; *buses leave this bus station every day for numerous destinations*; **subway station** = place where subway trains stop, where passengers get on or off; *there's a subway station just a few minutes' walk away*

(c) large main building for a service; *the fire station is just down the road from us*; *he was arrested and taken to the local police station*; **power station** = factory that produces electricity; *the power station chimneys can be seen from across the river*; **service station** = garage that sells gas and repairs automobiles; *luckily I broke down right outside a service station*; **TV station** *or* **radio station** = building where TV or radio programs are broadcast; *the station broadcasts hourly reports on snow conditions*

(d) *(in Australia)* **sheep station** = very large farm, specializing in raising sheep

2 *verb*
to place someone officially in a place; *soldiers were stationed in the border towns*; *police were stationed all along the route of the procession*

③ **stationary**
['steɪʃnəri] *adjective*
not moving, standing still; *he collided with a stationary vehicle*; *traffic is stationary for four miles on the freeway into Los Angeles* (NOTE: do not confuse with **stationery**)

③ **stationery**
['steɪʃnəri] *noun*
materials used when writing, such as paper, envelopes, pens, ink, etc.; *the letter was typed on his office stationery* (NOTE: no plural; do not confuse with **stationary**)

② **station wagon**
['steɪʃən 'wægən] *noun*
large automobile with a flat space behind the seats where parcels or suitcases can be put

③ **statistics**
[stə'tɪstɪks] *noun*
facts given in the form of figures; *we examined the sales statistics for the previous six months*; *government statistics show an increase in heart disease*

① **statue**
['stætʃu] *noun*
figure of a person or animal carved from stone, made from metal, etc.; *the statue of Abraham Lincoln is in the center of the square*

④ **status**
['steɪtəs] *noun*
(a) general position; **status inquiry** = check on a customer's credit rating; **legal status** = legal position
(b) social importance when compared to other people; *he has a low-status job on the subway*; *his status in the company has been rising steadily*; **status symbol** = thing which you use which shows that you are more important than someone else; *the chairman's automobile is a*

④ **statutory**
['stætʃətrɪ] *adjective*
imposed by law; *there is a statutory period of thirteen weeks before new employees are given permanent jobs*; **statutory holiday** = holiday that is fixed by law; **statutory sick pay** = payment made each week by an employer to an employee who is away from work because of sickness

① **stay**
[steɪ]
1 *verb*
(a) to remain, not to change; *the temperature stayed below zero all day*; *in spite of the fire, he stayed calm*; *I won't be able to stay awake until midnight*
(b) to stop in a place; *they came for lunch and stayed until after midnight*; *I'm kind of tired so I'll stay at home tomorrow*; *he's sick and has to stay in bed*
(c) to stop in a place as a visitor; *they stayed two nights in San Juan on their tour of Puerto Rico*; *where will you be staying when you're in New York?*; *my parents are staying at the Hotel Victoria*
2 *noun*
(a) time during which you live in a place; *my sister's here for a short stay*; *did you enjoy your stay in Montpelier?*
(b) **stay of execution** = delay in putting a legal order into effect; *the judge granted a stay of execution*

③ **stay away**
['steɪ ə'weɪ] *verb*
not to come or go to something; *she doesn't like parties, and stayed away*; *many voters are bored with elections and stayed away from the polls*

③ **stay in**
['steɪ 'ɪn] *verb*
to stop at home instead of going out; *we prefer to stay in rather than go and stand in line for hours to get into the movie theater*

③ **stay out**
['steɪ 'aʊt] *verb*
to remain away from home; *the girls stayed out until two o'clock in the morning*

② **stay put**
['steɪ 'pʊt] *phrase*
to stay where you are, not to move; *I'm not going to resign - I'm staying put!*; *stay put! - I'll go and get a doctor*

③ **stay up**
['steɪ 'ʌp] *verb*
not to go to bed; *we stayed up late to see the New Year in*; *little children are not supposed to stay up until midnight watching TV*

② **steadily**
['stedɪlɪ] *adverb*
not changing; regularly or continuously; *things have been steadily going from bad to worse*; *sales have increased steadily over the last two years*

② **steady**
['stedɪ]
1 *adjective*
(a) firm, not moving or shaking; *you need a steady hand to draw a straight line without a ruler*; *he put a piece of paper under the table leg to keep it steady*
(b) continuing in a regular way; *there is a steady demand for computers*; *the automobile was doing a steady seventy miles per hour*; *she hasn't got a steady boyfriend* (NOTE: **steadier - steadiest**)
2 *verb*
(a) to calm; *she took a pill to steady her nerves*
(b) to keep firm; *he put out his hand to steady the ladder*

② **steak**
[steɪk] *noun*
(a) thick slice of beef; *he ordered steak and potatoes*; *I'm going to grill these steaks*
(b) thick slice cut across the body of a big fish; *a grilled salmon steak for me, please!* (NOTE: do not confuse with **stake**)

① **steal**
[stil] *verb*
(a) to take something which belongs to another person; *someone tried to steal my purse*; *she owned up to having stolen the jewels*; *did the burglar steal all your CDs? - I'm afraid so*; *he was arrested for stealing, but the judge let him off with a fine*
(b) **to steal the show** = to do better than a star actor; *it was the little dog that stole the show*; *see also* THUNDER
(c) to move quietly; *he stole into the office and tried to find the safe*; **to steal away** = to go away very quietly; *he stole away under cover of darkness*; **to steal a glance at** = to look at quickly and secretly at; *while the boss wasn't looking she stole a glance at the papers on his desk* (NOTE: **stealing - stole** [stəʊl] **- stolen** ['stəʊlən] ; do not confuse with **steel**)

② **steam**
[stim]
1 *noun*
(a) moisture that comes off hot or boiling water; *clouds of steam were coming out of the kitchen*; **steam engine** = engine that runs on pressure from steam
(b) *(informal)* **to let off steam** = to get rid of energy by doing something vigorous; *we sent the children out to play in the backyard to let off steam*
2 *verb*
(a) to send off steam; *the kettle is steaming - the water must be boiling*
(b) to cook over a pan of boiling water by allowing the steam to pass through holes in a

container with food in it; *how are you going to cook the fish? - I'll steam it*
(c) to move by steam power; *the ship steamed out of the harbor*
(d) to go fast in a certain direction; *we were steaming along at 70 miles per hour when we had a flat tire*

① **steel**
[stil]
1 *noun*
strong metal made from iron and carbon; *steel knives are best for the kitchen*; *the door is made of solid steel*; **steel band** = band that plays West Indian music on steel drums of different sizes which make different notes; *we spent the evening dancing to music from a steel band*; **steel gray** = dark gray color, the color of steel; *steel gray will be fashionable next winter*
2 *verb*
to steel yourself to do something = to get ready to do something which is going to be unpleasant; *he steeled himself for a very awkward interview with the police* (NOTE: do not confuse with **steal**)

② **steep**
[stip]
1 *adjective*
(a) which rises or falls sharply; *the automobile climbed the steep hill with some difficulty*; *the steps up the church tower are steeper than our stairs at home*
(b) very sharp increase or fall; *a steep increase in interest charges*; *a steep fall in share prices*
(c) *(informal)* too much; *their prices are a bit steep*; *that's a bit steep!* (NOTE: **steeper - steepest**)
2 *verb*
(a) to soak in a liquid; *let the clothes steep in soap and water to get the stains out*
(b) to soak in a liquid to absorb its flavor; *the meat must steep in red wine and herbs for 24 hours*
(c) steeped in history = full of history, where many historical events have taken place; *New York is steeped in history*

② **steer**
['stɪər] *verb*
(a) to make an automobile, a ship, etc., go in a certain direction; *she steered the automobile into a ditch*; *the pilot steered the ship into harbor*
(b) to steer clear of = to avoid; *I steer clear of foods that contain a lot of fat*

① **steering wheel**
['stɪrɪŋ 'wil] *noun*
wheel that is turned by the driver to control the direction in which a vehicle travels; *the hitchhiker grabbed the steering wheel and tried to send the truck into the ditch*

② **stem**
[stem]
1 *noun*

(a) stalk, the tall thin part of a plant which holds a leaf, a flower, a fruit, etc.; **trim the stems before you put the flowers in water**
(b) main stalk of a plant or tree; *a standard rose bush with a tall stem*
(c) part of a wine glass like a column; *wine glasses with colored stems*
(d) from stem to stern = from the front of a boat to the back; *the boat was packed from stem to stern with tourists*
2 *verb*
(a) to stem from = to be caused by; *his health problems stem from an infection*
(b) to try to prevent something flowing or spreading; *first, try to stem the flow of blood*; *the police are trying to stem the rising tide of crime* (NOTE: **stemming - stemmed**)

③ **stencil**
['stensl] *noun*
sheet of cardboard or metal with a pattern cut out of it, so that if you place it on a surface and paint over it, the pattern will be made on the surface; *she decorated the bathroom with stencils of fish*

① **step**
[step]
1 *noun*
(a) movement of your foot when walking; *I wonder when the baby will take his first steps*; *take a step sideways and you will be able to see the castle*
(b) to take one step forward and two steps back = not to advance very quickly; **step by step** = gradually, a little at a time; *it's better to introduce the changes step by step*; *the book takes you step by step through Spanish grammar*
(c) regular movement of feet at the same time as other people; **in step** = moving your feet at the same rate as everybody else; **out of step** = moving your feet at a different rate from everybody else; *I tried to keep in step with him as we walked along*; *the recruits can't even march in step*; *one of the squad always gets out of step*; **in step with something** = at the same rate or speed as something; *house prices have risen in step with salaries*; **out of step with something** = moving at a different rate or speed from something; *wages have got out of step with the rise in the cost of living*
(d) the sound made by a foot touching the ground; *we heard soft steps outside our bedroom door*; *I can always recognize your father's step*
(e) one stair, which goes up or down; *there are two steps down into the kitchen*; *I counted 75 steps to the top of the tower*; *be careful, there's a step-up into the bathroom*
(f) one thing which is done or has to be done out of several; *the first and most important step is to find out how much money we can spend*; **to take steps to prevent something happening** =

to act to stop something from happening; *the museum must take steps to make sure that nothing else is stolen*

2 *verb*

to move forward, backward, etc., on foot; *he stepped out in front of a bicycle and was knocked down*; *she stepped off the bus into a pool of water*; *don't step back, there's a child behind you*; **to step on the brakes** = to push the brake pedal hard; *(informal)* **to step on the gas** = to drive faster; *step on the gas - we'll miss the train!*; *(informal)* **step on it!** = hurry up! (NOTE: **stepping - has stepped**)

③ **step in**
['step 'ɪn] *verb*

(a) to enter; *please step in and see what we have to offer*

(b) to do something in an area where you were not involved before; *everything was working fine until the manager stepped in*; *fortunately a teacher stepped in to break up the fight*

② **stereo**
['steriəʊ]

1 *adjective*

= STEREOPHONIC; *a stereo disk*

2 *noun*

(a) machine that reproduces sound through two different loudspeakers or headphones; *I bought a new pair of speakers for my stereo*; **car stereo** = system in an automobile which reproduces sound in stereo

(b) in stereo = using two speakers to give an impression of depth of sound

③ **stereophonic**
[steriə'fɒnɪk] *adjective*

referring to sound which comes through from two different channels and loudspeakers

④ **stereotype**
['steriətaɪp] *noun*

typical sort of person; *he fits the stereotype of the mad professor*

④ **sterling**
['stɜrlɪŋ]

1 *noun*

British currency; *the prices are quoted in sterling*; **the pound sterling** = official term for the British currency

2 *adjective*

(a) sterling silver = silver which has been tested to show that it has a standard high quality; *we gave her six sterling silver spoons*

(b) of a certain standard, especially of good quality; *she has many sterling qualities*; *this old coat has done sterling service over the years*

③ **stern**
[stɜrn]

1 *adjective*

serious and strict; *the judge addressed some stern words to the boys* (NOTE: **sterner - sternest**)

2 *noun*

back part of a ship; *the stern of the ship was damaged; see also* STEM (NOTE: the front part is the **bow**)

② **stew**
[stju]

1 *noun*

meal of meat and vegetables cooked together for a long time; *this lamb stew is a French recipe*

2 *verb*

to cook for a long time in liquid; *stew the apples until they are completely soft*

② **steward**
['stjʊəd] *noun*

(a) man who looks after passengers, and serves meals or drinks on a ship, aircraft, train, or in a club; *the steward served us drinks on deck*

(b) person who organizes public events such as horse races, etc.; *the stewards will inspect the course to see if the race can go ahead*

③ **stewardess**
[stjʊə'des] *noun*

woman who looks after passengers and serves food and drinks on a ship or aircraft; *the stewardess demonstrated how to put on the life jacket* (NOTE: plural is **stewardesses**)

① **stick**
[stɪk]

1 *verb*

(a) to glue or attach; *can you stick the tail on the donkey?*; *she stuck the stamp on the letter*; *they stuck a poster on the door*

(b) to be fixed or not to be able to move; *the automobile was stuck in the mud*; *the door sticks - you need to push it hard to open it*; *he was stuck in Little Rock without any money*

(c) to push something into something; *she stuck his hand into the hole*; *she stuck her finger in the jam to taste it*; *she stuck the ticket into her bag*; *she stuck a needle into her finger*

(d) to stay in a place; *stick close to your mother and you won't get lost*; **to stick together** = to stay together; *if we stick together they should let us into the club*; **to stick to your guns** = to keep to your point of view even if everyone says you are wrong (NOTE: **sticking - stuck** [stʌk])

2 *noun*

(a) thin piece of wood, thin branch of a tree; *he pushed the pointed stick into a hole*; *I need a strong stick to tie this plant to; see also* WRONG

(b) (walking) stick = strong piece of wood with a handle used as a support when walking; *since she had the accident she gets around on two sticks*; *at last mother has agreed to use a walking stick*

(c) hockey stick = curved piece of wood for playing hockey

(d) anything long and thin; *a stick of rock*; *a stick of chewing gum*

② **sticker**
['stɪkər] *noun*

small piece of paper or plastic which you can stick on something to show a price, as a decoration or to advertise something; *the salesman charged me more than the price on the sticker*; *she stuck stickers all over the doors of her wardrobe*

① **stick out**
['stɪk 'aʊt] *verb*

(a) to push something out; **to stick your tongue out at someone** = to make a rude gesture by putting your tongue out of your mouth as far as it will go; *that little girl stuck out her tongue at me!*

(b) to be further forward or extended away from something; *your wallet is sticking out of your pocket*; *the roof sticks out over the path*

(c) *(informal)* **to stick out like a sore thumb** = to be easily seen; *their house sticks out like a sore thumb because it is painted pink*

② **stick up**
['stɪk 'ʌp] *verb*

(a) to be further up above a surface or to extend beyond a surface; *the rack sticks up above the roof of the automobile*

(b) to put up a notice, etc.; *she stuck up a notice about the bake sale*

(c) *(informal)* **stick 'em up!** = put your hands up!

(d) **to stick up for someone** *or* **something** = to defend someone or something against criticism; *he stuck up for his rights and in the end won the case*; *will you stick up for me if I get into trouble at school?*

① **sticky**
['stɪkɪ] *adjective*

(a) covered with something which sticks like glue; *my fingers are all sticky*; *this stuff is terribly sticky - I can't get it off my fingers*

(b) with glue on one side so that it sticks easily; **sticky label** = label with sticky glue on one side which you can stick without licking

(c) *(informal)* difficult or embarrassing; *I'm in a kind of sticky situation here* (NOTE: **stickier - stickiest**)

① **stiff**
[stɪf]

1 *adjective*

(a) which does not move easily; *the lock is very stiff - I can't turn the key*; *I've got a stiff neck*; *she was feeling stiff all over after running in the race*

(b) *(brush)* hard; *you need a stiff brush to get the mud off your shoes*

(c) **bored stiff** = very bored; *he talked on and on until we were all bored stiff*; *I'm bored stiff with sitting indoors, watching the rain come down*

(d) difficult; *he had to take a stiff test before he qualified*

(e) formal, not friendly; *his attitude was very stiff toward her*

(f) strong, not weak; *they face stiff competition*; *a stiff breeze was blowing across the bay*; *his book received some stiff criticism in the press*;

stiff drink = alcoholic drink with very little water added (NOTE: **stiffer - stiffest**)

2 *noun*

(informal) dead body; *someone called to say there was a stiff on the sidewalk*

④ **stile**
[staɪl] *noun*

steps which allow people, but not animals, to get over a wall or fence; *the path led across the field to a stile*

① **still**
[stɪl]

1 *adjective*

(a) not moving; *stand still while I take the photo*; *if you want to see the rabbits keep still and don't make any noise*; *there was no wind, and the surface of the lake was completely still*

(b) *(of drinks)* not bubbly; *can I have a glass of still mineral water, please?*

2 *adverb*

(a) continuing until now; which continued until then; *I thought he had left, but I see he's still there*; *they came for lunch and were still sitting at the table at eight o'clock in the evening*; *weeks afterwards, they're still talking about the accident*

(b) *(with comparative)* we've had a cold fall, but they expect the winter will be colder still; **still more** = even more; *there were at least twenty thousand people in the football stadium and still more lining up to get in*

(c) in spite of everything; *it wasn't sunny for the picnic - still, it didn't rain*; *he still insisted on going on vacation even though he had broken his leg*

④ **stimulate**
['stɪmjʊleɪt] *verb*

to encourage someone or an organ to be more active; *we want to stimulate trade with the Middle East*; *I'm trying to stimulate the students*; *this drug stimulates the heart*

④ **stimulus**
['stɪmjʊləs] *noun*

thing that encourages someone or something to greater activity; *what sort of stimulus is needed to get the tourist trade moving?*; *a nerve which responds to stimuli* (NOTE: plural is **stimuli** ['stɪmjʊlaɪ])

① **sting**
[stɪŋ]

1 *noun*

(a) wound made by an insect or plant; *bee stings can be very painful*; *have you anything for wasp stings?*

(b) tiny needle, part of an insect or plant which injects poison into your skin; *he pulled out the sting which was stuck in her arm*

2 *verb*

(a) to wound with an insect's or plant's sting; *I've been stung by a wasp*; *she walked bare-legged through the woods and got stung by nettles*; *see also* NETTLE

(b) to give a burning feeling; *the antiseptic may sting a little at first*

(c) *(informal)* **to sting someone (for)** = to charge someone a lot of money; *he was stung for the football tickets*; *they stung me for $150* (NOTE: **stinging - stung** [stʌŋ])

① **stink**
[stɪŋk]
1 *noun*
(a) very nasty smell; *there's a terrible stink in the kitchen*

(b) *(informal)* **to create** *or* **make** *or* **kick up** *or* **raise a stink about something** = to complain vigorously about something; *the neighbors will kick up a stink if you damage their fence*
2 *verb*
(a) to make a nasty smell; *the office stinks of gas*

(b) *(informal)* to seem to be dishonest; *the whole affair stinks* (NOTE: **stank** [stæŋk] - **stunk** [stʌŋk])

② **stir**
[stɜr]
1 *noun*
(a) action of mixing the ingredients of something, or something which is cooking; *add the sugar and give the mixture a stir*; *you should give the sauce a stir from time to time*
(b) excitement; *the exhibition caused a stir in the art world*
2 *verb*
(a) to move a liquid or powder or something which is cooking, to mix it up; *he was stirring the sugar into his coffee*; *keep stirring the sauce, or it will stick to the bottom of the pan of the pan*

(b) to move about; *the baby slept quietly without stirring*; *I didn't stir from my desk all day*

(c) **to stir someone to do something** = to make someone feel that they ought to do something; *we must try to stir the committee into action* (NOTE: **stirring - stirred**)

② **stir up**
['stɜr ʌp] *verb*
to stir up trouble = to cause trouble; *the fans came with the deliberate intention of stirring up trouble*

② **stitch**
[stɪtʃ]
1 *noun*
(a) little loop of thread made with a needle in sewing or with knitting needles when knitting; *she uses very small stitches when sewing children's clothes*; *very fine wool will give you more stitches than in the pattern*

(b) *(informal)* clothes; *how can I go to the party - I haven't a stitch to wear*; **with not a stitch on** = completely naked; *I can't come now, I haven't a stitch on*

(c) small loop of thread used by a surgeon to attach the sides of a wound together to help it to heal; *she had three stitches in her arm*; *come back in ten days' time to have the stitches removed*

(d) sharp pain in the side of the body after you have been running; *I can't go any further - I've got a stitch*

(e) **in stitches** = laughing out loud; *his story about the school play had us all in stitches* (NOTE: plural is **stitches**)
2 *verb*
(a) to attach with a needle and thread; *she stitched the badge to his jacket*

(b) to sew the sides of a wound together; *after the operation, the surgeon stitched the wound*; *his finger was cut off in an accident and the surgeon tried to stitch it back on*

① **stock**
[stɒk]
1 *noun*
(a) supply of something kept to use when needed; *I keep a stock of typing paper at home*; *our stocks of food are running low*; *the factory has large stocks of coal*

(b) **in stock** = available in the store or warehouse; *we hold 2000 items in stock*; **out of stock** = not available in the store or warehouse; *we are out of stock of this item* or *this item is out of stock*; **to take stock** = to count the items in a warehouse; *they take stock every evening after the store closes*; **to take stock of a situation** = to assess how bad a situation is; *we need to take stock of the situation and decide what to do next*

(c) investments in a company, represented by shares; *we were advised to invest in gold stocks*; **stocks and shares** = shares in ordinary companies

(d) liquid made from boiling bones, etc., in water, used as a base for soups and sauces; *fry the onions and pour in some chicken stock*
2 *verb*
to keep goods for sale in a warehouse or store; *they don't stock this book*; *we try to stock the most popular colors*
3 *adjective*
normal, usually kept in a store; **stock size** = normal size; *we only carry shoes in stock sizes*; **stock argument** = argument that is frequently used; *she used the stock argument about higher salaries leading to fewer jobs*

④ **stock exchange**
['stɒk ɪks'tʃeɪndʒ] *noun*
place where stocks and shares are bought and sold; *he works on the New York Stock Exchange*; *shares in a closed corporation are not traded on the stock exchange*

① **stockholder**
['stɒkhəʊldər] *noun*
person who holds shares in a company; *the stockholders voted against the merger*

① **stocking**
['stɒkɪŋ] *noun*
long light piece of women's clothing which

covers all the leg and your foot; *she was wearing black shoes and stockings*; *the robbers wore stockings over their faces*; **Christmas stockings** = large colored stockings, which children hang up and that are filled with presents on Christmas Eve; **stocking stuffer** = little gift that can be put into a Christmas stocking

③ **stock market**
['stɒk 'mɑːrkɪt] *noun*
place where shares are bought and sold (i.e., a stock exchange); *the stock market crash of 1929*; **stock market value** = value of a company based on the current market price of its shares

③ **stock up with**
['stɒk 'ʌp wɪð] *verb*
to buy supplies for use in the future; *we'll stock up with food to last us over the holiday weekend*

② **stole, stolen**
[stəʊl *or* 'stəʊlən]
see STEAL

② **stomach**
['stʌmək]
1 *noun*
(a) part of the inside of the body shaped like a bag, into which food passes after being swallowed; *I don't want anything to eat - my stomach's upset or I have a stomach upset*; *he has had stomach trouble for some time*; *his eyes were bigger than his stomach* = he took too much food and couldn't finish it
(b) the middle of the front of the body; *he had been kicked in the stomach*
2 *verb*
to put up with, to tolerate; *they left the meeting because they couldn't stomach any more arguments*

① **stone**
[stəʊn]
1 *noun*
(a) very hard material, found in the ground, used for building; *all the houses in the town are built in the local gray stone*; *the stone carvings in the old church date from the 15th century*; *stone floors can be very cold* (NOTE: no plural in these meanings: **some stone, a piece of stone, a block of stone**)
(b) small piece of stone; *the children were playing at throwing stones into the pond*; *the beach isn't good for sunbathing as it's covered with very sharp stones*
(c) **precious stones** = stones, such as diamonds, which are rare and very valuable
(d) single hard seed inside a fruit; *count the cherry stones on the side of your plate*
2 *adverb*
completely; **stone cold** = very cold; *no wonder you're freezing, the radiators are stone cold*; **stone deaf** = completely deaf; *it's no use shouting - she's stone deaf*; **stone broke** = with no money at all

③ **stony**
['stəʊni] *adjective*
made of lots of stones; *they walked carefully across the stony beach* (NOTE: **stonier - stoniest**)

② **stood**
[stʊd]
see STAND

① **stool**
[stuːl] *noun*
small seat with no back; *when the little girl sat on the piano stool her feet didn't touch the floor*

② **stoop**
[stuːp] *verb*
to bend forward; *she stooped and picked something up off the carpet*

① **stop**
[stɒp]
1 *noun*
(a) end of something, especially of movement; *the police want to put a stop to automobile crimes*; **to come to a stop** *or* **to a full stop** = to stop moving; *the automobile rolled on without the driver, and finally came to a stop at the bottom of the hill*; *all the building work came to a stop when the money ran out*
(b) place where you break a journey; *we'll make a stop at the next service station*
(c) place where a bus or trolley lets passengers get on or off; *we have been waiting at the bus stop for twenty minutes*; *there are six stops between here and the town square*
(d) *(informal)* **to pull out all the stops** = to make every effort; *they pulled out all the stops to make sure the work was finished on time*
2 *verb*
(a) not to move anymore; *the motorcycle didn't stop at the red lights*; *the people in the line were very annoyed when the trolley went past without stopping*
(b) to make something not move anymore; *the police officer stopped the traffic to let the truck back out of the garage*; *stop that boy! - he's stolen my purse*
(c) not to do something anymore; *the office clock has stopped at 4:15*; *at last it stopped raining and we could go out*; *she spoke for two hours without stopping*; *we all stopped work and went home*; *the restaurant stops serving meals at midnight*
(d) **to stop someone** *or* **something (from) doing something** = to make someone or something not do something anymore; *the rain stopped us from having a picnic*; *how can the police stop people stealing cars?*; *can't you stop the children from making such a noise?*; *the builder couldn't stop the faucet dripping*
(e) to stay at a place for a short time; *can you stop at a newsstand on your way home and buy the evening paper?*

(f) to stay as a visitor in a place; *they stopped for a few days in Kingston; I expect to stop in New Jersey for the weekend*

(g) to stop at nothing = to do everything, whether good or bad, to succeed; *he'll stop at nothing to get that job;* **to stop short of doing something** = to stop just in time to avoid doing something; *he stopped short of admitting he was guilty*

(h) to stop an account = to stop supplying a customer until he has paid what he owes; **to stop payment on a check** *or* **to stop a check** to ask a bank not to pay a check that you have written (NOTE: **stopping - stopped**)

① **stop by**
['stɒp 'baɪ] *verb*
(informal) to visit someone for a short time; *he said he might stop by on his way home*

① **stoplight**
['stɒplaɪt] *noun*
traffic light, red, green and yellow lights for making the traffic stop and start; *to get to the police station, you have to make a left at the next stoplight*

① **stop off**
['stɒp 'ɒf] *verb*
to stop for a time in a place before going on with your journey; *we stopped off for a couple of nights in Dallas on our way to Mexico*

③ **stopper**
['stɒpər] *noun*
piece of glass, wood, etc., put into the mouth of a bottle or jar to close it; *put the stopper back in the jar*

② **stop up**
['stɒp 'ʌp] *verb*
to block; *he tried to stop up the hole in the pipe with some kind of cement*

② **storage**
['stɔːrɪdʒ] *noun*
(a) keeping in a store or warehouse; *we put our furniture into storage; we don't have enough storage space in this house;* **storage capacity** = space available for storage; **storage facilities** = equipment and buildings suitable for storage; **cold storage** = keeping food, etc., in a cold store to prevent it going bad; **to put a plan into cold storage** = to postpone work on a plan, usually for a very long time
(b) cost of keeping things in store; *storage costs us 10% of the value of the items stored*
(c) facility for storing data in a computer; *a hard disk with a storage capacity of 200 Mb*

① **store**
[stɔr]
1 *noun*
(a) shop, a place where you can buy things; *you can buy shoes in any of the big stores in town; does the store have a furniture department?;* **department store** = large store, with different sections for different types of goods; **general**

store = small (country) store that sells a wide range of goods
(b) supplies kept to use later; *we keep a big store of coal for the winter; they bought stores for their journey*
(c) place where goods are kept; *the goods will be kept in store until they are needed;* **cold store** = warehouse or room where supplies can be kept cold; **to be in store for someone** *or* **to have something in store for someone** = to be going to happen to someone; *she has a big surprise in store; we didn't know what would be in store for us when we surrendered to the enemy*
2 *verb*
(a) to keep food, etc., to use later; *we store (away) all our vegetables in the shed*
(b) to put something in a warehouse for safekeeping; *we stored our furniture while we were looking for a house to buy*
(c) to keep something in a computer file; *we store all our personnel records on computer*

① **storm**
[stɔrm]
1 *noun*
(a) high wind and very bad weather; *several ships got into difficulties in the storm; how many trees were blown down in last night's storm?; March and October are the worst months for storms;* **a storm of applause** = loud burst of cheering; *a storm of applause greeted the orchestra*
(b) by storm = (i) in a sudden rush or attack; (ii) with a great deal of excitement; *the soldiers took the enemy castle by storm; the pop group has taken the town by storm*
2 *verb*
(a) to rush about angrily; *he stormed into the store and demanded to see the manager;* **to storm off** *or* **out** = to go away or out in anger; *she stormed out of the meeting and called her lawyer*
(b) to attack suddenly and capture; *our troops stormed the enemy camp*

② **stormy**
['stɔrmi] *adjective*
when there are storms; *they are forecasting stormy weather for the weekend* (NOTE: **stormier - stormiest**)

① **story**
['stɔri] *noun*
(a) description that tells things that did not really happen but are invented by an author; *the book is the story of two children during the war; she writes children's stories about animals*
(b) description that tells what really happened; *she told her story to the journalist;* **it's a long story** = it is difficult to describe what happened
(c) lie, something which is not true; *nobody will believe such stories*
(d) whole floor in a building; *a twenty-story office block; the upper stories of the block caught fire* (NOTE: plural is **stories**)

③ **stout**
[staʊt]
1 *adjective*
quite fat; *the stout man had difficulty going up the stairs* (NOTE: **stouter - stoutest**)
2 *noun*
type of strong black beer

① **stove**
[stəʊv] *noun*
apparatus for heating or cooking; *the shed is heated by an oil stove*; *the milk boiled over and made a mess on the kitchen stove*; *we have an electric stove in the kitchen*

② **straight**
[streɪt]
1 *adjective*
(a) not curved; *Madison Avenue is a long straight street*; *the line under the picture isn't straight*; *she has straight black hair*; *stand up straight!*
(b) not sloping; *is the picture straight?*; *the shelf should be perfectly straight but it slopes slightly to the left*; *your necktie isn't straight*
(c) clear and simple; *I want you to give me a straight answer*; **a straight fight** = an election contest between two candidates only
(d) tidy; *can you get the room straight before the visitors arrive?*
(e) **to get something straight** = to understand clearly the meaning of something; *before you start, let's get this straight - you are not going to be paid for the work* (NOTE: **straighter - straightest**)
2 *adverb*
(a) going in a straight line, not curving; *the road goes straight across the plain for two hundred miles*; **to go straight on** *or* **to keep straight on** = to continue along this road without turning off it; *go straight on past the road junction and then make a left*; *keep straight on and you'll find the hospital just after the supermarket*; *the church is straight in front of you*
(b) immediately, at once; *wait for me here - I'll come straight back*; *if there is a problem, you should go straight to the manager*
(c) without stopping or changing; *she drank the milk straight out of the bottle*; *the cat ran straight across the road in front of the automobile*; *he looked me straight in the face*; *the plane flies straight to Washington*
(d) (alcohol) with no water or any other liquid added; *he drinks his whiskey straight*
(e) *(informal)* **to go straight** = to stop committing crimes; *after he left prison he went straight for six or seven months*
3 *noun*
(on a racetrack) part of the track which is straight; *the runners are coming into the final straight*

③ **straightaway**
[ˈstreɪtəweɪ] *adverb*
immediately; *he got my letter, and wrote back straightaway; as soon as he heard the news he straightaway phoned his wife*

① **straighten**
[ˈstreɪtn] *verb*
(a) to make straight; *she had surgery to straighten her nose*; *he straightened his necktie and went into the meeting*
(b) **to straighten up** = to stand straight after bending down; *he straightened up and looked at me*

④ **straightforward**
[streɪtˈfɔːwəd] *adjective*
(a) honest and open; *she refused to give a straightforward answer*
(b) easy, not complicated; *if you follow the instructions carefully, it's quite a straightforward job*

③ **straight off**
[ˈstreɪt ˈɒf] *adverb*
immediately, at once; *I'll start straight off with the most important question*

③ **straight out**
[ˈstreɪt ˈaʊt] *adverb*
directly, without hesitating; *she told him straight out that she didn't want to see him again*

② **strain**
[streɪn]
1 *noun*
(a) nervous tension and stress; *can she stand the strain of working in that office?*
(b) condition where a muscle has been stretched or torn by a sudden movement; *she dropped out of the race with muscle strain*
(c) force of pulling something tight; *can that small rope take the strain of the boat?*
(d) **to put a strain on** = to make something more difficult; *the strong dollar will put a strain on our exports*; *his drinking put a strain on their marriage*
(e) music, part of a tune; *they all sang to the strains of the guitar*
(f) variety, breed; *they are trying to find a cure for a new strain of the flu virus*; *he crossed two strains of rice to produce a variety which is resistant to disease*
2 *verb*
(a) to injure part of your body by pulling too hard; *he strained a muscle in his back or he strained his back*; *the effort strained his heart*
(b) to make great efforts to do something; *they strained to lift the piano into the van*
(c) to put pressure on something, to make something more difficult; *the mortgage payments will strain our budget*; *the argument strained our relations*
(d) to pour liquid away, leaving any solids behind; *boil the peas for ten minutes and then strain*

② **strand**
[strænd]
1 *noun*

one piece of hair, thread, etc.; *strands of hair kept blowing across her face*

2 *verb*

to leave someone or something alone and helpless; *her purse was stolen and she was stranded without any money; the captain stranded the ship on a beach*

① stranded
['strændɪd] *adjective*

alone and unable to move; *the blizzard left thousands of people stranded at the airport; the airlines are trying to bring back thousands of stranded tourists*

① strange
[streɪnʒ] *adjective*

(a) not usual; *something is the matter with the engine - it's making a strange noise; she told some very strange stories about the firm she used to work for; it felt strange to be sitting in the office on a Saturday afternoon; it's strange that no one spotted the mistake; a strange-looking young man was with her*

(b) which you have never seen before or where you have never been before; *I find it difficult getting to sleep in a strange room; we went to Japan and had lots of strange food to eat* (NOTE: **stranger - strangest**)

② strangely
['streɪnʒli] *adverb*

in a strange way; *your face seems strangely familiar, have we met before?; strangely enough, my birthday's on the same day as his*

① stranger
['streɪnʒər] *noun*

(a) person whom you have never met; *I've never met him - he's a complete stranger to me; children are told not to accept rides from strangers*

(b) person in a place where he has never been before; *I can't tell you how to get to the post office - I'm a stranger here myself*

① strap
[stræp]

1 *noun*

long flat piece of material used to attach something; *can you do up the strap of my backpack for me?; I put a strap around my suitcase to make it more secure*

2 *verb*

(a) to fasten something with a strap; *he strapped on his oxygen cylinder; the patient was strapped to a stretcher; make sure the baby is strapped into her seat*

(b) to wrap a bandage tightly around a limb; *she strapped up his ankle and told him to lie down* (NOTE: **strapping - strapped**)

④ strategic *or* strategical
[strə'tiːdʒɪk'l] *adjective*

referring to strategy; **strategic advantage** = position which gives an advantage over the enemy; *breaking the enemy's secret code gave us an enormous strategic advantage;* **strategic planning** = planning the future work of an organization

③ strategy
['strætədʒi] *noun*

planning of actions in advance; *their strategy is to note which of their rival's models sells best and then copy it; the government has no long-term strategy for dealing with crime;* **business strategy** = planning of how to develop your business

② straw
[strɔ] *noun*

(a) dry stalks and leaves of crops left after the grain has been harvested; *you've been lying on the ground - you've got bits of straw in your hair; the farm workers picked up bundles of straw and loaded them onto a truck*

(b) thin plastic tube for sucking up liquids; *she was drinking orange juice through a straw*

(c) **straw vote** *or* **straw poll** = rapid poll taken near voting day, to see how people intend to vote; *a straw poll of members of staff showed that most of them were going to vote for the city council's plan*

(d) *(informal)* **the last straw** = the final and worst problem in a series; *the children had been sick one after another, but the last straw was when the eldest girl caught the measles; that's the last straw* = I can't stand any more of this

① strawberry
['strɔbri] *noun*

common soft red summer fruit growing on low plants; *I picked some strawberries for dessert; a jar of strawberry jam* (NOTE: plural is **strawberries**)

② stray
[streɪ]

1 *adjective*

(a) which is wandering away from home; *we found a stray cat and brought it home*

(b) not where it should be; *he was killed by a stray bullet from a gunman*

2 *verb*

to wander away; *the sheep strayed onto the golf course; the children had strayed too far onto the rocks and couldn't get back*

3 *noun*

animal that is lost and wandering far away from home; *we have two female cats at home and they attract all the strays in the district*

③ streak
[strik]

1 *noun*

(a) line of color; *she's had blonde streaks put in her hair*

(b) particularly characteristic type of behavior; *she has a ruthless streak in her; it's his mean streak that makes him not buy any Christmas presents*

(c) **streak of lightning** = a flash of lightning

(d) period when a series of things happens; *I was on a winning streak, I won three times in a* *row*; *I hope our unlucky streak is coming to an end*; **a streak of luck** = a period when you are lucky; *his streak of luck continued as he won the lottery yet again*

2 *verb*

(a) to go very fast; *the rocket streaked across the sky*

(b) to mark with lines of color; *tears streaked down her face*

① **stream**
[strim]
1 *noun*
(a) little river; *can you jump across that stream?*
(b) things which pass continuously; *crossing the road is difficult because of the stream of traffic*; *we had a stream of customers on the first day of the sale*; *streams of refugees tried to cross the border*

2 *verb*
to flow continuously; *blood was streaming down his face*; *automobiles streamed out of the park*; *children streamed across the square*

① **street**
[strit] *noun*
(a) road in a town, usually with houses on each side; *it is difficult to park in our street on Saturday mornings*; *her apartment is on a noisy street*; *the school is in the next street*; **street map** *or* **street plan** = diagram showing the streets of a town, with their names; *you will need a street map to get around Brooklyn*
(b) *(used with names)* **I live on 42nd Street** (NOTE: abbreviated to **St.: 42nd St.**)
(c) Main Street = the main shopping street in a town; *his store is on Main Street*
(d) at street level = at the same height as the street; *the main entrance is at street level*

① **streetcar**
['stritkɑər] *noun*
public vehicle similar to a bus, that runs on rails laid in the street; *I take a streetcar from my apartment to the office*

① **strength**
[streŋθ] *noun*
(a) being strong; *she hasn't got the strength to lift it; you should test the strength of the rope before you start climbing*
(b) being at a high level; *the strength of the demand for the new automobile is surprising*; *the strength of the dollar increases the possibility of higher inflation*
(c) in strength = in large numbers; *the police were there in strength*; **at full strength** = with everyone present; *the department had several posts vacant, but is back to full strength again*; **in a show of strength** = to show how strong an army is; *in a show of strength, the government sent an aircraft carrier to the area*; **to go from strength to strength** = to get stronger and stronger; *under his leadership the party went from strength to strength*; **on the strength of** =

because of; *they employed him on the strength of the references from his previous employer* (NOTE: the opposite is **weakness**)

③ **strengthen**
['streŋθn] *verb*
(a) to make something stronger; *the sea wall is being strengthened to prevent another flood*; *this will only strengthen their determination to oppose the government*; *we are planning to strengthen airport security*
(b) to become stronger; *the wind is strengthening from the southwest* (NOTE: the opposite is **weaken**)

③ **stress**
[stres]
1 *noun*
(a) nervous strain caused by an outside influence; *she has difficulty coping with the stress of the office*; *people in positions of responsibility often have stress-related illnesses*
(b) force or pressure on something; *stresses inside the planet create earthquakes*; **stress fracture** = fracture of a bone caused by excessive force, as in some types of sport
(c) strength of your voice when you pronounce a word or part of a word; *in the word "emphasis" the stress is on the first part of the word* (NOTE: plural is **stresses**)

2 *verb*
to put emphasis on something; *I must stress the importance of keeping the plan secret*

③ **stressed**
[strest] *adjective*
worried and tense; *when you're feeling stressed it's better to try to get to bed early*; *if you feel stressed, just close your eyes and listen to some relaxing music*; *(informal)* **stressed out** = very worried and tense; *he's stressed out with his new job*

① **stretch**
[stretʃ]
1 *noun*
(a) long piece of land, road, etc.; *for long stretches of the Trans-Siberian Railway, all you see are trees*; *stretches of the river have been so polluted that bathing is dangerous*; **the final stretch** *or* **the home stretch** = the last stage of a race or journey; *he was far ahead of the other runners when they came to the final stretch*
(b) long period of time; *for long stretches we had nothing to do*; **at a stretch** = without a break; *he played the piano for two hours at a stretch*
(c) action of putting out your arms and legs as far as they will go; *I love to lie in bed and have a good stretch before I get up*
(d) by no stretch of the imagination = no one can possibly believe that; *by no stretch of the imagination can you expect him to win* (NOTE: plural is **stretches**)

2 *verb*

(a) to spread out for a great distance; *the line of cars stretched for three miles from the accident; the line stretched from the door of the movie theater right around the corner; white sandy beaches stretch as far as the eye can see*
(b) to push out your arms or legs as far as they can; *the cat woke up and stretched; the monkey stretched out through the bars and grabbed the little boy's cap; (informal)* to stretch your legs = to go for a short walk after sitting for a long time; *during the coffee break I went out into the garden to stretch my legs*
(c) to pull out so that it becomes loose; *don't hang your sweater up like that - you will just stretch it; these pants are not supposed to stretch*
(d) to make someone work or think hard

③ **stretch back**
['stretʃ 'bæk] *verb*
to go back over a long period; *his interest in music stretches back to when he was in elementary school*

③ **stretcher**
['stretʃər] *noun*
folding bed with handles, on which an injured person can be carried by two people; *some of the injured could walk, but there were several stretcher cases; the rescue team brought him down the mountain, strapped to a stretcher*

③ **stretch to**
['stretʃ 'tu] *verb*
to stretch something to the limit = to be almost too much for; *the new automobile is going to stretch my finances to the limit*

② **strict**
[strɪkt] *adjective*
(a) exact (meaning); *the files are in strict order of their dates*
(b) which must be obeyed; *I gave strict instructions that no one was to be allowed in; the rules are very strict and any bad behavior will be severely punished*
(c) insisting that rules are obeyed; *our parents are very strict with us about staying up late* (NOTE: **stricter - strictest**)

④ **strictly**
['strɪktli] *adverb*
(a) in a strict way; *all staff must follow strictly the procedures in the training manual*
(b) strictly confidential = completely secret; *what I am going to tell you is strictly confidential*
(c) strictly speaking = really, in reality; *strictly speaking, she's not my aunt, just an old friend of the family*

④ **stride**
[straɪd]
1 *noun*
long step; *in three strides he was across the room and out of the door;* to make great strides = to advance quickly; *doctors have made great strides in the treatment of cancer;* to take something in your stride = to deal with

something easily; *other people always seem to have problems, but she just takes everything in her stride*
2 *verb*
to walk with long steps; *she strode into the room carrying a whip; we could see him striding across the field* (NOTE: **striding - strode** [strəʊd])

① **strike**
[straɪk]
1 *noun*
(a) stopping of work by workers because of lack of agreement with management or because of orders from a labor union; *they all voted in favor of a strike; the danger of a strike was removed at the last minute;* general strike = strike of all the workers in a country; sit-down strike = strike where the workers stay in their place of work and refuse to leave; to take strike action = to go on strike; *the workers voted to take strike action;* strike ballot *or* strike vote = vote by workers to decide if a strike should be held
(b) to go out on strike *or* to go on strike = to stop work; *the workers went on strike for more money; the stewards and stewardesses are on strike for higher pay;* to call the workforce out on strike = to tell the workers to stop work; *the union called its members out on strike*
(c) military attack; *they launched an air strike against the enemy positions*
(d) *(in baseball)* pitched ball which is swung at and missed; *three strikes and you're out*
2 *verb*
(a) to stop working because of disagreement with management; *the workers are striking in protest against bad working conditions*
(b) to hit something hard; *he struck her with a bottle; she struck her head on the low door; he struck a match and lit the fire*
(c) *(of a clock)* to ring to mark an hour; *the church clock had just struck one when she heard a noise outside her bedroom door*
(d) to come to someone's mind; *a thought just struck me; it suddenly struck me that I had seen him somewhere before;* it strikes me that = I think that; *it strikes me that we may be charging too much*
(e) to surprise someone; *he was struck by the poverty he saw everywhere*
(f) to attack; *the police are afraid the killer may strike again; the illness struck without warning*
(g) to come to an agreement; *we expect to strike a deal next week; they struck a bargain and decided to share the costs* (NOTE: **striking - struck** [strʌk])

③ **strike off**
['straɪk 'ɒf] *verb*
to remove a name from a list because of bad behavior; *he was struck off the register of doctors*

① **strike out**
['straɪk 'aʊt] *verb*

(a) *(in baseball)* to fail to hit the ball three times; *the batter struck out*
(b) to fail at something; *I applied for the job, but I struck out*

④ **striker**
['straɪkər] *noun*
(a) worker who is on strike; *strikers surrounded the factory*
(b) player whose main task is to score goals; *his pass back to the goalkeeper was stopped by the opposition striker, who then scored*

② **striking**
['straɪkɪŋ]
1 *adjective*
noticeable, unusual; *she bears a striking similarity to my aunt*; *it is a very striking portrait of the president*
2 *noun*
hitting; **within striking distance** = quite close, near enough to hit; *the capital is within striking distance of the enemy guns*

① **string**
[strɪŋ] *noun*
(a) strong thin thread used for tying up parcels, etc.; *this string isn't strong enough to tie up that big package*; *she bought a ball of string*; *we've run out of string* (NOTE: no plural in this meaning: **some string; a piece of string**)
(b) long series of things, events; *she's been plagued with a string of illnesses*; *I had a string of phone calls this morning*
(c) thread on a musical instrument which makes a note when you hit it; *he was playing the violin when one of the strings broke*; *a guitar has six strings*; **string instrument** = musical instrument with strings which make the notes

③ **string along**
['strɪŋ ə'lɒŋ] *verb*
(a) to walk along in a line behind someone; *the teachers walked in front and the children strung along behind*
(b) to promise someone something to get him or her to cooperate with you; *he was just stringing her along - he never intended to marry her, but just wanted to get at her money*

③ **strings**
[strɪŋz] *noun*
(a) *(informal)* hidden conditions; **are there any strings attached?** = are there any hidden conditions?; *the bank loaned us the money with no strings attached*; *(informal)* **to pull strings** = to use your influence to make something happen; *her father pulled strings to get her the job*
(b) **the strings** = section of an orchestra with string instruments; *the work provides a lot of scope for the strings*; *see also* BRASS, WIND
(c) members of an orchestra who play string instruments; *the strings sit at the front of the orchestra, near the conductor*

① **strip**
[strɪp]
1 *noun*
(a) long narrow piece of cloth, paper, etc.; *he tore the paper into strips*; *houses are to be built along the strip of land near the church*; **magnetic strip** = layer of magnetic material on a plastic card, used for recording data
(b) **comic strip** *or* **cartoon strip** = cartoon story made of a series of small drawings inside little boxes side by side
(c) **landing strip** = rough place for planes to land; *the soldiers cut a landing strip in the jungle*
2 *verb*
(a) to take off your clothes; *strip to the waist for your chest X-ray*; *he stripped down to his underpants*
(b) to remove completely; *the wind stripped the leaves off the trees*; *first we have to strip the old paint off the cupboards*; *he was stripped of his position following the scandal about bribes* (NOTE: **stripping - stripped**)

② **stripe**
[straɪp] *noun*
(a) long line of color; *he has an umbrella with red, white and blue stripes*
(b) piece of colored cloth sewn to a soldier's jacket to show his rank; *he has just got his sergeant's stripes*

② **stroke**
[strəʊk]
1 *noun*
(a) gentle touch with your hand; *she gave the dog a stroke*
(b) sudden loss of consciousness; *she had a stroke and died*
(c) movement of a pen, brush, etc., which makes a line; *she can draw a cartoon with just a few strokes of the pen*
(d) act of hitting something, such as a ball; *it took him three strokes to get the ball onto the green*
(e) sound made when hitting something (such as a bell); **on the stroke of midnight** = when the clocks are striking twelve
(f) **stroke of luck** = piece of luck; *I had a stroke of luck yesterday - I found my purse which I thought I had lost*; *it was a stroke of luck that you happened to come along at that moment*; **he hasn't done a stroke of work all day** = he hasn't done any work at all
(h) style of swimming; *she won the 200 m breast stroke*
(i) person rowing who sits at the back of the boat and sets the pace for the others; *see also* BOW
2 *verb*
to run your hands gently over; *she was stroking the cat as it sat in her lap*

③ **stroll**
[strəʊl]
1 *noun*

short relaxing walk; *we went for a stroll by the river after dinner*

2 *verb*

to walk slowly to relax; *people were strolling in the park*; *on Sunday evenings, everyone strolls along the bank of the river*

① **strong**
[strɒŋ]

1 *adjective*

(a) (person) with a lot of strength; *I'm not strong enough to carry that box*

(b) which has a lot of force or strength; *the string broke - we need something stronger*; *the wind was so strong that it blew some shingles off the roof*; **strong currency** = currency that is high against other currencies (NOTE: the opposite is a **weak currency**)

(c) with a powerful smell, taste, etc.; *I don't like strong cheese*; *you need a cup of strong black coffee to wake you up*; *there was a strong smell of gas in the kitchen*

(d) strong drink = alcohol; *have an orange juice, or would you prefer something stronger?* (NOTE: **stronger - strongest**)

2 *suffix*

(used to show a number of people) *a 50-strong party of marines landed on the beach*; *a group of workers twenty strong*

3 *adverb*

going strong = still very active, still working; *she had a heart operation ten years ago and is still going strong*

③ **strongbox**
['strɒŋbɒks] *noun*

small heavy safe for keeping valuable documents, jewels, etc.; *thieves broke open the strongbox and stole the jewels*

② **strongly**
['strɒŋli] *adverb*

in a strong way; *the castle is strongly defended*; *they objected very strongly to the plan*

② **struck**
[strʌk] *see* STRIKE

③ **structural**
['strʌktʃrəl] *adjective*

referring to a structure; *the inspector reported several structural defects*; **structural unemployment** = unemployment caused by the changing structure of an industry or of society

② **structure**
['strʌktʃər]

1 *noun*

(a) way in which things are organized; *a career structure within a corporation*; *the company is reorganizing its discount structure*

(b) *(formal)* way in which something is built; *the structure of the bridge had been weakened by constant traffic*

2 *verb*

to arrange according to a certain system; *we've tried to structure the meeting so that there is plenty of time for discussion*

② **struggle**
['strʌgl]

1 *noun*

(a) fight; *after a short struggle the burglar was arrested*

(b) hard effort to do something because of difficulties; *setting up a new company during a recession was always going to be a struggle*; *her constant struggle to bring up her children*; *their struggle against illness*

2 *verb*

(a) to fight with an attacker; *two men were struggling on the floor*

(b) to try hard to do something difficult; *she's struggling with her math homework*; *she struggled to carry all the shopping to the car*; **to struggle to your feet** = to stand up with great difficulty; *after the blast from the bomb she struggled to her feet and started running*

② **stubborn**
['stʌbən] *adjective*

(a) not willing to change your mind; *he's so stubborn - he only does what he wants to do*

(b) difficult to remove; *to get rid of really stubborn stains you will need to use something stronger than regular soap*

① **stuck**
[stʌk] *see* STICK

① **student**
['stjudənt] *noun*

(a) person who is studying at a college or university; *all the science students came to my lecture*; *she's a brilliant student*; *two students had to take the exam again*

(b) boy or girl studying at high school

① **studio**
['stjudiəʊ] *noun*

(a) place where movies, broadcasts, recordings, etc., are made; *the movie was made at these studios*; *and now, back to the studio for the latest news and weather report*; *they spent the whole day recording the piece in the studio*

(b) very small apartment for one person, usually one room with a small kitchen and bathroom; *you can rent a studio overlooking the sea for $450 a week in high season*

(c) room where an artist paints; *she uses this room as a studio because of the good light*; **design studio** = independent firm which specializes in creating designs for companies

(d) place where photographers take photographs; *a studio photograph of the bride and bridegroom* (NOTE: plural is **studios**)

① **study**
['stʌdi]

1 *noun*

(a) work of examining something carefully to learn more about it; *the company asked the experts to prepare a study into new production techniques*; *the review has published studies on the new drug*; **nature study** = learning about plants and animals at school

(b) room in which someone reads, writes, works, etc.; *when he says he is going to his study to read, it usually means he's going to have little nap*

(c) studies = attending college or a university; *she interrupted her studies and went to work in Kenya for two years; he has successfully finished his studies*

2 *verb*

(a) to learn about a subject at college or a university; *he is studying medicine because he wants to be a doctor; she's studying French and Spanish in the modern languages department*

(b) to examine something carefully to learn more about it; *we are studying the possibility of setting up an office in New York; the government studied the committee's proposals for two months; doctors are studying the results of the screening program*

(c) to look at something carefully; *she was studying the guidebook*

② **stuff**
['stʌf]
1 *noun*

(a) substance, especially something unpleasant; *you've got some black stuff stuck to your shoe*

(b) *(informal)* things, equipment; *dump all your stuff in the living room; take all that stuff and put it in the trash can; all your photographic stuff is still in the back of my truck*

2 *verb*

(a) to push something into something to fill it; *he stuffed his pockets full of sweets for the children; the banknotes were stuffed into a small plastic bag*

(b) to put chopped onions, chopped meat, etc., inside meat or vegetables before cooking; *they served stuffed vine leaves as a starter; we had roast lamb stuffed with mushrooms*

(c) *(informal)* **to stuff yourself** = to eat a lot; *they were stuffing themselves on chocolate pudding*

(d) to fill the skin of a dead animal so that it looks alive; *there was a stuffed owl at the top of the stairs in the old castle*

(e) *(informal, rude)* **(go and) get stuffed** = go away, stop interfering; *you can tell the manager to go and get stuffed*

④ **stuffer**
['stʌfər] *noun*
stocking stuffer = little gift that can be put into a Christmas stocking

③ **stuffy**
['stʌfi] *adjective*
without any fresh air; *can't you open a window, it's so stuffy in here; I dislike traveling into town every day on stuffy underground trains* (NOTE: **stuffier - stuffiest**)

② **stumble**
['stʌmbl] *verb*
(a) to trip, to almost fall by hitting your foot against something; *he stumbled as he tried to get down the stairs in the dark*

(b) to walk about, staggering; *he was stumbling around in the basement, looking for the light switch*

(c) to stumble across something = to find something by accident; *I stumbled across this letter which someone had hidden*

(d) to make mistakes when reading; *he managed to stumble through the reading test; she read the TV news without stumbling over any of the foreign words*

② **stump**
[stʌmp]
1 *noun*
short piece of something left sticking up, such as the trunk of a tree that has been cut down; *after cutting down the trees, we need to get rid of the stumps*

2 *verb*

(a) *(informal)* to ask someone a difficult question which he can't answer; *the CEO was stumped when the committee asked him how many hours the average employee worked; today's puzzle has stumped me completely or has got me stumped*

(b) to campaign (for votes); *the candidate stumped all of Ohio*

③ **stun**
[stʌn] *verb*

(a) to knock someone out, to make someone lose consciousness with a blow to the head; *the blow on the head stunned him*

(b) to shock someone completely; *she was stunned when he told her that he was already married* (NOTE: **stunning - stunned**)

② **stung**
[stʌŋ] *see* STING

② **stunk**
[stʌŋk] *see* STINK

③ **stunning**
['stʌnɪŋ] *adjective*
extraordinary, wonderful and beautiful; *this is a stunning photograph of your mother; they have a stunning house*

② **stupid**
['stjuːpɪd] *adjective*

(a) not very intelligent; *what a stupid man!*

(b) not showing any sense; *it was stupid of her not to wear a helmet when riding her motorcycle; he made several stupid mistakes*

③ **sturdy**
['stɜrdi] *adjective*
strong, with good muscles; *she has two sturdy little boys* (NOTE: **sturdier - sturdiest**)

② **stutter**
['stʌtər]
1 *noun*
speech problem where you repeat the sound at the beginning of a word several times; *he is trying to cure his stutter*

2 *verb*

to repeat the same sounds when speaking; *he stuttered badly when making his speech*

① **style**
[staɪl] *noun*
(a) way of doing something, especially way of designing, drawing, writing, etc.; *the room is decorated in Chinese style*; *the painting is in his usual style*; *that style was fashionable in the 1940s*
(b) elegant or fashionable way of doing things; *she always dresses with style*; *they live in grand style*
(c) way someone behaves, thinks or lives; *it's not her style to forget an appointment*; *their style of life wouldn't suit me*

② **stylish**
['staɪlɪʃ] *adjective*
attractive and fashionable; *he drives a stylish sports car*; *we ate in a very stylish new restaurant*

② **sub**
[sʌb]   *(informal)*   =   SUBMARINE, SUBSCRIPTION, SUBSTITUTE

② **sub-**
[sʌb] *prefix meaning*
below, under

② **subject**
['sʌbdʒɪkt] *noun*
(a) thing which you are talking about or writing about; *he suddenly changed the subject of the conversation*; *the newspaper has devoted a special issue to the subject of pollution*
(b) thing shown in a painting, etc.; *the same subject is treated quite differently in the three paintings*
(c) area of knowledge which you are studying; *math is his weakest subject*
(d) to be the subject of = to be the person or thing talked about or studied; *the painter Chagall will be the subject of our lecture today*; *advertising costs are the subject of close examination by the auditors*
(e) *(grammar)* noun or pronoun that comes before a verb and shows the person or thing that does the action expressed by the verb; *in the sentence "the cat sat on the mat" the word "cat" is the subject of the verb "sat"*
(f) person who is born in a country, or who has the right to live in a country; *she is a British subject but a Canadian citizen*

④ **subjective**
[sʌb'dʒektɪv] *adjective*
seen from your own point of view, and therefore possibly biased; *this is a purely subjective impression of what happened* (NOTE: the opposite is **objective**)

④ **subject to**
1 *adjective* ['sʌbdʒɪkt 'tu]
(a) depending on something; *we want you to go on a study tour to Germany, subject to getting your parents' permission;* **the contract is subject to government approval** = the contract

will be valid only if it is approved by the government; **sale subject to contract** = sale that is not legal until a proper contract has been signed
(b) affected by; *the timetable is subject to change without notice*; *this jewelry is subject to import tax*; *after returning from the tropics he was subject to attacks of fever*
2 *verb* [sʌb'dʒekt 'tu]
to subject to = to make something or someone suffer something unpleasant; *the guards subjected the prisoners to physical violence*; *we were subjected to a mass of questions by reporters*

② **submarine**
[sʌbmə'rin]
1 *noun*
special type of ship which can travel under water; *the submarine dove before she was spotted by enemy aircraft*
2 *adjective*
which is under the water; *a submarine pipeline*

④ **submission**
[sʌb'mɪʃn] *noun*
(a) state of giving in or having to obey someone; *their plan was to starve the enemy into submission* (NOTE: no plural in this meaning)
(b) evidence, document, argument used in court; *in his submission, he stated that the city council had always acted within the law*

③ **submit**
[sʌb'mɪt] *verb*
(a) to submit to = to yield to; *he definitely won't submit to pressure from the committee*
(b) to put something forward for someone to examine; *you are requested to submit your proposal to the planning committee*; *he submitted a claim to the insurers*; *reps are asked to submit their expenses claims once a month*
(c) to plead in court; *the defense submitted that there was no case to answer* (NOTE: **submitting - submitted**)

④ **subordinate**
1 *adjective* [sə'bɔrdnət]
(a) under the control of someone else; less important; **subordinate to** = which is under the control of; *the new arrangement will make our department subordinate to yours*
(b) subordinate clause = clause in a sentence which depends on the main clause
2 *noun* [sə'bɔrdnət]
person who is under the direction of someone else; *his subordinates find him difficult to work with*
3 *verb* [sə'bɔrdneɪt]
to subordinate something to = to put something in a less important position than something else; *we were taught to subordinate our personal feelings to the needs of the state*

② subscription
[sʌbˈskrɪpʃn] *noun*
(a) money paid to a club for a year's membership; *he forgot to renew his club subscription*
(b) money paid in advance to a magazine for a series of issues; *did you remember to pay the subscription to the computer magazine?*; **to take out a subscription to a magazine** = to start paying for a series of issues of a magazine; **to cancel a subscription to a magazine** = to stop paying for a magazine

④ subsequent
[ˈsʌbsɪkwənt] *adjective*
(formal) which comes later; *the tropical storm and the subsequent floods stopped the baseball game*; *all subsequent reports must be sent to me immediately they arrive*

④ subsequently
[ˈsʌbsɪkwəntli] *adverb*
(formal) afterwards; *I subsequently discovered that there had been a mistake*; *what happened subsequently proved that our forecast had been correct*

④ subsidize
[ˈsʌbsɪdaɪz] *verb*
to help by giving money; *the government has refused to subsidize the automobile industry*

④ subsidy
[ˈsʌbsɪdi] *noun*
money given to help pay for something which is not profitable; *the government has increased its subsidy to the coal industry* (NOTE: plural is **subsidies**)

③ substance
[ˈsʌbstəns] *noun*
(a) solid or liquid material, especially one used in chemistry; *a secret substance is added to the product to give it its yellow color*; *toxic substances got into the drinking water*
(b) truth behind an argument; *there is no substance to the rumor that his business was controlled by a criminal gang*; *she brought documents to add substance to her claim*
(c) *(formal)* **a man of substance** = a rich man
(d) *(formal)* drug; *he was found to have certain illegal substances in his suitcase*; **substance abuse** = addiction to illegal drugs

④ substantial
[sʌbˈstænʃl] *adjective*
(a) large, important; *she was awarded substantial damages*; *he received a substantial sum when he left the company*; *a substantial amount of work remains to be done*
(b) large, which satisfies; *we had a substantial meal at the local diner*
(c) solid, strong; *this wall is too thin, we need something much more substantial*

④ substantially
[sʌbˈstænʃəli] *adverb*
(a) mainly, mostly; *their forecast was substantially correct*
(b) by a large amount; *the cost of raw materials has risen substantially over the last year*

② substitute
[ˈsʌbstɪtjut]
1 *noun*
person or thing that takes the place of someone or something else; *this type of plastic can be used as a substitute for leather*; *meat substitutes are often made from soy*; *I thought the substitute teacher was better than our normal teacher*; *when the goalkeeper was injured they sent in a substitute*
2 *verb*
to substitute something *or* **someone for something** *or* **someone else** = to put something or someone in the place of something or someone else; *he secretly substituted the fake diamond for the real one*; **to substitute for someone** = to replace someone; *who will be substituting for the sales manager when she's away on vacation?*

④ subtle
[ˈsʌtl] *adjective*
(a) not obvious or easily seen; *there's a subtle difference between the two political parties*
(b) difficult to analyze because of being complicated or delicate; *a sauce with a subtle taste of lemon*; *a subtler shade would be better than that bright color* (NOTE: **subtler - subtlest**)

① subtract
[sʌbˈtrækt] *verb*
to take one number away from another; *subtract 10 from 33 and you get 23* (NOTE: subtracting is usually shown by the minus sign - : **10 - 4 = 6**: say "ten subtract four equals six")

① subtraction
[sʌbˈtrækʃn] *noun*
act of subtracting one figure from another; *he tried to do the subtraction in his head*

③ suburb
[ˈsʌbɜrb] *noun*
residential area on the edge of a town; *he lives in a quiet suburb of Boston*; **the suburbs** = area all round a town where a lot of people live; *people who live in the suburbs find the air quality is better than downtown*

③ suburban
[səˈbɜrbən] *adjective*
referring to the suburbs; *this is a very suburban area - almost everyone commutes downtown each day*; *you can ride the train from this suburban station to the city*

③ subway
[ˈsʌbweɪ] *noun*
underground railway system; *the New York subway*; *it will be quicker to take the subway to Grand Central Station* (NOTE: the London equivalent is the **tube** *or* **Underground**)

② succeed
[sʌkˈsid] *verb*
(a) to do well or to be profitable; *his business has succeeded more than he had expected*

(b) to succeed in doing something = to do what you have been trying to do; *she succeeded in passing her driver's test*; *I succeeded in getting them to agree to my plan*
(c) to follow on after someone who has retired, left the job, etc.; *Mr. Smith was succeeded as chairman by Mr. Jones*

② **success**
[sʌkˈses] *noun*
(a) achieving what you have been trying to do; *she's been looking for a job in a library, but without any success so far*
(b) doing something well; *her photo was in the newspapers after her Olympic success*; *the new automobile has not had much success in the Japanese market*
(c) somebody or something that succeeds; *the launch of the new model was a great success*; *he wasn't much of a success as a manager*; *the heart operation was a complete success* (NOTE: plural is **successes**)

③ **successful**
[sʌkˈsesfəl] *adjective*
who or which does well; *he's a successful business man*; *she's very successful at hiding her real age*; *their selling trip to Japan proved successful*

③ **successfully**
[sʌkˈsesfəli] *adverb*
achieving what was intended; *the new model was successfully launched last week*; *she successfully found her way to the museum*

④ **succession**
[səkˈseʃn] *noun*
(a) series of the same sort of thing; *I had a succession of phone calls from my relatives*
(b) in succession = one after the other; *three people in succession have asked me the same question*; *he won the title five times in succession*

④ **successive**
[səkˈsesɪv] *adjective*
which come one after the other; *successive delays have meant that we are now ten months behind schedule*; *in three successive matches the goalkeeper was injured*

④ **successor**
[səkˈsesər] *noun*
person who takes over from someone; *Mr. Smith's successor as chairman will be Mr. Jones*; *he handed the keys of the safe over to his successor*

② **such**
[sʌtʃ]
1 *adjective*
(a) of this sort; *the police are looking for such things as drugs or stolen goods*
(b) no such = not existing; *there is no such day as April 31*; *someone was asking for a Mr. Simpson but there is no such person working here*

(c) such as = like; *some stores such as food stores are open on Sundays*
(d) very; so much; *there was such a crowd at the party that there weren't enough chairs to go round*; *it's such a shame that she's sick and has to miss her sister's wedding*; *she's such a slow worker that she produces about half as much as everyone else*; *these days, people can't afford to buy such expensive meals*
2 *pronoun*
this type of person or thing; *she's very competent, and is thought of as such by the management*; *the noise was such that it stopped me sleeping*

③ **suck**
[sʌk] *verb*
(a) to hold something with your mouth and pull at it (with your tongue); *the baby didn't stop sucking his thumb until he was six*
(b) to have something in your mouth which makes your mouth produce water; *he bought a bag of candy to suck in the automobile*
(c) to pull liquid into your mouth by using the muscles in your mouth; *she sucked the orange juice through a straw*; *she carries a bottle of apple juice everywhere and the baby sucks some when she's thirsty*
(d) *(informal)* to be dreadful; *this job sucks!*

② **sucker**
[ˈsʌkər] *noun*
(a) lollipop; *she gave the kid a strawberry-flavored sucker*
(b) *(informal)* person who is easily fooled; *I gave him the money - I'm such a sucker!*

③ **suck up**
[ˈsʌk ˈʌp] *verb*
(a) to swallow; *the new vacuum cleaner sucks up dust very efficiently*
(b) *(informal)* **to suck up to someone** = to say nice things to someone so as to get good treatment; *you should see the way he sucks up to the boss*

① **sudden**
[ˈsʌdən] *adjective*
(a) which happens very quickly or unexpectedly; *the sudden change in the weather caught us without any umbrellas*; *the bus came to a sudden stop*; *his decision to go to Canada was very sudden*
(b) all of a sudden = suddenly, quickly, giving you a shock; *all of a sudden the room went dark*

① **suddenly**
[ˈsʌdənli] *adverb*
quickly and giving you a shock; *the car in front stopped suddenly and I ran into the back of it*; *suddenly the room went dark*; *she suddenly realized it was already five o'clock*

③ **sue**
[su] *verb*
to take someone to court, to start legal proceedings against someone to get compensation for a wrong; *she is suing the*

driver of the other automobile for damages; he sued the company for $50,000 compensation; we are still debating whether to sue or not

② **suffer**

['sʌfər] *verb*

(a) to be in a bad situation, to do badly; *the harvest has suffered because of the bad weather; exports have suffered during the last six months*

(b) to receive an injury; *he suffered serious injuries in the accident*

(c) to feel pain; *he didn't suffer at all, and was conscious until he died*

(d) to suffer from = to have an illness or a fault; *she suffers from constant headaches; the company's products suffer from bad design; our automobile suffers from a tendency to use too much oil*

(e) not to suffer fools gladly = to be impatient with stupid people; *her main problem when answering customer complaints is that she doesn't suffer fools gladly*

② **sufferer**

['sʌfrər] *noun*

person who has a certain disease; *a new drug to help asthma sufferers or sufferers from asthma;* **fellow sufferer** = person who suffers from the same thing as you; *she often gets migraine headaches and likes to talk with fellow sufferers*

② **suffering**

['sʌfrɪŋ] *noun*

feeling pain over a long period of time; *the doctor gave him an injection to relieve his suffering;* **to put an animal out of its suffering** = to kill an animal which is very sick

④ **sufficient**

[sə'fɪʃənt] *adjective*

(formal) as much as is needed; *does she have sufficient funds to pay for her trip?; there isn't sufficient room to put the big couch in here; allow yourself sufficient time to get to the airport*

④ **sufficiently**

[sə'fɪʃəntli] *adverb*

(formal) enough; *he isn't sufficiently careful to use a chain saw; the climate is not sufficiently warm to grow orange trees here*

② **suffix**

['sʌfɪks] *noun*

letters added to the end of a word to make another word; *the suffix "-ly" can be added to an adjective to form an adverb such as "partially" or "suddenly"* (NOTE: plural is **suffixes**; the opposite, letters which are added in front of a word, is a **prefix**)

① **sugar**

['ʃʊgər] *noun*

(a) white substance that you use to make food sweet; *how much sugar do you take in your tea?; a spoonful of sugar will be enough; can you pass me the sugar, please?;* **brown sugar** = sugar which has not been made pure; **white sugar** = sugar which has been made pure; **powdered sugar** = fine powdered white sugar, used to cover cakes; *if you're in a hurry, just dust the cake with powdered sugar;* **sugar lump** *or* **lump of sugar** = cube of white sugar (NOTE: no plural: **some sugar; a bag of sugar; a lump of sugar; a spoonful of sugar**)

(b) *(informal)* a spoonful of sugar; *how do you take your coffee? - milk and one sugar, please*

② **suggest**

[sə'dʒest] *verb*

to mention an idea to see what other people think of it; *the chairman suggested that the next meeting should be held in October; might I suggest a visit to the museum this afternoon?; what does he suggest we do in this case?*

② **suggestion**

[sə'dʒestʃn] *noun*

idea that you mention for people to think about; *we have asked for suggestions from passengers; the company acted upon your suggestion; whose suggestion was it that we should go out in a boat?; I bought those shares at the suggestion of the bank*

③ **suicide**

['suːɪsaɪd] *noun*

(a) act of killing yourself; *whether her death was murder or suicide is not yet known;* **to commit suicide** = to kill yourself; *he killed his two children and then committed suicide;* **suicide note** = letter left by someone who has committed suicide; *her suicide note was left on the kitchen table;* **attempted suicide** *or* **suicide attempt** = trying to kill yourself, but not succeeding; *she is still in the hospital after her suicide attempt*

(b) political suicide = action which ends your political career; *by voting against the government he effectively committed political suicide*

① **suit**

[suːt]

1 *noun*

(a) set of pieces of clothing made of the same cloth and worn together, such as a jacket and pants or skirt; *a dark gray suit will be just right for the interview; the pale blue suit she was wearing was very smart;* **ski suit** = one-piece suit, or jacket and pants, for skiing

(b) one of the four sets of cards with the same symbol in a pack of cards; *clubs and spades are the two black suits and hearts and diamonds are the two red suits*

(c) to follow suit = to do what everyone else does; *she jumped into the pool and everyone else followed suit*

(d) = LAWSUIT

2 *verb*

(a) to look good when worn by someone; *green usually suits people with red hair; that hat doesn't suit her*

(b) to be convenient; *he'll only do it when it suits him to do it; Thursday at 11 o'clock will suit me fine*

② **suitable**
['suːtəbl] *adjective*
which fits or which is convenient; *the most suitable place to meet will be under the big clock in the main square; we advertised the job again because there were no suitable candidates; a blue dress would be more suitable for an interview; I'm looking for a suitable present for her 30th birthday; is this a suitable moment to discuss the office move?*

② **suitcase**
['suːtkeɪs] *noun*
box with a handle which you carry your clothes in when you are traveling; *I never pack my suitcase until the last minute; the customs officer made him open his three suitcases; (informal)* **to live out of a suitcase** = to travel so frequently, that you don't spend much time at home

③ **suite**
[swiːt] *noun*
(a) set of rooms, especially expensive rooms; *their offices are in a suite of rooms on the eleventh floor; they booked a suite at the best hotel;* **honeymoon suite** = specially attractive hotel rooms for honeymoon couples; **VIP suite** = specially luxurious suite at an airport or in a hotel, for very important people
(b) set of pieces of furniture; **bathroom suite** = bath, washbowl and toilet; *a new bathroom suite could cost over $4500;* **bedroom suite** = bed, chest of drawers and other furniture for a bedroom; **living room suite** = sofa and matching armchairs
(c) several short pieces of music played together as one item; *the "Planets Suite" by Gustav Holst* (NOTE: do not confuse with **sweet**)

④ **sulk**
[sʌlk] *verb*
to show you are annoyed by not saying anything; *they're sulking because we didn't invite them*

④ **sultana**
[sʌlˈtænə] *noun*
type of pale raisin with no seeds; *we will need sultanas for the Christmas cake*

① **sum**
[sʌm] *noun*
(a) quantity of money; *he only paid a small sum for the automobile; a large sum of money was stolen from his safe; we are owed the sum of $750;* **lump sum** = money paid in one payment, not in several small payments; *you can take part of your pension as a lump sum*
(b) simple problem in math; *she tried to do the sum in her head; see also* SUMS
(c) total of two or more figures added together; *the sum of all four sides will give you the distance around the field*

(d) sum total = total amount of something which may not be as much as you want; *the Royal Palace and the National Museum were closed, so we went to the Museum of the Army and that was the sum total of what we saw*

③ **summary**
['sʌməri]
1 *noun*
short description of what has been said or written, or of what happened, without giving all the details; *she gave a summary of what happened at the meeting; here's a summary of the book in case you don't have time to read it; it is 7:30 and here is a summary of the news* (NOTE: plural is **summaries**)
2 *adjective*
which happens immediately; *he was given a summary punishment*

① **summer**
['sʌmər] *noun*
hottest time of the year, the season between spring and the fall; *next summer we are going to Barbados; the summer in Australia coincides with our winter here in Washington, DC; I haven't any summer clothes - it's never hot enough here;* **Indian summer** = warm period in early fall; *we had an Indian summer this year in late September;* **summer vacation** = period during the summer when children do not go to school; vacations taken by workers during the period from June to September; *I'm starting my summer vacation on July 20; the weather was awful during our summer vacation;* **summer school** = classes held at a school, college or university during the summer vacation; *she is organizing a summer school in Florence on "Fifteenth Century Italian Art"*

② **summertime**
['sʌmətaɪm] *noun*
the time of year when it is summer; *it's summertime, and the farmers are out in the fields all day long*

③ **summit**
['sʌmɪt] *noun*
(a) top of a mountain; *it took us three hour's hard climbing to reach the summit*
(b) summit (meeting or conference) = meeting of heads of state or government leaders to discuss international problems; *the question was discussed at the last European summit*

④ **summon**
['sʌmən] *verb*
(a) *(formal)* to tell people to come to a meeting; *the president summoned a meeting of the supreme council; she was summoned to appear before the committee*
(b) to summon up courage = to force yourself to be brave enough to do something; *he summoned up enough courage to do his first flight all by himself;* **to summon up strength** = to manage to have enough strength to do

something; *he summoned up all his strength and climbed the last few feet to the top*

① **sums**
[sʌmz] *noun*
math, making simple calculations with figures; *she is much quicker at sums than her sister*

① **sum up**
[ˈsʌm ˈʌp] *verb*
(a) to make a summary of what has been said; *I'd just like to sum up what has been said so far*; *can you sum up the most important points in the speech for me?*
(b) *(of a judge)* to speak at the end of a trial and review all the evidence and arguments for the benefit of the jury; *I was surprised the judge did not mention that when he summed up* (NOTE: summing - summed)

① **sun**
[sʌn]
1 *noun*
(a) very bright star around which the Earth travels and which gives light and heat; *the sun was just rising when I got up*; *I'll try taking a photograph now that the sun's come out*; *don't stare at the sun, even with sunglasses on*
(b) light from the sun; *I'd prefer a table out of the sun*; *we're sitting in the shade because the sun's too hot*; *she spent her whole vacation just sitting in the sun*; **sunscreen** or **sunblock** = cream which you put on your skin to avoid getting burned by the sun; *it you're going to the beach don't forget to take the sunscreen*; **everything under the sun** = absolutely everything; *we talked about everything under the sun*
2 *verb*
to sun yourself = to sit in the sun and get warm; *the cat was sunning herself on the window ledge* (NOTE: sunning - sunned)

① **Sunday**
[ˈsʌndi] *noun*
the seventh day of the week, the day between Saturday and Monday; *last Sunday we went on a picnic*; *most stores are now open on Sundays*; *can we fix a lunch for next Sunday?*; *today is Sunday, November 19*; **in your Sunday best** = wearing your smartest clothes; *all the children came in their Sunday best*

① **sunflower**
[ˈsʌnflauər] *noun*
very large yellow flower on a very tall stem; *the children are having a competition to see who can grow the tallest sunflower*

② **sung**
[sʌŋ]
see SING

③ **sunglasses**
[ˈsʌnglæsɪz] *noun*
dark glasses worn to protect your eyes from the sun; *I always wear sunglasses when I'm driving*

① **sunk**
[sʌŋk]
see SINK

① **sunlight**
[ˈsʌnlaɪt] *noun*
light which comes from the sun; *sunlight was pouring into the room*; *there's not really enough sunlight to take a picture*; *sunlight is essential to give the body Vitamin D* (NOTE: no plural)

① **sunny**
[ˈsʌni] *adjective*
(a) with the sun shining; *another sunny day!*; *they forecast that it will be sunny this afternoon*
(b) where the sun often shines; *we live on the sunny side of the street*; *their sitting room is bright and sunny, but the dining room is dark*
(c) *(informal)* **sunny side up** = (egg) fried on one side without being turned over, so you can see the yellow center (NOTE: sunnier - sunniest)

① **sunset**
[ˈsʌnset] *noun*
time when the sun goes down in the evening; *at sunset, bats come out and fly around*

① **sunshine**
[ˈsʌnʃaɪn] *noun*
pleasant light from the sun; *we have had very little sunshine this July*; *she likes sitting in the sunshine* (NOTE: no plural)

③ **super**
[ˈsupər] *adjective (informal)*
(a) very good; *we had a super time in Hawaii*
(b) very large; *I ordered a super ice-cream sundae*

③ **superb**
[suˈpɜrb] *adjective*
marvelous, wonderfully good; *he scored with a superb shot from just outside the penalty area*; *I'll have another helping of that superb chocolate cake*

② **Super Bowl**
[ˈsupər ˈbəul] *noun*
championship football game played between two professional American teams that are the best in their divisions; *Detroit is this year's location for the Super Bowl*

④ **superficial**
[supərˈfɪʃl] *adjective*
(a) which affects only the top surface; *the damage was only superficial*; *she suffered a few superficial grazes but nothing serious*
(b) dealing only with the most obvious and simple matters; *I can't answer your question because I only have a very superficial knowledge of the subject*

② **superintendent**
[supərɪnˈtendənt] *noun*
(a) person who manages all the schools in a certain area; *the superintendent interviewed all the applicants for the teaching position*

(b) person who maintains a building; *go and see the superintendent about the leaking pipe*

③ **superior**
[su'pıəriər]
1 *adjective*
(a) of very high quality; *he gave her a very superior box of chocolates*; **superior to** = better than; *our products are superior to theirs*; *their distribution service is much superior to ours*
(b) in a higher rank; *soldiers should always salute superior officers*; **superior to someone** = of a higher rank than someone; *she is superior to him in the office management system*
(c) thinking you are better than other people; *those who live downtown imagine they are superior to those in the suburbs*
2 *noun*
person in a higher rank; *each manager is responsible to his superior* (NOTE: the opposite is **inferior**)

④ **superlative**
[su'pɜrlətɪv]
1 *noun*
form of an adjective or adverb showing the highest level when compared with another; *"biggest" is the superlative of "big"*; *put a few superlatives in the ad to emphasize how good the product is*
2 *adjective*
extremely good; *he's a superlative goalkeeper*

> COMMENT: superlatives are usually formed by adding the suffix -est to the adjective: "quickest" from "quick", for example; in the case of long adjectives, they are formed by putting "most" in front of the adjective: "most comfortable", "most expensive", and so on. Some superlatives are not regular, such as "worst" and "best". You can also form superlatives by adding phrases like "as possible": "as big as possible"

② **supermarket**
['supərmarkıt] *noun*
large store selling mainly food and household goods, where customers serve themselves and pay at a checkout; *we've got no coffee left, can you buy some from the supermarket?*; *we do all our shopping at the local supermarket*

④ **supervise**
['supərvaɪz] *verb*
to watch carefully, to see that work is well done; *she supervises all the new staff*; *our move to the new house was supervised by my wife*

④ **supervision**
[supər'vɪʒn] *noun*
act of supervising; *prisoners are allowed out under strict supervision to work on the prison farm*; *new staff work under supervision for the first three months*; *she is very experienced and can be left to work without any supervision*

② **supervisor**
['supərvaɪzər] *noun*
person who supervises work, a student, etc.; *if you have any questions, ask your supervisor*; *my supervisor says I am getting on very well*

① **supper**
['sʌpər] *noun*
light meal which you eat in the evening; *what do you want for your supper?*; **to have supper** = to eat an evening meal; *we'll have supper outside as it is still hot*; *we usually have supper at about 7 o'clock*; *come and have some supper with us tomorrow evening*

④ **supplement**
1 *noun* ['sʌplɪmənt]
(a) thing which is in addition, especially an additional amount; *the company gives him $300 per month as a supplement to his pension*; *you need to take a vitamin supplement every morning*
(b) additional section at the back of a book; *there is a list of U.S. presidents in the supplement at the back of the book*
(c) magazine which is part of a newspaper; *I read his article in the Sunday supplement*
2 *verb* ['sʌplɪment]
to add to; *we will supplement the regular staff with part-time people during the Christmas rush*

③ **supplier**
[sə'plaɪər] *noun*
person, company, or country which supplies; *they are major suppliers of spare parts to the automobile industry*; *a supplier of fertilizers* or *a fertilizer supplier*

② **supply**
[sə'plaɪ]
1 *noun*
(a) stock of something which is needed; *we have two weeks' supply of coal*; **in short supply** = not available in large enough quantities to meet the demand; *fresh vegetables are in short supply during the winter*; **the law of supply and demand** = general rule that the amount of something which is available is linked to the amount wanted by potential customers
(b) **supplies** = stock of food, etc., which is needed; *after two months at sea, their supplies were running out*; *the government sent medical supplies to the disaster area*; *we buy all our office supplies from one firm*
(c) something which is needed, such as goods, products or services; *the electricity supply has failed again*; *they signed a contract for the supply of computer equipment*; *rebel forces have cut off the town's water supply*
2 *verb*
to provide something which is needed; *details of addresses and phone numbers can be supplied by the store staff*; *he was asked to supply a blood sample*; *she was asked to supply the names of two references*; *they have signed a*

contract to supply data; **to supply someone with something** = to provide something to someone; *he supplies the hotel with cheese* or *he supplies cheese to the hotel*; *the local farm supplies the college with milk and cheese*

② **support**
[sə'pɔrt]
1 *noun*
(a) thing which stops something from falling; *they had to build wooden supports to hold up the wall*
(b) something which helps keep something else in place; *the strap will provide some support for your knee*
(c) encouragement; *the chairman has the support of the committee*; *she spoke in support of our plan*
(d) financial help, money; *we have had no financial support from the bank*
2 *verb*
(a) to hold something up to stop it falling down; *the roof is supported on ten huge pillars*
(b) to provide money to help; *we hope the banks will support us during the expansion period*
(c) to encourage; *which football team do you support?*; *she hopes the other members of the committee will support her*
(d) to accept; *the public will not support another price hike*
(e) to give help, to help to run; *the main computer system supports six PCs*

③ **supporter**
[sə'pɔrtər] *noun*
person who encourages; *it sounds a good idea to me - I'm surprised it hasn't attracted more supporters*

④ **supportive**
[sə'pɔrtɪv] *adjective*
who supports or gives encouragement to someone; *he is very supportive of his children*

② **suppose**
[sʌ'pəuz] *verb*
(a) to think something is probable; *where is the secretary? - I suppose she's going to be late as usual*; *I suppose you've heard the news?*; *what do you suppose they're talking about?*; *will you be coming to the meeting this evening? - I suppose I'll have to*; *I don't suppose many people will come*
(b) *(showing doubt)* what happens if?; *suppose it rains tomorrow, do you still want to go for a walk?*; *he's very late - suppose he's had an accident?*; *suppose I win the lottery!*; *(giving a doubtful yes) please can I go on the swing? - oh, I suppose so*; *(giving a doubtful no) it doesn't look as though anyone is coming to the meeting - I suppose not*

◇ **supposed to be**
[sə'pəuzd 'tə 'bi] *phrase*
(a) should, ought to; *the children were supposed to be in bed*; *how I am supposed to know where he is?*

(b) believed to be; *he's supposed to be a good dentist*; *the movie is supposed to be awful*

④ **supposedly**
[sə'pəuzɪdli] *adverb*
as you suppose; *she's supposedly going to phone us later*

② **supposing**
[sə'pəuzɪŋ] *conjunction*
what happens if?; *supposing it rains tomorrow, do you still want to go for a walk?*; *he's very late - supposing he's had an accident?*

④ **suppress**
[sə'pres] *verb*
(a) to limit something, such as a person's freedom; *the government suppressed the opposition movement and executed its leaders*
(b) to stop something being made public; *all opposition newspapers have been suppressed*; *they tried to suppress the evidence but it had already got into the newspapers*
(c) to stop yourself showing what you really feel; *she suppressed her feeling of disgust and tried to look happy*; *he couldn't suppress a smile*

② **supreme**
[su'prim] *adjective*
(a) greatest, in the highest position; *her dog was supreme champion*; *it meant one last supreme effort, but they did it*
(b) **Supreme Court** = highest court in a country; *the Supreme Court was asked to rule on his case*

① **sure**
[ʃuər]
1 *adjective*
(a) certain; *is he sure he can borrow his mother's car?*; *I'm sure I left my car keys in my coat pocket*; *it's sure to be cold in Russia in December*; *make sure* or *be sure that your computer is switched off before you leave*; *when taking a shower, please make sure that the shower curtain is inside the bathtub*
(b) which can be relied on; *it's a sure remedy for the flu*
(c) **sure of yourself** = confident that what you do is right; *he's only just starting in business, so he's still not very sure of himself* (NOTE: **surer - surest**)
2 *adverb*
(a) *(meaning yes)* can I borrow your automobile? - sure, go ahead!; *I need someone to help with this computer program - sure, I can do it*
(b) *(as emphasis) he sure was mad when he saw what they'd done to his automobile*
(c) **for sure** = certainly; *if you sell the house you'll regret it, and that's for sure!*
(d) **sure enough** = as was expected; *no one thought he would pass his exams and sure enough he failed*

② **surely**
['ʃʊərli] *adverb*
(a) *(used mostly in questions where a certain answer is expected)* of course, I'm certain; *surely they can't expect us to work on Sundays?*; *but surely their office is in San Francisco, not Los Angeles?*; *they'll surely complain if we give them more work to do*
(b) carefully; **slowly but surely** = gradually; *slowly but surely he caught up with the leading car in the race*

③ **surf**
[sɜrf]
1 *noun*
white waves breaking along a shore; *the surf is too rough for children to bathe*
2 *verb*
(a) to ride on breaking waves on a board; *it's too dangerous to go surfing today*
(b) **to surf the Internet** *or* **to surf the Net** = to explore Internet websites looking at the pages in no particular order

① **surface**
['sɜrfɪs]
1 *noun*
top part of something; *when it rains, water collects on the surface of the road*; *the surface of the lake was completely still*; *he stayed a long time under water before coming back to the surface*; *he seemed calm but under the surface he was furious*; *birds first appeared on the surface of the Earth millions of years ago*
2 *verb*
(a) to come up to the surface; *the bird dove and then surfaced a few yards further on*; *his fear of failure has surfaced again*
(b) to cover a road, etc., with hard surface material; *we've had the drive surfaced with concrete*; *the kitchen floor is supposed to be surfaced with material which doesn't stain*

④ **surge**
[sɜrdʒ]
1 *noun*
(a) sudden increase in the quantity of something; *the good weather has brought a surge of interest in camping*; *the TV commercials generated a surge of orders*
(b) sudden rising up of water; *the surge of the sea between the rocks*
(c) sudden increase in electrical power; *power surges can burn out computer systems*
(d) sudden rush of emotion; *he felt a sudden surge of anger at the thought of having been cheated*
2 *verb*
(a) to rise suddenly; *the waves surged up onto the rocks*
(b) to move in a mass; *the crowd surged (forward) onto the field*; *the fans surged around the pop star's limo*

① **surgeon**
['sɜrdʒən] *noun*

doctor who specializes in surgery; *she has been sent to see an eye surgeon*; **surgeon general** = head of the U.S. public health service; *see also* PLASTIC

③ **surgery**
['sɜrdʒəri] *noun*
treatment of disease which requires an operation to cut into or remove part of the body; *she had surgery to straighten her nose*; *the patient will need surgery to remove the scars left by the accident* (NOTE: no plural in this meaning); (NOTE: plural is **surgeries**)

③ **surgical**
['sɜrdʒɪkl] *adjective*
referring to surgery; **surgical gloves** = thin rubber gloves worn by a surgeon; *see also* SPIRIT

④ **surname**
['sɜrneɪm] *noun*
name of someone's family, shared by all people in the family; *her Christian name or first name is Anne, but I don't know her surname*

④ **surplus**
['sɜrpləs]
1 *adjective*
extra, left over; *surplus butter is on sale in the stores*; *we are holding a sale of surplus stock*; **surplus to requirements** = more than is needed; *these copper pipes are surplus to our requirements*
2 *noun*
extra stock; material left over; *the surplus of grain is being sold abroad* (NOTE: plural is **surpluses**)

① **surprise**
[sər'praɪz]
1 *noun*
(a) feeling when something happens which you did not expect to happen; *he expressed surprise when I told him I'd lost my job*; *to his great surprise, a lot of people bought his book*; *what a surprise to find that we were at school together!*
(b) unexpected event; *they baked a cake for her birthday as a surprise*; *what a surprise to see you again after so long!*
(c) **to take someone by surprise** = to shock someone by saying or doing something which they did not expect; *her question took him by surprise and he didn't know how to answer*
2 *adjective*
which is unexpected; *a surprise fall in the value of the dollar*; *they gave a surprise party for the retiring college president*
3 *verb*
(a) to make someone surprised; *it wouldn't surprise me if it rained*; *what surprises me is that she left without saying goodbye*
(b) to find someone unexpectedly; *she surprised the two boys smoking in the yard*

surprised
[sər'praɪzd] *adjective*
astonished; *she was surprised to see her former boyfriend at the party*; *we were surprised to hear that he's gotten a good job*

surprising
[sər'praɪzɪŋ] *adjective*
astonishing, which you do not expect; *there was a surprising end to the story*; *wasn't it surprising to see the two sisters together again?*; *it's hardly surprising she doesn't want to see you again after what you said*

surprisingly
[sər'praɪzɪŋli] *adverb*
in a way which surprises; *considering she's just had an operation she looks surprisingly fit*; *not surprisingly, goods of this quality are very expensive*; *the judge was surprisingly soft on the youths*

surrender
[sə'rendər]
1 *noun*
(a) giving in to an enemy because you have lost; *the surrender of the enemy generals led to the end of the war*
(b) giving up of an insurance policy before the final date when it should mature; **surrender value** = money which an insurer will pay if an insurance policy is given up
2 *verb*
(a) to give in to an enemy because you have lost; *our troops were surrounded by the enemy and were forced to surrender*
(b) *(formal)* to give up a ticket, insurance policy, etc.; *he was asked to surrender his passport to the police*

surround
[sə'raʊnd] *verb*
to be all around someone or something; *the president has surrounded himself with a group of advisers*; *floods had surrounded the village*

surrounded
[sə'raʊndɪd] *adjective*
with something all around; *the villa is outside the town, surrounded by vineyards*; *the surgeon, surrounded by his team of experts, started the operation at 9:30*; *the government collapsed, surrounded by scandals*

surroundings
[sə'raʊndɪŋz] *noun*
area around a person or place; *the surroundings of the hotel are very peaceful*; *she found herself in very unpleasant surroundings*

survey
1 *noun* ['sɜrveɪ]
(a) general report on a subject; general investigation by asking people questions; *we carried out a survey among our customers*; *the government has produced a survey of education needs*
(b) careful examination of a building to see if it is in good enough condition; *they asked for a survey of the house before buying it*; *the insurance company is carrying out a survey of the damage caused by the storm*; **damage survey** = a report on damage done
(c) taking accurate measurements of land, so as to produce a plan or map
2 *verb* [sər'veɪ]
(a) to ask people questions to get information about a subject; *roughly half the people we surveyed were in favor of the project*
(b) to make a survey of a building; *the insurance company brought in experts to survey the damage caused by the fire*
(c) to measure land in order to produce a plan or map; *they're surveying the area where the new airport will be built*
(d) to look at something so that you see all of it; *he stood on the roof of the palace surveying the crowd in the square*

survival
[sər'vaɪvəl] *noun*
continuing to exist; *the survival of the crew depended on the supplies carried in the boat*; *the survival rate of babies has started to fall*; **survival of the fittest** = the process of evolution of a species, by which the characteristics that help it to survive are passed on to its young, and those characteristics which do not help survival are not passed on

survive
[sər'vaɪv] *verb*
(a) to continue to be alive after an accident, etc.; *it was such a terrible crash, it was miracle that anyone survived*; *the president has survived two bomb attacks this year*; *he survived a massive heart attack*; *not all the baby pigs survived more than a few days*
(b) to continue to exist; *it is one of the three surviving examples of his work*
(c) to live longer than someone else; *he survived his wife by ten years*; *she had no surviving relatives*; *he is survived by his only son*

survivor
[sər'vaɪvər] *noun*
person who is still alive after an accident, etc.; *helicopters were sent out to look for survivors*

suspect
1 *adjective* ['sʌspekt]
which might be dangerous; *don't eat any of that fish - it looks a bit suspect to me*; **suspect package** = package that might contain a bomb or something harmful
2 *noun* ['sʌspekt]
person who is thought to have committed a crime; *the police arrested several suspects for questioning*
3 *verb* [sə'spekt]
(a) to suspect someone of doing something = to think that someone may have done something wrong; *I suspect him of being involved in the robbery*; *they were wrongly suspected of taking bribes*

(b) to guess, to think that something is likely; *I suspect it's going to be more difficult that we thought at first*; *we suspected all along that something was wrong*

③ **suspend**
[sə'spend] *verb*
(a) to hang something; *the ham is suspended in the smoke over a fire for some time, which gives it a particular taste*
(b) to stop something for a time; *work on the construction project has been suspended*; *sailings have been suspended until the weather gets better*
(c) to stop someone from doing something, such as working; *he has been suspended with full pay while investigations are continuing*

② **suspenders**
[sʌ'spendərz] *noun*
straps which go over your shoulders to hold up your pants; *he wore bright red suspenders with his jeans*

③ **suspense**
[sə'spens] *noun*
waiting impatiently for something to happen or for someone to do something; *friends and relatives of the passengers waited in suspense at the airport for news of the plane*

③ **suspicion**
[sə'spɪʃn] *noun*
(a) feeling that something is wrong, that someone has committed a crime; *his actions immediately aroused suspicion on the part of the police*; *the bank regards his business deals with considerable suspicion*; *they were arrested on suspicion of exporting stolen goods*
(b) general feeling that something is going to happen; *I have a suspicion that he's coming to see me because he wants to borrow some money*; *her suspicions proved to be correct when she saw the wedding announced in the paper*

② **suspicious**
[sə'spɪʃəs] *adjective*
(a) which seems to be wrong, dangerous or connected with a crime; *the police found a suspicious package on the station platform*; *that the secretary seemed to know all about the deal before everyone else was very suspicious*; *we became suspicious when we realized we hadn't seen him for three days*
(b) suspicious of = not trusting; *I'm suspicious of people who tell me they know a way of getting rich quickly*

④ **sustain**
[sə'steɪn] *verb*
(a) to make something continue; *how long can this level of activity be sustained?*
(b) to receive an injury; *he sustained severe head injuries*
(c) to give you strength; *you need a good breakfast to sustain you through the day*

④ **sustained**
[sə'steɪnd] *adjective*
which continues for a long time; *a sustained effort will be needed*

① **swallow**
['swɒləʊ]
1 *verb*
(a) to make food or liquid pass down your throat from your mouth to the stomach; *he swallowed his beer and ran back to the office*; *she swallowed hard and knocked on the door to the interview room*
(b) to accept something; *he finds being laid off hard to swallow*
2 *noun*
common bird with pointed wings and tail, which flies fast; *there are several swallows' nests under the roof*

④ **swallow up**
['swɒləʊ 'ʌp] *verb*
to make something disappear inside; *he stepped out of the door and was swallowed up in the crowd*; *more than half my salary is swallowed up in mortgage payments*

① **swam**
[swæm] *see* SWIM

① **swamp**
[swɒmp]
1 *noun*
area of land that is always wet, and the plants that grow in it; *you can't build on that land - it's a swamp*
2 *verb*
(a) to cover something with water; *the waves nearly swamped our little boat*
(b) swamped with = having so much, that it is impossible to deal with it all; *the office is swamped with work*; *the switchboard has been swamped with calls*

② **swan**
[swɒn] *noun*
large white water bird with a long curved neck; *the swans look so graceful swimming on the pond*; *as the swans stood by the edge of the water, they flapped their wings*

③ **swap**
[swɒp]
1 *verb*
to exchange something for something else; *can I swap my tickets for next Friday's show?*; *let's swap places, so that I can talk to Susan*; *after every game the players swapped shirts with the other team*; *they swapped jobs* = each of them took the other's job (NOTE: **swapping** *or* **- swapped**)
2 *noun*
(a) exchange of one thing for another; *I'll do a swap with you - one of my CDs for your T-shirt*
(b) swaps = things, such as stamps, coins, etc., which you have ready to exchange for others; *I have a few swaps left but nobody wants them*

② **swarm**
[swɔrm] *noun*
large group of insects, etc., flying around together; *a swarm of flies buzzed around the meat*

② **sway**
[sweɪ]
1 *verb*
(a) to move, bending in a smooth way from side to side; *the crowd swayed in time to the music*; *the palm trees swayed in the breeze*
(b) to have an influence on; *the committee was swayed by a letter from the president*
2 *noun*
to hold sway over someone = to hold power over someone; *he held sway in Russia for several years*

② **swear**
['sweər] *verb*
(a) to make a solemn public promise; *he swore he wouldn't touch alcohol again*; *the witnesses swore to tell the truth*; **to swear someone to secrecy** = to make someone swear not to tell a secret; *he was sworn to secrecy*
(b) to take an oath; **to swear someone in** = to make an official take an oath; *he was sworn in as governor*
(c) *(informal)* **I could have sworn** = I was totally sure; *I could have sworn I put my keys in my coat pocket*
(d) to shout curses; *they were shouting and swearing at the police*; *don't let me catch you swearing again!*
(e) *(informal)* **to swear by** = to believe completely in something; *he swears by a cough medicine used by his grandmother* (NOTE: **swearing - swore** [swɔr] **- sworn** [swɔrn])

② **sweat**
[swet]
1 *noun*
drops of salt liquid that come through your skin when you are hot or when you are afraid; *after working in the field all day he was covered in sweat*; *he broke out into a cold sweat when they called his name*; **sweat gland** = gland in the body that produces sweat; **no sweat!** = it's easy; don't worry about it
2 *verb*
to produce sweat; *he ran up the hill, sweating and red in the face*; *see also* LABOR

② **sweater**
['swetər] *noun*
knitted pullover with long sleeves; *you'll need a sweater in the evenings, even in the desert*

② **sweatshirt**
['swetʃɜrt] *noun*
thick cotton shirt with long sleeves; *a sweatshirt is comfortable if the evening is cool*

③ **sweatsuit**
['træksut] *noun*
pair of matching pants and top, in warm material, worn when practicing sports; *the runners were warming up in their sweatsuits*

① **Swede**
[swid] *noun*
person from Sweden; *the Swedes have a very high standard of living*

① **Sweden**
['swidən] *noun*
country in northern Europe, between Norway and Finland; *we went for a camping vacation in Sweden*; *summer evenings in Sweden can be quite cool* (NOTE: capital: **Stockholm**; people: **the Swedes**; language: **Swedish**; currency: **the Swedish krona**)

① **Swedish**
['swidɪʃ]
1 *adjective*
coming from Sweden; referring to Sweden; *have you bought the new Swedish stamps?*; *Swedish roads do not have as much traffic as ours*
2 *noun*
language spoken in Sweden; *can you translate this letter into Swedish, please?*; *their children spoke Swedish with their grandmother*

① **sweep**
[swip]
1 *verb*
(a) to clear up dust, dirt, etc., from the floor with a brush; *have you swept the kitchen floor yet?*
(b) **to sweep the board** = to win completely; *the American team swept the board in the Grand Prix*
(c) to move rapidly; *she swept into the room, with a glass of wine in her hand*; *the party swept to power in the general election*; *a feeling of anger swept through the crowd*; **to sweep past** = to go past quickly; *the president's automobile swept past*; *she swept past without saying a word*
(d) to follow a curve; *the freeway sweeps around the mountain*; *the road sweeps down to the harbor*
(e) **to sweep something away** = to carry something rapidly away; *the river flooded and swept away part of the village*; *she was swept away by the powerful current* (NOTE: **sweeping - swept** [swept])
2 *noun*
(a) act of clearing things with a brush; *I'll just give the hall floor a sweep*
(b) **to make a clean sweep of something** = (i) to clear something away completely; (ii) to win everything; *he made a clean sweep of all the old files*; *they made a clean sweep at the local government elections*
(c) wide open area; *the green sweep of the lawn running down to the lake*
(d) wide movement of your arm; *with a sweep of his arm he knocked all the glasses off the table*

① **sweet**
[swit]
1 *adjective*
(a) tasting like sugar, and neither sour nor bitter; *these apples are sweeter than those green ones*; **to have a sweet tooth** = to like sweet food; *he's very fond of puddings - he has a real sweet tooth!*
(b) charming, pleasant; *he sent me such a sweet birthday card*; *it was sweet of her to send me flowers*; *what a sweet little girl!*; *how sweet of you to help me with my baggage!* (NOTE: **sweeter - sweetest**)
2 *noun*
sweets = candy, foods that are made with sugar; *we are not allowed to eat sweets before dinner* (NOTE: do not confuse with **suite**)

③ **swell**
[swel]
1 *verb*
to get bigger, to make bigger; *more and more people arrived to swell the crowd outside the palace gates*; **to swell (up)** = to become larger or to increase in size; *she was bitten by an insect and her hand swelled (up)* (NOTE: **swelling - swollen** ['swələn] **- swelled**)
2 *adjective*
(informal) very good; *we had a swell time in New York City*; *that sounds like a swell idea*
3 *noun*
movement of large waves in the open sea; *the boat rose and fell with the swell*; *there's a heavy swell running*

① **swept**
[swept] *see* SWEEP

③ **swerve**
[swɜrv] *verb*
to move suddenly to one side; *she had to swerve to avoid the bicycle*

① **swift**
[swɪft]
1 *adjective*
rapid; *their phone call brought a swift response from the police* (NOTE: **swifter - swiftest**)
2 *noun*
little bird like a swallow but with shorter wings and tail, which flies very fast

① **swim**
[swɪm]
1 *noun*
moving in the water, using your arms and legs to push you along; *what about a swim before breakfast?*; *it's too cold for a swim*; **swimsuit** = clothing worn by women or children when swimming; *don't forget to bring your swimsuit*; **swim trunks** = short pants worn by men and boys when swimming; *he changed into his swim trunks*
2 *verb*
(a) to move in the water using your arms and legs to push you along; *she can't swim, but she's taking swimming lessons*; *she swam in*
the Caribbean Sea on vacation; *salmon swim up the rivers in spring time*
(b) my head is swimming = I feel dizzy; *my head was swimming after working at the computer all day*
(c) to swim against the tide = to do things differently from everyone else; *carry on as you are, even if you think you're swimming against the tide*
(d) swimming in *or* **swimming with** = in a lot of liquid; *a plate of pasta swimming in sauce*; *sausages swimming in maple syrup* (NOTE: **swimming - swam** [swæm] **- has swum** [swʌm])

① **swimming**
['swɪmɪŋ] *noun*
action of swimming; *swimming is my mom's favorite form of exercise*

② **swimming pool**
['swɪmɪŋ 'pul] *noun*
large pool for swimming; *the school has an indoor swimming pool*; *she swam two lengths of the swimming pool*

① **swing**
[swɪŋ]
1 *noun*
(a) movement of your arm forward and backward; **to take a swing at someone** = to try to hit someone; *someone took a swing at him with a stick*
(b) change in opinion which can be measured; *there was a swing of 10% to the socialists in the elections*
(c) to go with a swing = to go very well, to be very enjoyable; *the party went with a swing*; **to get into the swing of things** = to enjoy being involved; *he'd never been to a nightclub before but soon got into the swing of things*; **in full swing** = going very well; *when we arrived the party was in full swing*
(d) seat held by ropes or chains, to sit on and move backward and forward, usually outdoors; *she sat on the swing and ate an apple*
2 *verb*
(a) to move from side to side or forward and backward, while hanging from a central point; *she picked up the baby and swung him around and around*; *he swung up and down on the garden swing*; *a window swung open and a man looked out*
(b) to change direction or opinion; *the automobile swung off the road into the hotel parking lot*; *the voters swung to the right in Sunday's elections*; *he swung round to face the crowd*
(c) to move with a swing; *they were swinging the bags one after the other into the garbage van*; *he swung his suitcase up onto the rack* (NOTE: **swinging - swung** [swʌŋ])

① **Swiss**
[swɪs]
1 *adjective*

referring to Switzerland; *we eat a lot of Swiss cheese*; *the Swiss banking system protects the identity of its customers*

2 *noun*

a Swiss = a person from Switzerland; **the Swiss** = people from Switzerland; *the Swiss celebrate their national day on August 1*

① **switch**

[swɪtʃ]

1 *noun*

(a) small device that you push up or down to stop or start an electrical device; *the switch to turn off the electricity is in the closet*; *there is a light switch by the bed*

(b) sudden change in opinion; *a switch in government policy* (NOTE: plural is **switches**)

2 *verb*

(a) to do something quite different suddenly; *we decided to switch from gas to electricity*

(b) to exchange; *let's switch places*; *he switched flights in Montreal and went on to Calgary*; *the job was switched from our U.S. factory to China*

② **switchboard**

['swɪtʃbɔrd] *noun*

central point in a telephone system, where all lines meet; *you should phone the switchboard if you can't get the number you want*; *we have to stagger the lunch hour so that there is always someone on the switchboard*

④ **switch-hitter**

['swɪtʃˈhɪtər] *noun*

(in baseball) player who can bat both left-handed and right-handed; *the switch-hitter decided to bat right-handed*

③ **switch off**

['swɪtʃ ˈɒf] *verb*

(a) to make an electrical device stop; *don't forget to switch off the TV before you go to bed*; *she forgot to switch her automobile lights off or switch off her automobile lights*; *the electric kettle switches itself off automatically when it boils*

(b) *(informal)* to stop listening to what someone is saying; *if you talk too slowly, everyone starts to switch off*; *I just switched off once the discussion started getting too technical*

③ **switch on**

['swɪtʃ ˈɒn] *verb*

to make an electrical device start; *can you switch the radio on - it's time for the evening news?*; *when you put the light on in the bathroom, the fan switches itself on automatically*

③ **switch over to**

['swɪtʃ ˈəʊvərtu] *verb*

to change to something quite different; *we have switched over to gas for our heating*

① **Switzerland**

['swɪtsələnd] *noun*

European country, south of Germany, east of France and north of Italy; *many people go on skiing vacations in Switzerland*; *we went to Switzerland last summer* (NOTE: capital: **Berne**; people: **the Swiss**; languages: **French, German, Italian**; currency: **the Swiss franc**)

② **swollen**

['swəʊlən] *adjective*

much bigger than usual; *she can't walk with her swollen ankle*; *the swollen river burst its banks*; *see also* SWELL

② **swoop**

[swup] *verb*

to come down rapidly to make a sudden attack; *the planes swooped down low over the enemy camp*

① **sword**

[sɔrd] *noun*

weapon with a handle and a long sharp blade; *he rushed onto the stage waving a sword*

② **swore**

[swɔr] *see* SWEAR

③ **sworn**

[swɔrn] *adjective*

under oath; *in his sworn statement he said something quite different*; **sworn enemies** = people who will always be enemies; *see also* SWEAR

③ **swum**

[swʌm] *see* SWIM

② **swung**

[swʌŋ] *see* SWING

① **syllable**

['sɪləbl] *noun*

a whole word or part of a word which has one single sound; *there a three syllables in the word "sympathy"*

② **symbol**

['sɪmbl] *noun*

sign, letter, picture or shape that means something or shows something; *they use a bear as their advertising symbol*; *the crown was the symbol of the empire*; *the olive branch is a symbol of peace*; *Pb is the chemical symbol for lead*

③ **symbolic** *or* **symbolical**

[sɪmˈbɒlɪk *or* sɪmˈbɒlɪkl] *adjective*

used as a symbol; *an olive branch is symbolic of peace*

② **sympathetic**

[sɪmpəˈθetɪk] *adjective*

showing that you understand someone's problems; *I'm very sympathetic to her problems*; *he wasn't very sympathetic when I told him I felt sick*

③ **sympathize**

['sɪmpəθaɪz] *verb*

to sympathize with someone = to show that you understand someone's problems; *I sympathize with you, my husband snores too*; *I get back pains, and I sympathize with all fellow sufferers*

③ **sympathy**
['sɪmpəθi] *noun*
(a) feeling of understanding for someone else's problems, or after someone's death; *we received many messages of sympathy when my wife died*; *I find it difficult to express my sympathy when someone whom I hardly know dies*; *he had no sympathy for his secretary who complained of having too much work*
(b) agreement with or support for someone or something; *I have a good deal of sympathy with the idea*; **to come out on strike in sympathy** = to stop work to show that you agree with another group of workers who are on strike; *the postal workers went on strike and the telephone engineers came out in sympathy* (NOTE: plural is **sympathies**)

③ **symphony**
['sɪmfəni] *noun*
long piece of music in several parts, called "movements", played by a full orchestra; *a performance of Beethoven's Fifth Symphony*; *Smetana included themes from folk music in his symphonies* (NOTE: plural is **symphonies**)

③ **symptom**
['sɪmptəm] *noun*
(a) change in the way the body works, or change in the way the body looks, showing that a disease is present and has been noticed by the patient or doctor; *he has all the symptoms of measles*
(b) visible sign which shows that something is happening; *garbage everywhere on the sidewalks is a symptom of the cash crisis facing the town*

④ **syndicate**
1 *noun* ['sɪndɪkət]
group of people or companies working together to make money; *a U.S. investment syndicate*
2 *verb* ['sɪndɪkeɪt]
to produce an article, a cartoon, etc., which is then published in several newspapers or magazines; *his cartoon strip is syndicated across the U.S.*; *she writes a syndicated column on personal finance*

④ **syndrome**
['sɪndrəʊm] *noun*
(a) group of symptoms which taken together show that a particular disease or condition is present; *their daughter has Down's syndrome*
(b) general feeling or way of approaching a problem, etc.; *it's an example of the "let's go home early on Friday afternoon" syndrome*

④ **synthesis**
['sɪnθəsɪs] *noun*
producing something by combining a number of smaller elements; *the plan is a synthesis of several earlier proposals* (NOTE: plural is **syntheses**)

④ **synthetic**
[sɪn'θetɪk]
1 *adjective*
artificial, made by man; *a coat of synthetic fur*
2 *noun*
artificial or man-made material; *he used synthetics to create elegant gowns*

③ **syrup**
['sɪrəp] *noun*
(a) thick sweet liquid consisting of sugar, water and medicine or flavoring; *to make syrup, dissolve sugar in a cup of boiling water*; *cough syrup* = syrup with medicine added to relieve coughing
(b) fruit or plant juice boiled until thick; *I like maple syrup on pancakes*

③ **system**
['sɪstəm] *noun*
(a) group of things which work together; *the system of interstate highways or the interstate highway system*; **computer system** = set of programs, commands, etc., which run a computer; **the central nervous system** = the brain and the cord running down the spine, which link together all the nerves
(b) the body as a whole; *being made redundant gives a serious shock to the system*
(c) way in which things are organized; *I've got my own system for dealing with invoices*; **filing system** = way of putting documents in order for easy reference

④ **systematic**
[sɪstə'mætɪk] *adjective*
organized in a good way; *a more systematic approach is needed*; *he organized a systematic attempt to bring down the government*; *she ordered a systematic report on the distribution service*

④ **systematically**
[sɪstə'mætɪkli] *adverb*
in a systematic way; *go through the report again systematically*; *he systematically fired anyone who disagreed with him*

Tt

③ T, t
[ti]
twentieth letter of the alphabet, between S and U; *don't forget - you spell "attach" with two Ts*; **to dot the i's and cross the t's** = to settle the final details of an agreement

① table
['teɪbl]
1 *noun*
(a) piece of furniture with a flat top and legs, used to eat at, work at, etc.; *we had breakfast sitting round the kitchen table*; *he asked for a table by the window*; *she says she booked a table for six people for 12:30*; **to lay the table** *or* **to set the table** = to put knives, forks, spoons, plates, etc., on a table ready for a meal; *can someone set the table please, the food's almost ready*; *the table was laid for six*; **to clear the table** = to take away the dirty knives, forks, spoons, plates, etc., after a meal; *the waitress cleared a table for us and we sat down*
(b) list of figures, facts, information set out in columns; **table of contents** = list of contents in a book
(c) list of numbers to learn by heart how each number is multiplied; *he's learned his nine times table*
2 *verb*
to put items of information on the table before a meeting; *the report of the finance committee was tabled*; **to table a motion** = to put forward a proposal for discussion by putting details of it on the table at a meeting

① tablecloth
['teɪblklɒθ] *noun*
cloth that covers a table during a meal; *put a clean tablecloth on, please*; *the coffee stains on the tablecloth won't come out*

④ tablespoon
['teɪblspun] *noun*
(a) large spoon for serving food at table or measuring for cooking
(b) amount held in a tablespoon; *add two tablespoons of sugar*

① tablet
['tæblət] *noun*
small round pill taken as medicine; *take two tablets before meals*

② table tennis
['teɪbl 'tenɪs] *noun*
game similar to tennis, but played on a large table with a net across the center, with small round bats and a very light white ball; *do you want a game of table tennis?* (NOTE: also called **ping-pong**)

② tack
[tæk]
1 *noun*
(a) small nail with a wide head; **carpet tack** = nail for attaching a carpet to the floor; *(informal)* **to get down to brass tacks** = to start discussing the real problem
(b) movement of a sailboat in a certain direction as it sails against the wind; **to change tack** = to start doing something different; *originally he offered to pay the all costs of the party and then changed tack and asked everyone to pay for themselves*
2 *verb*
(a) to nail something down using tacks; *he tacked down the edge of the carpet*
(b) *(in a sailboat)* to change direction so that wind blows the sails from the other side; **they were tacking up the river** = they sailed up the river changing direction all the time because the wind was against them

③ tackle
['tækl]
1 *noun*
(a) equipment; *he brought his fishing tackle with him*
(b) *(in football)* catching and knocking down an opposing player
2 *verb*
(a) to grab someone to stop him doing something; *he tried to tackle the burglar himself*
(b) to try to deal with a problem or job; *you can't tackle a job like changing the central heating system on your own*; *you start cleaning the dining room and I'll tackle the kitchen*
(c) *(in football)* to catch and knock down an opposing player; *he was tackled before he could score*

④ tactic
['tæktɪk] *noun (often plural)*
(a) way of doing something so as to get an advantage; *his tactic is to wait until near closing time, when the supermarket reduces the price of all types of food*
(b) way of fighting a war; *guerrilla tactics were successful against the advancing army*

① tag
[tæg]
1 *noun*

(a) label, a piece of paper, plastic, etc., attached to something to show a price, contents, someone's name and address, etc.; **gift tag** = little label put on a parcel to show who it is for and who it is from; **name tag** = label with a name printed on it; *visitors to the factory are given name tags*; **price tag** = label with the price printed on it; *the automobile has a $75,000 price tag*

(b) children's game where the first child has to try to touch another one who then chases the others in turn; *they were playing tag on the school playground*

2 *verb*

(a) to attach a label to something; *these coats need to be tagged before you put them on the racks*; *we tag birds so that we can study their migration routes*

(b) *(informal)* to tag along behind someone = to follow close behind someone; *whenever we go out for a walk my sister insists on tagging along*

(c) to tag something on to something = to attach something at the end of something else; *he tagged on an extra section at the end of the letter* (NOTE: **tagging - tagged**)

② **tail**
[teɪl]
1 *noun*

(a) long thin part at the end of an animal's body, which can move; *all you could see was a slight movement of the cat's tail*; **to turn tail** = to turn round and run away; *as soon as they heard the dog barking, the burglars turned tail and ran off* (NOTE: do not confuse with **tale**)

(b) end or back part of something; *the tail of the line stretched around the corner and into the next street*; *they say it is safer to sit near the tail of an aircraft*

(c) **tails** = the side of a coin without the head of a president, etc., on it; **heads or tails** = throwing a coin in the air to see which side comes out on top; *let's toss heads or tails for the check!*

(d) long back part of a coat or shirt; *he tucked the tail of his shirt back into his pants*

(e) **tails** = man's evening dress, a black coat with a long tail, black pants, white bow tie, etc.; *all the men wore white ties and tails to the ball*

2 *verb*

to follow close behind someone; *the police tailed the truck from the harbor to the warehouse*

④ **tailcoat**
['teɪlkəʊt] *noun*
tails, a man's evening dress

④ **tail off**
['teɪl 'ɒf] *verb*

to become fainter or less; *he started speaking, but his voice tailed off into a whisper*; *the number of overseas visitors starts to tail off in September*

② **tailor**
['teɪlər]
1 *noun*

person who makes clothes for men, such as suits, coats, etc.; *he gets all his clothes made by a tailor*

2 *verb*

(a) to make clothes that fit closely; *she wore a tailored jacket*

(b) to adapt something to fit a special need; *the payments can be tailored to suit your requirements*; *this course is tailored to the needs of women going back to work*

③ **tailpipe**
['teɪlpaɪp] *noun*

the tube at the back of a motor vehicle from which gases produced by the engine are sent out into the air; *clouds of white smoke were coming out of the tailpipe*

① **take**
[teɪk]
1 *verb*

(a) to lift and move something; *she took the jar of jam down from the shelf*; *the waiter took the tablecloth off the table*

(b) to carry something to another place; *can you take this check to the bank for me, please?*

(c) to go with someone or something to another place; *he's taking the children to school*; *they took the automobile to the garage*; *we took a taxi to the hotel*

(d) to steal; *someone's taken my watch*

(e) to go away with something which someone else was using; *someone has taken the newspaper I was reading*; *who's taken my cup of coffee?*

(f) to use or occupy; *sorry, all these seats are taken*; **to take your seats** = to sit down; *please take your seats, the play is about to start*

(g) to do a test; *you must go to bed early because you'll be taking your examination tomorrow morning*; *she had to take her driver's test three times before she finally passed*

(h) to eat or to drink (often); *do you take sugar in your tea?*; *how do you take your coffee - black or with cream?*; *take the medicine three times a day after meals*

(i) to accept; *if they offer you the job, take it immediately*

(j) to do certain actions; *we took our vacation in September this year*; *she's taking a shower after going to the beach*; *she took a photograph or took a picture of the Statue of Liberty*; *she needs to take a rest*; **to take action** = to do something; *you must take immediate action if you want to stop people from stealing from the store*; **to take a call** = to answer the telephone; *I was out of the office so my secretary took the call*; **to take the chair** = to be chairman of a meeting; *in the absence of the chairman his deputy took the chair*; **to take dictation** = to write down what someone is saying; *the secretary was taking dictation from the chief* *executive officer*; **to take place** = to happen; *the reception will take place on Saturday*; **to take stock** = to count the items in a warehouse; **to take stock of a situation** = to examine the state of things before deciding what to do; *when we had taken stock of the situation, we decided the best thing to do was to sell the house*

(k) to need; *it took three strong men to move the piano*; *they took two days or it took them two days to get to Denver*; *when he wants to watch a TV show it never seems to take him long to finish his homework*

(l) to accept or to hold; *the ticket machine takes nickels, dimes and quarters*; *the elevator can take up to six passengers*

(m) to be successful, to have the right effect; **his kidney transplant has taken** = the transplant has been successful (NOTE: **taking - took** [tʊk] - **has taken** ['teɪkn])

2 *noun*
(a) money received in a store; *today's take was less than yesterday's*
(b) scene that has been filmed; *the actors took a break between takes*

④ **take after**
['teɪk 'æftər] *verb*
to look like a parent or relative; *she takes after her mother*

② **take away**
['teɪk ə'weɪ] *verb*
(a) to remove something or someone; *take those scissors away from little Nicky - he could cut himself*; *the ambulance came and took her away*; *the police took away piles of documents from the office*
(b) to subtract one number from another (NOTE: **take away** is usually shown by the minus sign - : **10 - 4 = 6**: say "ten take away four equals six")

① **take back**
['teɪk 'bæk] *verb*
(a) to go back with something; *if the pants are too short you can take them back to the store*; *if you don't like the color, you can take it back and change it*
(b) to accept something which someone has brought back; *I took my pants to the store where I had bought them, but they wouldn't take them back because I didn't have a receipt*
(c) to withdraw something which has been said, and apologize for it; *I take it all back - they're a marvelous team*

③ **take down**
['teɪk 'daʊn] *verb*
(a) to reach up and bring something down; *I took the jar down from the shelf*
(b) to bring something down which had been put up; *on January 6 we take down the Christmas decorations*; *they have finished the roof and are taking down their ladders*
(c) to write down; *the police officer took down his name and address*

③ **take in**
['teɪk 'ɪn] *verb*
(a) to bring inside something which was outside; *the boat was taking in water*; *in October they took in the lemon trees from the gardens*
(b) to understand; *I don't think she took in anything of what you said*
(c) to deceive; *thousands of people were taken in by the advertisement*
(d) to make a piece of clothing smaller; *can you take these pants in? - they're much too loose around the waist* (NOTE: the opposite in this meaning is to **let out**)

① **take off**
['teɪk 'ɒf] *verb*
(a) to remove, especially your clothes; *he took off all his clothes or he took all his clothes off*; *take your dirty boots off before you come into the kitchen*; *see also* HAT
(b) to remove or to deduct; *he took $35 off the price*
(c) *(of plane)* to leave the ground; *the plane took off at 4:30*
(d) to remove someone in a plane or helicopter; *the ship was listing badly and the crew had to be taken off by helicopter*
(e) to start to rise fast; *sales took off after the TV commercials*
(f) **she took the day off** = she decided not to work for the day

③ **takeoff**
['teɪkɒf] *noun*
(a) *(of an aircraft)* leaving the ground; *I always ask for a seat by the window, so that I can watch the takeoff*
(b) funny imitation of someone; *you should see his takeoff of the history professor*

③ **take on**
['teɪk 'ɒn] *verb*
(a) to agree to do a job; *she's taken on a part-time job in addition to the one she's already got*
(b) to agree to have someone as a worker; *the store has taken on four youngsters straight from school*; *we need to take on more staff to cope with the extra work*
(c) to fight someone; *it seems he is taking on the whole government*

① **take out**
['teɪk 'aʊt] *verb*
(a) to pull something out; *he took out a gun and waved it around*; *the dentist had to take his tooth out*
(b) to invite someone to go out; *I'm taking all the office staff out for a drink*
(c) **to take out insurance against theft** = to pay a premium to an insurance company, so that if a theft takes place the company will pay compensation; **to take out $75** = to remove $75 in cash from a bank account
(d) **the hot weather takes it out of you** = the hot weather makes you very tired; **to take it out**

on someone = to make someone suffer because you are upset or worried; *he keeps on taking it out on his secretary*

③ **takeout**
['teɪkaʊt]
1 *noun*
hot meal that you buy to eat back home; *we had Chinese takeout last night*
2 *adjective*
referring to a meal you buy to eat back home; *we had a takeout dinner last night*

② **take over**
['teɪk 'əʊvər] *verb*
(a) to start to do something in place of someone else; *Miss Black took over from Mr. Carter on May 1*; *thanks for looking after the switchboard for me - I'll take over from you now*; *when our history teacher was sick, the English teacher had to take over his classes*; *the Republicans took over from the Democrats*
(b) to buy a business by offering to buy most of its shares; *the company was taken over by a big group last month*

① **takeover**
['teɪkəʊvər] *noun*
(a) buying of a controlling interest in a business by buying more than 50% of the shares; *the takeover may mean that a lot of people will lose their jobs*; **takeover bid** = offer to buy all or most of the shares of a business so as to control it; **to make a takeover bid for a company** = to offer to buy most of the shares in a company; **hostile takeover** = takeover where the board of the company being bought do not recommend the sale and try to fight it
(b) occupying a capital city and removing the government; *many people were killed during the military takeover*

④ **take to**
['teɪk 'tu] *verb*
(a) to start to do something as a habit; *he's taken to looking under his bed every night to make sure no one is hiding there*; *she's recently taken to wearing sneakers to work*; **he took to drink** = he started to drink alcohol regularly
(b) to start to like someone; *she took to her boss right away*

④ **take up**
['teɪk 'ʌp] *verb*
(a) to occupy or to fill a space; *this sofa takes up too much room*; *being in charge of the staff sports club takes up too much of my time*
(b) to remove something which was down; *you will need to take up the carpets if you want to polish the floor*
(c) to start to do a certain activity, sport, etc.; *she was over fifty when she took up long-distance running*
(d) to take someone up on something = to accept an offer made by someone; *he asked me if I wanted two tickets to the show and I took him up on his offer*

③ **talcum powder**
['tælkʌm 'paʊdər] *noun*
soft powder with a pleasant scent, used to make the skin softer or to reduce rubbing; *she put some talcum powder between her toes*

① **tale**
[teɪl] *noun*
(literary) story; *a tale of a princess and her wicked sisters*; **old wives' tale** = old, and often silly, idea; *eating carrots won't make you see in the dark - that's just an old wives' tale* (NOTE: do not confuse with **tail**)

② **talent**
['tælənt] *noun*
(a) natural ability or skill; *she has a talent for getting customers to spend money*
(b) people with natural ability; *the club is always on the lookout for fresh talent*; **talent contest** = contest to find new performers, singers, etc.

④ **talented**
['tæləntɪd] *adjective*
with a lot of talent; *she's a very talented musician*

① **talk**
[tɔk]
1 *noun*
(a) conversation, discussion; *we had a little talk, and she agreed with what the committee had decided*; *I had a long talk with my father about what I should study at college*
(b) talks = negotiations; *we have entered into talks with the union leaders*
(c) lecture about a subject; *he gave a short talk about the history of the town*
(d) general rumor; *there has been talk of a change of government*
2 *verb*
to say things, to speak; *the guide was talking French to the group of tourists*; *I didn't understand what he was talking about*; *we must talk to the neighbors about their noisy dog - he kept me awake again last night*; *they're talking of selling their house and going to live by the sea*

① **talkative**
['tɔkətɪv] *adjective*
who likes to talk a lot or to gossip; *our new neighbors are not very talkative*

③ **talk into**
['tɔk 'ɪntu] *verb*
to talk someone into doing something = to persuade someone to do something; *the salesman talked us into buying a new automobile*

③ **talk over**
['tɔk 'əʊvər] *verb*
to discuss; *we've talked it over and decided not to leave*; *if you want to borrow money, go and talk it over with the bank manager*; *why don't you come and talk it over with your mother?*

③ **talk show**
['tɔk 'ʃəu] *noun*
TV show where famous people talk to the host;
*she has been invited to appear on the new talk
show*

① **tall**
[tɔl] *adjective*
(a) high, usually higher than normal; *the bank
building is the tallest building in Pittsburgh*;
can you see those tall trees over there?; *he's the
tallest boy in his class*; *how tall are you? - I'm
six foot two (6' 2")* *his brother is over six feet
tall*
(b) *(informal)* **tall order** = difficult task; *asking
all the staff to move to Oregon is a really tall
order* (NOTE: **taller - tallest**. Note also the use
with figures: **the tree is two meters tall; he's six
feet tall; tall** is used with people and thin things like
trees or skyscrapers; for things that are a long way
above the ground use **high: high clouds, a high
mountain**)

① **tan**
[tæn]
1 *adjective*
with a brown and yellow color; *he was wearing
tan shoes*
2 *noun*
(a) brown and yellow color; *do you have the
same shoes, but in tan?*
(b) brown color of the skin after being in the
sun; *she got a tan from spending each day on
the beach*
3 *verb*
to get brown from being in the sun; *she tans
easily - just half an hour in the sun and she's
quite brown* (NOTE: **tanning - tanned**)

② **tangerine**
['tændʒə'rin] *noun*
small orange with soft skin which peels easily;
there was a bowl of tangerines on the table

④ **tangible**
['tændʒəbl] *adjective*
which is real or noticeable; *have the
anti-pollution measures had any tangible
results?*; *there is no tangible evidence that he
was responsible for the crime*

② **tangle**
['tæŋgl]
1 *noun*
mass of threads, string, hair, etc., all mixed
together; *the tangle of shrubs in the backyard
needs clearing*; **in a tangle** = all mixed up; *all
my hair is in a tangle*
2 *verb*
(a) to get things mixed together in knots; *her
hair is so tangled that it's impossible to comb it*
(b) **to tangle with someone** = to get into an
argument with someone; *he often tangles with
his father*

② **tank**
[tæŋk] *noun*
(a) large container for liquids; *how much oil is
left in the tank?*; **gas tank** = container built into
an automobile, truck, etc., for holding gas;
water tank = tank for holding water
(b) armored vehicle with caterpillar tracks and
powerful guns(Caterpillar is a trademark); *tanks
rolled along the main streets of the town*

② **tanker**
['tæŋkər] *noun*
ship or truck for carrying liquids, especially oil;
an oil tanker ran onto the rocks in the storm; *a
gas tanker broke down on the freeway*

① **tap**
[tæp]
1 *noun*
(a) faucet, a device with a knob which, when
you twist it, lets liquid or gas come out; *he
washed his hands under the tap in the kitchen*;
she forgot to turn the gas tap off; **on tap** =
available when you need it; *we should have all
this information on tap*; **to turn a tap on** = to
allow water to run; **to turn a tap off** = to stop
water running
(b) little knock; *as a signal, he gave three taps
on the door*
2 *verb*
(a) to hit something gently; *she tapped him on
the knee with her finger*; *a police officer tapped
him on the shoulder and arrested him*
(b) to attach a secret listening device to a
telephone line; *the police tapped his phone
because they thought he was a spy*
(c) to take liquid out of something; *they tap the
maple trees in spring*; *he's going down to the
cellar to tap a barrel of beer*
(d) to take energy or resources and use them; *the
resources of Northern Siberia have not yet
been tapped* (NOTE: **tapping - tapped**)

① **tape**
[teip]
1 *noun*
(a) long narrow strip of cloth, plastic, etc.; *she
stitched tape along the bottom of his pants to
stop them fraying*; **tape measure** *or* **measuring
tape** = long strip of plastic marked in
centimeters or inches, etc., used for measuring;
*he took out a tape measure and measured the
length of the table*; **sticky tape** = strip of plastic
with glue on one side, used to stick things
together, etc.
(b) **magnetic tape** = special plastic tape on
which sounds and pictures can be recorded, also
used for recording computer data; *she lent me
her Beach Boys tape*; *I play a lot of tapes when
I'm driving by myself*; **on tape** = recorded on
magnetic tape; *we have the whole conversation
on tape*; **tape deck** = part of a stereo system,
which plays tapes
2 *verb*
(a) to record something on tape or on video; *the
whole conversation was taped by the police*; *I
didn't see the program because I was at work,
but I've taped it*

(b) to attach with sticky tape; *she taped up the box before taking it to the post office*

② **target**
['tɑrgɪt]
1 *noun*
(a) object that you aim at with a gun, etc.; *his last shot missed the target altogether*; *she hit the target three times in all*; **target practice** = practicing at shooting at a target; *he put an old can on top of the post and used it for target practice*
(b) goal that you try to reach; **to set targets** = to fix quantities that workers have to produce; **to meet a target** = to produce the quantity of goods or sales that are expected; *we need to set targets for our salesmen to meet*; **to miss a target** = not to produce the amount of goods or sales that are expected; *the factory missed its production targets again this year*; **target language** = language that a student is learning, the language into which something is translated; **target market** = market to which a company is planning to sell its service
2 *verb*
to aim at customers, possible markets, etc.; *the advertising campaign is targeting the student market*

④ **tariff**
['tærɪf] *noun*
(a) tax to be paid for importing or exporting goods; **to impose a tariff on something** = to make a tax payable when you buy something; **to lift tariff barriers** = to reduce import taxes
(b) list of prices for electricity, gas, water, etc.; *the new winter tariff will be introduced next week*

④ **tartan**
['tɑrtən] *noun*
cloth woven into a special Scottish pattern; *she wore a tartan kilt*; *my Scottish grandmother gave me a tartan rug*

② **task**
[tæsk] *noun*
(a) job of work which has to be done; *there are many tasks which need to be done in the garden*; *he had the unpleasant task of telling his mother about it*; **task force** = special group of people chosen to carry out a difficult task; *they sent in a task force to sort out the problem school*
(b) **to take someone to task for** = to criticize someone for; *she took him to task for not cleaning the bathroom*

② **taste**
[teɪst]
1 *noun*
(a) one of the five senses, by which you can tell differences of flavor between things you eat, using your tongue; *I've got a cold, so I've lost all sense of taste*
(b) flavor of something that you eat or drink; *the pudding has a funny or strange taste*; *do you like the taste of garlic?*; *this milkshake has no taste at all*
(c) being able to appreciate things that are beautiful; *my taste in music is quite different from hers*; *I don't share his taste for bright green shirts*; *she showed great taste in decorating her dining room*; **to someone's taste** = in a way that someone likes; *modern jazz is not to everyone's taste*
(d) very small quantity of food or drink, or other things; *this is a taste of what the country will be like under the new ruler*; **he's had a taste of prison** = he has been in prison once
2 *verb*
(a) to notice the taste of something with your tongue; *can you taste the onions in this soup?*; *she has a cold so she can't taste anything*
(b) to have a certain taste; *this cake tastes of soap*; *what is this green stuff? - it tastes like cabbage*; *the dessert tastes very good*
(c) to try something to see if you like it; *would you like to taste the wine?*; *she asked if she could taste the cheese before buying it*

① **tasty**
['teɪsti] *adjective*
with an especially pleasant taste; *I liked that pie - it was very tasty* (NOTE: **tastier - tastiest**)

① **taught**
[tɔt] *see* TEACH

① **tax**
[tæks]
1 *noun*
money taken by the government from incomes, sales, etc., to pay for government services; *the government is planning to introduce a tax on food*; *you must pay your tax on the correct date*; *the newspaper headline says "TAXES TO GO UP"*; **airport tax** = tax added to the price of an air ticket to cover the cost of running an airport; **income tax** = tax which is paid according to how much you earn; *income tax is deducted from your salary with each paycheck*; **sales tax** = tax on goods and services, added as a percentage to the invoiced sales price; **exclusive of tax** = not including tax; **inclusive of tax** = including tax; *all prices are shown inclusive of value-added tax* (NOTE: plural is **taxes**)
2 *verb*
(a) to put a tax on something or someone; *income is taxed at 25%*
(b) to pay tax on something; *he will be taxed heavily for the sports car*
(c) to demand a great deal; *moving all this furniture taxed her strength*
(d) *(formal)* **to tax someone with something** = to accuse someone of doing something; *she taxed him with neglecting her*

③ **taxation**
[tæk'seɪʃn] *noun*
action of imposing taxes; *money raised by taxation pays for all government services*; **direct taxation** = taxes (such as income tax)

which are paid direct to the government; **indirect taxation** = taxes (such as sales tax) which are added to the price of goods and not paid directly to the government

② **taxi**
['tæksi]
1 *noun*
automobile that you can hire with a driver; *can you call a taxi to take me to the airport?; why aren't there any taxis at the station today?; there are no buses on Sunday afternoons, so we had to take a taxi to the party* (NOTE: also often called a **cab** and sometimes **taxicab**)
2 *verb*
(of an aircraft) to go slowly along the ground before taking off or after landing; *the aircraft taxied out onto the runway*

③ **taxi driver**
['tæksi 'draɪvər] *noun*
person who drives a taxi; *the taxi driver helped me with my baggage*

② **taxpayer**
['tækspeɪər] *noun*
person who pays tax, especially income tax; *I don't think the government's plan will be very popular with taxpayers*

① **tea**
[ti] *noun*
(a) drink made from hot water that has been poured onto the dried leaves of a tropical plant; *can I have another cup of tea or some more tea?; I don't like tea - can I have coffee instead?*
(b) a cup of tea; *can we have two teas and two muffins, please*
(c) the dried leaves of a tropical plant used to make a warm drink; *we've run out of tea, can you put it on your shopping list?; put a spoonful of tea into the pot and add boiling water*
(d) dried leaves or flowers of other plants, used to make a drink; *mint tea*

① **tea bag**
['tibæg] *noun*
small paper bag with tea in it which you put into the pot with hot water; *I don't like weak tea - put another tea bag in the pot*

② **teach**
[titʃ] *verb*
(a) to give lessons, to show someone how to do something; *she taught me how to dance; he teaches math in the local school; she taught herself to type; who taught her to swim?*
(b) *(informal)* **to teach someone a lesson** = to punish someone for doing something wrong; *I've locked up her bike - it will teach her a lesson not to go out when she should be doing her homework; that'll teach you* = that will be a punishment for you; *that'll teach you for forgetting to wash the dishes* (NOTE: **teaching - taught** [tɔt])

① **teacher**
['titʃər] *noun*
person who teaches, especially in a school; *Mr. Jonas is our math teacher; the French teacher is sick today; he trained as an elementary school teacher; see also* PET

① **teaching**
['titʃɪŋ] *noun*
(a) work of being a teacher, of giving lessons; *the report praised the high standard of teaching at the college; he was working in a bank, but has decided to go into teaching instead;* **the teaching profession** = all teachers, taken as a group; *the teaching profession is often blamed by parents if their children do badly at school*
(b) **teachings** = political or moral ideas which are taught; *Christianity is based on the life and teachings of Jesus Christ; the teachings of Gandhi*

② **teacup**
['tikʌp] *noun*
cup for drinking tea; *she put the teacups and saucers on a tray; (informal)* **tempest in a teacup** = lot of fuss about something which is not important

② **teakettle**
['tiketl] *noun*
a container with a lid and spout, used for boiling water; *turn the gas up, the teakettle hasn't boiled yet; each bedroom has an electric teakettle, tea bags and packs of instant coffee;* **to put the teakettle on** = to start heating the water in a teakettle; *I've just put the teakettle on so we can all have a cup of tea*

① **team**
[tim]
1 *noun*
(a) group of people who play a game together; *there are nine people in a baseball team; he's a fan of the local hockey team; our college team played badly last Saturday*
(b) group of people who work together; *they make a very effective team; in this job you have to be able to work as a member of a team;* **management team** = all the managers who work together in a company; **sales team** = all representatives, salesmen and sales managers working together in a company; *he has a sales team of twenty people* (NOTE: the word **team** is singular, but can be followed by a singular or plural verb: **the team has** *or* **have come out of the changing room**)
2 *verb*
to team up with someone = to join someone to work together; *I teamed up with George to tackle the Mississippi project*

① **teapot**
['tipɒt] *noun*
pot which is used for making tea; *put two tea bags into the teapot and add boiling water*

② tear

1 *noun*

(a) [tɪər] drop of salt water that forms in your eye when you cry; *tears were running down her cheeks*; **in tears** = crying; *all the family were in tears*; **she burst into tears** = she suddenly started crying

(b) [teər] place where something has a hole in it from being ripped; *can you mend the tear in my jeans?*; *see also* WEAR AND TEAR

2 [teər] *verb*

(a) to make a hole in something by pulling; *he tore his pants climbing over the fence*; *my jacket is torn - can it be mended?*

(b) to pull something into bits; *he tore the letter in half*; *she tore up old newspapers to pack the cups and saucers*

(c) to go very fast; *he tore across the platform, but just missed his train*; *she grabbed the dress and tore out of the store* (NOTE: **tearing - tore** [tɔr] **- torn** [tɔrn])

③ tear down

[ˈteərˈdaʊn] *verb*

(a) to knock something down; *they tore down the old town hall and replaced it with a supermarket*

(b) to remove a piece of paper or cloth that is hanging up; *the crowd tore down the pictures of the president*; *the police tore down the opposition party's election posters*

③ tear gas

[ˈtɪərˈgæs] *noun*

gas that makes your eyes burn, used by police to control crowds; *in the end the police had to resort to using tear gas*; *the police used tear gas to clear demonstrators from outside the White House*

② tease

[tiz] *verb*

to say or do something to annoy someone on purpose; *he teased her about her thick glasses*; *stop teasing that poor cat*

① teaspoon

[ˈtispun] *noun*

(a) small spoon for stirring tea or other liquid or a measuring spoon for cooking (tsp); *can you bring me a teaspoon, please?*

(b) the amount contained in a teaspoon; *I take one teaspoon of sugar in my coffee*

③ tech

[tek] *noun*

(informal) technical school; *he's doing an engineering course at the local tech school*; *see also* HIGH TECH

④ technical

[ˈteknɪkl] *adjective*

referring to industrial processes or practical work; *don't bother with the technical details of how the machine works, just tell me what it does*; *the instructions are too technical for the ordinary person to understand*; **technical school** = secondary school or chollege, teaching technical skills; **technical subjects** = practical skills taught in schools or colleges, such as automobile maintenance, electrical engineering, etc.; **technical term** = specialized word used in a particular science, or trade

④ technically

[ˈteknɪkli] *adverb*

(a) in a technical way; *it's technically possible to make a lightbulb that would never wear out*

(b) technically (speaking) = according to the exact meaning; *technically he isn't a member of the club because he hasn't paid this year's subscription*

③ technician

[tekˈnɪʃn] *noun*

person who is a specialist in a particular area of industry or science; *she's a computer technician*; *we have a team of technicians working on the project*; **laboratory technician** = person who deals with practical work in a laboratory

③ technique

[tekˈnik] *noun*

way of doing something; *he developed a new technique for processing steel*; *she has a specially effective technique for dealing with complaints from customers*

③ technological

[teknəˈlɒdʒɪkl] *adjective*

referring to technology; *the company has reported making an important technological discovery*

④ technology

[tekˈnɒlədʒɪ] *noun*

use or study of industrial or scientific skills; *we already have the technology to produce such a machine*; *the government has promised increased investment in science and technology*; **introduction of new technology** = putting new electronic equipment into a business or industry; *see also* INFORMATION TECHNOLOGY

① teddy (bear)

[ˈtedɪ ˈbeər] *noun*

child's toy bear; *she won't go to bed without her teddy bear*; *the little boy held his teddy tight* (NOTE: the plural is **teddies**)

④ tedious

[ˈtidiəs] *adjective*

boring; *the lectures are so tedious I skip most of them*; *filing invoices is a tedious job but it has to be done*

④ teen

[tin] *noun*

(a) teens = age between 13 and 19; *she worked at the restaurant when she was in her teens*

(b) = TEENAGER

② teenage

[ˈtineɪdʒ] *adjective*

(a) *(also* **teenaged**) aged between 13 and 19; *he has two teenage(d) daughters*

(b) referring to young people aged between 13 and 19; *the federal government is trying to deal with the problem of teenage crime*; *the teenage market for the pop group's records is enormous*

① **teenager**
['tineɪdʒər] *noun*
young person aged between 13 and 19; *most of the people who come to the club are teenagers*

① **tee shirt** *or* **T-shirt**
['tiʃɜrt] *noun*
light shirt with no buttons or collar, usually with short sleeves; *no wonder you're cold if you went out in just a tee shirt*; *she was wearing jeans and a T-shirt*

① **teeth**
[tiθ]
see TOOTH

④ **telecommunications**
[telɪkəmjunɪ'keɪʃnz] *noun*
communication system using telephone, radio, TV, satellites, etc.; *thanks to modern telecommunications, the information can be sent to our office in Japan in seconds* (NOTE: also shortened to **telecoms** ['telɪkɒmz])

① **telephone**
['telɪfəʊn]
1 *noun*
machine that you use to speak to someone who is some distance away; *can't someone answer the telephone - it's been ringing and ringing*; *I was in the yard when you called, but by the time I got to the house the telephone had stopped ringing*; **by telephone** = using the telephone; *he booked his plane ticket by telephone*; *she reserved a table by telephone*
2 *verb*
to call someone using a telephone; *your wife telephoned when you were out*; *can you telephone me at ten o'clock tomorrow evening?*; *I need to telephone our office in New York* (NOTE: **telephone** is often shortened to **phone: phone call, phone book,** etc., but not in the expressions **telephone switchboard, telephone operator, telephone exchange**)

◇ **on the telephone**
['ɒn ðə 'telɪfəʊn]
speaking by telephone; *don't make such a noise - Daddy's on the telephone*; *William! - there's someone on the telephone who wants to speak to you*; *the sales manager is on the telephone all the time*

③ **telephone book** *or* **telephone directory**
['telɪfəʊn 'bʊk or daɪ'rektəri] *noun*
book that gives the names of people in a town with their addresses and telephone numbers; *the restaurant must be new - it isn't in the telephone book*; *look up his number in the telephone directory* (NOTE: is often shortened to **phone book**)

③ **telephone booth**
['telɪfəʊn 'buθ] *noun*
shelter with windows round it containing a public telephone; *call me from the telephone booth outside the diner, and I'll come and pick you up*; *there was a line of people waiting to use the telephone booth* (NOTE: often shortened to **phone booth**)

① **telephone number**
['telɪfəʊn 'nʌmbər] *noun*
number of one particular telephone; *what's the telephone number of the garage?*; *his telephone number's (612) 458-6307* (NOTE: is often shortened to **phone number**)

> COMMENT: The number (612) 458-0367 is pronounced "area code six one two, four five eight, zero three six seven". If the last four numbers end in 00, they are usually said as hundred; e.g. 458-6300 = "four five eight, sixty-three hundred". Similarly, if the last four numbers end in 000, they are often said as thousand; e.g. 458-6000 = "four five eight, six thousand".

① **telescope**
['telɪskəʊp]
1 *noun*
tube with a series of lenses for looking at objects that are very far away; *with a telescope you can see the ships very clearly*; *he discovered a satellite by using the telescope in his backyard*; **optical telescope** = telescope that uses mirrors and lenses to make the image and light coming from stars very much larger; **radio telescope** = telescope that uses radio waves to find or see stars and other objects in the sky
2 *verb*
to push together, so that one piece slides into another; *in the crash, several of the cars of the express train were telescoped*

② **televise**
['telɪvaɪz] *verb*
to broadcast something by television; *the debates in the House are now televised*; **the show is being televised live** = the show is being broadcast on TV as it takes place, and not recorded and broadcast later

① **television (TV)**
[telɪ'vɪʒən] *noun*
(a) sound and pictures that are sent through the air or along cables and appear on a special machine; *we don't watch television every night - some nights we go to to the bar*; *is there any basketball on television tonight?*; *Wednesday evening television programs are never very interesting*; *he stayed in his room all evening, watching television*; **cable television** = television system, where pictures are sent by cable
(b) piece of electrical equipment that shows television pictures; *we can't watch anything - our television has broken down*; *switch off the*

television - that program's stupid; when my husband comes home in the evening he just pours himself a beer, turns on the television and goes to sleep (NOTE: television is often written or spoken as **TV** ['ti 'vi])

② **television set (TV)**
[teli'vɪʒn 'set] *noun*
piece of electrical equipment that shows television pictures; *my father has bought a new television set or a new TV*

① **tell**
[tel] *verb*
(a) to say something to someone, for example a story or a joke; *she told me a long story about how she got lost in San Francisco; I don't think they are telling the truth*
(b) to give information to someone; *the police officer told them how to get to the post office; he told the police that he had seen the accident take place; don't tell my mother you saw me at the bar; nobody told us about the picnic*
(c) to tell someone what to do = to give someone instructions; *the teacher told the children to stand in a line; give a shout to tell us when to start*
(d) to notice; *he can't tell the difference between butter and margarine; you can tell he is embarrassed when his face turns red*
(e) to tell the time = to be able to read the time from a clock; *he's only three, but he can already tell the time* (NOTE: telling - told [təʊld])

③ **teller**
['telər] *noun*
employee who carries out a transaction for a customer at a bank, taking in or giving out money; *the bank teller cashed the checks for her*

③ **tell off**
['tel 'ɒf] *verb*
(informal) to speak to someone angrily about something wrong he or she has done; *the students were told off for being late; the teacher will tell you off if you don't do your homework*

② **temper**
['tempər]
1 *noun*
(a) state of becoming angry; *you have to learn to control your temper; he has a violent temper*
(b) general calm state of mind; *he lost his temper* = he became very angry; *she tried to keep her temper* = she tried to stay calm and not get angry
2 *verb*
(a) *(formal)* to temper something with = to make something have a less harsh effect; *we try to temper the strict prison regime with sports and educational activities*
(b) to make a metal hard by heating and cooling; *a tempered steel blade*

② **temperature**
['temprətʃər] *noun*
(a) heat measured in degrees; *the temperature of water in the swimming pool is 80°; temperatures in the Arctic can be very low; I can't start the automobile when the temperature is below zero; put the thermometer in the patient's mouth - I want to take her temperature*
(b) illness where your body is hotter than normal; *she's off work with a temperature; the doctor says he has a temperature and has to stay in bed*

② **tempest**
['tempest] *noun*
(formal) big storm; *(informal)* **tempest in a teacup** = lot of fuss about something which is not important

② **temple**
['templ] *noun*
(a) building for worship, usually Hindu or Buddhist, or ancient Greek or Roman, but not Christian or Muslim; *we visited the Greek temples on the islands*
(b) flat part of the side of the head between the top of the ear and the eye; *he had a bruise on his right temple*

④ **temporarily**
['temprərəli] *adverb*
for a short time only; *he's temporarily unemployed; I'm staying at my mother's temporarily while my apartment is being decorated*

③ **temporary**
['temprəri] *adjective*
which is not permanent, only lasting a short time; *she has a temporary job with a construction company; this arrangement is only temporary;* **temporary employment** = work that does not last for more than a few months; **temporary staff** = staff who are appointed for a short time; *we usually hire about twenty temporary staff during the Christmas period*

④ **tempt**
[temt] *verb*
(a) to try to persuade someone to do something, especially something pleasant or wrong; *can I tempt you to have another jelly doughnut?; they tried to tempt him to leave his job and work for them*
(b) to be tempted to = to feel like doing something; *he was tempted to send the food back to the kitchen; I am tempted to accept their offer*
(c) to tempt fate = to do something which could have bad results; *it would be tempting fate to buy that automobile without having had it checked by a garage*

④ **temptation**
[tem'teɪʃn] *noun*
being tempted; thing which tempts; *putting*

chocolates near the cash register is just a temptation for little children; the temptation is just to do nothing and hope the problem will simply go away

① **ten**
[ten]
(a) number 10; *in the market they're selling ten oranges for two dollars*; *she's ten (years old) next week*; *the next plane for Paris leaves at 10 (o'clock) in the evening*; **the ten hundreds (1000s)** = the years from 1000 to 1099 (NOTE: compare **the tenth century**)
(b) *(informal)* **ten to one** = very likely; *ten to one he finds out about the payment*
(c) *(informal)* **tens** = $10 bills or £10 notes; *he gave me two twenties and four tens*

③ **tenant**
['tenənt] *noun*
person or company that rents a room, apartment, house, office, land, etc., in which to live or work; *the previous tenants left the apartment in a terrible state*

① **tend**
[tend] *verb*
(a) **to tend to do something** = to be likely to do something; *she tends to lose her temper very easily*
(b) **to tend toward something** = to lean in a certain direction; *he's certainly not a conservative - if anything, he tends toward the liberals*
(c) to look after something; *his job is to tend the flower beds in front of the town hall*

④ **tendency**
['tendənsɪ] *noun*
way in which someone or something is likely to act; *the photocopier has a tendency to break down if you try to do too many copies at the same time*; *at parties, he has an unfortunate tendency to sit in a corner and go to sleep*

① **tender**
['tendər]
1 *adjective*
(a) (food) which is easy to cut or chew; *a plate of tender young beans*; **tender meat** = which can be chewed or cut easily; *the meat was so tender, you hardly needed a knife to cut it* (NOTE: the opposite is **tough**)
(b) delicate, easily damaged; *the baby has very tender skin*
(c) showing love; *the plants need a lot of tender loving care*
(d) which cannot stand frost; *keep the tender young plants in the greenhouse until June*
2 *noun*
(a) offer to do something at a certain price; **to put in a tender** *or* **to submit a tender for a job** = to offer to do work at a certain price
(b) **legal tender** = coins or notes which can be legally used; *old Confederate notes are no longer legal tender in the U.S.* (NOTE: no plural in this meaning)

(c) *(old)* vehicle carrying coal attached to a steam locomotive
3 *verb*
(a) **to tender for a job** = to offer to do work at a certain price; *the company is tendering for a construction job in Saudi Arabia*
(b) *(formal)* to offer; *he tendered his resignation*
(c) *(formal)* to offer money; *please tender the correct fare*

② **tennis**
['tenɪs] *noun*
game for two or four players who use rackets to hit a ball backward and forward over a net; *he's joined the local tennis club*; *would you like a game of tennis?*; *I won the last two tennis matches I played*; *tennis players have to be fit*; **tennis ball** = ball for playing tennis; *that onion's the size of a tennis ball*; **tennis court** = specially marked area for playing tennis; **tennis racket** = racket used to play tennis; **tennis shoes** = special light shoes worn when playing tennis or a lightweight sneaker

③ **tense**
[tens]
1 *adjective*
nervous and worried; *I always get tense before going to a job interview*; *the atmosphere in the hall was tense as everyone waited for the result of the vote* (NOTE: **tenser - tensest**)
2 *noun*
(grammar) form of a verb which shows the time when the action takes place; **future tense** = form of a verb which shows that something will happen; *"he will eat" and "he is going to eat" are forms of the future tense of the verb "to eat"*; **past tense** = form of a verb which shows that it happened before the present time; *"sang" is the past tense of the verb "to sing"*; **present tense** = form of a verb which shows the time we are in now; *the present tense of "to sit" is "he sits" or "he is sitting"*
3 *verb*
to become nervous and worried; *he tensed suddenly, as he heard a sound outside the window*

③ **tension**
['tenʃn] *noun*
(a) being tight; *you need to adjust the tension in your tennis racket before starting a game*
(b) state of nervous anxiety; *tension built up as we waited for the result*
(c) situation between countries or races who may be enemies; *there is tension in the area caused by fighting between different religious groups*

① **tent**
[tent] *noun*
shelter made of cloth, held up by poles and attached to the ground with ropes; *we went camping in Oregon and took our tent in the back of the station wagon*; *their tent was blown*

away by the wind; *the flower show was held in a tent in the grounds of the castle*; **to pitch a tent** = to put up a tent; *we pitched our tent in a field by a little mountain stream*

④ **tentative**
['tentətɪv] *adjective*
which has been suggested but not accepted, done in an uncertain way because you are not sure what will happen; *this is only a tentative suggestion*; *we suggested Wednesday May 10 as a tentative date for the wedding*; **tentative proposal** = proposal made to find out what the response is; *we put forward a tentative proposal for the committee to consider*

② **tenth (10th)**
[tenθ] *adjective & noun*
today is April tenth (April 10) that's the tenth phone call I've had this morning; *we spend a tenth of our income on food*; **the tenth century** = the period from 900 to 999 (NOTE: compare **the ten hundreds**; Note also that with dates **tenth** is usually written **10: July 10, 1935; April 10, 1991**: (say "April tenth"); with names of kings and queens **tenth** is usually written **X: King Charles X** (say "King Charles the Tenth")

② **term**
[tɜrm]
1 *noun*
(a) official length of time; *his term as president was marked by a lot of disagreement*; *she was sent to prison for a term of three years*; **in the long term** = for a long period from now; **in the short term** = for a short period from now; *in the long term, this investment should be very profitable*; **term of office** = period of time when someone has a position; *during his term of office as president*; *see also* LONG-TERM, SHORT-TERM
(b) one of the parts of a school or university year; *a school year can have three terms*; *the current term ends on December 15*
(c) word or phrase that has a particular meaning; *he used several technical terms which I didn't understand*; *some people use "hon" as a term of affection*
(d) *see also* TERMS
2 *verb*
(formal) to call something by a certain word; *you say it is acceptable behavior - I would term it shocking*

③ **terminal**
['tɜrmɪnl]
1 *adjective*
(a) in the last period of a fatal illness; *he has terminal cancer*; **terminal illness** = illness from which the patient will soon die
(b) at the end; **terminal shoot** = shoot at the end of a branch
2 *noun*
(a) building at an airport where planes arrive or depart; *the flight leaves from Terminal 4*

(b) building where you end a journey; **air terminal** = building in the center of a town where passengers arrive from an airport; **bus terminal** = place where buses begin or end their journeys; *buses leave the terminal every fifteen minutes*
(c) **electric terminal** = connecting point in an electric circuit; *the positive terminal of a battery is indicated by a plus sign*
(d) **computer terminal** = keyboard and monitor, attached to a main computer system

④ **terminate**
['tɜrmɪneɪt] *verb*
(formal) to finish, to come to an end; *the offer terminates on July 31*; *the flight from Paris terminates in New York*

③ **terms**
[tɜrmz] *noun*
(a) conditions which are agreed before something else is done; *we bought the store on very favorable terms*; *what are the terms of the agreement?*
(b) **to come to terms** = to reach an agreement; *when it became obvious that neither side would win, they came to terms*; **to come to terms with something** = to accept that something has happened and cannot be changed; *it took him some time to come to terms with the fact that he would never walk again*
(c) **terms of payment** = condition for paying something; *the terms of payment are 50% discount, with 60 days' credit*; **our terms are cash with order** = we will supply the goods you want if you pay cash at the same time as you place the order
(d) **terms of reference** = areas which a committee has to examine or discuss; *the terms of reference of the committee do not extend to EU policy*
(e) way of getting on with someone; *they're on bad terms with the people next door*; *the company is on good terms with all its suppliers*; **they're not on speaking terms** = they refuse to talk to each other
(f) **in terms of** = (i) expressed as; (ii) as regards; *how much is 5% per month in terms of an annual percentage rate?*; **we are talking in terms of a salary plus bonuses** = the job is offered with a salary plus bonuses

④ **terrace**
['terəs] *noun*
(a) flat area with a stone or tiled floor, which is raised above another area; *the guests had drinks on the terrace before going into dinner*
(b) **terraces** = rows of wide steps or areas of land; *in China, rice is grown on terraces*

① **terrible**
['terɪbl] *adjective*
(a) very bad; *we shouldn't have come to this party - the music's terrible*; *there was a terrible storm last night*

(b) frightening; *it must have been terrible to be in the car that plunged into the river*

② **terribly**
['teribli] *adverb (informal)*
(a) very; *I'm terribly sorry to have kept you waiting*; *the situation is terribly serious*
(b) in a very bad way; *the farmers are suffering terribly from drought*

② **terrific**
[tə'rifik] *adjective (informal)*
(a) wonderful; *we had a terrific time at the party*
(b) very big or loud; *there was a terrific noise and the whole building collapsed*

② **terrify**
['terifai] *verb*
to make someone very frightened; *the sound of thunder terrifies me*

④ **terrifying**
['terifaiŋ] *adjective*
very frightening; *a terrifying whirlwind hit the town*

③ **territorial**
[teri'tɔriəl] *adjective*
referring to territory; *they made territorial gains at the end of the war*; *territorial waters* = sea waters near the coast of a country, which are part of that country and which are governed by the laws of that country

② **territory**
['teritri] *noun*
(a) large stretch of land; land which belongs to a country; *they occupied all the territory on the east bank of the river*; *a group of soldiers had wandered into enemy territory*
(b) area visited by a salesman; *his territory covers the northern part of the country*
(c) area that an animal or bird thinks belongs only to it; *animals often fight to defend their territories* (NOTE: plural is **territories**)

② **terror**
['terər] *noun*
(a) great fear; *they live in constant terror of racist attacks*; *reign of terror* = period when law and order have broken down and people live in a continual state of fear
(b) *(informal)* naughty child; *their daughter's a little terror*
(c) *(informal)* **a terror for** = who insists on; *the new manager is a terror for clever uniforms in the store*

③ **terrorism**
['terərizm] *noun*
policy of using violence in a political cause; *acts of terrorism continued during the whole summer*; *the government has said that it will not give in to terrorism*

③ **terrorist**
['terərist]
1 *noun*

person who practices terrorism; *terrorists stormed the plane and told the pilot to fly to Rome*
2 *adjective*
referring to terrorism; *terrorist attacks have increased over the last few weeks*

① **test**
[test]
1 *noun*
(a) examination to see if you know something, etc.; *we had an English test yesterday*; *she passed her driver's test*
(b) examination to see if something is working well; *the doctor will have to do a blood test*; *it is a good test of the automobile's ability to brake fast*
2 *verb*
(a) to examine you to see if you can do something, etc.; *the teacher tested my spoken Spanish*
(b) to examine something to see if everything is working well; *we need to test your reactions to noise and bright lights*; *he has to have his eyes tested*; *she tested her new four-wheel drive in the snow*

② **testament**
['testəmənt] *noun*
(a) **last will and testament** = document written by someone which says what they want to happen to their property after they die; *this is the last will and testament of James Smith*
(b) **Old Testament** = the first part of the Bible, which deals with the origins and history of the Jewish people; **New Testament** = the second part of the Bible, which deals with the life of Jesus Christ, his teachings, and the early Christian church

② **testify**
['testifai] *verb*
to give evidence in court; *she testified against her former boss*; *he refused to testify because he was afraid*

③ **testimony**
['testiməni] *noun*
statement given in court about what happened; *the defense lawyers tried to persuade the jury that the manager's testimony was false*

④ **testing**
['testiŋ]
1 *adjective*
which is difficult to deal with; *this has been a testing time for the whole family*; *in the second interview they will ask you more testing questions*
2 *noun*
examining something to see if it works well; *during the testing of the engine several defects were corrected*

② **text**
[tekst] *noun*
(a) main written section of a book, not the notes, index, pictures, etc.; *it's a book for little*

children, with lots of pictures and very little text; **text processing** = using a computer to produce, check and change documents, reports, letters, etc.

(b) original words of a speech; *the text of the Gettysburg Address*

③ **textbook**
['tekstbuk] *noun*
book which students use to learn about the subject they are studying; *we are supposed to buy this English textbook*

③ **textile**
['tekstaɪl] *noun*
cloth; *they export textiles all over the world*; *the textile industry is influenced by world commodity prices*

② **text message**
['tekst 'mesɪdʒ] *noun*
message sent by telephone, using short forms of words, which appear on the screen of a cellular phone; *he sent me a text message asking me to meet him at the club tonight*

③ **texture**
['tekstʃər] *noun*
(a) the way in which a surface can be felt; *the soft texture of velvet*
(b) the way a substance is formed; *this bread has a light texture*; *the heavy texture of clay soil*

② **than**
[ðæn or ðən]
1 *conjunction (used to indicate an action or state which is being compared with something else) it's hotter this week than it was last week*
2 *preposition (used to link two parts of a comparison) his automobile is bigger than mine*; *she was born in New York City, so she knows it better than any other town*; *you can't get more than four people into this elevator*; *it's less than five miles to the nearest drugstore*

② **thank**
[θæŋk] *verb*
(a) to say or do something that shows you are grateful to someone for doing something for you; *she thanked the police officer for helping her to cross the street*; *don't forget to thank Aunt Ann for her present*; *"Thank you for your letter of June 25"*
(b) thank goodness! *or* **thank God!** *or* **thank heavens!** = expressions used to show relief; *thank goodness it didn't rain for the school fair!*; *thank God the ambulance turned up quickly!*

③ **thankful**
['θæŋkfəl] *adjective*
glad because a worry has gone away; *we'll all be thankful to get back into harbor safely*; *I'm thankful that the firemen arrived so quickly*; *see also* MERCY

① **thanks**
[θæŋks]
1 *noun*

word showing that you are grateful; *we sent our thanks for the gift*; *we did our best to help but got no thanks for it*; *the committee passed a vote of thanks to the secretary for having organized the meeting*; *many thanks for your letter of the 15th*
2 *interjection showing you are grateful*
do you want some more tea? - no thanks, I've had two cups already; *anyone want a lift to the station? - thanks, it's a long walk from here*

① **Thanksgiving (Day)**
[θæŋks'gɪvɪŋ] *noun*
American festival, celebrating the first harvest of the pilgrims who settled in the United States (celebrated on the fourth Thursday in November); *all the family will be here for Thanksgiving*

> COMMENT: the traditional menu for Thanksgiving dinner is roast turkey, bread stuffing, potatoes, cranberry sauce, and pumpkin pie

④ **thanks to**
['θæŋks 'tu] *preposition*
because of, as a result of; *thanks to the map which he faxed to us, we found his house without any difficulty*; *thanks to my father, she has a job*

① **thank you**
['θæŋk ju]
1 *interjection showing that you are grateful*
thank you very much for your letter of the 15th; *did you remember to say thank you to your grandmother for the present?*; *would you like another piece of cake? - no thank you, I've had enough*; **thank-you letter** = letter written to thank someone for something
2 *noun*
words which show you are grateful; *let's say a big thank-you to the people who organized the show*

② **that**
[ðæt]
1 *adjective (used to show something which is further away) can you see that white house on the corner over there?*; *do you remember the name of that awful hotel in Provincetown?* (NOTE: the opposite is **this**; the plural is **those**)
2 *pronoun*
that's the book I was talking about; *do you know who that is sitting at the next table?*
3 *relative pronoun*
where is the package that she sent you yesterday?; *can you see the man that sold you the ticket?*; *there's the suitcase that you left in the taxi!* (NOTE: when it is the object of a verb **that** can be left out: **where's the letter he sent you? here's the box you left in the bedroom.** When it is the subject, **that** can be replaced by **which** *or* **who**: **a house that has red windows** *or* **a house which has red windows**; **the man that stole the**

automobile *or* **the man who stole the automobile**)

4 *conjunction*

(a) *(after verbs like* hope, know, tell, say; *and adjectives like* glad, sorry, happy*); they told me that the manager was out*; *she said several times that she wanted to sit down*; *I don't think they knew that we were coming*; *I'm glad that the weather turned out fine*; *I am sorry that you have been kept waiting*

(b) *(after* so *or* such; + *adjective or noun) the restaurant was so expensive that we could only afford one dish*; *it rained so hard that the street was like a river*; *we had such a lot of work that we didn't have any lunch*; *there was such a long line that we didn't bother waiting* (NOTE: that is often left out: he didn't know we were coming; it's so hot in here we all want a drink of water)

5 *adverb*

(usually with negative) so, to such an extent; *you must remember him, it's not all that long ago that we had a drink with him*; *his new automobile is not really that big*

③ **thatched**

[θætʃt] *adjective*

covered with a straw roof; *he lives in a little thatched cottage*

② **thaw**

[θɔ]

1 *verb*

(a) to melt; *the ice is thawing on the village pond*

(b) to warm something which is frozen; *can you thaw the frozen peas?*

(c) to become less formal; *after a period of tension, relations between the two countries have begun to thaw*

2 *noun*

warm weather which makes snow and ice melt; *the thaw came early this year*

① **the**

[ðər] *before a vowel* [ði] *article*

(a) *(meaning something in particular) where's the book you brought back from the library?*; *that's the cat from next door*

(b) *(used with something of which only one exists) the sun came up over the hills*; *they want to land scientists on the moon*

(c) *(meaning something in general) there's nothing interesting on the television tonight*; *she refuses to use the telephone*; *the streets are crowded at lunchtime*; *many people were out of work during the 1990s*

(d) [ði] *(meaning something very special) it's the store for men's clothes*; *she's the doctor for children's diseases*; *that's not the Charlie Chaplin movie, is it?*

(e) *(used to compare) the more he eats, the thinner he seems to get*; *the sooner you do it, the better*; *this is by far the shortest way to New Orleans*; *she's the tallest person in the office*

① **theater**

[ˈθɪətər] *noun*

(a) building in which plays are shown; *I'm trying to get tickets for the theater tonight*; *what is the play at the local theater this week?*; *we'll have dinner early and then go to the theater*

(b) **movie theater** = building where movies are shown;

(c) **the theater** = (i) art of presenting plays on the stage; (ii) business of presenting plays on the stage; *I like the theater better than the cinema*; *she wants to work in the theater as a designer*

② **theft**

[θeft] *noun*

(a) stealing (in general); *we have brought in security guards to protect the hotel against theft*; *they are trying to stop theft by members of the public*

(b) act of stealing; *thefts in supermarkets have increased enormously*

① **their**

[ðeər] *adjective*

(a) belonging to them; *after the movie, we went to their house for supper*

(b) referring to them; *the family was eating their dinner when the fire broke out* (NOTE: do not confuse with **there, they're**)

① **theirs**

[ðeərz] *pronoun*

the one that belongs to them; *which car is theirs - the Ford?*; *she's a friend of theirs*; *the girls wanted to borrow my automobile - theirs wouldn't start*

① **them**

[ðem] *object pronoun*

(a) *(referring to a people or things which have been mentioned before) do you like meringue pies? - no, I don't like them very much*; *there's a group of people waiting outside - tell them to come in*

(b) *(referring to a singular, used instead of* him; *or* her*); if someone phones, ask them to call back later*

② **theme**

[θim] *noun*

(a) the main subject of a book or article; *the theme of the book is how to deal with illness in the family*

(b) main idea; *the theme of the exhibition is "The U.S.A. in the twenty-first century"*

(c) main tune in a piece of music; *the theme comes again at the end of the piece*; **theme park** = amusement park based on a single theme (such as Disneyland, etc.); *a visit to the theme park is included in the package tour*; **theme tune** *or* **theme song** = tune or song played several times in a movie or TV serial by which you can recognize it

③ **themselves**
[ðəm'selvz] *pronoun*
(a) *(referring to the same people or things that are the subject of the verb)* *cats always spend a lot of time cleaning themselves*; *it's no use going to the doctor's office - the doctors are all sick themselves*
(b) **by themselves** = all alone; *the girls were all by themselves in the tent*; *they did it all by themselves*

① **then**
[ðen]
1 *adverb*
(a) at that time in the past or future; *he had been very busy up till then*; *ever since then I've refused to eat duck*; *we're having a party next week - what a pity! I'll be in Oregon then*
(b) after that, next; *we all sat down, and then after a few minutes the waiter brought us the menu*; *it was a busy trip - he went to Brazil, then to Uruguay and finally to Argentina*
(c) and so, therefore; *if there isn't any fish on the menu, then we'll have to have a vegetarian dish*; *then he was already at home when you phoned?*
2 *adjective*
who or which existed at a certain time in the past; *the then secretary of education was a man called Travis*

④ **theoretical**
[θɪə'retɪkl] *adjective*
not proved or done in practice; *she has the theoretical power to dismiss any of the staff*

④ **theoretically**
[θɪə'retɪkli] *adverb*
in theory, but not in practice; *theoretically the treatment should work, but no one has ever tried it*; *it is theoretically possible for him to win the tournament, but very unlikely*

③ **theory**
['θɪəri] *noun*
(a) explanation of something which has not been proved but which you believe is true; *I have a theory which explains why the police never found the murder weapon*
(b) careful scientific explanation of why something happens; *Galileo put forward the theory that the Earth turns round the sun*; **the theory of evolution** = theory, explained by Charles Darwin, that species develop by a process of natural selection
(c) statement of general principles which may not apply in practice; **in theory** = in principle, though maybe not in practice; *in theory the treatment should work, but no one has ever tried it*; *in theory the results should be the same every time you do the experiment* (NOTE: plural is **theories**)

④ **therapist**
['θerəpɪst] *noun*
person who is specially trained to give therapy; *the therapist said I should rest my leg as much*

as possible; **occupational therapist** = person who treats patients by making them do certain activities and exercises

④ **therapy**
['θerəpi] *noun*
treatment of a patient to help cure a disease or condition; *they use heat therapy to treat muscle problems*; **group therapy** = type of treatment where a group of people with the same disorder meet together with a therapist to discuss their condition and try to help each other; **occupational therapy** = treating patients by using activities to help them deal with problems or disabilities, used especially for handicapped patients or patients suffering from mental illness; **speech therapy** = treatment to cure a disorder in speaking; *see also* HORMONE

① **there**
[ðeər]
1 *adverb*
(a) in that place; *is that black van still there parked outside the house?*; *where have you put the tea bags? - there, on the kitchen counter*
(b) to that place; *we haven't been to the museum yet - let's go there tomorrow*; *have you ever been to China? - yes, I went there last month*
(c) *(used when giving something to someone)* *there you are: two cheeseburgers and a lemonade* (NOTE: do not confuse with **their, they're**)
2 *interjection*
(a) *(showing pity)* *there, there, don't get upset*; *there, sit down for a little while and you'll soon feel better*
(b) *(showing you were right)* *there, what did I say? the plane's late*
(c) *(making a decision)* *if you don't want to come with me, I'll go all by myself, so there!*
3 *pronoun (used usually with the verb* **to be** *when the real subject follows the verb)* *there's a little door leading into the yard*; *there's someone at the door asking for you*; *there are some pages missing in my newspaper*; *were there a lot of people at the movie theater?*; *there seems to have been a lot of rain during the night*; *there isn't any jam left in the cupboard* (NOTE: when **there** comes at the beginning of a sentence, the following subject comes after the verb if the subject is a noun and not a pronoun: **there goes the bus** but **there it goes**)

④ **thereby**
[ðeə'baɪ] *adverb*
(formal) by doing that; *a truck crashed into the bridge, thereby blocking the road*; *the company lowered its prices, thereby winning a market share from its competitors*

③ **therefore**
['ðeərfɔr] *adverb*
for this reason; *I therefore have decided not to grant his request*; *they have reduced their*

prices, therefore we should reduce ours if we want to stay competitive

④ **thermal**
['θɜrməl] *adjective*
referring to heat; **thermal underwear** = thick underwear which keeps you warm; *it's December, so I'd better get out my thermal underwear*

① **thermometer**
[θə'mɒmɪtər] *noun*
instrument for measuring temperature; *put the thermometer in your mouth - I want to take your temperature*; *the thermometer outside shows 70°*

② **these**
[ðiz] *see* THIS

① **they**
[ðeɪ] *pronoun*
(a) *(referring to people or things)* *where do you keep the spoons? - they're in the right-hand drawer*; *who are those people in uniform? - they're police officers*; *the children played in the sun and they all got red*
(b) *(referring to people in general)* *they say it's going to be good weather this weekend*
(c) *(referring to a singular, used after someone, etc.)* *if someone else joins the line, they'll just have to wait* (NOTE: when it is the object, **them** is used instead of **they**: *we gave it to them*; *the police beat them with clubs*; also when it follows the verb to **be**: *who's that? - it's them!*)

③ **they'd**
[ðeɪd] = THEY HAD, THEY WOULD

① **they'll**
[ðeɪl] = THEY WILL

③ **they're**
[ðeər] = THEY ARE (NOTE: do not confuse with **their, there**)

② **thick**
[θɪk]
1 *adjective*
(a) bigger than usual when measured from side to side, not thin; *he cut a slice of bread which was so thick we couldn't toast it*; *the walls of the castle are three feet thick*; *some oranges have very thick skins*; *he took a piece of thick rope*
(b) close together; *they tried to make their way through thick jungle*; *the field was covered with thick grass*; *(informal)* **through thick and thin** = together, even when things are going badly; *she stuck with him through thick and thin*; *(informal)* **to be thick with (somebody)** = to have a close relationship with (somebody); *she is thick with the manager*; *(of two people)* **they're as thick as thieves** = they are great friends, they share each other's secrets
(c) *(of liquids)* which cannot flow easily; *if the paint is too thick add some water*; *a bowl of thick soup is just what we need on a cold day like this*

(d) which you cannot see through easily; *thick fog had closed the airport*
(e) *(informal)* stupid, not very intelligent; *he's a bit thick* (NOTE: **thicker - thickest**)
2 *adverb*
in a thick way; *put the plaster on thick so that it covers up the cracks*; *(informal)* **to lay it on thick** = to praise someone excessively; *it was laying it on a bit thick to say that she plays the violin like Menuhin*

② **thief**
[θif] *noun*
person who steals; *the police are certain they will catch the thief*; *see also* THICK (NOTE: plural is **thieves** [θivz])

③ **thigh**
[θaɪ] *noun*
part at the top of the leg between your knee and your hip; *she was wearing a very short skirt and everyone could see her thighs*

① **thin**
[θɪn]
1 *adjective*
(a) not fat; *the table has very thin legs*; *he's too thin - he should eat more*
(b) not thick; *a plate of thin sandwiches*; *the book is printed on very thin paper*; *the package was sent in a thin cardboard box*
(c) not placed or growing close together; *the audience is a bit thin tonight*; *the hill was covered with thin grass*; *see also* VANISH
(d) *(of liquid)* which flows easily, which has too much water; *all we had for lunch was a bowl of thin soup*; *add water to make the paint thinner*
(e) which you can see through; *they hung thin curtains in the windows*; *a thin mist covered the valley* (NOTE: **thinner - thinnest**)
2 *adverb*
in a thin way; *don't spread the butter too thin*
3 *verb*
(a) to make more liquid; *if you want to thin the soup just add some water*
(b) to become fewer; *the crowds began to thin by evening*
(c) **to thin out** = to make plants grow less close together; *these lettuces need to be thinned out*

① **thing**
[θɪŋ] *noun*
(a) something which is not living, which is not a plant or animal; *can you see that black thing in the soup?*; *what do you use that big blue thing for?*
(b) usually kind way of talking to or about a person or animal; *the lady in the candy shop is a dear old thing*; *you silly thing! - why on earth did you do that?*
(c) something in general; *they all just sat there and didn't say a thing*; *the first thing to do is to call an ambulance*; *that was a stupid thing to do!*; **a good thing** = something lucky; *it's a good thing there was no police officer on duty at the door*; **first thing in the morning** = as soon as

you get up; **last thing at night** = just before you go to bed; *first thing in the morning, he does his exercises*

(d) problem, worry; *I can't relax, it's just one thing after another*

(e) *(informal)* **to have a thing about something** = to have strong feelings about something; *he has a thing about spiders*; *she has a thing about men with beards*; **to have another thing coming** = to be waiting for something that will not happen; *if he thinks he's going to tell me how to do my job, he has another thing coming*

(f) *(informal)* **to do your own thing** = to be independent, to do what you want to do; *he listens to what the manager says but then goes away and quietly does his own thing*

② **things**
[θɪŋz] *noun*

(a) clothes, equipment; *did you bring your tennis things?*; *she left her painting things in the car*

(b) general situation; *things aren't going well at the office*; *he always takes things too seriously*

① **think**
[θɪŋk]
1 *verb*

(a) to use your mind; *we never think about what people might say, we always do what we think is right*; **to think twice** = to consider very carefully; *think twice before you sign that contract*

(b) to have an opinion; *I think San Diego is a nicer place to live in than Los Angeles*; *everyone thinks we're mad to go on vacation in December*; *according to the weather forecast, they think it's going to rain*; *he didn't think much of the movie*; *the gang is thought to be based in Chicago*

(c) to make a plan to do something; *we're thinking of opening an office in New York* (NOTE: **thinking - thought** [θɔt])

2 *noun*

period when you think, the act of thinking; *let me have a little think and I'll tell you what we should do*; *have a think about what I've just said*; *we really need to have another think about the plan*; *(informal)* **to have another think coming** = to be waiting for something that will not happen; *if he thinks he's going to tell me how to do my job, he has another think coming*

③ **think about**
[ˈθɪŋk əˈbaʊt] *verb*

(a) to have someone or something in your mind; *I was just thinking about you when you phoned*; *all she thinks about is food*

(b) to consider a plan in your mind; *have you ever thought about writing children's books?*; **to think twice about** = to consider very carefully; *I'd think twice about spending all the money you've saved*

(c) to have an opinion about something; *what do you think about the government's plans to increase taxes?*

③ **think back**
[ˈθɪŋk ˈbæk] *verb*

to remember something in the past; *think back to last Wednesday - do you remember seeing me sign the letter?*

② **thinking**
[ˈθɪŋkɪŋ] *noun*

process of reasoning about something; *I don't understand the thinking behind the decision*; **to my way of thinking** = my opinion is; *to my way of thinking, it shouldn't be allowed*

① **think of**
[ˈθɪŋk ˈɒv] *verb*

(a) to consider a plan in your mind; *we are thinking of going to Tennessee for a vacation*

(b) to remember something; *now I think of it, he was at the party last week*

(c) to have an opinion about something; *what do you think of the government's plans to increase taxes?*; *I didn't think much of the play*; *she asked him what he thought of her idea*; **to tell someone what you think of something** = to criticize; *he went up to her and told her exactly what he thought of her stupid idea*; **to think highly of someone** = to have a high opinion of someone; **to think nothing of doing something** = to consider something normal, easy; *she thinks nothing of working ten hours a day*; *(as a response to an apology)* **think nothing of it!** = please don't bother to thank me for it; **he thought better of it** = he changed his mind; *he was going to pay the whole bill himself, and then thought better of it*

③ **think out**
[ˈθɪŋk ˈaʊt] *verb*

to consider something carefully in all its details; *have you thought out all the implications of the plan?*; *they submitted a well thought-out design*

③ **think over**
[ˈθɪŋk ˈoʊvər] *verb*

to consider a plan or proposal very carefully; *that's the proposal: think it over, and tell me what you decide tomorrow*

③ **think up**
[ˈθɪŋk ˈʌp] *verb*

to invent a plan or new idea; *he thought up a mad plan for making lots of money*

① **third (3rd)**
[θɜrd]
1 *adjective*

(a) referring to three; *she came in third in the race*; *the bakery is the third shop on the right*; *it will be her third birthday next Friday*; *her birthday is on the third of March or March the third (March 3)* **the third century** = the period from 200 to 299 (NOTE: with dates **third** is usually written **3**: **May 3, 1921**: **June 3, 1896**: (say "June third"); with names of kings and queens **third** is usually written **III: King Henry III** (say "King Henry the Third")

(b) third party = any third person, in addition to the two main parties involved in a contract; *if possible we want to prevent third parties becoming involved in the dispute*; **third-party insurance** = insurance which pays compensation if someone who is not the insured person suffers a loss or injury

(c) *(followed by a superlative)* only two others are more; *this is the third longest bridge in the world*; *he's the third highest paid member of staff*

2 *noun*

one part out of three equal parts; *a third of the airline's planes are made in Europe*; *two-thirds of the staff works part-time*

① **thirsty**

['θɜrsti] *adjective*

feeling that you want to drink; *it's so hot here that it makes me thirsty*; **are you thirsty?** = would you like a drink? (NOTE: **thirstier - thirstiest**)

① **thirteen**

[θɜr'tin]

number 13; *he's only thirteen (years old), but he can drive a golf cart*; *she'll be thirteen next Monday*; **the thirteen hundreds (1300s)** = the period from 1300 to 1399 (NOTE: compare **the thirteenth century**)

① **thirteenth (13th)**

[θɜr'tinθ] *adjective & noun*

it's her thirteenth birthday on Monday; **Friday the thirteenth** = day which many people think is unlucky; **the thirteenth century** = the period from 1200 to 1399 (NOTE: compare **the thirteen hundreds**; Note also that with dates **thirteenth** is usually written **13 July 13, 1935; October 13, 1991:** (say "October thirteenth"); with names of kings and queens **thirteenth** is usually written **XIII: King Louis XIII** (say: "King Louis the Thirteenth")

② **thirtieth (30th)**

['θɜrtiəθ] *adjective & noun*

he came in thirtieth out of thirty-five in the race; *the thirtieth of March or March the thirtieth (March 30) it was my thirtieth birthday last week* (NOTE: with dates **thirtieth** is usually written **30: May 30, 1921: June 30, 1896:** (say "June thirtieth")

① **thirty**

['θɜrti] number 30; *he's thirty (years old) she must have more than thirty pairs of shoes*; *she and her partner are both in their thirties* = they are both aged between 30 and 39 years old; **the (nineteen) thirties (1930s)** = the period from 1930 to 1939 (NOTE: **thirty-one** (31), **thirty-two** (32), etc., but **thirty-first** (31st), **thirty-second** (32nd), etc.)

① **this**

[ðɪs]

1 *adjective & pronoun*

(a) *(used to show something which is nearer - in contrast to* **that***)*; *this is the store that was mentioned in the paper*; *this little girl is a friend of my daughter*; *I think we have been to this restaurant before*; *this is Angela Smith, our new sales manager*

(b) *(used to refer to a part of today, the recent past or a period of time which will soon arrive)* I *saw him on the train this morning*; *my mother is coming for dinner this evening*; *I expect to hear from him this week*; *he's retiring this August*; *this year, our sales are better than last year*; *they're going to Utah this summer* (NOTE: plural is **these**)

2 *adverb*

(informal) so much; *I knew you were going to be late, but I didn't expect you to be this late*

③ **thistle**

['θɪsl] *noun*

large wild plant with purple flowers, and leaves with prickles; *he sat down on a patch of thistles and jumped up again*

② **thorn**

[θɔrn] *noun*

sharp point on a plant; *most roses have sharp thorns*

③ **thorough**

['θʌrər] *adjective*

(a) very careful and detailed; *the police have carried out a thorough search of the woods*

(b) total; *they made a thorough mess of it*; *it was a thorough waste of time*

② **thoroughly**

['θʌrəli] *adverb*

(a) in a complete and careful way; *we searched the yard thoroughly but couldn't find his red ball*

(b) totally; *I'm thoroughly fed up with the whole business*

② **those**

[ðəuz] *see* THAT

③ **though**

[ðəu] *adverb & conjunction*

(a) in spite of the fact that; *though tired, she still kept on running*; *we don't employ any accounting staff, though many companies do*; **odd though it may seem** = although it may seem odd

(b) as though = as if; *his voice sounded strange over the telephone, as though he was standing in a cave*; *that shirt doesn't look as though it has been ironed*; *it looks as though there is no one in*

(c) even though = in spite of the fact that; *he didn't wear a coat, even though it was snowing*; *he wouldn't come with us, even though we asked him twice*; *we managed to make ourselves understood, even though no one spoke English*

② **thought**

[θɔt]

1 *noun*

(a) idea that you have when thinking; *he had an awful thought - suppose they had left the bathroom faucet running?*

(b) process of thinking; *he sat deep in thought by the window*

(c) opinion; *he expressed his thoughts on the subject in a letter to the newspaper*; **to have second thoughts about something** = to change your mind about something; *I think she's beginning to have second thoughts about accepting the job*; **on second thought** = having thought about it again; *I asked for coffee, but on second thought I think I'll have tea*

2 *verb*

see THINK

① **thoughtful**
['θɔtfəl] *adjective*

(a) being sensitive to what other people want; *it was very thoughtful of you to come to see me in the hospital*

(b) thinking deeply; *he looked thoughtful, and I wondered if there was something wrong*

① **thousand**
['θauzənd]

number 1000; *we paid three hundred thousand dollars ($300,000) for the house*; *thousands of people had their vacations spoiled by the storm* (NOTE: after numbers **thousand** does not take the plural ending **-s: two thousand, ten thousand**)

① **thousandth (1000th)**
['θəauzənθ]

1 *adjective*

referring to a thousand; *the tourist office gave a prize to their thousandth visitor*

2 *noun*

one part out of a thousand; *a thousandth of a second*

① **thread**
[θred]

1 *noun*

(a) long strand of cotton, silk, etc.; *a spider spins a thread to make its web*; *wait a moment, there's a white thread showing on your coat*

(b) **to lose the thread of a conversation** = to miss what the conversation is about

(c) ridge going around and around a screw or the inside of a nut; *it's difficult to tighten the nut because the thread is very worn*

2 *verb*

(a) to put a piece of cotton through the eye of a needle; *my eyesight is getting so bad, I can't even thread a needle*

(b) to make something go through a hole; *put the reel on the projector and then thread the end of the film through this slot*

(c) **to thread your way** = to go carefully between things; *she threaded her way through the piles of boxes*; *we threaded our way through the crowds of Christmas shoppers*

③ **threat**
[θret] *noun*

(a) warning that you are going to do something

unpleasant, especially if someone doesn't do what you want; *her former husband had been making threats against her and the children*; *the police took the threat to the president very seriously*; *do you think they will carry out their threat to bomb the capital if we don't surrender?*; **death threat** = warning to someone that he or she will be killed

(b) person or thing which may harm; *fast sports cars are a threat to other road users*

③ **threaten**
['θretn] *verb*

(a) to warn that you are going to do something unpleasant, especially if someone doesn't do what you want; *she threatened to go to the police*; *the teacher threatened her with punishment*

(b) to be likely to have a bad effect on something; *the collapse of the stock market threatened the exchange rate*

③ **threatening**
['θretnɪŋ] *adverb*

suggesting that something unpleasant will happen; *the weather looks threatening*; *the crowd made threatening gestures at the referee*

① **three**
[θri]

number 3; *she's only three (years old), so she can't read yet*; *come and see me at three (o'clock) three men walked into the bank and pulled out guns* (NOTE: **three** (3) but **third** (3rd))

③ **three-quarters**
[θri'kwɔrtərz]

1 *noun*

three fourths, 75%; *I'm three-quarters of the way through the book*; *about three-quarters of the members are in favor*; **three-quarters of an hour** = forty-five minutes; *we had to wait an hour and three-quarters*

2 *adverb*

75%, three-fourths; *the bottle was three-quarters full*

① **threw**
[θru] *see* THROW (NOTE: do not confuse with **through**)

③ **thrift**
[θrɪft] *noun*

(a) saving money and spending it carefully; *through hard work and thrift the family became rich* (NOTE: no plural in this meaning)

(b) private local bank which accepts and pays interest on deposits from small investors

① **thrill**
[θrɪl]

1 *noun*

feeling of great excitement; *it gave me a thrill to see you all again after so many years*; *the thrill of driving through a group of elephants*

2 *verb*

to make someone very excited; *we were thrilled to get your letter*

② **thrilling**
['θrɪlɪŋ] *adjective*
which makes you very excited; *it was thrilling to arrive in New York City for the first time*

① **throat**
[θrəʊt] *noun*
(a) tube which goes from the back of your mouth down the inside of your neck; *she got a fish bone stuck in her throat*; **sore throat** = infected throat, which is red and hurts when you swallow or speak; *she has a sore throat and has lost her voice*; **to clear your throat** = to give a little cough; *he cleared his throat and started to speak*; **a lump in your throat** = feeling unable to speak because you are so upset or so happy; *she had a lump in her throat as she saw her little girl dance across the stage*
(b) your neck, especially the front part; *he put his hands around her throat and pressed hard*

② **throne**
[θrəʊn] *noun*
chair on which a king or queen sits during ceremonies; **to succeed to the throne** = to become king or queen; *he succeeded to the throne when his grandfather died* (NOTE: do not confuse with **thrown**)

① **through**
[θru]
1 *preposition*
(a) across the inside of something; going in at one side and coming out of the other; *she looked through the open door*; *cold air is coming in through the broken window* ; *she pushed the needle through the ball of yarn*
(b) during a period of time; *they insisted on talking all through the movie*
(c) by; *we sent the package through the regular mail*; *we heard of his wedding through the newspaper*
(d) caused by; *we marked him as absent through illness*; *we missed the deadline through her forgetting to mark it in her diary*
(e) up to and including; **Monday through Friday** = from Monday to Friday inclusive
2 *adverb*
(a) going in at one side and coming out of the other side; *someone left the gate open and all the cows got through*
(b) speaking by telephone; *I can't get through to New York*; *can you put me through to the person who deals with customer complaints?*
(c) **to see something through** = to make sure that something is finished   (NOTE: do not confuse with **threw**; **through** is often used after verbs: **to go through, to fall through, to see through,** etc.)
3 *adjective*
(a) not stopping; **through traffic** = traffic which is going through a town and doesn't stop; *through traffic is being diverted to the bypass*
(b) **through with something** = finished using something, not wanting something anymore; *are you through with the newspaper?*; *she's through with her boyfriend*

③ **throughout**
[θru'aʊt] *preposition & adverb*
everywhere, all through; *throughout the country, floods are causing problems on the roads*; *heavy snow fell throughout the night*

① **throw**
[θrəʊ]
1 *verb*
(a) to send something through the air; *how far can he throw a baseball?*; *they were throwing stones through automobile windows*; *she threw the letter into the wastepaper basket*; *he was thrown into the air by the blast from the bomb*
(b) **to throw a party** = to organize a party; *they threw a reception for the prize winners*
(c) (*informal*) to shock; *what the boss said threw me* (NOTE: **throwing - threw** [θru] **- has thrown** [θrəʊn])
2 *noun*
(a) act of throwing; *her throw beat the world record*; *he hurt his back after a throw from his horse*
(b) **only a stone's throw from** = very near; *the hotel is only a stone's throw from the beach*
(c) piece of material which you put over a chair, use as a blanket, etc.; *she gave me a piece of old Chinese silk as a throw to cover the sofa*

① **throw away**
['θrəʊ ə'weɪ] *verb*
to get rid of something which you don't need anymore; *don't throw away those old newspapers - they may come in useful*; *she threw away all her winter clothes*

① **thrown**
[θrəʊn] *see* THROW

① **throw out**
['θrəʊ 'aʊt] *verb*
(a) to push someone outside; *when they started to fight, they were thrown out of the restaurant*
(b) to get rid of something which you don't need; *I'm throwing out this old office desk*
(c) to refuse to accept; *the proposal was thrown out by the planning committee*

① **throw up**
['θrəʊ 'ʌp] *verb*
(*informal*) to be sick, to bring up partly digested food from the stomach into the mouth; *the cat threw up all over the sofa*

③ **thru**
[θru]   *preposition,   adverb   &   adjective;* (*informal*) = THROUGH

③ **thrush**
[θrʌʃ] *noun*
brown bird with brown spots on its light-coloured breast; *thrushes sing beautifully* (NOTE: plural is **thrushes**)

④ **thrust**
[θrʌst]
1 *noun*

force which pushes; *the thrust of the rocket's engines pushed him back in his seat*
2 *verb*
to push suddenly and hard; *he thrust the newspaper into his pocket*; *she thrust the documents into her briefcase* (NOTE: **thrusting - thrust**)

④ **thud**
[θʌd]
1 *noun*
dull, heavy noise; *his head hit the ground with a thud*
2 *verb*
to make a dull noise; *a stone thudded into the wall behind him* (NOTE: **thudding - thudded**)

② **thumb**
[θʌm]
1 *noun*
(a) short thick finger which is slightly apart from the other four fingers on each hand; *the baby was sucking its thumb*; *she cried when she hit her thumb with the hammer*
(b) to be all thumbs = to be awkward when trying to do something with your hands; *can you help me untie this knot, I'm all thumbs!*; **rule of thumb** = easily remembered way of doing a simple calculation; *divide by eight and multiply by five is a useful rule of thumb when converting kilometers into miles*
(c) *(informal)* **thumbs up (sign)** = gesture to show that you approve, that things are all right; *he gave us the thumbs up to show that we were through to the next stage of the competition*; *(informal)* **thumbs down (sign)** = gesture to show you disapprove; *the project got the thumbs down from the minister*
(d) under someone's thumb = dominated by someone; *she has him under her thumb* = he has to do what she tells him to do
2 *verb*
(a) to thumb a lift = to ask an automobile driver or truck driver to take you as a passenger, usually by signaling with the thumb while holding a sign with your destination written on it; *her automobile broke down and she thumbed a lift from a passing motorist*
(b) to thumb through = to turn over pages; *I was just thumbing through this old accounts book*

① **thumbtack**
[ˈθʌmtæk] *noun*
pin with a large flat head, used for pinning papers to a wall or a surface; *she used thumbtacks to pin the poster to the door*; *he put a thumbtack on the teacher's chair*

③ **thump**
[θʌmp]
1 *noun*
dull noise; *there was a thump from upstairs as if someone had fallen out of bed*
2 *verb*

(informal) to hit someone or something hard with your fist; *he rushed up to the policeman and started thumping him on the chest*

① **thunder**
[ˈθʌndər]
1 *noun*
(a) loud noise in the air following a flash of lightning; *a tropical storm accompanied by thunder and lightning*; *he was woken by the sound of thunder*
(b) loud noise; *the thunder of horses on the road outside the house*; *he took his bow to a thunder of applause*; *(informal)* **to steal someone's thunder** = to spoil what someone is planning to do by doing it first, and so getting applauded for it
2 *verb*
(a) to make a loud noise in the air following lightning; *it thundered during the night*
(b) to make a loud noise like thunder; *trucks thundered past on the highway all night*
(c) to speak in a very loud voice; *"shut up" he thundered to the little boy in the back row*

② **thunderstorm**
[ˈθʌndəstɔrm] *noun*
storm with rain, thunder and lightning; *there was a terrible thunderstorm last night and our house was struck by lightning*; *don't take shelter under a tree during a thunderstorm*

① **Thursday**
[ˈθɜrzdeɪ] *noun*
day between Wednesday and Friday, the fourth day of the week; *last Thursday was Christmas Day*; *shall we arrange to meet next Thursday?*; *today is Thursday, April 14*; *the club meets on Thursdays* or *every Thursday*; *the 15th is a Wednesday, so the 16th must be a Thursday*

③ **thus**
[ðʌs] *adverb (formal)*
(a) in this way; *the two pieces fit together thus*
(b) as a result; *she is only fifteen, and thus is not eligible for the over-sixteens competition*

② **tick**
[tɪk]
1 *noun*
(a) sound made every second by a clock; *the only sound we could hear in the room was the tick of the clock*
(b) a mark made when checking or counting something; *the teacher put a tick by their names*
(c) small insect which lives on the skin and sucks blood; *dogs can be affected by ticks*
2 *verb*
to make a regular little noise; *all you could hear was the clock ticking in the corner of the library*; *watch out! that package is ticking!*

① **ticket**
[ˈtɪkɪt] *noun*
(a) piece of paper or card which allows you to travel; *they won't let you get on to the bus without a ticket*; *we've lost our plane tickets -*

how can we get to Chicago?; **season ticket** = ticket that you can use for a certain period of time for theater performances or sporting events; **one-way ticket** = a ticket for one journey from one place to another; **round-trip ticket** = ticket for a journey from one place to another and back again

(b) piece of paper which allows you to go into a movie theater, an exhibition, etc.; *can I have three tickets for the 8:30 show please?*; *we tried several theaters but there were no tickets left anywhere*

(c) piece of paper that a police officer gives to someone who has committed a traffic offense; *she got a ticket for speeding in the town center*; **parking ticket** = paper which you get when you leave an automobile parked wrongly, telling you that you will have to pay a fine; *if you leave your car without paying the meter you'll get a parking ticket!*

(d) receipt; *keep the ticket in case you want to exchange the pants later*; **sales ticket** = piece of paper showing a price

(e) a party's list of candidates for election to political office; *he ran for governor on the Republican ticket*

③ **ticket office**
['tɪkɪt 'ɒfɪs] *noun*
office where tickets can be bought (either for travel or for theaters or cinemas, etc.); *there was a long line at the ticket office*; *if the ticket office is closed you can buy a ticket on the train*

① **tickle**
['tɪkl]
1 *noun*
something in your throat that makes you cough; *I've got a nasty tickle in my throat*
2 *verb*
to touch someone in a sensitive part of the body to make them laugh; *she tickled his toes and he started to laugh*; *something is tickling me in the small of my back*; (*informal*) **tickled pink** = very much amused; *we were tickled pink to get our first letter from our little granddaughter*

④ **tick off**
['tɪk 'ɒf] *verb*
(*informal*) **to tick someone off** = to make (somebody) angry; *don't tick him off again*

② **tide**
[taɪd]
1 *noun*
(a) regular rising and falling movement of the sea; *the tide came in and cut off the children on the rocks*; *the tide is out, we can walk across the sand*; **high tide** *or* **low tide** = points when the level of the sea is at its highest *or* at its lowest; *high tide is at 6:05 P.M. today*; **the tide has turned** = the tide has started to go up or down
(b) **the tide of public opinion** = the general trend of feeling among the public
2 *verb*

to tide someone over = to help someone get through a difficult period; *can you lend me $75 to tide me over until payday?*

② **tidy**
['taɪdi]
1 *adjective*
(a) neat, in order; *I want your room to be completely tidy before you go out*; *she put her clothes in a tidy pile*
(b) (*informal*) quite large amount or sum; *when he dies his children will inherit a tidy sum* (NOTE: **tidier - tidiest**)
2 *verb*
to make something neat; *he tidied his room before he went to school*

① **tie**
[taɪ]
1 *noun*
(a) cord, string or rope used for tying; *we put a tie around the package*
(b) necktie, a long piece of colored cloth that men wear around their necks under the collar of their shirts; *he's wearing a blue tie with red stripes*; *they won't let you into the restaurant if you're not wearing a tie*
(c) something that links or unites; *he has family ties in New Orleans*
(d) result in a competition or election where both sides have the same score; *the result was a tie and the vote had to be taken again*; **there was a tie for second place** = two people were equal second (NOTE: also **draw** in a game)
2 *verb*
(a) to attach with string, rope, etc.; *the package was tied with a little piece of string*; *he tied his horse to the post*; *the burglars tied his hands behind his back*; *he's tied to his work* = he can never get away from it
(b) to have the same score as another team in a competition; *they tied for second place*; *they tied 2-2 so there will be a replay next week*
(c) to make a knot; *he tied a knot in his handkerchief to remind him*

② **tie up**
['taɪ 'ʌp] *verb*
(a) to put string or rope around something; *the package was tied up with thick string*; *you should tie that dog up or it will bite someone*
(b) **to be tied up** = to be busy; *I'm kind of tied up right now - can we try to meet next week sometime?*

① **tiger**
['taɪgər] *noun*
large wild animal of the cat family living mainly in India and China; it is yellow in color, with black stripes; *I bet you wouldn't dare put your hand into the cage and stroke that tiger*

② **tight**
[taɪt]
1 *adjective*
(a) fitting too closely; *these shoes hurt - they're too tight*

(b) packed close together; **tight fit** = situation where there is not enough space to fit; *we can get one more person into the taxi but it will be a tight fit*; **tight schedule** = a schedule where many meetings are very close together; *the doctor has a very tight schedule today and cannot fit in any more appointments*

(c) *(informal)* **money is tight** = there is not very much money available

(d) holding firmly; *keep a tight hold of the bag, we don't want it stolen* (NOTE: **tighter - tightest**)

2 *adverb*

(a) closely, firmly (shut); *make sure the windows are shut tight*

(b) to hold tight = to hold something firmly; *hold tight - we're about to take off*; **to sit tight** = to stay in one place without doing anything; **sleep tight!** = sleep well!

③ **tighten**

['taɪtn] *verb*

to make tight; to become tight; *I tightened the straps on my backpack*; **to tighten your belt** = to be ready to spend less, eat less, etc.; *the government warned that we must tighten our belts*

② **tightly**

['taɪtli] *adverb*

in a tight way; *she kept her eyes tightly shut*; *tie the string as tightly as you can*

③ **tights**

[taɪts] *noun*

piece of clothing made of thin material, covering your hips, legs and feet, worn by girls, women, dancers, etc.; *look - you've got a hole in your tights!*

③ **tile**

[taɪl]

1 *noun*

(a) flat piece of baked clay used as a covering for floors, walls or roofs; *the floor is covered with red tiles*; *we are putting white tiles on the bathroom walls*

(b) similar piece of another kind of material used to cover a floor, etc.; *they put cork tiles on the walls*; **carpet tiles** = square pieces of carpet which can be put down on the floor like tiles

2 *verb*

to cover the surface of a roof, a floor or a wall with tiles; *they have tiled the kitchen with red floor tiles*; *a white-tiled bathroom*

② **till**

[tɪl]

1 *preposition & conjunction*

until, up to the time when; *I don't expect him to be home till after nine o'clock*; *they worked from morning till night to finish the job*; *we worked till the sun went down*

2 *noun*

drawer for keeping cash in a store; *there was not much money in the till at the end of the day*

3 *verb*

(formal) to plow and cultivate soil, to make it ready for growing crops; *in some parts of the country farmers are still using horses to till the land*

② **tilt**

[tɪlt]

1 *noun*

(a) sloping position; *the table has a noticeable tilt*

(b) (at) full tilt = at full speed; *he was going full tilt when he tripped over*; *the automobile ran full tilt into a tree*

2 *verb*

(a) to slope; *the shelf is tilting to the right*; *you'll have to change places - the boat is tilting*

(b) to put in a sloping position; *he tilted the barrel over to get the last drops of beer out*

① **timber**

['tɪmbər] *noun*

(a) *(general)* wood cut ready for building; *these trees are being grown to provide timber for houses* (NOTE: no plural: for one item say **a piece of timber**)

(b) timbers = large pieces of wood used in building; *the roof was built with timbers from old ships*; *some of the timbers are rotten and need to be replaced*

① **time**

[taɪm]

1 *noun*

(a) particular point in the day shown in hours and minutes; *what time is it? or what's the time?*; *can you tell me the time please?*; *the time is exactly four thirty*; *departure times are delayed by up to fifteen minutes because of the volume of traffic*; **to tell the time** = to read the time on a clock or watch; *she's only three so she can't tell time yet*

(b) hour at which something usually happens; *the closing time for the office is 5:30*; *it's must be nearly time for dinner - I'm hungry*; *is it time for the children to go to bed?*; *see also* BEDTIME, DINNERTIME, LUNCHTIME, TEATIME

(c) amount of hours, days, weeks, etc.; *there's no need to hurry - we've got plenty of time*; *do you have time for a cup of coffee?*; *he spent all that time watching the TV*; *if the fire alarm rings, don't waste time putting clothes on - run out of the hotel fast*; *see also* FIND TIME

(d) certain period; *we haven't been to Canada for a long time*; *we had a letter from my mother a short time ago*; **in ... time** = during a period from now; *we're going on vacation in four weeks' time*; **to take time** = to need a certain amount of time; *it didn't take you much time to get dressed*; **to take your time** = to do something carefully and slowly; *don't hurry me, I like to take my time*; **to take time out to do something** = to stop doing something and do something else; *he took time out from his work to show me how to run the machine*; *your*

time's up = the amount of time allocated to you is over; *bring back your boat, your time's up*; *(informal)* **to do time** = to serve a prison sentence; *he's doing time for theft*
(e) system of hours on the clock; *New York City is on Eastern Standard Time during the winter*; **time difference** = difference in time between one time zone and another; *there is a five-hour time difference between New York and London*
(f) particular moment when something happens; *they didn't hear anything as they were asleep at the time*; *by the time the ambulance arrived the man had died*; *you can't do two things at the same time*; **for the time being** = temporarily; *for the time being I'm staying at my mother's while my apartment is being decorated*; **at times** = on some occasions; *at times I think he's quite mad*; *see also* SOMETIMES
(g) period when things are pleasant or bad; *everyone had a good time at the party*; *we had an awful time on vacation - the hotel was dreadful, and it rained without stopping for ten whole days*
(h) one of several moments or periods when something happens; *I've seen that movie on TV four times already*; *that's the last time I'll ask them to play cards*; *next time you come, bring your swimming things*; **time after time** = again and again; *I've told her time after time not to do it*
(i) times = multiplied by; *six times twenty is one hundred and twenty*; *this book is three times as expensive as that one*; *she's a hundred times more efficient than the old secretary*
(j) times = a period in the past; *in Elizabethan times, most men carried swords*; **behind the times** = not up-to-date, old-fashioned; *he's way behind the times* = he's very old-fashioned
2 *verb*
(a) to count in hours, minutes and seconds; *I timed him as he ran around the track*; *don't forget to time the eggs - they have to cook for only three minutes*; *the police cameras timed the automobile - it was going at more than 100 miles per hour*
(b) to choose the right moment; *she timed her vacation right - it was the hottest week of the year*

◇ **in time**
['ın 'taım] *phrase*
not late; *they drove fast and got to the station just in time to catch the train*; *you'll have to hurry if you want to be in time for the meeting*; *we got to the movie theater just in time for the start of the movie*; **in good time** = early, before the time needed; *we drove fast and got to the airport in good time*

◇ **on time**
['ɒn 'taım] *phrase*
happening at the expected time; *the plane arrived on time*; *she's never on time for meetings*; *you will have to hurry if you want to get to the wedding on time* *or* *if you want to be on time for the wedding*

③ **time limit**
['taım 'lımıt] *noun*
point in time by which something should be done; *we will set a time limit of two weeks for the project to be completed*

④ **timetable**
['taımteıbl]
1 *noun*
printed list which shows the times of classes in school, of trains leaving, etc.; *we have two English lessons on the timetable today*; *the airline has issued its summer timetable, and all the times have changed*; *according to the timetable, the train is ten minutes late*
2 *verb*
to schedule, to arrange the times for something; *you are timetabled to speak at 4:30*

③ **time zone**
['taım 'zəun] *noun*
one of 24 bands in the world in which the same standard time is used; *when you fly across the U.S.A. you cross several time zones*

④ **timing**
['taımıŋ] *noun*
controlling the time at which something happens; *the timing of the conference is very convenient, as it comes just before my summer vacation*; *that was good timing - to arrive just as I was opening a bottle of wine!*

① **tin**
[tın] *noun*
(a) soft metal with a color like silver; *bronze is a mixture of copper and tin*; *there have been tin mines in this area since Roman times*; **tin foil** = very thin sheet of metal used for wrapping food before cooking; *wrap the fish in tin foil before putting it on the barbecue grill*
(NOTE: Chemical element: chemical symbol: **Sn**; atomic number: **50**)
(b) any metal box; *keep the cookies in a tin or they'll go soft*; *she puts her spare coins into a tin by the telephone*

② **tingle**
['tıŋgl]
1 *noun*
sharp feeling like prickles; *it didn't hurt, I just felt a tingle in my leg*
2 *verb*
to have a sharp feeling like prickles; *it will tingle when I put the antiseptic on your cut*

③ **tinkle**
['tıŋkl]
1 *noun*
noise like the ringing of a little bell; *the gentle tinkle of cow bells in the mountain fields*
2 *verb*
to make a little ringing noise; *the little bell tinkled as she went into the shop*

① **tiny**

['taɪnɪ] *adjective*

very small; *can I have just a tiny bit more pudding?*; *the spot on her forehead is so tiny you can hardly see it*; *she lives in a tiny cabin in the mountains* (NOTE: **tinier - tiniest**)

② **tip**

[tɪp]

1 *noun*

(a) end of something long; *she reads Braille by touching the page with the tips of her fingers*; *he pushed the piece of wood into the river with the tip of his walking stick*; *(informal)* **it's on the tip of my tongue** = I'll remember it in a moment, I'm trying hard to remember it; **it's the tip of the iceberg** = it's only a small part of something (usually unpleasant) while the rest is hidden; *those errors in the accounts were just the tip of the iceberg - the staff had been stealing money and stock for years*

(b) money given to someone who has provided a service; *the taxi driver was annoyed because I only gave him 50 cents as a tip*; *the service hasn't been very good - should we leave a tip for the waiter?*; *the staff are not allowed to accept tips*

(c) advice on something which could be profitable; *he gave me a tip about a horse which was likely to win*; *she gave me a tip about a cheap restaurant just around the corner from the hotel*

2 *verb*

(a) to pour something out; *he picked up the box and tipped the contents out onto the floor*; *she tipped all the food out of the bag*

(b) to give money to someone who has helped you; *I tipped the waiter $2*; *should we tip the driver?* (NOTE: **tipping - tipped**)

① **tip over**

['tɪp 'əʊvər] *verb*

(a) to lean and fall over; *the truck tipped over in the wind*; *my cup tipped over and all the coffee spilled on to the tablecloth*

(b) to make something lean so that it falls over; *the wind was so strong that it tipped over the trailer*

① **tip up**

['tɪp 'ʌp] *verb*

(a) to lean and fall over; *the cup tipped up and all the tea went into the saucer*

(b) to turn something over so that the contents fall out; *he tipped up the bottle to see if there was any tomato sauce left inside*

① **tire**

['taɪər]

1 *noun*

ring made of rubber and a hard case, which is put around a wheel and which is filled with air; *check the pressure in the tires before starting a journey*; *they used an old tire to make a seat for the garden swing*; **snow tires** = special tires with thick treads, for use when driving on snow;

when renting an automobile in the winter, check if it has snow tires; **spare tire** = extra tire carried in an automobile in case you have a flat tire

2 *verb*

(a) to become tired; to make someone become tired; *he is getting old and tires easily*; *we went for a long bicycle ride to tire the children out*

(b) to tire of = to lose interest in something; *the children soon tired of playing with their toy soldiers*

① **tired**

['taɪərd] *adjective*

(a) feeling sleepy; *I'm tired - I think I'll go to bed*; *if you feel tired, lie down on my bed*

(b) feeling that you need rest; *we're all tired after a long day at the office*

(c) to be (sick and) tired of something = to be bored with something, to have had enough of something; *I'm sick and tired of waiting for the doctor*; *they're tired of always having to wash all the dishes*; **to get tired of something** = to become bored with something; *can't we do something else - I'm getting tired of visiting museums*

① **tired out**

['taɪərd 'aʊt] *adjective*

feeling very sleepy, feeling that you must have rest; *they were tired out after their long walk*; *come and sit down - you must be tired out*

① **tissue**

['tɪʃu] *noun*

(a) soft paper handkerchief; *there is a box of tissues beside the bed*

(b) tissue paper = thin soft paper used for wrapping glass and other delicate objects; *wrap the glasses in tissue paper before you put them away in the box*

(c) groups of cells which form an animal or plant; *animal tissue grown in a laboratory*; *they took a sample of tissue from the growth*

② **title**

['taɪtl] *noun*

(a) name of a book, play, painting, movie, etc.; *he's almost finished the play but hasn't found a title for it yet*; **title page** = page at the beginning of a book, which gives the title (usually in large letters), the name of the author and the name of the publisher; **title role** = part in a play or movie which gives the name to the play or movie; *she played the title role in "Mrs. Warren's Profession"*

(b) *(in sport)* official position of champion; *what are his chances of keeping the Formula One title for a second year running?*

(c) word (such as Dr., Mr., Professor, etc.) put in front of a name to show an honor or a qualification

(d) right to own a property; *he holds the title to the property*; **title deeds** = document showing who is the owner of a property

① **to**
[tu]
1 *preposition*
(a) *(showing direction or place)* **they went to the police station**; *do you know the way to the beach?*; *the river is to the north of the town*; *everyone take one step to the right, please*
(b) *(showing a period of time)* **the office is open from 9:30 to 5:30, Monday to Friday**; *she slept from 11:30 to 8:30 the following morning*
(c) *(showing time in minutes before an hour)* **get up - it's five to seven (6:55)** *the train leaves at a quarter to eight (7:45)* (NOTE: **to** is used for times between the half hour and o'clock: **3:35** = twenty-five to four; **3:45** = a quarter to four; **3:55** = five minutes to four. For times after the hour see **past**)
(d) *(showing person or animal that receives something)* **take the book to the librarian**; *pass the salt to your grandfather*; *you must be kind to cats*
(e) *(showing connection)* **they lost by twelve to nine**; *the exchange rate is six francs to the dollar*; *there are four keys to the office*; *in this class there are 28 children to one teacher*
(f) *(showing that you are comparing)* **do you prefer butter to margarine?**; *you can't compare canned pineapple to fresh fruit*
2 *(used before a verb)*
(a) *(following verbs)* **did you remember to switch off the light?**; *the burglar tried to run away*; *she agreed to go to work in Wisconsin*; *they all decided to go home early*
(b) *(showing purpose)* **the nurses came to help at the scene of the accident**; *the doctor left half an hour ago to go to the hospital*
(c) *(used after adjectives)* **I'd be glad to help**; *is the water OK to drink?*; *I'm sorry to be so late for the meeting*
(d) *(used after a comparison)* **she was too tired to do anything except sit down**
(e) *(used after nouns)* **this is the best way to do it**; *she had a sudden desire to lie down and go to sleep*
3 *adverb*
to come to = to become conscious again; *when he came to, he was lying on the floor of the church*

② **toast**
[təʊst]
1 *noun*
(a) slices of bread which have been cooked at a high temperature until they are brown; *can you make some more toast?*; **wheat toast** *or* **white toast** = toast made from wheat bread or white bread; *I always have a piece of wheat toast and marmalade for breakfast*; see also WARM (NOTE: no plural in this meaning: **some toast, a piece of toast** *or* **a slice of toast**)
(b) **to drink a toast to someone** = to take a drink and wish someone success; *let's drink a toast to the bride and bridegroom!*; *we all drank a toast to the future success of the company*

2 *verb*
(a) to cook bread, etc., in a toaster or under a grill, until it is brown; *we had toasted cheese sandwiches*
(b) to wish someone success and drink at the same time; *they all toasted the happy couple with champagne*

① **toaster**
['təʊstər] *noun*
electric device for toasting bread; *that slice of bread is too thick to fit in the toaster*

① **tobacco**
[tə'bækəʊ] *noun*
dried leaves of a plant used to make cigarettes and for smoking in pipes; *he bought some pipe tobacco*; *tobacco causes lung cancer* (NOTE: no plural)

① **today**
[tə'deɪ]
1 *noun*
(a) this day; *today's her sixth birthday*; *what's the date today?*; *there's a story in today's newspaper about a burglary on our road*
(b) this present time; *the young people of today have far more money than I had when I was their age*
2 *adverb*
on this day; *he said he wanted to see me today, but he hasn't come yet*; **today week** *or* **a week from today** = in exactly seven days' time; *a week from today, and we'll be sitting on the beach* (NOTE: no plural. Note also that when you refer to the morning or afternoon, etc., of **today**, you say **this morning, this afternoon**, etc.; the day before today is **yesterday** and the day after today is **tomorrow**)

③ **toddler**
['tɒdlər] *noun*
little child who has just learnt to walk; *he's been fascinated by cars ever since he was a toddler*

② **toe**
[təʊ]
1 *noun*
one of the five parts like fingers at the end of the foot; *she stepped on my toe and didn't say she was sorry*; **big toe** = the largest of the five toes; **little toe** = the smallest of the five toes; **to keep someone on their toes** = to keep someone ready or alert; *my job is to make sure the workers are always on their toes*
2 *verb*
to toe the line = to do what you are told to do; *he was fired because he refused to toe the line* (NOTE: do not confuse with **tow**)

② **TOEFL**
= TEST OF ENGLISH AS A FOREIGN LANGUAGE

① **together**
[tə'geðər] *adverb*
(a) doing something with someone else or in a group; *tell the children to stay together or they'll get lost*; *if you're going to the movie*

theater, and we're planning to go too, why don't we all go together?
(b) joined with something else, or with each other; *tie the sticks together with string*; *do you think you can stick the pieces of the cup together again?*; *if you add all the figures together, you'll get the total sales*; *we've had three sandwiches and three beers - how much does that come to all together?*; compare ALTOGETHER

① **toilet**
['tɔɪlət] *noun*
(a) bowl with a seat on which you sit to get rid of waste matter from your body; *there is a shower and toilet in the bathroom*; **to go to the toilet** = (i) to use a toilet to remove waste matter from the body; (ii) to remove waste matter from the body; *the kids all want to go to the toilet at the same time*; *Mom! the cat's been to the toilet on the living room carpet*; **toilet paper** = soft paper for wiping your bottom after going to the toilet; **toilet roll** = roll of toilet paper; **to flush a toilet** = to press a handle to make water flow through the toilet bowl to clear it; *don't forget to flush the toilet*
(b) room with this toilet bowl in it; *the ladies' toilet is at the end of the corridor*; *the men's toilets are downstairs and to the right*; *there's a public toilet at the train station*

③ **token**
['təʊkən] *noun*
(a) thing which is a sign or symbol of something; *please accept this small gift as a token of our thanks*; **by the same token** = in the same way; *you have every right to complain about him, but, by the same token, you mustn't get upset if he complains about you*; **token charge** = small charge which does not cover the real costs; **token gesture** = small action done to show that you intend to deal with a problem; *the motion criticizing the government was simply a token gesture by the opposition parties*; **token payment** = small payment to show that a payment is being made; **token strike** = short strike to show that the workers want to make a complaint about something; **token woman** or **token black** = woman or black person appointed to a position on a committee, etc., in an attempt to show that there is no sexual or racial discrimination
(b) piece of paper, card, etc., which is used in the place of money; *you can use these tokens to pay for meals*
(c) plastic or metal disk, used instead of money; *she put a token into the slot machine*

② **told**
[təʊld] *see* TELL

④ **tolerance**
['tɒlərəns] *noun*
(a) tolerating unpleasant behavior, etc.; *the police showed great tolerance faced with a crowd of youths throwing bottles and stones*

(b) allowing something to exist which you do not agree with; *tolerance of other people's views*
(c) ability of the body to stand the effect of a drug or a poison; *he has been taking the drug for so long that he has developed a tolerance to it*
(d) amount by which something can vary from a particular size; *the specifications allow for a tolerance of 0.005 mm*

④ **tolerate**
['tɒləreɪt] *verb*
(a) to allow something which you do not like to happen without complaining about it; *she does not tolerate singing in the classroom*
(b) to allow something which you do not agree with to exist; *opposition parties are not tolerated in that country*; *he is not known for tolerating people with opposing views to his*
(c) to accept the effect of a drug or a poison; *the body can tolerate small amounts of poison*

③ **toll**
[təʊl]
1 *noun*
(a) payment for using a service, usually a road, bridge or ferry; *you have to pay a toll to cross the bridge*; *there's an office at the bridge where the man collects the tolls*; **toll bridge** = bridge where you have to pay a toll to cross
(b) number of people hurt, of buildings damaged, etc.; **to take a toll of** = to destroy or damage; *the storm took a heavy toll of ships in the harbor*; *the wind took a toll of trees in the park*; **death toll** = number of people who have died; *the death toll in the disaster has risen to three hundred*
(c) solemn ringing of a bell; *the toll of the great bell could be heard across the fields*
2 *verb*
to ring a bell slowly, as for a funeral; *the bell was tolling as the coffin arrived at the church*

④ **toll call**
['təʊl 'kɔl] *noun*
long-distance telephone call; *I made a toll call to Seattle*

③ **toll free**
['təʊl 'fri] *adjective & adverb*
without having to pay the charge for a long-distance telephone call; *a toll-free number*; *to call someone toll-free*

② **tomato**
[tə'meɪtəʊ] *noun*
(a) small, round red fruit used in salads and cooking; *tomatoes cost 30 cents per pound*; *we had a salad of raw cabbage and tomatoes*; *someone in the crowd threw a tomato at the speaker on the platform*; **tomato sauce** = sauce made with tomatoes and herbs; *do you want tomato sauce with your spaghetti?*
(b) tomato plant, plant which produces tomatoes; *he planted six tomatoes in his back yard* (NOTE: plural is **tomatoes**)

① **tomorrow**
[tə'mɒrəʊ]
1 *adverb*

referring to the day after today; *are you free for lunch tomorrow?*; *I mustn't forget I have a dentist's appointment tomorrow morning*; *we are going to an Italian restaurant tomorrow evening*

2 *noun*

the day after today; *today's Monday, so tomorrow must be Tuesday*; *tomorrow is our tenth wedding anniversary*; **the day after tomorrow** = two days after today; *we're going to Paris the day after tomorrow*

② **ton**
[tʌn] *noun*

(a) measure of weight equal to 2000 pounds; *a ship carrying 1000 tons of coal*; *they harvested over one hundred tons of apples*; **metric ton** = 1000 kilograms

(b) *(informal)* **it weighs a ton** = it is very heavy; *your suitcase weighs a ton, what do you have in it?*; *(informal)* **tons of** = lots of; *I've tons of work to do*; *she got tons of cards on her twenty-first birthday*

③ **tone**
[təʊn]
1 *noun*

(a) way of saying something, or of writing something, which shows a particular feeling; *his tone of voice showed he was angry*; *she said hi in a friendly tone of voice*; *you could tell from the tone of his letter that he was annoyed*

(b) *(on the phone)* special noise that indicates something; *please speak after the tone*; **dial tone** = noise made by a telephone to show that it is ready for you to dial a number

(c) slight difference in color; *she prefers soft tones like pink or pale blue*

(d) **muscle tone** = normal slightly tense state of a healthy muscle; *exercising every day will improve muscle tone*

(e) general spirit of an area, a meeting, etc.; *having all those rusty old fridges and stoves in their front garden lowers the tone of the neighborhood*

(f) *(in music)* the difference in pitch between pairs of notes

2 *verb*

to prepare by exercise; *he toned his muscles at the gym*

① **tongue**
[tʌŋ] *noun*

(a) organ in your mouth, which can move and is used for tasting, swallowing and speaking; *the soup was so hot it burned my tongue*; **to say something with your tongue in your cheek** *or* **to say something tongue-in-cheek** = to say something which you do not mean seriously; **it's on the tip of my tongue** = I'll remember it in a moment, I'm trying hard to remember it

(b) similar part in an animal, used for food; *we had tongue for dinner*

(c) way of speaking; *she can have a sharp tongue when she wants to*

(d) language; **mother tongue** *or* **native tongue** = language which you spoke when you were a little child; *she speaks English very well, but Spanish is her mother tongue*

④ **tongue-twister**
['tʌŋtwɪstər] *noun*

phrase (like "she sells seashells on the seashore") which is difficult to say quickly

① **tonight**
[tə'naɪt] *adverb & noun*

the night or the evening of today; *I can't stop - we're getting ready for tonight's party*; *I'll be at home from eight o'clock tonight*; *I don't suppose there's anything interesting on TV tonight*

① **too**
[tu] *adverb*

(a) more than necessary; *there are too many people to fit into the elevator*; *I think we bought too much bread*; *it's too hot for us to sit in the sun*

(b) *(often at the end of a clause)* also; *she had some coffee and I had some too*; *she, too, comes from Canada* *or* *she comes from Canada too*

① **took**
[tʊk] *see* TAKE

② **tool**
[tul] *noun*

instrument which you hold in your hand to do certain work, such as a hammer, spade, etc.; *a set of tools for repairing the automobile*

② **tooth**
[tuθ] *noun*

(a) one of a set of hard white objects in the mouth which you use to bite or chew food; *children must learn to brush their teeth twice a day*; *I'll have to see the dentist - one of my back teeth hurts*; *the dentist took one of her teeth out*; **false teeth** = artificial plastic teeth which fit inside the mouth and take the place of teeth which have been taken out; **milk teeth** = a child's first twenty teeth, which are gradually replaced by permanent teeth; *see also* WISDOM TOOTH

(b) **to have a sweet tooth** = to like sweet food; *he's very fond of chocolate - he has a real sweet tooth!*; *don't put the chocolates next to her - she has a very sweet tooth*; **long in the tooth** = old; *she's getting a bit long in the tooth for riding a motorcycle*

(c) **armed to the teeth** = carrying lots of weapons; *the robbers were armed to the teeth*

(d) one of the row of pointed pieces on a saw, comb, zipper, etc.; *throw that comb away, half its teeth are broken* (NOTE: plural is **teeth** [tiθ])

① **toothbrush**
['tuθbrʌʃ] *noun*

small brush which you use to clean your teeth; *use your toothbrush twice a day*; *I forgot to pack a toothbrush; she gave him an electric toothbrush for his birthday* (NOTE: plural is **toothbrushes**)

① **toothpaste**
['tuːθpeɪst] *noun*

soft substance which you spread on a toothbrush and then use to brush your teeth; *she squeezed some toothpaste onto her brush; I must buy a small tube of toothpaste to take when I'm traveling* (NOTE: no plural: some **toothpaste**, a tube of **toothpaste**)

① **top**
[tɒp]
1 *noun*

(a) highest place, highest point of something; *he climbed to the top of the stairs and sat down; the bird is sitting on the top of the apple tree; look at the photograph at the top of page four*
(b) flat upper surface of something; *do not put coffee cups on the top of the computer; the car has a black top; a birthday cake with sugar and fruit on the top*
(c) cover for a jar, bottle, etc.; *take the top off the jar, and see what's inside; she forgot to screw the top back on the bottle*
(d) best position in a contest, a profession, etc.; *she came top in the competition*
(e) piece of clothing for the upper part of the body; *she packed three skirts and three matching tops*
2 *adjective*
(a) in the highest place; *the restaurant is on the top floor of the building; jams and marmalades are on the top shelf*
(b) best; *she's one of the world's top tennis players*
3 *verb*
(a) to put something on top; *strawberry shortcake topped with whipped cream*
(b) to do better than; *I don't think anyone else will top his score; (informal)* **to top it all =** on top of everything else; *to top it all, a pipe burst in the bathroom and the whole house was flooded* (NOTE: **topping - topped**)

◇ **on top**
phrase

on; *a birthday cake with sugar and fruit on top*

◇ **on top of**
phrase

(a) on; *he put the book down on top of the others he had bought; there is a roof garden on top of the hotel; do not put coffee cups on top of the computer*
(b) in addition to; *on top of all my office work, I have the clean the house and look after the baby*

② **topic**
['tɒpɪk] *noun*

subject of a discussion or conversation; *can we move on to another topic?;* **to bring up a topic =** to start to discuss something; *she brought up the topic of where to go on vacation*

④ **topical**
['tɒpɪkl] *adjective*

interesting at the present time; *the question of global warming is very topical*

③ **topple**
[tɒpl] *verb*

(a) to fall down; *he lost his balance and toppled forward*
(b) to make a government or dictator lose power; *the government was toppled after three days of street fighting*

③ **topple over**
['tɒpl 'əʊvər] *verb*

to fall down; *the bottle toppled over and smashed onto the floor*

③ **torch**
[tɔrtʃ]
1 *noun*

burning light, carried in the hand; *the demonstrators marched through the streets carrying flaming torches* (NOTE: plural is **torches**)
2 *verb*

to set fire to something on purpose; *rioting students torched the police station*

② **tore**
[tɔr] *see* TEAR

① **torn**
[tɔrn] *see* TEAR

① **tornado**
[tɔ'neɪdəʊ] *noun*

violent storm with a whirlwind; *a tornado struck the southern coast* (NOTE: plural is **tornadoes**)

③ **tortilla**
[tɔr'tijə] *noun*

round, flat bread made of corn or wheat flour; *tortillas are part of Mexican food*

② **torture**
['tɔrtʃər]
1 *noun*

making someone suffer pain as a punishment or to make them reveal a secret; *they accused the police of using torture to get information about the plot*
2 *verb*

to inflict mental or physical pain on someone; *the soldiers tortured their prisoners; the police officer tortured the girl by refusing to tell her where her mother was*

② **toss**
[tɒs]
1 *verb*

(a) to throw something up into the air, or to someone; *she tossed me her car keys;* **to toss a coin =** to throw a coin to decide something according to which side is on top when it comes down; *we tossed a coin and I had to wash the dishes;* **let's toss for it =** let's throw a coin in the air and the person who guesses right starts to play first or has first choice

(b) to move something about; *the waves tossed the little boat up and down*; **the horse tossed its head** = made a sharp movement of the head

2 *noun*

(a) act of throwing something into the air; *(in sport)* **to win the toss** = to guess correctly which side of the coin comes down on top and so have first choice or play first

(b) sharp movement up and down of the head; *with a toss of its head, the horse raced off*

Ⓞ **total**

['təʊtəl]

1 *adjective*

complete, whole; *the expedition was a total failure*; *their total losses come to over $600,000*

2 *noun*

whole amount; *the total comes to more than $1500*; **grand total** = final total made by adding several items

3 *verb*

(a) to add up to; *the bill totaled $900*; *he was declared bankrupt, with debts totaling more than $1.5 m*

(b) to destroy (something) completely; *she totaled the car in the accident*

④ **totally**

['təʊtəli] *adverb*

completely; *the house was totally destroyed in the fire*; *I had totally forgotten that I had promised to be there*; *he disagrees totally with what the first speaker said*

Ⓞ **touch**

[tʌtʃ]

1 *noun*

(a) one of the five senses, the sense of feeling with the fingers; *the sense of touch is very strong in blind people*

(b) contact, the passing of news and information; **to get in touch with someone** = to contact someone; *I'll try to get in touch with you next week*; **to lose touch with someone** = to lose contact with someone; *they used to live next door, but we've lost touch with them now that they've moved to Albany*; **to put someone in touch with someone** = to arrange for someone to have contact with someone; *the bank put us in touch with a local lawyer*; **to stay in touch with someone** = to keep contact with someone; *we met in Hong Kong thirty years ago but we have still kept in touch*; *see also* OUT OF TOUCH (NOTE: no plural in meanings (a) and (b))

(c) gentle physical contact; *I felt a light touch on my hand*

(d) very small amount; *he added a few touches of paint to the picture*; *there's a touch of frost in the air this morning*; **finishing touches** = final work to make something perfect; *we're just putting the finishing touches to the exhibition before we open tomorrow morning* (NOTE: plural in meanings (c) and (d) is **touches**)

2 *verb*

(a) to feel with your fingers; *the police officer touched him on the shoulder*; *don't touch that cake - it's for your mother*

(b) to be so close to something that you press against it; *his feet don't touch the floor when he sits on a big chair*; *there is a mark on the wall where the couch touches it*

(c) to eat or drink; *I never touch coffee*; *we never touch fruit which has not been washed*

(d) to make someone feel sad; *his sad song touched all the people in the church*

(e) *(informal)* **to touch someone for** = to try and get someone to lend or give you money; *how much did he touch you for?*

③ **touch down**

['tʌtʃ 'daʊn] *verb*

to land; *the plane touched down at 3r20*

② **touchdown**

['tʌtʃdaʊn] *noun*

(a) *(in football)* the act of carrying or catching the ball behind the other team's goal line for a score of six points; *he scored two touchdowns in the first quarter*

(b) landing of an aircraft or spacecraft

② **touched**

[tʌtʃt] *adjective*

grateful, pleased with; *she was touched to get your phone call on her birthday*

③ **touching**

['tʌtʃɪŋ] *adjective*

which affects the emotions; *a touching letter from my sister*

② **touch up**

['tʌtʃ 'ʌp] *verb*

to add a small amount of paint; *you will need to touch up the automobile where it has been scratched*

Ⓞ **tough**

[tʌf] *adjective*

(a) difficult to chew or to cut; *my steak's a bit tough - how's yours?* (NOTE: the opposite is **tender**)

(b) difficult; *the exam is extremely tough* (NOTE: the opposite is **easy**)

(c) strict; *the police are getting tough on drunk drivers*

(d) *(informal)* unfortunate; *it's tough that you can't come to the party*; *having three little children to look after is tough on the parents*; **tough luck!** = I'm sorry you have a problem, that you didn't win, that you didn't do well, etc., but there's nothing I can do to help you; *you've missed the last bus? - tough luck, you'll just have to walk* (NOTE: **tougher - toughest**)

② **tour**

[tʊər]

1 *noun*

(a) trip to various places coming back in the end to the place you started from; *there are so many tours to choose from - I can't decide which one to go on*; *she gave us a tour around the old castle*; **guided tour** = tour with a guide who

shows places to tourists; **package tour** = tour where everything (hotel, food, travel, etc.) is arranged and paid for before you leave
(b) journey on business to various places coming back in the end to the place you started from; *he is leading a group of businessmen on a tour of Italian factories*
(c) journey round various places where you perform, speak, etc.; *the pop group is on a European tour*; *the president went on a tour of the North East*
2 *verb*
(a) to go on vacation, visiting various places; *they toured the south of Florida*
(b) to visit various places to perform or speak; *the opera company toured Eastern Europe last year*

④ **tourism**
['tʊrɪzm] *noun*
business of providing travel, accommodation, food and entertainment for tourists; *tourism is the country's main source of income*

② **tourist**
['tʊrɪst] *noun*
person who goes on vacation to visit places away from his home; *the tourists were speaking in Spanish*; *there were parties of tourists visiting all the churches*; *this exhibition is always full of tourists*; **tourist bureau** *or* **tourist information office** *or* **tourist information center** = office which gives information to tourists about the place where it is situated; *you can get a map of the town from the tourist bureau*; **tourist class** = type of seating in an aircraft which is cheaper than first class; *he always travels first class, because he says tourist class is too uncomfortable*; *the tourist class fare is much less than the first class*; **tourist trap** = place which charges tourists too much; *it used to be a quiet little town, but now it's just a tourist trap*

② **tournament**
['tʊrnəmənt] *noun*
sporting competition with many games where competitors who lose drop out until only one is left; *my son is playing in a chess tournament this week*; *the golf tournament starts on Saturday*

③ **tow**
[təʊ]
1 *verb*
to pull an automobile or a ship which cannot move by itself; *the automobiles were towing trailers*; *they towed the ship into port*
2 *noun*
action of pulling something; *we got a truck to give us a tow to the nearest garage* (NOTE: do not confuse with **toe**)

② **toward** *or* **towards**
[twɔrd or twɔrdz] *preposition*
(a) in the direction of; *the crowd ran toward the police station*; *the bus was traveling south,*

toward the center of town; *the ship sailed straight toward the rocks*
(b) near (in time); *do you have any free time toward the end of the month?*; *the exhibition will be held toward the middle of October*
(c) as part of the money to pay for something; *he gave me $150 toward the cost of the hotel*
(d) in relation to; *she always behaved very kindly toward her dad*

② **towel**
['taʊəl] *noun*
large piece of soft cloth for drying; *there's only one towel in the bathroom*; *after washing her hair, she wound the towel round her head*; *I'll get some fresh towels*; **to throw in the towel** = to give up, not to continue a contest; **bath towel** = very large towel for drying yourself after having a bath; **beach towel** = colored towel used to dry yourself after swimming in the sea, and also for sitting on; **dish towel** = cloth that you use for drying plates, dishes, etc.; **towel rail** = bar of metal or wood in a bathroom on which you can hang a towel

② **tower**
['taʊər]
1 *noun*
tall construction; *the castle has thick walls and four square towers*; **control tower** = tall building at an airport where the radio station is
2 *verb*
to tower over = to rise very high above; *he towers over his wife who is very small*

② **town**
[taʊn] *noun*
place, larger than a village, where people live and work, with houses, stores, offices, factories, etc.; *there's no store in our neighborhood, so we do our shopping in the nearest town*; *the town is known for its chocolate*; *(informal)* **to go to town** = to spend a lot of money or time on something; *she really went to town buying furniture for the new house*; *(informal)* **to paint the town red** = to go out drinking and going to parties in town

③ **toxic**
['tɒksɪk] *adjective*
poisonous, harmful; *caution: this product is toxic*; **toxic waste** = waste which is poisonous or harmful to the environment; *environmentalists want to ban the dumping of toxic waste in the sea*

① **toy**
[tɔɪ]
1 *noun*
thing for children to play with; *we gave him a box of toy soldiers for Christmas*; *the children's toys are all over the living room floor*; *she won't let me play with any of her toys*
2 *verb*
to toy with something = to play with something (not seriously); *she wasn't hungry and only toyed with her food*

trace

[treɪs]

1 *noun*

(a) something which shows that something existed; *the police found traces of blood in the kitchen*; **without trace** = leaving nothing behind; *the automobile seems to have vanished without trace*

(b) very small amount; *there was a trace of powder on his coat*; *she showed no trace of anger*

2 *verb*

(a) to follow an animal's tracks; *we traced the fox back to its hole*

(b) to find where someone or something is; *they couldn't trace the letter*; *the police traced him to Chicago*; *I will try to trace your order with the production department*

(c) to copy a drawing, etc., by placing a sheet of transparent paper over it and drawing on it; *she traced the map and put it into her project on the history of the town*

trace element

[ˈtreɪs ˈeləmənt] *noun*

chemical element which a plant or animal needs to grow properly, but only in very small amounts

COMMENT: plants require traces of copper, iron, manganese and zinc; human beings need chromium, cobalt, copper, magnesium, manganese, molybdenum, selenium and zinc, but all in tiny quantities

track

[træk]

1 *noun*

(a) **tracks** = series of marks left by an animal's feet, marks left by wheels, etc.; *we followed the car tracks to the forest*; *those are the tracks of a deer*; **to make tracks for** = to go toward; *they made tracks for the nearest hotel*

(b) **to be on someone's track** = to follow someone; *the police are on his track*

(c) **to keep track of** = to keep an account, to keep yourself informed about; *I like to keep track of new developments in computer technology*; **to lose track of someone** *or* **something** = not to know where someone or something is; *we lost track of him after he went to work in New Mexico*; **we lost track of the time** = we didn't know what time it was

(d) rough path; *we followed a track through the forest*; **off the beaten track** = in a place which is away from main roads and not normally visited by many people; *our town is off the beaten track and so is very quiet*; **you're on the right track** = you're working the right way in order to succeed, you're doing the right thing; *we haven't solved the problem yet, but we're certainly on the right track*; **you're on the wrong track** = you're working in the wrong way

(e) path for races; **track events** = running competitions; **track shoes** = running shoes

(f) line of parallel rails for trains; *the trains will be late because of repairs to the track*; **single-track railroad** = railroad where trains go up and down the same rails but with places where two trains can pass; *(informal)* **to have a one-track mind** = to think about only one thing or to have only one thing which interests you

(g) one of the sections of music on a disk; *one of the tracks from their disk has been released as a single*

2 *verb*

to follow someone or an animal; *the hunters tracked the bear through the forest*; *we tracked the fox back to its hole*; *the police tracked the gang to an apartment in south Salem*

track down

[ˈtræk ˈdaun] *verb*

to track someone down = to follow and catch (a criminal); **to track something down** = to manage to find something; *I finally tracked down that file which you were looking for*

track suit

[ˈtræksut] *noun*

pair of matching pants and top, in warm material, worn when practicing sports; *the runners were warming up in their track suits*

tractor

[ˈtræktər] *noun*

heavy vehicle with large back wheels, used for work on farms; *he was driving a tractor across the field*; *we got behind a tractor driving through a small town and missed the meeting*

trade

[treɪd]

1 *noun*

(a) business of buying and selling; *the U.S.'s trade with Canada is up by 5%*; **export trade** = the business of selling to other countries; **import trade** = the business of buying from other countries; **free trade** = system where goods can go from one country to another without any restrictions; **to do a good trade in a range of products** = to sell a large number of a range of products

(b) people or companies that deal in the same type of product or service; *he is in the used-car trade*; **trade price** = special wholesale price paid by a retailer to a wholesaler or manufacturer

2 *verb*

(a) to buy and sell, to carry on a business; *the company has stopped trading*; *they trade in tobacco*

(b) to exchange something for something; *I'll trade the automobile for your motorcycle*

trade in

[ˈtreɪd ˈɪn] *verb*

to give in an old item, such as an automobile or washing machine, as part of the payment for a new one; *he traded in his old Chevrolet for a new model*

③ **trade-in**
['treɪdɪn] *noun*
(a) giving one thing for another
(b) thing given in place of another

③ **trademark** *or* **trade name**
['treɪdmɑrk or 'treɪd 'neɪm] *noun*
particular name, design, etc., which has been registered by the manufacturer and which cannot be used by other manufacturers; *Acme is a registered trademark*; *their trademark is stamped on every item they produce*

② **trader**
['treɪdər] *noun*
person who does business; *Arab traders crossed into India by boat*

③ **tradition**
[træ'dɪʃn] *noun*
beliefs, customs and stories that are passed from one generation to the next; *it's a family tradition for the eldest son to take over the business*; *according to local tradition, two murderers were hanged where the two roads meet*

④ **traditional**
[trə'dɪʃnəl] *adjective*
according to tradition; *on Easter Day it is traditional to give chocolate eggs to the children*; *villagers still wear their traditional costumes on Sundays*

① **traffic**
['træfɪk]
1 *noun*
(a) automobiles, trucks, buses, etc., which are traveling on a street or road; *I leave the office early on Fridays because I don't like driving through downtown in the hectic traffic*; *the lights turned green and the traffic moved forward*; *rush hour traffic is worse on Fridays*; **traffic offenses** = offenses committed by drivers of vehicles
(b) **traffic circle** = place where several roads meet, and traffic has to move in a circle around a central area
(c) **air traffic** = aircraft flying around; *air traffic around here will increase when they build the new airport*
(d) illegal trade; *the South American drugs traffic* (NOTE: no plural: **some traffic; a lot of traffic**)
2 *verb*
to deal in drugs, weapons, etc., illegally; *he made a fortune trafficking in guns* (NOTE: **trafficking - trafficked**)

③ **traffic jam**
['træfɪk 'dʒæm] *noun*
situation where automobiles, trucks, etc., cannot move forward on a road because there is too much traffic, because there has been an accident, because of repair works, etc.; *a truck was blown over, causing a big traffic jam*; *there are traffic jams on the roads out of the city every Friday evening*

③ **traffic lights**
['træfɪk 'laɪts] *noun*
red, green and yellow lights for making the traffic stop and start; *to get to the police station, you have to make a left at the next traffic lights*; *he drove across the intersection when the traffic lights were red* (NOTE: often shortened to just **lights**)

② **tragedy**
['trædʒədi] *noun*
(a) serious play, movie, or novel that ends sadly; *Shakespeare's tragedy "King Lear" is playing at one of the Broadway theaters*
(b) very unhappy event; *tragedy struck the family when their mother was killed in an automobile crash* (NOTE: plural is **tragedies**)

③ **tragic**
['trædʒɪk] *adjective*
(a) very sad; *a tragic accident on the freeway*
(b) referring to a tragedy; *one of the greatest tragic actors*

① **trail**
[treɪl]
1 *noun*
(a) tracks left by an animal, by a criminal, etc.; *we followed the trail of the bear through the forest*; *the burglars left in a red sports car, and a squad car was soon on their trail*
(b) path or track; *keep to the trail otherwise you will get lost*; **mountain trail** = path through mountains; **nature trail** = path through the countryside with signs to showing interesting features, such as plants, trees, birds or animals
(c) something that follows behind; *the vehicle left a trail of blue smoke*; *the dogs followed the trail of drops of blood to a warehouse*; *the storm left a trail of destruction across the south of the country*
2 *verb*
(a) to follow the tracks left by an animal or a person; *the police trailed the group across New Mexico*
(b) **to trail behind** = to follow slowly after someone; *she came in third, trailing a long way behind the first two runners*; *the little children trailed behind the older ones*
(c) **trailing plant** = plant whose stems hang down or lie along the ground
(d) to let something drag behind; *she stormed out, trailing her coat on the floor behind her*

② **trailer**
['treɪlər] *noun*
(a) small goods vehicle pulled behind an automobile; *we carried all our camping gear in the trailer*
(b) van with beds, table, washing facilities, etc., which can be towed by an automobile; **trailer park** = place where trailers are kept, usually permanently (NOTE: also called a **mobile home**)
(c) parts of a full-length movie shown as an advertisement for it; *we saw the trailer last*

week, and it made me decide not to see the movie

train
[treɪn]
1 *noun*
(a) engine pulling a group of coaches on the railway; *the train to Philadelphia leaves from platform 1*; *hundreds of people go to work every day by train*; *the next train to St. Louis will be in two minutes* ; **train set** = child's toy train with engines, coaches and rails; **train timetable** = list showing times of arrivals and departures of trains
(b) series of things, one after the other; *the police are trying to piece together the train of events which led to the accident*; **train of thought** = series of thoughts, one after the other; *my wife asked me to help with the baby, thus breaking my train of thought*
2 *verb*
(a) to teach someone or an animal how to do something; *she's being trained to be a bus driver*; *guide dogs are trained to lead blind people*
(b) to make a plant grow in a certain way; *we've trained the climbing rose up the wall*
(c) to become fit by practicing for a sport; *he's training for the 100 meters*; *she's training for the Olympics*

trainer
['treɪnər] *noun*
person who trains a sportsman or a team; *his trainer says he's in peak condition for the fight*

training
['treɪnɪŋ] *noun*
(a) being taught a skill; *the store is closed on Tuesday mornings for staff training*; *there is a ten-week training period for new staff*
(b) practicing for a sport; **to be in training** = to practice for a sport; *she's in training for the Olympics*

tram
[træm] *noun*
public transport vehicle, which runs on rails laid in the street; *you can take the tram from the station to the city center* (NOTE: also called a **streetcar**)

tranquil
['træŋkwɪl] *adjective*
calm or peaceful; *they were fishing in a tranquil lake*

tranquility
[træŋ'kwɪlɪti] *noun*
being calm or peaceful; *I like the peace and tranquility of the mountains*

transaction
[træn'zækʃn] *noun*
piece of business; *the whole transaction was conducted in French*; **cash transaction** = business which is paid for in cash

transfer
1 *noun* ['trænsfər]
(a) action of moving something or someone to a new place; *I've applied for a transfer to our New York branch*
(b) changing to another form of transport; **transfer passenger** = traveler who is changing from one aircraft or train or bus to another, or to another form of transport
2 *verb* [træns'fər]
(a) to move something or someone to another place; *the money will be transferred directly to your bank account*; *she transferred her passport from her purse to her jacket pocket*; *he's been transferred to our Dallas office*
(b) to change from one type of travel to another; *when you get to the airport at Mexico City, you have to transfer onto another flight* (NOTE: **transferring - transferred**)

transform
[trænz'fɔrm] *verb*
to change the appearance of someone or something completely; *after her marriage she was transformed*; *the frog was transformed into a handsome prince*

transistor
[træn'zɪstər] *noun*
device which can control the flow of electric current in a circuit; **transistor (radio)** = small pocket radio which uses transistors

transit
['trænzɪt] *noun*
(a) movement of passengers or goods on the way to a destination; *some of the party's baggage was lost in transit*; **goods in transit** = goods being transported from one place to another; **transit lounge** = waiting room in an airport where passengers wait for connecting flights; **transit passengers** = travelers who are changing from one aircraft to another
(b) **mass transit** = system for moving large numbers of people by public transportation around an urban area

transition
[træn'zɪʃn] *noun*
process of moving from one state to another; *she easily made the transition from being a poor student to a rich executive*

translate
[trænz'leɪt] *verb*
to put words into another language; *can you translate what he said?*; *he asked his secretary to translate the letter from the German agent*; *she translates mainly from Spanish into English, not from English into Spanish*

translation
[trænz'leɪʃn] *noun*
text which has been translated; *I read Tolstoy's "War and Peace" in translation*; *she passed the translation of the letter to the accounting department*

③ **translator**
['trænsleɪtər] *noun*
person who translates; *she works as a translator for the United Nations*

② **transmission**
[trænz'mɪʃn] *noun*
(a) radio or TV broadcast; *we interrupt this transmission to bring you a news flash*
(b) *(formal)* passing of disease from one person to another; *patients must be isolated to prevent transmission of the disease to the general public*
(c) *(in an automobile)* series of moving parts which pass the power from the engine to the wheels; *there's a strange noise coming from the transmission*

② **transmit**
[trænz'mɪt] *verb*
(a) to pass a disease from one person to another; *the disease was transmitted to all the people he came into contact with*; *the disease is transmitted by fleas*
(b) to send out a program or a message by radio or TV; *the message was transmitted to the ship by radio* (NOTE: **transmitting - transmitted**)

② **transparent**
[trænz'peərənt] *adjective*
(a) which you can see through; *the meat is wrapped in transparent plastic film*
(b) which is completely obvious; *his explanation was a transparent lie*
(c) clear and open about official actions; *the government insists on the importance all its actions being transparent*

② **transplant**
1 *noun* ['trænsplænt]
(a) act of taking an organ such as the heart, or tissue such as a piece of skin, and putting it into a patient to replace an organ or tissue which is not working properly or is damaged; *he had a heart transplant*
(b) organ or piece of tissue which is transplanted; *the kidney transplant was rejected*
2 *verb* [træns'plænt]
(a) to move a plant from one place to another; *you should not transplant trees in the summer*
(b) to put an organ or piece of tissue into a patient to replace an organ or tissue which is not working properly or is damaged; *they transplanted a kidney from his brother*

② **transport**
1 *noun* ['trænsport]
movement of goods or people in vehicles; *air transport is the quickest way to travel from one country to another*; *freight transport costs are getting lower*; *what means of transport will you use to get to the hotel?*
2 *verb* [træn'sport]
to move goods or people from one place to another in a vehicle; *the company transports millions of tons of goods by train each year*; *the*

visitors will be transported to the factory by helicopter

② **transportation**
[trænspɔr'teɪʃn] *noun*
action or means of moving goods or people; *the company will provide transportation to the airport*; **ground transportation** = buses, taxis, etc., available to take passengers from an airport to the town; **public transportation** = transport (such as buses, trains) which can be used by anyone; *the government's policy is to persuade people to use public transportation instead of their automobiles*; *how can we get there by public transportation?*

① **trap**
[træp]
1 *noun*
(a) device to catch an animal; *there is a mouse in the kitchen so we will put down a trap*
(b) device to catch a person by surprise; **police radar trap** = small radar device by the side of a road which senses and notes details of automobiles that are traveling too fast
(c) *(informal)* mouth; **keep your trap shut!** = don't say anything
2 *verb*
to catch or hold; *several people were trapped in the wreckage of the plane*; *he was trapped on video as he tried to break into the bank* (NOTE: **trapping - trapped**)

④ **trapdoor**
['træpdɔr] *noun*
door in a floor or in a ceiling; *there's a trapdoor leading to the roof*

① **trash**
[træʃ]
1 *noun*
useless things; *throw out all that trash from her bedroom* (NOTE: no plural)
2 *verb*
(a) to smash up; *someone trashed the telephones*
(b) to ruin someone's reputation; *she wrote an article trashing the pop singer*

③ **trash can**
['træʃkæn] *noun*
large plastic or metal container for household garbage; *they come to empty the trash cans once a week*; *she put the rest of the dinner in the trash can* (NOTE: also called a **garbage can**)

④ **trauma**
['trɔmə] *noun*
mental shock caused by a sudden unpleasant experience, which was not expected to take place; *she was in trauma after the crash*; *in court, he had to live through the trauma of the accident again*

④ **traumatic**
[trɔ'mætɪk] *adjective*
which gives a sharp and unpleasant shock; *witnessing an accident can be as traumatic as*

being involved in it; *I will never forget our traumatic arrival in India*

travel
['trævəl]
1 *noun*
(a) action of moving from one country or place to another; *air travel is the only really fast method of going from one country to another*; **travel insurance** = insurance taken out by a traveler against accident, loss of baggage, illness, etc. (NOTE: no plural in this meaning)
(b) **travels** = long journeys abroad; *she is someone he met on his travels in India*
2 *verb*
to move from one country or place to another; *he travels fifty miles by automobile to go to work every day*; *he has traveled across the United States several times on his motorcycle*; *the bullet must have traveled several yards before it hit the wall*

traveler
['trævlər] *noun*
person who travels; *travelers to Boston are experiencing long delays*

traveler's check
['trəvlərz 'tʃek] *noun*
check which you buy at a bank before you travel and which you can then use in a foreign country; *most stores here accept traveler's checks*; *the hotel will cash traveler's checks for you*

tray
[treɪ] *noun*
flat board for carrying food, glasses, cups and saucers, etc.; *he had his lunch on a tray in his bedroom*; *she bumped into a waitress who was carrying a tray of glasses*

treacherous
['tretʃrəs] *adverb*
(a) dangerous; *ice is making the roads very treacherous*
(b) not to be trusted; *he was shot by a treacherous bodyguard*

tread
[tred]
1 *noun*
(a) top part of a stair or step which you stand on; *the carpet on the bottom tread is loose*; *metal treads are noisy*
(b) pattern of lines cut into the surface of a tire; *you need to change your tires - the tread's worn*
(c) way of walking; *he walked up to the door with a firm tread*
2 *verb*
to step, to walk; *they tread a trail through the pasture*; *watch where you're treading - there's broken glass on the floor* (NOTE: **treading - trod** [trɒd] **- has trodden** ['trɒdən])

treasure
['treʒər]
1 *noun*
jewels, gold, or other valuable things; *the treasure was kept locked in a vault*; *buried treasure* = gold, silver, etc., which someone has hidden; *they are diving in the Caribbean Sea looking for Spanish treasure*; **treasure hunt** = game where clues lead you from place to place until you come to a hidden prize; *we organized a treasure hunt for the children's party*
2 *verb*
to value something; *I treasure the calm life of the fishing village where I live*; *she treasures her three cats and wouldn't part with them for anything*

treasury
['treʒri] *noun*
(a) **Treasury** = government department that deals with the country's finance; *all government departments have to have their spending plans approved by the Treasury*; **Secretary of the Treasury** *or* **Treasury Secretary** = member of the government in charge of finance
(b) place where treasure is kept; *robbers broke into the royal treasury and stole boxes of gold*

treat
[trit]
1 *noun*
special thing which gives pleasure; *it's always a treat to sit down quietly at home after a hard day working in the store*; **a treat in store** = special pleasant experience in the future; *if you've never seen this movie before you've got a treat in store*; **this is our treat** = we are paying the bill
2 *verb*
(a) to deal with someone; *she was badly treated by her uncle*; *it you treat the staff well they will work well*
(b) **to treat someone to something** = to give someone a special meal or outing as a gift; *come along - I'll treat you all to ice cream!*
(c) to look after a sick or injured person; *after the accident some of the passengers had to be treated in the hospital for cuts and bruises*; *she is being treated for rheumatism*
(d) to process in some way to make safe or to protect; *wastewater from households is treated before being put into the river*; *the wood has been treated to make it resistant to rot*

treatment
['tritmənt] *noun*
(a) way of behaving toward something or someone; *the report criticized the treatment of prisoners in the jail*; *what kind of treatment did you get at school?*; *we got VIP treatment when we visited China*
(b) way of looking after a sick or injured person; *he is having a course of heat treatment*; *the treatment for skin cancer is very painful*

treaty
['triti] *noun*
written legal agreement between two or more countries; *the treaty was signed in 1845*; *countries are negotiating a treaty to ban nuclear weapons* (NOTE: plural is **treaties**)

① **tree**
[tri] *noun*
(a) very large plant, with a thick trunk, branches and leaves; *the cat climbed up an apple tree and couldn't get down*; *in the fall, the trees in our park turn brown and red*; *he was sitting under a tree and was struck by lightning*
(b) **family tree** = table showing a family going back over many generations; *he's going through the local parish records to try to establish his family tree*

② **tremble**
['trembl]
1 *noun*
shaking movement; *there was a tremble in her voice*
2 *verb*
to shake because you are cold or afraid; *she was trembling with cold*; *I tremble at the thought of how much the meal will cost*

③ **tremendous**
[trɪ'mendəs] *adjective*
(a) enormous, very big; *there was a tremendous explosion and all the lights went out*; *there's tremendous excitement here in Florida as we wait for the election result*
(b) wonderful; *it would be absolutely tremendous if you won*; *her birthday party was tremendous fun*

④ **trend**
[trend] *noun*
general tendency; *there is a trend away from old-established food stores*; *the government studies economic trends to decide whether to raise taxes or not*

② **trial**
['traɪəl] *noun*
(a) court case held before a judge; *the trial will be heard next week*; **to stand trial** *or* **to be on trial** = to appear in court; *she stood trial, accused of murder*; *he's on trial for theft*
(b) act of testing something; *the new model is undergoing its final trials*; **on trial** = being tested to see if it is acceptable; *the system is still on trial*; **trial period** = time when a customer can test a product before buying it; *at the end of the trial period we weren't satisfied and sent the machine back*; **trial and error** = testing and rejecting various things until you find the one which works; *we found out the best way of working was simply by trial and error*
(c) game played to select the best players for a team; *trials to select the U.S. hockey team will be held this weekend*

③ **tribal**
['traɪbl] *adjective*
referring to tribes; *according to tribal custom the women sit in a different area from the men*; *their tribal lands were occupied by people from a neighboring tribe*

① **tribe**
[traɪb] *noun*
(a) group of people with the same race, language and customs; *she went into the jungle to study the primitive tribes*
(b) *(informal)* large family group; *they came with their tribe of children*

④ **tribunal**
[traɪ'bjunl] *noun*
specialist court which examines special problems and makes judgments; *a special tribunal has been set up to investigate these complaints*; **industrial tribunal** = court which decides in disputes between employers and workers; *the case of unfair dismissal went to the industrial tribunal*

③ **tribute**
['trɪbjut] *noun*
(a) words, flowers or gifts, etc., to show respect to someone, especially someone who has died; *tributes to the dead president have been received from all over the world*
(b) **to pay tribute to** = to praise; *speaker after speaker paid tribute to her work for charity*

① **trick**
[trɪk]
1 *noun*
clever act to deceive or confuse someone; *the recorded sound of barking is just a trick to make burglars think there is a dog in the house*; **to play a trick on someone** = to deceive or confuse someone; *he played a mean trick on his sister*; *my memory seems to be playing tricks on me*; *(informal)* **that should do the trick** = that should do what we want to be done; *"there, that should do the trick" he said as he tightened the last screw*
2 *adjective*
which deceives; *trick photography makes a tiny insect look like a giant monster*; **trick question** = question that is intended to deceive people
3 *verb*
to deceive, to confuse someone; *we've been tricked, there's nothing in the box*; **to trick someone into doing something** = to make someone do something which he did not mean to do by means of a trick; *he tricked the old lady into giving him all her money*; **to trick someone out of something** = to get someone to lose something by a trick; *she tricked the bank out of $150,000*; **to trick-or-treat** = to play a children's game on Halloween, where children visit houses asking for sweets, etc., otherwise they will play a trick

③ **trickle**
['trɪkl] *verb*
to flow gently; *water trickled out of the cave*

③ **tricky**
['trɪki] *adjective*
(a) difficult to do; *getting the wire through the little hole is quite tricky*

(b) *(informal)* who cannot be trusted; *he's a tricky individual* (NOTE: trickier - trickiest)

① **tricycle**
['traɪsɪkl] *noun*
a bicycle with three wheels, two at the back and one at the front; *a tricycle is best for little children because they can't tip over easily*

① **tried, tries**
[traɪd or traɪz] *see* TRY

④ **trifle**
['traɪfl] *noun*
(a) pudding made of cake or biscuits with jelly, jam, fruit, wine and cream; *do you want chocolate pudding or trifle for dessert?*
(b) a little bit; *it was a trifle warm, and he took his jacket off*

② **trigger**
['trɪgər]
1 *noun*
little lever which you pull to fire a gun; *he pointed the gun at her and pulled the trigger*
2 *verb*
to trigger something (off) = to start something happening; *the police are afraid the demonstration may trigger off a full-scale riot; the explosion was triggered by a spark*

④ **trillion**
['trɪljən] *noun*
(a) one million millions
(b) **trillions of** = a huge number of; *there were trillions of tiny fish in the lake*

② **trim**
[trɪm]
1 *adjective*
(a) tidy, cut short; *she always keeps her hedges trim*
(b) slim and fit; *he keeps himself trim by going for a long walk every day* (NOTE: trimmer - trimmest)
2 *verb*
(a) to cut something to make it tidy; *he trimmed the hedge in front of the house; ask the hairdresser to trim your beard*
(b) to cut back; to reduce; *to trim expenditures*
(c) to decorate; *she wore a white blazer trimmed with blue* (NOTE: trimming - trimmed)
3 *noun*
(a) cutting of your hair, a plant, etc.; *he went to the hairdresser's for a trim; can you give my beard a trim, please?*
(b) decoration on an automobile, a piece of clothing, etc.; *the car is white with a dark blue trim*

① **Trinidad & Tobago**
['trɪnɪdæd n tə'beɪgəʊ] *noun*
country in the Caribbean Sea, formed of two islands in the West Indies (NOTE: capital: **Port of Spain**; people: **Trinidadians**; language: **English**; currency: **Trinidad & Tobago dollar**)

② **Trinidadian**
[trɪnɪ'dædiən]
1 *adjective*
referring to Trinidad; *I met the Trinidadian ambassador*
2 *noun*
person from Trinidad; *Trinidadians are passionate about the game of cricket*

② **trio**
['triːəʊ] *noun*
(a) group of three things or people, especially a group of three musicians
(b) piece of music for three instruments (NOTE: plural is **trios**)

① **trip**
[trɪp]
1 *noun*
(a) short journey; *our trip to Orlando was canceled; we're going on a trip to the seaside;* **business trip** = journey to visit business contacts; **bus trip** = journey by bus; **day trip** = journey lasting one day
(b) *(slang)* sensation experienced after taking drugs; *she had a bad trip*
2 *verb*
to catch your foot in something so that you stumble and fall down; *she tripped as she was coming out of the kitchen with a tray of food; see also* TRIP OVER, TRIP UP (NOTE: tripping - tripped)

① **triple**
['trɪpl]
1 *verb*
to become three times as large; to make something three times as large; *output has tripled over the last year; we've tripled the number of visitors to the museum since we reduced the entrance fee*
2 *adjective*
with three parts; *the three brothers are marrying three sisters in a triple wedding*

② **trip over**
['trɪp 'əʊvər] *verb*
to catch your foot in something so that you stumble and fall; *she was running away from him when she tripped over a toy; he tripped over the wire and fell down the stairs*

② **trip up**
['trɪp 'ʌp] *verb*
(a) **to trip someone up** = to make someone fall down; *she put her foot out and deliberately tripped the waiter up*
(b) *(informal)* to make a silly mistake; *we tripped up badly in not inviting her to the party;* **to trip someone up** = to force someone to make a mistake; *he tried to trip me up by asking a question on a completely different subject*

② **triumph**
['traɪəmf]
1 *noun*
great victory, great achievement; *they scored a triumph in their game against the French; the bridge is a triumph of modern engineering;* **in triumph** = celebrating a great victory; *after the battle the army entered the city in triumph*

2 *verb*

(a) to win a victory, to achieve something; *she triumphed in the 800 meters*

(b) **to triumph over something** = to be successful in spite of difficulties which could have stopped you; *he triumphed over his disabilities to become world champion*; **to triumph over someone** = to win a victory over someone; *our local team triumphed over their old rivals*

③ **triumphal**

[traɪˈʌmfl] *adjective*

referring to triumph; *the team made a triumphal return to their hometown*; **triumphal arch** = large building over a road, to celebrate a victory; *there are the ruins of a triumphal arch in the center of the square*

③ **triumphant**

[traɪˈʌmfənt] *adjective*

happy because you have won; *he gave a triumphant wave as he crossed the finishing line*

③ **trod, trodden**

[trɒd or ˈtrɒdn] *see* TREAD

② **trolley**

[ˈtrɒli] *noun*

electric bus or streetcar; *I take a trolley from my apartment to the office*

① **troop**

[truːp]

1 *noun*

(a) **troops** = soldiers; *enemy troops occupied the town*

(b) large group of people; *she took a troop of schoolchildren to visit the museum*

2 *verb*

to go all together in a group; *after the play the whole cast trooped off to the local restaurant*; *all the students trooped into the hall*

① **trophy**

[ˈtrəʊfi] *noun*

prize given for winning a competition; *he has a display of trophies which he won at golf*; *our team carried off the trophy for the third year in a row* (NOTE: plural is **trophies**)

④ **tropic**

[ˈtrɒpɪk] *noun*

(a) **tropic of Cancer** = parallel running around the Earth at 23°28N; **tropic of Capricorn** = parallel running around the Earth at 23°28S

(b) **the tropics** = the hot areas of the world lying between these two parallels; *he lived in the tropics for ten years*; *people work more slowly in the tropics*

② **tropical**

[ˈtrɒpɪkl] *adjective*

(a) referring to hot countries; *in tropical countries it is always hot*; **tropical storm** = violent storm occurring in the tropics

(b) **tropical fish** = brightly colored little fish coming from hot countries; *I'm going to the*

library to find out how to take care of tropical fish

② **trot**

[ˈtrɒt]

1 *noun*

action of running with short regular steps; *let's start today's exercises with a short trot round the football field*

2 *verb*

to run with short regular steps; *she trotted down the path to meet us* (NOTE: **trotting - trotted**)

② **trouble**

[ˈtrʌbl]

1 *noun*

(a) problems, worries; *the trouble with old automobiles is that sometimes they don't start*; *looking after your cat is no trouble - I like animals*; *the children were no trouble at all*; *we are having some computer trouble or some trouble with the computer*; *he has his old back trouble again*; **it's asking for trouble** = it is likely to cause problems; *if you don't take out insurance, it's just asking for trouble*

(b) **to get into trouble** = to start to have problems with someone in authority; *he and his friends got into trouble with the police*; *she got her best friend into trouble*

(c) **to take the trouble to** = to make an extra effort and do something; *he didn't even take the trouble to write to thank us*; *if you had taken the trouble to look at the train timetable, you would have seen that there aren't any trains on Sundays*

2 *verb*

(a) to cause inconvenience; *can I trouble you for a light?*; *I'm sorry to have to trouble you with this, but I don't know how to switch my computer off*; **not to trouble to do something** = to make no effort to do something; *he didn't even trouble to tell us he was going to cut down the tree*

(b) to make someone worried; *I can see that there's something troubling him but I don't know what it is*

(c) to make an extra effort to do something; *he didn't even trouble to thank us for our gift*

① **troubled**

[ˈtrʌbld] *adjective*

(a) where there are problems; *he comes from a troubled family background*; *we live in troubled times*

(b) worried; *he has a troubled look on his face*; *they seem troubled but I don't know why*

③ **trough**

[trɒf] *noun*

long narrow open container for food or water for farm animals; *the pigs were eating at the trough*

② **trousers**

[ˈtraʊzərz] *noun*

clothes which cover your body from the waist down, split in two parts, one for each leg; pants; *he tore his trousers climbing over the fence*;

she was wearing a red sweater and gray trousers; *he bought two pairs of trousers in the sale* (NOTE: plural; to show one piece of clothing say **a pair of trousers**)

④ **trowel**
['trauǝl] *noun*

hand tool, like a large spoon, used in the garden; *she made holes with a trowel before planting her bulbs*

④ **truant**
['truǝnt] *noun*

to play truant = not to go to school when you should be there; *the boys played truant and went fishing*

③ **truce**
[trus] *noun*

agreement between two armies or enemies, etc., to stop fighting for a time; *when it got dark, they decided to call a truce*

① **truck**
[trʌk]
1 *noun*

goods vehicle for carrying heavy loads; *trucks thundered past the house all night*; *they loaded the truck with bricks*; **pickup truck** = truck with a cab for the driver and an open area in the back for the load
2 *verb*

to transport in a truck; *they trucked supplies to the refugees in the mountains*

③ **truck driver** *or* **trucker**
['trʌk 'draɪvǝr *or* 'trʌkǝr] *noun*

person who drives a truck; *a truck driver gave us a lift into town*

④ **truckload**
['trʌkloʊd] *noun*

amount of goods carried on a truck; *they delivered six truckloads of wood*

③ **trudge**
[trʌdʒ]
1 *noun*

long hard walk; *it was a long trudge through the mud back to the camp*
2 *verb*

to walk slowly with heavy footsteps; *he missed the bus and had to trudge down to the village to buy some milk*

① **true**
[tru] *adjective*

correct, right; *what he says is simply not true*; *it's quite true that she comes from Israel*; *is it true that he's been married twice?* (NOTE: **truer - truest**)

③ **truly**
['truli] *adverb*

(a) really; *he truly believes that was what happened*; *I'm truly grateful for all your help*; *do you love me, really and truly?*
(b) Truly yours = words written at the end of a slightly formal letter; *(informal)* **yours truly** =

me myself; *who had to pay for all the damage, why yours truly, of course!*

① **trumpet**
['trʌmpɪt] *noun*

(a) brass musical instrument which is played by blowing; *he plays the trumpet in the school orchestra*; *she practices the trumpet in the evenings*
(b) *(informal)* **to blow your own trumpet** = to boast about what you have done; *he's always blowing his own trumpet*

① **trunk**
[trʌŋk] *noun*

(a) thick stem of a tree; *he tried to measure around the trunk of the old oak tree*
(b) an elephant's long nose; *the elephant picked up the apple with its trunk*
(c) large box for storing or sending clothes, etc.; *they sent a trunk of clothes in advance to the new house*
(d) space at the back of an automobile, where you put baggage; *they packed all the boxes in the trunk*
(e) swim trunks = short pants worn by men and boys when swimming

① **trust**
[trʌst]
1 *noun*

(a) belief that something or someone is strong, will work well, etc.; *don't put too much trust in his skills as a driver*; **to take something on trust** = to take something without looking to see if it is all right; *we took his statement on trust*
(b) legal arrangement to pass valuables or money to someone to look after; *he left his property in trust for his grandchildren*
(c) company that manages money for its clients
2 *verb*

(a) to be sure of someone, to be confident that someone is reliable; *you can trust his instructions - he knows a lot about computers*; *I wouldn't trust him farther than I could kick him*
(b) *(informal)* **trust you to** = it is typical of you to; *trust him to be late!*; *trust them to forget to bring the food!*
(c) *(formal)* to hope or to believe; *I trust she will not get lost*
(d) to trust someone with something = to give something to someone to look after; *can she be trusted with all that cash?*

③ **trustee**
[trʌs'ti] *noun*

person who administers a trust or who directs a charity or other public institution; *the lease has to be agreed with the trustees of grandfather's estate*; *the director is appointed by the trustees of the museum*

① **truth**
[truθ] *noun*

thing which is true, a true story; *do you think he is telling the truth?*; *the police are trying to work out the truth about what happened; I don't think there is any truth in his story*

① **truthful**
['truːθfəl] *adjective*
(a) who always tells the truth; *she's a very truthful child*
(b) giving true facts; *to be truthful, I'm not quite sure where we are*

① **try**
[traɪ]
1 *verb*
(a) to make an effort to do something; *the burglar tried to climb up the tree; don't try to ride a motorcycle if you've never ridden one before; why don't you try to get a ticket yourself?*
(b) to test, to see if something is good; *you must try one of my mother's cookies; I tried the new toothpaste and I didn't like the taste; have you ever tried eating cheese with fruit?*
(c) to hear a civil or criminal case in court; *the case will be tried by a judge and jury*
2 *noun*
making an effort to do something; *she's going to have a try at water skiing; he had two tries before he passed his driver's test; let's give it a try = let's see if it works*

① **try on**
[traɪ 'ɒn] *verb*
to put on a piece of clothing to see if it fits; *you must try the pants on before you buy them; did you try on the shoes at the store?*

① **try out**
['traɪ 'aʊt] *verb*
(a) to test something, to see if it is good; *it's best to try a car out before you buy it*
(b) **to try out for** = to compete for a position or role; *she tried out for the swim team*

① **T-shirt** *or* **tee shirt**
['tiːʃɜrt] *noun*
light shirt with no buttons or collar, usually with short sleeves; *she was wearing jeans and a T-shirt; no wonder you're cold if you went out in just a T-shirt*

① **tube**
[tjuːb] *noun*
(a) long pipe for carrying liquids or gas; *he was lying in a hospital bed with tubes coming out of his nose and mouth; air flows down this tube to the face mask;* **inner tube** = rubber tube which is filled with air inside a tire
(b) soft container with a screw top that contains paste, etc.; *I forgot to pack a tube of toothpaste; she bought a tube of face cream; I need a tube of glue to mend the cup*
(c) *(informal)* television; *he's watching the tube*

③ **tuck**
[tʌk]
1 *verb*
to put into a narrow or small place; *the store is tucked away down a little lane; I offered him a*

$10 bill, which he tucked away into his shirt pocket
2 *noun*
little fold in a piece of cloth; *I put a tuck in the shirt to make it fit better around the waist*

② **tuck in**
['tʌk 'ɪn] *verb*
(a) to fold something around and push the ends in; *she tucked the blanket in around the baby* or *she tucked the baby in; he tucked his pants into his boots*
(b) *(informal)* to start eating in an enthusiastic way ; *after our long walk we all tucked into a huge lunch*

① **Tuesday**
['tjuːzdeɪ] *noun*
day between Monday and Wednesday, the second day of the week; *I saw him in the office last Tuesday; the club always meets on Tuesdays; shall we meet next Tuesday evening?; today is Tuesday, April 30; the 15th is a Monday, so the 16th must be a Tuesday*

② **tug**
[tʌg]
1 *verb*
to pull hard; *he tugged on the rope and a bell rang* (NOTE: **tugging - tugged**)
2 *noun*
(a) sudden pull; *he felt a tug on the line - he had caught a fish!*
(b) powerful boat that pulls other boats; *two tugs helped the ship get into the harbor*

① **tug-of-war**
[tʌgəv'wɔr] *noun*
competition in which two teams pull against each other on a rope; *there will be a tug-of-war between teams from the two villages*

② **tumble**
['tʌmbl]
1 *verb*
to fall; *he tumbled down the stairs head first; she arrived home late after the party and just tumbled into bed;* **to tumble dry** = to dry washed clothes in an automatic dryer
2 *noun*
fall; *she took a tumble on the ski slopes*

④ **tumor**
['tjuːmər] *noun*
swelling or growth of new cells in the body; *the doctors discovered a tumor in the brain* or *a brain tumor; the hospital diagnosed a tumor in the stomach*

② **tune**
[tjuːn]
1 *noun*
(a) series of musical notes which have a pattern that can be recognized; *he wrote some of the tunes for the musical; she walked away whistling a little tune*
(b) **to change your tune** = to change your way of thinking; *he used to say that managers had an easy life, but when he was promoted he soon*

changed his tune; *(informal)* **to the tune of $150** = at least $150; *we are paying rent to the tune of over $750 a week*
(c) in tune = with the correct musical tone; *the various sections of the orchestra weren't playing in tune*; **in tune with** = fitting in with, similar to; *his speech was in tune with the changing policies of the party*; **out of tune** = not fitting in with; *the wind instruments seem to be playing out of tune*
2 *verb*
(a) to adjust a radio to a particular station; *he keeps the radio tuned to the local radio station*
(b) to adjust a musical instrument so that it plays at the correct pitch; *the man has come to tune the piano*
(c) to adjust an automobile engine so that it works as efficiently as possible; *you'd use less gas if you had the engine properly tuned up*

② **tunnel**
['tʌnl]
1 *noun*
long passage under the ground; *the Channel Tunnel links Britain to France*; *the road around Lake Superior goes through a tunnel*; *they are digging a new tunnel for the subway*; *taking the tunnel through the mountains is quicker than driving up over them*; **tunnel vision** = (i) seeing only the area immediately in front of the eye; (ii) having the tendency to concentrate on only one aspect of a problem; *(informal)* **there's light at the end of the tunnel** = there is some hope that everything will be all right in the end
2 *verb*
to dig a long passage underground; *they decided to tunnel under the hill rather than build the road around it*

① **Turkey**
['tɜrki] *noun*
country in the eastern Mediterranean, south of the Black Sea; *Turkey lies partly in Europe and partly in Asia*; *we're going sailing off the coast of Turkey this summer* (NOTE: capital: **Ankara**; people: **the Turks**; language: **Turkish**; currency: **Turkish lira**)

① **turkey**
['tɜrki] *noun*
(a) large farm bird, similar to a chicken but much bigger, often eaten at Thanksgiving; *who's going to carve the turkey?*
(b) meat from this bird; *would you like another slice of turkey?*; *we had roast turkey and potatoes*

COMMENT: roast turkey is served with mashed potatoes, gravy and cranberry sauce, and forms the main part of the traditional Thanksgiving or Christmas meal

① **turn**
[tɜrn]
1 *noun*

(a) movement in a circle; *he gave the bottle top a couple of turns*; *don't forget to give the key an extra turn to lock the door*
(b) change of direction, especially of a vehicle; *the bus made a sudden turn to the left*; *see also* U-TURN
(c) road which leaves another road; *take the next turn on the right*
(d) doing something in order, one after the other; *you have to wait for your turn to see the doctor*; *it's my turn on the piano now; let me go now - no, it's my turn next*; **in turn** = one after the other in order; *each of the children will sing a song in turn*; **out of turn** = not in the correct order; *people don't like it if you go out of turn*
(e) to take turns *or* **to take it in turns** = to do something one after the other, to help each other; *they took it in turns to push the automobile or they took turns to push the automobile*
(f) the meat is done to a turn = properly cooked all through
(g) performance in a show; *their song and dance act is one of the most popular turns of the evening*
(h) to do a good turn = to do something to help; **one good turn deserves another** = if you do something to help someone they should do something to help you
2 *verb*
(a) to go around in a circle; *the wheels of the train started to turn slowly*; *be careful - the blades go on turning for a few seconds after the engine has been switched off*
(b) to make something go round; *turn the handle to the right to open the safe*
(c) to change direction, to go in another direction; *the automobile turned the corner too fast and hit a tree*; *the turn signal is blinking*; *the path turns to the right after the drugstore*; **the tide has turned** = the tide has started to go up or down
(d) to move your head or body so that you face in another direction; *can everyone turn to look at the camera, please*
(e) to change into something different; *leaves turn red or brown in the fall*; *when he was fifty, his hair turned gray*
(f) to go past a certain time; *it's turned nine o'clock, and they still haven't come home*; **she's turned sixty** = she is more than 60 years old
(g) to find a page in a book; *please turn to page 65*

① **turn around**
['tɜrn ə'raund] *verb*
to move your head or body so that you face in another direction; *he turned around when the police officer touched his shoulder*; *she turned around to see who was following her*

③ **turn away**
['tɜrn ə'wei] *verb*
(a) to send people away; *the restaurant is full,*

so we have had to turn people away
(b) to turn so as not to face someone; *he turned away because he didn't want to be photographed*

① **turn back**
['tɜːn 'bæk] *verb*
(a) to go back in the opposite direction; *the path was full of mud so we turned back and went home*
(b) to tell someone to go back; *the police tried to turn back the people who had no tickets*

① **turn down**
['tɜːn 'daʊn] *verb*
(a) to refuse something which is offered; *he was offered a job in Australia, but turned it down*; *she has turned down a job or turned a job down in the town hall*
(b) to make less noisy, less strong; *can you turn down the radio - I'm trying to work*

② **turn in**
['tɜːn 'ɪn] *verb*
(a) to take someone or something to someone in authority; *everyone was asked to turn in their guns*; *he caught the thief and turned him in to the police*
(b) *(informal)* to go to bed; *it's after eleven o'clock - time to turn in!*

② **turn into**
['tɜːn 'ɪntʊ] *verb*
(a) to change to become something different; *the wicked queen turned the prince into a frog*; *we are planning to turn this room into a museum*
(b) to change direction and go into something; *we went down the main road for a short way and then turned into a little lane on the left*

② **turn off**
['tɜːn 'ɒf] *verb*
(a) to switch off; *don't forget to turn the TV off when you go to bed*; *turn off the lights or turn the lights off - Pop's going to show the slides from his vacation*
(b) to leave a road you are traveling on; *you can turn off Main Street into one of the parking lots*; *when you get to the next crossroads turn off the main road and go down a little path toward the river*

② **turn on**
['tɜːn 'ɒn] *verb*
(a) to switch on; *can you turn the light on or turn on the light - it's too dark to read*; *turn on the TV or turn the TV on - it's time for the news*
(b) to attack someone suddenly; *the dog suddenly turned on the girl*; *the newspapers suddenly turned on the prime minister*

① **turn out**
['tɜːn 'aʊt] *verb*
(a) to force someone to go out; *they were turned out of their house when they couldn't pay the rent*
(b) to produce or make; *the factory turns out more than 10,000 automobiles a week*

(c) to switch off; *turn out the lights or turn the lights out - Pop's going to show the slides from his vacation*
(d) to happen in the end; *we got talking, and it turned out that she went to school with my brother*; *the party didn't start very well, but everything turned out all right in the end*
(e) to come out; *the whole town turned out to watch the cycling race*

① **turn over**
['tɜːn 'əʊvər] *verb*
(a) to roll over; *the truck went around the corner too fast and turned over*; *their boat turned over in the storm*
(b) to turn the page of a book; *turn over the page or turn the page over*; *she turned over two pages together*
(c) to have a certain amount of sales; *we turn over about three million dollars per year*

④ **turnover**
['tɜːnəʊvər] *noun*
(a) amount of sales of goods or services by a business; *our turnover is rising each year*
(b) staff turnover = changes in staff, with some leaving and new people coming; *high staff turnover is a sign that a company is in trouble*
(c) type of small sweet pie made with pastry and a fruit filling; *an apple turnover*

② **turnpike**
['tɜːnpaɪk] *noun*
main road where you have to pay tolls

④ **turn up**
['tɜːn 'ʌp] *verb*
(a) to arrive; *the food was spoiled because half the guests didn't turn up until nine o'clock*; *he turned up unexpectedly just as I was leaving the office*
(b) to be found; *the police searched everywhere, and the little girl finally turned up in an alley*; *the keys turned up in my coat pocket*
(c) to make louder, stronger; *can you turn up the radio or turn the radio up - I can't hear it*; *turn up the gas or turn the gas up, the potatoes aren't cooked yet*
(d) to unfold; *to keep warm he turned up his coat collar*

③ **tutor**
['tjuːtər]
1 *noun*
teacher, especially a person who teaches only one student or a small group of students; *his first job was as private tutor to some German children*
2 *verb*
to teach a small group of students; *she earns extra money by tutoring foreign students in English*

④ **tuxedo**
[tʌk'siːdəʊ] *noun*
(a) man's formal jacket, usually black, but sometimes white, worn with a bow tie

(a) man's formal black jacket and pants, worn to dances and formal dinners

① **TV**
['ti 'vi] *noun*
(a) television; *they watch TV every night*; *the TV news is usually at nine o'clock*; *some children's TV programs are very dull*; *the daughter of a friend of mine was on TV last night*; **cable TV** = television system where the programs are sent along underground cables; **satellite TV** = television system, where pictures are sent via space satellites; **TV lounge** = room in a hotel, hospital, etc., where residents can watch TV
(b) television set; *he's bought a portable TV*; *our TV is broken so we had to listen to the radio instead*; *we have a TV in our bedroom*

① **twelfth (12th)**
[twelfθ] *adjective & noun*
he came in twelfth out of two hundred in the competition; *it's her twelfth birthday next week*; **the twelfth century** = the period from 1100 to 1199 (NOTE: compare **the twelve hundreds**; Note also that with dates **twelfth** is usually written **12**: July 12, 1935; October 12, 1991: (say "October twelfth"); with names of kings and queens **twelfth** is usually written **XII**: King Louis XII (say: "King Louis the Twelfth")

① **twelve**
[twelv]
number 12; *she's twelve (years old) tomorrow*; *come over for a cup of coffee at twelve o'clock*; *there are twelve months in a year*; **the twelve hundreds** = the period from 1200 to 1299 (NOTE: **twelve o'clock at night** is midnight)

① **twentieth (20th)**
['twentiəθ] *adjective & noun*
she was twentieth out of twenty in the race; *today is June twentieth (June 20)* *it's her twentieth birthday on Wednesday*; **the twentieth century** = the period from 1900 to 1999 (NOTE: with dates **twentieth** is usually written **20**: July 20, 1935; October 20, 1991: (say "October twentieth"))

① **twenty**
['twenti]
number 20; *she's twenty (years old) next week*; **he's in his twenties** = he is between 20 and 29 years old; **the (nineteen) twenties (1920s)** = the years from 1920 to 1929; **the twenty-first century** = the period from the year 2000 to 2099; *(informal)* **twenties** = $20 bills or £20 notes; *he gave me two twenties and four tens*; *see also* VISION (NOTE: **twenty-one (21)**, **twenty-two (22)**, etc., but **twenty-first (21st)**, **twenty-second (22nd)**, etc.)

② **twice**
[twais] *adverb*
two times; *turn it off - I've seen that program twice already*; *twice two is four, twice four is eight*; *I'm fifteen, she's thirty, so she's twice as old as I am*

② **twin**
[twin] *adjective & noun*
(a) one of two babies born at the same time to the same mother; *he and his twin brother*; *she's expecting twins*; **identical twins** = twins who look exactly alike; *I'm not surprised you were confused, they're identical twins*
(b) **twin beds** = two single beds placed in a bedroom

③ **twinkle**
['twinkl] *verb*
(of stars, eyes) to shine with a little moving light; *we could see the lights of the harbour twinkling in the distance*

② **twirl**
[tw3rl] *verb*
to twist something round in your hand; *I wish I could twirl a stick like she does*

① **twist**
[twist]
1 *verb*
(a) to turn in different directions; *the path twisted between the fields*
(b) to wind something round something; *she twisted the string around a piece of stick*
(c) to bend a joint in the wrong way; *she twisted her ankle running to catch the bus*; *(informal)* **to twist someone's arm** = to put pressure on someone to persuade them to do what you want; *I had to twist his arm to get him to lend me his car*
2 *noun*
(a) thing which has been twisted; *put a twist of lemon (peel) in the drink*; *the twists and turns of the road through the mountains*; *it is difficult to follow the twists and turns of government policy*
(b) different way of telling a story; *he put a new twist on the story about the princess*

① **two**
[tu]
number 2; *there are only two peppermints left in the box*; *his son's only two (years old), so he can't read yet*; *she didn't come home until after two (o'clock)* **one or two** = some, a few; *only one or two people came to the exhibition* (NOTE: **two (2)** but **second (2nd)**)

④ **twofer**
['tufər] *noun*
two items for the price of one; *he got a twofer on neckties*

① **tying**
['taiiŋ] *see* TIE

② **type**
[taip]
1 *noun*
(a) sort or kind; *this type of bank account pays 10% interest*; *what type of accommodation are you looking for?*; **blood type** = classification of blood into a certain group; people with the same type of blood

(b) characters used in printing; *the chapter headings are in bold type* (NOTE: no plural in this meaning)
2 *verb*
to write with a typewriter; *please type your letters - your writing's so bad I can't read it*; *she only typed two lines and made six mistakes*

③ **typed**
[taɪpd] *adjective*
written on a typewriter; *we prefer to get typed applications rather than handwritten ones*

② **typewriter**
['taɪpraɪtər] *noun*
machine that prints letters or figures on a piece of paper when keys are pressed; *keep a cover over your typewriter when you are not using it*; **typewriter ribbon** = thin strip of material or plastic, with ink or carbon on it, used in a typewriter

③ **typhoon**
[taɪ'fun] *noun*
the name for a violent tropical storm in the Far East; *the typhoon caused immense damage in the regions along the coast* (NOTE: in the Caribbean Sea it is called a **hurricane**)

④ **typical**
['tɪpɪkl] *adjective*
having the usual qualities of a particular group or occasion; *describe a typical day at school*; *he's definitely not a typical bank manager*; **that's typical of him** = that's what he always does; *it's typical of them to be late*

③ **typically**
['tɪpɪkli] *adverb*
in a typical way; *I want to buy something which is typically Amish*; *typically, he arrived for dinner a hour late*

Uu

③ **U, u**
[ju]
twenty-first letter of the alphabet, between T and V; *the letter Q is always followed by a U*; **U-bend** = bend in a pipe shaped like a U; *see also* U-TURN

① **ugly**
['ʌgli] *adjective*
(a) not beautiful, not pleasant to look at; *what an ugly pattern!*; *the part of the town round the bus station is even uglier than the rest*; *the possibility of inflation reared its ugly head*; **ugly as sin** = very ugly
(b) **ugly mood** = dangerous mood; *the mood of the crowd turned ugly* (NOTE: **uglier - ugliest**)

④ **uh-huh**
[ə'hər] *interjection showing that you agree or that you have been listening*; *"Want to come?" - "Uh-huh!"*

④ **UK** *or* **U.K.**
[ju'keɪ] *abbreviation for* United Kingdom; *exports from the UK or UK exports rose last year*

④ **ultimate**
['ʌltɪmət]
1 *adjective*
last, final; *this is the ultimate game in the series*
2 *noun*
the most valuable or desirable thing; *our first-class cabins are the ultimate in traveling luxury*

④ **ultimately**
['ʌltɪmətli] *adverb*
in the end; *ultimately, the manager had to agree to refund her money*

① **umbrella**
[ʌm'brelə] *noun*
(a) round frame covered with cloth which you hold over your head to keep off the rain; *can I borrow your umbrella?*; *the company gives away umbrellas with red, green and white spots*; *as it was starting to rain, he opened his umbrella*; *the wind blew my umbrella inside out*; **beach umbrella** = a large umbrella to protect you from the sun
(b) **umbrella organization** = large organization which includes several other smaller ones

② **umpire**
['ʌmpaɪər]
1 *noun*
person who acts as a judge in a game to see that the game is played according to the rules; *the umpire ruled that the ball was out*; *he was fined for shouting at the umpire* (NOTE: umpires judge in tennis and baseball, but in most other games the person in charge is a **referee**)
2 *verb*
to act as umpire; *we don't think he umpired the match very fairly*

④ **UN**
['ju'en] *abbreviation for* United Nations; *UN peacekeeping forces are in the area*; *the U.S. Ambassador to the UN spoke in the debate*

③ **unable**
[ʌnˈeɪbl] *adjective*
(formal) not able (to do something); *I regret than I am unable to accept your suggestion; she was unable to come to the meeting* (NOTE: **be unable to** is rather formal; otherwise use **can't** or **couldn't**)

④ **unacceptable**
[ʌnəkˈseptəbl] *adjective*
which you cannot allow because it is too bad; *there were an unacceptable number of errors in the test; the terms of the contract are quite unacceptable*

④ **unanimous**
[juˈnænɪməs] *adjective*
with everyone agreeing; *there was a unanimous vote against the proposal; the jury reached a unanimous verdict of not guilty*

② **unarmed**
[ʌnˈɑrmd] *adjective*
with no weapons; *should policemen who patrol the streets be armed or unarmed?; **unarmed combat** =* fighting an enemy without using weapons; *soldiers practice unarmed combat*

② **unaware**
[ʌnəˈweər] *adjective*
unaware of *or* **unaware that** = not knowing; *he said he was unaware of any rule forbidding animals in the restaurant; she walked out of the restaurant with her boyfriend, unaware that the photographers were waiting outside*

② **unbearable**
[ʌnˈbeərəbl] *adjective*
which you cannot stand; *old people find this heat unbearable; the noise was unbearable and no one could work*

② **unbelievable**
[ʌnbɪˈlivəbl] *adjective*
incredible, which is difficult to believe; *it's unbelievable that she didn't know that the drugs were hidden in her suitcase; he has an unbelievable number of pop records*

④ **unbiased**
[ʌnˈbaɪəst] *adjective*
without any bias; *the court must be unbiased*

② **unbreakable**
[ʌnˈbreɪkəbl] *adjective*
which cannot be broken; *the windows are made of unbreakable glass*

② **uncertain**
[ʌnˈsɜrtən] *adjective*
(a) doubtful, not sure; *she is uncertain as to whether her father will come to stay; their plans are still uncertain*
(b) in no uncertain terms = rudely; *he told him in no uncertain terms what he could do with his offer*
(c) which will probably change for the worse; *she faces an uncertain future*

① **uncle**
[ˈʌŋkl] *noun*
brother of your father or mother; husband of an aunt; *he was brought up by his uncle in the Northwest Territories; we had a surprise visitor last night - old Uncle Charles*

④ **unclear**
[ʌnˈkliər] *adjective*
not clear; *the result of the election is still unclear - the two parties are neck and neck*

③ **Uncle Sam**
[ˈʌŋkl ˈsæm] *noun*
the U.S. government, represented by a tall man with a beard and top hat who wears the national colors; *all my extra income goes to Uncle Sam for taxes*

③ **uncomfortable**
[ʌnˈkʌmftəbl] *adjective*
(a) not comfortable, not soft and relaxing; *what a very uncomfortable bed!; plastic seats are very uncomfortable in hot weather*
(b) to feel uncomfortable about = to feel worried about; *I still feel uncomfortable about asking her to carry all that cash to the bank*

② **uncommon**
[ʌnˈkɒmən] *adjective*
strange or odd; rare; *it's a very uncommon bird in the north of Montana; it's not uncommon for us to have hundreds of phones calls during the morning*

③ **unconscious**
[ʌnˈkɒnʃəs]
1 *adjective*
not conscious, not aware of what is happening; *he was found unconscious on the street; she was unconscious for two days after the accident;* **unconscious of something** = not realizing something; *he was quite unconscious of how funny he looked*
2 *noun*
the unconscious = the part of the mind that stores thoughts, memories or feelings which you are not conscious of, but which influence what you do

② **uncover**
[ʌnˈkʌvər] *verb*
(a) to take a cover off something; *leaving the jars of jam uncovered will attract wasps*
(b) to find something which was hidden; *they uncovered a secret store of gold coins; the police have uncovered a series of secret financial deals*

④ **undeniable**
[ʌndɪˈnaɪəbl] *adjective*
which cannot be denied, which is quite clearly true; *there are undeniable tax advantages in working abroad; it is a undeniable fact that the climate is warming*

④ **undeniably**
[ʌndɪˈnaɪəbli] *adverb*
in an undeniable way, in a way which is quite

clearly true; *he is undeniably the best player in the team*

① **under**
['ʌndər] *preposition*
(a) in or to a place where something else is on top or above; *we all hid under the table; my pen rolled under the sofa; she can swim under water*
(b) less than a number; *no one wanted the old table - it was sold for under $15; it took under two weeks to sell the house; the train goes to Paris in under three hours; under half of the members turned up for the meeting*
(c) younger than; *she's a chief executive officer and she's still under thirty*
(d) according to; *under the terms of the agreement, the goods should be delivered in October*
(e) controlled by a ruler; *the country enjoyed a period of peace under the rule of the French* (NOTE: **under** is often used with verbs: **to look under, to go under,** etc.)

② **underclothes**
['ʌndərkləʊðz] *noun*
clothes that you wear next to the skin, under other clothes; *he ran out of the house in his underclothes; the doctor asked him to strip down to his underclothes*

④ **underestimate**
1 *noun* [ʌndər'estɪmət] estimate which is less than the actual figure; *the figure of $75,000 was a considerable underestimate*
2 *verb* [ʌndər'estɪmeɪt] to think that something is smaller or not as bad as it really is; *he underestimated the amount of time needed to finish the work; don't underestimate the intelligence of the average voter*

④ **underfoot**
['ʌndər'fʊt] *adverb*
on the ground; *it's very wet underfoot after the rain*

④ **undergo**
[ʌndər'gəʊ] *verb*
to suffer, to have something happen to you; *she will probably have to undergo another operation soon* (NOTE: **underwent** [ʌndər'went] - **undergone** [ʌndər'gɒn])

③ **undergraduate**
[ʌndər'grædjʊət] *noun*
college or university student who has not yet received a bachelor's degree; *the undergraduates signed up for their new classes*

② **underground**
['ʌndərgraʊnd]
1 *adverb*
(a) under the ground; *worms live all their life underground; if power cables were put underground they wouldn't spoil the scenery*
(b) **to go underground** = to go into hiding; *they had to go underground for a time until the police called off their search*
2 *adjective*

(a) under the ground; *there's an underground passage to the tower; the hotel has an underground parking lot*
(b) secret, hidden; *he was a member of an underground terrorist organization in the 1970s*
3 *noun*
UK subway, a railway in a town which runs under the ground; *take the underground to go to Oxford Circus*

① **underline**
['ʌndərlaɪn] *verb*
(a) to draw a line under a word, a figure; *he wrote the title and then underlined it in red*
(b) to emphasize; *this just underlines the urgent need for more medical supplies; I want to underline the fact that we need an experienced sales force*

④ **underlying**
[ʌndər'laɪɪŋ] *adjective*
which is the reason for everything; *it is difficult to solve the underlying problem of bad housing*

④ **undermine**
[ʌndər'maɪn] *verb*
to make weaker; *the documents undermined his case; our heavy industry has been undermined by the low labor costs in the Far East*

② **underneath**
[ʌndər'niθ]
1 *preposition*
under; *she wore a long green sweater underneath her coat; can you lie down and see if my pen is underneath the couch?*
2 *adverb*
under; *he put the box of books down on the kitchen table and my sandwiches were underneath!*
3 *noun*
base, the part of something which is under; *the underneath of the car is showing signs of rust*

① **underpants**
['ʌndərpænts] *noun*
short underwear for the part of the body from the waist to the top of the legs; *the doctor told him to strip down to his underpants; his wife gave him a pair of bright red white and blue underpants for his birthday*

③ **underpass**
['ʌndərpæs] *noun*
passage or crossing of a road and another road or railroad track which people can walk (as under a busy road); *there's an underpass from the bus station to the shopping center*

① **undershirt**
['ʌndərʃɜrt] *noun*
light piece of underwear for the top half of the body; *he wears a long-sleeve undershirt in winter; if you don't have a clean undershirt, wear a T-shirt instead*

① **understand**
['ʌndər'stænd] *verb*
(a) to know what something means; *don't try to talk English to Mr. Yoshida - he doesn't understand it*; *I hardly speak any Japanese, but I managed to make myself understood*
(b) to have information, to think something is true because someone has told you so; *we understand that they're getting married next month*; *it was understood that the group would meet at the bar*
(c) to have sympathy for someone; *she's a good teacher - she really understands children*
(d) to know why something happens or how something works; *I can easily understand why his wife left him*; *I still don't understand how to operate the new laser printer* (NOTE: understanding - understood ['ʌndər'stʊd])

④ **understandable**
['ʌndər'stændəbl] *adjective*
normal, which is easy to understand; *her response was quite understandable under the circumstances*

① **understanding**
['ʌndər'stændɪŋ]
1 *noun*
(a) ability to understand something; *my understanding of how the Internet works is severely limited*
(b) sympathy for someone else and their problems; *the boss showed no understanding when she told him about her financial difficulties*; *the aim is to promote understanding between the two countries*
(c) private agreement; *we reached an understanding with the lawyers*; *the understanding was that we would all go to the office after lunch*
(d) **on the understanding that** = on condition that, provided that; *we accept the terms of the contract, on the understanding that it has to be ratified by the whole board*
2 *adjective*
sympathetic; *his understanding attitude was much appreciated*

② **understood**
['ʌndər'stʊd] *see* UNDERSTAND

④ **undertake**
['ʌndər'teɪk] *verb*
(a) to agree to do something; *he has undertaken to pay her $150 a week for twelve weeks*
(b) to do something; *they undertook a survey of the market on our behalf* (NOTE: undertook ['ʌndər'tʊk] - has undertaken)

③ **under way**
['ʌndər 'weɪ] *adverb*
in progress; *the show finally got under way after a lot of delays*

③ **underwater**
['ʌndərwɔtər] *adverb*
under the surface of water; *she can swim well, even underwater*

① **underwear**
['ʌndərweər] *noun*
clothes worn next to your skin under other clothes; *it's December, so I'd better get out my thermal underwear*; *the nurse asked her to strip to her underwear and put on a hospital gown*; *each child will need to bring a change of underwear* (NOTE: no plural)

④ **underwent**
['ʌndər'went] *see* UNDERGO

② **undid**
['ʌn'dɪd] *see* UNDO

③ **undo**
['ʌn'du] *verb*
(a) to make something loose, which is tied or buttoned; *the first thing he did on getting home was to undo his necktie*; *undo your top button if your collar is too tight*; *wait a second, my shoe has come undone*
(b) to upset the good effect of something; *his remarks on TV undid all the good work done to increase racial cooperation* (NOTE: undid ['ʌn'dɪd] - has undone ['ʌn'dʌn])

④ **undoubted**
['ʌn'daʊtɪd] *adjective*
certain, true; *his undoubted enthusiasm for the project helped get it off the ground*

① **undress**
['ʌn'dres] *verb*
to take your clothes off; *the doctor asked the patient to undress*; *he got undressed; he undressed and got into the bath*; *they carried him upstairs, undressed him and put him to bed*

③ **uneasy**
['ʌn'izi] *adjective*
nervous and worried; *I'm kind of uneasy about lending her so much money* (NOTE: uneasier - uneasiest)

② **unemployed**
['ʌnɪm'plɔɪd]
1 *adjective*
without a job; *he was unemployed for about six months*
2 *noun*
the unemployed = people with no jobs; *the government is offering special grants to help the unemployed*

② **unemployment**
['ʌnɪm'plɔɪmənt] *noun*
lack of work; *the unemployment figures or the figures for unemployment are rising*; **mass unemployment** = situation where large numbers of people are out of work; **unemployment benefits** = money paid by the government to someone who is unemployed

① **uneven**
['ʌn'iːvn] *adjective*
not smooth, not flat; *don't try to put your tent up where the ground is uneven*

② **unexpected**
[ʌnɪkˈspektɪd] *adjective*
which is surprising and not what was expected;
we had an unexpected visit from the police; *his
failure was quite unexpected*

③ **unexpectedly**
[ʌnɪkˈspektɪdli] *adverb*
in an unexpected way; *just as the party was
starting his mother walked in unexpectedly*

① **unfair**
[ʌnˈfeər] *adjective*
not right, not fair; *it's unfair to expect her to do
all the housework while her sisters don't lift a
finger to help*; **unfair dismissal** = removing of a
person from his job for reasons which do not
appear to be reasonable; *he appealed to the
tribunal on the grounds of unfair dismissal*

② **unfortunate**
[ʌnˈfɔːrtʃənət] *adjective*
(a) which is not lucky; *he made some rather
unfortunate purchases on the stock exchange*
(b) which makes you sad; *it was very
unfortunate that she couldn't come to see us*
(c) embarrassing; *he made some very
unfortunate friendships when he was in the
army*; *she made some unfortunate remarks
about the bride's feet*

② **unfortunately**
[ʌnˈfɔːrtʃənətli] *adverb*
sadly, which you wish was not true;
*unfortunately, the train arrived so late that she
missed the meeting*

② **unfriendly**
[ʌnˈfrendli] *adjective*
not like a friend; *he answered in such an
unfriendly way that I wondered what I had
done to make him annoyed*

② **ungrateful**
[ʌnˈɡreɪtfəl] *adjective*
not grateful; *he's an ungrateful boy - he never
thanked me for his Christmas present*

③ **unhappily**
[ʌnˈhæpɪli] *adverb*
in a sad way; *she sat staring unhappily out of
the window*

① **unhappy**
[ʌnˈhæpi] *adjective*
sad, not happy; *he's unhappy in his job because
his boss is always criticizing him*; *she looked
very unhappy when she came out of the
hospital*; *the children had an unhappy
childhood* (NOTE: **unhappier - unhappiest**)

① **unhealthy**
[ʌnˈhelθi] *adjective*
not healthy; which does not make you healthy;
*sitting around smoking and not doing any sport
is very unhealthy*; *those children have a very
unhealthy diet* (NOTE: **unhealthier -
unhealthiest**)

③ **unidentified**
[ʌnaɪˈdentɪfaɪd] *adjective*
which you do not recognize, which you cannot
identify; *the photograph stayed in a drawer
unidentified for years*

② **uniform**
[ˈjuːnɪfɔːrm]
1 *noun*
special clothes worn by all members of an
organization or group; *he went to the costume
party dressed in a police officer's uniform*; *who
are those people in Russian army uniform?*;
what color is her school uniform?; *the staff all
wear yellow uniforms*; **in uniform** = wearing a
uniform; *the police officer was not in uniform
at the time*
2 *adjective*
all the same, never changing; *the supermarket
wants vegetables of uniform size and color*

④ **unify**
[ˈjuːnɪfaɪ] *verb*
to join separate countries or groups together to
form a single one; *the country was finally
unified after years of civil war*

② **union**
[ˈjuːnɪən] *noun*
(a) **labor union** = an organization that
represents workers who are its members in
discussions with employers about wages and
conditions of employment; *the staff are all
members of a labor union* or *they are labor
union members*; *the union called a meeting to
discuss the company's takeover by a Japanese
company*
(b) state of being joined together; *we support
the union of these various groups under one
umbrella organization*
(c) group of countries or independent states
which are linked into a federation; *the union
between England and Scotland is over 300
years old*; *see also* EUROPEAN UNION
(d) *(specifically)* the United States of America;
*the president will give his State of the Union
message in January*
(e) *(formal)* marriage; *their union will be
celebrated on November 1*

④ **unique**
[juˈniːk] *adjective*
different to everything else, the only one that
exists; *the stamp is unique, and so is worth a
great deal*; *he's studying the unique wildlife of
the island*

③ **unit**
[ˈjuːnɪt] *noun*
(a) one part of something larger; *if you pass
three units of the course you can move to the
next level*
(b) one piece of furniture, such as a cupboard, or
set of shelves, etc., which can be matched with
others; *the kitchen is designed as a basic set of
units with more units which can be added later*;
wall unit = cupboard that matches other units

and is attached to the wall; **corner unit** = unit that matches other units and fits into a corner

(c) monetary unit = main item of currency of a country (such as the dollar, peseta, pound, etc.); *the dollar is the monetary unit in the U.S.A. (this is a mutual fund in the US)*

(d) specialized section of a hospital; *she is in the intensive care unit; the burns unit was full after the plane crash*

(e) amount used to measure something; *kilos and pounds are units of weight*

(f) number one; *63 has six tens and three units*

① **unite**
[juˈnaɪt] *verb*
to join together into a single body; *the office staff united in asking for better working conditions; workers of the world, unite!*

① **united**
[juˈnaɪtɪd] *adjective*
joined together as a whole; *relief workers from various countries worked as a united team; they were united in their desire to improve their working conditions*

① **United Kingdom (UK)**
[juˈnaɪtɪd ˈkɪŋdəm] *noun*
independent European country, formed of England, Wales, Scotland and Northern Ireland; *he came to the United Kingdom to study; does she have a UK passport?; French citizens do not need work permits to work in the United Kingdom; see also* BRITISH, ENGLISH (NOTE: capital: **London**; people: **British**; language: **English**; currency: **pound sterling (£)**))

① **United Nations (UN)**
[juˈnaɪtɪd ˈneɪʃnz] *noun*
international organization including almost all independent states in the world, where member states are represented at meetings; *see also* GENERAL ASSEMBLY, SECURITY COUNCIL

① **United States of America (U.S.A.)**
[juˈnaɪtɪd steɪts ʌv əˈmerɪkər] *noun*
independent country, a federation of states (originally thirteen, now fifty) in North America, south of Canada and north of Mexico; *she now lives in the United States with her husband and two sons; the New Zealand student worked in the U.S.A. during her summer vacation; what is the largest city in the United States?; they came across to the United States by ship; he never had the chance to visit the United States; see also* AMERICAN (NOTE: capital: **Washington, DC**; people: **Americans**; language: **English**; currency: **U.S. dollar**)

④ **unity**
[ˈjuniti] *noun*
being one whole; *the aim of the government is to preserve national unity*

④ **universal**
[junɪˈvɜrsəl] *adjective*
which is understood or experienced by everyone; *there is a universal hope for world peace*; **Universal Product Code** = bar code, printed lines which can be read by a computer, used to check prices and inventory of retail products

② **universe**
[ˈjunɪvɜrs] *noun*
all space and everything that exists in it, including the Earth, the planets and the stars; *scientists believe the universe started as an explosion of matter*

② **university**
[junɪˈvɜːsɪti] *noun*
highest level of educational institution, which gives degrees to successful students, and where a wide range of specialized subjects are taught; *you need to do well at school to be able to go to a university; my sister is at a university* (NOTE: plural is **universities**)

① **unknown**
[ʌnˈnoʊn] *adjective*
(a) not known; *she was killed by an unknown attacker; the college received money from an unknown donor*

(b) unknown quantity = person whose ability and track record you know nothing about; *the new boss is something of an unknown quantity* (NOTE: the opposite is a **known quantity**)

③ **unless**
[ʌnˈles] *conjunction* if not; except if; *unless we hear from you within ten days, we will start legal action; I think they don't want to see us, unless of course they're ill*

③ **unlike**
[ʌnˈlaɪk] *adjective & preposition*
(a) totally different from; *he's quite unlike his brother*

(b) not normal, not typical; **it is unlike him to be rude** = he is not usually rude

① **unlikely**
[ʌnˈlaɪkli] *adjective*
(a) not likely; *it's unlikely that many people will come to the show*

(b) (story) which is probably not true; *he told some unlikely story about how his train ticket had been eaten by a dog*

③ **unlock**
[ʌnˈlɒk] *verb*
to open something which was locked; *I can't unlock the car door, I think I've got the wrong key*

② **unluckily**
[ʌnˈlʌkɪli] *adverb*
with bad luck; *unluckily a police car came past just as he was climbing out of the window*

① **unlucky**
[ʌnˈlʌki] *adjective*
not lucky, which brings bad luck; *many people think Friday 13 is unlucky; they say it's unlucky to walk under a ladder* (NOTE: unluckier - unluckiest)

④ **unmistakable**
[ʌnmɪsˈteɪkəbl] *adjective*
which is easily recognized, which cannot be
mistaken; *his old red Chevrolet is unmistakable*

① **unnecessary**
[ʌnˈnesəsəri] *adjective*
which is not needed, which does not have to be
done; *it is unnecessary for you to wear a suit to
the party*; *she makes too many unnecessary
phone calls*

③ **unofficial**
[ʌnəˈfɪʃl] *adjective*
not approved by an administration or by people
in power; *we have had some unofficial
meetings with people from the ministry*;
unofficial strike = strike by local workers
which has not been approved by the union

② **unpack**
[ʌnˈpæk] *verb*
to take things out of the boxes or cases in which
they were carried; *I've just come back from
Canada and I'm still unpacking*

② **unpleasant**
[ʌnˈplezənt] *adjective*
not nice, not pleasant; *there's a very unpleasant
smell in the kitchen*; *the boss is a very
unpleasant man and shouts at his secretary all
the time*; *try not to be unpleasant to the
waitress*

② **unpopular**
[ʌnˈpɒpjʊlər] *adjective*
not liked by other people; *the new working
hours were very unpopular with the staff*

④ **unravel**
[ʌnˈrævl] *verb*
(a) to undo something knitted; *she will have to
unravel the jumper to start knitting again*
(b) *(knitting or woven material)* to become
undone; *don't cut that bit of wool or the jumper
will unravel*
(c) to solve a mystery; *no one has ever been
able to unravel the mystery of what happened
to the money*

④ **unrest**
[ʌnˈrest] *noun*
protest by people to try to get political or
industrial change; *the announcement of the
election followed a period of unrest*; *the
government has sent in troops to deal with the
unrest in the south of the country* (NOTE: no
plural)

③ **unsealed**
[ˈʌnsild] *adjective*
which is not closed or stuck down; **unsealed
envelope** = envelope where the flap has not been
stuck down but is simply tucked inside; *the
information was sent in an unsealed envelope*
(NOTE: an envelope where the flap is stuck down is
a **sealed envelope**)

② **unselfish**
[ʌnˈselfɪʃ] *adjective*
thinking only of other people; *she was praised*
for her unselfish work for poor families

② **unsuccessful**
[ʌnsəkˈsesfəl] *adjective*
which does not succeed; *he was unsuccessful in
his attempt to get elected to the Senate*; *your
application for the job was unsuccessful*

② **untidy**
[ʌnˈtaɪdi] *adjective*
not tidy; *his bedroom is untidier than ever*;
*he'll never be promoted, he always looks so
untidy* (NOTE: **untidier - untidiest**)

① **untie**
[ʌnˈtaɪ] *verb*
to undo something which is tied with a knot;
*since her shoelaces are always untied, she'd be
better off wearing boots*; *someone untied the
boat and it drifted down the river*; *can you help
me untie this knot, it is very tight!*

② **until**
[ʌnˈtɪl]
1 *conjunction*
up to the time when; *she was perfectly well until
she ate the strawberries*; *he blew his whistle
until the police came*
2 *preposition & conjunction*
up to the time when; *I don't expect to be back
until after ten o'clock*; *until yesterday, I felt
very well* (NOTE: the word **till** has the same
meaning)

① **untrue**
[ʌnˈtruː] *adjective*
not true, false; *his story was quite untrue - the
jewels were not hidden in a teddy bear*

③ **unusual**
[ʌnˈjuːʒuəl] *adjective*
strange, not normal; *it is unusual to have rain at
this time of year*; *she chose a very unusual
color scheme for her sitting room*

② **unusually**
[ʌnˈjuːʒuəli] *adverb*
strangely, not as normal; *the weather is
unusually warm for January*; *unusually, she
didn't say very much at the dinner*

③ **unveil**
[ʌnˈveɪl] *verb*
(a) to take a cover off something, so as to open it
formally to the public; *the statue was unveiled
by the mayor*
(b) to reveal details of a new plan, etc.; *the
committee will unveil its proposals next week*

④ **unwarranted**
[ʌnˈwɒrəntɪd] *adjective*
which is not justified; *his criticisms were totally
unwarranted*

② **unwell**
[ʌnˈwel] *adjective*
sick, ill, not well; *she felt unwell and had to go
home* (NOTE: not used before a noun: **the baby
was unwell** but **a sick baby**)

① **unwilling**
[ʌn'wɪlɪŋ] *adjective*
not wanting to do something; *he was unwilling to pay any more; she was an unwilling member of the crew*

① **up**
[ʌp]
1 *adverb*
(a) in or to a high place; *put your hands up above your head; what's the cat doing up there on the cupboard?*
(b) to a higher position; *his temperature went up suddenly; the price of gas seems to go up every week*
(c) not in bed; *they stayed up all night watching movies on TV; he got up at six because he had an early train to catch; it's past eight o'clock - you should be up by now; she's getting better - the doctor says she will be up and about very soon*
(d) toward the north; *I'll be going up to Augusta next week*
(e) *your time's up* = you have had all the time allowed
2 *preposition*
(a) in or to a high place; *they ran up the stairs; she doesn't like going up ladders*
(b) along; *go up the street to the traffic lights and then make a right; the house is about two hundred yards up the road* (NOTE: that **up** is often used after verbs: **to keep up, to turn up,** etc.)
3 *verb*
(a) to raise prices, etc.; *they upped their offer to $1500*
(b) *(informal)* to stand up, to get up; *she upped and left him when she heard he had been seen with her best friend* (NOTE: **upping - upped**)
4 *noun*
the ups and downs of life in the army = the good and bad periods

④ **up-and-coming**
[ʌpən'kʌmɪŋ] *adjective*
(informal) becoming fashionable and likely to succeed; *they live in a very up-and-coming part of town; he's one of the most up-and-coming young executives, that would make him an up-and-comer*

③ **up and down**
[ʌp ənd 'daʊn]
1 *preposition*
in one direction, then in the opposite direction; *the police officer was walking up and down in front of the bank; she looked up and down the street but couldn't see her little boy*
2 *noun*
ups and downs = the times of good luck and bad luck; *his book describes the ups and downs of life in the army*

③ **up and running**
[ʌp ənd 'rʌnɪŋ] *adjective*
(informal) working; *he played an important role in getting the project up and running; the project is up and running at long last*

④ **update**
1 ['ʌpdeɪt] *noun*
latest information; *the manager gave us an update on the latest sales figures*
2 [ʌp'deɪt] *verb*
to add the latest information to something so that it is quite up-to-date; *she was asked to update the telephone list; the figures are updated annually; they have updated their guidebook to Europe to include current prices*

③ **up for**
['ʌp 'fɔr] *preposition*
(a) ready for; *my house insurance is up for renewal*
(b) *up for sale* = on sale, going to be sold; *he's put his apartment up for sale*

③ **up front**
[ʌp 'frʌnt] *adverb*
in advance; *money up front* = payment in advance; *they are asking for $150,000 up front before they will consider the deal; we had to put money up front before we could get them to sign the deal*

④ **upgrade**
[ʌp'greɪd] *verb*
(a) to improve the quality of something; *she has upgraded her computer*
(b) to put someone into a more important job; *his job has been upgraded to senior manager*

③ **uphold**
[ʌp'həʊld] *verb*
(a) *to uphold the law* = to make sure that laws are obeyed
(b) *(legal)* to reject an appeal and support an earlier judgment; *the appeal court upheld the decision of the lower court* (NOTE: **upholding - upheld** [ʌp'held])

④ **upkeep**
['ʌpkip] *noun*
cost of keeping a house, an automobile, etc., in good order; *we're forced to sell the house because its upkeep is so expensive; the upkeep of the automobile costs me more than $75 a week; how much are you getting from your former husband for the upkeep of the children?* (NOTE: no plural)

① **upon**
[ʌ'pɒn]
(a) *(formal)* on; *the church was built upon a low hill*
(b) likely to happen soon; *the summer vacation will soon be upon us again*

① **upper**
['ʌpər]
1 *adjective*
(a) higher or further up; *the upper slopes of the mountain are covered in snow; upper arm* = part of the arm from the shoulder to the elbow; *he had a rash on his right upper arm*

(b) more important; **upper house** *or* **upper chamber** = more senior of the two houses in a parliament; *the bill has been passed in the lower house and now goes to the upper house for further discussion* (NOTE: opposite is **lower**)

2 *noun*

top part of a shoe; *a pair of shoes with leather uppers and plastic soles*

③ **upright**
['ʌpraɪt]

1 *adjective*

standing straight up, vertical; *he got dizzy as soon as he stood upright; put your seats into the upright position for landing; she picked up the bottle and placed it upright on the table*

2 *noun*

(a) vertical post; *the goalkeeper was leaning against one of the uprights*

(b) piano with a vertical body (NOTE: the other type of piano, with a large horizontal body, is called a **grand piano**)

③ **uprising**
['ʌpraɪzɪŋ] *noun*

revolt; *an uprising against the government; the uprising was crushed by the army*

① **upset**
[ʌp'set]

1 *adjective*

(a) very worried, unhappy, anxious; *she gets upset if he comes home late*

(b) slightly sick; *she is in bed with an upset stomach*

2 *noun*

(a) slight illness; **stomach upset** = slight infection of the stomach; *she is in bed with a stomach upset*

(b) unexpected defeat; *there was a major upset in the tennis tournament when the number three seed was beaten in the first round*

3 *verb*

(a) to knock over; *he upset all the coffee cups*

(b) to make someone worried or unhappy; *don't upset your mother by telling her you're planning to go to live in Russia*

② **upside down**
['ʌpsaɪd 'daʊn] *adverb*

(a) with the top underneath; *don't turn the box upside down - all the papers will fall out; the automobile shot off the road and ended up upside down in a ditch; bats were hanging upside down from the branches*

(b) in disorder; *while he was out someone had searched his room, turning the place upside down*

② **upstairs**
[ʌp'steərz]

1 *adverb*

on or to the upper part of a building, bus, etc.; *she ran upstairs with the letter; I left my glasses upstairs; let's go upstairs onto the top deck - you have a much better view*

2 *adjective*

on the upper floors of a building; *we have an upstairs kitchen; we let the one of the upstairs offices to an accountant*

3 *noun*

the upper floors of a building; *the upstairs of the house needs decorating; compare* DOWNSTAIRS

① **up to**
[ʌp 'tu] *preposition*

(a) as many as; *the elevator will take up to six people*

(b) what are you up to these days? = what are you doing?

(c) it's up to you = it is your responsibility

(d) capable of doing something; *it's a very demanding job and I wonder if she's up to it*

① **up-to-date**
[ʌp tə' deɪt]

1 *adverb*

with the latest information; *I keep myself up-to-date on the political situation by reading the newspaper every day*

2 *adjective*

with very recent information; *I don't have an up-to-date timetable*

① **upward** *or* **upwards**
['ʌpwərd *or* 'ʌpwərdz]

1 *adjective*

moving toward a higher level; *the rocket's engines generate enormous upward thrust*

2 *adverb*

(a) toward the top; *the path went upward for a mile then leveled off*

(b) upward of *or* **upwards of** = more than; *upward of a thousand people answered the advertisement*

③ **uranium**
[jʊ'reɪniəm] *noun*

radioactive metal used in producing atomic energy (NOTE: Chemical element: chemical symbol: U; atomic number: 92)

④ **urban**
['ɜrbən] *adjective*

(a) referring to towns; *they enjoy an urban lifestyle*

(b) living in towns; *the urban fox has become common in many parts of the city*

② **urge**
[ɜrdʒ]

1 *noun*

strong wish to do something; *she felt an urge to punch him on the nose*

2 *verb*

(a) to advise someone strongly to do something; *he urged her to do what her father said; I would urge you to vote for the proposal; our lawyer urged us to be careful and avoid breaking the law*

(b) to urge someone on = to encourage someone to do better, to do more; *the runners were urged on by their supporters*

④ **urgency**
['ɜrdʒənsi] *noun*
being very important, needing to be done quickly; *there was a note of urgency in his voice*; *the police seem to have no sense of urgency*; **there's no great urgency** = there's no need to rush

③ **urgent**
['ɜrdʒənt] *adjective*
which is important and needs to be done quickly; *he had an urgent message to go to the police station*; *she had an urgent operation*; *the leader of the city council called an urgent meeting*; *this package is urgent and needs to get there tomorrow*

④ **urine**
['jʊərɪn] *noun*
wastewater which is passed out of the body; *he was asked to produce an urine sample for testing*

① **Uruguay**
['jʊərəgwaɪ] *noun*
country in Latin America, north of Argentina; *he's going to Uruguay on business* (NOTE: capital: **Montevideo**; people: **Uruguayans**; language: **Spanish**; currency: **Uruguayan peso**)

② **Uruguayan**
[jʊrə'gwaɪən]
1 *adjective*
referring to Uruguay; *Uruguayan exports to the U.S.A.*
2 *noun*
person from Uruguay

② **us**
[ʌs] *object pronoun (meaning me and other people)* *mother gave us each one dollar to buy ice cream*; *who's there? - it's us!*; *the company did well last year - the management have given us a bonus*

① **U.S.** *or* **U.S.A.**
['jues or 'jues'eɪ] *see* UNITED STATES (OF AMERICA); *they're thinking of coming to the U.S. on vacation next year*; *they spent three weeks traveling in the U.S.A.*

① **use**
1 *verb* [juz]
(a) to take a tool, etc., and do something with it; *did you use a sewing machine to make your curtains?*; *the car's worth quite a lot of money - it's hardly been used*; *do you know how to use a computer?*; *can I use this knife for cutting meat?*
(b) to take a service; *guests used the fire escape to get out of the building*; *she used the money she had saved to pay for a trip to Mexico*; *I don't use the subway much because I can walk to the office*; *we use second-class mail for all our correspondence*
(c) to take a substance and do something with it; *don't use this water for drinking*; *does this automobile use much gas?*; *turn down the heating - we're using too much gas*

(d) to take advantage of someone; *he works every evening until late - I think they're just using him*
2 *noun* [jus]
(a) purpose, being useful for something; *can you find any use for this piece of cloth?*
(b) being used; *the coffee machine has been in daily use for years*
(c) possibility of using something; *room 51 has no bathroom, but you have the use of the bathroom next door*; *the lounge is for the use of the hotel guests*; *don't worry, he'll soon recover the use of his arm*
(d) being useful; *he kept the old chair, thinking it might be of use some day*; *what's the use of telling the children to shut up - they never do what I say*; *it's no use just waiting and hoping that someone will give you a job*
(e) **to make use of something** = to use something; *he didn't make use of his phrase book once*; *you should make more use of your bicycle*

③ **used**
[juzd] *adjective*
which is not new; *a store selling used clothes*; *I bought a used car*

② **used to**
['juzd 'tu]
(a) **to be used to something** *or* **to doing something** = not to worry about doing something, because you do it often; *farmers are used to getting up early*; *we're used to hard work in this office*; *I'm not used to eating such a large meal at lunchtime*
(b) **to get used to something** *or* **to doing something** = to do something often or for a period of time, so that it is not a worry anymore; *she'll soon get used to her new job*; *we lived in Canada for six years, so we got used to very cold temperatures*; *even though he had to catch the 6:15 train for years, he never got used to getting up early*
(c) *(showing that something happened often or regularly in the past)* *there used to be lots of small stores in the town until the supermarket was built*; *when we were children, we used to go to West Virginia every year for our vacations*; *the police think he used to live in Seattle*; *he used to smoke a pipe*; *didn't she use to work in Oklahoma City?* (NOTE: the forms used in the negative and questions: **he used to work in Boston**; **he didn't use to work in Boston** *or* **he used not to work in Boston**; **didn't he use to work in Boston?**)

① **useful**
['jusfəl] *adjective*
who or which can help you do something; *I find these scissors very useful for opening letters*; *she's a very useful person to have in the office*; **to make yourself useful** = to do something to help

② **useless**
['juslǝs] *adjective*
which is not useful, which doesn't help; *these scissors are useless - they won't cut anything*; *I found it useless to try to persuade her to do something different*; *she's useless at numbers* = she is no good at math

③ **user**
['juzǝr] *noun*
person who uses a tool or a service; *we have mailed the users of our equipment about the possible design fault*; **user's guide** *or* **handbook** = book showing someone how to use something; *I find the computer user's guide very useful*

① **use up**
['juz 'ʌp] *verb*
to use all of something; *she's used up all the glue*; *paying for the house has used up all my savings*

② **usual**
['juʒʊǝl]
1 *adjective*
(a) which is done or used often; *she took her usual bus to the office*; *we'll meet at the usual time, usual place*; *his usual practice is to get up at 6:30 and run around the park*; *the usual hours of work are from 9:30 to 5:30*
(b) **as usual** = as is normal, in the usual way; *the mail was late today as usual*; *as usual, it rained for the school fair*; **business as usual** = everything is still working in the normal way in spite of difficulties; *although their warehouse burned down within twenty-four hours it was business as usual*
2 *noun*
(informal) drink or food which someone has most often in a restaurant, diner, etc.; *a glass of the usual, please*; *will you have your usual, sir?*

③ **usually**
['juʒǝli] *adverb*
very often, mostly; *there's usually someone in the office at 9 o'clock*; *we usually broil our*

chicken; *the restaurant is usually full on Friday evenings*

③ **utility**
[ju'tɪlɪti] *noun*
(a) how useful something is ; **utility room** = room in a house where you put the washing machine, freezer, etc.
(b) **utilities** = essential public services (such as electricity, gas, water, etc.)

④ **utilize**
['jutɪlaɪz] *verb*
(formal) to make use of something; *he's looking for a job where he can utilize his programming skills*

③ **utter**
['ʌtǝr]
1 *adjective*
complete, total; *the exhibition was an utter waste of time*; *he's an utter fool*
2 *verb*
to speak; to make a sound; *she only uttered a few words during the whole evening*

④ **utterly**
['ʌtǝrli] *adverb*
completely; *he was utterly worn out after the test*

④ **U-turn**
['jutɝn] *noun*
(a) turning round to go back in the opposite direction; *the squad car did or made a U-turn and went back to the hotel*; *U-turns are not allowed on this road*
(b) **to do a U-turn** = to change policy completely; *the newspapers were surprised at the government's U-turn on defense expenditures*; *the government has done a complete U-turn on retirees' rights*

Vv

③ **V, v**
[vi]
twenty-second letter of the alphabet, between U and W; *I know his name's Stephen but I don't know if it is spelled with a PH or a V (Stephen or Steven)*

② **vacancy**
['veɪkǝnsi] *noun*
(a) job that is not filled; *we have vacancies in several departments*; *we advertised a vacancy*

for a secretary in the local paper; **job vacancies** = jobs that are empty and need people to do them
(b) empty place, empty room; *all the hotels had signs saying "No vacancies"*

② **vacant**
['veɪkǝnt] *adjective*
(a) empty, available for you to use; *there are six rooms vacant in the new hotel wing*; *is the toilet vacant yet?*

(b) *(expression)* not showing any interest; *he sat with a vacant expression on his face*

① **vacation**
[vəˈkeɪʃn]
1 *noun*
holiday; *the family went on vacation in Canada*
2 *verb*
to take a holiday; *they are vacationing in Mexico*

② **vaccine**
[ˈvæksin] *noun*
substance which contains the germs of a disease and which is injected into a patient to prevent him or her getting the disease; *the hospital is waiting for a new batch of vaccine to come from the laboratory*; *new vaccines are being developed all the time*

③ **vacuum**
[ˈvækjuəm]
1 *noun*
(a) space which is completely empty of all matter, including air; *the experiment has to be carried out in a vacuum*; **vacuum-packed food** = food packed in a plastic envelope from which all air has been removed; *vacuum-packed cheese will keep for months*
(b) to create a vacuum = to empty a space completely; **power vacuum** = situation where there is no one left in control; *the death of the secretary of state creates a power vacuum in the government*
(c) working in a vacuum = working in a situation where you have no connection with anyone else
(d) = VACUUM CLEANER
2 *verb*
(informal) to clean using a vacuum cleaner; *she vacuums the hall every day*; *I must vacuum the living room before my mom arrives*

② **vacuum cleaner**
[ˈvækjuəm ˈklinər] *noun*
machine which cleans by sucking up dust; *our cat hides under the bed when she hears the vacuum cleaner*

④ **vague**
[veɪg] *adjective*
not clear, with no precise details; *he's very vague about what he wants to do after college*; *we've made some vague plans to go to the Bahamas in August* (NOTE: **vaguer - vaguest**)

④ **vain**
[veɪn] *adjective*
(a) which does not succeed; *she went to the club in the vain hope of finding him there*
(b) in vain = without any success; *we waited in vain for a bus and had to walk home*; **he did not die in vain** = his death had an immense effect on the people
(c) very proud of your appearance, clothes, achievements, etc.; *he's very vain, and is always combing his hair* (NOTE: do not confuse with **vein**; note: **vainer - vainest**)

④ **valedictorian**
[vælɪdɪkˈtɔriən] *noun*
student who has the highest grade average in a graduating class and who makes a speech at the graduation ceremony

④ **valid**
[ˈvælɪd] *adjective*
(a) which is acceptable because it is true; *that is not a valid argument or valid excuse*; *she made several valid points in her speech*
(b) which is legal and can be used for a time; *travelers must have a valid ticket before boarding the train*; *I have a season ticket which is valid for one year*; *he was carrying a valid passport*

① **valley**
[ˈvælɪ] *noun*
long piece of low land through which a river runs; *fog forms in the valleys at night*; *a lot of computer companies are based in Silicon Valley*

② **valuable**
[ˈvæljubl]
1 *adjective*
(a) worth a lot of money; *be careful, that glass is valuable!*; *the burglars stole everything that was valuable*
(b) useful, which helps; *she gave me some very valuable advice*
2 *noun*
valuables = items which are worth a lot of money; *you can deposit valuables in the hotel safe*

② **value**
[ˈvælju]
1 *noun*
(a) amount of money which something is worth; *he imported goods to the value of $500*; *the fall in the value of the yen*; *items of value can be deposited in the hotel safe overnight*; **to rise in value** = to become worth more; **to fall in value** = to become worth less; *houses have fallen in value in some parts of the country*; **good value (for money)** = a bargain, something which is worth the price paid for it; *that restaurant gives value for money*; *vacations in Italy are good value because of the exchange rate*
(b) quantity shown as a number; *what is the pressure value at the moment?*
(c) practical value = being useful; *the device is of no practical value at all*
2 *verb*
(a) to estimate the value of something in money; *the jewels have been valued at $5000*
(b) to consider something as being valuable; *she values her friendship with him*

③ **valve**
[vælv] *noun*
(a) device in a tube (in a machine) which allows air or liquid to pass through in one direction only; *the problem was caused by a faulty valve*; **safety valve** = valve which allows liquid, gas,

steam, etc., to escape if the pressure becomes too high

(b) piece of tissue in the heart, in a blood vessel, or other organ, which opens and closes to allow liquid to pass in one direction only; *surgery was needed to repair a valve in the heart*

② **van**
['væn] *noun*
covered goods vehicle; *a delivery van ran into the back of my automobile; our van will call this afternoon to pick up the goods*; security **van** = specially protected van for delivering cash and other valuable items; armored truck; *six gunmen held up the security van*

④ **vandal**
['vændl] *noun*
person who destroys property, especially public property, because they like doing that; *vandals have pulled the telephones out of the phone booths by the station*

① **vanish**
['vænɪʃ] *verb*
to disappear suddenly; *the rabbit vanished down a hole*; to vanish into thin air = to disappear completely; *all the money the investors had put into the company simply vanished into thin air*

④ **vanload**
['vænləʊd] *noun*
amount of goods carried in a van; *when we moved we had three vanloads of books*

② **vapor**
['veɪpər] *noun*
substance which you can see in the form of mist or a gas, usually caused by heating; *you can see water vapor rising from the swimming pool in cold weather*

③ **variable**
['veəriəbl]
1 *adjective*
which may change frequently; *the weather forecast is for variable winds; the weather can be very variable on the coast*
2 *noun*
thing which varies; *we have to take a great many variables into account*

③ **variation**
[veəri'eɪʃn] *noun*
(a) change from one state or level to another; *the variation in color or the color variation is because the cloth has been dyed by hand; there is a noticeable variation in temperature in the desert regions; the chart shows the variations in price over a period of six months*
(b) variations = short pieces of music which take the same theme but repeat it in different styles

③ **varied**
['veərɪd] *adjective*
made up of different sorts and kinds; *the menu isn't very varied - there are only three*

appetizers and two main courses; a varied program of music

③ **variety**
[və'raɪəti] *noun*
(a) differences; *her new job, unlike the old one, doesn't lack variety*; variety of = a lot of different sorts of things or people; *she's had a variety of boyfriends; we had a variety of visitors at the office today; we couldn't go on vacation this year for a variety of reasons*; variety is the spice of life = if you meet with lots of different people, visit lots of different places, etc., then this makes your life exciting
(b) different type of plant or animal in the same species; *do you have this new variety of rose?; is this a new variety of potato?*
(c) type of entertainment which includes several different short performances by different types of artist (such as singers, dancers, etc.); *at Christmas, the TV has nothing but a series of variety shows*

② **various**
['veəriəs] *adjective*
different; *the store sells goods from various countries; I'll be out of the office today - I have to see various suppliers*

④ **varsity**
['vɑrsɪti] *adjective*
relating to the main sports team in a university, college or school; *we went to the varsity baseball game*

③ **vary**
['veəri] *verb*
(a) to change what you do often; *it will help your digestion if you vary your diet*
(b) to be different; *prices of apartments vary from a few thousand dollars to millions*

③ **vast**
[væst] *adjective*
enormous, very large; *the plain was vast - it stretched as far as the eye could see; a vast tanker suddenly appeared out of the fog*

② **veal**
[vil] *noun*
meat from a calf; *we had roast veal for lunch*; veal cutlet = flat cake of ground veal, fried

④ **vegan**
['vɪgən] *noun*
person who does not eat meat, milk, butter, cheese, eggs or fish, but only eats vegetables and fruit and other non-animal products; *his wife is a vegan, so we'll make a special meal for her*

① **vegetable**
['vedʒɪtəbl] *noun*
(a) plant grown to be eaten, but not usually sweet; *we grow potatoes, carrots and other sorts of vegetables in the garden; what vegetables do you want with your meat? - beans and carrots, please; the soup of the day is vegetable soup*; green vegetables = vegetables which are green, especially spinach, etc.; *green vegetables are a good source of fiber in the diet;*

root vegetables = vegetables, such as carrots, of which you eat the roots
(b) vegetable oil = oil which is extracted from plants

④ **vegetarian**
[ˌvedʒɪˈteərɪən]
1 *noun*
person who eats only fruit, vegetables, bread, eggs, etc., but does not eat meat, and sometimes not fish; *our children are all vegetarians*; **strict vegetarian** = person who does not eat any animal products, including eggs and milk
2 *adjective*
not eating meat; *he is on a vegetarian diet*; *she asked for the vegetarian menu*; **vegetarian dish** = dish which does not contain meat

② **vehicle**
[ˈviːkl] *noun*
(formal) automobile, truck, bus, etc., a machine which carries passengers or goods; *goods vehicles can park at the back of the building*; *there are more and more motor vehicles on the roads every year*; **commercial vehicle** = vehicle which carries passengers or goods

③ **vein**
[veɪn] *noun*
(a) small tube in the body which takes blood from the tissues back to the heart; *the veins in her legs are swollen*; *compare* ARTERY
(b) mood shown in speaking or writing; *he went on in the same vein for twenty minutes*
(c) thin tube forming part of the structure of a leaf; *the veins are easily seen if you hold the leaf up to the light*
(d) thin layer of mineral in rock; *they struck a vein of gold* (NOTE: do not confuse with **vain**)

③ **velvet**
[ˈvelvət] *noun*
cloth made from silk, with on one side a soft surface like fur; *he wore a velvet jacket for dinner*

① **Venezuela**
[ˌvenɪˈzweɪlə] *noun*
country in the north of South America, on the Caribbean Sea; *he's going to Venezuela on business* (NOTE: capital: **Caracas**; people: **Venezuelans**; language: **Spanish**; currency: **bolivar**)

② **Venezuelan**
[ˌvenɪˈzweɪlən]
1 *adjective*
referring to Venezuela; *Venezuelan exports to Spain are increasing*
2 *noun*
person from Venezuela

④ **venture**
[ˈventʃər]
1 *noun*
business or commercial deal which involves risk; *the venture failed and all the partners lost money*; *she has started a new venture - a computer store*

2 *verb (formal)*
(a) to risk doing something dangerous; *she ventured into the cave*; *they ventured out into the snowstorm*
(b) to say something, even though other people may criticize you for saying it; *at last he ventured to say that the whole thing was a failure*

④ **venue**
[ˈvenjʊ] *noun*
agreed place where a meeting will be held; *what is the venue going to be for the exhibition?*; *the meeting will be held on Wednesday, May 10, but the venue has not been fixed yet*

② **verb**
[vɜːb] *noun*
(grammar) word that shows an action, being or feeling, etc.; *in the sentence "she hit him with her fist" the word "hit" is a verb*

④ **verbal**
[ˈvɜːbəl] *adjective*
(a) spoken; not written down; *the principal gave the boys a verbal warning*; **verbal abuse** = rude words; **verbal agreement** = agreement that is spoken (such as one made over the phone)
(b) *(grammar)* referring to a verb; *when you say "to X-ray" the noun has taken a verbal form*; **verbal noun** = noun formed from a verb (NOTE: in English, verbal nouns are formed from the "-ing " form of verbs, as in **cycling is good exercise; singing is very popular in Wales**)

③ **verdict**
[ˈvɜːdɪkt] *noun*
(a) decision of a magistrate or jury; *the jury returned a guilty verdict after one hour*; **to come to a verdict** *or* **to reach a verdict** = to decide whether the accused is guilty or not
(b) *(informal)* opinion, what you think about something; *she gave her verdict on the soup*

④ **verge**
[vɜːdʒ]
1 *noun*
edge; **on the verge of** = near to; *the company is on the verge of collapse*; *she was on the verge of a nervous breakdown*
2 *verb*
to verge on = to be close to; *his comments about her clothes verged on the offensive*

④ **versatile**
[ˈvɜːsətl or ˈvɜːsətaɪl] *adjective*
(a) *(person)* good at doing various things equally well; *he's very versatile - he can play the piano, the guitar and he's the lead singer as well*
(b) *(machine, material, etc.)* which is suitable for various uses; *the automobile is extremely versatile: it can be used on rough mountain tracks, but is equally suitable for town use*

② **verse**
[vɜːs] *noun*
(a) group of lines which form a part of a song or poem; *we sang all the verses of the school song*; *she read the first verse to the class*

(b) poetry, writing with words carefully chosen to sound attractive, set out in lines usually of a regular length; *he published a small book of verse*; *compare* PROSE (NOTE: no plural in this meaning)

(c) one short sentence from the Bible, each of which has a number; *the reading in church was some verses from Matthew*; **to give** *or* **to quote chapter and verse for something** = to say exactly where to find a piece of information

③ **version**
['vɜrʃn] *noun*
(a) description of what happened as seen by one person; *the victim told her version of events to the jury*
(b) type of a work of art, model of automobile, etc.; *this is the movie version of the novel*; *he bought the cheapest version available*
(c) translation; *here is the Chinese version of the book*

④ **versus**
['vɜrsəs or vi] *preposition (in a sports match, a civil court case)* against (NOTE: usually written **v.** *or* **vs.**: St. Louis Rams vs. Tennessee Titans; Reilly v. Internal Revenue Service)

④ **vertical**
['vɜrtɪkl]
1 *adjective*
standing or rising straight up; *he drew a few vertical lines to represent trees*; *we looked at the vertical cliff and wondered how to climb it*
2 *noun*
the vertical = position of something pointing straight up and down; *the ship was listing several degrees from the vertical*

① **very**
['veri]
1 *adverb (used to make an adjective or adverb stronger)* *it's very hot in the car - why don't you open a window?*; *can you see that tall pine tree over there?*; *the time seemed to go very quickly when we were on vacation*
2 *adjective*
exactly the right one, exactly the same; *she's the very person you want to talk to*; *the scene takes place at the very beginning of the book*; *he did his very best to get tickets*

◇ **very many**
['veri 'meni] *adjective*
a lot of; *very many small birds failed to survive the winter*; **not very many** = not a lot of; *there weren't very many visitors at the exhibition* (NOTE: **not very many** is used with things you can count: **not very many automobiles**)

◇ **very much**
['veri 'mʌtʃ]
1 *adverb*
greatly; *I don't like chocolate very much*; *thank you very much for your check*; *it's very much hotter today than it was yesterday*
2 *adjective*

not very much = not a lot of; *she doesn't have very much work to do at the office*; *they haven't got very much money* (NOTE: **not very much** is used with things which you cannot count: **not very much money**)

② **vessel**
['vesl] *noun*
(a) *(formal)* container for liquid; *experts on the Roman period think it was a form of ancient drinking vessel*; **blood vessel** = any tube which carries blood around the body; *arteries and veins are both blood vessels*
(b) ship; *vessels from all countries crowded into the harbor*; **merchant vessel** = commercial ship that carries a cargo

① **vest**
[vest] *noun*
short coat with buttons and without any sleeves, which is worn over a shirt and under a jacket; *he wore a pale gray vest with a black jacket*

② **vet**
[vet]
1 *noun*
(informal) veterinary surgeon; *we have to take the cat to the vet*; *the vet has an office on Main Street*
2 *verb*
to examine carefully; *all candidates have to be vetted by the chief executive officer* (NOTE: **vetting - vetted**)

③ **veteran**
['vetrən]
1 *noun*
(a) soldier, sailor, etc., who has fought in a war; *the veterans visited war graves on the 50th anniversary of the battle*; **Veterans Day** = November 11, when members of the armed forces who died in battle are remembered; *old soldiers were wearing their decorations for the Veterans Day parade*
(b) person who has a lot of experience; *he is a veteran of many takeover bids*
2 *adjective*
who has a lot of experience; *she's a veteran war correspondent*; *the veteran movie director died this week*

③ **veterinarian**
[vetərə'neəriən] *noun*
doctor who specializes in treating sick animals; *the veterinarian will examine the horses* (NOTE: abbreviated to **vet**)

④ **veterinary**
['vetrənri] *adjective*
referring to the treatment of sick animals; *he always wanted to study veterinary medicine*

③ **veto**
['vitəʊ]
1 *noun*
ban, order not to allow something to become law; *the president exercised his veto*; *the U.S. used its veto in the Security Council*; **power of veto** = power to forbid something; *the president*

has (the) power of veto over bills passed by Congress (NOTE: plural is **vetoes**)

2 *verb*

to forbid; *the proposal was vetoed by the president*; *the council has vetoed all plans to hold protest marches downtown*

④ **via**

['vaɪə] *preposition*

through; *we drove to New Mexico via Texas*; *we are sending the payment via our office in New York*; *the shipment is going via the Suez Canal*

④ **viable**

['vaɪəbl] *adjective*

able to work in practice; *the project is certainly viable*; **not commercially viable** = not likely to make a profit; *it is no longer viable to extract tin from these mines*

④ **vibrant**

['vaɪbrənt] *adjective*

(a) *(person)* full of energy; *a teacher with a vibrant personality*

(b) bright; *he likes vibrant blues and greens while I prefer browns and greys*

④ **vibrate**

[vaɪ'breɪt] *verb*

to move slightly, but rapidly and continuously; *the windows vibrate whenever a plane flies over the house*; *the new car vibrates more than the old one*

④ **vicar**

['vɪkər] *noun*

priest in charge of a parish; *we have to see the vicar to arrange a date for the wedding*

④ **vice**

[vaɪs] *noun*

(a) wicked way of living, especially involving sex; **vice squad** = police department dealing with sexual offenses, etc.

(b) particular form of being wicked; *jealousy is a vice*

(c) bad habit; *I have all the usual vices - I smoke, I drink, I drive too fast*

① **vice president**

['vaɪs'prezɪdənt] *noun*

(a) deputy to a president; *when President Kennedy was assassinated, Vice-President Johnson became president*

(b) one of the executive directors of a corporation

COMMENT: in the U.S.A., the Vice-President is the president (i.e. the chairman) of the Senate. He also succeeds a President if the President dies in office

③ **vicious**

['vɪʃəs] *adjective*

(a) cruel and wicked; *a vicious attack on an elderly lady*

(b) **vicious circle** = situation where one problem leads to another that is worse than the

first; *he found it hard to break out of the vicious circle of drugs, followed by crime and imprisonment*

③ **victim**

['vɪktɪm] *noun*

person who is attacked, who is in an accident; *the victims of the car crash were taken to the local hospital*; *she was the victim of a brutal attack outside her front door*; *earthquake victims were housed in tents*

④ **victimize**

['vɪktɪmaɪz] *verb*

to treat someone less fairly than others; *the prison governor was accused of victimizing young prisoners*; *she was victimized at school because she was fat*

③ **victor**

['vɪktər] *noun*

(formal) person who wins a fight, game or battle; *the victor ran around the track waving a flag*

① **victory**

['vɪktrɪ] *noun*

winning of a battle, a fight, a game, etc.; *they won a clear victory in the general election*; *the guerrillas won a victory over the government troops*; *the American victory in the Olympics*

① **video**

['vɪdiəʊ] *noun*

(a) electronic system which records, stores and reproduces pictures and sound; *using video, it is possible to show students the mistakes they have made and get them to correct them*

(b) text, film or graphics which can be viewed on a television or monitor; *he was watching a video of the movie*; *she borrowed the video from the public library*

④ **videotape**

['vɪdiəʊteɪp]

1 *noun*

magnetic tape on which pictures and sound can be recorded for playing back on a television set; *he made a videotape of the movie*

2 *verb*

to record pictures, a TV program or movie, etc., on tape; *I didn't see the program because I was at work, but I've videotaped it*

① **view**

[vju]

1 *noun*

(a) what you can see from a certain place; *you can get a good view of the sea from the church tower*; *we asked for a room with a sea view and were given one looking out over the train station*

(b) photograph or picture; *here is a view of our house taken last year*

(c) way of thinking about something; *in his view, the government ought to act now*; **point of view** = way of thinking; *try to see it from a teacher's point of view*; **to take a dim view of something** = not to think very highly of something; *he takes a dim view of members of staff turning up late for work*

(d) in view of = because of; *in view of the stormy weather, we decided not to go sailing*; (formal) **with a view to** = with the aim of; *they bought the store with a view to converting it into a restaurant*; **on view** = exhibited for people to look at; *the final year students' work is on view in the college art gallery*

2 *verb*

(a) to watch; *the president viewed the procession from a special stand*; *he viewed the fireworks on TV*

(b) to consider; *he views the change of government as a disaster for the country*

③ **viewer**

['vjuər] *noun*

(a) person who watches TV; *the program attracted ten million viewers*

(b) small device through which you can look at color slides; *she bought a little viewer to look at her slides*

④ **viewpoint**

['vjupɔint] *noun*

particular way of thinking about things; *his viewpoint is not the same as mine*; *she looks at the project from the viewpoint of a mother with young children*

④ **vigorous**

['vigrəs] *adjective*

very energetic, very strong; *he went for a vigorous run around the park*; *the plant has put out some vigorous shoots*

④ **villa**

['vilə] *noun*

large country house or seaside house, usually in a warm country; *he is staying in a villa on the Mediterranean*; *they are renting a villa in Greece for August*

① **village**

['vilidʒ] *noun*

small group of houses in the country, like a little town, with a church, and usually some stores; *they live in a little village in the Swiss Alps*; *the store in the village sells just about everything we need*; *they are closing the school in our village because there aren't enough children*

② **vine**

[vain] *noun*

climbing plant; *the sides of the hills are covered with vines*

② **vinegar**

['vinigər] *noun*

liquid with a sharp taste, made from sour wine, used in cooking; *vinaigrette is a mixture of oil and vinegar*

② **vineyard**

['vinjəd] *noun*

area planted with vines for making wine; *we visited vineyards in California and bought some wine*

④ **vintage**

['vintidʒ] *noun*

(a) fine wine made in a particular year; *1995 was a very good vintage*; *what vintage is it? - it's a 1968*; **vintage wine** = fine, expensive old wine made in a good year

(b) year when something was made; *the kitchen is equipped with a 1950 vintage oven*

(c) of typical high quality associated with a certain person; *the movie is vintage Laurel and Hardy*

③ **vinyl**

['vainl] *noun*

type of strong plastic sheet which can be made to look like other materials such as leather, tiles, etc.; *they covered the floor with vinyl tiles to look like marble*

② **violate**

['vaiəleit] *verb*

to break a rule, to go against the law; *the council has violated the planning regulations*; *the rebels violated the conditions of the peace treaty*; *the country has violated the international treaty banning the testing of nuclear weapons*

② **violence**

['vaiələns] *noun*

(a) action which is intended to hurt someone; *acts of violence must be punished*

(b) great force; *the violence of her reaction surprised everyone*

③ **violent**

['vaiələnt] *adjective*

(a) very strong; *the discussion led to a violent argument*; *a violent snowstorm blew all night*

(b) very severe; *he had a violent headache*

(c) who commits acts of violence; *he husband was a very violent man*; **violent death** = death caused by an act of violence; *she died a violent death*

③ **violently**

['vaiələntli] *adverb*

(a) roughly, with force; *this horse threw him violently onto the ground*; *she rolled the bottle violently across the table*

(b) strongly, with great feeling; *she violently rejected the accusations made against her*; *he reacted violently to the injection*; *the mushrooms made her violently sick*

② **violin**

[vaiə'lin] *noun*

string instrument played with a bow; *everyone listened to him playing the violin*

③ **VIP**

[viai'pi] = VERY IMPORTANT PERSON; *seats have been arranged for the VIPs at the front of the hall*; *we laid on VIP treatment for our visitors*; *we got VIP treatment when we visited China*; **VIP lounge** = special room at an airport for important travelers; **VIP suite** = specially luxurious suite at an airport or in a hotel, for very important people

④ **virgule**
['vɜrgjul] *noun*
printing sign (/) used to show an alternative; *all members/visitors must sign the register* (NOTE: also called **slash**)

④ **virtual**
['vɜrtʃuəl] *adjective*
almost, nearly; *the company has a virtual monopoly of French wine imports*

④ **virtually**
['vɜrtʃuəli] *adverb*
almost; *the price of these shirts has been reduced so much that we're virtually giving them away*; *it's virtually impossible to get tickets for the concert*

④ **virtue**
['vɜrtju] *noun*
(a) particularly good character; good quality; *hard work is his principal virtue*
(b) special thing which gives you an advantage; *the virtue of owning an automobile is that you have complete freedom of movement*
(c) *(formal)* **by virtue of** = as a result of; *by virtue of his father who was born in Boston he can claim U.S. nationality*

④ **virus**
['vaɪrəs] *noun*
(a) tiny cell that can only develop in other cells and often destroys them; *scientists have isolated a new flu virus*
(b) hidden routine placed in a computer program, which corrupts or destroys files; *you must check the program for viruses* (NOTE: plural is **viruses**)

> COMMENT: many common diseases such as measles or the common cold are caused by viruses; these diseases cannot be treated with antibiotics

④ **visa**
['vizə] *noun*
special stamp on a passport allowing you to enter a country; *she filled out her visa application form*; *he applied for a tourist visa*; *you will need a visa to go to China*; **entry visa** = visa allowing someone to enter a country; **multiple entry visa** = visa allowing someone to enter a country many times; **tourist visa** = visa which allows a person to visit a country for a short time on vacation; **transit visa** = visa which allows someone to spend a short time in one country while traveling to another country

③ **vise**
[vaɪs] *noun*
tool that screws tight to hold something, so that a workman can work on it; *he put the piece of wood in a vise before cutting it*

② **visible**
['vizbl] *adjective*
which can be seen; *the marks of the bullets were clearly visible on the armored car*; *everywhere in the forest there are visible signs of the effects of acid rain*; **visible imports** *or* **exports** = real products which are imported *or* **exported**; *compare* INVISIBLE

③ **visibly**
['vizibli] *adverb*
in a way which everyone can see; *she was visibly annoyed by the television cameras outside her house*

② **vision**
['viʒn] *noun*
(a) eyesight, your ability to see; *after the age of 50, the many people's vision begins to fail*; **field of vision** = area that you can see over clearly; **tunnel vision** = (i) seeing only the area immediately in front of the eye; (ii) having the tendency to concentrate on only one aspect of a problem; **twenty/twenty vision (20/20 vision)** = perfectly normal eyesight
(b) what you can see from where you are; *from the driver's seat you have excellent all-round vision*
(c) ability to look and plan ahead; *her vision of a free and liberal society*; *we need a man of vision as college president*
(d) thing which you imagine; *he had visions of himself stuck in New York City with no passport and no money*; *she had visions of him being arrested for drug smuggling*

① **visit**
['vizɪt]
1 *noun*
short stay with someone, short stay in a town or a country; *they had a visit from the police*; *we will be making a short visit to Chicago next week*; *the manager is on a business visit to China*; **to pay a visit to** = to go and see; *while we're in town, let's pay a visit to the local museum*; *we will pay my sister a visit on her birthday*
2 *verb*
to stay a short time with someone, to stay a short time in a town or country; *I am on my way to visit my sister in the hospital*; *they are away visiting friends in the north of the country*; *the group of tourists are going to visit the glass factory*; **visiting hours** *or* **visiting times** = times of day when friends are allowed into a hospital to visit patients; **visiting team** = opposing team that have come to play against the home team

① **visitor**
['vizɪtər] *noun*
(a) person who comes to visit; *how many visitors come to the museum each year?*; *we had a surprise visitor yesterday - the bank manager!*; **visitors' book** = book in which visitors to a museum or guests at a hotel write comments about the place; **visitors' bureau** *or* **visitor information center** = office that deals with visitors' questions; **health visitor** = nurse who visits people in their homes to check their health; **prison visitor** = member of a group of people who visit, inspect and report on conditions in a

prison; **summer visitor** = person or a bird that only comes to this country in the summer
(b) visitors = VISITING TEAM

③ **visual**
['vɪʒuəl] *adjective*
referring to seeing; **visual aids** = maps, slides, films, etc., used to illustrate a lecture; *using slides or other visual aids would make the lecture more interesting*; **visual arts** = arts such as painting, sculpture, etc., which can be seen, as opposed to music which is listened to; *photography is one of the visual arts*

③ **visualize**
['vɪʒuəlaɪz] *verb*
to have a picture of something in your mind; *I can just visualize myself driving a sports car on the freeway; can you visualize her as manager of the store?*

④ **vital**
['vaɪtl] *adjective*
(a) very important; *it is vital that the murderer should be caught before he commits another crime*; *oxygen is vital to human life*
(b) vigorous, energetic; *his vital energy comes out in his paintings*
(c) vital organs = the most important organs in the body (such as the heart, lungs or brain) without which a human being cannot live

① **vitamin**
['vaɪtəmɪn] *noun*
essential substance which is found in food and is needed for growth and health; *make sure your diet contains enough vitamins*

③ **vivid**
['vɪvɪd] *adjective*
(a) very lively, very like the real thing; *she has a vivid imagination*; *the play is a vivid picture of country life*; *I had a really vivid dream last night*; *she gave a vivid account of her experiences at the hands of the kidnap gang*
(b) very bright; *a field of vivid yellow flowers*; *the vivid colors of a Caribbean beach*

② **vocabulary**
[və'kæbjʊləri] *noun*
(a) words used by a person or group of persons; *reading stories to little children helps them expand their vocabulary*; *she reads a lot of French newspapers to improve her vocabulary*; *the dictionary will give you some of the specialist legal vocabulary you will need in your job*
(b) printed list of words; *there is a Spanish-English vocabulary at the back of the book* (NOTE: plural is **vocabularies**)

③ **vocal**
['vəʊkl] *adjective*
(a) referring to the voice; *singers need to do vocal exercises daily*; **vocal cords** = folds in the throat which are brought together to make sounds when air passes between them
(b) very loud (in protest); *the protesters were very vocal at the demonstration*

④ **vogue**
[vəʊg] *noun*
fashion; *are those silver shoes the latest vogue?*; *the vogue for wearing bright red suspenders seems to have disappeared*; **in vogue** = fashionable; *this year, black is back in vogue again*

① **voice**
[vɔɪs]
1 *noun*
(a) sound made when you speak or sing; *I didn't recognize his voice over the telephone*; *the chairman spoke for a few minutes in a low voice*
(b) to lose your voice = not to be able to speak; *she has a sore throat and has lost her voice*; **to raise your voice** = to start to shout; **at the top of your voice** = very loudly; *the little boy suddenly said "look at her funny hat" at the top of his voice*
2 *verb*
to tell what you think; *she voiced her objections to the plan*

② **voice mail**
['vɔɪs 'meɪl] *noun*
type of telephone answering system, where messages can be left for a person; *he wasn't in his office, so I left a message on his voice mail*

② **volcano**
[vɒl'keɪnəʊ] *noun*
mountain with a hole on the top through which red hot rocks, ash and gas can come out; *the volcano erupted last year* (NOTE: plural is **volcanoes**)

COMMENT: volcanoes occur along faults in the Earth's surface and exist in well-known chains. Some are extinct (they no longer erupt), but some are always active, in that they send out gas and smoke all the time. Volcanoes are popular tourist attractions: the best-known in North America is Mount St. Helen's in Washington State. In South America there are volcanoes all along the chain of the Andes, from Popocatapetl in Mexico to Aconcagua in Chile

② **volume**
['vɒljum] *noun*
(a) one book, especially one in a series; *have you read the third volume of his history of medieval Europe?*
(b) amount of sound; *she turned down the volume on the radio*; *he drives with the automobile radio on at full volume*
(c) capacity, amount which is contained inside something; *what is the volume of this barrel?*
(d) amount of something; *the volume of traffic on the freeway was far more than usual*

③ **voluntarily**
['vɒləntrəli] *adverb*
willingly; *he surrendered voluntarily to the police*

③ **voluntary**
['vɒləntri] *adjective*
(a) done because you want to do it, and without being paid; *many retired people do voluntary work*
(b) done willingly, without being forced; *he made a voluntary contribution to the fund*; **voluntary retirement** = situation where a worker asks to be made retired, usually in return for a large payment

② **volunteer**
[vɒlən'tɪər]
1 *noun*
(a) person who offers to do something without being paid or being forced to do it; *the school relies on volunteers to help with the fair*; *the information desk is manned by volunteers*; **volunteer organization** = organization which does not receive funds from the government but relies on contributions from the public or from business
(b) soldier who has asked to join the army, without being forced to do so; *the volunteers had two weeks' training and then were sent to the front line*
2 *verb*
(a) to offer to do something without being paid or being forced to do it; *he volunteered to collect the entrance tickets*; *will anyone volunteer for the job of washing the dishes?*
(b) to join the armed services because you want to, without being forced; *he volunteered for the U.S. Navy*
(c) to give information without being forced to do so; *she volunteered a statement to the police*

① **vote**
[vəʊt]
1 *noun*
(a) marking a paper, holding up your hand, etc., to show your opinion or who you want to be elected; *how many votes did you get?*; *there were only ten votes against the plan*; **to take a vote on a proposal** *or* **to put a proposal to the vote** = to ask people present at a meeting to say if they agree or do not agree with the proposal; **to cast a vote** = to vote; *the number of votes cast in the election was 125,458*
(b) act of voting; **vote of no confidence** = vote to show disapproval of the government, etc.; *they passed a vote of no confidence in the chairman*; **postal vote** = election where the voters send in their voting papers by mail; postal ballot; *the result of the postal vote will be known next week*
(c) the right to vote in elections; *only in 1920 were women given the vote*
(d) number of votes made by a group of voters; *no one knows where the youth vote will go*
2 *verb*
to mark a paper, to hold up your hand, etc., to show your opinion or who you want to be elected; *fifty percent of the people voted in the election*; *we all voted to go on strike*; **to vote for a proposal** *or* **to vote against a proposal** = to say that you agree or do not agree with a proposal; *twenty people actually voted for the proposal to knock down the old church*

③ **vote of thanks**
['vəʊt əv 'θæŋks] *noun*
situation where someone has done something and is given an official thank you by a vote of a whole committee; *she proposed a vote of thanks to the outgoing chairman*

② **voter**
['vəʊtər] *noun*
person who votes or who has the right to vote; *voters stayed at home because of the bad weather*; *the voters were lining up outside the polling stations from early morning*; **floating voter** = person who is not sure which party to vote for in an election; **register of voters** = list of the names of people who can vote in an election

④ **voucher**
['vaʊtʃər] *noun*
paper that is given instead of money; *enclosed is a voucher to be presented at the reception desk of the hotel when you arrive*; *with every $30 of purchases, the customer gets a cash voucher to the value of $3*

③ **vow**
[vaʊ]
1 *noun*
solemn promise; *he made a vow to visit the holy places in the Near East*; *she vowed to have her revenge but she died before she could keep her vow*
2 *verb*
(formal) to make a solemn promise to do something; *he vowed to pay the money back*

① **vowel**
['vaʊəl] *noun*
one of the five letters (a, e, i, o, u) which represent sounds made without using the teeth, tongue or lips; *"b" and "t" are consonants, while "e" and "i" are vowels* (NOTE: the letters representing sounds which are not vowels are **consonants**; note also that in some languages "y" is a vowel)

② **voyage**
['vɔɪdʒ] *noun*
long journey, especially by ship or spacecraft; *the voyages of Sir Francis Drake*; *the voyage of Explorer to Mars*

③ **vs.**
['vɜrsəs] *see* VERSUS

④ **vulnerable**
['vʌlnərəbl] *adjective*
who or which can easily be hurt; *the government is vulnerable to criticism*; *children of that age are particularly vulnerable*; *small babies are vulnerable to infection*

Ww

① **W, w**
['dʌbl ju]
twenty-third letter of the alphabet, between V and X; *"one" is pronounced as if it starts with a W*

③ **wag**
[wæg] *verb*
to move from side to side or up and down; *the dog ran up to him, wagging its tail* (NOTE: wagging - wagged)

② **wage** *or* **wages**
[weɪdʒ *or* 'weɪdʒɪz]
1 *noun*
money paid, usually in cash each week, to a worker for work done; *all work came to a stop when the firm couldn't pay the workers' wages*; *her wages can't keep up with the cost of living*; *the company pays quite good wages*; *she is earning a good wage or good wages in the pizza place*; **wage freeze** = period when wages are not allowed to increase; **basic wage** = normal pay without any extra payments; *the basic wage is $170 a week, but you can expect to earn more than that with overtime*; **hourly wage** *or* **wage per hour** = amount of money paid for an hour's work; *they are paid by the hour and the hourly wage is very low*; **living wage** = enough money to live on; *he doesn't earn a living wage*; **minimum wage** = lowest hourly wage that a company can legally pay its workers; *a statutory minimum wage has existed in some countries for years* (NOTE: used both in the singular and the plural: **he doesn't earn a living wage; her wages are $750 a week**)
2 *verb*
to **wage war on** = to fight against; *the government is waging war on poverty*; *the police are waging war on drug dealers*

① **wagon**
['wægn] *noun*
(a) *(old)* heavy cart pulled by horses
(b) *(informal)* **on the wagon** = not drinking alcohol; *he's been on the wagon for the last three months*

② **waist**
[weɪst] *noun*
(a) narrower part of the body between the bottom of the chest and the hips; *she measures 32 inches around the waist or she has a 32-inch waist*
(b) part of a piece of clothing such as a skirt, pants or dress, that goes around the middle of your body; *the waist of these pants is too small for me* (NOTE: do not confuse with **waste**)

① **wait**
[weɪt]
1 *verb*
(a) to stay where you are and not do anything until something happens or someone comes; *wait here while I call an ambulance*; *they had been waiting for half an hour in the rain before the bus finally arrived*; *wait a minute, my shoe is undone*; *don't wait for me, I'll be late*; *we gave our order half an hour ago, but are still waiting for the first course*; *the man didn't come on Friday, so we had to wait until Monday to have the fridge repaired*
(b) to **keep someone waiting** = to make someone wait because you are late; *the boss doesn't like being kept waiting*; *sorry to have kept you waiting!*
(c) to **wait on someone** = to serve food and drink to someone, especially in a restaurant; to **wait on someone hand and foot** = to do everything for someone; *he just sits around watching TV, and his mother waits on him hand and foot*
(d) to **wait a meal for someone** = not to serve a meal at the usual time because you are waiting for someone to arrive; *don't wait dinner for me, I'm going to be late*
2 *noun*
time spent waiting until something happens or arrives; *you've just missed the bus - you will have a very long wait for the next one*; to **lie in wait for someone** = to hide and wait for someone to come so as to attack him; *the lions were lying in wait in the long grass* (NOTE: do not confuse with **weight**)

② **waiter**
['weɪtər] *noun*
man who brings food and drink to customers in a restaurant; *the waiter still hasn't brought us the first course*; *shall we give the waiter a tip?*; **headwaiter** = person in charge of other waiters; *see also* WAITRESS

③ **waiting list**
['weɪtɪŋ 'lɪst] *noun*
list of people waiting for a service or medical treatment; *there is a waiting list of people hoping to get on the flight*

③ **waiting room**
['weɪtɪŋ 'rum] *noun*
room where you wait at a doctor's, dentist's or at a train station; *take a seat in the waiting room - the dentist will be free in a few minutes*

① **waitress**
['weɪtrəs] *noun*
woman who brings food and drink to customers in a restaurant; *the waitress brought us the menu; how much shall we give the waitress as a tip?*; *see also* WAITER (NOTE: plural is **waitresses**)

③ **wait up**
['weɪt 'ʌp] *verb*
not to go to bed because you are waiting for someone; *don't wait up for us - we'll be very late*

① **wake**
[weɪk]
1 *verb*
(a) to stop someone's sleep; *the telephone woke her or she was woken by the telephone; I banged on her door, but I can't wake her; he asked to be woken at 7:00*
(b) to stop sleeping; *he woke suddenly, feeling drops of water falling on his head* (NOTE: **waking - woke** [wəʊk] **- has woken**)
2 *noun*
(a) white waves following a boat as it goes through the water; *the ferry's wake rocked the little boat*
(b) in the wake of = following something, immediately after something; *the management has to decide what to do in the wake of the sales director's resignation*
(c) meeting of people before a funeral

② **wake up**
['weɪk 'ʌp] *verb*
(a) to stop someone's sleep; *he was woken up by the sound of the dog barking or the barking of the dogs woke him up*
(b) to stop sleeping; *she woke up in the middle of the night, thinking she had heard a noise; come on, wake up! it's past ten o'clock; he woke up to find water coming through the roof of the tent;* **wake-up call** = phone call from the hotel switchboard to wake a guest up
(c) to wake up to = to realize; *when is he going to wake up to the fact that he is never going to be promoted?*

① **Wales**
[weɪlz] *noun*
country to the west of England, forming part of the United Kingdom; *there are some high mountains in North Wales* (NOTE: capital: **Cardiff**; people: **the Welsh**; languages: **Welsh, English**)

① **walk**
[wɔk]
1 *verb*
(a) to go on foot; *the baby is ten months old, and is just starting to walk; she was walking along Main Street on her way to the bank; the protesters walked across the bridge; the visitors walked around the factory;* **to walk someone home** = to go with someone who is walking home; *it was getting late, so I walked her home*
(b) to take an animal for a walk; *he's gone to walk the dog in the fields*
(c) *(in baseball)* (i) to go to first base after the pitcher has thrown four balls; (ii) to throw four balls to a batter, allowing the batter to go to first base; *he walked and the player on first base then went to second base; the pitcher walked three players*
2 *noun*
(a) usually pleasant journey on foot; *let's all go for a walk in the park*
(b) going on foot; *it's only a short walk to the beach; it's only five minutes' walk from the office to the bank or the bank is only a minute's walk from the office*
(c) path where you can walk; *we spent three days walking along one of the long-distance walks in the hills*
(d) organized route for walking; *we went on a walk around Dickens' London; are you coming on the sponsored walk for refugees?*

③ **walk about**
['wɔk ə'baʊt] *verb*
to walk in various directions; *we walked about looking for a restaurant*

① **walker**
['wɔkər] *noun*
person who goes walking for pleasure and exercise; *he's an excellent walker, and goes walking in Oregon every summer*

③ **walk off**
['wɔk 'ɒf] *verb*
(a) to go away on foot; *she walked off and left him holding the shopping; the builders walked off the site because they said it was too dangerous*
(b) to walk off your dinner = to go for a walk to help you digest your dinner

③ **walk off with**
['wɔk 'ɒf wɪð] *verb*
(a) to win; *she walked off with first prize*
(b) to steal; *the burglar walked off with all my silver*

① **walk out**
['wɔk 'aʊt] *verb*
(a) to go out on foot; *she walked out of the house and down the street*
(b) to go out angrily; *he walked out of the restaurant, saying that the service was too slow*
(c) *(of workers)* to go on strike, to stop working and leave your office or factory; *the office staff walked out in protest*
(d) to walk out on someone = to leave someone suddenly; *she walked out on her husband and went to live with her mother; our head salesman walked out on us just as we were starting our fall sales campaign*

① **walk up**
['wɔk 'ʌp] *verb*
(a) to climb on foot; *I never take the elevator - I always walk up the three flights of stairs to my office*
(b) **to walk up to someone** = to come or go up to someone on foot; *she walked up to me and asked if I needed any help*

① **wall**
[wɔl] *noun*
(a) bricks, stones, etc., built up to make one of the sides of a building, of a room or to surround a space; *the walls of the restaurant are decorated with pictures of movie stars; there's a clock on the wall behind my desk; he got into the house by climbing over the garden wall; the garden is surrounded by an old stone wall*
(b) *(informal)* **to drive** *or* **send someone up the wall** = to make someone very annoyed; *the noise of the drilling in the road outside the office is driving me up the wall*
(c) **wall of silence** = plot by everyone to say nothing about what has happened; *the police investigation met with a wall of silence*
(d) **walls** = thick stone construction around an old town; *you can walk on the old town walls here*

① **wallet**
['wɒlɪt] *noun*
small flat leather case for credit cards and banknotes, carried in your pocket; *someone stole my wallet in the crowd; his wallet was stolen from his back pocket; don't leave your wallet on the automobile seat*

① **wallpaper**
['wɔlpeɪpər]
1 *noun*
paper with different patterns on it, covering the walls of a room; *the wallpaper was light green to match the carpet*
2 *verb*
to stick wallpaper on walls; *she spent the weekend wallpapering the dining room*

① **Wall Street**
['wɔl 'strit] *noun*
(a) street in New York City where the Stock Exchange is situated; *he walked along Wall Street, looking for the company's offices*
(b) American finance center in New York City; *Wall Street reacted cautiously to the interest rise* (NOTE: here the name of the street is used to mean the U.S. financial markets in general)

① **walnut**
['wɒlnʌt] *noun*
hard round nut with a wrinkled inside part; *he cracked the walnuts with his hammer; a scoop of toffee and walnut ice cream*

① **wander**
['wɒndər] *verb*
(a) to walk around without any particular aim; *they wandered around the town in the rain;* **to wander away** *or* **wander off** = to walk away from where you are supposed to be; *two of the party wandered off into the market*
(b) to stop thinking about the current problem and think about something else; *sorry - my mind was wandering, thinking about the garden;* **he is old and his mind is wandering** = he no longer thinks clearly

② **want**
[wɒnt]
1 *verb*
(a) to hope that you will do something, that something will happen, that you will get something; *she wants a new car for her birthday; where do you want to go for your vacation?; he wants to be a teacher; do you want any more tea?*
(b) to ask someone to do something; *the manager wants me to go and see him; I want those windows painted*
(c) to need; *with five children, what they want is a bigger house; the kitchen ceiling wants painting*
(d) to look for someone; *the bank manager has disappeared and is wanted by the police*
2 *noun*
(a) lack of something; **in want of something** = needing something; *the kitchen is in want of a good clean; he looks as though he's in want of a good meal;* **for want of something better** = as something better is not available; *for want of something better to do we went to the movie theater*
(b) something that you want very much; *their greatest want is for warm clothes;* **want ads** = small advertisements listed in a newspaper under special headings (such as "property for sale" or "jobs wanted"); **wants** = things needed; *their wants are too numerous to count*

④ **wanton**
['wɒntn] *adjective*
wild or undisciplined; *his wanton disregard for the rules; reports of wanton killing reach us every day*

① **war**
[wɔr] *noun*
(a) fighting between countries; *millions of soldiers and civilians were killed during the war; the two countries are at war;* **to declare war on a country** = to state formally that a war has begun against a country; **civil war** = situation inside a country where groups of armed people fight against each other or against the government; *see also* PRISONER OF WAR
(b) strong action against something; *the police have declared war on the drug dealers*
(c) argument between companies; **price war** *or* **price-cutting war** = competition between companies to get a larger market share by cutting prices; *right now there's a price war between the two airlines*

② **ward**
[wɔrd]
1 *noun*

(a) room or set of rooms in a hospital, with beds for patients; *the children's ward is at the end of the hall*; *she was taken into the accident and emergency ward*

(b) division of a town for administrative purposes; *he was elected councilor for the fifth ward*

(c) young person protected by a guardian or a court; **ward of court** = young child who is under the protection of the court

2 *verb*

to ward something off = to keep something away; *they keep a flock of geese in the warehouse to ward off thieves*

② **warden**

['wɔrdən] *noun*

(a) person in charge of an institution; *ask the warden if we can visit on Sundays*

(b) person who looks after or guards something; **park warden** *or* **game warden** = person who looks after a park or hunting and fishing laws; *the park warden told us not to let our dog run loose*

② **wardrobe**

['wɔrdrəub] *noun*

(a) clothes; *she bought a whole new wardrobe for her vacation*

(b) tall cupboard in which you hang your clothes; *he moved the wardrobe from the landing into the bedroom*

② **warehouse**

['weərhaus]

1 *noun*

large building where goods are stored; *our products are dispatched from the central warehouse to stores all over the country*

2 *verb*

to store goods in a warehouse; *they have offered to warehouse for us on a temporary basis*

③ **warfare**

['wɔrfeər] *noun*

fighting a war, especially the method of fighting; *the arguments between the countries soon developed into open warfare*; *the enemy resorted to guerrilla warfare*; *governments are trying to ban chemical warfare*

① **warm**

[wɔrm]

1 *adjective*

(a) quite hot; *the temperature is below freezing outside but it's nice and warm in the office*; *the children tried to keep warm by playing baseball*; *are you warm enough, or do you want another blanket?*; *the winter sun can be quite warm in February*

(b) pleasant and friendly; *we had a warm welcome from our friends*; *she has a really warm personality* (NOTE: **warmer - warmest**)

2 *verb*

(a) to make hotter; *come and warm your hands by the fire*; *if you're cold, I'll warm some soup*; *the greenhouse effect has the result of*

warming *the general temperature of the Earth's atmosphere*

(b) to become interested in something, to start to like someone; *she never really warmed to the subject of her college course*; *I think everyone is warming to the new boss*

③ **warming**

['wɔrmɪŋ] *noun*

making warmer; **global warming** = gradual rise in temperature over the whole of the Earth's surface, caused by the greenhouse effect

③ **warmly**

['wɔrmli] *adverb*

in a warm way; *they greeted us very warmly when we arrived*; *I warmly welcome the result of the election*; *wrap up warmly if you're going for a walk in the snow*

① **warmth**

[wɔrmθ] *noun*

(a) being or feeling warm; *it was cold and raining outside, and he looked forward to the warmth of his home*

(b) enthusiasm for something; *the management's lack of warmth for the project*

① **warm up**

['wɔrm 'ʌp] *verb*

(a) to make hotter; *a cup of coffee will soon warm you up*; *I'll just warm up some soup for supper*

(b) to practice or exercise; *the orchestra is warming up before the concert*; *the runners were warming up on the track*

② **warn**

[wɔrn] *verb*

(a) to inform someone of a possible danger; *we were warned to boil all drinking water*; *children are warned not to play on the frozen lake*; *the group was warned to look out for pickpockets*; *the guide warned us that there might be snakes in the ruins*

(b) to inform someone in advance; *the labor union has warned that there will be a strike tomorrow*; *the weather forecast warned of storms across the Gulf of Mexico* (NOTE: you warn someone **of** something, or **that** something may happen)

① **warning**

['wɔrnɪŋ]

1 *noun*

(a) information about a possible danger; *he shouted a warning to the children*; *the government issued a warning about traveling in some countries in the area*

(b) written or spoken notice to an employee telling him or her that they will be dismissed or punished if they don't stop behaving in a certain way; *when he was late for the third time this week, he got a written warning*

(c) **without warning** = unexpectedly; *the car in front braked without warning and I couldn't stop in time*

2 *adjective*

which informs about a danger; *red warning flags are raised if the sea is dangerous*; *warning notices were put up around the building site*

② **warrant**
['wɒrənt]
1 *noun*

official document from a court permitting someone to do something; *the judge issued a warrant for her arrest*
2 *verb*

(a) to guarantee that something is of good quality, will work properly, etc.; *all the spare parts are warranted for six months*
(b) to be a good reason for; *our sales in Louisiana do not warrant six trips a year to Baton Rouge by the sales director*

④ **warranty**
['wɒrənti] *noun*

guarantee, a legal document which promises that goods purchased will work properly or that an item is of good quality; *the automobile is sold with a twelve-month warranty*; *the warranty covers spare parts but not labor costs* (NOTE: plural is **warranties**)

② **warrior**
['wɒriər] *noun*

(formal) person who fights in battle; *thousands of warriors charged at the enemy, waving spears*

④ **wary**
['weəri] *adjective*

careful because of possible problems; *I am very wary of any of his ideas for making money*; *you should be wary of going on the ice in the spring* (NOTE: **warier - wariest**)

① **was**
[wɒz] *see* BE

① **wash**
[wɒʃ]
1 *verb*

(a) to clean using water; *cooks should always wash their hands before touching food!*; *he hates washing dishes*; *I must wash the car before we go to the wedding*
(b) **to wash your hands of someone** *or* **something** = to refuse to be responsible for something; *she's washed her hands of her son since he was put in prison for drug dealing*; *he's washed his hands of the whole affair*
(c) to flow or to make flow, often carrying something; *the waves washed the boat to the shore*; *the rain washes the soil down the hill*
2 *noun*

(a) action of cleaning, using water; *the car needs a wash* ; *he's in the bathroom, having a quick wash*
(b) laundry; *she asked me to hang the wash out to dry*; *(informal)* **it will all come out in the wash** = everything will work out correctly, in spite of various mistakes having been made;

don't worry too much about the mistakes in your report - it'll all come out in the wash

② **wash away**
['wɒʃ ə'weɪ] *verb*

to remove with water; *use a bucket of water to wash away the mud from under the automobile*; *several houses were washed away by the floods*

③ **washbowl** *or* **washbasin**
['wɒʃbəʊl or 'wɒʃbeɪsn] *noun*

container, with faucets, for holding water for washing your hands and face, usually attached to the wall of a bathroom; *each bedroom in the hotel has a washbowl*

① **wash down**
['wɒʃ 'daʊn] *verb*

(a) to wash with a large amount of water; *they washed down the van with buckets of water*; *the sailors were washing down the deck*
(b) to have a drink with food; *he had a pizza washed down by a glass of beer*

① **washing**
['wɒʃɪŋ] *noun*

(a) action of washing; *the washing of the kitchen floor seems to take ages*
(b) clothes which have been washed, or which are ready to be washed; *put the washing in the washing machine*; *she hung out her washing to dry* (NOTE: no plural)

② **washing machine**
['wɒʃɪŋ mə'ʃin] *noun*

machine for washing clothes; sometimes called a washer; *he took the clothes out of the washing machine and hung them up to dry* (NOTE: a machine for washing plates and glasses is a **dishwasher**)

① **wash off**
['wɒʃ 'ɒf] *verb*

to take off by washing; *wash the mud off your shoes before you come into the house*; *the stain won't wash off*

① **washroom**
['wɒʃrum] *noun*

room with a bath, a washbowl and usually a lavatory; *there is a liquid soap dispenser in the men's washroom*

① **wasn't**
[wɒznt] *see* BE

① **wasp**
[wɒsp] *noun*

insect that can sting; *wasps buzzed around the barnyard when she disturbed their nest*

② **waste**
[weɪst]
1 *noun*

(a) unnecessary use of time or money; *it is a waste of time asking the boss for a raise*; *that computer is a waste of money - there are plenty of cheaper models*
(b) garbage, things which are no use and are thrown away; *put all your waste in the trash can*; *the garbage collectors collect household*

waste once a week; **industrial waste** = garbage from industrial processes; *the company was fined for putting industrial waste into the river*; **kitchen waste** = garbage from the kitchen, such as bits of vegetables, cans, etc.; **nuclear waste** = radioactive waste from a nuclear reactor; *the disposal of nuclear waste is causing problems worldwide*; **waste pipe** = pipe that takes used or dirty water to the drains; *the waste pipe from the kitchen sink is blocked*; **to lay waste to** = to destroy (something) completely; *the kids laid waste to our clean yard* (NOTE: no plural; do not confuse with **waist**)

2 *verb*

to use more of something than you need; *don't waste time putting your shoes on - jump out of the window now*; *we turned off all the heating so as not to waste energy*

3 *adjective*

useless, ready to be thrown away; *we have heaps of wastepaper to take to the dump*; *waste products should not be dumped in the sea*

① **wastebasket**

['weɪstbæskɪt] *noun*

small box or basket where useless papers can be put; *he threw the letter into the wastebasket*

② **wastepaper**

['weɪstpeɪpər] *noun*

useless paper, paper which is thrown away as useless; *throw those papers into the wastepaper basket*

① **watch**

[wɒtʃ]

1 *noun*

(a) device like a little clock which you wear on your wrist; *she looked at her watch impatiently*; *what time is it? - my watch has stopped* (NOTE: plural in this meaning is **watches**)

(b) looking at something carefully; *visitors should be on the watch for pickpockets*; *keep a watch on the potatoes to make sure they don't burn* (NOTE: no plural for this meaning)

(c) period when a soldier or sailor is on duty; *the men on the night watch didn't see anything unusual*

2 *verb*

(a) to look at and notice something; *did you watch the TV news last night?*; *we went to the sports field to watch the football game*; *everyone was watching the children dancing*

(b) to look at something carefully to make sure that nothing happens; *watch the saucepan - I don't want the potatoes to burn*; *can you watch the baby while I'm at the hairdresser's?*

① **watch out**

['wɒtʃ 'aut] *verb*

(a) to be careful; *watch out! there's a car coming!*

(b) **to watch out for** = to be careful to avoid; *you have to watch out for children playing in the road*; *watch out for pickpockets!*

① **water**

['wɔtər]

1 *noun*

(a) common liquid (H_2O) which forms rain, rivers, lakes, the sea, etc., and which makes up a large part of the bodies of organisms, and which you drink and use in cooking, in industry, etc.; *can we have three glasses of water, please?*; *cook the vegetables in boiling water*; *is this water safe to drink?*; *you are advised to drink only bottled water*; *the water temperature is 60°*; **drinking water** = water that you can drink safely; **running water** = water that is available in a house through water mains and faucets; *I'm not sure that all the houses here have running water*; *there is hot and cold running water in all the rooms*; **under water** = (i) under the surface of water; (ii) covered by floods; *parts of the town are under water after the river flooded*

(b) *(phrases)* **to keep your head above water** = (i) to swim with your head out of the water; (ii) to be able to keep out of trouble; **to spend money like water** = to spend large amounts of money; *when they were furnishing the house they just spent money like water*; *(informal)* **it's all water under the bridge** = a long time has passed and the situation has changed completely; **like water off a duck's back** = having no effect at all; *he was told off several times for being late, but it was like water off a duck's back*

(c) mass of water forming a lake, river, sea, etc.; *they live right on the water's edge*; *when you fly across the lake, you realize how much water there is*; *living surrounded by water, they became good sailors* (NOTE: no plural for meanings (a), (b) and (c): **some water**; **a drop of water**)

(d) **waters** = areas of sea; **territorial waters** = sea near the coast of a country, which is part of that country and governed by the laws of that country; **in international waters** *or* **outside territorial waters** = in that part of the sea which is outside any country's jurisdiction; *the attack happened in U.S. territorial waters*

2 *verb*

(a) to pour water on the soil around a plant to make it grow; *because it is hot we need to water the garden every day*; *she was watering her bed of flowers*

(b) *(of your eyes)* to fill with tears; *(of your mouth)* to fill with water; *peeling onions makes my eyes water*; **to make your mouth water** = to look so good that your mouth fills with water; *the cake makes my mouth water*; *his new automobile made her mouth water*

(c) **to water something down** = to make a statement less radical; *their proposals were watered down a lot*

③ **watercolor**

['wɔtərkʌlər] *noun*

(a) paint which is mixed with water; *I used to*

paint in oils but now I prefer water-colors; he prefers using watercolors to oils
(b) picture painted using watercolors; *there is an exhibition of watercolors in the gallery; she bought a watercolor of the church*

② **watermelon**
['wɒtərmelən] *noun*
very large type of melon with red flesh and black seeds; *she cut the watermelon into slices; they sat in the shade eating slices of watermelon*

② **waterproof**
['wɒtərpruf] *adjective*
which will not let water through; *these boots aren't waterproof - my socks are soaking wet*

② **watertight**
['wɒtərtaɪt] *adjective*
made so that water cannot get in or out; *the food has to be kept in watertight containers*

① **wave**
[weɪv]
1 *noun*
(a) ridge of water on the surface of the sea, a lake or a river; *waves were breaking on the rocks; watch out for big waves on the beach; the sea was calm, with hardly any waves*
(b) up and down movement of your hand; *she gave me a wave* = she waved her hand to me
(c) regular curve on the surface of hair; *his hair has a natural wave*
(d) sudden increase in something; *a wave of anger surged through the crowd;* **crime wave** = increase in the number of crimes; **heat wave** = sudden spell of hot weather; *the temperature went up to 110° during the heat wave in San Francisco*
(e) groups of people, machines, etc., rushing forward; *wave after wave of soldiers attacked the fort; they sent in waves of planes to bomb the harbor*
(f) airwaves = way in which radio signals move through the air; *see also* LONG WAVE, MEDIUM WAVE, SHORTWAVE
2 *verb*
(a) to move up and down in the wind; *the flags were waving outside the town hall*
(b) to make an up and down movement of the hand (usually when saying goodbye); *they waved until the car was out of sight; they waved goodbye as the boat left the harbor;* **to wave to someone** = to signal to someone by moving your hand up and down; *when I saw him I waved to him to cross the road;* **to wave someone on** = to tell someone to go on by a movement of the hand; *the police officer waved the traffic on*
(c) *(of hair)* to have a wave; *I wish my hair would wave naturally*

① **wax**
[wæks]
1 *noun*
(a) solid substance made from fat or oil, used for making candles, polish, etc.; *she brought a can*

of wax polish and started to polish the furniture
(b) soft yellow substance made by bees to build their nests; *he separated the honey from the wax and put it into jars*
(c) soft yellow substance that forms in your ears
2 *verb*
to put wax polish on furniture, etc.; *she was waxing the dining room table*

① **way**
[weɪ]
1 *noun*
(a) path or road which goes somewhere; *they are our neighbors from across the way; I'll walk the first part of the way home with you*
(b) correct path or road to go somewhere; *do you know the way to the post office?; she showed us the way to the bus station; they lost their way and had to ask for directions; I'll lead the way - just follow me*
(c) on the way = during a journey; *I'll stop at the store on my way to the restaurant; she's on her way to the office;* **well on the way to** = nearly; *the repairs to the house are well on the way to being finished;* **to go out of your way to help someone** = to make a special effort to help someone
(d) to make way for = to provide or clear a space for somebody or something; *they chopped down hundreds of trees to make way for the freeway*
(e) to make your way = to go to (a place) with some difficulty; *can you make your way to passport control?; he made his way to the tourist information office*
(f) particular direction from here; *a one-way street; can you tell which way the wind is blowing?; this way please, everybody!*
(g) means of doing something; *my mother showed me the way to make marmalade; isn't there any other way of doing it?; he thought of a way of making money quickly; the way she said it implied it was my fault;* *(informal)* **to get your own way** = to do what you want to do, even if other people don't want you to do it; *she always seems to get her own way*
(h) to have it both ways = to take advantage from two courses of action; *he wants to have it both ways, but he'll soon realize he can't; you can't have it both ways - going out to the club every evening and saving money;* **in many ways** = almost completely; *in many ways, I think she is right;* **in some ways** = not completely; *in some ways she may be wrong*
(i) manner of behaving; *he spoke in a pleasant way; you will have to get used to the manager's funny little ways*
(j) distance; *the bank is quite a long way away; he has a long way to go before he qualifies as a doctor*
(k) space where someone wants to be or which someone wants to use; *get out of my way - I'm in a hurry; it's best to keep out of the way of the*

police for a moment; I wanted to take a shortcut, but there was a truck in the way
(l) progress, forward movement; **under way** = moving forward; *the project is under way at last*
(m) in a bad way = very sick; *she's in the hospital and in a really bad way*
2 *adverb*
(informal) far, a long distance away; *the bank is way beyond the general store; their financial problems started way back in 1992; the price was way too high for me;* **way over your head** = difficult to understand; *the book was way over my head*

◇ **by the way**
['baɪ ðə 'weɪ]
(used to introduce something which is not very important or to change the subject which is being talked about) **by the way, have you seen my keys anywhere?**

◇ **no way**
['nəʊ weɪ]
not at all; *can I have a table for lunch? - no way!; there's no way that the government is going to get involved*

◇ **out of the way**
['aʊt əv ðə 'weɪ]
(a) not near any large town; *the gas station is a bit out of the way*
(b) strange, unusual; *what she proposed was nothing out of the way*

① **way in**
['weɪ 'ɪn] *noun*
entrance; *this is the way in to the theater; the way in is through the gates*

① **way out**
['weɪ 'aʊt] *noun*
(a) exit; *this is the way out of the parking lot; he couldn't find the way out of the movie theater in the dark*
(b) way out of a difficulty = a solution to a problem; *the leave the country and live abroad was probably the easiest way out*

① **we**
[wi] *pronoun*
(a) *(used by a speaker referring to himself or herself and others)* *he said we could go into the exhibition; we were not allowed into the restaurant in jeans; we had a wonderful vacation - we all enjoyed ourselves enormously* (NOTE: when it is the object **we** becomes **us: we gave it to him; he gave it to us;** when it follows the verb to **be, we** usually becomes **us: who is it? - it's us!**)
(b) *(used instead of I)* **the royal we** = using "we" instead of "I"; *Queen Victoria of England said "we are not amused"*

② **weak**
[wik] *adjective*
(a) not strong; *after his illness he is still very weak; I don't like weak coffee*

(b) not good at, not having knowledge or skill; *she's weaker at science than at math; Spanish is his weakest subject; she gave the weakest of excuses for not finishing the work on time* (NOTE: do not confuse with **week;** note: **weaker - weakest**)

② **weaken**
['wikn] *verb*
to make or to become weak; *she was very weakened by the disease; if you remove that wall you'll weaken the whole structure; living outside the borough weakens his chances of getting a place in that school* (NOTE: the opposite is **strengthen**)

① **weakness**
['wiknəs] *noun*
(a) state of being weak; *the doctor noticed the weakness of her pulse* (NOTE: the opposite is **strength**)
(b) *(informal)* **weakness for** = liking for; *she has a weakness for tall men with dark hair; I have a weakness for doughnuts*

② **wealth**
[welθ] *noun*
riches, a large amount of money; *his wealth was inherited from his grandfather* (NOTE: no plural)

② **wealthy**
['welθi] *adjective*
very rich (person); *is she really wealthy?; 50% of the land is in the hand of the ten wealthiest families* (NOTE: **wealthier - wealthiest**)

② **weapon**
['wepən] *noun*
object such as a gun or sword, which you fight with; *the crowd used iron bars as weapons*

① **wear**
[weər]
1 *verb*
(a) to have (especially a piece of clothing) on your body; *what dress are you wearing to the party?; when last seen, he was wearing a blue raincoat; she's wearing her mother's earrings; she wears her hair very short*
(b) to become damaged or thin through being used; *the tread on the automobile tires is worn; I've worn a hole in the heel of my sock*
(c) to make somebody or something tired; *my son's constant questions wear my patience* (NOTE: **wearing - wore** [wɔr] **- has worn** [wɔrn])
2 *noun*
(a) *(formal)* clothes; *the menswear department is on the first floor*
(b) action of wearing clothes; *this jacket is suitable for summer wear; a little black dress is perfect for evening wear*
(c) amount of use which something may have; *the carpet on the stairs will have a lot more wear than the one in the bedroom*
(d) action of damaging something through use; **fair wear and tear** = damage through normal

use which is accepted by an insurance company; *the policy covers most forms of damage but not wear and tear to the machine*

① **wear off**
['weər'ɒf] *verb*
to disappear gradually; *the effects of the drug wore off after a few hours*

① **wear out**
['weər'aut] *verb*
(a) to use something so much that it is broken and useless; *walking across the U.S.A., he wore out three pairs of boots*
(b) to wear yourself out = to become very tired through doing something; *she wore herself out looking after the old lady; see also* WORN OUT

③ **weary**
['wɪəri] *adjective*
very tired; *we were all weary after a day spent walking around Boston*; **to grow weary of (doing) something** = to get tired of doing something; *we grew weary of always eating in the same restaurant* (NOTE: **wearier - weariest**)

② **weather**
['weðər]
1 *noun*
(a) conditions outside, i.e., if it is raining, hot, cold, windy, sunny, etc.; *what's the weather going to be like today?*; *the weather in Alaska is usually colder than here*; *rain every day - just normal spring weather!*; *if the weather gets any better, then we can go out in the boat*
(b) under the weather = miserable or unwell; *she's feeling a bit under the weather* (NOTE: no plural; do not confuse with **whether**)
2 *verb*
(a) *(of sea, frost, wind, etc.)* to wear down rocks, to change the color of wood, etc.; *the rocks have been weathered into curious shapes*; *the wooden fence was dark brown but now it has weathered to a light gray color*
(b) to survive a storm, crisis; *I don't know if we can weather this crisis without any extra cash*

② **weave**
[wiv] *verb*
(a) to make cloth by winding threads in and out; *the cloth is woven from the wool of local sheep*; *the new weaving machines were installed last week*
(b) to make something by a similar method, but using straw, etc.; *she learned how to weave baskets* (NOTE: **wove** [wəuv] **- has woven** [wəuvn])

② **web**
[web] *noun*
(a) net made by spiders to catch flies; *the garden is full of spiders' webs in the fall*
(b) *(Internet)* **the Web** = the World Wide Web, the thousands of web sites and web pages on the Internet, which users can visit; **web page** = single file of text and graphics, forming part of a web site; **web site** = collection of pages on the web which have been produced by one company or person and are linked together; *how many visitors placed an order on our web site last week?*

② **wed**
[wed] *verb*
to marry; *she wed her high school sweetheart* (NOTE: **wedding - wed** *or* **wedded**)

③ **we'd**
[wid]
= WE HAD, WE WOULD

② **wedding**
['wedɪŋ] *noun*
marriage ceremony, when two people are officially made man and wife; *they rang the church bells at the wedding*; *don't count on having good weather for your wedding*; *the movie ends with a wedding*; *this Saturday I'm going to John and Mary's wedding*; **church wedding** = a wedding held in a church, and performed by a priest; **civil wedding** = wedding which is performed by a magistrate, held at a City Hall or other place, but not a church; **silver wedding** = celebration when two people have been married for twenty-five years; **golden wedding** = celebration when two people have been married for fifty years; *it's my parents' golden wedding next Tuesday*; **white wedding** = wedding where the bride wears a white dress; **wedding anniversary** = date which is the date of a wedding in the past; *don't tell me that for once you remembered our wedding anniversary!*; **wedding cake** = special cake made with dried fruit, covered with icing, eaten at a wedding reception; *did you get a piece of wedding cake?*; **"Wedding March"** = piece of music by Mendelssohn played at weddings; *the organ played the "Wedding March" as the bride and bridegroom walked out of the church*; **wedding reception** = party held after a wedding, including meal, drinks, toasts, etc.; *the wedding reception was held in the gardens of the hotel*; **wedding ring** = ring that is put on the finger during the wedding ceremony

COMMENT: at a wedding, the bride is usually assisted by bridesmaids (young girls) and pages (little boys). The bridegroom is always helped by his best man, who is usually an old friend. The bride is "given away" by her father, that is, she goes into the church on his arm, and leaves the church on the arm of her new husband. Weddings are often on Saturdays; weddings are usually followed by the wedding reception, and then the bride and bridegroom go away on their honeymoon. The costs of the wedding are usually borne by the parents of the bride

③ **wedge**
[wedʒ]
1 *noun*

(a) solid piece of wood, metal, rubber, etc., that has a V-shape; *put a wedge under the door to hold it open*
(b) piece of anything with a V-shape; *a wedge of cheese*
2 *verb*
(a) to put a wedge under something fix it firmly open or shut; *she wedged the door open with a piece of wood*
(b) to force something into a small space; **to become wedged** *or* **to get wedged** = to become tightly stuck; *he got his head wedged between the bars of the cage*

① **Wednesday**
['wenzdi] *noun*
day between Tuesday and Thursday, the third day of the week; *she came for coffee last Wednesday*; *Wednesdays are always busy days for us*; *can we meet next Wednesday afternoon?*; *Wednesday July 24 would be a good date for a meeting*; *the 15th is a Tuesday, so the 16th must be a Wednesday*

② **weed**
[wid]
1 *noun*
wild plant that you do not want in a garden; *weeds grew all over the strawberry beds while he was on vacation*
2 *verb*
(a) to pull out plants that you do not want from a garden; *she spent all afternoon weeding the vegetable garden*
(b) **to weed out** = to remove something which is not wanted; *weed out any old newspapers you don't want and take them to the recycling center*

① **week**
[wik] *noun*
(a) period of seven days, usually from Monday to Sunday; *there are 52 weeks in the year*; *it's my aunt's 80th birthday next week*; *I go to the movie theater at least once a week*; **a week from now** *or* **a week today** = this day next week; *a week from now or in a week's time, I'll be on vacation*; **a week tomorrow** = in eight days' time; *a week tomorrow I'll be in Florida*; **yesterday week** = a week ago yesterday; *they came back from vacation yesterday week*; **what day of the week is it today?** = is it Monday, Tuesday, etc.?
(b) part of a seven day period, when people work; *he works a 35-hour week or he works 35 hours every week* (NOTE: do not confuse with **weak**)

① **weekday**
['wikdeɪ] *noun*
any of the days from Monday to Friday, when most offices are open (but not Saturday or Sunday); *the banks are only open on weekdays*; *there are many more trains on weekdays than on Sundays*

① **weekend**
['wikend] *noun*
Saturday and Sunday, or the period from Friday evening to Sunday evening; *we're going skiing for the weekend*; *why don't you come to spend next weekend with us in the country?*; *at weekends, we try to spend time in the garden*; **long weekend** = weekend, including Friday night and Sunday night; *we took a long weekend in the country*; **weekend break** = short vacation over a weekend; *we went away for a weekend break in Seattle*

② **weekly**
['wikli]
1 *adjective & adverb*
which happens or is published once a week; *we have a weekly paper that tells us all the local news*; *the weekly rate for the job is $375*; *do you pay the newspapers weekly?*
2 *noun*
magazine published once a week; *he gets a gardening weekly every Friday* (NOTE: plural is **weeklies**)

② **weep**
[wip] *verb*
(formal) to cry, to have tears coming out of your eyes; *seeing them cut down the trees to make a new freeway is enough to make you weep*; *my mother wept with joy when I came back safe and sound*; *crowds of weeping relatives followed the coffin* (NOTE: **weeping - wept** [wept])

① **weigh**
[weɪ] *verb*
(a) to use scales or a weighing machine to measure how heavy something is; *can you weigh this package for me?*; *they weighed his suitcase at the check-in counter*; *I weighed myself this morning*; **weighing machine** = device for weighing someone or something; *she placed the bag of candy on the weighing machine*
(b) to have a certain weight; *this piece of meat weighs 100 grams*; *the packet weighs twenty-five ounces*; *how much do you weigh?*; *he weighs 120 pounds*; *she only weighs 40 pounds*

① **weight**
[weɪt]
1 *noun*
(a) how heavy something is; *what's the maximum weight of a package the post office will accept?*; **to sell fruit by weight** = to sell for a certain price per pound; **gross weight** = weight of both the container and its contents; **net weight** = weight of goods without the packing material and container
(b) how heavy a person is; *his weight is less than it was a year ago*; **to lose weight** = to get thinner; *he's trying to lose weight*; **to put on weight** = to get fatter; *she's put on a lot of weight since her vacation*

(c) to pull your weight = to work as hard as everyone else; *the manager has the reputation for being ruthless with employees who don't pull their weight*; *(informal)* **to throw your weight about** = to use your authority to tell people what to do in a rude way; *she loves to throw her weight about at management meetings*; *she's worth her weight in gold* = she's a very useful person and we couldn't do without her

(d) something which is heavy; *if you lift heavy weights like big stones, you can hurt your back*; *do you have a weight to put on the papers to stop them blowing away?*; **that's a weight off my mind!** = that is something I need not worry about any longer

2 *verb*

(a) to attach something heavy to something; *they weighted down the sack with bricks and threw it into the river*

(b) to add an amount to a total to produce a certain result; *the figures are weighted to take account of seasonal variations* (NOTE: do not confuse with **wait**)

② **weird**
['wɪərd] *adjective*
strange, different from what is normal; *I don't like her new boyfriend - he's really weird*; *wasn't it weird that he called just when we were talking about him?*; *this meat has a weird taste* (NOTE: **weirder - weirdest**)

② **welcome**
['welkʌm]
1 *adjective*

(a) met or accepted with pleasure; *the rain was welcome after months of drought*; *a bowl of warm soup would be welcome*; *after a game of football he had a welcome hot shower or a hot shower was very welcome*

(b) **welcome to** = willingly allowed to; *you're welcome to use the library whenever you want*

(c) *(informal) (as a reply to "thank you")* **thanks for carrying the bags for me - you're welcome!**

2 *verb*

(a) to greet someone in a friendly way; *the staff welcomed the new secretary to the office*; *when we arrived at the hotel we were welcomed by a couple of barking guard dogs*

(b) to be glad to hear news; *I warmly welcome the result of the election*; *I would welcome any suggestions as to how to stop the water coming through the roof*

3 *noun*

action of greeting someone; *there was not much of a welcome from the staff when we arrived at the hotel*; **warm welcome** = a friendly welcome; *they gave me a warm welcome*

② **welfare**
['welfeər] *noun*

(a) providing comfort and freedom from want; *the club looks after the welfare of the elderly people in the town*; *we take the children to a*

child welfare agency; *the government has taken measures to reform the welfare system*

(b) money paid by the government to people who need it; *he exists on welfare payments*; *the family is on welfare*

① **well**
[wel]
1 *adverb*

(a) in a way that is satisfactory; *he doesn't speak Russian very well*; *our business is small, but it's doing well*; *is the new computer working well?*

(b) a lot (more); *he got back from the office late - well after eight o'clock*; *you should go to the Grand Canyon - it's well worth a visit*; *there were well over sixty people at the meeting*; *she's well over eighty*

(c) **as well** = also; *when my aunt comes to stay she brings her two cats and the dog as well*; *you can't eat a hamburger and a pizza as well*; **as well as** = not only, but also; *some newsstands sell food as well as newspapers*; *she ate a brownie as well as two scoops of ice cream*

(d) *(to emphasize)* *he may well be right*; *she's well aware of how serious the situation is*

2 *adjective*
healthy; *she's looking well after her vacation!*; *the secretary's not very well today - she's had to take off work*; *it took him some weeks to get well after his flu*

3 *interjection*
(which starts a sentence, and often has no meaning) *well, I'll show you round the house first*; *well now, we've washed the dishes so we can sit and watch TV*; *(showing surprise)* *well, well! what is Mr. Smith doing here!*

4 *noun*
very deep hole dug in the ground with water or oil at the bottom; *we pump water from the well in our garden*; *Texan oil wells*

① **well done**
['wel 'dʌn]
1 *interjection*
showing congratulations; *well done, Dallas Cowboys!*; *well done to all of you who passed the test!*

2 *adjective*
(meat) which has been cooked a long time; *can I have my steak well-done, please?*

③ **well-earned**
[wel'ɜrnd] *adjective*
which you have deserved; *after doing all that gardening I think I can take a well-earned rest*

② **well-known**
[wel'nəun] *adjective*
famous, known by a lot of people; *she lives next door to a well-known TV star*

④ **well-off**
[wel'ɒf] *adjective*
(informal) rich; *I thought his wife came from a well-off family*

② **well-paid**
['wel'peɪd] *adjective*
earning a good salary; *well-paid secretaries can earn really high salaries*; *what I want is not just a well-paid job but one that is interesting*

① **Welsh**
[welʃ]
1 *adjective*
referring to Wales; *we will be going climbing in the Welsh mountains at Easter*
2 *noun*
(a) the Welsh = the people of Wales; *the Welsh are proud of their language*; *the Welsh are magnificent singers*
(b) language spoken in Wales; *Welsh is used in schools in many parts of Wales*

① **went**
[went] *see* GO

② **wept**
[wept] *see* WEEP

③ **were, weren't**
[wɜr *or* wɜrnt] *see* BE

① **west**
[west]
1 *noun*
direction of where the sun sets; *the sun sets in the west and rises in the east*; *we live in a house to the west of the town*; *their house has a garden that faces west or a west-facing garden*; **the West** = (i) Western Europe and North America; (ii) area of the U.S. west of the Mississippi River
2 *adjective*
in or to the west; *she lives on the west coast*; *the west part of the town is near the river*; **west wind** = wind which blows from the west; *a cold west wind is blowing from the Rocky Mountains*
3 *adverb*
toward the west; *go west for about eight miles, and then you'll come to the national park*; *the river flows west into the ocean*

① **western**
['westərn]
1 *adjective*
from or in the west; *I have never visited the western states*; *the western part of Canada has wonderful mountains*; *see also* COUNTRY
2 *noun*
movie about cowboys; *she likes watching old westerns on TV*

① **wet**
[wet]
1 *adjective*
(a) covered in water or other liquid; *she forgot her umbrella and got wet walking back from the stores*; *the chair's all wet where he knocked over his beer*; *the baby is wet - can you change her diaper?*; **wet through** *or* **soaking wet** = very wet; *change your shirt - it's wet through*; *I was soaking wet after falling into the river*

(b) when it is raining; *the summer months are the wettest part of the year*; *there's nothing I like better than a wet Sunday in Rockport*
(c) not yet dry; *watch out! - the paint's still wet*
(d) *(informal)* **wet behind the ears** = young and inexperienced; *he may be wet behind the ears, but don't underestimate his competence!*
(e) *(informal)* **wet blanket** = a person or thing that ruins enjoyment; *don't invite Ben to the party - he's such a wet blanket!* (NOTE: **wetter - wettest**)
2 *verb*
(a) to make something wet; *the rain didn't really wet the soil*
(b) to sprinkle with water; *wet the shirt before you iron it*
(c) *(of child)* **to wet the bed** = to pass waste water from the body in bed and make it wet; *she's started to wet her bed*

① **we've**
[wiv] = WE HAVE

② **whale**
[weɪl] *noun*
(a) huge animal that lives in the sea; *you can take a boat into the mouth of the river to see the whales*
(b) *(informal)* **to have a whale of a time** = to enjoy yourself very much; *the children had a whale of a time at the zoo*

③ **wharf**
[wɔrf] *noun*
place by the sea where a ship can tie up to take on or put off cargo; *the fishing boats were tied up at the wharf* (NOTE: plural is **wharfs** *or* **wharves** [wɔrvz])

① **what**
[wɒt]
1 *adjective*
(asking a question) *what time is it?*; *what type of food does he like best?*
2 *pronoun*
(a) the thing which; *did you see what was in the box?*; *what we like to do most on vacation is just to visit old churches*
(b) *(asking a question)* *what's the correct time?*; *what did he give you for your birthday?*; *what's the name of the new diner on Main Street?*; *what's the Spanish for "table"?*; *what happened to his car?*
3 *adverb*
(a) *(showing surprise)* *what a huge meal!*; *what beautiful weather!*
(b) *(giving a reason)* *what with the children being sick one after another, and my husband being away, I've got my hands full at the moment*
4 *interjection*
(showing surprise) *what! the restaurant's full?*; *what! did you hear what he said?*; *I won the lottery! - What!* (NOTE: after **what** used to ask a question, the verb is put before the subject: **what's the time** but **they don't know what the time is**)

③ **what about**
[wɒt ə'baʊt] *phrase*
(showing a suggestion) what about having some lunch?; *they invited everybody - are you sure, what about Fiona?*

② **whatever**
[wɒt'evər] *pronoun*
(form of "what" which emphasizes)
(a) it doesn't matter what; *you can have whatever you like for Christmas*; *she always does whatever she feels like doing*; *I want that automobile whatever the price*
(b) *(in questions)* what, why; *whatever made him do that?*; *whatever does that red light mean?*; *I've sold the automobile - whatever for?*

② **what for**
['wɒt 'fɔr]
(a) why; *what are they all shouting for?*; *he's sold his automobile - what for?*; *what did he phone the police for?*
(b) for what use; *what's this red button for?*

④ **whatsoever**
[wɒtsəʊ'evər] *adjective & pronoun*
(form of "whatever" which emphasizes) **there is no truth whatsoever in the report**; *the police found no suspicious documents whatsoever*; **none whatsoever** = none at all; *do you have any idea why the computer suddenly stopped working? - none whatsoever* (NOTE: always used after a noun and after a negative)

① **wheat**
[wit] *noun*
cereal plant of which the grain is used to make flour; *after the storms much of the wheat lay flat on the ground*; *my mother uses wheat flour to make bread* (NOTE: no plural)

① **wheel**
[wil]
1 *noun*
(a) round piece which turns round a central point and on which a bicycle, an automobile, etc., runs; *the front wheel and the back wheel of the motorcycle were both damaged in the accident*; *we got a flat tire as well as a bent wheel*; **on wheels** = with wheels attached; *hospital beds are on wheels so they are easy to move*
(b) any similar round piece for turning; **steering wheel** = wheel which is turned by the driver to control the direction of a vehicle; *the steering wheel is on the left-hand side of American cars*; **to be at the wheel** = to be driving; *she was at the wheel when the automobile went off the road*; **to take the wheel** = to start to drive an automobile; *she took the wheel because her husband was falling asleep*
2 *verb*
(a) to push something along that has wheels; *he wheeled his motorcycle into the garage*; *she was wheeling her bike along the sidewalk*

(b) to wheel round = to turn round suddenly; *she wheeled round and went straight back to the counter*
(c) to fly in circles; *birds were wheeling above the fishing boats*
(d) to wheel and deal = to negotiate to make business deals

① **wheelbarrow**
['wilbærəʊ] *noun*
small cart with one wheel in front, and two handles, used to carry heavy loads; *he filled the wheelbarrow with soil and wheeled it to the end of the garden*

③ **wheelchair**
['wiltʃeər] *noun*
chair on wheels which people who cannot walk use to move around; *he manages to get around in a wheelchair*; *she has been confined to a wheelchair since her accident*; **wheelchair entrance** = special entrance with a slope instead of steps, which can be used by people in wheelchairs

① **when**
[wen]
1 *adverb*
(asking a question) at what time; *when is the last plane for Atlanta?*; *when did you last go to the dentist?*; *when are we going to get paid?*; *since when has he been wearing glasses?*; *I asked her when her friend was leaving* (NOTE: after **when** used to ask a question, the verb is put before the subject: **when does the movie start?** but **he doesn't know when the movie starts**; **when is he coming?** but **they can't tell me when he is coming**)
2 *conjunction*
(a) at the time that; *when he was young, the family was living in Vermont*; *when you go on vacation, leave your key with the neighbors so they can feed the cat*; *do you remember the day when we all went for a picnic in the park?*; *let me know when you're ready to go*
(b) after; *when the speaker had finished, he sat down*; *wash the plates when you've finished your breakfast*
(c) even if; *the salesman said the car was worth $7000 when he really knew it was worth only half that*
(d) although; *I said I knew nothing about it when in fact I'd known about it for some time*

③ **whenever**
[wen'evər] *adverb*
(a) at any time that; *come for a chat whenever you like*; *we try to see my mother-in-law whenever we can or whenever possible*
(b) *(form of "when" which emphasizes) whenever did she learn to drive?*

① **where**
[weər] *adverb*
(a) *(asking a question)* in what place, to what place; *where did I put my glasses?*; *do you know where the restaurant is?*; *where are the*

knives and forks?; *where are you going for your vacation?*

(b) *(showing place)* in a place in which; *stay where you are and don't move*; *they still live in the same house where they were living twenty years ago*; *here's where the wire has been cut*

(c) whenever; *use fresh tomatoes where possible* (NOTE: after **where** used to ask a question, the verb is put before the subject: **where is the bottle?** but **he doesn't know where the bottle is**)

④ **whereas**
[weər'æz] *conjunction*

(a) if you compare this with the fact that; *he likes tea whereas she prefers coffee*

(b) *(formal)* taking the following fact into consideration; *whereas the contract between the two parties states that either party may withdraw at six months' notice*

④ **whereby**
[weə'baɪ] *adverb*

(formal) by which; according to which; *a deed whereby ownership of the property is transferred*; *a teaching method whereby students can measure their own progress*

③ **wherever**
[weə'evər] *adverb*

(a) to or in any place; *you can sit wherever you want*; *wherever we go on vacation, we never make hotel reservations*; *the police want to ask her questions, wherever she may be*

(b) *(form of "where" which emphasizes)* *wherever did you get that hat?*

③ **whether**
['weðər] *conjunction*

(a) *(showing doubt, or not having reached a decision)* if; *do you know whether they're coming?*; *I can't make up my mind whether to go on vacation now or later*

(b) *(applying to either of two things)* both; *all employees, whether managers or regular staff, must take a medical test* (NOTE: do not confuse with **weather**)

① **which**
[wɪtʃ] *adjective & pronoun*

(a) *(asking a question)* what person or thing; *which dress are you wearing to the wedding?*; *which boy threw that stone?*

(b) **which is which** = what is the difference between the two; *there are two switches, one for the light and one for the fan, but I don't know which is which*

(c) *(only used with things, not people)* that; *we're going to the Chinese restaurant, which is next door to the office*

(d) **in which case** = if that is the case; *he's sick, in which case he'd better stay at home* (NOTE: with an object, **which** can be left out: **here's the bread we bought yesterday**)

③ **whichever**
[wɪtʃ'evər]
1 *pronoun*

(a) anything that; *you can take several routes, but whichever you choose, the journey will still take three hours*

(b) *(form of "which" which emphasizes)* no matter which; *take whichever one you want*
2 *adjective*

no matter which; *whichever newspaper you read, you'll get the same story*

① **while**
[waɪl]
1 *noun*

(a) some time; *it's a while since I've seen him*; **in a while** = in a short time, soon; *I'll be ready in a while*; **a little while** = a short period of time; *do you mind waiting a little while until a table is free?*; **quite a while** = a longer period of time; *he changed jobs quite a while ago*; **once in a while** = from time to time, but not often; *it's nice to go to have a Mexican meal once in a while*

(b) **it is worth while** = it is good to do, it may be profitable; *it's worth while keeping copies of your work, in case your computer goes wrong*; *it's well worth while trying to get a ticket for the show*; **to be worth someone's while** = to be worth doing; **it is worth your while** = it is worth the effort; *it's worth your while keeping copies of your work, in case your computer goes wrong*; **I'll make it worth your while** = I'll pay you a lot to do it; *it's an awful job, but if you agree to do it I'll make it worth your while*; *see also* WORTHWHILE
2 *conjunction*

(a) when, at the time that; *he tried to cut my hair while he was watching TV*; *while we were on vacation someone broke into our house*; *shall I clean the kitchen while you're having a bath?*

(b) *(showing difference)* *he likes meat, while his sister is a vegetarian*; *she only earns $180 a week while everyone else in the office earns twice that*; *everyone is watching TV, while I'm in the kitchen making the dinner*

(c) *(formal)* although; *while there may still be delays, the service is much better than it used to be*

② **whine**
[waɪn] *verb*

(a) to make a loud high noise; *you can hear the engines of the racing cars whining in the background*

(b) to complain with a loud high sound; *the dogs whined when we locked them up in the kitchen* (NOTE: do not confuse with **wine**)

① **whip**
[wɪp]
1 *noun*

(a) long, thin piece of leather with a handle, used to hit animals to make them do what you want; *riders use the whip to make their horses run faster*

(b) **to crack the whip** = to make everyone do what you want; *the boss had to crack the whip to get the job finished on time*

(c) member of a political party who manages members of the party serving in a legislative body; **majority whip** or **minority whip** = assistants to the majority or minority leaders in the House or Senate, whose responsibility is to make sure the members of their party vote for the vote

2 verb

(a) to hit someone or an animal with a whip; *he whipped the horse to make it go faster*

(b) to beat cream, eggs, etc., until firm; *whip the eggs and milk together*; *it is easier to whip cream if it is cold*

(c) to go quickly; *he whipped around to the store to buy some cigarettes*

(d) to do something quickly; *he whipped off his hat when he saw her coming toward him*; *she whipped out her checkbook* (NOTE: **whipping - whipped**)

② **whirl**
['wɜːrl] verb
to turn round quickly, to spin; *the children's paper windmills whirled in the wind*

① **whirlpool**
['wɜːrlpʊl] noun
stream of water that turns round and round very fast; *be careful, there are whirlpools in the river*

① **whirlwind**
['wɜːrlwɪnd] noun
column of air that turns round and round very fast; *whirlwinds come in the summer months and cause a huge amount of damage*

③ **whisk**
[wɪsk] noun
1 noun
kitchen tool used for whipping cream, eggs, etc.; *she was looking for the whisk to beat some eggs*
2 verb
(a) to move something very fast; *she whisked the plate of muffins away before I could take one*; *they came in, said hi to us, and whisked our daughter off to the restaurant*
(b) to beat cream, eggs, etc., very quickly; *next, whisk the mixture until it is smooth and has no lumps*; *I always whisk egg whites by hand*

② **whiskey or whisky**
['wɪski] noun
(a) strong alcoholic drink, made from grain; *Sam keeps a bottle of whiskey in the pantry*; *I don't like whiskey - I prefer beer*
(b) a glass of this drink; *she asked the bartender for two whiskeys* (NOTE: the spelling **whisky** is used when it is made in Scotland; the plural is **whiskies**)

② **whisper**
['wɪspər]
1 noun
quiet voice, words spoken very quietly; *she spoke in a whisper*
2 verb

to speak very quietly, to make a very quiet sound; *he whispered instructions to the other members of the gang*; *she whispered to the nurse that she wanted something to drink*

① **whistle**
['wɪsl]
1 noun
(a) high-pitched sound made by blowing through your lips when they are almost closed; *she gave a whistle of surprise*; *we heard a whistle and saw a dog running across the field*
(b) simple instrument that makes a high-pitched sound, played by blowing; *the referee blew on his whistle to stop the match*
2 verb
(a) to blow through your lips to make a high-pitched sound; *they marched along, whistling an Irish song*; *the porter whistled for a taxi*
(b) to make a high-pitched sound using a small metal instrument; *the referee whistled to stop the match*

① **white**
[waɪt]
1 adjective
of a color like snow or milk; *a white shirt is part of the uniform*; *a white automobile will always look dirty*; *her hair is now completely white*; **white Christmas** = Christmas when there is snow on the ground; **white goods** = large household electrical equipment like fridges and washing machines; **white meat** = pale meat like breast of chicken or turkey, opposed to red meat like beef; **white wine** = wine that is clear or slightly yellow; *I'll have a glass of white wine with the fish*; *(informal)* **white as a sheet** = completely white, very pale; *are you all right? - you look as white as a sheet* (NOTE: **whiter - whitest**)
2 noun
(a) color of snow or milk; *the white of the mountains stood out against the deep blue of the sky*
(b) person whose skin is pale; *whites are in the minority in African countries*
(c) pale-colored meat (on a chicken); *do you want a leg or some white?*
(d) white part of something; *the white of an egg*; *the whites of his eyes were slightly red*; *(informal)* **wait until you see the whites of their eyes** = wait until they are very close to you
(e) *(informal)* white wine; *a glass of house white, please*

① **White House**
['waɪt 'haʊs] noun
(a) building in Washington, D.C., where the President of the U.S.A. lives and works; *the President invited the Prime Minister to lunch at the White House*; *the new First Lady is planning to change the decorations in only a few rooms in the White House*
(b) *(informal)* the U.S. government, the

president himself; *a White House spokesman gave a statement to the press*; *White House officials refused to confirm the report*

② who
[hu] *pronoun*
(a) *(asking a question)* which person or persons; *who was the person who phoned?*; *who phoned?*; *who are you talking to?*; *who was she going home with?*; *who spoke at the meeting?*
(b) the person or the people that; *the men who came yesterday morning work for the electricity company*; *anyone who didn't get tickets early won't be able to get in*; *there's the taxi driver who took us home last night*; *do you remember the girl who used to work here as a waitress?* (NOTE: with an object, **who** can be left out: **there's the man I saw at the restaurant.** Note also that when **who** is used as an object, it is sometimes written **whom** [hum] : **whom are you talking about?** **the man whom I saw in the office,** but this is not common. After **who** used to ask a question, the verb is put before the subject: **who is that man over there?** but **I don't know who that man is over there**)

② whoever
[huˈevər] *pronoun*
(form of "who" which emphasizes) no matter who, anyone who; *whoever finds the umbrella can keep it*; *go home with whoever you like*

② whole
[həʊl]
1 *adjective*
all of something; *she must have been hungry - she ate a whole apple pie*; *we spent the whole winter in the south*; *a whole lot of people came down with the flu*
2 *noun*
all, everything; *she stayed in bed the whole of Sunday morning and read the newspapers*; *the whole of the north of the country was covered with snow*; *did you watch the whole of the program?* (NOTE: do not confuse with **hole**)
3 *adverb*
in one piece; *the penguin swallowed the fish whole*

③ wholesale
[ˈhəʊlseɪl]
1 *adverb*
buying goods from manufacturers and selling them in large quantities to traders who then sell them in smaller quantities to the general public; *he buys wholesale* (NOTE: the opposite is **retail**)
2 *adjective*
(a) in large quantities; *we get a wholesale discount from the manufacturer*
(b) on a large scale; *the wholesale killing of wild birds*

④ wholesaler
[ˈhəʊlseɪlər] *noun*
person who buys goods in large quantities from manufacturers and sells them to retailers; *the store doesn't buy direct from the manufacturer but from a wholesaler*

④ wholly
[ˈhəʊli] *adverb*
(formal) completely, totally; *I don't think she has wholly recovered from her illness*; *we were talking about two wholly different subjects* (NOTE: do not confuse with **holy**)

③ whom
[hum] *see* WHO

② who's
[huz] = WHO IS, WHO HAS

① whose
[huz] *pronoun*
(a) *(asking a question)* which belongs to which person; *whose is that automobile?*; *whose checkbook is this?*; *whose money was stolen?*
(b) of whom; *the family whose car was stolen*; *the girl whose foot you stepped on* (NOTE: do not confuse with **who's**)

① why
[waɪ]
1 *adverb*
(a) *(asking a question)* for what reason; *why did he have to call me in the middle of the TV movie?*
(b) *(giving reason)* she told me why she couldn't go to the party
(c) *(showing something else is preferred)* why go by car to New York when you can take a plane?*; *why don't we go for a picnic now that it's sunny?* (NOTE: after **why** used to ask a question, the verb is put before the subject: **why is the sky blue?** but **I don't know why the sky is blue**)
2 *interjection showing surprise*
why, if it isn't old Mr. Smith!

② wicked
[ˈwɪkɪd] *adjective*
(a) very bad; *what a wicked thing to say!*; *it was wicked of them to steal the birds' eggs*
(b) naughty; *she gave a wicked little laugh*
(c) *(informal)* very good; *they do a wicked line in muffins*

① wide
[waɪd]
1 *adjective*
(a) which measures from side to side; *the table is three feet wide*; *the river is not very wide at this point*
(b) extensive, enormous; *the store carries a wide range of imported goods*; *she has a wide knowledge of French painting* (NOTE: **wider - widest**)
2 *adverb*
(a) as far as possible, as much as possible; *she opened her eyes wide*; *the door was wide open so we just walked in*; *wide apart* = separated by a large space; *he stood with his legs wide apart*; *wide-awake* = very much awake; *at eleven o'clock the baby was still wide-awake*

(b) not on the target; *the shells fell wide of their target*; **to be wide of the mark** = to be very wrong; *he's wide of the mark when he says that the old automobile is worth $3000*

③ **widely**
['waɪdli] *adverb*
(a) by a wide range of people; *it is widely expected that he will resign*
(b) over a wide area; *pollution spread widely over the area around the factory*; *she has traveled widely in Europe*; **he is very widely traveled** = he has traveled in many places

③ **widen**
['waɪdn] *verb*
(a) to make wider; *we need to widen the road to take larger trucks*
(b) to become wider; *further along, the road widens to allow two automobiles to pass*

③ **widespread**
['waɪdspred] *adjective*
over a large area; *there were widespread floods in the south of the country*; *there is a widespread idea that exercise is good for you*

② **widow**
['wɪdəʊ] *noun*
woman whose husband has died and who has not married again; *she was left a widow at a very early age*

② **widower**
['wɪdəʊər] *noun*
man whose wife has died and who has not married again; *she married again, this time a widower aged 62*

② **width**
[wɪdθ] *noun*
(a) measurement of something from one side to another; *I need to know the width of the sofa*; *the width of the garden is at least forty feet* or *the garden is at least forty feet in width*
(b) distance from one side to another of a swimming pool; *she swam three widths easily*

① **wife**
[waɪf] *noun*
woman who is married to a man; *I know Mr. Jones quite well but I've never met his wife*; *they both came with their wives*; *see also* TALE
(NOTE: plural is **wives** [waɪvz])

② **wig**
[wɪg] *noun*
false hair worn on the head; *she wore a green wig for the party*; *in the movie, he wears a gray wig to make him look older*

① **wild**
[waɪld]
1 *adjective*
(a) living in nature, not in a zoo; *wild dogs wander over parts of Australia*; **wild animals** = animals that are living in natural surroundings, as opposed to pets or farm animals; *we watched a TV program on wild animals in Africa*

(b) **wild mountain scenery** = mountains with high rocks, waterfalls, etc.
(c) *(informal)* very angry; very excited; *he will be wild when he sees what I have done to the automobile*; *the fans went wild at the end of the match*; *(informal)* **to be wild about something** = to be very interested in something; *she's wild about motorbikes*; **beyond your wildest dreams** = even better than you could expect; *the results exceeded our wildest dreams*
(d) not thinking carefully; *she made a few wild guesses, but didn't find the right answer*; *they had the wild idea of walking across the Sahara*
2 *noun*
(a) **in the wild** = living in nature; *in the wild, elephants can live to a great age*
(b) **the wilds of** = the remote parts of; *they have a cabin in the wilds of the Rockies*
3 *adverb*
(a) freely; *in this zoo, animals can roam wild in the fields*
(b) without any control; *the crowds were running wild through the center of the town*

② **wilderness**
['wɪldərnəs] *noun*
wild country or desert, which is not cultivated and which has no inhabitants; *he spent years exploring the Arctic wilderness*

② **wildflower**
[waɪld'flaʊər] *noun*
flower that grows naturally, not a garden plant; *the book is full of pictures of wildflowers*

③ **wild-goose chase**
[waɪld 'gus 'tʃeɪs] *noun*
hopeless search; *they set off on a wild-goose chase for new kitchen furniture*

① **wildlife**
['waɪldlaɪf] *noun*
birds, plants and animals living free and not controlled by humans; *they spent the summer studying the wildlife in the national park*; **wildlife park** = large park surrounded by high fences, where wild animals are kept and are allowed to run wild inside (NOTE: no plural)

② **wildly**
['waɪldli] *adverb*
(a) in a wild way; *the crowd cheered wildly as the pop group started to sing*
(b) **wildly wrong** = completely wrong; *his prediction of a great summer was wildly wrong*

② **will**
[wɪl]
1 *verb, used with other verbs*
(a) *(to form the future)* *the party will start soon*; *will they be staying a long time?*; *we won't be able to come to dinner*; *if you ask her to play the piano, she'll say "no"*
(b) *(emphasizing)* *the dog will keep eating the cat's food*
(c) *(polite way of asking someone to do something)* *will everyone please sit down?*; *will*

someone close the curtains?; *(formal) won't you sit down?*

(d) *(showing that you are keen to do something)* *don't call a taxi - I'll take you home*; *the automobile will never start when we want it to*; *don't worry - I will do it* (NOTE: the negative: **will not** is usually written **won't** [wəʊnt]. The past is: **would**, negative: **would not**, usually written **wouldn't**. Note also that **will** is often shortened to **'ll: he'll =** he will)

2 *noun*

(a) power of the mind and character; **to work with a will =** to work very hard and willingly; **with the best will in the world =** however much you want to do something; *even with the best will in the world, I don't see how we can finish it in time*

(b) wish; **against your will =** without your agreement; *he was forced to pay the money against his will*; **of your own free will =** willingly, without being forced; *he signed the document of his own free will*; **at will =** whenever you want to; *visitors can wander around the gardens at will*

(c) legal document by which a person gives instructions as to what should happen to the property after he or she dies; *he wrote his will in 1984*; *according to her will, all her property is left to her children*; *has she made a will yet?*

① **willing**
['wɪlɪŋ] *adjective*
eager to help; *is there anyone who is willing to drive the bus?*; *I need two willing helpers to wash the truck*

③ **willingly**
['wɪlɪŋli] *adverb*
readily, in a eager way; *I would willingly do the shopping but my foot hurts too much*

② **willow**
['wɪləʊ] *noun*
tree with long thin branches often found near rivers; *she sat under an old willow, watching the river flow past*; **weeping willow =** type of large willow tree with long hanging branches

① **win**
[wɪn]
1 *noun*
beating someone in a game; *the local team has only had two wins so far this year*; *we're disappointed, we expected a win*
2 *verb*
(a) to beat someone in a game; to be first in a race; *I expect our team will win tomorrow*; *the local team won their match yesterday*; *she won the race easily*
(b) to get (a prize, etc.); *she won first prize in the art competition*; *he won two million dollars on the lottery*; *she's hoping to win a new automobile in a competition in the paper* (NOTE: **winning - won** [wʌn])

① **wind**
1 [wɪnd] *noun*

(a) air moving fast outdoors; *the wind blew two trees down in the park*; *there's no point trying to use an umbrella in this wind*; *there's not a breath of wind - the sailboats aren't moving at all*; **to run like the wind =** to run very fast; *he ran like the wind and won the race*; **windchill (factor) =** air temperature including the effect of the wind

(b) being able to breathe; **to get your wind back =** to breathe properly again after running fast; *just give me a moment to get my wind back and I'll give you the message*

(c) **wind instruments =** musical instruments that you have to blow to make a note; *he doesn't play any wind instrument, just the piano*; **wind section =** section of an orchestra with wind instruments; *the work provides a lot of scope for the wind section*; *see also* BRASS, STRINGS

(d) gas that forms in the stomach; *the baby is suffering from wind*

(e) **to get wind of something =** to hear a rumor about something; *somehow, our rivals got wind of our plan to expand our chain of stores*

2 [waɪnd] *verb*

(a) to turn a key, etc., to make a machine work; *do you need to wind (up) the clock twice a week?*

(b) to twist round and round; *he wound the towel around his waist*; *she wound the string into a ball* (NOTE: **winding - wound** [waʊnd])

③ **wind down**
['waɪnd 'daʊn] *verb*
to relax; *I need to wind down after the hectic day I've had*

② **windmill**
['wɪnmɪl] *noun*

(a) mill for grinding flour, driven by sails which turn when the wind blows; *they live in an old windmill by the sea*

(b) little toy made of folded paper, which turns in the wind; *the children all had little paper windmills*

② **window**
['wɪndəʊ] *noun*

(a) opening in a wall, door, etc., which is filled with glass; *when I fly, I always ask for a seat by the window, so that I can watch the landing and takeoff*; *I looked out of the kitchen window and saw a fox*; *it's dangerous to lean out of automobile windows*; *the burglar must have got in through the bathroom window*; **store window =** large window in a store where goods are displayed so that customers can see them; *she bought the dress she had seen in the store window*

(b) **window of opportunity =** short moment when the conditions for something are especially favorable

(c) section of a computer screen used to display special information; *open the command window to see the range of possible commands*

③ **window box**
['wɪndəʊ 'bɒks] *noun*
long narrow box for plants which is put on a
ledge outside a window; *she has a beautiful
display of flowers in her window boxes*

③ **windshield**
['wɪnʃild] *noun*
(a) glass window in the front of an automobile,
bus, truck, etc.; *the windshield broke when a
stone hit it; I can't see through the windshield -
it's raining so hard*
(b) screen on the front of a motorcycle; *the
windshield protects the rider from the rain*

③ **wind up**
['waɪnd 'ʌp] *verb*
(a) to turn a key to make a machine work; *when
did you wind up the clock or wind the clock up?*
(b) to turn a handle to make something go up;
wind up your window if it starts to rain
(c) to end up, to be finally; *they wound up
owing the bank thousands of dollars; we tried
several restaurants and wound up in one by the
train station*
(d) to finish; *the meeting wound up at five
o'clock*
(e) (*informal*) to make someone annoyed; *he
only did it to wind you up*

① **windy**
['wɪndi] *adjective*
when a strong wind is blowing; *we have a lot of
windy weather in March; dress warmly, it's a
cold windy day outside* (NOTE: **windier -
windiest**)

② **wine**
[waɪn]
1 *noun*
alcoholic drink made from grapes; *we had a
bottle of Chilean red wine; two glasses of white
wine, please; should we have some white wine
with the fish?*; **house wine** = special wine
selected by a restaurant, cheaper than other
wines on the wine list; **wine list** = list of wines
and other drinks available in a restaurant (NOTE:
usually singular: **some wine, a glass of wine.** Note
that the plural **wines** means different sorts of wine)
2 *verb*
to wine and dine someone = to invite someone
for an expensive meal; *he seems to spend most
of his time wining and dining potential
customers*

③ **wine glass**
['waɪn 'glæs] *noun*
glass for serving wine; *these wine glasses are
very expensive*

① **wing**
[wɪŋ] *noun*
(a) one of the two parts of the body which a bird
or butterfly, etc., uses to fly; *a brown butterfly,
with white spots on its wings; the birds were
soaring in the warm air currents, hardly
moving their wings; which part of the chicken
do you prefer, a leg or a wing?*

(b) (*informal*) **to take someone under your
wing** = to help someone by showing them what
to do, especially someone who is new to the
work or who is in training
(c) one of the two flat parts sticking from the
side of an aircraft, which hold the aircraft in the
air; *he had a seat by the wing, so could not see
much out of the window*
(d) part of a large building which leads off to the
side of the main building, often built as an
extension; *they are building a new wing for the
hospital*
(e) part of a political party which has a certain
tendency; *she is part of the right wing of the
party*

① **wink**
[wɪŋk]
1 *verb*
to shut and open one eye quickly, as a signal; *she
winked at him to try to tell him that everything
was going well*
2 *noun*
(a) opening and shutting one eye quickly; *she
gave him a wink to show that she had seen him
take the last piece of cake*
(b) (*informal*) **forty winks** = a very short sleep;
he closed his eyes and had forty winks; **hardly
sleep a wink** = almost not to sleep at all; *we
hardly slept a wink last night because of the
noise of the traffic outside*

① **winner**
['wɪnər] *noun*
(a) person who wins; *the winner of the race gets
a silver cup*
(b) something which is successful; *his latest
book is a winner*

① **winning**
['wɪnɪŋ] *adjective*
(a) which has won; *the winning team go on to
the next stage of the tournament; she had the
winning lottery ticket*; **winning post** = post
which indicates the end of a horse race; *the first
past the winning post was "White Lady"*
(b) pleasant, attractive; *she has a very winning
smile*

④ **win over**
['wɪn 'əʊvər] *verb*
to persuade someone who was previously
reluctant; *we argued with them, but finally won
them over*

① **winter**
['wɪntər]
1 *noun*
the coldest season of the year, the season
between fall and spring; *in some countries
winter usually means snow; it's too cold to do
any gardening in the winter; we're taking a
winter vacation in Mexico*; **winter sports** =
sports which are done in the winter, such as
skiing, skating, etc.
2 *verb*

to spend the winter in a place; *my parents winter in Florida*

③ **winterize**
['wɪntəraɪz] *verb*
to prepare something for winter weather; *you must winterize the car*

① **wipe**
[waɪp]
1 *verb*
to clean or dry with a cloth; *wipe your shoes with a cloth before you polish them*; *here's a tissue to wipe your nose*; *use the blue towel to wipe your hands*; *I'll wash the dishes, but someone else must wipe*
2 *noun*
action of cleaning or drying with a cloth; *she gave the table a quick wipe*

② **wipe out**
['waɪp 'aʊt] *verb*
(a) to kill, to destroy; *the huge waves wiped out half the villages along the coast*
(b) to remove completely; *the costs of moving to the new office have completely wiped out our profits*

③ **wipe up**
['waɪp 'ʌp] *verb*
to clean liquid that has been spilled, with a cloth; *wipe up that milk that you spilled on the floor*

① **wire**
['waɪər]
1 *noun*
(a) thin piece of metal or metal thread; *he used bits of wire to attach the apple tree to the wall*; *the basket is made of woven wire*
(b) **(electric) wire** = thin metal thread along which electricity flows, usually covered with colored plastic; *the wires seem to be all right, so there must be a problem with the dishwasher itself*; **live wire** = wire with electricity running through it; *be careful - that's a live wire*
(c) *(informal)* **to get your wires crossed** = to get two messages confused; *we seem to have got our wires crossed - I thought we were meeting today, and he thought it was tomorrow*
2 *verb*
to put in wires to carry electricity around a building; *the office has been wired for computers*

① **wisdom**
['wɪzdəm] *noun*
general common sense; *I doubt the wisdom of allowing her to go out alone at night*; **words of wisdom** = sound advice; *just a few words of wisdom: don't get involved!*

③ **wisdom tooth**
['wɪzdəm 'tuθ] *noun*
one of the four back teeth which only grow after the age of 20, or sometimes not at all

① **wise**
[waɪz]
1 *adjective*
(a) having intelligence and being sensible; *I don't think it's wise to ask her to invest all that*

money in his business; *it was a wise decision to cancel the trip*
(b) **to be none the wiser** = to know no more about it than you did before; *I read his report, and I'm still none the wiser*; *his complicated explanation left us none the wiser about how the system would work*
2 *verb*
(informal) **to wise someone up** = to make someone understand what is really happening (NOTE: **wiser - wisest**)

② **wisecrack**
['waɪzkræk] *noun*
sarcastic comment; *his wisecracks made us laugh*

① **wish**
[wɪʃ]
1 *noun*
(a) desire; *I have no wish to get involved*
(b) what you want to happen; **to make a wish** = to think of something you would like to have or to see happen; *close your eyes and make a wish*; *make a wish when you blow out the candles on your birthday cake*; **her wish came true** = what she wanted to happen did happen
(c) greetings; *best wishes for the New Year!*; *please give my good wishes to your family* (NOTE: plural is **wishes**)
2 *verb*
(a) to want something (which is almost impossible to have); *I wish I were blonde*; *I wish we didn't have to go to work on Christmas Day*; *I wish my birthday wasn't in June when I'm taking my exams*
(b) to want something to happen; *she sometimes wished she could live in the country*; *I wish some of you would help me with housework*; **I wouldn't wish it on anyone** = it is so awful, I wouldn't want anyone, even someone I don't like, to have it; *this flu is awful, it's not something I would wish on anyone*
(c) to hope something good will happen; *she wished him good luck in his interview*; *he wished me a Happy New Year*; *wish me luck - my interview is tomorrow*
(d) *(formal)* to want; *the principal wishes to see you in his study*

③ **wit**
[wɪt] *noun*
(a) being able to say clever and funny things; *his wit comes out all through his book*
(b) **wits** = intelligence; **at your wits' end** = not knowing what to do next; *they were at their wits' end when the builders reported even more structural problems in the house*; **to keep your wits about you** = to keep calm in a difficult situation and think hard what to do next; *don't panic, keep your wits about you, and everything will be all right*

① **witch**
[wɪtʃ] *noun*
(in children's stories) wicked woman believed to

have magic powers; *the wicked witch turned the prince into a frog* (NOTE: plural is **witches**)

① **with**

[wɪθ or wɪð] *preposition*

(a) *(showing things or people that are together)* *she came here with her mother; my sister is staying with us for a few days*

(b) *(showing something which you have)* *he went into the church with his hat on; you know the woman with blue eyes who works in the accounting department; they live in the house with the pink door*

(c) *(showing something which is used)* *he was cutting up wood with a saw; since his accident he walks with a stick; the crowd attacked the police with stones and bottles*

(d) because of; *her little hands were blue with cold; half the people in the office are ill with the flu*

(e) and; *he always has ice cream with apple pie; I want a sheet of paper with an envelope* (NOTE: **with** is used with many adjectives and verbs: **to agree with, to be pleased with**, etc.)

② **withdraw**

[wɪθˈdrɔ] *verb*

(a) to move back; *the crowd slowly withdrew as the soldiers advanced; he talked to the guests for a few moments, then withdrew into his library*

(b) to take back; *the old coins have been withdrawn from circulation*

(c) to take money out of a bank account; *you can withdraw up to $300 from any cash machine*

(d) to take back something which has been said; *she withdrew her offer to provide the food for the party* (NOTE: **withdrew** [wɪθˈdru] - **withdrawn**)

② **withdrawal**

[wɪθˈdrɔəl] *noun*

(a) removing money from a bank account; *she made three withdrawals last week*

(b) going back, doing the opposite of what you had said you would do; *his withdrawal from the election surprised his friends*

(c) **withdrawal symptoms** = unpleasant physical condition which occurs when someone stops taking a drug; *she is trying to give up smoking, and is having difficulty in coping with the withdrawal symptoms*

③ **withhold**

[wɪθˈhəʊld] *verb*

to refuse to let someone have something; *they suspect him of withholding important information from the police*; **withholding tax** = income tax deducted from an employee's salary before he or she is paid (NOTE: **withholding** - **withheld** [wɪθˈheld])

② **within**

[wɪˈðɪn] *preposition*

(a) *(in space or time)* in; *the house is within easy reach of the station; we are within walking distance of the store; I must go back for a checkup within three months; they promised to deliver the sofa within a week*; **within sight** = able to be seen; *we are almost there, the house is within sight; the ship sank within sight of land*

(b) **within the law** = legal; *is parking on the sidewalk within the law?*

③ **with it**

[ˈwɪð ɪt] *phrase*

(informal) knowing all about something; *she's very with it when it comes to what is happening on the fashion scene; I'm just not very with it today - I seem to be forgetting everything*

① **without**

[wɪˈðaʊt] *preposition*

(a) not with; *they came on a walking vacation without any boots; she managed to live for a few days without any food; he was stuck in Trenton without any money; they were fined for traveling without a ticket*

(b) not doing something; *she sang for an hour without stopping; they lived in the hut in the forest without seeing anybody for weeks*

(c) **without doubt** = certainly; *it is, without any doubt, his best movie ever*

④ **withstand**

[wɪθˈstænd] *verb*

to resist, to stand up to; *these plants can withstand the coldest winter; can a frame house withstand a hurricane?* (NOTE: **withstanding - withstood**)

① **witness**

[ˈwɪtnəs]

1 *noun*

(a) person who sees something happen or who is present when something happens; *the witness happened to be outside the house when the fire started*

(b) person who appears before a court or committee to give evidence; *the secretary appeared as a witness in the libel case*

(c) person who is present when someone signs a document; *the contract has to be signed in front of two witnesses; his sister signed as a witness*

(d) *(formal)* **to bear witness to** = to be evidence of; *his reaction bore witness to his interest in the matter* (NOTE: plural is **witnesses**)

2 *verb*

(a) to be present when something happens, and see it happening; *did anyone witness the accident?*

(b) to sign a document to show that you guarantee that the other signatures on it are genuine; *one of his colleagues witnessed his signature*

③ **witness stand**

[ˈwɪtnəs ˈstænd] *noun*

place in a courtroom where the witnesses give evidence; *he was called to the witness stand to answer questions from the prosecutor*

④ **witticism**
['wɪtɪsɪzm] *adjective*
clever and funny remark; *she made some witticisms about life in Washington D.C.*

③ **witty**
['wɪtɪ] *adjective*
clever and funny; *he made a witty speech at the wedding; she made some witty remarks which helped to keep everyone amused* (NOTE: wittier - wittiest)

② **wives**
[waɪvz] *see* WIFE

② **wobble**
['wɒbl]
1 *verb*
to move from side to side; *the children made the gelatin wobble in their bowls; don't wobble the table when I'm pouring coffee*
2 *noun*
shaking movement; *the front tire has a wobble*

② **wobbly**
['wɒblɪ] *adjective*
(a) shaking from side to side; *his bike has a wobbly back wheel; she sat on a wobbly armchair*
(b) *(of person)* not very steady; *she's a lot better, but still a bit wobbly on her feet*

③ **woke** *or* **woken**
[wəʊk *or* wəʊkn] *see* WAKE

① **woman**
['wʊmən] *noun*
adult female person; *the manager is an extremely capable woman; there were two middle-aged women in the seats next to ours; there are more and more women bus drivers; he still has no woman in his life* (NOTE: plural is women ['wɪmɪn])

① **won**
[wʌn] *see* WIN

① **wonder**
['wʌndər]
1 *verb*
(a) to want to know something; *I wonder why the room has gone quiet; she was wondering how many French francs you get for a U.S. dollar; if you don't ring home, your parents will start wondering what has happened*
(b) to think about something; *I wonder how I can earn more money; he's wondering what to do next;* **to wonder about** = (i) to think about; (ii) to worry about; *we've been wondering about moving house; I'm wondering about the children, they look very pale*
(c) *(asking a question politely)* *we were wondering if you would like to come for dinner on Saturday*
2 *noun*
(a) amazing thing; **to do wonders for** = to help make something better; *an evening out would do wonders to cheer him up; the cream did wonders for her skin problem;* **no wonder** = it isn't surprising; *it's no wonder you had*

difficulty in getting tickets for the show with so many tourists in New York City
(b) admiring feeling of surprise; *the little girl stared at the elephant in wonder*

② **wonderful**
['wʌndərfəl] *adjective*
very good, splendid; *they had a wonderful vacation by a lake in Canada; the weather was wonderful for the whole vacation; you passed your driver's test the first time? - wonderful!*

④ **wonderfully**
['wʌndərfəli] *adverb*
in a wonderful way; *the experiment worked wonderfully well*

① **won't**
[wəʊnt] *see* WILL NOT

④ **woo**
[wu] *verb*
(a) to try to get someone to support you, to vote for you, etc.; *the store is trying to woo customers with special offers*
(b) *(old)* to try to attract a girl to marry you

① **wood**
[wʊd] *noun*
(a) hard material which comes from a tree; *the kitchen table is made of wood; she picked up a piece of wood and put it on the fire; a wood floor would be just right for this room* (NOTE: no plural for this meaning: some wood, a piece of wood)
(b) many trees growing together; *the path goes straight through the wood; their house is on the edge of the woods; (informal)* **not to see the wood for the trees** = not to see what is important because you are concentrating only on details
(c) **woods** = area of land covered in trees; *they walked through the woods to the lake;* **we're not out of the woods yet** = we still have problems; *there's still so much to do to the house, we're not out of the woods yet*
(d) heavy wooden club, used in golf to hit the ball as far as possible; *he's trying a new wood* (NOTE: do not confuse with **would**)

① **woodchuck**
['wʊdtʃʌk] *noun*
small North American animal with short legs that digs its home underground (NOTE: also called a **groundhog**)

① **wooden**
['wʊdən] *adjective*
(a) made out of wood; *in the market we bought little wooden dolls for the children;* **wooden spoon** = spoon made of wood, used when cooking; *she used a wooden spoon to stir the sauce*
(b) *(of an actor, etc.)* being awkward and not natural when acting; *he was very wooden on stage*

① **woodland**
['wʊdlənd] *noun*
area of land covered in woods; *they walked through the woodlands to the lake; woodland birds are affected by climate change*

① **woodpecker**
['wʊdpekər] *noun*
bird with a long sharp beak which makes holes in trees to find insects under the bark; *she heard the woodpecker hammering and then saw it in the tree*

① **wool**
[wʊl] *noun*
(a) long threads of twisted hair, used to make clothes or carpets, etc.; *the carpet is made of wool; I need an extra ball of wool to finish this sweater*
(b) hair growing on a sheep; *the wool is cut from sheep in early summer;* **to pull the wool over someone's eyes** = to deceive someone by not telling them the true facts; *the real estate agent tried to pull the wool over our eyes about the house*

① **woolen**
['wʊlən] *adjective*
made of wool; *she was wearing a red woolen jumper*

② **woolly**
['wʊli] *adjective*
(a) made out of wool; *she wore a woolly hat*
(b) looking like wool; *little woolly clouds floated past in the sky* (NOTE: **woollier - woolliest**)

② **word**
[wɜrd] *noun*
(a) separate piece of language, either written or spoken; *this sentence has five words; he always has difficulty in spelling words like "though"; a word-for-word translation often doesn't make any sense*
(b) something spoken; *she passed me on the street but didn't say a word; I'd like to say a few words about Mr. Smith who is retiring today;* **to have a word with** = to speak to; *I must have a word with the manager about the service; the waitress had made so many mistakes, I had to have a word with her;* **to have words with someone** = to argue with someone; *he had words with his neighbor about the fence;* **without a word** = without saying anything; *she went out of the room without a word*
(c) something written; *we had a postcard with a few words from my sister in Canada; we've not heard a word from the lawyers*
(d) promise that you have made; **to give your word** = to promise; *he gave his word that the matter would remain confidential;* **to keep your word** = to do what you promised to do; *he kept his word, and the check arrived the next day;* **to take someone's word for it** = to accept what someone says as being true; *OK, I'll take*

your word for it, this is all the cash you have in the house
(e) **to breathe a word** = to mention something; *we want to keep the plan secret, so don't breathe a word to anyone;* **in other words** = to that is to say; *it's seven o'clock - in other words, time for dinner; I'm going on vacation next month, in other words I'll be away from the office for about four weeks;* **you took the words out of my mouth** = you've said exactly what I was going to say

③ **wore**
['wɔr] *see* WEAR

① **work**
[wɜrk]
1 *noun*
(a) something done using your strength or your brain; *there's a great deal of work still to be done; there's too much work for one person; she tries to avoid doing too much work in the house; if you've finished that piece of work, there's plenty more to be done; cooking for two hundred people every day is hard work;* **to have your work cut out to do something** = to find it difficult to do something; *they'll have their work cut out to get the job finished on time;* **he hasn't done a stroke of work all day** = he hasn't done any work at all
(b) job done regularly to earn money; *he goes to work every day on his bicycle; work starts at 9 A.M. and finishes at 5 P.M.; her work involves a lot of traveling; he is still looking for work*
(c) **at work** = working; *the roofers are still hard at work; she's at work today, but will have the day off tomorrow;* **out of work** = without a job; *hundreds of people were put out of work when the factory closed; she has been out of work for six months* (NOTE: no plural for meanings (a) and (b): **some work, a piece of work**)
(d) something which has been made, painted, written, etc., by someone; *an exhibition of the work of local artists; the complete works of Shakespeare;* **standard work** = book that is the recognized authority on a subject; *he's the author of the standard work on mountain birds*
2 *verb*
(a) to use your strength or brain to do something; *I can't work in the garden if it's raining; he's working hard at school, we're very pleased with his progress; work well and you'll soon get a better job;* **to set to work** = to start working; *if we all set to work early, we should finish the job this evening*
(b) to have a job; *she works in an office in Hartford; he used to work in his father's store; she had to stop working when her mother was sick*
(c) *(of machine)* to run; *the computers aren't working; the machine works by electricity*
(d) to make a machine run; *she works the biggest printing machine in the factory; do you*

know how to work the washing machine?
(e) to succeed; *will the plan work?*; *his plan worked well*; *if the cough medicine doesn't work, you'll have to see a doctor*
(f) to move a little; **to work loose** = to become loose by constant movement; *the nut holding the wheel must have worked loose*

③ **work at**
['wɜrk 'æt] *verb*
to work at something = to work hard; *if you want to become a tennis professional you will have to work at it*

③ **workbook**
['wɜrkbʊk] *noun*
book in which a student can write answers to exercises printed in the book

① **worker**
['wɜrkər] *noun*
(a) person who works in a certain way; *she's a good worker*; *he's a fast worker*
(b) person who works, especially in a certain job; *the factory closed when the workers went on strike*; *office workers usually work from 9:30 to 5:30*
(c) female bee which goes out to find pollen for the queen

④ **workforce**
['wɜrkfɔrs] *noun*
all the workers in an office or factory; *the management has made an increased offer to the workforce*; *the company cannot continue production with half its workforce off sick* (NOTE: no plural)

① **working**
['wɜrkɪŋ] *adjective*
referring to a job or to work; *the working population of a country*; *the unions have complained about working conditions in the factory*; **working breakfast** = breakfast where you discuss business; **working class** = group in society consisting of people who work with their hands, usually earning wages not salaries; **working life** = the years a person has worked; *I was a commuter all my working life*; **working week** = the part of the work when people usually go to their jobs; *the government is planning to reduce the working work to 35 hours*

③ **workings**
['wɜrkɪŋz] *noun*
(a) way or ways in which something works; *the workings of an automobile engine are a complete mystery to him*; *I wish I could understand the workings of local government!*
(b) workings = place where mineral has been dug; *that hole is the entrance to some old iron workings*

③ **workman**
['wɜrkmən] *noun*
man who works with his hands; *two workmen came to mend the gas heater* (NOTE: plural is **workmen**)

③ **work on**
['wɜrk 'ɒn] *verb*
to work hard to make something better; *you'll have to work on your math if you want to get through the exam*

① **work out**
['wɜrk 'aʊt] *verb*
(a) to calculate; *I'm trying to work out if we've sold more this year than last*; *the waiter couldn't work out the total check*
(b) to succeed; *everything worked out quite well in the end*
(c) to do exercises; *he works out every morning in the gym*

④ **workplace**
['wɜrkpleɪs] *noun*
place where work is done; *more work will get done if the workplace is in pleasant surroundings*

③ **works**
[wɜrks] *noun*
(a) factory; *the steelworks will be closed next week for the Christmas vacation*
(b) parts of a machine; *I looked inside the clock and there seems to be dust in the works*
(c) public works = constructions which benefit the public in general (such as highways, hospitals, etc.)
(d) *(informal)* **the works** = everything; *they have laid out new gardens in front of the city hall with colored lights, fountains - the works!*

② **workshop**
['wɜrkʃɒp] *noun*
very small factory where things are made or repaired; *he runs a workshop for repairing bicycles*; *the chairs are made in the workshop behind the store*

② **workstation**
['wɜrksteɪʃn] *noun*
desk with terminal, monitor, keyboard, etc., where a computer operator works; *the system has five workstations linked in a network*

③ **work up**
['wɜrk 'ʌp] *verb*
(a) to develop; *I find it difficult to work up any enthusiasm for my new job*
(b) to do some hard work to make something happen; *I'm doing some digging to work up an appetite*
(c) to work yourself up into a state = to make yourself annoyed and worried by something; *he's worked himself up into such a state about his finals*

① **world**
[wɜrld] *noun*
(a) the earth on which we live; *here is a map of the world*; *she flew around the world twice last year*; *he has to travel all over the world on business*; *an around-the-world ticket allows you to stop in several places*; **Old World** = Europe, Asia and Africa; **New World** = North and South America; **Third World** = countries of

Africa, Asia and South America which do not have highly developed industries; **World War** = war in which many countries all over the world take part

(b) to come into the world = to be born; **to bring a child into the world** = to give birth to a baby; **to be all alone in the world** = to have no family; *he isn't married, an only child, both his parents are dead, so he's all alone in the world; (informal)* **to be on top of the world** = to feel very happy; *she has a new boyfriend and is on top of the world;* **out of this world** = magnificent; *the cooking in the restaurant was out of this world;* **to think the world of someone** = to respect or love someone; *they think the world of their daughter;* **to do someone a world of good** = to make someone feel much better; *his vacation has done him a world of good*

(c) *(making a question stronger)* **who in the world is John Sparrow?** = do you have any idea who John Sparrow is?

(d) people with a particular interest or who work in a particular business; *he's very interested in the world of music; she wants to get into the world of big business*

(e) particular group of animals, etc.; *the insect world*

③ **World Series**
['wɜrld 'siriz] *noun*
series of professional baseball games played by the best teams of the major leagues; *they haven't won the World Series in twenty years*

② **worldwide**
[wɜrld'waid] *adjective & adverb*
over the whole world; *the company has a worldwide network of distributors; a worldwide energy crisis; the TV news program is available worldwide*

① **worm**
[wɜrm]
1 *noun*
(a) small animal which has no bones or legs and lives in the soil; *birds were on the grass looking for worms;* **the early bird catches the worm** = if you are the first to do something you will beat your rivals (NOTE: also called **earthworm**)
(b) similar tiny animal living inside an animal's body; *we had to give the dog a tablet to get rid of its worms*
2 *verb*
(a) to get through by twisting and turning; *they managed to worm their way into the exhibition*
(b) to worm something out of someone = to get information out of someone by continually asking questions; *they managed to worm the information out of her*
(c) to get worms out of an animal; *the cat needs to be wormed*

① **worn**
[wɔrn] *see* WEAR

① **worn out**
['wɔrn 'aut] *adjective*
(a) very tired; *he was worn out after the game of baseball; she comes home every evening, worn out after a busy day at the office*
(b) old and which has been used a lot; *the tires on the back wheels are worn out; she was wearing a pair of worn out trainers; see also* WEAR OUT

② **worried**
['wʌrid] *adjective*
anxious; *he had a worried expression on his face; she's looking worried; I'm worried that we may run out of gas;* **worried to death** = extremely worried; *they were worried to death about her*

② **worry**
['wʌri]
1 *noun*
(a) something which makes you anxious; *go on vacation and try to forget your worries*
(b) being anxious; *she is a great source of worry for her family*
2 *verb*
to be anxious because of something; *he's worrying about his driver's test; I worry when the children stay out late; don't worry, I'll be back on time; she's always pale and that worries me*

③ **worrying**
['wʌriŋ] *adjective*
which makes you worried; *there has been a worrying increase in the number of thefts*

② **worse**
[wɜrs]
1 *adjective*
(a) less good (as compared to something else); *it rained for the first week of our vacation, and the second week was even worse; I think this movie is worse than the one I saw last week; both children are mean - but the little girl is worse than her brother; both children are sick, and to make matters worse, their mother has broken her arm*
(b) more ill; *he's much worse since he started taking his medicine*
2 *adverb*
not as well; *he drives badly enough but his sister drives even worse* (NOTE: **worse** is the comparative of **bad, badly** and **ill**)
3 *noun*
something which is worse; *they thought their problems were over, but worse was to follow;* **to take a turn for the worse** = to suddenly become more ill; *everyone thought she was getting better and then she took a turn for the worse*

③ **worsen**
['wɜrsn] *verb*
to become worse; *I think the pain has worsened today; we are watching the worsening situation carefully*

③ **worse off**
['wɜrs 'ɒf] *adjective*
with less money than before; *the family is much worse off since he lost his job*

③ **worship**
['wɜrʃɪp]
1 *noun*
(a) praise and respect to God; *prayer is the most important part of worship*; **an act of worship** = a religious ceremony
(b) praise and love for someone or something; *her worship of her boss isn't healthy*; **hero worship** = excessive praise and love for someone who is considered a hero
2 *verb*
(a) to praise and respect God; *the ancient peoples worshipped stone statues of their gods*
(b) to take part in a church service; *they worship regularly in the parish church*
(c) to praise and love someone very much; *she absolutely worships her boyfriend* (NOTE: **worshipping - worshipped**)

① **worst**
[wɜrst]
1 *adjective*
worse than anything else; *this summer is the worst for fifty years*; *I think this is the worst movie he's ever made*
2 *adverb*
less well than anything or anyone else or than at any other time; *it's difficult to say which team played worst in the tournament*; *she works worst when she's tired*
3 *noun*
very bad thing; *the worst of the bad weather is past now*; **to prepare for the worst** = to get ready to have bad news; *your father was very badly injured - you must prepare for the worst* (NOTE: **worst** is the superlative of **bad** and **badly**)

① **worth**
[wɜrθ]
1 *adjective*
(a) to be worth = to have a certain value or price; *this ring's worth a lot of money*; *gold is worth more than silver*; *the house is worth more than $400,000*; *the automobile is worth $9000 on the used-car market*
(b) for all you are worth = with as much effort as possible; *they dug for all they were worth to try to find people trapped by the explosion*
(c) to be worth doing something = to find something good or helpful to do; *it's worth taking a map with you, as you may get lost in the little streets*; *his latest movie is well worth seeing*; *the old castle is well worth visiting or is well worth a visit*; *see also* WHILE
2 *noun*
value; *its worth will increase each year*; *can you give me thirty dollars' worth of gas?*

③ **worthwhile**
[wɜrθ'waɪl] *adjective*
which is worth the effort spent on it; *taking handicapped children to the coast is a very worthwhile project*; *was your trip to Los Angeles worthwhile?*

② **worthy**
['wɜrði] *adjective*
deserving; *it's a worthy cause, and I'm ready to help*; *the plan is worthy of careful consideration* (NOTE: **worthier - worthiest**)

① **would**
[wʊd] *verb used with other verbs*
(a) *(polite way of asking someone to do something)* *would you please stop talking?*; *would someone please tell me where the library is?*; *would you like some more tea?*
(b) *(past of "will")* *he said he would be here for lunch*; *she hoped she would be well enough to come*; *he wouldn't go even if I paid him*
(c) *(past of "will", showing something which often happens)* *he would bring his dog with him, even though we asked him not to*; *naturally the car wouldn't start when we were in a hurry*; *my husband forgot my birthday again this year - he would!*
(d) *(showing something which often happened in the past)* *every morning she would go and feed the chickens*; *he would always be there waiting outside the station*; *they would often bring us flowers*
(e) *(following a condition)* *I'm sure that if they could come, they would*; *I would've done it if you had asked me to*; *if she were alive, she would or she'd be a hundred years old today*; *if it snowed we would or we'd go skiing* (NOTE: the negative **would not** is usually written **wouldn't**. Note also that **would** is often shortened to **'d: she'd be a hundred, he'd stay at home.** Note also that **would** is only used with other verbs and is not followed by **to**)

① **would rather**
['wʊd 'ræðər] *verb*
to prefer; *I would rather live in New York than anywhere else*; *are you all going to pay? - we'd rather not*; *they'd rather we stayed at home than go with them*

② **wound**
1 [wund] *noun*
(a) cut made on someone's body, usually in fighting; *the soldier had a bullet wound in his leg*; *he was admitted to the hospital with a knife wound in his chest*
(b) hurt to someone's feelings; *the wounds caused by the divorce will take years to heal*
2 [wund] *verb*
(a) to hurt someone badly in a fight, a war; *two of the gang were wounded in the bank robbery*; *as a young soldier he was badly wounded*
(b) to hurt someone's feelings; *she was deeply wounded by what he said*
3 [waʊnd] *see* WIND

② **wove, woven**
[wəʊv or 'wəʊvn] *see* WEAVE

① **wrap**
[ræp]
1 *verb (usually* **wrap up***)*
(a) to cover something all over; *we're wrapping up the Christmas presents for the children; the package is wrapped (up) in brown paper; if you're cold, wrap yourself (up) in your blanket*
(b) to wear warm clothes; *wrap up warmly if you're going for a walk in the snow*
(c) *(informal)* to finish off; *that just about wraps up the points we have to make*
(d) **to wrap around** = to put right around something; *she wrapped her arms around the little boy; it's cold - wrap your scarf around your neck* (NOTE: **wrapping - wrapped** [ræpt])
2 *noun*
(a) piece of cloth that is put around the shoulders or the top part of the body; *she pulled her wrap closer around her*
(b) *(informal)* **to keep something under wraps** = to keep something secret; *the whole project is still under wraps*

④ **wrapped up in**
['wræpt 'ʌp ɪn] *adjective*
busy doing something, so that you don't notice anything else; *she is so wrapped up in her work she sometimes forgets to eat*

② **wrapping**
['ræpɪŋ] *noun*
paper, cardboard, plastic, etc., used to wrap something up; *the children tore the wrapping off the box; remove the wrapping before putting the dish in the microwave;* **wrapping paper** = brightly colored paper used to wrap presents; *I bought two rolls of Christmas wrapping paper*

① **wreck**
[rek]
1 *noun*
(a) ship which has been sunk or badly damaged; *divers have discovered the wreck of a Spanish treasure ship; the wreck of the "Mary Rose" was found in the sea near the Florida coast*
(b) anything which has been damaged and cannot be used; *the police towed away the wreck of the automobile; their new vehicle is now a total wreck*
(c) *(informal)* nervous, tired and worried person; *after the interview with the boss he was a nervous wreck; spend just two hours manning the complaints desk and you're reduced to a wreck*
2 *verb*
(a) to damage something very badly; *the ship was wrecked on the rocks in the storm; the building was wrecked by the explosion*
(b) to ruin something; *the children have caught measles and that has wrecked our plans to go to Florida*

② **wreckage**
['rekɪdʒ] *noun*

what is left of a building, ship, plane, etc., after it has been wrecked; *wreckage of the automobiles and trucks covered the freeway; the rescue team searched the wreckage of the hotel looking for survivors; clearing the wreckage from the railrod track will take several days* (NOTE: no plural)

③ **wrestle**
['resl] *verb*
to fight with someone to try to throw him to the ground; *the President's guards wrestled with the demonstrators*

② **wriggle**
['rɪgl] *verb*
to twist from side to side; *the baby wriggled in her father's arms; the worm wriggled back into the soil*

② **wring**
[rɪŋ] *verb*
to twist something, especially to get water out of it; *he wrung out his shirt before hanging it up to dry* (NOTE: do not confuse with **ring;** note: **wringing - wrung** [rʌŋ])

① **wrinkle**
['rɪŋkl] *noun*
(a) fold in the skin; *she has wrinkles round her eyes*
(b) line or crease in cloth, etc.; *he tried to iron out the wrinkles in his trousers*

① **wrinkled**
['rɪŋkld] *adjective*
full of lines or creases; *he was wearing a wrinkled old shirt*

① **wrist**
[rɪst] *noun*
joint between the arm and the hand; *he sprained his wrist and can't play tennis tomorrow; see also* SLAP

① **write**
[raɪt] *verb*
(a) to put words or numbers on paper, etc., with a pen, computer, etc.; *she wrote the address on the back of an envelope; someone wrote "down with the management" on the wall of the bank; write the reference number at the top of the letter; did you know she used to write for the "Washington Post"?; he wrote a book on keeping tropical fish*
(b) to write a letter and send it to someone; *have you written to your mom yet?; she writes to me twice a week; don't forget to write as soon as you get to your hotel; he wrote a letter to the management to complain about the service; don't forget to write a postcard when you get to New York;* *(informal)* **it's nothing to write home about** = it's not very special; *the food in the hotel is nothing to write home about* (NOTE: **writing - wrote** [raʊt] **- has written** ['rɪtn])

① **write back**
['raɪt 'bæk] *verb*
to answer by letter; *she got my postcard, and wrote back immediately*

① **write down**
['raɪt 'daʊn] *verb*
to write on paper, etc.; *she wrote down the registration number of the automobile*; *please write down all the necessary details on a piece of paper*

④ **write in**
['raɪt 'ɪn] *verb*
(a) to write a letter to an organization; *hundreds of people wrote in to complain about the program*
(b) to vote for a candidate whose name does not appear on the ballot paper, by writing his or her name there

④ **write-in**
['raɪtɪn] *noun*
(vote for a) candidate whose name is written by the voter onto the ballot paper; *the write-ins received about 3% of the vote*

③ **write off**
['raɪt 'ɒf] *verb*
(a) to cancel a debt; *the bank couldn't trace him so they had to write the debt off*
(b) to remove an asset from a company's accounts because it no longer has any value; *the automobile was written off* = the insurance company considered the automobile a total loss

② **write out**
['raɪt 'aʊt] *verb*
to write something in full; *can you write out a list of all the things you want?*; *to write out a check* = to write the words and figures on a check and then sign it

② **writer**
['raɪtər] *noun*
person who writes; *who is the writer of this letter?*; *she's the writer of books on gardening*

④ **write up**
['raɪt 'ʌp] *verb*
to write a text in full from notes which you have taken; *I took a lot of notes, and now I have to write them up for the local newspaper*

① **writing**
['raɪtɪŋ] *noun*
(a) something which is written; *please don't phone, reply in writing*; *put everything in writing, then you have a record of what has been done*
(b) *(informal)* **the writing is on the wall** = there are signs that a disaster is about to happen; *the writing is on the wall for old-fashioned butcher's shops*
(c) words written by hand; *his writing's so bad I can't read it*; *see also* HANDWRITING
(d) being a writer; *he earns his living from writing*
(e) *(formal)* **writings** = serious things written; *we studied the writings of Karl Marx*

① **written**
['rɪtn] *adjective*
which has been put in writing; *he had a written reply from the White House*; *see also* WRITE

① **wrong**
[rɒŋ]
1 *adjective*
(a) not correct; *he gave three wrong answers and failed the test*; *that's not the right time, is it? - no, the clock is wrong*; *you've come to the wrong house - there's no one called Jones living here*; *there is something wrong with the television*; *I must have pressed the wrong key - a message flashed up on the screen*; **wrong number** = telephone number which is not the one you wanted to dial; *we tried dialing several times, but each time got a wrong number*; *I want to speak to Mr. Cousin please - sorry, you've got the wrong number*
(b) **to get off on the wrong foot** = to start to do things the wrong way; **to get up on the wrong side of the bed** = to start the day badly; **to get the wrong end of the stick** = not to understand correctly what someone is saying
(c) not suitable; *you came just at the wrong time, when we were bathing the children*; *she was wearing the wrong sort of dress for a wedding*
(d) bad; *it's wrong to talk like that about her*; *cheating on exams is wrong*
(e) making someone worried; **what's wrong?** = what is the matter?; *what's wrong with my handwriting? - there's nothing wrong with it, it's just that I find it difficult to read*; **I hope nothing's wrong** *or* **there's nothing wrong, is there?** = I hope there is no problem
2 *adverb*
badly; *everything went wrong yesterday*; *she spelled my name wrong*; **don't get me wrong** = don't put the wrong meaning on what I'm trying to say; *don't get me wrong, I love him more than anyone else but at times he can be very annoying*
3 *noun*
(a) thing which is not right; *the group is campaigning against wrongs done to children in care*
(b) **to be in the wrong** = to have made a mistake; *I apologize - I was clearly in the wrong*

◇ **on the wrong side of**
[ɒn ðə 'rɒŋ saɪd əv] *phrase*
(a) going against; *he got on the wrong side of the law*
(b) *(informal)* older than; *she's on the wrong side of fifty*

① **wrote**
[rəʊt] *see* WRITE

② **wrung**
[rʌŋ] *see* WRING

Xx

① **X, x**
[eks]
(a) twenty-fourth letter of the alphabet, between W and Y
(b) *(sign showing that something is multiplied)* 3 *x 3 = 9* (NOTE: say "three times three equals nine")
(c) *(sign showing size)* **the table top is 24 x 36cm** (NOTE: say "twenty-four by thirty-six centimeters")
(d) *(sign used to indicate an unknown person)* **let's take the example of Mrs. X, who is a widow, 40 years old**
(e) mark of a cross; *to find the treasure, you have to find the spot marked "X" on the map*

① **Xmas**
['krɪsməs or 'eksməs] *noun (informal)* = CHRISTMAS

① **X-ray**
['eksreɪ]
1 *noun*
(a) **X-rays** = rays which go through the soft tissue, and allow the bones and organs in the body to be photographed; *the dentist took X-rays of his teeth; an X-ray examination showed the key was inside the baby's stomach; the X-ray department is closed for lunch*
(b) photograph taken with X-rays; *the X-ray showed that the bone was broken in two places; they will take an X-ray of his leg; she was sent to the hospital for an X-ray*
2 *verb*
to take an X-ray photograph of someone; *there are six patients waiting to be X-rayed; they X-rayed my leg to see if it was broken*

Yy

③ **Y, y**
[waɪ]
twenty-fifth letter of the alphabet, between X and Z; *not many words begin with a Y*

③ **yacht**
[jɒt] *noun*
(a) sailboat, used for pleasure and sport; **yacht club** = private club for people who sail yachts
(b) large luxurious motor boat; *she spent her vacation on a yacht in the Caribbean Sea*

② **Yankee**
['jæŋki] *noun (informal)*
(a) person from a northern U.S. state; *Southerners think Yankees speak too fast*
(b) person from New England; *Yankees make excellent clam chowder*
(c) person from the U.S.A.; *posters with "Yankees go home" appeared on the walls* (NOTE: in this meaning often abbreviated to **Yank**)

① **yard**
[jɑrd] *noun*
(a) measurement of length, 36 inches (= 0.914 meters); *the police station is only yards away from where the fight took place; can you move your car a couple of yards as it is blocking the entrance to our garage?; we need two 3-yard lengths of copper pipe;* **square yard** = measurement of area measuring one yard on each side
(b) area of land around a house; *we keep our bikes in the yard; let's have a barbecue in our back yard*
(c) large area where stores are kept outside, where trucks can pick up or put down loads; *he went to the railroad yard*

① **yarn**
[jɑrn] *noun*
long piece of wool used in knitting or weaving; *she sells yarn from the wool of her sheep*

② **yeah**
[jeər] *interjection (informal meaning)* YES

① **year**
[jɜr] *noun*
(a) period of time, lasting twelve months, from January 1 to December 31; *Columbus discovered America in the year 1492; the great celebrations which took place in the year 2000; last year we did not have a vacation; next year*

she's going on vacation in Australia; the weather was very bad for most of the year; **year in, year out** *or* **year after year** = every year, over a long period of time; *year in, year out he sends me a plant for my birthday;* **all year round** = working or open for the whole year; *the museum is open all year round; see also* NEW YEAR, NEW YEAR'S DAY

(b) a period of twelve months from a particular time; *we spent five years in Hong Kong; he died two hundred years ago today; she'll be eleven years old tomorrow; how many years have you been working for the company?*

(c) **years** = a long time; **I haven't seen him for years** = I haven't seen him for a very long time

(d) **school year** = period which starts in September and finishes in June; *the school year starts in September; it's her last year at college;* **tax year** = the twelve-month period on which taxes are calculated; *see also* CALENDAR, FINANCIAL, LEAP YEAR

② **yearbook**
['jɜrbʊk] *noun*
book that is produced annually by a school, has pictures of the students and details the activities and achievements of the year; *there is a picture of each of the students in the yearbook*

④ **yeast**
[jist] *noun*
living fungus used to make bread and alcohol; *yeast is a good source of Vitamin B*

① **yell**
[jel]
1 *verb*
to shout very loudly; *the police officer yelled to her to get out of the way*
2 *noun*
loud shout; *he gave a yell and everyone came running to see what he had found*

① **yellow**
['jeləʊ]
1 *adjective*
of a color like that of the sun or of gold; *his new automobile is bright yellow; she's wearing yellow shoes; at this time of year the fields are full of yellow flowers;* **yellow jacket** = type of yellow and black wasp (NOTE: **yellower - yellowest**)
2 *noun*
the color of the sun or gold; *do you have any hats of a lighter yellow than this one?; the yellow of the flowers against the rocks makes a very beautiful photograph*
3 *verb*
to become yellow; *the pages of the diary have yellowed with time but you can still read it*

③ **yellow pages**
['jeləʊ 'peɪdʒɪz] *noun*
section of a telephone directory printed on yellow paper, which lists businesses under various headings, such as computer stores,

banks, etc.; *he looked up "airlines" in the yellow pages*

③ **yelp**
[jelp] *verb*
(usually of animals) to give a short cry of pain or excitement; *the dogs were yelping in the back of the car*

④ **yen**
[jen] *noun*
(a) currency used in Japan; *it cost two thousand yen* (NOTE: no plural; usually written ¥ after figures: 2000¥)
(b) *(informal)* strong desire; *he has a yen to go walking along the Great Wall of China*

① **yes**
[jes] *adverb*
(word showing that you agree, accept, etc., the opposite of "no") *they asked her if she wanted to come and she said "yes"; anyone want more coffee? - yes, please; you don't like living in California? - yes I do!; didn't you work in Sacramento at one time? - yes, I did; I need a clear answer - is it "yes" or "no"?*

③ **yesterday**
['jestərdeɪ] *adverb & noun*
the day before today; *yesterday was March 1 so today must be the 2nd; she came to see us yesterday evening;* **the day before yesterday** = two days before today; *it rained the day before yesterday; the store only opened the day before yesterday*

① **yet**
[jet]
1 *adverb*
(a) already, until now; *has the manager arrived yet?; I haven't seen her yet this morning; don't throw the newspaper away - I haven't read it yet*
(b) **as yet** = up till now; *they have not managed to repair the fault as yet; as yet, he hasn't given me any explanation for being late*
(c) still, even; *the police charged and yet more fans were arrested; she ate yet another piece of cake*
(d) *(formal)* in the future; *all hope is not lost, we may yet win the championship*
2 *conjunction*
but, still; *he's very small and yet he can kick a ball a long way; it was starting to snow, and yet he went out without a coat*

④ **yew**
[ju] *noun*
large evergreen tree with flat green needles and poisonous red berries; *you often find yews growing near churches* (NOTE: do not confuse with **you**)

③ **yield**
[jild]
1 *noun*
(a) interest produced by an investment; *the yield on these bonds is higher than average*

(b) quantity of a crop or a product produced from a plant or from an area of land; *what is the normal yield per acre?*

2 *verb*

(a) to produce money; *the investment has yielded a good interest until now*

(b) to produce a crop or a product; *this variety of rice can yield up to 2 short tons per acre*; *the North Sea oil deposits yield 100,000 barrels a month*

(c) to produce a result; *their researches finally yielded the information they were looking for*

(d) to yield to someone = to give up, to give way; *(of traffic)* **to yield to another automobile** = to allow another automobile to go first; **to yield to pressure** = to give in to pressure; *the government yielded to pressure from the unions and did not proceed with the planned legislation*

③ **yogurt**
['jɒɡət] *noun*
milk which has become slightly sour after bacteria are added, often flavored with fruit; *a container of strawberry yogurt*; **plain yogurt** = yogurt without any flavoring

② **yolk**
[jəʊk] *noun*
yellow part inside an egg; *in my boiled egg, the yolk was soft and the white was hard*; *beat the yolks of three eggs and add sugar*

② **Yom Kippur**
['jɒm kɪ'pur] *noun*
Jewish holiday observed with fasting and prayer; *Yom Kippur is in October this year*

① **you**
[ju] *pronoun*
(a) *(referring to someone being spoken to)* **are you ready?**; *you look tired, you should rest a bit*; *if I give you my address will you give me yours?*; *hi, how are you?*; *are you both keeping well?*

(b) *(referring to anybody)* *you never know when you might need a pair of scissors*; *you have to be tall to be a basketball player*

(c) *(addressing someone directly)* *you with the red scarf over there, I need to see your ticket!*; *hey you! leave my bicycle alone* (NOTE: **you** is both singular and plural)

② **you'd**
[jud] = YOU HAD, YOU WOULD

① **you'll**
[jul] = YOU WILL

① **young**
[jʌŋ]
1 *adjective*
not old; *she's very young, she's only six*; *he became president when he was still a young man*; *my little brother's much younger than me* or *much younger than I am*; *in the afternoon there are TV programs for very young children*; *this is where your dad used to live when he was a young boy*; *your new haircut makes you look younger* (NOTE: **younger - youngest**)

2 *noun*
(a) young animals or birds; *animals fight to protect their young*

(b) the young = young people; *today, the young have great need of moral teaching* (NOTE: no plural)

① **youngster**
['jʌŋstər] *noun*
young person; *the youngsters went to the park to play baseball*

① **your**
[jɔr] *adjective*
belonging to you; *I hope you didn't forget to bring your toothbrush*; *this letter is for your brother*

① **you're**
[juər or jɔr] = YOU ARE

① **yours**
[jɔrz] *pronoun*
(a) belonging to you; *this is my automobile - where's yours?*; *my car's in the garage, can I borrow yours?*; **a friend of yours** = one of your friends; *you said she was a friend of yours, but she says she's never met you*

(b) *(greetings used at the end of a letter)* **Yours faithfully** = used as an ending for business letters, when addressed to no specific person; **Sincerely yours** = used as an ending to a letter addressed to a named person; **Truly yours** = words written at the end of a slightly formal letter; *(informal)* **Yours truly** = me myself; *who had to pay for all the damage, why yours truly, of course!*

① **yourself** *or* **yourselves**
[jɔr'self or jɔr'selvz] *pronoun*
(a) *(referring to "you" as a subject)* *why do you wash the automobile yourself, when you could easily take it to the car wash?*; *watch out for the broken glass - you might hurt yourself*; *I hope you are all going to enjoy yourselves*

(b) *(for emphasis)* *did you yourself see what happened?*

(c) by yourself *or* **by yourselves** = alone, with no one to help you; *will you be all by yourself at Christmas?*; *did you find your way back to the hotel all by yourself?* (NOTE: the plural **yourselves** refers to **you** as a plural subject)

① **youth**
[juθ] *noun*
(a) young person; *gangs of youths were causing trouble in the town*; *a youth, aged 16, was arrested for possessing drugs*

(b) period when you are young, especially the time between being a child and being an adult; *in his youth he was a great traveler*; *I haven't done that since the days of my youth!*

① **you've**
[juv] = YOU HAVE

Zz

③ **Z, z**
[ziː]
last and twenty-sixth letter of the alphabet; *he can say his alphabet from A to Z*

③ **zap**
[zæp] *verb (informal)*
(a) to destroy someone or something completely; *he used a spray to zap the insects; (on a computer) he zapped all the monsters and got to the end of the game*
(b) to expose something to radiation; *if you want the milk warm, zap it in the microwave* (NOTE: **zapping - zapped**)

① **zebra**
['ziːbrə] *noun*
African animal like a horse, with black and white stripes; *zebras' stripes help them hide in the long grass of the African bush* (NOTE: usually no plural: **a herd of zebra**)

④ **zenith**
['zeniθ] *noun*
(a) highest point, point of greatest achievement; *the soprano retired at the zenith of her career*
(b) highest point in the sky reached by the sun or moon; *the sun is now at its zenith*

② **zero**
['zɪərəʊ] *noun*
(a) number 0; *the code for international calls is zero one one (011)*
(b) freezing point of water on a thermometer; *the temperature stayed below zero for days*
(c) score of no points; *they lost ten - zero* (NOTE: plural is **zeros**)

② **zigzag**
['zɪgzæg]
1 *adjective & noun*
(line) which turns one way, then the opposite way
2 *verb*
to move from left to right, then from right to left; *the car zigzagged up the freeway until the police managed to stop it* (NOTE: **zigzagging - zigzagged**)

② **zillion**
['zɪljən] *noun*
(informal) a very large number; *there were about a zillion people at the airport*

② **zinc**
[zɪŋk] *noun*
hard bright light-colored metal; *iron coated with zinc is used for shed roofs* (NOTE: Chemical element: chemical symbol: **Zn**; atomic number: **30**)

④ **zinnia**
['zɪnɪə] *noun*
garden plant with brightly colored flowers; *the zinnias look pretty*

② **zip**
[zɪp]
1 *noun*
energy; *Grandpa had a lot of zip after his nap*
2 *verb*
(a) to zip up = to close something using a zipper; *she zipped up her coat; he zipped up his bag*
(b) to go fast; *automobiles were zipping past us on the freeway* (NOTE: **zipping - zipped**)

③ **ZIP code**
['zɪp 'kəʊd] *noun*
numbers used to indicate a postal delivery area in an address on an envelope; *don't forget the ZIP code - it's a very important part of the address*

② **zipper**
['zɪpər] *noun*
device for closing openings on pants, dresses, bags, etc., consisting of two rows of teeth which lock together; *the zipper on my coat is broken; can you do up the zipper at the back of my dress?*

② **zone**
[zəʊn]
1 *noun*
area or part which is different from others, or which has something special; *squad cars are patrolling the inner city zones; the town center has been made into a pedestrian zone;* **time zone** = one of 24 bands in the world in which the same standard time is used; *when you fly across the U.S.A. you cross several time zones*
2 *verb*
to divide a town into parts for planning purposes; *the land is zoned for industrial use*

① **zoo**
[zuː] *noun*
place where wild animals are kept, and where people can go to see them; *let's go to the zoo this afternoon; we went to the zoo to see the lions and elephants*

③ **zoom**
[zum]
1 *noun*
= ZOOM LENS
2 *verb*
(a) to go very fast, making sound; *automobiles were zooming past me on the highway*
(b) *(of prices, etc.)* to rise suddenly and sharply; *the exchange rate zoomed up last month*
(c) **to zoom in on something** = to focus a camera lens so that it makes a distant object appear to come closer; *he zoomed in on the yacht*

③ **zoom lens**
['zum 'lenz] *noun*
camera lens which allows you to change quickly from distant to close-up shots while still keeping in focus; *using a zoom lens can give you close-ups of lions from quite a long way away*